Psychology

Psychology

Eighth Edition

Lester A. Lefton
TULANE UNIVERSITY

Linda Brannon
MCNEESE STATE UNIVERSITY

BOSTON NEW YORK SAN FRANCISCO
MEXICO CITY MONTREAL TORONTO LONDON MADRID MUNICH PARIS
HONG KONG SINGAPORE TOKYO CAPE TOWN SYDNEY

Executive Editor: Carolyn Merrill
Editorial Assistant: Kate Edwards
Marketing Manager: Wendy Gordon
Developmental Editor: Kelly Perkins
Senior Editorial Production Administrator: Deborah Brown
Composition Buyer: Linda Cox
Manufacturing Buyer: Megan Cochran
Cover Administrator: Linda Knowles
Text Design and Electronic Composition: Deborah Schneck
Editorial Production Service: Susan McNally
Photo Researcher: Laurie Frankenthaler
Copy Editor: Susanna Brougham

For related titles and support materials, visit our online catalog at
www.ablongman.com

Library of Congress Cataloging-in-Publication Data

Lefton, Lester A.
Psychology / Lester A. Lefton, Linda Brannon. – 8th ed.
p. cm.
Includes bibliographical references and index.
ISN 0-205-34643-X
1. Psychology. I. Brannon, Linda II. Title

BF121.L424 2002
150–dc21

Printed in the United States of America

10 9 8 7 6 5 4 3 2 1 VHP 08 07 06 05 04 03 02

Photo credits appear on page 739, which should be considered an extension of the copyright page.

Brief Contents

Contents

6 Consciousness 188

7 Learning 220

8 Memory 262

9 Cognitive Psychology 298

10 Intelligence 330

16 Therapy 566

17 Psychology in Action 606

Preface

The **completely revised** eighth edition of *Psychology* is the result of a new and exciting partnership between Linda Brannon—the author of *Gender* (third edition, Allyn & Bacon) and co-author of a textbook on health psychology—and me, Lester Lefton. Linda's expertise in the fields of diversity and gender studies has been essential to the substantial integration of these issues in the eighth edition. Moreover, her engaging writing style and fresh approach to the field of general psychology have greatly enhanced every subject covered in the book. Together, we **thoroughly updated and rewrote** every chapter in order to bring the eighth edition of *Psychology* into the 21st century and to address the most recent topics and concerns in the field today.

Why This Book Was Written

The goal of this book is to help students appreciate the exciting field of psychology, to increase their knowledge, and to stimulate their interest and understanding of human behavior and mental processes. The complexity of psychology makes the task hard, but our love for this discipline makes the task a joy. To share our enthusiasm and appreciation for psychology, we have chosen to focus on four themes that help explain and present psychology.

Four Major Themes

The 21st-century world is diverse and increasingly more connected. Issues of diversity crop up everywhere in the field of psychology and help make it the varied, complicated, and challenging field that it is. We use the following themes to organize our presentation of diversity and interconnection in psychology:

- the complex relationship between nature and nurture
- the changing impact and definition of diversity
- the importance of evolutionary and biological topics within the field of psychology
- the relevance of psychology in students' everyday life and the importance of critical thinking

What's New in the Eighth Edition and Why

Because it is so important to keep current with new directions in psychology, we have **totally rewritten** the book based on our colleagues' reviews of the previous edition as well as reviews of our competitors. Though the seventh edition of *Psychology* was very well received by both students and the instructors, we felt that the eighth edition needed substantial revision in order to stay attuned to the needs of students and professors in the upcoming years. To achieve this goal, we wrote completely new opening stories that focus on current news events, updated or completely rewrote all the boxed features, and stayed up-to-date on new research and theories—making the eighth edition as current as possible.

Our Goals: Be an Active Learner

Because Linda and I both teach introductory psychology, we remain engaged with the course material and have, for years, experimented with various presentation methods. We share a mutual goal: to encourage the student to *be an active learner*. To accomplish this in the eighth edition, we did the following:

- Used a personal voice in our writing and shared our own points of view on various aspects of the field
- Added a new text feature called Be an Active Learner to encourage students to become actively involved in the learning process, to be responsible for their own learning, and to make psychology meaningful by linking information they are learning to their own life experiences, which is a theme of our text
- Emphasized and expanded upon aspects of psychology that might be particularly relevant to students' lives in a new feature called Psychology in Action
- Added a new Point/Counterpoint feature to each chapter, encouraging students to actively consider psychological controversies on their own
- Included interactive figures, labeled For the Active Learner
- Let real-life students and recent grads tell how they use psychology in their own lives in a new feature called Student Voices

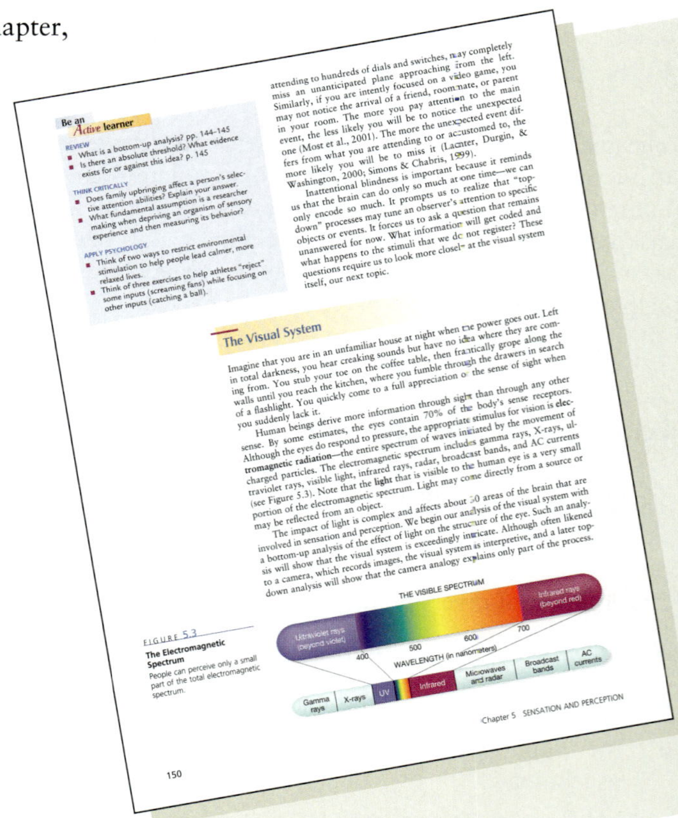

Be an *Active* learner

REVIEW

- What is a bottom-up analysis? pp. 144–145
- Is there an absolute threshold? What evidence exists for or against this idea? p. 145

THINK CRITICALLY

- Does family upbringing affect a person's selective attention abilities? Explain your answer.
- What fundamental assumption is a researcher making when depriving an organism of sensory experience and then measuring its behavior?

APPLY PSYCHOLOGY

- Think of two ways to restrict environmental stimulation to help people lead calmer, more relaxed lives.
- Think of three exercises to help athletes "reject" some inputs (screaming fans) while focusing on other inputs (catching a ball).

attending to hundreds of dials and switches, may completely miss an unanticipated plane approaching from the left. Similarly, if you are intently focused on a video game, you may not notice the arrival of a friend, roommate, or parent in your room. The more you pay attention to the main event, the less likely you will be to notice the unexpected one (Most et al., 2001). The more the unexpected event differs from what you are attending to or accustomed to, the more likely you will be to miss it (Lachter, Durgin, & Washington, 2000; Simons & Chabris, 1999).

Inattentional blindness is important because it reminds us that the brain can do only so much at one time—we can only encode so much. It prompts us to realize that "top-down" processes may tune an observer's attention to specific objects or events. It forces us to ask a question that remains unanswered for now. What information will get coded and what happens to the stimuli that we dc not register? These questions require us to look more closel– at the visual system itself, our next topic.

The Visual System

Imagine that you are in an unfamiliar house at night when the power goes out. Left in total darkness, you hear creaking sounds but have no idea where they are coming from. You stub your toe on the coffee table, then frantically grope along the walls until you reach the kitchen, where you fumble through the drawers in search of a flashlight. You quickly come to a full appreciation of the sense of sight when you suddenly lack it.

Human beings derive more information through sight than through any other sense. By some estimates, the eyes contain 70% of the body's sense receptors. Although the eyes do respond to pressure, the appropriate stimulus for vision is **electromagnetic radiation**—the entire spectrum of waves initiated by the movement of charged particles. The electromagnetic spectrum includes gamma rays, X-rays, ultraviolet rays, visible light, infrared rays, radar, broadcast bands, and AC currents (see Figure 5.3). Note that the **light** that is visible to the human eye is a very small portion of the electromagnetic spectrum. Light may come directly from a source or may be reflected from an object.

The impact of light is complex and affects about ;0 areas of the brain that are involved in sensation and perception. We begin our analysis of the visual system with a bottom-up analysis of the effect of light on the structure of the eye. Such an analysis will show that the visual system is exceedingly intricate. Although often likened to a camera, which records images, the visual system is interpretive, and a later top-down analysis will show that the camera analogy explains only part of the process.

FIGURE 5.3 **The Electromagnetic Spectrum** People can perceive only a small part of the total electromagnetic spectrum.

150 Chapter 5 SENSATION AND PERCEPTION

New Features to the Eighth Edition

We also updated **all** the features in the book and added several brand-new features for the eighth edition.

Point/Counterpoint

The new *Point/Counterpoint* feature focuses on controversial issues in psychology, such as ethics in animal research, whether men are naturally promiscuous, whether homosexuality is biologically based or learned, and whether Ritalin really helps people with ADHD. We discuss both sides of the issue and present the latest research results.

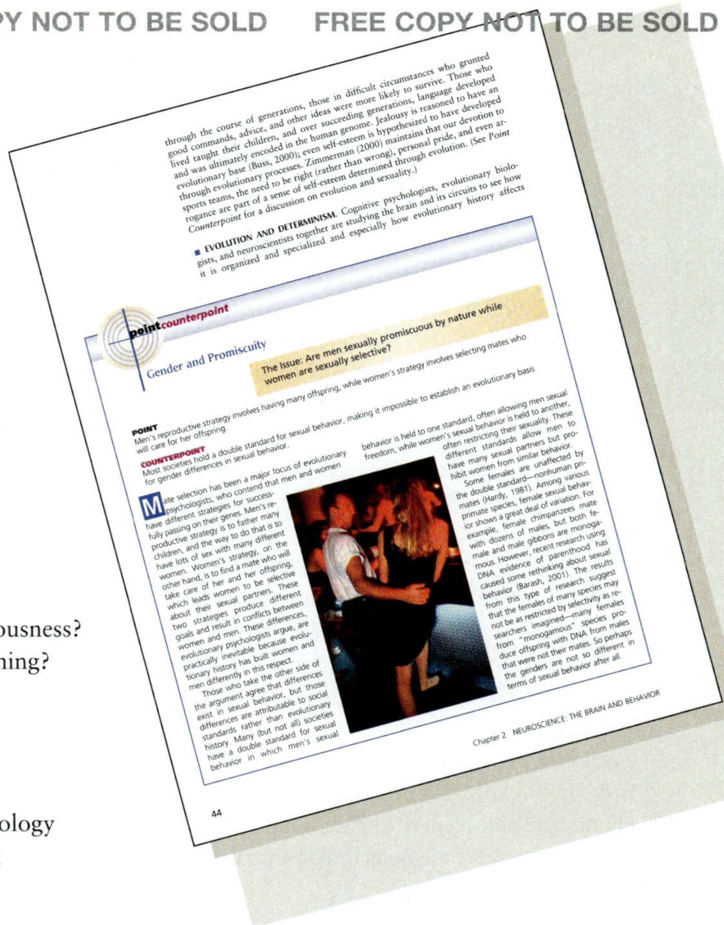

Chapter 1	Research with Nonhuman Animals
Chapter 2	Gender and Promiscuity
Chapter 3	Ritalin—Use or Abuse?
Chapter 4	Adolescent Medical Decision Making
Chapter 5	Does Subliminal Advertising Work?
Chapter 6	Is Hypnosis an Altered State of Consciousness?
Chapter 7	Men and Women—Differences in Learning?
Chapter 8	Recovered Memories
Chapter 9	Can Computers Think?
Chapter 10	One or Many Intelligences?
Chapter 11	The Basis of Homosexuality
Chapter 12	Freud's Continuing Relevance to Psychology
Chapter 13	Do Television Program Content Rating Systems Work?
Chapter 14	Alternative Medicine
Chapter 15	Multiple Personality Disorder—Is It Real?
Chapter 16	Controlled Drinking and Alcoholism
Chapter 17	The Internet and Social Isolation

Be an Active Learner

Be an Active Learner reminds students to pause, answer questions, and think about what they have just learned. Some questions review material the students have just read, others encourage students to think critically, yet others ask students to apply what they have learned to their own lives.

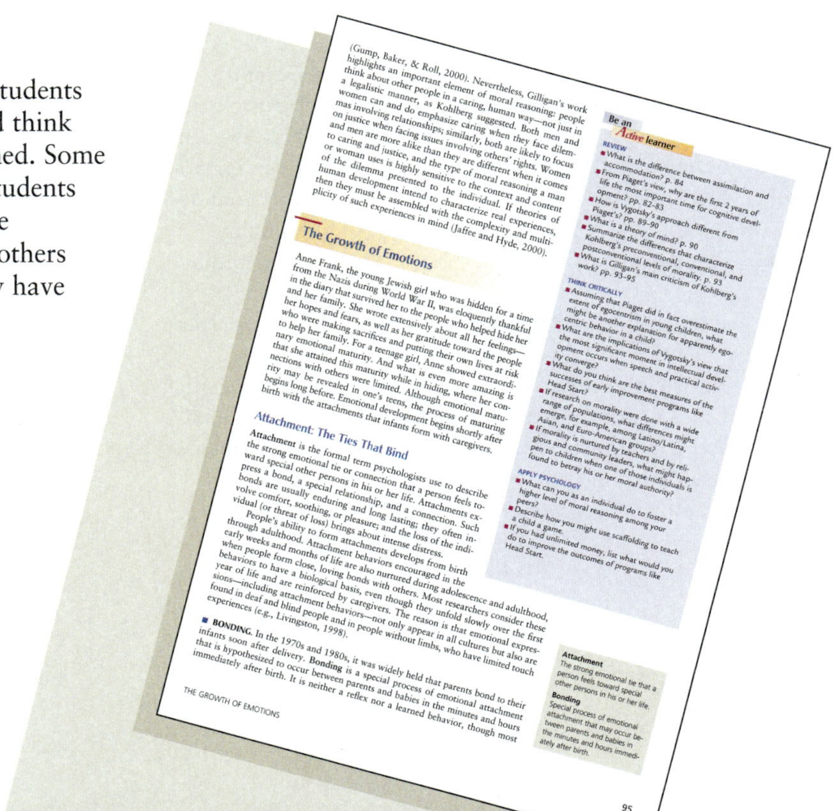

Introduction to Research Basics

We believe that research is a cornerstone of psychology, and the eighth edition of *Psychology* reflects an increased emphasis on its role. We reviewed every citation from the seventh edition and revised and updated all citations that correspond to the latest research in the field. We kept citations of classic studies from the history of psychological research.

We also believe that the research method should be contextualized within a book and that it is more important to focus on the analysis process rather than on actual data. To accomplish this, Linda Brannon has updated and rewritten the research information that appeared in Chapter 1. It now appears as a series of research lessons—one per chapter—called Introduction to Research Basics. Each box highlights a different research method used in psychological research, and connects it with chapter-related content. These boxes, as a group, stand as a series of lessons in research methodology.

		Research Method
Chapter 1	To Sleep, Perchance to Experiment	Experimental
Chapter 2	Correlation Is Not Causation	Correlational
Chapter 3	Understanding the Danger	Cross-Sectional Study
Chapter 4	Sibling Influences During Early Adolescence	Longitudinal and Cross-Sectional
Chapter 5	Have You Ever Smelled a Color?	Experimental
Chapter 6	Caught in a Maze	Descriptive
Chapter 8	Testing Very Long-Term Memory	Ex Post Facto Design
Chapter 9	Acquiring a First Language	Naturalistic Observation
Chapter 10	Seeing What You Expect to See	Experimental
Chapter 11	Sex Surveys	Survey and Sampling
Chapter 12	Are Personality Traits Stable?	Longitudinal Study
Chapter 13	Internet Use and Sociability	Ex Post Facto Design
Chapter 14	Racism and Reactivity	Experimental
Chapter 15	Cross-Cultural Factors in a Diagnosis	Case Study
Chapter 16	Prevention Instead of Treatment?	Experimental
Chapter 17	Sex Discrimination in Employment Interviews	Meta-Analysis

Psychology in Action

Psychology in Action boxes focus on how psychology can be applied to everyday life. We want students to leave their general psychology class with more than just memorized facts; we want them to gain a pronounced appreciation for the relationship between the theory they have learned and the lives they are leading.

psychology in action

Seeing Violence, Doing Violence

430

Chapter 12 PERSONALITY AND ITS ASSESSMENT

Chapter 1	Using Psychological Knowledge to Improve Performance
Chapter 2	Left-Handed in a Right-Handed World
Chapter 3	Children Read Emotional Cues Well
Chapter 3	Gender Stereotypes
Chapter 4	The Legacy of Divorce
Chapter 6	Sentenced to Meditate
Chapter 7	Getting Rid of Phobias
Chapter 7	Creating Fluid, Flexible Thinking
Chapter 8	Improving Justice
Chapter 9	Be a Critical Thinker
Chapter 9	Deaf People and Cochlear Implants
Chapter 10	The Abecedarian Intervention
Chapter 11	Lie Detectors and Emotion
Chapter 12	Seeing Violence, Doing Violence
Chapter 13	Why We Listen to What "They" Say
Chapter 14	Psychology and the Aftermath of September 11
Chapter 15	Preventing Suicide
Chapter 16	Choosing a Therapist
Chapter 16	A Token Economy
Chapter 17	Who Is at Risk for Excessive Drinking?

Student Voices

Student Voices is a new feature, found in the margins of the text. Current college students and recent graduates discuss why studying psychology is important to them and how they actively apply it in their own lives.

student voices

Katie LaRoche
Saint Anselm College

198

Chapter 6 CONSCIOUSNESS

Features That Have Stood the Test of Time

Brain and Behavior

The *Brain and Behavior* box reinforces one of the main themes of the text: the important role of biological and evolutionary topics within the rapidly changing field of psychology. The box introduces students to the role of recent research and touches upon topics such as geography and dyslexia, the aging brain and Alzheimer's disease, and neuroimaging and mental disorders.

Chapter 1	We've Come a Long Way
Chapter 2	The Special Case of Twins
Chapter 3	Critical Periods
Chapter 4	The Prevalence of Eating Disorders
Chapter 5	Geography and Dyslexia
Chapter 5	Seeing Pain
Chapter 6	Drug Addiction
Chapter 7	Conditioning in Addicts
Chapter 8	The Aging Brain and Alzheimer's Disease
Chapter 9	Is Cognition Hardwired in Any Way?
Chapter 10	Art, Creativity, and Intelligence
Chapter 11	Experiencing and Recognizing Fear
Chapter 12	The Genetics of Personality Traits
Chapter 13	Biological Aspects of Human Aggression
Chapter 14	Psychoneuroimmunology
Chapter 15	Neuroimaging and Mental Disorders—It's All in Your Brain
Chapter 16	A Best-Selling Medication—Prozac
Chapter 17	Forensic Psychology—DNA and the Law

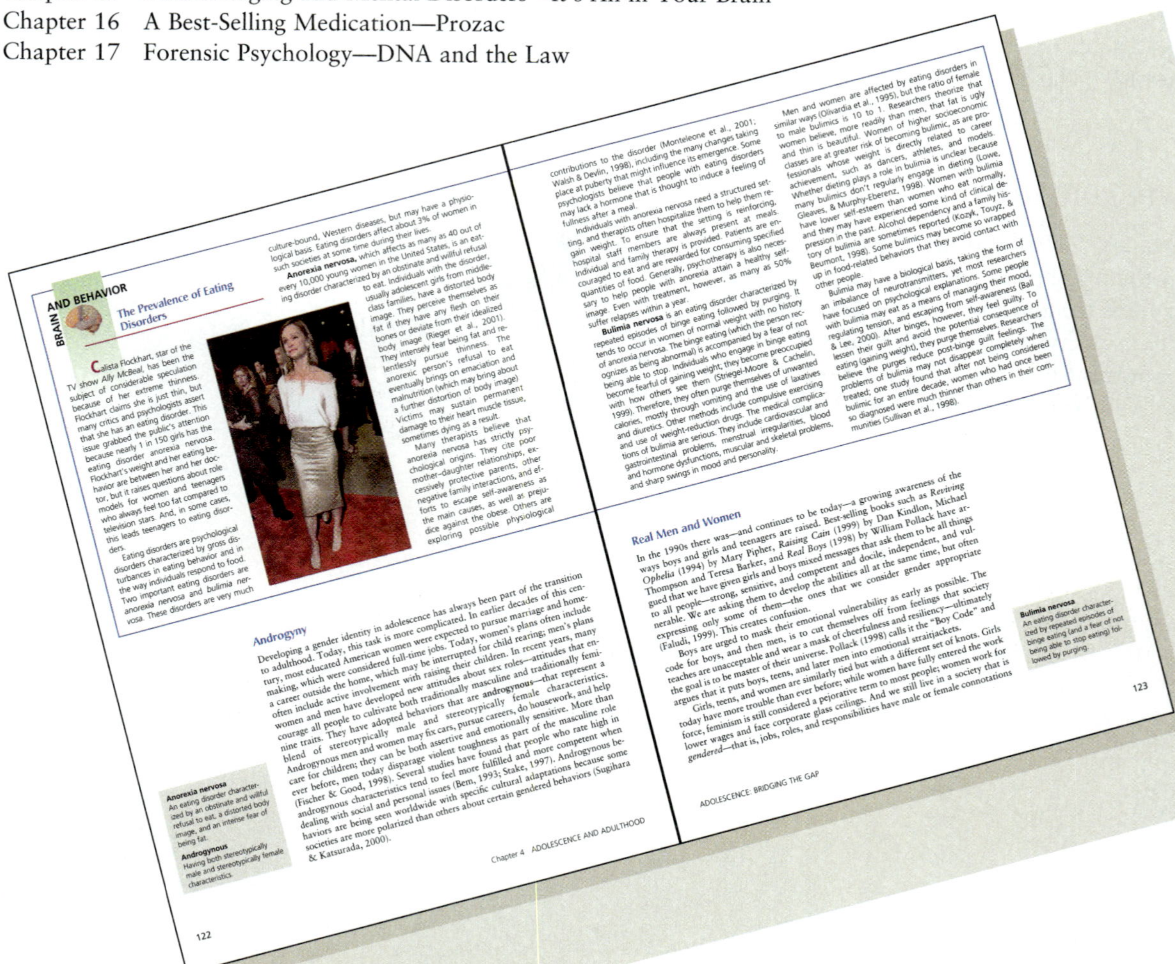

Building Tables

This feature, popular in previous editions, synthesizes the information presented in each chapter in a chart that provides a review at a glance. Aptly named, *Building Tables* build fact upon fact to ensure that students retain the most important concepts from each chapter.

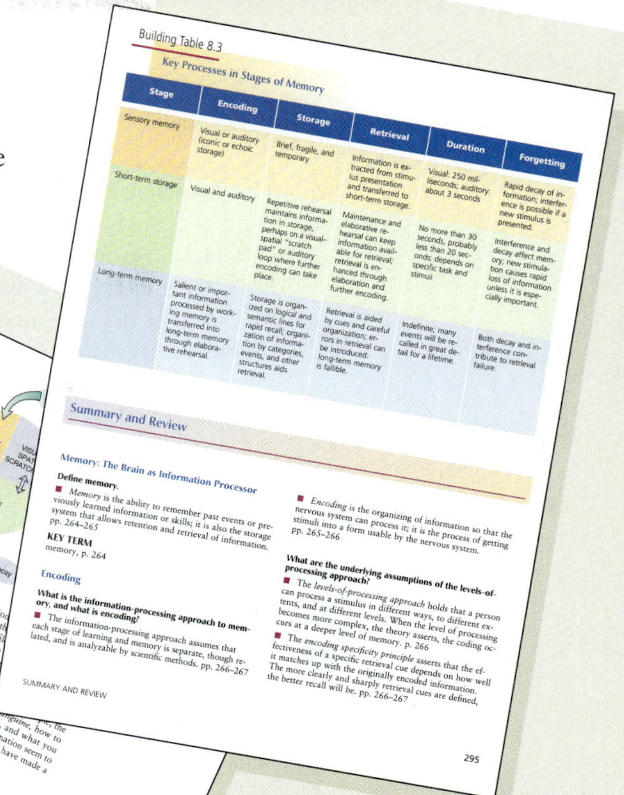

Reorganization of the Eighth Edition

The chapters on child development and on adolescent and adult development now follow the chapter on brain and behavior, in order to underscore the importance of development in the study of psychology and to introduce the complex relationship between nature and nurture. However, every chapter in the book has been written so that it can either stand alone or be read in sequence with others. Also, every chapter has been rewritten with the aim of providing a more structured approach, with a smoother, more cohesive flow of information. We have attempted to match the internal structure of each chapter with the way teachers present material.

Twentieth-Century American Artwork

Art and psychology can both be viewed as windows to the soul. The eighth edition capitalizes on this connection by drawing students into each chapter through the visual language of the 20th-century American artist. A carefully chosen piece of art appears at the beginning of each chapter, representing the glorious diversity of modern psychology. The art selections span the portfolios of a varied group of 20th-century artists. Both men and women are represented, as well as artists of various ethnicities and those who are famous as well as less well known. The idea is this: When students view the works of artists such as Jonathan Greene, Ruby Pearl, Andy Warhol, Margarett Sargent, and Jacob Lawrence, we want them to *feel* psychology as it moves through our modern age.

Supplements for Instructors

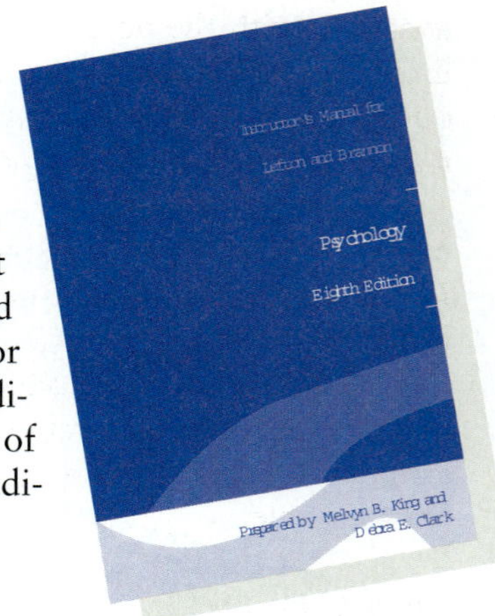

The *Instructor's Resource Manual,* written by Melvyn B. King of State University of New York–Cortland and Debra E. Clark, has been completely revamped for this edition. Each chapter begins with a valuable grid correlating the text to every print and media supplement available. King and Clark continue to correlate ancillary materials and instructor resources throughout their detailed lecture outlines. In addition, the *Instructor's Resource Manual* contains a wealth of activities, handouts, and numerous additional teaching aids.

Margaret Condon and Therese Scheupfer of Northeastern Illinois University have developed a lengthy *Test Bank*. Many of the items have been classroom-tested. More than 2,000 multiple-choice questions are available; to make the items more challenging to students, the authors have added a fifth answer option to each question. In addition, they have crafted numerous true/false, short answer, and longer essay questions to flesh out this robust *Test Bank,* which is also available on a dual platform CD-ROM. This computerized version is available with Tamarack's easy-to-use TestGen software, which lets you prepare tests for printing as well for network and online testing and has full editing capability for Windows and Macintosh.

The Allyn & Bacon Introduction to Psychology Transparency Set contains 200 full-color transparencies and is available upon adoption of the text from your local Allyn & Bacon sales representative.

The Allyn & Bacon Interactive Video, a 90-minute tape with on-screen critical thinking questions, has been developed to accompany Psychology. The accompanying video user's guide offers suggestions for using the video in class and contains a summary of each video segment.

Course Compass, BlackBoard, WebCT—Allyn & Bacon's course management systems—combine premium online content with enhanced class management tools such as quizzing and grading, syllabus building, and results reporting. See *www.abinteractive.com* for more information.

The *Digital Media Archive* 3.0 is a CD-ROM that contains hundreds of full-color digitized images, as well as video clips, audio clips, web links, activities, and lecture outlines to enhance introductory psychology lectures.

A *PowerPoint CD-ROM* presentation for Windows, which includes an electronic copy of the *Instructor's Resource Manual,* as well as a link to the book's companion website, was prepared by Albert M. Bugaj of University of Wisconsin–Marinette and is available to adopters of the book.

A *Companion Website* was designed to accompany this eighth edition. Access is available with the purchase of a new textbook; available on this free site is an online study guide, which includes chapter learning objectives and multiple-choice questions. The site also contains video, interactive activities, and web links. See *www. ablongman.com/lefton8e* for a sample of the site.

Mind Matters CD-ROM was developed by James Hilton of the University of Michigan and Charles Perdue of West Virginia University, this CD-ROM is available to be packaged with your text. A unique learning tool, the CD-ROM helps students explore psychology by combining interactivity with clear explanation, fostering active learning and reinforcing core concepts. Visit *www.abacon.com/mindmatters* for sample activities. Both a print copy and a downloadable copy of a *Faculty Guide* are available.

Allyn & Bacon Video Library makes available to instructors an extensive videotape library. Please see your local Allyn & Bacon sales representative for details regarding the video policy.

Supplements for Students

Grade Aid, a workbook by Andy Ryan, a police psychologist who teaches at the University of South Carolina, actively involves students in the learning process. For each chapter, *Grade Aid* features chapter summaries, learning objectives, activities and exercises, practice tests, and short answer/essay questions, to help students grasp the concepts in the text.

iSearch for Psychology contains material on conducting web searches and critically evaluating and documenting Internet sources. It also contains material specific to using the Internet in the study of psychology through Internet activities, as well as lists of URLs related to the discipline. The *iSearch* also contains an access code for entrance to ContentSelect, Pearson Education's online database of peer reviewed and discipline-specific journals. Students can conduct online research anywhere and any time they have an internet connection.

Psych Tutor, a service of Allyn & Bacon, provides free tutoring for students who purchase a new text. Qualified college psychology instructors tutor students on all material covered in the text, including art and figures. The Tutor Center provides tutoring assistance by phone, fax, e-mail, and the Internet, during Tutor Center hours. Students who bought used books can purchase the Psych Tutor for $25 at *www.aw.com/tutorcenter.*

Premium Resource CD combines a compilation of chapter-specific video clips with critical thinking questions, and links directly to the companion website. Clips include coverage of such topies as the human genome project, anorexia, alcoholism in teens, a gender study, hypnosis, lucid dreaming, phobias, and more.

Acknowledgments

We thank the following people who prepared special marketing reviews to assist us in gauging trends in the field and to provide us with their own valuable input to our draft manuscript of the eighth edition:

Lee Fernandez, Modesto Junior College
Alicia Grandey, Pennsylvania State University
Emmett Lampkin, Kirkwood Community College
Jerry Marshall, Green River Community College
Mark Mitchell, Clarion University
Merryl Patterson, Austin Community College

We also thank the following people who reviewed the seventh edition in preparation for our writing of the eighth edition:

Joseph Bilotta, Western Kentucky University
Victor Broderick, Ferris State University
Brad Caskey, University of Wisconsin–River Falls
Stephen Chew, Samford University
David Coddington, Midwestern State University
Patrick R. Conley, University of Illinois–Chicago
Randolph R. Cornelius, Vassar College
Orlando Correa, Hartford Community College
Tamara J. Ferguson, Utah State University
Scott Geller, Virginia Polytechnic Institute and State University
Judy Gentry, Columbus State Community College
Harvey Ginsburg, University of Southwest Texas State
Ronald Jacques, Brigham Young University–Idaho
James Johnson, Illinois State University–Normal
Edward Harmon Jones, University of Wisconsin–Madison
Tracy L. Kahan, Santa Clara University
Kevin Keating, Broward Community College
Melvyn B. King, SUNY–Cortland
Stephen Klein, Mississippi State University
Gary Levy, University of Wyoming
Michele Lewis, Northern Virginia Community College
Fred Medway, University of South Carolina
Jeffrey Mio, California State Polytechnic University–Pomona
Margie Nauta, Illinois State University
Shannon Rich, Texas Woman's University
Deborah Richardson, University of Georgia
Larry Rosenblum, University of California–Riverside
Alan Searleman, St. Lawrence University
Michael Selby, California Polytechnic State University
N. Clayton Silver, University of Nevada–Las Vegas
Pamela Stewart, Northern Virginia Community College–Annandale
W. Scott Terry, University of North Carolina–Charlotte
Michelle Tomarelli, Texas A&M University
German Torres, SUNY–Buffalo
Kim Ujcich, Middle Tennessee State University
Lisa Whitten, SUNY–Old Westbury
Michael Zickar, Bowling Green State University

We owe a huge debt of thanks to the people at Allyn and Bacon for their support, guidance, and assistance. Carolyn Merrill's confidence, management, support, and careful handling have been essentially important for both of us. A first-class editor and publisher, she is also a first-class person. Kelly Perkins and Anne Weaver helped us think creatively and write carefully; their insights were helpful. Allyn and Bacon's production department reinvigorated the eighth edition with the professional skills of designer/page maker Deborah Schneck and copy editor Susanna Brougham. Susan McNally facilitated the process of production at a time that we appreciated a calm, smooth, and methodical force. We also thank Joyce Nilsen and Marcie Mealia for their dedicated efforts in selling our book.

Students always deserve thanks because they teach us, and we acknowledge that situation and thank them for doing so. We thank Grant Bursek and Chris May who helped in library research. We thank several staffers, including Maxine Cogar and Pat Harrison, who helped us with logistical support. We also owe thanks to our colleagues in our psychology departments, who offered expert advice and cheerleading, each at the appropriate times. Several colleagues were especially helpful to me (LB), including Jess Feist, Diana Odom Gunn, Patrick Moreno, Cam Melville, Dena Matzenbacher, and Jan Disney.

We have friends and relatives who have supported and inspired us in various ways through the years, and their love, encouragement, and friendship mean a great deal to us. I (LL) thank Gene and Lois Green, Al and Susan Waxenberg, Stephen and Nancy Guerrera, Marcy and Jason Mallett. I also thank Frank Provenzano, Len Rosen, Ed Caress, Sandi Kirschner, and Bill Barke—each in his or her own way has helped me enormously. I thank my friend, mentor, and teacher Arnold Rubin for his enduring support; his untimely passing has left a gulf in many people's lives. And my love to my daughters, Sarah and Jesse, who inspire and bring me pride every day.

Our spouses deserve special recognition. Linda Lefton and Barry Humphus have encouraged and supported us in this daunting task, and they deserve even more than the love and thanks that we offer. They are our friends, lovers, and spouses—they are our best friends. What more can we say?

Lester A. Lefton
Linda Brannon

Two Careers in Psychology

I love teaching psychology. I hope my students here at Tulane University like the way I do it. My teaching technique and style began over three decades ago. My career in psychology began with a survey of sexual attitudes that I conducted in high school. I passed out questionnaires to the juniors and seniors, who were to respond anonymously. Then I spent days poring over, collating, and summarizing the data—which I, of course, found fascinating.

At Northeastern University in Boston, I majored in psychology and was particularly interested in clinical psychology. I took courses in traditional experimental psychology—learning, physiology, perception—but especially enjoyed abnormal psychology, child development, and personality. While in college, I worked in a treatment center for emotionally disturbed children. The work was hard, emotionally grueling, and stressful, and the pay wasn't particularly good—thus, the direct delivery of mental health services began to lose some of its appeal for me. Later, as a laboratory assistant, I collected and analyzed data for a psychologist doing research in vision. In contrast to my counseling experience, hunting for answers to scientific questions and collecting data were activities that held my interest.

My graduate studies at the University of Rochester included research in perception, and I studied visual information processing. In graduate school, my intellectual skills were sharpened and my interests were focused and refined. After earning my PhD, I became a faculty member at the University of South Carolina. My research in cognitive psychology involved studying perceptual phenomena such as eye movements. Now at Tulane University, I teach, do research, and write psychology textbooks. My goal is to share my excitement about psychology in the classroom, in my textbooks, and in professional journals.

Over time, my interests have changed, as I'm sure yours will. At first, I was interested in the delivery of mental health services to children. Later, I focused on applied research issues, such as eye movements among learning-disabled readers. But my primary focus remains in basic research issues. My evolving interests have spanned the three major areas in which psychologists work: applied research, human services, and experimental psychology—topics I present throughout the text.

I am married to a wonderful woman and have two daughters. I have applied in my family life much of what I have learned in my profession. My family hasn't been angry about it, although from time to time my "psychologizing" about issues can be annoying, I'm sure. I'm an avid bicyclist and computer hacker and occasional photographer. My life has generally revolved around my work and my family—not necessarily in that order. You'll probably gather that from many of the stories and examples I relate in this text.

I invite you to share in my excitement and my enthusiasm for psychology. Stay focused, read closely, and think critically. As you read, think about how the text relates to your own experiences—drawing personal connections to what you read will make it more meaningful. And please feel free to write me: *Lefton@tulane.edu.* Good luck!

Lester Lefton

My career in psychology began when I kept taking psychology courses as an undergraduate at the University of Texas at Austin. I was going to be a drama major, but I just couldn't stay away from the psychology courses because I was intrigued by how people understand the world in terms of language. Other areas of psychology, such as social psychology and child development, were almost equally exciting. Deciding which one to pursue was difficult, but I chose the program in human experimental psychology at the University of Texas at Austin.

During my years in graduate school, I was involved in researching language and cognitive processes. I spent many hours in the laboratory, collecting and analyzing data, and attempting to understand. The results of research studies fascinated me. I loved the data, and the printouts, and the patterns that the analyses revealed.

Toward the end of my doctoral studies, I got to teach a course in introductory psychology, and I also discovered that I loved teaching. When I finished my doctoral degree, I went to McNeese State University in Lake Charles, Louisiana. McNeese emphasizes teaching, and I taught a variety of courses, specializing in experimental psychology and biopsychology as well as continuing to teach introductory psychology.

In the early 1980s, I became interested in the developing field of health psychology. Along with Jess Feist, one of my colleagues in the department of psychology, I began to write a textbook for this new area. The result is *Health Psychology: An Introduction to Behavior and Health,* which is now in its fifth edition.

When I was a graduate student, a minority of students were women, but that situation changed, bringing changes to the entire field of psychology. It was exciting to be part of that transition and to watch women come into the discipline in large numbers. My research interest turned to gender issues, and an editor at Allyn and Bacon persuaded me that I should write a textbook on the topic. *Gender: Psychological Perspectives* is the result, and the course that I teach on the psychology of gender is one of my favorites.

I teach, do research in the area of gender, and write textbooks. In 1998, I was selected to be Distinguished Professor of the year at McNeese State University. I am married to a terrific guy, Barry Humphus, who has encouraged and helped me do things I did not think I could do, such as write three textbooks. I love movies (and movie trivia) and find wine both delicious and fascinating. I am an occasional hiker and reluctant jogger.

My students never stop teaching me, and I am grateful to them. Both Lester and I invite you to share our excitement and enthusiasm for psychology. If you want to tell me anything, contact me at *lbrannon@lightwire.net.*

Linda Brannon

Psychology

1 What Is Psychology?

Jacob Lawrence, *The Library*, 1960

Imagine this scene: A group of people are discussing how to accomplish a commonly agreed upon goal. This is not always a respectful discussion, and some group members criticize and even insult others as they disagree about what they need to do next. Some members form partnerships or alliances but do not always tell the truth or keep their promises to their buddies. Too often members compete rather than cooperate, and many express their emotions in unpleasant and sometimes even violent ways. When violence occurs, it is usually perpetrated by a man. When someone cries, it is usually a woman. Indeed, the women and men often behave in ways considered stereotypical for their gender.

Over the past few years, this type of scene has occurred again and again on the popular new type of television show called Reality TV. These programs place groups of people in unusual and often competitive situations, and viewers watch them interact. On *Real World, Survivor, Big Brother,* and *Temptation Island,* human behavior is big entertainment. It can be intriguing to see how the players/actors/participants "use psychology" to influence others and gain advantage; their actions, words, and emotions can seem genuine and spontaneous.

chapter outline

■ *On* Real World, Survivor, Big Brother, *and* Temptation Island, *human behavior is big entertainment.*

Viewers find such shows compelling in part because they want to understand human behavior and relationships. However, Reality TV actually tells incredibly little about real people. For one thing, the cast does not represent the range of humanity—cast members are usually chosen for their good looks, taut bodies, charisma, or energy. Events are scripted to maximize entertainment value, encouraging viewers to root for certain characters and dislike others. Also, the settings scarcely resemble reality—few people inhabit remote islands, live in multi-million-dollar homes, or compete every day for cash prizes. In fact, there may be a danger in taking Reality TV seriously. The characters might be mistaken for models of "ideal people," though their behavior and values rarely seem ideal as they often tell untruths, taunt others, feign kindness, or try to win at any cost. Also, these programs often ridicule values that most Americans embrace; for example, *Temptation Island* shows no respect for faithfulness in a committed relationship. Although it little resembles reality, Reality TV might influence some viewers' ideas and behaviors.

Popular culture, including television, has created and nurtured some exaggerated ideas of what psychology is and what psychologists do. For example, one image of a research psychologist is a man in a white coat, running rats through a maze. Though such experiments do in fact take place, today the researcher is almost as likely to be a woman, and the white coat is not necessary. During the 1940s and 1950s, white rats were the most common experimental subjects in research on learning, the most popular focus of research at the time. But this has changed—humans have replaced rats as the most common participants in psychology research, and learning is only one of many areas of study in psychology. Psychology is a much more varied field than the image implies.

Another typical picture shows a patient lying on a couch while a therapist, steeped in the theories of Sigmund Freud, quietly takes notes. Again, this image only partly reflects reality: Freud was important in pioneering therapeutic methods to help people understand and deal with problems, and many psychologists offer therapy to individuals. Yet the ideas of Freud reflect only one part of the history and theory of psychology, and Freud's therapeutic techniques are not used by many psychologists today. This image is also too limited.

A third analysis of psychology holds that, when all is said and done, psychological understanding is nothing more than common sense about how people behave. Actually, common sense is usually based on hindsight and casual observation. **Psychology** is the science of human behavior and mental processes, and it differs from common sense precisely because it is a science. Rather than casual observation,

Psychology
The science of behavior and mental processes.

psychologists use rigorous, systematic observation that yields comprehensive theories and reliable knowledge. The many subfields of psychological research have produced information on how people grow up and become independent, how people interact in relationships, and how they learn and remember, sleep and dream, perceive the world, and live fulfilling lives. Psychology also explores perplexing issues such as violence, drug abuse, and other problem behavior. This exciting field is daily stretching the boundaries of what we know about people, their relationships, and their inner world of thought and feeling.

■ *During the 1940s and 1950s, white rats were the most common experimental subjects in research on learning.*

Reality TV may give the illusion of studying human behavior, but psychology is the science that actually does so. Those who want to understand real human behavior and relationships will need to look farther than the TV set. Taking courses in psychology and studying this book will be a good way to begin. In this chapter we will discuss the discipline of psychology, its role as a science, its history, and its future. And you will see there are recurring themes.

Four Recurring Themes in Psychology

Throughout this book, we will introduce you to the world of psychology through the use of four key organizing themes. The first emphasizes the *action-oriented* quality of research and practice in psychology. Psychologists generate knowledge and ideas, and then they put them to use. How can they improve memory, learning, or social adjustment? How can they help people manage their lives and relationships? Questions like these will be addressed in the main text and in features called *Psychology in Action.*

The second theme involves the relationship between *the brain and behavior*. The structure and function of the brain, and the rest of the nervous system, have a huge impact on personality, communication, physical health, emotions, and many other areas of life. Current studies of the brain include how the brain changes over the life span and how drugs affect it, both positively and negatively. Because the brain is so central to human thought and behavior, it has long been closely studied by psychologists. Features called *Brain and Behavior* will highlight this fascinating topic.

The interaction of *nature* and *nurture* is the third theme that we will return to again and again. Nature (our biological and genetic composition) and nurture (the many elements of the environment we live in) both have important roles in shaping human thought and behavior. A lively debate concerning which is more influential, and how the two elements work together, has a long history in psychology, and continues today. This book will focus on how nature and nurture interact to affect intelligence, sexual behavior, and other areas, presenting the latest research and theories.

Finally, we will take into account the range of *human diversity* as we study psychology. Gender, ethnicity, social class, sexual orientation, age, religion, and other identities and influences play important roles in shaping people's ideas and actions. Not too long ago, many psychologists focused

Be an *Active* learner

REVIEW

- Why is psychology considered a science and not just common sense? pp. 5–6
- What makes psychology an action-oriented discipline? p. 6

THINK CRITICALLY

- Why must psychologists consider the interaction of nature and nurture rather than choosing one over the other?
- How would ignoring diversity limit psychology?

APPLY PSYCHOLOGY

- Watch several episodes of Reality TV and make notes on how the participants "use psychology" on each other. Keep these notes and compare this portrayal of psychology to the information you learn as you read this book.

their studies only on people of European or European American descent, believing that they set the norm for humanity. Fortunately, this is no longer the case. Today psychologists try to eliminate such bias from their research and appreciate how *cultural context* can affect areas such as child development, relationships, and personality. This book will often feature cross-cultural research and the experiences of diverse groups of people.

What Is This Science of Psychology?

Psychologists use scientific principles, methods, and procedures to develop an organized body of knowledge and to predict how people will behave. Psychology is considered a social and behavioral science because it deals with both human behavior and mental processes. *Mental processes* include thought and ideas as well as more complex reasoning processes. Psychologists make inferences about mental processes by observing *overt actions,* directly observable and measurable movements or the results of such movements. Overt actions include a range of behaviors: walking and gesturing, social interactions such as talking to someone, and emotional responses such as laughing. These behaviors are called overt because they are directly observable. Certain physiological reactions, such as heart rate and patterns of brain activity, must be measured with instruments, but the instruments make these responses observable.

Psychologists place so much emphasis on behavior that they have declared the years 2000–2010 the "Decade of Behavior." Through their national organization, the American Psychological Association (APA), psychologists launched an initiative to focus attention on the contributions of the behavioral and social sciences in addressing many of society's daunting challenges—including child abuse and neglect, violence against women, safety and security in our communities, and the critical issue of health care. Closely related to these goals are educating people to learn and think critically, training workers to be more efficient and productive, and sensitizing people to the scope of diversity. Achieving these goals will require the application of an extensive knowledge base, which psychologists have built through scientific research. Psychologists often think of themselves as detectives, sifting through data and theories in an orderly way to uncover the causes of behavior.

Like other modern sciences, psychology is based on two premises—empiricism and theory development. According to the principle of **empiricism,** knowledge must be acquired through careful observation rather than from logic or intuition. Collecting useful empirical data requires researchers to set aside their personal biases and strive to be objective. After gathering and studying such data, psychologists are able to formulate theories. A psychological **theory** is a collection of interrelated ideas and observations that together describe, explain, and predict behavior and mental processes. Empirical observation leads to theories; thus, empirical data and theories are the basics of psychology.

Three Principles of Scientific Endeavor

Empiricism
The view that knowledge should be acquired through observation and often an experiment.

Theory
A collection of interrelated ideas and facts put forward to describe, explain, and predict behavior and mental processes.

Psychology is committed to empiricism—the view that knowledge is acquired through observation. Careful observation requires trying to be objective, gathering information systematically, and maintaining a healthy skepticism when studying behavior and mental processes. By following these basic principles, psychologists become scientific researchers. These principles can also help you be a critical thinker in your daily life.

■ **OBJECTIVITY.** For psychologists, objectivity means evaluating research and theory on their merits, without preconceived ideas and without allowing personal bias to enter the process. By becoming aware of and putting aside personal bias, researchers are better able to make objective observations and fair evaluations. This requirement is very difficult because, like everyone else, scientists are people with feelings and convictions, who live in a particular social context. Psychologists must set aside personal views about people and society when entering the laboratory, which is not easy. But when researchers bring their biases into their research, they fail to be good scientists. Unfortunately, the history of psychology (and other sciences) is filled with instances of bias. For example, during the 19th century, the intelligence of people of African descent was assumed to be lower than that of European peoples. This prejudiced view led to scientific research that supported this opinion. A neurologist named Morton found that people of African descent had smaller brains and were thus less intelligent than those of European descent (Gould, 1996). That view was wrong; brain size does not vary with ethnic background. Morton saw what he expected to see rather than what his data showed. His research was contaminated because he failed to be objective.

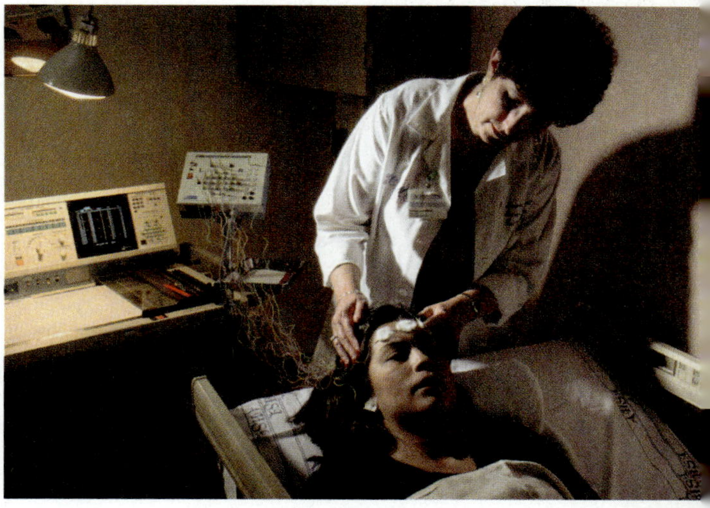

■ *Certain physiological reactions, such as patterns of brain activity, must be measured with instruments to be observable.*

■ **SYSTEMATICITY.** To do scientific research, one must be systematic—that is, a plan is necessary for gathering data. People who gather information without a systematic plan are doing casual observation rather than collecting scientific data. For example, a person who believes that seatbelt use is dangerous can find information to support that view. Citing cases in which people have been thrown free of automobile crashes can appear to support the belief that seatbelts are dangerous. However, a systematic collection of information from many accident reports leads to the conclusion that seatbelts save rather than endanger lives. A systematic method of collecting data is essential to good science, and many such methods exist. The experimental method is a favorite, both of psychologists and other researchers.

■ **HEALTHY SKEPTICISM.** One needn't be a scientific researcher to realize that although life is full of incredible events, people's reports of strange phenomena must be taken with a grain of salt. This caution also applies to scientific research. It is easy to be skeptical about stories of alien abduction, but information presented at scientific meetings or appearing in research journals is often not viewed with the same skepticism. It should be. Psychologists maintain a healthy skepticism: a cautious view of data, hypotheses, and theory until results are repeated, verified, and established over time. Healthy skepticism applies to all phases of scientific inquiry.

The Scientific Method in Psychology

As they develop theories that describe, explain, predict, and manage behavior, psychologists use the same method as other scientists. The **scientific method** is the technique used in psychology to discover knowledge about human behavior and mental processes; it involves *stating the problem, developing a hypothesis, designing a study, collecting and analyzing data,* and *drawing conclusions and reporting results.*

Let's consider these five basic steps of the scientific method as an overview of how psychologists (and other scientists) do their work.

Scientific method
In psychology, the techniques used to discover knowledge about human behavior and mental processes; in experimentation, the scientific method involves stating the problem, developing hypotheses, designing a study, collecting and analyzing data (which often includes manipulating some part of the environment to better understand existing conditions that led to a behavior or phenomenon), replicating results, and drawing conclusions and reporting results.

■ **STATE THE PROBLEM.** Psychologists must first ask questions that can be answered, that is, questions that are stated in a way that allows investigation. Psychologists refine some of the techniques used by other scientists in order to deal with the subtleties of human behavior. The typical scientific research process in psychology is systematic and begins with a specific, narrowly defined question. For

introduction to research basics

To Sleep, Perchance to Experiment

Let's walk through a research study looking at some of the key processes. Imagine that you were a researcher interested in sleep, especially the effects of sleep loss. Robert Stickgold and his colleagues (Stickgold, James, & Hobson, 2000) were such researchers; they were interested in the effects of sleep deprivation, specifically its effects on memory. They chose an *experimental design* to investigate this question.

HYPOTHESIS Initially researchers form a *hypothesis,* a tentative statement or idea expressing a relationship between two variables. The hypothesis for the sleep deprivation study was that participants deprived of sleep would show poorer memory than those allowed to sleep after learning.

VARIABLES Stickgold and his colleagues trained participants on a visual memory task in which participants had to recall a specific visual pattern after a brief presentation of the pattern, a time lapse, and the presentation of a different pattern. This task is confusing and difficult, and people tend to improve slowly with practice. The researchers manipulated the timing of participants' sleep. Therefore, sleep deprivation was the *independent* (manipulated) *variable.* The *dependent variable* was the participants' performance on the visual memory task.

PARTICIPANTS The participants in the study were 133 people between the ages of 18 and 25.

CONTROL AND EXPERIMENTAL GROUPS The sleep deprivation study compared two groups of participants, one of which was allowed to sleep after learning the visual memory task; the other was not.

PROCEDURE The participants all learned the same task, which took between 60 and 90 minutes. The participants who were deprived of sleep stayed awake for 30 hours and then were tested on the task. The participants who were allowed to sleep normally were also tested again after the same time interval.

RESULTS Those participants who were deprived of sleep for 30 hours after learning showed poorer memory for the task than those participants who slept. By comparing the performance on the task (the dependent variable) of the experimental and control groups, the researchers determined that the independent variable (sleep deprivation) was responsible for the difference in the dependent variable between the groups.

CONCLUSIONS A study of this type allows researchers to infer that sleep is important in memory formation. The participants who had slept showed better memory for the task they learned than those who were not allowed to sleep. This research certainly has implications for college students and studying—the common practice of staying awake late at night to study may not be as wise as it seems because

instance, if you ask an overly broad question such as "What is the mind?" you will make little headway toward an answer. But questions such as "Does the type of reward affect children's willingness to practice a musical instrument?" or "Does St.John's wort work as well as Prozac in treating depression?" can be investigated.

Hypothesis
A tentative statement or idea expressing a causal relationship between two events or variables that is to be evaluated in a research study.

Experiment
A procedure in which a researcher systematically manipulates and observes elements of a situation in order to test a hypothesis and make a cause-and-effect statement.

Variable
A condition or characteristic of a situation or a person that is subject to change (it varies) within or across situations or individuals.

■ **DEVELOP A HYPOTHESIS.** In the second step of the scientific method, psychologists make an educated guess about the answer to the question they've posed. Such a formulation is called a **hypothesis**—a tentative statement or idea expressing a relationship concerning events or variables included in a research study. A hypothesis might put forth that rewards will prompt children to practice a musical instrument.

Most often, a hypothesis emerges from a theory, which psychologists have developed based on their current knowledge and past research. As previously defined, a *theory* is a collection of interrelated ideas and information that describes, explains, and predicts behavior and mental processes. For example, theories of reinforcement address the power of different types of reinforcement, including positive reinforcement (reward). A theory must organize data well, and it must suggest testable predictions (hypotheses) that can be used to check the theory. Such testing usually occurs within the context of a well-designed research study.

■ **DESIGN A STUDY.** Next, researchers choose an approach to test the hypothesis. They identify key variables and responses, and then choose a technique that will help them answer the question that prompted the study. Psychological research

sleep deprivation interferes with forming memories for learned information. In addition, the sleep deprivation study indicated that making up lost sleep does not improve memory—the experimental group participants, even after being allowed to sleep, still did not show the same memory improvement that occurred in participants from the control group. Therefore, sleeping can boost memory, and the timing of sleep is an important factor in its benefits.

LIMITATIONS AND PROBLEMS Even successful studies have limitations. For example, the study on sleep deprivation used young adults as participants, and that choice in itself is a limitation. Psychology research tends to include small samples of participants. A **sample** is a group of participants who represent a larger group. In this case, the larger group is all young adults between the ages of 18 and 25. The extent to which this age group differs from the general population limits the ways in which research can generalize their results. What holds true for young adults may not be true for the general population. Therefore, the sampling process represents a limitation for psychology research.

Good experiments allow researchers to draw conclusions about cause and effect relationships between independent and dependent variables. Though this basic plan is simple, arranging for two (or more) groups to be equal in all-important ways except for the independent variable and choosing and measuring an appropriate dependent variable are not easy tasks. Before researchers can suggest that one situation causes another, they have to be sure that several specific conditions are met. A relationship between the variables is not sufficient to determine that one caused the other. *Correlational studies* demonstrate a relationship between two variables, but correlated variables may not be causally related. This caution is an important one. The Introduction to Research Basics box in Chapter 2 describes correlational studies and emphasizes how these studies do not allow researchers to determine causation.

Bias can enter the research process at many points, and researchers must be careful in making design choices to minimize these biases. They pay close attention to how the data are collected and to whether the results of a study are repeatable in additional experiments. To make meaningful causal inferences, researchers must create situations in which they can limit the likelihood of obtaining a result that is simply a chance occurrence or caused by irrelevant factors. Only by using carefully formulated experiments can researchers make sound interpretations of results and cautiously extend them to other situations.

We will present some of the problems that plague research design and show how scientists solve these problems in Introduction to Research Basics boxes throughout the book. We have concentrated on the experimental method because researchers favor this method, but scientific research in psychology includes a variety of methods, each with advantages and limitations. Other methods of inquiry will be presented in the Introduction to Research Basics boxes, along with their strengths and limitations.

The research process is central to psychological inquiry, but it can be applied to your own thinking. Indeed, thinking critically—not only about psychology research but also about other issues—can make you a more effective student.

often takes the form of an **experiment**—a procedure in which researchers systematically manipulate and observe elements of a situation in order to answer a question and, usually, to establish a cause and effect relationship. In addition, they must define their terms and determine how to make measurements.

Researchers must select the variables to include in a study. A **variable** is a condition or a characteristic of a situation or a person that is subject to change (it varies) either within or across situations or individuals. In an experiment, there are two types of variables—independent variables and dependent variables. The **independent variable** is the variable that the experimenter directly and purposely manipulates to see what changes occur as a result of the manipulation. The **dependent variable** is the behavior or response that is expected to change because of manipulation of the independent variable. For example, researchers who believe that a reward influences behavior might manipulate the presence of the reward, the type of reward, the amount of reward, or the timing of reward as the independent variable. A researcher could arrange for some children who are learning to play a musical instrument to receive a reward for practicing at home while others receive no reward. The behavior that the researcher wants to change would be the dependent variable. In this example, time spent practicing is the dependent variable.

Researchers try to be as precise as possible in defining independent and dependent variables. To do so, they often use an **operational definition,** a definition of a variable in terms of the set of methods or procedures used to measure or study that variable. Saying that *reward* is the independent variable is not very precise;

Sample
A group of participants who are assumed to be representative of the population about which an inference is being made.

Independent variable
The variable in a controlled experiment that the experimenter directly and purposely manipulates to see how the other variables under study will be affected.

Dependent variable
The variable in a controlled experiment that is expected to change because of the manipulation of the independent variable.

Operational definition
A definition of a variable in terms of the set of methods or procedures used to measure or study that variable.

many definitions of *reward* are possible. Using an operational definition, researchers would need to specify that the reward was a 1-ounce candy bar or 30 minutes of access to a video game, delivered to the child upon completion of one hour of practice. In addition, the researcher could operationalize the definition of *dependent variable,* time spent practicing, by measuring the number of minutes that the children spend playing their musical instruments (and not just time spent in the practice room).

Researchers must determine whether it is actually the change in the manipulated variable—not some unknown extraneous (outside) factor—that causes a change in the dependent variable. To examine such an issue, researchers often use more than one group of participants so that they can make a comparison. **Participants** are individuals who take part in experiments and whose behavior is observed and recorded. (In previous decades, psychologists called participants *subjects,* but that term is now reserved for nonhumans.) The attributes that participants must have in common depend on what the experimenter is testing. For example, in the study on rewards for musical practice, the participants must be children who are learning to play a musical instrument.

Once the participants are known to be comparable on important attributes, they are assigned randomly to either the experimental or the control (comparison) group. *Random assignment* means that the participants are assigned by lottery rather than on the basis of any particular characteristic, preference, or situation that might have even a remote possibility of influencing the outcome. The **experimental group** is the group of participants who receive the new treatment. Thus, some psychologists refer to the experimental group as the *treatment group.* The **control group** is the comparison group—the group of participants who are tested on the dependent variable in the same way as the experimental group but who do not receive the new treatment. In the study with rewards for practice, one group might receive a favorite food or permission to play video games for half an hour as a reward, while the others receive no reward for practicing.

If the researcher is confident that all the children were equally reluctant to practice before the beginning of the experiment—that is, that the two groups are truly comparable—then he or she can conclude that the manipulation is the cause of the experimental group's change in level of practicing. Unless the researcher uses comparable groups, the effect of the treatment will not be clear, and few real conclusions can be drawn from the data. In addition, if some extraneous, irrelevant variable enters the experiment, then the experiment can also be impossible to interpret clearly. *Extraneous variables* are factors that affect the results of an experiment but that are not of interest to the experimenter. Examples of an extraneous variable are the parents' encouragement for practicing, the music teachers' behavior during lessons, and the children's initial motivation to learn. When extraneous variables intrude during an experiment (or just before it), they may *confound results*—make the data difficult to interpret.

COLLECT AND ANALYZE DATA. After researchers have specified the key variables, chosen the participants, and considered ways of controlling for extraneous variance, they conduct the study, hoping it will yield interpretable, meaningful results. Techniques for data collection must be carefully chosen so as not to bias the results in favor of one hypothesis or another. The data collected must also be organized, coded, and simplified in a way that allows a reasonable set of conclusions to be drawn. When a researcher has gathered 10,000

student voices

Stephanie Stevens
Utah Valley State College

When I was 17, I started a job working with psychologists. I started just answering phones, modifying forms for the therapists... a lot of paperwork. I then started scoring tests and helping out with research projects. In working closely with the psychologists and seeing the impact they made on other people's lives, I fell in love with it.

Be an *Active* Learner

REVIEW
- Identify three key principles to which scientists must be committed. pp. 6–7
- Describe the steps in the scientific method. pp. 7–11
- Distinguish between independent and dependent variables and between control and experimental groups. pp. 9–10

THINK CRITICALLY
- How can researchers introduce personal bias into an experiment?
- What problems can arise when considering research done on rats and generalizing its conclusions to humans?

APPLY PSYCHOLOGY
- You may have read that scientists have hypothesized that estrogen replacement therapy may lessen a woman's chances of developing Alzheimer's disease, a progressive degenerative disorder affecting memory. What questions would you ask, and what issues would concern you, in testing this hypothesis?

observations on 300 participants, something must be done to organize all the information. Psychologists usually use statistical methods to help summarize and condense the data.

Researchers want to be sure that the differences they find are meaningful, and they use statistics to allow them to conclude whether the results they have obtained are significant. For psychologists, a **significant difference** is a difference that is statistically unlikely to have occurred because of chance alone and is inferred to be most likely due to the systematic manipulation of variables by the researcher. For example, if the data collected from the study on reward and musical practice increased the time that children spent practicing, the researchers would want to conclude that these differences occurred because of the rewards and that the difference is big enough to be important. The results are significantly different only if they could not be due to chance, to the use of only one or two participants, or to individual differences among participants. If experimental results are not statistically significant, they do not confirm the hypothesis and are not as informative as results that do offer confirmation. (As Chapter 5 discusses, rewards are very powerful in changing behavior, and a reward program can have a large effect on willingness to practice.)

■ **DRAW CONCLUSIONS AND REPORT RESULTS.** After the results are organized and the statistics have been calculated, researchers then organize their ideas and observations in order to make predictions about behavior. They begin to draw conclusions about results and relate those conclusions to the data that they have collected. Ultimately, researchers report their results to the scientific community by publishing their study—they report their findings along with their interpretations of what the results mean.

Critical Thinking: An Active Learning Process

For nearly the first 75 years of the history of psychology, most research participants were 18-year-old first-year college students primarily of European American ethnic backgrounds. Researchers assumed that the differences between this sample and all other people were not important. But this thinking was really quite shortsighted; women do not necessarily respond in the same way as men in many circumstances; older adults and children don't respond in the same ways as do 18-year-olds. And members of various ethnic groups bring different thoughts and perspectives to research situations. Psychologists eventually realized that male European American college freshmen were not always representative; they realized this as part of the critical thinking process. Psychologists, like all scientists, are trained to think, to evaluate research critically, and to put their results into a meaningful framework. Psychologists follow a traditional approach to evaluating research. Their *critical thinking* consists of evaluating evidence, sifting through choices, assessing outcomes, and deciding whether conclusions make sense. To benefit from this textbook, you might find it helpful to use the same critical thinking skills and framework in order to follow psychologists' logic, to understand their approach, and to evaluate their research. When you think critically, you are being open-minded but evaluative. You reject glib generalizations; you determine the relevance of information and look for biases and imbalances, as well as for objectivity and testable, repeatable results. A critical thinker identifies central issues and makes careful conclusions. A critical thinker maintains a skeptical and questioning attitude. A critical thinker also has to tolerate some uncertainty and be patient—to accept that all the answers do not come at once.

When thinking critically about research, you sort through information as a detective does, trying to be objective, questioning the hypotheses and conclusions, avoiding oversimplification, and considering all the arguments, objections, and

Participant
An individual who takes part in an experiment and whose behavior is observed as part of the data collection process; previously known as a *subject*.

Experimental group
In an experiment, a group of participants to whom a treatment is given.

Control group
In an experiment, the comparison group—the group of participants who are tested on the dependent variable in the same way as those in the experimental group but who do not receive the treatment.

Significant difference
In an experiment, a difference that is unlikely to have occurred because of chance alone and is inferred to be most likely due to the systematic manipulations of variables by the researcher.

student voices

Christopher J. May
Tulane University

My interest in psychology was partially fueled by the enigmas that the mind presents. The workings of the brain are largely unknown. As such, the mind represents one of the greatest unsolved mysteries, and one that couldn't be closer to home.

counterarguments. You evaluate all assumptions and actively seek out conflicting points of view. You revise your opinions when the data and conclusions call for it. Whenever you have to evaluate a research study in this text, in the popular press, or in a psychological publication, you might find it helpful to focus on five research criteria: *purpose, methodology, participants, repeatability,* and *conclusions.*

1. *Purpose.* What is the purpose of the research? What is the researcher trying to test, demonstrate, or prove? Has the problem been clearly defined? Is the researcher qualified to conduct this research?
2. *Methodology.* Is the methodology—the design of study—the most appropriate one for the topic? Has the method been properly and carefully executed? Does the experiment include a properly constituted control or comparison group? Have variables been carefully and clearly defined? Has the researcher followed ethical guidelines (see p. 17)?
3. *Participants.* Was the sample of participants properly chosen and carefully described? How was the sample selected? Does the sample accurately reflect the characteristics of the population of individuals about which the researcher would like to make generalizations? Will any generalizations be possible from this study?
4. *Repeatability.* Are the results repeatable? Has this researcher shown the same finding more than once? Have other investigators made similar findings? Are the results clear and unambiguous—that is, not open to criticism because of poor methodology? What additional evidence will be necessary to convince other researchers to support the conclusions?
5. *Conclusions.* How logical are the conclusions of the study, and what implications and applications does it suggest? Do the researcher's data support them? Has the researcher gone beyond the data, drawing conclusions that might fit a predisposed view rather than conclusions that follow logically from the data? What implications do the data have for psychology as a science and as a profession? Does the research have any implications for you as an individual? Has the researcher considered alternative explanations of the results?

Think again about the sleep deprivation experiment described earlier. Let's use the five criteria to evaluate this research. The participants were young adults deprived of sleep after learning a visual memory task, and they were compared to young adults who slept a normal amount after learning. Both groups were tested on their memory for the task.

- *Was the purpose of the study clear?* The purpose was to assess the effect of sleep deprivation on memory formation.
- *Was the methodology appropriate?* The method involved depriving one group of participants of sleep for 30 hours after the learning task (the experimental group) and comparing them to participants who sleep normally (the control group).
- *Was the sample of participants properly chosen?* The participants were young adults who were in good health. A reasonable generalization from their memory performance to the performance of other people of similar age is possible.
- *Are the results repeatable?* If the results were obtained with several groups of participants, and if the results were consistent within each of those groups, the repeatability of the results would seem likely. This aspect of the study remains to be tested.
- *How logical are the conclusions?* The conclusions that can be drawn from such a research study have some limits. There was only one age group—young

adults. The learning task was visual memory, and verbal learning might differ. No generalizations could be applied to children, older adults, or people with chronic mental illness. The results of the study do not contradict common sense, and they add to our understanding of factors that relate to memory formation.

Thinking critically is not a negative process—it is not the same as thinking cynically. Being critical should not lead you to doubt all research and find fault with all procedures. Instead, thinking critically can lead you to distinguish the faults from the strong points of studies. It can also help you appreciate the advantages while recognizing the limitations of the research method used. You can also apply your critical thinking skills to nonacademic material. When a TV commercial tells you that 9 out of 10 doctors recommend Brand Whatever, apply critical thinking to that claim. What kinds of doctors, for what kind of ailment, for patients of what age, and for what extent of usage?

As you read this text, evaluate research findings. We will present the research in ways that will allow you to evaluate it critically and draw your own conclusions. Also, each chapter contains several Be an Active Learner boxes, containing critical thinking questions. These questions suggest new ideas and perspectives for you to consider as you evaluate the research studies presented. Though not the only places in the text where you should use your critical thinking skills, they definitely encourage you to be evaluative.

Avoiding Ethnocentrism and Other Forms of Bias

Researchers must be careful to avoid subtle but significant biases that would influence research results. These include gender, racial, ethnic, and cultural biases. At any stage of the research endeavor, an experimenter can influence the results and their interpretation by making assumptions about people, how they tend to think or act, and how they might be affected by the variable under study. Such assumptions also often affect researchers' attitudes about whether to report findings such as gender or ethnic differences among participants. Psychologists must scrutinize the research questions they pose because their own cultural view may determine which issues they consider important. For example, school violence became a topic of great public and research interest in 1998, after a series of school shootings in suburban schools. These shootings did not signal the beginnings of school violence, but rather a change in the conventional wisdom concerning school violence—that it was a problem of urban, inner-city schools populated mostly by ethnic minority students. When similar problems appeared in largely White, middle-class, suburban schools, public attention and research funding skyrocketed, which reflects a cultural bias.

Because research studies are used to draw conclusions and make generalizations about people, it is important to understand that enormous differences exist among individuals and groups. The young and the old may behave differently under similar conditions; research done only on men may yield different results from research done only on women. People are not all alike and do not all behave in the same way, even when placed in the same situation.

Ethnocentrism

Individuals, groups, and institutions often see the world from their point of view only and have trouble recognizing that their outlook is not the only vantage point from which to view the world. Individuals and groups tend to believe that their own group is superior to other cultural groups and that their group—whatever that group might be—is the standard, the reference point against which other people and groups should be judged. We refer to this tendency as **ethnocentrism.** It implies the granting

Ethnocentrism
Tendency to believe that one's own group is the standard, the reference point against which other people and groups should be judged.

of superiority to one's own group characteristics and a devaluation of nearly everyone else. Ethnocentrism should be avoided in research and in life because it leads to *institutional racism*—the creation of policies, procedures, operations, and culture of public or private institutions that reinforce and promote individual prejudices and ethnocentric behaviors (Huff, 1997).

Many people may be largely unaware that they hold ethnocentric (sometimes called *monocultural*) beliefs about their own superiority. Historically, psychology in the United States reflected such a bias, having adopted a largely European American worldview as normative because most psychologists shared this background. Uncritically accepting the values of their culture, needless to say, affected psychologists' view of child development, social relationships, and psychological abnormalities. Today, psychologists have become especially sensitive to such biases and work to develop an awareness and understanding of ethnic and other forms of diversity.

Race, Ethnicity, Culture, and Social Class

The word *race* can mean dissimilar things to different groups. For some theorists—especially those who are biologically oriented—there exist natural, physical divisions among humans that are hereditary, reflected in body type, and are roughly captured by terms such as Black, White, and Asian. According to this view, one's parents, body type, and skin color determine one's membership within a genetically defined racial group. Yet research from genetics laboratories shows strong evidence that the observable traits or characteristics of human beings, for example, hair color or weight, are not necessarily genetic. Furthermore, there is greater genetic variation *within* populations, for example, within those groups typically labeled Black and White, than *between* these populations. The truth is there are no genetic characteristics possessed by all Blacks; similarly, there is no gene or cluster of genes common to all Whites. One's race is not determined by a single gene or gene cluster—these findings counter the assumption that race reflects fundamental genetic differences. For these reasons, race as a construct, while widely used, is less valuable to psychologists than ethnicity, which is a psychological variable and affects behavior in fundamental ways.

Ethnicity refers to common traits, background, and allegiances, which are often culture-, religion-, or language-based, shared by a group of people; ethnicity is learned from family, friends, and experiences. Families of Asian American descent, for example, bring to the American experience a wealth of different worldviews and different ways of bringing up children, based on their particular heritages (Korean, Chinese, Japanese, or Vietnamese, for example). The ethnic makeup of the U.S. population is changing rapidly. In the past decade, the Latino/Latina population has grown to 35 million people, largely of Mexican origin; the African American population also increased to 35 million people; and the Asian population grew to 12 million (U.S. Bureau of the Census, 2001). Like people in any large population, members of an ethnic group reflect a wide range of individual differences. Cultural values and ideas within a group differ, each person's subjective sense of being in a group differs, and the overall experience of being a minority individual differs—for example, it represents powerlessness and discrimination for some individuals but pride and uniqueness for others.

Culture reflects a person's ethnic background, religious and social values, artistic and musical tastes, and scholarly interests. Culture is the unwritten social and psychological guidebook that each of us learns and uses to interpret our world. A number of cultural factors shape behavior, values, and even mental health; culture has a direct bearing on the nurturing of families and especially the upbringing of children. Though it helps bind individuals together into groups, culture is not static—neighborhoods, economies, and governments change over time, and local culture eventually follows. Certainly, changes in communication and technology are shifting many cultures that have remained relatively unaltered for hundreds of years.

For example, attitudes toward domestic violence are changing throughout the world. The centuries-long tradition of husbands being allowed to beat their wives is being challenged in the United States, Canada, western Europe, Latin America, Africa, and Asia. These changes reflect an expanding worldview partly due to changes in communication technology and the spread of electronic media such as radio, television, and the Internet.

■ *In today's world of global travel and communications, many societies are sharing values, ideas, and traditions.*

Culture can also be described as promoting either an individualist or collectivist outlook. *Individualist cultures* (like that of the United States) stress personal rather than group goals and value individual freedom and autonomy; *collectivist cultures* (like those in many Asian countries) favor group needs (including those of family, coworkers, and religious and political groups) over individual ones. Collectivist cultures value a tightly knit social fabric and a willingness to go along with the group (Oysterman, Coon, & Kemmelmeier, 2002). The origins of such preferences are often religious in nature but permeate many aspects of the culture (Sampson, 2000).

The impact of individualist and collectivist cultures appears prominently in child-rearing techniques—individualist cultures stress exploration, creativity, and achievement for children, whereas collectivist cultures foster duty, obedience, and conformity. Of course, no society is made up entirely of people who adhere to a single set of cultural values. Most societies represent a wide range of cultural values; for example, in U.S. society the South is more collectivist (think family ties, church life, and shared sense of oppression after the Civil War) than is the Mountain West, which tends to be more individualistic (think rugged, self-reliant farmers and cowhands) (Vello & Cohen, 1999). Furthermore, in today's world of global travel and communications, many societies are sharing values, ideas, and traditions. In the end, cultural values within a population are strong but not homogeneous, and so research on culture will help people understand both their differences *and* commonalities.

Closely tied to culture is a person's social class, which refers to a person's education, income, and occupational status or prestige. The U.S. class structure is not as rigid as it was in the 19th century or as in some non-Western countries, and class distinctions are somewhat fuzzy in the United States. But Americans do fall into several socioeconomic classes. Among these classes are the lower class, whose members are economically poor and poorly educated; the middle class, which includes a wide range of income and educational levels; and the upper class, whose wealth comes from inheritance and who are well educated. The concept of socioeconomic class is not the same as ethnicity or culture, and people in the same socioeconomic class may be of the same or different ethnicities and cultural backgrounds. For example, people who work in manufacturing automobiles on a production line are in the middle class, but they may be from any ethnic background, male or female, and of varying cultural values. Social class affects people's view of the world and their behavior. Participants in psychology research are often college students, and people in the lower class do not attend college as often as those in other social classes. Therefore, psychology research has overlooked social class differences as a variable in research and has excluded people in the lower classes from much of its research. For example, socioeconomic class would be an important variable in a study of tobacco use among high school students; overlooking this factor may lead to conclusions that are not true or, at a minimum, not generalizable.

Gender, Sexual Orientation, Age, and Disability

During the first three-quarters of the 20th century, women's roles in scholarship and universities were restricted. Although some female faculty members taught and did research in psychology, they were rarely prominent in their departments. Nor was the role of sex and gender an important variable in psychology research.

Today, psychologists conduct research in which gender is a variable. That research has shown that women may react differently than men in the same situations. Thus a person's sex can be a crucial factor to consider when choosing a research study sample. For example, some early research on morality showed that, in general, women see moral situations differently than men do; research on communication styles, aggression, and love shows differences between men and women, and in some situations, those differences are large. Further, more than half of the people seen by mental health practitioners are women—although this may be because men with mental health problems are less likely to seek therapy. Today, most psychologists see gender as an important variable in research; as a consequence, researchers seek to understand how, when, and why such differences come to exist and their influence on behavior.

Sexual orientation is different from sexual behavior because it refers to feelings and self-concept. Persons may or may not express their sexual orientation in their behaviors. Three sexual orientations are commonly recognized: *homosexual,* attraction to individuals of one's own sex; *heterosexual,* attraction to individuals of the other sex; or *bisexual,* attractions to members of both sexes. Persons with a homosexual orientation are sometimes referred to as gay (both men and women) or as lesbian (women only). Psychologists and psychiatrists agree that being gay or lesbian in and of itself is unrelated to psychological disturbance or maladjustment—that is, sexual orientation is not a basis for diagnosis of illness, mental disorders, or emotional problems. In 1973, the weight of empirical data, coupled with changing social standards and the development of a politically active gay community in the United States, led the American Psychiatric Association to remove homosexuality from its diagnostic manual. In 1987, that decision was supported by a vote of the membership, and in 1997, the leaders reaffirmed that decision.

People with homosexual or bisexual orientations have long been stigmatized, but the American Psychological Association has worked vigorously to eradicate that stigma (Division 44, 2000). It has sought to decrease *homophobia*—discomfort from being near or in contact with homosexuals. It has also sought to fight *heterosexism*—an ideological system that denies, denigrates, and stigmatizes any nonheterosexual form of behavior, identity, relationship, or community.

Older people constitute a growing percentage of the general population. More than 30 million Americans are age 65 or older, and the aging of the baby boomer generation born between 1946 and 1964 means that the number of older people will continue to rise. Psychologists are developing programs that focus on the special needs of older people for social support, physical and psychological therapy, and continuing education.

Disability is a social construct that can be viewed from different perspectives—medical, moral, and social. Most Western cultures consider disability according to a medical model (such as individuals whose medical condition means they need a wheelchair). A moral model of disability regards disability as the result of sins or transgressions; even today, in some cultures disability is connected with feelings of guilt and shame, which may extend to the entire family. This model blames the disabled for their disability. This model is not prevalent today, especially in the United States. Instead, the disability community employs a social model, which considers individuals as disabled in specific circumstances and in specific ways. This view emphasizes the context of the disability and the adaptions that individuals and institutions can make to allow disabled persons to function in society. People with disabilities need to be considered with special care and sensitivity. Programs that focus on their special needs for social support, physical and psychological therapy, and

student voices

Lacie Michel
Southeastern Louisiana University

"Hello, and thanks for participating in our study!" As an undergraduate research assistant, as soon as I had spoken these words for the first time, I knew this statement would become a fundamental part of my future. Now I have completed my master's in psychology and plan on pursuing my Ph.D.

continuing education are being developed by psychologists, who are incorporating people with disabilities as participants in human research and considering the sensibility and voices of those with a broad array of disabilities—visual, hearing, cognitive, learning, psychiatric, and physical challenges such as paralysis of limbs.

Diversity Within and Between Groups

The differing perspectives on day-to-day behavior held by diverse groups in society have not always been appreciated, understood, or even recognized in psychological theory or research. For example, psychologists take Freud to task for developing a personality theory that can now be seen as clearly sexist. (We will be evaluating Freud's theory in Chapter 12.) In Freud's day, however, most people accepted sexist beliefs without much question. Further, ethnic minorities and special groups such as older people were rarely—if ever—included in psychological research studies, even though these studies were intended to represent the general population. Today, psychologists seek to study all types of individuals and groups in order to make valid conclusions based on scientific evidence. They see cultural diversity as an asset for both theorists and researchers; they also recognize that they must research, learn about, and theorize about this diversity in order to help individuals optimize their potential. It is crucial to realize, though, that *there are usually more differences within a group than between groups.* For example, intelligence test scores differ more among Asian Americans than they do between Asian Americans and any other ethnic group (Geary et al., 1999).

Individual circumstances exist, and people's unique experiences can make many generalizations virtually impossible. Individuals—even those who are members of special populations—often behave just as the general population does, but perhaps with a slight twist or variation. Here is the key point to remember as you read this book: although people are very much alike and share many common, even universal, experiences and behaviors, every individual is unique; each person's behavior reflects his or her distinctive life experiences. Psychology considers the influence of different groups but concentrates on individual behavior and thought.

Ethics in Psychological Research

Ethics in research comprises the rules concerning proper and acceptable conduct that investigators use to guide their research; these rules govern the treatment of nonhuman animals, the rights of human beings, and the responsibilities of investigators. Guided by images from movies and television, people sometimes imagine psychologists with evil motives, performing unethical experiments on human participants and nonhuman animals in secret laboratories, avoiding the rules of ethical scientific conduct. Of course, this image is incorrect. Most psychologists work in university laboratories and work under rules of ethical conduct formulated by the U.S. government and the American Psychological Association (1992).

Most research in psychology is conducted using human participants, and ethics is an important priority. Before a study begins, participants must give the researcher their **informed consent**—their agreement to take part in the experiment and their acknowledgment, through a signature on a document, that they understand the nature of their participation in the research and have been fully informed about the general nature of the research, its goals, and its methods. Participants cannot be coerced to do things that would be physically harmful to them, that would have negative psychological effects, or that would violate standards of decency. The investigator is responsible for ensuring the ethical treatment of the participants in a research study; the participants are free to decline to participate or to withdraw at any time without penalty. In addition, any information gained in an experimental situation is

Ethics
Rules of proper and acceptable conduct that investigators use to guide psychological research; these rules concern the treatment of animals, the rights of human beings, and the responsibilities of investigators.

Informed consent
The agreement of participants to take part in an experiment and their acknowledgment, expressed through their signature on a document, that they understand the nature of their participation in upcoming research and have been fully informed about the general nature of the research, its goals, and its methods.

considered strictly confidential. At the end of the project, the participants must go through a postexperiment interview, sometimes referred to as debriefing. **Debriefing** is a procedure that informs participants about the true nature of an experiment, including hypotheses, methods, and expected or potential results. Debriefing is done *after* the experiment so that the validity of the responses is not affected by participants' knowledge of the experiment's purpose.

Is it ever acceptable for researchers to deceive human participants in psychological studies? Imagine a situation in which a researcher tricks a person into believing that she is causing another person pain. Is this procedure acceptable? Or is

point*counterpoint*

Research with Nonhuman Animals

The Issue: Should nonhuman animals be used in research?

POINT
The use of nonhuman animals is necessary for research to progress.

COUNTERPOINT
The use of nonhuman animals in research is ethically unacceptable.

Some people believe that animal research puts nonhuman animals through unfair and painful treatments, violating their basic rights and subjecting them to cruelty. They argue that animal researchers take it for granted that nonhuman animals are inferior to human beings and assert that this is a faulty assumption. Animal rights advocates also question whether the information scientists learn from animals is even relevant to human research because enormous variations exist between species in reaction to specific techniques, medicines, or manipulations. A further concern is how carefully federal guidelines on the treatment of animals in research are actually carried out in labs and research facilities. Many religions, Buddhism included, assert that people cannot be hunters, fishers, trappers, or slaughterhouse workers; adherents are not allowed to kill animals, even when doing so will lead to discoveries that will prolong human life.

Advocates of animal research argue that using nonhuman animals in research studies allows experimenters to isolate simple aspects of behavior and to eliminate the complex distractions and variables that arise in studies involving humans. The use of animals also enables researchers to conduct studies that could not ethically be done with human beings. Furthermore, because most animals have shorter life spans than humans do, experimenters can control and observe an animal's entire life history, perform autopsies to obtain information, and study several generations within a short period of time. Research with animals has helped psychologists understand many aspects of behavior, including eating, learning, perception, and motivation. In addition, for many diseases, such as multiple sclerosis, cancer, and Alzheimer's disease, animal research and experimentation have brought almost daily breakthroughs and raised legitimate hopes for cures (Mehlhorn, Holborn, & Schliebs, 2000). The federal government has strict guidelines for the treatment of research animals, and the American Psychological Association (APA) has its own stringent ethical regulations on the humane care and appropriate treatment of animals used in research.

Only a small percentage of psychological research (8%) is done on nonhuman animals, but certain areas of scientific research, such as biology and medicine, rely heavily on nonhuman animals. Researchers who use animals argue that there is no realistic, viable alternative for nonhuman animals in the research they do, and this research enhances human welfare. Animal research results in treatments and cures of animal diseases, but humans benefit more than the nonhuman animals do. At present, research with nonhuman animals continues throughout the scientific community, but the controversy over this practice also continues.

it acceptable for a researcher to try to change a participant's views of social or political issues? The answer to these questions is generally no. Researchers must not use deception unless the study has overriding scientific, educational, or practical value. And even then, two key procedures must be followed: obtaining informed consent and providing feedback about the true nature of the experiment.

Some psychologists believe deception is unacceptable under *any* circumstances. They assert that it undermines the public's belief in the integrity of scientists and that its costs outweigh its potential benefits. Other psychologists argue that deception is necessary to their research. For example, cheating is difficult to study if participants know that the study is about cheating. Most psychologists do not conduct research that involves deception; those who do are especially careful to use informed consent and extensive feedback to minimize potentially harmful effects. Whenever deception is necessary to achieve some legitimate scientific goal, psychologists go to extraordinary lengths to protect the well-being, rights, and dignity of participants; anything less is considered a violation of APA guidelines (Fisher & Fryberg, 1994).

Some psychologists study behavior by first observing it in nonhuman animals and then generalizing the principles to human behavior. Research with both nonhuman animals and human beings is extensive, and all of it must be governed by ethical considerations. The use of nonhuman animals in research has become a controversial issue, and psychology is part of that debate (see the Point/Counterpoint box).

The ethical guidelines from the American Psychological Association reflect the amount and diversity of psychological research. The formulation of these guidelines dates to the 1960s, but psychology research began in the late 19th century. At that time, psychology was very different than it is now. Next, we'll examine the early principles of psychology and how they influence today's perspectives.

Be an *Active* learner

REVIEW

- Why must psychologists consider the cultural context in which behavior occurs? pp. 13–15
- Why is ethnicity a more useful concept than race in psychology research? p. 14
- In what ways can the gender of participants in experimental research affect results? pp. 16–17

THINK CRITICALLY

- Why is sample size so important in psychological research?
- As psychologists increasingly consider themselves to be biomedical researchers, what kind of special training in ethics might they need?
- What do you think is the most important thing researchers should do to promote the welfare of animals used in research?

APPLY PSYCHOLOGY

- Imagine a research study testing the effects of a low dosage of a medication that helps relieve anxiety. The participants are 50 men who suffer from job-related stress. What would be the limitations of such a study? Would you say that such a study is poorly designed, or that it has a flawed methodology? Why?

Psychology: A Young Discipline

The history of psychology is short—dating back just over 100 years. Beginning in the late 19th century, inquiry in philosophy and physiology evolved into psychology. Early psychology was characterized by schools of thought that viewed the emerging science in different ways and voiced some of the controversies that remain in the field today.

The Early Traditions

STRUCTURALISM. Before Wilhelm Wundt, the field of psychology simply did not exist. Wundt (1832–1920) (pronounced "Voont") founded the first psychological laboratory in Leipzig, Germany, in 1879. One of Wundt's major contributions was teaching his students to use the scientific method when asking psychological questions (Vermersch, 1999). Wundt wanted to understand the mind, and he attracted students from Europe and from the United States who were also interested in this problem.

Englishman Edward B. Titchener (1867–1927) helped popularize Wundt's initial ideas, along with his own, in the United States and the rest of the English-speaking world. Titchener espoused **structuralism**, the school of psychological thought

Debriefing
A procedure to inform participants about the true nature of an experiment after its completion.

Structuralism
The school of psychological thought that considered the structure and elements of immediate, conscious experience to be the proper subject matter of psychology.

that considered the structure and elements of immediate, conscious experience to be the proper subject matter of psychology. Instead of exploring the broad range of behavior and mental processes that psychologists consider today, the structuralists tried to observe only the inner workings of the mind to determine the simple elements of conscious experience. They felt that all conscious experience could ultimately be reduced to simple elements or blends of those simple elements.

To discover these elements, structuralists used the technique of **introspection,** or *self-examination,* in which an individual describes and analyzes thoughts as they occur. In the process of formulating this technique, they also conducted some of the first experiments in psychology. For example, they studied the speed of thought by observing reaction times for simple tasks.

By today's standards, the structuralists focused too narrowly on individuals' conscious experiences. They used such restrictive techniques that the school made little progress in describing the nature of the mind. Their focus was also narrow in terms of those who studied psychology—almost all were wealthy White men. Structuralist psychology excluded not only women and people from most ethnic groups but also children, the mentally ill, and those with impaired mental capabilities. The minds that they sought to understand came from a narrow range of humans.

■ **FUNCTIONALISM.** Before long, a new perspective developed, bringing with it a new, more active way of thinking about behavior. Built on the basic concepts of structuralism, **functionalism** was the school of psychological thought that tried to explore not just the mind's structures but how and why the mind *functions* and is related to consciousness. It also sought to understand how people adapted to their environment. This approach included a wider variety of topics and questions. Functionalism became very popular, especially in the United States.

With William James (1842–1910) at its head, this lively new school of psychological thought was the first American attempt to explain behavior. James, a physician and professor of anatomy at Harvard University, was charming, informal, outgoing, and vivacious, and especially well liked by his students. He argued that knowing only the contents of consciousness (structuralism) was too limited; a psychologist also had to know how those contents functioned and worked together. Through such knowledge, the psychologist could understand how the mind (consciousness) guided behavior. In 1890, James published *Principles of Psychology,* in which he described the mind as a dynamic set of continuously evolving elements. In this work, he coined the phrase *stream of consciousness,* describing the mind as a river, always flowing, never remaining still.

James broadened the scope of psychology by studying nonhuman animals, by applying psychology in practical areas such as education, and by experimenting on overt behavior, not just mental processes. Despite this broadening, the definition of psychology remained the same—the study of consciousness, and psychologists were still almost exclusively white and male.

■ **GESTALT PSYCHOLOGY.** Functionalism was never as popular in Europe as it was in the United States, but structuralism had challengers in Europe, too. One such approach was **Gestalt psychology**—the school of psychological thought that argued that it is necessary to study a person's total experience, not just parts of the mind or behavior (*Gestalt* is a German word that means "configuration"). It was a radical departure from structuralism in terms of its emphasis and explanations of the mind. Gestalt psychologists such as Max Wertheimer (1880–1943) and Kurt Koffka (1886–1941) suggested that conscious experience is more than simply the sum of its individual parts. Arguing that each mind organizes the elements of experience into something unique, by adding structure and meaning to incoming stimuli, Gestalt psychologists analyzed the world in terms of perceptual frameworks. They proposed that people mold simple sensory elements into patterns through which they interpret the world. By analyzing the whole experience—the

Introspection
A person's description and analysis of what he or she is thinking and feeling or what he or she has just thought about.

Functionalism
The school of psychological thought that was concerned with how and why the conscious mind works; an outgrowth and reaction to structuralism, its main aim was to know how the contents of consciousness functioned and worked together.

Gestalt [gesh-TALT] psychology
The school of psychological thought that argued that behavior cannot be studied in parts but must be viewed as a whole; the focus was on the unity of perception and thinking.

patterns of a person's perceptions and thoughts—psychologists could understand the mind and its workings.

Gestalt psychology exerted a major influence in several areas of psychology—especially social psychology, cognitive psychology, and therapy. Gestalt psychology's emphasis on perception affected theory and research on how people view each other and the social situation. Gestalt psychology's emphasis on how perception affects thought laid the foundation for studies of cognitive psychology. A Gestalt-oriented therapist dealing with a "problem" family member might try to see how the "part" (the person seen as the problem) could be better understood in the context of the "whole" (the family configuration). Despite its influence, the Gestalt school does not exist in today's psychology. Indeed, only certain influences remain from all of these early schools of psychological thought.

From Past to Present

The early schools of psychology focused on the mind and how it functioned. It was not until the mid-1920s that learning became a major topic of interest, and it was not until the 1940s and 1950s that the roles of free will and self-expression were included in psychology by the humanistic perspective. The 1970s saw the emergence of cognitive psychology, which stresses thinking and thought processes.

The early schools were dominated by a narrow focus of ideas by men and by Europeans and European Americans. The early schools led to different "points of view" of psychology—different ways of looking at human behavior and mental processes—that we often refer to as perspectives. Some perspectives have been far more influential than others; some have faded from psychology, and others are still vital forces in the field. As you read further in this book, you will see over and over again how these perspectives appear in and shape current psychological study and thought. Table 1.1 provides a brief summary of these perspectives.

TABLE 1.1

Perspectives on Psychological Issues

Perspective	Main Idea	Main Issue, Emphasis, or Technique
Psychoanalytic	Maladjustment is a consequence of anxiety resulting from unresolved conflicts and forces of which a person may be unaware.	Techniques to explore unconscious processes that direct daily behavior
Humanistic	Each human being's experience is unique, and humans have free will to determine their destiny.	Promoting self-actualization—the ultimate level of psychological development
Behaviorist	Predicting and controlling human behavior through the principles of learning is the goal of psychology.	The study of observable behaviors and how behavior is conditioned
Cognitive	Human beings engage in certain behaviors because of the thoughts and ideas they hold.	The role of thought in day-to-day behaviors, including problem solving
Evolutionary	Over the course of many generations, human behavior has adapted in ways that allow the species to survive.	The organization, specialization, and evolution of neural structures
Biopsychological	Heredity and biological structures affect mental processes and behavior, and physical mechanisms affect emotions, feelings, thoughts, desires, and sensory experiences.	Genetic abnormalities, central nervous system problems, brain damage, hormonal changes, and brain structures
Social–Cultural	Social and cultural context influences a person's behavior, thoughts, and feelings.	A special focus on culture and social setting, complementary to studies of the person and the psychological issue at hand

■ *Sigmund Freud was an early pioneer in the treatment of emotional problems.*

■ **THE PSYCHOANALYTIC PERSPECTIVE.** Sigmund Freud was an early pioneer in the treatment of emotional problems, hypothesizing that the mind includes a large region he called the unconscious. Working from the premise that unconscious mental processes direct daily behavior, he developed techniques to explore those unconscious processes; these techniques include free association and dream interpretation. He emphasized that childhood experiences influence future adult behaviors and that sexual energy fuels day-to-day behavior.

Freud created the **psychoanalytic approach**—the perspective that assumes that emotional problems are a consequence of anxiety resulting from unresolved conflicts and forces of which a person may be unaware. Psychoanalysis is the therapeutic technique associated with this approach. When this approach was introduced in the United States, most psychologists ignored it. But, by the 1920s, when the United States was growing intellectually and emerging from some of the social and sexual strictures of the Victorian era, the influence of the psychoanalytic approach spread rapidly. Soon it was so widely studied that it threatened to eclipse research-based laboratory psychology (Hornstein, 1992). Chapter 12 discusses Freud's theory of personality, and Chapter 16 describes the therapeutic technique of psychoanalysis.

■ **THE BEHAVIORIST PERSPECTIVE.** American psychology in the 1920s moved from studying the contents of the mind (structuralism and functionalism) to studying overt, directly observable behavior. At the forefront of that movement was John B. Watson (1878–1958), the founder of behaviorism. **Behaviorism** is the school of psychological thought that rejects the study of the contents of consciousness and focuses instead on describing and measuring only what is observable, either directly or through assessment instruments.

Watson was an upstart—clever, brash, and defiant. He contended that behavior, not the private contents of the mind, is the proper subject matter of psychology. According to Watson, psychologists should study only activities that can be objectively observed and measured; prediction and control should be the goals of psychology. Watson rejected the work of Wundt and most other early psychologists; he argued that psychologists should put the study of consciousness behind them.

After Watson, other American researchers extended and developed behaviorism to such a degree that it became the dominant and only acceptable view of academic psychology in the United States from the 1920s until the 1950s. Among those supporting the study of behaviorism, and certainly the most widely recognized, was Harvard psychologist B. F. Skinner (1904–1990). In the 1940s, Skinner attempted to explain the causes of behavior by cataloging and describing the relationships among events in the environment (stimuli), a person's or animal's reactions (responses), and the conditions of the learned connection between the two (conditioning). Skinner is arguably the most influential psychologist ever trained in the United States. According to Skinner, our environment completely determines what we do—we control our actions about as much as a rock in an avalanche controls its path. Skinner's behaviorism led the way for thousands of research studies on conditioning and human behavior, which focused on stimuli and responses and the controlling of behavior through learning principles. Today, behaviorists are beginning to study a wider range of human behavior including mental phenomena such as decision making and maladjustment, but the basic learning principles that Skinner developed are among the most prominent influences in psychology.

Psychoanalytic [SYE-ko-an-uh-LIT-ick] approach
The perspective developed by Freud, which assumes that psychological maladjustment is a consequence of anxiety resulting from unresolved conflicts and forces of which a person may be unaware; includes the therapeutic technique known as psychoanalysis.

Behaviorism
The perspective that rejects the study of the contents of consciousness and focuses on describing and measuring only what is observable either directly or through assessment instruments.

Humanistic psychology
The perspective that emphasizes the uniqueness of each human being and the idea that human beings have free will to determine their destiny.

■ **THE HUMANISTIC PERSPECTIVE.** Another important perspective that has influenced modern psychology is **humanistic psychology**—the perspective that emphasizes the uniqueness of each person's experience and the idea that human beings have free will to determine their destiny. Stressing individual free choice, the humanistic approach arose in the late 1940s and early 1950s. Humanistic psychologists see people as inherently good and as conscious, creative, and born with an innate desire to fulfill themselves; they believe that psychoanalytical theorists misread people as fraught with inner conflict and that behaviorists are too narrowly focused on stimulus–response reactions. Humanistic psychologists focus on individual uniqueness and decision-making ability; they assume that inner psychic forces contribute positively to establishing and maintaining a normal lifestyle.

Proponents of the humanistic view, which was especially popular during the 1950s and 1960s, such as Abraham Maslow (whom we will meet in Chapter 11), and therapists who use the view such as Carl Rogers, believe that human beings have the desire to achieve a state of **self-actualization.** Self-actualization is the ultimate level of psychological development. The self-actualized person attempts to minimize ill health, attain a superior perception of reality, feel a strong sense of self-acceptance, and function fully as human beings. Such people experience life to the fullest, live in the present (rather than brooding about the past or dreading the future), and trust their own feelings. Humanistic psychologists think that people create their own perceptions of the world, actively choose their own life experiences, and interpret reality in ways that lead toward becoming self-actualized. Thus, for humanists, self-actualization is not only an optional state but also an instinctual and motivational need.

student voices

Lauren Swenson

University of Miami-Coral Gables

I still do not know what it is that draws me to psychology. Still, from expanding my knowledge of this science I have come to a better understanding of human nature, and find myself applying what I have learned to daily life experiences.

■ **COGNITIVE PSYCHOLOGY.** As both an outgrowth of behaviorism and a reaction to it, psychologists in the 1960s and 1970s developed **cognitive psychology**—the perspective that focuses on the mental processes and activities involved in perception, learning, memory, and thinking. So many theories developed, and so many psychologists embraced them, that talk arose of a cognitive revolution taking place within the discipline. Cognitive psychology currently exerts a strong influence on psychological thinking. Cognitive psychology encompasses theory on both symbolic thought processes and the physiological processes that underlie thought; for example, cognitive theories have been put forth to explain how the brain operates like a computer.

The cognitive perspective asserts that human beings engage in behaviors, both worthwhile and maladjusted, because of ideas and thoughts. Cognitive psychologists may be clinicians working with troubled clients to help them achieve more realistic ideas about the world and then change their thoughts and behavior to adjust to the world more effectively. For example, a cognitively oriented clinician might work to help a client realize that her distorted thoughts about her own importance are interfering with her ability to get along with coworkers. Cognitive psychologists may also be researchers who study intelligence, memory, perception, and other mental processes.

Because cognitive psychology spans many psychological fields and research traditions, it is hard to identify a single person who could be called its leader. However, psychologists Albert Bandura, Albert Ellis, Aaron Beck, George Miller, Ulric Neisser, Elizabeth Loftus, and Richard Lazarus have all taken prominent roles, and we will encounter their work in later chapters.

Self-actualization
The fundamental human need to strive to fulfill one's potential, thus, a state of motivation, according to Maslow; from a humanist's view, the ultimate level of psychological development in which a person attempts to minimize ill health, be fully functioning, have a superior perception of reality, and feel a strong sense of self-acceptance.

Cognitive psychology
The perspective that focuses on the mental processes and activities involved in perception, learning, memory, and thinking.

Today's Perspectives

Psychology in the early 21st century is diverse, both in terms of the perspectives it encompasses and the people it involves. The behaviorist orientation continues as a strong force in psychology; regardless of their research interests, many psychologists classify themselves as behaviorists. Cognitive psychology also continues to be a perspective that many psychologists identify as their own. New perspectives, such as evolutionary psychology, have grown within psychology, and the biopsychology perspective has grown more prominent in recent years.

■ **THE EVOLUTIONARY PERSPECTIVE.** Is your choice of a mate shaped by your evolutionary history? Do people seek out certain types of partners because some inborn preference pushes them to find specific characteristics attractive? Are women selective about their sex partners while men are driven to select many partners? Some **evolutionary psychologists** think so. The evolutionary psychological perspective seeks to explain and predict behaviors by analyzing how the human brain developed over hundreds of thousands of years, how it functions, and how that evolutionary history affects human behaviors today.

Evolutionary psychology assumes that the behavioral tendencies that help organisms adapt, be fit, and survive are the ones that will be passed on to successive generations, because adaptable, fit individuals have a greater chance of reproduction. Basing their ideas upon the work of Charles Darwin, the 19th-century naturalist who proposed that adaptation and survival of the fittest are mechanisms that produce an evolution of species, contemporary researchers such as David Buss, Douglas Kenrick, Leda Cosmides, and John Tooby have argued that human beings have evolved not only physically, but also psychologically. Evolutionary psychologists argue that significant portions of human behaviors and mental abilities have evolved slowly over time, leaving the human brain with specific abilities, such as the ability to learn and to acquire language. Other common human behaviors that interest evolutionary psychologists include the expression of humor and emotions, parenting behaviors, and social interactions. Sex and mating behaviors are also thought to be shaped by evolutionary history. From an evolutionary perspective, human beings seek out mates so as to reproduce—accordingly, men seek out women who will be fertile and bear them children, and women seek out men who will be good providers to feed and shelter them and their children. Evolutionary psychologists hypothesize that these mate-selection strategies lead to large differences between women and men. Women have few chances for reproduction because they produce few ova, but men have many opportunities because they produce millions of sperm. These differences, evolutionary psychologists argue, have produced women who are selective in choosing sex partners, whereas men want to have sex with many women. These different strategies maximize the reproductive possibilities for both but also result in conflict between women and men. This conflict is a side effect of our evolutionary heritage.

The idea that the development of the brain is influenced by innate mechanisms is not a new one. William James, the first American psychologist and the leading proponent of functionalism, spoke at length of instincts in his classic book *Principles of Psychology*. James referred to instincts as specialized neural circuits that are common to every member of a species and are a product of that species' evolutionary history. Today, cognitive psychologists, evolutionary biologists, and neuroscientists are studying those neural circuits—investigating the organization of these circuits, speculating about how they might have evolved to be adaptive in humanity's history, and researching how these circuits affect behavior today. These investigators assume that the brain is a physical system whose operation is governed by a biochemical process, which can be organized and modified in a regular fashion. They further assume that natural selection and a species' evolutionary history can determine how the brain currently operates. This means that the history of a species, over millennia, modifies the structure of the brains of members of the species. The design of the brain and its functioning have been shaped by previous experiences—not only those in an individual's lifetime, but also those of the species. From an evolutionary perspective, this constant change serves as an adaptive mechanism allowing individuals, and their brains, to continue to evolve.

Evolutionary psychology
The psychological perspective that seeks to explain and predict behaviors by analyzing how the human brain developed over time, how it functions, and how input from the social environment affects human behaviors; it seeks to explain human behavior by considering how behavior is affected from the vantage point of evolutionary biology.

Biopsychology perspective
The perspective that examines psychological issues in light of how biological factors affect mental processes and behavior and that focuses on how physical mechanisms affect emotions, feelings, thoughts, desires, and sensory experiences; often focusing on the molecular and cellular level it is also known as the *neuroscience perspective*.

■ **THE BIOPSYCHOLOGY PERSPECTIVE.** Researchers are increasingly turning to biology to explain behavior, acknowledging that biology and behavior interact in important ways. The **biopsychology perspective**, also referred to as the *neuroscience* *perspective,* examines psychological issues in light of how biological structures affect mental processes and behavior and how behavior can change brain function and structure. The biopsychology perspective often focuses on the molecular and cellular levels of the nervous system, for example, within the visual, auditory, or motor areas of the brain. Researchers with a biological perspective study behavior related to genetic abnormalities, central nervous system problems, brain damage, and hormonal changes. Each day brings ground-breaking research from the biological perspective. Some of this research has investigated whether a person's biological heritage affects depression, learning disabilities, or sexual orientation. Michael Gazzaniga (perception), Roger Sperry (brain organization), Carla Shatz (connections in the nervous system during development), Mary Bartlett Bunge (plasticity and regeneration), Irving Gottesman (schizophrenia), Patricia Goldman-Rakic (neural basis of learning), and

BRAIN AND BEHAVIOR

We've Come a Long Way

In the movie, *Girl, Interrupted,* Winona Ryder played Boston-area writer Susanna Kaysen, whose life had been interrupted by an 18-month stay in a mental hospital. When Kaysen attempted suicide in the late 1960s at age 18, she was hospitalized, and her experiences formed the basis for the book that became the movie. She received a diagnosis of borderline personality disorder, and her lengthy hospitalization often felt like a prison sentence.

Ryder felt a kinship with Kaysen and her experience because Ryder had also been hospitalized for mental problems. Their experiences, however, were very different, and those differences reflect changes in treatment for mental problems (Schorow, 2000). Ryder voluntarily checked herself into a mental hospital when she was 19 because she felt depressed and anxious. Unlike Kaysen, she left after a few days, found a therapist, worked on her problems, and got on with her life.

In the 1960s, long-term hospitalization was common; Kaysen's 18-month hospitalization was not unusual. Nor was her diagnosis as a borderline personality disorder, a label often given to young women with suicidal thoughts and self-destructive and inappropriate behavior. The lengthy hospitalization and the diagnosis are less common today. The escalating cost of hospitalization has been a major factor in briefer treatments and shorter hospital stays. In addition, adolescent girls now have a variety of resources that they can consult to help them cope with problems, including school and community mental health personnel and support groups (including online support groups on the Internet). A suicide attempt, however, is always considered serious and most likely a sign of depression, a disorder in which a person becomes overwhelmingly sad and dejected and loses interest in most of life's activities. Depression and other psychological disorders are now considered treatable. Perhaps most important from a psychologist's point of view, specific brain mechanisms are known to be involved in many disorders, including depression, and medication can be part of an effective program.

Ryder's experience with treatment is as typical of current approaches as Kaysen's treatment was for that time. Today's therapists combine talk-based treatment with high-tech diagnostic tools and medication. When they are taking medications such as Prozac (Chapter 16), changes in people's brain processes can be tracked (Chapter 9). And people can learn to cope with the stressors in their lives (Chapter 14) and better meet the demands of adolescence and adulthood (Chapter 4). All of this has come about because psychologists now better understand the links between brain and behavior.

Brain–behavior connections relating to depression are quite dramatic and have prompted the development of medications that act on brain chemicals to help people who are depressed (Gherovici, 2000; Valenstein, 1998). Such connections may be important in other areas of behavior as well—and an understanding of them may allow the development of techniques or medications to help you sleep, adjust to time changes, or remember things better. We've come a long way in recognizing brain–behavior relationships, and such relationships have become an essential part of psychology.

Be an *Active* learner

REVIEW

- Identify the key assumptions underlying each school or perspective of psychological thought. pp. 21–25
- What makes the evolutionary perspective such a departure from other schools of psychological thought? pp. 23–26

THINK CRITICALLY

- Some structuralists approached psychology as a natural science of the mind (similar to how chemists approach atoms and molecules). What problems arise from this approach?
- Which psychological perspective is most likely to be free of cultural biases? Why?
- Which perspective would argue for the existence of "human nature" and which would be most strongly opposed?

APPLY PSYCHOLOGY

- The behaviorist John B. Watson ultimately went into the advertising business—and many students who study psychology have that as a potential goal. How might you apply behaviorist principles within advertising? List ideas that a behaviorist might use to sell a product or promote a political candidate.
- Some behaviors are pleasurable yet dangerous—such as mountain climbing. Using an evolutionary perspective, explain the persistence of such behavior over generations.

Robert Plomin (intelligence) are often cited as leaders in biopsychology. You'll be hearing more about their work later.

The biological perspective is especially important in studies of sensation and perception, memory, and many types of behavior problems. The biological approach has become more prominent in research on psychological disorders such as schizophrenia, which has a genetic component, and alcoholism, which may also have biological underpinnings. The growing importance of the biological perspective has lifted it to a prominent position in psychology. We will revisit it many times, on many topics, in later chapters—especially in the *Brain and Behavior* boxes.

■ **THE SOCIAL AND CULTURAL PERSPECTIVE.** Today, psychologists realize that complex relationships exist among the factors that affect both overt behavior and mental processes. Recognizing and paying attention to social and cultural factors allows a researcher or practitioner to view a problem from diverse orientations. For example, consider depression, the disabling psychological disorder that affects 10%–20% of men and women in the United States at some time in their lives (Chapter 15 discusses depression at length). From a biological perspective, depression is related to changes in brain chemistry. From a behavioral point of view, people learn to be depressed and sad because of faulty reward systems in their environment. From a psychoanalytic perspective, people become depressed because their early childhood experiences caused them to form a negative outlook on life. From a cognitive perspective, depression is fostered by the interpretations (thoughts) an individual adopts about a situation.

But a practitioner sensitive to social situations and culture recognizes the complex nature of depression, and how behaviors associated with depression occur in a social context and in response to social circumstances. For example, people experience depression after personal loss, and the death of friends or family members is associated with depressed mood. Furthermore, women are typically expected and allowed to express sadness, whereas the male gender role restricts men from showing this emotion. Therefore, the social and cultural perspective takes these circumstances into account when considering depression.

Who Are These People Called Psychologists?

Sometimes people mistakenly assume that psychologists primarily assist those suffering from debilitating mental disorders, such as schizophrenia and severe depression. Actually, there is a world of variety in what psychologists do. Psychologists study nearly every aspect of life, not only to understand how people behave but also to help them lead happier, healthier, more productive lives. All psychologists consider research and theory to be the cornerstones of their approach, but they work in different settings with different objectives. Some psychologists have private practices or work in clinics or hospitals, testing and providing therapy, much like the popular image of psychologists. Other psychologists do research on a wide variety of topics, and many research psychologists combine this work with teaching in colleges or universities. Some psychologists combine teaching and research with providing therapy or counseling services.

Psychologists, then, are professionals who study behavior and use behavioral principles in scientific research or in applied settings. Most psychologists have advanced degrees, usually a PhD (doctor of philosophy). Many psychologists also train for an additional year or two in a specialized area such as mental health, physiology, or child development.

People are often unsure about the differences that characterize psychologists, psychiatrists, and psychoanalysts. All are mental health practitioners who help people with serious emotional and behavioral problems, but each takes a different perspective and each has different training. **Clinical psychologists** are psychologists who provide diagnosis and treatment of emotional and behavioral problems. These psychologists usually have a PhD in psychology and work in hospitals, clinics, or private practices. They typically hold a psychosocial view, believing that problems stem from emotional and social sources. **Counseling psychologists** also work with people who have behavioral or emotional problems. When counseling psychology began, these psychologists worked in helping people handle career planning and marriage, family, or parenting problems. In recent years, clinical and counseling psychology have become more similar. Now, counseling psychologists use psychotherapy and other therapies as well as administering psychological tests. According to many practitioners and researchers, counseling and clinical psychology are converging.

In contrast, **psychiatrists** are physicians with MD degrees who have chosen to specialize in the treatment of mental or emotional disorders. Patients who see psychiatrists may have physical as well as emotional problems. As physicians, psychiatrists can prescribe medications and admit patients for hospitalization. The American Psychological Association (APA) and its membership endorse and are pursuing the development of curricula to prepare psychologists to prescribe medications (Sammons et al., 2000). This change would decrease the differences between clinical psychology and psychiatry.

Clinical psychologists generally have more extensive training than psychiatrists do in research, assessment, and psychological treatment of emotional problems. Their nonmedical perspective differentiates their role from that of psychiatrists in hospital settings and encourages them to examine social and interpersonal variables more than psychiatrists do. Psychiatrists are physicians and thus use a medical approach, which often involves making assumptions about behavior—for example, that abnormal behavior is diseaselike in nature—which psychologists do not make. Clinical psychologists and psychiatrists often see a similar mix of clients and often work together as part of a mental health team. Most clinical psychologists and psychiatrists support collaborative efforts. However, disagreements can arise due to their different points of view.

Psychoanalysts are the reason for the association of psychology, Freud, and couches. Ironically, most psychoanalysts are not psychologists (and neither was Freud). Instead, psychoanalysts are usually psychiatrists. In addition to medical school, they have training in the technique of psychoanalysis, which Sigmund Freud (1856–1939) developed as a way to help people understand and resolve emotional problems. This treatment involves the analysis of unconscious motivation and dreams, and the assumption is that current life problems can be traced to the unconscious and to childhood experiences. To resolve these problems, patients must access these unconscious problems and bring them to consciousness, which can include lying on a couch and talking about the patient's life and problems. In strict Freudian psychoanalysis, a course of daily therapy sessions is required; the patient's treatment may last several years. Today, psychoanalytic institutes accept trainees who are not physicians, but the majority of psychoanalysts are medical doctors rather than psychologists.

As you may have gathered from these descriptions, the three kinds of practitioners may treat similar clients. However, their training and assumptions often vary, resulting in differences in their choice of treatment. Although the image of psychology as treatment is the most prominent one, psychology is much more.

Psychologist
Professional who studies behavior and uses behavioral principles in scientific research or in applied settings.

Clinical psychologist
Mental health practitioner who views behavior and mental processes from a psychological perspective and who assesses and treats persons with serious emotional or behavioral problems or conducts research into the causes of behavior.

Counseling psychologist
Mental health practitioner who assists people who have behavioral or emotional problems, through the use of testing, psychotherapy, and other therapies. This profession shares much ground with clinical psychology.

Psychiatrist
Physician (medical doctor) specializing in the treatment of patients with mental or emotional disorders.

Psychoanalyst
Psychiatrist or, occasionally, nonmedical practitioner who has studied the technique of psychoanalysis and uses it in treating people with mental or emotional problems.

What Psychologists Do

Human services psychologists, such as clinical and counseling psychologists, use behavioral principles in providing services such as therapy, testing, and counseling. They try to help people solve problems and promote well-being. And psychologists don't just help people with problems. In addition to counseling and clinical psychology, community and school psychologists also provide services. Some psychologists provide services to well-adjusted people, such as career counseling and assistance with community projects. Some psychologists help individuals improve their interpersonal skills and provide them with knowledge about self-help techniques; others work with professional athletes and musicians to improve their public performances. These subfields, along with their focuses, appear in Table 1.2.

Applied psychologists conduct research and then use their findings to solve practical problems. Many use psychological principles in businesses, government, and institutions such as hospitals.

TABLE 1.2

Subfields of Psychology and Their Focus

Field	Focus	Further Information
Applied Research		
Engineering psychology	Person–machine interface	Chapter 17
Educational psychology	Classroom behavior and learning; school performance	Chapter 17
Forensic psychology	Legal issues in court and correctional system; treating prison inmates	Chapter 17
Health psychology	Behavior as a factor in physical health	Chapter 14
Sport psychology	The role of sports in a healthy lifestyle; preparation of athletes for competition	Chapter 17
Industrial/organizational psychology	Employee evaluation, personnel selection, employee motivation, work behavior, management–labor relations, program evaluation	Chapter 17
Human Services Psychology		
Clinical psychology	Helping people with behavior problems	Chapter 16
Counseling psychology	Helping people with behavior problems	Chapter 16
Community psychology	Helping communities develop resources and social support to promote health	Chapter 17
Behavioral medicine	Helping people with physical illness adapt to and cope with their condition	Chapter 14
School psychology	Administer and interpret tests; develop communication among teachers, students, parents, and administrators	Chapter 17
Experimental Psychology		
Biopsychology	Relationship between nervous system and behavior	Chapter 2
Cognitive psychology	Thought processes, especially learning, memory, and perception	Chapter 9
Developmental psychology	Emotional, physical, and intellectual changes that occur through the lifespan	Chapters 3 and 4
Social psychology	How people interact; how groups affect individuals	Chapter 13

psychology *in action*

Using Psychological Knowledge to Improve Performance

Lorraine Finn is one of the new breed of baseball coaches. She isn't a mom or a gym teacher; she's married, young, athletic, and focused on one thing and one thing only—winning. Lorraine coaches a Little League team in the afternoon, a high school team in the early evening, and an insurance company's senior league on weekends. She has a mantra that she repeats over and over: "Keep your eye on the ball." And she means this literally and figuratively. She constantly reminds players to watch the ball. "You can't hit what you don't see," she says. Figuratively, what she is telling her players, young and old, is to focus on the task at hand—to play as well as they can.

In some ways, Lorraine thinks of herself as the president of a company trying to motivate employees. Her job, she feels, is to keep her players engaged, working hard, enjoying the challenge, and ultimately winning the game. Lorraine minored in psychology in college, completing 21 credit hours because she found the subject so relevant. Among other things, she studied learning, motivation, health, psychology, and personality. She found many psychological concepts applicable to her day-to-day life, and especially to coaching baseball. Lorraine is a lot like businessman Herb Kelleher.

Herb Kelleher is the chairman and CEO of Southwest Airlines, the fourth largest airline in the United States, in terms of profitability. His motto is "Low costs, high spirits"—and it works. Kelleher adopted a short-haul, high-frequency, low-fare strategy. Known for on-time performance, terrific baggage handling, and few customer complaints, the airline focuses on people first—Southwest Airlines looks for employees with a sense of humor, a sense of service, and no bad attitudes. Kelleher, considered the extrovert-in-chief, has a motivation style that can't be beat.

People like Finn and Kelleher help keep people motivated and performing. The best performances occur, they would argue, when people aren't thinking about the performance—instead, good work occurs when the worker maintains a state of effortless concentration. It's a matter of not trying too hard but simply focusing on the action itself.

You may be wondering what psychology can do for you in your daily life. Psychology might seem to be just another academic subject, a set of theories and concepts to be learned in order to pass an exam and complete a course requirement. Not so. Psychology can be applied to everyday life in an endless variety of ways, as you'll see throughout this book. An understanding of the processes of learning and thinking (Chapters 7 and 9) can be helpful in developing ways to mute your judgmental side and allow your natural abilities to come through. Knowledge of the principles of motivation and emotion (Chapter 11) can also be helpful.

You use psychological principles all the time, as do Lorraine Finn and Herb Kelleher. They have taken key ideas—"Keep your eye on the ball" and "Low cost, high spirits" and made them the organizing and motivating theme of their work. And it works. The way we as individuals can improve our performances—indeed, improve our lives—is by understanding basic psychological processes like motivation.

Experimental psychologists try to identify and understand the basic elements of behavior and mental processes. Theirs is an approach, not a specific field. That is, experimental psychologists use a set of *techniques* to examine a wide variety of topics. Applied psychologists attempt to provide practical help and advice to improve specific situations, whereas experimental psychologists focus on basic research issues. Experimental psychology covers many areas of interest, some of which overlap with fields outside psychology. These areas of interest appear in Table 1.2.

Making Psychology a Career

As we saw at the beginning of this chapter, psychology is a field of practice and research. Many psychologists directly help others through the delivery of mental health services. But an equal number of psychologists seek to generate knowledge, apply that knowledge, or do both; they focus on research and discovery. Psychologists ask questions of research that ultimately inform practice.

Like many students, when I (L. L.) was first attracted to psychology as a career, it was because I had a desire to help others. Psychology is an optimistic profession—and psychologists unabashedly admit to this bias. Psychologists generally adopt the view that human beings can change and that trying to feel, do, or be better is productive. My goal was just that—to help people achieve more in life—and so psychology and I were a match.

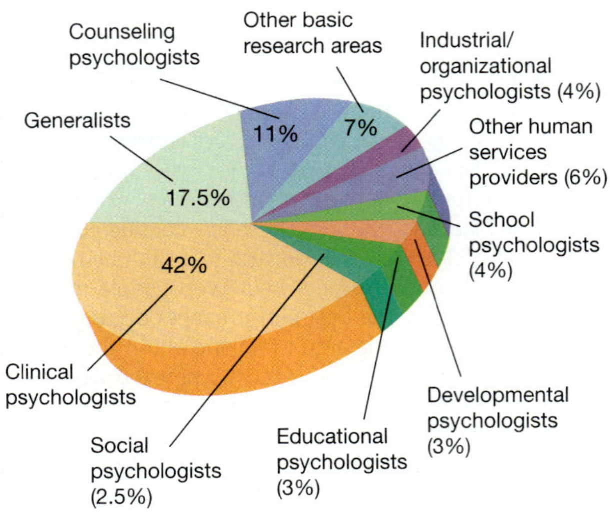

FIGURE 1.1

What Psychologists Do

Of the members of the American Psychological Association who work in the field of psychology, the majority are involved in the delivery of human services—as clinical, counseling, and school psychologists and as other human services providers. The rest focus on research, teaching, and application in university settings, government, and business. (*Data provided by American Psychological Association, 1995.*)

When I (L. B.) was first attracted to psychology, I was interested in understanding people's thought processes. I was fascinated with designing experiments and collecting and analyzing data. Experimental psychologists are struck with the differences among people and how they behave differently, even in similar situations. I wanted to understand human behavior—and so psychology and I were also a match.

Psychology attracts many college students who like the idea of understanding human behavior and helping others. The causes and implications of behavior intrigue these students; they realize that psychology is part of the fabric of daily life. After business administration, psychology is the second most popular undergraduate major—every year, about 33,000 college graduates major in psychology. Today's psychology students are increasingly female, ethnically diverse, and interested in a variety of subfields within psychology. And there is good news for students who go on to graduate school: almost all of the approximately 4,300 recipients of a doctoral degree in psychology each year find jobs related to their training. If you are considering the field of psychology, you'll be glad to hear that unemployment among psychologists is low and likely to remain so.

Training, of course, is the key to employment. A psychologist who (1) obtains a PhD in clinical psychology from an accredited university, (2) does an internship in a state hospital, and (3) becomes licensed to practice will encounter a wide variety of job opportunities in both the private and public sectors. Individuals with bachelor's or master's degrees usually do not have the same job opportunities that doctoral-level psychologists have. Some states grant credentials to psychologists with master's degrees, allowing them to work in the private and public sector, providing services. In those states that allow only psychologists with doctoral degrees to be licensed, those with master's or bachelor's degrees may provide services in hospitals, clinics, or agencies if they work under the supervision of a licensed psychologist.

It varies slightly from year to year, but for the past decade, about 67% of the members of the American Psychological Association work in delivering human services. About 48% are clinical psychologists who work in clinics, community mental health centers, health maintenance organizations, veterans' hospitals, public hospitals, and public and private mental health hospitals (see Figure 1.1). The remainder are private practitioners who maintain offices and work in schools, universities, businesses, and numerous other public and private settings.

Most psychologists employed by hospitals spend their time in the direct delivery of human services, including individual and group therapy. Business, government, and industry employ about 6% of the working psychologists. About 33% of the APA's members are employed by universities, nearly half of them in psychology departments. University psychologists spend most of their time researching and teaching.

The Changing Face of Psychology

Until the 1960s, psychology was a profession made up principally of men, mostly white men. In 1950, women received only 14.8% of all doctorate degrees in psychology. The first women in psychology received training similar to that of their male colleagues but were much less likely to achieve equivalent professional status. Women such as Mary Whiton Calkins and Margaret F. Washburn were leaders; William James, one of the first American psychologists, in 1895 praised Calkins for one of the best PhD examinations that he had ever seen, and Margaret Floyd Washburn served as APA president in 1921. Leta Stetter Hollingworth was an eminent psychologist who made important contributions to the psychology of women, clinical psychology, and educational psychology (particularly the psychology of the highly gifted). But despite the achievements of these women, their accomplishments are footnotes in the history of psychology.

But that situation has changed dramatically. As a helping profession with deep scientific roots, psychology now attracts, trains, and retains women and members of ethnic minorities. For example, women now earn 73% of bachelor's degrees in psychology and make up 66% of new doctorates in psychology. Seventy-one percent of new PhDs in clinical psychology are women. In academics, about 35% of full-time faculty are women (APA, 2001). In psychology, as in other careers, women are more likely than men to be employed on a part-time basis (Pion et al., 1996), which has a negative impact on their career advancement.

Today, research by and about women is prominent in psychology. You will hear the voices of female researchers throughout this text. The list of female researchers and practitioners is exceedingly long, but some of the more prominent are Judith Wallerstein and Mavis Hetherington, who have studied the impact of divorce on children; Florence Denmark, who has criticized sexist bias in research methods; Judith Rodin, who has done important work on eating and eating disorders; Elizabeth Loftus, who has studied the ability of eyewitnesses to remember accurately; Sandra Scarr, who studies intelligence; Kay Redfield Jamison, a national researcher, author, and advocate for those who suffer from mood disorders; and Elizabeth Spelke who studies infant thought processes. Women are presidents of national, regional, and local psychological organizations, and their thoughts and work are prominent in psychological journals. In APA's 108-year history, only nine women have been elected president of the association: Mary Whiton Calkins (1905), Margaret Floyd Washburn (1921), Anne Anastasi (1972), Leona E. Tyler (1973), Florence L. Denmark (1980), Janet T. Spence (1984), Bonnie R. Strickland (1987), Dorothy W. Cantor (1996), and Norine G. Johnson (2001).

The outlook for ethnic minorities in psychology is not as optimistic as that for women. Individuals from ethnic minorities comprise only 28% of the membership of the American Psychological Association (APA, 2001). Despite vigorous recruiting efforts on the part of universities, African Americans and Latinos/Latinas each receive only about 5% of the new doctoral degrees in psychology each year and have consistently done so for at least a decade. Many early African American psychologists faced harsh discrimination. Still, they overcame the odds; they earned doctoral degrees, published scientific research, and made lasting contributions to the discipline.

■ *African-American students receive about 5% of doctoral degrees in psychology each year.*

Gilbert Haven Jones was the first African American holder of a PhD to teach psychology in the United States. Albert S. Beckham was a clinician who published studies in the 1930s of socioeconomic status and adolescence among ethnic minority groups. Inez Prosser and Howard H. Long are also among the distinguished African American psychologists who published in the 1930s. Francis C. Sumner, who chaired the psychology department at Howard University, is considered the father of African American psychology. Kenneth Clark, former president of the APA, achieved national prominence for his work on the harmful effects of segregation. The works of Mamie Phipps Clark on self-esteem and racial identification (with her husband,

Kenneth Clark) have become classics. African American Gail Elizabeth Wyatt conducts research in the United States and Jamaica, and has been recognized for her distinguished contributions to research, scholarship, and writing in the areas of ethnicity and culture and especially her accounts of female sexuality among African Americans.

Individuals of Latino/Latina origin earn only 5% of doctoral degrees in psychology, and the role of Latinos/Latinas in the history of psychology is not well documented. Martha Bernal was the first Latina to earn a PhD in psychology in the United States. We do know that prominent Latino/Latina psychologists have focused on a variety of psychological issues. Manuel Barrera has done important work in community psychology, especially on social support systems. R. Diaz-Guerrero has examined cultural and personality variables among Latinos/Latinas. Jorge Sanchez conducted exemplary research on the role of education in the achievements of members of different ethnic minority groups and on biased test scores and intelligence testing. Counseling psychologist Melba J. T. Vasquez has been a Latina activist and educator. Psychologist Clarissa Pinkola Estés became the first Mexican American author to make the *New York Times* best-seller list with her 1992 book *Women Who Run with the Wolves: Myths and Stories of the Wild Woman Archetype.* And Salvador Minuchin, along with his collaborator Jorge Colapinto, has a highly successful family therapy training program that emphasizes hands-on experience, online supervision, and the use of videotapes to learn and apply the techniques of structural family therapy.

Diversity strengthens psychology. Research and theory become more complete when they embrace the multicultural nature of human beings. On a practical level, the effectiveness of the helping professions is enhanced when practitioners understand their clients. The variety of psychologists' research interests and their wide-ranging socioeconomic and ethnic backgrounds are contributing to a greater recognition of diversity among people—and this diversity is a strength that today's psychologists not only recognize but celebrate.

Be an *Active* learner

REVIEW

- What is the difference between a psychologist and a psychiatrist? p. 27
- Identify the focuses of applied research, human services psychology, and experimental psychology. p. 28
- What differences in approach characterize experimental psychologists and applied psychologists? p. 28

THINK CRITICALLY

- If you were to seek help for a marital conflict, what would be the key reason for choosing a psychologist rather than a psychiatrist?
- What forces once restricted women's achievement in psychology? What has changed to alter that situation?
- Why are ethnic minorities underrepresented in psychology?

APPLY PSYCHOLOGY

- List the kinds of problems you think people should seek help for. Keep this list tucked into this page, and add to it as you study each chapter of the text—you'll probably find that your list is a great deal longer and more detailed by the end of the course.

Summary and Review

Four Recurring Themes in Psychology

What themes characterize psychology?

■ Although television and movies portray psychology in various inaccurate ways, psychology is a science. *Psychology* is defined as the science of behavior and mental processes. p. 6

■ Four themes recur in this textbook: (1) psychology is an active, action-oriented discipline of research and practice; (2) knowledge of the brain and its relationship to behavior are central to understanding psychology; (3) human behavior is a complex mix of our biological heritage and our experience in the environment; and (4) behavior occurs within a cultural context, and diversity is an important part of psychology. pp. 5–6

KEY TERMS

psychology, p. 4

What Is This Science of Psychology?

What is included in the definition of psychology?

■ Psychology includes behavior and mental processes. Psychologists observe many aspects of human functioning—overt actions, social relationships, mental processes, emotional responses, and physiological reactions. All of these actions are directly observable, but measuring instruments may be required for observation of physiological responses such as heart rate or brain activity. p. 6

Identify the two premises upon which psychology (and other sciences) is based.

■ The principle of *empiricism* holds that knowledge must be acquired through observation. Empirical observation in psychology leads to *theory,* a collection of interrelated ideas and observations that describe, explain, and predict behavior and mental processes. p. 6

Identify three principles of science.

■ As social scientists, psychologists must strive to be objective, evaluating research and theory on their merits, without preconceived ideas. Psychologists are concerned with gathering data from the laboratory and the real world in systematic ways—that is, according to a plan rather than casual observation. Psychologists maintain a healthy skepticism: a cautious view of data, hypotheses, and theory until results are repeated, verified, and established over time. pp. 6–7

Describe the steps in the scientific method.

■ The discipline of psychology is committed to objectivity, systematicity, and healthy skepticism. In their research, psychologists use the *scientific method* to organize their ideas and to develop theories that describe, explain, predict, and help manage behavior. The scientific method's five basic steps are stating a problem clearly, developing a hypothesis, designing a study, collecting and analyzing data, and drawing conclusions and reporting results. pp. 7–11

Describe an experiment and indicate its key components.

■ An *experiment* is a procedure in which a researcher systematically strives to discover and describe the relationship between variables. Only controlled experiments allow researchers to draw conclusions that can be expressed as cause-and-effect statements. A *variable* is a characteristic of a situation or person that is subject to change or that differs within or across situations or individuals. The experimenter directly and purposely manipulates an independent variable. The *dependent variable* is expected to change because of manipulations of the independent variable. An *operational definition* specifies the procedures used to measure or study variables. pp. 8–9

■ A *hypothesis* is a tentative statement or idea expressing a causal relationship between two events or variables that are to be evaluated in a research study. p. 8

■ A *significant difference* is one that is statistically unlikely to have occurred because of chance alone. p. 10

What are key elements of the experimental research process?

■ There are two types of variables in any controlled experiment: independent variables and dependent variables. Participants are individuals who take part in experiments and whose behavior is observed and recorded. They serve in the experimental group—the group of participants to whom a new treatment is given; or they serve in the control group—the comparison group who are tested on the dependent variable in the same way as the experimental group but who do not receive the new treatment. Extraneous variables are factors that affect the results of an experiment but are not of interest to the experimenter. Careful experimental design can avoid this problem. pp. 8–10

KEY TERMS

empiricism, p. 6; theory, p. 6; scientific method, p. 7; hypothesis, p. 8; experiment, p. 8; variable, p. 8; sample, p. 9; independent variable, p. 9; dependent variable, p. 9; operational definition, p. 9; participant, p. 11; experimental group, p. 11; control group, p. 11; significant difference, p.11

Critical Thinking: An Active Learning Process

What is critical thinking?

■ Critical thinking involves evaluating evidence, sifting through choices, assessing outcomes, and deciding whether conclusions make sense. When evaluating research studies, critical thinkers focus on five research criteria: purpose, methodology, participants, repeatability, and conclusions. pp. 11–13

Avoiding Ethnocentrism and Other Forms of Bias

What is ethnocentrism?

■ *Ethnocentrism* is the tendency to believe that one's own group is the standard, the reference point against which other people and groups should be judged. Psychology has held a European bias but currently strives to eliminate ethnocentrism as well as bias based on gender, sexual orientation, age, and disability. pp. 13–14

KEY TERMS

ethnocentrism, p. 13

Ethics in Psychological Research

Describe the ethical considerations in psychological research.

■ *Ethics* in research comprises the rules of conduct that investigators use to guide their research; these rules concern the treatment of nonhuman animals, the rights of human beings, and the responsibilities of investigators. The APA has strict ethical guidelines for animal research, but this research remains controversial. Human participants cannot be coerced to do things that would be physically harmful, that would have other negative effects, or that would violate standards of decency. In addition, any information gained in an experimental situation is considered strictly confidential. Human participants must give *informed consent* to a researcher and must undergo *debriefing* following an experiment so that they understand the true nature of the research. In general, researchers must not use deception unless a study has overriding scientific, educational, or practical value. pp. 17–19

KEY TERMS

ethics, p. 17; informed consent, p. 17; debriefing, p. 19

Psychology: A Young Discipline

Identify the key assumptions underlying each early school of psychological thought.

■ Psychology became a field of study in the mid-19th century. *Structuralism,* espoused by Titchener and others, focused on the contents of consciousness as revealed through *introspection* and was the first true school of psychological thought. *Functionalism,* led by James and others, emphasized how and why the mind works. *Gestalt psychology,* in contrast to structuralism and functionalism, focused on perceptual frameworks and suggested that conscious experience is more than simply the sum of its individual parts. pp. 19–21

Identify the main ideas underlying psychoanalytic, behaviorist, humanistic, and cognitive psychology.

■ The *psychoanalytic approach* developed by Freud is the school of psychological thought that assumes that psychological maladjustment is a consequence of anxiety resulting from unresolved conflicts and forces of which a person may be unaware; its therapeutic technique is psychoanalysis. Watson, the founder of *behaviorism,* argued that the proper subject of psychological study was observable behavior. Skinner took up the behaviorist banner through much of the 20th century. *Humanistic psychology* arose in response to the psychoanalytic and behavioral views, and stresses free will and *self-actualization. Cognitive psychology* focuses on perception, memory, learning, and thinking and asserts that human beings engage in both worthwhile and maladjusted behaviors because of their ideas and thoughts. pp. 21–23

Identify key themes in today's perspectives on psychological thought.

■ *Evolutionary psychology* analyzes how specific behaviors, over the course of many generations, have led to adaptations that allow a species to survive; it explains human behavior by also considering how behavior is affected from the point of view of evolutionary biology. The *biopsychological perspective* examines how biological factors affect and are affected by mental processes and behavior, especially at the molecular and cellular level. *The social and cultural view* acknowledges the complex cultural factors and social relationships affect behavioral and mental processes and combines theories and techniques as appropriate to the situation. pp. 23–26

KEY TERMS

structuralism, p. 19; introspection, p. 20; functionalism, p. 20; Gestalt psychology, p. 20; psychoanalytic approach, p. 22; behaviorism, p. 22; humanistic psychology, p. 22; self-actualization, p. 23; cognitive psychology, p. 23; evolutionary psychology, p. 24; biopsychology perspective, p. 24

Who Are These People Called Psychologists?

Distinguish the various types of professionals in psychology.

■ *Psychologists* are professionals who study behavior and use behavioral principles in scientific research or in applied settings. Most psychologists have an advanced degree, usually a PhD. *Clinical psychologists* provide services to people with emotional and behavioral problems; *counseling psychologists* provide similar services. A *psychiatrist* is a physician who has specialized in the treatment of mental or emotional disorders. *Psychoanalysts* are usually psychiatrists; they have training in the specialized Freudian technique of psychoanalysis for treating people with emotional problems. pp. 26–27

Identify the focuses of human services psychology, applied research, and experimental psychology.

■ The three main fields of psychology are human services, applied research, and experimental psychology. All three consider research and theory to be the cornerstone of the psychological approach. Human services psychologists focus on helping individuals solve problems and on promoting their well-being. Applied researchers use research to solve practical problems. Experimental psychologists usually focus on teaching and research. pp. 27–28

In what fields are psychologists likely to be employed?

■ About 67% of psychologists who are members of the APA work in human services fields such as clinical, counseling, and school psychology. Most of the rest of the APA membership work in universities, businesses, and government, doing research, teaching, and evaluating programs. In recent years, psychology has attracted more women in graduate training and careers, but African Americans and Latino/Latina Americans remain underrepresented in psychology. p. 29–32

KEY TERMS

psychologist, p. 27; clinical psychologist, p. 27; counseling psychologist, p. 27; psychiatrist, p. 27; psychoanalyst, p. 27

2 Neuroscience: The Brain and Behavior

Santiago Hernandez, *Reflector,* 1996

All the instructions for making a human being are packed within a surprisingly small number of genes—about 30,000. The genetic instructions for making a person take up less than one inch of the six-foot-long strand of DNA that is packed inside nearly every cell in the human body. This information takes up merely 1 percent or so of the human genome. The genes can each produce one or, in some instances, several proteins—and the unique combinations of these proteins define individuals.*

On February 16, 2001, human genome researchers published the map of the human genome—all the heritable traits carried in each cell of the human body. The sequencing and mapping of the human genome are considered the beginning of a new era in science. But what effect does mapping the human genome have on psychology? What does understanding genetics have to do with understanding behavior? Is it possible that at conception a switch, gate, or hormonal trigger is pulled that determines whether an individual will be outgoing, shy, musical, or happy? Are sexual urges determined before birth?

Your dreams, problem-solving abilities, friendships, and anxieties all have a biological basis. All behaviors and

chapter outline

mental processes are in some way mediated by the neurons in our brains. While each of us may have a unique take on the world, with our own values and viewpoints, our ideas are coded, stored, processed, evaluated, and turned into mental processes or behaviors through the actions of the nervous system. In this chapter, we examine how the issues and findings from biology relate to human behavior and mental processes. Beginning with the smallest of the biological building blocks of behavior—genes and neurons—we will progress to the structure and functioning of the brain. We will focus on how biological processes affect behavior; this focus is coming to dominate thinking in the field of psychology, and some insist that psychology is now rooted in brain science (Kolb, 1999). However, any simple interpretation that genes determine behavior is incorrect (McGuffin, Riley, & Plomin, 2001); complex behaviors result from the interplay between environment and many genes (Plomin & Crabbe, 2000).

Genetics and Evolutionary Psychology

Does genetic makeup actually set a person up to be depressed, schizophrenic, or anxious? Biologists first began to examine this question, and many more, through the study of genetics, focusing on issues such as how blue eyes, brown hair, height, and a tendency to develop diabetes or high blood pressure are transmitted from one generation to the next. **Genetics** is the study of *heredity*, which is the biological transmission of traits and characteristics from parents to offspring. Psychologists know that some behaviors show high degrees of **heritability**, the genetically determined proportion of a trait's variation among individuals in a population. The heritability of some traits such as height is fairly obvious. Children with two tall parents have an excellent probability of being tall, but even a highly heritable trait like height depends on the environment to develop. Children with tall parents will be tall only if they get proper nutrition while they are growing. For people without tall parents, even a good diet will not make them tall. When scientists say that a trait is heritable, especially when they attach a percentage to that heritability—for example, 50%—they mean that 50% of the variation (differences) within *a group* of people is attributable to heredity.

Genetics
The study of heredity, which is the biological transmission of traits and characteristics from parents to offspring.

Heritability
The genetically determined proportion of a trait's variation among individuals in a population. Often expressed as a number between zero and 1, it refers to the percentage of variation in a population that is ascribed to genetics.

Nature
A person's inherited characteristics, determined by genetics.

Nurture
A person's experiences in the environment.

Nature and Nurture

Psychologists know that biology generally and heredity specifically play a role in shaping human behavior. However, there is a complex interplay between biology and experience, between inherited genes and encounters in the world—that is, between nature and nurture. **Nature** consists of a person's inherited characteristics determined by genetics; **nurture** refers to a person's experiences in the environment.

Those who consider nurture more important than nature suggest that experience, training, and effort are more significant than inheritance in determining behavior. John B. Watson, a pioneer in the field of behaviorism (which we will examine further in Chapter 7) believed that nurture was all-important. Watson's strong opinion of the importance of nurture is not shared by most contemporary psychologists, who acknowledge that both nature and nurture contribute to behavior. For example, people with special talents must be given opportunities to express and develop them. If Mozart had not had access to musical instruments, his talent would never have become apparent.

Psychologists know that biological makeup affects people's behavior. But how important is genetic inheritance for behavior? And how are genes translated into behavior? One major mode of influence is through changes to the brain. Over tens of thousands of years, human brains have evolved to meet environmental demands, resulting in a highly organized, complex brain that controls our behavior. Each new experience is stored away and may possibly affect later behavior. Genetic endowment provides the framework for behavior; within that framework, experiences ultimately shape what individuals feel, think, and do.

To understand the genetic component of behavior, it is necessary to understand the basics of genetics; so, let's take a closer look at the key factors in genetics. But keep in mind that the study of genetics (a biological approach) and the study of human interactions (a social approach) are not antagonistic fields (Cacioppo et al., 2000). Instead, they are complementary; biology and behavior are both part of a two-way interaction, with influence going each way.

Chromosome
Microscopic strands of DNA found in the nucleus of every body cell and carrying the self-replacing genetic information in their basic functional units, the genes.

Gene
The functional unit of hereditary transmission, consisting of DNA.

Genotype
A person's genetic makeup fixed at birth.

Phenotype
A person's observable characteristics shaped by genes and the environment.

The Basics of Genetics

Each human cell normally contains 23 pairs of chromosomes (46 chromosomes in all). **Chromosomes** are microscopic strands of deoxyribonucleic acid (DNA) found in the nucleus (center) of every body cell (see Figure 2.1). Chromosomes carry the self-replicating genetic information in their basic functional units, known as genes—thousands of which line up along each chromosome. **Genes** are the fundamental units of hereditary transmission, consisting of DNA. Genes provide templates that allow protein production, which doesn't sound very impressive, but these functions control various aspects of a person's physical makeup, including eye color, hair color, and height—and they influence behavior as well. Genetically determined characteristics are controlled by pairs of genes, located in parallel positions on chromosome pairs. Both of these corresponding genes influence the same trait, but they may carry different forms of the genetic code for that trait. One gene is *dominant* over the other, which is called *recessive*. The dominant gene is expressed, and the recessive is not. For example, if an individual's two genes for eye color carry the genetic codes for blue and brown, the individual will be brown-eyed, because the brown version of the gene is *dominant*. Only when both genes in the pair are the recessive versions of the gene will the recessive gene exert its influence (blue eye color, for example).

A **genotype** is a person's genetic makeup and is fixed at conception; but a genotype may or may not appear in observable characteristics—**phenotypes.** Consider eye color again; a mother and a father may both have brown eyes, but they may each also carry a recessive gene for blue eyes. Thus, their genotype includes a gene for blue eyes, but their phenotype is brown-eyed. We see many more brown-eyed than blue-eyed people because brown is dominant and is expressed in the phenotype when it is present in the genotype. The two brown-eyed parents may have offspring with brown eyes (very likely) or blue eyes (far less likely). Sometimes changes in genotypes occur in ways that are not expected, are not always evident in phenotype, and create unusual characteristics of body or

FIGURE 2.1
Building Blocks of Genetics
Each of the trillions of cells in the human body has 23 pairs of chromosomes in its nucleus. Each chromosome is essentially a long, threadlike strand of DNA, a giant molecule consisting of two spiraling and cross-linked chains. Resembling a twisted ladder and referred to as a double helix, each DNA molecule carries thousands of genes—the basic building blocks of the genetic code—which direct the synthesis of all the body's proteins.

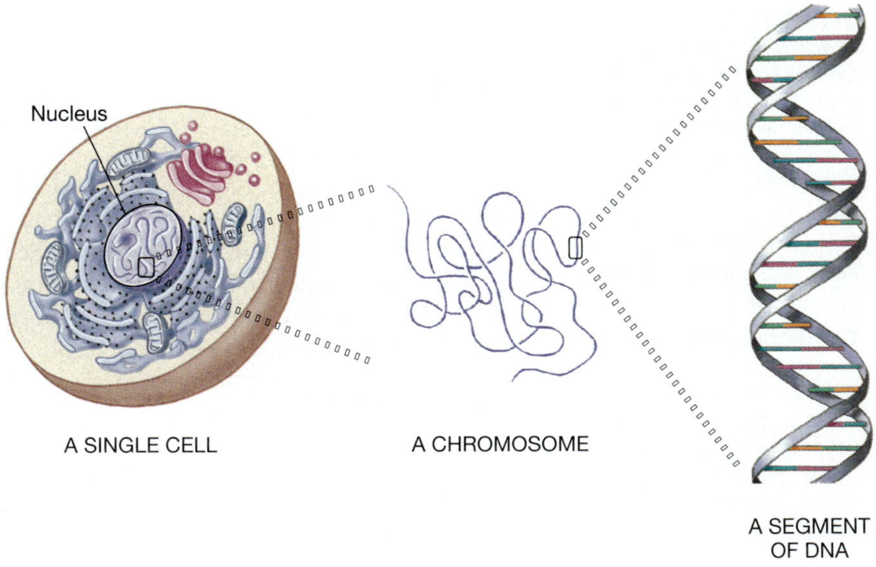

behavior—we call these unexpected changes in gene replications **mutations.** Mutations are principal sources of diversity in the human gene pool; some mutations cause desirable changes, but most do not.

Eye color is a simple trait compared to traits like "intelligence" or "jealousy," and so you can see that analyzing the origin of traits can be complicated. In its simplest form it works like this: Each parent's sperm or ovum (egg) contains 23 chromosomes—half of the total of 46 contained in all other body cells. Of these 23 pairs of chromosomes, 22 carry the same types of genetic information in both men and women, and the 23rd pair determines a person's sex. In women, the 23rd pair contains two X chromosomes; in men, it contains one X and one Y chromosome. At the moment of conception, a sperm and an ovum, each containing 23 chromosomes, combine, and the chromosomes form 23 new pairs. There are 8,388,608 possible ways for the 23 pairs of chromosomes to form, with 70,368,744,000,000 possible combinations of genes. You can see that the chance of any two individuals being exactly alike is exceedingly slim.

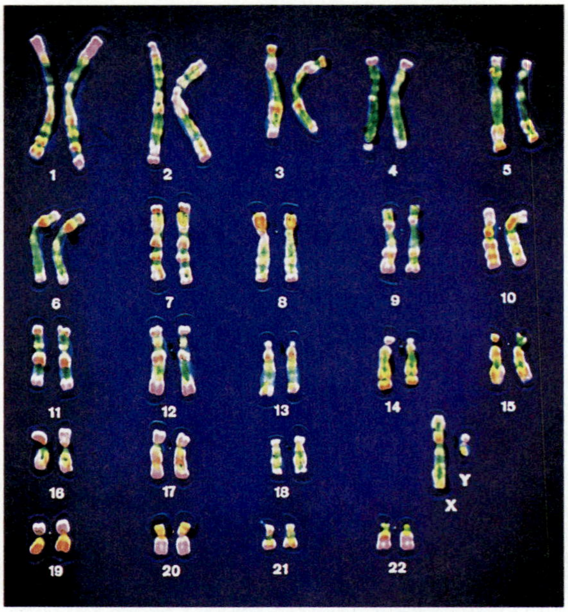

■ *The Y chromosome in these 23 pairs of human chromosomes means this person is male.*

Mapping the Genome

Biologists have mapped the human **genome**—the total DNA blueprint of heritable traits contained in every cell of the body. **Genetic mapping** involves dividing the chromosomes into smaller fragments that can be characterized, and ordering (mapping) the fragments to reflect their respective locations on specific chromosomes. The DNA is a double-stranded molecule built of four simple building blocks, called bases, which are grouped together in long strings. Resembling a twisted ladder and referred to as a *double helix,* the steps of the spiral ladder comprise pairs of these bases. The human genome consists of more than 3 billion base pairs, and the sequence of these bases of strings constitutes the genetic code. There are about 30,000 to 40,000 human genes—the truth is that genes are simply chemicals that direct the production of other chemicals. This information is converted into proteins, which act as enzymes and catalysts that turn various chemicals into still others, some of which affect behavior. So, each unique DNA sequence in each person may produce enzymes that influence an individual to feel sad or behave erratically—and this varies from location to location, sequence to sequence, and person to person. Thus, each person's heredity and response are unique, despite each human being's similarity to others.

It is important to recognize that human beings all share a very similar gene pool. Contrary to popular belief, differences among groups of people who are geographically distant, ethnically diverse, and considered of different races show little genetic variation—99.9% of DNA sequences found in the human genome are the same for all people (Venter et al., 2001). But that one-tenth of one percent makes for some interesting differences among us!

Researchers have identified the exact location or sites of genes contributing to muscular dystrophy, Huntington's disease, sickle cell anemia, some cancers, and learning problems, such as dyslexia (Peltonen & McKusick, 2001). Some researchers even argue that the nature of family social interactions has a genetic basis, because elements of personality, maladjustment, and language acquisition may be genetically determined (O'Connor & Plomin, 2000; O'Connor et al., 2000).

In 2001 the focus of research shifted from demonstrating the existence of genetic influence to exploring its extent and significance. Of course, researchers in this area face the crucial question of what to do with the expanding knowledge of the human genome. When scientists understand the basic genetic and biological mechanisms plus their relationship to behavior, they will be better able to predict situations in which maladjustment and behavior disorders may occur. Yet this ability to

Mutations
Unexpected changes in the gene replication process that are not always evident in phenotype and create unusual and sometimes harmful characteristics of body or behavior.

Genome
The total DNA blueprint of heritable traits contained in every cell of the body.

Genetic mapping
Dividing the chromosomes into smaller fragments that can be characterized and ordered (mapped) so that the fragments reflect their respective locations on specific chromosomes.

BRAIN AND BEHAVIOR

The Special Case of Twins

One of the best ways psychologists have to assess the contributions of nature and nurture is to study twins. Twins make ideal participants for such studies because they begin life in the same uterine environment and share similar patterns of nutrition and other prenatal influences. **Fraternal twins** (dizygotic twins) occur when two sperm fertilize two ova (eggs) and the two resulting *zygotes* (fertilized eggs) implant themselves in the uterus and grow alongside each other. The genes of these twins are not identical, so these twins are only as genetically similar as any brothers and sisters are. Fraternal twins can be of the same or different sexes. About 12 sets of fraternal twins occur in every 1,000 births. **Identical twins** (monozygotic twins) occur when one zygote splits into two identical cells, which then separate and develop independently into two genetically identical organisms, always of the same sex. Only 4 sets of identical twins occur in every 1,000 births.

Twins' genetic factors (nature) are fixed; but if the twins grow up in different families, their environments (nurture) differ. By comparing psychological characteristics of identical twins reared apart, researchers can assess the extent to which environment affects behavior and perhaps untangle a bit more of the nature–nurture interaction. They ask the question "How much of the difference, or variability, between twins (or between any two individuals, for that matter) is due to inherited characteristics?"

It's a complex picture. There are striking similarities in identical twins, even those separated for their entire lives (Wright, 1997), which supports the role of heredity. But a long and famous series of studies, called the *Minnesota adoption studies,* shows that young adopted twins are similar intellectually and in personality to other children in their *adoptive* families. This finding suggests that family environment exerts a great influence on young children. By adolescence, however, there is greater variation. Experiences outside the family are then playing a more powerful role (Wright, 1999). All families are interactive systems where genetics intermingle with a complex world. Turkheimer (2000, p. 161) said it well: "Genes and environments are both causal inputs into an interactive developmental system."

predict will no doubt create some difficult ethical dilemmas: If a particular pattern of genes is found to be associated with aggressiveness, how should society respond? Would it be desirable or ethical to screen newborns to identify those at risk of developing schizophrenia? Could this information be used to justify terminating pregnancies? Medical ethicists and psychologists argue that genetic screening cannot and should not be used for such purposes. Ethical considerations and legislation to guard people's rights must be high on the agenda of genetic researchers. Those who carry on the ethical debate must consider that genetics only lays the framework for behavior; because many events, life experiences, and cultural influences affect us, genetic influences must not be considered the sole determiner of behavior. Genes may bias us to respond in a specific way—for example, to feel lonely—but genes do not determine what a person who feels lonely will do about it (McGuire & Clifford, 2000).

Each Human Being Is Unique

With the exception of identical twins, every human being is genetically unique. Although each of us shares traits with our brothers, sisters, and parents, none of us is identical to them or to anyone else. The reason for this uniqueness is that a large number of genes determine, or at least influence, each person's physical, cognitive, and emotional characteristics. (See *Brain and Behavior* above.)

Fraternal twins
Twins that occur when two sperm fertilize two eggs; fraternal twins are only as genetically similar as any brothers or sisters are.

Identical twins
Twins that occur when one zygote splits into two identical cells, which then separate and develop independently; identical twins have exactly the same genetic makeup.

introduction to research basics

Correlation Is Not Causation

Many people believe that genetic inheritance determines behavior in much the same way that it determines eye color. But scientists can draw conclusions about what causes a particular behavior only based on evidence gained through experiments. Very few genetic studies, especially those conducted with human participants, are experimental. Instead, genetic researchers use a variety of methods that can be classified as *descriptive research,* which measures variables and attempts to develop an understanding of these variables and the relationships that may exist among them. Tyrone Cannon and his colleagues (1998) conducted a descriptive study with pairs of twins to determine the relative contributions of heredity and environment to schizophrenia, a serious behavior disorder characterized by delusions and hallucinations as well as problems in thought and personal relationships.

DESIGN This study was a **correlational study,** a type of descriptive research design that establishes the degree of relationship between two variables. Cannon and his colleagues wanted to establish the degree of relationship between diagnoses of mental disorders in pairs of twins. A correlation exists between two variables when an increase in the value of one variable is regularly accompanied by an increase or a decrease in the value of a second variable. Correlations are measured using the **correlation coefficient,** a number that expresses the degree and direction of a relationship between two variables. Correlation coefficients range from –1 (a perfect negative correlation) to +1 (a perfect positive correlation). Any correlation coefficient greater or less than 0, regardless of its sign, indicates that the variables are somehow related. The closer the correlation coefficient is to 1, the stronger the relationship.

HYPOTHESIS Schizophrenia will show a stronger relationship in identical than in fraternal twins; that is, if one twin of an identical twin pair exhibits symptoms of the disorder, the other will be likely to exhibit symptoms as well. In fraternal twins, if one twin exhibits symptoms, the other should be no more likely to exhibit symptoms than other siblings do.

PARTICIPANTS Participants were a total of 7,873 pairs of same-gender twins born in Finland between 1940 and 1957.

PROCEDURE Researchers screened records of inpatient and outpatient treatment as well as disability pension records for diagnoses of psychological disorders to determine the prevalence of schizophrenia in this population of twins.

RESULTS The prevalence of schizophrenia was 2% for this population of twins in Finland. The correlation between diagnoses of schizophrenia for identical (monozygotic) twins was .84, whereas the correlation for fraternal (dizygotic) twins was .34. Additional correlational analysis led Cannon and his colleagues to conclude that 83% of the variation in schizophrenia is due to inherited factors. This estimate is higher than that of previous studies.

LIMITATIONS Although the correlation between twin pairs was high, especially for identical twins, the relationship of genetic inheritance and schizophrenia is far from perfect. If schizophrenia were genetically *determined,* 100% of identical twins would be schizophrenic when one member of the pair was, but around half are not. This strength of correlation definitely suggests that inherited factors are involved in the development of schizophrenia, but factors other than genetics contribute to it as well (Plomin & Crabbe, 2000).

Correlations between behavior and genetics are never sufficient to indicate that genes cause behavior. That is, *correlated events are not necessarily causally related.* We say that we have a *correlation,* or that two events are *correlated,* when the increased presence (or absence) of a particular situation or condition is regularly associated with a high (or low) presence of another situation, or condition. That relationship exists between degree of genetic relationship and schizophrenia in affected families. To demonstrate causation, other research is necessary, and behavioral genetics researchers are gathering data that would causally link specific genes to schizophrenia (Brzustowicz et al., 2000). These links may produce information concerning how genes affect neurotransmitters, causing them to produce behavioral abnormalities, or how genes affect brain structure, producing the behaviors symptomatic of schizophrenia. These specific links are necessary to demonstrate that genes cause schizophrenia. Research in the near future may succeed in establishing these links, but correlational research does not have the power to show causal relationships.

Behavioral traits such as temperament and intelligence and disorders such as Alzheimer's disease and schizophrenia also have genetic components; this is why psychologists are especially interested in heredity. The field of *behavioral genetics* focuses on the influence of genes on behavior. Behavioral geneticists ask questions about whether human characteristics such as shyness, impulsiveness, or intelligence have a genetic, inherited basis. If they do, then to what extent is a given behavior inherited or biological in origin, and to what extent is it learned or due to experience?

Researchers thus talk of the *heritability* of a trait or behavior. Many heritable characteristics exist and vary among individuals in a population—intelligence, dancing ability, and height are just a few examples. Such characteristics require a genetic contribution from both parents, and how heritable a trait or characteristic is reflects estimates of how much of the variation in a *group* is due to genetic differences in that group (not in a specific person). We will take a closer look at heritability and behavior in Chapter 10.

A dozen or so genes predispose individuals to insulin-dependent diabetes; we say that such disorders are *multigenic*. Behavioral genetics researchers such as Robert Plomin argue that because most traits are determined by multiple genes, we cannot say that gene number 6 causes reading disability, but rather contributes to it. Gene number 6 may carry markers for disability that every person has, but the significant variation among individuals means that reading disability is expressed to a greater degree in some individuals than in others. So, some people will show greater expression of the genes for reading problems than other people will. So too with alcoholism and substance abuse; some people are far more likely to become addicted and dependent than are other individuals, or even more likely to exhibit delinquency (McGue, 1999; Taylor, Iacono, & McGue, 2000). This idea is important from a behavioral genetic point of view because it asserts that people are not simply "alcoholic," or "depressed," or "dyslexic"; rather, everybody has the potential of expressing those characteristics, but the unique combination of genes contributes to *how much* of those traits will be expressed for each individual.

The Evolutionary Approach to Psychology

The human genome did not emerge in its present form and remain unchanged over time. Rather, we know that human beings evolved, and through that selection process, our genes have their present configuration. If you accept that human behavior is influenced by our genetic heritage, then understanding our evolutionary history is an important aspect of learning about our current behavior. **Evolutionary psychology** is the psychological perspective that seeks to explain and predict behaviors by analyzing how the human brain developed over time and how evolutionary history affects the behavior of humans today; it seeks to explain human behavior by considering how behavior is affected from the vantage point of evolutionary biology. Evolutionary psychologists argue that significant portions of human behaviors and mental abilities have endowed the human brain with specific selected abilities, such as the ability to learn, to acquire language, and to choose suitable mates.

■ **NATURAL SELECTION.** Evolutionary theory in biology assumes that natural selection is a key factor in changes that appear in different organisms over time. **Natural selection** is the principle that those characteristics and behaviors that help organisms adapt, be fit, and survive are the ones that will be passed on to successive generations, because flexible, fit individuals have a greater chance of reproduction. Using ideas such as survival of the fittest, these researchers argue that traits have evolved slowly over time, and this has led to humans with distinct physiological mechanisms that push them toward certain behaviors and away from others. When a trait or inherited characteristic has increased in a population, evolutionary researchers say that an **adaptation** has occurred—and it occurred to help solve a problem of survival or reproduction. Evolutionary psychologists argue that certain psychological traits were not always what they are today; they assert that these traits are clear adaptations and represent evolved heredity. Evolution has created an instinct in human beings to protect their offspring from danger; there is a natural—evolutionary psychologists assert, genetically coded—tendency for parents to protect their young from danger (Geary, 2000). In doing so they ensure the survival of the species. Another example comes from the development of communication: in the early stages of human evolution, communication consisted merely of grunts. But

Correlational study
A type of descriptive research design that establishes the degree of relationship between two variables.

Correlation coefficient
A number that expresses the degree and direction of a relationship between two variables, ranging from −1 (a perfect negative correlation) to +1 (a perfect positive correlation).

Evolutionary psychology
The psychological perspective that seeks to explain and predict behaviors by analyzing how the human brain developed over time and how evolutionary history affects the behavior of humans today; it seeks to explain human behavior by considering how behavior is affected from the vantage point of evolutionary biology.

Natural selection
The principle that those characteristics and behaviors that help organisms adapt, be fit, and survive will be passed on to successive generations, because flexible, fit individuals have a greater chance of reproduction.

Adaptation
A trait or inherited characteristic that has increased in a population because it solved a problem of survival or reproduction.

through the course of generations, those in difficult circumstances who grunted good commands, advice, and other ideas were more likely to survive. Those who lived taught their children, and over succeeding generations, language developed and was ultimately encoded in the human genome. Jealousy is reasoned to have an evolutionary base (Buss, 2000); even self-esteem is hypothesized to have developed through evolutionary processes. Zimmerman (2000) maintains that our devotion to sports teams, the need to be right (rather than wrong), personal pride, and even arrogance are part of a sense of self-esteem determined through evolution. (See *Point Counterpoint* for a discussion on evolution and sexuality.)

■ **EVOLUTION AND DETERMINISM.** Cognitive psychologists, evolutionary biologists, and neuroscientists together are studying the brain and its circuits to see how it is organized and specialized and especially how evolutionary history affects

point*counterpoint*

Gender and Promiscuity

The Issue: Are men sexually promiscuous by nature while women are sexually selective?

POINT
Men's reproductive strategy involves having many offspring, while women's strategy involves selecting mates who will care for her offspring.

COUNTERPOINT
Most societies hold a double standard for sexual behavior, making it impossible to establish an evolutionary basis for gender differences in sexual behavior.

Mate selection has been a major focus of evolutionary psychologists, who contend that men and women have different strategies for successfully passing on their genes. Men's reproductive strategy is to father many children, and the way to do that is to have lots of sex with many different women. Women's strategy, on the other hand, is to find a mate who will take care of her and her offspring, which leads women to be selective about their sexual partners. These two strategies produce different goals and result in conflicts between women and men. These differences, evolutionary psychologists argue, are practically inevitable because evolutionary history has built women and men differently in this respect.

Those who take the other side of the argument agree that differences exist in sexual behavior, but those differences are attributable to social standards rather than evolutionary history. Many (but not all) societies have a double standard for sexual behavior in which men's sexual behavior is held to one standard, often allowing men sexual freedom, while women's sexual behavior is held to another, often restricting their sexuality. These different standards allow men to have many sexual partners but prohibit women from similar behavior.

Some females are unaffected by the double standard—nonhuman primates (Hrdy, 1981). Among various primate species, female sexual behavior shows a great deal of variation. For example, female chimpanzees mate with dozens of males, but both female and male gibbons are monogamous. However, recent research using DNA evidence of parenthood has caused some rethinking about sexual behavior (Barash, 2001). The results from this type of research suggest that the females of many species may not be as restricted by selectivity as researchers imagined—many females from "monogamous" species produce offspring with DNA from males that were not their mates. So perhaps the genders are not so different in terms of sexual behavior after all.

current thought processes. They all assume that the brain is a system whose function is governed by biological processes, whose evolutionary history influences how the brain currently operates. Evolutionary theory does not hold that behavior is determined or controlled exclusively by innate mechanisms (Buss, 1999). All human behavior occurs within some context, and the cultural environment of behavior is a necessary component for an evolutionary explanation of behavior because environment shapes physiological as well as psychological characteristics.

Evolutionary psychologists are quick to point out that the approach does not assert a *behavioral determinism* whereby evolutionary history determines behavior in an inalterable way (Buss, 1999; Caporael, 2001). Culture and environment affect behavior, and individuals are capable of change throughout their lives. Over time individuals develop new, different connections among brain cells that did not exist at birth. Furthermore, connections that existed at birth and in childhood may have disappeared. Basically, adult brains are not only capable of reorganizing themselves, but do so throughout a person's lifetime. Our brains are constantly being organized and reorganized, forming new and useful connections. We see evidence for such reorganization after a person has an accident or stroke and then recovers the ability to speak, read, or walk—despite the damage to the brain tissue that was the basis for that behavior (Rossini & Pauri, 2000). From an evolutionary perspective, all of this makes sense—connections that are useful survive, grow, and mature, and those that don't get used are pruned away.

Evolution is a continuous process, adapting to new obstacles as they appear and then moving on to solve the next obstacle that comes along. The design of the brain and its functioning is shaped by previous experiences—not only those in an individual's lifetime, but also those of the species. From an evolutionary perspective, this constant change serves as an adaptive mechanism allowing individuals, and their brains, to continue to evolve (Fernald & White, 2000). As Low (2000, p. 245) says, "Our evolved tendencies interact with today's novel environments." Psychologists strive to understand current behavior, and evolutionary psychologists believe that studying the challenges faced in human prehistory offers a way to understand contemporary behavior. Yet scientists like Paul Ehrlich (2000) caution us to remember that we are not captives to our genes and that biology and evolution only make sense within the context of a culture.

KEY QUESTIONS. What is exciting about evolutionary psychology is that it addresses questions that psychology has ignored in the past. It not only wants to understand mating and reproduction—behaviors closely associated with natural selection—but also how human beings have developed coping mechanisms, self-esteem, creativity, problem-solving abilities, and even a sense of awareness of ourselves, consciousness. In some ways, evolutionary psychology is going beyond the question of how the mind works, asking how it got to work the way it does, why, and where might it go next.

Like most new ideas, evolutionary psychology has proponents and critics. Proponents like David Buss (1999, 2000), Douglas Kenrick (2001), and Leda Cosmides and John Tooby (1999) assert that this new approach helps explain unanswered questions: issues of jealousy, aggression, and development. But critics like Stephen Jay Gould (1997, p. 60) maintain that evolutionary psychology goes too far in its explanations: "there are many evolutionary biologists who view everything that happens in evolution—every feature, every

Be an *Active* learner

REVIEW

- What is the distinction between nature and nurture? pp. 38–39
- What is heritability? p. 38
- Distinguish between genotypes and phenotypes. p. 39
- Define natural selection. p. 43

THINK CRITICALLY

- What fundamental characteristic of identical twins makes them ideal participants in studies of nature versus nurture?
- What potential environmental influences can alter people's inherited characteristics? Can such influences be limited? Should they be?
- Can you think of a behavior that evolutionary approaches might better explain than traditional psychological approaches? Explain your answer.

APPLY PSYCHOLOGY

- The effort to understand the biological characteristics associated with particular gene patterns has ethical implications. What if scientists find genes strongly associated with criminality, for example? What should be done with this knowledge?
- Automobiles have not been part of human history long enough to produce an evolutionary adaptation to them, yet we are able to deal with automobiles. What evolved abilities help us deal with them? Give another example of how evolved abilities are used to master other challenges in modern society.

behavior—as directly evolved for adaptive benefit. And that just doesn't work." Another type of criticism comes from Jerry Coyne (2000, p. 27), who points out the problems with taking an evolutionary approach to behavior: "Unlike bones, behavior does not fossilize, and understanding its evolution often involves concocting stories that sound plausible but are hard to test."

Like all appealing theories, evolutionary psychology will go through refinements and changes in focus; if it is a good, workable theory that explains data and phenomena well, it will stand the test of time (Ketelaar & Ellis, 2000). For now, evolutionary psychology is opening a brave new world of questions just as behavioral geneticists are unlocking the keys to how genes express themselves.

Communication in the Nervous System

The nervous system provides a means of internal communication as well as an interface for communication with the outside world. Even the simplest task requires smooth functioning of the nervous system. In some ways, the nervous system acts like an air traffic controller, watching, sending, receiving, processing, interpreting, and storing vital information. Many psychologists study how the electrical and chemical signals in the brain represent and transmit such information. By studying how the nervous system's components work together and how they are integrated, psychologists learn a great deal about the nature and diversity of behavior.

The **nervous system** consists of the structures and organs that facilitate communication in the body and allow all behavior and mental processes to take place. The nervous system has two subdivisions: the *central nervous system* (the brain and spinal cord) and the *peripheral nervous system* (all the other parts). We'll examine these two subdivisions shortly. First, however, you need to understand how communication proceeds within the system as a whole. The nervous system is composed of hundreds of billions of cells, each of which receives information from hundreds to thousands of others. The most elementary unit in the nervous system is the neuron, which is where we will begin.

Nervous system
The structures and organs that facilitate electrical and chemical communication in the body and allow all behavior and mental processes to take place.

Neuron
The single cell that is the basic building block of the nervous system and comprises dendrites (which receive neural signals), a cell body (which generates electrical signals), and an axon (which transmits neural signals); also known as a *nerve cell.*

Afferent neurons
Neurons that send messages to the spinal cord and brain.

Efferent neurons
Neurons that send messages from the brain and spinal cord to other structures in the body.

Dendrites
Thin, bushy, widely branching fibers that extend outward from the neuron's cell body and that receive signals from neighboring neurons and carry them back to the cell body.

Axon
A thin, elongated structure that transmits signals from the neuron's cell body to the axon terminals, which pass them on to adjacent neurons, muscles, or glands.

The Neuron

The basic building block of the nervous system is a single cell—the **neuron,** or nerve cell. There are billions of neurons throughout the body (as many as 100 billion in the brain alone), differing in shape, size, and function. Neurons are often grouped together in bundles; these bundles of neuron fibers are called *nerves* if they are in the peripheral nervous system and *tracts* if they are in the central nervous system.

■ **TYPES OF NEURONS.** All of the neurons in your body are not active at once. Nonetheless, each neuron is always ready to convey information and signals. Nerve pathways allow signals to flow (1) to the brain and spinal cord *from* the sense organs and muscles, and (2) from the brain and spinal cord *to* the sense organs and muscles, carrying messages that initiate reactions and behavior. Two types of neurons are involved in this two-way neuronal firing: **afferent neurons** (from the Latin *ad,* "to," and *ferre,* "carry") carry messages to the spinal cord and brain; **efferent neurons** (from the Latin *ex,* "out of," and *ferre,* "carry") carry messages from the brain and spinal cord to other structures in the body (see Figure 2.2).

There are three other subcategories of neurons: sensory neurons, motor neurons, and interneurons. *Sensory neurons* are afferent neurons that convey information from the body's sense organs to the brain and spinal cord. *Motor neurons* are efferent neurons that carry information from the brain and spinal cord to the muscles and glands. *Interneurons* connect other types of neurons. The interneurons form a network that allows the other neurons to interact with one another, and they outnumber sensory or motor neurons. The millions of neurons that work together are surrounded by *glial cells,* which nourish the neurons and help hold them in place. Glial cells are small—and ten times more numerous than sensory or motor neurons or interneurons. They constitute about 90% of the cells in the brain, and are important in forming connections between neurons (Ullian et al., 2001). In addition, glial cells help insulate the brain from toxins and also help to form the *myelin sheath.* Many neurons, especially the longer ones, are *myelinated,* covered with a thin white substance (the myelin sheath). Myelinated neurons conduct signals faster than unmyelinated neurons.

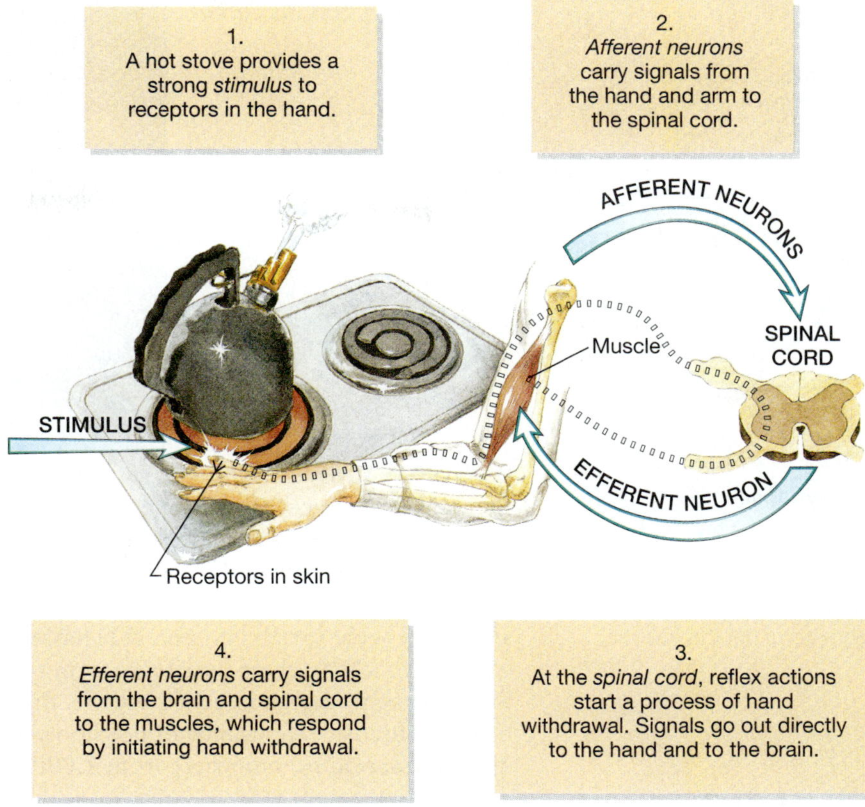

FIGURE 2.2

The Action of Afferent and Efferent Neurons

■ **PARTS OF A NEURON.** Typically, neurons are composed of four primary parts: dendrites, a cell body, an axon, and axon terminals (see Figure 2.3). **Dendrites** (from the Greek word for "tree," because of their branchlike appearance) are thin, bushy, widely branching fibers that extend outward from the neuron's cell body. Dendrites are the principal signal reception sites for neurons—they receive signals from neighboring neurons and carry them to the cell body (Kennedy, 2000). At the *cell body,* the signals are transformed and then continue to travel along the axon. The **axon** is a thin, elongated structure that transmits signals from the neuron's cell body to the *axon terminals* (the end points of each neuron). Axons also have branches at their endings.

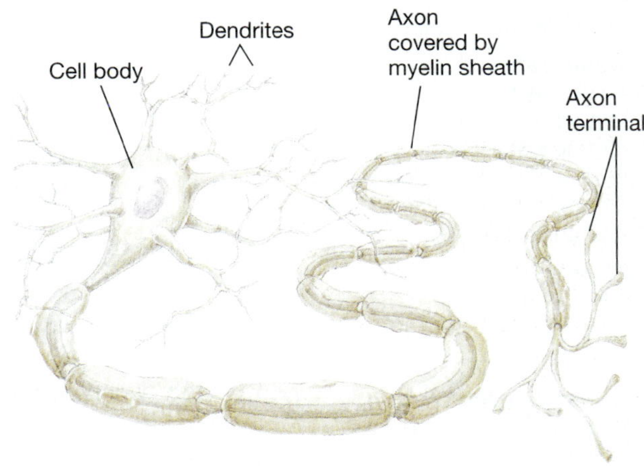

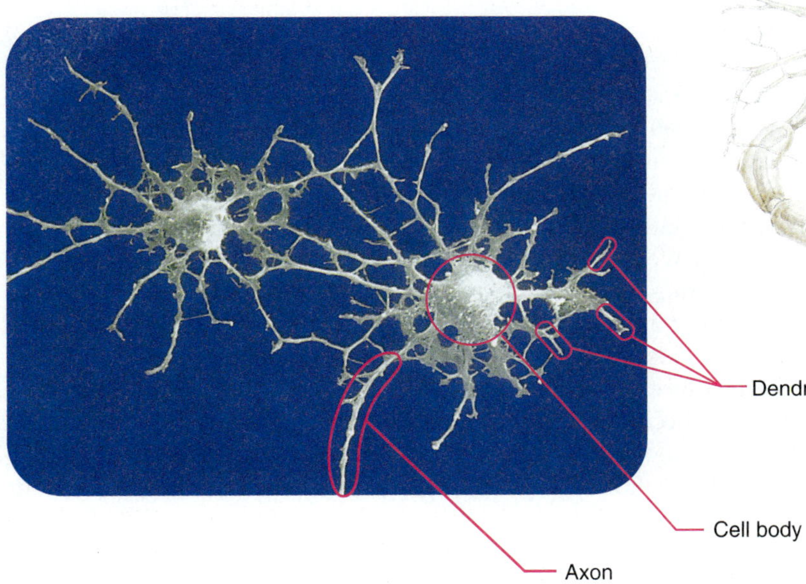

FIGURE 2.3

The Basic Components of a Neuron

Neurons appear in many forms, but all possess the basic structures shown here: a cell body, an axon (with myelin sheath and axon terminals), and dendrites.

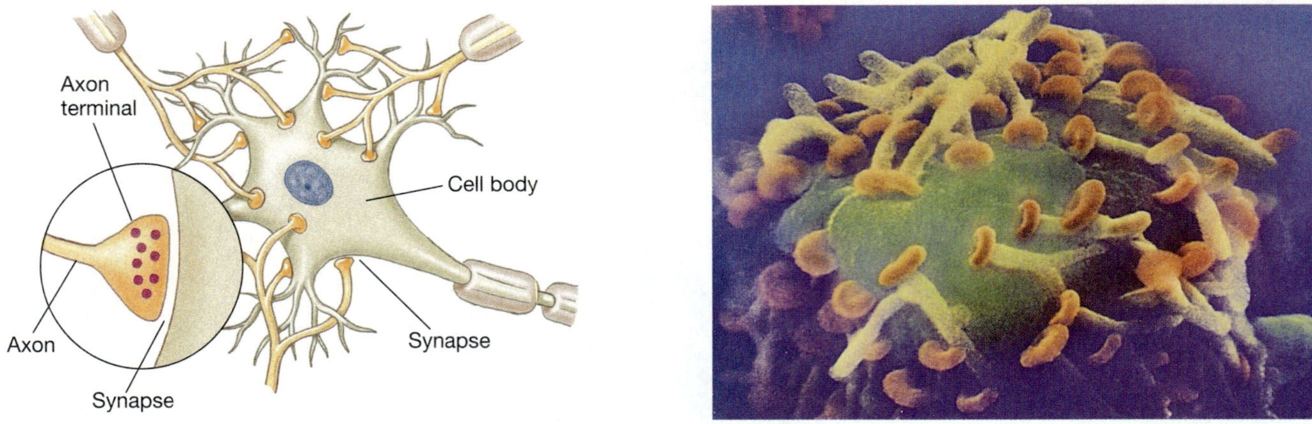

FIGURE 2.4
The Synapse
The synapse is very small. Chemicals released by the axon terminals cross the synapse to stimulate the cell body or the dendrites of another neuron.

Synapse [SIN-apps]
The microscopically small space between the axon terminals of one neuron and the receptor sites of another neuron.

Action potential
An electrical current that is sent down the axon of a neuron and is initiated by a rapid reversal of the polarization of the cell membrane; also known as a *spike discharge.*

All-or-none
Either at full strength or not at all; the basis on which neurons fire.

Refractory period
Amount of time needed for a neuron to recover after it fires; during this period, an action potential will not occur.

Neurotransmitter
Chemical substance that resides in the axon terminals within synaptic vesicles and that, when released, moves across the synaptic space and binds to a receptor site on an adjacent cell.

■ **NEURONAL SYNAPSES.** The axon terminals (the orange buttonlike structures in the photo) of almost all neurons lie very close to receptor sites (dendrites, cell body, or axons) of other neurons. The microscopically small space between the axon terminals of one neuron and the receptor sites of another is called a **synapse** (see Figure 2.4). This small region may hold the key to understanding how the nervous system allows the wide variability seen in behavior. You can think of many neurons strung together in a long chain as a relay team sending signals, conveying information, or initiating some action in a cell, muscle, or gland. Each neuron receives information from hundreds to thousands of neighboring neurons and may "synapse on" (transmit information to) anywhere from 1,000 to 10,000 other neurons.

■ **ELECTROCHEMICAL PROCESSES.** How do neurons communicate? What kinds of signals do they transmit? Neuroscientists know that the neural impulse is electrochemical in nature. Activity within neurons is electrical; between neurons, the message is chemical. Understanding the electrochemical processes of neural transmission is essential to understanding the role of neurons in behavior. The electrical process is created by the existence of an extremely thin cell membrane (less than 0.00001 millimeter thick) that is partially permeable. That is, there are channels, or "gates," in this membrane through which some particles can pass but others cannot, resulting in charged particles being trapped either inside or outside the neuron. The neuron is normally in a resting state, in which its interior is negatively charged relative to its exterior environment. The difference in electrical charge between the inside and the outside of the cell creates a state of *polarization* across the cell membrane. The result of this polarization is a neuron that is charged, ready and waiting to activate.

■ **ACTION POTENTIAL.** Each neuron has a *threshold,* a level of stimulation required for activation. When a neuron is stimulated by others to the point where it reaches its threshold, changes occur very rapidly. At this point, the "gates" of the cell membrane open, the membrane becomes fully permeable, positively charged ions rush through the membrane into the neuron, and a rapid reversal of electrical polarity occurs (see Figure 2.5). We say that the neuron is depolarized and an action potential has formed. The **action potential,** or *spike discharge,* is an electrical current that travels down the axon of a neuron, initiated by a rapid reversal of the polarization of the cell membrane. This event is often described as "firing," and the image is a good one to describe this explosive discharge.

A neuron does not necessarily *fire,* or produce an action potential, every time it is stimulated. If the threshold is not reached, the cell will not fire. Level of stimulation is important for firing. For example, a bright flash from a camera will stimulate more cells in the visual areas of the brain than the flicker of a candle. When a neuron fires, it generates an action potential in an **all-or-none** fashion—that is, the firing of the neuron, like the firing of a gun, occurs either at full strength or not at all.

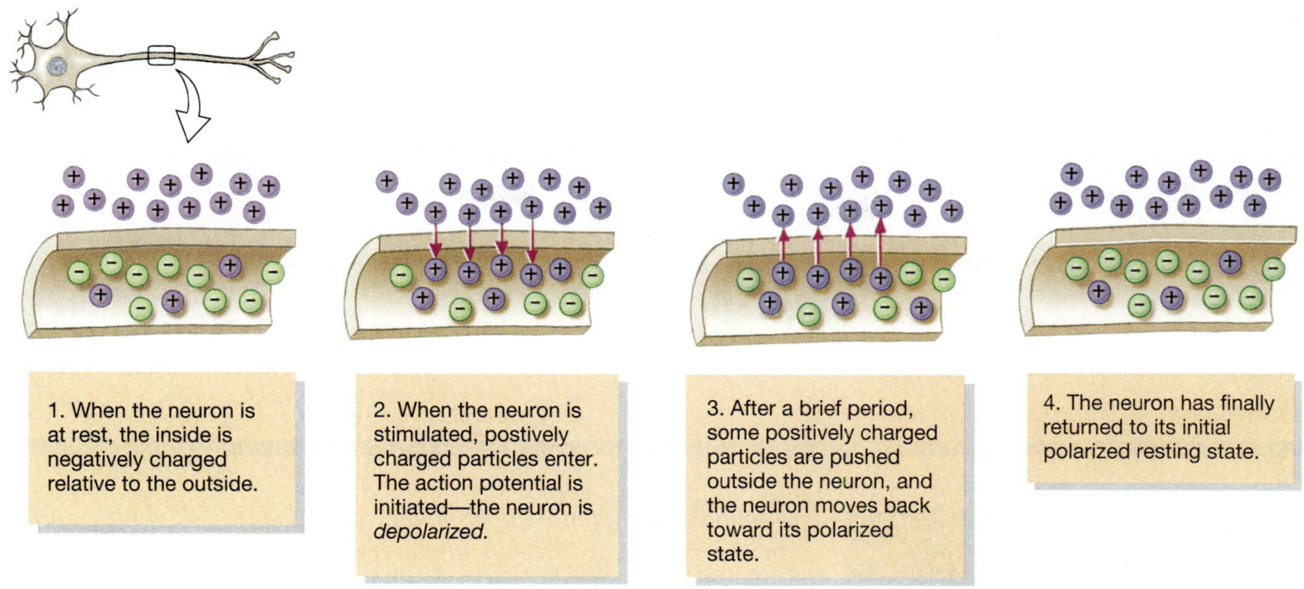

FIGURE 2.5

Generation of an Action Potential

Action potentials occur in 2 to 4 milliseconds (thousandths of a second); therefore, neurons cannot normally fire more than 500 times per second. After each firing, a neuron needs time to recover (generally just a few thousandths of a second); the time needed for recovery is called the **refractory period.** During this period, normal levels of stimulation will not produce an action potential.

Neurotransmitters and Behavior

When an action potential moves down to the end of an axon, it initiates the release of **neurotransmitters**—chemical substances that reside in the axon terminals within synaptic vesicles (small storage structures in each axon terminal). The neurotransmitters are the basis of the chemical part of neural transmission. These chemicals are released into the synapse, move across the synaptic space, and bind to receptor sites on adjacent neurons, thereby communicating with that cell (see Figure 2.6). We will examine the various types of neurotransmitters shortly.

When a neurotransmitter has affected an adjacent cell, it has accomplished its main mission; the neurotransmitter is then neutralized either by an enzyme or taken back up by the neuron that released it in a process called *reuptake.* Sometimes neurotransmitters excite receiving neurons, or cause them to fire more easily; sometimes they inhibit receiving neurons, or cause them to fire less easily. A change in the membrane potential of a neuron after it has received neurotransmitters from another neuron is called a *postsynaptic*

FIGURE 2.6

Major Steps in Neuronal Transmission

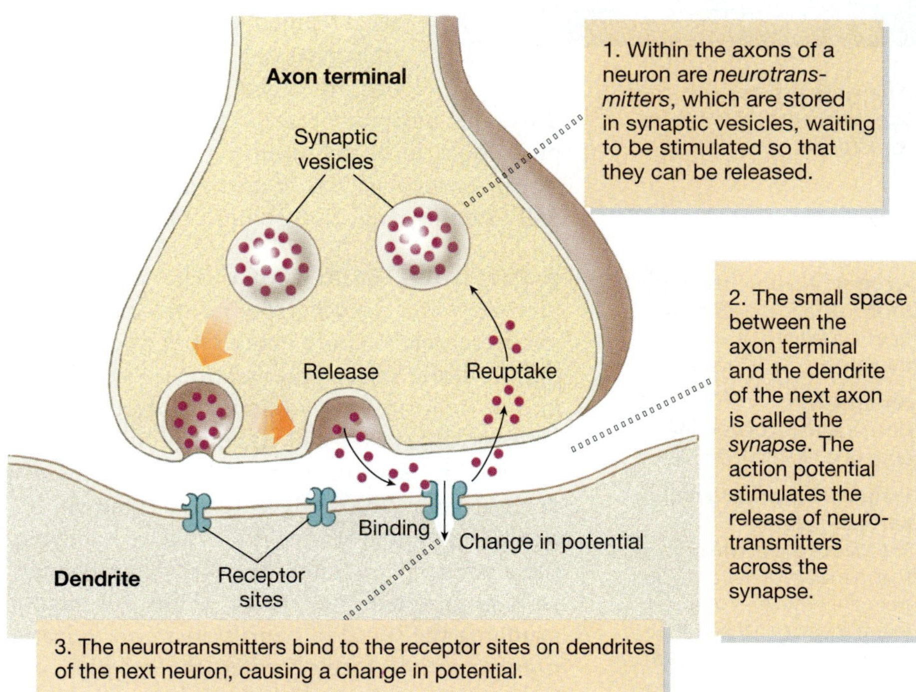

TABLE 2.1

Five Key Neurotransmitters

Neurotransmitter	Location	Effects
Acetylcholine	Brain, spinal cord, autonomic nervous system, selected organs	Excitation in brain and autonomic nervous system; excitation or inhibition in certain organs
Norepinephrine	Brain, spinal cord, selected organs	Inhibition in brain; excitation or inhibition in certain organs
Dopamine	Brain	Inhibition
Serotonin	Brain, spinal cord	Inhibition
GABA	Brain, spinal cord	Inhibition

■ *Strenuous exercise and stress are experiences that release endorphins.*

potential. An *excitatory postsynaptic potential (EPSP)* makes it easier for the neuron to fire; an *inhibitory postsynaptic potential (IPSP)* makes it harder for the neuron to fire. Because hundreds to thousands of neurons synapse on a single cell, a single neuron can receive both EPSP and IPSP at once (Abbott et al., 1997).

There are a large number of neurotransmitters; at least 50 have been identified. One of them, gamma-aminobutyric acid (GABA), is involved in virtually every behavior, including anxiety states. Another important neurotransmitter, *serotonin,* is distributed throughout the brain and is especially important in regulating sleep. The most well studied neurotransmitter, however, is *acetylcholine,* which is found in neurons throughout the brain and spinal cord. Acetylcholine is crucial to excitation of the skeletal muscles, the muscles that allow you to move. It is also important in functions such as memory, learning, and sexual behavior. The memory problems associated with Alzheimer's disease (to be discussed in Chapter 8) include an inability to produce sufficient amounts of acetylcholine. Table 2.1 describes five key neurotransmitters and their effects.

Cells contain other substances that are not neurotransmitters but act in similar ways; for example, neuropeptides act much like neurotransmitters. The effects of one type of naturally produced neuropeptide called *endorphins* are similar to those of morphine. Indeed, opiate drugs like morphine exert their effects by occupying endorphin receptors. As morphine does in hospitalized patients, endorphins inhibit certain synaptic transmissions—particularly those involving pain—and generally make people feel good. We will examine pain, endorphins, and pain management in more detail in Chapter 5.

Agonist [AG-oh-nist]
Chemical that mimics or facilitates the actions of a neurotransmitter.

Antagonist
Chemical that opposes the actions of a neurotransmitter.

Peripheral [puh-RIF-er-al] nervous system
The part of the nervous system that carries information to and from the central nervous system through spinal nerves attached to the spinal cord and through 12 cranial nerves.

■ **PSYCHOPHARMACOLOGY.** The study of how drugs affect the body is called pharmacology, and *psychopharmacology* is the study of how drugs affect behavior. Researchers study many types of drugs to learn the physiological mechanisms that underlie behavioral reactions. Psychopharmacological research may hold the key to treating drug addiction and other behavior problems. Such research may uncover drugs that will effectively block the addictive properties of drugs such as cocaine and lead to more successful forms of treatment for addiction (Robinson & Berridge, 2000). Research has shown that many common drugs alter the amount of a neurotransmitter released at synapses; other drugs alter the way neurotransmitters operate; yet other drugs change the speed at which neurotransmitters are disabled after release. Thus, for example, a drug may change behavior by changing the speed of neurotransmitter release, which increases the number of action potentials formed when the released neurotransmitter is excitatory or decreases the number of action potentials when the neurotransmitter is inhibitory.

Chemicals can also be used to mimic or facilitate the actions of neurotransmitters; such chemicals are called **agonists.** When an agonist is present, it is as if the neurotransmitter itself has been released. Other chemicals, called **antagonists,** oppose the actions of specific neurotransmitters. When an antagonist is present, receptor sites are blocked, and the neurotransmitter cannot have its usual effect. Schizophrenia, a disabling mental disorder, is often treated with antagonists. Neurons that normally respond to dopamine are blocked from doing so by being exposed to certain drugs that act as antagonists, and symptoms of schizophrenia are thereby diminished. (We will discuss dopamine and schizophrenia in more detail in Chapter 15.) Some drugs block the reabsorption, or reuptake, of neurotransmitters from their receptor sites. This blocking of reuptake has proved highly useful in the treatment of depression, which affects millions of people worldwide.

When neurons fire, information is transferred from the sense organs to the brain and then from the brain to the muscular system and the glands. If psychologists knew precisely how this transfer occurred, they could more successfully predict and manage the behavior of people with neurological damage, mood disorders, or epilepsy, for example. However, the firing of neurons and the release of neurotransmitters do not in themselves completely explain the biological bases of human behavior. The firing of individual neurons presents a close-up look at the function of the nervous system, but a wider view of brain structure is necessary to understand the relationship between brain and behavior. We turn next to that view of the brain and nervous system.

Be an *Active* learner

REVIEW

- Describe the electrical portion of neural transmission. p. 48
- Describe the path of a neural impulse from one neuron to another. pp. 47–48
- What is the difference between excitatory and inhibitory postsynaptic potentials? pp. 49–56

THINK CRITICALLY

- Should scientists try to apply their increasing knowledge of neuronal transmission to improve the human body—perhaps creating one that would not experience pain?
- What is the disadvantage of the increasing availability of drugs for the treatment of mental disorders?

APPLY PSYCHOLOGY

- If you worked for a pharmaceutical company, could you "design" a drug that would help people better manage their own behavior? If you could do so, what would you make this drug do?

The Organization of the Nervous System

It is a dark, wet evening; you are driving down a deserted road, listening to some 1980s oldies. A car appears out of nowhere, heading straight toward you. You swerve, brake, swerve again, pump the brakes, and then pull over to the side of the road—all within a matter of seconds. Your nervous system has controlled each of these reactions on a second-by-second basis, allowing you to avoid a crash. Psychologists must understand the organization and functions of the nervous system and its mutually dependent systems and subdivisions to explain such complex behavior. The central nervous system consists of the brain and spinal cord; the peripheral nervous system connects the central nervous system to the rest of the body. Let's examine both systems in some detail.

- *Both the somatic and autonomic divisions of the peripheral nervous system are involved in swerving to avoid a crash.*

The Peripheral Nervous System

The **peripheral nervous system** is the part of the nervous system that carries information to and from the central nervous system through spinal nerves attached to the spinal cord and through 12 cranial nerves, which carry signals directly to and from the brain. The peripheral nervous system contains all the nerves that are not in the central nervous system; its nerves lie in the *periphery,* or outer parts, of the body. It is subdivided, and its two major divisions are the somatic nervous system and the autonomic nervous system.

■ **THE SOMATIC NERVOUS SYSTEM.** The **somatic nervous system** is the part of the peripheral nervous system that both responds to the external senses of sight, hearing, touch, smell, and taste and acts on the outside world. Generally considered to be under the individual's voluntary control, the somatic nervous system is involved in perceptual processing (processing information gathered through the senses) and in control of movement and muscles. The somatic nervous system consists of both sensory (afferent) and motor (efferent) neurons, carrying information from the sense organs to the brain and from the brain and spinal cord to the muscles under conscious control. It is the somatic nervous system that allows you to see an oncoming car and get out of its way.

■ **THE AUTONOMIC NERVOUS SYSTEM.** The **autonomic nervous system** is the part of the peripheral nervous system that controls the vital and automatic activities of the body, such as heart rate, digestive processes, blood pressure, and functioning of internal organs. In contrast to the somatic nervous system, the autonomic nervous system operates continuously and involuntarily (although the technique of biofeedback, discussed in Chapter 6, allows partial voluntary control). The system is called *autonomic* (from the Greek word meaning "independent") because many

FIGURE 2.7

The Two Divisions of the Autonomic Nervous System

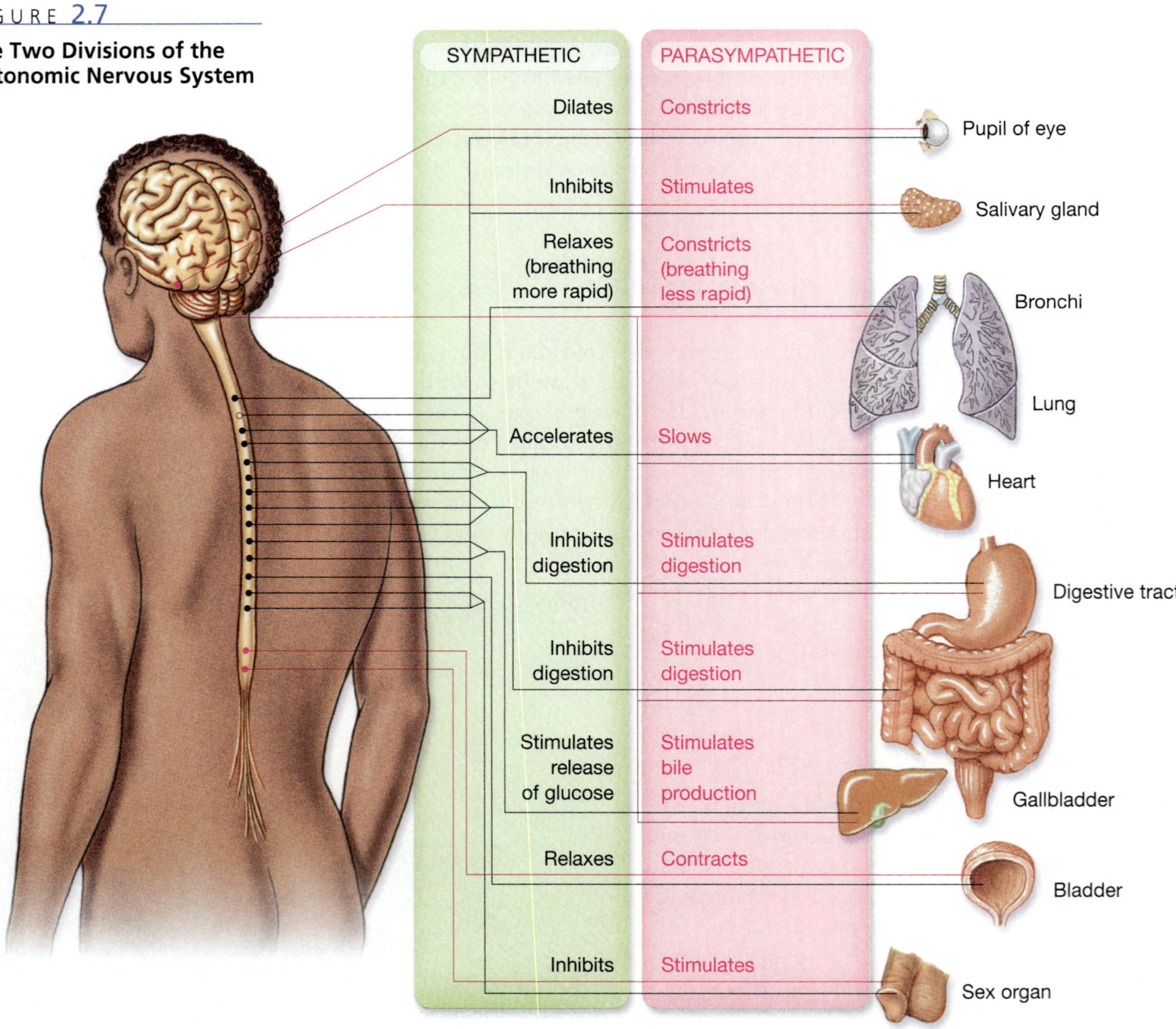

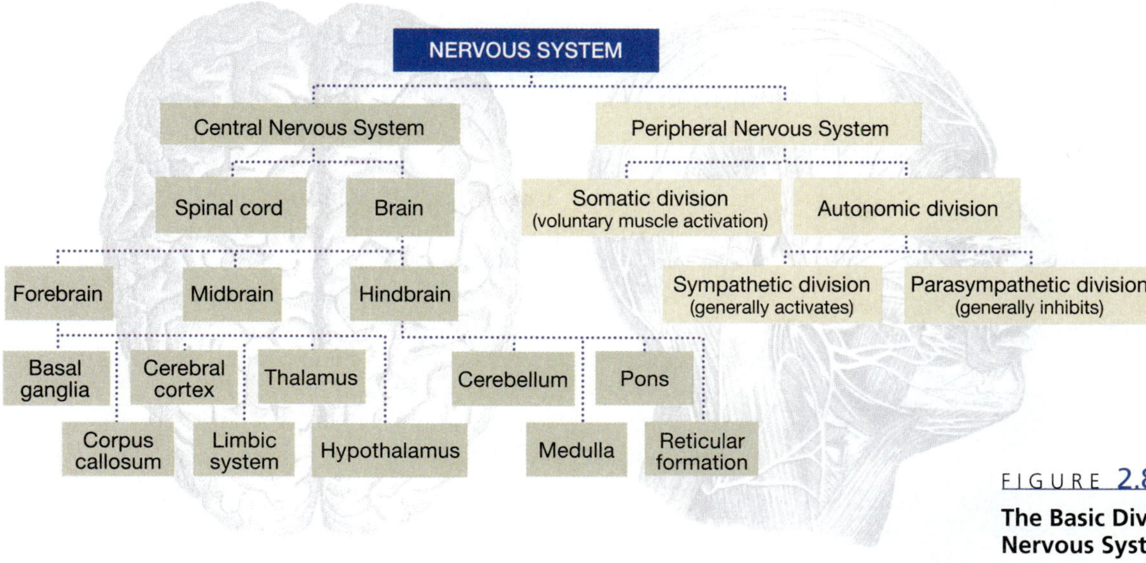

FIGURE 2.8

The Basic Divisions of the Nervous System

of its subsystems are self-regulating, focused on the utilization and conservation of energy resources. The autonomic nervous system consists of two divisions: the sympathetic nervous system and the parasympathetic nervous system, which work together to control the activities of muscles and glands (see Figure 2.7).

The **sympathetic nervous system** is the part of the autonomic nervous system that responds to emergency situations by activating bodily resources to handle these emergencies. Activation results in a sharp increase in heart rate and blood pressure, slowing of the digestive processes, dilation of the pupils, and general preparation for an emergency, like a possible head-on collision with a car. Together, these bodily changes are sometimes called the *fight-or-flight response*. These changes are usually accompanied by an increased flow of epinephrine, or adrenaline, which is a substance released by the adrenal gland and then regulated by a set of neurons in the hypothalamus and brain stem. Increased activity of the sympathetic nervous system is what makes your heart pound and your mouth go dry when your car narrowly misses hitting an oncoming car.

When the sympathetic nervous system is active and the organism is in a fight-or-flight state, the somatic nervous system is also activated. For example, when attempting to avoid a crash with another car, a driver must initiate a series of motor movements to steer, brake, and possibly shift gears. The driver's adrenal gland is stimulated by the sympathetic nervous system; the burst of energy produced by epinephrine (released by the adrenal gland) affects the somatic nervous system, making the driver's muscles respond strongly and rapidly. Thus, changes in the sympathetic nervous system can produce rapid changes in the organism's somatic nervous system; these changes are usually seen in emotional behavior and in stress reactions (discussed in detail in Chapters 11 and 14).

The **parasympathetic nervous system,** which is active most of the time, is the part of the autonomic nervous system that controls the normal operations of the body, allowing digestion and normal respiration (breathing) and heart rate. In other words, it keeps the body running smoothly. This system calms everything down and moves responses back to normal after an emergency. Parasympathetic activity does not show sharp changes from minute to minute.

The Central Nervous System

The **central nervous system** is the other major division of the nervous system. Consisting of the brain and the spinal cord, it serves as the body's main processing system for information (see Figure 2.8).

Somatic [so-MAT-ick] nervous system
The part of the peripheral nervous system that carries information from sense organs to the brain and from the brain and spinal cord to skeletal muscles, and thereby affects bodily movement; it controls voluntary, conscious, sensory, and motor functions.

Autonomic [au-toe-NOM-ick] nervous system
The part of the peripheral nervous system that controls the vital and automatic activities of the body, such as heart rate, digestive processes, blood pressure, and functioning of internal organs.

Sympathetic nervous system
The part of the autonomic nervous system that responds to emergency situations by activating bodily resources needed for major energy expenditures.

Parasympathetic [PAIR-uh-sim-puh-THET-ick] nervous system
The part of the autonomic nervous system that controls the normal operations of the body, such as digestion, blood pressure, and respiration.

Central nervous system
One of the two major parts of the nervous system, consisting of the brain and the spinal cord.

■ *For people such as actor Christopher Reeve, spinal cord damage results in loss of voluntary control over muscles.*

Although exactly how the brain functions still remains a mystery, neuroscientists know that the brain operates through many mutually dependent systems and subsystems to affect and control behavior. As noted earlier, millions of brain cells are involved in the performance of even simple activities. When you walk, for example, the visual areas of the brain are active and your sight guides you, the brain's motor areas help make your legs move, and the cerebellum helps you keep your balance. The central nervous system, communicating with the muscles and glands under the control of the brain, allows all these things to happen so effortlessly.

The brain is the control center, but it receives much of its information from the spinal cord, the main communication line to the rest of the body, and from the cranial nerves. The **spinal cord,** contained within the spinal column, receives signals from the sensory organs, muscles, and glands and relays these signals to the brain. *Spinal reflexes*—automatic responses that are controlled almost solely by the spinal cord—do not involve the brain. The knee jerk, elicited by a tap on the tendon below the kneecap, is a spinal reflex. Most sensory signals make their way up the spinal cord to the brain for further analysis, but the knee jerk response happens at the level of the spinal cord, before the brain has had time to register and act on the tap.

The spinal cord's importance comes primarily from its function in relaying information to and from the brain. When a person's spinal cord is severed, the information exchange between the brain and the muscles and glands stops below the point of damage. Spinal reflexes still operate, but individuals who suffer spinal cord damage, like actor Christopher Reeve, lose voluntary control over muscles in the parts of their bodies below the site of the injury. This shows that the spinal cord serves a key communication function between the brain and the rest of the body; it is the chief trunk line for neuronal activity. Let's turn next to the brain itself.

The Organization of the Brain

A person's intelligence, personality traits, and ability to communicate through language reside in a small organ protected by the skull—the brain. The human brain is highly evolved, complex, and specialized. It is this specialization that allows humans—in contrast to other animals—to think about the past and the future and to communicate possibilities. Scientists have studied its structure, its functions, its interconnections, and what happens to it when it is damaged, yet they still have much to learn.

Spinal cord
The portion of the central nervous system that is contained within the spinal column and transmits signals from the sensory organs, muscles, and glands to the brain, controls reflexive responses, and conveys signals from the brain to the rest of the body.

Brain
The part of the central nervous system that is located in the skull and that regulates, monitors, processes, and guides other nervous system activity.

Five Principles Governing Brain Organization

The **brain** is the part of the central nervous system that regulates, monitors, processes, and guides other nervous system activity. Located in the skull, the human brain is an organ weighing about 3 pounds and is often described as having three main divisions: the hindbrain, the midbrain, and the forebrain.

These specialized systems operate separately but often work together; in general they follow five key operating principles (Amaral, 2000). *First,* each system involves several brain regions that carry out different types of information processing. *Second,* there are identifiable pathways, groups of neurons bundled together, that project from one area of the brain to the next. *Third,* each part of the brain projects to the next in an orderly fashion, creating what are called topographically organized regions that can be mapped spatially. *Fourth,* the brain is hierarchically organized; that is, it is organized in a logical sequence usually starting off with simple cells, projecting to more complex areas of the brain, and ultimately winding up with the most complex processing taking place in the forebrain—and most of the major connections can be followed or mapped. *Last,* the brain systems are organized so that one side of the brain controls the other side of the body. Although we are not sure why, most brain structures are bilaterally symmetrical (the same on both sides) and cross over and control operations on the other side of the body.

Many brain activities are localized in one specific area, but some are not. For example, most speech and language activity can be pinpointed to a specific area, usually on the left side of the brain (Damasio & Damasio, 2000). Other activities occur in both hemispheres, such as visual activity in the visual cortex of both sides of the brain as well as in subcortical structures.

The Brain's Main Divisions

Initially, the brain forms three divisions—hindbrain, midbrain, and forebrain—and we usually refer to brain organization this way. But during the prenatal period the top and bottom sections divide again, ultimately forming five major divisions. As a general principle, the structures lower in the brain tend to be responsible for basic, reflexive functions, and those toward the top are involved in more complex and abstract mental functions.

In examining the brain, we begin where the spinal cord and the brain meet. As we move higher up and toward the top of the brain, we find structures with more complicated but less essential functions. The cortex—the deeply fissured gray surface matter that covers the cerebral hemispheres—exhibits the highest complexity of functioning. The cortex is the location of thought processing—one of the most advanced abilities of humans.

The Hindbrain and Midbrain

Every time Tiger Woods wins another golf tournament, it is a tribute to his cerebellum. If his cerebellum functioned even slightly less proficiently, he would be a duffer rather than a champion. The **hindbrain** (refer to the foldout) consists of the medulla, the reticular formation, the pons, and the cerebellum. The structures of the hindbrain receive afferent signals from other parts of the brain and from the spinal cord; they interpret the signals and either relay the information to more complex parts of the brain or immediately cause the body to act.

The hindbrain includes the **medulla,** the dense package of nerves lying just above the spinal cord that controls heartbeat and breathing and through which many afferent and efferent signals pass. Within the medulla is a latticelike network of nerve cells, *the reticular formation,* which controls a person's state of arousal. Damage to it can result in coma and death, and its normal function controls waking and sleeping. The reticular formation extends into and through the pons and the midbrain, with projections toward the cortex.

The **pons** provides a link between the lower brain and the rest of the brain; like the medulla, the pons affects sleep and dreaming. The **cerebellum** (or "little brain"), a structure attached to the back surface of the brain stem, influences balance, coordination, and movement, including single joint actions such as the flexing of an elbow or knee. The cerebellum constitutes only 10% of the total volume of the brain but contains more than half of its neurons! The cerebellum allows you to walk in a straight line, type accurately on a keyboard, and coordinate the many movements involved in dancing—and if you're Tiger Woods, hit a golf ball better than almost anyone ever has. The cerebellum may also be involved in some types of thinking and learning, although its functions in these areas are not yet clearly established (Thach, 1998).

Hindbrain
The most primitive organizationally of the three functional divisions of the brain, consisting of the medulla, the reticular formation, the pons, and the cerebellum.

Medulla [meh-DUH-lah]
The most primitive and lowest portion of the hindbrain; controls basic bodily functions such as heartbeat and breathing.

Pons
A structure of the hindbrain that provides a link between the medulla and the cerebellum and the rest of the brain; it affects sleep and dreaming.

Cerebellum [seh-rah-BELL-um]
A large structure that is attached to the back surface of the brain stem and that influences balance, coordination, and movement.

The hindbrain consists of the cerebellum, the medulla, the reticular formation, and the pons.

Structures of the brain

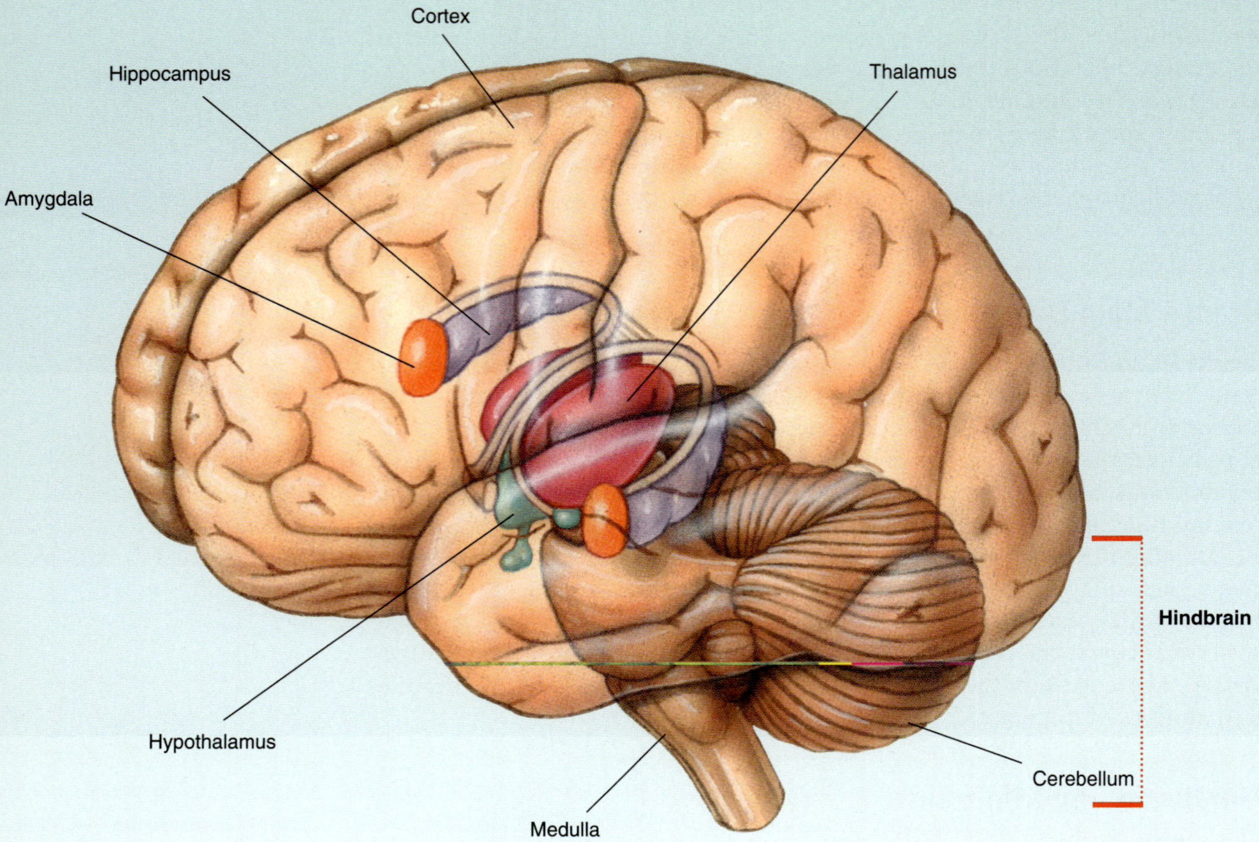

The forebrain is the largest and most complex of the three major sections of the brain. It encompasses the thalamus, the hypothalamus, the hippocampus, the amygdala, the basal ganglia (not shown here), the corpus callosum, and the cortex.

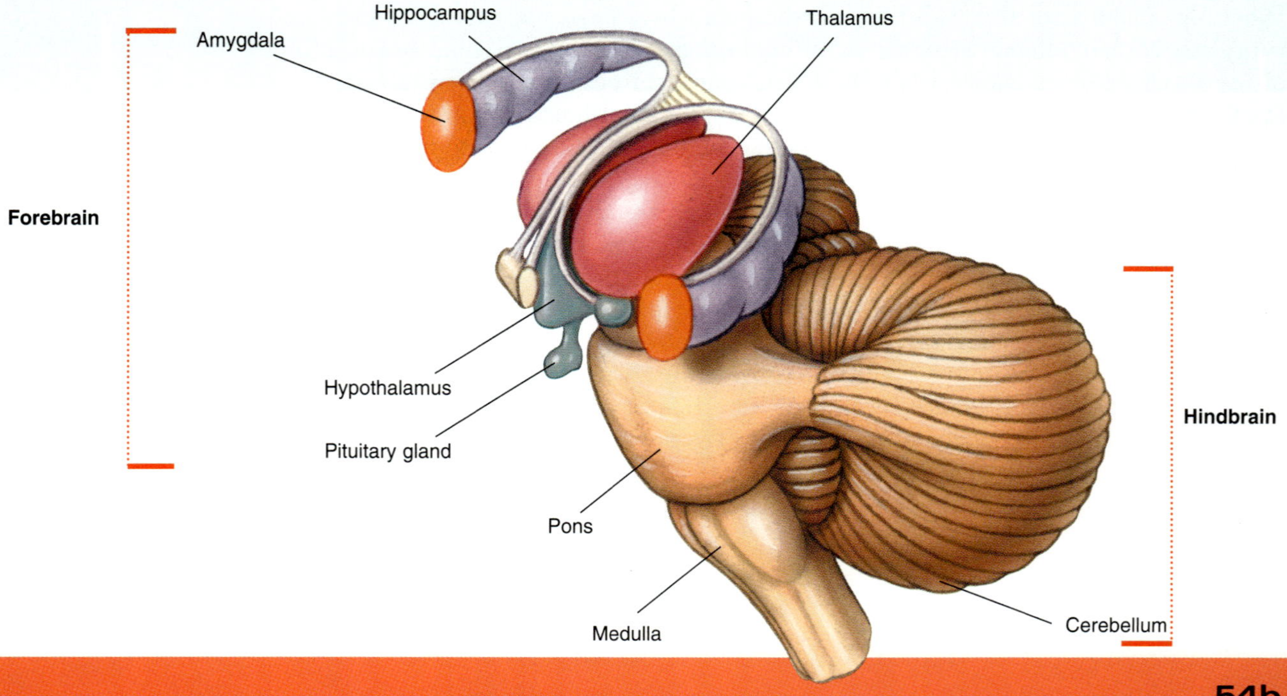

THE Human Brain

The human brain is divided into three major sections: the forebrain, the midbrain, and the hindbrain. Each of these is revealed in progressively more detail here.

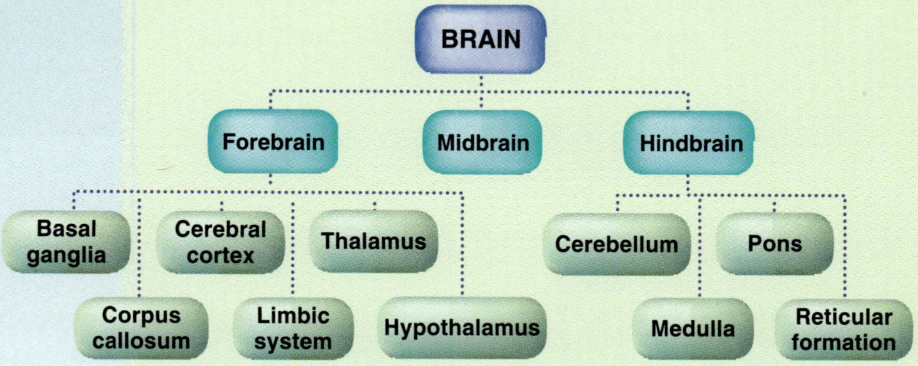

The midbrain, located between the forebrain and the hindbrain, consists of several major structures, as well as a number of smaller but important nuclei (collections of cell bodies). The reticular formation extends from the hindbrain into the midbrain.

The human brain—a cross-section

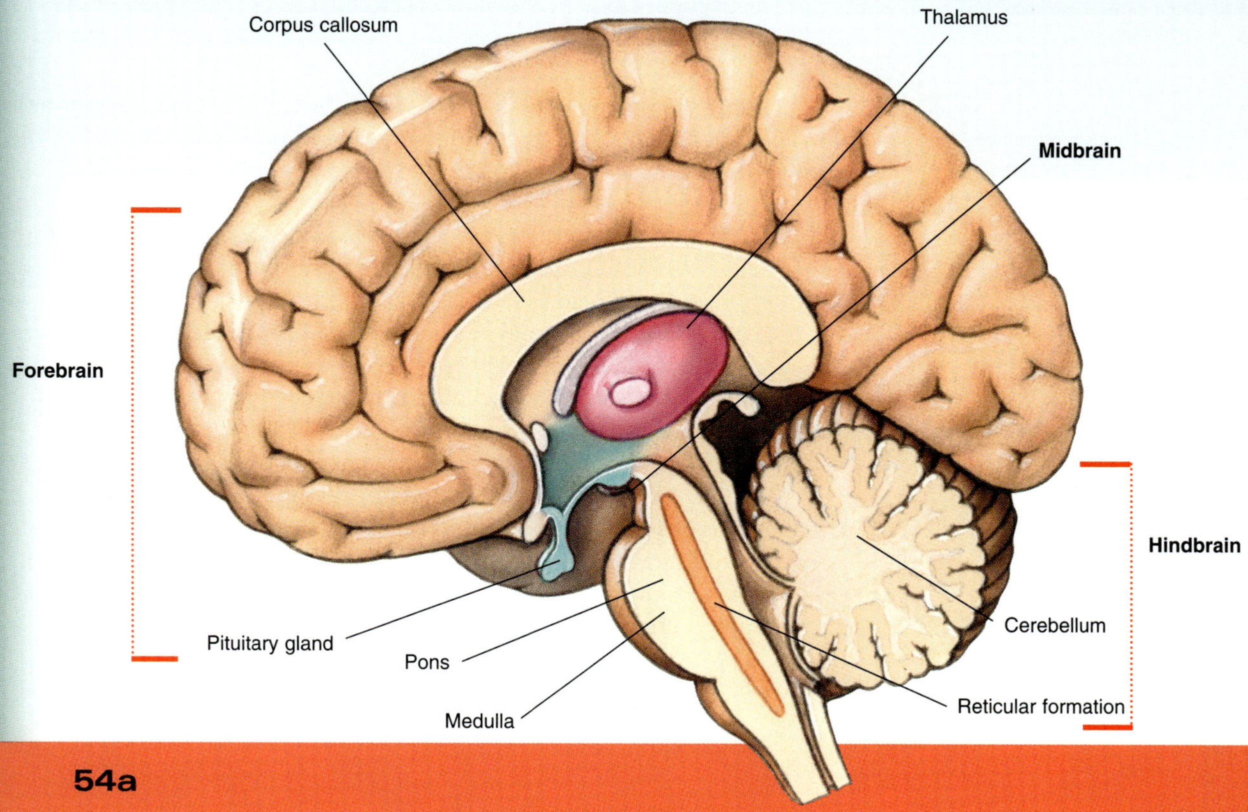

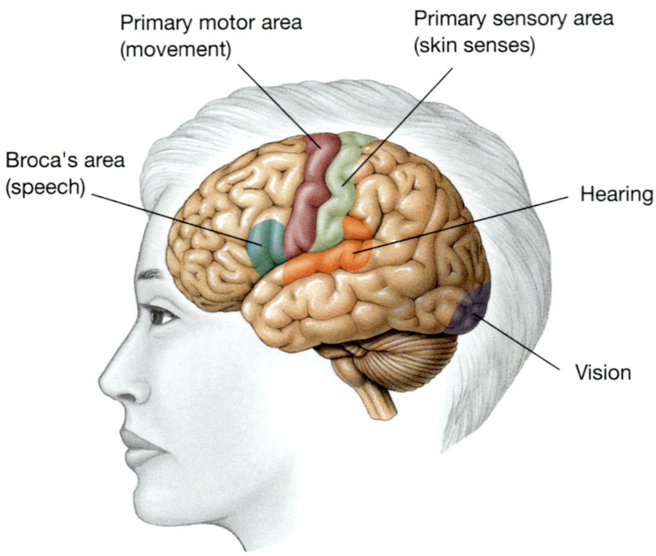

Specific areas of the brain control and influence both sensory and motor functions.

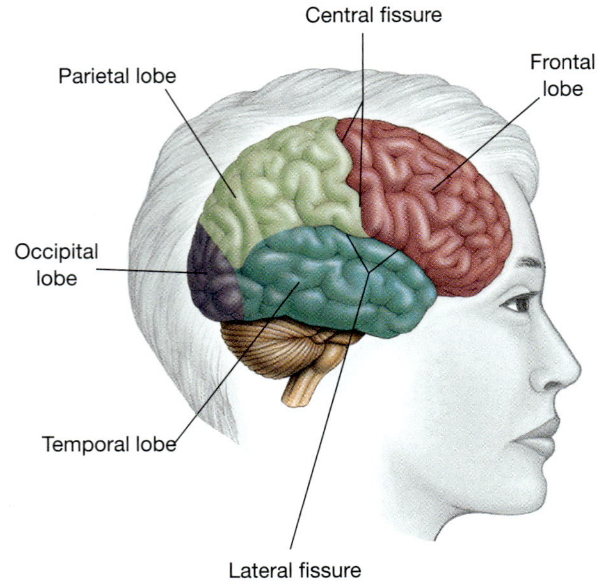

The *lateral fissure* divides the temporal lobe from the parietal lobe; the *central fissure* divides the frontal lobe from the parietal lobe.

FIGURE 2.9

The Cortex and the Lobes of the Brain

The cortex is the exterior covering of the cerebral hemispheres. It consists of four major lobes and the association cortex. The cortex plays a special role in behavior because it is directly involved in thought.

The **midbrain** (refer to the foldout) consists of nuclei (collections of cell bodies) that receive afferent signals from other parts of the brain and from the spinal cord. Like the hindbrain, the midbrain interprets the signals and either relays the information to a more complex part of the brain or causes the body to act at once. One portion of the midbrain governs smoothness of movement, another temperature regulation, and yet another reflexive movement. Movements of the eyeball in its socket, for example, are controlled by the *superior colliculus,* a structure in the midbrain. The reticular formation continues in the midbrain.

Midbrain
The second level of the three organizational structures of the brain, which receives afferent signals from other parts of the brain and from the spinal cord, interprets the signals, and either relays the information to a more complex part of the brain or causes the body to act at once; considered important in the regulation of movement.

Forebrain
The largest, most complicated, and most advanced organizationally and functionally of the three divisions of the brain, with many interrelated parts including the thalamus and hypothalamus, the limbic system, the basal ganglia and corpus callosum, and the cortex.

The Forebrain

The **forebrain** consists of divisions that are the most organizationally and structurally advanced; they are also the largest and most complicated of the brain structures because of their many interrelated parts.

■ **THE THALAMUS AND HYPOTHALAMUS.** The **thalamus** (refer to the foldout) acts primarily as a routing station for sending information to other parts of the brain, although it probably also performs some interpretive functions. Nearly all sensory information proceeds through this large structure before going to other areas of the brain. The **hypothalamus,** which is relatively small (the size of a pea) and located just below the thalamus, has numerous connections with the rest of the forebrain and the midbrain and affects many complex behaviors, such as eating, drinking, and sexual activity. We will examine its influence on eating in more detail in Chapter 11.

The largest structure in the human brain consists of the left and right cerebral hemispheres. The hemispheres consist of a covering, the cortex, underlying white matter, and three other structures (hippocampus, amygdala, and the basal ganglia). The two sides of the brain are interconnected by the corpus callosum. Each of these structures is important for psychology.

TABLE 2.2

The Lobes of the Brain

	Location	Function
Frontal lobe	In front of the central fissure; contains the motor cortex and Broca's area	Memory Movement Speech and language production
Parietal lobe	Behind frontal lobe	Sense of touch and body position
Temporal lobe	Below lateral fissure and parietal lobe	Speech, hearing, and some visual information processing
Occipital lobe	Back of the brain, next to and behind parietal and temporal lobes	Visual sense
Association cortex	Areas between parietal, temporal, and occipital lobes	Believed to be responsible for complex behaviors that involve thinking and sensory processes

■ **THE CORTEX.** The exterior covering of the hemispheres, called the **cortex** (or *neocortex*), is about 2–3 millimeters thick and consists of six thin layers of cells. It is *convoluted,* or wrinkled. These **convolutions,** folds in the tissue of the cerebral hemispheres and the overlying cortex, have the effect of creating more surface area within a small space. The overall surface area of the human cortex is at least 1.5 square feet. Human beings have a highly developed cortex, but most other mammals' brains are less deeply convoluted. The cortex plays a special role in behavior because it is intimately involved in thought.

A traditional way to study the cortex is to consider it as several *lobes,* or areas, named after the overlying cranial bones—*frontal, parietal, temporal,* and *occipital*—each with characteristic structures and functions. The four lobes are well defined by prominent fissures or what are called sulci (very deep furrows, or folds)—the *lateral fissure* and the *central fissure.* These easily recognizable fissures are like deep ravines that run among the convolutions, separating the lobes. The *frontal lobe* is in front of the central fissure; the *parietal lobe* is behind it. Below the lateral fissure and the parietal lobe is the *temporal lobe.* And at the back of the head, behind the parietal and temporal lobes, is the *occipital lobe.* Figure 2.9 illustrates the various lobes; Table 2.2 describes each lobe and its primary functions.

■ **THE LIMBIC SYSTEM.** One of the most complex and least understood structures of the brain is the **limbic system** (see Figure 2.10 on the following page). This system, located deep within the temporal lobe, is an interconnected group of structures (including parts of the cortex, thalamus, and hypothalamus) that influence emotions, memory, social behavior, and brain disorders such as epilepsy. Included within the limbic system are the hippocampus and the amygdala. In human beings, the *hippocampus* is involved in learning, memory, navigating about the world, and some emotional functions (Maguire et al., 1998).

The *amygdala* is also involved in emotional behaviors. Stimulation of the amygdala in animals, for instance, produces attack responses; surgical removal of the amygdala in human beings was once a radical way of treating people who were extremely violent. The amygdala is now considered important in learning, in the recognition of fear, and in a wide range of other emotions (Damasio, 1999).

Stimulation of several areas of the limbic system in rats produces what appear to be highly pleasurable sensations. Olds and Milner (1954) discovered that rats, when given small doses of electrical current in some of the limbic areas as a reward for bar pressing, chose bar pressing over eating, even after having been deprived of food for long periods. The researchers called the areas of the brain being stimulated *pleasure centers;* researchers have recently investigated the link

Thalamus
A large structure of the forebrain that acts primarily as a routing station to send information to other parts of the brain but probably also performs some interpretive functions; nearly all sensory information proceeds through the thalamus.

Hypothalamus
A relatively small structure of the forebrain, lying just below the thalamus, which acts through its connections with the rest of the forebrain and the midbrain and affects many complex behaviors, such as eating, drinking, and sexual activity.

Cortex
The convoluted, or furrowed, exterior covering of the brain's hemispheres, which is about 2 millimeters thick, consists of six thin layers of cells, and is divided into several lobes, or areas, each with characteristic structures; thought to be involved in both sensory interpretation and complex thought processes; also known as the *neocortex.*

Convolutions
Folds in the tissue of the cerebral hemispheres and the overlying cortex.

Limbic system
An interconnected group of structures (including parts of the cortex, thalamus, and hypothalamus) located deep within the temporal lobe and influencing emotions, memory, social behavior, and brain disorders such as epilepsy.

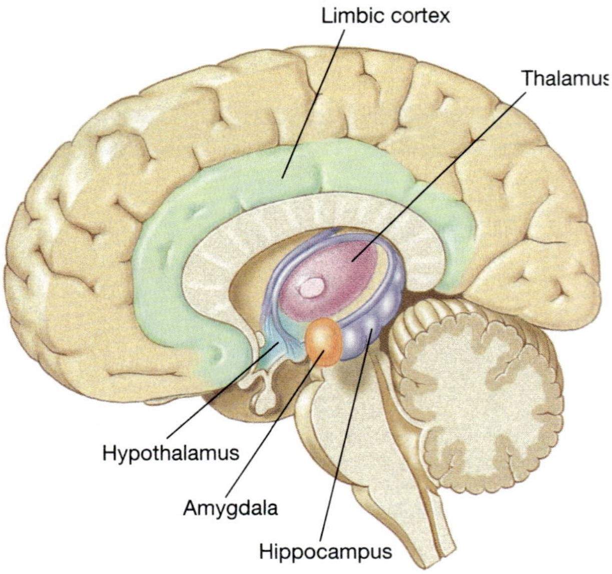

FIGURE 2.10
Principal Structures of the Limbic System

between addictive behaviors and stimulation of this brain system (Wise, 1996).

THE BASAL GANGLIA AND CORPUS CALLOSUM. The *basal ganglia* are a series of nuclei located deep in the forebrain to the left and right of the thalamus. They link the thalamus and the cortex. They control movements and posture, and their degeneration is associated with Parkinson's disease. Parts of the basal ganglia influence muscle tone and initiate commands to the cerebellum and to higher brain centers. Damage to this important neurological center can have severe consequences including muscular rigidity and tremors; in addition parts of the basal ganglia are involved in cognitive functions.

The left and right cerebral hemispheres have few connections, but the major one is the *corpus callosum.* This structure is a thick band of 200 million or so nerve fibers, which provide connections that convey information between the two cerebral hemispheres; damage to it results in essentially two separate brains within one skull. We'll return to the corpus callosum shortly.

The Brain at Work

In the 18th century, phrenology was very popular. Phrenologists measured the size and proportions of heads and analyzed the locations of bumps and other prominent features; their reasoning was that features on the skull were associated with certain kinds of thoughts. Today, scientists are still striving to understand the brain and how it works, but the methods of study have changed. Knowledge of the brain and its relationship to behavior comes in part from the study of *neuroanatomy*—the structures of the nervous system. Some neuroanatomists study the brains of people who have died of tumors, brain diseases, and trauma (injury) to the brain, hoping to correlate the type of brain damage with the loss of specific abilities, such as seeing, reading, or writing. Observing the behaviors and mental processes of individuals with damage caused by accidents, strokes, or brain tumors provides further information. Neuroanatomists who study behavior often use a technique called *ablation.* In ablation studies, after anesthetizing an animal (the ethical rules of research with nonhuman animals require anesthesia for surgery to prevent unnecessary pain), researchers remove or destroy a portion of an animal's brain and study the animal to determine which behaviors change. Today, in addition to ablation, researchers have an exciting variety of techniques that allow them to study a living brain without harming the subjects of their studies. Therefore, it is now possible to study a living, functioning human brain using EEGs, MRIs, and CT and PET scans. Still other researchers study brain–behavior relationships by watching animals or children as they interact with their environment and solve problems.

Monitoring Neuronal Activity

To understand neural function, researchers must study a living nervous system; dissection will not reveal anything about how brains work. Researchers have taken several approaches to this problem, including studying the function of a single neuron and using sophisticated technology to see the brain as it works.

One measuring technique is *single-unit recording,* in which researchers insert a thin wire, needle, or glass tube containing an electrolyte solution into or next to a single neuron to measure its electrical activity. Scientists usually perform this type of recording technique on the neurons of rats, cats, or monkeys. Such studies are invasive and damaging, so researchers use anesthesia or other medications to minimize any potential pain or discomfort to the animals. Because neurons fire extremely rapidly, the data are often fed into a computer, which averages the number of times the cell fires in 1 second or 1 minute. There are widely scattered neuronal clusters that act together, in synchrony, and identifying all of them is a task of Herculean proportions. But synchronized firing of neurons is essential to movement and perception; synchronized output from widely spaced neurons may be at the heart of perception and thought and of consciousness itself (Crick & Koch, 1998; Riehle et al., 1997; Rodriguez et al., 1999). Synchronized firing of diverse cells allows both specialization of different brain regions and combination of neuronal output for higher-order thinking.

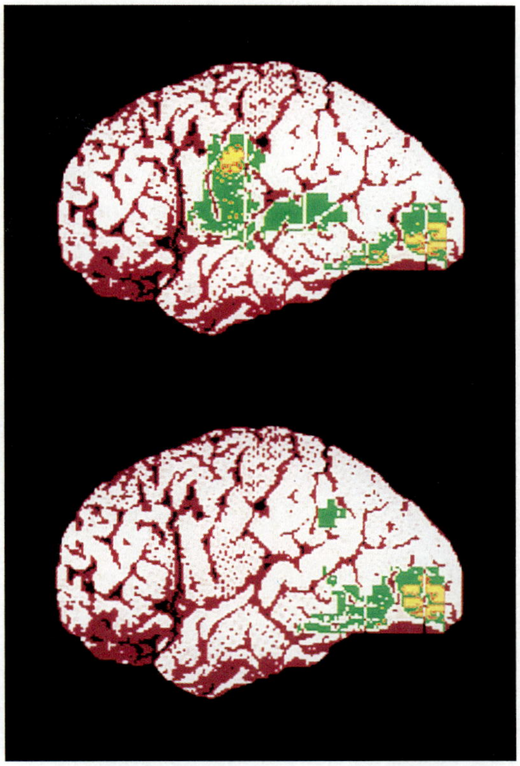

■ *PET scans reveal varying activity in different areas of the brain for reading aloud (top) versus reading silently (bottom).*

Another technique, *electroencephalography,* can measure electrical activity in the nervous systems of either nonhuman animals or humans. As the photo shows, this technique produces a graphic record of brain-wave activity called an **electroencephalogram,** or **EEG** (*electro* means "electrical," *encephalon* means "brain," and *gram* means "record"). Small electrodes placed on the scalp record the activity of thousands of neurons beneath the skull to produce an EEG. EEGs, which are generally analyzed by computer, are used for a variety of purposes, including the assessment of brain damage, epilepsy, tumors, and other abnormalities. In addition, this technique has been very important in the investigation of sleep.

In healthy human beings, EEGs show a variety of characteristic brain-wave patterns, depending on the level and kind of mental activity the person engages in. Researchers usually describe brain waves in terms of their *frequency* (the number of waves in a unit of time) and *amplitude* (the relative height or size of the waves). If people are awake, relaxed, and not engaged in active thinking, their EEGs are predominantly composed of *alpha waves,* which occur at a moderate rate (frequency) of 8 to 12 cycles per second and are of moderate amplitude. When people are excited, their brain waves change dramatically from alpha waves to *beta waves,* which are of high frequency and low amplitude. At different times during sleep, people show varying patterns of high-frequency and low-frequency waves correlated with dreaming activity and restorative functions, both of which are discussed in Chapter 6.

Important techniques for measuring the activity of the nervous system have emerged in the last two decades: CT, PET, and MRI scanning. **CT (computerized tomography) scans** are computer-enhanced X-ray images of the brain (or any area of the body) in three dimensions—essentially a series of X-rays that show photographic slices of part of the brain or body. CT scans are especially helpful in locating specific damaged areas or tumors in the brain, but people must be very still while being scanned, so this technique is not very helpful in revealing function.

PET (positron emission tomography) tracks radioactive markers injected into the bloodstream, enabling researchers to monitor marked variations in cerebral activity, which are correlated with mental processes. PET scans are a relatively new tool for neuroscientists, but research is proceeding rapidly. For example, the PET scan technique allowed researchers to find a relationship between blood flow and cognitive activity (Koski & Petrides, 2001). Specific brain regions have been found to be associated with specific types of memory or thought processes (Anderson et al., 2000), and those areas show more blood flow for some tasks (for example, recall compared to recognition) than do other areas (Cabeza & Nyberg, 2000). The potential of PET scans has yet to be fully unleashed, but researchers are using them

Electroencephalogram [ee-LECK-tro-en-SEFF-uh-low-gram] (EEG)
A graphical record of brain-wave activity obtained through electrodes placed on the scalp.

CT (computerized tomography) scans
Computer-enhanced X-ray images of the brain (or any area of the body) in three dimensions—essentially a series of X-rays that show photographic slices of the brain (or other part of the body).

PET (positron emission tomography)
Imaging technique that tracks radioactive markers injected into the bloodstream, enabling researchers to monitor marked variations in cerebral activity, which are correlated with mental processes.

to study a wide range of psychological coding processes as well as disorders such as schizophrenia (Andreasen, 1997). PET scans have several disadvantages, including resolution that is too poor to precisely locate activated brain regions. They also expose participants to radiation, and the equipment for PET scans is expensive and not widely available.

MRI (magnetic resonance imaging) uses magnetic fields instead of X-rays to produce brain scans that have far greater clarity and resolution than CT scans. MRI can distinguish brain parts as small as 1 or 2 millimeters, providing highly detailed images of the brain's tissue and having the power to reveal many kinds of abnormalities. MRIs are not invasive—nothing needs to be injected—and no radiation is involved, making MRI scans preferred over CT or PET scans in many situations.

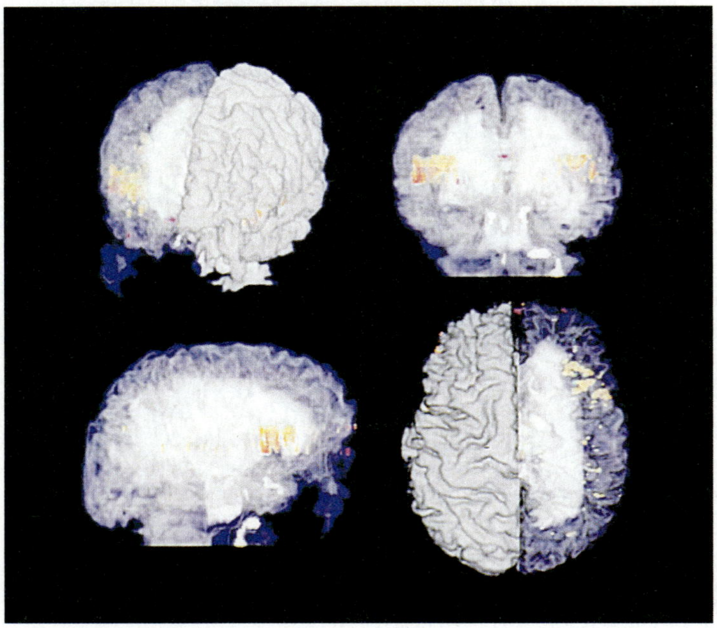

■ *MRI images register changes in brain metabolism, reflecting the areas of the brain that are active during specific tasks.*

A variation of MRI allows observation of the functioning of the brain. **Functional MRI (fMRI)** is an imaging technique that registers changes in the metabolism (energy consumption) of cells in various regions of the brain and thus allows observation of activity in the brain *as it takes place.* A person performs a particular task while the imaging is taking place. The area of the brain responsible for this task experiences an increase in metabolism that ultimately shows up on the fMRI image as a color change. By having a person perform specific tasks, it is possible to locate the corresponding regions of brain activation (e.g., Reichle, Carpenter, & Just, 2000). Unlike PET, which requires a break between scans (to allow radioactive traces to leave the system), fMRI allows for alternating experimental conditions in the same individual—a distinct and important advantage. And the newest fMRI techniques are exploiting its ability to track changes in brain activity over time (Mitchel et al., 2000; Ng et al., 2000).

Typically, a researcher will image the brains of two or more participants under different experimental conditions and then compare the images and activity of the brains in the different conditions and between the two people (e.g., Dupont et al., 2000). Often the participants in one group are healthy individuals and those in a different group have some type of disorder; often the tasks are cognitive ones that require participants to read, imagine, or perhaps calculate. Research shows that specific brain sites are indeed affected by specific tasks. For example, one study that used the fMRI technique showed that individuals with the reading disability dyslexia use their brains differently than, and not as well or efficiently as, individuals without dyslexia (Shaywitz et al., 1998). These researchers asked participants, both normal readers and those with dyslexia, to do tasks such as naming letters and identifying words. Among participants with normal reading ability, the expected areas of the brain became active, notably the visual cortex, the angular gyrus, and the left temporal-parietal area (Wernicke's area). People with dyslexia showed little activity in these areas but activity in other places not typically associated with reading. The researchers asserted that the brain activation patterns provided a "neural signature" for the impairment—that is, a way of identifying and diagnosing it (Fullbright et al., 1997). This example demonstrates the promise of fMRI to investigate brain functioning that accompanies behavior (Speck et al., 2000). Table 2.3 summarizes four important imaging techniques.

MRI (magnetic resonance imaging)
Imaging technique that uses magnetic fields instead of X-rays to produce scans of great clarity and high resolution, distinguishing brain parts as small as 1 or 2 millimeters.

fMRI (functional magnetic resonance imaging)
Imaging technique that allows observation of brain activity as it takes place by registering changes in the metabolism (energy consumption) of cells in various regions of the brain.

Remember that imaging techniques such as PET and fMRI do not detect mental activity directly—rather, they measure changes in blood flow or metabolism that are related to energy consumption by brain cells. Nevertheless, these techniques, especially fMRI, are creating a revolution in neuroscience—allowing researchers not

TABLE 2.3

Four Important Imaging Techniques

Technique	Function and Application
CT (computerized tomography)	Produces computer-enhanced, three-dimensional, X-ray images of the brain (or any part of the body), essentially a series of X-rays showing photographic slices of the brain (or other part of the body)
PET (positron emission tomography)	Tracks radioactive markers injected into the bloodstream, enabling researchers to monitor marked variations in cerebral activity, which are correlated with mental processes
MRI (magnetic resonance imaging)	Uses magnetic fields instead of X-rays to produce highly detailed images of brain tissue that have far greater clarity and resolution than CT scans; can distinguish brain parts as small as 1 or 2 millimeters in size
fMRI (functional MRI)	Registers changes in the metabolism (energy consumption) of cells in various regions of the brain and thus allows observation of activity in the brain as it takes place

only to explore anatomy but also to learn how the brain operates (see Table 2.3). For example, researchers have been able to show that small brain lesions (small areas of damaged brain tissue, often due to disease or injury) are common in elderly people and are a natural part of aging. Further, researchers are establishing tentative links among brain lesions, illness, neurochemistry, and depression. Even newer techniques are being developed, including one that induces a lesionlike disruption of brain activity that allows researchers to investigate attention, discrimination, and plasticity. This noninvasive technique is called *transcranial magnetic stimulation (TMS)* (Harmer et al., 2001). TMS is the application of a brief magnetic pulse to the scalp to induce changes in the local electrical activity in the underlying surface of the brain. Today researchers are exploring TMS as a research tool, a diagnostic tool, an adjunct used along with other brain imaging techniques, and for treatment for various psychiatric disorders (Burns & Stuart, 2000; Corthout et al., 2000).

Lawyers are now using various brain scans as part of the defense in some criminal trials. For example, an attorney may assert that PET scans show damage to the client's brain that traditional neurological tests could not have found. In one California case, a diagnosis of a mental disorder, confirmed through a PET scan, kept a man from going to the gas chamber.

One caution is necessary when considering all studies involving imaging techniques—the warning that we raised earlier concerning the correlation between a diagnosis of schizophrenia and a history of schizophrenia in the family. Just because there is a correlation between two events, in these cases brain activity and behavior, does not mean one *causes* the other in a simple way. Research on brain activity such as that from PET and fMRI studies must be analyzed with caution because many parts of the brain become active simultaneously and neural circuits are widely interconnected. Understanding the causality in these complex patterns will not be simple.

Brain Specialization—The Left and Right of Things

Are there specific places in the brain that control specific behaviors and thoughts? Does one side of the brain have more control over certain behaviors (for example, hand preference—see *Psychology in Action*) than the other side does? Some science writers have concluded that brain hemisphere dominance may affect your choice of occupation, and even your worldview. Let's explore the evidence.

■ **SPLITTING THE BRAIN.** Many body organs or structures are bilaterally symmetrical; that is, parts of the left and right half of the body, such as arms, legs, and

Psychology *in Action*

Left-Handed in a Right-Handed World

What do James Garfield, Harry Truman, Gerald Ford, Ronald Reagan, George Bush Sr., and Bill Clinton have in common? Aside from being presidents of the United States, all are (or were) left-handed, as were Joan of Arc, Alexander the Great, and C. P. E. Bach. So are Lisa Kudrow, Bruce Jenner, and Monica Seles. In fact, about 10% of the population is left-handed, depending on how you define left-handed. People's handedness—left-handedness especially—affects their lives in many ways.

Hand preference is probably controlled by at least two gene pairs that control brain dominance and handedness (Klar, 1996), but cultural beliefs about hand preference also shape hand use. Parents reinforce right-handed behavior, and the world is set up for right-handers. School desks are made to support your right arm and hand for writing. Computers come equipped with a mouse built for someone right-handed. Safety levers on mechanical equipment are placed for right-handers. Until recent decades, lefties were discriminated against and heavily encouraged to switch hands. Sometimes that encouragement took the form of a rap on the knuckles when students used their left hands.

Despite recent accommodations such as a specially designed (and more expensive) computer mouse, which has buttons that are reversible for lefties, the world is still structured for the right-handed. Perhaps as a consequence, left-handed people are more likely to have accidents (Coren & Previc, 1996). Their accidents may be more frequent and severe, which may be why they also suffer more pain from accidents (Coren & Previc, 1996). Coren has even argued that left-handed people die at a younger age (Halpern & Coren, 1991), but other research (Hicks et al., 1994) failed to find a survival advantage for right-handers.

But there is no controversy over the discrimination against left-handers and the convenience of being right-handed. Despite accommodations to the lefties of the world, the work and home environments are organized for righties, and this affects the way lefties live and work in both minor and major ways. End right-handed oppression! Lefties of the world, unite!

kidneys, are the same on each side. In such instances, each member of the pair does pretty much the same thing. The cerebral hemispheres are an exception to this bilateral symmetry. The right and left cerebral hemispheres show some differences in function.

In most human beings one cerebral hemisphere, usually the left, is specialized for the processing of speech and language; the other, usually the right, appears better able to handle spatial, musical, and drawing tasks. Although studies of brain activity yield a complex picture of brain function and brain structure, evidence of hemispheric specialization exists. For example, research using MRI scans supports a left–right distinction for pitch and music perception and indicates a difference between individuals who have perfect pitch and the rest of us (Schlaug et al., 1995).

What happens to behavior and mental processes when connections between the left and the right sides of the brain are cut? Since the early 1970s, Nobel Prize winner Roger Sperry (1913–1994) and Michael Gazzaniga have been at the forefront of research in cerebral organization, specializing in what happens when the two cerebral hemispheres are surgically severed (Gazzaniga, 2000). These studies have involved **split-brain patients**—many of whom are people with uncontrollable, life-threatening epilepsy who have undergone an operation to sever the corpus callosum (the band of fibers that connects the left and right hemispheres of the brain), which prevents seizures from spreading to both hemispheres. After the operation, testing revealed that there was little or no perceptual or cognitive interaction between the hemispheres; the patients seemed to have two distinct, independent brains, each with its own abilities. Studies of split-brain patients are invaluable to scientists seeking to understand how the brain works—in particular, how the left and right sides function together and separately.

Split-brain patients
People whose corpus callosum, which normally connects the two cerebral hemispheres, has been surgically severed.

Each cerebral hemisphere is neurologically connected to the opposite side of the body; thus, the left hemisphere normally controls the right side of the body (Johnson, 1998). The split-brain operation does not affect this crossing over of information between the body and the brain, but it does limit the internal communication between the two hemispheres. Split-brain patients are unable to use the speech and language capabilities located in the left cerebral hemisphere to describe activities carried out by

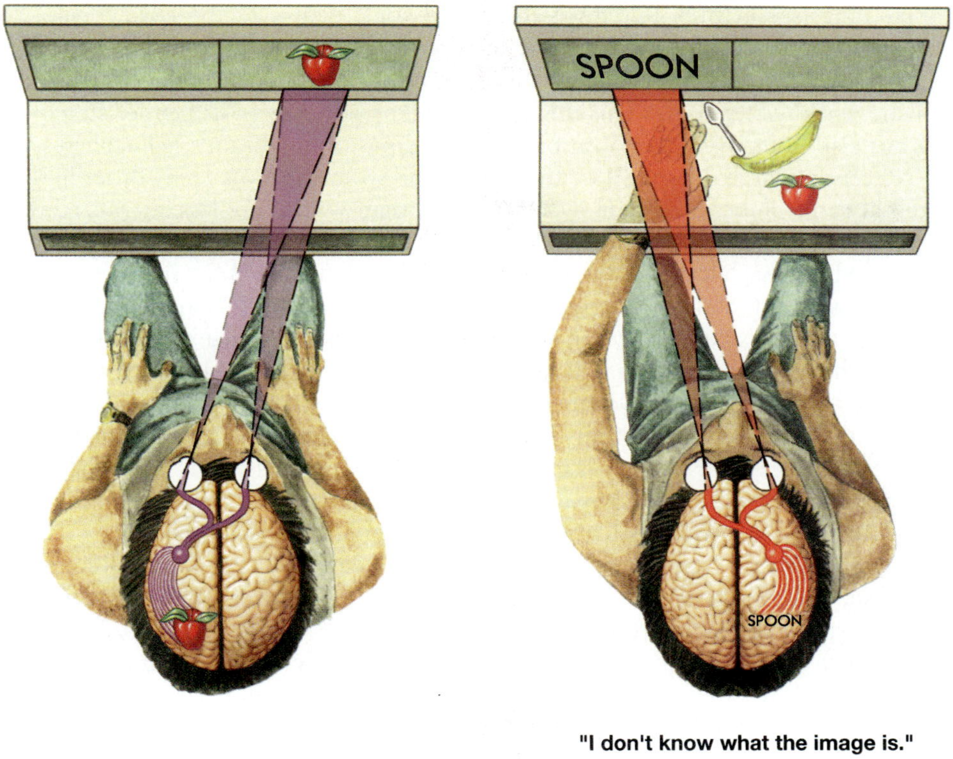

FIGURE 2.11

The Effects of Severing the Corpus Callosum

Imagine that a man whose corpus callosum (but not his optic nerves) has been severed is staring directly before him at a screen on either side of which a researcher can flash words or pictures. The researcher flashes a picture of an apple on the right side of the screen. The man is able to name the image because it has been sent via his optic nerves only to his brain's left hemisphere—where verbal processing occurs. When the researcher flashes the word *spoon* on the left side of the screen, the man's optic nerves send an image exclusively to his right hemisphere—which predominantly processes nonverbal stimuli. Now, because the right hemisphere is nonverbal, when the man is asked to name what he sees on the screen, he is unable to name the image as the word *spoon*. If he is asked to use his right hand, which is controlled by the left hemisphere, to pick out the object named on the screen (a spoon) from several objects, by touch alone, he will not be able to do so because his right hemisphere has been severed from his left and cannot communicate with it. However, if the man is asked to use his left hand to touch the object named on the screen, he can do so. The left hand is controlled by the right hemisphere, which is spatially adept and has been exposed to the word *spoon*.

the right one. When stimulus information is presented exclusively to a participant's left hemisphere (by presenting it in the right visual field while a participant stares straight ahead), the person can describe the stimulus (tell whether two items are identical) and can perform matching tasks in essentially normal ways. But when the same stimulus is presented to the right cerebral hemisphere, the person is unable to describe the stimulus verbally (a left-hemisphere task) because the right hemisphere cannot access the language capabilities of the right. (See Figure 2.11.)

Studies of split-brain patients have revealed that some brain functions are localized in one hemisphere and that many more abilities draw from a complex interconnection of structures (Metcalfe, Funnell, & Gazzaniga, 1995; Walsh, 2000). The growing body of brain imaging research shows that many activities that were considered exclusively left-brain (such as listening to someone speaking) or right-brain functions (such as listening to music) actually involve both hemispheres (Doty, 1999; Waldie & Mosley, 2000).

There is no doubt that both human beings and other animals exhibit lateralization and specificity of functions. Unfortunately, the popular press and TV newscasters oversimplify the specificity of functions and, in some cases, overgeneralize their significance to account for school problems, marital problems, artistic abilities, and even baseball batting averages. One example in the popular misconception of hemispheric specialization is that the right hemisphere is "creative." This belief is an overgeneralization from the right hemisphere's abilities in spatial visualization and drawing. The right hemisphere *is* better at drawing, but not necessarily more creative than the left; it depends on the task. For example, the right hemisphere is not capable of creative writing, and both hemispheres must work together to produce poetry—the left hemisphere must find the words and the right hemisphere must construct the meter. Typically, the two hemispheres work together in everyday tasks; for example, the left side of the brain may recognize a stimulus, but the right side is necessary to put that recognition into context (Doty, 2000).

■ **GENDER AND THE BRAIN.** People's misconceptions of brain hemispheric specialization have also led to theories on gender differences. Although there *are* studies indicating that men and woman have differences in their cerebral hemisphere

student voices

Julie Piccirillo,
Lynn University

I want to pursue a career in the neuropsychological and forensics area, trying to understand why some people commit certain acts and why others can control their actions. I want to dedicate my time to figuring out if the result of people's actions in life are due to genetics or are the result of psychological or sociocultural causes.

functioning (see below), this research has led some people to the false conclusion that there are masculine and feminine sides of the brain. The left side is seen as logical and rational and thus masculine, and the right side is considered emotional and holistic and thus feminine. This theory is mistaken not only in its gender stereotyping but also in its overgeneralization of the findings on the brain's hemispheres.

Recent research does indicate that men's and women's brains may differ in their cerebral hemispheres. The best evidence shows that women are less lateralized than men (Springer & Deutsch, 1998). Men have their language functions more strongly lateralized in the left hemisphere and their spatial functions in the right, while women have both abilities distributed in both hemispheres. PET and fMRI imaging has confirmed these differences in studies where men and women have solved problems as their brain functions are scanned. For example, when asked to decide on rhyming words (a language-related task), men's brains became active in their left hemispheres and women's brains became active in both hemispheres (Shaywitz et al., 1995). Similarly, a study that imaged men's and women's brains while they were read a passage from a novel showed the same left-hemisphere activation for men but activity in both hemispheres for women (Phillips et al., 2000).

Do these studies indicate that women's and men's brains function differently? And if so, does one gender's brain function "better" than the other gender's? Recent research suggests that there is no clear answer to the first question—while some studies such as the rhyming study and the listening study discussed above do show gender differences, the results are still considered inconclusive. For example, the differences demonstrated in the rhyming study reflected average differences between the brains of men and women, but not every individual in this study conformed to the pattern typical of his or her gender. That is, individuals varied in their pattern of brain activation—about 40% of the women showed an activation pattern typical of men. This point leads to an important caution to keep in mind—individual variation is much larger than the gender differences between men's and women's cerebral hemispheres. The second question is far easier to answer: these studies have not shown a performance difference in the tasks; rather, they have shown only a difference in brain activation patterns. Both men and women were able to perform the same tasks equally well.

Plasticity and Change

Does your brain stay the same from birth to death, or can it change through experience or simply through the passage of time? Basic brain organization begins well before birth, but details of brain structure and functions, particularly in the cerebral cortex, are subject to continued growth and development. What happens in one cell affects what happens to neighboring cells, so psychologists recognize that the brain is still *malleable* (teachable), especially during the formative years. This ability to change is often referred to as *plasticity*. Within limits, the nervous system can be modified and fine-tuned by experience acquired over years (Kaas, 2000)—and the brain can be trained to relearn, or to compensate for loss through an accident or some other brain trauma (Mesulam, 2000). The relearning typically involves some type of brain reorganization that establishes new representations of information in the brain (Gilbert et al., 2000).

Experience with specific stimuli reinforces the development of neural structures. You can liken the developing brain to a highway system that expands with use. Less-traveled roads are abandoned, but popular ones are broadened and new ones are expanded. When neural structures are used, reused, and constantly updated, they become faster and more easily accessed (Martin et al., 2000). During both early fetal and early infant development, the majority of neural links, connections, and interconnections are established (Neville & Bavelier, 2000). If the links are not used, they disappear (Colman, Babekura, & Lichtman, 1997). Such elaboration and reorganization may occur (Musso et al., 1999) but are more likely when organisms are placed in complex, superenriched (e.g., visually stimulating) environments (Elkind, 1999; Kempermann & Gage, 1999). One study showed that children with language-based learning impairments could be taught to use repetitive and adaptive training exercises to overcome their problems. The exercises are assumed to change neuronal structures and allow improvement in speech and language processing (Merzenich et al., 1996).

Changes in the brain are not surprising for young organisms, but plasticity is less expected in aging ones. As human beings grow older, their central nervous systems do not function as well as before. For example, the numbers of neurons and receptors decrease. In addition, some learning tasks become more difficult for aging animals, including humans. Research has attempted to identify whether changes in brain functioning can be correlated with changes in learning (McCandliss, Posner, & Givón, 1997).

Can damage done to the nervous system be repaired? Injury to the brain early in an organism's life is devastating, but the extent and permanence of the damage depend on the nature of the injury, the age at which it takes place, and whether the organism is exposed to positive factors, such as an enriched environment (Kolb & Gibb, 1999) and training that can compensate. Human beings are amazingly adaptable and can adjust to a changing world by reorganizing both brain structure and behavior (Kolb, 1999).

Hormones and Glands

People imagine that hormones control many behaviors, from sexual activity to cravings for sugar. Indeed, legal arguments have been made that hormones make people commit crimes. What are these chemicals, what do they do, and how do they affect behavior?

Hormones are chemicals that are produced by the endocrine glands and regulate the activities of specific organs or cells; a hormone travels through the bloodstream to target organs containing cells that respond specifically to that hormone. **Endocrine glands** are ductless glands that secrete hormones into the bloodstream (rather than into a duct that goes to the target organ). Figure 2.12 shows the location of several endocrine glands. The endocrine system is similar to the nervous system in providing a means of internal communication using chemical signals, but

Hormones
Chemicals that are produced by the endocrine glands and regulate the activities of specific organs or cells.

Endocrine [END-oh-krin] glands
Ductless glands that secrete hormones directly into the bloodstream, rather than through a specific duct, or opening, into a target organ.

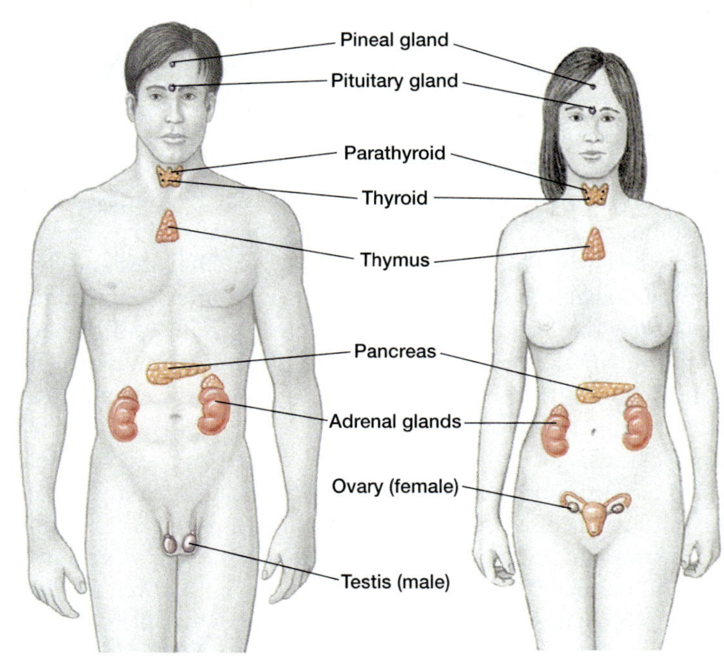

FIGURE 2.12

The Endocrine Glands

The endocrine glands are situated throughout the body. Though small in size, they exert enormous influences on behavior.

FIGURE 2.13

The Pituitary Gland

The pituitary gland is often called the body's master gland because it regulates many of the other endocrine glands. Located at the base of the brain, the pea-sized pituitary gland affects behavior indirectly through control of other glands and directly through release of hormones—including growth hormones and sex hormones—into the bloodstream.

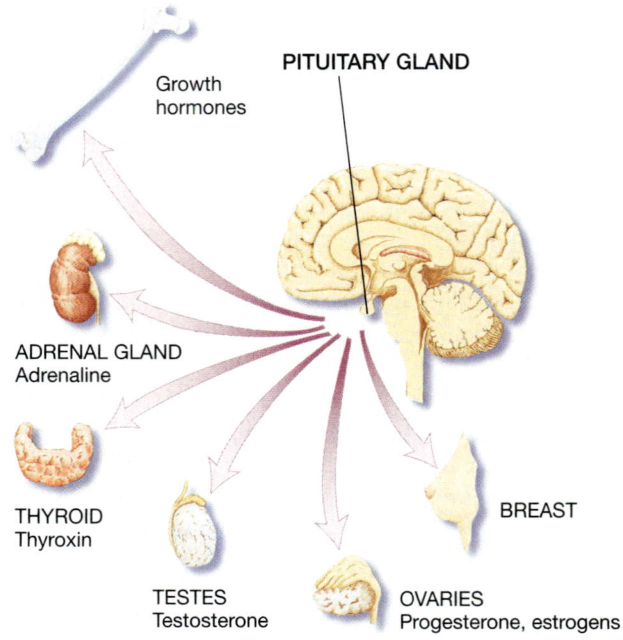

hormone action is slower. Endocrine glands are interconnected with the brain, and each hormone affects other glands and eventually, behavior. The brain initiates the release of hormones, which affect the target organs, which in turn affect behavior, which in turn affects the brain, forming a complex interaction.

The **pituitary gland** is often called the body's master gland because it regulates the actions of many other endocrine glands. The pituitary is located at the base of the brain and is closely linked to the hypothalamus, and one of its major functions is the control of growth hormones (see Figure 2.13). This gland produces hormones that act on other glands and influence growth and development, body metabolism, and sexual behavior.

The steroid hormones called androgens and estrogens are produced by the gonads—the ovaries and testes. These hormones affect sexual behavior, beginning before birth. These hormones control the prenatal development of the reproductive system, prompt the onset of puberty and sexual maturity, and are essential for fertility. People often assume that androgens, especially testosterone, are the basis for aggression and the reason that men are more aggressive than women are. But the relationship between testosterone and aggression is complex. For example, most men who take anabolic steroids (synthetic testosterone) do not become more aggressive (Pope, Kouri, & Hudson, 2000).

The pancreas is an endocrine gland involved in regulating the body's sugar levels through the production of **insulin**, the hormone that facilitates the transport of sugar from the bloodstream into body cells. When blood sugar is high, people feel energetic, and low levels produce fatigue and weakness. Diabetes and hypoglycemia are two problems associated with insulin, and both can influence behavior. Diabetes mellitus occurs when the pancreas fails to produce insulin and the body can no longer metabolize sugar. Errors in the opposite direction result in hypoglycemia, overproduction of insulin that results in low blood sugar levels and the accompanying feelings of fatigue and weakness.

The adrenal glands, located just above the kidneys, produce adrenaline (epinephrine), which has a dramatic effect on behavior. Imagine that someone cuts you off in traffic, and you become furious and begin chasing the offender in your car. Prompted by the stress and anger, the sympathetic division of your autonomic nervous system goes into action. Part of that action affects your adrenal medulla to produce epinephrine, which allows you to react quickly and possibly contributes to any tendency to do violence.

Pituitary [pit-YOU-ih-tare-ee] gland
The body's master gland, located at the base of the brain and closely linked to the hypothalamus; regulates the actions of other endocrine glands and controls growth hormones.

Insulin
Hormone that is produced by the pancreas and facilitates the transport of sugar from the blood into body cells, where it is metabolized.

Be an *Active* learner

REVIEW

- Describe the subdivisions of the autonomic nervous system. pp. 52–53
- Identify and describe the three main areas of the brain. pp. 54–55
- Identify the differences betwen PET and fMRI. pp. 59–60
- Why is the corpus callosum so essential to effective communication in the brain? pp. 62–63
- Under what circumstances is neural plasticity the greatest? p. 64
- What are the major endocrine glands and the hormones they produce? pp. 65–66
- Why are researchers justified in concluding that the pituitary is the master gland? p. 66

THINK CRITICALLY

- What might be one possible function of the convolutions of the cortex?
- Given that the brain's plasticity allows it to be sensitive to change, what—if anything—can individuals do to optimize their own growth and potential?
- What are the differences between hormones and neurotransmitters?
- Insulin has often be identified as a potential cause of obesity. When people eat sugar-laden food, they overproduce insulin, their blood sugar drops to very low levels, and this causes them to eat some more. How can this problem be solved in a society that binges on "super-sized" meals laden with sugar and fat?

APPLY PSYCHOLOGY

- Write a paragraph describing the responses a person feels when placed in a difficult situation and feels threatened, for example, is faced with an attacker. Describe in detail what happens to the person's body.
- In hypoglycemia a person produces insulin in too great a quantity, which results in very low blood sugar levels. Devise a diet and program of eating to help such an individual better manage his or her own insulin production.

Summary and Review

Genetics and Evolutionary Psychology

What do we mean by heritability?

■ When scientists say that a trait is *heritable,* especially when they attach a percentage to that heritability, they mean that a percentage of the variation (differences) among a *group* of people is attributable to heredity. p. 38

What is the distinction between nature and nurture?

■ Psychologists generally assert that human behavior is influenced by both *nature* (heredity) and *nurture* (environment). Psychologists study the biological bases of behavior to better understand how these two sets of variables interact. pp. 38–39

What is genetics, and why do psychologists study it?

■ *Genetics* is the study of heredity—the biological transmission of traits and characteristics from parents to offspring. *Chromosomes* carry each person's inherited genetic makeup. Each chromosome contains thousands of *genes,* made up of DNA. Genes are the basic unit of heredity. The 23rd pair of chromosomes determines the sex of a fetus. pp. 39–40

■ One's *genotype* is one's genetic makeup and is fixed at birth; but one's genotype may or may not be seen in observable characteristics. One's observable characteristics are one's *phenotype,* shaped by genotype and by the environment. Changes in gene replication produce *mutations,* which are the principal source of genetic diversity. pp. 39–40

What is the human genome, and why is it important?

■ The *genome* is the total DNA blueprint of heritable traits contained in every cell of the body. *Genetic mapping* involves dividing the chromosomes into smaller fragments that can be characterized, and ordering (mapping) the fragments to reflect their respective locations on specific chromosomes. Researchers have identified the exact location or sites of genes contributing to an array of traits; they argue that the nature of family social interactions has a genetic basis because elements of personality, maladjustment, and language acquisition may be genetically determined (at least in part). pp. 40–41

Why do we study identical twins?

■ *Identical twins* share exactly the same genetic heritage; they come from one ovum and one sperm and are always the same sex. *Fraternal twins* are produced by two ova and two sperm and therefore can be both male, both female, or one of each. They share genetic characteristics to the same extent as other siblings do. Studying identical twins allows researchers to clarify the effects of nature and nurture on developmental processes. p. 41

What is evolutionary psychology, and why has it become so important?

■ *Evolutionary psychology* is the psychological perspective that seeks to explain and predict behaviors by analyzing how the human brain developed over time, how it functions, and how input from the social environment affects human behaviors; it seeks to explain human behavior by considering how behavior is affected from the vantage point of evolutionary biology. p. 43

■ Evolutionary theory assumes that natural selection shapes physiology and behavior—*natural selection* is the principle that among the range of behaviors that occurs those that help organisms adapt, be fit, and survive are the ones that will be passed on to successive generations, because flexible, fit individuals have a greater chance of reproduction. When a trait or inherited characteristic increases in the population, adaptation has occured. p. 43

- From an evolutionary perspective a person's current state of evolutionary development reflects traits and behaviors that have enabled survival in the world. p. 45

KEY TERMS

genetics, p. 38; heritability, p. 38; nature, p. 38; nurture, p. 38; chromosome, p. 39; genes, p. 39; genotype, p. 39; phenotype, p. 39; mutations, p. 40; genome, p. 40; genetic mapping, p. 40; identical twins, p. 41; fraternal twins, p. 41; correlational study, p. 43; correlation coefficient, p. 43; evolutionary psychology, p. 43; natural selection, p. 43; adaptation, p. 43

Communication in the Nervous System

Describe the structures and processes that allow communication in the nervous system.

- The basic unit of the *nervous system* is the *neuron,* or nerve cell, made up of *dendrites,* a cell body, an *axon,* and axon terminals. Afferent neurons carry messages to the spinal cord and brain; efferent neurons carry messages from the brain to organs and muscles. The space between the axon terminals and another neuron is the *synapse.* pp. 46–48
- The *action potential* is caused by the stimulation of the neuron. If there is enough stimulation at the cell body, an action potential occurs (a rapid reversal of cell membrane potential). The neuron fires in an *all-or-none* fashion and has a *refractory period,* during which it cannot fire. The action potential moves down the axon and stimulates the release of *neurotransmitters,* chemicals that reside in the axon terminal's synaptic vesicles. The neurotransmitters move across the synaptic space and bind to receptor sites on neighboring cells, thereby conveying information to them. pp. 48–50

What is the focus of psychopharmacology?

- Psychopharmacology is the study of how drugs affect behavior. Research often focuses on agonists and antagonists. An *agonist* is a chemical that mimics or facilitates the action of a neurotransmitter, usually by occupying receptor sites. An *antagonist* is a chemical that opposes the action of a neurotransmitter, usually by blocking it from occupying receptor sites. pp. 50–51

KEY TERMS

nervous system, p. 46; neuron, p. 46; afferent neuron, p. 46; efferent neuron, p. 46; dendrites, p. 46; axon, p. 46; synapse, p. 48; action potential, p. 48; all-or-none, p. 48; refractory period, p. 48; neurotransmitter, p. 48; agonist, p. 50; antagonist, p. 50

The Organization of the Nervous System

Describe the subdivisions of the nervous system.

- The nervous system is composed of two subdivisions: the central and peripheral nervous systems. The *central nervous system* consists of the brain and the *spinal cord.* The *peripheral nervous system* carries information to and from the spinal cord and brain through spinal and cranial nerves. The peripheral nervous system is further subdivided into the *somatic* and *autonomic nervous systems.* The autonomic nervous system has two subdivisions: the *sympathetic* and *parasympathetic nervous systems,* which have different functions. pp. 51–54

KEY TERMS

peripheral nervous system, p. 50; somatic nervous system, p. 53; autonomic nervous system, p. 53; sympathetic nervous system, p. 53; parasympathetic nervous system, p. 53; central nervous system, p. 53; spinal cord, p. 54

The Organization of the Brain

What are the major sections of the brain, and what are its structures?

- The *brain* is divided into three key sections: the hindbrain, the midbrain, and the forebrain (which includes the cortex). p. 55
- The *hindbrain* consists of four main structures: the *medulla,* the reticular formation, the *pons,* and the *cerebellum.* pp. 55–56
- The *midbrain* is made up of nuclei that receive afferent signals from other parts of the brain and from the spinal cord, interpret them, and either relay the information to other parts of the brain or cause the body to act at once. pp. 55–56
- The *forebrain* is the largest and most complicated brain structure; it comprises the *thalamus* and the *hypothalamus,* the *limbic system,* the basal ganglia, the corpus callosum, and the *cortex.* The *convolutions* are folds in the tissue of the cerebral hemispheres and the cortex. The lateral fissure and the central fissure divide the cortex into lobes. pp. 56–57

KEY TERMS

brain, p. 54; hindbrain, p. 55; medulla, p. 55; pons, p. 55; cerebellum, p. 55; midbrain, p. 56; forebrain, p. 56; thalamus, p. 57; hypothalamus, p. 57; limbic system, p. 57; cortex, p. 57; convolutions, p. 57

The Brain at Work

Describe several techniques for studying brain activity and functions.

- One technique for measuring the activity of the nervous system is single-unit recording, in which scientists record the activity of a single cell by placing an electrode within or next to the cell. Another technique uses graphical records of brain-wave patterns, called *electroencephalograms (EEGs),* to assess neurological disorders and the types of activities that occur during thought, sleep, and other behaviors. pp. 58–59

■ Three significant techniques for measuring the activity of the nervous system have been developed in the past two decades. *CT (computerized tomography) scans* are computer-enhanced X-ray images. *PET (positron emission tomography) scans* use radioactive markers to allow researchers to capture an image showing which brain areas are most active during various mental processes. *MRI (magnetic resonance imaging) scans* use magnetism rather than radiation and furnish a higher resolution image than CT scans. *Functional magnetic resonance imaging (fMRI)* is an imaging technique that allows researchers to observe brain activity as it takes place, while a participant performs a task. pp. 58–61

How does the function of the left and right hemisphere differ?

■ Research shows that in most human beings, one cerebral hemisphere—usually the left—is specialized for processing speech and language; the other—usually the right—appears better able to handle spatial, musical, and drawing tasks. pp. 61–62

■ Normal cerebral hemispheres are connected to each other by the corpus callosum. *Split-brain patients* have their cerebral hemispheres surgically disconnected and as a result, they cannot internally access their left hemisphere language functions from their right hemisphere or their right hemisphere spatial capabilities from their left. pp. 62–63

KEY TERMS

electroencephalogram (EEG), p. 59; CT scans, p. 59; PET scans, p. 59; MRI scans, p. 60; fMRI scans, p. 60; split-brain patient, p. 62

Hormones and Glands

How does the endocrine system affect behavior?

■ The *endocrine glands* are a group of ductless glands that affect behavior by secreting *hormones* into the bloodstream. Each gland may influence different aspects of behavior, but all are governed by the *pituitary gland.* The pituitary gland is appropriately referred to as the master gland because of its central role in regulating hormones. Another important gland is the pancreas, which regulates the body's sugar levels by producing *insulin.* pp. 65–66

KEY TERMS

endocrine glands, p. 64; hormones, p. 64; pituitary gland, p. 66; insulin, p. 66

3 Child Development

Milton Avery, *Child's Supper*, 1945

Almost every day newspapers tell us of children who have survived being lost in the woods on camping trips, who have found their way home from a mall after getting lost there, or who have fallen down narrow wells only to be successfully retrieved 12 hours later. Children are marvelously resilient; they bounce back from scrapes, bruises, and emotional bumps with astonishing speed. Though many kids do not experience what our society considers an "ideal upbringing" (staying close to home, living in a nuclear family with mom and dad plus 2.2 children), most children grow up to be happy and productive, leading emotionally fulfilling lives. Not only that, but children with special needs—those with learning disabilities, physical challenges, and emotional problems—on the whole, wind up doing okay.

Having been lost and frightened for a few hours, having lived with one parent, two, or an extended family, or have experienced violence in a neighborhood does not determine who a child will become—but it does influence development. Home interactions are crucial in developing a child's personality. They aren't the only influence—biological factors certainly weigh in heavily—but they are nevertheless important. Psychologists know that essential

chapter outline

developmental processes take place in the early years of life. They also know that children develop differently. Some are cognitively advanced; others are average or slow. But when and to what extent any person attains developmental milestones is affected by a complex interaction of nature and nurture. The process begins before birth and continues throughout life.

Part of our goal for this chapter is to examine normal developmental processes in children, including diverse interacting areas such as physical, cognitive, moral, emotional, and social development. We will also see how genetic makeup interacts with the environment to produce individuals who are unique. And you will begin to understand why parents affect development so profoundly.

Key Issues and Research Designs

Developmental psychology is the study of lifelong, often age-related, processes of change in the physical, cognitive, moral, emotional, and social domains of functioning; such changes are rooted in biological mechanisms that are genetically controlled (for example, maturational processes involved in the growth of the nervous system), as well as in social interactions. Developmental psychologists study all of these changes—biological, maturational, and social—to find out how people grow and become transformed from young children to mature, functioning adults and to learn what causes those changes.

Developmental psychologists recognize that development involves gains and losses over time, because people can respond in either positive or negative ways to life's experiences. They also recognize that development must be viewed from multiple perspectives and within a historical and cultural context. Researchers acknowledge that the interaction of genetics and the environment is a complex issue and that there is considerable diversity in developmental and maturational growth (Baltes, 1998). Developmental psychologists have focused on a few key issues, theories, and research methods to unravel the causes of behavior. Their goal is always the same: to describe, explain, predict, and potentially help manage human development.

Issues in Developmental Psychology

Several key issues help developmental researchers order their questions and shape their point of view. Three of the most important of these are nature versus nurture, stability versus change, and continuity versus discontinuity.

Developmental psychology The study of the lifelong, often age-related, processes of change in the physical, cognitive, moral, emotional, and social domains of functioning; such changes are rooted in biological mechanisms that are genetically controlled, as well as in social interactions.

■ **NATURE OR NURTURE?** One way to look at individual development is to consider to what extent the developing person's abilities, interests, and personality are determined primarily by biological influences (*nature*) or primarily by environmental influences (*nurture*). The impact of nature and nurture underpins many of the issues we will be discussing. Separating biological from environmental causes of behavior is a complicated matter; the answer to any specific question about human behavior usually involves the interaction between nature and nurture.

To assess the roles played by genetics and environment, researchers have studied identical twins (people with the same genetic makeup) who have been raised in different environments, and they have found extraordinary similarities between such siblings (Wright, 1997). In one such study, researchers found an identical twin who was an accomplished storyteller with a collection of amusing anecdotes; when his twin brother, whom the researchers located later, was asked if he knew any funny stories, he leaned back with a practiced air and launched into one. Other twins shared interests in dogs, smoked the same cigarettes, or had the same political opinions. One pair of twins shared a phobia of the ocean; at the beach, both would enter the water backward, and then only up to their knees. This study included twin firefighters, twin gunsmiths, and twins who obsessively counted things. The study by Lykken and colleagues (1992) and another by McCourt and colleagues (1999) argue that genetics plays an especially important role in human development.

■ Mark Newman (left) and Gerald Levey—fraternal twins separated at birth—lived for 31 years, never knowing each other existed. Here, they pose with Dr. Nancy Segal, co-director of the University of Minnesota project on Twins Reared Apart, a project that studies the similarities of separated twins' lives.

Evolutionary psychologists go a step further. They suggest that development of an individual from birth through maturity involves the expression of evolved gradual changes in interaction with the social environment; they feel that different adaptations are necessary at different times in the course of development. They conclude that individual differences in development are the result of predictable, adaptive responses to environmental pressures that existed in human prehistory, and not the result of idiosyncratic events (Bjorklund & Pellegrini, 2000). So intelligence is fostered and develops in response to environmental demands; mothers and fathers differentially invest time and energy in their offspring, and this becomes an adaptation—those who have been nurtured more have a greater chance of surviving and reproducing. Attachment, gender differences, mate choices—all developmental issues to an extent—have thus evolved to help human beings adapt (Geary & Bjorklund, 2000).

But not all psychologists or parents agree; they believe that environment plays an equally crucial role. Their idea is that *unique* experiences in and outside of the home affect an individual's development in profound ways (Reiss et al., 2000). Many parents think they can enhance their children's environment and optimize the likelihood of their living successful and satisfying lives; but, of course, the opposite can and sometimes does occur. Sometimes ineffectual parenting occurs, which elicits antisocial behavior from children—the consequence is a family often torn by strife and anxiety. When this occurs, it is hard to discern who is "at fault"; so researchers think of the family as a system and the interaction among the family members according to a *transaction model* in which parents, children, and situations mutually influence one another (Little, 2000).

■ **STABILITY OR CHANGE?** Do individuals stay pretty much the same throughout their lives—cognitively, emotionally, and socially—or do they change and adapt in response to events in their environment? The issue of stability versus change is a recurring theme in developmental psychology. It is closely associated with the nature–nurture issue, because when a researcher assumes that stability exists, he or she often assumes that stable traits—for example, shyness—are inherited and genetically determined. Those who favor an environmental view are more likely to believe that people change over the course of a lifetime because of unique life events—for example, the loss of a sibling in a car accident.

■ **CONTINUITY OR DISCONTINUITY?** A third issue revolves around whether development is continuous or discontinuous. Some see development as *continuous,* as a process of gradual growth and change, with skills and knowledge added one bit at a time and one skill building on another. But development can also be viewed as *discontinuous,* with growth, maturation, and understanding of the world occurring at various critical periods and with changes appearing abruptly. For example, one day a child cannot walk, but the next day she takes several steps.

Developmental Theories

Most developmental psychologists have a theoretical orientation—a point of view that allows them to describe, explain, and predict behavior. Developmental theories give shape and order to sets of data about physical, cognitive, and social development. Some developmental theories date back to early psychologists; others are modern versions of earlier ideas; still others involve breaking new ground, looking at development and maturation from unique vantage points. These theories reflect the diversity of the discipline of psychology.

■ **THE PSYCHOANALYTIC APPROACH.** One of the earliest modern theories of development was Freud's. As you will see when we discuss personality in Chapter 12, Freud believed that early childhood experiences, especially those occurring before the age of 6, shape each person's biologically based urges. Interestingly, Freud never studied children; his theories developed out of studies of adults with psychological problems. We'll have much more to say about Freud later. Erik Erikson, whom we will discuss in detail in Chapter 4, took Freud's view and built on it to make it less gender-biased, more focused on normal personality development and development across the life span, and more sensitive to social and cultural influences on development.

■ **BEHAVIORISM.** In sharp contrast to the psychoanalytic tradition, behaviorism strongly influenced developmental psychology from the 1920s through the 1940s. Clark Hull focused on drive-reduction theories, attempting to discern how people are motivated by biological needs. Such theories later lent support to B. F. Skinner's behaviorism, which focused on the antecedents of behavior and reinforcers. Behaviorists have claimed that a child's development can proceed in any number of directions, depending entirely on his or her unique experiences. Behaviorism has been expanded to incorporate cognitive views of behavior.

■ **COGNITIVE THEORY.** The development of cognition has received careful attention from a number of researchers. The leading figure in this field, whom we will discuss in much more detail later, is Jean Piaget. Like Freud, Piaget strongly emphasized biological factors, believing that development occurs in a biologically determined sequence, but he also emphasized that development is a process of adaptation to the world, in which a child accommodates to its ever-changing demands. Piaget developed an exceedingly influential theory of cognitive development (Flavell, 1996). Closely linked to Piaget's theory is a cognitive theory that views human beings as problem solvers who attempt to make sense of the world; this *information-processing perspective* looks more closely at processes such as attention, memory, and problem solving and offers a different explanation of why young children think differently than older children. Most information-processing approaches see people as active decision makers, responding to environmental demands; these approaches attempt to explain how brain systems are hard-wired to lead people to think and act in the way they do.

Research Designs

Good researchers know that the method they use to study a problem often influences the results. In order to interpret what results might mean, a researcher must take into account the particular research design used. In developmental research, two widely used designs are the cross-sectional and the longitudinal. A psychologist using a *cross-sectional research design* compares many individuals of different ages to determine how they differ on some important dimension. The psychologist using a *longitudinal research design* studies a specific group of individuals at different ages to examine changes that have occurred over a long period of time.

Each research design has its advantages and disadvantages. For example, the cross-sectional design suffers from the fact that the participants' backgrounds differ;

they may have learned various things in different ways. Further, a participant's behavior, performance in a specific task, or ability may reflect a predisposition, a liking of the task, or some other variable unrelated to changes that come from development or aging. Most important, the age groups that are being examined may have had different life experiences—for example, one generation may have received substantially less education than the next, and education level will affect results on standardized tests. Individual differences are impossible to assess with the cross-sectional design.

But the longitudinal research design also has problems. For one thing, it requires the researcher to have access to the same people repeatedly, but some participants may move, withdraw from the study, or even die. Also, after repeated testing on the same task (even though the tests are months or years apart), participants may do better because of practice. Moreover, longitudinal research sometimes takes years to complete; during that time, important changes may occur in the participants' personal or social environment. Finally, such research is time-consuming and expensive. Figure 3.1 shows a comparison of the cross-sectional and longitudinal research designs.

FIGURE 3.1

Cross-Sectional and Longitudinal Research Design

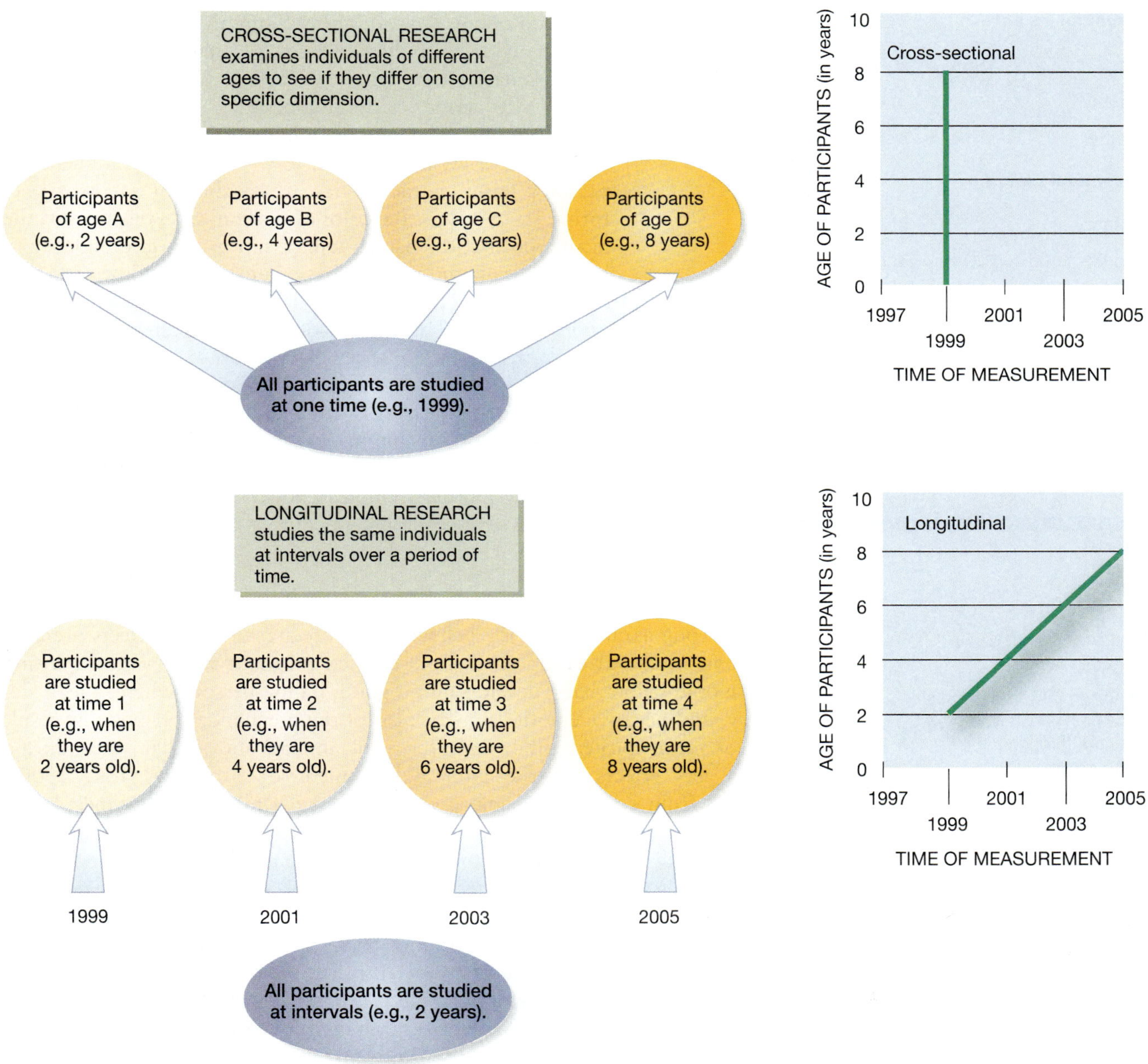

Physical Development

Psychologists refer to developmental events that occur before birth as *prenatal;* those that occur in the month after birth are *neonatal.* Both terms derive from the Latin word *natus,* meaning "born."

Prenatal Development

The lifelong journey of human development begins with conception. Conception occurs when an ovum and a sperm join in a woman's fallopian tube to form a **zygote**—a fertilized egg. Within 10 hours of conception, the zygote divides into four cells. During the next 5 days or so, the zygote floats down the fallopian tube and implants itself in the wall of the uterus. From implantation until the 49th day after conception, the organism is called an **embryo.** Then, from the 8th week until birth, the organism is called a **fetus.** On the average, maturation and development of a full-term human infant require 266 days, or about 9 months; this length of time is often divided into three *trimesters* (3-month periods). Table 3.1 summarizes the prenatal (before birth) and postnatal (after birth) periods of development.

TABLE 3.1

Life Stages and Approximate Ages in Human Development

Life Stage	Approximate Age
Prenatal period	
Zygote	Conception to day 5 to 7
Embryo	To day 49
Fetus	Week 8 to birth
Postnatal period	
Infancy	Birth to 18 months
Toddlerhood	18 months to 3 years
Early childhood	3 to 6 years
Middle childhood	6 to 13 years
Adolescence	13 to 20 years
Young adulthood	20 to 40 years
Middle adulthood	40 to 65 years
Late adulthood	65 plus

Although the prenatal environment—especially the mother's diet (Widerstrom, 1999)—can have an influence, a person's basic characteristics are established as the zygote forms; these include the color of the hair and eyes, the sex, the likelihood that the person will be tall or short, a tendency to be fat or lean, and perhaps basic intellectual abilities and personality traits. There, the cells begin the process of *differentiation:* organs and other parts of the body begin to form. Some cells form the *umbilical cord*—a group of blood vessels and tissues that connect the zygote to the placenta. The **placenta** is a mass of tissue that is attached to the wall of the uterus and acts as the life support system for the fetus. It supplies oxygen, food, and antibodies and eliminates wastes—all by way of the mother's bloodstream. Table 3.2 summarizes the major physical developments during the prenatal period.

Harmful Environmental Effects

Zygote [ZY-goat]
A fertilized egg.

Embryo [EM-bree-o]
The prenatal organism from the 5th through the 49th day after conception.

Fetus [FEET-us]
The prenatal organism from the 8th week after conception until birth.

Placenta [pluh-SENT-uh]
A mass of tissue that is attached to the wall of the uterus and connected to the developing fetus by the umbilical cord; it supplies nutrients and eliminates waste products.

People have long assumed that the behavior of a pregnant woman affects prenatal development. Medieval European doctors advised pregnant women that uplifting thoughts would help a baby develop into a good, happy person, whereas fear, despondency, and negative emotions might disrupt the pregnancy and possibly result in a sad or mean-spirited child. Research with animals shows that stress during pregnancy has effects on the later development of offspring (Lin, 2000). Generalizing from such data, some pregnant women strap portable tape players around their abdomens and play soothing music to their unborn child, in the hope that the child will gain a benevolent perspective on the outside world.

While a fetus may not be affected by the mother's condition to the extent suggested by medieval doctors, the quality of the life support system provided by the mother does influence the embryo and fetus from conception until birth. Environmental factors such as diet, infection, radiation, and drugs affect both the mother and the baby. The developing child is especially vulnerable in certain *critical periods,* during which it is maturing rapidly and is particularly sensitive to the environment. Although the basic architecture of the brain is in place well before

TABLE 3.2

Major Developments During the Prenatal Period

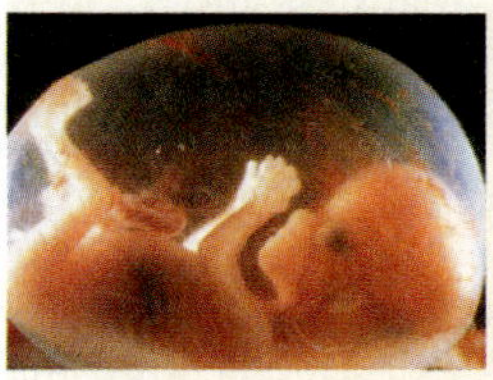

11 weeks

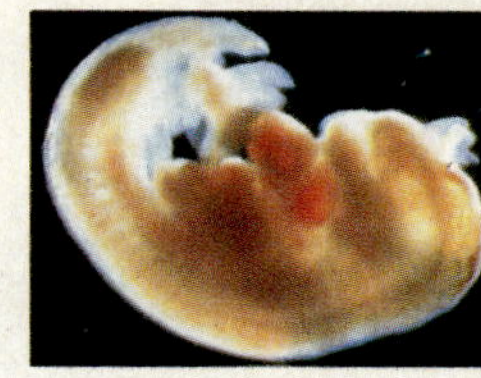

4 weeks

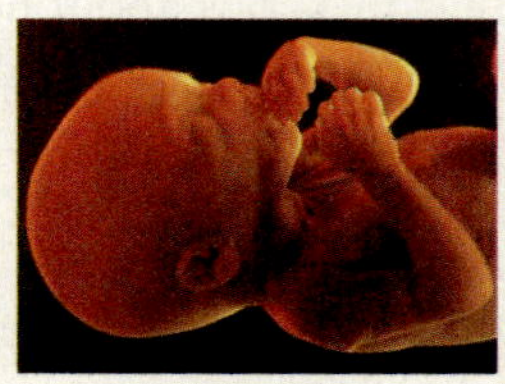

20 weeks

	Age	Size	Characteristics
First trimester 1–12 weeks	1 week	150 cells	Zygote attaches to uterine lining.
			Placental circulation established.
	2 weeks	Several thousand cells	Heart and blood vessels begin to develop. Basics of brain and central nervous system form.
	3 weeks	1/10 inch	Kidneys and digestive tract begin to form. Rudiments of ears, nose, and eyes are present.
	4 weeks	1/4 inch	Arms and legs develop. Jaws form around mouth.
	6 weeks	1/2 inch	
	8 weeks	1 inch, 1/30 ounce	Bones begin to develop in limbs. Sex organs begin to form.
	12 weeks	3 inches, 1 ounce	Gender can be distinguished. Kidneys are functioning, and liver is manufacturing red blood cells. Fetal movements can be detected by a physician.
Second trimester 13–24 weeks	16 weeks	6 1/2 inches, 4 ounces	Heartbeat can be detected by a physician. Bones begin to calcify.
	20 weeks	10 inches, 8 ounces	Mother feels fetal movements.
	24 weeks	12 inches, 1 1/2 pounds	Vernix (white waxy substance) protects the body. Eyes open; eyebrows and eyelashes form; skin is wrinkled. Respiratory system is barely mature enough to support life.
Third trimester 25–38 weeks	28 weeks	15 inches, 2 1/2 pounds	Fetus is fully developed but needs to gain in size, strength, and maturity of systems.
	32 weeks	17 inches, 4 pounds	A layer of fat forms beneath the skin to regulate body temperature.
	36 weeks	19 inches, 6 pounds	Fetus settles into position for birth.
	38 weeks	21 inches, 8 pounds	Fetus arrives at full term—266 days from conception.

birth, individual connections between neurons are subject to considerable influence or damage in infancy.

Substances that can produce developmental malformations (birth defects) during the prenatal period are known as **teratogens.** In the United States, birth defects are the leading cause of death during the first year of life. If the mother drinks alcohol in early and middle pregnancy, the baby is more likely to be born prematurely, to have a lower birthweight, and to suffer from mental retardation or attention-deficit/hyperactivity disorder (Ponnappa & Rubin, 2000). Maternal drinking during pregnancy is the leading known cause of mental retardation in newborns. Each year, about 10,000 infants are born with physical signs or cognitive disabilities associated with maternal drinking. Research shows that mothers who drink more than 3 ounces of 100-proof liquor per day during pregnancy are significantly more likely to have children with deficits in intelligence test scores at age 4 (Kelly, Day, & Streissguth, 2000; Streissguth et al., 1999).

Studies show that many drugs affect prenatal development. High doses of aspirin, caffeine, or tobacco all have negative effects (Barr et al., 1990). Cigarette smoking constricts the oxygen supply to the fetus. Babies born to mothers who smoke cigarettes tend to be smaller and may be at increased risk for cleft palate and

Teratogen [ter-AT-oh-jen] Substance that can produce developmental malformations (birth defects) during the prenatal period.

■ *Studies show that nicotine and alcohol are not advised for prenatal development.*

perhaps a slightly lower IQ. Certain drugs, including tranquilizers, can produce malformations of the head, face, and limbs as well as neurological disorders (Goldstein & Sundell, 1999). And, in recent years, hundreds of thousands of infants have been born addicted to crack and other drugs. Drugs may have an especially strong influence during the embryonic stage of development, when the mother may not realize she is pregnant; this is usually considered a critical period.

Newborns Come Well Equipped

Newborns grow rapidly—seemingly almost overnight—and they are not nearly as helpless as many people believe. At birth, infants can hear, see, smell, and respond to the environment in adaptive ways; in other words, they have good sensory systems. They are also directly affected by experience. Psychologists try to find out exactly how experience affects infants' perceptual development. In doing so, they need to discover how infants think, what they perceive, and how they react to the world. Researchers want answers to various questions about newborns' perceptual world: What are a child's inborn abilities and reflexes? When do inborn abilities become evident? How does the environment affect the emergence of inborn abilities?

■ **GROWTH.** An infant who weighs 7.5 pounds at birth may weigh as much as 20 or 25 pounds by 12 months. At 18 months, a child is usually walking and beginning to talk. For psychologists, infancy continues until the child begins to represent the world abstractly through language. Thus, *infancy* is the period from birth to about 18 months.

The rapid growth that occurs in the early weeks and months after birth is quite extraordinary and mirrors embryonic development in important ways. A newborn's head is about one-fourth of its body length; a 2-year-old's is only one-fifth. The head develops early, and motor development, control, and coordination progress from the head to the feet. This pattern of growth is called the *cephalocaudal trend* (from the Greek word *kephalé,* "head," and the Latin word *cauda,* "tail"). Following another pattern—the *proximodistal trend*—maturation and growth progress from the center (proximal part) of the body outward to the extremities (the more distant, or distal, part). That is, the head and torso grow before the arms, legs, hands, and feet do. Thus, a newborn's head is about the same circumference as the torso, and an infant's arms and legs are quite short, relatively speaking—but these change very quickly (see Figure 3.2).

FIGURE 3.2

The Cephalocaudal Trend of Growth

Body proportions change dramatically from fetal stages of development until adulthood. *(Berk, 1994.)*

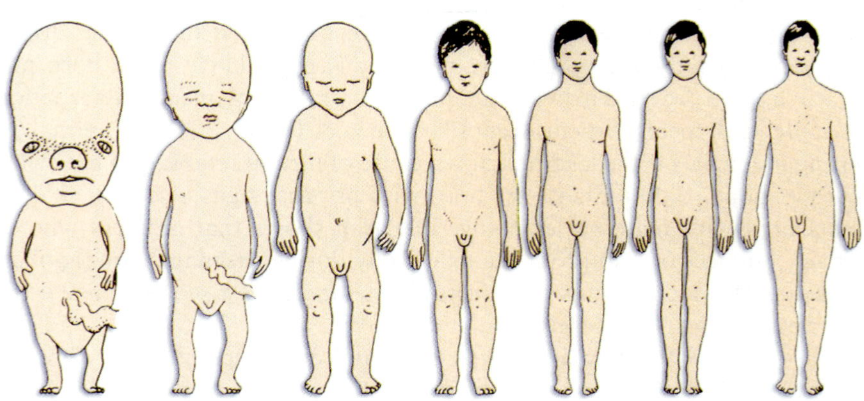

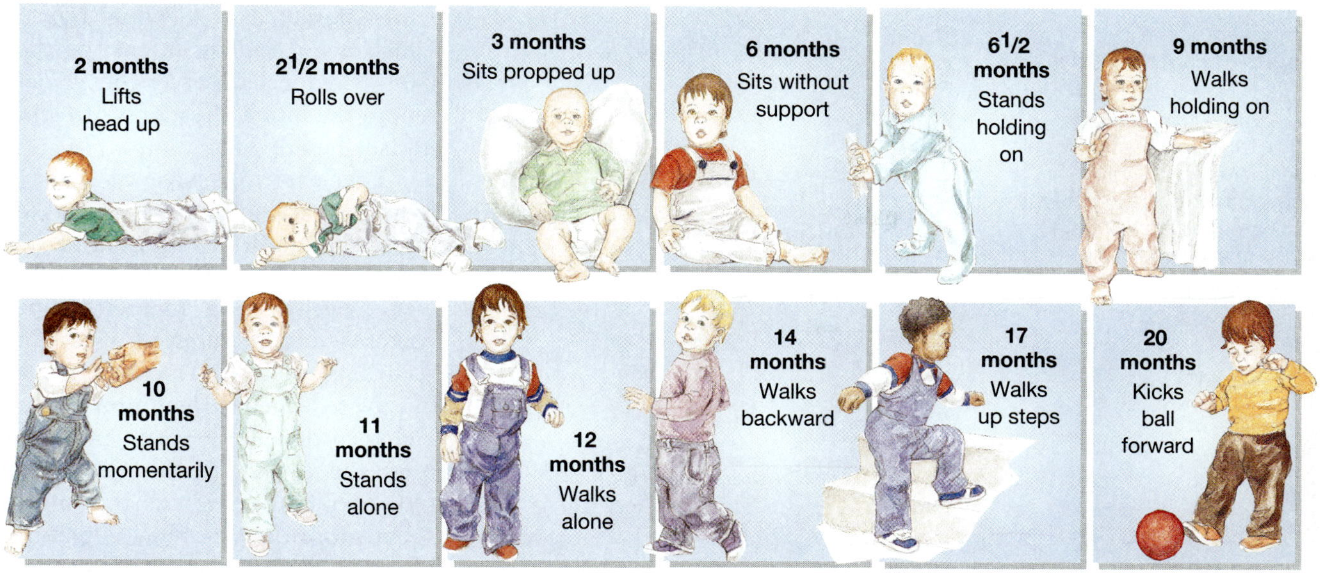

FIGURE 3.3

Development of Motor Skills in the First 2 Years

Infants typically develop motor skills in the sequence shown here. Normal, healthy infants may reach any of these milestones earlier or later than these average ages.

During the period of infancy and childhood (up through about age 13 years), the child grows physically from a being that requires constant care, attention, and assistance to a nearly full-size independent person. By 13 months, children can walk, climb, and manipulate their environment—skills that often lead to the need for a variety of safety features in the home. There is significant variability in the age at which children begin to walk or climb. Some do so early; others are slow to develop these abilities. The age at which these specific behaviors first occur seems unrelated to any other major developmental milestones. Figure 3.3 shows the major achievements in motor development in the first 2 years.

■ **NEWBORNS' REFLEXES.** Touch the palm of a newborn baby, and you'll probably find one of your fingers held in the surprisingly firm grip of a tiny fist. The baby is exhibiting a reflexive reaction. Babies are born with innate *primary reflexes*—unlearned responses to stimuli. Some, such as the grasping reflex, no doubt helped ensure survival in humanity's primate ancestors; most of these reflexes disappear over the course of the first year of life. Physicians use the presence or absence of primary reflexes to assess neurological status at birth and to evaluate rate of development during infancy. One primary reflex exhibited by infants is the **Babinski reflex**—a fanning out of the toes in response to a touch on the sole of the foot. Another is the **Moro reflex**—outstretching of the arms and legs and crying in response to a loud noise or an abrupt change in the environment. Newborns also exhibit the **rooting reflex**—turning the head toward a light touch (such as of a breast or hand) on their lips or cheek. They show the **sucking reflex** in response to a finger or nipple placed in their mouth and a vigorous **grasping reflex** in response to an object touching the palms of their hands or their fingers.

At first, an infant's abilities and reflexes are biologically determined. Gradually, learned responses, such as reaching for desired objects, replace reflex reactions. The baby's experiences in the environment become more important in determining development. The complex interactions between nature and nurture follow a developmental timetable that continues throughout life.

■ **INFANT PERCEPTION: FANTZ'S VIEWING BOX.** A mountain of research on infant perception shows that newborns have surprisingly well-developed perceptual systems. Robert Fantz (1961) did some of the earliest work on infant perception.

Babinski reflex
Reflex in which a newborn fans out the toes when the sole of the foot is touched.

Moro reflex
Reflex in which a newborn stretches out the arms and legs and cries in response to a loud noise or an abrupt change in the environment.

Rooting reflex
Reflex that causes a newborn to turn the head toward a light touch on lips or cheek.

Sucking reflex
Reflex that causes a newborn to make sucking motions when a finger or nipple is placed in the mouth.

Grasping reflex
Reflex that causes a newborn to grasp vigorously any object touching the palm or fingers or placed in the hand.

FIGURE 3.4

Results of Fantz's Study

Using a viewing box to observe newborns' eye movements, Fantz (1961) recorded the total time infants spent looking at various patterns. He found that they looked at faces or patterned material much more often than they looked at plain fields.

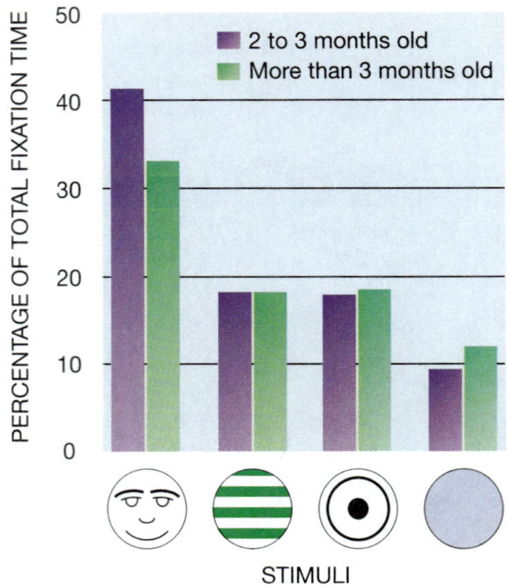

Fantz designed a viewing box in which he placed an infant; he then had a hidden observer or camera record the infant's responses to stimuli (see Figure 3.4).

The exciting part of Fantz's work was not so much that he asked interesting questions but that he was able to get "answers" from the infants. By showing infants various patterns and pictures of faces and recording their eye movements, he discovered their visual preferences. He recorded how long and how often the infants looked at each pattern or picture. Because the infants spent more time looking at pictures of faces than at patterns of random squiggles, Fantz concluded not only that they could see different patterns but also that they preferred faces.

Other researchers confirm that infants prefer complex visual fields over simple ones, curved patterns over straight or angular ones, and normal human faces over random patterns or faces with mixed-up features (Quinn, Brown, & Streppa, 1997). Even in the first few months of life, babies can discriminate among facial features and prefer attractive faces to less attractive ones (Rubenstein, Kalakanis, & Langlois, 1999; Slater et al., 2000). Newborns look at pictures of their parents more than at pictures of strangers (de Haan & Nelson, 1997; Fullmer, 1999). Babies as young as 3 months of age can discern a caregiver's shift of attention by observing the person's eyes and can then shift their own attention to the same object or event (Hood, Willen, & Driver, 1998).

At about 4 to 8 weeks, an infant may sleep for 4 to 6 hours during the night, uninterrupted by the need to eat, a change that weary parents usually welcome. When awake, infants smile at the caregiver and listen attentively to human voices. Between 6 and 9 months, infants begin to crawl, giving them more freedom to seek out favorite people. The ability to crawl is accompanied by important changes in behavior; in fact, some researchers assert that crawling is what allows critical behavior changes to occur (Bertenthal, Campos, & Kermoian, 1994).

By 7 months, infants can recognize happy faces and sounds and can discriminate among them (Soken & Pick, 1999). According to Arlene Walker-Andrews (Walker-Andrews, 1997; Walker-Andrews & Dickson, 1997), they recognize emotional expressions. Using a procedure similar to Fantz's, Walker-Andrews (1986) observed 5- and 7-month-old infants who saw films of people with angry or happy facial expressions making angry or happy sounds. (The lower third of each face was covered so that the infants could not match the sounds to the lips.) She recorded which images the infants looked at and how long they looked at them as an index of their interest and of whether there was incongruity between face and sound. Results showed that 7-month-old infants could tell when the sound and facial expression did not match, but 5-month-olds could not. This research supports the idea that infants can make such judgments and suggests a timetable by which they develop the ability to discriminate among facial expressions.

Critical Period
The time in the development of an organism when it is especially sensitive to certain environmental influences; outside of that period the same influences will have far less effect.

Infant perception is quite good; it follows a maturational timetable, but there are discontinuities in perceptual development. At first, babies attend to the most prominent features in the world; as time passes, they attend to, recognize, and respond to the world based on their recognition of people and situations—they begin to make more cognitive-based perceptual decisions (Reznick, Chawarska, & Betts, 2000).

BRAIN AND BEHAVIOR

Critical Periods

In a public briefing from the National Research Council, researcher Jack Shonkoff argued that early experiences that affect brain development lay the foundations for intelligence, emotional health, and moral development; but he also argued that the focus on a period from birth to age 3 is too narrow. "The neurological window of opportunity does not slam shut at age 3 or 5 . . . the disproportionate focus on 'zero to three' begins too late and ends too soon" (Shonkoff, 2000).

For sure there are critical periods for brain development. Attachments to other people—especially caregivers, usually moms and dads—forms at an early point in life, usually before the age of 3 (we will study attachment later in this chapter). But the window for forming attachments is probably wider than most have thought (Thompson, 2000; Thompson & Nelson, 2001). In the area of cognitive development, missed opportunities in the first 3 years may be missed opportunities indeed (Ramey & Sackett, 2000). In general, researchers assert that specific learning is not what is essential in the first 3 or 4 years—rather, children are prepared to learn through stimulation. But must specific tasks, skills, or knowledge be learned at a specific age—a critical period—or remain unlearned? A **critical period** is a time in the development of an organism when it is especially sensitive to certain environmental influences; outside of that period the same influences will have far less effect.

Newport and her colleagues studied second-language learning and found that this learning is harder later in life (Johnson, Shenkman, Newport, & Medin, 1996; Landau et al., 2000). Young children acquire a second language with greater ease and fewer mistakes than adults do. Furthermore, the neural systems underlying learning a second language show differences depending on the age of learning. For children under the age of 4, brain responses tend to be isolated in the left hemisphere—where you would expect them to be. But for children over age 4, there is much more right-hemisphere activity. Of course, language is not a single system; it involves sounds, words, meaning, and grammar, and emerges at different times. Brain organization is structured, ready for language at a young age—a critical period—and later learning deviates from this inherent pattern, both in physiology and in efficiency (Neville & Bavelier, 2000; Weber-Fox & Neville, 1999)

The brain continues to develop throughout life, but it is especially plastic during childhood. Children before puberty have the most plastic brains, and so it is not surprising that second-language acquisition grows more difficult after that period (Gao, Levine, & Huttenlocher, 2000; Huttenlocher, 1998, 1999). People continue to grow and develop throughout life, but brain development and chemistry are most sensitive and most plastic and easily changed in the younger developmental years.

■ **THE VISUAL CLIFF.** Walk and Gibson conducted a classic developmental research study in 1961. They devised the *visual cliff method* to determine the extent of infants' depth perception. In this method, a researcher uses a glass surface, half of which is covered with a checkerboard pattern, and places on it an infant who can crawl. The same checkerboard pattern is placed several feet below the transparent half of the glass surface. Infants can crawl easily from the patterned area onto the transparent area. Infants with poorly developed depth perception should be willing to crawl onto the transparent side as often as onto the patterned side. Conversely, infants with well-developed depth perception should refuse to crawl onto the transparent side, even when encouraged to do so by their mothers. Walk and Gibson found that 9-month-olds avoided the transparent surface, thus demonstrating that depth perception is well developed at this age.

■ *Walk and Gibson designed the visual cliff method to test the extent of infants' depth perception.*

■ **EVOLUTION AND NEWBORN PREPAREDNESS.** Newborns enter the world with the ability to experience, respond to, and learn from the environment. Their sensory systems are well formed but still developing; this development is strongly shaped by experience, which ultimately alters brain connections permanently (Simion & Butterworth, 1998) (see *Brain and Behavior* above). Newborns are thus biologically equipped and ready to perceive and experience the world; their brains develop, neurons interconnect, and this neuronal development continues for several years. Recall from Chapter 2 that although most of the connections are present at birth, the proper functioning of the system is sensitive to and depends on experience. Without proper and varied perceptual experiences, brain development is less than optimal. So, while evolution may have prepared a newborn to experience the world, a newborn and infant's interactions with the world shape its ability to cope effectively. And newborns and infants are active explorers of their world, not passive vessels into which experience is poured. Infants experiment; infants explore, and infants learn—it is this active, cognitive maturation that allows for and promotes survival, growth, development, and an increasing cognitive maturity.

The Development of Thought

Why are some cars made with child-proof locks and windows? Why do parents use gates to guard stairs and gadgets to keep kitchen cabinets closed? Why are young children's toys made so that small parts cannot come off? Because children are inquisitive and much more intelligent than many people give them credit for. Even 3-month-olds can learn the order of a list of items and, when given age-appropriate prompts, remember that information a day later (Gulya et al., 1998).

Infants' physical development is visible and dramatic; for example, to the delight of caregivers, babies sometimes respond by imitating their facial expressions (pursed lips, stuck-out tongues)—although research in this area is controversial, and the findings are not always consistent (Forman & Kochanska, 2001). The cognitive changes that occur in slightly older children are sometimes less visible, but no less dramatic. Children are continually developing, both physically and cognitively; they focus their attention on coping with an ever-expanding world. As they mature, they can determine causes of events. Much of this ability is cognitively based and develops following a timetable that is rooted in brain growth and development (Peltzer-Karpf & Zangel, 2001). Figure 3.5 shows some of the many cognitive activities of the first 12 months.

Without question, the 20th century's leading researcher and theorist on the cognitive development of children and adults was Jean Piaget; his work laid the foundation for an understanding of the development of thought and still dominates the field of developmental psychology.

Jean Piaget's Insights

Swiss psychologist Jean Piaget (1896–1980) came to believe that the fundamental development of all cognitive abilities takes place during the first 2 years of life; many psychologists and educators agree. Piaget devised ingenious procedures for examining the cognitive development of young children; he looked at what children did well, what mistakes they made, and when and how they gained insights into the world. Piaget's theory focuses on *how* people think instead of on *what* they think, making it applicable to people in all cultures. Perhaps Piaget's greatest strength, however, was his description of how a person's inherited capacities interact with the environment to produce cognitive functioning. What Piaget did best was focus on the details of children's cognitive life; he observed them in minute detail and noticed discontinuities in their abilities at various ages. Piaget's explanations of cognitive development focus, to a great extent, on its direction and development. He explains how a person changes from a self-centered infant to an independent thinker as an adolescent.

Be an *Active* learner

REVIEW

- What are the fundamental differences between the cross-sectional and longitudinal research designs? pp. 74–75
- Distinguish between a zygote, embryo, and fetus. p. 76
- Can infants see the way adults do? p. 78

THINK CRITICALLY

- What survival value might each of the primary reflexes have had for humans' ancestors?
- What survival function might infants' preference for human faces have?
- What are the implications of the idea of critical periods for our knowledge of when babies develop language?

APPLY PSYCHOLOGY

- Imagine that you are a parent and want to take advantage of critical periods in your child's life. What might you do to enhance your child's reading abilities? musical talents?

1 week

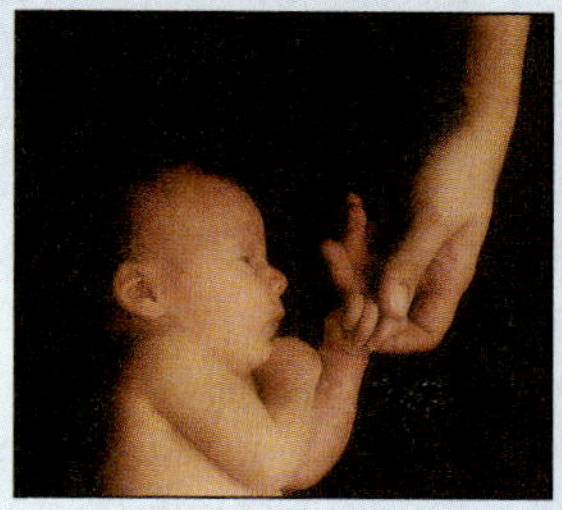

- See patterns, light, and dark
- Are sensitive to the location of a sound
- Distinguish volume and pitch
- Prefer high voices
- Will grasp an object if they touch it accidentally
- Stop sucking to look at a person momentarily

1 month

- Become excited at the sight of a person or a toy
- Look at objects only if in their line of vision

- Prefer patterns to plain fields
- Coordinate eyes sideways, up, and down
- Follow a toy from the side to the center of the body

2 months

- Prefer people to objects
- Stare at human faces; become quiet at the sound of a human voice
- Are startled at sounds and make a facial response
- Perceive depth
- Coordinate eye movements
- Reach out voluntarily instead of grasping reflexively
- Discriminate among voices, people, tastes, and objects

3 months

- Follow moving objects
- Glance from one object to another
- Distinguish near objects from distant objects
- Search with eyes for the source of a sound
- Become aware of self through exploration
- Show basic signs of memory

4 to 7 months

- See the world in color and with near-adult vision
- Pull dangling objects toward them
- Follow dangling or moving objects
- Turn to follow sound and vanishing objects
- Visually search out fast-moving or fallen objects
- Begin to anticipate a whole object when shown only part of it
- Deliberately imitate sounds and movements
- Recall a short series of actions
- Look briefly for a toy that disappears

8 to 12 months

- Put small objects into containers and pull them out of containers

- Search behind a screen for an object after they see it hidden there
- Hold and manipulate one object while looking at another object
- Recognize dimensions of objects

FIGURE 3.5

Infants' Perceptual and Cognitive Milestones

(Clarke-Stewart, Friedman, & Koch, 1985)

Although psychologists were initially skeptical of Piaget's ideas and some criticisms persist, many researchers have shown that his assumptions are generally correct and can be applied cross-culturally. But there are also dissenters (notably Russian psychologist Lev Vygotsky, whose theories we will consider a bit later) who stress society's role in shaping thought processes. Piaget put considerable emphasis on biology, asserting that cognitive development depends on the interaction between biological changes that take place within a child and experiences and that it follows the same path in all social environments.

■ **PIAGET'S CENTRAL CONCEPTS.** Piaget believed that what changes during development is the child's ability to make sense of experience. He called organized ways of interacting with the environment and experiencing the world a **schema** (*schemata* in the plural). You can think of a schema as a *mental structure;* in a way, a schema is a generalization a child makes based on comparable occurrences of various actions, usually physical, motor actions. Schemata guide thoughts based on prior experiences; they thus serve as the building blocks of cognitive growth.

Piaget argued that a schema could change through three processes: adaptation, assimilation, and accommodation. Initially, children develop schemata for motor behaviors, for example, realizing that reaching out and touching an object will cause it to move. Basic schemata combine, resulting in more complex ones. Schemata develop because a child realizes that action brings results; those results, in turn, may affect the child's future behavior. So, a child reaches out, touches a mobile, the bells that are attached to the mobile make a sound, the mobile changes position—and the child observes that a specific action has influenced the world. This entire process is called *adaptation.* As adaptation continues, a child organizes his or her schemata into more complex mental representations, linking one scheme with another. Ultimately, children develop schemata about play, make-believe, and the permanence of objects. For a child to develop schemata and more complex mental structures, two other important processes must occur: assimilation and accommodation.

Both children and adults use assimilation and accommodation to deal with new schemata. **Assimilation** is the process by which a person absorbs new ideas and experiences and incorporates them into existing mental structures and behaviors. **Accommodation** is the process of modifying previously developed mental structures and behaviors to adapt them to new experiences. A child who learns to grasp a ball demonstrates assimilation by later grasping other round objects. This assimilated behavior then serves as a foundation for accommodation. The child can learn new and more complex behaviors such as grasping forks, crayons, and sticks by modifying the earlier response—for example, by widening or narrowing the grasp. The two processes of assimilation and accommodation alternate in a never-ending cycle of cognitive growth, throughout the four stages of development that Piaget described. These stages and processes are part of an active construction of reality—babies and young children piece together their own view of the world, rather than just absorbing what adults teach them. The complexity of a child's schemata depends upon how well and how much the child assimilates or accommodates information. Piaget asserts that children are thus active in their own cognitive development.

Four stages of cognitive development are central to Piaget's theory. Piaget believed that just as standing must precede walking, some stages of cognitive development must precede others. For example, if a parent presents an idea that is too advanced, the child will not understand, and no real learning will take place. A 4-year-old who asks how babies are made will probably not understand a full, biologically accurate explanation and will not learn or remember it. If the same child asks the question a few years later, the more realistic and complex explanation will be more meaningful and more likely to be remembered. Piaget's stages are associated with approximate ages. The exact ages for each stage vary from person to person, but children in all cultures go through these same stages. Piaget acknowledged the complex interaction of environmental influences and genetic inheritances; nevertheless, he felt strongly that the order of stages was invariant. The four developmental stages he proposed are the sensorimotor stage, the preoperational stage, the concrete operational stage, and the formal operational stage.

Schema
In Piaget's view, a specific mental structure; an organized way of interacting with the environment and experiencing it—a generalization a child makes based on comparable occurrences of various actions, usually physical, motor actions (*schemata* in the plural).

Assimilation
According to Piaget, the process by which new ideas and experiences are absorbed and incorporated into existing mental structures and behaviors.

Accommodation
According to Piaget, the process by which existing mental structures and behaviors are modified to adapt to new experiences.

■ **THE SENSORIMOTOR STAGE.** Piaget considered the **sensorimotor stage,** which extends from birth to about age 2, to be the most significant, because the foundation for all cognitive development is established during this period. Consider the enormous changes that take place during the first 2 years of life. Newborns are totally dependent, reflexive organisms. Within a few weeks, infants learn some simple habits. They smile at their mothers or caregivers; they seek visual or auditory stimulation; they reach out and anticipate events in the environment, such as the mother's breast or a bottle. At 2 to 3 months, infants develop some motor coordination skills (Thelen, 2000) and a memory for past events, and they are able to predict future visual events (Diedrich et al., 2001; Gulya et al., 1998). According to Piaget, the acquisition of memory is a necessary foundation for further cognitive development.

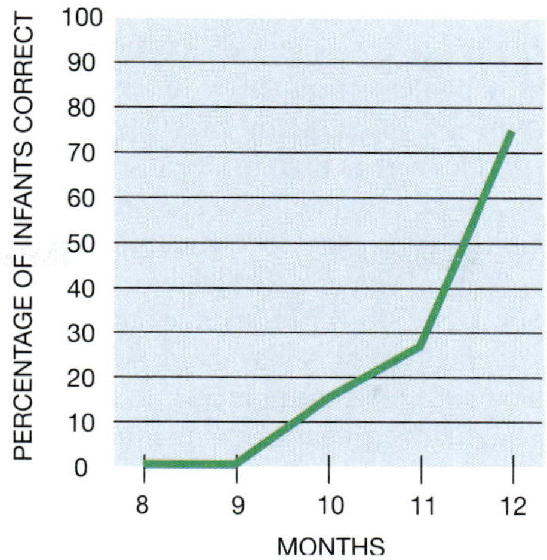

FIGURE 3.6

Object Permanence

Object permanence is the ability to know that an object continues to exist even when out of view. Research shows that the ability to remember the location of an object that is subsequently hidden improves over time. Most 1-year-olds can remember where an object has been hidden even after a delay of seven seconds. (*Fox, Kagan, and Weiskopf, 1979*)

By the age of 6 to 8 months, infants seek new and more interesting kinds of stimulation. They can sit up and crawl. No longer willing to merely watch what goes on around them, they begin to attempt to manipulate their environment. Piaget called this attempt "making interesting sights last"—that is, infants try to make interesting events recur. Karen Wynn (1998) suggests that even at this age infants have some very basic numerical reasoning abilities that lay the foundation for further development of arithmetic reasoning. At about 8 months, infants have intentions, and they attempt to overcome obstacles in order to reach goals. They can crawl to the other side of a room to reach a cat or a toy or follow a parent into the next room.

From about 9 months on, babies develop **object permanence**—the realization that objects continue to exist even when they are out of sight (see Figure 3.6). Prior to the development of object permanence, when the caregiver leaves the room and the baby can no longer see her, she no longer exists. After object permanence develops, the baby realizes that she is just out of view. Although the exact age at which object permanence becomes evident has not yet been established, Renée Baillargeon (Hespos & Baillargeon, 2001) has shown the existence of object permanence for some tasks in 4-month-olds—earlier than Piaget believed possible (see also Von Hofsten, Feng, & Spelke, 2000). In general, researchers assert that infants have knowledge of the physical world and a specialized learning ability that guides their acquisition of such knowledge, with various aspects of object permanence evolving gradually throughout the sensorimotor stage (Meltzoff & Moore, 2001; Spelke et al., 1992).

In the second half of the sensorimotor stage (from about 12 to 24 months), children begin to walk, talk, and use simple forms of logic. Object permanence is more fully developed; a child can now follow a ball that rolls away and can search for her or his mother after she has left the room. Children also begin to use language to represent the world, an ability that takes them beyond the concrete world of visual imagery. By age 2, a child can talk about dolly, doggy, cookies, going bye-bye, and other people, objects, and events. No longer an uncoordinated, reflexive organism, the child has become a thinking, walking, talking human being. Simultaneously, children may become manipulative and difficult to deal with. Parents often describe this stage as the terrible twos; it is characterized by the use of the ever-popular "No!" The child's behavior may vacillate between charming and awful. This vacillation and the emergence of annoying new habits, such as being difficult to dress and bathe, are signs of normal development, marking the beginning of the stage of preoperational thought.

Sensorimotor stage
The first of Piaget's four stages of cognitive development (covering roughly the first 2 years of life), during which the child develops some motor coordination skills and a memory for past events.

Object permanence
The realization of infants that objects continue to exist even when they are out of sight.

THE PREOPERATIONAL STAGE. In the **preoperational stage,** which lasts from about age 2 to age 6 or 7, children begin to represent the world symbolically. As preschoolers, they play with objects in new ways and try to represent reality through symbolic thought, by playing "let's pretend." But they continue to think about specifics rather than in the abstract and cannot deal with thoughts that are not easily visually represented. They make few attempts to make their speech more intelligible if a listener does not understand or to justify their reasoning, and they may develop behavior problems such as inattentiveness, belligerence, and temper tantrums. During this stage, adults often begin trying to teach children how to interact with others, but major social changes will not become fully apparent until the next stage of development.

A key element of the preoperational stage—which affects a child's cognitive and emotional behavior—is egocentrism, or self-centeredness. Present in the sensorimotor stage, but especially apparent in the preoperational stage, **egocentrism** is the inability to perceive a situation or event except in relation to oneself. Children are unable to understand that the world does not exist solely to satisfy their interests and needs. They respond to questions such as "Why does it snow?" with answers such as "So I can play in it." Children still cannot put themselves in anyone else's position.

At the end of Piaget's preoperational stage, children are just beginning to understand the difference between their ideas, feelings, and interests and those of others. This process of **decentration**—the process of changing from a totally self-oriented point of view to one that recognizes other people's feelings, ideas, and viewpoints—continues for several years. The concepts of egocentrism and decentration are widely recognized as central to Piaget's theory. However, few contemporary researchers have incorporated these ideas into their conceptions of how development proceeds.

Piaget held that children's understanding of space and their construction of alternative visual perspectives are limited during the preoperational stage. Recent evidence, however, suggests that Piaget may have underestimated the spatial–perspective abilities of children. Researchers have found that even 5-year-olds can solve certain visual and spatial problems previously thought to be solvable only by children 9 to 10 years old or older (Newcombe & Huttenlocher, 2000). Also, 4-year-olds are able to represent and remember the past.

Preoperational stage
Piaget's second stage of cognitive development (lasting from about age 2 to age 6 or 7), during which the child begins to represent the world symbolically.

Egocentrism [ee-go-SENT-rism]
Inability to perceive a situation or event except in relation to oneself; also known as *self-centeredness.*

Decentration
Process of changing from a totally self-oriented point of view to one that recognizes other people's feelings, ideas, and viewpoints.

Concrete operational stage
Piaget's third stage of cognitive development (lasting from approximately age 6 or 7 to age 11 or 12), during which the child develops the ability to understand constant factors in the environment, rules, and higher-order symbolic systems.

Conservation
Ability to recognize that objects can be transformed in some way, visually or physically, yet still be the same in number, weight, substance, or volume.

THE CONCRETE OPERATIONAL STAGE. The **concrete operational stage** is Piaget's third stage of cognitive development, lasting from approximately age 6 or 7 to age 11 or 12; during this stage, a child develops the ability to understand constant factors in the environment, rules, and higher-order symbolic systems such as arithmetic and geography. Children in this stage attend school, have friends, can take care of dressing and feeding themselves, and may take on household responsibilities. They can look at a situation from more than one viewpoint. They have gained sufficient mental maturity to be able to distinguish between appearance and reality and to think ahead one or two moves in checkers or other games. During this stage, children discover constancy in the world; they learn rules and understand the reasons for them. For example, a child learns not to build a sandcastle right at the water's edge, because the rising tide will inevitably destroy it.

Cognitive and perceptual abilities continue to develop as children mature and, slowly and in different ways, begin to grasp ever more difficult concepts. For example, at around age 7, children come to realize the connectedness of their thoughts, and they become especially conscious of their inner mental life and its unpredictability at times (Flavell, Green, & Flavell, 2000).

The hallmark of this stage is an understanding of **conservation**—the ability to recognize that objects can be transformed in some way, visually or physically, yet still be the same in number, weight, substance, or volume. This concept has been the subject of considerable research. In a typical conservation task, a child is shown three beakers or glasses. Two are short and squat and contain the same amount of

1. A child examines two glasses of juice and sees that they are the same.

2. A researcher pours the contents of one glass into a taller and narrower glass.

3. The child is asked to choose the glass that has "more" in it. Children who have not yet developed the ability to conserve choose the taller glass and often declare, "It has more in it; it's bigger."

FIGURE 3.7

Development of Conservation

Conservation is the ability to recognize that an object that has been transformed is still the same object, regardless of any changes it has undergone.

liquid (water or juice); the other is tall, narrow, and empty (see Figure 3.7). The experimenter pours the liquid from one short, squat glass into the tall, narrow one and asks the child, "Which glass has more juice?" A child who does not understand the principle of conservation will claim that the taller glass contains more, believing that the act of pouring somehow adds volume. A child who is able to conserve liquid quantity will recognize that the same amount of liquid is in both the tall and the short glasses.

A child who has mastered one type of conservation (for example, conservation of liquid quantity) often cannot immediately transfer that knowledge to other conservation tasks. For example, the child may not understand that two stacked weights weigh the same as the two weights placed side by side. A child who masters the concept of conservation realizes that specific facts are true because they follow logically, not simply because they are observed. Thus, the child infers that the tall glass *must* contain the same amount of liquid as the short glass because no liquid was added or taken away when the contents of the short glass were poured into the tall one (see *Introduction to Research Basics* on p. 88).

■ **THE FORMAL OPERATIONAL STAGE.** The formal operational stage is Piaget's fourth and final stage of cognitive development (beginning at about age 12), during which the individual can think hypothetically, can consider future possibilities, and can use deductive logic. Unlike children in the concrete operational stage, whose thought is still tied to immediate situations, adolescents can engage in abstract thought. They can form hypotheses that allow them to think of different ways to represent situations, organizing them into various possible relationships and outcomes. The cognitive world of adolescents is full of informal theories of logic and ideas about life; they are able to undertake scientific experiments requiring the formation and testing of hypotheses.

Formal operational stage
Piaget's fourth and final stage of cognitive development (beginning at about age 12), during which the individual can think hypothetically, can consider future possibilities, and can use deductive logic.

By age 12, about the beginning of adolescence, the egocentrism of the sensorimotor and preoperational stages has for the most part disappeared, but another form of egocentrism has developed. According to Inhelder and Piaget (1958), "The adolescent goes through a phase in which he [or she] attributes an unlimited power to his [or her] own thoughts so that the dream of a glorious future or of transforming the world through ideas (even if this idealism takes a materialistic form) seems to be not only fantasy, but also an effective action which in itself modifies the

introduction to research basics

Understanding the Danger

According to Piaget's theory of cognitive development, children have cognitive limitations during the preoperational stage. These limitations prevent children from having a full understanding of many concepts, and Lockman and Summers (1999) believed that these cognitive limitations would influence children's understanding of poison and its dangers.

DESIGN Lockman and Summers designed a **cross-sectional study,** a type of research design that compares individuals of different ages to determine how they differ on a particular important dimension. Cross-sectional studies are one way to study age-related differences (see p. 75 for more on this method and another way to research age-related differences).

HYPOTHESIS Lockman and Summers hypothesized that younger children would have a less complete understanding of the concept of poison than older children.

PARTICIPANTS Of the 426 children who participated, 189 were 4 years old, and 237 were 7 years old. None of these children had experienced any type of education about poison.

PROCEDURE The researchers asked the children two questions about poison: they asked for the definition of poison and whether or not there was any poison in the children's homes.

RESULTS The 4-year-olds and 7-year-olds showed different understandings of the concept of poison. This difference was not large in terms of the definition—76.4% of 4-year-olds and 96.4% of 7-year-olds were able to define or give an example of poison. However, 86.8% of the younger children said that they did not know whether any poison existed in their homes or believed that none was present; only 8% of the older children shared this opinion.

CONCLUSIONS Although young children may learn the definition of poison and be able to say that poison is dangerous, their cognitive limitations prevent them from fully realizing the immediacy of the dangers they face. Both parents and poison prevention educators need to understand children's cognitive capabilities to protect children more effectively.

empirical world" (pp. 345–346). The egocentrism and naive hopes of adolescents eventually decrease as they face and deal with the challenges of life. Piaget's stages of cognitive development are summarized in Figure 3.8.

PUTTING PIAGET IN PERSPECTIVE. Parents, educators, and psychologists can enhance children's cognitive development by understanding how mental abilities develop. Piaget recognized that parental love and parent–child interactions are always important to a child's development, but he asserted that they are *essential* in the first 2 years of life. For a child to develop object permanence, to learn how to make interesting sights last, and to develop the rudiments of numerical reasoning, it is necessary for caregivers to provide abundant physical and cognitive stimuli, especially stimuli that move and change color, shape, and form. Research confirms that children and animals given sensory stimulation during their early months develop more quickly both cognitively and socially than those not given such stimulation. Parents and educators who agree with Piaget have devoted their efforts to ensuring that the first years of life are ones in which stimulation is plentiful, curiosity is encouraged, and opportunities for exploration are maximized. An enriched environment is one in which the child has the freedom to manipulate objects and see them from many vantage points; expensive toys are not necessary—variety is the key. From Piaget's point of view, stimulation and manipulation optimize children's potential.

Although Piaget's ideas have had an enormous influence on developmental psychology, some researchers have problems with his approach on three fronts. He may have underestimated children's' cognitive development; he miscalculated the ages of transitions; and he placed too great an emphasis on the individual and deemphasized much of the social world. Psychologist Rochel Gelman argues that Piaget tended to underestimate younger children's abilities. For example, Shatz and Gelman (1973) found that 2-year-olds change the length of their sentences depending on whom they are talking to, using shorter sentences, for example, when

Cross-sectional study
A type of research design that compares individuals of different ages to determine how they differ on an important dimension.

FIGURE 3.8

Piaget's Stages of Cognitive Development

speaking to younger children. The researchers point out that being decentered enough to make such a shift in point of view is a sign of cognitive maturity. Many other researchers claim that Piaget may have overestimated the degree of egocentrism in young children. Baillargeon asserts that Piaget also underestimated the spatial–perceptual abilities of infants. She holds that abilities such as understanding what actually happens to objects when they are hidden, which Piaget saw as developing at 18 months, can be seen at 6 months of age (Miller & Baillargeon, 1990). More recently, Baillargeon (1998) has argued that infants are born with specialized learning mechanisms that allow for the acquisition of knowledge about the physical world. Other researchers agree, pointing out strong genetic effects on cognitive abilities early in development (Price et al., 2000; Rowe, Jacobson, & Van den Oord, 1999)—this is an interesting assertion that needs further research.

■ **ECOLOGICAL SYSTEMS THEORY.** Perhaps the newest type of developmental theory to have had a wide impact is *ecological systems theory.* Developed by a number of researchers, with Urie Bronfenbrenner at the forefront, this approach argues that children develop within a system of complex human relationships and that those relationships exist within both immediate environments such as families and neighborhoods and larger environments such as communities, states, and countries. This approach stresses the role of culture and of social relationships between individuals and within the larger society. According to the ecological systems approach, behavior and development must be studied cross-culturally because people do not live in a social vacuum. You will see that Bronfenbrenner is not alone in espousing this approach. Lev Vygotsky, who stressed that dialogues between children and members of society fuel child development, argued the same thing over 70 years ago.

Vygotsky's Sociocultural Theory: An Alternative to Piaget

Piaget saw the child as an organism that is self-motivated to understand the world. The child, he held, is a busy constructor of reality, making interesting sights last, inventing games, and learning abstract rules. But Lev Vygotsky (1896–1934) saw the child as not alone in this task but part of a social world filled with communication, with the self and with others. Vygotsky believed that children are constantly trying to extract meaning from the social world and to master higher-order concepts (Bruner, 1997). At first, children's mental life expresses itself in interactions with other people. Later, children engage in private speech (talking to themselves) to plan and guide their own behavior; when they use such speech, they do better in various tasks (Winsler, Carlton, & Barry, 2000). It is important to note that Piaget believed

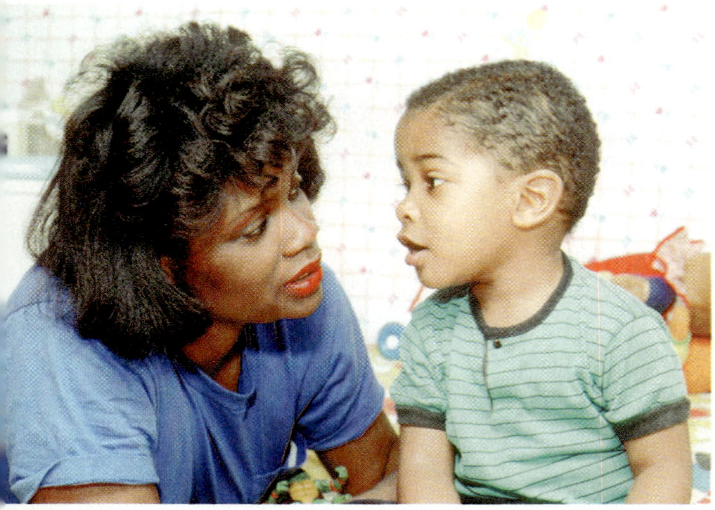

■ *Vygotsky's work focused on the importance of verbal interchange.*

that private speech was egocentric and did not involve taking the perspective of others. Vygotsky suggested just the opposite: private speech helps a child understand his or her world and that of other people. For Vygotsky (1934/1962), even the earliest speech is essentially social and useful; in fact, he asserted that social speech comes first, followed by private speech, then inner speech (thinking in words). Vygotsky wrote: "The most significant moment in the course of intellectual development . . . occurs . . . when speech and practical activity, two previously completely independent lines of development, converge" (Vygotsky, 1930/1978, p. 24).

To a great extent, Vygotsky's work focused on trying to understand what he called "culturally patterned dialogue." Vygotsky emphasized extracting meaning from the world, especially through verbal interchanges, and he was particularly interested in examining the culture and the situation—the context—through which meaning is extracted. Vygotsky's approach can be considered sociocultural (Bruner, 1997).

Vygotsky was especially concerned—perhaps overly concerned, according to Bruner (1997)—with how adults provide information about culture to children. From a Vygotskian perspective, skills and knowledge are culture-bound (Meadows, 1998). In Chapter 7, we consider the role of cooperative learning in education and see that when students cooperate in teams, they do better; Vygotsky's theory predicts such a result. He held that when children are presented tasks that are outside of their current abilities, they need the help of culture and society—usually parents—to accomplish them. When more skilled individuals help a child, the child then incorporates those new skills and ideas into his or her repertoire of behavior. In this interactive process, which Vygotsky called *scaffolding,* an adult sets up a structure for a child. As the child learns, the adult provides less help or makes the task slightly harder so that the child engages in more complex analysis and learning (Meadows, 1998; Stringer, 1998).

Theory of Mind

Piaget investigated how and when children develop intellectual abilities; Vygotsky extended the study of children's intellectual development by considering its social context. Recently, developmental theorists have been focusing on how and when children acquire theories about causation, including the causes of human behavior.

Adults use their knowledge of the world to construct informal and formal theories to explain behavior, other people's and their own. Adults are aware of their theories of human behavior and can articulate them: they say that people do what they do because of internal mental states, such as desires and beliefs. Joe climbed up on the kitchen counter because he "wanted" cookies; Jill looked for her glasses in the study because she "thought" she left them on her desk. Thus, adults possess and apply a **theory of mind**—an understanding of mental states such as feelings, desires, beliefs, and intentions and of the causal role they play in human behavior.

Theory of mind
An understanding of mental states such as feelings, desires, beliefs, and intentions and of the causal role they play in human behavior.

When do children first develop a theory of mind? Research indicates that children have little awareness of their own and other people's mental processes until about age 3, but it does develop at about this point (Wellman, Phillips, & Rodriguez, 2000). A typical research study in this area focuses on a situation like this: a child and two adults are in a room, with some object such as a ball in a box. One adult leaves the room, and the other moves the object, into a basket, for example. The child is then asked where the person who left the room will expect the object to be when he or she returns. A child who has developed a theory of mind will correctly predict that the person will look for the object where it last was (in the box), because the person will believe that it should still be there, not knowing that it was moved. A younger child, who has not yet developed a theory of mind, will say that the person coming back into the room will look for the object in its new location (in the basket). Before the age of 2 or 3, children are not able to set aside their own knowledge of the situation and realize that the person who left the room does not know that the object was moved. Developmental researchers say that they don't yet have a theory of mind.

The concept of theory of mind has stimulated many lines of research, including studies of infant and child attention, infant desires, and the role of brain development in cognitive maturation. But, according to some researchers, acquisition of a theory of mind is not an automatic developmental process. Astington (1999) asserts that children do not acquire such an understanding on their own; rather, through participation in social activities, they come to share their culture's way of seeing and talking about people's relations to one another and to the world. How and when children develop a theory of mind is partly determined by their interactions with others, especially family—a key variable in the development of intelligence (Cutting & Dunn, 1999). But it develops in all cultures, although not necessarily at the same pace (Tardif & Wellman, 2000). Thus, the notion that social relationships play a crucial role in cognitive development—which, as we saw earlier, was first introduced by Vygotsky—continues to influence developmental theory and research. As the next section shows, the psychologists who advised the federal government to begin Project Head Start in the 1960s agreed that an enriched social environment could help children develop cognitively.

Thought in a Social Context

Does growing up in an enriched environment facilitate learning and discovery? Can tutoring children one-on-one give them a leg up? Today, programs like JUMP-START attempt to do just that (Garnet, 1998). Such programs assume that if you give a child individual help and a supportive environment, it makes a difference. In a way, it all began with Project Head Start—Head Start was initiated in the 1960s in an effort to break the poverty cycle by raising the social and educational competency of disadvantaged preschool children. Today, Project Head Start enrolls about 750,000 children a year, most of them from the neediest families—mostly African American (65%) and from lower socioeconomic classes (Schnur, Brooks-Gunn, & Shipman, 1992). Head Start has served 13 million children and is often referred to as a milestone in psychology.

Project Head Start has shown great successes when a low teacher-pupil ratio is in place and the program is sustained for more than a year or two.

Project Head Start gives preschool children an enriched environment. Children attend a school with a low teacher–student ratio and are provided nutritional and medical services. Children receive focused, individual attention; efforts are made to build their self-confidence and self-esteem. The emphasis is on basic skills that may lead to more complex learning strategies, and preschoolers experience the joy of learning. Parent involvement is central; parents work on school boards and in the classroom and also receive related social services such as family counseling

Research on programs like Head Start has led to important conclusions about early interventions and experiences and their effects on children's lives. Ramey (1999) outlines several important findings: interventions need to begin early in development and continue for a long period of time; intensive programs (more hours per week) are better than nonintensive ones; direct intervention (rather than intervention through parental training) works best; programs that use multiple routes to enhance development are especially effective; individual differences must be emphasized, and so it is essential to find the right fit between children and programs; and environmental support at home and in the community is necessary for lasting and effective early intervention. Psychologists and educators know how to enhance Head Start and other similar programs; society just has to find the will and the resources to do it.

student voices

Suzanne Collins

St John's University

I found work as a family service worker for a daycare program. I saw so many of the things I learned in school making a difference in these families' lives. For example, a special ed teacher and I created a reading program to improve pre-literacy and social skills. This inspired me to apply to grad school, where I am working on my doctorate, specializing in early childhood interventions.

Moral Reasoning

Few children make it to adolescence without squabbling with a sibling over the "borrowing" of a sweater, a toy, or a couple of dollars. The adult in charge usually tells them to stop fighting and makes it clear that such behaviors and the resulting squabbles are unacceptable. As children grow, they develop the capacity to assess for themselves what is right or wrong, acceptable or unacceptable. From childhood on, individuals develop **morality**—a system of learned attitudes about social practices, institutions, and individual behavior used to evaluate situations and behavior as right or wrong, good or bad.

Children learn from their parents the behaviors, attitudes, and values considered appropriate and correct in their family and culture. Morality is also nurtured by teachers, by religious and community leaders, and by friends. But it is especially nurtured by daily interactions with caregivers in dialogues and conversations large and small (Laible & Thompson, 2000; Walker, Hennig, & Krettenauer, 2000). As children mature, they acquire attitudes that accommodate an increasingly complex view of reality. Your moral views when you were a 10-year-old probably differ from your views today. The U.S. Supreme Court has restricted adolescents' rights to make important life decisions—in part because the court believes adolescents lack moral maturity. But do they? Or is the reasoning and judgment of a child, a preteen, or an adolescent as sound as that of an adult? Today researchers are showing that children and teenagers need to and can be involved in making good decisions about their own health care (Ranelli, Bartsch & London, 2000).

Morality
A system of learned attitudes about social practices, institutions, and individual behavior used to evaluate situations and behavior as right or wrong, good or bad.

■ **PIAGET AND KOHLBERG.** Piaget examined children's ability to analyze questions of morality and found the results to be consistent with his ideas about cognitive development. Young children's ideas about morality are rigid and rule-bound; children expect justice to depend on particular actions. When playing a game, a young child will not allow the rules to be modified. Older children, on the other hand, recognize that rules are established by social convention and may need to be altered, depending on the situation. They have developed a sense of *moral relativity,* which allows them to recognize that situational factors affect the way things are perceived and that people may or may not receive their just reward or punishment (Piaget, 1932).

According to Piaget, as children mature, they move away from inflexibility and toward relativity in their moral judgments; they develop new cognitive structures and assimilate and accommodate new ideas. When young children are questioned about lying, for example, they respond that it is always bad, under any circumstances—a person should never lie. At some time between the ages of 5 and 12, however, children come to recognize that lying may be permissible in some circumstances—for example, lying to a bully so that he will not hurt a friend.

Piaget's theory of moral development was based on descriptions of how children respond to specific kinds of questions and the ages at which they switch and use other forms of answers. The research of Harvard psychologist Lawrence Kohlberg (1927–1987) grew out of Piaget's work. Kohlberg believed that moral development generally proceeds through three levels, each of which is divided into two

TABLE 3.3

A Comparison of Piaget and Kohlberg on Moral Development

Piaget	Kohlberg
Sensorimotor and preoperational (birth–6 or 7 years)	Level 1—*Preconventional morality*
	Stage 1: Obedience and punishment orientation
	Stage 2: Egocentric orientation
Concrete operational (7–11 or 12 years)	Level 2—*Conventional morality*
	Stage 3: Good-child orientation
	Stage 4: Authority and social order
Formal operational (12 years and beyond)	Level 3—*Postconventional morality*
	Stage 5: Contractual–legalistic orientation; societal needs considered
	Stage 6: Conscience or principle orientation

stages. The central concept in Kohlberg's theory is that of justice. In his studies of moral reasoning, Kohlberg presented stories involving moral dilemmas to people of various ages and asked them to describe what the stories meant to them and how they felt about them (Kohlberg, 1969). Table 3.3 compares Piaget and Kohlberg's theories on moral development.

In one of Kohlberg's stories, Heinz, a poor man, stole a drug for his wife, who would have died without it. Presented with the story of Heinz, children at level 1, *preconventional morality,* either condemn Heinz's behavior as unacceptable or they come up with some reason that is acceptable. They base their decisions about right and wrong on the likelihood of avoiding punishment and obtaining benefits. A child in this stage might say that Heinz should not have taken the drug because he might get caught. People at level 2, *conventional morality,* have internalized society's rules and say that Heinz broke the law by stealing and should go to jail. School-age children who are at level 2 conform in order to avoid the disapproval of other people. At this stage, a 10-year-old might choose not to try cigarettes because his parents and friends disapprove of smoking. Considerations of the implications of a person's behavior also govern level 2 judgments: Why did the person do it? What will the consequences be for that person and for others? Does the act violate important laws and rules? Only people who have reached level 3, *postconventional morality,* can see that although Heinz's action was illegal, the ethical dilemma is complex (see Figure 3.9 on the following page). As individuals move toward level 3 they become better able to move beyond fixed rules and laws and focus on principles. At level 3 morality, people make judgments on the basis of their perception of the needs of society, with the goal of fulfilling social contracts and maintaining community welfare and order.

Not all adults reach level 3. In the advanced stage of level 3, people make judgments on the basis of personally created moral principles—rather than societal teachings. Moral objection to legally sanctioned behaviors is associated with this stage—for example, a person can believe that it is morally wrong to kill a person for any reason even if convicted of a crime and sentenced to death. Research shows that such reasoning may incorporate a sense of virtue and religiosity (Walker & Pitts, 1998).

■ **MEN AND WOMEN: CAROL GILLIGAN'S WORK.** Criticisms of Kohlberg's pioneering research came from Carol Gilligan (1982, 1995, 1997), who found that people look at more than justice when they analyze moral conflicts. She discovered that people are also concerned with caring, with relationships, and with connections with other people. Though Kohlberg and his colleagues had not generally reported

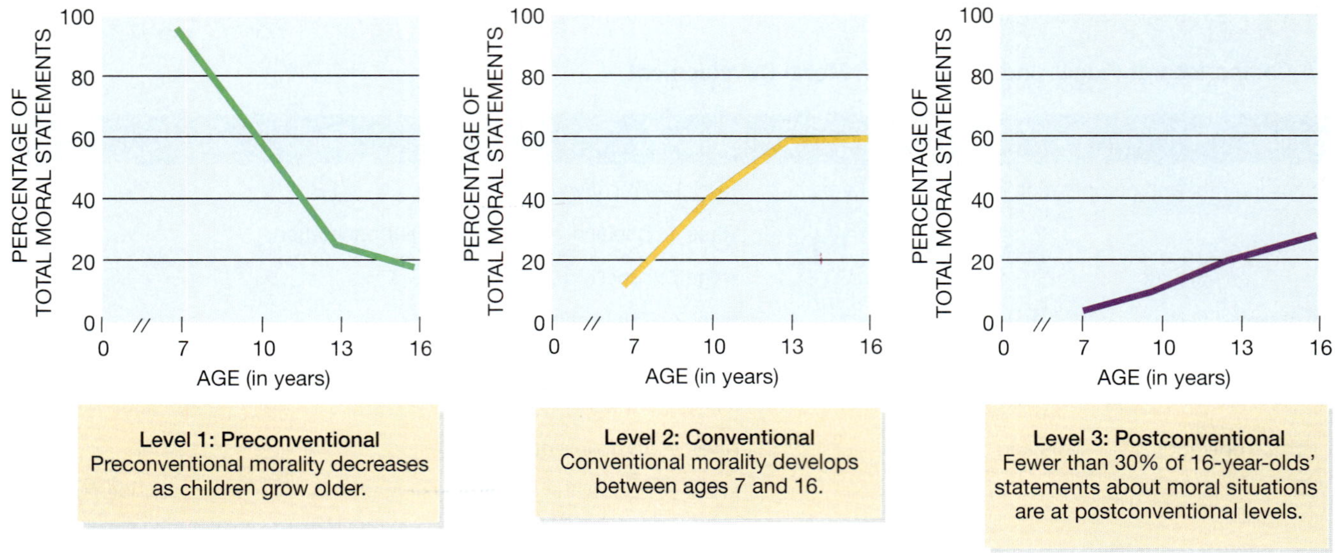

FIGURE 3.9

Development of Morality over Time

In Kohlberg's theory of morality, a distinct progression of moral development emerges over a child's life. Children do not often achieve the highest, or postconventional, levels of moral reasoning.

any differences between men and women, Gilligan criticized Kohlberg for developing his theory based solely on research with boys and men. When Gilligan studied women, she found gender differences in moral reasoning.

Differences between men and women on behaviors or mental processes are referred to as *gender differences*. Psychologists used to refer to such differences as sex differences. We make a distinction between the terms *sex* and *gender*. **Sex** refers to the biologically based categories of male and female. **Gender**, by contrast, refers to a socially and culturally constructed set of distinctions between masculine and feminine sets of behaviors that is promoted and expected by society. It turns out that there is a complicated relationship between sex and gender because biologically based characteristics are affected by cultural events in a person's life; be that as it may, the distinction is widely used and is a good shorthand (Fausto-Sterling, 2000).

Gilligan noted differences between girls and boys in their inclinations toward caring and justice. She found that girls are more concerned with care, relationships, and connections with other people—she hypothesized a feminine orientation to moral issues. As younger children, girls gravitate toward a morality of caring, whereas boys gravitate toward a morality of justice. Gilligan asserts that the difference between boys' and girls' approaches to morality is established by gender and by the child's relationship with the mother. Because of the gender difference between boys and their mothers, boys see that they are essentially different from other people, whereas girls develop a belief in their similarity (connectedness) to others. Gilligan asserts that the transition to adolescence is a crucial time, during which girls develop their own voice—a voice too often muted and suppressed (Brown, 1998; Gilligan, 1997). Gilligan shows that boys respond to Kohlberg's story of Heinz by indicating that sometimes people must act on their own to do the right thing; girls tend to say that Heinz's relationship with his wife is more important than obeying the law. Like Kohlberg, Gilligan argues that the development of a morality of caring follows a time course: initially, the child feels caring only toward herself, then later toward others as well, and ultimately (in some people) a more mature stage of caring for truth develops. Gilligan's work has influenced psychologists' evaluations of morality. Yet her approach fosters a continuation of gender stereotyping—women as nurturing, men as logical—and despite widespread acceptance of her view that Kohlberg's work is biased against women, surprisingly little research evidence supports that view (Fisher & Bredemeier, 2000; Miller & Bersoff, 1999). Moreover, Gilligan's work has been limited to White, middle-class children and adults; it needs a broader, more multicultural basis and such research has been forthcoming with a wide range of populations including Hispanic men and women

Sex
The biologically based categories of male and female.

Gender
A socially and culturally constructed set of distinctions between masculine and feminine sets of behaviors that is promoted and expected by society.

(Gump, Baker, & Roll, 2000). Nevertheless, Gilligan's work highlights an important element of moral reasoning: people think about other people in a caring, human way—not just in a legalistic manner, as Kohlberg suggested. Both men and women can and do emphasize caring when they face dilemmas involving relationships; similarly, both are likely to focus on justice when facing issues involving others' rights. Women and men are more alike than they are different when it comes to caring and justice, and the type of moral reasoning a man or woman uses is highly sensitive to the context and content of the dilemma presented to the individual. If theories of human development intend to characterize real experiences, then they must be assembled with the complexity and multiplicity of such experiences in mind (Jaffee and Hyde, 2000).

Be an *Active* learner

REVIEW

- From Piaget's view, why are the first 2 years of life the most important time for cognitive development? pp. 82–83
- What is the difference between assimilation and accommodation? p. 84
- How is Vygotsky's approach different from Piaget's? pp. 89–90
- What is a theory of mind? p. 90
- Summarize the differences that characterize Kohlberg's preconventional, conventional, and postconventional levels of morality. p. 93
- What is Gilligan's main criticism of Kohlberg's work? pp. 93–95

THINK CRITICALLY

- Assuming that Piaget did in fact overestimate the extent of egocentrism in young children, what might be another explanation for apparently egocentric behavior in a child?
- What are the implications of Vygotsky's view that the most significant moment in intellectual development occurs when speech and practical activity converge?
- What do you think are the best measures of the successes of early improvement programs like Head Start?
- If research on morality were done with a wide range of populations, what differences might emerge, for example, among Latino/Latina, Asian, and Euro-American groups?
- If morality is nurtured by teachers and by religious and community leaders, what might happen to children when one of those individuals is found to betray his or her moral authority?

APPLY PSYCHOLOGY

- What can you as an individual do to foster a higher level of moral reasoning among your peers?
- Describe how you might use scaffolding to teach a child a game.
- If you had unlimited money, list what would you do to improve the outcomes of programs like Head Start.

The Growth of Emotions

Anne Frank, the young Jewish girl who was hidden for a time from the Nazis during World War II, was eloquently thankful in the diary that survived her to the people who helped hide her and her family. She wrote extensively about all her feelings—her hopes and fears, as well as her gratitude toward the people who were making sacrifices and putting their own lives at risk to help her family. For a teenage girl, Anne showed extraordinary emotional maturity. And what is even more amazing is that she attained this maturity while in hiding, where her connections with others were limited. Although emotional maturity may be revealed in one's teens, the process of maturing begins long before. Emotional development begins shortly after birth with the attachments that infants form with caregivers.

Attachment: The Ties That Bind

Attachment is the formal term psychologists use to describe the strong emotional tie or connection that a person feels toward special other persons in his or her life. Attachments express a bond, a special relationship, and a connection. Such bonds are usually enduring and long lasting; they often involve comfort, soothing, or pleasure; and the loss of the individual (or threat of loss) brings about intense distress.

People's ability to form attachments develops from birth through adulthood. Attachment behaviors encouraged in the early weeks and months of life are also nurtured during adolescence and adulthood, when people form close, loving bonds with others. Most researchers consider these behaviors to have a biological basis, even though they unfold slowly over the first year of life and are reinforced by caregivers. The reason is that emotional expressions—including attachment behaviors—not only appear in all cultures but also are found in deaf and blind people and in people without limbs, who have limited touch experiences (e.g., Livingston, 1998).

Attachment
The strong emotional tie that a person feels toward special other persons in his or her life.

Bonding
Special process of emotional attachment that may occur between parents and babies in the minutes and hours immediately after birth.

■ **BONDING.** In the 1970s and 1980s, it was widely held that parents bond to their infants soon after delivery. **Bonding** is a special process of emotional attachment that is hypothesized to occur between parents and babies in the minutes and hours immediately after birth. It is neither a reflex nor a learned behavior, though most evolutionary psychologists claim that it is genetic. Pediatricians Marshall Klaus and John Kennell (1983) believe that a mother is in a state of heightened sensitivity to her child immediately after delivery and that she begins to form a unique and specific attachment to her child. Research shows that mothers recognize their infants by smell, touch, and sound (Kaitz et al., 1992), and that infants similarly recognize their mothers (Leon, 1992). Klaus and his colleagues argue that babies should have as much physical and emotional contact as possible with their mothers and fathers; keeping parents and infants together in the hospital shortly after birth, in rooming-in arrangements, should be the rule, not the exception. Despite the popular appeal of this concept, research has failed to confirm Klaus and Kennell's contentions that the period immediately after birth is special for attachment (Eyer, 1992).

ATTACHMENT IN INFANTS. John Bowlby (1907–1990) was one of the first modern psychologists to study the close attachment between mothers and their newborns. Bowlby (1977) argued that the infant's emotional tie with the caregiver evolved because it promotes survival. Bowlby asserted that an infant's very early interactions with its parents are crucial to normal development. Some psychologists consider the establishment of a close and warm parent–child relationship one of the major accomplishments of the first year of life. Formation of attachment is considered a pivotal developmental event that helps an infant develop basic feelings of security.

By the age of 7 or 8 months, attachment to the caregiver may become so strong that his or her departure from the room causes a fear response, especially to strangers; this response is known as *separation anxiety* and reflects insecurity on the part of the infant. When infants fear that the principal caregiver, usually the mother, may not be consistently available, they become clingy and vigilant (Ainsworth, 1979; Bowlby, 1988). In attempting to analyze attachment to parents, researchers have used a procedure called the *strange situation technique,* in which babies from 12 to 24 months old are observed with parents, separated from them briefly, and then reunited. Although attachment theory has been criticized for being largely based on behaviors observed during stressful situations that are somewhat artificial, research with the strange situation technique shows that most babies (about 60%) are secure; they are distressed by a parent leaving but are easily comforted. Other babies (about 20%) are neither distressed by separations nor comforted by reunions—these babies are categorized as *avoidant* and are considered to have an insecure attachment. Still other babies (about 15%) are *resistant;* these babies seek closeness with the parent, become angry when separated from the parent, and then show mixed feelings when reunited. Last, some babies (about 5%) are characterized as *disoriented;* they show confused, contradictory attachment behaviors and may act angry, sad, or ambivalent at any time.

Researchers find that attachment between babies and parents or caregivers who are affectionate and responsive makes emotional and cognitive development smoother.

Researchers find that time spent with babies enables secure attachments (Scher & Mayseless, 2000) and that secure babies have caregivers who are affectionate and especially responsive (Isabella, 1998). According to some researchers, this relationship makes cognitive and emotional development smoother (Call, 1999). Not all researchers agree, and cross-cultural studies show significant variations among cultures (e.g., Tronick, Morelli, & Ivey, 1992). Children who have not formed warm, close attachments early in life lack a sense of security and become anxious and overly dependent. Those who have close attachments require less discipline and are less easily distracted (Foote, Eyberg, & Schuhmann, 1998). When researchers examined relationships between older children and mothers, they found a positive correlation with ratings of attachment by the mothers.

Once established, early attachment is fairly stable. Babies are resilient (Kier & Lewis, 1997), and brief separations from parents, as in child-care centers, do not adversely affect attachment (Waters, Hamilton, & Weinfield, 2000). Influential psychologist Mary Ainsworth (1979) asserts that early attachment affects the child's later friendships, relations with relatives, and enduring adult relationships; other research confirms that people's relationships as adults are related to the attachment styles they had as children (Brennan, Clark, & Shaver, 1998).

There is little doubt that attachment is important, but does it determine who we become? Human beings have an amazing ability to adapt, survive, and negotiate the future. Michael Lewis (1997, 1998) cautions that researchers often overestimate the long-term effects of attachment, and that separation anxiety at age 1 has little to do with adjustment at age 18, let alone at age 35. Lewis studied a group of individuals at age 1 and again at age 18 in terms of attachment to family and friends; he found that secure attachment did not protect children from later maladjustment, nor did insecure attachment predict later trouble. Thus, early attachment probably doesn't determine adjustment as an adult, because too many life events, chance circumstances, and good and bad decisions can also affect the life course. For example, research shows that divorce affects children's social development, regardless of their attachment status as infants (Lewis, Feiring, & Rosenthal, 2000). The truth is that when there is conflict between parents, child adjustment suffers (Grych et al., 2000); there is significant variation, and some children are more vulnerable than others, but in the end conflict and divorce usually have negative effects on feelings of attachment. Adult children of divorce trust less and have diminished expectations about relationships (Wallerstein, Lewis, & Blakeslee, 2000).

■ **WHAT ABOUT CHILD CARE?** According to earlier traditions, mothers were expected to provide child care. But the trend toward mothers being employed outside their homes necessitates other arrangements. Child-care situations are becoming increasingly diverse as parents seek alternative arrangements for their children, but child-care centers provide care for about 30% of preschool children whose mothers are employed outside the home (see Figure 3.10).

Maternal employment and day care have become the topic of many heated arguments and a great deal of guilt on the part of mothers. Does the research suggest negative consequences for leaving children in the care of someone other than a parent? This question is difficult to answer because many variables influence the placement of a child into day care, including the family's economic resources (some families hire nannies rather than put children into day care), the child's age, the security of the child's attachment to parents, and the stability of the child-care arrangement. Some research has suggested negative effects of current child-care practices (Kim 1997), but the majority of studies find minimal effects. Broberg and his colleagues (1997) assert that being in day care did not place children at any disadvantage. Other research found virtually no difference in personality or attachment between children cared for at home and children who had

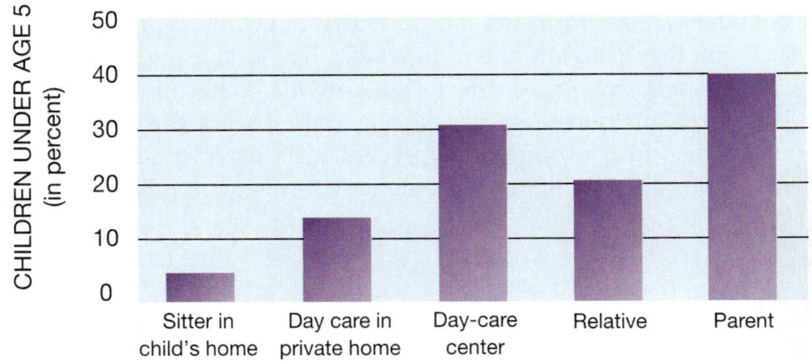

FIGURE 3.10

Arrangements for Child Care, 1995

This figure shows the distribution of child-care arrangements in 1995 for children under age 5 who were not in school. *(Scarr, 1998)*

psychology *in action*

Children Read Emotional Cues Well

Adults are not the only ones who can accurately read other people's moods and feelings—it turns out that many children are able to assess their own feelings and can read their parents' emotions pretty well too. Preschoolers with this ability are less likely to have serious learning or behavior problems in later years, according to psychologist Carroll E. Izard (Izard et al., 2001). Izard found that the ability to read others' emotions at age 5 predicted the youngsters' social behavior and academic competence at age 9. Furthermore, the effects were evident after the researchers took into consideration the child's verbal ability, temperament, and personality.

A child's inability to perceive emotional cues from others may also interfere with teacher–child rapport and the teacher's expectations of the child. It follows naturally that children who cannot grasp others' feelings may have poorer social relationships in the playground and the classroom; this may also affect their academic performance when working in teams by creating a lack of cooperation.

What cues do children read? Sometimes they are direct verbal statements—"I'm happy that you are here," "Your work is great," or "We don't want to play with you." Other cues are nonverbal, for example, not being picked for a team, being chosen last, or overlooking someone's extra effort in a task. Reading a cue is like watching a dance in which the partners are constantly signaling their intentions to one another. When the partners are together, the exchange and relationship proceed well. When they are apart, it becomes much harder to communicate effectively. And conversations and relationships are affected by the transmission of a wide range of subtle emotional cues, especially with body language. A teacher or parent might lean forward and gaze attentively, as if to say, "I'm interested. Tell me more." Or, if the adult's eyes are gazing somewhere else while the child is talking, the message might be "I'm not listening to you."

In the end, children, and then later adults, become expert in the interpretation of verbal and nonverbal information, and people depend on this near-automatic skill to make relationships meaningful.

received day care (Erel, Oberman, & Yirmiya, 2000; NICHD Early Child Care Research Network, 1997).

A comprehensive, multiyear study by Harvey (1999) assessed the cognitive, academic, behavioral, and emotional development of more than 6,000 children whose parents were both employed outside the home. The study tracked 12,600 mothers and their children, interviewing them each year starting in 1979, and it concluded that there were no permanent negative effects. The large sample size and the longitudinal nature of the study make it an important piece of evidence that parental employment and child care do not have significant negative effects—if the care is of high quality. Sandra Scarr (1998, p. 95) concludes: "Widely varying qualities of child care have been shown to have only small effects on children's current development and no demonstrated long-term impact, except on disadvantaged children, whose homes put them at developmental risk."

EVOLUTIONARY PERSPECTIVES. In a very real sense, one of the seminal figures in attachment theory, John Bowlby, was an evolutionary psychologist. Bowlby argued that the infant's attachment with the caregiver *evolves* because it *promotes survival.* Children who have strong attachments with their parents are more likely to grow up to be confident adults, form attachments to other people, reproduce, and pass on their genes to another generation. But, of course, like so many adaptations that people make, a person's environment bears on how his or her biological endowment plays out. Poverty, malnutrition, war, famine, and disease can all influence childhood attachment—thus, evolutionary psychologists assert that attachment is an evolved adaptation that facilitates a reproductive strategy (see Belsky, 1999).

Temperament

My (L.L.) daughter Jesse was born an inspector—she touched and tasted everything within reach, climbed out of her crib, and dangerously explored her world. She was like this as soon as she could navigate. She examined everything and everyone, including her sister! She got along well with her sister; both had and still have fairly easygoing dispositions and have never had any major quarrels. They read each other's moods well (see *Psychology in Action* on p. 98). But conflicts between siblings are common, and on occasion quite pronounced. The truth is that, because of temperament differences, siblings often don't get along, and some parents can't or don't know how to smooth things over (Brody, 1998).

Are children with aggressive or difficult temperaments more likely to use and abuse drugs in their teenage and adult years? Researchers say yes.

Temperament refers to early-emerging and long-lasting individual differences in disposition and in the intensity and especially the quality of emotional reactions. Some psychologists believe that each person is born with a specific temperament—easygoing, willful, outgoing, or shy, to name but a few. Newborns, infants, and children, like the adults they will eventually grow to be, are all different from one another. Generalizations from one child to all children are impossible, and even generalizations from a sample of children must be made with caution. So many variables can affect a child's growth and development that researchers painstakingly try to separate all the important ones. Alexander Thomas and Stella Chess (1977), in their pioneering work in the New York Longitudinal Study, point out that temperament is not fixed and unchangeable. Nevertheless, along with many other researchers, they argue that temperament refers to a complex set of processes—not a single thing—and that temperament refers to the way in which behavior is expressed, independent of the content of behavior or the motivation for behavior. Temperament is biologically based, moderately stable across time and over situations, but not necessarily invariant across time or situations. Further, the expression of temperament can be influenced by biological, developmental, and contextual factors. With these cautions in mind, let's look at some studies of temperament.

Data from the New York Longitudinal Study show that children tend to fall into four broad categories: easy (40% of children), difficult (10%), slow-to-warm-up (15%), and unique (35%). Easy children are happy-go-lucky and adapt easily to new situations; difficult children are resistant to environmental change and often react poorly to it; slow-to-warm-up children respond slowly, have low-intensity responses, and are often negative. Many children are unique, showing a varied blend of emotional reactions.

Many researchers contend that some specific initial temperamental characteristics may be biologically based. For example, Jerome Kagan and his colleagues found that 2- and 3-year-olds who were *extremely* inhibited—that is, cautious and shy—tended to remain that way for 4 more years. They also found physiological evidence that these children may be more responsive (by showing an increase in autonomic nervous system activity, for example) to change and unfamiliarity (Kagan, 1997b; Woodward et al., 2000). During the earliest months of life, some infants smile or reach out to a new face and readily accept being held or cuddled. Others are more inhibited. Still others exhibit extreme reticence, even distress, in the presence of strangers. Such xenophobic infants (those who fear strangers) may turn out to be inhibited, meek, and wavering as adults (Caspi & Roberts, 2001). Researchers know, however, that infant behaviors are not necessarily stable over time and may not be evident in later behavioral styles (except for very extreme cases—intense shyness or diffidence, for example). Further, what parents observe (social wariness with unfamiliar people) is different from the shyness that teachers observe (concern about social evaluation by peers), and so shyness—social inhibition and anxiety—varies in

Temperament
Early-emerging and long-lasting individual differences in disposition and in the intensity and especially the quality of emotional reactions.

point*counterpoint*

Ritalin—Use or Abuse?

The Issue: Is Ritalin Use a Good Thing?

POINT
Ritalin is a useful drug that helps manage children with various disorders and helps them learn.

COUNTERPOINT
Ritalin is an overprescribed, powerful drug that has unwanted side effects.

Doctors prescribe it, parents pass it out to children, and school nurses supervise the administration of it because all believe the pill will calm children and stop their disruptive behavior. It is methylphenidate. Best known by the brand name Ritalin, methylphenidate (METH-el-FEN-i-date) was introduced in 1956 and is a stimulant in the same class as amphetamines. Experts agree that it affects the midbrain, the part of the brain that controls impulses.

Advocates of Ritalin assert that the drug is a blessing and that it has helped those with attention-deficit/hyperactivity disorder (ADHD) concentrate. People diagnosed with ADHD are unable to sit still, plan ahead, finish tasks, or be fully aware of what's going on around them. To their family, classmates, or coworkers, they seem to exist in a cyclone of disorganized or harried activity. One of the most common mental disorders among children, it affects 3% to 5% of all children, perhaps as many as 2 million children in the United States. Two to three times more boys than girls are affected, and on average, at least one child in every classroom in the United States needs help for the disorder (National Institutes of Health, 1998).

Ritalin allows the patient to focus better on the task at hand (Jerome & Segal, 2001). Besides its use in treating the symptoms of ADHD, Ritalin is also prescribed for mild to moderate depression and in some cases of emotional withdrawal among elderly people. Initially Ritalin was used for children who were so restless that they were unreachable and unteachable. The National Institutes of Health (1998) support "the efficacy of stimulants and psychosocial treatments for ADHD and the superiority of stimulants relative to psychosocial treatments." The benefits of Ritalin are so strong that advocates say withholding the pills is a form of

different situations (Eisenberg et al., 1998). The fit between the temperament of an infant and the caregiver is critical. Some caregivers can do well with a calm infant but are inundated by an irritable one. Sometimes an interaction style familiar to a caregiver from caring for other children may not suit. The shared irritation can impair good socialization.

Biological factors play a key role in shyness (McEwen, 1999). Studies of identical twins on a range of emotional dimensions, especially temperament, also show support for a strong genetic component (DiLalla & Jones, 2000; Stroganova et al., 2000; Warren, Schmitz, & Emde, 1999). Even maternal actions, such as time spent in daylight during pregnancy, may have an effect; Gortmaker and colleagues (1997) found that short exposure to daylight during pregnancy was associated with a higher likelihood of shy behavior in offspring. Further evidence for a biological predisposition comes from studies of basic physiological responsivity—infants' heart rates in response to a distracting stimulus are known to predict temperament (Huffman et al., 1998). However, shyness is influenced by culture; in one cross-cultural study, researchers found that shyness among native Chinese students helps them gain acceptance from teachers; the opposite tends to be true for students in Western countries (Chen, 2000). Western culture also has a controversial relationship with drug treatment for many disorders (see *Point/Counterpoint* above).

In addition, shyness and other aspects of temperament can be changed; human behavior is the product of deliberative thought processes as well as biological forces. Imagine a child who is shy or diffident and not easy to coax into

neglect. Those who claim diet, exercise, or other treatments work just as well are kidding themselves, say believers. A typical parental comment is the following:

> His homework took 3 hours—even with me helping him—to do because his mind was in the sky. He was a genius at video games, but not at homework. He was also at the point of being held back in school. He shed tears because he could not control himself; he hated the way he acted. I was always getting complaints about his spontaneous outbursts. And then he took Ritalin—and everything changed.

But the situation is not all rosy. Critics say doctors who work with teachers to keep boisterous children in line misdiagnose students. As awareness of ADHD has grown, the characterization of the disorder now encompasses a much broader range of behaviors—an increasing number of children seem to have conditions that meet the definition of ADHD.

Ritalin production has increased by more than 700% since 1990. Since then disorders for which Ritalin is prescribed have jumped an average of 21% per year. Over the past five years alone, the number of prescriptions for Ritalin in the United States has jumped to 11.4 million from 4.5 million, including about 11% of all boys in the United States. Researchers claim a disturbing reliance upon the drug to solve problems that have other solutions (McCubbin & Cohen, 1999).

Ritalin is classified as a Schedule II drug—on a par with cocaine, morphine, and metamphetamines—thus, there is potential for abuse or dependence. Ritalin is widely misused by drug addicts, and it has associated with it a large number of suicides and emergency room admissions (Young, Longstaffe, & Tenenbein, 1999). The National Institutes of Health caution that "stimulant treatments may not 'normalize' the entire range of behavior problems, and children under treatment may still manifest a higher level of some behavior problems than normal children." They also note that there are no long-term studies testing stimulants or psychosocial treatments lasting several years (NIH, 1998; also Snider, Frankenberger, & Aspenson, 2000).

Of course, an ADHD diagnosis can and often does lead to medication, special education facilities, and parental support groups. Today, children and teenagers with ADHD may be placed in a special classroom, and eventually get non-timed college admission tests—about 40,000 SAT tests are administered this way each year. Are the ADHD diagnosis and the Ritalin treatment being used for the wrong reasons? by overzealous parents? by well-meaning physicians? (Pozzi, 2000).

Is Ritalin effective? Yes, it is. Can it help children and teenagers with ADHD? Yes, it can. Are mistakes made in diagnosing ADHD? Of course. Is there overdiagnosis? Yes. Overdiagnosis usually occurs when a doctor is inexperienced, untrained, pressured, or predisposed to "find" ADHD. We need careful controlled research into the impact and long-term effects of Ritalin—and those studies are still a few years away. We also need physician, teacher, and parent education into ADHD and the use of Ritalin.

social situations. Researchers today suggest that such a disposition will affect parent–child interactions and parental discipline practices, and, ultimately, the child's socialization. As Greenspan argues (1997), the qualities we often value more than any others—empathy, creativity, honor, the ability to love and trust—stem from relationships, not genes, and from how, over time, caregivers relate to their children. Indeed, researchers assert that a child's conscience emerges because of these interactions and the growth of self-understanding (Stilwell, Galvin, & Kopta, 2000). Clearly, a child's temperament affects his or her interactions with parents in important ways and may determine in part how the parents treat the child—there is a reciprocal and mutually reinforcing influence. Parents recognize that they affect their child's temperament and personality—and they are right (Hesse & Main, 2000). They assume that their child-rearing practices strongly influence development and that a child who might be categorized as difficult by Thomas and Chess (1977) may, if treated with patience, become easy as an adolescent. But researchers also know that children with aggressive or difficult temperaments are more likely to use and abuse drugs in their teenage and adult years. Researchers are identifying temperament risk factors and behaviors that predict drug abuse (Chassin et al., 2001).

Be an *Active* learner

REVIEW

- How do psychologists know that children experience attachment? pp. 95–97
- Cite evidence that some traits, such as shyness, are inborn. p. 101

THINK CRITICALLY

- Describe some ways in which physical and emotional development might interact.
- What are the implications for later emotional development of cross-cultural differences in responsiveness toward infants?

APPLY PSYCHOLOGY

- As a parent, what critical variables might you consider if your child is prescribed Ritalin by a physician?

Social Development

Any bookstore has shelves lined with how-to books on child rearing, written by physicians, parents, psychologists, and others. The variety of approaches and the number of experts show that ideas about child rearing are complicated and constantly changing. As society changes, so do beliefs and practices related to children's social development and ideas about how children form a sense of identity and self. As children move cognitively from being egocentric to a point of perceiving themselves as different from the rest of the world, they also develop the ability to think about social relationships. As we will see, children develop socially in not one but many environments.

The family is the first social environment. Regardless of culture, parents respond positively to what they judge as good behaviors in children and negatively to bad ones. Although cultural differences exist (there is extensive scheduling of daytime childhood behaviors in France and noninterference and acceptance by Swedish parents, for example), parents worldwide respond to their children in similar ways (McDermott, 2001). Although parents exert a powerful influence on children, theirs is not the sole influence. Some such as Harris (1998) assert that a child has many environments, especially his or her play groups, which exert profound effects on social development.

Early Social Development and Child Rearing

Social development begins soon after birth, with the development of an attachment between parents and their newborn. The nature of a child's early interactions with parents is a crucial part of personality development. Infants have a great need to be hugged, cuddled, nurtured, and made to feel good. Eventually, the most important job for parents is teaching their children how to become independent and how to interact with others.

■ **THE ROLE OF FATHERS.** I (L.L.) think of myself as a good dad. I often took charge of child care, changed diapers, and attended to my daughters' needs. But I probably didn't spend as much time with them as my wife did, and I may not have been as communicative as she was. Typical patterns of how mothers and fathers interact with their children are indeed changing. During the past three decades, women have entered the work force in unprecedented numbers and, in so doing, have changed the structure and fabric of family life. Few fathers stay home to provide child care, but women, who traditionally did spend more time at home, are spending less time with their young children due to women's careers. Are fathers taking up the slack in caring for children? Do fathers engage in basic caregiving activities, play, or both?

A father's involvement is important; his affection is important—and the research asserts that it is as important as love from mothers (Rohner, 1998; Silverstein & Auerbach, 1999). Today's fathers are more interested in their newborns and may be involved in their upbringing from the first moments of life, as evidenced by the fact that many more fathers are present in the delivery room when their children are born than was true in previous generations. In general, fathers are affectionate and responsive caregivers; they are concerned with their children's welfare (Fagan, 1997). Still, some men view parenting as a voluntary activity and themselves as helpers or assistants to their partners, whom they consider the primary caregivers. Fathers sometimes assert that they spend limited time with their children, but that this time is "quality" time.

Research on the quality and quantity of interactions between fathers and their children showed that some fathers spent significant time with their children, but most spent very little (Black, Dubowitz, & Starr, 1999). Some spent quality time (time devoted to active involvement with a child, as opposed to merely being present in the room with the child); others did not. Seventy-two percent had daily contact. Play turns out to be a prominent feature of the time men spent with their infants; in fact, the men were twice as likely to be involved in play as in basic caregiving activities (Hoosain & Roopnarine, 1995).

The quality of the time a father spends with his children is affected by the mother's attitudes (Beitel & Parke, 1998). For example, if mothers are highly supportive of a father's involvement, father involvement may be high or low, depending on the father, his work schedule, and his predispositions. But if a mother opposes or does not support of father involvement, the father will not be involved regardless of his individual disposition.

■ *Sharing is more likely after entry into kindergarten, which helps lead to a breakdown of egocentrism.*

Ethnicity is also a factor in fathering. African American families have their own unique ways of dealing with child care, as do Latino/Latina families, Asian American families, and European American families, and more cross-cultural research is needed to understand these patterns. Other factors also enter the picture, such as work schedules—a father's involvement has as much to do with each parent's work schedule as anything else (Averett, Gennetian, & Peters, 2000).

Although fathering is clearly good for children, it is also good for men—it enhances their self-esteem and feelings of competence. Children do not benefit merely from the presence of a father—fathers have to take part in family life.

■ **THE FIRST TWO YEARS.** In the first year of life, social interactions among children are limited; infants are largely egocentric and are basically unable to recognize any needs other than their own. By about the second half of the first year, children exhibit strong attachments to parents and other caregivers, along with fear of strangers.

As early as 9 months, infants show they like to play games by indicating their unhappiness when an adult stops playing with them (Ross & Lollis, 1987). They play by themselves; but as they grow older, especially after 2 years of age, they engage in more social play with other children (Howes & Tonyan, 1999).

By the end of their second year, children have begun to understand that they are separate from their parents—they are developing a sense of self. They begin to learn to interact with other people. They may play alongside other children, but they prefer to play with an adult rather than with another 2-year-old—gradually, however, they begin to socialize with their peers (Howes & Tonyan, 1999).

■ **SHARING.** The noted pediatrician Benjamin Spock once said that the only two things children will share willingly are communicable diseases and their mother's age. Actually, from age 2 until they begin school, children vacillate between quiet conformity and happy sharing, on the one hand, and stubborn negative demands and egocentric behavior, on the other. Because sharing is a socially desirable behavior, learning to share becomes a top priority when children enter a day-care center, nursery school, or kindergarten.

Although young children know that people experience mental states (Dad or Mom is in a bad mood, for example) (Wellman, Phillips, & Rodriguez, 2000), very young children still do not understand the concept of sharing—particularly the idea that if you share with another child, the other child is more likely to share with you. In a laboratory study of sharing, researchers observed pairs of children separated by a gate. Initially, one child was given toys and the other wasn't; then the situation was reversed. The researchers found that none of the children shared spontaneously; however, 65% shared a toy when their mothers asked them to. Moreover, a child who was deprived of a toy after having shared one often approached the child who now had the toy. One child even said, "I gave you a toy. Why don't you give me one?" Children do not initiate sharing at a young age; but once they share, they seem to exhibit knowledge about reciprocal arrangements. Of course, sharing is more likely among children who are friends because they have had more frequent social interaction and make more attempts at conflict resolution (Newcomb, Bukowski, & Bagwell, 1999). Sharing is also more likely after entry into kindergarten, which helps lead to a breakdown of egocentrism.

psychology *in action*

Gender Stereotypes

People have preconceived ideas and biases about many things, ranging from attraction to revulsion, from like to hate, and from desire to disinterest. Why do we have such biases—especially when thinking about men or women? It turns out that people like to categorize events and situations into neat packages. We often use "mental shortcuts" to help make sense of the world. Using such shortcuts helps us avoid or reduce information overload; people are "cognitive misers," processing events superficially unless they are motivated to do otherwise. This is especially true when it comes to looking at the behavior of men and women and results in gender stereotypes.

A **gender stereotype** is a fixed, overly simple, sometimes incorrect idea about traits, attitudes, and behaviors of males or females. Gender stereotyping leads people to ignore individual differences and to expect specific patterns of behavior based on gender. Young boys receive baseball gloves; young girls get Barbie dolls. Boys wear blue; girls wear pink. And these distinctions have an impact at an early age (Levy, 1999; Levy, Sadovsky, & Troseth, 2000). Is this a problem?

It can be, especially when gender stereotyping leads to ignoring individual differences, bias, and discrimination. The mechanisms of gender stereotyping can seem harmless and be subtle. Boys tend to be assigned chores that take them away from people (such as yard work and walking the dog), whereas girls tend to be assigned in-house activities. As a consequence, some researchers assert, girls interact more with people and may therefore become more nurturing, but they have fewer opportunities for inventive, active play. As a result of their experiences, boys may excel at manipulating objects and tools but lack in nurturance. And both girls and boys may receive approval and praise for their "gender-appropriate" behaviors, which reinforces those behaviors (Fagot, Rogers, & Leinbach, 2000). Not only is reinforcement important, but also children learn and adopt gender-based ideas merely by watching and reading about the behavior of adults of their own sex (LaRossa et al., 2000; Martin 2000; Schmitt, Anderson, & Collins, 2000). Of course, television is also a source of endless hours of gender stereotypes—ideas that are often exaggerated, especially in children's cartoons (Kinder, 1999; Thompson & Zerbinos, 1997).

A caution: we must remember that extremes in people's behavior often jump out. If you have a mild preexisting view about men exhibiting a specific behavior and then observe a man exhibiting that behavior (especially if it is an extreme case of it), you will remember that behavior, and that it was a man. You will notice, remember, and confirm your preexisting bias, and it may develop into a full-blown stereotype.

Starting at age 3 and continuing for several years, children prefer same-sex playmates and limit their interactions with the other gender. According to Eleanor Maccoby (1998), this characteristic cuts across a variety of situations and is difficult to change. Gender segregation does not happen solely because children have been given "boy" toys or "girl" toys; nor does it result solely from inborn temperamental differences that lead to rough-and-tumble play for boys and more sedate play for girls (Theimer, Killen, & Stangor, 2000). Rather, children spend some years actively avoiding the other sex, and at times, insulting them ("Boys are dumb," "Girls are retarded"). Children with widely different personalities are drawn together solely on the basis of their sex. Maccoby (1998) asserts that gender differences are minimal when children are observed individually but become more evident in social situations.

Both biological and environmental influences contribute to gender differences in children. However, gender differences in behavior are small and obvious only in certain situations, such as on the playground (Maccoby, 1998). As parents consider the implications of research on gender differences, they must use critical thinking skills. They should foster, among other things, children's achievement, moral values, and self-esteem. None of these is sex-based; both boys and girls can and should be taught to reason and solve problems; all children should be taught basic human values and made to feel they are worthwhile.

Gender Roles

Earlier we drew a distinction between sex and gender (see p. 94); the division focuses on biological traits dealing with reproductive capacity (sex) and behavioral and mental process that are constructed and reinforced by society (gender). Everyone acknowledges that women differ from men—but women *and* men are powerful, resourceful, sensitive, intuitive, and analytical. Yet they exhibit those abilities in different circumstances (Hales, 1999). To an important extent, the study of gender differences is an investigation of when, how, and why those abilities are revealed.

A generation ago, many parents tended to tenaciously encourage "masculine" traits such as athletic prowess in their sons and "feminine" traits such as popularity in their daughters. Parents accepted, promoted, and vigorously reinforced gender-based social environments. Today, many parents de-emphasize gender-based interests in their children, seeking to reduce or eliminate society's tendency to stereotype people on the basis of sex.

When young people are given equal schooling, measures of academic performance for boys and girls tend to be equal. Socially, both men and women value intelligence and a sense of humor in the other sex. But men and women differ in their biological makeup, and their experiences are not the same. Researchers must place gender differences within meaningful contexts in order to analyze them. This means looking at how parents treat children as a function of their biological sex, how schools and religious institutions establish and reinforce gender-specific behaviors, and how society views the influence of gender in the daily life of children and young adults (Hannover, 2000; Tiedemann, 2000). We must also remember that children are active learners and take part in learning about gender and gendered behaviors (Martin, 1999).

Modern medical technology has allowed parents to know the sex of their child during prenatal development, which allows parents to begin treating their children differently on the basis of their sex before the child is born; and so from the beginning, girls and boys have different life experiences. As Collins suggests, parental influences on child development are neither unambiguous nor insubstantial (Collins et al., 2000). We see their impact from the beginning—for example, relatively few Americans have gender-neutral names such as Pat, Terry, Chris, or Lee (Van Fleet & Atwater, 1997). Moms and dads agonize over picking just the right name, one that will send the right signals and will be gender-appropriate. Some psychologists assert that the way parents talk to and treat boys and girls creates special problems. For example, Pollack (1998) argues that parents have such strong expectations about how boys should behave—independent, strong, and tough—that the pressure of these expectations puts them at risk for various psychological problems. The truth is that many parents put similar, but different, pressure on girls—to be independent, strong, and feminine. Children today sometimes get mixed messages, and they certainly have high expectations placed on them, far more than when children were expected to be "seen but not heard" (Maccoby, 1998). See *Psychology in Action* to further explore the role of gender in shaping behavior.

student voices

Ashlyn Inderbitzen
Modesto Junior College

I chose psychology as my major because I want to be able to help children cope with their feelings and work out their problems so they can become well-rounded adults. I feel I can be someone they will be able to trust, rely on, and talk to.

Erik Erikson and the Beginning of the Search for Self

Developing an awareness of the self as different from others is an important step in early childhood social development. Self-perception begins when the child recognizes that he or she is separate from other people, particularly the mother; the self becomes more differentiated as a child develops an appreciation of his or her own inner mental world. Ideally, as children develop a concept of themselves, they develop self-esteem and significant attachments to others. Such cognitive, and then social, changes do not take place in isolation. They are influenced by the nature of a child's early attachments, by the cultural world surrounding the child, by the family's and society's

Gender stereotype
A fixed, overly simple, sometimes incorrect idea about traits, attitudes, and behaviors of males or females.

TABLE 3.4

Erikson's First Four Stages of Psychosocial Development

Stage	Approximate Age	Important Event	Description
1. Basic trust versus basic mistrust	Birth to 12–18 months	Feeding	The infant must form a loving, trusting relationship with the caregiver or develop a sense of mistrust.
2. Autonomy versus shame/doubt	18 months to 3 years	Toilet training	The child's energies are directed toward the development of physical skills, including walking and controlling the sphincter. The child learns control but may develop shame and doubt if not handled well.
3. Initiative versus guilt	3 to 6 years	Independence	The child continues to become more assertive and to take more initiative but may be chastised for being too forceful, which can lead to guilt feelings.
4. Industry versus inferiority	6 to 12 years	School	The child must deal with demands to learn new skills or risk a sense of inferiority, failure, and incompetence.

child-rearing practices, and by how the child is taught to think about the causes of events in the world (Waters, Hamilton, & Weinfield, 2000). The construction of an identity—a self—occurs slowly and gradually and is affected by myriad variables.

Perhaps no one studied the challenges of social development and self-understanding more closely than the psychoanalyst Erik H. Erikson (1902–1994). With sharp insight, a linguistic flair, and a logical, coherent approach to analyzing human behavior, Erikson, who studied with Freud in Austria, developed a theory of *psychosocial stages of development;* each of his stages contributes to the development of a unique self and helps define how a person develops a role, attitudes, and skills as a member of society. According to Erikson, a series of basic psychological conflicts determines the course of development. His theory is noted for its integration of individual disposition and environment with historical forces in the shaping of the self. Erikson's theory describes a continuum of stages, each involving a dilemma and a crisis, through which all individuals must pass. Each stage can have either a positive or a negative outcome. New dilemmas emerge as a person grows older and faces new responsibilities, tasks, and social relationships. A person may experience a dilemma as an opportunity and face it positively or may view the dilemma as a catastrophe and fail to cope with it effectively.

Table 3.4 lists the first four psychosocial stages in Erikson's theory, with their age ranges and the important events associated with them. These four stages cover birth through age 13. (We will look at Erikson's later stages, covering adolescence and adulthood, in Chapter 4.)

Stage 1 (birth to 12–18 months) involves the development of basic *trust versus basic mistrust.* During their first months, according to Erikson, infants make distinctions about the world and decide whether it is a comfortable, loving place in which they can feel basic trust. At this stage, they develop beliefs about people's essential trustworthiness. If their needs are adequately met, they learn that the world is a predictable and safe place. Infants whose needs are not met learn to distrust the world.

During stage 2 (18 months to 3 years), toddlers must resolve the crisis of *autonomy versus shame and doubt.* Success in toilet training and other tasks involving control leads to a sense of autonomy and more mature behavior. Difficulties dealing with control during this stage result in fears and a sense of shame and doubt.

Stage 3 of Erikson's theory (3 to 6 years) is that of *initiative versus guilt,* when children begin to exercise their own inventiveness, drive, and enthusiasm. During this stage, they either gain a sense of independence and good feelings about themselves or develop a sense of guilt, lack of acceptance, and negative feelings about themselves. If children learn to dress themselves, clean their rooms and accomplish other similar tasks, and develop friendships with other children, they can feel a sense of mastery; alternatively, they can be dependent or regretful.

During stage 4 (6 to 12 years), children must resolve the issue of *industry versus inferiority.* Children either develop feelings of competence and confidence in their abilities or experience inferiority, failure, and feelings of incompetence.

Erikson's theory asserts that children must go through each stage, resolving its crisis as best they can. Many factors have a bearing on the successful navigation of these stages. Of course, children grow older whether or not they are ready for the next stage. A person of any age may still have unresolved conflicts, opportunities, and dilemmas from previous stages. These can cause anxiety and discomfort and make resolution of advanced stages more difficult. Because adolescence is such a crucial stage for the formation of a firm identity, the environment surrounding an adolescent becomes especially important. We will turn to this topic in the next chapter.

Be an *Active* learner

REVIEW

- Identify two important variables that affect the quality of child care. pp. 97–98
- What is a gender stereotype? pp. 104–105

THINK CRITICALLY

- Why do you think that gender differences are minimized when children are observed individually?
- What does Erikson's theory have in common with Piaget's theory?

APPLY PSYCHOLOGY

- Should employers provide day care for their employees' children? If yes, what might be the implications for workers and employers? If no, why not?

Summary and Review

Key Issues and Research Designs

What is developmental psychology?

- *Developmental psychology* is the study of the lifelong, often age-related, processes of change in the physical, cognitive, emotional, moral, and social domains of functioning; these changes are rooted in genetically controlled biological mechanisms as well as in social interactions. p. 72

What are some issues in the study of human development and some methods of studying development?

- A key issue in development involves considering the extent to which a person's abilities, interests, and personality are determined by biological or genetic influences (by nature) or by environmental influences (by nurture). The issue of stability versus change is closely associated with that of nature versus nurture. Many researchers assume that stable traits are inherited and genetically determined, whereas those favoring an environmental view are more likely to believe that people change with life's events. A continuous view sees development as a process of gradual growth and change, but development can also be viewed as discontinuous, with growth, maturation, and understanding of the world occurring at various key periods and change appearing abruptly. pp. 72–73
- With a cross-sectional research design, researchers compare people of different ages to determine if they differ on some important dimension. With a longitudinal design, researchers study a group of people, usually of the same age, over a period of time to determine whether changes have occurred. pp. 74–75

KEY TERM

developmental psychology, p. 72

Physical Development

Distinguish between an embryo and a fetus.

- Conception occurs when an ovum and a sperm join in a woman's fallopian tube to form a *zygote*—a fertilized egg. p. 76
- The *placenta* is a mass of tissue that is attached to the wall of the uterus and acts as the life-support system for the fetus. p. 76

- From about the 5th through the 49th day after conception, the prenatal organism is called an *embryo;* from that point until birth, it is called a *fetus.* p. 76
- In the first months of life, an embryo is especially sensitive to teratogens. A *teratogen* is a substance that can produce developmental malformations; common teratogens include alcohol and other drugs. p. 77

How is a newborn equipped to deal with the world?

- A newborn comes prepared with a set of primary reflexes, among them the *Babinski reflex,* the *Moro reflex,* the *rooting reflex,* the *sucking reflex,* and the *grasping reflex.* Newborns also have surprisingly well-developed perceptual systems. p. 79
- During a *critical period,* an organism is especially sensitive to environmental influences. pp. 76–77

KEY TERMS

zygote, p. 76; embryo, p. 76; fetus, p. 76; placenta, p. 76; teratogen, p. 77; Babinski reflex, p. 79; Moro reflex, p. 79; rooting reflex, p. 79; sucking reflex, p. 79; grasping reflex, p. 79; critical period, p. 80

The Development of Thought

What is the difference between Piaget's concepts of assimilation and accommodation?

- Piaget's theory focuses on *how* people think, instead of on *what* they think. His theory includes the concept of the *schema,* a mental structure that helps a child make sense of experience. Piaget identified two processes that enable the individual to gain new knowledge: assimilation and accommodation. *Assimilation* is the process of incorporating new information into existing understanding. *Accommodation* is the process of modifying one's existing thought processes and framework of knowledge in response to new information. p. 84

Describe Piaget's stages of cognitive development.

- Piaget believed that cognitive development occurs in four stages, each of which must be completed before the next stage begins. In the *sensorimotor stage,* covering roughly the first 2 years of life, the child develops some motor coordination skills and a memory for past events; the rudiments of intelligence are established. pp. 84–89
- *Object permanence* is the realization that objects continue to exist even when they are out of sight. p. 85
- The *preoperational stage* lasts from about age 2 to age 6 or 7, when the child begins to represent the world symbolically. *Egocentrism,* the inability to perceive a situation or event except in relation to oneself, flourishes in this stage. At the end of the preoperational stage, children begin the process of *decentration,* gradually moving away from self-centeredness. p. 86
- *Conservation* is the ability to recognize that objects can be transformed in some way, visually or physically, yet still be the same in number, weight, substance, or volume. p. 87
- The *concrete operational stage* lasts from approximately age 6 or 7 to age 11 or 12; the child develops the ability to understand constant factors in the environment, rules, and higher-order symbolic systems. pp. 86–87
- The *formal operational stage* begins at about age 12, when the individual can think hypothetically, consider future possibilities, and use deductive logic. pp. 87–88

How is Vygotsky's approach different from Piaget's?

- Vygotsky saw the child as part of an active social world in which communication with others and self-speech (private speech) help the child understand his or her world and that of other people. Vygotsky held that when children are presented with tasks that are outside of their current abilities, they need the help of society to accomplish them. pp. 89–90

How do Piaget's and Kohlberg's views of the development of morality differ?

- *Morality* is a system of learned attitudes about social practices, institutions, and individual behavior that people use to evaluate situations and behavior as right or wrong, good or bad. Piaget and Kohlberg studied moral reasoning, focusing on how people make moral judgments about hypothetical situations. Their theories differ in that Piaget thought of the stages of moral development as discrete, whereas Kohlberg viewed them as overlapping. Kohlberg proposed that children's interactions with parents and friends may influence their conceptions of morality. pp. 92–93

What was Gilligan's main criticism of Kohlberg's work?

- Whereas Kohlberg showed that young children base their decisions about right and wrong on the likelihood of avoiding punishment and obtaining rewards, Gilligan found that children also focused on caring, relationships, and connections with other people. Most important, Gilligan found some differences between boys and girls. As young children, girls gravitate toward a morality of caring, while boys tend toward a morality of justice. pp. 93–95

KEY TERMS

schema, p. 84; assimilation, p. 84; accommodation, p. 84; sensorimotor stage, p. 84; object permanence, p. 85; preoperational stage, p. 86; egocentrism, p. 86; decentration, p. 86; concrete operational stage, p. 86; conservation, p. 86; formal operational stage, p. 87; theory of mind, p. 90; morality, p. 92; sex, p. 94; gender, p. 94

The Growth of Emotions

What is attachment, and why is it important?

- *Attachment* is the strong emotional tie that a person feels toward special other persons in his or her life. p. 95
- *Bonding* is a special process of emotional attachment theorized to occur between parent and child in the minutes and hours immediately after birth; bonding is a controversial idea that is widely accepted but has little research support. pp. 95–96

■ Bowlby was one of the first to study the close attachment between mothers and their babies and to show that babies separated from their mothers exhibit characteristic responses he identified as secure, avoidant, resistant, and disoriented. Once established, early attachment is fairly permanent. Verbal exchanges between child and caregiver help establish ties, teach language, inform infants about the world, and socialize them. pp. 96–98

How permanent is temperament?

■ *Temperament* refers to early-emerging and long-lasting individual differences in disposition and in the intensity and especially the quality of emotional reactions. Temperament is not fixed and unchangeable, although many researchers contend that some specific initial temperamental characteristics may be biologically based. pp. 98–101

KEY TERMS

attachment, p. 94; bonding, p. 95; temperament, p. 99

Social Development

When do children begin to develop a sense of self?

■ By the end of their second year, children have begun to understand that they are separate from their parents—they are developing a sense of self. Very young children do not understand the concept of sharing—particularly the idea that sharing with another child makes the other child more likely to share too. p. 103

What are gender stereotypes?

■ A *gender stereotype* is an expectation of specific behavior patterns based on a person's gender. Parents reinforce children selectively based on their gender to some extent, especially at young ages, but gender differences in behavior are small and are apparent only in certain situations, such as on the playground and in groups. pp. 104–105

Describe Erikson's stage theory of psychosocial development.

■ Erikson described psychosocial development throughout life as a series of stages during which people resolve various psychosocial issues. His theory suggests that at each stage a successful or unsuccessful resolution of a dilemma determines personality and social interactions. The first four stages are basic trust versus basic mistrust, autonomy versus shame and doubt, initiative versus guilt, and industry versus inferiority. pp. 105–106

KEY TERMS

gender stereotype, p. 105

4 Adolescence and Adulthood

Jonathan Green, *Boy by the Sea,* 1995

Professional wrestling attracts 32 million viewers every week; it is one of the most popular events on television. The performers are part athlete, part variety show comedians who combine fake violence and sexual innuendo, taking them to dramatic extremes. Pubescent boys are especially lured to this mixture of sex, shock, and violence, where each competition resembles an orgy of excitement and action.

No longer do wrestling promoters claim that the bouts are legitimate; indeed, to reassure the public that they will not see real violence, the promoters admit that wrestling is theatrical. Story lines are now developed for wrestlers—shadowy and complicated, these characters helped catapult wrestling to new prominence. Of course, wrestling obviously meets some need on the part of viewers, especially teenage boys and their dads.

In play and in life, boys have always been admired for their physical prowess—for example, who can run the longest distance in the shortest time? Through daring acts, boys also gain admiration, prestige, and self-esteem. And the stereotypes of what it means to be a boy or man are as strong today as they have ever been. Might some boys watch professional wrestling because they fear

chapter outline

being weak and slow, and might violence on television give a boy an outlet for accumulated fear, anger, or shame (Pollack, 1998)? While psychologists like William Pollack (1998) argue that we as a society should create violence-free zones and encourage acts of caring and empathy; in reality, television and other media sources, including video games and the Internet, are saturated with violence, sex, and yes, professional wrestling.

Human experience and development are influenced by an array of events including a person's biological inheritance, life experiences, and thoughts—and, to a certain extent, chance. And there is great variability in how specific events—professional wrestling and churchgoing alike—affect individuals. For example, moving from one state to another changes people's lives; a divorce is unsettling; a death in the family can be devastating; winning the lottery can jolt a person from poverty and anonymity to luxury and fame. So, in addition to normal, predictable developmental changes, once-in-a-lifetime events can permanently alter physical, social, and personality development. *Normative* life events are those that are typical for most men and women in a culture; they are commonly experienced major events, such as having children or retiring from work. Other life events are *idiosyncratic;* they are unique to an individual, such as the death of a sibling or a major health problem. Idiosyncratic life events are often compelling, but because normative life events affect most people, psychological theories have focused on them.

This chapter discusses some of the developmental changes that occur during adolescence and adulthood and traces the psychological processes underlying these changes. As you read, remember that a person's *chronological age* (age in years) is sometimes different from his or her *functional age* (age the person acts or seems). For example, some adolescents act older and wiser than their age-matched peers.

Adolescence: Bridging the Gap

In Western culture, the transition from childhood to adulthood brings dramatic cognitive, social, and emotional changes. Generally, this transition occurs between the ages of 12 and 20, a period known as *adolescence,* which bridges childhood and adulthood but is like neither of those states. **Adolescence** is the period extending from the onset of puberty to early adulthood. **Puberty** is the time when the reproductive system matures; it begins with an increase in the production of sex hormones, which signals the end of childhood. Although adolescents are in many ways like adults—they are nearly mature physically and mentally, and their moral development is fairly advanced—their emotional development may be far from complete, and generally they have not yet become self-sufficient economically. Their stages of development—cognitive, physical, and emotional—just have not caught up with one another.

Adolescence
The period extending from the onset of puberty to early adulthood.

Puberty
The period during which the reproductive system matures; it begins with an increase in the production of sex hormones, which signals the end of childhood.

Viewing Adolescence in Multiple Contexts

Adolescence is often referred to as a time of storm and stress brought on largely by raging hormones—and for some adolescents this is the case. It is a popular stereotype that adolescents are in a state of conflict resulting in part from a lack of congruity among the various aspects of their development—physical, cognitive, social, and emotional. There is some truth to this image. Most adolescents have normal conflicts, such as with parents, and some have atypical problems, such as poverty or parental alcoholism; what may compound these problems is that adolescents' coping mechanisms, or ways of dealing with such stressors, may not yet have evolved sufficiently. Consider alcohol abuse. Most adolescents know that underage drinking is illegal and that drinking is potentially deadly when combined with driving. Yet most are not mature enough to stand up to peer pressure and make a conscious decision not to drink—especially those youths who are at high risk because of poverty, absent parents, or alcoholism in the home (Dishion, McCord, & Poulin, 1999; Taubman-ben Ari, 2000).

Storm and stress do not give the whole picture of adolescence, however. Most adolescents go through this period of multiple changes without significant psychological difficulty (Arnett, 1999; Larson, 2000). Although spurts of hormones do affect adolescents' reactions, nonbiological factors seem to be especially important in moderating the effects of hormones on adolescents' moods (Archibald, 2000). Adolescence may be a challenging life period, just as adulthood is, but relatively few adolescents have serious difficulties (Roesser, Eccles, & Sameroff, 2000), and most psychologists agree that adolescence is not typically marked by great psychological turmoil. This does not mean that adolescence is conflict-free or that parent–child relationships do not change during this period; what it does mean is that adolescence does not *have* to be a stressful time (Galambos & Tilton-Weaver, 2000; Sagrestano et al., 1999). Most adolescents experience healthy emotional and social development during these years, and the frequency and intensity of conflicts decrease as adolescents grow older (Collins & Laursen, 2000).

While it is almost a cliché for a teenager in the United States to feel that "no one understands me," it is difficult to imagine a teenager growing up in the jungles of New Guinea expressing the same sentiment; her focus during the teen years is not on self-expression but on learning specific skills. Thus, the problems of adolescence must be considered in a cultural context. Even when adolescents grow up in the same country, they experience life's joys and disappointments in different ways. Some American teenagers come from disadvantaged economic groups, perhaps from a Chicago ghetto or a Native American reservation. Some grow up in luxury, perhaps in a wealthy suburb of Los Angeles. Others are exposed to racial prejudice, alcohol and other drug abuse, violence, nonsupportive families, or other stressors that lead them to feel a lack of control over their lives (Kilpatrick et al., 2000). In the end, the culture in which a teen grows and matures affects his or her overall view of the world, daily attitudes, as well as specific behaviors. Whether you view religion and the agriculture as inseparable, whether you view life as an unending process, or whether you view men and women as equals is determined by your culture.

■ *Cultural context affects the process of development and the problems adolescents encounter.*

Unfortunately, most research on adolescence has been conducted on White, middle-class American teenagers. But researchers now understand that the life experiences of various ethnic and cultural groups are not alike. Each year, more studies compare the experiences of different groups and sensitize both professionals and the

Just before the onset of sexual maturity, boys and girls experience significant growth spurts with girls maturing earlier.

public to cultural differences among groups as well as to the diversity that exists within groups. Remember, there is often more diversity within a given group than between groups.

Physical Development in Adolescence

The words *adolescence* and *puberty* are often used interchangeably, but in fact they mean different things. As noted earlier, puberty is the period during which the reproductive system matures. The age when puberty begins varies widely; some girls begin to mature physically as early as age 8, and some boys at 9 or 10 (Wilson, 1992). The average age at which individuals reach sexual maturity—the first menstruation for a girl, the first ejaculation for a boy—is 13, plus or minus a year or two (on average, girls enter puberty a year or two before boys). Just before the onset of sexual maturity, boys and girls experience significant *growth spurts,* gaining as much as 5 inches in height in a single year.

By the end of the first or second year of the growth spurt, changes have occurred in body proportions, fat distribution, bones and muscles, and physical strength and agility. In addition, the hormonal system has begun to trigger the development of secondary sex characteristics. **Secondary sex characteristics** are the genetically determined physical features that differentiate the sexes but are not directly involved with reproduction. These characteristics help distinguish men from women—for example, beards and chest hair in males, breasts in females. (Primary sex characteristics are the external genitalia and their associated internal structures, all of which are present at birth.) Boys experience an increase in body mass and a deepening of the voice, as well as the growth of pubic, underarm, and facial hair. Girls experience an increase in the size of the breasts, a widening of the hips, and the growth of underarm and pubic hair. Puberty ends with the maturation of the reproductive organs, at which time boys produce sperm and girls begin to menstruate. The first ejaculation for boys and the first menstrual cycle for girls (called *menarche*) are usually memorable events. The order and sequence of these physical changes are predictable, but, as noted earlier, the age at which puberty begins and the secondary sex characteristics emerge varies widely from person to person. Over the past 30 years, many girls have been reaching puberty at younger and younger ages, and this has put increasing pressure on them to choose situations and activities that go together with their physical growth—regardless of their emotional development at that age.

Puberty has received a good deal of research attention. For example, researchers have found that as boys pass through puberty, they feel more positive about their bodies, whereas girls are more likely to have negative feelings. Puberty itself does not create psychological maladjustment. However, adolescence means beginning to emerge as an adult, socially and sexually, and this requires significant adjustment. New forces affect the self-image of adolescents, and although these forces create new stresses, most adolescents perceive their new status as desirable. Physical maturation has implications for social development, because young people often gravitate to and choose environments and activities that complement their genetic tendencies (Collins et al., 2000). While they may eventually attain independence and clear thinking, we know that adolescents often make bad decisions, take risks, and are vulnerable to abuse of alcohol and other drugs (Spear, 2000).

Researchers find that in junior high school, early-maturing adolescents enjoy several advantages, including increased confidence, superior athletic prowess, greater

Secondary sex characteristics
The genetically determined physical features that differentiate the sexes but are not directly involved with reproduction.

Imaginary audience
A cognitive distortion experienced by adolescents, in which they see themselves as always "on stage" with an audience watching.

sexual appeal, and higher expectations from teachers and parents (Prokopcakova, 1998). But some early-maturing adolescents seem to be at a disadvantage, in part because peers often treat them as outsiders (Archibald, 2000; Ge, Conger, & Elder, 1996). But such differences in adolescence seem to have little long-term negative consequences; in fact, the stresses of being an early or late maturer may help teenagers become adept at coping. Many who were at a disadvantage during their school years become self-assured adults. So many factors go into the making of a self-assured adult that psychologists are really not sure how significant the impact of early or late maturation is.

During the teen years, the brain continues to consolidate circuits and hard-wire various abilities—physical ones like catching baseballs, mental ones like doing algebra problems, and artistic ones like playing piano. It is important to remember that the brain is still maturing during the adolescent years, making new connections and interconnections. In young adulthood the brain is still organizing, pruning neural cells that are inoperative and no longer useful, and reorganizing often used, important circuits (Casey, Giedd, & Thomas, 2000). In a real way, it is organizing itself into executive-like functions to operate in a fully efficient manner.

Cognitive Development in Adolescence

Teenagers often make poor decisions; they can be moody, clueless when reading teachers' or parents' intentions, have poor self-control, drive automobiles like trucks in a desert, seem to be driven more by hormones than common sense, and can be awkward and falling all over their limbs. They have trouble balancing their textbooks, checkbooks, and social lives. It's all about coordinating mind and body and about harnessing and coordinating their cognitive, thought abilities.

As children mature, they develop cognitively in rather complex ways, often in uncoordinated fits and starts. Piaget and Vygotsky showed that children's cognitive development has both biological and social components (see Chapter 3). And cognitive development does not stop in adolescence. Most adolescents are in the formal operational stage. Because they can think about the world abstractly and develop hypotheses, they learn new cognitive strategies. Teenagers expand their vocabularies, seek out creative solutions, and make full use of their higher mental functions. Problem solving often becomes a focus for adolescent thought. Many adolescents become egocentric, idealistic, and critical of others—at least for some time. And, as the next section points out, cultural backgrounds can be another factor influencing adolescents' cognitive development.

Adolescents often believe the world is focused around their individual lives—as if they are always "on stage."

Developing new cognitive abilities—moving into Piaget's stage of formal operations—is quite liberating for adolescents. But this newfound ability to understand the world and its subtleties is not always easy on adolescents, as they sometimes become argumentative and difficult. Part of the problem, from Piaget's view, is that teenagers become wrapped up in themselves and in their own thoughts—in short, quite egocentric. This egocentrism leads to two cognitive distortions. The first is the **imaginary audience**—the feeling adolescents have that they are always "on stage." "Everyone will be watching," thinks a teenager, referring to his or her first date, dance, or debate. If the adolescent egocentrically believes the world is attending critically to her or his life, she or he will go to great lengths to avoid calling attention to herself or himself (Vartanian, 2000).

Not only do adolescents believe that they are on stage, but they also develop an inflated sense of their own importance. This cognitive distortion is called the

personal fable—the belief that they are so special and unique that other people cannot understand them and that risky behaviors, such as unsafe sex, which might harm other people, will not harm them. The personal fable can lead to tragedy, such as when a teen thinks that he or she can drive after drinking. As we saw in Chapter 3, according to Inhelder and Piaget (1958), adolescents go through a phase in which they attribute an unlimited power to their own thoughts.

The imaginary audience and the personal fable may not be so much a return to childhood egocentrism as a side effect of cognitive growth and the ability to think about thinking. Adolescent egocentrism may be a bridging mechanism that allows adolescents to take on new roles, break away from parents, and integrate new views of the self—and so they may even be evident, to some extent, in adults (Frankenberger, 2000).

Cognitive differences between male and female adolescents are minimal. There are some observed sex differences—for example, on certain tests (such as the SAT), males as a group outperform females in mathematics (Park, Bauer, & Sullivan, 1998). However, when certain socioeconomic and cultural variables are controlled, these differences are very small. And it's important to remember that they are overall group differences, having no bearing on any individual's achievements.

■ **ARE THERE ETHNIC DIFFERENCES?** Which group does best in school: Latinos/Latinas, Asian Americans, or African Americans? It is widely believed that students of Asian American descent do better, thanks to cultural values that stress achievement. Researchers have found that this belief is accurate: culture does affect achievement in direct and indirect ways. Students in Asian nations spend more classroom time on academic subjects than do students in the United States; it is not surprising that their math scores are higher (Stigler & Baranes, 1988). Further, families and teachers in Asian societies tend to treat all students as equal, emphasizing effort more than innate abilities—whereas in many Western cultures more attention is given to innate cognitive strengths. In addition, in Asian and other non-Western societies, success is often attributed to external factors and failure to internal factors such as ability; the reverse is true in Western societies (Kivilu & Rogers, 1998).

■ *Excessivly permissive parenting often leads to troubles during adolescence; whereas authoritative parents are less often associated with troubles during adolescence.*

Parental behavior is also important. Adolescents whose parents are *authoritative*—not rigidly authoritarian but accepting, warm, democratic, and firm—achieve more in school than their peers (Steinberg et al., 1992). But peer interactions also turn out to be facilitative; strong peer support for academics can make up for a lack of positive parenting, and peer groups can be a source of positive support (Turner, 1999; Ungar, 2000).

Regardless of ethnic background, adolescents from authoritative homes functioned better socially than those from permissive or neglectful homes. In school performance, Steinberg found a slight difference among ethnic groups: authoritative parenting seemed to make more of a difference to White teenagers than to African American or Asian American ones. Why would authoritativeness benefit African Americans and Asian Americans less in academic performance than in social development? The difference in academic versus social development may have to do with sharply differing worldviews. The researchers found that all of the students believed a good education would pay off, but Asian Americans in particular had been taught to fear the consequences of a poor education. In contrast, African American students were more likely to be optimistic and believe that life could have positive outcomes despite a poor education. Obviously, students who believe that they can

Personal fable
A cognitive distortion experienced by adolescents, in which they believe they are so special and unique that other people cannot understand them and risky behaviors will not harm them.

point*counterpoint*

Adolescent Medical Decision Making

The Issue: Should adolescents be allowed to make life and death decisions?

POINT
Adolescents are cognitively mature and can and should make their own medical decisions.

COUNTERPOINT
Adolescents may be mature but do not have the context of life experience to make life-and-death decisions.

Imagine that you are a 16-year-old who for the past 7 years has been suffering with leukemia. You've gone through chemotherapy twice, done a bone marrow transplant, and had a seemingly endless number of blood transfusions. Despite aggressive treatment efforts, your condition has deteriorated and hope is running out.

This situation and ones similar to it occur in hospitals every day when adolescents and adults cope with chronic conditions like leukemia and cystic fibrosis. There often comes a point at which many patients conclude that death is preferable to the suffering and the difficult treatment procedures that often offer little hope. Adults make the decision for themselves, usually in consultation with family and friends. But if you were a teenager, your view and wishes may be completely ignored. Parents have power over medical decision making. But should they? Are adolescents capable of making informed decisions about their lives and health? There are sharp divisions of opinion on this matter.

On one hand, research shows that adolescents in general are capable of making health decisions and providing informed consent. The argument is that adolescents above age 12 or 13 have the cognitive capacities to make knowledgeable decisions because they are cognitively mature. Most states also allow teenagers who are on their own on the basis of marriage, parenthood, or military service the authority to consent to medical treatment. Still other states allow minors to make *some* types of medical decisions. Adolescents argue, and most parents agree, that they are capable of informed, intelligent decision making. Yet the majority of states does not allow adolescents to refuse various treatments—especially when the decision involves the potential loss of life.

There is another side to this issue—adolescents take risks, often ill-informed risks. So most states have laws that suggest that minors under the age of 21 are incapable of understanding, deliberating, and making important health care decisions. Thus, there is a focus on whether agreements to treatment are made knowingly, intelligently, and voluntarily. It's often been argued that adolescents, and many adults for that matter, don't meet these three criteria. Those who oppose adolescents making these decisions argue that there are scant research data to prove that adolescents are emotionally or cognitively mature enough to make life-and-death decisions. For example, do teenagers see all the options that adults see? Are teenagers fully aware of the consequences of their decisions? Do teenagers value what adults value, and are they looking at multiple options concurrently? In the end, are teenagers careful decision makers (Fischhoff & Bruine de Bruin, 1998)?

We know that adolescents make risky decisions and favor their own experience and anecdotal evidence over systematic factual information (Havemann et al., 1997). As a consequence, society draws a line at age 18 or 21 (depending on the state) and says that if you're younger than this age, you can't make the decision. Those who argue against adolescent decision making say that children need a protected period during which they can develop self-control, maturity, and the ability to make difficult decisions. They argue that children have limited world experience and that intellect should not be the only criterion. They further argue that if adolescents can make health care decisions, why can they not make decisions about when they will drive, when they will come home, and when they shall vote? In the most extreme, approval of "adolescent freedom" could even make a child's membership in a family voluntary.

In the end, mature children should not be ignored in the decision-making process. The American Medical Association asserts that physicians who treat minors have an ethical duty to promote the autonomy of minor patients by involving them in the medical decision-making process to a degree commensurate with their abilities. Parents should include their children and adolescents in the process, both to get their active support and to teach them how to make such decisions. The fact is, most parents do both, and it's only in fairly extreme circumstances that parents overrule adolescents. For now, the law limits adolescent decision making.

introduction to research basics

Sibling Influences During Early Adolescence

Brothers and sisters are obviously important for children as they grow and develop, but psychologists have not devoted a great deal of research to the influence of siblings. Recently, two groups of researchers have studied the influence of siblings during early adolescence; one group used a longitudinal study and the other conducted a cross-sectional study. These two methods use different approaches to studying age-related changes in developmental psychology (see page 75 in Chapter 3).

STUDY 1 Susan McHale and her colleagues (McHale et al., 2001) explored the impact of the sex of the sibling and siblings' gender-role orientations as influences on gender-related behaviors during middle childhood and early adolescence.

DESIGN This was a **longitudinal study,** a research method that examines a specific group of individuals at different ages, to discover changes that occur over time. This method falls within descriptive research techniques because the researchers do not manipulate variables; instead, they measure existing variables. Longitudinal studies are difficult to conduct; repeated measurements require locating a suitable selection of participants and following them over time. But though these studies are expensive and difficult, they give researchers helpful information about developmental trends.

HYPOTHESIS Older siblings' gender-role attitudes and behavior will influence their younger siblings to adopt similar attitudes and behaviors.

PARTICIPANTS Participants were 198 firstborn and second-born siblings and their parents. With the exception of two adopted Asian children, all were White and members of the working class or middle class, and they resided in rural areas, towns, and small cities.

PROCEDURE The research involved 3 years of data collection; by the third year of the study, the second-borns were approximately the same age that the firstborns had been in year 1.

The researchers conducted home interviews with mothers, fathers, and the children; in addition, participants filled out a daily diary of activities. McHale and her colleagues assessed parents' and children's gender-role attitudes as well as their sex-typed personality qualities and interest in sex-typed leisure activities to determine the patterns of influence.

RESULTS In general, firstborn siblings' behaviors in year 1 predicted second-born children's behaviors in year 3. That is, there seemed to be a modeling effect for the second-born children. Among firstborns, parental influence was more evident, and firstborns changed in ways that made them different from (rather than similar to) their siblings. In addition, the gender of the sibling made a difference; for example, girls with younger brothers reported less traditional attitudes than those with younger sisters. Also, boys with less traditional mothers became less traditional over time.

succeed without doing well in school will devote far less energy to academic pursuits than will those who are more fearful of the negative consequences of school failure. A child's worldview, taught by his or her parents and reinforced by peers, shapes future success (Chen & Lan, 1998). When it comes to school, distinctly different cultural views may alter motivation, performance, and later success in life and work.

Emotional and Social Development in Adolescence

Show me (L.L.) ten teenagers and I will show you ten distinct personalities. American teenagers have grown in a society that has extolled individual expression rather than conformity. Today's teenagers are also a generation whose parents have divorced at alarming rates and the economic gap between the very rich and the very poor has widened. With that said, it is not surprising that early childhood social interactions, as well as advances in cognitive development, profoundly affect adolescent social adjustment.

Teenagers in the United States spend a great deal of time alone—more so than in previous generations—whether while listening to music, surfing the Internet, or watching cable. They have an unprecedented number of opportunities to succeed, and fail—as well as to be lonely and feel isolated (Sanders et al., 2000). Children whose early adjustment is poor are less likely to make good

Longitudinal study
A research method that focuses on a specific group of individuals at different ages to examine changes that have occurred over time.

Cross-sectional studies
A type of research design that compares individuals of different ages to determine how they differ.

CONCLUSIONS Research using interviews and questionnaires—even longitudinal research that reveals developmental patterns—cannot provide conclusions concerning causality (what causes a behavior). However, the results from McHale and her colleagues suggest that sibling influences operate in ways that make children from the same family both similar (in the case of younger siblings) and more different (older siblings). Families are complex interactive systems that include influences from parents and siblings. Each child experiences a unique pattern of interactions. Many of us can appreciate this idea as we look at our brothers and sisters and wonder why they are so different from the way we are. This study demonstrated some ways in which these differences may develop.

STUDY 2 AmyKay Cole and Kathryn Kerns (2001) also studied the influence of siblings during early adolescence. Cole and Kerns focused on a comparison of three different ages and examined sibling interactions, with special attention to the gender composition of sibling pairs.

DESIGN Cole and Kerns used a cross-sectional rather than a longitudinal approach. **Cross-sectional studies** are a type of research design that compares individuals of different ages to determine how they differ. Researchers who want to contrast behavior at different ages often use this approach because it produces results more quickly than the longitudinal approach does. Cole and Kerns used this cross-sectional design to study intimacy, companionship, and conflict in preadolescent children and their siblings.

HYPOTHESIS Cole and Kerns hypothesized that the older participants and participants in same-gender pairs would have more intimate relationships and less conflict with their siblings than younger participants and those in mixed-gender pairs.

PARTICIPANTS Participants were 60 students in 4th grade, 44 students in 6th grade, and 66 students in 8th grade. All had at least one sibling.

PROCEDURE Participants filled out questionnaires that assessed the quality of their relationship with their sibling and the activities they and their siblings did together.

RESULTS Cole and Kerns found significant age differences for interactions with siblings, but not exactly as they had predicted. As predicted, intimacy was highest for 8th graders, but lower for 6th graders than for 4th graders. Gender composition of sibling pairs also produced differences, especially between pairs of brothers and pairs of sisters. Brother pairs were lowest in intimacy and in conflict resolution; sibling pairs that included a girl showed higher intimacy levels.

CONCLUSIONS Younger children have relationships with less intimacy than older children, and girls show more intimacy than boys. For siblings and friendships, boys engage in companionship-type activities and conflict. That is, the patterns of interactions between siblings during early adolescence showed similarities to the developmental patterns and gender differences seen in friendships. Cole and Kerns noted that the cross-sectional design of their study is one of its limitations, and in order to understand the developmental pattern of sibling interactions, a longitudinal study would be necessary.

adolescent adjustments, social and otherwise. Indeed, the suicide rate for adolescents is high, and has increased in recent decades (see Figure 4.1). When Cairns and Cairns (1994, 2000) tracked 695 young people growing up over a 14-year period, they saw early patterns of social adjustment manifest themselves as the years went by. These researchers argue that the trajectories of social development do not change much; troubled boys and girls tend to stay troubled, and happy and well-adjusted children are more likely to stay well adjusted. But, as mentioned earlier, regardless of their previous adjustment, teenagers' egocentrism—in the form of the imaginary audience and the personal fable—complicates their emotional and social adjustment.

Adolescents develop a self-image based on beliefs about themselves that are both cognitively and emotionally based, but other people also form expectations and beliefs about adolescents, which have an impact (Cairns & Cairns, 1994, 2000). Thus, an adolescent's personality and sense of self-esteem are affected by childhood experiences, events such as the timing of puberty and how peers and parents react to that timing, and stage of cognitive development. Self-esteem is also affected by ethnic identity, religion, and involvement in community service (Youniss, McClellan, & Yates, 1999).

FIGURE 4.1

The Suicide Rate for Adolescents and Young Adults Ages 15–24 Years Old Has Increased Dramatically. (*Centers for Disease Control and Prevention*)

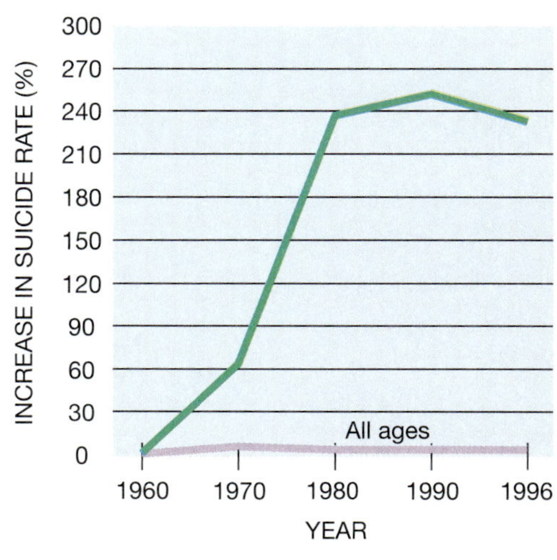

Parents and teachers can help troubled children and both early- and late-maturing adolescents develop a stronger sense of self-esteem. For example, research shows that involvement in athletics can be a buffer against the initially negative feelings about body image that can sometimes arise during this period. For both girls and boys, increased time spent playing sports is associated with higher satisfaction with body image and higher self-ratings on strength and attractiveness. Physical activity is associated with higher achievement, weight reduction, improved muscle tone, and stress reduction, all of which foster a positive self-image (Kirshnit, Richards, & Ham, 1988).

There are sharp individual differences in the development of adolescent self-esteem. In contrast to middle or later adolescence, early adolescence is associated with lower self-esteem and with feelings of insecurity, inadequacy, and shyness. Widespread publicity has claimed that this problem affects girls more than boys, but research shows that gender differences in self-esteem are small and in some countries and ethnic groups, no gender difference exists (Kling et al., 1999). Adolescent girls face many barriers to achievement, but very low self-esteem is not a big problem.

Two important sources of influence on self-esteem and personality are parents and peers. There is no question that adolescents are responsive to parental influence (Otto, 2000; Resnick et al., 1997). Psychologists and parents disagree about the relative importance of peers versus parents (Harris, 1998), but most studies indicate that adolescents' attitudes fall somewhere between those of their parents and those of their peers (Bukowski, Sippola, & Hoza, 1999; Paikoff et al., 1997). As Chapter 3 pointed out, the influence of peer groups is especially formidable—especially in the middle years of adolescence. *Peer groups* are people who identify with and compare themselves to one another. They often consist of people of the same age, gender, and ethnicity, although adolescents may change their peer group memberships and may belong to more than one group. As adolescents spend more time away from parents and home, they experience increasing pressure to conform to their peer groups' values regarding society, government, religion, music—and even fast-food restaurants. The desire for conformity especially affects same-sex peer relations (Bukowski, Sippola, & Newcomb, 2000). Peers constantly pressure one another to conform to behavioral standards, including standards for dress, social interaction, and even forms of rebellion, such as shoplifting and drug taking. Most important, peers influence the adolescent's developing self-concept. And adolescents are vulnerable; those who are unpopular can be victimized, which only further erodes self-esteem and creates withdrawal and a range of problems (Hodges et al., 1999).

Parents and their child-rearing style undoubtedly affect an adolescent's self-esteem and self-confidence (Neumark-Sztainer et al., 2000). Are they authoritative, nurturing, and at the same time firm, or are they heavy-handed and dictatorial, or perhaps more interested in being their child's pal and thus too permissive? Both parents and peers set standards by which the adolescent judges his or her own behavior. These three sources of influence (parents, peers, and self-interpretation) can establish self-esteem and self-confidence and allow an individual to attain good social and emotional adjustment. Some of that social adjustment is gender-based, as we'll discover next.

Who Am I? The Search for Gender Identity

Sex and gendered behaviors matter a great deal in both childhood and adulthood (Maccoby, 1998, 2000). Being a man or a woman in any culture carries with it certain roles. Men and women have different expectations for themselves and for members of the other sex, and those expectations often create inequality. Discrimination against women has decreased, but White men still dominate in the United States and many other Western societies (Rhode, 1997). Women still experience serious disparities in employment opportunities, pay, status, and access to leadership roles. This is a societal problem, which stems from society's definition and value of gender roles.

We saw in Chapter 3 that gender differences are differences between males and females in behavior or mental processes. Extensive research has revealed few important biologically determined behavioral or cognitive differences between the sexes (Geary, 1998). Although girls often reach developmental milestones earlier than boys do, this difference between the sexes usually disappears by late adolescence (Cohn, 1991). On the other hand, experience and learning—the way a person is raised and taught—have a profound impact on behaviors.

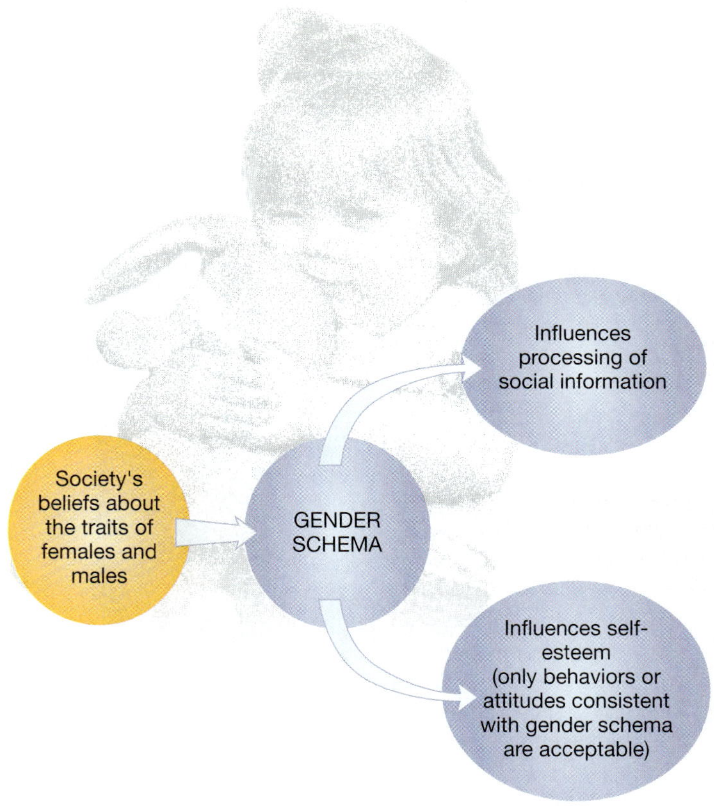

FIGURE 4.2

Gender Schema Theory

According to gender schema theory, children and adolescents use gender as an organizing theme for classifying and interpreting their perceptions about the world.

■ **GENDER IDENTITY.** As noted earlier, a key feature of adolescence is that it is a period of transition and change. Adolescents must develop their own identity, a sense of themselves as independent, mature individuals. One important aspect of identity is **gender identity**—a person's sense of being male or female. Children develop some sense of gender identity by age 3. By age 4 or 5, children realize that their gender identity is permanent; that is, they know that they will always be the sex that they are, but children as old as 6 or 7 can be confused about the constancy of gender. Some children in early elementary school believe that changing their hair, clothing, or behavior will alter their sex.

Consider the experience that adolescents have when their bodies change in appearance very rapidly, sometimes in unpredictable ways. During the transition to adulthood, adolescents often try out various types of behaviors, including those relating to male–female relationships and dating. Some adolescents become extreme in their orientation toward maleness or femaleness. Boys, especially in groups, may become overtly aggressive; girls may act submissively and be especially concerned with their looks. This exaggeration of traditional male or female behaviors, called *gender intensification,* is often short-lived, and it may be related to the increased self-esteem that boys feel during adolescence and the decreased self-esteem that girls experience (Aube et al., 2000; Kremen & Block, 1998).

Many psychologists believe that while children and adolescents are developing their gender identity, they attempt to bring their behavior and thoughts into conformity with generally accepted gender-specific roles. **Gender schema theory** asserts that children and adolescents use sex as an organizing theme to classify and interpret their perceptions about the world and themselves (Bem, 1985; Maccoby, 2000). (A *schema* is a conceptual framework that organizes information and makes sense of the world. See Figure 4.2 for a description of gender schema theory.) Young children decide on appropriate and inappropriate gender behaviors by processing a wide array of social information. They develop shorthand concepts of what boys and girls are like; then they try to behave in ways that are consistent with those concepts (Levy, 1999). Thus, they show preferences for sex-related toys, activities, and vocations. In fact, children's and, later, adolescents' self-esteem and feelings of worth are often tied to their gender-based perceptions about themselves, many of which are determined by identification with the same-gender parent or by what they see as society's view of gender roles (Hudak, 1993).

Gender identity
A person's sense of being male or female.

Gender schema theory
The theory that children and adolescents use gender as an organizing theme to classify and interpret their perceptions about the world and themselves.

BRAIN AND BEHAVIOR

The Prevalence of Eating Disorders

Calista Flockhart, star of the TV show *Ally McBeal,* has been the subject of considerable speculation because of her extreme thinness. Flockhart claims she is just thin, but many critics and psychologists assert that she has an eating disorder. This issue grabbed the public's attention because nearly 1 in 150 girls has the eating disorder anorexia nervosa. Flockhart's weight and her eating behavior are between her and her doctor, but it raises questions about role models for women and teenagers who always feel too fat compared to television stars. And, in some cases, this leads teenagers to eating disorders.

Eating disorders are psychological disorders characterized by gross disturbances in eating behavior and in the way individuals respond to food. Two important eating disorders are *anorexia nervosa* and *bulimia nervosa.* These disorders are very much culture-bound, Western diseases, but may have a physiological basis. Eating disorders affect about 3% of women in such societies at some time during their lives.

Anorexia nervosa, which affects as many as 40 out of every 10,000 young women in the United States, is an eating disorder characterized by an obstinate and willful refusal to eat. Individuals with the disorder, usually adolescent girls from middle-class families, have a distorted body image. They perceive themselves as fat if they have any flesh on their bones or deviate from their idealized body image (Rieger et al., 2001). They intensely fear being fat and relentlessly pursue thinness. The anorexic person's refusal to eat eventually brings on emaciation and malnutrition (which may bring about a further distortion of body image). Victims may sustain permanent damage to their heart muscle tissue, sometimes dying as a result.

Many therapists believe that anorexia nervosa has strictly psychological origins. They cite poor mother–daughter relationships, excessively protective parents, other negative family interactions, and efforts to escape self-awareness as the main causes, as well as prejudice against the obese. Others are exploring possible physiological

Androgyny

Developing a gender identity in adolescence has always been part of the transition to adulthood. Today, this task is more complicated. In earlier decades of this century, most educated American women were expected to pursue marriage and homemaking, which were considered full-time jobs. Today, women's plans often include a career outside the home, which may be interrupted for child rearing; men's plans often include active involvement with raising their children. In recent years, many women and men have developed new attitudes about sex roles—attitudes that encourage all people to cultivate both traditionally masculine and traditionally feminine traits. They have adopted behaviors that are **androgynous**—that represent a blend of stereotypically male and stereotypically female characteristics. Androgynous men and women may fix cars, pursue careers, do housework, and help care for children; they can be both assertive and emotionally sensitive. More than ever before, men today disparage violent toughness as part of the masculine role (Fischer & Good, 1998). Several studies have found that people who rate high in androgynous characteristics tend to feel more fulfilled and more competent when dealing with social and personal issues (Bem, 1993; Stake, 1997). Androgynous behaviors are being seen worldwide with specific cultural adaptations because some societies are more polarized than others about certain gendered behaviors (Sugihara & Katsurada, 2000).

Anorexia nervosa
An eating disorder characterized by an obstinate and willful refusal to eat, a distorted body image, and an intense fear of being fat.

Androgynous
Having both stereotypically male and stereotypically female characteristics.

contributions to the disorder (Monteleone et al., 2001; Walsh & Devlin, 1998), including the many changes taking place at puberty that might influence its emergence. Some psychologists believe that people with eating disorders may lack a hormone that is thought to induce a feeling of fullness after a meal.

Individuals with anorexia nervosa need a structured setting, and therapists often hospitalize them to help them regain weight. To ensure that the setting is reinforcing, hospital staff members are always present at meals. Individual and family therapy is provided. Patients are encouraged to eat and are rewarded for consuming specified quantities of food. Generally, psychotherapy is also necessary to help people with anorexia attain a healthy self-image. Even with treatment, however, as many as 50% suffer relapses within a year.

Bulimia nervosa is an eating disorder characterized by repeated episodes of binge eating followed by purging. It tends to occur in women of normal weight with no history of anorexia nervosa. The binge eating (which the person recognizes as being abnormal) is accompanied by a fear of not being able to stop. Individuals who engage in binge eating become fearful of gaining weight; they become preoccupied with how others see them (Striegel-Moore & Cachelin, 1999). Therefore, they often purge themselves of unwanted calories, mostly through vomiting and the use of laxatives and diuretics. Other methods include compulsive exercising and use of weight-reduction drugs. The medical complications of bulimia are serious. They include cardiovascular and gastrointestinal problems, menstrual irregularities, blood and hormone dysfunctions, muscular and skeletal problems, and sharp swings in mood and personality.

Men and women are affected by eating disorders in similar ways (Olivardia et al., 1995), but the ratio of female to male bulimics is 10 to 1. Researchers theorize that women believe, more readily than men, that fat is ugly and thin is beautiful. Women of higher socioeconomic classes are at greater risk of becoming bulimic, as are professionals whose weight is directly related to career achievement, such as dancers, athletes, and models. Whether dieting plays a role in bulimia is unclear because many bulimics don't regularly engage in dieting (Lowe, Gleaves, & Murphy-Eberenz, 1998). Women with bulimia have lower self-esteem than women who eat normally, and they may have experienced some kind of clinical depression in the past. Alcohol dependency and a family history of bulimia are sometimes reported (Kozyk, Touyz, & Beumont, 1998). Some bulimics may become so wrapped up in food-related behaviors that they avoid contact with other people.

Bulimia may have a biological basis, taking the form of an imbalance of neurotransmitters, yet most researchers have focused on psychological explanations. Some people with bulimia may eat as a means of managing their mood, regulating tension, and escaping from self-awareness (Ball & Lee, 2000). After binges, however, they feel guilty. To lessen their guilt and avoid the potential consequence of eating (gaining weight), they purge themselves. Researchers believe the purges reduce post-binge guilt feelings. The problems of bulimia may not disappear completely when treated; one study found that after not being considered bulimic for an entire decade, women who had once been so diagnosed were much thinner than others in their communities (Sullivan et al., 1998).

Real Men and Women

In the 1990s there was—and continues to be today—a growing awareness of the ways boys and girls and teenagers are raised. Best-selling books such as *Reviving Ophelia* (1994) by Mary Pipher, *Raising Cain* (1999) by Dan Kindlon, Michael Thompson and Teresa Barker, and *Real Boys* (1998) by William Pollack have argued that we have given girls and boys mixed messages that ask them to be all things to all people—strong, sensitive, and competent and docile, independent, and vulnerable. We are asking them to develop the abilities all at the same time, but often expressing only some of them—the ones that we consider gender appropriate (Faludi, 1999). This creates confusion.

Boys are urged to mask their emotional vulnerability as early as possible. The code for boys, and then men, is to cut themselves off from feelings that society teaches are unacceptable and wear a mask of cheerfulness and resiliency—ultimately the goal is to be master of their universe. Pollack (1998) calls it the "Boy Code" and argues that it puts boys, teens, and later men into emotional straitjackets.

Bulimia nervosa
An eating disorder characterized by repeated episodes of binge eating (and a fear of not being able to stop eating) followed by purging.

Girls, teens, and women are similarly tied but with a different set of knots. Girls today have more trouble than ever before; while women have fully entered the work force, feminism is still considered a pejorative term to most people; women work for lower wages and face corporate glass ceilings. And we still live in a society that is *gendered*—that is, jobs, roles, and responsibilities have male or female connotations (nurses are women, firefighters are men, for example). Pipher (1994) notes that the protected era that we once called adolescence has grown shorter, and the suffering that girls experience has grown stronger and is evident daily in eating disorders and depression. Today, adolescent girls are at greater risk for psychological disorders than ever before, are pressured to excel and be tough—be as good as the boys—and at the same time convey a waiflike image of feminine sexuality. The problem is that waiflike, sexual, strong, independent, and competent all don't usually go together—and certainly not for all girls, teenagers, and women.

Adolescent boys and girls are trapped. "By century's end," Faludi (1999, p. 451) writes, "the dictates of a consumer and media culture had trapped both men and women in a world in which top billing mattered more than building, in which representation trumped production, in which appearances were what counted." In Faludi's view, it's no longer enough just to be a traditional man who works hard, raises a family, and leads a good life. Today men, like women, have developed a hunger for stardom, for the role of the "leading" man. The dilemma men face, Faludi argues, is not so different from the forces straitjacketing women: the culture has taken from them much of their depth and relegated them to the status of ornaments.

In the end, men and women are being held to a near impossible standard of manhood or womanhood. The challenge for parents, educators, and psychologists is to allow children and teenagers to blossom fully, to emerge as adults unhindered by destructive emotional straitjackets of exaggerated gender stereotyping. Real boys and girls, real men and women all need to be able to be strong, independent, happy, sad, lonely, and unhappy. They have to be allowed to express their humanity openly as individuals, not in a highly gendered, emotionally constricted context.

Who Are My Friends?

When you like someone who likes you, there is a good chance that you call yourselves friends. Although some people have many friends and others have few, most people, at one time or another, find someone with whom they share values, ideas, and thoughts. At its simplest, a friendship is a close emotional tie between two peers (Kerns, 1998). Most teenagers report having between three and five good friends. As much as 29% of adolescents' waking hours are spent with friends; among adults, for a whole range of reasons, the time spent interacting with friends drops to 7%. If you had lots of friends as a child, you are more likely to have lots of them as an adult, even if you don't spend a great deal of time with each one of them.

According to Hartup and Stevens (1997), there are some important developmental consequences of having or not having friends. Children and adolescents who have friends tend to be more socially competent than those who do not. Having friends provides someone to confide in, to be afraid with, and to grow with, and friendship sets the stage for intimacy with adults. Elementary school children tend to form same-gender friendships; cross-gender friendships are rare. Adolescent friendships can contribute to sharing and intimacy, although they can also be filled with conflict over social or political issues, drugs, gangs, and sexual behavior—when friendships fall apart, a child's self-confidence is undermined (Keefe & Berndt, 1996).

Among adults, friendships between women differ from those between men; and both differ from a friendship between a man and a woman. In Western cultures, expectations for specific gender-based behaviors often control male–female interactions in friendship. Women talk more about family, personal matters, and doubts and fears than men do; men talk more about sports and work than do women. Women in general find friendships more satisfying than men do (Bleske & Buss, 2000); nevertheless, men experience and seek intimacy and support in friendships (Botschner, 1996).

Many researchers report that intimacy and shared values are the key variables that define a friendship. Ideally, close friends participate as equals, enjoy each other's company, have mutual trust, provide mutual assistance, accept each other as they are, respect each other's judgment, feel free to be themselves with each other, understand each other in fundamental ways, and are intimate and share confidences (Bender, 1999).

From a developmental point of view, friends are an important resource from childhood through old age, both cognitively and emotionally (Hartup & Stevens, 1997). But not all friendships are alike, and the meaning of a friendship is often buried below the surface conversation of shopping, school, or jobs.

■ **FRIENDS, THEN LOVERS: EVOLUTIONARY APPROACHES.** We may seek friends who share interests; we may also be shaped heavily by popular culture. But evolutionary psychologists assert that our current behavior—including our self-esteem—is shaped through the process of natural selection and a series of adaptations that are ultimately coded in the genome. For example, those whom we seek out as mates and have children with is, at least in part, under evolutionary control—or so say evolutionary psychologists. They assert that those whom we are sexually drawn to is an evolved adaptation. From their view, men seek out as many women as they can to mate with, especially women who are fertile—men are polygamous (Hinsz, Matz, & Patience, 2001). Women have evolved to seek out a man who can provide status, wealth, and security for them and their offspring; accordingly, they will be far more selective with whom they mate, tending to be monogamous. Thus, our genetic code, at its present state of evolution, makes men far more sexually promiscuous than women. The key from an evolutionary perspective is that this occurs due to natural selection.

Critics of evolutionary approaches are quick to point out that evolutionary psychology is nondevelopmental in its nature—it does not track changes in individuals over time, nor does it explain how evolution may express itself differently in different environments (think city living versus agrarian societies). In addition, our environment has grown more complex than it has ever been before, and evolution may be able to exert only so much of an influence; this is reflected in the sexual behavior of adolescents.

Sexual Behavior During Adolescence

Sex. It fascinates and it captivates. It is biological and it is cultural. It happens a lot for some and it happens very little for others. It is important to recognize and appreciate the fact that girls and women and boys and men tend to view sex and sexual behavior somewhat differently. For example, you will get many different answers if you ask,

■ *Most American adolescents view sexual intimacy as an important and normal part of growing up.*

- What constitutes sex?
- Is oral sex, sex?
- How many partners do you want to have in a lifetime?
- How often do you have sex?

Roy Baumeister and Dianne Tice (2001) point out that men tend to estimate and women tend to count; the former leads to high numbers of partners and encounters, the latter, low numbers. Any careful reading of the facts shows discrepancies and so data about human sexual behaviors—especially frequency data—must be viewed with careful analysis and critical thinking.

What changes in adolescent sexual behavior have occurred? American adolescents view sexual intimacy as an important and normal part of growing up; premarital

Be an *Active* learner

REVIEW

- How do the imaginary audience and the personal fable affect adolescent behaviors? pp. 115–116
- What is gender-schema theory? p. 121
- Are today's teenagers being held to a near impossible standard of manhood or womanhood? How? pp. 123–124
- Broadly characterize sexual behavior in adolescence. 124–126

THINK CRITICALLY

- Why do you think that teenagers have arguments with parents? Are such arguments necessary? productive?
- How do you think an increase in androgyny might affect adolescent friendships? How might it change the nature of courting? of marriage?
- If, as some researchers claim, anorexia has a physiological basis, why do you think it is less prevalent in other cultures?

APPLY PSYCHOLOGY

- As an adult who has gone through adolescence, is your personality pretty much the same, or have you gone through major changes? Explain your answer.
- Who do you think was more influential in your life, parents or peers? Were peers more influential in some areas than others?

heterosexual activity has become increasingly common among adolescents. Adolescents are having sexual experiences at younger ages than in previous decades, in part because knowledge and use of contraception are becoming more widespread, thus reducing the fear of pregnancy and diseases like AIDS. Today, adolescents consider sexual behavior normal in an intimate relationship (Graber, Britto, & Brooks-Gunn, 1999). Fifty-five percent of male teenagers have intercourse by age 18, and the same percentage of White female adolescents do so by just a year later, age 19 (Gates & Sonenstein, 2000). Among African Americans, 60% of boys have intercourse by age 16, and 60% of girls do so by age 18. There are great individual differences with regard to age at first intercourse and the subsequent frequency of intercourse. It is not uncommon for a teenager to have first intercourse at age 14 or 15 and then not to have sexual relations again for a year or two (Coley, Chase-Lansdale, & Lindsay, 1998; Laumann & Mebad, 2001).

More acceptant attitudes about adolescent sexual behavior have brought about increased awareness of the problems of teenage pregnancy. Each year in the United States, more than 500,000 unmarried teenage girls become pregnant. Adolescent pregnancy rates vary substantially with ethnicity; for example, Whites have substantially lower rates than do Latinos/Latinas or African Americans (Coley & Chase-Lansdale, 1998). The more engaged students are with schooling, the less likely they are to become pregnant (Manlove, 1998). The consequences of child bearing for teenage mothers are serious. Teenage mothers are more likely to smoke and to have low-birthweight infants; they are also less likely to receive timely prenatal care. Furthermore, a young woman's chances of obtaining education and employment become more limited if she becomes a mother, and many young mothers are forced to rely on public assistance. Most studies indicate that women who bear children early in their lives will not achieve economic equality with women who postpone parenthood until they are adults (Furstenberg & Hughes, 1995); adolescent pregnancy is also associated with abuse of alcohol and other drugs and with depression (Martin, Hill, & Welsh, 1998).

Current studies show that, despite the threat of AIDS, high school and college students still engage in regular sexual activity, often without appropriate protection. Comprehensive school-based health care programs that emphasize the complete picture of sexuality (attitudes, contraception, motivation, and behavior) reduce the risks of pregnancy in teenagers. But, for many parents and teenagers, such programs are controversial.

Adulthood: Years of Stability and Change

The life experience of an American adult today is also different from that of adults in other cultures. Americans have some things in common with people from other Western cultures, but very few with people in third world countries. These cultural differences have not been widely studied. In addition, until the 1970s, developmental psychologists in the United States concentrated largely on White middle-class infants and children.

Psychologists are now focusing on development across cultures and throughout the life span. They are recognizing that a person encounters new challenges in every stage of life. Researchers study adult development by looking at the factors

Building Table 4.1

Major Changes in Important Domains of Adult Functioning

Age	Physical Change	Cognitive Change	Work Roles	Personal Development	Major Tasks
Young adulthood, ages 18–25	Peak functioning in most physical skills	Cognitive skills high on most measures	Choice of career, which may involve several job changes	Conformity; task of establishing intimacy	Separate from family; form partnership; begin family; find job; create individual life pattern
Early adulthood, ages 25–40	Good physical functioning in most areas; health habits during this time establish later risks	Peak period of cognitive skill on most measures	Rising work satisfaction; major emphasis on career or work success; most career progress steps made	Task of passing on skills, knowledge, love (generativity)	Rear family; establish personal work pattern and strive for success
Middle adulthood, ages 40–65	Beginning signs of physical decline in some areas (strength, elasticity of tissues, height, cardiovascular function)	Some signs of loss of cognitive skill on timed, unexercised skills	Career reaches plateau, but higher work satisfaction	Increase in self-confidence, openness	Launch family; redefine life goals; redefine self outside of family and work roles; care for aging parents

that contribute to stability or change, to a sense of accomplishment or feelings of despair, and to physical well-being or diminished functioning. Think about the years after retirement, which can be a time of stability—bringing feelings of completion and well-being, or a difficult, unhappy time—full of physical and emotional troubles. Researchers also examine the differences between men and women, with emphasis on the unique experiences of women in American culture. Research studies and theories are recognizing and focusing on cultural diversity. And psychologists are now aware that a person's career is also a defining characteristic of adulthood. Adults spend an enormous amount of time and energy on their careers, and this aspect of adulthood has been examined relatively little by psychologists.

The end of the story is relatively good: as people age from adolescence to adulthood, and ultimately to old age, they become psychologically healthier (Carstensen & Charles, 1998; Jones & Meredith, 2000). Building Table 4.1 summarizes the major changes in important functional domains during young, early, and middle adulthood.

Physical Changes

One hundred years ago, only about half of all Americans who reached age 20 lived beyond age 65. Today, a higher percent of people live well into their 70s and beyond, but psychologists know relatively little about those middle years from 20 to 70. Psychologists study childhood physical development extensively but in comparison pay little attention to adult physical development. Although physical development in adulthood is slower, less dramatic, and generally less visible than that in childhood and adolescence, it does occur.

■ **FITNESS CHANGES.** Most of the adult years are characterized by health and fitness; the leading cause of death, for example, for people ages 25–44 is accidental

psychology *in action*

The Legacy of Divorce

Divorce is tough on everybody—plain and simple. It is difficult on the adults and on the children. The rate varies in every state and community, and it varies within ethnic groups, but in general the wake of divorce is often unhappiness, sometimes poverty, and an emotional impact on the children that can last well into adulthood.

We have long thought that divorce—the dissolution of a marriage—is supposed to end unhappiness between two adults and thus create a better home environment for adults and children; its also supposed to be tough for the first few years then gradually improve. However, Judith Wallerstein and her colleagues Julia Lewis and Sandra Blakeslee (2000) have studied a group of 131 children of divorce, tracing them through a 25-year history. They argue that the idea of better home lives and ultimately happy kids is a myth. Wallerstein asserts that children in postdivorce families are unhappy, more aggressive, and at high risk for a variety of problems. Not only that, but the impact of divorce is long-lasting—postdivorce adjustment takes a long time, and the impact of divorce lasts well into adulthood.

Adult children of divorce told Wallerstein and her colleagues that the hardest part for them was not the breakup, with all of its anger and court proceedings, but rather fear and anxiety concerning the future. It initiated worries about finances, how and with whom free time and holidays will be spent, and most of all, worry about trust and love. Will Mom or Dad's new spouse be caring? As a teen or adult, can you find a man or a woman who will be faithful and loving? Or will your relationship replicate your parents'? These children of divorce envied intact families.

These results are not unknown to adults; so many people have gone through divorce that its legacy is known. But the data show that our greater freedom through divorce is a two-edged sword, especially for the children—the cost for them is lifelong uneasiness with family where relationships are considered fragile and perhaps unreliable.

Wallerstein concludes that the impact of divorce on children is greatest in their later adulthood. In her book, entitled *The Unexpected Legacy of Divorce,* she makes a compelling argument. Further research on her conclusions will follow, but it is important to realize that her predictions are not the same for all families, all children, and all elements of society. For example, in a study of African American and European American mothers following divorce, well-being was affected by income levels and social support—the stronger the social support network, the faster and better did the moms cope with the transition (McKelvey & McKenry, 2000). Furthermore, well-respected researcher E. Mavis Hetherington (Hetherington & Kelly, 2002) argues that the effects of divorce are not so devastating and that children of divorce ultimately function well. Hetherington does not claim divorce does not take its toll, but rather that the havoc and later effects of divorce are often overstated and affect only 25% of children. While Wallerstein paints a sobering picture, psychologists are hard at work creating parenting workshops and postdivorce counseling workshops and helping educate parents and their children about the possibilities and strategies for happiness and success. They are also counseling couples and families to help people navigate marriage with all of its struggles and complexities. It is important to recognize that not all people follow the same paths in divorce and some find critical moments to turn the difficulties of divorce into opportunities for their children. Good, clear parenting can buffer children from negative effects of divorce (Hetherington & Kelly, 2002)

injury—for example, from motor vehicle crashes. Psychologists often speak of *fitness* as involving both a psychological and a physical sense of well-being. Physically, human beings are at their peak of agility, speed, and strength between ages 18 and 30. From 30 to 40, there is some loss of agility and speed. And between 40 and 60, even greater losses occur (Merrill & Verbrugge, 1999). In general, strength, muscle tone, and overall fitness deteriorate gradually from age 30 on. People become more susceptible to disease because their immune systems lose efficiency and thus the ability to fight disease. Respiratory, circulatory, and blood pressure problems are more apparent; lung capacity and physical strength are significantly reduced. Decreases in bone mass and strength occur, especially in women after menopause; the resulting condition is called *osteoporosis.*

■ **SENSORY CHANGES.** In early adulthood, most sensory abilities remain fairly stable. As the years pass, however, adults must contend with almost inevitable sensory losses. Reaction time slows. Vision, hearing, taste, and smell require a higher level of stimulation than they did at a younger age. Older people, for example, usually are unable to make fine visual discriminations without the aid of glasses, have limited capacity to adapt to darkness, and are at greater risk for glaucoma, cataracts, and retinal detachment. Older adults often have some degree of hearing loss, especially in the high-frequency ranges. By age 65, many people can no longer hear very high-frequency sounds, and some are unable to hear ordinary speech. Hearing loss is greater for men than for women.

Adults often experience some degree of hearing and visual loss as they age.

SEXUAL CHANGES. In adults of both sexes, advancing years bring changes in sexual behavior and desire as well as physical changes related to sexuality. For example, in the child-rearing years, women's and men's sexual desires are sometimes moderated by the stresses of raising a family and juggling a work schedule. Women often experience an increase in sexual desire in their 30s and 40s, but men achieve erections less rapidly at that age. For women, midlife changes in hormones lead to the cessation of ovulation and menstruation at about the ages of 50–52, a process known as menopause. Menopause is generally seen as a transition, after which women no longer have to deal with birth control issues; some women, however, perceive it as the beginning of old age and an end to youthful femininity (Avis, 1999). At about the same age, men's testosterone levels decrease, their ejaculations become weaker and briefer, and their desire for sexual intercourse typically decreases from adolescent levels (Rowland et al., 1993). Nevertheless, older people continue to engage in sexual activities and to find them enjoyable, and significant percentages find their sexual activities more satisfying than when they were younger (National Council on Aging, 1998). According to the National Council on Aging, sex remains a significant part of life for many older Americans. Nearly half of all Americans age 60 or older engage in sexual activity at least once a month. If older people are not active sexually, it is usually because they lack a partner or have a disabling medical condition. As with their younger counterparts, however, there is considerable variation from person to person.

THEORIES OF AGING. Although the average life span has been lengthening, psychologists and physicians have been examining the behavior and physiological changes that accompany aging only since the early 1970s. Three basic types of theories—based on heredity, external factors, and physiology—have been developed to explain aging. Although each emphasizes a different cause for aging, most likely aging results from a combination of all three.

Genes determine much of a person's physical makeup; thus, it is probable that *heredity*, to some extent, determines how a person ages and how long he or she will live. There is much evidence to support this claim. For example, long-lived parents tend to have long-lived offspring. However, researchers still do not know exactly *how* heredity exerts its influence on the aging process; they only know that there are multiple mechanisms of aging, some of them hereditary (Jazwinski, 1996).

One promising area of study has been apoptosis, the process by which cells kill themselves. Normal human cells have a limited capacity to proliferate, which is most likely mediated by telomeres. *Telomeres* are end segments of DNA responsible for aging of the cell (Bodnar et al., 1998). After a certain finite number of cell divisions, time on the biological clock runs out; the cells "age" and stop dividing. The research shows that human cells grow older each time they divide because their telomeres shorten; in a way they are "chewed up" just a bit with each successive cell division. If a chromosome does not have telomeres of the proper length, the cell will not divide. This finding is still somewhat controversial but holds promise for an explanation of aging.

External, or lifestyle, factors also affect how long a person will live. For example, people who live on farms live longer than those in cities; normal-weight people live longer than overweight people; and people who do not smoke cigarettes, who are not constantly tense, who wear seatbelts, and who are not exposed to disease or radiation live longer than others. Because these data on external factors are often obtained from correlational studies, cause-and-effect statements cannot be based on them; it is reasonable to assume, however, that external factors such as disease, smoking, and obesity affect a person's life span.

Several theories use *physiological explanations* to account for aging. Because a person's physiological processes depend on both hereditary and environmental factors, these theories rely on both concepts. The *wear-and-tear theory* of aging claims that the human organism simply wears out from overuse, like a machine (Hayflick, 1996); this idea has intuitive appeal but little research support. What little research does exist focuses on how the body uses its energy stores and indicates that the more active a life a person lives, the less efficient may be the body's use of energy and the faster the aging process (Levine & Stadtman, 1992). A related theory, the *homeostatic theory,* suggests that the body's ability to adjust to stress and other variations in internal conditions decreases with age. For example, as the ability to maintain a constant body temperature decreases, cellular and tissue damage occurs, and aging results. Similarly, when the body can no longer control the use of sugar through the output of insulin, signs of aging appear. On the other hand, aging may be the *cause* of deviations from homeostasis, rather than the result.

It is also important to distinguish between primary and secondary aging. *Primary aging* is the normal, inevitable change that occurs in every human being and is irreversible and progressive. Such aging happens despite good health, and it can make a person more vulnerable to American society's fast-paced and sometimes stressful lifestyle. *Secondary aging* is aging that is due to extrinsic factors such as disease, environmental pollution, and smoking. Lack of good nutrition is a secondary aging factor that is a principal cause of poor health and aging among the lower-income elderly in the United States.

Cognitive Changes

Changes in intellectual functioning that occur with age are pretty small. Up to the age of 65, there is little decline in learning or memory; motivation, interest, and recent educational experience (or lack of it) are more important than age with regard to a person's ability to master complex knowledge (Willis & Schaie, 1999). Although many people believe that declines in intellectual functioning are drastic and universal, they are not. Researchers do agree that certain cognitive abilities, especially in mathematics and memory functions, begin to deteriorate in many people after age 60.

Although most research indicates that cognitive abilities and memory functions typically decrease with advancing age (Anstey et al., 2001), many of the changes are of little importance for day-to-day functioning (Meinz & Salthouse, 1998; Salthouse, 1999; Schaie, 2000). For example, overall vocabulary decreases only slightly. Moreover, some of the changes observed in laboratory tasks (for example, reaction-time tasks) are small and can be forestalled or reversed through cognitive interventions. Yet there is no doubt that the brain encodes information differently in the young than in the old.

Researchers generally acknowledge that some age-related decrements do occur, especially after age 65 (e.g., Hambrick, Salthouse, & Meinz, 1999; Salthouse, 2000; Sharit & Czajia, 1999); however, such effects are often less apparent in cognitively active individuals. Many researchers suggest a "use it and you are less likely to lose it" approach (Hultsch et al., 1999; Kliegel et al., 2001). When deficits do occur, older individuals can compensate to optimize their performance. The truth is that most Americans are aging well and that with appropriate health care and social support systems, older individuals can do just fine, especially in everyday situations.

Social Changes

Social changes in adulthood follow a fairly predictable order. Younger adults focus on the issues of developing a sense of identity, a career direction, an intimate relationship, and often parenthood. Middle-age adults focus on caregiving of children and older parents, role changes, and planning for retirement. Older adults must address changing roles, retirement, loss of friends or spouse, changing friendships and relationships, physical change, caregiving, and eventual death.

Some people—perhaps the more poetic—think of life as a journey along a road from birth to death. The concept of a journey recalls Erik Erikson's stage theory, in which people move through a series of stages and must resolve a different dilemma in each stage in order to develop a healthy identity (see Chapter 3, pp. 105–106).

■ **ERIKSON REVISITED.** An important aspect of Erikson's stage theory is that people progress through well-defined stages from the beginning of life to the end, at each stage attempting to solve a particular dilemma. People move toward greater maturity as they pass from stage to stage. Stages 1–4 focus on childhood. Let's now consider the stages that begin with adolescence.

Erikson's stage 5, *identity versus role confusion,* marks the end of childhood and the beginning of adolescence. According to Erikson, the growth and turmoil of adolescence create an "identity crisis." The major task for adolescents is to resolve that crisis successfully by forming an *identity*—a sense of who they are, where they perceive themselves to be going, and what their place is in the world. Adolescents have to form a multifaceted identity that includes vocational choices, religious beliefs, gender roles, sexual behaviors, and ethnic customs. The task is quite daunting, which is one reason why adolescence is such a critical stage of development. From Erikson's view, the failure to form an identity leaves the adolescent confused about adult roles and unable to cope with the demands of adulthood, including the development of mature relationships with members of the opposite sex (Erikson, 1963, 1968). The special problems of adolescence—which sometimes include rebellion, suicidal feelings, and drug abuse—must also be dealt with at this stage and are tied up with identity (Belgrave, Brome, & Hampton, 2000).

■ *In Erickson's "intimacy versus isolation" stage, young adults begin to relate emotionally to others and commit to a lasting relationship.*

Stage 6 (young adulthood) *involves intimacy versus isolation.* Young adults begin to select other people with whom they can form intimate, caring relationships. Ideally, they learn to relate emotionally to others and commit to a lasting relationship; the alternative is to become isolated.

In stage 7 (middle adulthood), *generativity versus stagnation,* people become more aware of their mortality and develop a concern for future generations. They now hope to convey information, love, and security to the next generation, particularly

TABLE 4.1

Erikson's Last Four Stages of Psychosocial Development

Stage	Approximate Age	Important Event	Description
5. Identity versus role confusion	Adolescence	Peer relationships	The teenager must achieve a sense of identity that encompasses occupation, gender roles, sexual behavior, and religion.
6. Intimacy versus isolation	Young adulthood	Love relationships	The young adult must develop intimate relationships or suffer feelings of isolation.
7. Generativity versus stagnation	Middle adulthood	Parenting and work	Each adult must find some way to contribute to and support the next generation.
8. Ego integrity versus despair	Late adulthood	Reflection on and acceptance of one's life	Ideally, the person arrives at a sense of acceptance of oneself as one is and a sense of fulfillment.

their own children. They do so through caring acts that foster growth such as career mentoring (Bradley & Marcia, 1998). As adults, they try to influence their family and the world; otherwise, they stagnate and become self-absorbed. Generativity is, of course, not limited to middle adulthood. Research shows that people in early adulthood also experience it (Stewart & Vanderwater, 1998).

In stage 8 (late adulthood), *ego integrity versus despair,* people conduct a life review and assess whether their existence is meaningful, happy, and cohesive or wasteful and unproductive. Many individuals never arrive at stage 8, and some who do are filled with regrets and a feeling that time is too short. Those who successfully resolve the conflict inherent in this stage feel fulfilled, with a sense that they understand, at least partly, what life is about.

Table 4.1 summarizes the last four stages of Erikson's theory.

■ **LEVINSON'S LIFE STRUCTURES.** Another noted theorist, Daniel Levinson, has devised a different stage theory of adult development. He agrees that people go through stages and that they have similar experiences at key points in their lives. Unlike Erikson, however, Levinson does not see life as a journey toward some specific goal such as ego integrity. Rather, he believes that a theory of development should lay out the eras during which individuals work out various developmental tasks. These tasks may not be the same for all individuals and do not lead to a specific end.

Levinson (1978) suggests that as people grow older, they adapt to the demands and tasks of life. He describes four basic eras in the adult life cycle, each with distinctive qualities and different problems, tasks, and situations. The four eras outlined by Levinson are adolescence, early adulthood, middle adulthood, and late adulthood.

During *adolescence* (ages 4–17), young people enter the adult world but are still immature and vulnerable. During *early adulthood* (ages 18–45), they make their first major life choices regarding family, occupation, and style of living. The much-discussed midlife crisis occurs at the end of early adulthood. In fact, Levinson calls particular attention to it, asserting that most adults experience such a crisis in their early 40s. During this time, people often realize that their lives are half over—that if they are to change their lives, they must do so now. (This era is similar to Erikson's stage of generativity versus stagnation.) The term *midlife crisis* may be a misnomer. Levinson himself (1980) suggests that the event should more properly be called a *midlife transition*—a change that may be more difficult for some individuals than others. The word *transition* suggests that a person has reached a time in life when old ways of coping are giving way to new ones and old tasks have been accomplished. A person in transition faces new challenges and responsibilities, which often require reassessment, reappraisal, and the development of new skills. A *crisis,* in contrast, occurs when old ways of coping become ineffective and a person is helpless—not knowing what to do and needing new, radically different coping strategies. Crises are often perceived as painful turning points in people's lives. Not everyone experiences the infamous midlife crisis, but most people pass through at least one midlife transition (Rosenberg, Rosenberg, & Farrell, 1999).

Middle adulthood spans the years from 46 to 65. Adults who have gone through a midlife crisis learn to live with the decisions they made during early adulthood. Career and family are usually well established. People experience either a sense of satisfaction, self-worth, and accomplishment or a sense that much of their life has been wasted. Levinson's fourth and final stage, *late adulthood,* covers the years from age 65 on. During retirement, many people relax and enjoy the fruits of their labors. Children, grandchildren, and even great-grandchildren can become the focus of an older person's life.

Levinson's stage theory has a bit more of a rigid timetable than does Erikson's, and it focuses on developmental tasks, or themes. Levinson realizes that not all adults succeed in every era, at every task, or achieve feelings of independence. Who does and under what conditions are not clear. Levinson's theory is an alternative to Erikson's, but both suffer from being hard to evaluate experimentally and difficult to apply in making predictions about future behavior. A major shortcoming is that the theory was based on information gathered from a small sample of middle-class men between the ages of 35 and 45. Levinson developed his theory by studying 40 men in detail over several years. He interviewed the men weekly for several months and again after 2 years. Their wives were interviewed, and extensive biographical data were collected. Levinson's original study did not consider women, which is a limitation of his theory.

student voices

Summer Mansur
Oklahoma Christian University

After college I plan to get a master's in social work and then become licensed for children's therapy. Not only will I get to maximize my talents of communication and children, I can still be a mother, which is a top priority for me. Having children will only make me a more experienced counselor. With my own practice, I can balance home and work very well.

GENDER DIFFERENCES IN ADULT STAGES. Women follow life stages similar to those of men. But as children, women are taught different values, goals, and approaches to life, which are often reflected later in their choice of vocations, hobbies, and intellectual pursuits. Women have traditionally sought different careers, although this is changing. In the field of law, for example, women now comprise more than half of all law school students and about 40% of medical students. However, female attorneys often choose careers that do not follow the traditional associate–partnership ladder chosen by men. Levinson, in a follow-up book, *The Seasons of a Woman's Life* (1996), points out the complexities of women's lives based on his interviews with a small sample of women. According to Levinson, women must deal with contradictory roles and responsibilities, which make their lives more complex and difficult to understand than men's. Career women and homemakers go through the same sequence of stages, but these stages differ in their details.

Some women tend to experience transitions and life events at later ages and in less orderly sequences than men do. In addition, women experience events such as midlife transitions differently than men; whereas some men approach a midlife crisis at age 40 as a last chance to hold on to their youth, many women see it as a time to reassess, refocus, and revitalize their creative energies (Apter, 1995; Levinson, 1996). Stewart and Ostrove (1998) suggest that midlife brings women an increased sense of personal identity, personal efficacy, and capacity for generativity—women of this age are doing well and feeling both vigorous and well adjusted.

Women still face discrimination in the workplace, and society continues to be ambivalent in its expectations for women. They still have the primary burden of family responsibilities, especially child care; in the aftermath of a divorce, the woman usually gets physical custody of the children. Women often must juggle multiple roles, which can bring great satisfaction but which also places enormous burdens on

Be an *Active* learner

REVIEW

- What are the major sensory, physical, cognitive, and social changes that occur during adulthood? pp. 127–131
- In each of Erikson's eight stages, people face dilemmas. What are the consequences of a poor outcome at any one stage? pp. 131–132
- Why is the term *midlife crisis* a misnomer? pp. 132–133
- Why do some women experience transitions and life events at later ages and in less orderly sequences than men do? p. 133

THINK CRITICALLY

- What might be the implications of the finding that women follow a different developmental progression than do men?
- With so many people divorcing, what interventions might psychologists implement on a societal level to help decrease the divorce rate?
- Of how much importance are chance encounters in life? Why?

APPLY PSYCHOLOGY

- Write a brief set of hints to help parents better communicate with their teenage children; keep in mind that parents themselves are developing.
- What can individuals do as adults to help prepare themselves for retirement years? Make a list of at least five specific things that people in middle adulthood (ages 45–60) can do to get ready for growing older.

them (Kubicek, 2000; Napholz, 2000; Park & Liao, 2000). The assumption of sole child-care responsibility after divorce has sharp economic consequences that alter a woman's lifestyle, mental health, and course of life stages. Obvious life-stage differences exist for men and women—whether they are upper, middle, or lower class—but even greater differences exist *within* groups of demographically similar men or women.

CHANCE ENCOUNTERS. Life isn't always an orderly sequence of planned events that follows for men and women the way that day follows night. The reality is that many events are unplanned, chance happenings. A chance encounter may lead to an outcome that is not anticipated. It may generate new ideas, relationships, and careers; it may result in a change in direction and path of a person's life. Small events may have a big impact; a club meeting, a tropical storm "party," or a church retreat may lead to new insights, relationships, or pathways that were unpredicted, unplanned for.

Personality Development

A basic tenet of most personality theories is that, regardless of day-to-day variations, an individual's personality remains stable over time. That is, despite deviations from normal patterns of development, the way a person copes with life tends to remain fairly consistent throughout her or his lifetime. But personality may also be sensitive to the unique experiences of the individual, especially during the adult years. The adult years are filled with great personal challenges and opportunities and therefore require people to be innovative, flexible, and adaptive. Positive changes during adulthood—the development of a sense of generativity, the fulfillment of yearnings for love and respect—usually depend on some degree of success during earlier life stages. Adults who continue to have an especially narrow outlook are less likely to experience personality growth in later life.

Women have undergone special scrutiny since the early 1970s. As we have seen, researchers now recognize that the profession of psychology was male-dominated through the 1950s and generated a host of personality theories based on studies of men. Not surprisingly, these failed to address women's personality and development issues. Personality researchers acknowledge that contemporary women face challenges in the work force and the home that were not conceived of three decades ago. These challenges have given rise to the "supermom" phenomenon—women trying to achieve home, family, career, and personal satisfaction, all within the same span of years. Serious research into the psychological life of women is just beginning to emerge.

Aspects of personality development are discussed in further detail in Chapter 12.

Late Adulthood: Growing Older, Growing Wiser

As we grow older, we age experientially as well as physically; that is, we gather experiences and usually expand our worldview. Nevertheless, in Western society, growing older is not always easy, especially because of the negative stereotypes associated with the aging process. Today, however, people are healthier than ever before, are approaching their later years with vigor, and often look forward to second and sometimes third careers. In general, being over age 65 brings with it new

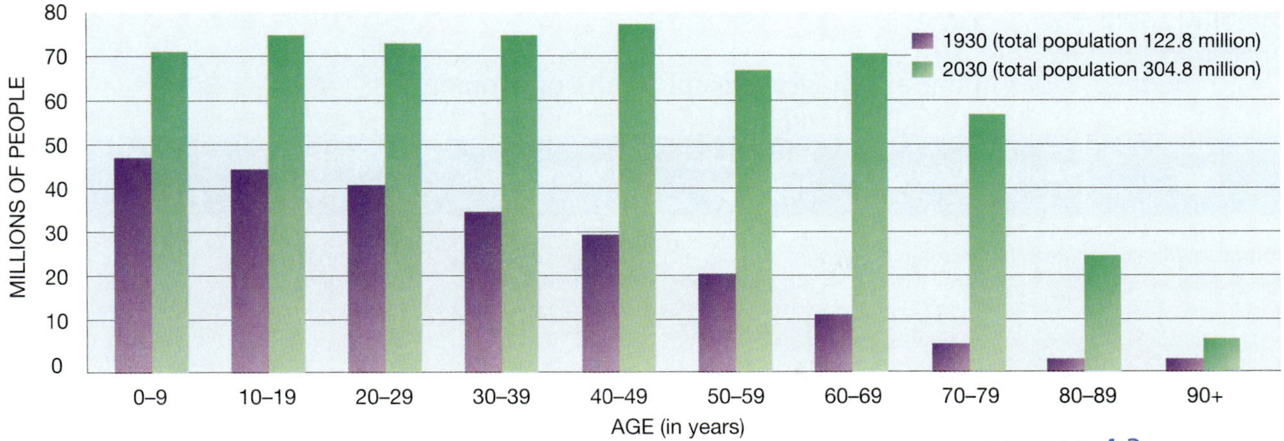

FIGURE 4.3

A Nation Growing Older

In the year 2030, the U.S. population will be distributed fairly evenly among 10-year age groups ranging from birth through 69. However, the number of elderly people in the United States will have increased sharply with the aging of the baby boomers.

developmental tasks—retirement, coping with health issues, and maintenance of an adequate standard of living.

How older people view themselves depends in part on how society treats them. Many Asian and African cultures greatly respect the elderly for their wisdom and maturity; in such societies, gray hair is a mark of distinction, not an embarrassment. In contrast, the United States is a youth-oriented society in which people spend a fortune on everything from hair dyes to facelifts to make themselves look younger. However, because the average age of Americans is increasing, how the elderly are perceived by their fellow Americans and how they perceive themselves may be changing.

Approximately 12% of the U.S. population—or more than 33 million Americans—is 65 years old or older. According to the U.S. Bureau of the Census, the proportion of elderly people is expected to increase to between 20% and 25% of the total population by 2030, and the number of Americans over age 65 will exceed 60 million by then and 78 million by 2050 (see Figure 4.3). At present, the average life expectancy at birth in the United States is about 76 years, and the oldest of the old—those over 85—are the most rapidly growing elderly age group. Life expectancy is different for men and women, however. Women live about 6 years longer than men, on average.

For many people, the years after age 60 are filled with new activities and interests. Both men and women enjoy doing things that they may have had to forgo earlier because of family commitments. Financially, two-thirds of American retirees are covered by pension plans provided by their employers, and virtually all receive Social Security checks. Socially, most older people maintain close friendships, stay in touch with family members, and are quite intact emotionally (Carstensen & Charles, 1998; Jones & Meredith, 2000). Some, however, have financial problems, and others experience loneliness and isolation because many of their friends and relatives have died or they have lost touch with their families. In the United States, there are now as many people over the age of 60 as there are under the age of 7, yet funding for programs to support the health and psychological well-being of older people is relatively limited.

■ *For many individuals, the years after age 60 are filled with new activities and interests.*

Building Table 4.2

Major Changes in Important Domains of Adult Functioning

Age	Physical Change	Cognitive Change	Work Roles	Personal Development	Major Tasks
Young adulthood, ages 18–25	Peak functioning in most physical skills	Cognitive skills high on most measures	Choice of career, which may involve several job changes	Conformity; task of establishing intimacy	Separate from family; form partnership; begin family; find job; create individual life pattern
Early adulthood, ages 25–40	Good physical functioning in most areas; health habits during this time establish later risks	Peak period of cognitive skill on most measures	Rising work satisfaction; major emphasis on career or work success; most career progress steps made	Task of passing on skills, knowledge, love (generativity)	Rear family; establish personal work pattern and strive for success
Middle adulthood, ages 40–65	Beginning signs of physical decline in some areas (strength, elasticity of tissues, height, cardiovascular function)	Some signs of loss of cognitive skill on timed, unexercised skills	Career reaches plateau, but higher work satisfaction	Increase in self-confidence, openness	Launch family; redefine life goals; redefine self outside of family and work roles; care for aging parents
Late adulthood, ages 65–75+	Significant physical decline on most measures	Small declines for virtually all adults on some skills	Retirement	Integration of ideas and experiences, perhaps self-actualization; task of ego integrity	Cope with retirement; cope with declining health; redefine life goals and sense of self

Myths, Realities, and Stereotypes

There is a widely held myth that older people are less intelligent than younger people, less able to care for themselves, inflexible, and sickly. The reality is that many elderly people are as competent and capable as they were in their earlier adulthood. They work, play golf, run marathons, socialize, and stay politically aware and active. Most older adults maintain a regular and satisfying sex life (Bretschneider & McCoy, 1988) and good mental health. Some people conduct life's activities in a frail, disorganized manner, even when young; others, although chronologically old, are youthful, vigorous, and happy (Carstensen & Charles, 1998; Jones & Meredith, 2000). How engaged the older adults become in life is a key factor; the willingness to persevere, cope, and stay involved seems central to a happy set of elderly years (Nair, 2000). Building Table 4.2 extends the overview of major changes in important functional domains through late adulthood.

Ageism
Prejudice against the elderly and the resulting discrimination against them.

■ **AGEISM.** Stereotypes about the elderly have given rise to **ageism**—prejudice against the elderly and the discrimination that follows from it. Ageism is prevalent in the job market, in which older people are not given the same opportunities as their younger coworkers, and in housing and health care. It is exceptionally prevalent in the media—on television and in newspapers and magazines—and in everyday language (Schaie, 1993). Schmidt and Boland (1986) examined everyday language to learn how people perceive older adults. They found interesting differences. For example, *elder statesman* implies that a person is experienced, wise, or perhaps conservative. However, *old statesman* might suggest that a person is past his prime, tired, or useless. The phrase *old people* may allude to positive traits of older adults—for example, being the perfect grandparent—or to negative qualities such as grouchiness or mental deficiencies. What does *old* mean?

Older people who are perceived as representing negative stereotypes are more likely to suffer discrimination than those who appear to represent more positive stereotypes. This means that an older person who appears healthy, bright, and alert is more likely to be treated with the same respect shown to younger people. By contrast, an older adult who appears less capable may not be given the same treatment. In Chapter 13, you'll see that first impressions have a potent effect on people's behavior. This seems to be particularly true for older people. Ageism can be reduced if people recognize the diversity that exists among aging populations.

■ *To date, there is no effective method of prevention, cure, or treatment for Alzheimer's disease.*

Health in Late Adulthood

Many people lead not only happy but also healthy lives well into late adulthood. Of course as people age various aches, pains, and a certain slowing of responses occur. While some older people have serious problems with arthritis, hypertension, and some orthopedic problems, many lead active, relatively healthy lifestyles. Nevertheless there are problems for some older individuals. One of those problems is dementia.

Many cognitive deficits are caused by brain disorders, sometimes termed *dementias,* which occur only in *some* older people. **Dementias** are impairments of mental functioning and global cognitive abilities in otherwise alert individuals, causing memory loss and related symptoms, and typically having a progressive nature (that is, growing worse over time). Dementia usually involves a loss of function in at least two areas of behavior, including language, memory, visual and spatial abilities, and judgment, which significantly interferes with a person's daily activities. It is important to point out that dementia is not a normal part of the aging process. Dementias are caused by abnormal disease processes and can affect younger as well as older persons. Only 0.4% of people age 60 to 65 suffer from dementias. The percentage increases to 3.6% of people age 75 to 79 and to 23.8% of those age 85 to 93 (Selkoe, 1992). Memory loss from dementia often occurs first for recent events and later for past events. Additional symptoms of dementias include loss of language skills, reduced capacity for abstract thinking, personality changes, and loss of a sense of time and place. Severe and disabling dementias affect about 1.5 million Americans. With the increasing number of elderly citizens, these statistics are on the rise.

Reversible dementias, which can be caused by malnutrition, alcoholism, or toxins (poisons), usually affect younger people. *Irreversible dementias* are of two types: multiple infarct dementia and Alzheimer's disease. *Multiple infarct dementia* is usually caused by two or more small strokes (often by ruptures of small blood vessels in the brain); it results in damage to the brain and a loss of function.

Alzheimer's disease is a chronic and progressive disorder of the brain and the most common cause of degenerative dementia in the United States. Named after Dr.

Dementia
Impairment of mental functioning and global cognitive abilities in otherwise alert individuals, causing memory loss and related symptoms and typically having a progressive nature.

Alzheimer's [ALTZ-hy-merz] disease
A chronic and progressive disorder of the brain that is the most common cause of degenerative dementia.

FIGURE 4.4

Incidence of Dementia, by Age, Caused by Alzheimer's Disease or Strokes

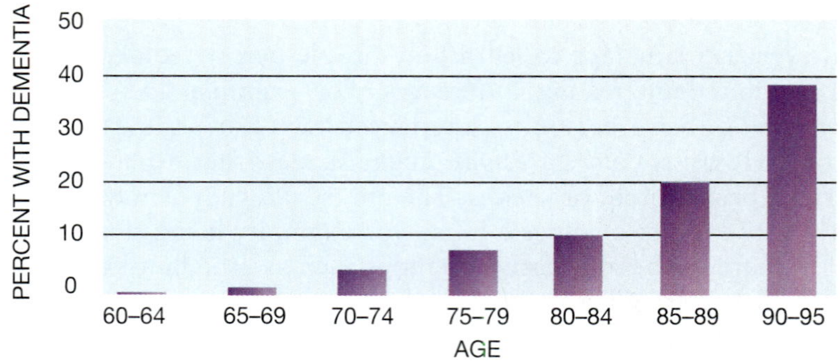

Alois Alzheimer, a German physician who first studied its symptoms, it could well be the most widespread neurological disorder of all time (see Figure 4.4).

People of all kinds can be victims of Alzheimer's disease, and all confront an unkind fate. In addition to memory loss, language deterioration, poor visual/spatial skills, and indifferent attitudes characterize this disease. It accounts for about 50% of the cases of progressive memory loss in aging individuals. (Vascular dementia and other similar disease processes account for 10%–20%, and depression for about 1%–5%. The other causes are metabolic, infectious, traumatic, inflammatory, and mass lesion disorders.)

As the population grows older, the number of cases of Alzheimer's disease increases. Currently, there are about 4 million diagnosed Alzheimer's patients in the United States and nearly 20 million worldwide; in addition, there are an untold number of undiagnosed cases. Because Alzheimer's is a degenerative disease, its progression cannot be stopped; it is irreversible and ultimately ends in death. To date, there is no fully effective method of prevention, treatment, or cure.

Scientific findings about possible causes of the disease come from a wide variety of sources, and it is generally argued that there are multiple routes to the disease. Not only do researchers not know the exact causes of Alzheimer's disease, but also no one has developed an effective treatment. Research is showing that there may be specific genes on specific chromosomes that cause nearly all of the cases of early-onset familial Alzheimer's; such research may lead to an understanding of the biochemical causes of the disease (Sherrington et al., 1995). The discovery of these genes may lead to diagnostic tests that can be offered individuals who are at risk because of family history.

As individuals age, there are changes in sleep patterns with people sleeping less and not as well; older people are more likely to suffer from arthritis, and osteoporosis (where bones to become weak and brittle) makes them more susceptible to accidents. The heart beats more slowly, the lungs lose capacity, arteries become less flexible, and digestive processes become less efficient. Further, slowing of cell division reduces the response of the immune system—the immune system is thus less effective, and so infections are more likely to occur and latent illnesses can be activated.

Death and Dying

People's overall health deteriorates as they age. For men, the probability of dying doubles in each decade after midlife. In some people, blood pressure rises, cardiac output decreases, and the likelihood of stroke increases, often as a result of cardiovascular disease, which also affects intellectual functioning by decreasing blood flow to the brain (Riegel & Bennett, 2000). Some individuals experience what is known as *terminal drop*—a rapid decline in intellectual functioning in the year before death. However, although there is evidence for the terminal drop, no satisfactory method exists for predicting death on the basis of poor performance on intelligence

Thanatology
The study of the psychological and medical aspects of death and dying.

Be an *Active* learner

REVIEW

- Describe ageism and its impact on older individuals. pp. 136–137
- What is dementia? p. 137
- What are the effects of Alzheimer's disease? pp. 137–138

THINK CRITICALLY

- How might the cognitive changes associated with aging influence the health and well-being of older adults?
- Why do you think people are living to older and older ages? What are new challenges that very old people face that old people of previous generations did not have to deal with?
- What special emotional problems might need to be addressed when a terminally ill person enters a hospice program?

APPLY PSYCHOLOGY

- Write a paragraph that describes the oldest person you know. Does the person's health and behavior fit the stereotypes that most people have about older people?
- How would you define successful aging? Make a list of at least five criteria for successful aging.

or neuropsychological tests or through genetic tests (Pedersen & Reynolds, 1998). While twin studies of health and aging exist, little evidence suggests that genetics, more than lifestyle and environmental variables, is a determining factor in age-related deficits (Pedersen & Svedberg, 2000).

If you are young, perhaps an adolescent, you are more likely than older people to die from an auto accident or AIDS. But the majority of the population die at an older age, and the leading causes of death in the United States are heart disease, cancer, strokes, and accidents; in fact, 7 out of 10 older Americans die from one of the first three of these causes. The number of Americans who succumb to heart disease has decreased because of improved health, reduced smoking, and positive lifestyle changes. Rates of strokes are significantly lower among men and women who do not smoke, who manage their high blood pressure, and who regularly exercise. But cancer remains the second leading cause of deaths; despite good cure rates, half of all cancers are found in men and women over the age of 65. A healthy lifestyle decreases the likelihood of disease, and research shows that older adults who exercise have increases in self-esteem (Tiggemann & Williamson, 2000).

In part because of the increasing age of the U.S. population, **thanatology,** the study of the psychological and medical aspects of death and dying, has become an interdisciplinary specialty. Researchers and theorists in several areas—including theology, law, history, psychology, sociology, and medicine—have come together to better understand death and dying. For psychologists, dealing with the process of dying is especially complicated because people do not like to talk or think about death. Nevertheless, considerable progress has been made toward understanding the psychology of dying.

Summary and Review

Adolescence: Bridging the Gap

Distinguish between puberty and adolescence.

■ *Puberty* is the period during which the reproductive system matures; it signals the end of childhood. There is considerable variation among individuals as to its time of onset. *Adolescence* is the period extending from the end of childhood (often defined as the onset of puberty) to early adulthood. p. 112

What are the major changes experienced by adolescents?

■ *Secondary sex characteristics* are the genetically determined physical features that differentiate the sexes but are not directly involved with reproduction. Examples are bodily hair patterns, pitch of voice, and muscle development. p. 114

■ Changes in intellectual abilities, body proportions, and sexual urges (together with changing relationships with parents and peers) create enormous challenges for adolescents. For some, the changes are problematic emotionally. Adolescents also develop cognitive distortions, especially the *imaginary audience* and the *personal fable,* in which they see themselves as "on stage" all the time and so special and unique that other people cannot understand them. The challenges of adolescence, however, must be considered in a cultural context, because most of the research on adolescence has been conducted with White, middle-class American teenagers—who are clearly not representative of all adolescents. pp. 115–118

Describe some factors that influence cognitive and social development in adolescence, especially with respect to gender similarities and differences.

■ Cognitive differences between male and female adolescents are minimal, but social differences are significant. Adolescents develop a self-image based on a set of beliefs about themselves; other people also generate expectations and beliefs about adolescents, and these beliefs affect them. The influence on adolescents of peer groups, people who identify with and compare themselves to one another, is formidable. pp. 118–120

■ *Gender identity* is a person's sense of being male or female. Parents are the first and most important forces acting to shape gender identity; they influence a child from birth. Peers and schools are other important sources of influence. *Gender schema theory* asserts that children and adolescents use gender as an organizing theme to classify and interpret their perceptions about the world and themselves. pp. 120–121

■ Most people adopt gender role stereotypes—beliefs about which gender-based behaviors are appropriate and acceptable for each gender; such beliefs are strongly regulated and reinforced by society. But *androgyny*, in which some stereotypically male and some stereotypically female characteristics are apparent in one individual, is more common today than in the past. p. 123

■ Eating disorders are psychological disorders marked by gross disturbances in eating behavior and in responses to food. *Anorexia nervosa* is an eating disorder characterized by the obstinate and willful refusal to eat, a distorted body image, and an intense fear of being fat. *Bulimia nervosa* involves repeated episodes of binge eating accompanied by fear of not being able to stop eating. Bulimics often purge themselves of unwanted calories by vomiting and using laxatives and diuretics. pp. 122–123

What is friendship?

■ Friendship is a close emotional tie between peers. Close friends ideally interact as equals, enjoy each other's company, have mutual trust, provide mutual assistance, accept each other as they are, respect each other's judgment, feel free to be themselves with each other, understand each other, and share confidences. High schoolers typically report having three to five good friends. Adolescents spend as much as 29% of their waking hours with friends. Among adults in Western cultures, expectations for specific gender-based behaviors often control male–female interactions in friendship. pp. 124–125

How have adolescent sexual behavior and attitudes changed in recent years?

■ More so than previous generations, today's adolescents view sexual intimacy as a normal part of growing up. Premarital heterosexual activity has become more common among adolescents, especially 13- to 17-year-olds. More relaxed attitudes concerning adolescent sexual behavior have brought about increased awareness among adolescents about contraception and pregnancy. Yet teen pregnancy is still widely prevalent; thus, increased awareness does not imply that the problem is being solved. pp. 125–126

KEY TERMS

adolescence, p. 112; puberty, p. 112; secondary sex characteristics, p. 114; imaginary audience, p. 114; personal fable, p. 114; gender identity, p. 121; gender schema theory, p. 121; androgynous, p. 122; anorexia nervosa, p. 122; bulimia nervosa, p. 123

Adulthood: Years of Stability and Change

Describe Erikson's last four stages of psychosocial development.

■ Erikson's stage 5, identity versus role confusion, marks the end of childhood and the beginning of adolescence; adolescents must decide who they are and what they want to do in life. Stage 6 (young adulthood) is characterized by intimacy versus isolation; young adults begin to select other people with whom they can form intimate, caring relationships. In stage 7 (middle adulthood), generativity versus stagnation, people become more aware of their mortality and develop a particular concern for future generations. Finally, in stage 8 (late adulthood), ego integrity versus despair, people decide whether their existence is meaningful, happy, and cohesive or wasteful and unproductive. pp. 131–132

Describe Levinson's theory of adult development.

■ According to Levinson's stage theory of adulthood, all adults live through the same developmental periods, though people go through them in their own ways. His theory of adult development (which was generated from data on men) describes four basic eras: adolescence, early adulthood, middle adulthood, and late adulthood. Each has distinctive qualities and different life problems, tasks, and situations. pp. 132–133

Differentiate between life transitions and crises.

■ Nearly everyone has life transitions, but not everyone experiences them as crises. A transition suggests that a person has reached a time in life when old ways of coping are giving way to new ones. A crisis occurs when old ways of coping become ineffective, and a person feels helpless and frustrated. pp. 132–133

Do women's life stages parallel men's?

■ Women do not necessarily follow the same life stages as men. Women tend to experience transitions and life events at later ages and in less orderly sequences than those reported by Levinson. p. 133

Describe the effects of aging.

■ Physical development and aging continue throughout adulthood. In general, strength, muscle tone, and overall fitness deteriorate from age 30 on. There are also sensory changes, including slower reaction time after age 65. Sexual behavior and desire typically change, and physical changes related to sexuality occur in adults of both sexes. pp. 127–129

- Primary aging is the normal, inevitable change that occurs with age and is irreversible, progressive, and universal. Secondary aging is aging that is due to extrinsic factors such as disease, environmental pollution, and smoking. p. 130
- Most research indicates that cognitive abilities decrease somewhat with advancing age, but many of the late-life changes are of little importance for day-to-day functioning and affect only some people. p. 130

Late Adulthood: Growing Older, Growing Wiser

Who are older people, and how is life different in late adulthood?

- In general, being over age 65 classifies a person as being aged. Approximately 12% of the U.S. population—more than 33 million Americans—are age 65 or older. p. 134
- *Ageism* is discrimination on the basis of age, often resulting in the denial of rights and services to the elderly. p. 136
- Brain disorders called *dementias* involve losses of cognitive abilities and mental functioning. Currently, there are about 4 million diagnosed Alzheimer's patients in the United States. *Alzheimer's disease* is a degenerative disorder whose progression cannot be stopped; it is irreversible and ultimately ends in death. Individuals who suffer from Alzheimer's disease slowly lose their memory. Within months, or sometimes years, they lose their speech and language functions. Eventually, they lose all memory and bodily control. pp. 137–138

KEY TERMS

ageism, p. 136; dementia, p. 137; Alzheimer's disease, p. 137; thanatology, p. 138

5 Sensation and Perception

Alexander Calder, *Untitled,* 1947

A picture of three-time Tour de France winner Lance Armstrong hangs on my (LL) bulletin board. I look at the photo every day and it gives me a bit of inspiration. Some days I'm inspired because of his sheer talent as an athlete (something that I'm not); other days, it's because at a young age Armstrong learned a valuable lesson about life (that it's not all about winning); and other days I think about his ability to withstand pain and adversity in his illness (cancer) and his bike rides (the longest and toughest known). Lance—I call him Lance—used psychological processes to overcome the difficulties of chemotherapy, surgery, and the punishing pain of the Tour de France. Most people know that pain is a signal of damage to the body or impending damage, but Lance was able to turn it off, endure it, and overcome—it was a matter of mind over body. Lance Armstrong's achievements are not only ones of moral courage, but they are psychological ones as well that show that one's situation, culture, family background, and ultimately, one's belief all affect the ability to experience, endure, and in some cases overcome pain. (You might want to read Lance's autobiography, *It's Not About the Bike* (2000), if you'd like to see how to harness some of the techniques he used in times of adversity and competition.)

chapter outline

Psychologists are interested in pain because it involves one of the five senses, because it helps us understand the human condition, and because it is a model of how human beings process information—from a sharp stimulus, to the receptors, and to experience. Psychologists pay particular attention to the beginnings and ends of the process—either from the stimulus (such as a sharp object) or the response (the pain that is felt) on how they record the information.

■ *Lance Armstrong overcame cancer to win the Tour de France for the third time. He is an example of the psychological power to endure.*

The Perceptual Experience

Whenever you are exposed to a stimulus in the environment—a word on a page or a breeze through your hair—the stimulus initiates an electrochemical change in sensory receptors in your body. That change in turn initiates the processes of sensation and perception. Psychologists study sensation and perception because what people sense and perceive determines how they will understand and interpret the world. Such understanding depends on a combination of stimulation, past experiences, and current interpretations. Although the relationship between perception and culture has not been extensively researched, it is clear that culture can affect perception—by establishing what people believe, pay attention to or ignore, and expect in their environments. For example, composers have long known that a person exposed only to Western music will find non-Western melodies unfamiliar and dissonant.

FIGURE 5.1

Bottom-up and Top-down Processing

Bottom-up perceptual processing builds from an analysis of individual stimulus to perception. Top-down processing begins with a perception, then determines the exact "fit" with features that are discernable.

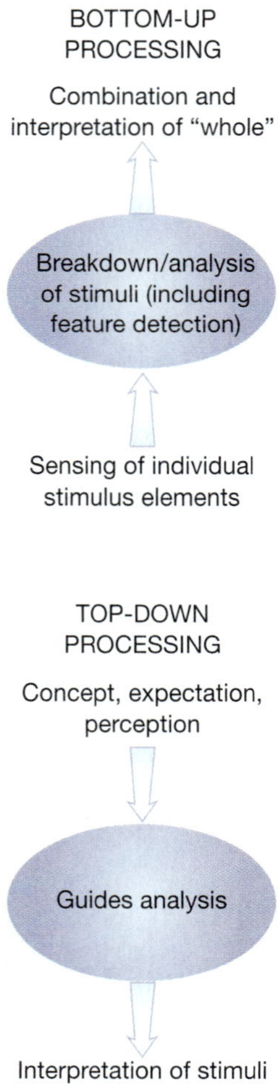

Sensation and Perception: Definitions

Traditionally, psychologists have studied sensation and perception together—as we do in this chapter. **Sensation** is the process in which the sense organs' receptor cells are stimulated and relay initial information to higher brain centers for further processing. **Perception** is the process by which an organism selects and interprets sensory input so that it acquires meaning. Thus, sensation provides the stimulus for further perceptual processing. For example, when light striking your eyeball initiates electrochemical changes, you experience the sensation of light. But your interpretation of the pattern of light and its resulting neural representation as an image are part of perception.

Some researchers who examine sensation and perception start at the most fundamental level of sensation—where the stimulus meets the receptors—and work up to more complex perceptual tasks involving interpretation. This approach is often called *bottom-up analysis*. Other researchers examine perceptual phenomena starting from the more complex level—not surprisingly, called *top-down analysis*. This type of analysis focuses on aspects of the perceptual process such as selective attention and active decision making, which are top-down processes. Perception is more than a reflexive discrimination process; rather, it involves integration of current sensory experiences with past experiences and even cultural expectations.

These two approaches, from the top down and from the bottom up, are both useful, because sensation and perception are not accomplished merely by the firing of a single group of neurons but involve whole sets of neurons, as well as previous experiences and stimulation that occurs at the eyes, ears, or other sense organs. Today, perceptual psychologists generally think in terms of *perceptual systems*—the sets of structures, functions, and operations by means of which people perceive the world around them. And psychologists know that perceptual systems interact. Sensory and perceptual processes rely so heavily on each other that many researchers think about them together (Pylyshyn, 1999). So sensation and perception together form the entire process through which an organism acquires sensory input, converts it into electrochemical energy, and interprets it so that it gains organization, form, and meaning. Through this complex process people explore the world and discover its rules. Doing so involves the nervous system and one or more (Macaluso, Frith, & Driver, 2000) of the perceptual or sensory systems: vision, hearing, taste, smell, and touch.

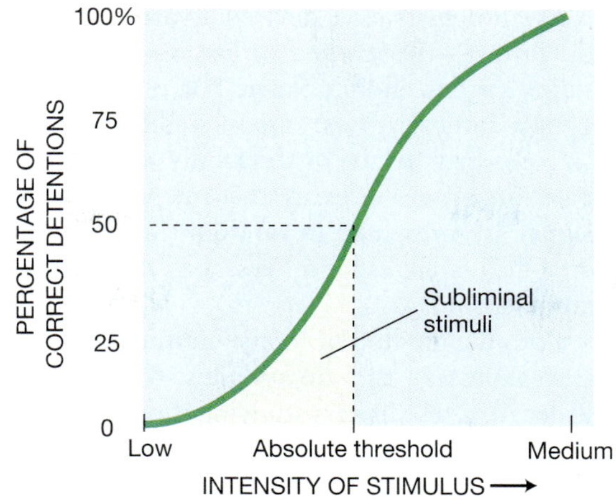

FIGURE 5.2

Absolute Threshold

When stimuli are detectable less than 50% of the time, they are considered subliminal.

Psychophysics

Although perceptual systems differ, they share a common process. In each case, the environment provides an initial stimulation. Receptor cells translate that stimulus into neural impulses, and the impulses are then sent to specific areas of the brain for further processing. Psychologists who study this process are using **psychophysics**—the subfield of psychology that focuses on the relationship between physical stimuli and people's conscious experiences of them.

Psychophysical studies attempt to relate the physical dimensions of stimuli to psychological experiences. This effort often begins with studying sensory thresholds. A *threshold* can be thought of as a dividing line, a point at which things become different. In perception, a threshold is the value of a sensory event at the point where things are perceived as different. Early researchers, such as Ernst Weber and Gustav Fechner, investigated absolute thresholds, the minimum levels of stimulation necessary to excite a perceptual system, such as vision. They asked, for example, what minimum intensity of light is necessary to make a person say, "I see it," or what minimum pressure is necessary for a person to feel something against the skin. It turns out that a true absolute threshold is impossible to determine, because no two individuals see, hear, or feel at exactly the same intensity. The absolute threshold for vision, or any other sense, is thus an average of the responses of a range of normal people. So, for a psychologist, the **absolute threshold** is the statistically determined minimum level of stimulation necessary to excite a perceptual system (see Figure 5.2). When perception takes place below the threshold of awareness we say there is **subliminal perception** taking place—but more on that in just a bit. Closely related is the *difference threshold*—the amount of change necessary for an observer to report 50% of the time that a value of a stimulus (say, a sound) has changed (has become louder or softer) or is different from another value (is the chirping of a cricket rather than a bird).

Sensation
Process in which the sense organs' receptor cells are stimulated and relay initial information to higher brain centers for further processing.

Perception
Process by which an organism selects and interprets sensory input so that it acquires meaning.

Psychophysics
Subfield of psychology that focuses on the relationship between physical stimuli and people's conscious experiences of them.

Absolute threshold
The statistically determined minimum level of stimulation necessary to excite a perceptual system.

Subliminal perception
Perception below the threshold of awareness.

Psychologists have devised a variety of methods for studying perceptual thresholds. In one—the *method of limits*—various values of a signal are presented in ascending or descending order. For example, a psychologist may present a light of very low intensity, then one of slightly higher intensity, and so on. A participant's task is to say when he or she finally sees the light—or, in the case of descending limits, no longer sees it. In another method—the *method of constant stimuli*—values of a signal are presented in random (not ascending or descending) order; the participants' task is to respond "yes" or "no," indicating that they have either detected a stimulus or not.

Both the method of limits and the method of constant stimuli have methodological weaknesses—they do not allow for key factors in the human observer. In the past few decades, researchers studying thresholds have used signal detection theory. **Signal**

point*counterpoint*

Does Subliminal Advertising Work?

The Issue: If a stimulus is presented subliminally, can it affect your behavior?

POINT
Subliminal messages affect consciousness, brain organization, and ultimately behavior.

COUNTERPOINT
Claims about the effects of subliminal perception, and any learning that results from it, are exaggerated and overblown—the effects are subtle at most.

In the 2000 presidential election there was a television ad that for a fraction of a second flashed the word "rats" in large capital letters on the screen. The intent of the ploy—denied by the ad makers—was to associate the other candidate with the most reviled of rodents. The ad makers were trying to use subliminal perception. Subliminal perception is perception that takes place below the threshold of awareness. If a stimulus is presented so quickly or at such a low intensity that you cannot consciously perceive it, can it affect your behavior? Do subliminal messages work?

Subliminal perception is possible. In fact, many cognitive scientists take unconscious perception for granted and build theories around it (Draine & Greenwald, 1999). Evidence exists for subliminal effects in a variety of experimental settings (Monahan, Murphy, & Zajonc, 2000). The presentation of a threatening or fearful message may raise the perceptual threshold above normal levels, making it harder for the participant to perceive subsequent subliminal words or images. Some researchers suggest that the unconscious or some other personality variable acts as a censor. For example, Pratkanis (2001) asserts that if an aggressive or sexual message is presented subliminally to participants, it will affect their subsequent behavior—so unconscious processes are indeed at work. Balay and Shevrin (1988) suggest that a stage beyond sensory or perceptual awareness affects the perceptual process. They maintain that subliminal perception can be explained in terms of nonperceptual variables such as motivation, previous experience, repetition, and unconscious or critical censoring processes that influence perceptual thresholds. So, in some controlled situations, subliminal stimuli can influence perception, attitudes, and behavior (Bogren, Bogren, & Thorell, 1998; Damian, 2001).

In the real world, however, we are constantly faced with many competing sensory stimuli. Therefore, what grabs our attention depends on many variables, such as the importance, prominence, and interest of a stimulus. Should we fear mind control by advertisers? The answer is probably no, because advertisements have to compete with so many other stimuli (Schredl et al., 1999; Trappey, 1996). Can backward speech in rock songs be interpreted and understood? Again, the answer is no (Begg, Needham, & Bookbinder, 1993). Can tapes listened to while you are asleep help you learn Greek or Latin? Once more, the answer is no (Moore, 1995).

In the end, subliminal perception, and any learning that results from it, is subtle at most (Channouf, 2000; Smith & Rogers, 1994) and is strongly affected by variables such as expectation, motivation, previous experience, personality, and learned, culturally based behaviors (Miller, 2000; Pratkanis, 2001). However, most psychologists argue that more research is needed to determine exactly what is taking place when subliminal perception occurs and to what degree subliminal stimuli can influence us.

detection theory holds that an observer's perception depends not only on the intensity of a stimulus but also on the observer's motivation, on the criteria he or she sets, and on the background noise. For example, when you are worried about a loved one being late, you listen especially carefully for cars that may be coming down the street. Your perception also depends on the criteria you set for determining that a signal is present—the criteria that lead you to say, "Yes, I detect the signal—the sound of a car." Finally, your perception also depends, according to signal detection theory, on the *noise* (the unstructured, constant background activity) in the environment; for example, the noise of children playing in the street, birds chirping, and a TV in the next apartment all make it more difficult to detect the sound of a car. In addition to manipulating the actual signal intensity, therefore, researchers have manipulated motivation levels (by offering varying rewards for detection), discrimination criteria (for example, by telling participants to be *very* sure before they say they can detect the signal), and levels of noise. It turns out that each variable affects a person's willingness to say, "Yes, I detect the signal." This important finding lends support to the idea that there is no finite or absolute threshold—individuals' responses vary, although each individual is consistent within a type of situation.

Selective Attention

If you think that most drivers keep their eyes on the road, you're wrong. Today people behind the wheel are peering at their CD player, Palm Pilot, cell phone, kids in the back seat, and even the sports page. We've seen men and women eating, combing their hair, and checking their clothing, all while driving at 65 miles per hour. If you think that you can attend to the road just because your eyes are open, you are wrong—and the accident rate due to inattention is frightening. The senses require attention, and that is an active process. Attending to too many things or failure to attend by being bored creates accidents (Gray & Regan, 2000). In fact, many perception researchers assert that there is no perception without attention (Mack & Rock, 1998). Attention has long been a key element in the study of sensation and perception because researchers have always recognized its complex role.

■ *The cocktail party phenomenon states that while a person often cannot discern the content of conversations, a person can usually hear his or her name.*

Consider what happens when you face competing tasks that require attention. For example, have you ever tried to study while listening to quiet music? You may have thought that the music barely reached your threshold of awareness. Yet you may have found your attention wandering. Did melodies or words start to interrupt your studying? Research on attention shows that human beings constantly extract signals from the world around them. Although we receive many different messages at once, we can usually attend to only a single selected one.

Because people can pay attention to only one or two things at a time, psychologists sometimes call the study of attention the study of *selective attention.* Early researchers in this area discovered the *cocktail party phenomenon,* whereby a person who cannot discern the content of conversations across a crowded and noisy room can nevertheless hear his or her name mentioned by someone in the crowd.

Signal detection theory
Theory that holds that an observer's perception depends not only on the intensity of a stimulus but also on the observer's motivation, on the criteria he or she sets for determining that a signal is present, and on the background noise.

Perceptual psychologists are interested in the complexities of the processes through which people extract information from the environment. These psychologists hope to answer this question: which stimuli do people choose to attend to? They focus on the *allocation* of a person's attention. For example, in selective-listening experiments, participants wearing a pair of headphones receive different messages simultaneously in each ear. Their task is often to shadow, or repeat, a message heard in one ear. Typically, they report that they are able to listen to a speaker in *either* the left ear or the right ear (but not both) and provide information about the content and quality of that speaker's voice.

The filter theory and the attenuation theory are two of the several theories about how people are able to listen selectively. The *filter theory* states that human beings possess a limited capacity to process information and that perceptual "filters" screen out information presented to one or the other of the two ears. The *attenuation theory* states that all the information a person receives is analyzed but that intervening factors inhibit (attenuate) attention so only selected information reaches the highest centers of processing. Hundreds of selective-listening studies have examined the claims of the competing theories, and recent research favors attenuation theory (Cowan & Wood, 1997). But regardless of whether people filter or attenuate information, selective-attention studies show that human beings must select among the available stimuli. It is impossible, for example, to pay attention to four lectures at once. A listener can extract information from only one speaker at a time. Admittedly, you can do more than one task at a time—for example, you can drive a car and sing along to your favorite CD—but you cannot use the same sensory channel (such as vision) for several tasks simultaneously. You cannot drive a car, read a book, and look at photographs at the same time because you have to direct your attention (Kastner et al., 1998).

Focusing on one stimulus or activity while trying to ignore other stimuli can be hard, but it is not impossible. Kerri Strugg, the Olympic gymnast, landed a near perfect vault while ignoring severe ligament pain from a previous vault, by focusing her attention on the sight of the apparatus while ignoring the pain in her leg; Strugg's efforts show that we can "reject" some inputs while focusing on other inputs, and research shows that this is indeed possible (Martino & Marks, 2000). Clearly, both the auditory and visual systems have limited capacities. People have limited ability to divide their attention between tasks and must allocate their perceptual resources for greatest efficiency. This becomes especially true when we recognize that we do processing from many modalities at the same time (sight and hearing, for example) and that they affect one another (McDonald & Ward, 2000). But what happens when it is not necessary to divide your attention? What occurs when stimuli in the environment are restricted?

■ *People have limited ability to divide their attention between tasks—such as driving, drinking coffee, and talking on the phone.*

Restricted Environmental Stimulation

Imagine utter loneliness ... darkness ... a complete lack of light and sound. Imagine being in an isolation tank where you don't have to adapt to the light—because there is absolutely none. This was the situation described in a compelling novel, a page-turner by Paddy Chayefsky called *Altered States*. I recommend it to all of my students; it raises provocative questions about human perceptual systems and consciousness—and the relationship between the two.

In 1954, neurophysiologist John Lilly enlisted modern technology to find out what would happen if the brain were deprived of all sensory input—if a person were to be placed in a situation much like that described by Chayefsky. Lilly actually constructed an isolation tank that excluded all light and sound and was filled with heavily salted water, which helps the body to float. In this artificial sea, deprived of all external stimuli, Lilly experienced dreams, reveries, hallucinations, and other altered mental states. Throughout the ages, mystics of all kinds have claimed to achieve such trance states by purposely limiting their sensory experiences—taking vows of silence, adhering to austere lifestyles, meditating while sitting as still as a stone for hours, and so on.

Psychologists refer to what Lilly experienced as restricted environmental stimulation. And some researchers argue that there are psychological benefits to be derived from sensory restriction (deprivation)—isolation from sights, sounds, smells, tastes, and most tactile stimuli. The benefits may have been exaggerated, but such restriction can have profound effects on animals and humans. One team of researchers (Bexton, Heron, & Scott, 1954) studied the effects of sensory restriction by isolating individual college students in a comfortable but dull room. The researchers allowed the students to hear only the continuous hum of an air conditioner; the participants wore translucent plastic visors to limit their vision and tubes lined with cotton around their hands and arms to limit sensory input to their skin. The results were dramatic. Within a few hours, the participants' performance on tests of mental ability was impaired. The students became bored and irritable, and many said they saw "images."

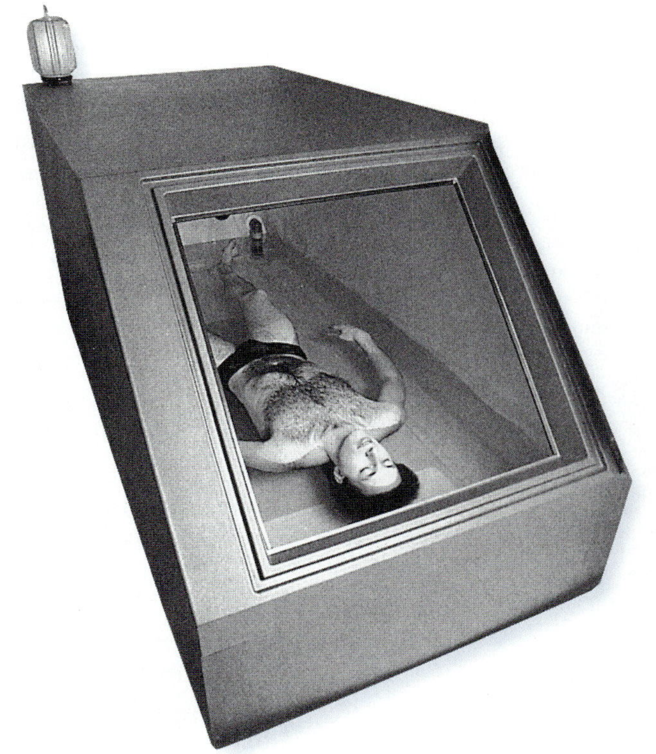

▪ *An isolation tank removes all external stimuli and may alter an individual's mental state.*

Several fascinating follow-up studies placed participants in identical conditions except that they were told that the sensory restriction would serve as an aid to meditation. How do you think this information affected their responses? The participants did not hallucinate or become irritable; in fact, their mental abilities actually improved (Lilly, 1956; Zuckerman, 1969). These studies suggest that people do not necessarily become bored because of lack of stimulation. Rather, when people evaluate their situation as monotonous, they become bored. Given the opportunity to relax in a quiet place for a long time, many people meditate; they find the "deprivation" relaxing. Such findings indicate the need for caution in interpreting data from sensory deprivation studies involving human beings, because participants approach these situations with powerful expectations.

Sensory restriction has proved to have positive effects on some people (Harrison & Barabasz, 1991). Many participants experience a profound relaxation in an environment of extreme sensory restriction (Sakata et al., 1995; Suedfeld, 1998), which can be highly effective in modifying some habits, such as smoking, and in treating problems such as obesity (Suedfeld, 1990) and addiction (Borrie, 1991). Men, older individuals, and people with strongly religious backgrounds may be more likely to benefit than others, and some people may be adversely affected. Further, previous experience with sensory restriction may produce a cumulative effect; that is, each time a person experiences the restricted environment, it may have a greater effect. In general, the benefits of restricted environmental stimulation are probably underestimated (Steel et al., 1995; Suedfeld, 1990).

Inattentional Blindness

When you drive down the road, listen to a concert, or watch a favorite movie, you display an inability to detect unexpected objects; you show *inattentional blindness.* Research on this phenomenon shows that unless you pay attention, you can miss even the most conspicuous events around you (Scholl, 2000). For example,while people paid close attention to a visual scene with sports figures in it, a figure in a gorilla suit appeared, pounded its chest, and then disappeared—and it went completely unnoticed (Most et al., 2001; Simons & Chabris, 1999)!

Experimental research on attention shows that when you pay rock-solid attention to an object, a scene, or an event, other (unexpected) events go unnoticed (Simons, Franconeri, & Reimer, 2000). This means that an airline pilot, closely

Be an *Active* learner

REVIEW

- What is a bottom-up analysis? pp. 144–145
- Is there an absolute threshold? What evidence exists for or against this idea? p. 145

THINK CRITICALLY

- Does family upbringing affect a person's selective attention abilities? Explain your answer.
- What fundamental assumption is a researcher making when depriving an organism of sensory experience and then measuring its behavior?

APPLY PSYCHOLOGY

- Think of two ways to restrict environmental stimulation to help people lead calmer, more relaxed lives.
- Think of three exercises to help athletes "reject" some inputs (screaming fans) while focusing on other inputs (catching a ball).

attending to hundreds of dials and switches, may completely miss an unanticipated plane approaching from the left. Similarly, if you are intently focused on a video game, you may not notice the arrival of a friend, roommate, or parent in your room. The more you pay attention to the main event, the less likely you will be to notice the unexpected one (Most et al., 2001). The more the unexpected event differs from what you are attending to or accustomed to, the more likely you will be to miss it (Lachter, Durgin, & Washington, 2000; Simons & Chabris, 1999).

Inattentional blindness is important because it reminds us that the brain can do only so much at one time—we can only encode so much. It prompts us to realize that "top-down" processes may tune an observer's attention to specific objects or events. It forces us to ask a question that remains unanswered for now. What information will get coded and what happens to the stimuli that we do not register? These questions require us to look more closely at the visual system itself, our next topic.

The Visual System

Imagine that you are in an unfamiliar house at night when the power goes out. Left in total darkness, you hear creaking sounds but have no idea where they are coming from. You stub your toe on the coffee table, then frantically grope along the walls until you reach the kitchen, where you fumble through the drawers in search of a flashlight. You quickly come to a full appreciation of the sense of sight when you suddenly lack it.

Human beings derive more information through sight than through any other sense. By some estimates, the eyes contain 70% of the body's sense receptors. Although the eyes do respond to pressure, the appropriate stimulus for vision is **electromagnetic radiation**—the entire spectrum of waves initiated by the movement of charged particles. The electromagnetic spectrum includes gamma rays, X-rays, ultraviolet rays, visible light, infrared rays, radar, broadcast bands, and AC currents (see Figure 5.3). Note that the **light** that is visible to the human eye is a very small portion of the electromagnetic spectrum. Light may come directly from a source or may be reflected from an object.

The impact of light is complex and affects about 30 areas of the brain that are involved in sensation and perception. We begin our analysis of the visual system with a bottom-up analysis of the effect of light on the structure of the eye. Such an analysis will show that the visual system is exceedingly intricate. Although often likened to a camera, which records images, the visual system is interpretive, and a later top-down analysis will show that the camera analogy explains only part of the process.

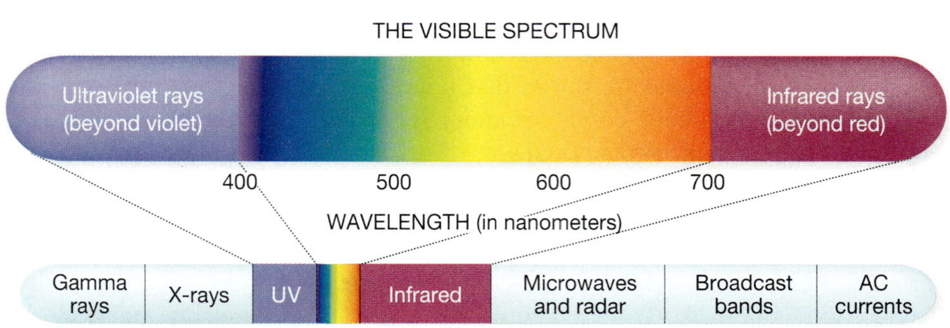

FIGURE 5.3

The Electromagnetic Spectrum

People can perceive only a small part of the total electromagnetic spectrum.

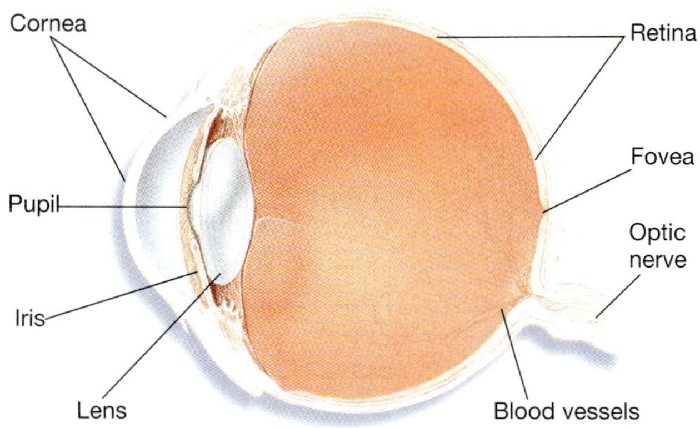

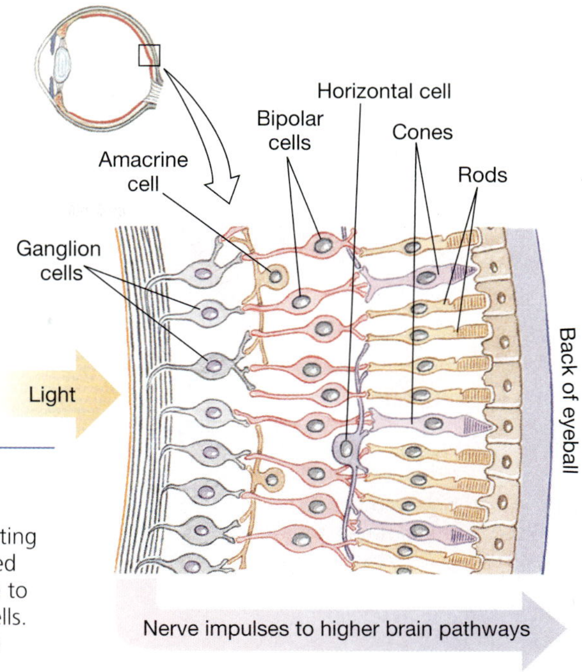

FIGURE 5.4

The Main Structures of the Eye

The photoreceptors of the retina are connected to higher brain pathways through the optic nerve. Light filters through layers of retinal cells before hitting the receptors (rods and cones), located at the back of the eyeball and pointed away from the incoming light. The rods and cones pass an electrical impulse to the bipolar cells, which in turn relay the impulse back out to the ganglion cells. The axons of the ganglion cells form the fibers of the optic nerve. (*Dowling & Boycott, 1966*)

The Structure of the Eye

Figure 5.4 shows the major structures of the human eye. Light first passes through the *cornea*—a small, transparent bulge covering both the *pupil* (the dark opening in the center of the eye) and the pigmented *iris*. The iris either constricts to make the pupil smaller or dilates to make it larger. Behind the pupil is the *lens*, which is about 4 millimeters thick. Together, the cornea, the pupil, the iris, and the lens form images in much the same way as a camera shutter and camera lens do. The *retina*, which lines the back of the eye, is like the film in a camera: it captures an image. Constriction of the iris makes the pupil smaller, improving the quality of the image on the retina and increasing the depth of focus—the distance to the part of the visual field that is in sharp focus. The action of the lens also helps control the amount of light entering the eye.

When people's eyeballs are not perfectly shaped, their vision is affected. People with elongated eyeballs are **myopic**, or *nearsighted;* they see clearly things that are close but have trouble seeing objects at a distance, because the image of an object falls short of the retina. **Hyperopic**, or *farsighted*, people have shortened eyeballs. They see objects at a distance clearly but have trouble seeing things up close, because the image of an object is focused behind the retina.

The *retina* consists of 10 layers of cells. Of these, the most important are the **photoreceptors** (the light-sensitive cells), the bipolar cells, and the ganglion cells. After light passes through several layers of bipolar and ganglion cells, it strikes the photoreceptor layer, which consists of *rods* (rod-shaped receptors) and *cones* (cone-shaped receptors); these will be described in detail later. In this layer, the light breaks down *photopigments* (light-sensitive chemicals), which causes an electrochemical change in the rods and cones. The process by which the perceptual system analyzes stimuli and converts them into electrical impulses is **transduction**, or *coding*. After transduction of the light stimulus by the retina, the resulting electrical energy is transferred back out to the next major layer, the *bipolar cells*.

■ **RODS AND CONES.** Each eye contains more than 120 million rods and 6 million cones. These millions of photoreceptors do not have individual pathways to the higher visual centers in the brain. Instead, through the process of *convergence*, electrochemical signals from many rods come together onto a single bipolar cell. At the

Electromagnetic [ee-LEK-tro-mag-NET-ick] radiation
The entire spectrum of waves initiated by the movement of charged particles.

Light
The small portion of the electromagnetic spectrum that is visible to the human eye.

Myopic [my-OH-pick]
Able to see clearly things that are close but having trouble seeing objects at a distance; nearsighted.

Hyperopic [HY-per-OH-pick]
Able to see objects at a distance clearly but having trouble seeing things up close; farsighted.

Photoreceptors
The light-sensitive cells in the retina—the rods and the cones.

Transduction
Process by which a perceptual system analyzes stimuli and converts them into electrical impulses; also known as *coding*.

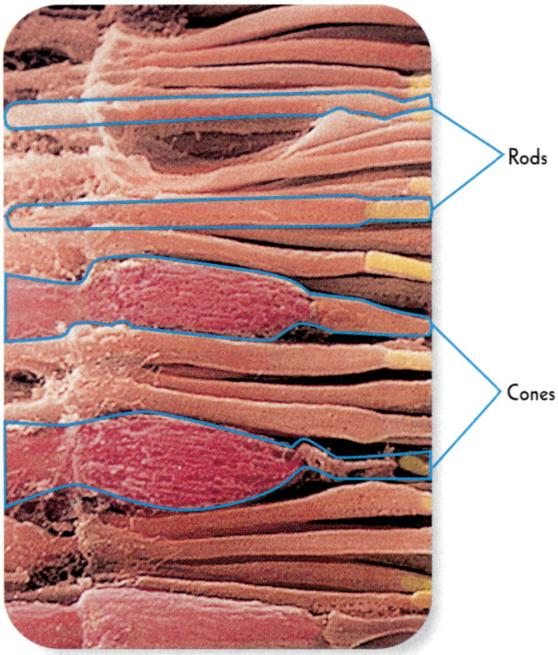

■ *Cones are packed tightly in the center of the retina and used for day vision, while rods are found on the rest of the retina and are predominantly used for night vision.*

same time, hundreds of cones synapse and converge onto other bipolar cells. From the bipolar cells, electrochemical energy is transferred to the *ganglion cell layer* of the retina. Dozens of bipolar cells synapse and converge onto each ganglion cell (there are about 1 million ganglion cells). The axons of the ganglion cells make up the *optic nerve,* which carries information that was initially received by the rods and cones to the brain. Still further coding takes place at the brain's **visual cortex,** or *striate cortex.* The visual cortex, the most important area of the brain's occipital lobe, further processes information from the *lateral geniculate nucleus* (one of the major visual projection areas in the visual system—see page 154).

The *duplicity theory of vision* (sometimes called the *duplexity theory*), which is now universally accepted, asserts that there are two separate receptor systems in the retina: the rods and the cones. It also states that rods and cones are structurally different and accomplish different tasks. Cones are for the most part tightly packed in the center of the retina, at the *fovea,* and are used for day vision, color vision, and fine visual discrimination. Rods (together with some cones) are found on the rest of the retina (the periphery) and are used predominantly for night vision (see Figure 5.5). The functioning of the cones is demonstrated in the visual acuity test you take when you apply for a driver's license. A *visual acuity* test measures the resolution capacity of the visual system—the ability to see fine details. Cones principally me-

FIGURE 5.5

The Distribution of Rods and Cones and the Blind Spot

The center of the retina (the fovea) contains only cones. At about 18° of visual angle (a measure of the size of images on the retina), there are no receptors at all. This is the place where the optic nerve leaves the eye, called the blind spot. Because the blind spot for each eye is on the nasal side of the eyeball, there is no loss of vision; the two blind spots do not overlap. *(Pirenne, 1967)*

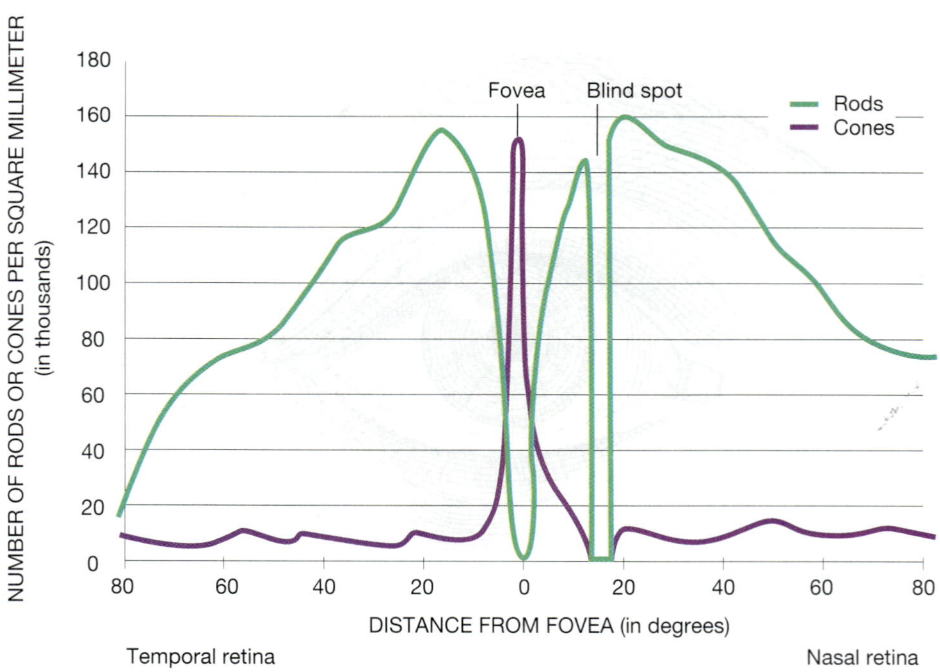

diate this ability. You do best on such a test in a well-lit room (cones operate at high light levels) and when looking directly at the test items (again, more cones are in the center of the retina than in any other place).

Your eyes are always in some state of light or dark adaptation. Rods and cones are sensitive to light, but they are less sensitive in a well-lit room than they are after having been in the dark. **Dark adaptation** is the increase in sensitivity to light that occurs when the illumination level changes from high to low. In dark adaptation, chemicals in the photoreceptors (rods and cones) regenerate and return to their original state, increasing the eyes' light sensitivity. If you go from a well-lit lobby into a dark theater, for example, you experience a brief period of low light sensitivity, during which you are unable to distinguish empty seats. Your ability to discern objects and people in the theater increases with each passing moment. Within 30 minutes, your eyes will have almost fully adapted to the dark and will be far more light sensitive. Of course, after leaving a dark theater and returning to the afternoon sunlight, you must squint or shade your eyes until they become adapted to the light.

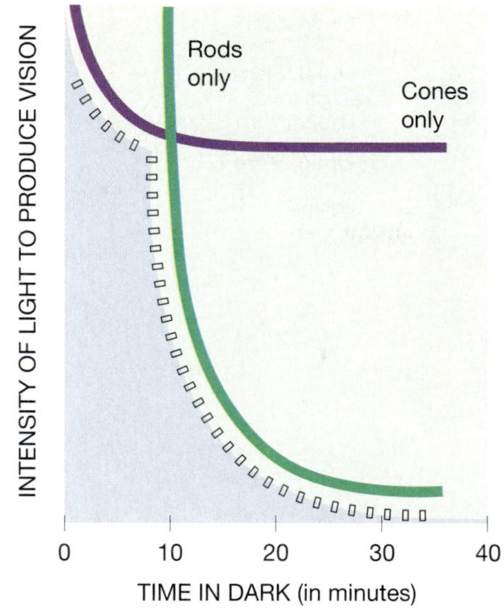

FIGURE 5.6

A Dark Adaptation Curve

The dashed line represents a typical overall dark adaptation curve. The two solid lines represent separate dark adaptation for rods and cones. Most dark adaptation occurs within 10 minutes. Rods, however, continue to adapt for another 20 minutes, reaching greater levels of sensitivity.

Figure 5.6 shows a dark adaptation curve. The cones determine the first part of the curve; the second part is determined by the rods. The speed at which the photochemicals in these receptors regenerate determines the shape of the two parts of the curve. The data for such curves are obtained from experiments with participants who possess only rods or cones. Typically, a participant is first shown bright light for 2 minutes. The light is then turned off, and the participant waits in a totally dark room for 15 seconds. Next, a very dim test spot of light is turned on for half a second, and the participant is asked if he or she sees it. Usually, the participant will report seeing the test spot only after several successive presentations, because dark adaptation occurs gradually. This is why, when you are driving at night, you may have trouble seeing clearly for a brief time after a car drives toward you with its high beams on; the photochemicals in the rods take some time to regenerate.

■ **HIGHER PATHWAYS.** As electrical impulses leave the retina through the optic nerve, they proceed to higher centers of the brain, including the lateral geniculate nucleus and the visual cortex (also called the striate cortex) (see Figure 5.7 on the following page). These connections are quite specific. Knowledge about the way visual structures are connected to the brain aids not only psychologists but also physicians, who can determine, for example, whether a stroke victim with poor vision has a blood clot that is obstructing circulation in one hemisphere of the brain.

Each eye is connected to both sides of the brain, with half of its optic nerve fibers going to the left side of the brain and the other half connecting to the right side. The point at which the crossover of half the optic nerve fibers from each eye occurs is called the **optic chiasm** (see Figures 5.7 and 5.8 on the following page). This crossover of impulses allows the brain to process two sets of signals from an image and helps human beings perceive form in three dimensions. Severing of the optic nerves at the optic chiasm results in tunnel vision—a condition in which peripheral vision is severely impaired and a person can see only items whose images fall on the central area of the eye, the fovea.

Visual cortex
The most important area of the brain's occipital lobe, which receives and further processes information from the lateral geniculate nucleus; also known as the *striate cortex.*

Dark adaptation
The increase in sensitivity to light that occurs when the illumination level changes from high to low, causing chemicals in the rods and cones to regenerate and return to their inactive state.

Optic chiasm [KI-azm]
Point at which half of the optic nerve fibers from each eye cross over and connect to the other side of the brain.

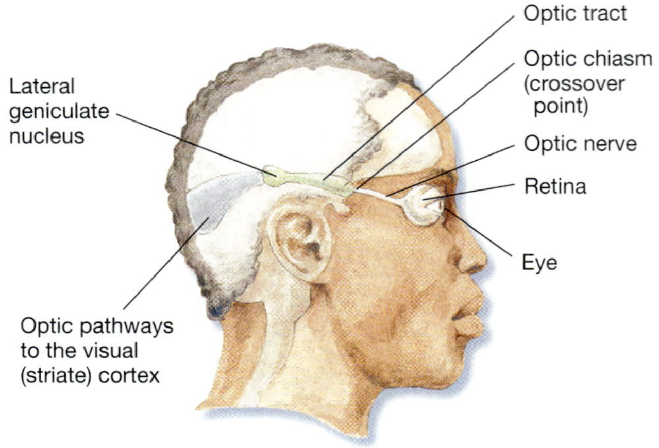

FIGURE 5.7

The Major Components of the Visual System

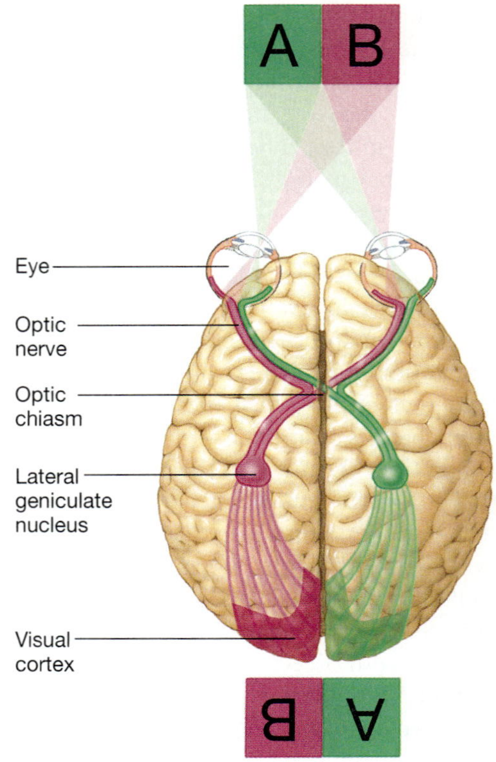

FIGURE 5.8

A Visual Image Projected to Both Hemispheres of the Brain

The Electrochemical Basis of Perception

You can probably find your way around your room in the dark; you know where light switches and doorknobs are. You can reach out and touch just about any object when you need it. Your memory for object locations and how to reach out is coded electrochemically, and scientists know which neurons are involved (Graziano, Hu, & Gross, 1997). In fact, vision and all other perceptual processes are electrochemical in nature. When receptors in the perceptual systems are stimulated, the information is coded and sent to the brain for interpretation and further analysis. Using this basic information about electrochemical stimulation, researchers are working on a visual prosthesis—a device to help the blind see—that bypasses the eyes and directly stimulates the visual cortex (Bak et al., 1990).

■ **RECEPTIVE FIELDS.** Scientists in a wide range of related fields have carried out research on the organization of vision and electrical coding for a long time. For example, Von Senden (1932) reported case histories of people who were born with cataracts (which cloud vision) and had them removed in adulthood. These individuals, seeing clearly for the first time as adults, experienced several deficiencies. For example, they were unable to recognize simple forms presented in an unfamiliar color or context. Some time later, Hirsch and Spinelli (1971) conducted a series of experiments in which they controlled the visual experiences of newborn kittens. The kittens wore goggles that let them perceive either vertical lines or horizontal lines. When the goggles were later removed, kittens raised with only horizontal experiences bumped into vertical chair legs but could leap into a horizontal chair seat; kittens raised with only vertical experiences had problems with horizontal surfaces. Such studies indicate that although most of the connections in the visual system are present in newborns, the proper functioning of the system depends on the organism's experiences, the task given, and even the other senses (Creem & Proffitt, 2001; Macaluso, Frith, & Driver, 2000).

Current knowledge about how the brain processes electrochemical signals comes from studies of single cells and of receptive fields and associated pathways.

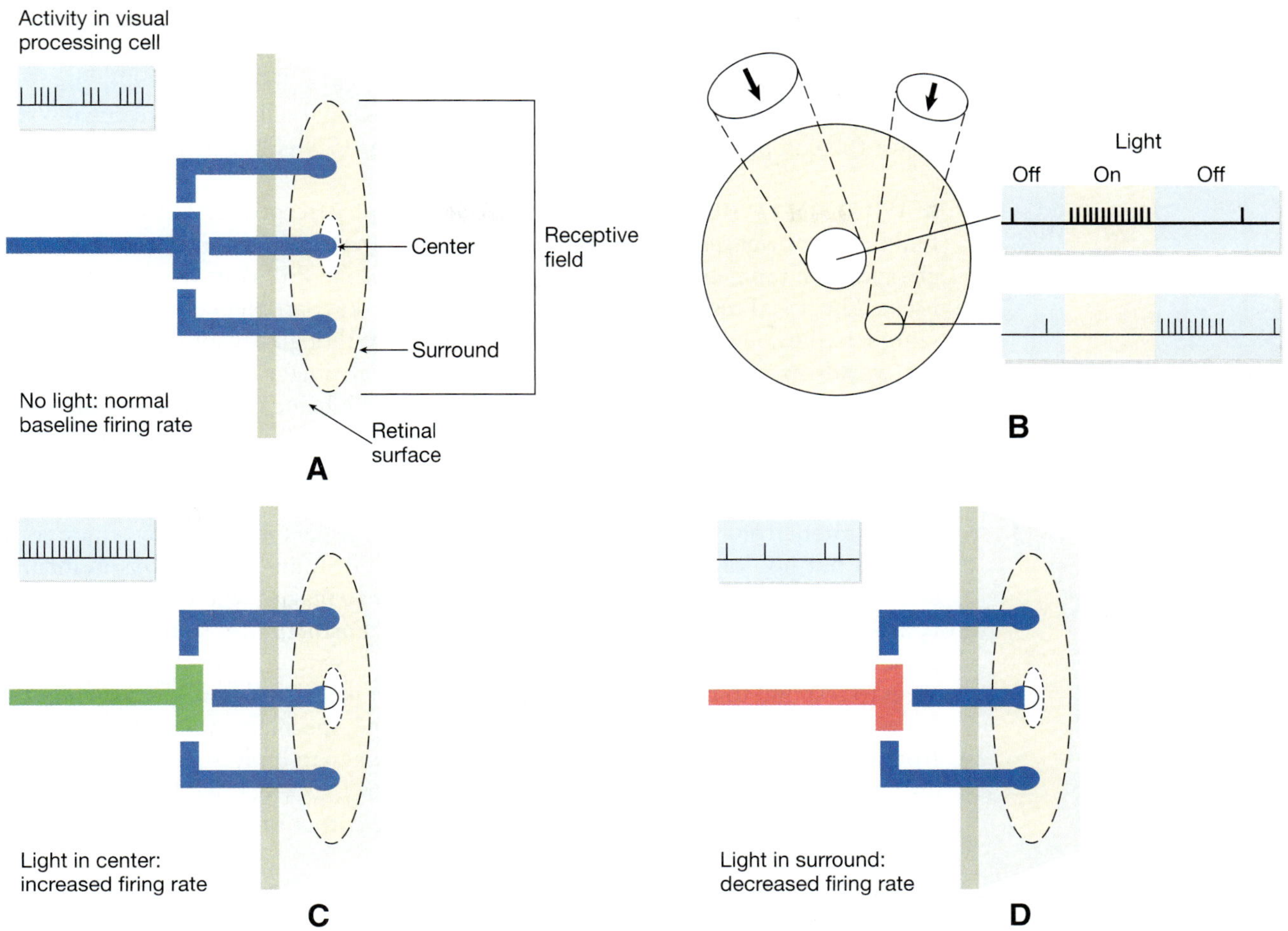

Receptive fields are the areas of the retina that, when stimulated, produce a change in the firing of cells in the visual system. For example, specific cells in the retina will fire, or become active, if a vertical line is presented to a viewer but not if a horizontal line is presented. Many perceptual psychologists refer to these stimulated visual system cells as *feature detectors*. Hubel and Wiesel (1962; 2000) found receptive fields that are sensitive to features of a stimulus line, such as its position, length, movement, color, and intensity (see Figure 5.9). Hubel and Wiesel characterized the feature detectors as simple, complex, or hypercomplex cells. *Simple cells* respond to the shape and size of lights that stimulate the receptive field. *Complex cells* respond most vigorously to the movement of light in one direction (e.g., Taylor et al., 2000). *Hypercomplex cells* are the most specific; they respond only to a line of the correct length and orientation that moves in the proper direction (e.g., Anderson et al., 2000; Blakemore & Campbell, 2000). From Hubel and Wiesel's point of view, electrical coding becomes increasingly more complex as information proceeds through the visual system (Anderson et al., 2000; Sonnenborg, Anderssen, & Arendt-Nielson, 2000). The work of Hubel and Wiesel earned them a Nobel Prize in 1981 and has been supported and extended by other noted researchers (see B. B. Lee, 1999).

FIGURE 5.9

Receptive Fields

Hubel and Wiesel (1962) found cells fire when stimulated in the center of their receptive field but do not fire when stimulated outside the center area. (A) Receptive fields in the retina are often circular with a center-surround arrangement. Light striking the center of the field produces the opposite result of light striking the surround. (B) Here, light in the center produces increased firing in the visual cell (C) and light in the surround produces decreased firing. (D)

Scientists now know that receptive fields also help link visual perception of space to body movements—as when Jackie Chan judges just the right time to leap from a helicopter to a floating barge, or when you see a ball and then slide to catch it (Graziano & Gross, 1994). Receptive fields are associated not only with every area of the visual cortex but with some nonvisual areas as well (Polonsky et al., 2000); for example, receptive fields stimulate cells in the parietal cortex, which is adjacent to the visual cortex and is associated with the control of movement (Corbetta & Vereijken, 1999). Receptive fields not only help you recognize vertical

Receptive fields
Areas of the retina that, when stimulated, produce a change in the firing of cells in the visual system.

and horizontal lines and balls flying through the air, but they also seem to be critically involved in the recognition of faces and other common objects (Allison et al., 1994). Receptive fields may be linked together in complex ways (B. B. Lee, 1999), and probably not by direct, strong connections between individual cells—the perceptual system is just too complicated and flexible (Crick & Koch, 1998; Heeger, 1999).

■ **WHAT AND WHERE.** Remember that the task of perception is difficult; a face, a building, a flower may all be seen from different angles and distances, and these can change from moment to moment. Yet an image of the President from any view still looks like the President. Herein lies a central, key problem for perception researchers: how does the brain perceive constancy though sensory input—views of the world—is constantly changing? Data about an image are probably kept in a storage location for a brief time while other data are being collected, and then these are integrated (e.g., Tenenbaum, de Silva, & Langford, 2000). Part of these data are based on information about what and where.

We know that the visual system processes an object's form and color (*what* it is) separately from its spatial location (*where* it is). A person can know where something is but not know what it is. Mecklinger (2000) found distinctions in memory stores, and "what" information affects our ability to make "where" discriminations (Carlson-Radvansky, Covey, & Lattanzi, 1999). Furthermore, some neurons seem to be tuned to detect either "what" information *or* "where" information; other cells seem to respond to both what and where an object is. Kilgard and Merzenich (1998) have found high degrees of "what" and "where" specificity for cells in the prefrontal cortex and suggest that they may hold the key to understanding how we get around, by linking objects (what) to places (where), as when we follow directions according to landmarks such as "the Kmart at the corner of 2nd and Main" (Rybak et al., 1998).

Researchers' study of electrochemical changes in the visual system shows that the brain simultaneously processes many components of an image—what it is, where it is, when it is perceived, colors, movement, and so on (Deco & Schürmann, 2000). Such simultaneous processing of information taking place in multiple locations of the brain is referred to as *parallel processing,* in contrast to *serial processing,* which occurs in a step-by-step, linear fashion. Parallel processing allows for fast recognition of complexities in the world; it also explains why brain-damaged individuals can recognize some elements of a scene and not others. It helps explain why people with reading disabilities can be smart and astute, able to play the piano and draw, but unable to make sounds correspond to letters. The representation and interpretation of the world happen in multiple brain locations, and some of those locations may not be operating well or efficiently, or even be primarily visual (Frey & Hinton, 1999; Kreiman, Koch, & Fried, 2000).

■ *Women and men tend to use different strategies to find their way in the world. Men's strategy relies more on geography and directions, whereas women's navigation uses landmarks.*

■ **GENDER DIFFERENCES—AN EVOLUTIONARY PERSPECTIVE.** Boys and girls are more alike than different on most visual tasks. But when it comes to spatial abilities—tasks that require the perception of a relationship of parts to a whole—boys have an edge in mental rotation of three-dimensional objects and perhaps in map reading, puzzles, and mazes (McBurney et al., 1997). When it comes to remembering where something is, women excel. Early researchers thought that the differences might have emerged because men were exposed to and trained in map reading and other tasks—a strong environmental point of view. But evolutionary researchers have asserted that as human beings evolved, men predominately hunted while women foraged—human beings were hunter-gatherers. Over time and through the process of natural selection, these hunter-gatherer activities fostered spatial (hunting) skills in men and spatial remembering (gathering) skills in women (Silverman et al., 2000).

If evolutionary theory is correct, it has some implications for everyday life. For example, women and men tend to use different strategies to find their way in the world. Men's strategies rely more on geography and directions, whereas women use landmarks in navigation (Schmitz, 1999). Men's use of geography and directions may be related to their proficiency in spatial orientation. Some researchers have related people's ability to find their way to spatial ability. Much of this research focuses on gender differences. The results from some studies show that men are more confident and learn to find their way around an unfamiliar place faster than women do (Schmitz, 1999; Silverman et al., 2000), but other researchers find that, despite the difference in strategies, women and men do equally well in navigating the world (Malinowski, 2001). Thus, the support for gender differences based on evolutionary theory is not clear.

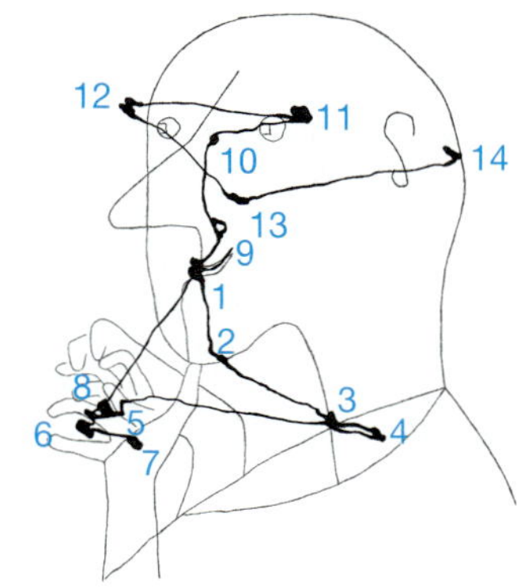

FIGURE 5.10

Patterns of Eye Movement

Eye movements made by a person viewing a drawing adapted from Paul Klee's *Old Man Figuring.* The numbers show the order of the visual fixations. Lines between the numbers represent saccades, which occupied about 10% of the viewing time. The remainder of the time was spent fixating.

Eye Movements

Your eyes are constantly in motion. They search for familiar faces in a crowded classroom, scan the headlines on a page in a newspaper, or follow a baseball hit high into right field for a home run. You notice when someone else is eyeing something over your shoulder and when someone is fixating on a spot on top of your head (is there a spider there?). Research on eye movements reveals what people are looking at, how long they look at it, and perhaps where they will look next. It also helps psychologists understand the visual link with auditory processing and sentence production (Griffin & Bock, 2000) and some visual problems, such as reading disabilities. Zangwill and Blakemore (1972) studied the eye movements of a man who had difficulty reading. They found that he was moving his eyes from right to left across the page, rather than in the usual left-to-right direction. Eye movements also depend on the context in which they are measured. The eye movements of a reader are different from those of someone keyboarding text, even when both are examining the same material. The keyboarder is processing the text merely in order to transcribe it, not to absorb its meaning, as the reader is doing (Inhoff, Starr, & Shindler, 2000). Thus, when researchers study eye movements, they work from the bottom up and from the top down, from the physiology and nature of the actual movements to the functions they perform (Schiller, 1998).

Saccades are the most common type of eye movement—in fact, your eyes make at least 100,000 saccades per day. These are rapid voluntary movements of the eyes when you are reading, driving, or looking for an object. The eye can make only four or five saccades in a second. Each movement of the eye takes only about 20 to 50 milliseconds, but there is a delay of about 200 to 250 milliseconds before the next movement can be made. During this delay, the eye fixates on some part of the visual field. People use eye *fixations* to form representations of the visual world, probably by integrating successive glances into memory. This integration requires that observers move their eyes, pay attention to key elements of a visual scene, and exert careful, systematic control over eye movements (Rayner, Reichle, & Pollatsek, 2000) (see Figure 5.10).

Eye movements have been used to determine the *perceptual span*—the size of the region a person sees when fixating visually; for example, the perceptual span is the number of letters you see when you fixate on a specific point on this page. Research shows that people use information gathered by both central vision (at the fovea) and peripheral vision (at noncentral regions of the eye) to determine the location of their next eye movements; this information ultimately affects the size of

Saccades [sack-ADZ]
Rapid voluntary movements of the eyes.

FIGURE 5.11

Spectral Sensitivity Curve

The average observer's sensitivity to visible light during daylight reaches a peak at 555 nanometers. Thus, the normal human eye is more sensitive to yellow wavelengths than to red or blue. The curve in the graph is called a *spectral sensitivity curve.*

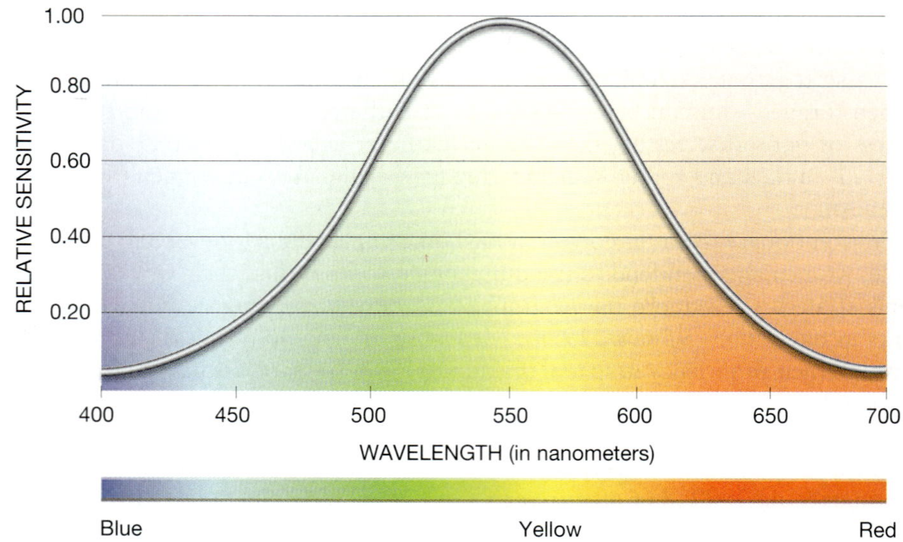

the perceptual span (Machado & Rafal, 2000; Rayner, 1998). Like so many other psychological phenomena, the size and nature of the perceptual span depend on the situation and personal variables. People also tend to direct their gaze to a point just to the left of center of words when they are reading. This site (left of center) may help them make inferences about the rest of the word and even where they will look next (Inhoff, Starr, & Shindler, 2000). A key benefit of this whole line of research is that eye movements can reveal a great deal about cognitive processes in general, and about reading and language in particular.

Hue
The psychological property of light referred to as color, determined by the wavelengths of reflected light.

Brightness
The lightness or darkness of reflected light, determined in large part by the light's intensity.

Saturation
The depth and richness of a hue determined by the homogeneity of the wavelengths contained in the reflected light; also known as *purity.*

Trichromatic [try-kroe-MAT-ick] theory
Visual theory, stated by Young and Helmholtz, that all colors can be made by mixing the three basic colors: red, green, and blue; also known as the *Young-Helmholtz theory.*

Color blindness
The inability to perceive different hues.

Opponent-process theory
Visual theory, proposed by Herring, that color is coded by stimulation of three types of paired receptors; each pair of receptors is assumed to operate in an antagonistic way so that stimulation by a given wavelength produces excitation (increased firing) in one receptor of the pair and also inhibits the other receptor.

Color Vision

Think of all the different shades of blue (navy blue, sky blue, baby blue, royal blue, turquoise, aqua). If you are like most people, you have no trouble discriminating among a wide range of colors. Color depends on the wavelengths of the visible light that stimulates the photoreceptors. It has three psychological dimensions: hue, brightness, and saturation. These dimensions correspond to three physical properties of light: wavelength, intensity, and purity.

When people speak of the color of an object, they are referring to its **hue**—whether the light reflected from the object looks red, blue, orange, or some other color. *Hue* is a psychological term, because objects themselves do not possess color. Rather, a person's perception of color is determined by how the eyes and brain interpret reflected wavelengths. In the visible spectrum, a different hue is associated with each range of wavelengths. Light with a wavelength of 400–450 nanometers looks blue; light with a wavelength of 700 nanometers looks red.

The second psychological dimension of color is **brightness**—how light or dark the hue of an object appears. Brightness is affected by three variables: (1) the greater the intensity of reflected light, the brighter the object; (2) the longer the wavelength of reflected light, the less bright the object; (3) the nearer the wavelengths are to the range of 500 to 600 nanometers, the more sensitive the photoreceptors (see Figure 5.11). This is why school buses are often painted yellow—it makes them more visible to motorists.

The third psychological dimension of color is **saturation,** or *purity*—the depth and richness of the hue, determined by the homogeneity of the wavelengths contained in the reflected light. Few objects reflect light that is totally pure. Usually objects reflect a mixture of wavelengths. Pure, saturated light has a narrow band of wavelengths and, thus, a narrow range of perceived color. A saturated red light with no blue, yellow, or white in it, for example, appears as a very intense red. Unsaturated colors are produced by a wider band of wavelengths. Unsaturated red light can appear to be light pink, dark red, or rusty brown, because its wider range of wavelengths makes it less pure (see Figure 5.12).

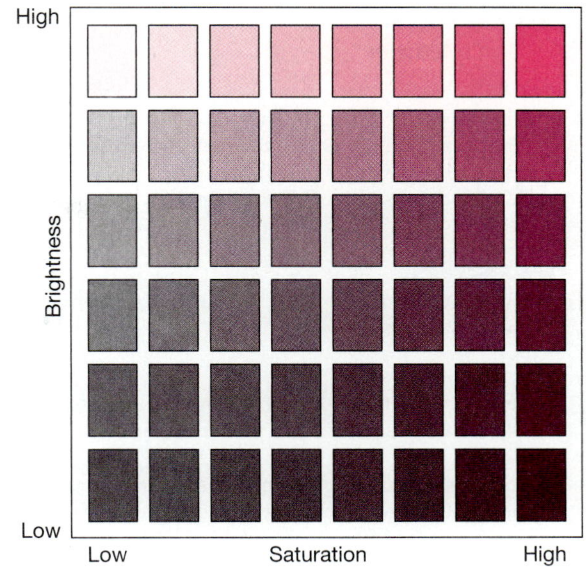

FIGURE 5.12

Hue, Brightness, and Saturation

These colors have the same dominant wavelength (hue) but different saturation and brightness.

■ **THEORIES OF COLOR VISION.** How does the brain code and process color? Two 19th-century scientists, Thomas Young and Hermann von Helmholtz, working independently, proposed that different types of cones provide the basis for color coding in the visual system. *Color coding* is the ability to discriminate among colors on the basis of differences in wavelength. According to the **trichromatic theory,** or the *Young-Helmholtz theory,* mixing three basic colors—red, green, and blue—can make all colors. (*Trichromatic* means "three colors"—*tri* meaning "three," and *chroma,* "color.") All cone cells in the retina are assumed to respond to all wavelengths of light; but there are three types of cones that are especially likely to respond to red, green, or blue wavelengths (see Figure 5.13). The combined neural output of the red-sensitive, green-sensitive, and blue-sensitive cones provides the information that enables a person to distinguish color. If the neural output from one type of cone is sufficiently greater than that from the others, that type of color receptor will have a stronger influence on a person's perception of color. Because each person's neurons are unique, it is likely that each of us sees color somewhat differently.

Unfortunately, the trichromatic theory does not account for some specific visual phenomena. For example, it does not explain why some colors look more vivid when placed next to other colors (color contrast). It does not explain why people asked to name the basic colors nearly always name more than three. Further, the trichromatic theory does not do a good job of explaining aspects of **color blindness**—the inability to perceive different hues (described below). For example, many people with color blindness cannot successfully discriminate colors in two areas of the visual spectrum. In 1887, to solve some of the problems left unsolved by the trichromatic theory, Ewald Herring proposed another theory of color vision—the **opponent-process theory.** This theory assumes that there are six basic colors to which people respond and that there are three types of receptors: red–green, blue–yellow, and black–white. Every receptor fires in response to all wavelengths; but in each pair of receptors, one fires more strongly in response to one wavelength. Strong firing in response to red, for example, is accompanied by weak firing in response to green. Opponent-process theory explains color contrast and color blindness better than the trichromatic theory does.

Both the trichromatic theory and the opponent-process theory have received support from research (e.g., Hurvich & Jameson, 1974). Physiological studies of the retina do show three classes of cones. Thus, the trichromatic theory seems to describe accurately the coding at the retina (Marks, Dobell, & MacNichol, 1964). Support for the opponent-process theory comes from microelectrode studies of the lateral geniculate nucleus in monkeys. Cells in this nucleus respond differently to various wavelengths. When the eye is stimulated with light of a wavelength between 400 and 500 nanometers, some cells in the lateral geniculate nucleus decrease their rate of firing. If the eye is stimulated with

FIGURE 5.13

Three Types of Cones

Each of the three types of cones in the eye has peak sensitivity in a different area of the visible spectrum. Thus, certain cells are more responsive to some wavelengths than to others. *(MacNichol, 1964)*

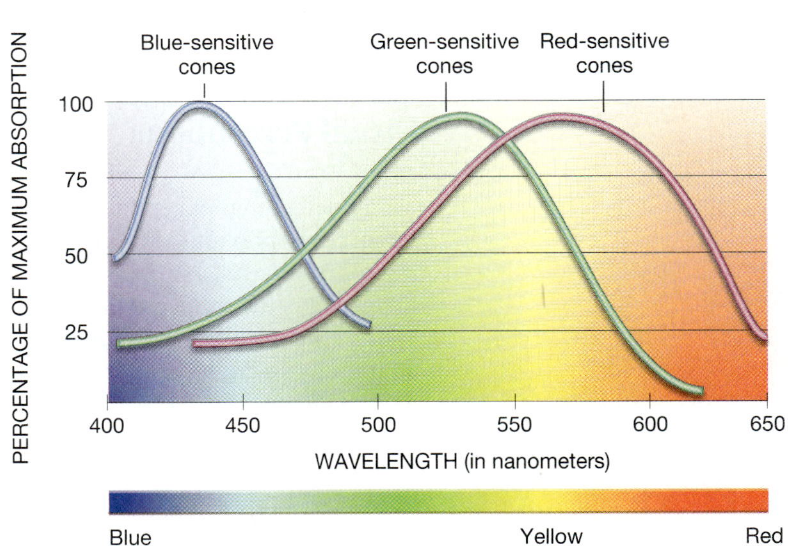

Be an
Active learner

REVIEW
- What does it mean to be myopic. p. 151
- What are three important differences between rods and cones? pp. 151–153
- Descibe the process of dark adaptation p. 153

THINK CRITICALLY
- Why do you think boys and girls might vary on some visual tasks?

APPLY PSYCHOLOGY
- Design an invention—a pair of glasses—that can help a partially color-blind person to see color better.
- How might you design a better pair of everyday corrective lenses? What might ensure better vision?

light of a longer wavelength, their firing rate increases (DeValois & Jacobs, 1968). This change is predicted by the opponent-process theory. Exactly how color information is transferred from the retina to the lateral geniculate nucleus remains to be discovered (Engel, 1999).

COLOR BLINDNESS. In 1794, John Dalton, formulator of the atomic theory of matter, believed he had figured out why he couldn't distinguish his red stockings from his green ones. He reasoned that something blue in his eyeball absorbed red light and prevented him from seeing red. Although Dalton was the first to try to describe color blindness scientifically, he was not the first—or the last—person to suffer from it. In fact, about 30 million Americans have some type of color perception problem.

Most human beings have normal color vision and can distinguish among about 100 different hues; they are considered trichromats. **Trichromats** are people who can perceive all three primary colors and thus can distinguish any hue. A very few people (less than 1%) do not see any color. These people, known as **monochromats,** are totally color-blind and cannot discriminate among wavelengths, often because they lack cones in their retinas (Boynton, 1988). The lack of the specific color-absorbing pigment or chemical in the cones makes accurate color discriminations impossible. Fortunately, most people with color vision deficiencies (about 8% of men and 1% of women) are only partially color-blind (Nathans, 1989). **Dichromats** are people who can distinguish only two of the three basic colors; they have difficulty distinguishing between either red and green or blue and yellow. About 2% of men cannot discriminate between reds and greens (Wyszecki & Stiles, 1967). What does the world look like to a person who is a dichromat? Such a person sees all the colors in a range of the electromagnetic spectrum as similar.

The full role of genetics in color blindness is not clear, but this perceptual problem is transmitted genetically from mothers to their male offspring. The fact that more men than women are color-blind is due to the way this genetic information is coded and passed on to each generation. Color blindness results from inherited alterations in the genes that are responsible for cone pigments; these genes are located on the X chromosome. Since girls have two X chromosomes and boys have only one, a girl will be color-deficient only if she inherits the defective gene from both parents. Boys who inherit an X chromosome with a defective gene will have deficient color vision.

Visual Perception

Many perceptual experiences depend on past events as well as current stimulation. Integrating previous experiences with new events makes perceptual encounters more meaningful. For example, only through experience do children learn that an object stays the same size and shape when it is moved farther away from them. Of course, our daily perceptions do not always lead to truth—the Mojave Desert looks as flat as can be for as far as the eye can see and makes some people (they even have their own society—the Flat Earth Research Society) believe that the earth is flat. In this section, we look at a range of visual perceptual phenomena that rely heavily on the integration of past and current experiences to develop a true perception of the world.

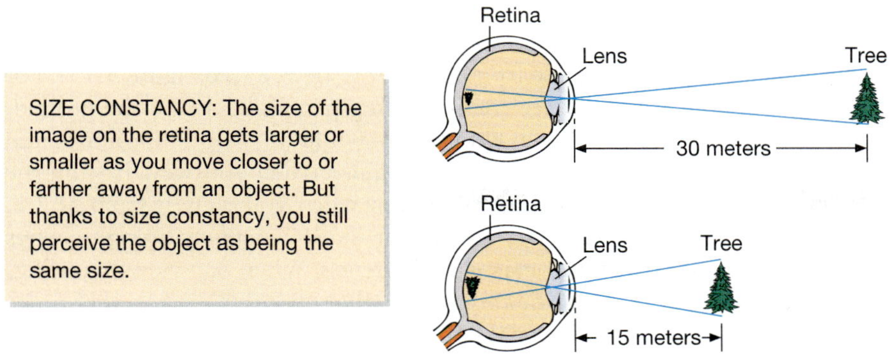

FIGURE 5.14

Perceptual Constancies

Size constancy is the perceptual system's ability to recognize that an object remains the same size regardless of its distance from an observer or the size of its image on the retina. *Shape constancy* is the perceptual system's ability to recognize a shape despite changes in the angle or position from which it is viewed.

Perception of Form: Constancy

If your friend is wearing dark glasses that conceal much of her face, you will probably still recognize her. Similarly, impressionist artists count on people's ability to infer a complete object from dots of paint on canvas, and cartoonists use exaggerated features to portray well-known people. Understanding how human beings perceive form and space helps architects to design buildings and designers to create furniture and clothes. Perception of form involves the interpretation of stimuli conveying information about size, shape, and depth to create a unified image. Two important aspects of form perception are recognizing forms at a distance and recognizing forms that appear to have changed size or shape.

■ **SIZE CONSTANCY.** People can generally judge the size of an object, even if the size of its image on the retina changes. For example, you can estimate the height of a 6-foot man who is standing 50 feet away and casts a small image on the retina; you can also estimate his height from only 5 feet away, when he casts a much larger image on the retina. **Size constancy** is the ability of the visual perceptual system to recognize that an object remains constant in size regardless of its distance from the observer or the size of its image on the retina. Infants attain size constancy by the age of 6 months and probably as early as 4 months.

Three variables determine the ability to maintain size constancy: (1) previous experience with the true size of objects, (2) the distance between the object and the person, and (3) the presence of surrounding objects. As an object moves farther away, the size of its image on the retina decreases and its perceived distance from the viewer increases (see Figure 5.14). These two effects always work together. Moreover, as an object moves away, its perceived size does not change in relation to that of objects around it. This is why knowing the size of surrounding objects helps people determine a perceived object's distance from them as well as its actual size. Hollywood special effects artists have used the brain's tendency to judge an object's size by comparing it with surrounding objects to convince moviegoers that, for example, a 6-inch clay model of an ape is the giant King Kong.

Trichromats [TRY-kroe-MATZ]
People who can perceive all three primary colors and thus can distinguish any hue.

Monochromats [MON-o-kroe-MATZ]
People who cannot perceive any color, usually because their retinas lack cones.

Dichromats [DIE-kroe-MATZ]
People who can distinguish only two of the three basic colors.

Size constancy
Ability of the visual perceptual system to recognize that an object remains constant in size regardless of its distance from the observer or the size of its image on the retina.

■ **SHAPE CONSTANCY.** Another important aspect of form perception is **shape constancy**—the ability of the visual perceptual system to recognize a shape despite changes in its orientation or the angle from which it is viewed (see Figure 5.15). For example, even though you usually see trees standing perpendicular to the ground, you can recognize a tree that has been chopped down and is lying in a horizontal position. Similarly, an ice cream cone looks triangular when you view it from the side; yet you perceive it as an ice cream cone even when you view it from above, where it appears more circular than triangular. But shape constancy doesn't always hold up; in some instances, distance makes a difference. When one views paintings where features are reduced to small squares, that is, the squares taken together make up features, it turns out that our ability to perceive shapes (for example, eyes, mouths, or doors) depends on the distance from which we view them (Pelli, 1999). We're not sure why yet, but this phenomenon violates the generally held rules about shape constancy.

Depth Perception

For centuries, Zen landscape artists have used the principles of depth perception to create seemingly expansive, rugged gardens out of tiny plots of land. Although a Zen landscape can be used to fool the eye, you normally judge distances accurately when you drive a car, catch a ball, or take a picture. Depth perception allows you to estimate your distance from an object and the distance between that object and another one. Closely associated with these two tasks is the ability to see in three dimensions—that is, to perceive height, width, and depth. Both monocular cues (using one eye) and binocular cues (using two eyes) are used in depth perception. Binocular cues predominate at close distances, and monocular cues are used for distant scenes and two-dimensional fields of view, such as paintings. These cues are operative and evident even in infants (Sen, Yonas, & Knill, 2001). Because the visual system is still plastic (modifiable) early in life, where and how depth information is coded depends on an infant's experiences. Research shows, for example, that binocular depth information is coded at different places if there is a deprivation of depth experiences (Trachtenberg, Trepel, & Stryker, 2000).

■ *Zen landscape artists use the principles of depth perception to create seemingly expansive, rugged gardens out of small plots of land.*

■ **MONOCULAR DEPTH CUES.** Depth cues that do not depend on the use of both eyes are **monocular depth cues** (see Figure 5.15). Two important monocular depth cues arise from the effects of motion on perception. The first cue, *motion parallax,* occurs when a moving observer stares at a fixed point. The objects behind that point appear to move in the same direction as the observer; the objects in front of the point appear to move in the opposite direction. For example, if you stare at a fence while riding in a moving car, the trees behind the fence seem to move in the same direction as the car (forward) and the bushes in front of the fence seem to move in the opposite direction (backward). Motion parallax also affects the speed at which objects appear to move. Objects at a greater distance from the moving observer appear to move more slowly than objects that are closer. The second monocular depth cue derived from movement is the *kinetic depth effect.* Objects that look flat when stationary appear to be three-dimensional when set in motion. When two-dimensional projections—such as images of squares or rods shown on a computer screen—are rotated, they appear to have three dimensions.

Shape constancy
Ability of the visual perceptual system to recognize a shape despite changes in its orientation or the angle from which it is viewed.

Monocular [mah-NAHK-you-ler] depth cues
Depth cues that do not depend on the use of both eyes.

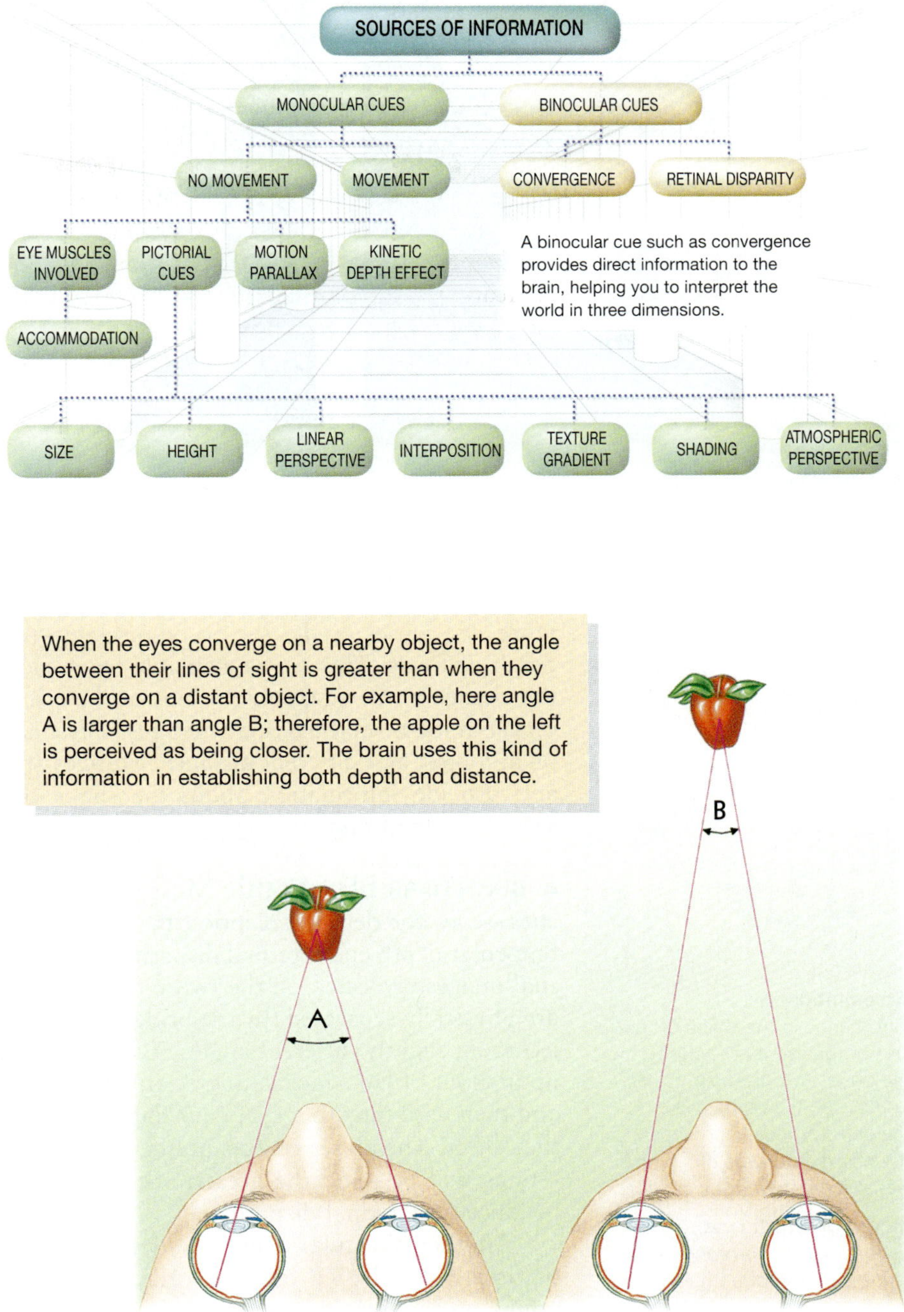

FIGURE 5.15

Depth Perception

The ability to see in three dimensions—height, width, and depth—depends on both monocular and binocular cues.

Other monocular depth cues arise from the stimulus itself; these are often seen in photographs and paintings. For example, because of the depth cue of *linear perspective,* larger or taller objects are usually perceived to be closer than smaller ones, particularly in relation to surrounding objects. In addition, because distant objects appear to be closer together than nearer objects, a painter shows distance by making parallel lines converge as they recede. Another monocular cue for depth is *interposition.* When one object blocks out part of another, the first appears to be closer. A fifth monocular cue is *texture;* surfaces that have little texture or detail seem to be in the distance. Artists often use the additional cues of *highlighting* and *shadowing.* Highlighted (light) objects appear close; shadowed (dark) objects appear to be farther away. In addition, the perceptual system picks up other information from shadowing, including the curvature of surfaces (Cavanagh & Leclerc, 1989). Still another monocular depth cue is *atmospheric perspective,* which relates to the wavelengths of reflected light. Distant mountains often look blue, for example, because long (red) wavelengths are more easily scattered as they pass through the air, allowing more short (blue) wavelengths to reach our eyes. Leonardo da Vinci used this phenomenon in his paintings; he even developed an equation for how much blue pigment to mix with the close-up color of an object to make the object appear as far away as he wished. Similarly, Michelangelo's figures seem to float off the ceiling of the Sistine Chapel because he used color so effectively to portray depth.

■ *Mountains in the distance often look blue because of the monocular depth cue, atmospheric perspective. Similarly, Michelangelo's figures seem to float off the ceiling of the Sistine Chapel because he used color so effectively to portray depth.*

Another monocular depth cue that is not derived from the stimulus is accommodation. If a person looks from one object to another that is at a different distance, the lenses of the eye accommodate—that is, change shape to adapt to the depth of focus. This cue is available from each eye separately. **Accommodation** is the change in the shape of the lens of the eye that enables the observer to keep an object in focus on the retina when the object is moved or when the observer focuses on an object at a different distance. Muscles attached to the lens control this change and provide information about the shape of the lens to the higher processing systems in the brain.

Accommodation
The change in the shape of the lens of the eye that enables the observer to keep an object in focus on the retina when the object is moved or when the observer focuses on an object at a different distance.

Binocular depth cues
Cues for depth perception that require the use of both eyes.

Retinal disparity
The slight difference between the visual images projected on the two retinas.

Convergence
The movement of the eyes toward each other to keep visual stimulation at corresponding points on the retinas as an object moves closer to the observer.

Illusion
A perception of a physical stimulus that differs from measurable reality or from what is commonly expected.

■ **BINOCULAR DEPTH CUES.** Most people, even infants, also use **binocular depth cues**—cues for depth perception that require the use of both eyes. One important binocular depth cue is **retinal disparity,** which is the slight difference between the visual images projected on the two retinas. Retinal disparity occurs because the eyes are physically separated (by the bridge of the nose), which causes them to see an object from slightly different angles. To see how retinal disparity works, hold a finger up in front of your face and look at some object across the room first with one eye and then with the other eye; your finger will appear in different positions relative to the object. The closer objects are to the eyes, the farther apart their images on the retinas will be—and the greater the retinal disparity. Objects at a great distance produce little retinal disparity.

Another binocular depth cue is convergence. **Convergence** is the movement of the eyes toward each other in order to keep visual stimulation at corresponding points on the retinas as an object moves closer to the observer. Like accommodation, convergence is controlled by eye muscles that convey information to the brain. For objects beyond 20 or 30 feet away, the eyes are aimed pretty much in parallel, and the effect of convergence diminishes.

Illusions

At some time, you have probably seen what looks like water ahead on the road, only to find it has disappeared when you drive by that point. You most likely also have seen railroad tracks that appear to converge in the distance. When normal visual process and depth cues seem to break down, you experience an optical illusion. An **illusion** is a perception of a physical stimulus that differs from measurable reality or from what is commonly expected.

A common illusion is the *Müller-Lyer illusion,* in which two lines of equal length with arrows on the ends appear to be of different lengths. A similar illusion is the

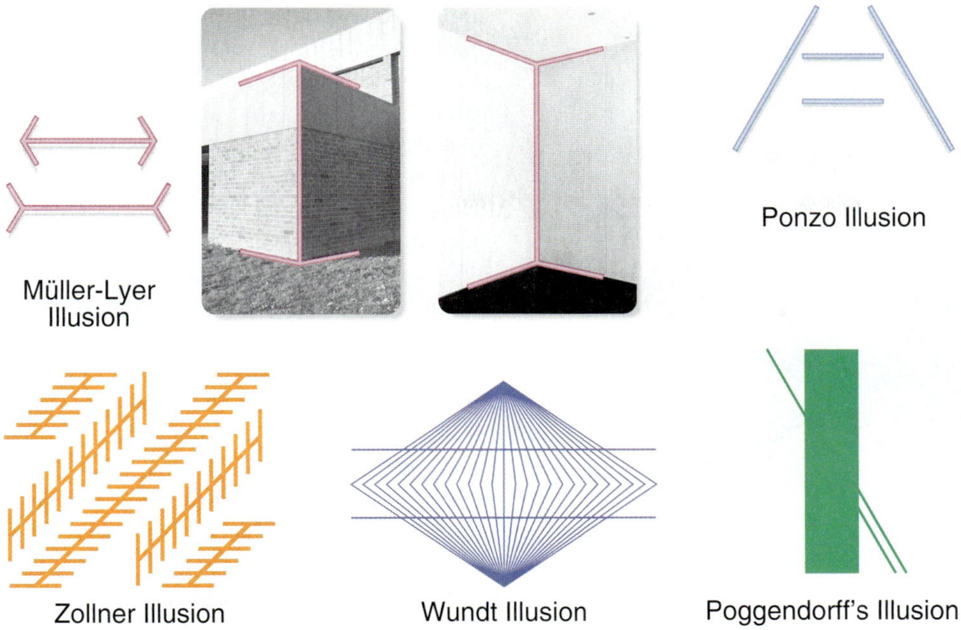

FIGURE 5.16

Five Well-Known Illusions

In the Müller-Lyer and Ponzo illusions, lines of equal length appear to differ in length. The photos with the Müller-Lyer illusion show how the arrows can represent a "near corner" and a "far corner." In the Zollner illusion, the short lines make the longer ones seem not parallel, even though they are. In the Wundt illusion, the center horizontal lines are parallel, even though they appear bent. In the Poggendorff illusion, the line disappears behind a solid and reappears in a position that seems wrong.

Ponzo illusion (sometimes called the railroad illusion), in which two horizontal lines of the same length, bracketed by slanted lines, appear to be of different lengths. (See Figure 5.16 for examples of these two illusions and three others; Figure 5.17 presents another perceptual phenomenon.) The *moon illusion* is a natural illusion. Although the actual size of the moon and the size of its image on the retina do not change, the moon appears about 30% larger when it is near the horizon than when it is overhead. The moon illusion is quite striking—in just a few minutes, the moon appears to change from quite large to quite small. The moon illusion is even seen in photographs and paintings (Suzuki, 1998).

How do visual illusions work? No completely satisfactory explanations have been found. Recent theories account for these illusions in terms of the backgrounds against which the objects are seen. These explanations assume that the observer has had previous experiences with a particular stimulus and has well-developed perceptual constancies. For example, the moon illusion is explained by the fact that, when seen overhead, the moon is against a featureless background, whereas at the horizon, objects are close to it. Objects in the landscape provide cues about distance that change the observer's perception of the size of the moon (Baird, Wagner, & Fuld, 1990; Restle, 1970). To see how the moon illusion depends on landscape cues, try this: when the moon is at the horizon, bend over and look at it from between your legs. Since that position screens out some of the horizon cues, the magnitude of the illusion is reduced.

The Ponzo illusion is similarly accounted for by the linear perspective provided by the slanted background lines. The Müller-Lyer illusion occurs because of the angles of the short lines attached to the ends of the longer lines. Short lines angled like arrow tails are often

FIGURE 5.17

For the Active Learner: Impossible Figures

Many types of drawings trick the perceiver because they portray *impossible figures*. Notice that the longer you stare at this drawing by M. C. Escher, the more visually confusing is the arrangement of its components.

■ Researchers have found that people who grew up in cultures that do not emphasize lines, angles, and geometry, view illusions differently.

interpreted as far corners—corners distant from the observer. Short lines angled like arrow heads are commonly interpreted as corners that are close to the observer. Therefore, lines with far-corner angles attached to them appear longer because their length is judged in a context of distance.

These are not the only ways of explaining illusions. Some researchers assert that the moon appears to be different in size on the horizon and overhead because people judge its size the same way they judge that of other moving objects that pass through space. Because the moon does not get closer to them, they assume it is moving away. Objects that move away get smaller; hence the illusion of a change in the size of the moon (Reed, 1984). This explanation focuses on constancies but also takes account of movement and space.

■ **CROSS-CULTURAL RESEARCH ON ILLUSIONS.** Each person brings a lifetime of experiences to his or her perceptions. This becomes especially clear from research conducted cross-culturally. Cross-cultural research on illusions, for example, shows that the Müller-Lyer and Ponzo (railroad) illusions are perceived differently by different cultures. Leibowitz (1971) conducted a series of studies on the Ponzo illusion, using both American participants and participants from Guam, where there are no railroads and perspective cues are far less prevalent than in the United States. Leibowitz had his participants judge the Ponzo illusion presented as simple line drawings and also in photographs. He found that the illusion was more pronounced for the American participants as he added more pictorial depth cues. The participants from Guam showed few differences when more pictorial cues were added. There were other differences between the groups; for example, the participants from Guam viewed depth differently than did their American counterparts. The different cultures viewed the world in dissimilar ways.

Other illusions have been investigated with different cultural groups. For example, Pedersen and Wheeler (1983) compared the reactions of two groups of Navajos to the Müller-Lyer illusion. One group lived in rectangular houses; these participants had extensive experience with corners, angles, and oblique lines. The other group lived in traditional Navajo round houses, similar to the Zulu round house shown in the photo, and their early experiences included far fewer encounters with angles. The researchers found that those who lived in angular houses were more susceptible to the Müller-Lyer illusion, which depends on angles. Some researchers say such illusions depend on the *carpenter effect,* because in Western cultures carpenters use lines, angles, and geometry to build houses.

Cross-cultural research is exciting and illuminating, although still limited in extent. For psychologists to develop truly comprehensive theories of perception, they must incorporate cross-cultural differences into their research.

Prosopagnosia: The Inability to Recognize Faces

Cindy Crawford, Leo DeCaprio, and Matt Damon all have distinctive faces. So do Bill Clinton, Condoleezza Rice, and Richard Nixon. Faces define and differentiate people. Whether a person's eyes, teeth, or hair present facial "landmarks" is un-

introduction to research basics

Have You Ever Smelled a Color?

Occasionally a phenomenon presents itself to a psychologist that is mildly mystifying. Such topics are often difficult to assess experimentally. But not completely—consider synesthesia.

Synesthesia is a bizarre phenomenon in which sensory images or qualities of one modality, such as vision, are transferred to another modality, such as taste or hearing (Marks, 2000; Ramachandran, 2000a). To a synesthetic person, a sip of lemonade may take on a green color as well as a sour-sweet flavor, or a soprano's aria may take on visual form that changes in shape, size, and color. In synesthesia, therefore, a stimulus produces two kinds of responses at the same time: the principal sensory experience that is normally associated with the stimulus and a second experience in another modality (Armel & Ramachandran, 1999). In synesthesia we hear shapes, see colors as sound, and may perceive a shirt as noisy (Martino & Marks, 2001).

The incidence of synesthesia is estimated to be approximately 1 in 25,000 individuals. There is probably a genetic component; it runs in families, and 15% of people with synesthesia have an immediate family history of other neurological abnormalities, including dyslexia, autism, and attention-deficit disorder. Typically, the synesthetic individual is female, left-handed, and of normal intelligence (Groffman, 1999).

Two synesthesia researchers, Vilayanur Ramachandran and Edward Hubbard (2001), investigated the phenomenon by looking at a specific form of synesthesia called "colored number synesthesia."

DESIGN The researchers used an *experimental design* in which they varied the presentation of materials as the *independent variable* and measured participants' perceptions of grouping of items as the *dependent variable.*

HYPOTHESIS Ramachandran and Hubbard hypothesized that people with synesthesia would be influenced by the perceptual qualities of visual displays prompted by their synesthesia as well as by the primary sensory properties.

PARTICIPANTS Two individuals with colored number synesthesia served as participants. Most experiments in psychology test many participants, but colored number synesthesia is rare, and these researchers wanted to explore this interesting phenomenon. An additional 20 participants without synesthesia served as comparisons.

PROCEDURE The participants completed a series of perceptual tests. In one, Ramachandran and Hubbard created a pattern that consisted solely of computer-generated *2*s and *5*s, which would appear as shapes such as triangles or circles to individuals with colored number synesthesia. In another experiment, the researchers compared perceptual groupings based on Arabic versus Roman numerals.

RESULTS The results were compelling. The participants with synesthesia were strongly influenced by this ability in their perceptions of the materials. In the experiment with *2*s and *5*s, the page just looked like a jumble of numbers to the comparison participants. But to the synesthetic participants, the shapes made of *2*s leapt out as perceptual groups because of the colors they evoked. In the experiment with Roman versus Arabic numerals, the Arabic numerals induced the perception of color, but the Roman numerals did not. Thus, the form of the numbers is a critical characteristic of this type of synesthesia.

CONCLUSIONS Ramachandran and Hubbard assert that the phenomenon of synesthesia is a real perceptual process rather than an associative effect of memory from childhood or a metaphor. Furthermore, they argue that a part of the brain known as the fusiform gyrus, which deals with color, may be cross-wired to a nearby area of the brain that deals with numbers, producing these specific cross-mode perceptions. This wiring is unusual, but they suggest that it is more common among artists and poets than others. Their results suggest that synesthesia is a real phenomenon, one that can and should be investigated, and that probably has a unique physiological basis. The research has just begun.

clear, but the perception of faces is a unique process. We all engage in the perceptual task of discerning, analyzing, remembering, and recognizing faces. Even in the first weeks of life, newborns are able to distinguish faces from other objects, and they quickly develop the ability to recognize their principal caregiver's face (Mondloch et al., 1999).

Research on brain structure shows that there is something about face perception that distinguishes it from other kinds of perception. Some interesting evidence comes from studies of agnosia. People with **agnosia** have normal, intact perceptual systems for detecting color, shape, and motion, and they have no verbal, memory, or intellectual impairment. And yet they are unable to recognize

Agnosia
An inability to recognize a sensory stimulus that should be recognizable because perceptual systems for detecting color, shape, and motion are normal and intact and there are no verbal, memory, or intellectual impairments.

things the way they should be able to. Agnosia usually occurs because of injury to the brain from an accident, or perhaps from a stroke. When a patient has agnosia, he or she can see stimuli but cannot name them. When presented with an object—a cup or a candle, for example—a person with agnosia is unable to name the object. Some visual agnosias are very specific—for example, color agnosia, movement agnosia, and object agnosia.

Is it possible that there are special regions of the brain responsible for *prosopagnosia*—the inability to recognize faces? Does the brain include a "face detector"? There are several lines of evidence supporting this notion. First, research shows that certain brain cells are activated by facial stimuli and not by other stimuli (Renault et al., 1989). Some individual cells have been found (around the temporal lobes) that respond best to faces, sometimes even to faces in a particular orientation, such as frontal or profile. Unfortunately, the appealing idea of "one face, one neuron" is somewhat flawed, because we simply do not have enough neurons in our brains to ensure that every face, every scene, is represented by an individual neuron. People are normally skilled at recognizing faces, but when faces are distorted, turned upside-down, or otherwise taken out of the usual perspective, face recognition is far more difficult (Farah et al., 1998; McNeil & Warrington, 1993), though still possible.

Researchers study agnosia in general, and prosopagnosia in particular, because it helps them understand specific areas of the brain. But such study also leads to the conclusion that our visual system is made up of interacting and interdependent parts that create a whole visual experience. Some tasks require very specific object recognition, but other tasks, such as face perception, require a more holistic, interactive analysis that depends on both sides of the brain (Rumiati & Humphreys, 1997) and the brain as a whole (Macaluso, Frith, & Driver,

FIGURE 5.18

Gestalt Laws

Gestalt principles are the organizing elements humans use to group perceptual fragments into the coherent wholes by which they perceive the world. *(Beck, 1966)*

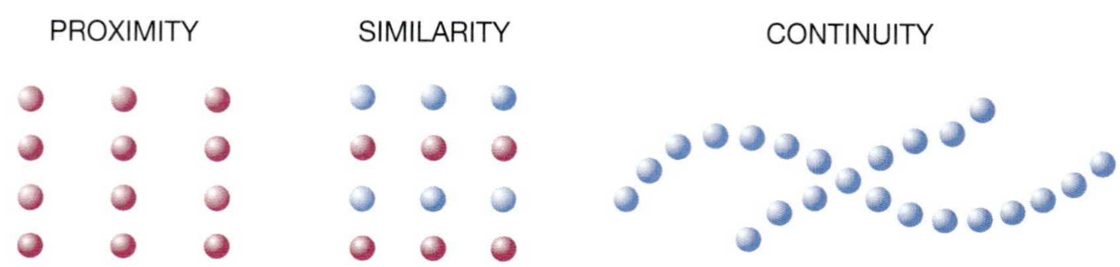

According to the Gestalt law of proximity, the circles on the left appear to be arranged in vertical columns because items that are close together tend to be perceived as a unit. According to the law of similarity, the red and blue circles in the middle appear to be arranged in horizontal rows because similar items tend to be perceived in groups. According to the law of continuity, an observer can predict where the next item should occur in the arrangement on the right because the grouping of items projects lines into space.

The law of Prägnanz: Items or stimuli that *can* be grouped together as a whole *will* be. These 16 dots are typically perceived as a square.

In a study asking people to divide these objects into two groups, Beck (1966) found that participants generally placed the boundary between upright and tilted *Ts* rather than between the backward *Ls* and the upright *Ts* because the latter appear more similar. Beck argued that this result supports the law of Prägnanz.

2000). The whole-versus-part distinction as it relates to prosopagnosia continues to be a cutting-edge research issue that may ultimately help specify relationships between brain and behavior.

Gestalt Laws of Organization

Gestalt psychologists suggest that conscious experience is more than the sum of its parts. They argue that the mind organizes the elements of experience to form something unique; each individual views the world in terms of perceptual frameworks. Analyzed as a whole experience, the patterns of a person's perceptions make sense. The first Gestalt psychologists—including Max Wertheimer, Kurt Koffka, and Wolfgang Köhler—greatly influenced early theories of form perception. These psychologists assumed (wrongly) that human perceptual processes *solely* reflect brain organization and that they could learn about the workings of the brain by studying perception. Researchers now know, of course, that the relationship between brain structure and function is much more complex—perception is a process that not only represents stimuli but reflects past experiences as well.

The early Gestaltists focused their perceptual studies on how people experience form and organization. These early researchers believed people organize each complex visual field into a coherent whole rather than seeing individual, unrelated elements. That is, they believed people see groups of elements, not fragments or parts. According to this idea, called the **law of Prägnanz,** items or stimuli that *can* be grouped together and seen as a whole, or a form, *will* be seen that way; viewers see the simplest shape consistent with available information. So, for example, people tend to see the series of 16 dots in the lower left portion of Figure 5.18 as a square. Not only did Gestaltists believe that perception is organized by grouping and form, but they also assumed that retinal stimulation was directly reflected in physiological processing.

The law of Prägnanz was based on principles of organization for the perception of figures, especially contours, which help define *figure–ground relationships.* Gestalt psychologists focused on the nature of these relationships, contending that people perceive *figures* (the main objects of sensory attention—the foregrounds) as distinct from the *grounds* (the backgrounds) on which they are presented (see Figure 5.19). Gestalt psychologists developed the following series of laws, the first three of which are illustrated in the upper part of Figure 5.18, for predicting which areas of an ambiguous pattern would be seen as the figure (foreground) and which as the ground (background):

- *Law of proximity:* Elements close to one another in space or time will be perceived as groups.
- *Law of similarity:* Similar items will be perceived in groups.
- *Law of continuity:* A string of items will project the probable location of the next item.
- *Common fate principle:* Items that move or change together will be perceived as a whole.
- *Law of closure:* Parts of a figure that are not presented will be filled in by the perceptual system.

Beck (1966) conducted a well-known study that examined Gestalt principles (see the lower right part of Figure 5.18). However, Beck's work showed that Gestalt principles are vague: they apply whether participants choose orientation

FIGURE 5.19

The Figure–Ground Relationship

For the Active Learner: Gestalt psychologists studied the figure–ground relationship. In this drawing, figure and ground can be reversed. Try it yourself. You'll notice that you can see either two faces against a white background or a goblet against a dark background.

Law of Prägnanz [PREG-nants]
The Gestalt notion that when items or stimuli *can* be grouped together and seen as a whole, they *will* be.

Be an *Active* learner

REVIEW

- Why can people generally judge the size of an object, even if the size of its image on the retina changes? p. 161
- Explain how monocular and binocular depth cues help people see depth. pp. 162–164
- How do perceptual psychologists account for the moon illusion? pp. 165–166
- What is *agnosia?* pp. 167–168

THINK CRITICALLY

- What did Gestalt psychologists mean when they said that "the whole is greater than the sum of its parts"?
- How do you think culture influences the experience of synesthesia?

APPLY PSYCHOLOGY

- If you were to design a robot, and the robot had "what" and "where" detectors, what other types of visual sensors might you add to it? Why?
- Could a computer be trained to distinguish between real phenomena and human illusions? What would a developer have to do to teach a computer to experience illusion?

or shape to break up the figure, but they do not explain why orientation predominated in Beck's study. Apparently, not all people use the same criteria in applying Gestalt laws under the same circumstances. Nor are Gestalt laws always consistent with current knowledge of brain organization—for example, when viewing a figure made up of other smaller figures, people vary a good deal as to whether they pay attention to the larger figure or the smaller ones (Rock & Palmer, 1990). Furthermore, the fact that cells that process "what" and "where" information are located throughout the brain shows that processing is multistage and complex—not merely bottom up, but also top down. Nevertheless, early investigations by Gestaltists offered enough glimpses into the true nature of perception that they continue to influence perceptual psychologists, serving as springboards to further research.

Hearing

You may have heard the oft-repeated statement that blind people can hear better than sighted individuals—and at least on some perceptual tasks, it turns out to be true (Bavelier et al., 2000; Rosenbluth, Grossman, & Kaitz, 2000). Although our sense of sight is powerful and gives texture to our experience, we rely enormously on our sense of hearing for many perceptual experiences, even more than on sight. Nevertheless, though most of us take hearing for granted, the task of listening is exceedingly complex. Consider music. Listening closely to modern music by composers such as Philip Glass is delightful and intriguing—and sometimes a real challenge for Western ears—because so much is going on at once, and for many the music sounds dissonant. The listener must simultaneously process the sounds, rhythms, and intensities produced by more than 20 instruments playing at once. Like seeing, hearing is a complex process that involves converting physical stimuli into a psychological experience based on physical stimulation and past cultural experiences.

FIGURE 5.20

The Frequency and Amplitude of Sound Waves

A person's psychological experience of sound depends on the frequency and amplitude of sound waves.

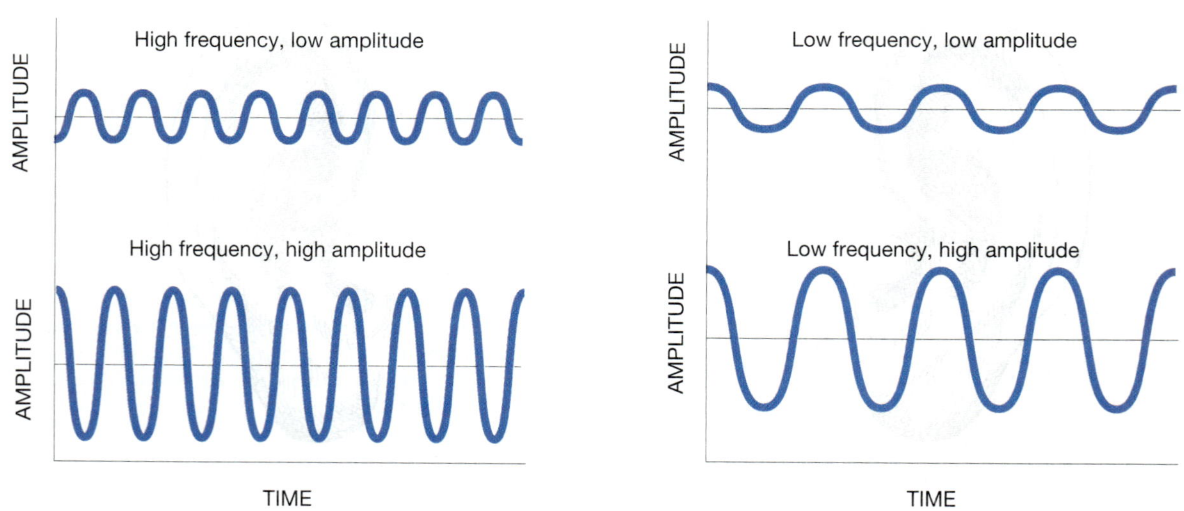

High-frequency sound waves have a large number of complete cycles per second and a high pitch; they can be of low amplitude (soft sound) or high amplitude (loud sound).

Low-frequency sound waves have a small number of complete cycles per second and a low pitch; they can be of low amplitude (soft sound) or high amplitude (loud sound).

Sound

When a tuning fork is struck or a stereo system booms out a bass note, sound waves are created and air is moved. You can place your hand in front of a stereo speaker and feel the displacement of the sound waves when the volume rises. The movement of the air and the accompanying changes in air pressure (physical stimuli) cause a listener's eardrum to move back and forth rapidly. The movement of the eardrum triggers a series of electromechanical and electrochemical changes that the person experiences as sound. **Sound** is the psychological experience that occurs when changes in air pressure affect the receptive organ for hearing; the resulting tones, or sounds, vary in frequency and amplitude. Sound is often thought of in terms of two psychological aspects, pitch and loudness, which are associated with the two physical attributes of frequency and amplitude.

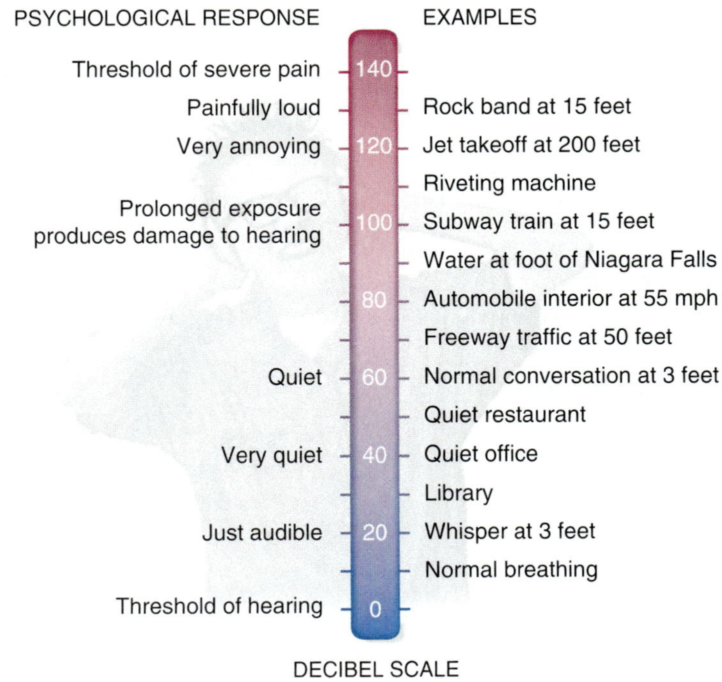

FIGURE 5.21

Psychological Responses to Various Sound Intensities

High-amplitude sound waves, such as those generated by a rock band, have greater energy than low-amplitude waves and a greater impact on the sensitive structure of the ears.

As shown in Figure 5.20, **frequency** is the number of complete changes in air pressure occurring during a given unit of time. Within 1 second, for example, there may be 50 complete changes (50 cycles per second) or 10,000 complete changes (10,000 cycles per second). Frequency is usually measured in hertz (Hz); 1 Hz equals 1 cycle per second. Frequency determines the pitch, or *tone*, of a sound; **pitch** is the psychological experience that corresponds with the frequency of an auditory stimulus. High-pitched tones usually have high frequencies. When a piano hammer strikes a short string on the right-hand end of a piano keyboard, the string vibrates at a high frequency and sounds high in pitch; when a long string (at the left-hand end) is struck, it vibrates less frequently and sounds low in pitch.

Amplitude, or *intensity*, is the total energy of a sound wave, which determines the loudness of the sound. High-amplitude sound waves have more energy than low-amplitude waves; they apply greater force to the ear (see Figure 5.20). Amplitude is measured in *decibels*. Every increase of 20 decibels corresponds to a tenfold increase in perceived intensity. (Decibels are measured on a logarithmic scale, which is exponential, not linear; thus, increases in sound intensity measured in decibels are quite large.) As Figure 5.21 shows, normal conversation has an amplitude of about 60 decibels, and sounds above 120 decibels are painfully loud.

Amplitude and frequency are not correlated. A low-frequency sound can be very loud or very soft; that is, it can have either high or low amplitude. Middle C on a piano, for example, can be played loudly or softly. The frequency (and thus the pitch) of the sound stays the same—it is still middle C; only its amplitude (and corresponding loudness) varies. The psychological perception of loudness depends on other factors, such as background noise and whether the person is paying attention to the sound. Another psychological dimension, *timbre*, is the quality of a sound—the specific mixture of amplitudes and frequencies that make up the sound. People's perceptions of all these qualities depend on the physical structure of their ears.

Sound
The psychological experience that occurs when changes in air pressure stimulate the receptive organ for hearing; the resulting tones, or sounds, vary in frequency and amplitude.

Frequency
The number of complete changes in air pressure occurring per unit of time; measured in hertz (Hz), or cycles per second.

Pitch
The psychological experience that corresponds with the frequency of an auditory stimulus; also known as tone.

Amplitude
The total energy of a sound wave, which determines the loudness of the sound; also known as *intensity*.

The Structure of the Ear

The receptive organ for *audition*, or hearing, is the ear: it translates physical stimuli (sound waves) into electrical impulses that the brain can interpret. The ear has three major parts: the outer ear, the middle ear, and the inner ear. The tissue on the outside of the head is part of the outer ear. The eardrum (*tympanic membrane*) is the boundary between the outer and middle ear. When sound waves enter the ear, they

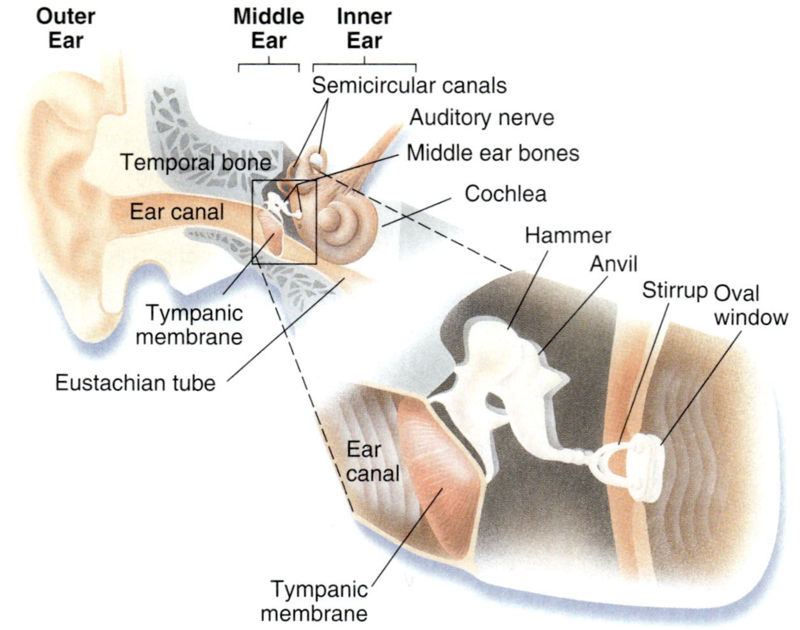

FIGURE 5.22

The Major Structures of the Ear

produce changes in pressure on the eardrum. The eardrum responds to these changes by vibrating.

The middle ear is quite small. Within it, tiny bones (*ossicles*) known as the *hammer, anvil,* and *stirrup* help convert the relatively large forces striking the eardrum into small forces. Two small muscles are attached to the ossicles; these muscles contract involuntarily when they are exposed to intense sounds. They help protect the delicate mechanisms of the inner ear from the damaging effects of an intense sound that could overstimulate them (Borg & Counter, 1989). Ultimately, the middle ear bones stimulate the *basilar membrane,* which runs down the middle of the *cochlea,* a spiral tube in the inner ear. Figure 5.22 shows the major structures of the middle and inner ear, and Figure 5.23 depicts the basilar membrane.

In the cochlea, which is shaped like a snail's shell and comprises three chambers, sound waves of different frequencies stimulate different areas of the basilar membrane. These areas, in turn, stimulate the hair cells, which initiate the electrical coding of sound waves. That is, these cells are responsible for the transduction of mechanical energy into electrochemical energy—neural impulses. The hair cells are remarkably sensitive. Hudspeth (1983), for example, found that hair cells respond when they are displaced as little as 100 picometers (trillionths of a meter).

Neural impulses make their way through the brain's auditory system in much the same way as visual information proceeds through the visual system. The impulses proceed through the auditory nerve to the midbrain and finally to the auditory cortex. Studies of single cells in the auditory areas of the brain show that some cells are more responsive to certain frequencies than to others. Katsuki (1961) found cells that are highly sensitive to certain narrow frequency ranges; if a frequency is outside their range, these cells might not fire at all. This finding is analogous to the findings reported by Hubel and Wiesel, who discovered receptive visual fields in which proper stimulation brought about dramatic changes in the firing of a cell; there is a highly structured cellular organization in the auditory system, comparable to that of the visual system.

FIGURE 5.23

The Basilar Membrane

In this view, the cochlea has been unwound and cut open to reveal the basilar membrane, which is covered with thousands of hair cells. Pressure variations in the fluid that fills the cochlea cause oscillations to travel in waves along the basilar membrane, stimulating the hair cells.

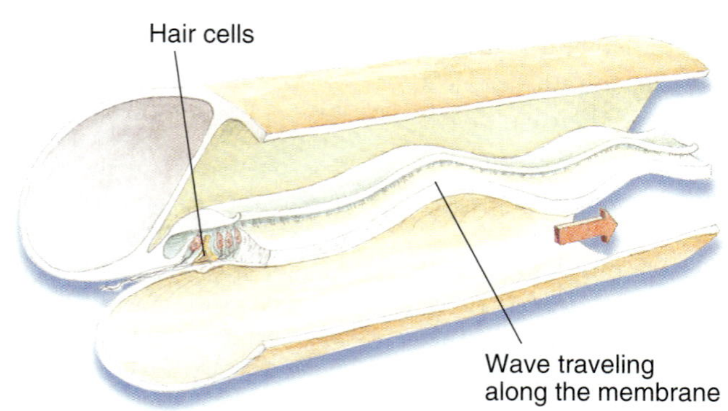

Theories of Hearing

Most theories of hearing fall into two major classes: place theories and frequency theories. *Place theories* claim that the analysis of sound occurs in the basilar membrane, with different frequencies and intensities affecting different parts (places) of the membrane. Such theories assert that each sound wave causes a traveling wave on the basilar membrane, which in turn causes displacement of hair cells on the membrane. The displacement of individual hair cells triggers specific information about pitch.

In contrast, *frequency theories* maintain that the analysis of pitch and intensity occurs at higher centers (levels) of processing, perhaps in the auditory area of the cortex, and that the basilar membrane merely transfers information to those centers. These theories suggest

BRAIN AND BEHAVIOR

Geography and Dyslexia

When it comes to dyslexia, researchers have tended to focus on the visual side of the reading process, thinking that dyslexia is more a visual disorder than one of hearing or speech. In fact, it is often called reading disability. But might dyslexia have as much to do with where a person is raised and what language the person speaks as it does with genetics, the brain, and the visual system?

It turns out that there is far more dyslexia in the United States than in Italy—twice as much. It also turns out that Italian is one of the easiest languages to learn and process. English is harder because it consists of 44 different sounds that can be combined in 1,100 ways. In Italian, every time you see two letters in combination, they sound the same; in English, words that sound alike are spelled differently (such as *to, two,* and *too*); also, words that are spelled alike may sound different (such as *bough* and *enough*). Since dyslexics have trouble differentiating sounds, the complexity of these spelling patterns adds to their burden—at least compared with Italian. The correspondence between letters, speech sounds, and whole-word sounds in English is often highly ambiguous.

In studies that used PET scans, Paulesu and his colleagues (Paulesu et al., 2000, 2001) found that Italian-speaking students showed greater and faster brain activation than did English-speaking students in areas associated with sound processing. The brains of Italians and Americans are the same, but the occurrence of dyslexia is different. The researchers concluded that since Italian orthography (the way letters represent the sound of a language in a specific spelling system) is consistent, it enables reliable and easy conversion of words to sounds, resulting in correct pronunciation.

Perhaps the difference between Italians and Americans in the rate of occurrence and severity of dyslexia may somewhat reflect how language is taught—for example, using phonics. Research shows that the visual process of reading is as much an auditory process because it involves the mapping of sounds. We may learn with further research that phonics is the best method for teaching some languages, but not others.

that the entire basilar membrane is stimulated and its overall rate of responding is somehow communicated to higher centers for analysis.

Like the theories that attempt to explain color vision, both place theories and frequency theories present theoretical problems. And neither type of theory explains all the data about pitch and loudness. For example, the hair cells do not act independently (as place theories suggest) but instead act together (as frequency theories suggest). And the rate at which hair cells fire is not fast enough to keep up with sound waves (which typically have frequencies of 1,000 to 10,000 cycles per second), as frequency theories suggest.

To get around the difficulties, modern researchers have developed theories of auditory information processing that attempt to explain pitch in terms of both specific action in parts of the basilar membrane and generalized frequency analyses at higher levels. Theories that seem at odds with one another can work together to explain pitch and loudness when the best parts of them are combined. (Does this remind you of the debate over the trichromatic and opponent-process theories of color vision discussed earlier?)

Sound Localization

How do you know where to turn when you hear a baby crying? Although not as direction-sensitive as many animals, human beings have amazingly efficient sound-localization (direction-determining) abilities. Researchers have learned much about these abilities by presenting sound through headsets, with one sound going to one ear and another sound to the other ear. Such experiments have revealed that two key factors influence sound localization: interaural time differences and interaural intensity differences. Because you have two ears, a sound produced to the left of your head will arrive at the left ear before the right. Thus, you have an *interaural time difference.* In addition, the sound will reach the two ears at different intensities. A sound produced at your left will be perceived as slightly more intense by the

Be an
Active learner

REVIEW

- What is the impact of sounds of varying frequency? pp. 170–171
- How does a person locate a sound? pp. 173–174
- How do psychologists define hearing loss? p. 174

THINK CRITICALLY

- Is perception a psychological or physical experience? Explain your answer.
- What makes a natural hearing experience as compared with one through earphones, for example?

APPLY PSYCHOLOGY

- What is the potential impact of an inner ear infection?
- Can you design a device that might be developed so as to create the most natural hearing possible for the deaf?

left ear than the right; thus, there is an *interaural intensity difference*. These two pieces of information are analyzed in the brain at nuclei (collections of cell bodies) that are especially sensitive to time and intensity differences between the ears.

Time and intensity differences are not the sole factors that determine sound localization, however. What happens when the sound source is just in front of you, and thus is equidistant from your two ears? It turns out that head and body movements help resolve the source of a sound. You rotate your head and/or move your body when you are unsure of the source of a sound. In addition, the external ear has ridges and folds that bounce sounds around just a bit, creating slight delays that help you localize sounds. Finally, visual cues and previous experiences help in localizing sounds in space.

Hearing Impairments

Sixteen percent of adults and more than one-third of people over age 60 have a hearing loss. In total, about 13 million people in the United States have hearing impairments, ranging from minor hearing loss to total deafness. Older individuals are often discriminated against because of their hearing problems. The numerous causes of hearing impairments include both environmental and genetic factors, which can lead to varying degrees of conduction deafness, sensorineural deafness, or a combination of the two (Vahava et al., 1998).

Conduction deafness is deafness resulting from interference with the transmission of sound to the neural mechanism of the inner ear. The interference may be caused by something temporary, such as a head cold or a buildup of wax in the outer ear canal. Or it may be caused by something far more serious, such as hardening of the tympanic membrane, destruction of the tiny bones within the ear, or diseases that create pressure in the middle ear. If sound can somehow be transmitted past the point of the conduction problem, hearing can be improved.

Sensorineural deafness is deafness resulting from damage to the cochlea, the auditory nerve, or higher auditory processing centers. The most common cause of this type of deafness is ongoing exposure to very high-intensity sound, such as that of gunshots, industrial noise, orchestras, bands, or jet planes. Musicians are at high risk, but listening to even moderately loud music for longer than 15 minutes a day can cause permanent hearing loss.

An audiometer, which presents sounds of different frequencies through a headphone, is used to evaluate hearing; results are presented as an *audiogram*, which is a graph showing hearing sensitivity at selected frequencies. The audiogram of the person whose hearing is being tested is compared with that of an adult with no known hearing loss. One less technical way to assess hearing is to test a person's recognition of spoken words. In a typical test of this sort, a person listens to a tape recording of speech sounds that are standardized in terms of loudness and pitch. Performance is rated in terms of the number of words the participant can repeat correctly at various intensity levels. Nonmedical personnel often administer these types of tests and then refer individuals who may have hearing problems to a physician.

You can easily see that there are many similarities in the perceptual mechanisms for hearing and vision. In both perceptual systems, physical energy is transduced into electrochemical energy, coding takes place at several locations in the brain, and impairments can affect people's abilities. Nevertheless, the auditory system, like the visual system, is plastic and can be trained and retrained after an accident or some other trauma, especially in young animals or humans (Klinke et al., 1999).

Conduction deafness
Deafness resulting from interference with the transmission of sound to the neural mechanism of the inner ear.

Sensorineural [sen-so-ree-NEW-ruhl] deafness
Deafness resulting from damage to the cochlea, the auditory nerve, or higher auditory processing centers.

Taste and Smell

Smell is the sense that people appreciate the least and yet has an enormous impact on behavior. The sense of smell is a direct pathway to the brain from the external world. It takes only seconds for a scent to enter the nose, stimulate sensory receptors, and then further activate emotions and even memories. There are many ways to view the sensory world we live in, but few offer such subtle discriminations and delights as smell and its close associate, taste. Tastes and smells evoke feelings. We become enchanted with the scent of a lover, the smell of home cooking, or the taste of a gourmet meal. Tastes and smells evoke memories of past events—Thanksgiving dinner, gnocchi during that summer in Italy, or the dentist's office. Perfume makers accordingly mingle dozens of substances to make perfumes that will evoke pleasant thoughts and feelings—and make some money!

Try the following experiment. Cut a fresh onion in half and inhale its odor while holding a piece of raw potato in your mouth. Now chew the potato. You'll most likely find that the potato tastes like an onion. This experiment demonstrates that taste and smell are closely linked. Food contains substances that act as stimuli for both taste and smell.

There is one taste most people have a special fondness for—sweetness. Babies prefer sweet foods, and so do great-grandmothers. But researchers know that a sweet tooth involves a craving for more than the taste of sugar. People with a sweet tooth crave candy, cake, ice cream, and sometimes liquor. Their bodies perceive the sweetness and learn that it is associated with many foods that are high in carbohydrates. Carbohydrates act almost as sedatives. So your cravings for some substances—your desire to taste or smell or eat or drink them—are affected by a number of variables, including the chemical composition of the substance, what it ultimately does to you, and your previous experiences with it.

student voices

Grant Bursek

George Washington University

For as long as I can remember I have been interested in psychology. I was fascinated by optical illusions and wanted to know how they worked. When I woke up in the morning I wanted to understand why I dreamed about monsters chasing me through a baseball game. In high school I wanted to know why some of my friends were natural leaders and others were content to follow. Psychology held all the answers to my questions.

Taste

I remember the first time I (L.L.) was in a wine store. My father wanted some wine to serve with dinner. I was overwhelmed by the quantity of wines, and the store owner allowed me (and I was only 16) to sample a variety: Cabernet Sauvignon, Merlot, Syrah, and Pinot Noir. The Cabernet was too strong, the Syrah too sweet, and the Pinot Noir was bland in comparison. Dad finally decided on a white wine; it was a Chardonnay and it tasted of oak with a slightly sweet pear flavor.

Taste is so complex that it is usually studied from the bottom up. Taste is a chemical sense. Food placed in the mouth is partially dissolved in saliva, which releases chemicals in the food that stimulate the *taste buds,* the primary receptors for taste stimuli (see Figure 5.24 on the following page). When substances contact the taste buds, you experience taste. The taste buds are found on small bumps on the tongue called *papillae.* Each hill-like papilla is separated from the next by a tiny trench, or moat; located on the wall of this moat are the taste buds, which can be seen only under a microscope. Each taste bud (human beings have about 10,000 of them) consists of 5 to 150 *taste cells.* These cells last only about 10 to 14 days and are constantly being renewed.

Although psychologists do not know exactly how many tastes there are, most agree that there are four basic ones: sweet, sour, salty, and bitter. Most foods contain more than one primary taste; Hawaiian pineapple pizza, for example, offers a complex array of taste stimuli and also stimulates the sense of smell. All taste cells are sensitive to all taste stimuli, but some cells are more sensitive to some stimuli than to others. (In this regard, they are much like the cones in the retina, which are sensitive to all wavelengths but are especially sensitive to a specific range of wavelengths.) By isolating stimuli that initiate only one taste sensation, psychologists have found that some regions of the tongue seem to be more sensitive than others

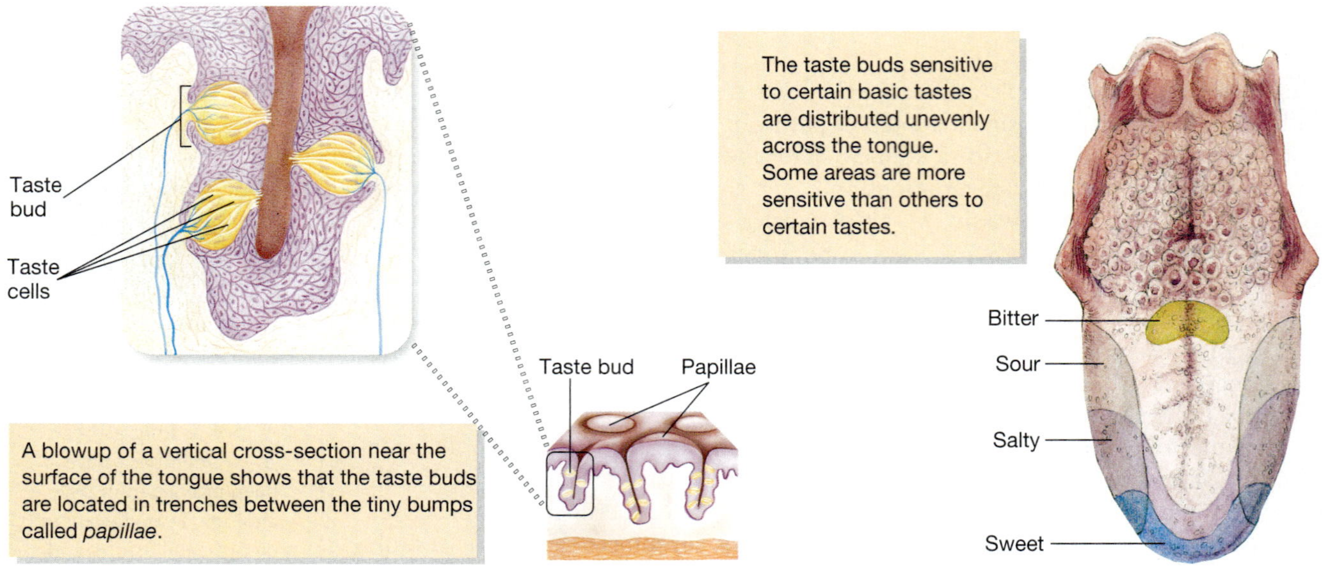

FIGURE 5.24

Taste Buds on the Surface of the Tongue

to particular taste stimuli. The tip of the tongue, for example, is more sensitive to sweet tastes than the back of the tongue is, and the sides are especially sensitive to sour tastes.

Some people are more sensitive to tastes than others, and sensitivity seems to be genetically determined. In fact, there are vast differences in taste sensitivity—with some individuals even being considered nontasters, most being considered medium tasters, and some being considered supertasters. Well-known taste researcher Linda Bartoshuk (Bartoshuk, 2000; Bartoshuk et al., 1996) investigated the taste buds of the different groups. She found that nontasters had as few as 11 buds per square centimeter on the tip of the tongue, whereas supertasters had as many as 1,100 taste buds per square centimeter. Supertasters taste sweet things as too sweet, bitter things as too bitter, and so forth. Nontasters cannot distinguish among basic tastes and require additional samplings to discern a flavor. Interesting, and not yet explained, is the finding that women are more likely to be supertasters.

- *Each taste bud consists of 5 to 150 taste cells. These cells last only about 10 to 14 days and are constantly being renewed.*

The taste of a particular food depends not only on its chemical makeup and the number of taste buds you have, but also on your past experiences with this or similar foods, on how much saliva is being mixed into the food as you chew, and on how long you chew the food. Food that is chewed well has a stronger taste. Food that rests on the tongue for a long time loses its ability to stimulate. This phenomenon is called *sensory adaptation,* or the temporary decrease in responsiveness of a receptor, often due to repeated high levels of stimulation. A food that loses its texture by being mashed up, or blended, with other foods has less taste and is less appealing to most adults. Thus, a taste experience, much like other perceptual experiences, depends not only on a sensory stimulus but also on the frequency and intensity of past experiences (Friedrich & Laurent, 2001).

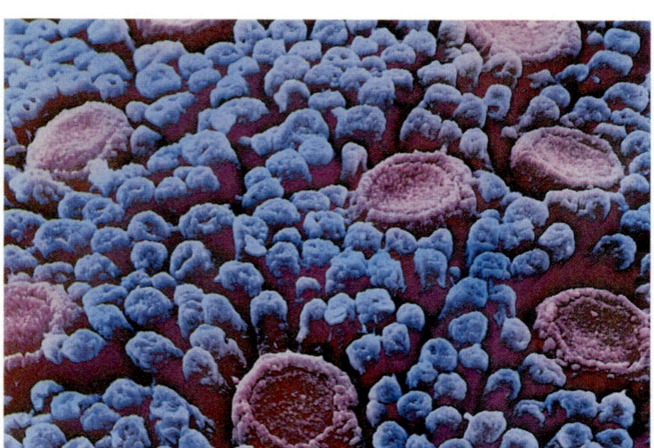

Smell

There's a good reason, other than etiquette, not to talk when your mouth is full—you lose some of the smells that help you experience the taste of food. The nose is the external section of the olfactory system, and it houses a complex array of receptors that transmit signals to key areas of the brain and allow us to smell (Scott et al., 2001; Vroon, 1997). Try eating chunks of raw potato and raw onion while holding your nose, and you will quickly see that they taste alike, as do chunks of carrot and apple. Smell is such an important sense that those who lose it permanently feel disabled. Like the sense of taste, **olfaction**—the sense of smell—is a chemical sense. That is, the stimulus for smell is a chemical in the air. The human olfactory system is remarkably sensitive: humans can distinguish approximately 10,000 different scents and can recognize a smell from as few as 40 or 50 molecules of the chemical. For the sensation of smell to occur, the molecules must move toward the receptor cells located on the walls of the nasal passage. This happens when you breathe molecules in through your nostrils or take them in through the back of your throat when you chew and swallow. When a chemical substance in the air moves past the receptor cells, it is partially absorbed into the mucus that covers the cells, thereby initiating the process of smell.

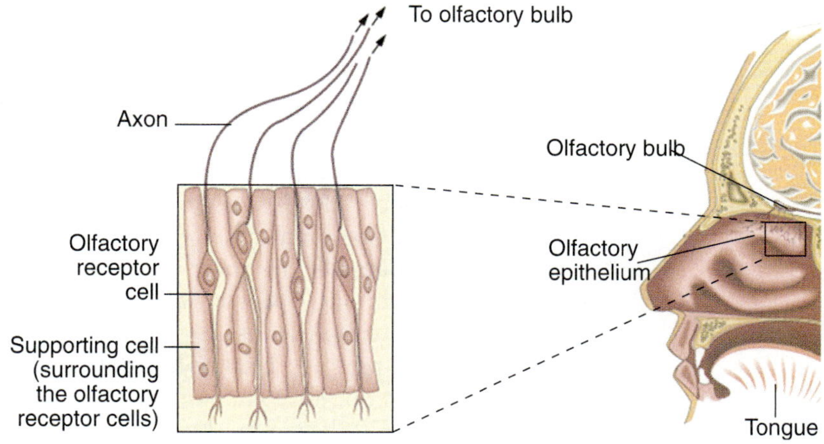

FIGURE 5.25
The Olfactory System

For human beings to perceive smell, information must be sent to the brain. At the top of the nasal cavity is the *olfactory epithelium* (see Figure 5.25), a layer of cells that contains the olfactory receptor cells—the nerve fibers that process odors and transmit information about smell to the olfactory bulbs (the enlargements at the end of the olfactory nerve) and on to higher centers of the brain. There can be as many as 30 million olfactory receptor cells in each nostril, which is what makes the olfactory system so sensitive and the electrochemical coding so complicated (Laurent, 1999; Scott et al., 2001; Wilson, 2000). The sensitivity of the human sense of smell is dramatically illustrated by perfume manufacturing, which is a complex process. Perfume makers may combine hundreds of substances to make one new perfume; dozens of perfumes have the same basic scent, varying only slightly. The manufacturer's task is to generate a perfume that has a distinctive *top note*—the first impact of its smell. Other substances in the mixture produce a *middle note* and an *end note*. The middle note follows after the top note fades away; the end note is long-lasting and persists for some time after the top and middle notes have disappeared.

Theories of smell involve both the stimulus for smell and the structure of the olfactory system. Some theories posit a few basic smells; others suggest that there are many—including flowery, foul, fruity, resinous, spicy, and burned. Psychologists have not agreed on a single classification system for smells, nor do they completely understand how odors affect the receptor cells. Research into the coding of smell is intense, and biopsychologists make headway each year; for example, they have shown that our memory for odors is long-lasting, odors can evoke memories of past events and childhood, and memory of smell is affected by language and emotional times in our lives (Engen & Engen 1997; Herz & Engen, 1996). So, a smell experience depends not only on a sensory stimulus but also on past experiences, including frequency and intensity (Friedrich & Laurent, 2001). Researchers are also studying whether and how odors affect human behavior. We consider this issue next.

■ **SMELL AND COMMUNICATION.** Animals secrete *pheromones* (pronounced FER-uh-moans)—chemical substances that are detected as scents by other animals and act as a means of communication. In fact, scents released by one animal may even influence the physiology of another animal.

Pheromones are widely recognized as initiators of sexual activity among animals. For example, female silkworms release a pheromone that can attract male silkworms from miles away. Similarly, when female salamanders are sexually receptive, they

Olfaction [ole-FAK-shun]
The sense of smell.

emit a highly odorous substance that attracts males (Rollman, 2000); rats and elephants behave similarly (Fornai & Orzi, 2001; Rasmussen & Krishnamurthy, 2000).

Many animals emit pheromones to elicit specific behavioral reactions; others, notably dogs and cats, use scents from their urine and scent glands to maintain territories and identify one another. Beavers attempt to keep strangers out of their territory by depositing foul-smelling substances emitted by sacs near the anus. Reindeer have scent glands between their toes that leave a trail for the rest of the herd. Communication via pheromones is found throughout the animal world. But do human beings share this ability?

Although people have always believed that a kind of "chemistry" exists between close friends, few really believed that one person's secretions might alter another person's behavior. Until relatively recently, scientists assumed that human beings do not communicate through smell. However, ground-breaking research in the 1970s began to change psychologists' thinking about smell and communication. McClintock (1971) found that the menstrual periods of women living in a college dormitory who were either roommates or close friends became roughly *synchronous*. That is, after the women lived together for several months, their menstrual cycles began and ended at about the same time. McClintock began to question whether the synchronization of the menstrual cycles was due to some type of chemical message. More recent experimental research (Jacob & McClintock, 2000; Stern & McClintock, 1998) found that women emit a whole array of chemical signals that affect synchronicity and behavior.

The effects of pheromones on animals are profound, but the role of pheromones in human life remains somewhat obscure and even controversial. Nevertheless, perfume makers have been working frenetically to make a perfume with pheromone-like capabilities. Is it reasonable for them to assert that perfumes, like pheromones, can attract members of the other sex? Probably not. Pheromones are not likely to be as powerful for human beings as they are for animals, because so many other environmental stimuli affect human behavior, attitudes, and interpersonal relations (Cacioppo et al., 2000).

The Skin Senses

Your skin, an organ of your body, contains a wide range of receptors for relaying information about the *skin senses*—pain, touch, and temperature. In each case, a stimulus is converted into neural energy, and then the brain interprets that energy as a psychological experience. Skin receptors ultimately send information to the somatosensory cortex of the brain.

Touch

The skin is more than just a binding that holds your body together. It is the location of your *sense of touch*—your tactile system. The skin of an adult human being measures roughly 2 square yards and comprises three layers: the epidermis, the dermis, and the hypodermis. The top layer, the *epidermis* (*epi* means "outer"), consists primarily of dead cells and varies in thickness. It is thin on the face and quite thick on the elbows and the heels. The epidermis is constantly regenerating; in fact, all of its cells are replaced every 28 days or so. The layer underneath the epidermis—the *dermis* (from *derma,* "skin")—contains live cells as well as a supply of nerve endings, blood, hair cells, and oil-producing (sebaceous) glands. Together, the dermis and epidermis are resilient, flexible, and quite tough. They protect the body against quick changes in temperature and pressure, and the epidermis in particular guards against pain from small scratches, cuts, and bumps. The deepest layer—the *hypodermis* (*hypo* means "under")—is a thick, insulating cushion.

The specialized receptors for each of the skin senses—pain, touch, and temperature—vary in shape, size, number, and distribution. For example, the body has many more cold receptors than heat receptors; it has more pain receptors behind the knee than on the top of the nose. The most sensitive areas of the hand have as many as 1,300 receptors per square inch.

The skin sense receptors appear to interact with one another; sometimes one sensation seems to combine with or change to another. Thus, increasing pressure can become pain. Similarly, an itch seems to result from a low-level irritation of nerve endings in the skin; however, a tickle can be caused by the same stimulus and can produce a reflexlike response—a response that is also dependent on psychological and social variables, as the next section points out. Further, people are far more sensitive to pressure in some parts of their bodies than in other parts (compare your fingers to your thigh); the more sensitive areas, such as the neck and the back of the knees, have more receptors than do the less sensitive areas. Complicating matters further, women have greater sensitivity to some pain stimuli than do men and are better able to discriminate among painful stimuli (Berkley, 1997).

Many of your determinations of how something feels are relative. When you say a stimulus is cold, you mean it is cold compared to normal skin temperature. When you say an object is warm, you mean it feels warmer than normal skin temperature. When you feel a child's head with the back of your hand and say the child has a fever, you are comparing normal skin temperature to a sick child's elevated skin temperature (and you wouldn't make such a determination immediately after coming indoors on a winter day when it was 20°F outside).

student voices

Jennifer M. Chen
Harvard University

Psychology shows up even in popular TV—I was watching an episode of *CSI,* and the investigators mentioned the (inattentional blindness) study in which subjects who are tracking white-shirted basketball players don't notice a man in a gorilla suit enter the scene. I said to my parents, "Hey, that's true!"

■ **BEING TICKLED.** There's no one who hasn't been tickled at some point in his or her life. Some of us are especially ticklish. We smile, laugh, squirm, and sometimes howl when tickled. But why?

Nineteenth-century speculations suggested that people laugh and are ticklish because of a "pleasant state of mind." But recent research is showing that tickling and its results are in part physical but in larger part psychological. People respond to a light touch on the sole of the foot or on the spine, but if they anticipate the touch, if they are with a friend or relative, or if there is an element of surprise, the response is much stronger. That's why people can't tickle themselves—there is no element of surprise, and tickling requires a social interaction and a psychological tension that requires at least two people (Claxon, 1975).

Think back to your childhood. When your mom or dad said, "I'm going … to … *tickle* you!" and started to wiggle her or his fingers, you were likely to wiggle and giggle even before you were touched. Once you were actually tickled, you may have convulsed in laughter. Those of us who laugh easily at humor are more likely to respond to tickling (Harris & Christenfeld, 1997), our physiological responses to tickling are likely to be stronger when we are with friends (Christenfeld et al., 1997), and we are more likely to experience touch as tickling if we feel comfortable with our bodies and are disposed to perceive pleasurable stimuli (Ruggieri et al., 1983).

Our response to humor and our ability to be tickled seem to be somewhat related. Both tickling and humor are universal behaviors found in human beings and in some chimpanzees. These behaviors occur at an early age and can be linked to specific neural pathways—these are elements of an evolved response. Indeed, the responses to both humor and tickling may serve an evolutionary purpose. Some evidence suggests that those with a humorous outlook on life may live longer (Weisfeld, 1993). Be tickled and live longer? Well, not exactly—but you'll have more fun!

Pain

Everyone has experienced acute pain at one time or another: a severe headache, the pain of childbirth, dental or arthritic pain, or perhaps a kidney stone or appendicitis.

For most of us, pain comes and then goes, and we look back, thankful for the relief. Pain is a perceptual experience with particular negative qualities (Wall, 2000). Pain is the most common symptom that doctors deal with, but despite its association with illness and disease, pain is adaptive and necessary. In rare cases, children have been born without the ability to feel pain, which places them in constant danger. Their encounters with caustic substances, violent collisions, and deep cuts elicit no painful responses that could teach them to avoid such experiences. Further, they do not recognize serious conditions that would send most of us to the doctor for attention—for example, broken bones, deep burns, or the sharp pains that signal appendicitis.

Studying pain is difficult because pain can be elicited in so many ways. For example, hunger or the flu may cause stomach pains, a cavity or an abscess can cause a toothache, and headaches can be caused by stress or eyestrain. Myriad kinds of pain exist, including sunburn pain, pain from terminal cancer, labor pains, lower back pain, pain from frostbite, and even pain in a "phantom limb" after trauma or surgery. Psychologists use several kinds of stimuli to study pain. Among them are chemicals, extreme heat and cold, and electrical stimulation.

Most researchers believe the receptors for pain are free nerve endings. *Free nerve endings* are the microscopic ends of afferent neurons that are distributed throughout the body's tissues and are not connected to any specific sensory organ. There are various types of these receptors, each especially sensitive to a certain type of intense or potentially harmful stimulation. Some areas of the body are more sensitive to pain than others. For example, the sole of the foot and the ball of the thumb are less sensitive than the back of the knee and the neck. Also, though an individual's pain threshold remains fairly constant, different individuals show varying sensitivities to pain. Some people have a low threshold for pain; they will describe a comparatively low-level stimulus as painful. Others have a fairly high pain threshold. When you experience pain, you know where it hurts, how much it hurts, and the quality of the pain (sharp, burning, localized); your body responds with autonomic nervous system activity—increased heart rate and blood pressure, sweating, and so forth. You then, in turn, respond in a certain way, depending on whether you are frightened, anxious, or merely annoyed.

You can see that the perception of pain is both physical and psychological; much depends on a person's attitudes, previous experiences, and culture (Keefe & France, 1999). For example, athletes often report not feeling the pain of an injury until after the competition has ended. Some cultures teach individuals to be stoical about pain and to endure individual suffering without complaint; in Western cultures, many people believe that pain and suffering are ennobling. Also, boys and girls within Western cultures are often taught to respond differently to pain (Wall, 2000) (see Table 5.1).

TABLE 5.1

Variables That Affect the Perception of Pain

Biological	Psychological	Environmental
Stimulation of free nerve endings Heightened sensitivity because of lowered thresholds Actions of endorphins Diseases of organs	Cognitive factors involving beliefs about meaning of pain Cultural beliefs and expectations about how to react to difficult situations including pain	Environmental stressors that increase or decrease pain perception through release of hormones Cultural learning experiences that produce beliefs and expectations (learning experiences may occur through classical and operant conditioning or observation) Painful physical stimuli including accidents and toxins

What allows pain suppression? How does the body process, interpret, and stop pain? Neuromatrix theory may offer an answer.

NEUROMATRIX THEORY. One explanation of how the body processes pain is the *neuromatrix theory* developed by Ronald Melzack (1999). The theory takes into account the sizes, level of development, and interplay of

BRAIN AND BEHAVIOR

Seeing Pain

Early studies of pain subjected people to stimuli such as cold water, asked participants how painful it was, and recorded how long they could withstand the pain. But today measures of pain have taken a distinctly biological emphasis. We still stimulate people with hot and cold, but now we also record brain activity during painful stimulation and watch the brain "light up" through PET and fMRI scans (see pp. 58–61). Researchers like A. Vania Apkarian and his colleagues have done fMRI studies to isolate where in the brain activity becomes greatest in response to a pain in young and middle-age adults (Bolanowski et al., 2000; Grachev & Apkarian, 2000).

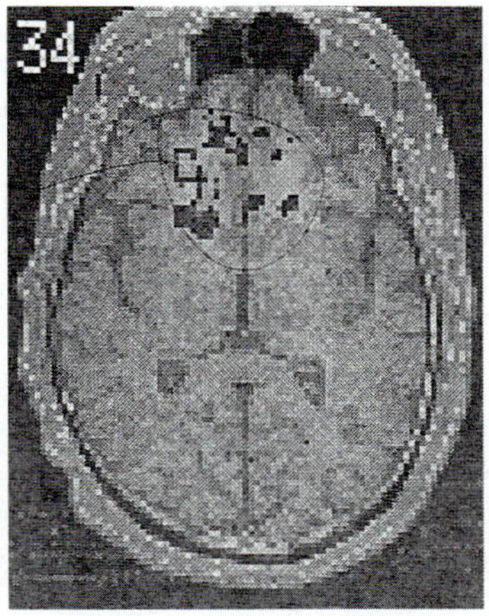

The impact of a physical measure of pain, in addition to traditional measurers of perceived pain, allows physicians to ensure that treatments are appropriate, that drugs are not over- or under-used, and that medical insurance will pay for treatments that otherwise may have been dismissed as complaints from cranky patients.

Until research like that of Apkarian and of Karen Davis (2000), researchers never had pictures of pain as it took place and never had been able to so precisely localize it and watch its time course. We can now track the pain of patients who are otherwise uncommunicative because of accidents, trauma, and stroke—and thus relieve their pain. This includes patients with Alzheimer's disease, those with severe disabling mental disorders like schizophrenia, and those suffering from the "phantom" pain that exists after a limb is amputated (Davis et al., 1998).

cells that initiate pain sensations; it also considers inhibitory cells that can diminish pain sensations. The theory contends that the brain possesses a neural network, the body–self neuromatrix (BSN), that integrates inputs to produce an output pattern that we experience as pain. The BSN comprises a widely distributed neural network and is determined by genetic and sensory influences. Melzack refers to this neuromatrix pattern as a neurosignature. The neurosignature output of the neuromatrix—patterns of nerve impulses of varying temporal and spatial dimensions—is produced by neural programs genetically built into the neuromatrix.

Multiple inputs act on the neuromatrix programs, including (1) sensory inputs; (2) visual and other sensory inputs that influence the interpretation of the situation; (3) emotional inputs from other areas of the brain; (4) neural self-modulation; and (5) the activity of the body's stress-regulation systems.

If the theory is correct (and the research is still being done), then the brain has been prewired to realize that its body is going to have a right arm. Even if the right arm is amputated, the brain is still prewired to believe that the arm is there. If the brain believes that limb is there, it might tell the limb to move by stimulating key neural pathways in the neuromatrix. Since the limb is not there, and the brain receives no sensory feedback, it will increase the strength of its stimulation, thus causing what we call phantom pain (Schultz & Melzack, 1999).

■ **ENDORPHINS.** There have been some exciting breakthroughs in research on pain receptors and the nature of pain. Consider, for example, the study of endorphins. **Endorphins** (from *endogenous,* meaning "naturally occurring," and *morphine,* an opiate painkiller) are painkillers that are produced naturally in the brain and the pituitary gland. There are many kinds of endorphins, and they help regulate several bodily functions, including blood pressure and body temperature (Koob, Wall, & Bloom, 1989). Endorphins also can produce euphoria and a sense of well-being—to an even greater extent than morphine does. Engaging in athletic activities can bring about an increased endorphin level. During and after running, runners often report experiencing "runner's high," a sensation many believe is related to the body's

Endorphins [en-DOR-finz] Painkillers produced naturally in the brain and the pituitary gland.

increased endorphin level. Exercise can increase endorphin levels, but intense exercise is required, and many who experience the "runner's high" are exhilarated over accomplishment rather than through endorphins.

Endorphins bind themselves to receptor sites in the brain and spinal cord, thereby preventing pain signals from passing on to higher levels of the nervous system. Some endorphins increase tolerance to pain, and others actually reduce pain sensations. *Enkephalin,* for example, is a brain endorphin that blocks pain signals (Blum et al., 2000; Samoriski & Greoss, 2000). Another endorphin, nocistatin, is being tested on a variety of painful conditions, and scientists may eventually be able to produce it synthetically (Okuda-Ashitaka et al., 1998). Morphine occupies endorphin receptors in the nervous system and is extremely effective in controlling pain.

■ **ACUPUNCTURE.** Many people who suffer chronic, unrelieved pain have sought help from acupuncture (Olausson & Sagvik, 2000). Initially developed in China thousands of years ago, *acupuncture* is a technique that uses long, slender needles, inserted into the body at specific locations, to relieve particular kinds of pain. Controlled studies of acupuncture have yielded varying results. Acupuncture seems to help when needles are placed near the site of pain; this contrasts to the traditional Chinese view that the key sites are located along life-force meridians found on acupuncture charts (Wall, 2000). It is possible that the needles stimulate endorphins that may help block the pain (Murray, 1995) or alter serotonin levels (Nash, 1996) that affect and alleviate pain or other problems (Bernstein, 2000). For some people, acupuncture may be a reasonable option and an effective treatment (Pan et al., 2000). The National Institutes of Health concludes that acupuncture may be effective with some kinds of pain—migraines, arthritis, and postoperative pain from dental surgery—but that more research is needed because controlled studies on acupuncture are inconclusive.

■ **PAIN MANAGEMENT.** Usually the pain resulting from a headache, toothache, or small cut is temporary and can be alleviated with a simple pain medication such as aspirin. For millions of people, however, aspirin is not enough (Ezzo et al., 2000). For those who suffer from constant pain caused by back injury, arthritis, or cancer, drug treatment either is not effective or is dangerous because of the high dosages required; in addition, each type of pain may require a different treatment (Fishbain, 2000). Sometimes painkillers are not prescribed because of fear of addiction—a fear that is often exaggerated by caring, well-meaning family and friends (Wall, 2000).

New technologies emerge every few years to help people manage pain. Leaders in pain research reason that something must happen at the site of an injury to trigger endorphin production. What if a drug could stop the whole pain perception process at the place where the injury occurred? In an effort to find such a compound, researchers are studying the receptor sites in skin tissue and observing how chemicals bind to them. The compounds they discover may not relieve pain completely but may be effective in combination with other pain medications, such as aspirin.

Practitioners who deal with pain recognize that although it may arise initially from physical complaints, it sometimes continues even after the physical cause abates because it provides other benefits to the sufferer (Gatchel & Turk, 1999). For example, pain may provide the sufferer with attention, which is reinforcing, or it may act as a distraction from other problems. Chapter 14 discusses pain management that focuses on helping people cope with pain regardless of its origins and on increasing a patient's pain-controlling skills.

Hypnosis (which will be examined in more detail in Chapter 6) has been used to treat pain. Patients may be instructed to focus on other aspects of life and may be told that their pain will be more bearable after the hypnotic session. Although some claim that two-thirds of patients who are considered highly susceptible to suggestion can experience some relief of pain through hypnosis, the National Institutes of Health concluded that a more accurate estimate was 15%–20%.

■ *Riding a rollercoaster usually affects your vestibular sense—the sense of bodily orientation and postural adjustment.*

Anxiety and worry can make pain worse. People who suffer from migraine headaches, for example, often make their condition worse by becoming fearful when they feel a headache coming on. Researchers find that biofeedback training, which teaches people how to relax and cope more effectively, can help those who suffer from chronic pain or migraine headaches gain some relief—although, again, results are mixed. (Biofeedback will be discussed further in Chapter 6.) Other treatments, closely related to biofeedback, involve cognitive coping strategies (discussed in Chapter 16). A negative attitude can make pain worse. Cognitive coping strategies teach patients to have a better attitude about their pain. Patients learn to talk to themselves in positive ways, to divert attention to pleasant images, and to take an active role in managing their pain and transcending the experience.

Kinesthesis and the Vestibular Sense

If you are a dancer or another type of athlete, you rely mightily on your body to provide you with information about hand, arm, and leg movements. You try to keep your balance, be graceful, and move with coordination and smoothness. Two sensory systems allow for skilled, accurate, and smooth movement—the often ignored, but vitally important, kinesthetic and vestibular systems.

Kinesthesis is the awareness aroused by movements of the muscles, tendons, and joints. It is what allows you to touch your finger to your nose with your eyes closed, leap over hurdles during a track-and-field event, and dance without stepping on your partner's feet. The study of kinesthesis provides information about bodily movements. The movements of muscles around your eye, for example, help you know how far away objects are. Kinesthesia and other internal sensations (such as an upset stomach) are *proprioceptive cues* (kinesthesia is sometimes called *proprioception*)—sensory cues that come from within the body.

The **vestibular sense** is the sense of bodily orientation and postural adjustment. It helps you keep your balance and sense of equilibrium. The structures essential to these functions are in the ear. Vestibular sacs and semicircular canals, which are linked indirectly to the body wall of the cochlea, provide information about the orientations of the head and the body. The vestibular sense allows you to walk on a balance beam without falling off, to know which way is up after diving into the water, and to sense that you are turning a corner when riding in a car, even when your eyes are closed.

Kinesthesis [kin-iss-THEE-sis]
The awareness aroused by movements of the muscles, tendons, and joints.

Vestibular [ves-TIB-you-ler] sense
The sense of bodily orientation and postural adjustment.

Rapid movements of the head bring about changes in the semicircular canals. These changes induce eye movements to help compensate for head changes and changes in bodily orientation. They may also be accompanied by physical sensations ranging from pleasant dizziness to unbearable motion sickness. Studies of the vestibular sense help scientists understand what happens to people during space travel and under conditions of weightlessness.

Extrasensory Perception

Sights, sounds, tastes, smells, touches, and even pain are all part of the normal sensory experience of human beings. Some people, however, claim there are other perceptual experiences that not all human beings recognize as normal. People have been fascinated by *extrasensory perception* (ESP) for hundreds of years. The British Society for the Study of Psychic Phenomena has investigated reports of ESP since the 19th century. Early experimenters tested for extrasensory perception by asking participants to guess the symbols on what are now called ESP cards, each marked with a star, a cross, a circle, a square, or a set of wavy lines. One of the most consistently successful guessers once guessed 25 cards in a row, an event whose odds of happening by chance are nearly 300 quadrillion to 1.

ESP includes telepathy, clairvoyance, precognition, and psychokinesis. *Telepathy* is the transfer of thoughts from one person to another. *Clairvoyance* is the ability to recognize objects or events, such as the contents of a message in a sealed envelope, that are not discernible by normal sensory receptors. *Precognition* is unexplained knowledge about future events, such as knowing when the phone is about to ring. *Psychokinesis* is the ability to move objects using only one's mental powers.

Experimental support for the existence of ESP is generally weak, and results have not been repeated very often. Moreover, ESP phenomena such as "reading people's minds" or bending spoons through mental power cannot be verified by experimental manipulations in the way that other perceptual events can be. In addition, the National Research Council has denounced the scientific merit of most of these experiments. These criticisms do not mean that ESP does not exist. Research using scientific methods continues, including new techniques such as the use of sophisticated electronic detection devices. Attempts to relate ESP phenomena to traditional psychology (as is common in nations of the former Soviet bloc) are underway. However, most psychologists see so much trickery and falsification of data and so many design errors in experiments on this subject that they remain skeptical.

Be an *Active* learner

REVIEW

- Why do we call taste and smell chemical senses? pp. 177–178
- What is the olfactory epithelium? p. 177
- Are human beings directly affected by pheromones? Explain your answer. pp. 179–180
- Why is the study of pain so complicated? pp. 179–180

THINK CRITICALLY

- How and why are smell and taste so intertwined?
- How might the study of endorphins be relevant to your life?
- If menstrual cycles of women living together can become synchronized, what happens when a man is introduced onto a dorm floor? Two men?

APPLY PSYCHOLOGY

- What can people do to help alleviate seemingly uncontrollable pain through traditional means?
- What could you do to enhance your sense of smell?

Summary and Review

The Perceptual Experience

How does the study of the psychological aspects of perception help explain individuals' attending to and attaching meaning to stimuli?

■ *Sensation* is the process in which the sense organs' receptor cells are stimulated and relay initial information to higher brain centers for further processing. pp. 144–145

■ *Perception* is the process through which people attach meaning to sensory stimuli by means of complex processing mechanisms. Each perceptual system operates in a similar way; although all are different, they share common processes. pp. 144–145

■ *Psychophysics* is the study of the relationship between physical stimuli and people's conscious experience of them. Psychophysical techniques allow researchers to study and approximate the *absolute threshold*—the statistically determined minimum level of stimulation necessary to excite a perceptual system. p. 145

■ If a visual or auditory stimulus is presented so quickly or at such a low level that a person cannot consciously perceive it, psychologists say that it is presented subliminally. Research on *subliminal perception* is controversial, and many researchers maintain that it can be explained in terms of nonperceptual variables such as motivation, previous experience, and unconscious or critical censoring processes. p. 145

■ The cocktail party phenomenon, which allows a person to hear his or her name spoken across a crowded and noisy room, is a basic finding of selective attention studies, which show that people have a limited capacity to pay attention to stimuli. p. 147

■ Studies of sensory deprivation and especially of sensory restriction have shown that profound relaxation can occur in an environment of extreme sensory restriction. pp. 148–149

KEY TERMS

sensation, p. 145; perception, p. 145; psychophysics, p. 145; absolute threshold, p. 145; subliminal perception, p. 145; signal detection theory, p. 147

The Visual System

Describe the structures of the visual system.

■ The main structures of the eye are the cornea, pupil, iris, lens, and retina. The retina is made up of 10 layers, of which the most important are the *photoreceptors*, the bipolar cells, and the ganglion cells. The axons of the ganglion cells make up the optic nerve. p. 151

What is the duplicity theory of vision?

■ The duplicity theory of vision states that rods and cones are structurally unique and are used to accomplish different tasks. That is, the two types of receptors have special functions and operate differently: cones are specialized for color, day vision, and fine acuity, and rods are specialized for low light levels but contribute little to color vision or acuity. pp. 152–153

What do receptive fields tell researchers about the perceptual process?

■ *Receptive fields* are areas on the retina that, when stimulated, produce changes in the firing of cells in the visual system. Cells at the lateral geniculate nucleus and the visual cortex are called feature detectors, and some of them are highly specialized—for example, for detecting motion or color. pp. 154–156

What are the trichromatic and opponent-process theories of color vision?

■ The three psychological dimensions of color are *hue, brightness,* and *saturation.* They correspond to the three physical characteristics of light: wavelength, intensity, and purity. Young and Helmholtz's *trichromatic theory* of color vision states that all colors can be made by mixing three basic colors and that the retina has three types of cones. Herring's *opponent-process theory* states that color is coded by a series of receptors that respond either strongly or weakly to different wavelengths of light. pp. 158–160

■ *Color blindness* is the inability to perceive different hues; many people with color blindness cannot successfully discriminate colors in two areas of the visual spectrum. p. 160

KEY TERMS

electromagnetic radiation, p. 151; light, p. 151; myopic, p. 151; hyperopic, p. 151; photoreceptors, p. 151; transduction, p. 151; visual cortex, p. 153; dark adaptation, p. 153; optic chiasm, p. 153; receptive fields, p. 155; saccades, p. 157; hue, p. 157; brightness, p. 158; saturation, p. 158; trichromatic theory, p. 158; color blindness, p. 158; opponent-process theory, p. 158; trichromats, p. 161; monochromats, p. 161; dichromats, p. 161

Visual Perception

What are size constancy and shape constancy?

■ *Size constancy* is the ability of the perceptual system to recognize that an object remains constant in size regardless of its distance from the viewer or the size of the retinal image. *Shape constancy* is the ability of the visual perceptual system to recognize a shape despite changes in its orientation or the angle from which it is viewed. pp. 161–162

What kinds of depth cues help people see depth?

■ The *monocular depth cues* include motion parallax, the kinetic depth effect, linear perspective, interposition, texture, highlighting and shadowing, atmospheric perspective, and *accommodation*. The two primary *binocular depth cues* are *retinal disparity* and *convergence*. pp. 162–164

What is an illusion?

■ An *illusion* is a perception of a physical stimulus that differs from measurable reality or from what is commonly expected. pp. 164–166

What did the Gestalt psychologists contribute to scientists' understanding of perception?

■ According to a Gestalt idea called the *law of Prägnanz*, stimuli that *can* be grouped together and seen as a whole, or a form, *will* be seen that way. Using the law of Prägnanz as an organizing idea, Gestalt psychologists developed principles of organization for the perception of figures, especially figure–ground relationships. pp. 169–170

KEY TERMS

size constancy, p. 161; shape constancy, p. 162; monocular depth cues, p. 162; accommodation, p. 164; binocular depth cues, p. 164; retinal disparity, p. 164; convergence, p. 164; illusion, p. 164; agnosia, p. 167; law of Prägnanz, p. 169

Hearing

What are the key characteristics of sound?

■ *Sound* refers to the psychological experience of changes in pressure in a liquid or gaseous medium—usually air. The *frequency* and *amplitude* of a sound wave determine in large part how a listener will experience a sound. p. 171

Describe the anatomy of the ear and how sound is processed.

■ The ear has three main parts: the outer ear, the middle ear, and the inner ear. The eardrum (tympanic membrane) is the boundary between the outer ear and the middle ear. Tiny bones (ossicles) in the middle ear stimulate the basilar membrane in the cochlea, a tube in the inner ear. Place theories of hearing claim that the analysis of sound occurs in the inner ear; frequency theories claim that the analysis of pitch and intensity takes place at higher centers of processing. pp. 171–172

■ Because you have two ears, you can locate the source of sound. A sound produced to the left of the head will arrive at the left ear before the right. This creates an interaural time difference. In addition, a sound produced to the left will be slightly more intense at the left ear than the right; thus, there is an interaural intensity difference. pp. 173–174

Distinguish between conduction deafness and sensorineural deafness.

■ *Conduction deafness* results from interference in the delivery of sound to the neural mechanism of the inner ear. *Sensorineural deafness* results from damage to the cochlea, the auditory nerve, or higher auditory processing centers. p. 174

KEY TERMS

sound, p. 171; frequency, p. 171; pitch, p. 171; amplitude, p. 171; conduction deafness, p. 174; sensorineural deafness, p. 174

Taste and Smell

Describe the anatomy of the tongue and explain how it allows for taste differences.

■ The tongue contains thousands of bumps, or papillae, each of which is separated from the next by a moat. The taste buds are located on the walls of these moats. Each taste bud consists of many taste cells. All taste cells are sensitive to all taste stimuli, but certain cells are more sensitive to some stimuli than to others. pp. 175–176

Why are taste and smell called chemical senses?

■ For taste or smell to occur, chemicals must come into contact with the receptor cells. For the sense of smell, the receptors are located on the walls of the nasal passage. When a chemical substance in the air moves past these receptor cells, it is partially absorbed into the mucus that covers the cells, thereby initiating the process of smell. The olfactory epithelium contains the olfactory receptor cells—the nerve fibers that process odors and enable an individual to perceive smell. pp. 177–178

KEY TERM

olfaction, p. 177

The Skin Senses

Describe the anatomy of the skin.

■ The skin is made up of three layers. The top layer is the epidermis. The layer underneath the epidermis is the dermis. The deepest layer, the hypodermis, is a thick insulating cushion. The skin sense receptors appear to interact with one another; sometimes one sensation seems to combine with or change to another. pp. 178–179

What theory of pain is most prominent now?

■ A widely accepted explanation of how pain sensations are processed is that the brain possesses a neural network, the body–self neuromatrix (BSN), that integrates inputs to produce the output pattern of pain. The BSN comprises a widely distributed neural network; Melzack refers to this neuromatrix pattern as a neurosignature. The neurosignature output of the neuromatrix is produced by neural programs genetically built into the neuromatrix. pp. 180–181

What are the body's naturally produced painkillers?

■ *Endorphins* are painkillers that are produced naturally in the brain and the pituitary gland. They help regulate several bodily functions, including blood pressure and body temperature. Stress, anticipated pain, and athletic activities bring about an increased level of endorphins. pp. 181–182

KEY TERMS

endorphins, p. 181

Kinesthesis and the Vestibular Sense

What sense involves the orientation of the entire body?

■ *Kinesthesis* is the awareness that is aroused by movements of the muscles, tendons, and joints. One kinesthetic sense is the *vestibular sense*—the sense of bodily orientation and postural adjustment—which helps you keep your balance and sense of equilibrium. p. 183

KEY TERMS

kinesthesis, p. 183; vestibular sense, p. 183

Extrasensory Perception

Is there a "sixth sense"—ESP?

■ ESP includes telepathy, clairvoyance, precognition, and psychokinesis. Experimental support for the existence of ESP is generally weak. Psychologists remain skeptical about ESP because they see so much trickery and falsification of data, as well as experimental design errors. p. 184

6 Consciousness

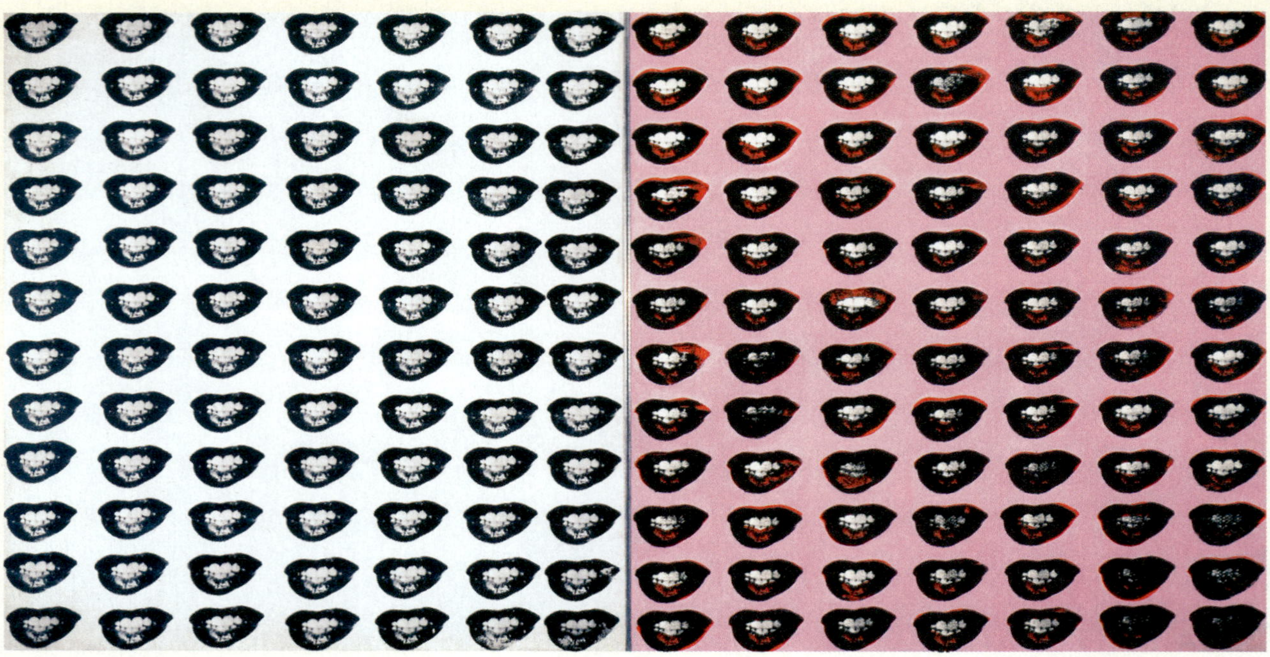

Andy Warhol, *Marilyn Monroe's Lips,* 1962

Many people have proclaimed that they are "dead tired," but very few actually die from lack of sleep. Members of one Italian family, however, are among those who do. This family has a genetic defect that produces a failure to be able to sleep. The affected individuals usually develop symptoms in their 50s. They feel exhausted but cannot sleep; they sweat profusely; their pupils become constricted; they lose weight. As the disease progresses, they become confused and begin to hallucinate. Sometimes they fall into a very light sleep, but this sleep neither refreshes them nor prevents their continuing degeneration. After several months, they fall into a coma and die (Max, 2001).

The history of this disorder goes back to the 1700s and has affected dozens of members of this family. In 1986, the disorder was named fatal familial insomnia (FFI), and the genetics of the disorder were established. Many puzzles remain. Not all family members who have the gene develop the disorder; some develop it earlier than middle age. Even more puzzling is the brain deterioration that underlies the disorder. In the brains of those who have died from FFI, the thalamus is filled with small holes, though the thalamus is seen mostly as a relay station for sensory information; it is not one of the brain structures believed to be important for sleep.

chapter outline

This mysterious sleep disorder is only one of the many puzzles of sleep. Most people do not die when they fail to sleep, mostly because the urge to sleep is so strong that they eventually are overtaken by sleep. Almost everyone has the opposite problem of those with FFI—we all sleep, even when we want to stay awake. This situation highlights the most important puzzle: the reason for sleep. Why is it necessary for us to spend time unconscious? What about sleep is so important that we must sleep or die? This question remains unanswered, but researchers have discovered the answers to other important questions about sleep and other states of consciousness.

Consciousness

> Introduction to Psychology: The theory of human behavior... Is there a split between mind and body, and, if so, which is better to have? Special consideration is given to a study of consciousness as opposed to unconsciousness, with many helpful hints on how to remain conscious. (Allen, 1983)

Woody Allen's humorous college catalog description of an introductory psychology course actually includes several elements that are relevant in the consideration of consciousness. His description pointed out the mind–body distinction and the concept of the unconscious, both of which are important issues. However, Allen's definition of psychology as human behavior is the modern one; the earliest definition of psychology was the study of the mind and consciousness.

Early psychologists, such as Wilhelm Wundt, studied little else but the topic of consciousness. In the late 1880s, Wundt and his students had research participants report their conscious experience while sitting still, while working, and while falling asleep. For these psychologists, the study of consciousness defined their field. At the turn of the century, Sigmund Freud (whom we will study in more depth in Chapter 12) made the study of consciousness much more complex. He proposed that the conscious level of the mind was small in comparison to the unconscious, which houses a person's underlying needs, wishes, and desires that influence feelings and behavior. According to Freud, people are aware of the information in their conscious but not of what is in the unconscious.

Then, in the 1920s, behaviorists such as John B. Watson argued that consciousness should be eliminated as a subject of psychological study—because it is not a physical structure that can be examined and measured. As the behavioral approach came to dominate American psychology, the study of consciousness and thought was all but abandoned. In the 1960s and 1970s, the emergence of cognitive psychology led psychologists to consider the phenomenon of consciousness once again. The emergence of evolutionary psychology in the 1990s and research advances in neuroscience made consciousness an active area of interest.

Defining Consciousness

Consciousness
The general state of being aware of and responsive to events in the environment, as well as one's own mental processes.

The study of consciousness in psychology has had its ups and downs, but defining **consciousness** always has posed problems for psychologists. Despite the problems, let's begin by defining consciousness as the general state of being aware of and responsive to events in the environment, as well as to one's own mental processes. Almost all psychologists agree that a person who is conscious is aware of the immediate environment; for example, you are conscious when you listen to a lecture (at least we instructors hope so!). But consciousness also refers to inner awareness and includes your knowledge of your own thoughts, feelings, and memories (sentience).

One focus of Woody Allen's course description has a long tradition: the notion that the mind and the body are separable. The doctrine of *dualism* dates back to the 17th-century French philosopher René Descartes, who asserted that the mind and body are completely separate things and interact only to a limited degree. Dualism has come to be well accepted and has even crept into our language: the statement "these athletes are prepared in both mind and body" suggests that the mind and body are separate entities requiring different preparations. Today, almost all psychologists reject dualistic ideas. The mind does not exist independent of the body. Psychologists (and most others) accept that our mental life has a physiological basis rooted in the brain—a view referred to as *materialism* (or *reductionism*). Not only is materialism the dominant perspective among today's psychologists, but they also take a less black-and-white view of "conscious" versus "unconscious." They assert that people are more aware of certain mental processes and less aware of others. For example, when you drive along a very familiar route, you may suddenly realize that you've gone several miles seemingly without being aware of what you passed. You know the route so well that you can drive automatically, or with less awareness. Cognitive psychologists generally do not speak about the unconscious but instead refer to controlled (deliberate or aware) versus automatic (and less aware) processes.

Most psychologists—including the early structuralists, Freud, and today's evolutionary psychologists—have acknowledged that people experience different *levels* of consciousness. They agree that consciousness can be seen as a continuum—ranging from the alert attention required to read this textbook to dreaming, hypnosis, or drug-induced states. According to this view of consciousness, a person who is not paying attention or is not alert may be said to be conscious, but not "as conscious" as one who is vigilant and alert. Researchers who favor this view of a continuum of awareness suggest, for example, that a person who is drinking heavily temporarily enters a lower (deeper) *level* in the range of consciousness—that of intoxication. A person who is in a state of consciousness that is dramatically different from ordinary awareness and responsiveness is said to be in an *altered state of consciousness*.

Not only are there various levels of consciousness, but some people are more able than others to think about their own thinking—a process called *metacognition*—which may allow them to access levels of consciousness or thought processes that are not available to other people. Researchers examine consciousness and metacognition by asking individuals to track their consciousness, their levels of alertness, and their moods in some detail over a period of days or even weeks. Not surprisingly, there is a rhythm to consciousness, and we will consider this cycle of alertness later in this chapter.

What is the function of consciousness? Clearly, consciousness allows us to monitor our bodily and mental states. It also allows us, to a certain extent, to control those states by taking certain actions. For example, when you feel anxious, you can breathe more deeply. When you are falling asleep at your desk, you can stretch, yawn (to take in some extra oxygen), and perhaps blink. The extent to which consciousness allows us to monitor and control our daily activities depends on how aware we are, whether we are at a low level of consciousness (such as asleep) or in some altered state accessed through hypnotism, meditation, or drug use.

student voices

Chau M. Le
Century College

Psychology more than anything has taught me to listen more intimately to my own thoughts, which has helped me overcome many trials in my life, such as counseling my parents through their divorce.

Theories of Consciousness

As in other areas of psychology, theory guides research about consciousness, and also as in other areas of psychology, opposing views have generated a great deal of controversy. On the one hand, some theorists maintain that consciousness will never

■ *Evolutionary theorist Steven Pinker argues that the mind is what the brain does.*

be explained; the mind is beyond human comprehension. On the other hand, some theorists assert that consciousness comes from the workings of the brain; consciousness is what the brain does. This latter view fits within the materialist or reductionist view because it holds that consciousness can be reduced to the physical apparatus of the brain. Between these two views is another view, which holds that consciousness can be understood, but a new approach is needed (Chalmers, 1996). This view holds that neither science nor philosophy has formulated principles that can explain consciousness, but more work may lead to success.

Those theorists who believe that consciousness is beyond understanding are the intellectual descendants of René Descartes, the 17th-century French philosopher. Those who take this view can be termed *mysterians* (Chalmers, 1996). One theorist who fits into this category is Colin McGinn (1999), who contends that consciousness is the ultimate mystery. Humans will never understand the mind because their minds are not built that way; the human mind cannot analyze itself.

Many theorists who have taken the materialist or reductionist approach to consciousness come from the neuroscience perspective, which holds that the mind and consciousness emerge from the brain at work. Theorists who take this position reject dualism and make no distinction between the workings of the brain and the mind. Antonio Damasio's *Descartes' Error* (1994), as the title suggests, argues that Descartes was wrong to believe that the mind and body function according to different principles. Damasio contends that the mind is firmly grounded in the brain, and highly complex brains become conscious. Similarly, Daniel Dennett (1991, 1996) asserts that human beings have access to many sources of information, which together create conscious experiences. He argues that the brain creates multiple drafts (copies) of experiences, which are constantly being reanalyzed. According to Dennett, the brain develops a sense of consciousness as well as a sense of self through this constant updating and reanalysis of experience. Taking this argument even further, Allan Hobson (1999) contends that not only the brain but the entire body is part of conscious experience. This view turns Descartes' dualism around, holding that consciousness and the body form a seamless, functioning whole.

Consciousness is an important issue in evolutionary psychology. Evolutionary theorists such as Leda Cosmides and John Tooby (1997) and Steven Pinker (1997) take the materialist position, maintaining that the mind is what the brain does—nothing more. In addition, evolutionary psychologists explain consciousness as an adaptation that gave humans a survival advantage. According to this view, the mind is a set of systems for computation, designed by natural selection to solve the kinds of problems our ancestors faced in their foraging way of life. Pinker argues that the "problem" of consciousness can be broken into three issues: sentience, access, and self-knowledge. *Sentience* refers to subjective experience and awareness—feelings. *Access* refers to the ability to report on the content and product of rational thought—to take deliberate, reasoned actions based on memory, rational ideas, and past experiences. *Self-knowledge* refers to the ability of individuals to recognize that their experiences are uniquely their own and to be aware that they are experiencing as they are doing it. Sentience is difficult to assess, but access and self-knowledge are cognitive activities that can be analyzed from a variety of vantage points, including the physiological, such as through fMRI scans and even biofeedback. From Pinker's view, such an analysis is crucial, because it is the only way for scientists to understand the true nature of consciousness. Remember, Pinker argues that the mind is a neural computer, fitted by natural selection with systems for reasoning.

Circadian [sir-KAY-dee-an] rhythms
Internally generated patterns of body functions, including hormonal signals, sleep, blood pressure, and temperature regulation, which have approximately a 24-hour cycle and occur even in the absence of normal cues about whether it is day or night.

Evolutionary psychologists see consciousness as only part of what the mind does; much of the mind's function is guided by brain functions that are outside awareness (Cosmides & Tooby, 1997). Complex neural circuits underlie functions such as vision, which seem simple and automatic. These processes are arranged so that we are not aware of some and do have conscious awareness of others. Thus, evolutionary psychologists see a variety of levels of consciousness, all of which can be traced to neural circuitry that has been selected for during evolution. The result is our current multilevel consciousness.

The problem of consciousness is a classic one in philosophy, and some philosophers do not believe that neuroscience and evolutionary theory are on the right track to solve the puzzle of consciousness. David Chalmers (1996) is one of the philosophers who believe that neuroscience will not be the answer to the origins of consciousness. He contends that the problems that neuroscience will solve are the "easy problems," whereas the existence of consciousness is the "hard problem." Chalmers considers consciousness a problem of another order, separate from issues of physiology, but he does not believe that this problem is unsolvable, as the mysterians do. He accepts that a solution is possible, but the current research in neuroscience will not provide it.

Thus, the larger issues are difficult to frame, and the answers are far from complete. To work toward a more complete overall understanding of consciousness, researchers often focus on particular states of consciousness. So, in the remainder of this chapter, we will look at many of those states. Some of them are desirable and normal; others alter human behavior in less desirable ways. We begin with a very familiar state of consciousness—sleep.

Be an *Active* learner

REVIEW

- What is the dualist position? p. 191
- What are the key characteristics of consciousness? pp. 190–191
- Compare the view that consciousness comes from the working of the brain to Descartes' view. pp. 191–193

THINK CRITICALLY

- Why might neuroscience researchers and philosophers have different views of consciousness?
- What functions of consciousness are important from an evolutionary point of view?

APPLY PSYCHOLOGY

- What are the advantages of having consciousness?
- Over the next week, list the things you do on "automatic pilot," and then analyze the things these situations have in common. Where do they occur? Are you alone or with others? What types of activities cause you to go into this altered state of consciousness?

Sleep

The Italian family whose members die because they cannot sleep are very unusual. Most people—indeed, most creatures—sleep. Some animals are awake during daylight and sleep at night, whereas other have the opposite cycle, but cycles of sleep and waking are the rule.

The Sleep–Wakefulness Cycle: Circadian Rhythms

In the casinos of Las Vegas, it is difficult to tell night from day. Activity is at fever pitch 24 hours a day, and there are no windows and few clocks. It is as if there *is* no day or night. But even in Las Vegas, people sleep. People sleep everywhere; it is inescapable. Humans and other animals seem to have an internal biological clock that controls the sleep–wakefulness cycle. This clock runs on about a 24-hour cycle; thus, the term *circadian* arose from the Latin *circa diem* ("around a day"). **Circadian rhythms** are internally generated patterns of body functions, including hormonal signals, sleep, blood pressure, and body temperature, which vary over approximately a 24-hour cycle. Even in places such as Las Vegas, when normal cues about whether it is day or night are missing, circadian rhythms still operate.

■ *Light is an important cue for regulating circadian rhythms.*

■ *Jet lag is a problem with circadian rhythms, which may create safety problems for pilots.*

Light is not essential for maintaining circadian rhythms, but it is an important cue. Light helps keep the biological clock in sync (Boivin et al., 1996). When time cues (clocks, natural light windows, temperature changes as the sun goes down) are missing from the environment for a long time, circadian rhythms still operate (Lavie, 2001). Early research indicated that when cues were absent, the cycle lengthened; but when all factors are controlled, the 24-hour cycle varies by only a few minutes (Lavie, 2001).

You can see the impact of circadian rhythms when your routine is thrown off by having to work through the night and sleep during the day—your body's clock no longer matches your work clock. This disruption is apparent for airline pilots, police, and health-care workers—some of the approximately 10 million Americans who work at night (Beers, 2000). When you put in long hours that stretch through the night and into the dawn, and especially when these hours are not regular, you become less attentive, think less clearly, and may even fall asleep on the job. Thus, employers, workers, and consumers need to be aware of the potential decreases in efficiency of night workers who vary their schedules, especially airline pilots and health-care workers. Their inattentiveness and errors can have serious safety consequences. Research shows that light therapy can help; exposure to bright light, even during sleep, can help reset circadian rhythms (Campbell & Murphy, 1998; Lavie, 2001). This possibility offers relief for those whose jobs call for constantly readjusting their internal clock.

Another problem with circadian rhythms is jet lag. If you travel by jet from, say, New York City to London, the trip will take about 6 hours. If you leave at 9:00 P.M., you will arrive in London 6 hours later—at 3:00 A.M.—as far as your body is concerned. It will seem very late at night. But local London time will be 8:00 A.M. You will experience exhaustion and disorientation—*jet lag*. You might have the urge to sleep during the first day, which will make you stay up at night and keep your circadian rhythm out of sync with London time. This experience will affect your performance in ways similar to the experience of people who work at night on a shifting schedule.

What should you do to minimize the effects of a shifting schedule or jet lag? Your body takes time to accommodate, so no instant cure is available (Dement, 1999). But you can make adjustments that ease a transition. Shifting schedules are very difficult to manage because your body's circadian rhythms adjust slowly while your schedule may change every week or two. Your adjustment will be more successful if your schedule shifts slowly or not at all; that is, working nights allows you to adapt, but shifting does not. Getting over jet lag also takes time, but your trip may be too short for your body to make the adjustment. In that case, William Dement (1999) advises staying with your own time zone and trying to schedule your trip to accommodate your body's established schedule.

If you need to make an adjustment for weeks rather than a few days, you can speed the adjustment process in two ways. One is through light exposure, which promotes wakefulness. Any level of light can be helpful, but the best is bright sunlight. To promote sleep, the hormone melatonin can be useful (Brown, 1994). This hormone is produced by the pineal gland in the brain, rises before people fall asleep, and helps keep the biological clock in sync (Middleton, Arendt, & Stone, 1997). Small doses of melatonin tend to promote sleep and can help shift the biological clock toward sleep.

Electroencephalogram [eel-ECK-tro-en-SEFF-uh-low-gram] (EEG)
Graphical record of brain-wave activity obtained through electrodes placed on the scalp and forehead.

Rapid eye movement (REM) sleep
Stage of sleep characterized by high-frequency, low-amplitude brain-wave activity, rapid and systematic eye movements, more vivid dreams, and postural muscle paralysis.

Non–rapid eye movement (NREM) sleep
Four distinct stages of sleep during which no rapid eye movements occur.

Sleep Stages: REM and NREM Sleep

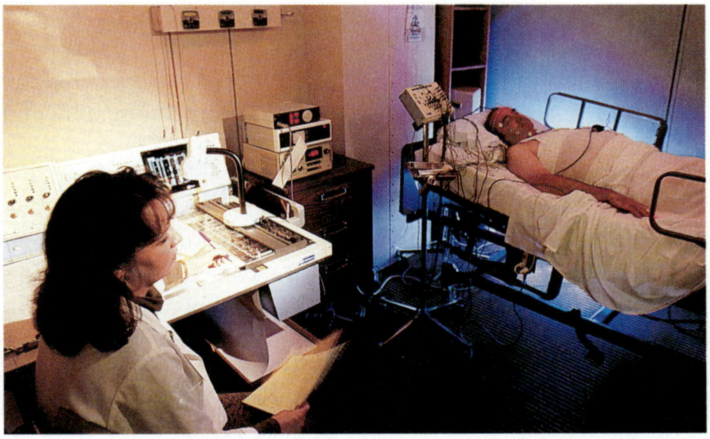

■ *Researchers in sleep laboratories study the EEG patterns of sleeping participants.*

Until the 1950s, the assumption was that consciousness had two levels: awake and asleep. When early sleep researchers such as Eugene Aserinsky, Nathaniel Kleitman, and William Dement studied the sleep—wakefulness cycle, they found that sleep consists of five different stages. By using **electroencephalograms (EEGs)**—graphic records of brain-wave activity obtained through electrodes placed on the scalp and forehead—these researchers found that sleep included a variety of different levels of consciousness.

Researchers working in sleep laboratories study the EEG patterns that occur in the brain while participants sleep. They make these recordings by gluing measuring electrodes to participants' scalps and allowing them to sleep (no easy task for the participants). The electrodes measure the electrical activity of neurons in the brain, and the waveforms reflect the brain's activity. EEG waves vary in two ways: in *frequency* and *amplitude*. The frequency shows the number of waves per second, and the amplitude indicates the height of the waves. Both of these factors are important in determining brain activity and stages of sleep. Recordings of the brain waves of sleeping participants have revealed five different stages of sleep, which occur in a cycle throughout a night's sleep.

The most dramatic finding of early sleep research was **rapid eye movement (REM) sleep**—characterized by high-frequency, low-amplitude brain-wave activity and systematic eye movements (Aserinsky & Kleitman, 1953). REM sleep occurs only after people go through four stages of **non–rapid eye movement (NREM)** sleep. During an 8-hour sleep period, people typically progress through five full cycles of the five stages of sleep, each cycle lasting approximately 90 minutes (see Figure 6.1).

Figure 6.1 shows the distinctive brain-wave patterns of wakefulness, the four stages of NREM sleep, and REM sleep in a normal adult. The waking brain-wave pattern exhibits high-frequency, low-amplitude waves, which indicate a lot of different

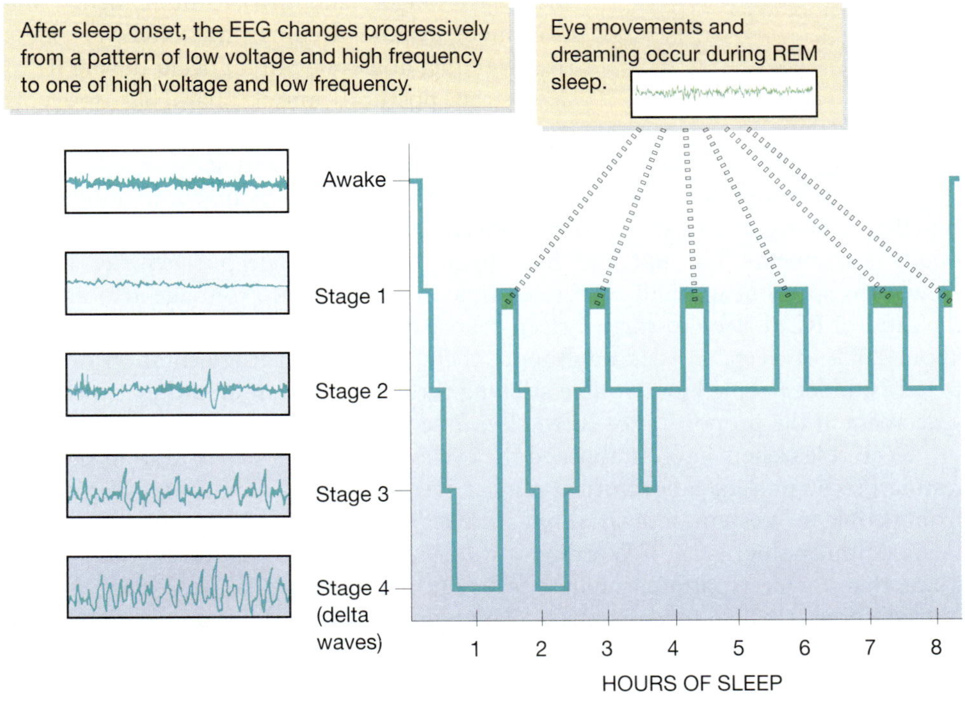

FIGURE 6.1

EEG Activity During Sleep

EEGs show distinctive and characteristic patterns during the wakeful state, REM sleep, and each of the four NREM sleep stages. Most people complete about five sleep cycles per night. (Dement, 1972)

types of brain activity. Stages 1 through 4 of NREM sleep reflect increasing relaxation of body activity and slower EEG activity; heart rate slows, blood pressure lowers, and respiration slows. EEG activity indicates lower levels of brain arousal. In addition, people become more difficult to awaken as they progress through the stages of NREM sleep.

In stage 1, light sleep, the brain waves are low amplitude and are relatively fast, with mixed frequencies. Sleepers in stage 1 can be awakened easily. Stage 2 sleep shows low-amplitude, nonrhythmic brain-wave activity, but sleepers in stage 2 are in deeper sleep than those in stage 1. Stage 3 sleep shows brain waves that are slower and higher in amplitude than those in stage 2, including some low-frequency, high-amplitude waves called *delta waves*. Stage 4 sleep, the deepest sleep, has over 50% delta waves. This stage of sleep is the lowest level of arousal that people normally experience. Sleepers take about 30 to 40 minutes to go through these NREM stages. When sleepers leave stage 4, they move back through stages 3, 2, and sometimes stage 1, and then nearly awaken before going into REM sleep.

REM sleep is very different from NREM sleep, not only in the presence of eye movements but also in body and brain arousal. In REM sleep, breathing and heart rate increase, eye movements become rapid, and EEG waves are high in frequency and low in amplitude. Indeed, REM sleep is difficult to distinguish from waking on the basis of brain or physiological arousal. But in some sense, people are even more soundly asleep because they are more difficult to awaken. In addition, people experience paralysis of the postural muscles during REM sleep; they make small movements, but they cannot sit up, stand, or walk during this sleep stage. These seemingly contradictory indications have led to the term *paradoxical sleep* to describe REM sleep (Jouvet, 1999).

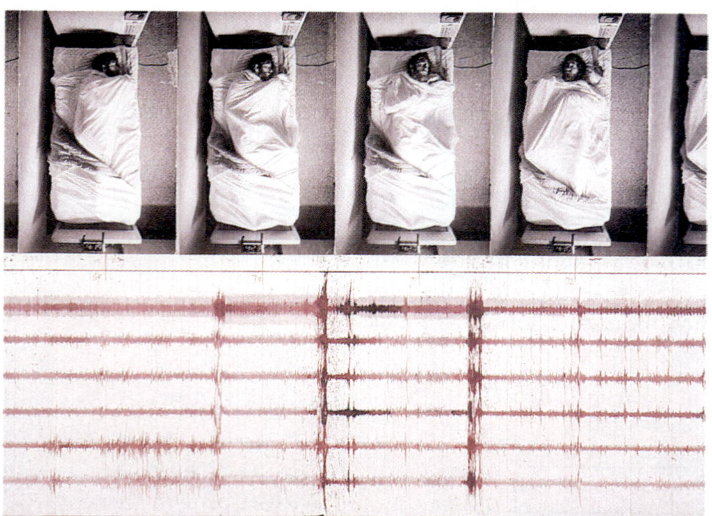

■ *During REM sleep, breathing and heart rate increase, eye movements become rapid, and EEG waves are high frequency and low amplitude.*

When awakened from a REM period, sleepers are more likely to report that they were dreaming than when awakened from other stages. Early research on sleep and dreaming suggested that dreams occurred only during REM sleep, but, in fact, dreams occur during all stages of sleep (Foulkes, 1996). REM dreams tend to be more vivid, last longer, and involve more detail and movement than dreams in NREM sleep. Sleepwalking, however, cannot occur during REM sleep—the postural muscle paralysis prevents walking, so the popular notion that sleepwalkers are acting out a dream is wrong.

Sleep cycles develop before birth, and they continue to change into adulthood. Initially, sleeping fetuses show no eye movements. Later, they show eye, facial, and bodily movements but not the five distinct stages of sleep (Dement, 1999). Newborns spend nearly half their sleep time in REM sleep. From age 1 to age 10, the ratio of REM sleep to stage 4 sleep decreases dramatically, accounting for only about 25% of sleep. In later adulthood, there is increased fragmentation of sleep patterns; older people have trouble sleeping through the night, and they experience a decrease in the proportion of REM sleep (see Figure 6.2).

Sleep researchers have established the cyclic pattern that occurs during sleep by testing people in sleep laboratories. Almost everything we know about sleep comes from people in Western, industrialized societies, which may give us a biased view of sleep. Anthropologist Carol Worthman studies sleep in other cultures, and she has found that our sleep patterns and habits may not be universal (Bower, 1999). People in traditional tribal cultures in Africa, Paraguay, Pakistan, and Indonesia have very different sleep habits from those of people in the United States. In these societies, sleep is more social, and people sleep in groups rather than alone or in couples;

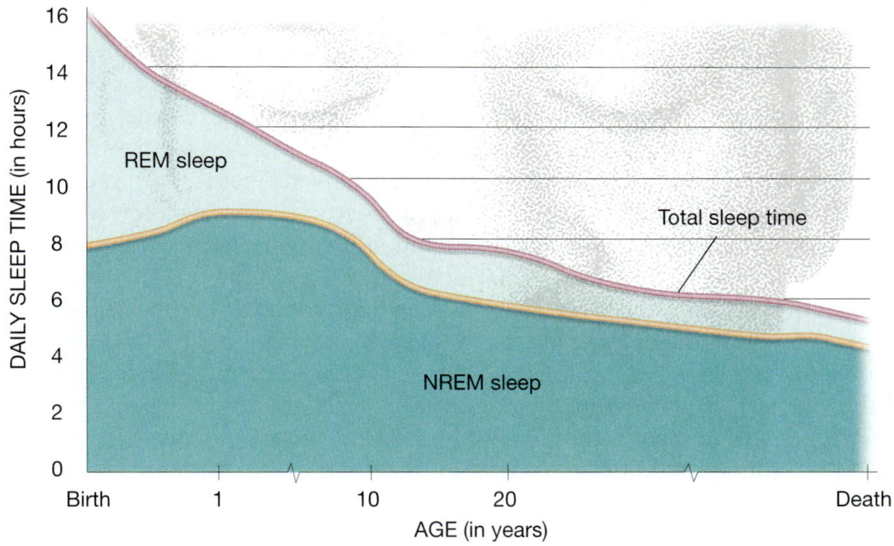

FIGURE 6.2

Changes in Sleep Patterns over a Lifetime

Children spend more time in REM sleep than adults do; the proportion of time spent in REM sleep decreases every year. NREM sleep accounts for nearly half of a newborn's sleep time. In adulthood, 80–85% of sleep is NREM. *(Roffwarg, Muzio, & Dement, 1966)*

babies sleep with their mothers. Noise is part of the sleep environment, and there are no thick, comfortable mattresses. Yet people in these cultures sleep well—they tend to complain about getting too much rather than too little sleep. Not only do sleep habits of people in these cultures differ, but sleep patterns also vary. People in these cultures experience the five stages of sleep, but they spend more time in stages 1 and 2 and less in the deeper stages of 3 and 4. This difference may allow them to wake more easily in less protected environments. This cross-cultural research shows how easy it can be to overgeneralize laboratory research and how variable even biologically based activities like sleep can be.

Sleep Deprivation

In January 1964, at age 17, Randy Gardner made history by setting a world's record by staying awake for more than 260 hours—just short of 11 days. He enlisted two friends to help keep him awake, and he took no stimulants, not even coffee. After 2 days, sleep researcher William Dement began supervising Gardner's progress, much to the relief of his parents. Although Gardner did not suffer any serious physical symptoms, there were marked psychological effects. On day 2, he had trouble focusing his eyes. On day 3, he experienced mood changes. On day 4, he was irritable and uncooperative; he also began to hallucinate. By day 6, Gardner had some memory lapses and difficulty speaking. By day 9, his thoughts and speech were sometimes incoherent. On day 10, blurred vision became more of a problem, and he was regularly forgetting things. Mornings were his most difficult time. Despite these behavioral changes, Randy never became violent or behaved in a socially deviant manner.

- *Researchers studied Randy Gardner as he experienced 260 hours of sleep deprivation.*

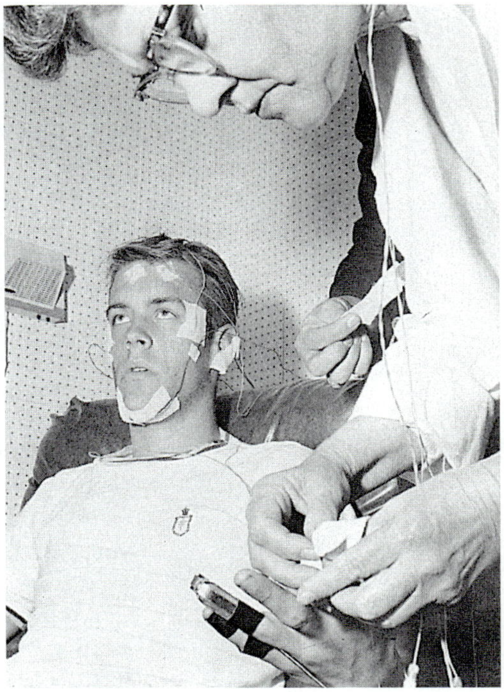

One of the most interesting aspects of Randy Gardner's adventure is what happened to his sleep after his deprivation. Dement followed up by monitoring and observing Gardner for several days to see how well he recovered, what happened to his sleep patterns, and whether he made up for the sleep he had lost. Dement found that for the 3 nights following his deprivation, Gardner slept an extra 6.5 hours; on the 4th night, he slept an extra 2.5 hours (Gulevich, Dement, & Johnson, 1966; Johnson, Slye, & Dement, 1965). Therefore, Randy did not make up all the sleep that he lost in his 11 days of sleep deprivation.

Randy Gardner's experience was unusual in terms of the length of his sleep deprivation, but going without sleep is a part of many

student voices

Katie LaRoche
Saint Anselm College

Becoming involved in sleep research, I learned how to use an EEG and read sleep patterns. My involvement found me helping to present this research at regional and national psychological conferences.

people's lives. According to the National Sleep Foundation (Harvey, 2000), 67% of adults in the United States get less than the recommended amount of sleep; 43% say that sleepiness interferes with activities in their lives, including work performance. People miss sleep in order to work, but they also neglect sleep in order to have fun, such as partying and watching TV. What are the effects of sleep deprivation? How much harm does going without sleep cause, especially at typical levels such as a few hours per night? If Randy Gardner's experience is typical, missing a few hours' sleep doesn't cause many problems, but many hours of deprivation produce major problems in functioning.

Some of the results from research on sleep deprivation are not at all surprising, but other results point to how drastically sleep deprivation can affect performance. The obvious result is that the longer people go without sleep, the sleepier they get and the worse their performance becomes (Devoto et al., 1999). One night of total sleep deprivation affects motor performance and memory (Forest & Godbout, 2000). But even a few hours of missed sleep can affect performance. A study that made this point in a dramatic way compared driving performance for people who were deprived of various amounts of sleep compared to those who had drunk various amounts of alcohol (Arnedt et al., 2001). The results showed that even low levels of alcohol impair driving ability, and sleep deprivation is comparable to drinking in its effects on driving. Indeed, driving skills worsen after staying awake only 3 hours longer than usual.

Do these results about sleep deprivation and driving explain the underlying reason for many traffic accidents? Research with long-haul truckers suggests that sleep deprivation is a serious safety problem. A team of researchers (Mitler et al., 1997) undertook a study of long-haul truck drivers to assess this safety issue. The researchers reasoned that such truckers, whose livelihood depends on delivering goods in a timely fashion, would sleep less than they needed to and that their sleep patterns would be altered in ways that would impair their driving skills. To do this study, these researchers had to conduct round-the-clock physiological monitoring while the truckers were on the job, which is an interesting contrast to the typical laboratory sleep research. The participants were driving 10 to 13 hours per day, and performance on the various measures was repeatedly tested over a 5-day period on over 200 trips totaling 204,000 miles.

The truckers averaged just over 5 hours of sleep per 24-hour period, which is about 2 hours less than what they reported as their ideal amount of sleep. The monitoring revealed that sleepiness was a substantial problem. For 7% of the time while they were actually driving, drivers exhibited signs of being in the first stage of sleep. In addition, 56% of the participants had at least one 6-minute period of drowsiness. The most likely times for such drowsy episodes were late at night and early in the morning, or between 11:00 P.M. and 5:00 A.M.

Truckers are not the only people who neglect sleep and engage in activities that can be dangerous. Airline and ship pilots, health-care workers, police, and those who monitor nuclear facilities can endanger the lives of others by their sleepiness. But millions of people endanger their own and others' lives by driving while drowsy; 60% of young adults admit that they have done so, and 17% say they have dozed off while driving (Harvey, 2000).

Pioneering sleep researcher William Dement (1999) argues that the modern world experiences massive sleep deprivation and that we suffer because of our sleepiness. He describes this problem as *sleep debt*. Think of your sleep needs as a checkbook, with the total amount of sleep having to be in balance at the end of a week. After sleep deprivation, you owe your body sleep time. If you don't pay up, you pay the price in terms of sleepiness, trouble with concentration and attentiveness, poor mood, and lack of judgment which may put you in danger.

What about complete sleep deprivation? What happens when people do not sleep at all? We know relatively little about this topic, for obvious reasons of ethics. Researchers cannot completely deprive people of sleep to see what happens, but we do know what happens to rats and to those with fatal familial insomnia: they die. Rats completely deprived of sleep die after two to three weeks of complete sleep deprivation (Rechtschaffen, 1998). Some of the symptoms in sleep-deprived rats are similar to those experienced by the Italian family with FFI—they show signs of terrible exhaustion, they lose the ability to regulate body temperature, and they lose weight. Sleep is obviously important, but what does it do?

Why Do We Sleep?

Researchers have established what happens during sleep but not why we sleep. Several theories attempt this task, but none is completely satisfactory (Rechtschaffen, 1998). The most obvious approach is to say that we sleep because we are tired—sleep provides some type of restorative function. If so, researchers have not identified what sleep restores. And fatigue does not relate directly to the need for sleep. Bedridden hospital patients, for example, sleep about the same amount of time as people who are on their feet all day. Heavy exercise seems to increase the need for sleep on any particular day, but these variations are not large (Youngstedt, O'Connor, & Dishman, 1997). And people can be exhausted and yet unable to sleep; an extreme example is the members of the Italian family afflicted with fatal familial insomnia.

The evolutionary approach is not very successful in explaining sleep. The adaptive advantage of spending hours per day unconscious is difficult to explain. The argument that forced unconsciousness keeps creatures out of danger can be countered with the point that being unconscious increases vulnerability. In addition, while we are asleep, we are not able to do other things that would increase our survival advantage, such as gather food, care for children, or have sex (Rechtschaffen, 1998). Therefore, considering the evolutionary cost of sleep *raises,* rather than answers, questions about why we sleep.

Another theory emphasizes sleep as part of circadian rhythms and emphasizes the brain mechanisms underlying the regulation of sleep and waking (Lavie, 2001). The circadian theory of sleep takes a broad approach, examining the cross-species differences and similarities in amount of sleep and sleep stages. This theory explains the mechanisms of sleep better than the underlying reasons of why sleep seems necessary.

Some theories of sleep concentrate on the stages of sleep, especially on REM sleep. One theory within this group holds that REM activity is important to memory formation, but two opposing camps disagree over what involvement REM has in memory. One version proposes that REM sleep is necessary to eliminate unnecessary and mistaken neural connections formed during waking (Crick & Mitchison, 1983), whereas another version hypothesizes that REM activity is important to memory formation (Stickgold et al., 2000). Yet another theory holds that REM plays an essential role in neural maturation, pointing to the finding that infants and babies spend more time in REM sleep than adults and older people do (Dement, 1999). This theory of sleep shows promise but leaves a great deal about sleep and its other stages unexplained.

No single theory has yet explained why we sleep, and perhaps none ever will. Perhaps one theory alone would be inadequate for this task anyway. Sleep serves multiple functions, and thus, several theories may be necessary to explain those various functions (Rechtschaffen, 1998).

Is There a Sleep Switch?

What makes you go to sleep, and what wakes you? If your life is like mine (LB), you probably feel that "exhaustion" is the clear answer to the first part of that question, and "the alarm clock" answers the second. Those answers may be true for many of us, but they don't tell the whole story. If we could sleep whenever we wanted and as much as we needed, we would still go to sleep and wake up. Indeed, the research on circadian rhythms shows that people maintain a rhythmic cycle of sleeping and waking, even when they are removed from their normal lives and deprived of cues about day and night. Is there a physiological structure that regulates and initiates sleep and wakefulness? Researchers suggest that there may be a certain brain structure that "turns on" sleep and another that "turns on" waking. Like cells in the visual system, which are activated when exposed to certain stimuli, these specialized brain cells may be selectively active.

Sherin and colleagues (1996) found that cells in the brains of sleeping rats seemed to turn on or off, depending on the stage of sleep. The specific area of the brain in which these cells are located is the front region of the hypothalamus, called the *ventrolateral preoptic area,* or the VLPO. In rats that were deprived of sleep for 9 to 12 hours, the researchers found that a key protein was present throughout most of the brain but not in the VLPO; in contrast, in rats that were not sleep-deprived, the protein was found in the VLPO but not in the rest of the brain. Further research has confirmed the importance of the VLPO in promoting sleep and has added information about how this area might work (Gallopin et al., 2000). The neurons in the VLPO produce GABA, an inhibitory neurotransmitter (see Table 2.1, p. 50). In addition, cells in the VLPO have connections to other locations in the brain and may be related to not only the control of sleep but also wakefulness.

Researchers have known for years that a collection of neurons in the *suprachiasmic nucleus* (SCN) (an area just above where the optic nerves meet and cross) is essential to the regulation of circadian rhythms. Dement (1999) argues that the biological clock actually promotes waking, which he calls clock-dependent alerting. The function of this internal clock helps us wake at two times during the 24-hour day: once in the early morning and again in the evening. Its effect is weak during the afternoon. Dement says that these effects explain why we are drowsy in the afternoon, feeling as if we just can't make it until bedtime, but start to feel more alert as the evening progresses. The longer we stay awake, the sleepier we get, so the effects of alerting are overtaken by sleepiness, so we sleep. Connections between the VLPO and the SCN are likely to be part of this regulation, but research must establish this connection and identify the neurotransmitters that allow it to occur.

Sleep Disorders

Do you snore so loudly that you keep others awake or fall asleep at inappropriate times, such as when driving a car? Do you ever have trouble falling asleep, or find yourself sleepwalking? If you answer yes, you have a sleep disorder. Many sleep disorders exist; some are not dangerous, but others are life threatening.

People who fall asleep suddenly and unexpectedly have a disorder known as *narcolepsy.* In addition to daytime sleepiness, people with narcolepsy experience muscle weakness as they fall uncontrollably into sleep, and their sleep stages do not follow the normal cycle. This disorder affects about 1 in 2,000 people and can cause them to have a very restricted life—they never know when they will have an attack. Narcolepsy has a genetic component (Takahashi, 1999), and an effective drug treatment has recently been developed (Dement, 1999).

Another sleep disorder, *sleep apnea,* is even more serious. This sleep disorder causes airflow to stop for at least 15 seconds; the sleeper stops breathing and chokes, and then wakens briefly. Loud snoring is a symptom of sleep apnea. People with this disorder often have as many as 100 apnea episodes in a night. Rather than waking, they may choke and die, making this disorder life threatening. Because their sleep is interrupted so often, people with apnea are exceedingly sleepy. They may have memory losses, severe headaches, and work-related accidents. About 20% of the population experience sleep apnea to the extent that their lives and health are affected (Dement, 1999). Middle-aged, overweight men are at increased risk, but even children can have apnea. Several therapies have been effective in treating apnea, including a machine that affects airway pressure and minor surgery. Both approaches help clear the airway so that people can breathe normally during sleep.

Insomnia, problems in going to sleep or maintaining sleep, is a very common sleep disorder. As many as 1 in 10 people reports insomnia at some time in their lives, often caused by anxiety or depression. Some people who complain about insomnia have trouble going to sleep, tossing and turning for hours; others can go to sleep but wake up and can't get back to sleep. They may actually sleep as much as those who do not complain of insomnia, but their quality of sleep tends to be poor and they do not feel rested (Dement, 1999). People with insomnia tend to be listless and tired during the day and desperate to get some sleep, which may lead them to try sleeping pills or other drugs. In years past, sleeping pills were usually *barbiturates,* which produced dependency and altered the stages of sleep by reducing the proportion of REM sleep (Webb & Agnew, 1975). (Recall that the body's normal response to sleep deprivation is to *increase* REM sleep.) Today, less dangerous sleeping pills have been developed, but physicians are very reluctant to prescribe medication to help people sleep, especially for those who have chronic insomnia. Various researchers have proposed behavioral methods that do not rely on drugs to help people manage their sleep problems; among these methods are relaxation training, thought restructuring, and self-hypnosis (e.g., Morin et al., 1994).

Night terrors, another sleep disorder, consist of panic attacks that occur within an hour after a person falls asleep. Sitting up abruptly in a state of sheer panic, a person with a night terror may scream, breathe rapidly, and experience a state of total fright, yet the person is not fully conscious. Night terrors are not vivid nightmares; they occur in NREM sleep, usually in stage 4. They are especially common in young children between the ages of 3 and 8. They usually disappear as a child grows older. Although night terrors appear to be extremely frightening, they are not symptoms of any psychological disorder, and are often forgotten (except by the startled and concerned parents). The cause of night terrors is not fully established, but they may be a result of an electrochemical overload of some part of the brain during NREM sleep.

Sleepwalking is a disorder that tends to run in families and is common among children. A sleepwalker appears both asleep and awake at the same time—a sleepwalking child may reach out to a parent for a hug, navigate a darkened room, avoid a piece of furniture, walk into the street, or seem to be trying to accomplish a task—yet still be asleep. More boys sleepwalk than girls, and children who sleepwalk tend to outgrow it as they mature. Brain activity of sleepwalkers, when recorded with an EEG, shows stage 4 sleep. Research shows that different parts of a sleepwalker's brain display different levels of activity: motor portions of the brain are active; higher-level cognitive portions show little activity. Contrary to popular belief, there is no danger in waking a sleepwalker. More likely, you may not be able to wake the sleepwalking individual because he or she is so deeply asleep (Dement, 1999).

Sleep disorders like sleepwalking can be dangerous if the sleepwalker does dangerous things (such as fall down stairs or walk into the street), but the disorder itself does not signal a problem and causes no direct damage. Sleep disorders like apnea are very dangerous, however. Not only are people with apnea in danger of dying in their sleep, but they also experience sleepiness that can cause other dangers. William Dement contends that doctors are not very sensitive to the possibility of sleep disorders and miss many diagnoses, with huge implications for health and well-being.

Be an *Active* learner

REVIEW

- What are circadian rhythms and what affects them? pp. 193–194
- Differentiate between REM and NREM sleep, and characterize the various sleep stages. pp. 195–197
- How common is sleep deprivation? What are its effects? p. 198
- Describe three different theories of the function of sleep. p. 199
- What brain structures regulate sleep and wakefulness? p. 200
- What is the most common sleep disorder? the most dangerous? pp. 200–201

THINK CRITICALLY

- How has sleep been affected by societal and technological changes that began in the 20th century?
- What does the research on sleep deprivation reveal about the reasons for sleep?
- How can the evolutionary view explain sleep disorders?

APPLY PSYCHOLOGY

- Calculate your current sleep debt, and make a schedule that would allow you to pay back this debt. How difficult would it be for you to carry out this schedule?
- You probably know someone who experiences sleepwalking. Devise a plan to prevent this person from harming him- or herself.

Insomnia
Problems in going to sleep or maintaining sleep.

Dreams

Why do some people rarely remember their dreams while other people can recall theirs in vivid detail? Do dreams contain hidden meanings and mysterious symbols to be deciphered? Sometimes lifelike, sometimes surreal, and sometimes incoherent, dreams may seem to replay a person's life history or venture into the unknown. Dreams have long occupied an important place in psychology, but only since the 1950s have they come under close scientific scrutiny. Dream research is difficult to conduct. In addition, because the data from dream research are always memories of past events, they are sometimes difficult to quantify and verify (Koulack, 1991), and this is especially true with youngsters, who have difficulty reporting dreams from their own perspective (Foulkes & Kerr, 1994).

What Is a Dream?

A **dream** is a state of consciousness that occurs during sleep and is usually accompanied by vivid visual imagery, although the imagery may also be tactile or auditory. Dreams are associated with REM sleep—about 80% of the time people are awakened from REM, they report a dream. Dreams also occur during NREM sleep, when they tend to be less visual and less bizarre and to contain less action imagery (Casagrande et al., 1996). NREM dreams, such as the dreams that occur at the beginning of sleep (Vogel, 1991), are more like waking thoughts (Foulkes, 1985).

Although we cannot assume that REM sleep guarantees dreaming, research from sleep labs (Hobson, 1999) suggests that people tend to forget dreams when they do not wake during or soon after the dream, so it is likely that most people dream every night, probably several times. REM dreams last from a few seconds to several minutes. The first REM period (and likely the first dream) of a typical night occurs about 90 minutes after a person has fallen asleep and lasts for 10 minutes. More dreaming occurs during the second part of the night than at the beginning (Casagrande et al., 1996; Hobson, 1999). If we dream in 80% of REM periods, the total would be three or four dreams per night, 365 days per year. The average person is likely to have more than 100,000 dreams in a lifetime. However, people remember only a few of their dreams. Usually, they recall a dream because they woke in the middle of it or because the dream had powerful emotional content or imagery.

The Content of Dreams

Sometimes the content of a dream is related to day-to-day events, to an unfulfilled desire, or to an unpleasant experience. Sometimes a person experiences the same dream or a sequence of related dreams over and over again. Dreams are mostly visual, and most are in color. Most dreams focus on events and people with whom the dreamer comes into contact frequently—family, friends, or coworkers. Common dream themes include sex, aggressive incidents, and misfortunes or worries. Sounds and other sensations from the environment that do not awaken a sleeper are often incorporated into a dream. For example, when a researcher sprayed water on the hands of sleepers, 42% of those who did not awaken later reported dreaming about swimming pools, baths, or rain (Dement & Wolpert, 1958).

PET scans show that not all areas of the brain are equally active during REM, which may account for some of the differences between imagery during waking and dreaming. Braun and his colleagues (1998) found that the primary visual cortex is nearly shut down during REM sleep, but that other visual areas are highly active. This lack of integration of visual areas may account for some of the confused nature of dreams and their bizarre, disconnected content. Without interpretation from important visual areas, dreaming is like looking at a map that doesn't show key exits, roads, or directional arrows.

Dream
A state of consciousness that occurs during sleep, usually accompanied by vivid visual, tactile, or auditory imagery.

TABLE 6.1

Theories of Dreaming

Psychodynamic Theory	Jungian Theory	Physiological Model	Cognitive Model
Psychodynamic theorists such as Freud view dreams as expressions of desires, wishes, and unfulfilled needs that exist in the unconscious.	Jungian theorists see dreams not only as expressions of needs and desires, but as reflections of people's collective unconscious.	Biological models of dreaming view dreams as combinations of neural signals that are randomly generated and see analysis of dreams as inappropriate.	Cognitive theorists view dreams as a continuation of waking cognitive processes; dreams have no hidden meaning and reflect people's everyday concerns.

When Lester's younger daughter was 6 years old, she told him about a dream in which she was being chased by a monster. In the dream, she realized that she was dreaming, and so she turned around and made friends with the monster. Like Lester's daughter, people sometimes report that they are aware of dreaming while it is happening; this type of dream is called a **lucid dream.** Most people have had a lucid dream at one time or another, particularly as children. Often people who have experienced a lucid dream report that they felt as though they were inside and outside the dream at the same time. Most people have little or no control over their dreams, but Stephen LaBerge has worked toward understanding and developing people's ability to experience lucid dreams, claiming that many benefits accompany the ability to control your dreams (LaBerge & Gackenbach, 2000).

Dream Theories

Psychologists have developed a number of theories to explain dreaming. Some believe that dreams express desires and thoughts that may be unacceptable to the conscious mind. Many therapists who interpret and analyze dreams assume that dreams represent some aspect of the personality that is seeking expression; this view—widely held—suggests that dreams put emotions into a context and that dreaming allows the safe expression of emotions (Hartmann, 1995, 1996). Some psychologists find dreams meaningless. Others see much symbolism in dreams and assert that the content of a dream hides its true meaning. Thus, theories of dreaming vary throughout the range of possible differences—from the view that dreams are the road to an understanding of our most hidden wishes to the position that dreams have no meaning. The suggested meaning of a dream depends on the psychologist's orientation. (See Table 6.1.)

■ **PSYCHODYNAMIC VIEWS.** Sigmund Freud described dreams as "the royal road to the unconscious." For Freud, a dream expressed desires, wishes, and unfulfilled needs that exist in the unconscious (see Chapter 12 for more on Freud and the unconscious). In his book *The Interpretation of Dreams* (1900/1953), Freud spoke about the manifest and latent content of dreams. The **manifest content** of a dream consists of its overt story line, characters, and setting—the obvious, clearly discernible events of the dream. The **latent content** of a dream is its deeper meaning, usually involving symbolic, hidden meaning, and repressed or obscured ideas and wishes. These wishes might make the dreamer uncomfortable if they were expressed overtly. Freud would say that at the latent level, a dream about a tunnel is definitely *not* about a tunnel. You will see in Chapters 12 and 16 that Freud used dreams extensively in his theory of personality and in his treatment approach.

Carl G. Jung (1875–1961) was trained in the Freudian approach to therapy and personality analysis, and he, too, considered dreams a crucial means for understanding human nature. However, Jung took it for granted that a dream was nature's way of allowing humans access to their own unconscious. He believed that an individual's

Lucid [LOO-sid] dream
Dream in which the dreamer is aware of dreaming while it is happening.

Manifest content
The overt story line, characters, and setting of a dream—the obvious, clearly discernible events of the dream.

Latent content
The deeper meaning of a dream, usually involving symbolism, hidden meaning, and repressed or obscured ideas and wishes.

■ *Jung believed that the mandala represented a person's inner striving for unity.*

dreams express his or her deepest feelings in an uncensored form; they were a dreamer's attempt to make sense of life's tasks, compensate for unconscious urges, and predict the future (McLynn, 1997). Jung asserted that dreams give visual expression to instincts and that all humans share in the **collective unconscious,** a storehouse of primitive ideas and images inherited from one's ancestors. These inherited ideas and images, whose representations emerge in dreams, are termed *archetypes,* and are emotionally charged and rich in meaning and symbolism. The photo shows one especially important archetype—the *mandala,* a mystical symbol, often with a circular pattern, that in Jung's view represents a person's inner striving for unity. Dream analysis is also important in Jungian therapy, with a focus on understanding and accepting one's humanity. We will consider this approach in more detail in our study of personality in Chapter 12.

Today, psychoanalytic theorists still see dreams as keys to the unconscious, but they also suggest that dreams integrate past experiences with current ones to produce a structure of ideas and feelings that are organized so as to help restore psychological balance. Thus, theorists such as Fosshage (1997) assert that dreams speak to the dreamer and tell stories of the person's ongoing psychological transformation. These ideas appeal to many, but little research supports them (Blagrove, 1996).

■ **COGNITIVE VIEWS.** Some contemporary researchers believe that dreams are connected to reality, have meaning, and even have a "grammar" of their own, without having a hidden, or latent, content. These cognitive researchers (e.g., Foulkes, 1985, 1996) suggest that dreams reflect the same kind of thinking that people do when they are awake—they express current wishes, desires, and issues with which a person is dealing. Foulkes (1990) argues that the creation of a dream depends on active, integrative intelligence and that studying the content of dreams allows researchers to learn more about development, intelligence, and language, as well as how cognitive processes develop. According to this view, not only do we dream of what is currently concerning us, but our culture and language affect dream content; for example, the dream content of those who are bilingual is related to the language that was dominating their waking hours before sleep (Foulkes et al., 1993).

Consistent with the cognitive view, a cross-cultural study demonstrated that life events affect dream content (Punamäki & Joustie, 1998). This study compared the dreams of Finnish and Palestinian children, whose cultures vary a great deal in the attitudes toward dreams (as well as in many other ways). In addition, the study compared the dreams of Palestinian children living in Gaza, an area where opposition to Israeli occupation is strong and there is violence and the threat of violence, to children living in Galilea, a peaceful area. Few differences in dreams appeared in children from the two cultures, but the life events made a difference for dream content. As expected, the Palestinian children living in violent neighborhoods reported far more dreams of persecution and aggression than did the Palestinians from nonviolent areas or the Finnish children. Although the researchers found no difference in dream content between Palestinian and Finnish children, which fails to support an effect of culture on dream content, this study did show that daily life experiences for the children living with violence intrude vividly on dreams.

■ **BIOLOGICAL VIEWS.** Researchers know that dreaming is neither solely a right-hemisphere nor solely a left-hemisphere function—both hemispheres of the brain are involved (McCormick et al., 1997). But both sides of the brain may not be operating simultaneously or even in congruence. Is it possible that this lack of coordination means that dreams have no underlying meaning and are just random fleeting images? Two researchers from Harvard Medical School, Allan Hobson and Robert McCarley (1977), proposed that dreams (and, for that matter, all consciousness)

Collective unconscious
Jung's theory of a shared storehouse of primitive ideas and images that are inherited from one's ancestors; these inherited ideas and images, called *archetypes,* are emotionally charged and rich in meaning and symbolism.

Descriptive studies
A type of research method that allows researchers to measure variables so that they can develop a description of a situation or phenomenon.

introduction to research basics

Caught in a Maze

Have you ever had a dream about being caught in a giant maze, trying to find your way out? If you have, maybe some of the corridors in the maze ended in dead ends, and you weren't sure where you were going. If so, you aren't alone—rats have similar dreams, at least the ones in the Massachusetts Institute of Technology laboratory of Kenway Louie and Matthew Wilson (2001). These two researchers conducted a descriptive study in which they compared the pattern of neural activity during maze learning with the pattern during REM sleep. They wanted to determine if the two types of patterns were similar enough to conclude that the rats were dreaming of their daytime maze-running activities.

HYPOTHESIS Neural activity in the hippocampus, a brain structure involved in memory formation, will be similar during REM sleep and during maze running.

DESIGN The design was a descriptive study using correlation. **Descriptive studies** are a type of research method that allows researchers to measure variables so that they can develop a description of a situation or phenomenon. Louie and Wilson wanted to know the degree of relationship between the firing patterns of neurons in the hippocampus during maze running and during REM sleep. This method allowed them to make some inferences about dream content in nonhuman animals, a topic that has been difficult to study because rats can't report their dreams. However, rats do have the same five sleep stages that humans experience, including REM sleep.

PROCEDURE Louie and Wilson measured the pattern of activation in the rats' hippocampus (see Chapter 2, p. 56) and then compared that pattern to the activation in the hippocampus during REM sleep. These researchers placed 4 rats in a circular maze and made recordings from neurons in their brains during this activity. Then they made neural recordings of over 40 REM periods in the rats that had run the maze.

RESULTS Some REM periods showed brain activity that was not at all similar to the pattern during maze running, but about half of the REM periods showed a very similar pattern of activity in the hippocampus. The researchers measured the similarity by using a correlation statistic (see Chapter 2 for a more detailed explanation of this technique) to determine the degree of association between neural activity during maze running and during REM sleep. They found patterns that seem to be so similar that they could be considered neural "signatures" of this specific activity.

CONCLUSIONS These researchers believe that the rats are replaying their maze experiences during their dreams. The replay was the same length as the experience of traversing the maze, and the researchers could match the patterns of activity closely. Not only does this research tell us that rats dream but that both rat and human dreams may serve to consolidate memory. One version of the biological theory of dreaming holds that REM sleep is important for memory formation, and this research strengthens that claim.

have a physiological basis; dream content has no hidden meaning, or indeed, much meaning at all. They argue that during periods of REM sleep, the parts of the brain responsible for long-term memory, vision, audition, and perhaps even emotion are spontaneously *activated* (stimulated) by cells in the hindbrain, especially the pons. The cortex tries to *synthesize,* or make sense out of the messages. This attempt to make sense is part of a human tendency to create sense and order, but the content of dreams is unimportant, whereas the activity of REM is very important (Hobson, 1989, 1999). Research supports the activation more than the synthesis part of the theory. A growing body of research (Stickgold et al., 2000) shows that REM activity is important to memory formation, so the neural activity of REM may be essential in daily "housecleaning" for the cerebral cortex, scanning previous memories, refreshing storage mechanisms, and maintaining active memories (see *Introduction to Research Basics*). Dreams may have no hidden meaning, but most people (including most psychologists) have trouble accepting that dreams are meaningless because their content is so related to personal experience.

Be an *Active* learner

REVIEW

- How do researchers know when people dream? p. 202
- Which sleep disorders might have serious implications for day-to-day behavior? pp. 200–201

THINK CRITICALLY

- What, if anything, would happen to you if you cut your normal daily amount of sleep by 2 hours for a period of several months?
- Keep a notepad at your bedside, and record several nights' dreams immediately on awakening. (Otherwise, you're likely to forget them by the time you have breakfast.) Which theory of dreaming seems to explain your dreams best? Why?

APPLY PSYCHOLOGY

- Record several of your dreams, and try to analyze at least one using Freudian, Jungian, cognitive, and biological approaches to dream analysis.

Controlling Consciousness: Biofeedback, Hypnosis, and Meditation

Can you learn to control your own consciousness? Can you manipulate your mental states to achieve certain bodily reactions? Some people's personal experience suggests that you can, and research confirms these possibilities. For centuries, people have learned to relax and breathe in special ways to decrease the experience of pain—for example, during childbirth. Contestants have won marathons through intense mental concentration that allowed them to endure especially difficult physical ordeals. Laboratory research also shows that people can bring some otherwise autonomic bodily states (see Chapter 2), such as blood pressure, heart rate, and blood vessel constriction, under conscious control through the technique of biofeedback.

Biofeedback

■ *Biofeedback uses electronic equipment to measure physical responses, such as muscle tension or EEG activity which allows the person to learn to control those responses.*

Imagine a special clinic where people could be taught to treat themselves for headaches, high blood pressure, stress-related illnesses, even nearsightedness. By learning conscious control of what are normally involuntary reactions, patients might be able to cure themselves. Biofeedback allows some of these possibilities.

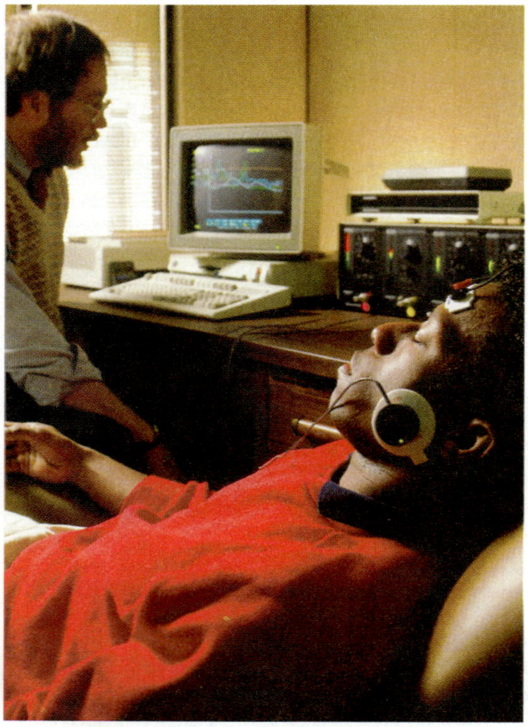

Physicians and psychologists once assumed that most biological functions, especially those involving the autonomic nervous system, could not be controlled voluntarily except through drugs or surgery. Since the 1960s, however, studies have explored the extent to which people can learn to control these functions through biofeedback. **Biofeedback** is a process through which people receive information about the status of a physical system and use this feedback information to learn to control the activity of that system. The process usually uses electronic equipment to measure the status of a system, such as blood pressure, and to give immediate feedback to the person being monitored about the activity level. A well-known psychologist, Neal E. Miller, was one of the first researchers to train rats to control certain physical responses, such as heart rate. Miller's research (1969) indicated that rats can be trained to either raise or lower their heart rate, and Miller suggested that human beings might be able to learn the same techniques and benefit from them.

We do not normally control functions such as heart rate and blood flow and may not have any conscious awareness of these physical processes. But biofeedback machines provide that awareness, which allows us to learn conscious control. A relaxed person viewing his or her own brain waves on a monitor, for example, can increase the frequency of those waves by receiving the appropriate type of feedback. Similarly, a participant whose heart rate is displayed on a monitor can see the rate decrease as he or she relaxes, thereby learning about the physiological states that allow the body to relax. The person can learn which behaviors relax the heart and lower blood pressure and, in time, can learn to reproduce those behaviors and control heart rate and blood pressure.

Biofeedback
A process through which people receive information about the status of a physical system and use this feedback information to learn to control the activity of that system.

People can learn to control physical reactions that are normally not under conscious control (which makes a good party trick), but how useful is biofeedback? The technique has been used to treat a variety of disorders, including chronic headaches, muscle tension problems, back pain, and high blood pressure. Although people can learn to control their blood pressure, biofeedback is not a practical strategy for managing high blood pressure. Its greatest success is in helping people manage

point*counterpoint*

Hypnosis and States of Consciousness

The Issue: Is hypnosis an altered state of consciousness?

POINT
Hypnosis is an altered state of consciousness characterized by suggestibility, relaxation, and concentration.

COUNTERPOINT
Hypnosis involves no alteration of consciousness.

Some authorities, including Ernest Hilgard (1965; Hilgard & Hilgard, 1994), define hypnosis as an altered state of consciousness during which the person's consciousness is divided or dissociated. In this state, people are more highly suggestible, and they can control physiological processes that they cannot during normal waking, such as pain perception.

Other authorities, including Theodore X. Barber (1991), contend that hypnosis is not an altered state of consciousness. Instead, some people have a trait that makes them more prone to follow suggestions. This view rejects the notion that an induction is necessary; all of the effects associated with hypnosis can be achieved without it. Those who accept this view believe that hypnosis is more like playing the role of a hypnotized person than attaining an altered state of consciousness.

These two views are incompatible, and there is research support for both. The definition of hypnosis as an altered state of consciousness received support from a study in which researchers used PET brain imaging technology to study people during hypnosis (Rainville et al., 1999). This study compared people during relaxation, hypnosis, and hypnosis with suggestions about suppressing pain. While hypnotized, people's brains showed a complex pattern of changes, including increased activation of the frontal lobes, especially the areas involved in language, and the occipital cortex, which is involved in vision and imagery. In addition, the participants showed changes in brain activation in an area of the cerebral cortex that is associated with attention. This study suggests that people who are hypnotized experience an altered state of consciousness, as reflected by a distinct pattern of brain activity.

Barber's studies (1991), however, show that participants who undergo hypnotic induction and participants given task-motivating instructions (such as to concentrate deeply, fix their attention, or breathe deeply) perform similarly. Typically, more than half of the participants in experimental groups showed responsiveness to task suggestions, in contrast to 16% in control groups that were given no special instructions. From the results, Barber concluded that task-motivating instructions are almost as effective as hypnotic induction in increasing participants' responsiveness.

A third definition for hypnosis proposes that hypnosis is a state of focused attention that allows people to relax and learn to control bodily functions (Olness, 1993). This definition concentrates on the characteristics associated with and the benefits that can be derived from hypnosis. So, in the end, we have three views of hypnosis—and the research continues.

chronic headaches, especially migraine headaches (Compas et al., 1998). Many of its benefits are related to relaxation, and other consciousness-controlling techniques are often as effective as biofeedback.

Hypnosis

"You are falling asleep. Your eyelids are becoming heavy. The weight on your eyes is becoming greater and greater. Your muscles are relaxing. You are feeling sleepier and sleepier. You are feeling very relaxed." These instructions are typical of those used in *hypnotic induction*—the process used to hypnotize people. The induction procedure is fairly standard, but almost everything else about hypnosis is controversial, including its definition (see *Point/Counterpoint*).

Hypnosis was first used as a treatment in the late 1700s in France by Franz Anton Mesmer. His work was discredited, and hypnosis fell into disfavor. Since that time, hypnosis has gone through cycles of acceptance and rejection. At the present

■ *Most people do not achieve a hypnotic state as easily as the popular image suggests, and most hypnotized people do not do bizarre or unconventional things.*

time, opinions are divided not only on the definition of hypnosis but also on its uses. The agreement is greater on the characteristics associated with hypnosis and with hypnotized people.

The movie image of hypnosis is different from the actual hypnotic state. In the movies, the hypnotist swings a gold watch while saying "you are getting sleepy," and the weak-willed subject loses the ability to maintain control, falling completely under the power of the hypnotist. Almost everything about this image is incorrect; the only accurate part is that hypnotic inductions usually contain the suggestion that the participant is getting sleepy. Despite that suggestion, hypnosis is not the same as any stage of sleep (Rainville et al., 1999).

People who are hypnotized are not weak-willed or unintelligent. Those who are good hypnotic subjects tend to have good visual imagery ability and are able to become absorbed in imaginative experiences (Sheehan & Robertson, 1996). The ability to concentrate is also related to how easily people can be hypnotized (Crawford, 1994), so intelligence is positively rather than negatively related to the ability to be hypnotized. In the movies, people usually fall into a deep trance immediately, but in real life, most people do not. Practice is a factor in hypnosis; good hypnotic subjects need practice to attain a deep hypnotic state, and even those who are not good hypnotic subjects can improve with practice.

Suggestibility is also a factor in hypnosis, but there is controversy over whether hypnosis produces increased suggestibility or whether suggestibility is a characteristic of those who can be hypnotized. This difference of opinion relates to the controversy over the definition of hypnosis, as *Point/Counterpoint* details. However, the popular image of suggestibility during hypnosis is also incorrect. Suggestibility increases when a person is hypnotized (Braffman & Kirsch, 1999; Rainville et al., 1999), but most people do not do bizarre or unconventional things as a result of hypnotic suggestion. Nor does the suggestibility extend beyond hypnosis, and the power of *posthypnotic suggestion* is not as strong as people imagine. That is, when a hypnotist makes suggestions about behavior to be performed at a later time, the hypnotized person is not destined to carry out those suggestions. In one study, people responded at a higher rate to a verbal request by the experimenter than to the posthypnotic suggestion (Barnier & McConkey, 1998). Therefore, hypnosis is not a very effective technique to lose weight, stop smoking, or break other bad habits because posthypnotic suggestions are not very effective in altering behavior.

Other effects popularly associated with hypnosis are also less powerful than people imagine. Heightened memory is another effect supposedly associated with hypnosis, but the evidence for this effect is weak, especially for *age regression* under hypnosis. In the movies, hypnotized people sometimes recall early childhood experiences that they had consciously forgotten, but these effects are most likely re-creations of those experiences rather than memories of them (Spiegel, 1998). In fact, memory can be distorted by hypnosis. The increased suggestibility associated with hypnosis can make a hypnotized person vulnerable to suggestions by the hypnotist, which can result in memory distortion. For this reason, hypnosis is a poor choice for helping witnesses recall details of a crime—they may remember things that they did not see (Loftus, 2000). The problem of memory distortion during hypnosis has become extremely controversial in connection with the phenomenon of *recovered memories* from women who have, often under hypnosis, remembered childhood sexual abuse (a topic covered in more detail in Chapter 8).

Meditation
The use of a variety of techniques including concentration, restriction of incoming stimuli, and deep relaxation to produce a state of consciousness characterized by a sense of detachment.

What uses, then, does hypnosis have? The technique is used in psychotherapy and in health-care settings to help people relax and to assist in pain control. A great deal of research has concentrated on hypnosis and pain, and the effects are real (Spiegel, 1998). Hypnosis has been used to help people control a variety of types of pain, ranging from childbirth and dental pain to burn and cancer pain. Hypnosis is also used in combination with other treatments to help people cope with stress, focus energy, and deal with anxiety and traumatic experiences. The effects produced by hypnosis are greater than the effects of expectancy, and brain imaging studies of hypnotized people offer the possibility of understanding how the brain functions during hypnosis.

Meditation

Meditation has become an important daily routine for one of my (LB) former students. He was in prison when he decided that meditation provided a way to think and behave in a more productive way. He had been arrested before, had problems with drug use, and behaved impulsively in a number of ways. Now he has a college degree and holds a management-level job. He says that meditation is an important part of his life, and he meditates every day. He is not alone is believing in the benefits of meditation (see *Psychology in Action*).

Meditation involves concentration and deep relaxation.

Meditation is the use of a variety of techniques including concentration, restriction of incoming stimuli, and deep relaxation to produce a state of consciousness characterized by a sense of detachment and relaxation. For centuries, meditation has been used to alter consciousness and help relieve health problems. Those who practice it take a variety of approaches and use a variety of positions—sitting, lying down, or reclining. Practitioners report that it can

psychology ***in action***

Sentenced to Meditate

People who choose meditation often report life-changing experiences as a result of their practice of it. But what about people who do not choose meditation but instead have it forced on them? Many would guess that these circumstances would make for a low likelihood of success, especially if the people who are forced to meditate are prisoners. The experience of a group of judges and offenders defies these predictions. The Enlightened Sentencing Project, a panel of eight judges in Missouri, routinely sentences offenders to meditation practice (King, 2000). Although meditation is usually not the only part of a sentence, it has been part of probation for over 100 offenders. Judge David Mason first saw the benefits of meditation in 1996, and other judges joined him in this unusual sentencing strategy.

Probationers report that their lives have changed, and judges receive glowing reports from probationers' family and friends. The main benefits are in the areas of self-control and self-esteem, and judges, probationers, family, and friends see the benefits. One probationer said that nothing had worked for him like meditation. "If it worked for me, it can work for anybody. My entire outlook on life has changed." Judge Henry Autrey is equally enthusiastic, saying that his probationers who practice meditation have shown life changes that he has rarely seen in other probationers (*Latest News,* 2001).

Probationers are not the only offenders who can benefit from meditation. Charles Flinton (1998) studied a group of young men who were incarcerated in a camp for juvenile delinquents. He involved one group of these young men in an 8-week meditation program to determine the effect of meditation on factors related to criminal behavior, including anxiety. When he compared the meditators to other prisoners who had not been involved in the meditation program, he found that even this brief program had an impact on anxiety and feelings of being in control of their lives. Perhaps such results will impress more judges, and the Enlightened Sentencing Project will not be the only bench handing down sentences to meditate.

Be an *Active* learner

REVIEW

- What happens during biofeedback that allows people to gain control of autonomic processes? p. 206
- Which characteristics of hypnosis are undisputed? Which are controversial? pp. 207–209
- What do the different types of meditation have in common? p. 210

THINK CRITICALLY

- Evaluate who would be the better hypnotic subject—an elderly person or a child.
- How would you go about demonstrating that hypnosis and meditation are different states of consciousness?

APPLY PSYCHOLOGY

- If you wanted to try biofeedback, hypnosis, or meditation to help you control stress, which would be the easiest to do? Which would be the most economical approach?
- Your roommate smokes and would like to quit. He asks you if you would recommend hypnosis as a therapy for quitting. What is your advice?

reduce anxiety, tension headaches, backaches, asthma, and the need for sleep, and research has confirmed some of these benefits. It can also increase self-awareness and feelings of inner peace (Andresen, 2000). Meditation is not relaxation—rather, relaxation is a by-product of meditation.

Practitioners distinguish among several types of meditation, but much of the recent research has concentrated on *mindfulness meditation*. All meditation techniques aim to induce an altered state of awareness and direct the focus of attention away from the outside world through intense concentration. A person begins *mindfulness meditation* by trying to empty the mind and just be still. As random and intrusive thoughts arise, the person notices them (becomes mindful of their content) without reacting to them, judging them, or dwelling on them. They eventually become mere wisps of thought that pass through consciousness while the meditator remains serene. Eventually, a mindful meditator becomes aware that reactions to thoughts cause suffering, and that one can entertain thoughts without having to react.

In *concentrative meditation*, a meditator concentrates on a visual image or a mantra (a word or a phrase repeated over and over). When the mind wanders to a random thought, the meditator brings the mind back to the image or mantra, without paying attention to the content of the thought. In this case, the image or mantra is the important thing. Concentrative meditation is closely tied to religions such as Tibetan Buddhism, Zen Buddhism, and Hinduism.

Supporters of meditation claim that it is a unique state, capable of causing profound physiological and psychological changes. They argue that mindfulness meditation produces a different mode of cognitive processing, by training people to maintain awareness of ongoing events and increase their attention. Detractors argue that meditation is nothing more than relaxation. Research indicates that meditation is an altered state of consciousness. A study measured EEGs during two different types of meditation, mindfulness and concentrative, and compared these two types of meditation to relaxation (Dunn et al., 1999). The results showed that the three states were associated with different EEG patterns.

Many controlled studies have shown that meditators can alter their physiological responses and improve their psychological functioning by reducing anxiety (Miller et al., 1995), reducing stress (Murphy, 1996), and coping with serious illness (Speca et al., 2000). In addition, the benefits of meditation extend to a variety of problems, including people who are in legal trouble, as my former student and the people who are sentenced to meditate have demonstrated.

Altering Consciousness with Drugs

Drug
Any chemical substance that, in small amounts, alters biological or cognitive processes or both.

Psychoactive [SYE-koh-AK-tiv] drug
A drug that alters behavior, thought, or perceptions by altering biochemical reactions in the nervous system, thereby affecting consciousness.

There is no doubt that the United States is a drug-using culture. At least one-third of all U.S. citizens between the ages of 18 and 74 regularly use some kind of consciousness-altering drug that changes both brain activity and daily behavior. Americans take drugs to wake up in the morning, to relieve the pain they feel during the day, to relax, and to get to sleep. These drugs may be legal or illegal; they may be used responsibly or abused with tragic consequences. A **drug** is any chemical substance that, in small amounts, alters biological or cognitive processes or both. Many widely used drugs are **psychoactive drugs**, which are drugs that alter behavior, thought, or perceptions by altering biochemical reactions in the nervous system, thereby affecting consciousness. The United States is not alone in its use of psychoactive drugs. Indeed, using drugs to alter consciousness is common to almost all cultures. Some cultures restrict drugs to ceremonial or religious uses; others permit drug use as a way to manage emotions and moods; others allow drugs as a way to increase social interaction; still others condone drug use as a way to improve performance. Drugs that are condoned by one culture may be condemned by another, but drug use occurs throughout the world and has existed throughout history.

Many psychoactive drugs are associated with the properties of tolerance or dependence or both. **Tolerance** is the characteristic of requiring higher and higher doses of a drug to produce the same effect. **Dependence** occurs when the drug becomes part of the body's functioning and produces *withdrawal* when the drug is discontinued. Tolerance and dependence can be dangerous, especially in combination. The term *addiction* is usually used to describe this combination of tolerance and dependence. But drug use and abuse are more than a matter of drug properties. Societal attitudes, family circumstances, genetic background, friends' drug use, and personal attitudes influence a person's reasons for using (or avoiding) drugs. Not all people who use drugs abuse them. Therefore drug use and abuse fit into complex individual and social circumstances. Let's first consider psychoactive drugs and their effects and then examine drug use and abuse.

Psychoactive Drugs

For drugs to alter behavior and cognitive processes, they must affect the nervous system. Most do so by crossing into the brain and influencing the action of neurotransmitters. These drugs cross the **blood–brain barrier,** a mechanism that prevents certain molecules from entering the brain but allows others to cross. In the brain, psychoactive drugs can produce a variety of effects, including inhibiting, stimulating, or altering neural activity. These changes occur through a variety of actions that affect neurotransmitters, including the more rapid release of neurotransmitters and the increase of neurotransmitter effects by slowing their breakdown. In addition, some drugs can occupy the same receptor sites as brain neurotransmitters, which will then mimic the effect of the neurotransmitter. Psychoactive drugs, then, alter consciousness by affecting brain chemicals and neural transmission. There are many different types of psychoactive drugs, but they can be classified according to their effects.

■ **SEDATIVE–HYPNOTICS.** Drugs that have inhibitory effects are classified as **sedative–hypnotics,** defined as a class of drugs that relax and calm a user and, in higher doses, induce sleep (sometimes they are referred to as *depressants*). These drugs function to depress neural activation. Many widely used (and abused) drugs fit into this classification, including alcohol, tranquilizers, barbiturates, and opiates. Alcohol is clearly the most commonly used drug in this category. Indeed, many people have trouble recognizing that alcohol is a drug because it is legal and people can obtain it without a medical prescription.

However, alcohol meets the definition of a psychoactive drug: it crosses the blood–brain barrier and produces both tolerance and dependence. Alcohol molecules can pass into the brain and affect it globally, depressing brain function. Alcohol is a depressant, and its effects include a dampening of arousal and a decrease in inhibitions; it encourages some behaviors that are normally under tight control (Stritzke, Lang, & Patrick, 1996). For example, it may diminish people's social inhibitions and make them less likely to restrain aggressive impulses (Ito, Miller, & Pollock, 1996). These effects can cause problems, but its effects on coordination and reaction time are its main hazards. These effects vary, depending on the amount of alcohol in the bloodstream and the gender and weight of the user (see Figure 6.3). After equal amounts of alcohol consumption, women have higher blood alcohol levels than men do, even allowing for differences in body weight (Frezza et al., 1990; Friel et al., 1999).

Tolerance
The characteristic of requiring higher and higher doses of a drug to produce the same effect.

Dependence
The situation that occurs when the drug becomes part of the body's functioning and produces withdrawal symptoms when the drug is discontinued.

Blood–brain barrier
A mechanism that prevents certain molecules from entering the brain but allows others to cross.

Sedative–hypnotic
Any of a class of drugs that relax and calm a user and, in higher doses, induce sleep; also known as a depressant.

FIGURE 6.3

Relationship Between Alcohol Consumption and Blood Alcohol Level, by Gender and Weight

Note that 1.0 ounce of alcohol is equivalent to 2 glasses of wine, 2 cans of beer, or 1 mixed drink. *(Ray & Ksir, 1993)*

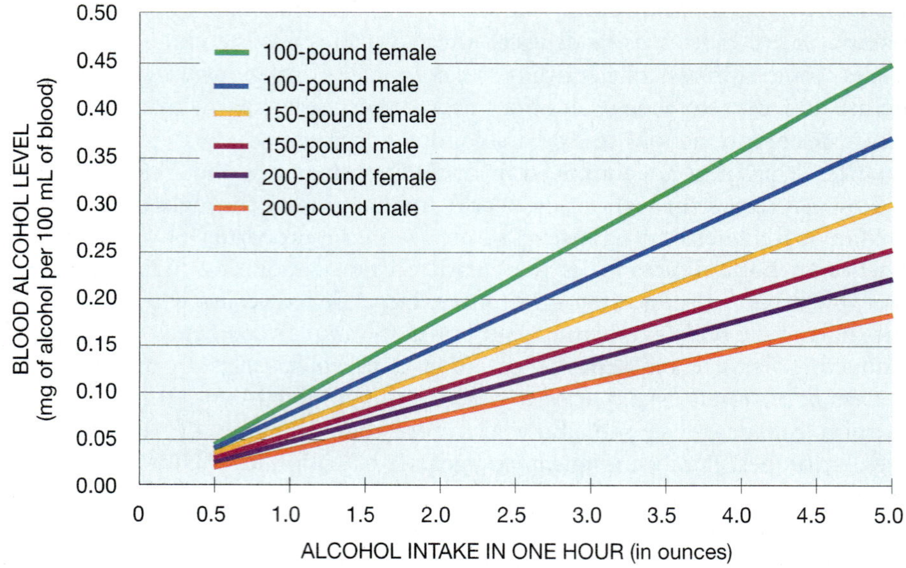

With increasing amounts of alcohol in the bloodstream, people typically exhibit progressively slower responses; they often exhibit severe motor disturbances, such as staggering and slurred speech. A blood alcohol level greater than 0.10 (0.1 milligram of alcohol per 100 milliliters of blood) usually indicates that the person has consumed too much alcohol to function responsibly, but lower levels of alcohol also affect behavior. In most states, a blood alcohol level of 0.10 legally defines intoxication; police officers may arrest drivers who are found to have this level of blood alcohol. Table 6.2 shows the behavioral effects associated with various blood alcohol levels.

Other drugs in the sedative–hypnotic category are not as widely used as alcohol, but their effects are similar: in low doses, they relax or calm people, and in high doses, they induce sleep, unconsciousness, or even death. These drugs include barbiturates, tranquilizers, and opiates. Some of these drugs are legally available by prescription and have legitimate medical uses, but they are also used illegally for their psychoactive effects. These effects include the relaxation that is common to this class of drugs; some people experience euphoria (a "high") when they use these drugs, but others find their effects unpleasant.

The **opiates** are drugs derived from the opium poppy, including opium, morphine, and heroin. Current medical use of opiates includes pain relief, for which they are the most effective drugs. In the brain, opiates occupy endorphin receptors. *Endorphins* are neurochemicals that the brain manufactures; they provide a naturally occurring mechanism for pain relief. When opiates occupy endorphin receptors, they mimic

TABLE 6.2

Behavioral Effects Associated with Various Blood Alcohol Levels

Blood Alcohol Level*	Behavioral Effects
0.05	Lowered alertness, impaired judgment, release of inhibitions, feelings of well-being or sociability; slowed reaction times and impaired motor function
0.10	Markedly slowed reaction time and impaired motor function, less caution
0.15	Large, consistent increases in reaction time
0.20	Marked depression in sensory and motor capability, decidedly intoxicated behavior
0.25	Severe motor disturbance and impairment of sensory perceptions
0.30	In a stupor but still conscious—no comprehension of events in the environment
0.35	Lack of consciousness equivalent to that of surgical anesthesia; lethal dose for about 1% of adults
0.40	Lethal dose for about 50% of adults

**In milligrams of alcohol per 100 milliliters of blood*

the effect of endorphins. Opiates produce a high tolerance and dependence, and many of those who use these drugs for pleasure become addicted (but few people who receive opiates in the hospital for pain relief do).

■ Alcohol meets the definition of a psychoactive drug because it alters thought and behavior and produces both tolerance and dependence.

■ **STIMULANTS.** A **stimulant** is any drug that increases alertness, reduces fatigue, and elevates mood. Drugs in this category also tend to increase blood pressure, heart rate, and metabolic rate as well as decrease appetite. The examples that people tend to think of in this category are amphetamines and cocaine, but the category also includes caffeine and nicotine. These drugs act on the peripheral as well as the central nervous system, and all have tolerance and dependence properties. People who need a cup of coffee to wake up in the morning rarely think of themselves as drug addicts, but they may be dependent on caffeine to perform this normal function; and they experience withdrawal when coffee is unavailable, which meets the definition of drug dependence. Their addiction is socially acceptable and easy to satisfy, but they are still dependent on a psychoactive drug.

People who are dependent on caffeine experience fewer problems than those who are dependent on nicotine, amphetamines, or cocaine. *Nicotine* is the addictive drug in tobacco, and tobacco use is a major health problem in the United States and many other countries (National Center for Health Statistics, 2000). Nicotine is not the main health risk associated with tobacco, but it is the ingredient that makes quitting tobacco use so difficult (Kluger, 1996). Nicotine does not have very strong tolerance properties, but dependence on it is strong, and withdrawal symptoms are unpleasant.

Amphetamines also produce a strong dependence, but they also have strong tolerance properties. Like other stimulants, amphetamines produce arousal and alertness. People often take them for these effects or as an appetite suppressant. Some people react strongly to these drugs, getting more than they wanted—prolonged wakefulness and agitation rather than alertness. Continued use can lead not only to dependence but also to altered thoughts, especially unfounded feelings of suspiciousness and even symptoms like those of schizophrenia (see Chapter 15 for a description of these symptoms).

Like other stimulants, *cocaine* produces increased alertness, but it also acts as an anesthetic. Those properties were actually the reason for its initial use in Europe and the United States, but its potential for abuse soon became evident. A smokable form of cocaine, *crack,* is less expensive and thus more widely used (the name comes from the crackling sound that often occurs when the drug is heated). Cocaine takes effect rapidly and produces positive feelings, and these two attributes can lead to abuse of cocaine. Because the effects are short-term, people have the urge to use more cocaine.

■ **PSYCHEDELIC DRUGS.** A consciousness-altering drug that affects moods, thoughts, memory, judgment, and perception and that is consumed for the purpose of producing those results is called a **psychedelic drug.** (The term *psychedelic* means "mind-expanding.") Psychedelic drugs are sometimes called *hallucinogens,* although many psychedelic drugs do not cause hallucinations. Their principal action is creating altered perceptions and producing vivid imagery. The impact of psychedelics varies widely, depending on the individual user as well as the drug. A range of drugs from LSD to Ecstasy falls within this category. Lysergic acid diethylamide, or LSD, produces altered perceptions of visual and auditory stimuli and sometimes changes in time and distance perception.

Ecstasy is the common term for methylenedioxymethamphetamine, or MDMA (also called "Adam," "X-TC," "X," or "E"). It is also a psychedelic, although it is derived from methamphetamine. MDMA was synthesized over 80 years ago but became

Opiates
Drugs derived from the opium poppy, including opium, morphine, and heroin.

Stimulant
A drug that increases alertness, reduces fatigue, and elevates mood.

Psychedelic drugs
Consciousness-altering drugs that affect moods, thoughts, memory, judgment, and perception and that are consumed for the purpose of producing those results.

popular in the 1980s as part of the "club rave scene." Ecstasy affects the neurotransmitter serotonin, causing massive release of it. Along with the overabundance of serotonin comes feelings of well-being, happiness, and a kinship with others. Controversy exists over its hazards, with some arguing that it is harmless and others insisting that it can kill (Beech et al., 2000). The massive serotonin release may produce prolonged problems with that neurotransmitter, and the hazard is greater for women than for men (Reneman et al., 2001). Deaths have been linked to Ecstasy use, many of which are probably due to impurities that occur in its manufacture and others due to problems in body temperature regulation directly related to Ecstasy use.

In contrast to synthetic Ecstasy, marijuana is completely natural—the dried leaves and flowering tops of the *Cannabis sativa* plant, whose active ingredient is *tetrahydrocannabinol* (THC). It is the most widely used of the psychedelic drugs, and 33% of adolescents and adults in the United States have used marijuana (U.S. Bureau of the Census, 2000). People's reactions to marijuana vary even more than to other psychoactive drugs. Some people experience elation and a feeling of well-being; some just feel sleepy; others experience feelings of paranoia and nausea. Like alcohol, marijuana affects judgment and coordination, presenting dangers associated with driving and other situations in which reaction time, judgment, and perception are important.

Although researchers agree that marijuana produces neither tolerance nor dependence, there is little agreement over its dangers. Some people use marijuana to the point that it interferes with their lives; they seem to have a dependence on it despite its lack of physical dependence properties. Since its rise to popular use during the 1960s, millions of people have used this drug and believe that its risks are equivalent to those of alcohol. Many of these people see no reason why marijuana is illegal while alcohol is legal. One faction is pushing for the legalization of marijuana, pointing to its benefits and medical uses. Others believe that marijuana is a "gateway" drug that leads to the use of other, more dangerous drugs and argue that it should remain illegal.

Drug Use and Abuse

Although our society is filled with drug users, most of those people do not consider themselves drug abusers. Part of that reasoning depends on the legality and acceptability of the drug they use, and those two factors are related. People often reserve the classification of "drug" for the substances that require prescriptions or are obtained illegally, and they have trouble thinking of other substances, such as alcohol, tobacco, or over-the-counter medications, as drugs. This thinking leads people to overestimate the dangers of the substances they consider drugs and to underestimate the hazards of the substances they fail to classify as drugs. Both types of thinking can lead to problems.

In discounting the hazards of legally available and socially acceptable substances, people overlook the problems associated with alcohol and tobacco. These two substances present the biggest drug problems in the United States (and also in many other countries). The legal availability and social acceptability of these substances contribute to their widespread use. For example, about 80% of adolescents and adults in the United States have tried alcohol and 70% have tried cigarettes; 51% are current drinkers and 27% are current smokers (U.S. Bureau of the Census, 2000; see Figure 6.4). Adults between the ages of 21 and 39 are the heaviest drinkers, but young adults between 18 and 25 are more likely to be binge drinkers who consume at least 5 drinks on one occasion. This pattern of drinking is especially dangerous because it produces drunkenness, with its associated hazards.

Contrasted with the widespread use of these legal drugs, no illegal drug is a close comparison. Marijuana is the most commonly used illegal drug—33% have tried it, and 5% are current users. Combining the categories of amphetamines, cocaine, sedatives, tranquilizers, opiates, and hallucinogens yields a total of 2.3% of people age 12 and older who currently use any of these drugs. Those numbers may not sound right to you—it may seem as if practically everyone you know has tried some illegal drug, and many are current users. Adolescents and young adults use both legal and illegal drugs at higher rates than the general population, so your perception and the statistics may both be correct. For example, 44% of 18- to 25-year-olds have tried marijuana, and 13% are current users; 10% have tried cocaine, and 2% are current users. While these numbers do not indicate that *everyone* is using illegal drugs, the figures reflect more widespread drug use for adolescents and young adults than for younger or older people. The small percentage of people using illegal drugs can still cause big problems, but the use of legal, socially acceptable drugs is a much larger social and health problem.

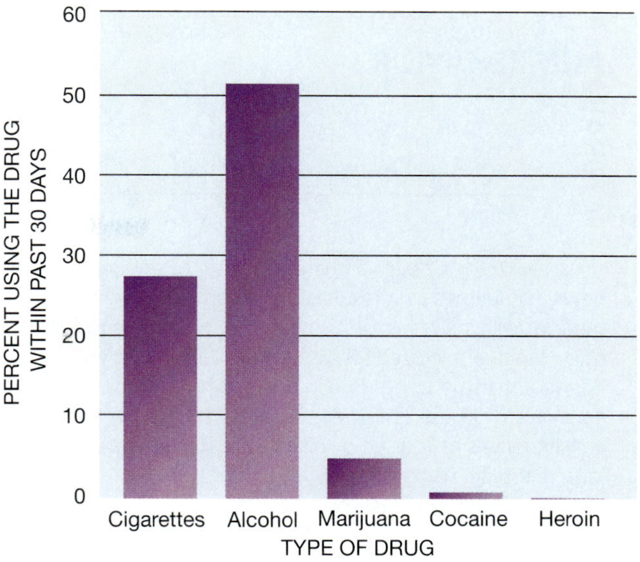

FIGURE 6.4

Percent of Americans over Age 12 Who Have Used Various Drugs Within the Past 30 Days *(U.S. Bureau of the Census, 2000, p.141)*

Some psychoactive drugs produce direct physical damage, but most of the problems associated with drug use are indirect rather than direct effects of the drug. Nicotine is not an especially dangerous drug, but smoking tobacco is a major cause of disease and death (National Center for Health Statistics, 2000). The damage from using most psychoactive drugs comes largely from the alterations to consciousness and the resulting changes in perception, reactions, judgment, and behavior. That is, their psychoactive properties produce their main hazards. For example, alcohol use can cause liver damage, but the primary hazard of alcohol use is its relationship to increased risk of accidents. Smoking marijuana is more damaging to the lungs than smoking tobacco, but again, increased risk of accidents is the greatest danger of marijuana use. These risks are substantial—unintentional injury is the leading cause of death for people under age 35, and drug use contributes to accidental injury and death (U.S. Bureau of the Census, 2000). Therefore, any psychoactive drug use can present dangers, but some people abuse these drugs and experience problems as a result. (Table 6.3 lists commonly used drugs and their efects.)

WHAT IS SUBSTANCE ABUSE? What is the difference between drug use and drug abuse? Some authorities define the use of any illegal drug as substance abuse, but some of those who use illegal drugs experience few problems. Others, however, ruin their lives and the lives of those around them. The impact on people's lives is one way to gauge use versus abuse; people who experience negative effects as a result of their drug use cross the line into abuse.

A **substance abuser** is a person who overuses and relies on drugs to deal with everyday life. Most substance abusers use alcohol or tobacco, but the whole range of psychoactive drugs and combinations of these drugs presents possibilities for substance abuse. A person is a substance abuser if all three of the following statements apply:

- The person has used the substance for at least a month.
- The use has caused legal, personal, social, or vocational problems.
- The person repeatedly uses the substance even in situations when doing so is hazardous, such as when driving a car.

Missing work or school, spending too much money on drugs, damaging personal relationships, and getting into legal trouble are all signs of substance abuse. When substance abusers try to decrease or quit their drug use, they experience withdrawal symptoms if the substance tends to cause dependence. **Withdrawal symptoms** are the reactions experienced when a substance abuser stops using a drug with dependence properties. Withdrawal symptoms are typically the opposite of the

Substance abuser
A person who overuses and relies on drugs to deal with everyday life.

Withdrawal symptoms
The reactions experienced when a substance abuser stops using a drug with dependence properties.

BRAIN AND BEHAVIOR

Drug Addiction

Actor Robert Downey Jr. has often been in the news, sometimes as a result of his award-winning acting but more often as a result of his drug use. He seems to want to quit. He has apologized for his behavior and publicly stated his intention to stop using drugs. Yet he gets arrested again and again for drug use. Downey has experienced many negative consequences as a result of his drug abuse. He has lost good jobs; his wife divorced him, and he can no longer see his son; he has spent a good deal of time in drug rehabilitation programs; he has been arrested many times; he has spent time in prison. But as of this writing, Downey doesn't seem to be able to stop using drugs.

Why do some people use drugs to the point of destroying their lives? Saying that they are addicted is not really an answer. Like Downey, many drug abusers have gone through drug rehabilitation (and many have also spent time in prison), where they go through withdrawal and "kick the habit," only to return to drug use. Obviously, the drug's dependence properties are not the only explanation for drug addiction. Research is beginning to develop another answer: drugs produce changes in the brain that make staying away from drugs difficult.

Alan Lesher, director of the National Institute on Drug Abuse, lists 72 risk factors that may encourage drug use (Powledge, 1999). These risk factors range from the street price of drugs to having drug-using family and friends. Downey's life certainly has exposed him to some of these risk factors. When he was 6 years old, his father (director Robert Downey Sr.) gave him marijuana, thinking it was cute to see his 6-year-old smoking a joint (Lemonick, 2000). Another risk for drug use is depression, and Downey has reported that he is depressed. However, he could be depressed as a result of his drug use. Downey has used cocaine and amphetamines, both stimulants, and withdrawal from stimulant use produces symptoms similar to depression.

Lesher does not discount the influence of risk factors for initiation into drug use, but he believes that repeated drug use alters brain function in ways that make it difficult to quit (Lemonick, 2000). These alterations seem to involve the neurotransmitter dopamine and, what's more interesting, they may be common to all drug abuse. In addition, this same brain mechanism's importance may extend beyond its role in drug abuse; dopamine and this brain system may relate to the experience of all types of pleasurable stimulation. That is, the brain mechanism that underlies drug addiction may be the brain's "reward circuit" (Powledge, 1999).

Despite their different modes of action, many drugs seem to affect dopamine availability in the synapse (Powledge, 1999). Drugs like cocaine block the reabsorption of dopamine by neurons, which allows dopamine to stay in the synapse longer and have a prolonged effect. Amphetamines cause neurons to release more dopamine, which also prolongs dopamine's effects. Nicotine, alcohol, and opiates all seem to affect dopamine in some way.

According to this view, the brain "learns" to be addicted through repeated exposure to a drug. This learning forms associations between taking the drug and the pleasurable and powerful emotions the drug produces. With these brain circuits well established through practice, a person becomes a drug addict, always prone to cope with stressful situations by using drugs. This situation does not mean that drug abusers will always use drugs but that their brains are primed to respond to drugs. Abusers have long experience with using drugs as a way to cope with many situations—both the physiology and the learned associations push a drug abuser in this direction. Thus, relapse is always a risk. Avoiding drugs is only one step in the recovery process. It is also important to break the learned associations between drug use and the pleasurable emotional states associated with drug use; some therapies address this issue (Powledge, 1999).

Can Robert Downey Jr. give up drugs? Yes—thousands of people with drug abuse problems as serious as his have done so. But this task is difficult, and Downey has a brain with a drug habit and a style of coping that has relied on taking drugs. Both of these factors will make his recovery a difficult process.

drug's effects. For example, the effects of alcohol are decreased levels of activation, so the withdrawal effects are increased levels of activation, including agitation and physical arousal (the "shakes"). Although substance abusers usually like the effects of the drug they use, the opposite effects are not as pleasant. Of course, one way to stop these unpleasant symptoms is to use more drugs. Repeated drug use is often considered addiction (see *Brain and Behavior*).

TABLE 6.3

Commonly Used and Abused Drugs

Type of Drug	Examples of Drug	Effects of Drug	Causes Tolerance?	Causes Physiological Dependence?
Sedative–hypnotics	Alcohol	Reduces inhibitions; slows reactions	Yes	Yes
	Barbiturates (e.g., Seconal)	Reduce tension; induce sleep	Yes	Yes
	Tranquilizers (e.g., Valium)	Alleviate tension; induce relaxation	Yes	Yes
	Opium, Morphine, Heroin	Alleviate pain and tension; alter perception	Yes	Yes
Stimulants	Caffeine	Increases alertness	Yes	Yes
	Amphetamines	Increase excitability, alertness, and talkativeness; decrease appetite	Yes	Yes
	Cocaine	Increases alertness, decreases fatigue, stimulates sexual arousal	Yes	Yes
	Nicotine	Increases alertness and metabolism	Yes	Yes
Psychedelics	Marijuana	Changes mood and perception	No	No
	LSD	Changes perception	No	No
	Ecstasy	Produces sense of well being and connection to others	No	Possibly

A great variety of social and individual factors have an impact on drug use and abuse. Indeed, the list includes dozens of factors, such as family members' drug use, peer group drug use, personal beliefs in the dangers of drugs, age, ethnic background, and education. All of these factors (and many more) relate to drug use, but none specifically predicts who will become a drug abuser and who will use drugs in socially accepted, responsible ways.

A great deal of publicity has been devoted to genetic factors in drug abuse, especially alcohol abuse. Alcoholism is not inherited, but genetic factors do relate to the metabolism of alcohol (Li, 2000). These genetically controlled metabolic factors create what is known as a *genetic predisposition,* inherited factors that make it more likely that people with these genetic factors will develop a problem. A genetic predisposition differs from a direct inheritance. Factors that are inherited, such as eye color, require no set of environmental circumstances for their expression. People with the double recessive genes for blue eyes will have blue eyes. People who inherit the combination of genes that predisposes them to problem drinking will not necessarily develop drinking problems. For example, people who do not drink cannot have drinking problems. Those who live in cultures that forbid alcohol are less likely to develop problem drinking, regardless of their genetic predisposition. Therefore, a genetic predisposition is a risk factor for alcohol abuse (and possibly other drug problems), but it does not specifically predict problem drug use.

Why, then, do people use (and abuse) drugs? From an evolutionary point of view, drug use (and especially abuse) is a puzzle (Nesse, 1997). If consciousness is an adaptive advantage, then alterations to that consciousness are maladaptive. Psychoactive drugs have a variety of effects that put

Be an *Active* learner

REVIEW

- What is a psychoactive drug? p. 210
- What is the difference between tolerance and dependence? p. 211

THINK CRITICALLY

- If you were a psychologist evaluating whether someone was a substance abuser, what would you look for?
- If psychoactive drugs act through the brain's reward circuits, are drugs necessary for the experience of a "high"?

APPLY PSYCHOLOGY

- Evaluate the binge drinking on your campus—under what circumstances is it most common? How acceptable is it? What, if any, are the differences between the drinking styles of men and women?

people in danger, which is clearly maladaptive. Yet people in almost every culture in the history of the world have used some substance that alters their consciousness. The mechanisms of drug action make use of existing brain chemicals and pathways to exert their effects. A leading view of psychoactive drug action is that these substances act through the brain's "reward system," as noted in *Brain and Behavior.* So in a sense, we have brains that are built to respond to psychoactive drugs. The challenge, then, is to manage these altered states of consciousness.

Summary and Review

Consciousness

What are the key characteristics of consciousness?

■ *Consciousness* is a general state of being aware of and responsive to events in the environment, as well as one's own mental processes. Theories of consciousness attempt to explain the underlying basis of self-awareness. Consciousness can range from alert attention to dreaming, being hypnotized, or being in a drug-induced state. Altered states of consciousness differ from waking in terms of brain and body activation. pp. 190–193

KEY TERM
consciousness, p. 190

Sleep

Describe the cycles of sleep and wakefulness.

■ A biological clock that ticks within each person controls the sleep–wakefulness cycle; *circadian rhythms* are internally generated bodily rhythms. When time cues such as daylight and clocks are removed from the environment, circadian rhythms still function. pp. 193–194

■ Recordings of the brain waves of participants in sleep research using EEGs have revealed distinct cycles of sleep. Each cycle has four stages of *non–rapid eye movement (NREM)* sleep plus *rapid eye movement (REM) sleep.* During NREM sleep, the brain and body decrease in levels of activation and arousal. During REM sleep, rapid and systematic eye movements occur, and the brain and body experience a high level of arousal. A full sleep cycle lasts about 90 minutes, so five complete sleep cycles occur in an average night's sleep. pp. 195–197

■ Despite extensive knowledge about sleep stages, the reason for sleep remains a mystery. p. 199

What are the characteristics of common sleep disorders?

■ Snoring loudly, sleepwalking, and falling asleep at inappropriate times may be signs of sleep disorders. People who fall asleep suddenly and unexpectedly have a sleep disorder known as narcolepsy. Loud snoring is a symptom of sleep apnea. *Insomnia* is the inability to fall asleep or to maintain sleep throughout the night. This problem may be caused by anxiety or depression. Sleepwalking can put the sleepwalker at risk of injury but is otherwise not dangerous. pp. 200–201

KEY TERMS
circadian rhythms, p. 193; electroencephalogram (EEG), p. 195; rapid eye movement (REM) sleep, p. 195; non–rapid eye movement (NREM) sleep, p. 195; insomnia, p. 201

Dreams

What is a dream?

■ A *dream* is a state of consciousness that occurs during sleep and is usually accompanied by vivid visual imagery, although the imagery may also be tactile or auditory. Dreams are associated (although not perfectly) with REM sleep, and REM dreams tend to be vivid. Some people experience lucid dreams in which they are aware that they are dreaming. The first dream of a typical night occurs 90 minutes after a person has fallen asleep and lasts for approximately 10 minutes. pp. 202–203

How have key theorists explained dreaming?

■ For Freud, a dream expressed desires, wishes, and unfulfilled needs that exist in the unconscious—he referred to dreams as "the royal road to the unconscious." Freud made a distinction between a dream's *manifest content* (its overt story line, characters, and settings) and its *latent content* (its deeper meaning, usually involving symbolism, hidden meaning, and repressed or obscured ideas and wishes). p. 203

■ Jung took for granted the idea that a dream is nature's way of allowing humans access to their own unconscious, and he saw dreams as the language through which an individual expresses his or her own deepest feelings in an uncensored form. He asserted that each person shares in the *collective unconscious,* a storehouse of primitive ideas and images in the unconscious that are inherited from one's ancestors. pp. 203–204

■ Cognitive theorists believe that dreams show the same type of cognitive processes that occur during waking, and dream content reflects areas of concern to the dreamer. p. 204

■ Hobson believes that dreams have a biological basis

and that, during periods of REM sleep, the parts of the brain responsible for long-term memory, vision, audition, and perhaps even emotion are spontaneously activated (stimulated) by cells in the hindbrain, especially the pons. The cortex attempts to organize, or make sense out of, the random stimuli. pp. 204–205

KEY TERMS

dream, p. 202; lucid dream, p. 203; manifest content, p. 203; latent content, p. 203; collective unconscious, p. 204; descriptive studies, p. 204

Controlling Consciousness: Biofeedback, Hypnosis, and Meditation

Describe the characteristics of three key means of controlling consciousness.

■ *Biofeedback* is a process through which people receive information about the status of a physical system and use this feedback information to learn to control the activity of that system. Learning conscious control of autonomic processes is possible, and biofeedback has been used as a therapeutic technique, especially to control headaches. pp. 206–207

■ *Hypnosis* remains controversial, including its definition. Some authorities see it as an altered stated of consciousness, but others do not. Hypnosis can produce special effects such as relaxation, increased concentration, and pain reduction, but its effectiveness in memory enhancement and as a treatment for smoking and dieting is questionable. pp. 207–209

■ Meditation produces a state of consciousness characterized by a sense of detachment and relaxation. The types of meditation are mindfulness and concentrative; both induce an altered state of awareness. People using mindfulness meditation focus on trying to empty the mind and just be still. Concentrative meditation involves use of a visual image or a mantra; when the mind wanders to random thoughts, the meditator brings it back to the image or mantra without paying attention to the content of the thoughts. Meditation techniques are often used to help in stress management. pp. 209–210

KEY TERMS

biofeedback, p. 206; meditation, p. 208

Altering Consciousness with Drugs

What are the different properties of drugs?

■ A *drug* is any chemical substance that alters normal biological processes. A *psychoactive drug* is a drug that alters behavior, thought, or emotions by crossing the blood–brain barrier and altering biochemical reactions in the nervous system, thereby affecting consciousness. Some drugs produce *tolerance,* the characteristic of requiring higher and higher doses of a drug to produce the same effect, or *dependence,* the situation that occurs when the drug becomes part of the body's functioning and produces withdrawal when the drug is discontinued. Drugs that produce this combination are often referred to as addictive. pp. 210–211

How do psychoactive drugs affect the nervous system and behavior?

■ *Sedative–hypnotics* include alcohol, barbiturates, and *opiates.* These drugs all relax and calm users. All produce both tolerance and dependence. pp. 211–213

■ *Stimulants* are drug that increase alertness, reduce fatigue, and elevate mood. This category includes caffeine, nicotine, cocaine, and amphetamines. These drugs also produce tolerance and dependence. pp. 211–213

■ *Psychedelic drugs* such as LSD, Ecstasy, and marijuana are consciousness-altering drugs that affect moods, thoughts, memory, judgment, and perception and that are consumed for the purposes of producing those results. These drugs do not produce tolerance or dependence, but are still abused. pp. 213–214

What is the difference between substance use and abuse?

■ Many people use various substances, but not all users are abusers. *Substance abusers* have used a drug for at least 1 month; have experienced legal, personal, social, or vocational problems as a result of their drug use; have used the drug in situations when doing so is hazardous; and experienced withdrawal symptoms if they are dependent on the drug they abuse. pp. 215–216

■ Many social and personal factors relate to substance use and abuse, but specific predictions about who will abuse drugs are not possible. Underlying brain mechanisms involving the neurotransmitter dopamine may be a common factor for drug abuse. pp. 217–218

KEY TERMS

drug, p. 210; psychoactive drug, p. 210; tolerance, p. 211; dependence, p. 211; blood–brain barrier, p. 211; sedative–hypnotic, p. 211; opiate, p. 213; stimulant, p. 213; psychedelic drugs, p. 213; substance abuser, p. 215; withdrawal symptoms, p. 215

7 Learning

Lyonel Feininger, *Architecture II, The Man of Potin,* 1921

The warm, comforting, almost hypnotic voice says:

Irritability, sadness, sudden mood changes, tension, bloating. If you suffer from many of these symptoms month after month and they clearly interfere with your daily activities and relationships you could have PMDD. PMDD, premenstrual dysphoric disorder, is a distinct medical condition that is characterized by intense mood and physical symptoms right before your period.

Sarafem can help. Doctors can treat PMDD with Sarafem, the first and only prescription medication for PMDD.

Advertising is powerful. Through full-page advertisements in glossy magazines or TV images of beautiful people walking through idyllic meadows, an advertiser—in this case, one promoting the products of a drug company—tries to influence your behavior. You are coaxed to talk to your doctor, your mother, or your next-door neighbor about this brand-new drug, Sarafem. In fact, this fine, safe, and effective medication is Prozac, a familiar drug renamed and repackaged as a pink and lavender capsule.

chapter outline

The "buzz" about Sarafem, which spreads as "experts" and "everyday people" espouse its virtues, does the advertising industry proud—sales of Sarafem have soared. But from a psychologist's point of view, a certain type of learning is occurring—the advertiser wants people to learn certain information about a drug and then behave in a certain way—buy, or at least inquire about, the drug. Advertising plays on our ability to learn.

Psychologists know that people can be taught new behaviors and new associations. In fact, most human behaviors can be learned, unlearned, and modified; humans exhibit few totally reflexive behaviors. Unlike the proverbial dog, we *can* be taught new tricks. Even some of our behaviors that may have a genetic basis can be changed through diligence and effort. The ability to think about past events and to modify future behavior is part of what distinguishes human beings from other organisms: we can learn and even think about and reflect on what we learn.

Learning is at the core of psychology. It affects personality, social behavior, and development. Much learning takes place effortlessly, simply as a result of experience. By the time we reach adulthood, experience has taught us a large number of simple, predictable associations. We know, for example, that a long day at the beach may result in a painful sunburn and that a gas station should be our next stop when the fuel gauge reads empty. We have also learned many complicated processes, such as how to drive a car and how to appreciate music ranging from Bach to Phish. Some people learn socially deviant behaviors, such as stealing and drug abuse.

In general, learning is the process by which people acquire new knowledge and is a key concern of psychology. Psychologists define **learning** as a relatively permanent change in an organism that occurs as a result of experiences in the environment and that is often *exhibited in overt behavior*. This last point means that, because the internal processes of learning cannot be seen, psychologists study the *results* of learning. To do so, they may examine overt behavior such as solving an algebra problem or throwing a ball. They may also measure physiological changes in areas such as brain-wave activity, heartbeat, and temperature. This definition of learning has three other important parts: (1) experiences in the environment, (2) change in the organism, and (3) permanence.

Behavior is always being modified; new experiences affect learning, and what is learned may be forgotten. And, along with the external environment, an organism's internal motivation, abilities, and physiological state influence its ability to learn. For example, if you are tired, learning the material in this chapter will be especially difficult. Also, practice and repeated experiences ensure that you will readily exhibit newly acquired learning. Furthermore, when learning has occurred, physiological changes—for example, in synapse organization or levels of dopamine—have occurred as well, so that after you learn, you're no longer the same.

The factors that affect learning are often studied by using animals as subjects, because the genetic heritage of animals is easy to control and manipulate and because all details of their life history and environmental experiences can be known. Although some psychologists claim that different processes underlie animal and human learning, most believe—and experiments show—that the processes are similar. Differences do become apparent, however, when complex behaviors and the use of language are being studied.

Learning
Relatively permanent change in an organism that occurs as a result of experiences in the environment.

As you read this chapter, ask yourself whether you favor particular study spots or associate fear and other emotions with specific places. Chances are that you will begin to see in yourself a whole range of learned associations that shape your daily interactions. You will see how your experiences and the resulting associations illustrate the three basic learning processes that are covered in this chapter: classical conditioning, operant conditioning, and cognitive learning.

Pavlovian, or Classical, Conditioning Theory

Psychologists often use the term *conditioning* in a general sense, to mean learning. But more precisely, **conditioning** is a systematic procedure through which associations and responses to specific stimuli are learned. It is one of the simplest forms of learning. For example, consider what generally happens when you hear the theme from *The X-Files*. You expect that something supernatural or otherworldly will appear on your TV screen, because the theme music introduces a program that usually includes aliens or weird events—and if you're a fan of the show, you probably feel a pleasant sense of anticipation. You have been *conditioned* to feel that way. In the terminology used by psychologists, *The X-Files* theme music is the stimulus, and your excitement and anticipation are the response. A *stimulus* is an event, usually a detectable input (music, for example) that has an impact on an organism; a *response* is the reaction of an organism (anticipation or fear, for example) to a stimulus.

When psychologists first studied conditioning, they found relationships between specific stimuli and responses. They observed that each time a certain stimulus occurs, the same reflexive response, or behavior, follows. For example, the presence of food in the mouth leads to salivation; a tap on the knee results in a knee jerk; a bright light in the eye produces contraction of the pupil and an eye blink. A **reflex** is an automatic behavior that occurs involuntarily in response to a stimulus and without prior learning and usually shows little variability from instance to instance. Conditioned behaviors, in contrast, are learned. Dental anxiety—fear of dentists, dental procedures, and even the dentist's chair—is a widespread conditioned behavior (Merckelbach et al., 1999; White, 2000). Many people have learned to respond with fear to the stimulus of sitting in a dentist's chair, since they associate the chair with pain (Liddell & Locker, 2000). A chair by itself (a neutral stimulus) does not elicit fear, but a chair associated with pain becomes a stimulus that can elicit fear. This is an example of conditioning.

■ *When your eye is exposed to intense light, it responds by reflex: your pupil contracts and your eye blinks.*

Conditioned behaviors may occur so automatically that they appear to be reflexive. Like reflexes, conditioned behaviors are involuntary; unlike reflexes, they are learned. In classical conditioning (to be defined shortly), previously neutral stimuli such as chairs and buzzers become associated with specific events and lead to responses such as fear and anxiety.

In 1927, Ivan Pavlov (1849–1936), a Russian physiologist, summarized a now-famous series of experiments in which he uncovered a basic principle of learning—conditioning. His study of conditioning began quite accidentally while he was studying saliva and gastric secretions in the digestive processes of dogs. He knew it is normal for dogs to salivate when they eat (salivation is a reflexive behavior that aids digestion) but he found that the dogs were salivating *before* they tasted their food. Pavlov reasoned that this might be happening because the dogs had learned to associate the trainers, who brought them food, with the food itself. Anxious to know more about this form of learning, Pavlov abandoned his research on gastric processes and redirected his efforts into studying the salivary reflex of dogs.

Conditioning
Systematic procedure through which associations and responses to specific stimuli are learned.

Reflex
Automatic behavior that occurs involuntarily in response to a stimulus and without prior learning and usually shows little variability from instance to instance.

Terms and Procedures

The terminology and procedures associated with Pavlov's experiments can seem confusing, but the basic ideas are actually quite straightforward. Let's explore them systematically. What Pavlov described was **classical conditioning**, or *Pavlovian conditioning*, in which an originally neutral stimulus, through repeated pairing with a stimulus that naturally elicits a response, comes to elicit a similar or even identical response. For example, when a bell, buzzer, or light (a neutral stimulus) is associated with the presentation of food, a stimulus that normally brings about a response (salivating), the neutral stimulus over time comes to elicit the same response as the normal stimulus. Pavlov termed the stimulus that normally produces the reflexive response the **unconditioned stimulus** (as its name implies, it elicits the relevant response without conditioning). He termed the response to this stimulus the **unconditioned response**. The unconditioned response occurs involuntarily, without learning, in response to the unconditioned stimulus.

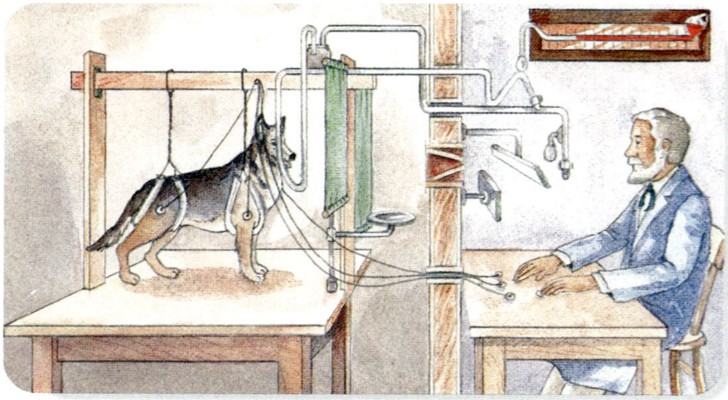

FIGURE 7.1
Pavlov's Experimental Setup

Pavlov started his study of conditioning in dogs with a relatively simple experiment—teaching the dogs to salivate in response to a bell. First, he surgically moved each dog's salivary gland to the outside of the dog's cheek to make the secretions of saliva accessible. He attached tubes to the relocated salivary glands so that he could collect and then measure precisely the amount of saliva produced by the food—the unconditioned stimulus. The dog was restrained in a harness and isolated from all distractions in a cubicle (see Figure 7.1). Then Pavlov introduced a bell—the new stimulus (see Figure 7.2). He called the bell a neutral stimulus because the sound of a bell is not normally related to salivation and generally elicits only a response of

FIGURE 7.2
The Three Stages of Classical Conditioning

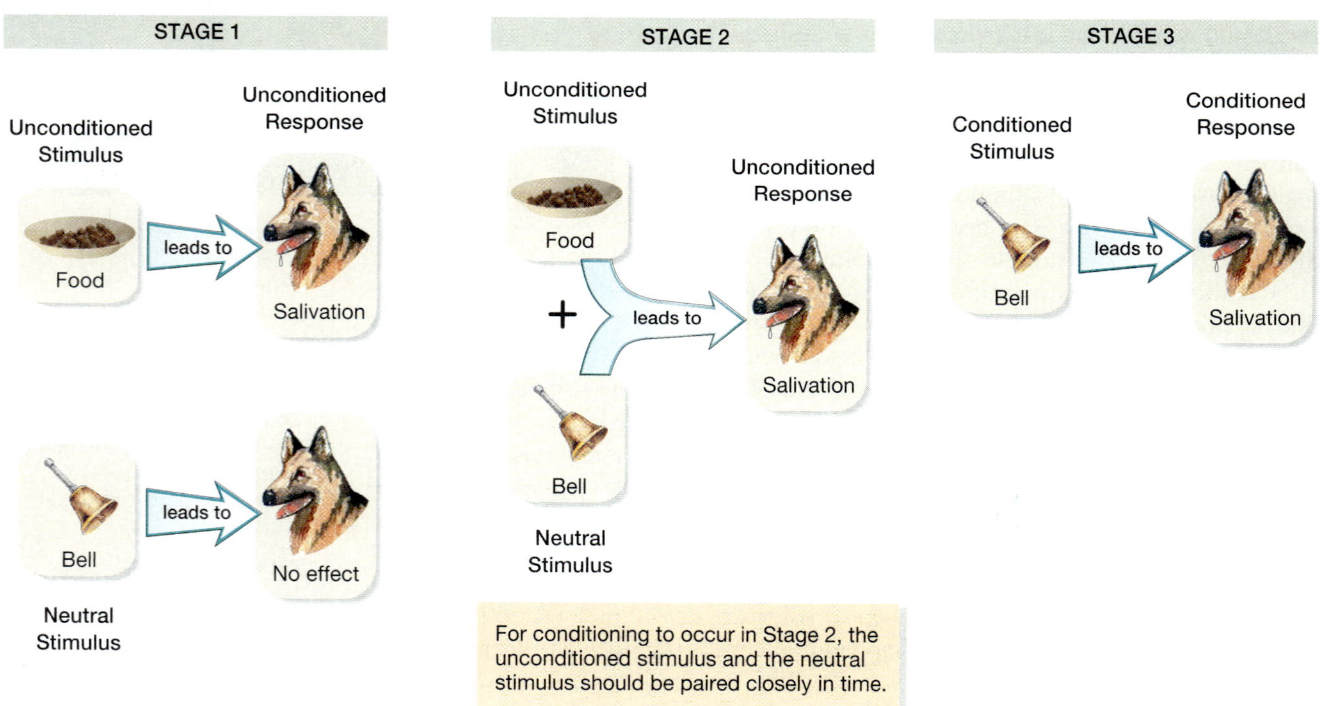

orientation (an attempt to locate the sound) or attention. Pavlov measured the amount of saliva the dog produced when a bell was rung by itself; the amount was negligible. He then began the conditioning process by ringing the bell and immediately placing food in the dog's mouth. After he did this several times, the dog salivated in response to the sound of the bell alone.

Pavlov reasoned that the dog had associated the bell with the arrival of food. He termed the bell, which elicited (or produced) salivation as a result of learning, a conditioned stimulus. A **conditioned stimulus** is a neutral stimulus that, through repeated association with an unconditioned stimulus, becomes capable of eliciting a conditioned response. As its name implies, a conditioned stimulus becomes capable of eliciting a response because of (conditional on) its pairing with the unconditioned stimulus. He termed the salivation—the learned response to the sound of the bell—a **conditioned response** (the response elicited by a conditioned stimulus). (Pavlov originally called the conditioned response a "conditional" response because it was conditional on events in the environment—it depended on them. An error in translating his writings created the term used most often today—conditioned response.) From his experiments, Pavlov discovered that the conditioned stimulus (the bell) brought about a similar but somewhat weaker response than the unconditioned stimulus (the food). The process of classical conditioning is outlined in Figure 7.2.

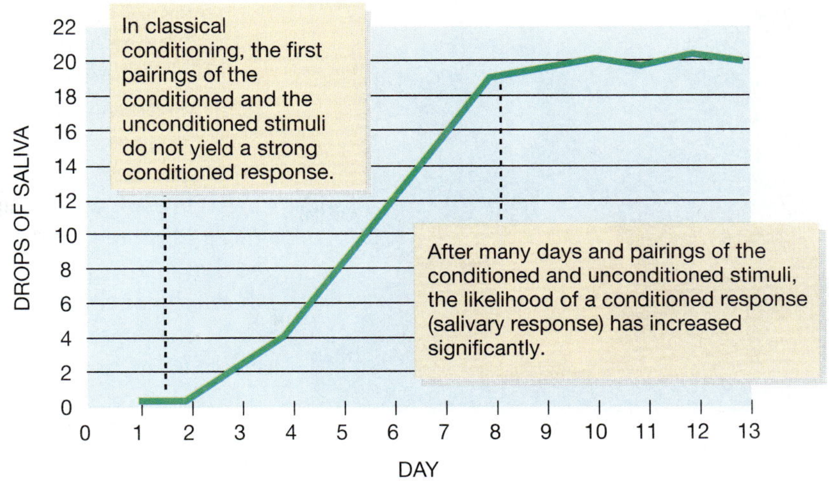

FIGURE 7.3

A Typical Acquisition Curve

The key characteristic of classical conditioning is the use of an originally neutral stimulus (here, a bell) to elicit a response (here, salivation) through repeated pairing of the neutral stimulus with an unconditioned stimulus (here, food) that elicits the response naturally. On the first few trials of such pairings, conditioning is unlikely to occur. With additional trials, there is a greater likelihood that conditioning will occur. After dozens or even hundreds of pairings, the neutral stimulus yields the conditioned response. Psychologists generally refer to this process as an *acquisition process* and say that an organism has *acquired* a response. Figure 7.3 shows a typical acquisition curve.

Classical conditioning occurs regularly in the everyday world. You may have learned to associate the distinctive smell of a sandalwood aftershave with a cousin whom you see infrequently but think of warmly. If you walk into a room and smell his unique brand, you may think of him or expect him to be there. Classical conditioning doesn't always involve associations of positive things. When you enter a dentist's office, your heart rate may increase and you may begin to feel anxious because of learned associations you have developed. When classical conditioning occurs, behavior changes.

Classical conditioning
Conditioning process in which an originally neutral stimulus, by repeated pairing with a stimulus that normally elicits a response, comes to elicit a similar or even identical response; also known as Pavlovian conditioning.

Unconditioned stimulus
Stimulus that normally produces a measurable involuntary response.

Unconditioned response
Unlearned or involuntary response to an unconditioned stimulus.

Conditioned stimulus
Neutral stimulus that, through repeated association with an unconditioned stimulus, begins to elicit a conditioned response.

Conditioned response
Response elicited by a conditioned stimulus.

Classical Conditioning in Humans

After Pavlov's success with conditioning in dogs, psychologists were able to see that conditioning also occurs in human beings. Marquis (1931) showed that classical conditioning occurs in infants. Marquis knew that when an object touches an infant's lips, the infant immediately starts sucking, because the object is usually a nipple, from which the infant gets milk. The nipple, an unconditioned stimulus, elicits sucking, an unconditioned response. After repeated pairings of a sound or light with a nipple, infants were conditioned to suck when only the sound or light was presented.

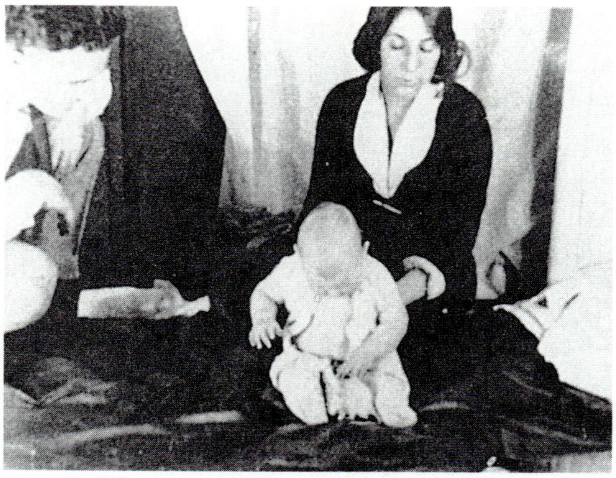

In their now famous experiment, Watson and Rayner gave baby Albert a white rat to play with. However, after Watson and Rayner repeatedly paired the rat (conditioned stimulus) with a loud noise (unconditioned stimulus), Albert learned to associate the two and grew afraid of the rat.

Sucking is one of many reflexive behaviors of human beings; thus, it is one of many responses that can be conditioned. For example, newborns respond reflexively to loud noises. (We examined newborns' reflexes in Chapter 3.) A loud noise naturally elicits a startle response—an outstretching of the arms and legs and associated changes in heart rate, blood pressure, and breathing. Through conditioning procedures, all kinds of neutral stimuli can become conditioned stimuli that elicit a reflexive response of this sort. A puff of air delivered to the eye, for example, produces the unconditioned response of an eye blink. When a light or buzzer is paired with the puff of air, it will eventually elicit the eye blink by itself; this conditioned eye blink is a robust response, one that is retained for long periods of time, particularly among younger adults (Solomon et al., 1998). This effect can be produced in many other animals besides humans.

The complex process of learning is not automatic; it depends on a whole array of events, including an organism's past experiences with the conditioned and unconditioned stimulus. This is especially true for complex conditioned responses. Both pleasant and unpleasant emotional responses can be classically conditioned. Consider this example: if a child who is playing with a favorite toy is repeatedly frightened by a sudden loud noise, the child may be conditioned to be afraid each time he or she sees the toy. John B. Watson and Rosalie Rayner explored this type of relationship in 1920 in a now-famous experiment with an 11-month-old infant named Albert. (Today, such an experiment would be considered unethical.) Albert was given several toys and a live white rat to play with. One day, as he reached for the rat, the experimenters suddenly made an ear-splitting noise that frightened the child. After repeated pairing of the noise and the rat, Albert learned the relationship. The rat served as a conditioned stimulus and the loud noise as the unconditioned stimulus; on each subsequent presentation, the rat evoked a conditioned response of fear in Albert.

As another example, beer commercials apply conditioning principles by featuring attractive people enjoying their favorite beer while frolicking on a warm, sunny beach or socializing in a cozy ski chalet. The producers hope that when viewers associate the can of beer (a neutral stimulus) with an unconditioned stimulus that naturally elicits a positive emotional response (the pleasant scene), the beer will similarly elicit a positive response. In other words, they hope to condition people to feel good whenever they think about this beer.

Higher-Order Conditioning

After a neutral stimulus becomes a conditioned stimulus, it generally elicits the conditioned response whenever it is presented. Another phenomenon that may occur is **higher-order conditioning**—the process by which a neutral stimulus takes on conditioned properties through pairing with a conditioned stimulus. Suppose a dog is conditioned to associate a light with a mildly loud, high-pitched siren. On seeing the light, the dog will exhibit fear; the light has become a conditioned stimulus that elicits a fear response. If a bell is now paired with or presented just before the light, the new stimulus (the bell) can also take on properties of the conditioned stimulus (the light). After repeated pairings, the dog associates the two events (the light and the bell), and either event by itself will elicit a fear response. When a third stimulus—say, an experimenter in a white lab coat—is introduced, the dog may learn to associate the experimenter with the bell or light. After enough trials, the dog may show a conditioned

Be an *Active* learner

REVIEW

- What is a conditioned behavior? pp. 223–224
- Does learning have to be exhibited in overt behavior? Explain your answer. p. 222

THINK CRITICALLY

- Provide examples of higher-order conditioning from your own experience.

APPLY PSYCHOLOGY

- How might you increase the likelihood that higher-order conditioning will take place? Give an example.

fear response to each of the three stimuli: the light, the bell, and the experimenter (Pavlov, 1927; Rescorla, 1977, 1998, 2001).

Thus, higher-order conditioning permits increasingly remote associations, which can result in a complex network of conditioned stimuli and responses. At least two factors determine the extent of higher-order conditioning: (1) the similarity between the new stimulus and the original conditioned stimulus, and (2) the frequency and consistency with which the two stimuli are paired. You can see that successful pairing of conditioned and unconditioned stimuli—that is, successful classical conditioning—is influenced by many variables.

Key Variables in Classical Conditioning

Classical conditioning is not as simple a process as Pavlov might have thought. As noted earlier, such learning is not automatic; it depends on a matrix of events, including an organism's past experiences with the conditioned and unconditioned stimuli as well as key variables concerning those stimuli. For example, how bright must the oil light in your car be? How loud does the buzzer have to be? How long does the bell have to ring? How sinister must movie music be? How many times must someone experience pain in a dentist's chair, and how strong does the pain have to be? As with other psychological phenomena, situational variables affect whether and under what conditions classical conditioning will occur. Cultural variables are also important; though the principles of conditioning are the same in every culture, what constitutes a fear-producing stimulus, for example, varies from culture to culture and even from person to person.

Some of the most important variables in classical conditioning are the strength and timing of the unconditioned stimulus and the frequency of its pairings with the neutral stimulus. When these variables are optimal, conditioning occurs easily.

Strength, Timing, and Frequency

■ **STRENGTH OF THE UNCONDITIONED STIMULUS.** A puff of air delivered to the eye will easily elicit a conditioned response to a neutral stimulus paired with it, but only if the puff of air (the unconditioned stimulus) is sufficiently strong. Research shows that when the unconditioned stimulus is strong and constantly elicits the reflexive (unconditioned) response, conditioning to a neutral stimulus is likely to occur. On the other hand, when the unconditioned stimulus is weak, it is less likely to elicit the unconditioned response, and conditioning to a neutral stimulus is unlikely to occur. Thus, pairing a neutral stimulus with a weak unconditioned stimulus will not reliably lead to conditioning.

■ **TIMING OF THE UNCONDITIONED STIMULUS.** For conditioning to occur, an unconditioned stimulus must usually be paired with a neutral stimulus close enough in time for the two to become associated; that is, they must be temporally contiguous (close in time). For optimal conditioning, the neutral stimulus should occur a short time (often cited as one-half second) before the unconditioned stimulus and overlap with it, particularly for reflexes such as the eye blink. (In Pavlov's experiment, conditioning would not have occurred if the bell and the food had been presented an hour apart.) The two stimuli may be presented together or separated by a brief interval. Some types of conditioning can occur despite fairly long delays, but the optimal time between the two stimuli varies from one study to another and depends on many things, including the type of conditioned response sought (e.g., Cunningham et al., 1999).

Higher-order conditioning
Process by which a neutral stimulus takes on conditioned properties through pairing with a conditioned stimulus.

■ **FREQUENCY OF PAIRINGS.** Occasional or rare pairings of a neutral stimulus with an unconditioned stimulus, even at close intervals, usually do not result in conditioning; generally speaking, frequent pairings that establish a relationship between the unconditioned and the conditioned stimulus are necessary. If, for example, food and the sound of a bell are paired on every trial, a dog will be conditioned more quickly than if the stimuli are paired on every other trial. The frequency of the natural occurrence of the unconditioned stimulus is also important. If the unconditioned stimulus does not occur frequently but is always associated with the conditioned stimulus, more rapid conditioning is likely because one stimulus predicts the other (Rescorla, 1988). Once the conditioned response has reached its maximum strength, additional pairings of the stimuli do not increase the likelihood of a conditioned response. There are exceptions to this general rule, though, in which specific one-time pairings can produce learning.

Predictability

A key factor determining whether conditioning will occur is the predictability of the association of the unconditioned and conditioned stimuli. Closeness in time and regular frequency of pairings promote conditioning, but these are not enough. Predictability—the ability to anticipate future events—turns out to be a central factor in facilitating conditioning (Rescorla, 1988).

Pavlov thought that classical conditioning was based on timing. Research has shown, however, that if the unconditioned stimulus (such as food) can be predicted by the conditioned stimulus (such as a bell), then conditioning is rapidly achieved. Conditioning depends more on the reliability with which the conditioned stimulus predicts the unconditioned stimulus. Pavlov's dogs learned that bells were good predictors of food; the conditioned stimulus (bell) reliably predicted the unconditioned one (food), and so conditioning was quickly achieved.

In Rescorla's view, what an organism learns through conditioning is the predictability of events—bells predicting food, light predicting puffs of air to the eye, dentist chairs predicting pain. An organism learns that there is some sort of relationship between the conditioned and unconditioned stimuli. Many learning researchers consider predictability a cognitive concept; human beings and many animals make predictions about the future based on past events in a wide range of circumstances (Siegel et al., 2000). As you will see in the next two chapters (on memory and cognition), such thought is based on simple learning but becomes more complex. You'll also see how the predictability and relationship of events become important in phenomena such as extinction and spontaneous recovery, considered next.

Extinction and Spontaneous Recovery

Some conditioned responses last for a long time; others disappear quickly. Much depends on whether the conditioned stimulus continues to predict the unconditioned one. Consider the following: What would have happened to Pavlov's dogs if he had rung the bell each day but never followed it with food? What would happen if you went to the dentist every day for 2 months, but the dentist only brushed your teeth with pleasant-tasting toothpaste and never drilled?

If a researcher continues Pavlov's experiment by presenting the conditioned stimulus (bell) but no unconditioned stimulus (food), the likelihood of a conditioned response (salivation) decreases with every trial; the response undergoes extinction. In classical conditioning, **extinction** is the procedure of withholding the unconditioned stimulus—presenting the conditioned stimulus alone. This procedure gradually reduces the probability (and often the strength) of a conditioned response. Imagine a study in which a puff of air is associated with a

Extinction
In classical conditioning, the procedure of withholding the unconditioned stimulus and presenting the conditioned stimulus alone, which gradually reduces the probability of the conditioned response.

Spontaneous recovery
Recurrence of an extinguished conditioned response, usually following a rest period.

buzzer that consistently elicits the conditioned eye-blink response. If the unconditioned stimulus (the puff of air) is no longer delivered in association with the buzzer, the likelihood that the buzzer will continue to elicit the eye-blink response decreases over time (see Figure 7.4). When presentation of the buzzer alone no longer elicits the conditioned response, psychologists say that the response has been *extinguished* (Rescorla, 2001a, b).

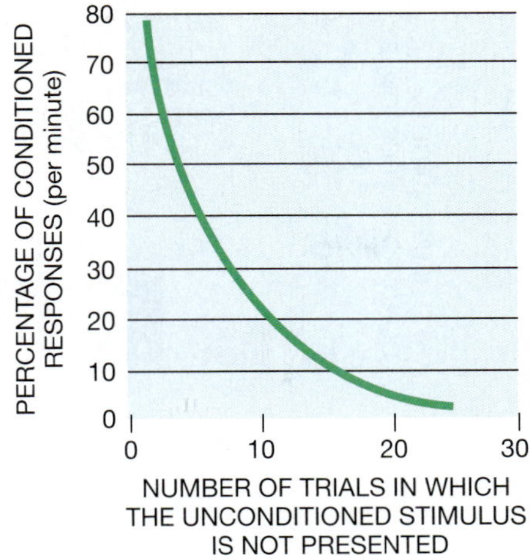

FIGURE 7.4

A Typical Extinction Curve

Numerous experiments have demonstrated that the percentage of times an organism displays a conditioned response decreases over a number of trials in which the unconditioned stimulus is not presented. When presentation of the unconditioned stimulus alone no longer elicits the conditioned response, the response has been extinguished.

But an extinguished conditioned response may not be gone forever. It can recur, especially after a rest period, and this recurrence is termed **spontaneous recovery**. If the dog whose salivation response has been extinguished is placed in the experimental situation again after a rest period of 20 minutes, its salivary response to the bell will recur briefly (although less strongly than before). This behavior shows that the effects of extinction are not permanent and that the learned association is not totally forgotten (see Figure 7.5).

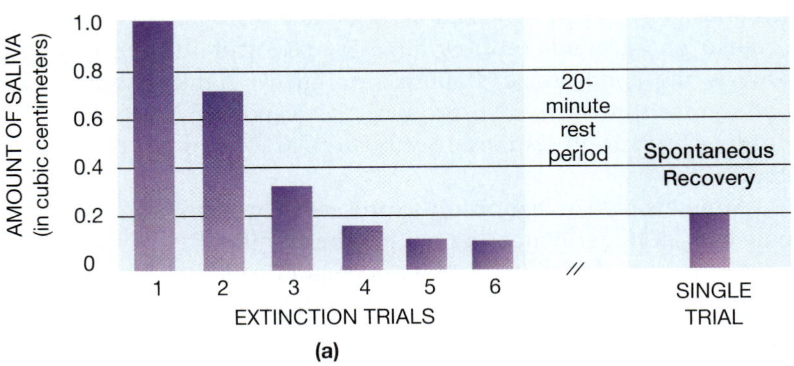

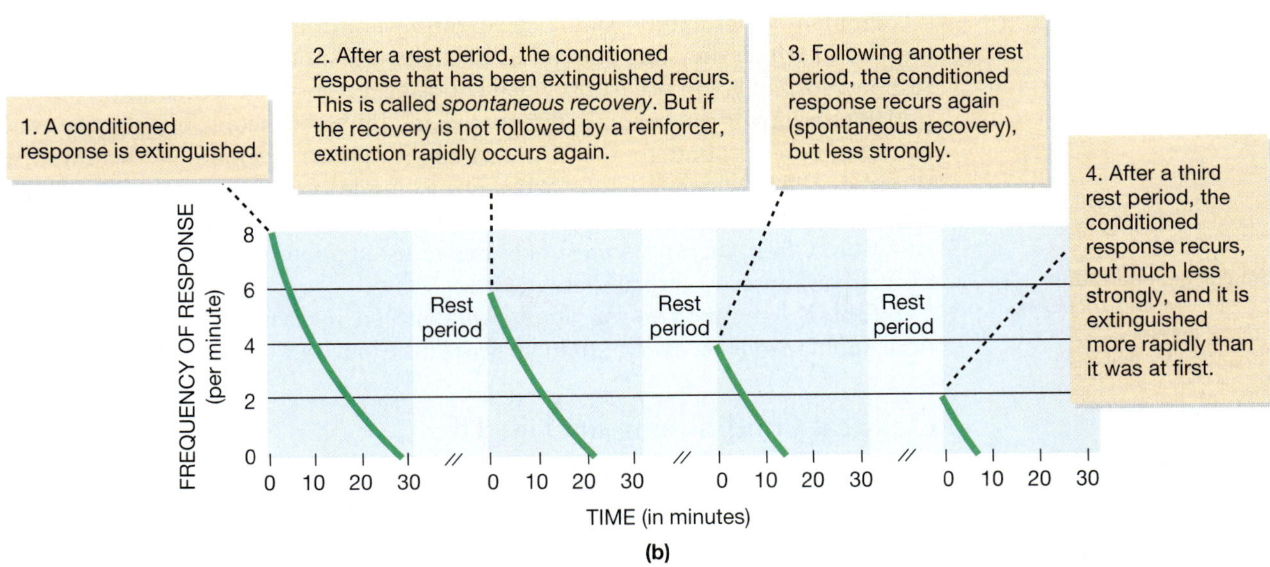

FIGURE 7.5

The Process of Spontaneous Recovery

The graph in part (a) shows some of Pavlov's actual data from an experiment published in 1927. Pavlov brought about extinction in a series of six trials by omitting the presentation of the unconditioned stimulus; but after a 20-minute rest period, spontaneous recovery occurred.

FIGURE 7.6

Stimulus Generalization

Stimulus generalization occurs when an organism (an animal or a human being) exhibits a conditioned response to a stimulus that is similar but not identical to the original conditioned stimulus. In this experiment, a pigeon was trained to respond to a tone of 1,000 Hz by pecking a key. Later, the pigeon was presented with tones of different frequencies so that the experimenter could determine whether it would respond to those dissimilar frequencies. Results showed that the percentage of responses decreased as the tone's frequency became increasingly different from the training frequency. *(Jenkins & Harrison, 1960)*

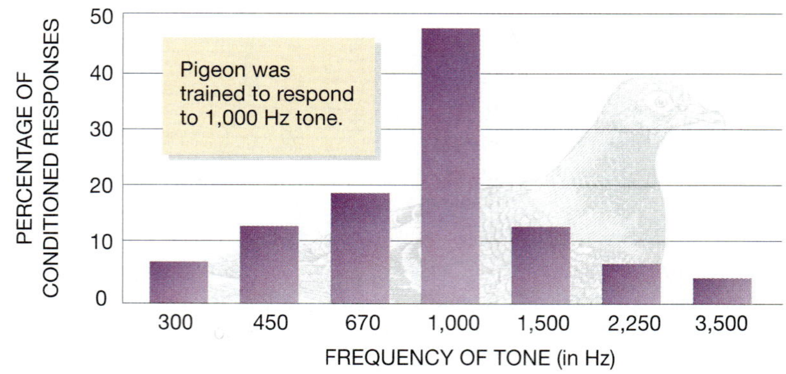

Stimulus Generalization and Stimulus Discrimination

Imagine that a 3-year-old child pulls a cat's tail and gets a painful scratch in return. It will not be surprising if the child develops a fear of that cat; but the child may actually develop a fear of all cats, and even of dogs and other four-legged animals. Adults may respond in a similar way—through a process that psychologists call stimulus generalization.

Stimulus generalization occurs when an organism develops a conditioned response to a stimulus that is similar but not identical to the original conditioned stimulus. The extent to which an organism responds to a stimulus similar to the original one depends on how alike the two stimuli are. If, for example, a loud tone is the conditioned stimulus for an eye-blink response, somewhat lower but similar tones will also produce the response. A totally dissimilar tone will produce little or no response. See Figure 7.6 for another example of stimulus generalization.

Stimulus discrimination is the process by which an organism learns to respond only to a specific stimulus and not to other stimuli. Pavlov showed that animals that have learned to differentiate between pairs of stimuli display frustration or even aggression when discrimination is made difficult or impossible. He trained a dog to discriminate between a circle and an ellipse and then on successive trials changed the shape of the ellipse to look more and more like the circle. Eventually, the animal was unable to discriminate between the shapes but randomly chose one or the other; it also became aggressive.

Human beings exhibit similar disorganization in behavior when placed in situations in which they feel compelled to make a response but don't know how to respond correctly. On occasions when choosing a response becomes difficult or impossible, behavior can become stereotyped and limited in scope; people may choose either not to respond to the stimulus or always to respond in the same way (Lundin, 1961; Maier & Klee, 1941). For example, a supervisor confronted by an angry employee may either respond in kind, by blowing up, or withdraw from the situation. Often, therapists must help maladjusted people learn to be more flexible in their responses to difficult situations.

Table 7.1 summarizes four important concepts in classical conditioning: extinction, spontaneous recovery, stimulus generalization, and stimulus discrimination.

Stimulus generalization
Process by which a conditioned response becomes associated with a stimulus that is similar but not identical to the original conditioned stimulus.

Stimulus discrimination
Process by which an organism learns to respond only to a specific stimulus and not to other stimuli.

Classical Conditioning in Daily Life

I (L.L.) have to admit it. I respond to the sound of music with classically conditioned responses over and over again: Play the national anthem, and I well up with pride. Play the soundtrack from the latest romantic film, and I get teary-eyed. All of us become conditioned to respond to all kinds of stimuli, and much of that conditioning

TABLE 7.1

Four Important Concepts in Classical Conditioning

Property	Definition	Example
Extinction	The process of reducing the probability of a conditioned response by withholding the unconditioned stimulus (the reinforcer)	An infant conditioned by the stroking of its lips to suck in response to a light is no longer given the unconditioned stimulus of stroking the lips; the infant stops sucking in response to the conditioned stimulus.
Spontaneous recovery	The recurrence of an extinguished conditioned response following a rest period	A dog's conditioned salivary response has been extinguished. After a rest period, the dog again salivates in response to the conditioned stimulus, though less than before.
Stimulus generalization	The occurrence of a conditioned response to stimuli that are similar but not identical to the original conditioned stimulus	A dog conditioned to salivate in response to a high-pitched tone also salivates in response to a somewhat lower-pitched tone.
Stimulus discrimination	The process by which an organism learns to respond only to a specific reinforced stimulus	A goat is conditioned to salivate only in response to lights of high intensity, not to lights of low intensity.

is Pavlovian classical conditioning. Let's consider some important examples that have helped psychologists understand both human behavior and conditioning.

■ **THE GARCIA EFFECT.** My daughter Sarah has hated mustard ever since her sixth birthday party. After the guests left the party, we sat down for ham sandwiches with lettuce and mustard. Two hours later, she was ill—fever, vomiting, chills, and swollen glands. It was the flu. But as far as Sarah was concerned, it was the mustard that had made her sick; 19 years later, she still refuses to eat mustard.

This association of mustard and nausea is an example of a conditioned taste aversion. In a famous experiment, John Garcia gave animals specific foods or drinks and then induced nausea (usually by injecting a drug or by exposing the animals to radiation). He found that after only one pairing of a food or drink (the conditioned stimulus) with the drug or radiation (the unconditioned stimulus), the animals avoided the food or drink that preceded the nausea (e.g., Garcia & Koelling, 1971; Linberg et al., 1982).

Two aspects of Garcia's work startled the research community. First, Garcia showed that a conditioned taste aversion could be established even if the nausea was induced several hours after the food or drink had been consumed. This contradicted the previously held assumption that the time interval between the unconditioned stimulus and the conditioned stimulus must be short, especially for conditioning to occur quickly. More recent research confirms Garcia's finding (De La Casa & Lubow, 2000; Grigson, 2000). Garcia also showed that not all stimuli could become associated. He tried to pair bells and lights with nausea to produce a taste aversion in rats, but he was unable to do so—learning depended on the relevance of the stimuli to each other. This led Garcia to conclude that "strong aversions to the smell or taste of food can develop even when illness is delayed for hours after consumption [but] avoidance reactions do not develop for visual, auditory, or tactile stimuli associated with food" (Garcia & Koelling, 1971, p. 461). The appropriateness of stimuli may depend on whether they "belong" together in nature: bells and nausea have little to do with each other; smells and nausea are far more likely to be related in the real world, and so a smell might quickly become a conditioned stimulus for nausea (Hollis, 1997). Ultimately, Garcia's work disproved two accepted principles of learning.

Conditioned taste aversion, sometimes called the *Garcia effect*, has survival value and practical applications. In one trial (instance), through classical conditioning,

■ *Conditioned taste aversion, or the Garcia effect, has been used successfully to deter coyotes from attacking sheep.*

animals associate a food with illness—and then they avoid that food. For example, coyotes often attack sheep and lambs. Garcia laced lamb meat with a substance that causes a short-term illness and put the food on the outskirts of sheep ranchers' fenced-in areas. Coyotes who ate the lamb meat became sick and developed an aversion to it. After this experience, they approached the sheep as if ready to attack but nearly always backed off (e.g., Garcia et al., 1976). By using conditioned taste aversion, Garcia deterred coyotes from eating sheep.

■ **LEARNING AND CHEMOTHERAPY.** Cancer patients often undergo chemotherapy, and an unfortunate side effect of the therapy is vomiting and nausea. The patients often develop a lack of appetite and lose weight. Is it possible that they lose weight because of a conditioned taste aversion? According to researchers some cancer patients become conditioned to avoid food (Montgomery et al., 1998; Montgomery & Bovbjerg, 1997). They check into a hospital, have a meal, are given chemotherapy, become sick, and thereafter avoid the food that preceded the therapy. Schafe and Bernstein (1996) report on research with children and adults who were going to receive chemotherapy. Bernstein's research showed that patients given foods before therapy developed specific aversions to those foods; control groups who were not given any food before their therapy did not develop taste aversions.

Patients develop the food aversions even when they know it is the chemotherapy that induces the nausea. Bernstein suggested an intervention based on learning theory: patients could be given a "scapegoat" food, such as candies with a particular flavor, just before chemotherapy; then, any conditioned aversion that developed would be to an unimportant and easily avoided food rather than to nutritious foods. When Bernstein (1988, 1991) tried this procedure, she found that both children and adults were far less likely to develop food aversions to nutritious foods.

■ **CONDITIONING OF THE IMMUNE SYSTEM.** Classical conditioning explains a wide range of human behaviors, including some physical responses to the world, such as accelerations in heart rate and changes in blood pressure. Substances such as pollen, dust, animal dander, and mold initiate allergic reactions in many people. Cat fur, for example, may naturally elicit an allergic reaction, such as an inability to breathe, in someone with asthma. Asthma attacks, like other behaviors, can be conditioned to occur. If Lindsay's asthmatic friend has *always* found cat fur in Lindsay's house (a regular pairing), classical conditioning theory predicts that even if all the cat hair is removed, the asthmatic friend may have an allergic reaction when she enters Lindsay's house. (A conditioned stimulus, the house, predicts an unconditioned response, the allergic reaction.) Researchers have shown that people with severe allergies can have an allergic reaction after merely seeing a cat, even if there is no cat fur present, or upon entering a house that used to have a cat, even long after the cat's demise.

Even the body's immune system can be conditioned. Normally, the body releases disease-fighting antibodies when toxic substances appear in the blood. This is an involuntary activity that is not controlled by the nervous system. In a striking series of studies, animals that had fatal autoimmune lupus were classically conditioned in a way that altered their immune responses (Ader, 1997, 2000; Ader & Cohen, 1993). The experimenters paired a sweet-tasting solution with a drug that produced illness and, as a side effect, also suppressed the immune response. The

BRAIN AND BEHAVIOR

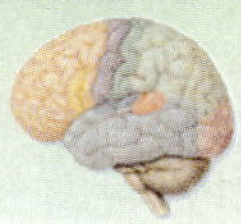

Conditioning for Drug Addicts

Drug abuse cannot be blamed on any one event, person, family, or set of circumstances; drug seeking will not be accounted for by one approach (Drummond, 2001). We know that drug dependence is a physiological phenomenon. Initially most illegal and abused drugs produce a feeling the user finds positive, followed upon withdrawal by an unpleasant effect—this happens because the brain "demands" more of the drug to feel good or go back to "normal." This cycle of pleasure and need leads to repeated use and may result in addiction—users learn to use drugs to satisfy the physiological needs created by the drug (O'Brien et al., 1998). They learn to place confidence in their drug of choice—like alcohol—rather than in work, family, or other areas of life (O'Brien et al., 1998). After extensive and repeated use, alcoholics and other drug abusers resent people and events that do not fit in with their drug use.

In addition, and making matters worse, we also know that drug users become conditioned. For example, when addicts inject heroin, their bodies produce an antiopiate substance to protect them from an overdose; this is a natural response. Siegel (1999) argues that if the addict always injects the drug in the same room, the place itself may serve to initiate an antiopiate response, without any use of the drug. That is, the location of heroin use can serve as a conditioned stimulus for the antiopiate response. When the user injects the drug in a different location, the well-developed antiopiate response does not occur—the body is not doing something that it has become accustomed to. As a consequence, the user may inject too much of the drug, leading to an overdose. The stimulus for the increased use may have been merely the location of the drug consumption (Baptista et al., 1998).

A comprehensive theory of drug use, abuse, tolerance, and withdrawal will have to incorporate the neurobiology of addiction (Koob, 2000) and environmental cues (Carter & Tiffany, 1999) and bodily reactions that are Pavlovian in origin. Addicts' bodies react not only to effects of the drug but also in an anticipatory way to the sight of needles, drugs, and locations (Losa, 1999; Siegel & Allen, 1996).

animals quickly learned to avoid the sweet-tasting substance that seemed to predict nausea. When later presented with the sweet-tasting substance alone, they avoided it but still showed a reduction in immune system response. The experimenters had classically conditioned an immune system response that was thought to have no interconnection to the nervous system (Hiramoto et al., 1997). This is an intriguing finding that is further explored in *Brain and Behavior*.

Pavlov's Understanding Reinterpreted

When Pavlov was busy measuring salivation, he had no reason to consider the complex array of variables that psychologists now think about in connection with classical conditioning. Pavlov thought in terms of simple associations between paired stimuli. Today, researchers also consider the relevance of a stimulus, as well as its appropriateness, predictability, and ability to create higher-order associations. Pavlov laid the foundation for later studies of emotion and thought because he showed that organisms learn associations about events in the environment. But these associations are more complex than Pavlov ever appreciated.

Pavlov focused on actual, observable stimuli and responses; today, researchers are considering how imagined stimuli—thoughts that we have about events—can evoke a response (Dadds et al., 1997). Do thoughts about airplane disasters cause people to avoid air travel? This broader view of conditioning may lead to a better understanding of how behavior can be established and maintained by thoughts, images, and anticipation of events, all of which can lead to conditioned and sometimes nonproductive, even abnormal responses.

Be an *Active* learner

REVIEW

- What key variables affect learning? pp. 227–228
- If a conditioned stimulus is presented without an unconditioned stimulus, what happens? p. 227

THINK CRITICALLY

- What led Garcia to conclude that taste aversion can occur after one trial or one instance? What other examples of learning could occur after one trial or one instance?

APPLY PSYCHOLOGY

- Drug abuse is seen by many as a psychological and physical problem. Psychologically, what are some conditioned responses that might lead to drug overdoses among addicts?

Building Table 7.1

Types of Learning: Classical Conditioning

Type of Learning	Procedure	Result	Example
Classical conditioning	A neutral stimulus (such as a bell) is paired with an unconditioned stimulus (such as food).	The neutral stimulus becomes a conditioned stimulus-it elicits the conditioned response.	A bell elicits a response from a dog.

Building Table 7.1 summarizes some of the key elements of classical conditioning. Although classical conditioning explains a wide range of phenomena, not all behaviors result from such associations. Many complex behaviors result from another form of learning—operant conditioning—which focuses on behavior and its consequences. Operant conditioning is discussed next.

Operant Conditioning

An organism can be exposed to bells, whistles, or lights and may form associations between stimuli and events—but in these kinds of situations the organism, the learner, has little control over the events. A light is presented before food is delivered, and an association is formed. But what happens when a child is scolded for playing with and breaking a valuable camera or receives a pat on the back after doing well in class? Does learning take place? From the point of view of many learning psychologists, the consequences of a person's behavior have powerful effects that change the course of subsequent behavior. Unlike classical conditioning, this view sees the organism as actively operating on and within the environment and, as a result, experiencing rewards or punishments. Let's explore this distinction further because it helps explain the how and why of what we do.

The Pioneers: B. F. Skinner and E. L. Thorndike

In the 1930s, B. F. Skinner (1904–1990) began to change the way psychologists think about conditioning and learning. Skinner questioned whether the passive Pavlovian (classical) conditioning that focused on reflexive, automatic responses should be studied at all. Instead, he focused solely on an organism's observable behavior and did not consider thought processes, consciousness, brain–behavior relationships, and the mind to be proper subject matter for psychological research. At best, private events—thoughts, feeling, and emotions—are the early stages of overt behavior and are not readily accessible for scrutiny. Skinner's early work was in the tradition of such strict behaviorists as Watson, although Skinner ultimately modified some of his own most extreme positions. His 1938 book, *The Behavior of Organisms*, continues to have an impact on studies of conditioning.

Operant [OP-er-ant] conditioning
Conditioning in which an increase or decrease in the probability that a behavior will recur is affected by the delivery of reinforcement or punishment as a consequence of the behavior; also known as *instrumental conditioning*.

According to Skinner, most behaviors can be explained through operant conditioning, rather than through Pavlov's classical conditioning. Skinner used the term *operant conditioning* because the organism *operates* on the environment, with every action followed by a specific event, or consequence. **Operant conditioning**, or *instrumental conditioning*, is conditioning in which an increase or decrease in the probability that a behavior will recur is affected by the delivery of reinforcement or punishment as a consequence of the behavior. The conditioned behavior is usually voluntary, not reflexive, as in classical conditioning. Another key difference between classical conditioning and operant conditioning is that a consequence *follows*, rather than coexists with, the behavior.

Consider what happens when a boss rewards and encourages her overworked employees by giving them unexpected cash bonuses. If the bonuses improve morale and induce the employees to work harder, then the employer's conditioning efforts will be successful. In turn, the employees could condition the boss's behavior by rewarding her paying of bonuses with further increases in productivity, thereby encouraging her to continue giving bonuses.

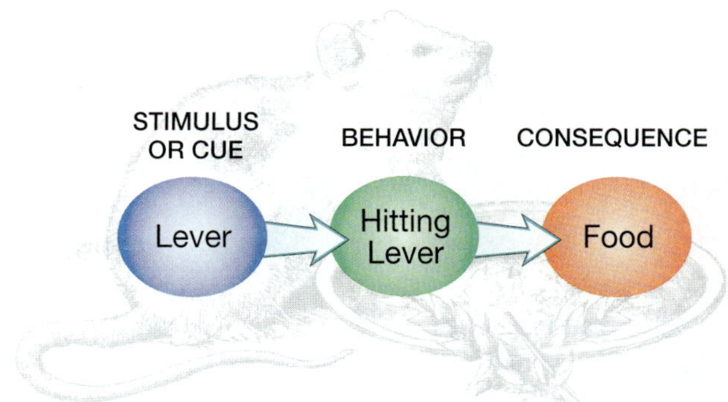

FIGURE 7.7

The Process of Operant Conditioning

Operant conditioning is different from classical conditioning in that the behavior to be conditioned (such as hitting a lever) is reinforced after it occurs.

In the laboratory, researchers have studied similar sequences of behaviors followed by rewards. One of the most famous experiments was conducted by the American psychologist E. L. Thorndike (1874–1949), who pioneered the study of operant conditioning during the 1890s and first reported on his work in 1898. Thorndike placed hungry cats in boxes and put food outside the boxes. The cats could escape from the boxes and get food by hitting a lever that opened a door in each box. The cats quickly performed the behavior Thorndike was trying to condition (hitting the lever), because doing so (at first by accident and then deliberately) gave them access to food. Because the response (hitting the lever) was essential to (instrumental in) obtaining the reward, Thorndike used the term *instrumental conditioning* to describe the process and called the behaviors *instrumental behaviors*.

Although Skinner spoke of operant conditioning and Thorndike of instrumental conditioning, the two terms are often used interchangeably. What is important is that both Skinner and Thorndike acknowledged that first the behavior is *emitted* (displayed) and then a consequence (for example, a reward) follows. This is unlike classical (Pavlovian) conditioning, in which there is first a change in the environment (for example, bells and food are paired) and then the conditioned behavior (usually a reflexive response) is *elicited* (see Figure 7.7).

In operant conditioning, such as in Thorndike's experiment with cats, the type of consequence that follows the behavior is a crucial component of the conditioning, because it determines whether the behavior is likely to recur. The consequence can be either a reinforcer or a punisher. A reward acts as a *reinforcer*, increasing the likelihood that the behavior targeted for conditioning will recur; in Thorndike's experiment, food was the reinforcer for hitting the lever. A *punisher*, on the other hand, decreases the likelihood that the targeted behavior will recur. If a piercing alarm is sounded each time a cat touches a lever, the cat quickly learns not to touch the lever. Parents use a reinforcer when they make use of the family car contingent on responsible behavior. A teenager on a date is more likely to return home at an appropriate hour if doing so will ensure future use of the car. (We will discuss reinforcement and punishment—consequences—in more detail later in this chapter.)

The Skinner Box and Shaping

Much of the research on operant conditioning has used an apparatus that most psychologists call a Skinner box—even though Skinner himself never approved of the name. A **Skinner box** is a box that contains a responding mechanism (often a lever or a bar) and a device capable of delivering a consequence to an animal in the box whenever it makes a desired response (one the experimenter has chosen). In experiments that involve rewards, the delivery mechanism is often a small lever or bar in the side of the box; the animal receives a food reward for pressing it. Punishment sometimes takes the form of electric shocks delivered through a grid on the floor of the box.

Skinner box
Named for its developer, B. F. Skinner, a box that contains a responding mechanism and a device capable of delivering a consequence to an animal in the box whenever it makes the desired response.

In a traditional operant conditioning experiment, a rat that has been deprived of food is placed in a Skinner box. The rat moves around the box, seeking food or

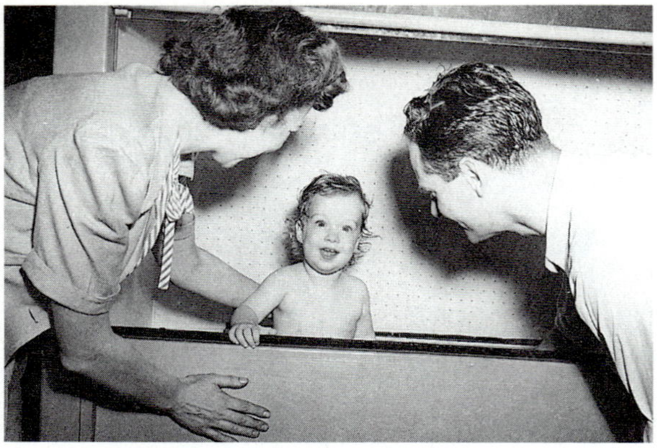

■ *Skinner believed so strongly in controlled environments that he devised a living space for his infant daughter. Known as the "baby box," this space allowed Skinner to shape his daughter's behavior in certain ways, for example, to determine how she would respond if she was uncomfortable. Although Skinner's daughter grew up quite normally, ethical questions were raised about manipulating children this way.*

a means of escape; eventually, it stumbles on the lever and presses it. Immediately following that action, the experimenter delivers a pellet of food into a cup. The rat moves about some more and happens to press the lever again; another pellet of food is delivered. After a few trials, the rat learns that pressing the lever brings food. A hungry rat will learn to press the lever many times in rapid succession to obtain food. Today, psychologists use computerized devices to quantify behavior such as bar pressing and to track the progress an organism makes in learning a response.

Teaching an organism a complex response takes many trials because most organisms need to be taught in small steps, through *shaping*. **Shaping** is the gradual process of selectively reinforcing behaviors that come closer and closer to (that approximate) a desired response. To teach a hungry rat to press a bar in a Skinner box, for example, a researcher begins by giving the rat a pellet of food each time it enters the half of the box where the bar is located. Once this behavior is established, the rat receives food only when it touches the wall where the bar is located. Next, it receives food only when it approaches the bar—and so on, until it receives food only when it actually presses the bar. At each stage, the reinforced behavior (entering the half of the box nearest the bar, touching the wall that has the bar, and so on) more closely approximates the desired behavior (pressing the bar). The sequence of stages used to elicit increasingly closer approximations of a desired behavior is sometimes called the *method of successive approximations* (which means basically the same thing as *shaping*).

Shaping is effective for teaching animals new behaviors; for example, shaping is used to train a dog to sit on command. The trainer generally does this by pushing down on the dog's rear while verbally commanding, "Sit!" and then immediately giving the dog a treat. With a treat as reinforcer following the sitting, the dog begins to sit with less and less pressure applied to its rear; eventually, it sits on command.

Shaping is also helpful in teaching people new behaviors. For example, were you taught how to hit a baseball? If so, you were probably first taught, with reinforcing praise from your coach, how to hold the bat correctly, then how to swing it, then how to make contact with the ball, how to shift your weight, how to follow through, and so on. Similarly, a father who wants his son to make his bed neatly will at first reinforce *any* attempt at bed making, even if the results are sloppy. Over successive weeks, the father will reinforce only the better attempts, until finally he reinforces only neat bed making. Patience is important, because it is essential to reinforce all steps toward the desired behavior, no matter how small. Shaping embodies a central tenet of behaviorism: reinforced behaviors recur. Skinner is the individual responsible for forcefully advancing that notion; psychologists attribute to him the idea that various consequences can redirect the natural flow of behavior. Among the most important of these consequences is reinforcement.

Reinforcement: A Consequence That Strengthens a Response

Shaping
Selective reinforcement of behaviors that gradually approach (approximate) the desired response.

Reinforcer
Any event that increases the probability of a recurrence of the response that preceded it.

To really understand operant conditioning, you need to study the basic principles of reinforcement. To psychologists, a **reinforcer** is any event that increases the probability of a recurrence of the response that preceded it. Thus, a behavior followed by a desirable event is likely to recur. Examples of reinforcement abound in daily life: a person works hard at his job and is rewarded with high pay; a student studies long hours for an examination and is rewarded with a top grade; sales agents call on hundreds of clients and sell lots of their products; young children behave appropriately and receive affection and praise from their parents. The specific behaviors of working hard, studying a great deal, calling on clients, and behaving appropriately are established because of reinforcement. Such behaviors can be made to recur by using either or both of two kinds of reinforcers: positive and negative.

■ Pet owners can use shaping to teach animals to obey. Each time this dog makes a closer approximation to the owner's goal of having it sit, she rewards it with a treat.

■ **POSITIVE REINFORCEMENT.** Most people have used positive reinforcement at one time or another. **Positive reinforcement** is the presentation of a stimulus after a particular response in order to increase the likelihood that the response will recur. When you are teaching your dog tricks, you reward it with a biscuit or a pat on the head. A parent who is toilet training a 2-year-old may applaud when the child uses the toilet rather than messing his diaper; the applause is a reinforcer. The dog and the child continue the behaviors because they have been rewarded with something desirable; their behaviors have been positively reinforced.

Some reinforcers are more powerful than others, and a reinforcer that rewards one person may not have reinforcing value for another. A smile from an approving parent may be a powerful reinforcer for a 2-year-old; high grades may be the most effective reinforcer for a student; money may be effective for one adult, a trip to Hawaii for another, prestige or status for someone else.

■ **NEGATIVE REINFORCEMENT.** Whereas positive reinforcement increases the probability of a response through delivery of a stimulus, **negative reinforcement** increases the probability of a response through removal of a stimulus, usually an *aversive* (unpleasant or noxious) one. Negative reinforcement is still reinforcement because it strengthens or increases the likelihood of a response; its reinforcing properties are associated with removal of an unpleasant stimulus. For example, suppose a rat is placed in a maze whose floor is an electrified grid that delivers a shock every 50 seconds, and the rat can escape the shock by turning to the left in the maze. The behavior to be conditioned is turning to the left in the maze; the reinforcement is termination of the painful stimulus. In this case, negative reinforcement—termination of the painful stimulus—increases the probability of the response (going left) because that response removes the unpleasant stimulus.

Noxious or unpleasant stimuli are often used in animal studies of escape and avoidance. In *escape conditioning*, a rat in a Skinner box receives a shock just strong enough to cause it to thrash around until it bumps against a bar, thereby stopping the shock. In just a few trials, the rat learns to press the bar to escape being shocked, to bring an unpleasant situation to an end. In *avoidance conditioning*, the same apparatus is used, but a buzzer or some other cue precedes the shock by a few seconds. In this case, the rat learns that when it is presented with a stimulus or cue such as a buzzer, it should press the bar to avoid the shock—to prevent it from occurring. Avoidance conditioning generally involves escape conditioning as well: first the animal learns how to escape the shock by pressing the bar; then it learns how to avoid the shock by pressing the bar when it hears the buzzer that signals the oncoming shock.

In avoidance conditioning, the organism learns to respond in such a way that the noxious stimulus is never delivered. For example, to avoid receiving a bad grade on an English exam, a student may study before the exam. And when an adult develops an overwhelming fear of plane crashes, the person may avoid air travel entirely. Thus, avoidance conditioning can explain both adaptive behaviors, such as studying before an exam, and irrational fears, such as the fear of flying.

Most children master both escape and avoidance conditioning at an early age; appropriate signals from a disapproving parent often elicit a response intended to forestall punishment. Similarly, just knowing the possible effects of an automobile accident makes most cautious adults wear seat belts. Both positive and negative reinforcements *increase* the likelihood that an organism will repeat a behavior. If the reinforcement is strong enough, is delivered often enough, and is important enough to the organism, it can help maintain behaviors for long periods.

Positive reinforcement
Presentation of a stimulus after a particular response in order to increase the likelihood that the response will recur.

Negative reinforcement
Removal of a stimulus (usually an aversive one) after a particular response to increase the likelihood that the response will recur.

■ **THE NATURE OF REINFORCERS.** The precise nature of reinforcers is somewhat murky. Early researchers recognized that anything that satisfies biological needs is a powerful reinforcer. Later researchers defined as reinforcers things that satisfy various nonbiological needs—for example, conversation relieves boredom, and sounds relieve sensory deprivation. Therapists and learning theorists know, for example, that something that acts as a reinforcer for one person may not do so for another person (especially if that person is from a different culture) or for the same person on another day. Therefore, they are very careful about identifying aspects of a client's life—or a rodent's environment—that act as reinforcers. If someone were to offer you a reinforcer to perform some fairly difficult task, what would be the most effective reinforcer? Do reinforcers change with a person's age and experiences, or do they depend on how often the person has been reinforced? Today, researchers are trying to discover what reinforcers will work best in practical settings such as the home and the workplace (Farmer-Dougan, 1998).

A reinforcer that is known to be successful may work only in specific situations. The delivery of food pellets to a hungry rat that has just pressed a lever increases the likelihood that the rat will press the lever again. But this reinforcer works only if the rat is hungry; the food pellets are not reinforcing for a rat that has just eaten. Psychologists studying learning and conditioning create the conditions for reinforcement by depriving animals of food or water before an experiment. In doing so, they motivate the animals and allow the food or water to take on reinforcing properties. In most experiments, the organism is motivated in some way. Chapter 11 discusses the role of an organism's needs, desires, and physiological state in determining what can be used as a reinforcer.

A **primary reinforcer** is a reinforcer that has survival value for an organism (for example, food, water, or the termination of pain); its value does not have to be learned. Food can be a primary reinforcer for a hungry rat, water for a thirsty one. A **secondary reinforcer** is a neutral stimulus (such as money or grades) that initially has no intrinsic value for the organism but that becomes rewarding when linked with a primary reinforcer. Many of our pleasures are secondary reinforcers that have acquired value—for example, leather coats keep us no warmer than cloth ones, and sports cars take us where we want to go no faster than four-door sedans.

Secondary reinforcers are generally used to modify human behavior. Approving nods, unlimited use of the family car, and job promotions are secondary reinforcers that can establish and maintain a wide spectrum of behavior. Salespeople may work 72-hour weeks when their manager, using basic psychology, offers them bonuses for increasing their sales by a specific percentage during a slow month. The manager may reason that increasing the amount of the secondary reinforcer (money) may promote better performance (higher sales). Research shows that increasing or decreasing the amount of a reinforcer can significantly alter an organism's behavior.

Primary reinforcer
Reinforcer (such as food, water, or the termination of pain) that has survival value for an organism; this value does not have to be learned.

Secondary reinforcer
Any neutral stimulus that initially has no intrinsic value for an organism but that becomes rewarding when linked with a primary reinforcer.

Superstitious behavior
Behavior learned through coincidental association with reinforcement.

■ **SUPERSTITIOUS BEHAVIORS.** Because reinforcement plays a key role in the learning of new behaviors, parents and educators intentionally and regularly try to reinforce children and students. But what happens when a person or animal is *accidentally* rewarded for a behavior—when a reward has nothing to do with the behavior that immediately preceded it? Under this condition, people and animals may develop **superstitious behavior**—behavior learned through coincidental association with reinforcement. Superstitious behavior often represents an attempt to gain some control of a situation that may be unpredictable. For example, a baseball player may try to extend his hitting streak by always using the same "lucky" bat or engaging in small, often repetitive rituals (Bleak & Frederick, 1998). Many superstitious behaviors—including fear responses to the number 13, black cats, and walking under ladders—are centuries old and have strong cultural associations. Individual superstitious behaviors generally arise from the purely random, coincidental association of some object or event and a particular behavior. Thus, a person who happens to wear the same pair of shoes in three bicycle races and wins the races may come to believe there is a causal relationship between wearing that pair of shoes and winning.

■ **ELECTRICAL BRAIN STIMULATION.** Until the 1950s, researchers assumed that reinforcers were effective because they satisfied some need or drive in an organism, such as hunger. Then James Olds (1955, 1969) found an apparent exception to this assumption. He discovered that rats find electrical stimulation of specific areas of the brain to be rewarding in itself. Olds implanted an electrode in the hypothalamus of each rat and attached the electrode to a stimulator that provided a small voltage. The stimulator was activated only when the rat pressed a lever in a Skinner box. Olds found that the rats pressed the lever thousands of times in order to continue the self-stimulation. In one study, the rats pressed it at a rate of 1,920 times per hour (Olds & Milner, 1954). Rats even crossed an electrified grid to get to the lever and obtain this stimulation. Animals that were rewarded with brain stimulation performed better in a maze, running faster with fewer errors. And hungry rats often chose the self-stimulation over food.

Stimulation of specific areas of the brain initiates different drives and activities. In some cases, it reinforces behaviors such as bar pressing; in others, it increases eating, drinking, or sexual behavior. Psychologists are still not sure how electrical stimulation reinforces a behavior such as lever pressing but they do know that certain neurotransmitters play an important role. The area of the brain stimulated (initially thought to be the medial forebrain bundle but now recognized to include large parts of the limbic system), the state of the organism, its particular physiological needs, and the levels of various neurotransmitters are all important. A hungry rat, for example, will self-stimulate faster than a rat that is not hungry. In addition, a hungry rat will generally choose electrical brain stimulation over food but not to the extent of starving itself.

student voices

Kevin Warneke
Century College

I enrolled in intro psych to get a better feel for how to deal with kids because I had been teaching men's chorus at my old high school. The chapter about how to discipline and teach kids, and to use positive reinforcement has been a huge step in learning to be a teacher.

Punishment: A Consequence That Weakens a Response

You already know that consequences—whether rewards or punishments—affect behavior. Clearly, rewards can establish new behaviors and maintain them for long periods. How effective is punishment in manipulating behavior? **Punishment** is the process of presenting an undesirable or noxious stimulus, or removing a desirable stimulus, to decrease the probability that a preceding response will recur. Punishment, unlike reinforcement, aims to *decrease* the probability of a particular response. Thus, people commonly use this technique to try to teach children and pets to control their behavior. For example, when a dog growls at visitors, its owner chastises it; when a child writes on the walls with crayons, the parents may scold her harshly or make her scrub the walls. In both cases, people indicate displeasure by delivering a stimulus intended to suppress an undesirable behavior.

Researchers use the same technique to decrease the probability that a behavior will recur. They deliver a noxious or unpleasant stimulus, such as a loud piercing alarm, when an organism displays an undesirable behavior. If an animal is punished for a specific behavior, the probability that it will continue to perform that behavior decreases.

Another form of punishment involves removal of a pleasant stimulus. For example, if a teenager stays out past her curfew, she may be grounded for a week. If a child misbehaves, he may be forbidden to watch television that evening. One effective punishment is the *time-out*, in which an individual is removed from an environment containing positive events or reinforcers. For example, a child who hits and kicks may have to sit in a corner with no toys, television, books, or people.

Thus, punishment can involve either adding a noxious stimulus, such as scolding, or subtracting a positive stimulus, such as watching TV. In both cases, the aim

Punishment
Process of presenting an undesirable or noxious stimulus, or removing a desirable stimulus, to decrease the probability that a preceding response will recur.

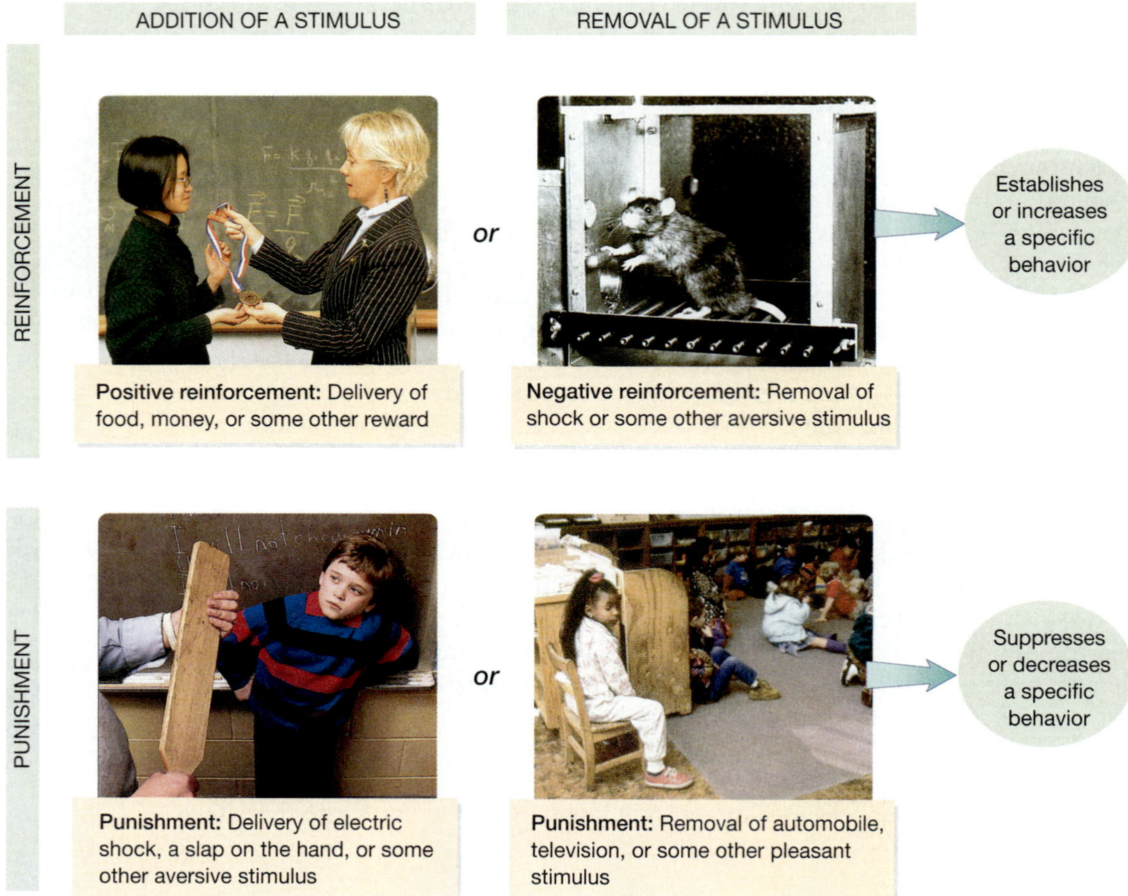

FIGURE 7.8

Effects of Reinforcement and Punishment

is to decrease the likelihood of a behavior. (See Figure 7.8 for a summary of the effects of adding or subtracting a reinforcer or punisher; also, see Figure 7.9 for a comparison of punishment and negative reinforcement.)

■ **THE NATURE OF PUNISHERS.** Like reinforcers, *punishers* can be primary or secondary. A **primary punisher** is a stimulus that is naturally painful or unpleasant to an organism; two examples are a piercing high-pitched sound to an animal and visible parental rage to a small child. A **secondary punisher** is any neutral stimulus that initially has no intrinsic negative value for an organism but acquires punishing qualities when linked with a primary punisher. Examples are the word "No," a shake of the head, or indifference. Secondary punishers can be effective means of controlling behavior, especially when used in combination with reinforcers for desired behaviors. But, as with reinforcement, what is punishing for one person or in one culture may not have the same properties for another person or in another culture. A show of indifference may punish some behaviors for some people, but a display of disapproval from a stern authority figure may be a far more powerful punishment for others. Fathers may be more powerful disciplinarians in some cultures than others; similarly, guilt as a punishing device is used in some cultures more than others. And in collectivist societies, stern disapproval from one's group may be far more powerful than it would be in individualist societies that focus on individual self-esteem and inner strength.

Primary punisher
Any stimulus or event that is naturally painful or unpleasant to an organism.

Secondary punisher
Any neutral stimulus that initially has no intrinsic negative value for an organism but acquires punishing qualities when linked with a primary punisher.

■ **PUNISHMENT PLUS REINFORCEMENT.** Psychologists have long known that punishment by itself is not an effective way to control or eliminate behavior. Punishment can suppress simple behavior patterns; once the punishment ceases,

FIGURE 7.9

Comparison of Negative Reinforcement and Punishment

Punishment involves the presentation of an aversive stimulus to decrease the likelihood of a behavior recurring. Negative reinforcement encourages a behavior by removing an aversive stimulus. Thus, punishment and negative reinforcement have opposite effects on behavior.

however, animals and human beings often return to the previous behavior. To be effective, punishment must be continuous, and the desired alternative behavior should be reinforced at the same time. Therefore, those who study children's classroom behavior recommend a combination of punishment for antisocial behavior and reinforcement for prosocial behavior. A combination of private reprimands for disruptive behaviors and public praise for cooperative behaviors is often the most effective method for controlling classroom behavior.

■ **LIMITATIONS OF PUNISHMENT.** A serious limitation of punishment as a behavior-shaping device is that it suppresses only existing behaviors. It cannot be used to establish new, desired behaviors. Punishment also has serious social consequences (Clutton-Brock & Parker, 1995). If parents use excessive punishment to control a child's behavior, for example, the child may try to escape from the home so that punishment cannot be delivered. Further, children who receive physical punishments often demonstrate increased levels of aggression when they are away from the punisher. Punishment may control a child's behavior while the parents are nearby, but it may also alienate the child from the parents.

Research also shows that children imitate aggression. Thus, parents who punish children physically are likely to have children who are physically aggressive (Grusec, Goodnow, & Kuczynski, 2000). A child may strike out at the person who administers punishment in an attempt to eliminate the source of punishment, sometimes inflicting serious injury. Punishment can also bring about generalized aggression. For example, human beings who have been punished are often hostile and aggressive toward other members of their group. This is especially true of prison inmates, whose hostility is well recognized, and of class bullies, who are often the children most strictly disciplined by their parents or teachers. Skinner (1988) believed that punishment in schools is unnecessary and harmful; he advocated nonpunitive techniques, which might involve developing strong bonds between students and teachers and reinforcing school activities at home (Comer & Woodruff, 1998). In general, disciplinary techniques that lead to a perception of control on the part of the child being disciplined—a sense of how to avoid future discipline—are much more likely to prevent recurrence of undesired behavior, even when the disciplining agent (teacher or parent) is not around.

Be an *Active* learner

REVIEW

- How could a roommate's lack of cleanliness be altered to a more desirable behavior? p. 236
- What events are most likely to ensure that a behavior will be repeated, especially in children? p. 237
- What is the difference between a primary and secondary reinforcer? p. 238

THINK CRITICALLY

- What is negative reinforcement? How is it different from positive reinforcement in terms of its results in affecting long-term behavior?

APPLY PSYCHOLOGY

- Your neighbor tells you, "Punishment just doesn't work with my kids anymore. I keep escalating the punishments, and they keep acting worse and worse! I don't know what to do!" What do you think is going on, and what would you advise your neighbor to do?

FIGURE 7.10

The Magnitude and Delay of Reinforcement

(a) As the amount of a reinforcer (its strength or magnitude) increases, the time it takes an organism to reach a goal usually decreases. (b) As a delay is placed between a response and reinforcement, the probability that a behavior will occur decreases. Short delays (or no delays) between a response and reinforcement increase the chances that a behavior will recur.

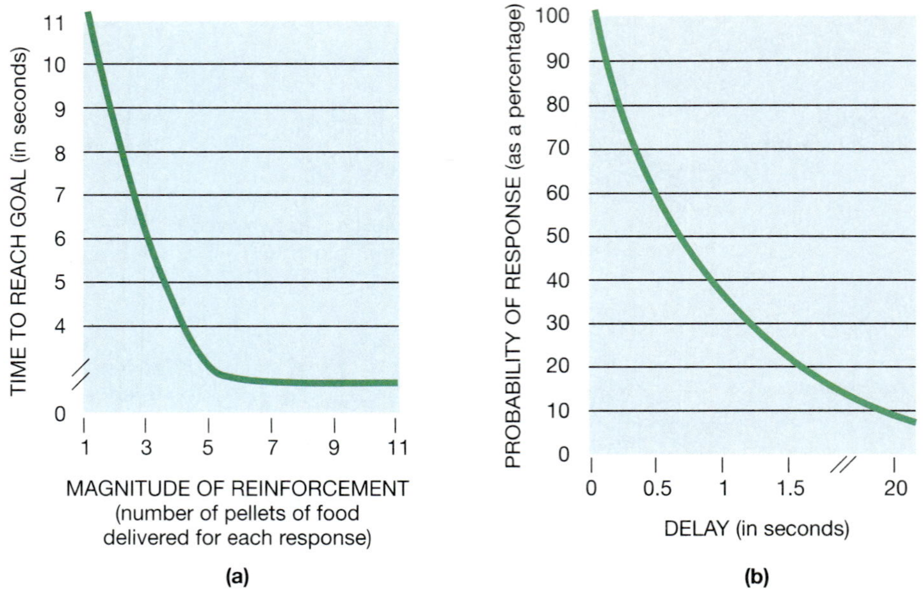

Further, if punishment is delivered inconsistently or without reference to the organism's behavior or culture (Rudy & Grusec, 2001), it may lead to **learned helplessness**, the reaction of a person or animal that feels powerless to control the punishment and so stops making any response at all (LoLordo & Taylor, 2001; Maier, Peterson, & Schwartz, 2000; Schwartz, 2000; Shatz, 2000; Springer 2000).

Key Variables in Operant Conditioning

As with classical conditioning, many variables affect operant conditioning. Most important are the strength, timing, and frequency of consequences (either reinforcement or punishment).

Strength, Timing, and Frequency

■ **STRENGTH OF CONSEQUENCES.** Studies comparing productivity with varying amounts of reinforcement show that the greater the reward, the harder, longer, and faster a person will work to complete a task (see Figure 7.10). For example, if you ran a lawn-mowing company, the more money you received for mowing lawns, the more lawns you would want to mow. Similarly, the stronger the punishment, the more quickly a behavior can be suppressed and the longer it will remain suppressed. If you knew you would get a $200 ticket for speeding, you would be far more likely to obey the speed limit.

The strength of a consequence can be measured in terms of either time or degree. For example, the length of time a child stays in a time-out chair without positive reinforcements can affect how soon and for how long an unacceptable behavior will be suppressed. Thus, for a given child, a 2-minute stay might not be as effective as a 10-minute stay. Likewise, a half-hearted "Please don't do that, sweetie" is not as effective as a firm "Don't do that again."

Learned helplessness
The behavior of giving up or not responding to punishment, exhibited by people or animals exposed to negative consequences or punishment over which they have no control.

Punishment, whatever its form, is best delivered in moderation; too much may be as ineffective as too little. If too much punishment is delivered, it may cause panic, decrease the likelihood of the desired response, or even elicit behavior that is contrary to the punisher's goals.

■ **TIMING OF CONSEQUENCES.** Just as the interval between presenting the conditioned stimulus and the unconditioned stimulus is important in classical conditioning, the interval between a desired behavior and the delivery of the consequence (reward or punishment) is important in operant conditioning. Generally, the shorter the interval, the greater the likelihood that the behavior will be learned (again, see Figure 7.10).

■ **FREQUENCY OF CONSEQUENCES.** How often do people need to be reinforced? Is a paycheck once a month sufficient? Will people work better if they receive reinforcement regularly or if they receive it at unpredictable intervals? Up to this point, our discussion has generally assumed that a consequence follows each response. But what if people are reinforced only some of the time, not continually? When a researcher varies the frequency with which an organism is reinforced, the researcher is manipulating the *schedule of reinforcement*—the pattern of presentation of the reinforcer over time. The simplest and easiest reinforcement pattern is *continuous reinforcement*—reinforcement for every occurrence of the targeted behavior. However, most researchers, or parents for that matter, do not reinforce a behavior every time it occurs; rather, they reinforce occasionally or intermittently. What determines the timetable for reinforcement? Schedules of reinforcement generally are based either on intervals of time or on frequency of response. Some schedules establish a behavior quickly; however, quickly established behaviors are more quickly extinguished than are behaviors that are slower to be established. (We'll discuss extinction in operant conditioning further in the next section.) Researchers have devised four basic schedules of reinforcement; two are *interval schedules* (based on time periods), and two are *ratio schedules* (based on work output).

Interval schedules can be either fixed or variable. Imagine that a rat in a Skinner box is being trained to press a bar in order to obtain food. If the experiment is on a **fixed-interval schedule**, the reward will follow the first bar press that occurs after a specified interval of time. That is, the rat will be given a reinforcer if it presses the bar at least once after a specified time interval and will receive the same reward regardless of whether it works a great deal (presses the bar repeatedly) or just a little. As Figure 7.11 shows, a fixed-interval schedule produces a scalloped graph. Just after reinforcement (shown by the tick marks in the figure), both animals and human beings typically respond slowly; just before the reinforcement is due, there is an increase in performance. Under a **variable-interval schedule**, the reinforcer is

Fixed-interval schedule
A reinforcement schedule in which a reinforcer (reward) is delivered after a specified interval of time, provided that the required response occurs at least once in the interval.

Variable-interval schedule
A reinforcement schedule in which a reinforcer (reward) is delivered after predetermined but varying amounts of time, provided that the required response occurs at least once after each interval.

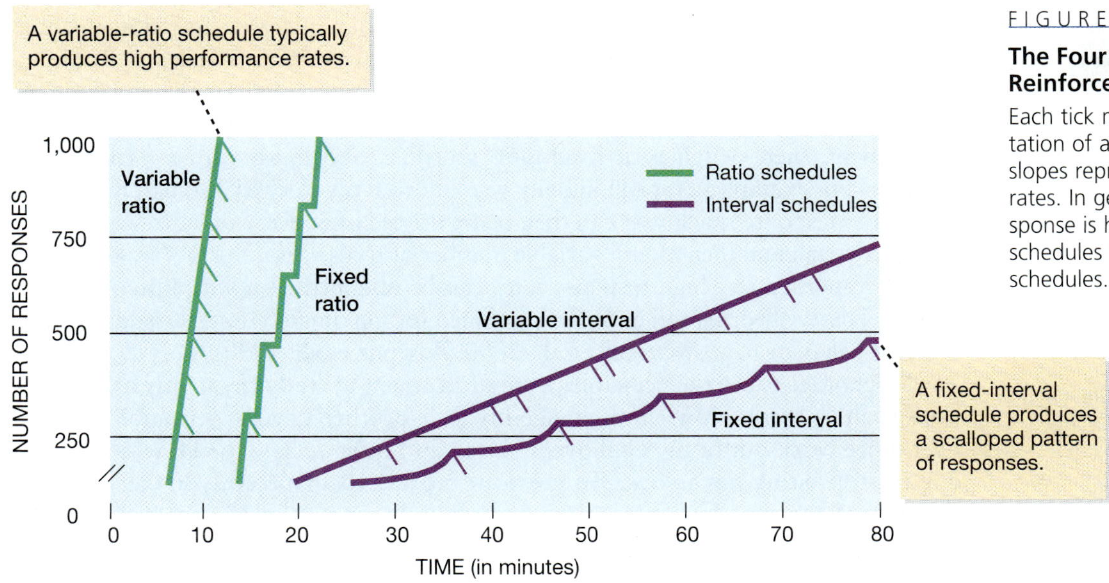

FIGURE 7.11

The Four Basic Types of Reinforcement Schedules

Each tick mark indicates presentation of a reinforcer. Steep slopes represent high work rates. In general, the rate of response is higher under ratio schedules than under interval schedules.

TABLE 7.2

Types of Reinforcement Schedules

Schedule	Description	Effect
Fixed-interval	Reinforcement is given for the first response after a fixed time.	Response rate drops right after reinforcement but then increases near the end of the interval.
Variable-interval	Reinforcement is given for the first response after a predetermined but variable interval.	Response rate is slow and regular.
Fixed-ratio	Reinforcement is given after a fixed number of responses.	Response rate is fast and regular.
Variable-ratio	Reinforcement is given after a predetermined and variable number of responses.	Response rate is regular and high.

delivered after predetermined but varying amounts of time, as long as an appropriate response is made at least once after each interval. The organism may be reinforced if it makes a response after 40 seconds, after 60 seconds, and then after 25 seconds. Rats reinforced on a variable-interval schedule work at a slow, regular rate; the graph of a variable-interval schedule does not have the scalloped effect of a fixed-interval graph. The work rate is relatively slow because the delivery of the reinforcer is tied to time intervals rather than to output.

Ratio schedules, which can also be either fixed or variable, are based on output instead of time. In a **fixed-ratio schedule**, the organism is reinforced for a specified number of responses (amount of work). For example, a rat in a Skinner box might be reinforced after every 10th bar press. In this case, the rat will work at a fast, regular rate. It has learned that hard work brings regular delivery of a reinforcer. Variable-ratio schedules can bring about very high rates of response. A **variable-ratio schedule** reinforces the responder for a predetermined but variable number of responses (amount of work). Thus, a rat learns that hard work produces a reinforcer, but it cannot predict when the reinforcer will be delivered. Therefore, the rat's best bet is to work at a regular, high rate, thereby generating the highest available rate of response. Sales agents for insurance companies know that the more prospects they approach, the more insurance they will sell. They may not know who will buy, but they do know that a greater number of selling opportunities will ultimately result in more sales. Similarly, gamblers pour quarters into slot machines because they never know when they will be reinforced with a jackpot. Table 7.2 summarizes the four schedules of reinforcement.

An efficient way to teach a response is to begin with a continuous schedule of reinforcement, then switch to a fixed-ratio schedule, and finish with a variable-ratio schedule. For example, a rat can initially be reinforced on every trial so that it will learn the proper response quickly. It can then be reinforced after every other trial, then after every fifth trial, and then after a variable number of trials. Once the rat has learned the desired response, very high response rates can be obtained even with infrequent reinforcers. These schedules can easily be combined for maximum effect, depending on the targeted behavior (e.g., Worsdell et al., 2000; Zarcone et al., 1999).

Fixed-ratio schedule
A reinforcement schedule in which a reinforcer (reward) is delivered after a specified number of responses has occurred.

Variable-ratio schedule
A reinforcement schedule in which a reinforcer (reward) is delivered after a predetermined but variable number of responses has occurred.

Psychologists use the principles of reinforcement to study frequently asked questions such as these: How can I change my little brother's rotten attitude? How can I get more work out of my employees? How do I learn to say no? How do I get my dog to stop biting my ankles? To get your brother to shape up, you can shape his behavior. Each time he acts in a way you like, however slightly, reward him with praise or affection. When he behaves annoyingly, withhold attention or rewards and ignore him. Continue this pattern for a few weeks; as he becomes more pleasant, show him more attention. Remember, reinforced behaviors tend to recur [but so do phobias (see *Psychology in Action*).]

Most workers get paid a fixed amount each week. They are on a fixed-interval schedule—regardless of their output, they get their paycheck. One way to increase productivity is to place workers on a fixed-ratio schedule. A worker who is paid by the piece, by the report, by the page, or by the widget is going to produce more pieces, reports, pages, or widgets than one who is paid by the hour and whose productivity therefore does not make a difference. Automobile salespeople, who are known for their persistence, work for commissions; their pay is linked to their ability to close a sale. Research in both the laboratory and the business place shows that when pay is linked to output, people generally work harder.

psychology *in action*

Getting Rid of Phobias

Have you ever heard of the following terms?

Claustrophobia—fear of enclosed spaces
Technophobia—fear of technology
Sciophobia—fear of shadows
Decidophobia—fear of making decisions
Nyctophobia—fear of night
Electrophobia—fear of electricity
Topophobia—fear of performing (stage fright)
Tropophobia—fear of moving or making changes

We all have fears, but most of them are manageable. Fear becomes a phobia when we lose control over our ability to control fear about a particular situation or object. Formally, we define a *phobia* as an anxiety disorder involving excessive irrational fear of, and consequent avoidance of, specific objects or situations. People with a phobic disorder exhibit avoidance and escape behaviors, show increased heart rate and irregular breathing patterns, and report thoughts of disaster and severe embarrassment. Many psychologists agree that phobias are established (learned) and maintained by the release a person receives from escaping or avoiding the feared circumstances.

Millions of Americans suffer from phobias. But the outlook for them has improved greatly. In fact, people with simple phobias can often find relief in a matter of weeks. Psychologists use a variety of techniques usually linked to their viewpoint about the cause of the disorder. But it turns out that many of these techniques share a common feature: they all require that patients meet head-on the source of their discomfort and then *learn* a new response. The therapy is usually (but not always) behavioral and the key word is *learn.*

One behavioral technique, systematic desensitization, requires the client to learn formal, deep-muscle relaxation. It is up to the client to categorize situations that cause anxiety. An individual who fears snakes, for example, might place "holding a snake" at the top of the inventory of things that make him anxious and "viewing a snake from across the room" at the bottom of the list.

The client is then asked to imagine the least fear-provoking scene from his list. At the same time, he or she is asked to relax. By remaining comfortable while at the same time imagining the feared situation, the client may weaken the association between the situation and feelings of anxiety. Once the client has become thoroughly comfortable imagining the least threatening situation, he or she moves up the list and conquers each level of fear in turn.

Of course exposure to such situations gradually lets the client get used to it—that is, the client ultimately learns that there is no real danger. Gradually, slowly, the anxiety is extinguished. Some therapists believe that the more quickly such exposure takes place, the more quickly the phobia will be eliminated. There is some evidence that treatment is most effective when systematic desensitization of thoughts is used along with real life, or "in vivo," exposure. Programs using in vivo exposure techniques have become widely used in the treatment of simple phobias. But there is a catch—often, clients with phobias have trouble getting better because they avoid the object or situation that elicits the anxiety, and even the therapy that deals with the phobia.

Behavior therapy techniques to help clients confront and overcome their fears use principles of learning. For example, in cognitive-behavior therapy, clients with phobias are trained to become aware of their own negative thought statements such as, "I'll die if I go there" or "I can't do it." They learn to replace such thoughts with positive coping statements such as "Of course, I can do it." (We will have more to say about cognitive-behavior therapy in Chapter 16.) In general, phobia treatment programs that are based on learning principles are widely available and effective.

Of course, not every form of treatment is appropriate for every patient or client. Some phobia programs offer psychotherapy, behavior therapy, and medications. And sometimes a combination of these treatments is necessary. Because phobias are so widespread, you likely know someone who suffers from one. Effective treatment is available. Encourage the person to seek help.

Stimulus Generalization and Stimulus Discrimination

Stimulus generalization and *stimulus discrimination* occur in operant conditioning much as they do in classical conditioning. The difference is that in operant conditioning the reinforcement is delivered only after the animal correctly discriminates between the stimuli. For example, suppose an animal in a laboratory is shown either a vertical or a horizontal line and is given two keys to press—one if the line is vertical, the other if the line is horizontal. The animal gets rewards for correct responses. The animal will usually make errors at first; but after repeated presentations of the vertical and horizontal lines, with reinforcements given only for correct responses, the animal will learn to discriminate between stimuli. Stimulus discrimination can also be established with colors, tones, and more complex stimuli.

The processes of stimulus generalization and discrimination are evident daily. Children often make mistakes by overgeneralizing. For example, a baby who knows that cats have four legs and a tail may call all four-legged animals "cat." With experience and with guidance and reinforcement from parents, the child will learn to discriminate between dogs and cats, based on body size, shape, fur, and sounds. Similarly, once you may have been unaware of distinctions among various impressionist artists, but after several viewings, you may have learned to recognize the works of Renoir, Monet, and Pissarro.

Many practitioners feel that irrational fears develop because of generalizations that people make from one area of life to another. Some people with phobias develop them after first suffering from spontaneous panic attacks—feelings of intense, overwhelming terror accompanied by symptoms such as sweating, shortness of breath, or faintness. These attacks seem to occur randomly and without warning, making it impossible for a person to predict what situation will trigger such a reaction. They then generalize from the previous circumstance (that was associated with panic) to other similar situations.

Extinction and Spontaneous Recovery

In operant conditioning, if a reinforcer or punisher is no longer delivered—that is, if a consequence does not follow an instrumentally conditioned behavior—the behavior either will not become well established or, if it is already established, will undergo extinction (see Figure 7.12). **Extinction**, in operant conditioning, is the process by which the probability of an organism's emitting a response is reduced when reinforcement no longer follows the response. One way to measure the extent

FIGURE 7.12

The Process of Extinction

When an organism's behavior is no longer reinforced, the likelihood that the organism will continue to respond decreases; psychologists say that the behavior has undergone extinction. Extinction is seen with both animals and human beings. In one study, C. D. Williams found that a child was throwing tantrums at bedtime to get attention. Williams instructed the parents to pay no attention to the tantrums. After several days, the number of minutes the child cried decreased to zero. A week later, an aunt put the child to bed; when the child made a fuss (spontaneous recovery), the aunt reinforced the child with attention. The parents then had to initiate a second extinction process. (Williams, 1959)

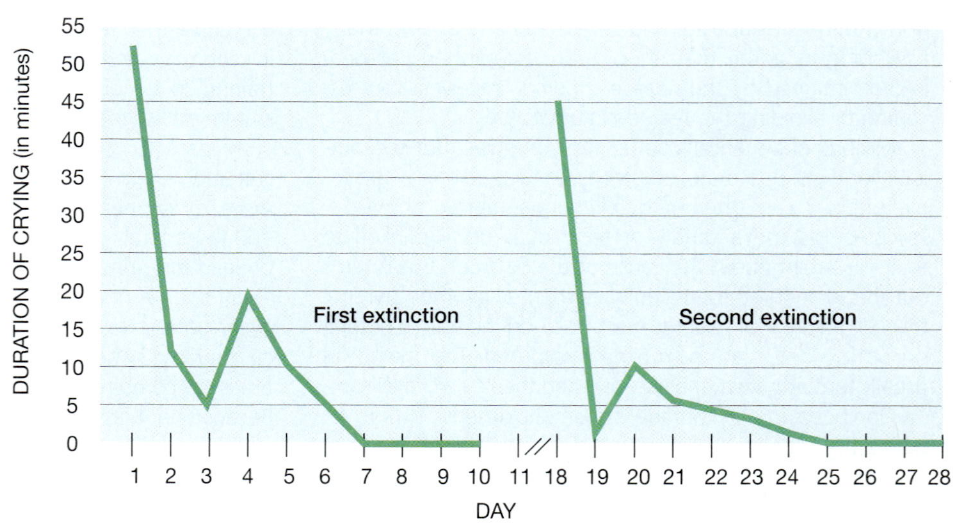

of conditioning is to measure how resistant a response is to extinction. *Resistance to extinction* is a measure of how long it takes, or how many trials are necessary, before extinction occurs. Suppose, for example, that a pigeon is trained to peck a key whenever it hears a high-pitched tone. Pecking in response to the high-pitched tone brings reinforcement, but pecking in response to a low-pitched tone does not. If the reinforcement process ceases entirely, the pigeon will eventually stop pecking the key. If the pigeon has been on a variable-ratio schedule and thus expects to work for long periods before reinforcement occurs, it will probably keep pecking for a very long time before stopping. If it has been on a fixed-interval schedule and thus expects reinforcement within a short time, it will stop pecking after just a few unreinforced trials.

People also show extinction; many parents know that when they stop reinforcing a child's misbehaviors with lots of attention (even if that attention consists of scolding), the misbehaviors often decrease. Note that the decrease in response is not always immediately apparent, however. When a reinforcer is withheld, organisms sometimes work harder—showing an initial increase in performance. In such cases, the curve depicting the extinction process shows a small initial increase in performance, followed by a decrease.

As in classical conditioning, *spontaneous recovery* also occurs in operant conditioning. If an organism's conditioned response has undergone extinction and the organism is given a rest period and then retested, the organism will show spontaneous recovery of the response. If the organism is put through this sequence several times, its overall response rate in each session will decrease. After one rest period, the organism's rate will almost equal what it was when the conditioned response was reinforced. However, after a dozen or so rest periods (with no reinforcements), the organism may make only one or two responses; the level of spontaneous recovery will have decreased markedly. Eventually, the response will disappear completely.

People also show spontaneous recovery. When you answer a question in class, reinforcement or punishment often follows: the instructor may praise you for your intelligence or grill you about your lack of understanding. However, if the instructor stops reinforcing correct answers or does not call on you when you raise your hand, you will probably stop responding (your behavior will be extinguished). After a vacation, you may start raising your hand again (spontaneous recovery), but you will quickly stop if your behavior remains unreinforced. Instructors learn early in their careers that if they want to have lively classes, they need to reinforce not just correct answers but also attempts at correct answers. In doing so, they help shape their students' behavior.

Table 7.3 on the following page summarizes four important concepts in operant conditioning: extinction, spontaneous recovery, stimulus generalization, and stimulus discrimination.

Operant Conditioning in Daily Life

Our world is full of reinforcers and punishers. We can work for rewards such as money. We can volunteer our time for worthy causes such as the Red Cross, homeless shelters, and AIDS research. Of course, sometimes people feel that they are helpless in the face of the punishers. The costs of living keep rising; random violence seems to increase; the environment is in serious trouble. But, by and large, most of us feel in control of our reinforcers and punishers. We know that many rewards and punishments are contingent on our behaviors. Each of us, to various extents, experiences operant conditioning in daily life.

Extinction
In operant conditioning, the process by which the probability of an organism's emitting a response is reduced when reinforcement no longer follows the response.

■ **INTRINSICALLY MOTIVATED BEHAVIOR.** Psychologists have shown that reinforcement is effective in establishing and maintaining behavior. But some behaviors are intrinsically rewarding—they are pleasurable in themselves. People are likely to

TABLE 7.3

Four Important Concepts in Operant Conditioning

Property	Definition	Example
Extinction	The process of reducing the probability of a conditioned response by withholding the reinforcer after the response	A rat trained to press a bar stops pressing when this behavior is no longer reinforced.
Spontaneous recovery	The recurrence of an extinguished conditioned response following a rest period	A rat's continued bar-pressing behavior has undergone extinction; after a rest period, the rat again presses the bar.
Stimulus generalization	The process by which an organism learns to respond to stimuli that are similar but not identical to the original conditioned stimulus	A cat presses a bar when presented with either an ellipse or a circle.
Stimulus discrimination	The process by which an organism learns to respond only to a specific reinforced stimulus	A pigeon presses a key only in response to red lights, not to blue or green ones.

repeat *intrinsically motivated behaviors* for their own sake; for example, they may work on craft projects for the feeling of satisfaction they bring. People are likely to perform *extrinsically motivated behaviors*, such as working for a paycheck, for the sake of the external reinforcement alone. Interestingly, if a person is offered reinforcement for an intrinsically motivated behavior, performance may actually decrease. Imagine, for example, that a man does charity work because it makes him feel good. Being paid could cause the man to lose interest in the work because it would no longer offer the intrinsic reinforcement of feelings of selflessness. A student pianist may lose her desire to practice if her teacher enters her in a competition; practice sessions become ordeals, and the student may wish to stop playing altogether. For every person and in every culture, reinforcers differ and are determined by a host of learning experiences. Chapter 11 considers this issue at greater length, especially the topic of the potential hidden costs of rewards.

■ **BEHAVIORAL SELF-REGULATION.** *Behavioral regulation theorists* assume that people and animals will choose, if possible, activities that seem optimal to them. Rats, for example, will spend their time eating, drinking, and running on a wheel—activities they find pleasurable. An experiment by Bernstein and Ebbesen (1978) showed that human beings readjust their activities in a systematic manner. The researchers paid participants to live in an isolated room 24 hours a day, 7 days a week, for several weeks. The room had all the usual amenities of a home—bed, tables, bathroom, books, cooking utensils, and so forth. The experimenters observed the participants through a one-way mirror and recorded their baseline activity—the frequency of their specific behaviors when no restrictions were placed on them. The researchers found, for example, that one participant spent nearly twice as much time knitting as studying. The experimenters used the participant's baseline activity to determine the reinforcer—in this case, knitting.

The experimenters then imposed a contingency. In the case of the participant who liked to knit, for example, they insisted that she study for a specific amount of time before she could knit. If she studied only as much as she did before, she would be able to

■ *Weight Watchers, an organization that emphasizes behavioral self-regulation, helps its members control their weight by encouraging them to analyze and amend their own eating habits.*

Building Table 7.2

Types of Learning: Classical Conditioning and Operant Conditioning

Type of Learning	Procedure	Result	Example
Classical conditioning	A neutral stimulus (such as a bell) is paired with an unconditioned stimulus (such as food).	The neutral stimulus becomes a conditioned stimulus—it elicits the conditioned response.	A bell elicits a response from a dog.
Operant conditioning	A behavior is followed by a consequence—either reinforcement or punishment.	The behavior increases or decreases in frequency.	A rat will press a bar 120 times per hour to achieve a reward or to avoid punishment.

knit for much less time. As a consequence, the woman altered her behavior so that she could ultimately spend more time knitting. She began to study for longer periods of time—eventually more than doubling the time she spent studying.

Other techniques of behavioral self-regulation are derived from the basic learning principles of reinforcement. According to Wing and her colleagues (Jeffery et al., 2000; Tate, Wing, & Winett, 2001; Wing & Jeffery, 1999), if individuals with medical conditions that require daily attention are to regulate themselves, they must observe, evaluate, and then reinforce their own behaviors. The researchers assert that when people *self-observe* the target behavior, they are better able to *self-evaluate* their progress. After evaluating their progress, it is crucial that they receive *reinforcement* for adhering to their medical regimen—perhaps by going out to a concert with a friend or buying themselves a present. When these procedures are followed, adherence to the medical regimen improves.

Behavioral self-regulation has other practical applications. It is effective within classrooms (Winsler et al., 2000) and in other social situations where it can modulate disruptive behavior (Cavalier, Ferretti, & Hodges, 1997). Members of the diet program Weight Watchers may be told to keep track of when and what they eat, when they have the urge to eat, and what feelings or events precede those urges. The program's organizers seek to help people identify the events that lead to eating so that they can control it. The aim is to help people think clearly, regulate themselves, and thus manage their lives better. This decision process and the focus on thinking are clearly seen in studies of cognitive learning, considered next.

Building Table 7.2 summarizes key points of comparison between classical and operant conditioning.

Be an *Active* learner

REVIEW

- What are the most effective reinforcement schedules? pp. 243–245
- How can researchers measure extinction to show whether learning exists? pp. 246–247

THINK CRITICALLY

- Would you agree or disagree with the view that all intrinsically motivated behaviors must at some point have been reinforced? Why?
- Why is record in baseline activity important in research?

APPLY PSYCHOLOGY

- Physiologically, are there ways in which a person might facilitate learning and consolidation? Explain your answer.

The Biology That Underpins Learning

This chapter is about learning and experiences in the environment that shape behavior, yet it is impossible to consider learning without recognizing the complex interplay of a person's biological heritage with their day-to-day experiences, the role of evolution, and how learning is coded.

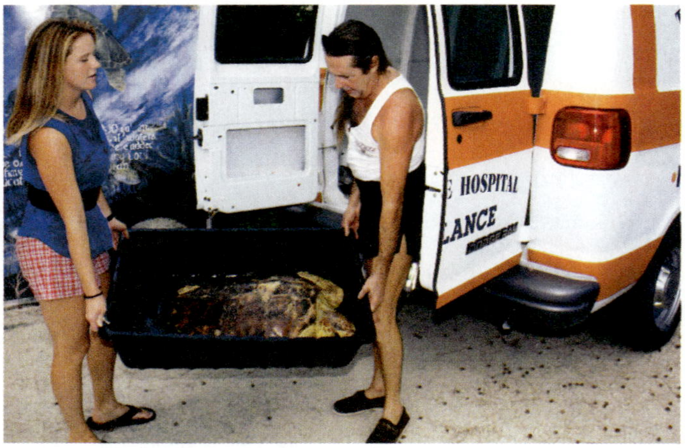

■ *These wildlife rehabilitators are transporting an injured turtle to an animal hospital, with the hopes of ultimately releasing it back into the wild.*

Nature and Nurture

Our *nature* consists of our inherited characteristics determined by genetics; our *nurture* refers to our experiences in the environment. We established in Chapters 1 and 2 that there is a complex interplay of nature and nurture and they are complementary, not antagonistic, processes (Cacioppo et al., 2000). Through day-to-day experiences people choose and mold their own environments. But animals are different; their environment may change or even be lost to them because of human activity such as residential or industrial development. This can lead to controversy. What do you do with displaced wild animals? Animal lovers who deal with such issues focus on wildlife rehabilitation. Wildlife rehabilitation involves caring for injured, ill, orphaned, and displaced wild animals with the goal of releasing them into their natural habitat. A rehabilitator strives to maintain all animals in a wild condition and release them as soon as appropriate. But does caring for wild animals, away from their natural habitats, make them less afraid of humans and thus less animal-like? Is the learning that develops through this nurture appropriate for wild animals?

It can be difficult to discern which behaviors derive from nature and which from nurture. For example, cheetahs must quickly devour their kill, unless they want to share it with lions and hyenas—is this behavior learned or innate? This research question has yet to be fully answered, but it may hold the key to aid us to understand human evolution and learning.

Are Evolutionary Theory and Learning Theory Incompatible?

At first blush it might seem that evolutionary theory, with its emphasis on evolved psychological mechanisms, focuses on built-in behavior patterns that have taken root in organisms over successive generations and have become part of the genome (see Chapters 1 and 2). Evolutionary theory is largely biological in focus and may seem to exclude consideration of the central concern of learning theory—changes that occur in an organism due to experiences in life. (Remember that we define *learning* as a relatively permanent change in an organism that occurs *as a result of experiences in the environment*.) Yet learning theory and evolutionary theory are more compatible than they might appear.

Evolutionary theory does not rule out learning, and evolution does not strictly determine behavior—in fact, genes and the genome do not code for any specific behavior (Petrinovich, 1997). Indeed, humans and other animals must be capable of learning or they would not be very adaptive. Genetically determined tendencies are modified by the environment, and so evolutionary theory recognizes differences in societies and distinct, even unique learning patterns in different cultures. Nevertheless, all human beings exhibit some characteristics everywhere in the world—for example, all human beings smile. That human beings learn and adapt is a key evolved psychological mechanism. This mechanism helps human beings survive and allows us to look toward the future, evaluate the past, and not feel hopelessly locked into a determined, rule-bound set of behaviors.

Evolutionary theory asserts that evolution is continuously setting the framework for human learning, and throughout life individuals adapt to their surroundings; some do so better than others. In the long run, those that adapt and learn the best will survive and reproduce. Thus learning and evolutionary theory are more compatible than many think.

Learning and the Nervous System

Whenever learning occurs, there is a relatively permanent change in behavior; and this change is reflected in the nervous system. Donald O. Hebb (1904–1985), a Canadian psychologist, was one of the first to suggest that, with each learning situation, the structure of the brain changes. He argued that certain groups of neurons act together, and their synaptic transmissions and general neural activity form a recurring pattern—he referred to such a group of coordinated neurons as a *reverberating circuit*. The more the circuit that represents a concept or experience is stimulated, the better that concept or experience will be remembered and the more the structure of the brain is altered.

Remember that learning is a process that occurs because of unique interactions among hundreds of thousands of neurons in the brain. Using this fact, Hebb (1949) suggested that stimulation of particular groups of neurons causes them to form specific patterns of neural activity. The evolution of a temporary neural circuit into a more permanent circuit is known as *consolidation*. According to Hebb, consolidation serves as the basis of learning and memory. If Hebb is correct, then when people first sense a new stimulus, only temporary changes in neurons take place; but repetition of the stimulus causes consolidation, and the temporary circuit becomes a permanent one.

Many psychologists today believe that the consolidation process provides the key to understanding learning—that individual differences in ability to learn (or remember) may be due to differing abilities to consolidate neural circuits (Gabriel & Talk, 2001; Nadel & Bohbot, 2001; Vianna et al., 2001). Confirmation of this notion comes from studies using electroconvulsive shock therapy (discussed in Chapter 15) to disrupt consolidation, which results in impaired learning and memory in both human beings and animals. Further support comes from studies showing that recent (less consolidated) memories are more susceptible to loss through amnesia than are older (more consolidated) memories (Craik, 2001; Parkin, 2001; Winocur, McDonald, & Moscovitch, 2001).

The consolidation process may even play a role in the brain's physiological development. Researchers have compared the brains of animals raised in enriched environments, where toys and other objects are available for the animals to play with and learn from, with the brains of animals raised in deprived environments. The brains of animals raised in rich environments have more elaborate networks of nerve cells, with more dendrites and more synapses with other neurons (Greenough et al., 1999). This means that stimulating a neuron over and over again may cause it to branch out and become more easily accessible to additional synaptic connections. These findings may indicate that when key neurons are stimulated, the events that cause the stimulation may be better remembered and more easily accessed—this may be part of the reason why practice makes perfect (McGaugh, 1999; O'Mara, Commins, & Anderson, 2000). Although there has been less work done with human beings in this area, Jacobs and his colleagues (1993) found that people with more education have more dendritic elaboration; and Scheibel's research team (1990) found that parts of the body that are used more (fingers versus the wall of the chest) have more elaborate dendritic organization in the brain.

If a neuron is stimulated and fires, the biochemical processes involved make it more likely to respond again later; further, its number of dendrites increases because of previous stimulation (Baudry, 1998; Beaulieu & Colonnier, 1989). Synaptic plasticity allows associations to be learned (Moser et al., 1998; Tracy et al., 1998); repetition, as in repeated pairings of a conditioned and unconditioned stimulus in classical

Be an *Active* learner

REVIEW

- Does evolutionary theory rule out learning as a process? pp. 250–251
- What is a Hebbian reverberating circuit? p. 251

THINK CRITICALLY

- How might the consolidation process make learning possible?
- Why is synaptic plasticity in learning so important?

APPLY PSYCHOLOGY

- The effort to map the human genome may have key findings for learning theory. What could be done with this new knowledge? In what ways might we rethink how we go about teaching school children based upon such knowledge?

conditioning, may make learning and remembering easier (Kandel & Abel, 1995)—a conception that fits perfectly with Hebb's original suggestions.

Not only does a single neuron have many synaptic sites on its dendrites, but also it can be active in more than one network of functions. Some neurons may be involved in more activities and exert a stronger influence than others—for example, those neurons involved in behaviors in which visual and motor activities interact may become especially elaborate. Alkon (1989) showed that there is extensive interaction between a neuron's synaptic sites and those of other neurons. He argued that the spread of electrical and chemical activity from one site to another is critical for initiating learning and memory. He asserted that a given neuron can receive and store a huge number of different incoming signals. More recently, Alkon has been developing mathematical and computer models to simulate neuronal encoding for memory. This exciting work also extends Hebb's ideas.

Also in its infancy, but very promising, is the finding that specific genes are necessary for the formation of learning and memory. One research team has isolated a gene, dubbed the *CREB gene*, which is crucial in the consolidation process. Without this gene, certain proteins are not activated and memories are fleeting (Bourtchuladze et al., 1994; Duman et al., 2000; Impey, 1999). The genetic causes of memory and memory loss are yet to be fully understood; the presence of the CREB gene is only one link in the complex chain of events from experience to recall, but it seems to be an essential one.

student voices

Tina Malsbender
Century College

Our teacher talked about the experiment where you blow into an infant's eyes after you ring a bell, and after a while the infant would learn to close his eyes every time the bell was rung, even if you didn't blow anymore. I experimented with my host family's baby. Then their 3-year old started begging, "Do it to me!" so I ended up blowing into his eyes for 5 minutes—and was too exhausted to continue my experiment.

Cognitive Learning

"Enough!" Patrick shouted, after 4 grueling hours of trying to write a program for his personal computer. The program was full of bugs, all resulting from the same basic problem—but he didn't know what the problem was. After dozens of trial-and-error manipulations, Patrick turned off the computer and went off to study for his history exam. Then, while staring at a page in the text, he noticed a phrase set off by commas—and suddenly he realized his programming mistake. He had mistakenly put commas in his program's if–then statements. It was correct English, but incorrect computer syntax.

Patrick solved his problem by thinking. His discovery was not a matter of simple conditioning of a simple response with a simple reinforcer. As you've seen, learning researchers have actively focused on learning that involves reinforcement. Studies by Pavlov, Thorndike, and Skinner revealed that conditioning processes require a reinforcer for behavior to be maintained. Much of the learning literature has focused on stimuli and responses and their relationship, timing, and frequency. But is a reinforcer always necessary for learning? Can a person learn new behaviors as a result of thinking or using the imagination? Are there gender differences (see *Point/Counterpoint*)? These questions are problematic for traditional learning researchers—but not for cognitive psychologists or learning researchers with a cognitive emphasis.

Thinking about a problem allows you to solve the problem and makes other behaviors possible; thus, thinking and imagination become crucial to learning and problem solving (Skinner, 1989). The importance of thinking—the focus of cognitive research—is evident even in early learning studies and will be demonstrated over and over again as we examine areas of psychology such as motivation, maladjustment, and therapy. Some of the most famous psychologists of the early 20th century examined learning when reinforcement was not evident and behavior was not observable. These early studies focused on insight and latent learning, and some of them led to modern studies of cognitive mapping. Recent research has focused on generative learning and observational learning, as well as problem solving, creativity, and concept formation (which we will cover in Chapter 9). All of this work indicates that there are many different aspects to what is learned and how learning takes place.

point_counterpoint_

Men and Women–Differences in Learning

The Issue: Do men and women learn differently?

POINT
There is no evidence that men and women learn differently.

COUNTERPOINT
Men and women have different cognitive styles, which lead them to learn differently.

Although many people believe that men and women think in very different ways, psychologists have been able to find little evidence that learning varies by gender. Psychologists have found small differences in abilities—girls and women have advantages on some verbal tasks, and men and boys have the advantage on some spatial tasks (Halpern, 1997). These differences in abilities can be manifested as differences in interests, such as course choices, college majors, and careers, but abilities are not the same as the process of learning.

Psychologists have been assessing cognitive learning styles for decades; in doing so, they have found that males and females are taught to learn differently. Boys and girls are taught different behavior on the playground, at home, and in the classroom—and these behaviors influence the way they learn. In general, boys are taught to win, whereas girls are encouraged to enjoy the game and the process of playing and are taught to get along, communicate, and cooperate (Kohn, 1993). As a consequence, girls and women tend to feel more comfortable in cooperative learning situations, whereas boys and men tend to prefer a classroom hierarchy with a leader who is in charge. Some research has supported these gender differences (Galotti et al., 1999; Knight, Elfenbein, & Martin, 1997), but other research (Severiens & Ten Dam, 1997) suggests that gender role rather than gender is the factor related to these preferences. The notion that men's and women's learning styles differ led to the creation of same-sex classes, with the argument that each sex needs to use its own style for most effective learning.

At George Washington University's Mount Vernon campus, women are taking classes called "Women in Power" and "Women in Business," as well as traditional literature and math classes in which the students are all women.

Some educators argue that female students work better in groups, in cooperative efforts that stimulate connections among their ideas and emphasize critical thinking (Gillies & Ashman, 1996). Critical thinking, which focuses on integrating ideas rather than memorizing information, is at the core of such efforts. Same-sex settings appear to be better for women when it comes to problem solving (Inzlicht & Ben-Zeev, 2000).

Research on the role of learning styles confirms some differences between men and women—although there are still more differences among women and among men than between men and women. Gender differences in learning styles tend to be small, to be focused on a narrow range of abilities, and to emerge primarily when special types of processing are encouraged by test developers, teachers, or employers (Meyers-Levy & Maheswaran, 1991). Men's and women's preferences for different learning styles do not mean that each is incapable of either; in fact, men and women are almost identical in their ability to learn (Galotti et al., 1999).

Insight

When you discover a relationship among a series of events, you may say that you have had an *insight*. Insights are usually not taught but rather are discovered. Like Patrick's discovery of his extra commas, many learning experiences involve both sustained thought and insight.

Discovering the sources of insight was the goal of researchers working with animals during World War I. Wolfgang Köhler, a Gestalt researcher, showed that chimpanzees were capable of achieving insights about how to retrieve food that was beyond their reach. The chimps discovered that they could pile up boxes or make a long stick out of several shorter ones. They were never reinforced for these specific behaviors; insight showed them how to get the food. Insight results from thought, without direct reinforcement. Once a chimp learns how to pile boxes, or once Patrick realizes his comma error, the insight is not forgotten, and no further instruction or training is necessary. The role of insight is often overlooked in studies of learning; however, it is an essential element in problem solving (discussed in Chapter 9).

Latent Learning

After a person has an insight, learns a task, or solves a problem, the new learning is not necessarily evident. Researchers in the 1920s placed hungry rats in a maze and recorded how many trials it took the rats to reach a particular spot, where food was hidden. It took many days and many trials, but the hungry rats learned the mazes well. Other hungry rats were put into the maze but were not reinforced with food on reaching the same spot; instead, they were merely removed from the maze. A third group of hungry rats, like the second group, were not reinforced at first but, after 10 days, were given food on reaching the goal. Surprisingly, after 1 day of receiving reinforcement, the rats in the third group were reaching the goal with few errors. During the first 10 days of maze running, they must have been learning something but not showing it. Receiving a reward gave them a reason to use what they had learned.

Researchers such as E. C. Tolman (1886–1959) argued that the rats were exhibiting **latent learning**—learning that occurs in the absence of direct reinforcement and that is not necessarily demonstrated through observable behavior. Tolman showed that when a rat is given a reason (such as food) to show learning, the behavior will become evident. In other words, a rat—or a person—that is given no motivation to do so may not demonstrate learned behavior even if learning has occurred. Tolman's work with rats led him to propose the idea that animals and human beings develop (or *generate*) a kind of mental map of their world, which allows them to navigate a maze or city streets. Tolman's idea of latent learning was especially significant because the definition of learning at that time was strictly behavioral—observable behavior was an essential part of the definition. Tolman laid the foundation for later studies of latent learning (e.g., Prados, Chamizo, & Mackintosh, 1999) and of generative learning, learning to learn, and cognitive maps. We will consider each in turn.

Generative Learning

Modern cognitive psychology is changing the way in which educational psychologists think about classroom learning. According to most cognitive psychologists, in addition to organizing new information in neural structures resembling maps, each individual gives a unique meaning to information being learned. The individual uses his or her existing cognitive maps to interpret the new information. Cognitive psychologists thus see learning as a *generative process*—that is, the learner generates (constructs) meaning by building relationships between familiar and unfamiliar events (Wittrock, 2000). According to the *generative learning model*, when people are exposed to new information or experiences, their perception is affected by their existing knowledge or previous experiences. They then generate meaning about (or interpret) the new information or experiences in ways that are consistent with their prior learning. In other words, they access existing ideas and link new ideas and experiences to them. As a result, their brain structures are modified. These modifications are encoded in memory and can be accessed later to interpret additional new information. Generative learning is thus seen as a constructive process—a process of constantly remodeling and building on existing knowledge.

Latent learning
Learning that occurs in the absence of direct reinforcement and that is not necessarily demonstrated through observable behavior.

According to the generative learning model, classroom learning is not so much a matter of engaging in activities and receiving external reinforcement from the teacher or even of receiving knowledge that is transferred from the teacher to the learner. Rather, it is the result of an active process in which the learner plays a critical role in generating meaning. No one else can build relationships between what the learner already knows and what he or she is currently learning. As a result, what each person actually learns is unique to that person.

Learning to Learn and Cooperative Learning

Most college seniors believe they are much better students than they were when they started college. What makes the difference? How do students learn to learn better? Today, educators and cognitive researchers are focusing on *how* information is learned, as opposed to *what* is learned.

Human beings learn how to learn; they learn specific strategies for particular topics, and they devise general rules that depend on their goals. The techniques for learning how to fish are different from those for learning a foreign language or those for learning mathematics. Researchers argue that lack of effective learning strategies is a major cause of low achievement by university students (Lin, McKeachie, & Naveh-Benjamin 1999; McKeachie, 1999). They suggest that students can benefit from using certain general cognitive techniques:

- *Elaboration.* Translating concepts into one's own language and trying actively to relate new ideas to old ones
- *Attention.* Focusing one's concentrative abilities and staying on task
- *Organization.* Developing skills that allow one to perform the tasks of learning and concept formation in an orderly manner
- *Scheduling.* Developing routine times for studying (this turns out to be a key element of both organization and managing anxiety)
- *Managing anxiety.* Learning to focus anxiety on getting a task done, rather than becoming paralyzed with fear
- *Expecting success.* Developing an expectation of success rather than failure
- *Note taking.* Acquiring the skills necessary to take notes that will be a worthwhile learning tool
- *Learning in groups.* Developing cooperative learning styles that make the most of interactions with other students

Making students aware of the processes used in learning and remembering is vitally important. This awareness (thinking about thinking and learning about learning) is called *metacognition.* When students think about their own learning, they do better; when they act strategically to modify their own strategies, they learn more (Wynn-Dancy & Gillam, 1997) and are able to do better across a curriculum (Perkins & Grotzer, 1997). Different subjects require different learning strategies. Students can better grasp history, chemistry, or economics if they understand *how* to go about studying each of these topics. After people learn *how* to learn, the differences become obvious; indeed, some researchers think of creativity as a metacognitive process involving thinking about one's own thoughts (Pesut, 1990).

Individual learning can also be enhanced through techniques that involve cooperative learning. In the past, many American teachers attempted to motivate students by having them compete against

Research shows that—no matter their age—many students learn more and have more fun when collaborating in a group, rather than learning individually.

one another. However, research shows that cooperative interactions among students—not just between students and teachers or between students and books—play a significant role in real learning. Cooperation helps students think about how they learn. There is no question that classroom learning has changed. No longer are students taken to task for helping one another with their work, because they are now expected to collaborate in the learning process—breaking down barriers between learner and teacher. Teachers who overlook student-to-student teaching may be failing their own courses (Kohn, 1993).

In fact, studies show that forming teams of students in which no one gets credit until everyone understands the material is far more effective than competitive or individualized learning. Whether the students are preschoolers or college age, studying English or physics, they have more fun, enjoy the subject matter more, and learn more when they work together (Karabenick & Collins, 1997). Students' achievements and attitudes are both improved through cooperative learning (Leikin & Zaslavsky, 1997; Whicker, Bol, & Nunnery, 1997). Another approach to improving learning skills is described in the *Psychology in Action.*

Cognitive Maps

Some people are easily disoriented when visiting a new city; others seem to acquire an internal map quickly. These internal maps are sometimes called *cognitive maps*—mental representations that enable people to navigate from a starting point to an unseen destination. How are these cognitive maps learned? Travel routes can be learned through simple associations: this street leads to that street, that street runs past the pizza parlor, and then you go left. But researcher Gary Allen (2000a) asserts that learning routes is not just rote memorization of turns and signs, but involves perceptual and cognitive factors. He devised a series of studies to demonstrate this (Allen, Kirasic, & Spilich, 1997; Allen & Willenborg, 1998). Slides taken during an actual walk through an urban neighborhood were shown in sequential order to a group of research participants; the same slides were shown in random order to a second group. All participants were then asked to make judgments about the distance from the beginning of the walk to a variety of specific locations. Amazingly, the participants who viewed the random presentation made judgments that were almost as good as those of the participants who saw the slides in the correct sequence. How did they do it?

Allen contended that the participants formed a cognitive map by using visual information that overlapped from slide to slide to piece together a map of the neighborhood. (Without the overlap among the scenes, the pictures would have appeared to have shown different neighborhoods.) The participants tried to place the randomly ordered slides in sequence mentally by paying attention to particular parts of the visual world shown in previous slides. They attempted to impose order on a collage of perceptual information.

Allen's research showed that in determining routes, human beings pay attention to the landmarks they find most useful. People learn the value of various types of landmarks during childhood. In one study, Allen and his colleagues discovered that young children do not realize the value of landmarks in the same way adults do. As they gain experience, children are more likely to notice landmarks that identify where choices need to be made. Allen made a strong case for perceptual and cognitive influences on the learning of routes. His research suggests that people learn routes by dividing them into segments and then integrating those segments, along with useful landmarks, into cognitive maps (Allen, 2000a); in many cases, those map-reading abilities are better for men than women (Allen, 2000b). Being active processors of information helps people form cognitive maps—which may be spatial or geographical but may also involve other types of information, such as the organizational structure of a company or the links and pages of a website. Thus, the study of cognitive maps may have broad implications for the study of thought.

psychology *in action*

Creating Fluid, Flexible Thinking

If you drive to school or work the same way every day, you probably use shortcuts that you think get you there sooner. People develop shortcuts in a whole array of behaviors, and some researchers (as we will see in Chapter 13) believe that mental shortcuts help account for a limited view of learning. We can learn new routes to work, and new ways to view the world, if we take novel approaches to learning.

Some researchers and practitioners argue that people need to be more flexible in their approach to learning and not be mindless or passive. Ellen Langer has argued that even the classroom basics of reading, writing, and arithmetic need to be taught "mindfully." Langer (1997, 2001) argues that essential information must be placed in a context and used in novel and important ways in order for learners to make the most of it. Mathematics, for example, can be shown to be important in music, logic, and writing. She has taken on the educational community in arguing that students must take an active role in learning to become aware adults (Langer & Moldoveanu, 2000). She has identified seven myths that stunt people's intellectual and learning growth and keep them trapped in tight categorical thinking:

1. *The basics should become second nature.* She argues that people "overlearn" basic information and skills so much that they don't really think about key ideas.
2. *Paying attention means staying focused.* Langer contends that noticing new, diverting ideas and events is important to help a learner place information in multiple contexts.
3. *Delaying gratification is important.* Educators often take the fun out of learning by saying students should learn now and have fun later. Rather, according to Langer, learning is fun, and it should be encouraged as fun.
4. *Rote memorization is necessary.* Memorized material is often not retained. When students critically analyze and think about information—rather than merely memorizing—they learn it better and remember it.
5. *Forgetting is a problem.* Sometimes forgetting information can free you to learn new, more important, or more relevant information. Drive the same route every day, so to speak, and you won't consider other alternatives.
6. *Intelligence is knowing skills and information.* Intelligence, for Langer, is thinking flexibly and looking at the world from many perspectives.
7. *There are right and wrong answers.* From Langer's view, what is correct is context-dependent. Is there a correct way to drive to school? It depends on what your goals are—getting there quickly, a scenic drive, the fewest turns? Is capitalism the correct way to run an economic system? If you are a Westerner, you will view capitalism differently than if you live in a more socialist country.

The truth is that people do need to learn the basics and to memorize some key pieces of information, but how they learn and what they do with the basics is what Ellen Langer is concerned about. Langer would say, for example, that everyone needs to know how to read, but students need to think about what they are reading. Teachers can help children develop thinking skills by asking them questions such as "Was this a good ending?" and "Do you think that if Hamlet had been a princess, rather than a prince, the story would have unfolded differently? Why?"

Langer worries that people may become trapped by categories and distinctions that are context-dependent and become oblivious to alternative aspects of the situations they encounter (Langer, 1992). Researchers and educators are reviewing Langer's ideas. Let's hope they'll be flexible enough to consider them.

The Theory of Observational Learning

A truly comprehensive learning theory of behavior must be able to explain how people learn behaviors that are not taught through reinforcement. For example, everyone knows that smoking cigarettes is unhealthy. Smokers regularly try to stop smoking, and most people find the first experience with smoking unpleasant. Nonetheless, 12-year-olds light up anyway. They inhale, cough for several minutes, and feel nauseated. There is no doubt that it is a punishing experience for them, but they try again. Over time, they master the technique of inhaling and, in their view, look "cool" smoking a cigarette. That's the key to the whole situation: the 12-year-olds observe other people with cigarettes, think they look cool, want to look cool themselves, and therefore imitate the smoking behavior.

Such situations present a problem for traditional learning theorists, whose theories give a central role to the concept of reinforcement. There is little reinforcement in establishing smoking behavior; instead, there is punishment (coughing and nausea).

Building Table 7.3

Types of Learning: Classical Conditioning, Operant Conditioning, and Observational Learning

Type of Learning	Procedure	Result	Example
Classical conditioning	A neutral stimulus (such as a bell) is paired with an unconditioned stimulus (such as food).	The neutral stimulus becomes a conditioned stimulus—it elicits the conditioned response.	A bell elicits a response from a dog.
Operant conditioning	A behavior is followed by a consequence—either reinforcement or punishment.	The behavior increases or decreases in frequency.	A rat will press a bar 120 times per hour to achieve a reward or to avoid punishment.
Observational learning	An observer attends to a model to learn a behavior.	The observer learns a sequence of behaviors and becomes able to perform them at will.	After watching TV violence, children are more likely to show aggressive behaviors.

Nonetheless, the behavior recurs. To explain this type of learning, Stanford University psychologist Albert Bandura has contended that the principles of classical and operant conditioning are only two of the many ways in which people learn.

During the past 30 years, Bandura's ideas, known as observational learning theory, or *social learning theory*, have expanded the range of behaviors that can be explained by learning theory (Woodward, 1982). **Observational learning theory** suggests that organisms learn new responses by observing the behavior of a model and then imitating it. This theory focuses on the role of thought in establishing and maintaining behavior. Bandura and his colleagues conducted important research to confirm their idea that people can learn by observing and then imitating the behavior of others (Bandura, 1969, 1977b; Bandura, Ross, & Ross, 1963). In their early studies, these researchers showed a group of children some films with aggressive content (an adult punched an inflated doll); they showed another group of children some films that had no aggressive content. They then compared the play behavior of both groups. The researchers found that the children who had viewed the aggressive films tended to be aggressive afterward, whereas the other children showed no change in behavior. Bandura's research and many subsequent studies have shown that observing aggression teaches children how to be aggressive. Children do not perform the aggressiveness they have learned when they also see the aggressive model being punished (Goldstein, 2001). Building Table 7.3 compares observational learning with the other two major types of learning discussed in this chapter: classical conditioning and operant conditioning.

Everyday experience also shows that people imitate the behavior of others, especially those whom they hold in high esteem. Parents regularly say to children, "Now watch me..." or "Yes, that's the right way to do it." They provide a seemingly endless string of situations for children to watch and copy, and then reinforce the children for imitation (Masia & Chase, 1997). Children emulate soldiers dressed in army fatigues, carry toy machine guns, and pretend to launch missiles. Countless young girls became interested in ice skating after watching 16-year-old Sarah Hughes steal the gold in the 2002 Winter Olympics in Salt Lake City. Unfortunately, not all observational learning is positive. Alcohol and other drug use often begins when children and teenagers imitate people they admire.

Observational learning theory
Theory that suggests that organisms learn new responses by observing the behavior of a model and then imitating it; also known as *social learning theory*.

Laboratory studies of observational learning show that people can learn new behaviors merely by observing them, without being reinforced. For example, in a study by Bernal and Berger (1976), participants watched a film of other participants being conditioned to produce an eye-blink response. The filmed participants had a puff of air delivered to their eyes; this stimulus was paired with a tone. After a number of trials, the filmed participants showed an eye-blink response to the tone alone. The participants who watched the film also developed an eye blink in response to a tone. Other studies show that people who stutter can decrease their stuttering by watching others decrease their stuttering (Martin & Haroldson, 1977). Even children who fear animals can learn to be less fearful by watching other children interact with animals (Bandura & Menlove, 1968).

A key point to remember is that if a person observes an action that is punished, the person will not imitate that action—at least not right away. Children who observe aggression that is punished do not immediately behave aggressively; nevertheless, they may learn aggressive responses and evince them in the future. Learning may take place through observation, but performance of specific learned behaviors may depend on a specific setting and a person's expectations about the effect of exhibiting the learned behaviors.

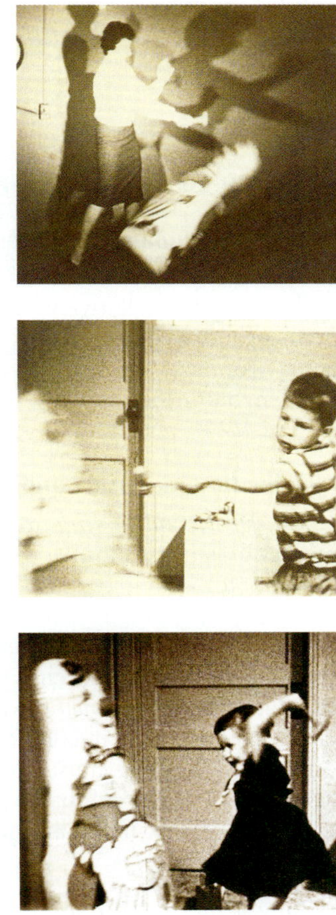

After watching an adult take aggressive action against a Bobo doll, children imitated the aggressive behavior.

KEY VARIABLES IN OBSERVATIONAL LEARNING. Whether a person learns a behavior depends on the extent to which he or she actually does it—a child who directly experiences smoking, for example, is far more likely to remember and copy the behavior than a child who merely hears about it or watches a film showing it. Direct experience will always be a far more potent way for a person to remember and learn. In real-world learning situations—classrooms, playgrounds, and homes—children and adults learn best when they are engaged in doing and observing. They are reinforced in some cases, observe and imitate in other cases, and sometimes change the way they are learning in midstream. Greeno (1989) maintains that all learning is active, takes place within a context, constantly changes, and depends on the active participation (whether undertaken consciously or unconsciously) of the learner.

Given that people can learn through many sources, psychologists know that the effectiveness and likelihood of learning are affected by certain key elements. One is the *type and power of the model* employed. Nurturing, warm, and caring models, for example, are more likely to engage and be imitated than indifferent, angry ones; authoritative parents are more likely to be imitated than passive ones. In a classroom, children are more likely to participate with and imitate peers whom they see as powerful and dominant.

Another element is the *learner's personality and degree of independence*. Dependent children are more likely to learn from and imitate models than are independent children. Generally, the less self-confidence a person has, the more likely the person is to imitate a model.

A third factor is the *situation*. People are more likely to imitate others when they are uncertain about correct behavior. A teenager going on a first date, for example, takes cues about dress from peers and imitates their behavior. A person who has never before been exposed to death and watches a family member or close friend die may not know what to say or how to express feelings. Watching other people express their grief provides a model for behavior. But not everyone learns well, and there are sharp differences in how people learn.

Be an *Active* learner

REVIEW

- According to observational learning theorists, why is reinforcement not crucial in the learning process? p. 254
- Who are the best types of models for a behavior that is to be learned through observational learning? pp. 258–259

THINK CRITICALLY

- Do you think learning in a history class or a biology laboratory is facilitated through active participation in activities? Explain your answer.

APPLY PSYCHOLOGY

- As a leader, how can a person be a better model for a company and its employees?
- Do you think collaboration is especially effective for younger or older students? Why?

Summary and Review

Pavlovian, or Classical, Conditioning Theory

Identify the fundamental difference between learning and reflexes.

■ *Learning* is a relatively permanent and stable change in an organism that occurs as a result of experiences in the environment. In contrast, *reflexes* are behaviors that occur involuntarily, quickly, and without prior learning. pp. 222–223

Describe how classical conditioning works.

■ *Classical conditioning* involves the pairing of a neutral stimulus (for example, a bell) with an *unconditioned stimulus* (for example, food) so that the *unconditioned response* (for example, salivation) becomes a *conditioned response*. In *higher-order conditioning*, a second neutral stimulus takes on reinforcing properties by being associated with the *conditioned stimulus*. For classical conditioning to occur, the unconditioned stimulus and the conditioned stimulus must usually be presented in rapid succession, and the conditioned stimulus must predict the occurrence of the unconditioned stimulus. pp. 223–227

KEY TERMS

learning, p. 222; conditioning, p. 223; reflex, p. 223; classical conditioning, p. 225; unconditioned stimulus, p. 225; unconditioned response, p. 225; conditioned stimulus, p. 225; conditioned response, p. 225; higher-order conditioning, p. 227

Key Variables in Classical Conditioning

What are the most important variables in classical conditioning?

■ The most important variables in classical conditioning are the strength, timing, and frequency of the unconditioned stimulus. p. 227–228

How may conditioned responses vary depending on the situation?

■ *Extinction* is the process of reducing the likelihood of a conditioned response by withholding the unconditioned stimulus (not pairing it with the conditioned response). *Spontaneous recovery* is the recurrence of an extinguished conditioned response, usually following a rest period, which shows that previously learned associations are not totally forgotten. pp. 228–229

■ *Stimulus generalization* is the process by which a conditioned response becomes associated with a stimulus similar to, but not the same as, the original conditioned stimulus. In contrast, *stimulus discrimination* is the process by which an organism learns to respond only to a specific stimulus and not to other stimuli. p. 230

What are the key findings in studies of conditioned taste aversion?

■ It takes only one pairing of a food or drink (the conditioned stimulus) with a nausea-inducing substance (the unconditioned stimulus) to make organisms avoid the food or drink that preceded the nausea—to develop a conditioned taste aversion. Taste aversion can be learned even if the nausea is induced several hours after the food or drink has been consumed; this is important because learning theorists had previously assumed that it was essential for the two events to occur close together in time. pp. 231–232

KEY TERMS

extinction, p. 228; spontaneous recovery, p. 228; stimulus generalization, p. 230; stimulus discrimination, p. 230

Operant Conditioning

What takes place in operant conditioning?

■ *Operant conditioning* is conditioning in which an increase or decrease in the probability that a behavior will recur is determined by whether the behavior is followed by a reward or a punishment. A key component of operant conditioning is reinforcement. *Shaping* is selectively reinforcing behavior that gradually approximates a desired behavior. pp. 234–236

How do reinforcement and punishment work?

■ A *reinforcer* is any event that increases the probability that the response that preceded it will recur. *Positive reinforcement* increases the probability that a desired response will occur by introducing a rewarding or pleasant stimulus. *Negative reinforcement* increases the probability that a desired behavior will occur by removing an aversive stimulus. p. 237

■ *Primary reinforcers* have survival value for the organism; their value does not have to be learned. *Secondary reinforcers* are neutral stimuli that initially have no intrinsic value for the organism but that become rewarding when they are paired with a primary reinforcer. p. 238

■ Punishment, unlike reinforcement, decreases the probability of a particular response. *Punishment* is the process of presenting an undesirable or noxious stimulus, or removing a positive, desirable stimulus, to decrease the probability that a preceding response will recur. p. 239

KEY TERMS

operant conditioning, p. 234; Skinner box, p. 235; shaping, p. 236; reinforcer, p. 236; positive reinforcement, p. 237; negative reinforcement, p. 237; primary reinforcer, p. 238; secondary reinforcer, p. 238; superstitious behavior, p. 238; punishment, p. 239; primary punisher, p. 240; secondary punisher, p. 240; learned helplessness, p. 242

Key Variables in Operant Conditioning

What are the most important variables affecting operant conditioning?

■ The most important variables affecting operant conditioning are the strength, timing, and frequency of consequences. Strong consequences delivered quickly yield high work rates. But consequences do not have to be continuous. Studies have shown that consequences, especially reinforcers, can be intermittent. *Fixed-interval* and *variable-interval schedules* provide reinforcement after fixed or variable time periods; *fixed-ratio* and *variable-ratio schedules* provide reinforcement after fixed or variable amounts of work. Variable-ratio schedules produce the highest work rates; fixed-interval schedules induce the lowest work rates. pp. 243–245

Distinguish between extrinsic and intrinsic motivation.

■ Psychologists have shown that reinforcement (extrinsic motivation) is effective in establishing and maintaining behavior. But some behaviors are intrinsically motivated; they are performed because they are pleasurable in themselves. Behavioral regulation theorists assume that organisms make choices, if possible, to engage in those activities that seem optimal to them. If they are prevented from performing a desired activity, they will readjust their activities. pp. 247–248

KEY TERMS

fixed-interval schedule, p. 243; variable-interval schedule, p. 243; fixed-ratio schedule, p. 244; variable-ratio schedule, p. 244; extinction, p. 244

The Biology That Underpins Learning

Are learning theory and evolution incompatible?

■ Evolutionary theory does not mean, nor demand, genetic determinism. Genetically determined tendencies are modified by learning and so evolutionary theory recognizes differences in societies and distinct, even unique learning patterns. p. 250

What is a reverberating circuit?

■ Hebb argued that certain groups of neurons act together, and their synaptic transmissions form a recurring pattern—he referred to such a group of coordinated neurons as a reverberating circuit. The evolution of a temporary neural circuit into a more permanent circuit is known as consolidation. pp. 251–252

Cognitive Learning

What is the focus of cognitive learning psychologists?

■ Cognitive learning psychologists focus on thinking processes and on thought that helps process, establish, and maintain learning. Some of the early studies focused on insight and latent learning. When you discover a relationship characterizing a series of events, psychologists say that you have had an insight. *Latent learning* is learning that occurs in the absence of any direct reinforcement and that is not necessarily demonstrated through observable behavior, though it has the potential of being exhibited. pp. 252–253

What fundamental assumptions do observational learning theorists make about the learning process?

■ *Observational learning theory* (also called social learning theory) suggests that organisms learn new responses by observing the behavior of a model and then imitating it. This theory has expanded the range of behaviors that can be explained by learning theorists and focuses on the role of thought in establishing and maintaining behavior. p. 258

■ Some key variables in observational learning are the type and power of the model, the learner's personality and degree of independence, and the situations in which the learning occurs. p. 259

KEY TERMS

latent learning, p. 254; observational learning theory, p. 258

8 Memory

Jonathan Green, *Colored Clothes,* 1996

What if one of your friends told you that he had been abducted by aliens? After you accepted that he was not kidding (and was completely sober), would you believe this story? What if he could tell you details about the experience and seemed frightened by it? Psychiatrist John Mack was in a similar situation: his patients told him stories of how they had been abducted by aliens and what had happened during these abductions. Rather than treat these patients for delusions, this Harvard professor of psychiatry came to the point where he believed them.

Mack wrote about the experiences of his patients in *Abduction: Human Encounters with Aliens* (1994). Mack's patients' reports of alien abductions are very similar to episodes of *The X-Files.* People report that they have been kidnapped and have encountered small, gray-skinned aliens who performed experiments on them. These memories do not always appear immediately after the experience but instead may come out weeks or months later and then only as part of their experience in therapy, often under hypnosis.

This situation raises a number of difficult questions concerning these *recovered memories.* Are these memories real recollections of events or imagined occurrences, possibly even created during hypnosis? What memory

chapter outline

processes do we use when we "remember" things that never happened? How different is this situation from what happens to you every day—at least in terms of memory distortion? How accurate are your memories, and how are they formed? How are you able to remember?

Chapter 7 pointed out that learning is a *relatively* permanent change in an organism that occurs as a result of experience and is often, but not always, expressed in overt behavior. Memory is the ability to recall past events, images, ideas, or previously learned information or skills; memory is also the storage system that allows a person to retain and retrieve previously learned information. **Memory** and learning are two ways of looking at the process of acquiring information, storing it, and using it. We call the acquisition part learning and the storage, and later access to learned information, memory.

Memory: The Brain as Information Processor

Memory is not some physical structure found in one corner of the brain, with some people having more and others having less of it. Rather, memory is an ability and a process, and it can be examined from many different perspectives. Information in memory must be obtained through interaction with the environment (nurture), but memory capacity is part of the biological equipment (nature). The memory process is an example of the interaction of nature and nurture.

Traditionally, psychologists have considered memory as a type of storage and have sought to understand its structure and limits. Early memory studies, at the beginning of the 20th century, focused on factors related to how quickly people learned and forgot lists of nonsense words. Physiological psychologists thought of the brain as a huge map with certain areas that code vision, others that code auditory events, and still others that code and store memories. Their research goal was to discover the spatial layout and associated functions of the brain. After World War II, research became more practical, focusing on variables such as how the organization of material affects retention. Today, research still focuses on understanding the complex processes of memory but also considers practical issues, including how people can code information and use memory aids, imagery, and other learning cues to retrieve information from memory more effectively. Researchers are also using brain imaging techniques to study the brain in the process of remembering and pinpointing the specific areas that become more active when people remember.

In this age of computers and information technology, it is not surprising that researchers have likened the brain to a computer—an information processor. This analogy has guided the study of memory since the 1960s and 1970s, when researchers began to recognize the brain's complex interconnections and information-processing abilities. The truth, of course, is that human brains are not computers; nor do they work exactly as computers do. In some ways they work better and in other ways not as well. They make mistakes, and they are influenced by biological, environmental, and interpersonal events. Nevertheless, enough similarities exist between human brains and computers for psychologists to discuss learning and memory in terms of information processing.

Psychologists use the term *information processing* to refer to organizing, interpreting, and responding to information coming from the environment. The information-

Memory
The ability to recall past events, images, ideas, or previously learned information or skills; the storage system that allows for retention and retrieval of previously learned information.

Encoding
The organizing of information so that the nervous system can process it.

processing approach typically focuses on the flow of information, beginning with the sensory systems, where information from the outside world originates. This approach describes and analyzes a sequence of stages for key memory processes, assuming that the stages and processes are separate, though related. Although psychologists once considered memory a step-by-step, linear process, they now recognize that many of these steps take place simultaneously, in parallel.

■ *Researchers have compared the brain to computers—both are information processing systems.*

Virtually every approach to understanding memory offered by researchers has proposed that memory involves three key processes. The names of these processes derive from information technology and will sound familiar to you if you know how computers work. The first process is *encoding;* the second is placement of information in some type of *storage,* either temporary or permanent; the third is making the information available through *retrieval.* We will use this three-process model to guide our exploration of memory. You will see that memory involves all three of these processes.

Encoding

I (LB) tell my students to think of memory as a filing cabinet, and how well that filing cabinet works depends on several factors. The filing cabinet can be very useful if you have a good system of organization so that when you file information away, you will know how to retrieve it. You need folders and a code for each folder that will allow you to find the folder in the cabinet. If you put information in a folder and file it away in the cabinet without labeling the folder, your filing cabinet will be a good way to get folders off your desk, but little more. Coding is critical.

The conversion of sensory stimuli into neural impulses is a type of coding, the first step of encoding and establishing a memory. *Encoding* means getting information into the system to be processed and converting it into a usable form. In terms of memory, **encoding** is the organizing of sensory information so that the nervous system can process it, much as a computer programmer devises code that a computer can understand. The sensory information can be of any type: visual, auditory, olfactory, and so on.

The role of *attention* is important for encoding (Brown & Craik, 2000). In general, *attention* refers to the process of directing mental effort to some features of the environment and not to others. People can focus their attention on one idea, one event, one person, or one memory task, or they can shift their attention among several tasks or events. Divided attention during encoding interferes with the process, and people who are forced to divide their attention during encoding tend to perform more poorly during retrieval; they experience a type of memory failure we can describe as encoding failure. Such failures are very common because many stimuli compete for a person's attention.

Take Home Tip *for the Active Learner*

Do you listen to your favorite radio station while studying? If you do—and you later find your test scores are not what you'd hoped—you could be suffering from encoding failures. Listening to music, watching TV, and participating in other such activities can divide your attention and make encoding less effective. Another study strategy that divides attention is switching from subject to subject. If you are studying for two big tests—one on Shakespeare's plays and one on precalculus, stick with Shakespeare until you feel confident you have learned the material. Then switch to precalc'.

Researchers also want to know about processes that occur once information enters memory, for example, how a person recalls information so as to make inferences. Even the monitoring of one's own awareness and memory, a process

FIGURE 8.1

For the Active Learner: Levels of Processing

If your last name begins with one of the letters A *through* K: Examine the following list of words, counting the number of letters with only curves (such as *C* and *S*) versus the number of letters with only straight lines (such as *K* and *N*). Do not count letters with a combination of curved and straight lines (such as *B* and *R*).

If your last name begins with one of the letters L *through* Z: Examine the following list of words, analyzing their meaning and trying to determine any possible relationships among them.

FINGERPRINTS
INVESTIGATION
SUSPECT
NEWSPAPER
MIDNIGHT
ATTORNEY
NEPHEW
MOTIVE
ARREST
INHERITANCE
KITCHEN

called *metacognition*, has become a focus of research. We encode various kinds of information in a range of ways and to different extents. The type and extent of encoding affect what we remember.

Levels of Processing

Does the human brain encode and process some information in a different way than it does other information? Do thinking processes depend on the different types of analysis? Researchers Fergus Craik and Robert Lockhart (1972) argued that the brain can encode and process stimuli (information) in different ways, to different extents, and at different levels. They called their theory the **levels-of-processing approach.** You can see how this works by examining the example in Figure 8.1. If you follow the first set of instructions to examine these words while looking for the letters with curves versus straight lines, you will focus on the shape of the letters, and you will analyze them in these sensory terms. If you follow the instructions to try to understand what property the words have in common, you will do a different type of analysis, which relates to the meaning and properties of the words. The second type of instructions makes you encode, analyze, and store the words at a deeper level. According to this view of encoding, how information is processed determines how it will be stored for later retrieval.

Cognitive psychologists began to equate the level of processing with the depth of analysis involved. When the level of processing becomes more complex, they theorized, the code goes deeper into memory. Thus, the memory for the lines and shapes of the letters may be fleeting and short-lived, the memory for the words themselves may last longer, and the memory for the underlying relationship among the words may last the longest. (If you followed the directions above, you can demonstrate one effect of this last type of processing for yourself, later in this chapter.)

Encoding is not a discrete step that happens all at once, before memory stores information. Rather, some levels of encoding happen quickly and easily, whereas other levels take longer and are more complex. You may continue to encode information while previously encoded information is being stored. According to Craik and Lockhart, encoding of various memory levels involves different operations, and various kinds of information are stored in different ways and for different durations.

The levels-of-processing approach generated an enormous amount of research. It explains why you retain some information, such as your family history, for long periods, whereas you quickly forget other information, such as the dry cleaner's phone number. It shows that when people are asked to encode information in only one way, they do not encode it in other ways. For example, when people are asked to encode words not for meaning, but only so that they can quickly repeat them (say, to remember a list of items to buy at the supermarket), they can later recall very few of them.

However, some researchers did not fully accept the levels-of-processing approach, which dealt primarily with establishing memories. These researchers suggested that recall differences originate from how memories are elaborated on, or made distinctive. For example, the link between encoding and the later process of retrieval is explained by the **encoding specificity principle,** which states that the effectiveness of a specific retrieval cue depends on how well it matches up with the originally encoded information. The more sharply your retrieval cues are defined and the more closely they are paired with memory stores, the better your recall will be and the less likely you will be to experience retrieval failures. For example, our students sometimes fail to recognize us when they meet us in the grocery store or at the movies, but they always

Take Home Tip *for the Active Learner*

Becoming an active learner can boost your memory. When you interact with new information in an active way, it becomes personally meaningful. Find ways to connect yourself, your knowledge, and your life experiences to the material you are encoding. By asking and answering your own questions and organizing information in ways that make sense to you, you encode it at a deeper level of processing. Once you are engaged in active learning, facts become more than facts—they become meaningful and stay with you. For example, reading is a fairly passive process, but highlighting important information makes the process more active and more personal. Thinking of personal examples of the principles from each section you read is another way to make abstract concepts more concrete and more personal.

recognize us on campus. On campus, we match the circumstances in which they know us, but off campus, we do not, which leads some of them to experience retrieval difficulties because of the type of encoding they have done (presuming, of course, that they are not intentionally avoiding us).

Derived from the encoding specificity principle is the idea of **transfer-appropriate processing,** which occurs when the initial processing of information is similar to the process of retrieval. When there is a close relationship between encoding and retrieval in terms of the form of the information (whether it is visual, auditory, or in some other form) and the processing required, retrieval improves. Researchers have given participants instructions to encode words either for sound or for meaning; when participants code for sound but then are asked to recall the meaning, they perform worse than when they are asked to code for sound and to recall sound (Franks et al., 2000; Morris, Bransford, & Franks, 1977; Rajaram, Srinivas, & Roediger, 1998).

The levels-of-processing research and its subsequent refinements and extensions shape the way cognitive researchers think about memory. These researchers argue that the way information is encoded relates to how it is stored, processed, and later recalled. They are aware that encoding processes are flexible; they are affected by both the cues provided and the demands of the retrieval tasks. The processes of encoding are also affected by preconceived biases people have; humans tend to notice and encode information that confirms beliefs they already hold—a tendency called *confirmation bias* (Jonas et al., 2001). This tendency to "see what you expect to see" is a powerful force in allowing people to retain inaccurate beliefs.

Take Home Tip *for the Active Learner*

When you study for a test, you should study in the same way you will be tested. If a test will be in essay format, study by writing essays rather than by underlining text. If a test will consist of geometry problem sets, study by doing problem sets rather than studying proofs or principles.

Levels-of-processing approach
Theory of memory that suggests that the brain processes and encodes stimuli (information) in different ways, to different extents, and at different levels.

Encoding specificity principle
Notion that the effectiveness of a specific retrieval cue depends on how well it matches up with the originally encoded information.

Transfer-appropriate processing
Initial processing of information that is similar in modality or type to the processing necessary in the retrieval task.

Neuroscience and Encoding

Memories are retained because they take some form in the brain. Researchers are exploring the neurobiological bases of memory, and recent developments in brain imaging have boosted this knowledge. Positron emission tomography (PET) and functional magnetic resonance imaging (fMRI) (described in Chapter 2) have allowed researchers to examine the brain during the process of encoding.

The frontal lobes constitute about one-third of the brain; the prefrontal lobes with their overlying cortex are the large areas on the left and right at the very front of the brain, behind the forehead. The drive to understand the roles of specific brain areas began years ago, but only recently have researchers identified specific memory functions of the prefrontal cortex. Endel Tulving and his colleagues showed that the left prefrontal cortex is used more in *encoding* of new information into memory, whereas the right prefrontal cortex is involved more in memory *retrieval* (Nyberg, Cabeza, & Tulving, 1996; Tulving et al., 1994). Research using PET and fMRI imaging shows that when participants engage in various tasks, left and right brain scans are quite different—that is, there is different blood flow in different portions of the prefrontal cortex (Courtney et al., 1998; Craik et al., 1999).

Researchers have long known that the temporal lobes of the cerebral cortex are related to memory (Squire & Kandel, 1999), and brain imaging studies have furnished more specific knowledge of how the temporal lobes interact with other brain structures. An fMRI study demonstrated that the posterior (back) part of the medial (middle) temporal lobes are activated during the encoding process, but a different partof the temporal lobes becomes active during retrieval (Gabrieli et al., 1997). This research provides neurological

Be an *Active* learner

REVIEW

- What are the key assumptions of the information-processing approach to memory? pp. 264–265
- What is the underlying assumption of the levels-of-processing approach? pp. 266–267

THINK CRITICALLY

- Much of the research on encoding as a factor in retrieval has been done on memory for verbal information. How might encoding as a factor in retrieval apply to memory for skills and motor performance?

APPLY PSYCHOLOGY

- What changes would you have to make in your study strategies to allow the encoding specificity principle to improve your studying?

FIGURE 8.2

Areas of the Brain Involved in Encoding

The prefrontal cortex and the temporal lobes are involved in the process of encoding.

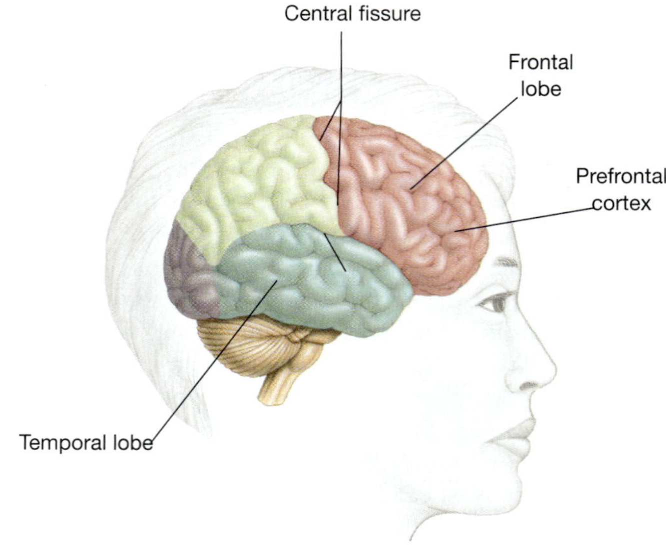

confirmation that encoding and retrieval are different processes with different underlying brain centers.

Researchers have also examined the pattern of brain activation during encoding by using PET imaging and also found that encoding activated the medial temporal lobe (Anderson et al., 2000). In addition, the left prefrontal cortex became active, but this activation was not the same for all participants—older adults showed some different brain activation, which may be related to their decreased encoding ability and memory problems.

Storage

To continue the analogy of memory as a filing cabinet, the storage capacity consists of the drawers of the cabinet. Once a folder is created and labeled, it is filed away in a drawer. If the drawer is open, the information is more readily accessible than if the drawer is closed. **Storage** is the process of maintaining or keeping information readily available; it also refers to the locations where information is held, which researchers call *memory stores.* The duration of storage may be a few seconds or many years, but if people have access to information they no longer sense, then memory is involved. For example, if you look up a telephone number, go to the telephone, and dial the number while no longer looking at it, then memory is involved, even if only for seconds.

Researchers have conceptualized a three-stage model for memory storage: (1) sensory memory, (2) short-term storage, and (3) long-term memory. *Sensory memory* is a very brief storage based on the sensory systems. When you hear a song, see a photograph, or touch a piece of silk, sensory memory starts. This very brief storage allows for attention and coding processes to begin. Our filing cabinet analogy has no equivalent of sensory memory. Information from sensory memory may pass into *short-term storage,* which is limited both in how long information can stay and how much information can fit. This storage is similar to a computer's random access memory (RAM), holding information for processing. Another similarity between your memory and your computer's RAM is fragility—information in short-term storage is easily lost, just as it is when the electricity goes off unexpectedly in your computer. Similarly, if you look up a telephone number but do not dial it immediately, you quickly lose that information. In a computer, information is stored for longer periods of time on the hard disk or on a floppy disk. In the brain, information is stored in *long-term memory,* from which a person can recall, retrieve, and reconstruct previous experiences.

Storage
Process of maintaining or keeping information readily available; also, the locations where information is held, or *memory stores.*

Sensory Memory

As George Sperling demonstrated in the early 1960s, **sensory memory**, sometimes called the *sensory register*, is the storage mechanism that performs initial encoding and provides brief storage of sensory stimuli. The brief image of a stimulus appears the way lightning does on a dark evening: the lightning flashes, and you retain a brief visual image of it. In his experiments, Sperling (1960) briefly presented research participants with a visual display consisting of three rows of letters, which they saw for only a fraction of a second. He asked the participants to recite the letters, and they typically responded by reciting 3 or 4 letters from the first row. This limit for their performance suggests that they record only 3 or 4 items in their sensory register. But when he cued them (with a tone that varied for each row), Sperling found that participants were able to recall three out of four letters from any of the rows. This result suggests that the sensory register records a complete picture. When Sperling delayed the cue signaling which row to report, recall decreased, which suggests that sensory memory fades very rapidly (see Figure 8.3). From Sperling's studies and others that followed, researchers concluded that we have a brief (250 milliseconds, or 0.25 second), rapidly fading sensory visual memory. Although some researchers have challenged the existence and physiological basis of sensory memory (Sakitt & Long, 1979), most researchers still see it as the first stage of encoding (Healy & McNamara, 1996).

■ *When lightning flashes, you retain a brief visual image of it in sensory memory.*

Sensory memory captures a visual, auditory, tactile, or chemical stimulus (such as an odor) in a form the brain can interpret. Consider the visual system. The initial coding usually contains information in the form of a picture. Sensory memory establishes the visual stimulus in the form of neural impulses and stores it for 0.25 second in an almost photographic manner. This visual sensory representation is sometimes called an *icon,* and the storage mechanism is called *iconic storage.* For the auditory system, the storage mechanism is called *echoic storage;* it holds an auditory representation for about 3 seconds.

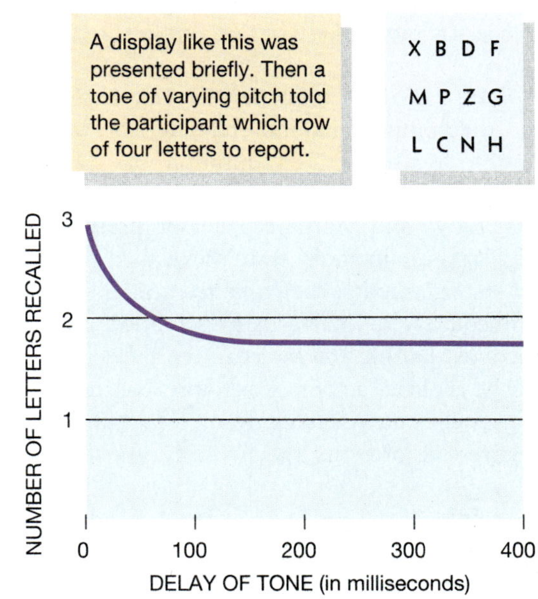

FIGURE 8.3

Sperling's Discovery of a Visual Sensory Memory

The graph plots participants' accuracy in reporting a specified row of letters. At best, participants recalled about three out of the four letters in a row. As the tone was delayed, the accuracy of recall decreased. But note that there were no further decreases in accuracy when the tone was delayed more than 200 milliseconds. *(Based on data from Sperling, 1960, p. 11.)*

Sensory memory lasts very briefly. Once information is established there, it must be transferred elsewhere for additional encoding and storage, or it will be lost. For example, when you locate a phone number on a rapidly scrolling computer screen, the number is established in your visual sensory memory (iconic storage); but unless you quickly transfer it to short-term storage by repeating it over and over to yourself, writing it down, or associating it with something else in your memory, you will forget it. Building Table 8.1 on the following page summarizes key processes in sensory memory.

Sensory memory
Mechanism that performs initial encoding and brief storage of sensory stimuli; also known as the *sensory register.*

Building Table 8.1

Key Processes in Sensory Memory

Stage	Encoding	Storage	Retrieval	Duration	Forgetting
Sensory memory	Visual or auditory (iconic or echoic storage)	Brief, fragile, and temporary	Information is extracted from stimulus presentation and transferred to short-term storage.	Visual: 250 milliseconds; auditory: about 3 seconds	Rapid decay of information; interference is possible if a new stimulus is presented.

Short-Term Storage

Once captured in sensory memory, stimuli either fade or are transferred to a second stage—short-term storage. Initially, researchers spoke of *short-term memory,* to emphasize its brief duration. After extensive research, however, the nature of short-term storage became clearer, and researchers began to recognize its active nature, giving it the term *working memory.* Both terms apply to the brief, fragile storage that occurs between sensory memory and long-term memory, but people who use the term *short-term memory* have a slightly different conceptualization of that storage from those who use the term *working memory* (Baddeley, 2000; Kail & Hall, 2001). We use the term *short-term storage* as a general term to refer to this type of brief memory; we use the terms *short-term memory* and *working memory* to refer to research on those specific topics. In the filing cabinet analogy, short-term storage would be equivalent to the information on the desk, before it went into the cabinet. When you are working with the information, creating the folder, and deciding what to use as a label, that process is more like what occurs in short-term storage than is the filing cabinet.

Memory span
The number of items that a person can reproduce from short-term memory, usually consisting of one or two chunks.

Chunks
Manageable and meaningful units of information organized in such a way that they can be easily encoded, stored, and retrieved.

Rehearsal
Process of repeatedly verbalizing, thinking about, or otherwise acting on or transforming information in order to keep that information active in memory.

Maintenance rehearsal
Repetitive review of information with little or no interpretation.

Elaborative rehearsal
Rehearsal involving repetition and analysis, in which a stimulus may be associated with (linked to) other information and further processed.

■ **EARLY RESEARCH ON SHORT-TERM MEMORY.** Thousands of researchers have studied the components and characteristics of storage in short-term memory. Early research focused on its duration, its capacity, and its relationship to rehearsal. Researchers had studied memory and retrieval for decades, but it was not until 1959 that Lloyd and Margaret Peterson presented experimental evidence for the existence of a separate memory store they called short-term memory. In a laboratory study, the Petersons asked participants to recall a three-consonant sequence, such as *xbd,* either immediately following its presentation or after a time interval ranging from 1 to 18 seconds. During the interval, the participants had to count backward by threes; the purpose of this activity was to prevent them from repeating (rehearsing) the consonant sequence. The Petersons wanted to examine recall when rehearsal was not possible. Figure 8.4 presents their results. As the interval between presentation and recall

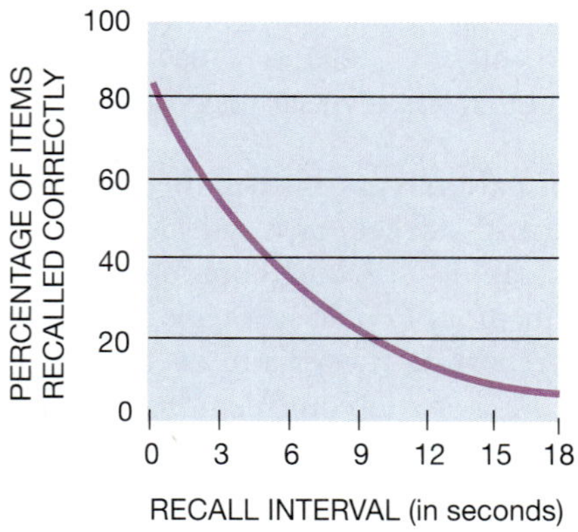

FIGURE 8.4
Results of Peterson and Peterson's Classic Experiment
Peterson and Peterson (1959) found that when they delayed the report of three-letter syllables by having subjects count backward, accuracy of recall decreased over the first 18 seconds.

increased, accuracy of recall decreased, until it fell to levels that could have been due to chance. The Petersons' experiment, like many others that followed, showed that information contained in short-term memory is available for 20–30 seconds at most. After that, the information must be transferred to long-term memory, or it will be lost.

In 1956, George Miller argued that human beings can retain about seven (plus or minus two) items in short-term memory. The number of items a person can reproduce from short-term memory is the **memory span.** But what constitutes an "item" is not consistent. For example, a person can recall about 5 letters, about 5 words, and about 5 sentences. Therefore, people can group information in ways that expand short-term memory capacity. The groupings are called **chunks**—manageable and meaningful units of information organized in a familiar way for easy encoding, storage, and retrieval. Short-term memory will hold one or two chunks. Many people remember their Social Security number in three chunks (a really difficult task for short-term memory) and telephone numbers in two chunks (a much easier task). When telephone companies began to use 10 digits in telephone numbers, people had trouble remembering them because of their short-term memory limit. But because they could think of area codes as chunks, people got around those limits and dealt with 10-digit dialing. Chunks can be organized on the basis of meaning, past associations, rhythm, or some arbitrary strategy a person devises to help encode large amounts of data (Brown & Craik, 2000). Determining what constitutes a chunk is sometimes difficult, though, because what is perceptually or cognitively grouped together by one individual may be grouped differently by other individuals.

Take Home Tip
for the Active Learner

The chunking memory technique works well with numbers, letters, and words, as you have read. However, it can also be effective in remembering ideas, which you can also group together. For example, if you were studying for a test on this chapter, you could "chunk together" a list of factors that increase recall, to help you remember them on test day. Another chunk might be factors that contribute to forgetting.

Researchers agree that a key operation—rehearsal—is especially important in memory. Rehearsal usually involves more than simply repeating information to keep it from decaying. **Rehearsal** is the process of repeatedly verbalizing, thinking about, or otherwise acting on or transforming information in order to keep that information active in memory. Psychologists distinguish two important types of rehearsal: maintenance and elaborative. **Maintenance rehearsal** is the repetitive review of information with little or no interpretation. This shallow form of rehearsal involves only the physical stimuli, not their underlying meaning. It generally occurs just after initial encoding has taken place—for example, when you repeat a phone number just long enough to dial it. **Elaborative rehearsal** involves repetition plus analysis, in which the stimulus may be associated with (linked to) other information and further processed. When a grocery shopper attempts to remember the things he needs in order to make dinner, he may organize them in a meaningful mental pattern, such as according to the aisles where the items are displayed in the supermarket. Elaborative rehearsal, during which information is made personally meaningful, is especially important in the encoding processes. This type of rehearsal allows information to be transferred into long-term memory. Maintenance rehearsal alone is usually not sufficient to allow information to be permanently stored. In general, information held in short-term memory is either transferred to long-term memory or lost.

■ *Maintenance rehearsal is adequate to keep information active in memory, but elaborative rehearsal allows information to be transferred to long-term memory.*

For example, you can repeat the term *suprachiasmic nucleus* until you can recognize it and connect it with the regulation of circadian rhythm, but to remember this term and its meaning beyond the date of the test on that section, you need to do more. One strategy would be to analyze the term, breaking it down into parts and developing an understanding of each one. *Chiasm* means "intersection," and it refers to the place in the brain where the optic nerves from each eye come together. *Supra* means "above," and

Take Home Tip *for the Active Learner*

If you want to remember something, there is no substitute for rehearsal. Maintenance rehearsal, in which you simply repeat information without attaching any meaning to it, will facilitate recognition or rote recall if you do not have to remember the information for very long. However, if you want to remember ideas for a long time, you need to understand them, and this requires the use of elaborative rehearsal. With elaborative rehearsal, you generate meaning as you repeat and think about the material you are learning.

nucleus is a formation of neurons within the brain. So the term *suprachiasmic nucleus* describes a brain structure that lies above the optic chiasm. Though it requires some work, this level of elaboration will boost memory for this information.

THE EMERGENCE OF WORKING MEMORY. Until the 1970s, psychologists used the term *short-term memory* to refer to memory that lasts for less than a minute. In the 1970s researchers Alan Baddeley and Graham Hitch (1974, 1994) began to reconceptualize short-term memory as a more complex type of brief storage they called *working memory*. Their model contains several substructures that operate simultaneously to maintain information while it is being processed. Earlier psychologists often concentrated on single memory tasks, trying to understand the stages of encoding, storage, and retrieval. But the concept of working memory goes beyond individual stages to describe the active integration of both conscious processes (such as repetition) and unconscious processes. This model of memory emphasizes how human memory meets the demands of real-life activities such as listening to the radio, reading, and mentally calculating the sum of 74 plus 782.

Working memory is the storage mechanism that temporarily holds current or recent information for immediate or short-term use. In working memory, information is not simply stored; it is further encoded and then maintained for about 20–30 seconds while active processing takes place. A person may decide that a specific piece of information is important; if it is complicated or lengthy, the person will need to actively rehearse it to keep it in working memory. As we saw earlier, *rehearsal* is the process of repeatedly verbalizing, thinking about, or otherwise acting on or transforming information in order to keep it in memory.

The addition of new information may also *interfere* with the recall of other information in working memory. Baddeley and Hitch (1974) demonstrated the limited capabilities of several components, or subsystems, of working memory by having participants recall digits while doing some other type of reasoning task. If one subsystem is given a demanding task, the performance of the others will suffer. One subsystem in working memory encodes, rehearses, and holds auditory information such as a person's name or phone number. Another subsystem is a visual–spatial scratch pad or blackboard, which stores visual and spatial information, such as the appearance and location of objects, for a brief time and then is erased to allow new information to be stored. A third subsystem is a central processing mechanism, something like an executive who balances the information flow and allows people to solve problems and make decisions. This executive controls the processing flow and adjusts it when necessary. Research shows that the type of information being processed by working memory affects the accuracy of the processing (Kruley, Sciama, & Glenberg, 1994). For example, reading a passage consisting entirely of words presents different requirements from reading a passage with both words and pictures, and the central processing mechanism must make adjustments for the different types of information being processed.

Figure 8.5 illustrates the now widely accepted view of short-term storage as working memory. Building Table 8.2 summarizes key processes in the first two stages of memory.

Working memory
Storage mechanism that temporarily holds current or recent information for immediate or short-term use and that is composed of several subsystems: an auditory loop to encode and rehearse auditory information, a visual–spatial "scratch pad" for visual information, and a central processing mechanism, or executive, that balances and controls information flow.

Long-term memory
Storage mechanism that keeps a relatively permanent record of information.

Long-Term Memory

Information about names, faces, dates, places, smells, and events is stored in relatively permanent form in **long-term memory.** In contrast to the limitations of sensory and short-term storage, long-term memory is indefinite; much of it lasts a lifetime. The capacity of long-term memory also seems unlimited; the more information a

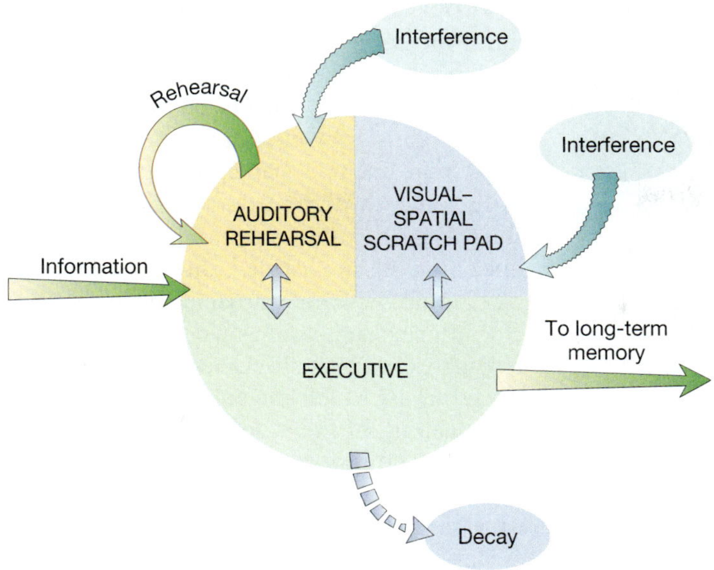

FIGURE 8.5

Working Memory

In working memory, active processing occurs. Information is held in either a visual–spatial scratch pad or auditory loop, depending on the type of input. This information is monitored by an executive, or central processing mechanism.

person acquires, the easier it is to acquire more information. Using our filing cabinet analogy, we can say that long-term memory includes all the folders in the cabinet. And, as in a filing cabinet, information can be lost ("misfiled") or unavailable for some other reason (the drawers can get stuck). In contrast to a filing cabinet, the information in human memory is active rather than passive in storage and subject to distortion—as if the memos in the folder had morphed into photographs of the office staff while in the cabinet.

A wide variety of information is stored in long-term memory—for example, the words to "The Star-Spangled Banner," the meaning of the word *sanguine,* how to operate a CD player, the place where your psychology class meets, and what you did to celebrate your high school graduation. Different types of information seem to be stored and called on in different ways. On this basis, psychologists have made a number of distinctions among the types of memory.

Building Table 8.2

Key Processes in the First Two Stages of Memory

Stage	Encoding	Storage	Retrieval	Duration	Forgetting
Sensory memory	Visual or auditory (iconic or echoic storage)	Brief, fragile, and temporary	Information is extracted from stimulus presentation and transferred to short-term storage.	Visual: 250 milliseconds; auditory: about 3 seconds	Rapid decay of information; interference is possible if a new stimulus is presented.
Short-term storage	Visual and auditory	Repetitive rehearsal maintains information in storage, perhaps on a visual–spatial "scratch pad" or auditory loop where further encoding can take place.	Maintenance and elaborative rehearsal can keep information available for retrieval; retrieval is enhanced through elaboration and further encoding.	No more than 30 seconds, probably less than 20 seconds; depends on specific task and stimuli	Interference and decay affect memory; new stimulation causes rapid loss of information unless it is especially important

■ *Procedural memory includes motor skills such as skating.*

■ **PROCEDURAL AND DECLARATIVE MEMORY.** **Procedural memory** is memory for skills, including the perceptual, motor, and cognitive skills required to complete complex tasks (see Figure 8.6). Driving a car, in-line skating, or cooking a meal involves a series of steps that include perceptual, motor, and cognitive skills—and thus procedural memory. Acquiring such skills is usually time-consuming and difficult at first; but once the skills are learned, they are relatively permanent and automatic. **Declarative memory** is memory for specific information, such as who Theodore Kaczynski is (a terrorist known as the Unabomber), which member of the group REM left the band (drummer Bill Berry), and the meaning of the word *sanguine* (hopeful and confident). Declarative memories may be established quickly, but the information is more likely to be forgotten over time than is the information in procedural memory. Not all declarative memories are the same, and some researchers subdivide declarative memory into episodic and semantic memory.

FIGURE **8.6**

Procedural and Declarative Long-Term Memory

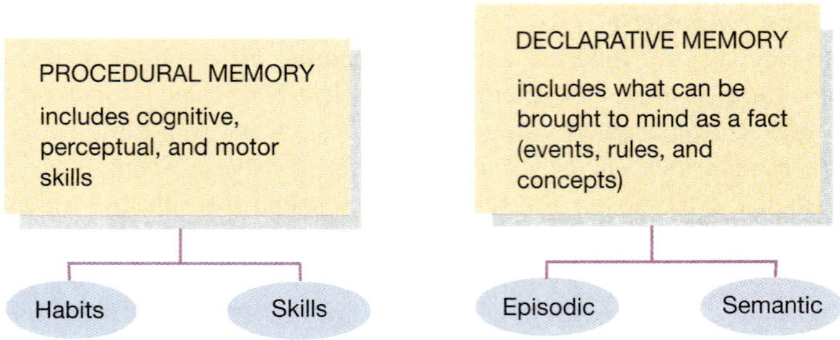

Procedural memory
Memory for skills, including the perceptual, motor, and cognitive skills required to complete complex tasks.

Declarative memory
Memory for specific information.

Episodic [ep-ih-SAW-dick] memory
Memory of specific, personal events and situations (episodes) tagged with information about time.

Semantic memory
Memory of ideas, rules, words, and general concepts about the world.

Explicit memory
Conscious memory that a person is aware of, such as a memory of a word in a list or an event that occurred in the past.

Implicit memory
Memory a person is not aware of possessing; considered an almost unconscious process, implicit memory occurs almost automatically.

■ **EPISODIC AND SEMANTIC MEMORY.** **Episodic memory** is memory of specific personal events and situations (episodes), tagged with information about time. An episodic memory includes where, when, and how you obtained the information, plus chronological dating or tagging, so you know the sequence of events within your episodic memory. Examples include having breakfast this morning, the movie you saw last night, and what you did on vacation two summers ago. Episodic memory is often highly detailed: you may recall not only the plot of the movie you saw last night and who starred in it, but also the temperature of the theater, the smell of the popcorn, what you were wearing, who accompanied you, and many other details of the experience.

Episodic memory about ourselves—our own personal story—can be termed *autobiographical memory*. In some sense, we *are* our autobiographical memories; we need these memories to construct a personal view of self (Fivush, 2001). People's autobiographical memories can last for many years (Neisser & Libby, 2000); when autobiographical memory is lost, people lose some of their personal sense of self. This type of long-term memory storage is durable and fairly easy to access if a helpful retrieval cue, such as a smell associated with the event, is available. These memories are also subject to a variety of distortions (which we will consider in a later section). A defining characteristic of autobiographical memories is their organization by temporal markers, such as what happened the summer after you graduated from high school (Shum, 1998).

Semantic memory is memory for ideas, rules, words, and general concepts about the world. It is your personal, generalized knowledge, based on a set of concepts about the world, about previous events, experiences, and learned information. It is not time-specific; it refers to knowledge that may have been gathered over days or weeks, and it continues to be modified and expanded over a lifetime. Your knowledge of what a typical horse looks like comes from semantic memory; knowledge of your last encounter with a horse is episodic memory. Semantic memory develops earlier in childhood than does episodic memory (Tulving, 1993; Wheeler, 2000).

After looking at this photo, you remember things you notice (explicit memory) but also details you do not recall noticing (implicit memory).

EXPLICIT AND IMPLICIT MEMORY. **Explicit memory** is conscious memory that a person is aware of, such as a memory of a word in a list or an event that occurred in the past; most of the memory tasks we have been looking at require explicit recall of information. Both semantic and episodic memory is explicit, consisting of voluntary, active memory store. When you tap semantic memory, you are accessing explicit memory. In contrast, **implicit memory** is memory a person is not aware that he or she possesses; considered an almost unconscious process, implicit memory is accessed almost automatically and unintentionally.

For example, you may remember things that you are supposed to remember (explicit memories), but you are also likely to recall things you did not deliberately attempt to learn—the color of a book you are studying or the name of the book's publisher, the size of a piece of cake you were served, or perhaps the make of a computer in the office of a professor you have visited (implicit memories). Implicit memory occurs without conscious awareness; it demonstrates that people can learn without intentional effort (Boronat & Logan, 1997), and what they learn explicitly and how they are asked to recall it may affect their implicit memories (Nelson, McKinney, & Gee, 1998). Lending physiological support to the explicit/implicit distinction is the finding that these memory stores seem to be found in different locations in the brain (Fleischman et al., 1997).

The distinction between explicit and implicit memory adds another dimension to researchers' understanding of long-term memory, suggesting that memory storage is varied and complex. These distinctions also suggest that these different types of memory may have differing representations in the brain and that the functioning of one system is independent of others.

PRACTICE. Obviously, practice is a factor in storage, but research indicates that the timing of practice is an important factor. In one 1978 study, Baddeley and Longman wanted to learn which of two types of practice resulted in more optimal learning and retention: intensive practice at one time (massed practice) or the same amount of practice divided into several intervals (distributed practice). To answer this question, they taught postal workers to touch-type.

The participants were divided into four groups, each member of which practiced the same number of hours, using either distributed practice or massed practice. One group practiced typing 1 hour a day; the second practiced 2 hours a day; the third practiced 1 hour twice a day; the fourth practiced 2 hours twice a day. Given the same total number hours of practice, did the distribution of those practice hours make a difference? The dependent variable was how well they learned to type—that is, the number of accurate keystrokes per minute. A typing test showed that distributed practice (typing 1 hour a day for several days) was most effective. From this experiment and others, researchers have learned that the effectiveness of distributed practice depends on many variables, including the method, order, and speed of presentation. Distributed practice is especially effective for perceptual motor skills, where eye–hand coordination is important.

Take Home Tip *for the Active Learner*

When you study, distribute your practice and rehearsal over time. For optimum learning, you should study each subject for a relatively short time every day or every other day, instead of trying to cram all your studying into one long session, right before a test. Distributing your study time instead of cramming will increase the amount of material you can learn and remember *without* increasing your total study time.

Neuroscience and Storage

Using both PET and fMRI, researchers can now identify the neural machinery that underlies brain functions, and some of the most exciting research involves studies of the neural activity and brain locations associated with working memory. The visual–spatial scratch pad of working memory is embodied physically in the brain. When Smith and others (1995) had participants engage in either a spatial memory task or an object memory task, the spatial task activated only right-hemisphere prefrontal regions, whereas the object task activated primarily left-hemisphere regions. In later research, Smith (1997) found different working memory subsystems for spatial, object, and verbal information. Further, other researchers (Gabrieli et al., 1997; Jonides et al., 1997) showed that as a working-memory task grew more difficult, participants' brain scans became more active, especially in the prefrontal cortex. This and other results (Nyberg & Cabeza, 2000) suggest that the prefrontal cortex may be the place where this coordinating, or executive, function of working memory is carried out.

One patient with brain damage has been very important in focusing attention on the brain mechanisms underlying the transition of information from short-term storage to long-term memory. Brenda Milner (1966) reported the case of H. M., a man whose brain was damaged as a result of surgery to control his epilepsy. His short-term storage was intact, but he was unable to form new long-term declarative memories. As long as H. M. was able to rehearse information and keep it in short-term storage, his recall performance was normal. However, as soon as he could no longer rehearse, his recall became poor. That is, his ability to shift information from short-term to long-term storage was impaired. (His procedural memory was not so severely affected, and he was able to learn new skills.) Milner's account of this case provides support for a neurological distinction between short- and long-term memory and focused researchers' attention on the role of the *hippocampus,* a brain structure in the temporal lobes. Subsequent research has shown that this brain structure is an important component in memory formation, especially the transfer of information from short-term to long-term storage (Zola & Squire, 2000). (For a more common example of this memory problem, see *Brain and Behavior*.)

The process of changing a temporary memory to a permanent one is called **consolidation,** and this concept plays an important role in one of the leading theories of neuroscience and storage. Canadian psychologist Donald Hebb (1904–1985) presented one of the major physiological theories of memory. Hebb (1949) suggested that when groups of neurons are stimulated, they form patterns of neural activity. When specific groups of neurons fire frequently, this activity establishes regular neural circuits through the process of consolidation. According to Hebb, this process must occur for short-term memory to become long-term memory. When key neurons and neurotransmitters are repeatedly stimulated by various events, those events may be better remembered and more easily accessed—this may be part of the reason that practiced behaviors are so easily recalled (Kandel & Abel, 1995).

If a neuron is stimulated, the biochemical processes involved make it more likely to respond again later; this increase in responsiveness is referred to as *long-term potentiation,* a phenomenon that is especially evident in areas of the brain such as the hippocampus. In addition, clear evidence exists that specific protein synthesis occurs just after learning and that long-term memory depends on this synthesis (Squire & Kandel, 1999). Psychologists now generally accept the idea that the structure of synapses changes after learning, and especially after repeated learning experiences. As Hebb said, "Some memories are both instantaneously established and permanent. To account for the permanence, some structural change seems necessary" (1949, p. 62).

Consolidation [kon-SOL-ih-DAY-shun]
The process of changing a short-term memory to a long-term one.

If the changes in the physical brain that form the basis for memory occur at the level of the synapse, then no one brain structure should be specifically associated with long-term memory. This conclusion seems true—researchers worked for years trying

BRAIN AND BEHAVIOR

The Aging Brain and Alzheimer's Disease

Will your memory decline as you get older? Is memory loss an inevitable consequence of aging? As people age, they often lose some memory abilities but not others. The largest problems come from storage of long-term episodic memories, but sensory memory and implicit memory tasks show little decline in healthy older people (Balota, Dolan, & Duchek, 2000). However, several diseases can devastate memory, and Alzheimer's disease is the most disastrous and, unfortunately, the most common.

Alzheimer's disease is a degenerative disease of the brain, and its diagnosis can only be confirmed after death, during an autopsy. An examination of neurons in the brain, especially in the medial temporal and frontal lobes, will show a pattern of *neurofibrillary tangles* (tangled bundles of neurons) as well as a buildup of *plaque* (tissue that interferes with the function of neurons). The underlying cause of Alzheimer's disease is unknown, but one rare version is linked to a defective gene, and all versions may have some genetic involvement.

Problems with memory are the most prominent feature of Alzheimer's disease and the most common complaint among Alzheimer's patients (Hodges, 2000). The symptoms of early Alzheimer's disease include problems with forming new memories. This pattern is not surprising, considering the damage that is occurring to the medial temporal lobes and the hippocampus. People with more advanced Alzheimer's are unable to retrieve large areas of personal memory. They lose their past more completely than people with other types of memory loss.

The progress of Alzheimer's disease affects other parts of the brain, damaging other memory systems. Working memory is less affected than other memory systems, but intact working memory helps keep people functioning in the present, not the past. Alzheimer's patients typically have impairments in semantic memory, which means they forget items of general knowledge. This type of memory loss is more devastating than personal memory loss because it means that these individuals may forget important information that they need to get along in the world, such as what keys are and what belongs in a kitchen. In addition, Alzheimer's disease can produce deficits in procedural memory, so patients may not only forget what a fork is but also how to eat. Other types of memory loss rarely affect procedural memory.

People with advanced Alzheimer's disease are unable to care for themselves and need constant care. The population of the United States and many other industrialized countries is aging, and age is the leading risk factor for Alzheimer's disease. Few people younger than 65 are affected, but as many as 50% of those over 85 are (Evans et al., 1989). Thus, this devastating disease may affect as many as 6 million people in the United States by the year 2040.

to find a structure in the cerebral cortex that formed the specific brain basis for memory. They failed. Although complete agreement has not been reached, many authorities now accept that memory is distributed throughout the brain rather than localized in one spot. As we have seen, structures in the medial temporal lobe, including the hippocampus, are critically important in forming long-term storage, but the temporal lobes are not the site of long-term memory (Markowitsch, 2000). Therefore, the picture of long-term memory in the brain is extremely complex. Memories are distributed over the cerebral cortex and even in lower brain structures, and their encoding and retrieval activate pathways that include the prefrontal cortex and the medial temporal lobes.

Be an *Active* learner

REVIEW

- What evidence shows that sensory memory is temporary and fragile? pp. 269–270
- How does the idea of working memory expand the initial conception of short-term memory? p. 272
- What structures are important for memory storage in the brain? pp. 276–277

THINK CRITICALLY

- In terms of memory systems, why does reading a book about tennis not help your tennis game?
- Do you think it makes evolutionary or adaptive sense to have memory representations all over the brain? Or would it be better if memory were located in a specific place? Explain your reasoning.

APPLY PSYCHOLOGY

- Analyze how you typically study for tests, and compare your strategy to the recommendations from the research on storage in long-term memory. Then list some ways in which you could become a more effective learner.

Retrieval

If memory is like a filing cabinet, then retrieval is like the process of opening the drawer and finding a folder that has been filed. The retrieval operation usually goes smoothly; you know which drawer to open and you can find the folder, pull it out, and see the information, which matches the coded label. Likewise, most memory retrieval is fairly easy; we consciously and explicitly try to remember something, and it becomes available more or less effortlessly. But things *can* get in the way of remembering—you realize when you take a test and cannot remember a fact or concept, even though you know that you have "filed it away." Like everyone, you experience many retrieval failures, situations in which you "know that you know" the information yet cannot access it.

Retrieval is the process by which stored information is recovered from memory. Recalling your Social Security number, remembering the details of an assignment, and listing the names of all Seven Dwarfs are retrieval tasks. A person may encode information quickly, deal with the information in working memory, and enter the information into long-term memory. But once information is coded and stored, the person must be able to retrieve the information and use it in a meaningful way. It turns out that the ability to retrieve information depends on how retention is measured and how the information is encoded and stored.

Retention: Measures of Retrieval

Are you a fan of *The Weakest Link,* or do you prefer *Who Wants to Be a Millionaire?* Does your preference relate to the difference in difficulty of the two? These two television shows are similar—both require participants to retrieve information that they have stored in memory. They differ in rules and format, but a major difference is the way that each asks participants to access information. *The Weakest Link* asks participants to recall information by reproducing it, whereas *Who Wants to Be a Millionaire?* requires participants to recognize information. Psychologists use these two measures of *retention,* plus another method called *relearning.* When a person retains information, presumably he or she has acquired (learned) something that was not there previously, and this retained information can later be retrieved.

■ **RECALL.** In recall tasks, participants have to retrieve previously presented information. Not only *The Weakest Link* but also fill-in-the-blank and essay exams require the recall of information. In experiments, the information usually comprises strings (lists) of digits or letters. A typical study might ask participants to remember 10 items, one of which is presented on a screen every half-second. The participants would then try to repeat the list of 10 items at the end of the 5-second presentation period.

Three widely used recall tasks are free recall, serial recall, and paired associate tasks. In *free recall tasks,* participants are to recall items in any order, much as you might recall the items on a grocery list. *Serial recall tasks* are more difficult; the items must be recalled in the order in which they were presented, as you would recall the digits in a telephone number. In *paired associate tasks,* participants are given a cue to help them recall the second item of a pair of items. In the learning phase of a study, the experimenter might pair the words *tree* and *shoe.* In the testing phase, participants would be presented with the word *tree* and would have to respond with the correct answer, *shoe.*

■ **RECOGNITION.** In a multiple-choice test, as in *Who Wants to Be a Millionaire?,* you are asked to recognize relevant information. Psychologists have found that recognition tasks can help them measure subtle differences in memory ability better than recall tasks can. That's because although a person may be unable to recall the details of a previously learned fact, he or she may recognize them. Asked to name

Retrieval
Process by which stored information is recovered from memory.

the capital of Maine, more people would succeed on *Millionaire* than on *Weakest Link*. The chance of answering correctly is better when presented with four names to choose from: Columbus, Annapolis, Helena, or Augusta (final answer: Augusta).

■ **RELEARNING.** No current game show uses relearning as a memory task—it wouldn't make a very exciting show. This technique assesses memory by measuring how long it takes to relearn material that a participant has learned previously. The rationale for this assessment is that rapid relearning indicates some residual memory. For example, let's say you receive a list of 12 words to memorize, and you work with them until you can recite them perfectly. You report back two days later and are asked to recall the list. Unless you have rehearsed the list during the 2-day interval, your performance will be far from perfect. However, you will quickly relearn the material, indicating that you have some memory of the items, even though you could not recall them.

Retrieval Success and Failure: Encoding Specificity

Some contemporary researchers assert that every memory is retained and available but that some memories are less accessible than others. Think of the filing cabinet analogy: some of the folders in the cabinet cannot be found (perhaps because they are misfiled, or perhaps the drawer gets stuck temporarily); retrieval is difficult or impossible. When retrieval of information is blocked, the information is effectively forgotten, but it is not gone—just inaccessible. (For a view on how long information can be accessible, see *Introduction to Research Basics*).

Research on retrieval focuses on how people encode information and on the cues that help them recall it—the interaction between encoding and retrieval. If you are given a cue for retrieval that relates to some aspect of the originally stored information, retrieval will be easier, faster, and more accurate. For example, if we asked you what stage of sleep is usually associated with dreams, you might find it fairly easy to recall because you may have known about the association between REM and dreaming even before you studied Chapter 6. But if we asked you which brain structure is associated with the regulation of the sleep–wake cycle, the task would be much harder because the term *suprachiasmic nucleus* is much less familiar than *REM*. Retrieval cues make recall easier. This evidence supports the *encoding specificity principle,* which asserts that the effectiveness of a specific retrieval cue depends on how well it matches up with information in the original encoded memory (see p. 266). This principle predicts that people who encode information under one set of circumstances should find it easier to retrieve that information under the same circumstances. This prediction is supported by the phenomenon of state-dependent learning and retrieval.

■ *The millionaire character in Charlie Chaplin's movie* City Lights *remembers Charlie only when he is intoxicated, which is known as state-dependent learning.*

■ **STATE-DEPENDENT LEARNING AND RETRIEVAL.** Psychologist Gordon Bower (1981) used the following story to describe a phenomenon known as *state-dependent learning:*

> When I was a kid I saw the movie *City Lights* in which Charlie Chaplin plays the little tramp. In one very funny sequence, Charlie saves a drunk from leaping to his death. The drunk turns out to be a millionaire who befriends Charlie, and the two spend the evening together drinking and carousing. The next day, when sober, the millionaire does not recognize Charlie and even snubs him. Later the millionaire gets drunk again, and when he spots Charlie, treats him as his long-lost

introduction to research basics

Testing Very Long-Term Memory

Most memory research takes place in a laboratory, with participants who learn a selection of material and then have their memory tested. The testing for memory typically occurs within minutes. Sometimes, researchers test after hours or days have elapsed, but studies of longer retention are rare because keeping track of participants is such a problem. Harry Bahrick solved that problem by finding material that many people had already learned at the same time in their lives and testing their memory for that material years later. He has used this approach in a number of studies, including memory for photos in high school yearbooks and memory for courses taken in high school and college (Bahrick, 2000). This approach has allowed Bahrick to study memory in real-life contexts, over time spans as long as 50 years.

DESIGN Bahrick's (1984) approach is not experimental. His research method is a type of descriptive study called an **ex post facto study,** a type of design that contrasts groups of people who differ on some variable of interest to the researcher. He did not manipulate the information presented to participants as typical memory researchers do when they vary the type of material (nouns or numbers) or amount of information (10 or 20 words) participants must memorize. Instead, he chose participants who already had the experiences of interest, such as studying a foreign language, and he tested them. This approach may look like an experiment because the participants are tested in a lab, but it has important differences. By choosing participants who already differ, researchers such as Bahrick do not manipulate an independent variable but instead choose participants with the appropriate level of the variable they select. This variable is called a *subject variable* because it describes characteristics of the subjects (participants) in the study. Because the researchers do not manipulate an independent variable, they have no possibility of exerting control over other variables, so they are restricted from making conclusions about cause and effect relationships. However, this approach can tell about differences among people with varying characteristics, which was Bahrick's goal.

HYPOTHESIS Bahrick hypothesized that people who had completed more Spanish courses would have better retention of Spanish, even many years later. That is, he hypothesized that practice would be a factor in very long-term memory. In addition, he hypothesized that the amount of time that elapsed would show a relationship to memory.

PARTICIPANTS Bahrick found 733 volunteers who agreed to complete a Spanish reading, vocabulary, and grammar examination and to furnish background information about their coursework and grades (along with permission to verify this information). These participants had taken at least one Spanish course during high school or college. This instruction took place between 2 months and 50 years prior to testing.

PROCEDURE Bahrick grouped participants according to the time that had passed since their last Spanish instruction. He also assessed how much Spanish instruction each person had received, creating a procedure to make coursework equivalent to college semesters and placing participants in 10 different categories of instruction. These 10 categories were the levels of his subject variable, amount of Spanish instruction. Bahrick determined that most of the participants did not practice Spanish after they finished the courses, so rehearsal was not a factor in his study.

RESULTS Bahrick found that both elapsed time and amount of Spanish instruction were important factors in memory. He found that, regardless of the age of the participants or how long ago they had studied Spanish, the greatest memory loss occurs within 3 to 6 years after completing the last Spanish course. Retention then remains constant for several decades, but declines again after about 30 years.

The number of courses completed was also an important factor in memory. The best predictor of memory for Spanish was the number of Spanish courses completed.

CONCLUSIONS Even without rehearsal or great personal relevance, some information in semantic long-term memory persists for 25 years or longer. Original training is the best predictor of retention in long-term memory. So practice, indeed, does seem to make memory permanent—for at least 30 years.

Ex post facto study
A type of design that contrasts groups of people who differ on some variable of interest to the researcher.

State-dependent learning
The tendency to recall information learned while in a particular physiological state most accurately when one is again in that physiological state.

> companion. So the two of them spend another evening together carousing and drinking and then stagger back to the millionaire's mansion to sleep. In the morning, of course, the sober millionaire again does not recognize Charlie, treats him as an intruder, and has the butler kick him out by the seat of his pants. The scene ends with the little tramp telling the camera his opinion of high society and the evils of drunkenness. (p. 129)

The millionaire remembers Charlie only when he is intoxicated, the same state he was in when he originally met him. Psychologists find that information learned while a person is in a particular state is recalled most accurately when the person is again in that state. Thus, this phenomenon is known as **state-dependent learning,** and includes state-dependent retrieval. This dependence of retrieval on learning state is associated with states involving drugs, time of day (Holloway, 1977), traumatic experiences (Perry, 1999), and language spoken (Schrauf, 2000).

In a typical study of state-dependent learning, Weingartner and colleagues (1976) had four groups of participants learn and recall lists of words. The control group learned and recalled the words while sober; a second group learned and recalled while intoxicated; a third group learned while sober and recalled while intoxicated; a fourth group learned while intoxicated and recalled while sober. The results showed that participants recalled the words best when they were in the state in which they had learned them. (This is not to say that memory works better when you're drunk! All else being equal, recall is better in sober individuals.)

A widely accepted explanation for state-dependent learning and retrieval focuses on how states affect the storage–retrieval process. According to this view, when the person's state at the time of encoding matches the state at the time of retrieval, access is facilitated; when the states do not match, retrieval is not as easy (Brown & Craik, 2000; Schramke & Bauer, 1997). For example, when you study for an examination with music in the background but are tested in quiet conditions, your recall may not be as good. This effect extends to mood; studying after exercise, when in a good mood, or when well rested is likely to lead to better recall (Eich, 1995; Izquierdo & Medina, 1997).

Take Home Tip *for the Active Learner*

When you study, match the conditions under which you will be tested, including factors such as background noise, lighting, time of day, number of people present, and your state of alertness. If you cannot, then study under varying conditions so that your encoding will not be strongly related to any one set of retrieval conditions.

Flashbulb Memory

Where were you when you heard about the attacks on the World Trade Center and the Pentagon? How did you hear about these events? What were you doing? What were your first thoughts? Do you remember those details more vividly than you remember what you had for lunch two days ago? These terrorist attacks made a life-long impression on most Americans as well as many people around the world. Are these public, dramatic events the basis of a special kind of memory?

Your memories of seeing or hearing about the terrorist attacks on the United States on September 11, 2001, may be the type of major event that is referred to as *flashbulb memory.* Such events are dramatic, and memory of them tends to be vivid.

Brown and Kulik (1977) were the first to research this type of memory. They argued that there is a special type of memory for events that have a critical level of emotional impact and what they called *consequentiality.* Most people immediately understand the concept of flashbulb memory and can identify personal examples. The attacks on the World Trade Center are examples, but the Columbine shootings and the death of Princess Diana are also dramatic, public events that many people put into the category of flashbulb memory. The types of events that are likely to be flashbulb memories vary among countries. For example, people living in the United Kingdom are more likely to have such a memory for the resignation of Prime Minister Margaret Thatcher than are residents of North America (Conway et al., 1994). Thus, more Europeans than Americans have flashbulb

■ *Millions of people have a flashbulb memory for this emotionally charged event.*

memories of the death of Princess Di, but this event is the type of public, emotionally charged event that prompts the formation of these memories. The concept of flashbulb memories has not only generated a great deal of research but also has prompted debate over its validity.

The concept of flashbulb memory holds that people will have complete, detailed, accurate memories from such events. Brown and Kulik argued that a special memory mechanism creates flashbulb memories, which explains their special characteristics. Other psychologists argue that the processes of encoding and retrieval can account for flashbulb memories, just as for other memories (Schooler & Eich, 2000); the emotional component of these memories makes them more distinctive (affecting encoding) and more often rehearsed (affecting retrieval).

Another point of argument involves the accuracy of flashbulb memories. Brown and Kulik argued that the special mechanism for creating these memories should make them very accurate—just like the photograph made by the flashbulb. Researchers approached the topic by focusing on some public event that generated emotion; they collected people's memories of various events (earthquakes, assassinations, and the space shuttle *Challenger* explosion) and compared the detail and accuracy to those of other memories. Results indicate that flashbulb memories are far from perfectly accurate, and they change over time, but people still retain the feeling of vividness for these memories (Koriat, Goldsmith, & Pansky, 2000). Thus, flashbulb memories are probably created by the same mechanisms that form other memories. They are certainly vivid, but other emotionally charged personal memories share the level of detail and persistence of flashbulb memories.

■ *Men's memory tends to be better for hardware than for groceries.*

Gender and Memory

Although many people believe that the differences between women and men extend to every type of behavior, research shows very few differences in memory. For example, no gender differences appeared in a study involving recalling pictures and words (Ionescu, 2000). Women were slightly better than men at recalling the names and faces of their high school classmates after as many as 50 years, but Bahrick's analysis (2000) of that difference held that women were better at learning the information, not at recall. This gender difference in attention and learning is probably the basis of any differences in memory—men and women attend to different types of information. Differential attention leads to encoding differences and thus to retrieval differences.

The factors that prompt gender differences in attention conform to gender stereotypes. For example, one study asked women and men to memorize a shopping list and the directions of how to get to a particular place (Herrmann, Crawford, & Holdsworth, 1992). The results showed the expected stereotypical differences: women performed slightly better on the shopping list and men on the directions. But the study showed that memory could be manipulated along stereotypical lines. Of the participants who received information that the shopping list related to groceries, women did better, but for participants who were told that the list pertained to hardware, men's memory for the items was better. Therefore, memory efficiency can be manipulated not only by attention but also by how well the memory task matches gender-stereotypical information.

Primacy effect
The more accurate recall of items presented at the beginning of a series.

Recency effect
The more accurate recall of items presented at the end of a series.

What Facilitates Retrieval?

Study the list of words in Figure 8.7 for 45 seconds, trying to memorize them in the order in which they appear. After 45 seconds, cover the list and write down as many of the words as you can, in the order that they appeared.

Long-term memory studies have brought forth some interesting findings about retrieval and have generated hundreds of other studies focusing on factors that can facilitate or inhibit accurate recall. Two of these factors are (1) primacy and recency effects and (2) imagery. You may be able to see both in your performance on the list you just memorized.

FIGURE 8.7

For the Active Learner: Memory Retrieval Activity

Study this list of words for 45 seconds, especially focusing on their order. After 45 seconds, cover the list and write down as many of the words as you can, in the order that they appeared. Then return to the text to find out what your performance on this task says about your memory.

horse
cabin
water
field
model
apple
heart
scene
constitutional
earth
bugle
night
voice
ocean
child
movie
grape

■ **PRIMACY AND RECENCY EFFECTS.** In a typical memory experiment, a participant may be asked to do something very similar to the memory task you just attempted: study a list of words and recall as many of the items as possible so that the researcher can determine whether the information was transferred from short-term storage to long-term memory. If the list is 30 or 40 items long, such experiments typically show an overall recall rate of 20%, but memory is not even throughout the list. Recall is higher for words at the beginning of a series than for those in the middle, a phenomenon termed the **primacy effect.** This effect occurs because no information related to the task at hand is already stored in short-term storage; at the moment a person begins a new task, attention to new stimuli is at its peak. In addition, words at the beginning of a series get to be rehearsed more often, allowing them to be transferred to long-term memory. Thus, the primacy effect is associated with long-term memory processes. Examine your recall of the list—you probably recalled "horse," "cabin," and "water," but possibly not "heart," "bugle," or "night."

However, recall is *even higher* for words at the end of a series—a phenomenon termed the **recency effect.** These more recently presented items are still being held in short-term storage, where they can be actively rehearsed without interference as they are encoded for long-term memory. The recency effect is thus thought to be related to short-term storage. Examine your recall list again—did you recall "movie" and "grape"? Figure 8.8 is a graph showing the recall rate for words in various positions in a list. It is called a *serial position curve* and presents the probability of recall as a function of an item's position in a list (series) of presented items.

There is an exception, however: the serial position curve occurs in lists of items in which the items are all fairly similar. When one item in a list differs from the others—an adjective in a series of common nouns or a longer word in a series of short ones—the one different item is learned more easily. This is the phenomenon called the

Take Home Tip *for the Active Learner*

People tend to have trouble retrieving information in the middle of a long list, so arrange your studying so that you don't attempt to learn the equivalent of a long list. Instead of forcing yourself to endure a long, drawn-out study session, take a short break (5–10 minutes) after you have studied for 20–30 minutes. Taking breaks will enhance your learning and memory because it will increase the number of times that the primacy and recency effects can work for you.

You can also make the von Restorff effect work for you by highlighting an important idea in your text or notes—it will stand out from everything else and therefore be more easily remembered (unless you highlight the whole page!). You can also use the von Restorff effect by exaggerating the meaning of the important idea or by making it seem funny or bizarre. For example, if you are having trouble remembering the term *von Restorff effect,* think of a *van Resting off* the edge of a cliff.

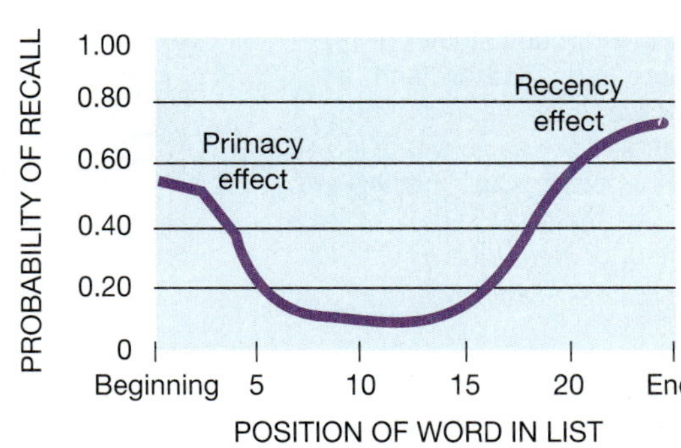

FIGURE 8.8

A Serial Position Curve

The probability of recalling an item is plotted as a function of its serial position on a list of items. Generally, the first several items are fairly likely to be recalled (the primacy effect), and the last several are recalled very well (the recency effect).

Kosslyn had subjects imagine elephants, flies, and rabbits. An imagined rabbit appeared small in size next to an elephant.

Next to a fly, however, an imagined rabbit appeared large in size.

FIGURE 8.9

Kosslyn's Imagery Studies
(Kosslyn, 1975)

von Restorff effect. Did you recall the world "constitutional"? If you did, you illustrated the von Restorff effect.

■ **IMAGERY.** People use perceptual imagery every day as a long-term memory retrieval aid. **Imagery** is the creation or recreation of a mental picture of a sensory or perceptual experience. People constantly invoke images to recall things they did, said, read, or saw. You may have used imagery to help you memorize the list at the beginning of this section; those words have images that are easy to create. People's imagery systems can be activated by visual, auditory, or olfactory stimuli or by other images (Tracy & Barker, 1994). Imagery helps you answer questions such as these: Which is darker green, a pea or a Christmas tree? Which is bigger, a tennis ball or a baseball? Does the person you met last night have brown eyes or blue?

One technique researchers use to study imagery is to ask participants to imagine objects of various sizes—for example, an animal such as a rabbit next to either an elephant or a fly. In a 1975 study by Stephen Kosslyn of Harvard University, participants reported that when they imagined a fly, plenty of room remained in their mental image for a rabbit. However, when they imagined an elephant, it took up most of the space. One particularly interesting result was that the participants required more time and found it harder to see a rabbit's nose when the rabbit was next to an elephant than when it was next to a fly, because the nose appeared to be extremely small in the first instance (see Figure 8.9).

FIGURE 8.10

The Speed of Thought
The speed of thought can be assessed through studies of mental rotation. Shepard and Metzler (1988) asked participants to see as quickly as possible whether visual stimuli were in fact the same stimuli, but rotated, or were different stimuli. *(Shepard & Metzler, 1971)*

Although they are mental, not physical, phenomena, images have "edges" like those on a photograph—points beyond which visual information ceases to be represented (Kosslyn, 1987). These and other properties of mental images have been useful in a wide variety of studies designed to measure the nature and speed of thought (see, for example, Figure 8.10).

Imagery
The creation or re-creation of a mental picture of a sensory or perceptual experience.

Imagery is an important perceptual memory aid. In fact, a growing body of evidence suggests that it is a means of preserving perceptual information that might otherwise decay. According to Allan Paivio (1971), a person told to remember two

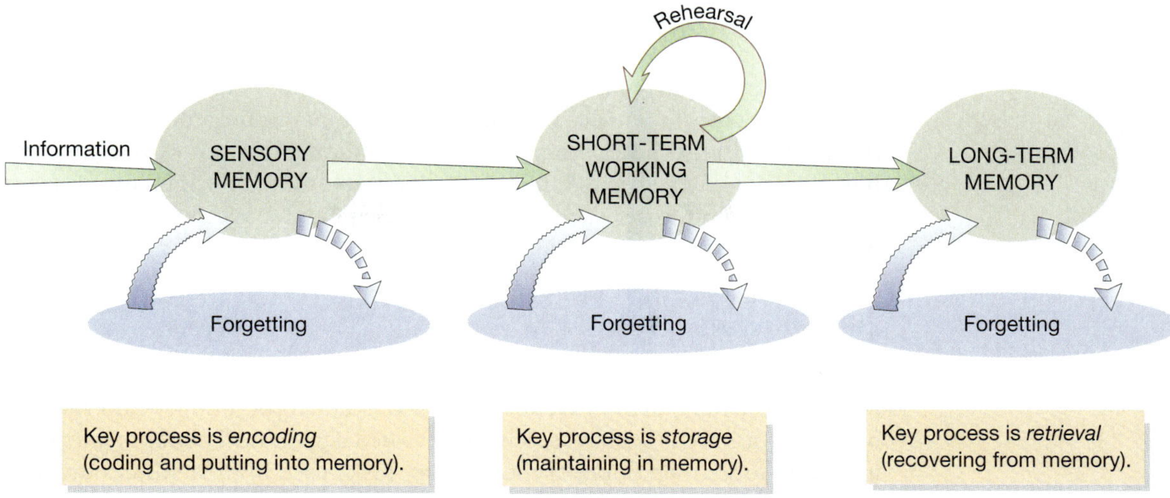

FIGURE 8.11

Encoding, Storage, and Retrieval in Memory

When information enters the memory's information-processing system, it proceeds from sensory memory to short-term storage and then to long-term memory.

words may form an image combining those words. Someone told to remember the words *house* and *hamburger*, for example, might form an image of a house made of hamburgers or of a hamburger on top of a house. When the person is later presented with the word *house*, the word *hamburger* will be easy to retrieve because the imagery aided retrieval. Paivio suggests that words paired in this way become conceptually linked, with the image as the crucial factor.

How images facilitate recall and recognition is not yet fully understood, but one possibility is that an image may add another code to semantic memory. With two codes, semantic and imaginal, a person has two ways to access previously learned information. Some researchers argue that imagery, verbal encoding mechanisms, and semantic memory operate together to encode and to aid in retrieval (Marschark et al., 1987).

Figure 8.11 presents an overall view of the memory processes of encoding, storage, and retrieval.

Take Home Tip *for the Active Learner*

Some people are good at creating images, but for those of us who are not, a rhyme can help: *one is a bun, two is a shoe, three is a tree, four is a door, five is a hive, six is sticks, seven is heaven, eight is a gate, nine is a vine, and ten is a hen.* Now you can use your memory of this rhyme to learn other material by creating an image that attaches the new material to the items in the rhyme. Make the image unusual so it will be memorable, and picture the image. If the order of the items is important, you have to stick to the order in the rhyme, but otherwise you can rearrange the list to maximize the outrageous imagery. For example, if you have to remember to get milk, peanut butter, apples, and mouthwash at the store, create images that pair each item with one on the list. For the association between milk and bun, imagine opening a package of buns and pouring milk into the package so that they are wet, soggy, and disgusting; picture that image. Then think about polishing your shoes with peanut butter, spreading it evenly over the shoes. Create an image for each item. To recall the items, all you have to do is think, "One is a bun," and your image of milk-soaked buns should prompt your memory. "Two is a shoe," which should prompt you to retrieve... .

Be an *Active* learner

REVIEW

- What techniques have researchers used to assess memory retrieval? pp. 278–279
- What evidence do some researchers cite when arguing that flashbulb memories do not result from a unique type of memory process? pp. 281–282
- How do primacy and recency effects influence memory retrieval? p. 283

THINK CRITICALLY

- Is flashbulb memory more explicit or implicit? Explain.
- What makes unusual imagery better than ordinary images as memory aids?

APPLY PSYCHOLOGY

- Can you see any differences in memory for the women and men in your family? Do stereotypical gender differences apply? Give examples.
- Provide three examples of how imagery can assist retrieval, drawing these examples from the classes you are taking now.

Forgetting: When Memory Fails

Quick! Name your first-grade teacher. Recite your Social Security number. Tell where you went on your last vacation. Did you have any problems in remembering the answers to these questions? In general, your memory serves you amazingly well, but we tend to take good memory for granted and to complain about memory lapses. Everyone experiences memory failures, and forgetting has been a topic in psychology since its early years.

Early Studies

Starting with the pioneering work of Hermann Ebbinghaus and others in the latter part of the 1800s, many psychologists have studied forgetting—and their work has not been forgotten! Such research has revealed a great deal about memory processes, including forgetting. Some of the memory tasks used in their studies involved paper and pencil, but most merely involved the experimenter, a participant, and some information to be learned.

■ *Hermann Ebbinghaus was the first researcher to investigate memory scientifically.*

■ **EBBINGHAUS AND FORGETTING.** Hermann Ebbinghaus (1850–1909) studied how well people retain stored information. Ebbinghaus earnestly believed that the contents of consciousness could be studied by scientific principles. He tried to quantify how quickly participants could learn, relearn, and forget information. Ebbinghaus was the first person to investigate memory scientifically and systematically, which made his technique as important as his findings.

In his early studies, in which he was both researcher and participant, Ebbinghaus assigned himself the task of learning lists of letters in order of presentation. First, he strung together groups of three letters to make nonsense syllables such as *nak, dib, mip,* and *daf* because he believed that nonsense syllables carry no previous associations to contaminate the measurement of learning. Next, he recorded how many times he had to present lists of these nonsense syllables to himself before he could remember them perfectly. Ebbinghaus found that when the lists were short, his learning was nearly perfect after one or two trials. When they contained more than seven items, however, he had to present them over and over to achieve accurate recall.

Later, Ebbinghaus did learning experiments with other participants, using the technique of *relearning.* He had them learn lists of syllables and then, after varying amounts of time, measured how quickly the participants relearned the original list, which he called the *saving method,* because what was initially learned was not totally forgotten. Ebbinghaus's research showed that forgetting occurs very rapidly. Recall falls from perfect performance to less than 50% correct within 20 minutes. After the first several hours, forgetting levels off to a very slow decrease, indicating that most forgetting occurs quickly. (See Figure 8.12, which shows Ebbinghaus's "forgetting curve.")

Schema [SKEEM-uh]
A conceptual framework that organizes information and allows a person to make sense of the world.

Decay
Loss of information from memory as a result of disuse and the passage of time.

■ **BARTLETT AND FORGETTING.** In 1932, English psychologist Sir Frederick Bartlett reported that when college students tried to recall stories they had just read, they changed them in several interesting ways: they shortened and simplified details, a process Bartlett called *leveling;* they focused on or emphasized certain details, a process he called *sharpening;* and they altered facts to make the stories fit their own views of the world, a process he called *assimilation.* In other words, the students constructed memories that distorted the events.

Contemporary explanations of this distortion have centered on the reconstructive nature of the memory process—memory retrieval is more like a reconstruction

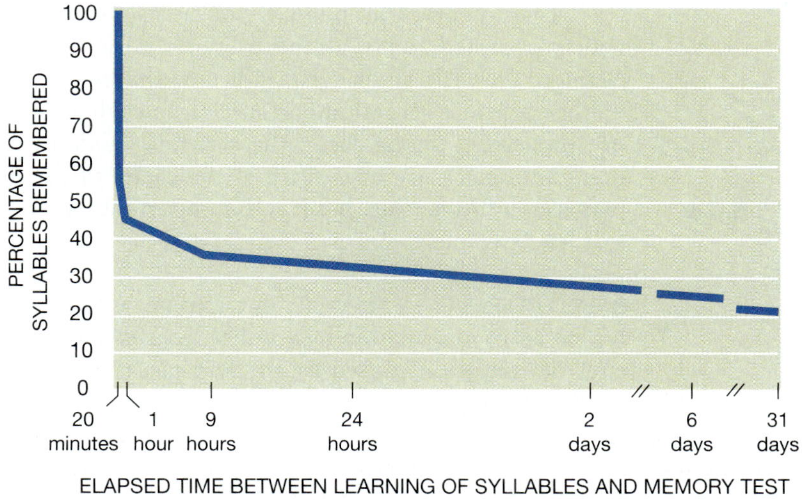

FIGURE 8.12

Ebbinghaus's Forgetting Curve

Ebbinghaus found that most forgetting occurs during the first 9 hours after learning.

than a replay. This reconstructive process occurs partly because people develop a **schema**—a conceptual framework that organizes information and allows a person to make sense of the world. Because people cannot remember *all* the details of an event or situation, they keep key facts and lose minor details. Schemas group together key pieces of information. In general, people try to fit an entire memory into some framework that will be available for later recall. Distortion is important in forgetting, but so is the type of decay that Ebbinghaus researched.

Key Causes of Forgetting

Daniel Schacter (2001) wrote about the types of problems that can plague memory, referring to them as "sins of memory." Schacter's memory sins include factors that affect the reasons that people fail to retrieve information when they need it and the processes that make memory inaccurate. Two processes, decay and interference, account for several "memory sins" and can affect both short-term storage and long-term memory. (See Figure 8.13.)

■ **DECAY OF INFORMATION. Decay** is the loss of information from memory as a result of disuse and the passage of time. Decay theory asserts that unimportant events fade from memory, and details become lost, confused, or fuzzy if not called up every once in a while. Another way to look at decay theory is this: memory exists in the brain in a physiological form known as a *memory trace.* With the passage of time and a lack of active use, the trace disintegrates or fades and is lost.

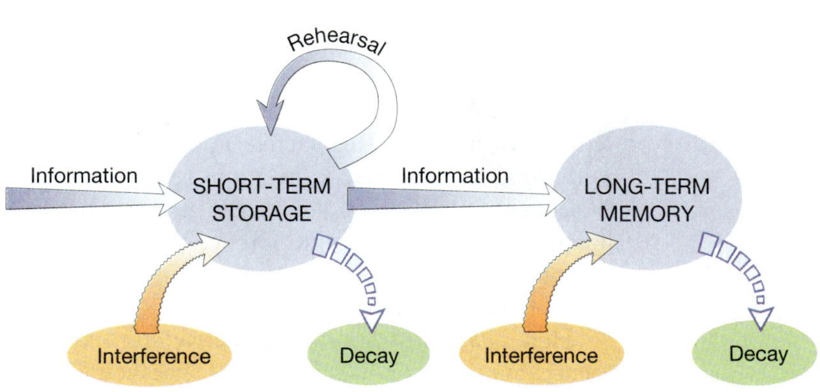

FIGURE 8.13

Decay and Interference in Short-Term and Long-Term Storage

The transfer of information from short-term storage to long-term memory is crucial for accurate recall at a later time. Note that decay and interference affect both stages of storage.

Take Home Tip
for the Active Learner

This text is providing you with a great deal of new information. Interference will be a problem, but you can prevent interference by organizing your studying. For example, pay attention to the headings and subheadings within chapters. Attending to the outline of chapters or sections can help you understand the organization of the material, which can minimize the impact of interference.

Decay theory was popular for many years but is not widely accepted today as the primary cause of forgetting. Many of the early studies that indicated that memories decay did not consider several important variables that affect memory processes, among them, the rate and mode of stimulus presentation. Decay does form a small part of the final explanation of forgetting, but it is less important than other factors, such as interference.

■ **INTERFERENCE IN MEMORY. Interference** is the suppression of one bit of information by another received either earlier or later or confusion caused by the two pieces of information. Interference theory suggests that the limited capacity of short-term storage makes it susceptible to interference from, or confusion among, other learned items. That is, when competing information is stored in short-term storage, the crowding that results affects a person's memory for particular items. The person experiences encoding failure—a memory failure attributable to encoding problems. For example, if you look up a friend's home telephone number and then look up her cell phone number as well, the second number will probably interfere with your ability to remember the first one. Moreover, interference in memory is more likely to occur when a person is presented with a great deal of new information. Situations that present an overload of information tend to produce encoding failures.

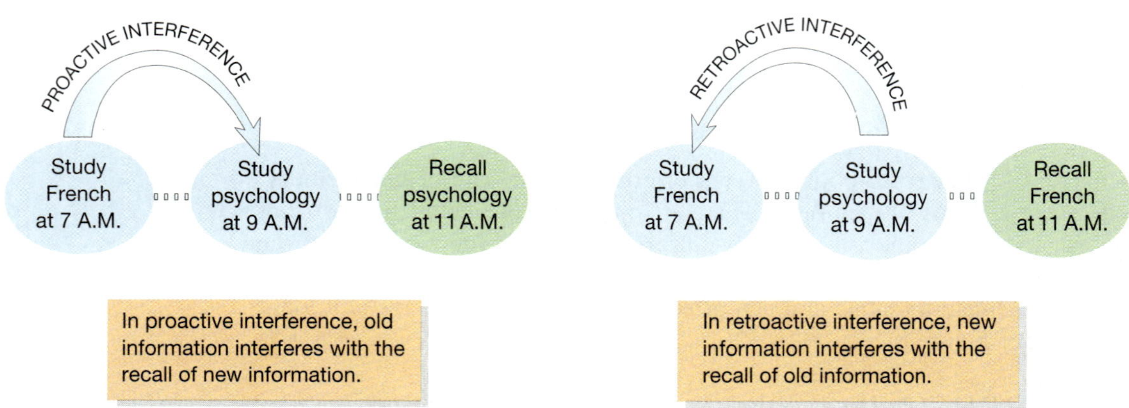

FIGURE 8.14

Proactive and Retroactive Interference

In memory, proactive and retroactive interference occur when information interferes with (inhibits recall of) other information.

Research on interference theory shows that the extent and nature of a person's experiences with a learning task both before and after learning are important. For example, someone given a list of nonsense syllables may recall 75% of the items correctly. However, if the person had earlier been given 20 similar lists to learn, the number of items correctly recalled would be lower; the previous lists would interfere with recall. If the person were subsequently given additional lists to learn, recall would also be lower. Psychologists call these interference effects proactive and retroactive interference (or inhibition). **Proactive interference,** or *proactive inhibition,* is a decrease in accurate recall of information as a result of the effects of previously learned or presented information. **Retroactive interference,** or *retroactive inhibition,* is a decrease in accurate recall as a result of the subsequent presentation of different information. Figure 8.14 illustrates both types of interference. Proactive and retroactive interference help explain most failures to recall information in long-term memory.

Take Home Tip
for the Active Learner

If you have a choice about when to make a speech or when to be interviewed, go first or last if you want to be remembered.

Here is an illustration of proactive and retroactive interference: Suppose you hear a series of speeches, each 5 minutes

■ *Listening to a series of speeches, you will be most likely to recall the first and last ones.*

long. According to psychological research on interference, you will be most likely to remember the first and last speeches. There will be no proactive interference with the first speech and no retroactive interference with the last speech. Your memory of the middle speeches, however, will suffer from both proactive and retroactive interference. Political campaign managers attempt to capitalize on these effects in scheduling their candidates' speeches. For example, they urge the candidates to speak both very early in the campaign and very late, just before people vote. If several candidates are to speak back-to-back, knowledgeable campaign managers try to schedule their candidates either first or last.

■ **INTERFERENCE IN ATTENTION.** According to Schacter (2001), interference in attention is responsible for one of the most annoying types of memory failure—absentmindedness. This problem plagues almost everyone, even people who have excellent memories, because this type of interference prevents information from getting into long-term memory.

Absentmindedness is encoding failure. You really can't remember where you put your keys because that information is not there to retrieve. This problem is common because the competition for attention leads us to ignore some stimuli at critical points in the flow of information through the memory system, and we do not remember where we put our keys, book, really important paper, glasses, wallet, and so forth.

When people try to attend to more than one thing at a time, their attention is divided, which is another form of interference in attention. Divided attention presents a problem for both encoding and retrieval processes, but these effects are not equal: distraction during encoding is a much bigger problem than during retrieval (Brown & Craik, 2000).

Interference in attention may be the underlying explanation for people's poor identification of individuals from ethnic groups other than their own. The old saying that "They all look alike" is not correct. People can perceive subtle differences in faces, but they do not necessarily use this ability. According to research by Daniel Levin (2000), people have a tendency to attend to and encode more detailed face information when the faces are from people in their own ethnic group, rather than other ethnic groups. The memory failure is really an encoding problem that originated at the level of attention. "They" all look alike because we do not attend to enough detail to remember the differences that characterize their faces.

For many years, interference in attention was used to explain what is called the *Stroop effect* (Stroop, 1935). The Stroop test is a procedure in which people

Interference
Suppression of one bit of information by another received either earlier or later or the confusion of two pieces of information.

Proactive [pro-AK-tiv] interference
Decrease in accurate recall of information as a result of the effects of previously learned or presented information; also known as *proactive inhibition*.

Retroactive [RET-ro-AK-tiv] interference
Decrease in accurate recall of information as a result of the subsequent presentation of different information; also known as *retroactive inhibition*.

FIGURE 8.15

For the Active Learner: Stroop Effect

Read the words in each column as fast as you can.

A	B	C
red	blue	green
green	red	yellow
blue	green	blue
yellow	yellow	red
blue	red	blue
red	blue	green
yellow	yellow	red
green	red	blue
blue	blue	green
red	green	yellow
green	yellow	red
blue	red	yellow
yellow	blue	green
green	yellow	blue

are presented with the names of colors, printed in ink that is not the same as the color named. Figure 8.15 illustrates the Stroop effect. When people read column A, naming the word, most people find it difficult to attend to the word and ignore the color of ink (the Stroop effect). Their performance is slower and has more errors than for column B, when the words are in standard, black ink, or in column C, when the words are printed in the same color ink as the name of the word. The color of the ink produces interference. This explanation has been popular—but attention, rather than interference, is now considered more important in explaining the Stroop effect (MacLeod, 1991).

Special Types of Forgetting

Psychologists have learned that special kinds of forgetting are not easily explained by decay or interference. These problems are not symptomized by the inability to retrieve information from memory. Instead, these "sins of memory" lead to remembering incorrectly.

■ **EYEWITNESS TESTIMONY.** The police and the courts have generally accepted *eyewitness testimony* as some of the best evidence. Eyewitnesses are people who saw a particular crime occurring, often have no bias or grudge, and are sworn to tell (and recall) the truth. Eyewitness testimony is considered very credible and is often a factor that increases the chance of a conviction. But can the witness to an accident or crime accurately report the facts of the situation to the police or the courts? The answer is yes and no; eyewitnesses can be accurate, and many of their identifications are correct. But eyewitnesses make mistakes. The growing availability of DNA evidence has demonstrated how often eyewitnesses are incorrect (see the *Psychology in Action* box).

■ *Memories are subject to interference, distortion, and error, which can lead eyewitnesses to make mistakes.*

psychology *in action*

Improving Justice

For 20 years psychologists investigated the processes that can influence the accuracy of eyewitness accounts. According to Kathryn Foxhall (2000, p. 36) "the police departments haven't exactly knocked the door down to find out what law enforcement was doing wrong in getting testimony to convict people." That situation began to change when DNA evidence showed that eyewitnesses were mistaken almost as often as the psychological research indicated. A big change occurred in 1996, when the Department of Justice convened a panel to study the problem of inaccuracy among witnesses and to make recommendations to law enforcement concerning witnesses.

The guidelines developed by this expert panel provide detailed instructions for law enforcement personnel so that they can obtain the best quality of information from witnesses (U.S. Department of Justice, 1999). Many of the guidelines represent applied versions of research findings from the studies on eyewitness testimony. For example, one recommendation is to avoid biased questions. The guidelines suggest using open-ended questions that allow witnesses to put information in their own words rather than asking questions that include a limited number of choices. For example, an interviewer should say, "Tell me about the crash," rather than "Was it the white car that ran the red light?" Another recommendation is to ask witnesses to use drawings and gestures rather than rely exclusively on verbal recall. This recommendation allows witnesses to draw on various modes of encoding in their retrieval.

The inclusion of psychologists and their expertise in eyewitness recall marks what psychologist Gary Wells (in Foxhall, 2000) describes as a high point in the involvement of psychologists in law enforcement. More than 60 wrongfully convicted people have been exonerated by using DNA evidence, and many were convicted on the basis of eyewitness testimony. These guidelines represent a beginning for improving justice.

If memory is a reconstructive process, as many psychologists contend, then it is not a literal reproduction of the past; memory is not a storehouse of information but a perception of the past (Koriat et al., 2000). Researchers with this view have explored a variety of real-life memory problems, including eyewitness accuracy, beginning in the 1970s with Elizabeth Loftus (1975, 1979). She investigated the accuracy of eyewitness testimony and the circumstances that lead witnesses to make mistakes. One of her early studies presented a video of a traffic crash and asked people to answer questions about what they saw. Loftus found that the wording of questions influenced the witnesses' reports. For example, witnesses who answered the question, "How fast were the cars going when they contacted each other?" gave significantly lower speed estimates than the witnesses who answered the question, "How fast were the cars going when they crashed into each other?" All participants saw the same videotape, but they were influenced by the wording of the questions. This distortion of memory is sometimes referred to as the *misinformation effect.*

To complicate matters, the memories of eyewitnesses often become enhanced over time (recall Bartlett's theory of assimilation). Harvard law professor Alan Dershowitz (1986) asserts that the memories of witnesses—particularly those with a stake in the eventual outcome—tend to get more detailed with the passage of time. Dershowitz calls this process *memory enhancement* and argues that it occurs when people fit their hazy memories into a coherent pattern that seems realistic and likely. Ironically, the more detailed a witness's report is (even about irrelevant details), the more credible that witness is assumed to be, even if the witness is recalling things inaccurately (Bell & Loftus, 1989).

Not only are witnesses inappropriately credible, they are also overly confident—even when they are wrong. Unfortunately, accuracy and confidence in one's accuracy are not strongly related; people can have a great deal of confidence that they saw something when, in fact, they did not (Koriat et al., 2000; Sporer et al., 1995). When a person feels that another eyewitness has corroborated an identification, the witness's confidence increases. However, when another witness identifies someone else, that confidence quickly decreases (Luus & Wells, 1994). Even repeated interrogation of a witness can modify the witness's memory—enhancing the recall of

pointcounterpoint

Recovered Memories

The Issue: Are recovered memories real?

POINT

The process of repression leads to motivated forgetting, and these memories represent traumatic events in people's past.

COUNTERPOINT

Recovered memories are usually false memories that occur through suggestion rather than recall.

The concept of motivated forgetting is critical to the controversy over recovered memories. If motivated forgetting can occur, then these repressed memories can resurface and the memories can be recovered. This process is exactly what some people claim has happened: as adults, people can recover the memories of childhood abuse or prior alien abduction. The debate over recovered memories has become intense and divisive, sometimes pitting clinical psychologists against researchers.

The memory researchers typically draw from laboratory studies that demonstrate everyday memory processes as well as errors and distortions in retrieval. Based on this type of research, some memory researchers have asserted that victims of sexual abuse could not forget their childhood events for long durations (Garry & Loftus, 1994; Pendergrast, 1997) and that there is nothing special about a traumatic memory (Shobe & Kihlstrom, 1997).

Clinicians and researchers have accused each other of acting improperly. The clinicians who have worked with patients claim that the laboratory research cannot be generalized to patients because laboratory research is restricted from presenting traumatic events and studying the memory consequences (Pope, 2000). Generalizing laboratory research to traumatized patients is not valid. Researchers have accused misguided therapists of helping people "recover" events that never occurred, such as the accusations concerning psychiatrist John Mack and his patients who recalled alien abductions.

Three key questions need to be addressed: First, can someone forget horrible experiences and remember them years later? Second, is there a potential physiological basis for such recall? And third, is memory fallible? Clinical psychologists are concerned with the first issue; physiologists, the second; and memory researchers, the third.

The third question is the easiest to answer. Yes, memory is fallible in a number of ways, including remembering events that never took place. People can be led on and can attribute information to the wrong source; people can fail to retrieve information that is in their long-term memory, and they can believe that they experienced something that they did not.

In answer to the second question, there may be perceptual and physiological explanations for these memory errors (Payne et al., 1997; Schacter, 1997). Even more interesting, true memories may produce different patterns of brain activity than do false memories (Cabeza et al., 2001; Fabiani, Stadler, & Wessels, 2000).

The first question is the most difficult to answer, and researchers and clinicians have furnished different answers. Let's look at the areas of agreement. Without any question, many women and men have been sexually abused as children, and this abuse can be a factor in psychological problems, both during childhood and continuing into adulthood (Knapp & VandeCreek, 2000). No facet of the recovered memory controversy should minimize or discount the reality of the problem of sexual abuse during childhood.

Many abused children do not talk about the situation. Failing to tell someone is not the same as failing to remember (and this situation could also apply to alien abductees). Many people tell therapists about sexual abuse because their therapist may be the first person who has asked or the first person who is trusted. Thus, allegations of sexual abuse during childhood may first appear years later, but this situation is not part of the recovered memory controversy. These memories were not recovered because they were never lost; they simply were not disclosed.

Most victims of sexual abuse remember the experience, but all do not. And some of those who remember are patients in therapy. These cases are the center of the recovered memory debate. According to a review of surveys of therapists, patients with recovered memories of abuse are rare, but they exist (Knapp & VandeCreek, 2000). Also, a question by the therapist concerning sexual abuse during childhood is not a sufficient suggestion to create a false memory. Suggestive techniques, especially those involving hypnosis, are ways to create false memories, making Mack's patients' memories of alien abduction more suspect than many of the patients who recall childhood sexual abuse.

some details and inducing the person to forget other details—even when the questioning contains no misinformation (Shaw, Bjork, & Handal, 1995). A witness may recall the type of gun used in a robbery after a police interview but become confused over the color of the coat the robber was wearing. When the questions are leading, the bias is strong, and people sometimes cannot distinguish their reconstructed memories from the events they actually experienced. After the third interview, the witness may not be able to distinguish between what she witnessed and inferences she made on the basis of questions that came up in the interviews.

The research on eyewitness testimony suggests that memory is routinely inaccurate. People reconstruct events, and those reconstructions can vary sharply from what occurred. This type of error is definitely one of the "sins" of memory, but a related memory issue has generated even more controversy: can traumatic events lead people to experience a special type of forgetting in which the memory is buried in the unconscious and then later recovered?

MOTIVATED FORGETTING. Freud (1933) was the first to suggest formally the idea of *motivated forgetting*—that frightening, traumatic events might be forgotten simply because people want (or need) to forget them. He stated that such memory loss occurs through *repression*—the burying of traumatic events in the unconscious, where they remain but are inaccessible. The status of the concept of repressed memories gained more attention when the topic of sexual abuse of children began to gain widespread publicity; the topic of alien abduction has added to this controversy (see *Point/Counterpoint*).

Most researchers agree that motivated forgetting probably is a real phenomenon, but it is not the type of phenomenon that can be investigated experimentally in a laboratory. It would be unethical to attempt to traumatize participants, and it would require follow-ups over time to determine if the experience had resulted in repression. Clinical psychologists have experience in dealing with people who have lived through traumatic events, both in childhood and later in life, but some researchers are reluctant to accept clinical evidence (Pope, 2000). Thus, the phenomenon of motivated forgetting due to repression is accepted, but many psychologists are critical of its use in the debate over recovered memories of childhood abuse (and alien abduction).

To further complicate this complex area, repression is not necessary for the creation of false memories, nor are such memories unique to traumatic experiences. In Figure 8.1, we asked you to examine a group of words to illustrate levels of processing, but your memory for this list can also illustrate another memory phenomenon. Without looking at the list again, identify which of the following words were on that list—SWEET, NEEDLE, ARREST, HOMICIDE. If you followed the set of instructions to analyze the meaning and relationship among the words, you will probably say that SWEET and NEEDLE were not on the list, which is correct. You are also likely to say that the other two words appeared on the list. That is not correct; only one of those words—ARREST—was part of the list. People tend to identify the other two words as part of that list because HOMICIDE has a conceptual relationship with the 12 words on that list (Roediger & McDermott, 1995). If you misidentified this word, you have experienced a false memory. It wasn't related to a personal trauma, and your forgetting wasn't motivated in any way, but it demonstrates how everyone is subject to the memory processes that can lead to false memories.

Why are our memories so vulnerable to interference, distortion, and error? The adaptive benefits of memory are obvious, so the evolutionary benefit of memory is clear. However, some of that benefit is negated by memory problems, which seem difficult to reconcile in an evolutionary framework. Perhaps the problems of memory are not so serious (Anderson & Schooler, 2000). The same processes that produce memory problems may have advantages, or alternatively, these errors are not

student voices

Kate Cook
Simon's Rock College

As a nonfiction writer, I rely heavily on my ability to recall the past. It is crucial that I remember details of moments (the afternoon light through a window or the crisp smell of a campfire or the slight give of kneading dough to create a complete picture for my readers. My psychology training has helped me to understand the processes of memory more completely.

so damaging as to hamper reproductive success. For example, most of the information that we cannot recall is not critically important, at least in a life-threatening way, and we seem to be able to retrieve the information that is important at any given time. We forget information such as the function of the suprachiasmic nucleus all too often during a test, but we do not forget that walking into traffic is dangerous. Indeed, even people with profound types of memory loss rarely lose memory to the extent that they endanger themselves.

Neuroscience and Forgetting: Studies of Amnesia

Much of the early work on the neuroscience of memory began with the study of patients in hospitals who for one reason or another had developed **amnesia,** the inability to remember information. Daytime TV dramas (the soaps) frequently portray people with amnesia, but the presentation is rarely accurate. Amnesia occurs much more often on television than anywhere else. The standard TV scenario involves a person who has sustained a blow to the head, who wakes up in the hospital and cannot remember who he (or she) is or how he got to the hospital. The amnesia persists for weeks or months (depending on the plot development of the show). In reality, many people who sustain a blow to the head are indeed knocked unconscious, taken to the hospital, and wake up not remembering how they got there (after all, they were unconscious when transported to the hospital). However, relatively few forget who they are, and this type of amnesia very rarely persists for weeks or months.

There are two basic kinds of amnesia: retrograde and anterograde. **Retrograde amnesia** is the inability to remember events and experiences that preceded a damaging event, such as a blow to the head. The loss of memory can cover a period ranging from a few minutes to several years. Recovery tends to begin quickly and over the next days to weeks, memory returns, with earlier events being remembered before more recent ones. This type of amnesia is the real version of what appears on the soaps.

Anterograde amnesia is the inability to remember events and experiences that occur *after* an injury or brain damage; that is, anterograde amnesia is the inability to form new memories. People suffering from anterograde amnesia are stuck in the lives they lived before being injured; new events are often completely forgotten. The case of H. M. (see p. 276) is an example of anterograde amnesia. People with anterograde amnesia are able to learn some new information, but they tend to be much better at forming new procedural memories than declarative memories (Squire & Kandel, 1999). H. M. could meet someone for the hundredth time, yet believe the individual to be a perfect stranger, but he was able to learn new motor skills. Interestingly, he would have no recall of the experience of practicing such a skill, so he would believe that he could not perform the task he had learned.

The existence of different types of amnesia produced by different types of brain damage supports the view that memory is extremely varied. Many types of coding exist, and many types of memories are formed. These memories may be affected by a range of physical events, past experiences, and current ones—thus, memory is as much a process as it is an event or thing.

Building Table 8.3 summarizes key processes in the three stages of memory.

Be an *Active* learner

REVIEW

- What are the differences between Ebbinghaus's and Bartlett's approaches to forgetting? pp. 286–287
- Describe the differences between proactive and retroactive interference. p. 288
- Distinguish retrograde from anterograde amnesia. p. 294

THINK CRITICALLY

- At what point in the investigation of a crime is it most critical to the witness to correctly identify a perpetrator? Why?
- What types of evidence would you need in order to accept as valid the recovered memories of alien abductions? Would this evidence differ from that needed to validate recovered memories of childhood sexual abuse? If so, are the differing standards reasonable and objective?

APPLY PSYCHOLOGY

- What type of study and testing environment will minimize interference in encoding and retrieving memory, and how can you build such an environment?

Amnesia [am-NEE-zhuh]
Inability to remember information (typically all events within a specific period), usually due to physiological trauma.

Retrograde [RET-ro-grade] amnesia
Loss of memory of events and experiences that preceded an amnesia-causing event.

Anterograde amnesia
Loss of memory for events and experiences occurring from the time of injury forward.

Building Table 8.3

Key Processes in Stages of Memory

Stage	Encoding	Storage	Retrieval	Duration	Forgetting
Sensory memory	Visual or auditory (iconic or echoic storage)	Brief, fragile, and temporary	Information is extracted from stimulus presentation and transferred to short-term storage.	Visual: 250 milliseconds; auditory: about 3 seconds	Rapid decay of information; interference is possible if a new stimulus is presented.
Short-term storage	Visual and auditory	Repetitive rehearsal maintains information in storage, perhaps on a visual–spatial "scratch pad" or auditory loop where further encoding can take place.	Maintenance and elaborative rehearsal can keep information available for retrieval; retrieval is enhanced through elaboration and further encoding.	No more than 30 seconds, probably less than 20 seconds; depends on specific task and stimuli	Interference and decay affect memory; new stimulation causes rapid loss of information unless it is especially important.
Long-term memory	Salient or important information processed by working memory is transferred into long-term memory through elaborative rehearsal.	Storage is organized on logical and semantic lines for rapid recall; organization of information by categories, events, and other structures aids retrieval.	Retrieval is aided by cues and careful organization; errors in retrieval can be introduced: long-term memory is fallible.	Indefinite; many events will be recalled in great detail for a lifetime.	Both decay and interference contribute to retrieval failure.

Summary and Review

Memory: The Brain as Information Processor

Define memory.

■ *Memory* is the ability to remember past events or previously learned information or skills; it is also the storage system that allows retention and retrieval of information. pp. 264–265

KEY TERM
memory, p. 264

Encoding

What is the information-processing approach to memory, and what is encoding?

■ The information-processing approach assumes that each stage of learning and memory is separate, though related, and is analyzable by scientific methods. pp. 266–267

■ *Encoding* is the organizing of information so that the nervous system can process it; it is the process of getting stimuli into a form usable by the nervous system. pp. 265–266

What are the underlying assumptions of the levels-of-processing approach?

■ The *levels-of-processing approach* holds that a person can process a stimulus in different ways, to different extents, and at different levels. When the level of processing becomes more complex, the theory asserts, the coding occurs at a deeper level of memory. p. 266

■ The *encoding specificity principle* asserts that the effectiveness of a specific retrieval cue depends on how well it matches up with the originally encoded information. The more clearly and sharply retrieval cues are defined, the better recall will be. pp. 266–267

What is the neurological basis of encoding?

■ PET and fMRI brain imaging techniques indicate that the prefrontal cortex and areas in the medial temporal lobes are involved in encoding, but different areas are important for retrieval. pp. 267–268

KEY TERMS

encoding, p. 264; levels-of-processing approach, p. 267; encoding specificity principle, p. 267; transfer-appropriate processing, p. 267

Storage

Describe the role of sensory memory.

■ *Storage* refers to the process of maintaining information as well as the locations where information is held. p. 268

■ *Sensory memory* is the mechanism that performs initial encoding and brief storage of sensory information. Once information is established in sensory memory, it must be transferred elsewhere for additional encoding or it will be lost. pp. 269

Describe short-term storage.

■ Short-term storage was initially conceptualized as *short-term memory*, which maintains a limited amount of information (7 plus or minus 2 items) for about 20–30 seconds. *Working memory* is a more recent conceptualization that is seen as consisting of three subsystems: an auditory loop to encode and rehearse auditory information; a visual–spatial scratch pad, and a central processing mechanism, or executive, that balances the information flow. p. 270

What is rehearsal?

■ The limited number of items that can be reproduced easily after presentation is called the *memory span*. The immediate memory span usually contains one or two *chunks*—manageable and meaningful units of information. p. 271

■ *Rehearsal* is the process of repeatedly verbalizing, thinking about, or otherwise acting on or transforming information in order to remember it. *Maintenance rehearsal* is the repetitive review of information with little or no interpretation; this shallow form of rehearsal involves the physical stimulus, not its underlying meaning. *Elaborative rehearsal* involves repetition in which the stimulus may be associated with other events and further processed; this type of rehearsal is usually necessary to transfer information to long-term memory. pp. 271–272

What is long-term memory, and what are the different types of long-term storage?

■ *Long-term memory* is the storage mechanism that keeps a relatively permanent record of information. It is divided into procedural memory and declarative memory. *Procedural memory* is memory for the perceptual, motor, and cognitive skills necessary to complete complex tasks; *declarative memory* is memory for specific facts, which can be subdivided into episodic and semantic memory. pp. 272–274

■ *Episodic memory* is a personal memory for specific events and situations, including time sequence. *Semantic memory* is memory of generalized knowledge of the world, including ideas, rules, and general concepts based on experiences and learned knowledge. pp. 274–275

■ *Explicit memory* is conscious memory that a person is aware of, such as memory of a word in a list or an event that occurred in the past; generally speaking, most recall tasks require participants to recall explicit information. Explicit memory is a voluntary, active memory store. In contrast, *implicit memory* is memory a person is not aware of possessing; considered an almost unconscious process, implicit memory occurs unintentionally and almost automatically. p. 275

What is the neurological basis of memory storage?

■ Structures in the prefrontal cortex and the medial temporal lobes are important for working memory, and the hippocampus, a structure in the medial temporal lobes, is critical in transferring memories from short-term to long-term storage. *Consolidation* is the term that describes this transformation. The repeated stimulation of neurons may produce changes in the synapses of neurons and long-term potentiation, which may be the underlying neurological basis for memory. pp. 276–277

KEY TERMS

storage, p. 268; sensory memory, p. 269; memory span, p. 270; chunks, p. 270; rehearsal, p. 270; maintenance rehearsal, p. 270; elaborative rehearsal, p. 270; short-term memory, p. 270; working memory, p. 272; long-term memory, p. 272; procedural memory, p. 272; declarative memory, p. 274; episodic memory, p. 274; semantic memory, p. 274; explicit memory, p. 274; implicit memory, p. 274; consolidation, p. 276

Retrieval

What are recall, recognition, and relearning?

■ *Retrieval* is the process by which stored information is recovered from memory. Recall, recognition, and relearning can be used to assess retrieval success. Recall is reproducing the details of a situation or idea and placing them together in a meaningful framework (usually without any cues or aids). Recognition is remembering whether one has seen a stimulus before—whether the stimulus is familiar. After information has been learned, relearning can determine how long it takes to reacquire the information. pp. 278–279

How does a person's physiological or emotional state affect retrieval?

■ Physiological and emotional states affect retrieval. *State-dependent learning* is the tendency to recall information learned in a particular physiological or emotional state most accurately when one is again in that state.

Flashbulb memories are vivid memories associated with a state of emotional arousal. p. 281

Does gender relate to memory?

■ Gender is not a very important factor in memory, but gender stereotypes have an impact on attention, which can affect memory. p. 282

What distinguishes the primacy effect from the recency effect?

■ The *primacy effect* is the more accurate recall of items presented first in a series; the *recency effect* is the more accurate recall of items presented last. p. 283

What is imagery?

■ *Imagery* is the cognitive process of creating a mental picture of a sensory event. People's imagery systems can be activated by visual, auditory, or olfactory stimuli. pp. 284-285

KEY TERMS

retrieval, p. 278; ex posto facto study; p. 280; state-dependent learning, p. 280; primacy effect, p. 282; recency effect, p. 282; imagery, p. 284

Forgetting: When Memory Fails

How and why is information lost from memory?

■ Memory distortions occur in part because people develop a schema, a way to organize information, that fails to include all details of a situation. pp. 286–287

■ *Decay* is the loss of information from memory as a result of disuse and the passage of time. According to interference theory, the limited capacity of short-term storage makes it susceptible to *interference. Proactive interference* is a decrease in accurate recall as a result of the effects of previously learned or presented information. *Retroactive interference* is a decrease in accurate recall as a result of the subsequent presentation of different information. pp. 287–288

What do eyewitness testimony and recovered memories reveal about the memory process?

■ Both types of memory processes show that memory is subject to errors, including distortion and suggestibility. These errors indicate that memory is more of a reconstruction than a replay. Everyone is subject to these memory problems, but memory is an adaptive process that has many more advantages than disadvantages. pp. 290–293

Distinguish retrograde from anterograde amnesia.

■ *Amnesia* is the inability to remember information, usually because of some physiological trauma (such as a blow to the head). *Retrograde amnesia* is the inability to remember events that preceded a traumatizing event; *anterograde amnesia* is the inability to remember events that occur after such an event. p. 294

KEY TERMS

schema, p. 286; decay, p. 286; interference, p. 289; proactive interference, p. 289; retroactive interference, p. 289; amnesia, p. 294; retrograde amnesia, p. 294; anterograde amnesia, p. 294

9 Cognitive Psychology

Stuart Davis, *Abstraction,* 1937

The past decade has produced a massive number of news stories—the Clinton–Lewinsky scandal, the Gore–Bush fight for the White House, and the attack on the World Trade Center, to name just a few key events. These remarkable stories grab our attention, making us want to know more. The Clinton–Lewinsky humiliation dragged the nation through the sexual escapades of our president and brought about his impeachment. The World Trade Center attacks led to an all-out war on terrorism. When such events occur, most of us gain information and then form our opinions by reading newspapers, watching television, and logging on to the Web. These are typical ways of finding out how our world and our country are changing.

chapter outline

Psychologists find it compelling to study how news is reported and received. They observe how the media operate, track the biases that emerge in reporting news, and observe how people's opinions are shaped. Newspapers, and the media in general, have been criticized for viewing the world in ways that promote liberal political views, disparage conservative views, and ignore nontraditional values. The media is regularly criticized for being sexist, racially prejudiced, pro-gay, ageist, anti-environmental, and biased toward a Western worldview—among other things. When we read newspapers and listen to television, we often find "our" views missing—the commentators are too conservative, too liberal, or in general too polarized to reflect our view. Careful listeners, critical thinkers, and good scientists try to make good decisions about issues in science and politics. Yet we know that our thoughts are affected by a number of variables. For example, in considering how to respond to terrorism—most recently, terror that emerged as part of an Islamic jihad—people often have trouble overcoming preconceived ideas and tend to cling to old, often wrong beliefs despite contradictory evidence. The truth is that people rely on past experience and are reluctant to listen with an open mind to new information (especially information that might require questioning their own beliefs). Thus people often harbor ideas that are ill-informed or just plain wrong. We have a name for this phenomenon—confirmation bias—which we'll discuss later.

Every day, each of us faces and tries to sort out problems both small and large. Researchers attempt to learn how we do this, to better understand thought and help people maximize their potential. Researchers try to break down thought and language into their constituent parts, analyzing each step separately. Some biologists and even many neuroscientists assert that psychologically complex phenomena such as speech and language must be analyzed according to the laws of evolution, molecular biology, and physics (Wilson, 1998). But the truth is—and most social scientists agree on this point—that human behavior, especially thought and language, is far too complex, original, and spontaneous to be explained simply in terms of molecules, genes, and DNA. Human behavior is so complex and varied that no single field of study or theoretical approach can explain it.

In searching for a comprehensive theory of psychology—one that accounts for individual differences—research has recognized that thought and language are separate, but closely related, aspects of human behavior. Thought allows human beings to reflect on and assess the past and to develop new ideas and technology. Language provides human beings with a unique vehicle for expressing thoughts about the past, present, and future. This chapter therefore covers both cognition (thought) and language, the symbolic system people use to communicate their thoughts verbally. Let's take the next step toward understanding human behavior.

Cognitive Psychology: An Overview

How are a tiger and a domestic cat similar? Who is the U.S. Secretary of State? How do you make an omelet? Answering each of these questions requires a different mental procedure. To answer the first question, you probably formed mental images of both felines and then compared the images. In answering the second question, you may simply have recalled the right name from recent news stories. The third question may have required you to mentally review the preparation of an omelet and describe each step. The thinking you used to answer all three questions required the use of knowledge, language, and images.

Cognitive psychology
The study of the overlapping fields of perception, learning, memory, and thought, with a special emphasis on how people attend to, acquire, transform, store, and retrieve knowledge.

Cognitive psychology is the study of the overlapping fields of perception, learning, memory, and thought; it is the study of how people attend to, acquire, transform, store, and retrieve knowledge. Cognitive psychology includes the topics of consciousness, learning, and memory, which we discussed in the past three chapters, and it is basic to other topics, such as intelligence (Chapter 10). In this chapter, we will focus on two core subjects of cognitive psychology: thought and language. The word *cognition* derives from the Latin *cognoscere*, "to know." Cognitive psychologists are interested primarily in mental processes that influence the acquisition and use of knowledge as well as the ability to *reason*—to generate logical and coherent ideas, evaluate situations, and reach conclusions. Cognitive researchers assume that mental processes exist, that people are active processors, and that cognitive processes can be studied using techniques that measure the speed and accuracy of responses.

In the 1920s, behaviorism—with its focus on directly observable behavior—became the main force in psychology, and there was little reference to internal cognitive processes. Discussion of and research on such "mentalistic" phenomena as imagery were avoided. In the late 1950s and early 1960s, the brain itself began to be compared to a computer, and research into thought began again in earnest. This research in the decades after World War II was incredibly wide-ranging and attempted to answer questions that the behaviorists of the 1920s could not address adequately.

■ *Is a penguin or a blue jay closer to your idea of a typical bird?*

It is sometimes hard to pinpoint exactly what cognitive psychology is. This chapter demonstrates the breadth of cognitive psychology and its growth since its origins in the 1950s. We begin with the study of concept formation, which is crucial for all cognition.

Concept Formation: The Process of Forming Mental Groups

Each day, we all solve problems, make decisions, and reason logically, often following steps that are complicated but orderly. Many researchers conceive of reasoning itself as an orderly process that takes place in discrete steps, one set of ideas leading to another. To perform this process, people need to be able to form, manipulate, transform, and interrelate concepts. **Concepts** are the mental categories people use to classify events and objects according to common properties. Many objects with four wheels, a driver's seat, and a steering wheel are automobiles; "automobiles" is a concept. More abstract is the concept of "justice," which has to do with legality and fairness. "Animal," "computer," and "holiday" are all examples of concepts that have various *exemplars*, or specific instances; so there are many kinds of animals, for example, dogs, giraffes, and whales. The study of *concept formation* is the examination of the way people organize and classify events and objects, usually in order to solve problems.

FIGURE 9.1

Classification Tasks

These tasks require choosing from alternatives that share certain properties. For example, in a typical classification task for children, the objective is to circle the picture that is most like the sample.

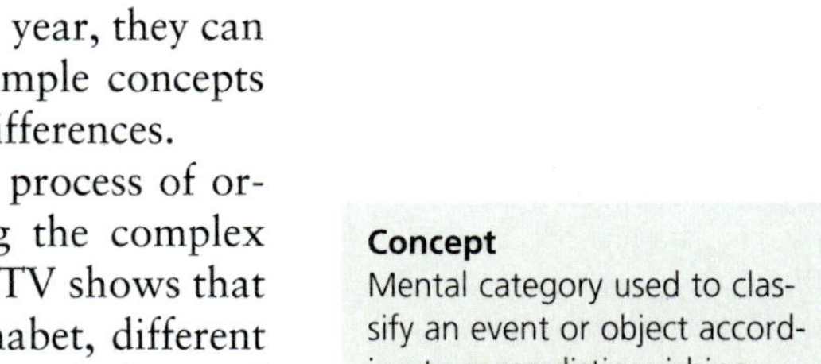

Concepts make people's experience of the world more meaningful by helping them organize their thinking. Individuals develop progressively more complex concepts throughout life. Early on, infants learn the difference between "parent" and "stranger." Within a year, they can discriminate among objects, colors, and people and comprehend simple concepts such as "animal" and "flower." By age 2, they can verbalize these differences.

Much of what young children learn involves *classification*—the process of organizing things into categories—which is crucial to understanding the complex world (see Figure 9.1). Think back to your early school years and to TV shows that taught basic language skills. You were taught the letters of the alphabet, different colors, farm animals and their sounds, and shapes such as triangles, circles, and squares. This process of developing concepts through classification continues

Concept
Mental category used to classify an event or object according to some distinguishing property or feature.

throughout life. It involves separating dissimilar events, finding commonalities, and then grouping similar items together (Ariely, 2001). But what is the best way to study the processes by which children and adults classify and organize information?

As a type of thinking, concept formation is relatively easy to study in controlled laboratory situations. Psychologists design laboratory studies whose objective is to observe participants forming and using concepts through a wide range of tasks. If you were a participant in such an experiment, you might be asked to respond to simple questions, such as "Is this card red, blue, or yellow?" Other tasks become more complex—"Is a bicycle a toy or a vehicle?" (well, it depends on whether it is a kiddy bike or a motorized one, for example). Even more complicated concept formation tasks can be devised in which subtleties between categories are hard to discern—for example, you could be asked to distinguish between a big house, a mansion, a street, a drive, and a boulevard. The experimenter might time your responses and also ask you to express your thought processes out loud.

A key requirement for laboratory studies of concept formation is that participants be able to form rules—statements of how stimuli are related. In a common task used in laboratory investigations of concept formation, an experimenter tells the participants that something about the stimuli to be presented makes them similar. Participants are asked to identify this characteristic—this rule about the relationship between the stimuli. Each time a stimulus is presented, participants are told whether or not the item has the characteristic being targeted. For example, suppose the first stimulus is a picture of a large bird. The experimenter says that it is a *positive instance* (an example that has the characteristic under study). The participant now knows that the concept being studied is most likely largeness or being a bird. The second picture shows a small red bird; the experimenter says that this, too, is a positive instance; the participant now knows that size is not important. The third picture shows a large blue bird; it, too, is a positive instance. Although the concept could be the ability to fly or being an animal, the participant may guess that the relevant concept is being a bird. When, on the fourth trial, the picture is of a small blue toy car and the experimenter says it is a *negative instance* (not an example of the concept), the participant might say with conviction that "bird" is the concept being described. The laboratory example we have just considered allows careful examination of how people form or recognize concepts. But concepts are not always clear-cut. For example, you know that a professor is a teacher and a high school instructor is a teacher, but are ministers teachers? How about den leaders or the president of the United States? Each of these individuals acts as a teacher from time to time. Or consider the concept "family." One concept of a family is Mom, Dad, and 2.4 kids. But what of single-parent families, blended families, adoptive families, communal families, single-gender families, and extended families? Some researchers consider a family to be any group of people who care about each other in significant ways. You can see that concepts are often fuzzy. Often you must think about concepts carefully to understand and define them.

Be an *Active* learner

REVIEW

- What is the fundamental difference between a positive and a negative instance in concept formation? p. 302
- What are prototypes, and how do people use them? p. 302

THINK CRITICALLY

- Cognitive psychology is expansive in scope. How is this a strength of the field? How is it a weakness?

APPLY PSYCHOLOGY

- If you were designing a course to help people develop concept formation skills, what exercises might you include?

Eleanor Rosch has asserted that when people are presented with *fuzzy concepts*, they tend to define them in terms of *prototypes*, or best examples of a class of items (Rosch, 1978). A **prototype** is an abstraction, an idealized pattern of an object or idea that is stored in memory and used to decide whether similar objects or ideas are members of that class of items. A high school English teacher may be a prototype of "teacher"; ministers, den leaders, and psychologists are also examples, but not "best" examples. Some concepts have easily defined prototypes; others are hard to define. When you think about the concept "furniture," you easily recognize that chairs, sofas, and tables are good examples (or *exemplars*). But telephones, stoves,

Prototype
An abstraction, an idealized pattern of an object or idea that is stored in memory and used to decide whether similar objects or ideas are members of the same class of items.

pianos, and mirrors are all furniture as well; therefore, finding a prototype that truly embodies the essence of "furniture" is not an easy task. The concept "computer modem" is much less fuzzy; there may be a few shapes and sizes, but nearly all computer modems do the same thing, in pretty much the same way. Of course, many variables affect how easily concepts are defined, including properties of the concept as well as an individual's unique experiences with its exemplars. These experiences help people build strategies and solve problems.

Problem solving
The behavior of individuals when confronted with a situation or task that requires insight or determination of some unknown elements.

Problem Solving: Confronting Situations That Require Solutions

You are generally unaware of your cognitive processes; you don't usually think about thinking. And yet you are thinking all the time—sorting through choices, deciding where to go, what to do, and when to do it. When you think, you engage in a wide variety of activities, from daydreaming to planning your next few steps on a mountain path.

We have learned many associations, have distinct memories, and are able to categorize and distinguish among objects, events, and concepts. We often, for example, have exemplars in memory of various physics problems (or algebra or chemistry for that matter). When presented with a new problem, we often recall that last problem and see if its solution (or one very similar to it) will work. So our concept formation abilities form the basis for our problem-solving abilities.

■ *Coaches use heuristics when relating the moves they believe are most likely to succeed, based on past experience. A coach might ask, "What move has usually enhanced our strategic position in the game?"*

Human beings are wonderful at **problem solving,** at confronting and resolving situations that require insight or determination of some unknown elements. Because you can form concepts and group things together in logical ways, you are able to organize your thoughts and attack a problem. How can you manage to study for your psychology exam when you have an English paper due tomorrow? How can you fit all your clothes and other belongings into your room's tiny closet? What should you do when your car gets a flat tire on the interstate? These are all problems to be solved. Your approaches to these dilemmas represent some of the highest levels of cognitive functioning. Psychologists believe the process of problem solving has stages, summarized in Figure 9.2 (e.g., Knoblich & Ohlsson, 1999).

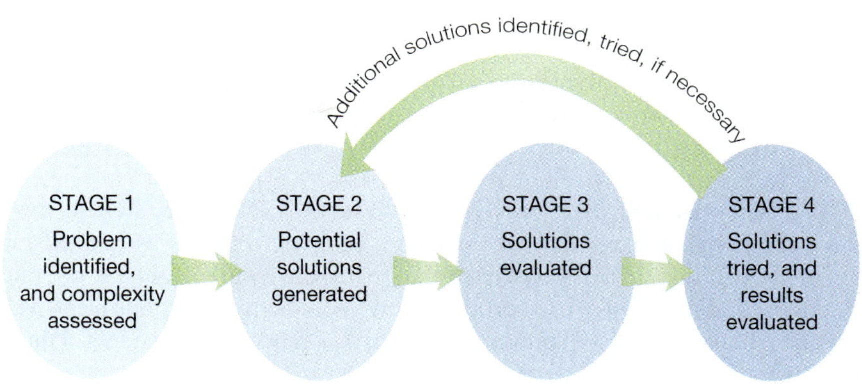

FIGURE 9.2
Stages in Problem Solving
Problem solving can be conceived of as a four-stage process.

There are huge differences in people's problem-solving abilities, but psychologists can help individuals become more effective problem solvers. It turns out that when people (or machines, for that matter) solve problems, they tend to use two basic approaches: algorithms and heuristics. An **algorithm** is a procedure for solving a problem by implementing a set of rules over and over again until the solution is found. An algorithm, if performed correctly, *guarantees* a correct solution. Many mathematics problems (for example, finding a square root) can be solved by using an algorithm. Algorithms are also used for a wide variety of real-life tasks, from increasing the yield of a recipe (say, by doubling each ingredient) to writing a computer program (even a relatively simple program requires several algorithms). To implement an algorithm, you follow the rules regarding which task to implement at which point in the procedure. For example, an algorithm for doubling a recipe might be as follows: "Find the recipe's list of ingredients. Find the amount of a given ingredient, multiply that amount by 2, and use the product as the new amount for that ingredient. Repeat this procedure for each ingredient listed in the recipe." It's monotonous, but it works. However, because you *must* follow every step in an algorithm in order to use it, the necessary time and effort may make algorithms impractical for some purposes. Human problem solvers learn to use rules-of-thumb so that they do not have to follow algorithms rigidly. These rules-of-thumb are integral to heuristic problem-solving strategies.

Heuristics are sets of strategies that act as flexible guidelines—not strict rules and procedures—for discovery-oriented problem solving. A heuristic *may* quickly lead you to a correct solution, but it does not guarantee one. Heuristics reflect the processes used by the human brain; they involve making rough guesses and subjective evaluations that might be called hunches or intuitions (Rumelhart, 1997). For example, the coach of a hockey team might evaluate the team's first-period performance and intuit that different plays might better its chances against that opponent.

Algorithm [AL-go-rith-um] Procedure for solving a problem by implementing a set of rules over and over again until the solution is found.

Heuristics [hyoo-RISS-ticks] Sets of strategies, rather than strict rules, that act as guidelines for discovery-oriented problem solving.

Subgoal analysis Heuristic procedure in which a problem is broken down into smaller steps, each of which has a subgoal.

Means–ends analysis Heuristic procedure in which the problem solver compares the current situation with the desired goal to determine the most efficient way to get from one to the other.

Backward search Heuristic procedure in which a problem solver works backward from the goal or end of a problem to the current position, in order to analyze the problem and reduce the steps needed to get from the current position to the goal.

Functional fixedness Inability to see that an object can have a function other than its stated or usual one.

Most heuristic approaches focus on the goal that is to be achieved. In one approach called **subgoal analysis,** a problem is taken apart or broken down into several smaller steps, each of which has a subgoal. For example, the writing of an essay could be broken into subgoals such as formulating the problem, doing library research, and drafting an outline. In **means–ends analysis,** the person compares the current situation or position with the desired end (the goal) to determine the most efficient *means* for getting from one to the other—for example, she might recognize that getting out of debt first means cutting up credit cards. The objective is to reduce the number of steps needed to reach the goal. A **backward search** involves working backward from the goal, or endpoint, to the current position, both to analyze the problem and to reduce the steps needed to get to the goal. Some problems are most easily solved by starting at the objective and working backward toward the opening or beginning position. People often solve puzzles using this approach, because there are usually a smaller number of choices at the end than at the beginning of a puzzle. This strategy reduces the near infinite number of options available from the opening of the puzzle.

Barriers to Problem Solving

People's problem-solving abilities vary, and they may be subject to certain limitations, among which are functional fixedness and mental set. Researchers study these limitations to gain a better understanding of the processes of problem solving.

■ **FUNCTIONAL FIXEDNESS: COGNITION WITH CONSTRAINTS.** When my (LL) daughter Sarah was 4 years old, we went on a camping trip. It was raining and she wanted to sleep in the car but complained that there was no pillow. I took her raincoat out of the back seat, rolled it up, and it instantly became a pillow. She slept soundly. Sarah was exhibiting a basic human characteristic—functional fixedness. **Functional fixedness** is the inability to see that an object can have a function other than its stated

FIGURE 9.3

The Two-String Problem

In the two-string problem, the person must set one string in motion in order to tie the strings together. This solution illustrates that sometimes, in order to solve problems, people need to overcome functional fixedness and use tools in new ways.

or usual one. When people are functionally fixed, they have limited their conceptual framework; they see too few functions for an object. In many ways, this fixedness constitutes a barrier to problem solving.

Studies of functional fixedness show that the name or meaning given to an object or tool often limits its function (German & Defeyter, 2000). In a typical study, a research participant is presented with a task and provided with tools that can be used in various ways. One laboratory problem used to show functional fixedness is the two-string problem (see Figure 9.3). In this task, a person is put in a room that has two strings hanging from the ceiling and some objects lying on a table. The task is to tie the two strings together, but it is impossible to reach one string while holding the other. The only solution is to tie a weight (one of the objects on the table) to one string and set it swinging back and forth, then take hold of the second string and wait until the first string swings within reach. This task is difficult for some people because their previous experiences with objects may prevent them from considering them as potential tools in an unusual situation.

■ **MENTAL SET.** Psychologists have found that most individuals are flexible in their approaches to solving problems. In other words, they do not use preconceived, or "set," solutions but think about objects, people, and situations in new ways. A flexible approach would allow an astronaut to make an air-filtering device out of duct tape and other spare parts (as in a scene from the film *Apollo 13*). This kind of solution requires limber thought processes. However, sometimes people develop a rigid strategy, or approach, to certain types of problems (Wiley, 1998).

Creative thinking requires breaking out of one's *mental set*—limited ways of thinking about possibilities. Having a mental set is the opposite of being creative. Prior experience predisposes a person to make a particular response in a given situation. In an increasingly complex and changing world, such limitations are problematic. Figure 9.4 offers a problem that is difficult because it requires you to overcome a mental set. Draw no more than four lines that will run through all nine dots—without lifting your pen from the paper. The answer is provided in Figure 9.5 on page 306.

Here's another example of mental set shown in this well-known, oft-repeated riddle. A boy is rushed into an emergency room at the local hospital. Dr. Suarez cries out, "Oh no, my son! What happened?" A few second later Dr. Sonnenschein looks at the same child in the ER and says something similar, such as "Oh no, my son!"

Whose child is he?

Did the hospital make a mistake? Or is Dr. Suarez, a woman, married to Dr. Sonnenschein, a man? Or did a gay couple adopt the child? Our mental set for

FIGURE 9.4

For The Active Learner: The Nine-Dot Problem

Because people tend to group things in familiar ways, it is hard for them to overcome their psychological set to connect the nine dots as instructed.

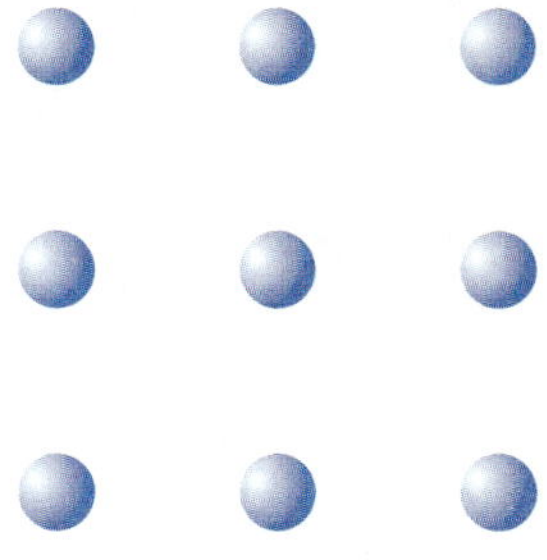

Try to connect all nine dots with no more than four lines, without lifting your pen from the paper.

psychology *in action*

Be A Critical Thinker

Every day, you have to make judgments, classify ideas, and follow logic—that is, engage in reasoning—to solve problems. Being able to think critically will improve your reasoning and thus your problem-solving skills. Besides the guidelines presented in Chapter 1 (pp. 12–13), several other tips can make you a better critical thinker:

Don't fixate on availability. Things that come to mind quickly are not necessarily the best solutions to problems. Don't choose the first answer just because it's there.

Don't generalize too quickly. Just because most elements in a group follow a pattern does not mean all elements in the group will follow the pattern. For example, just because the florist removed the thorns from most of the red roses you bought for Valentine's Day does not mean he didn't miss one.

Don't settle for an easy solution. People often settle for a solution that works, even though other solutions may work even better. Look at all the alternatives.

Don't choose a solution just because it fits preexisting ideas. People often accept ideas too quickly when they conform to previously held views. This is a serious mistake for researchers, who need to be open to new ideas, a state of mind that often requires conscious effort.

Don't fail to consider any possible solution. If you do not evaluate *all* of the available alternatives, you are likely to miss the correct, or most logical, answer.

Don't be emotional. Sometimes people become emotionally tied to a specific idea, premise, or conviction. When this happens, the likelihood of being able to critically evaluate the evidence drops sharply. Critical thinkers are cool and evaluative, not headstrong and emotional.

physicians being men and for the traditional composition of nuclear families helps define a mental set that limits the ability to solve this riddle easily.

Psychology in Action offers suggestions for overcoming barriers to problem solving and improving your critical thinking skills.

FIGURE 9.5

For The Active Learner: The Nine-Dot Solution

Here is a creative solution to the nine-dot problem presented in Figure 9.4. Note that you have to think beyond the typical mental set of seeing the nine dots as forming a square.

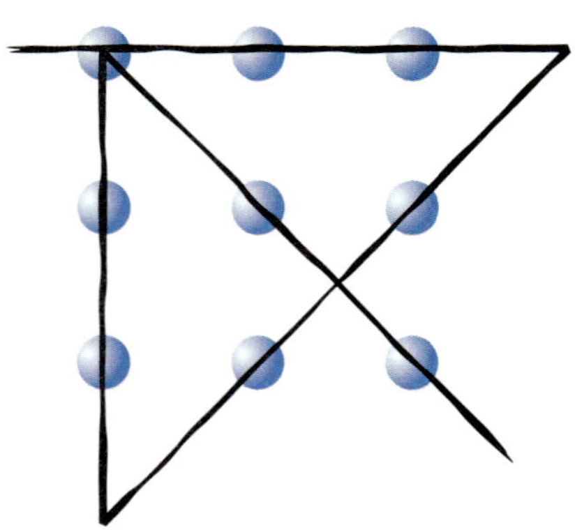

Creative Problem Solving

The owners of a high-rise professional building were deluged with complaints that the building's elevators were too slow. The owners called in a consultant, who researched the problem and discovered that, indeed, tenants often had to wait several minutes for an elevator. Putting in new, faster elevators would cost tens of thousands of dollars, more than the owners could afford. Eventually, the consultant devised a creative solution that ended the complaints but cost only a few hundred dollars: he installed wall mirrors at each elevator stop. Evidently, being able to check out one's appearance while waiting made the time go faster.

Creativity is a feature of thought and problem solving that includes the tendency to generate or recognize high-quality ideas that are original, novel, and appropriate (Sternberg, 2001b). An *original response* to a problem is one that doesn't copy or imitate another response; that is, it originates from the problem solver. A *novel response* is a response that is new or that has no precedent. Unless an original and novel response is also an appropriate response to a given problem, however, psychologists do not call it creative. An *appropriate response* is a response that is reasonable in terms of the situation. Two important questions in studies of creativity are how people can become more creative in their thinking and who is likely to be creative (Mumford et al., 2001; Sternberg, 2000a).

Creativity
A feature of thought and problem solving that includes the tendency to generate or recognize ideas considered to be high-quality, original, novel, and appropriate.

According to well-known creativity researcher Mihalay Csikszentmihalyi (2001), creative individuals are those who have changed the surrounding culture in some way that involves original thinking. Csikszentmihalyi asserts that creativity is the process of redefining or transforming a domain (either a professional field or an area of interest such as gardening, music, or painting) or creating a new domain.

But he also acknowledges, and indeed stresses, the idea that individuals work and create within a culture; creativity is culture dependent—in the West, creativity is often measured as a work product, but in Eastern traditions creativity is often seen as a process of finding inner truth (Lubart, 1999).

When people sort through alternatives to try to solve a problem, they attempt to focus their thinking, discarding inappropriate solutions until a single appropriate option is left. In this way, they *converge* on an answer (or use convergent thinking skills). **Convergent thinking** is narrowing down choices and alternatives to arrive at a suitable answer. **Divergent thinking,** in contrast, is widening the range of possibilities and expanding the options for solutions; doing so lessens the likelihood of functional fixedness or mental set. Guilford (1967) defined creative thinking as divergent thinking. According to other psychologists, any solution to a problem that can be worked out only with time and practice is not a creative solution. To foster creativity, people need to rethink their whole approach to a task. Successful executives and entrepreneurs know this to be the case (McClelland, 1998), and those who develop new technologies, products, and services are often well rewarded for their creativity.

Another way to stimulate creative problem solving is a technique called brainstorming. In **brainstorming,** people consider all possible solutions without making any initial judgments about the worth of those solutions. This procedure can be used to generate alternative solutions to problems as diverse as how a city can dispose of its waste and what topic should be selected for a group project. The rationale behind brainstorming is that people will produce more high-quality ideas if they do not have to evaluate the suggestions immediately. Brainstorming attempts to release the potential of the participants so as to increase the diversity of ideas and promote creativity.

Convergent thinking
In problem solving, the process of narrowing down choices and alternatives to arrive at a suitable answer.

Divergent thinking
In problem solving, the process of widening the range of possibilities and expanding the options for solutions.

Brainstorming
Problem-solving technique that involves considering all possible solutions without making prior evaluative judgments.

■ **EXPERTISE IN PROBLEM SOLVING.** There is a difference between people who are creative problem solvers and those who are termed expert problem solvers. The former often use domain-free knowledge—they just have good overall, creative strategies for problem solving. Expert problem solvers have domain- or area-specific knowledge, which is often—but not always—an advantage (Wiley, 1998). The idea is simple: experts (such as experts in computers or auto maintenance) have spent hundreds of hours learning everything they can about specific computers or cars. They often can see nuances that a novice cannot. Their problem solving is "grounded" in experience and training.

■ **THE INVESTMENT THEORY OF CREATIVITY.** Robert Sternberg has developed a novel approach to studying creativity. He argues that a person brings six interactive resources to problem solving: intelligence, thinking style, knowledge, personality, motivation, and environment. People sometimes use their creativity to develop a solution that others have ignored or dismissed when dealing with a problem. These creative thinkers may later promote, or "sell," their idea, and their independent work may pay off. This notion of working on undervalued problem solutions, marketing them, and implementing them led Sternberg to call this approach an *investment theory of creativity* (Sternberg & Lubart, 1999). Sternberg contrasts this approach with traditional ideas that often define truly creative people as those with exceptionally high levels of certain personality attributes.

In the end, to be creative you have to be intelligent and willing to redefine problems, analyze ideas, take some sensible risks, see clever connections between ideas, and convince other people that the ideas are good—unexamined ideas produce little societal change (Sternberg, 2001a).

Be an *Active* learner

REVIEW

- What are the important differences between heuristics and algorithms? p. 304
- Identify and describe three research-proven ways of improving problem-solving abilities. pp. 304–305
- Characterize the investment theory of creativity. p. 307

THINK CRITICALLY

- What mental habits might you develop in order to break through functional fixedness when you need to solve a problem?
- What kinds of situations cause people to become irrational when they try to solve a problem?

APPLY PSYCHOLOGY

- In school settings, people solve theoretical problems and answer questions that might be divorced from reality (such as how to solve the problem of worldwide poverty in one year). How does this approach facilitate problem solving? Or does it? Explain your answer.

Reasoning and Decision Making

Deciding whether to go for a run at lunchtime, have a sandwich and soft drink, or catch up on my correspondence is a daily decision for me (LL). Each choice carries with it benefits, and each has costs; but because I make this decision day in and day out, the process usually occurs quickly. And more often than not, I choose the sandwich rather than the run or the emails. But how do I make such decisions? When cognitive psychologists study *thinking*, they generally attempt to study the systematic day-to-day processes of reasoning and decision making (Galottie, 1990). **Reasoning** is the purposeful process by which a person generates logical and coherent ideas, evaluates situations, and reaches conclusions. The system or principles of reasoning used to reach valid conclusions or make inferences is called **logic.** You can think about reasoning as either an ordered process or an unstructured process in which ideas and beliefs are continuously updated (Rips, 1990)—both approaches are valid, and people use both types of reasoning.

Decision making means assessing and choosing among alternatives. You make decisions that involve the probability of some event (will my friends want to go on this trip with me?) and others that involve expected value (how important is *this* trip, rather than some other one?). Your decisions vary from the trivial to the complex—what to eat for breakfast, which courses to take, what career to pursue. The trivial decisions are usually made quickly, without much effort or even conscious thought. The complex ones require conscious, deliberate, effortful consideration.

■ *Diverse worldviews affect how people in the East and the West solve problems.*

Some students have trouble with the distinction between problem solving and decision making. Think of it like this: both focus on making a good rational solution, but problem solving involves the self-generation of options followed by choosing the best one; decision making often involves narrowing options presented to you.

Psychologists have devised numerous approaches for looking at decision-making processes. We examine estimating probabilities used in situations in which the answer or decision is uncertain.

Uncertainty: Estimating Probabilities

How do people decide what to wear, where to go on vacation, or how to answer a question on the SAT? How do they decide when something is bigger, longer, or more difficult than something else? Many decisions are based on formal logic, some on carefully tested hypotheses, and some on educated guesses. An *educated guess* is one based on knowledge gained from past experience—often from a prototype (see p. 304). When you see dark thunderheads, for example, you may guess that it will rain (perhaps, in your mind, a prototypical rainy day begins with dark thunderheads)—but you cannot be 100% sure. Weather forecasts express likelihood of rain as a percentage—that is, as a probability, based on past experiences.

People make probability estimates about all types of events and behaviors. They guess about the likelihood of a Democratic or a Republican victory in an election or of their favorite team's chances in the playoffs. On the basis of past experience, they estimate the probability that they will stay on their diet or get stuck in a traffic jam on the way to work. People can judge whether a particular event increases or decreases the probability of another event. When several factors are involved, their effects may compound or mitigate one another to alter the probability of an outcome.

Reasoning
The purposeful process by which a person generates logical and coherent ideas, evaluates situations, and reaches conclusions.

Logic
The system or principles of reasoning used to reach valid conclusions or make inferences.

Decision making
Assessing and choosing among alternatives.

For example, the probability that there will be rain when there are thunderclouds, high winds, and low barometric pressure is much higher than the probability of rain when it is merely cloudy.

Research participants asked to make probability judgments about the real world, particularly about fairly rare events such as airplane crashes, are less likely to make accurate judgments than are participants who are given laboratory problems (Chase, 2000). People do not always behave logically; because of their mood or lack of attention, they may act irrationally, ignore key pieces of data, and thus make bad (or irrational) decisions that are not based on probability. The further in the future the event, and the more variables that could come into play, the more likely people will be to make bad predictions (Olsen, 1997). Sometimes, people's worldviews color their probability decision making. For example, having strong religious or political views can influence a person's strategies and decision estimates.

Finally, people are not machines or computers; their past experiences, personalities, and cultural backgrounds can influence their thought processes—sometimes in unpredictable ways. However, cognitive psychologists have suggested ways for individuals to become the most efficient learners and thinkers they can be, and researchers have found that people can be taught to weigh costs and benefits more accurately and to be less influenced by their frames of reference (Bayster & Ford, 2000; Blount & Larrick, 2000). One way to break out of traditional frames of reference is to use analogies. When researchers examined how students could best learn scientific concepts, they found that analogies and metaphors are especially useful. Students can learn factual details well through traditional teaching methods, but analogies—especially creative ones—provide conceptual bridges that facilitate learning, memory, and concept development.

Barriers to Sound Decision Making

In the same way that people's problem solving can be hampered by mental sets, their decision making can be hindered by a range of stumbling blocks. By studying and learning about those limitations, we hope to overcome some of them.

■ **THE GAMBLER'S FALLACY.** If you know about probability, you know that people have misconceptions about the probabilities of events. A common fallacy is the *gambler's fallacy*—the belief that the chances of an event's occurring increase if the event has not recently occurred. This fallacy has brought millions of dollars to the casinos of Las Vegas and Atlantic City. In reality, *every time* you flip a coin, the chance of getting "heads" is 1 in 2, or 0.5—regardless of what happened on the last flip, or the last ten flips; and every pull of a slot machine has the same likelihood of making you a winner, regardless of what happened—or didn't happen—on the last pull.

■ *Playing chess was one of the first human activities that researchers tried to duplicate with computers.*

■ **BELIEF IN SMALL NUMBERS.** Limiting the number of observations we make because of a *belief in small numbers* also contributes to poor decision making. A small sample of observations is likely to be highly variable and not reflective of the larger population. However, the truth is that people are willing to draw conclusions from a small sample—say 10 neighbors—and assume that such a sample is representative of an entire town, state, or country.

■ **THE AVAILABILITY HEURISTIC.** Although my (LL) wife knows that flying in planes is quite safe—safer than walking through the parking lot of a nearby shopping mall—she is still hesitant to fly for fear of an (unlikely) malfunction and subsequent crash. Like my wife, most people overestimate the probability of unusual events occurring in their lives and may make poor decisions based on those probabilities. The overestimation of the probability is probably due to the wide media attention given to infrequent catastrophic events; information about them is more "available" than other information, and it is easy to think of examples. Psychologists refer to the *availability heuristic*—the tendency to judge the probability of an event by how easy it is to think of examples of it. The number of fatalities due to plane crashes, tornadoes, and icebergs is overestimated.

■ **OVERCONFIDENCE.** People often become overconfident and overestimate the soundness of their judgments and the accuracy of their knowledge. Such *overconfidence* is another major stumbling block to sound decision making. Imagine the surprise of a student when he was rejected from the only law school he applied to. He neglected to apply to other schools because he was sure—convinced—that he would get into his first choice. Individuals become so committed to their ideas and beliefs, especially political ones, that they are often more confident than correct and, when challenged, may become even more rigid and inflexible. For example, a person who believes that the only solution to local traffic problems is new roads may refuse to even consider mass transit as an alternative solution.

■ **THE CONFIRMATION BIAS.** Perhaps the greatest challenge to making good decisions is that people tend to cling to beliefs despite contradictory evidence; psychologists call this phenomenon the *confirmation bias*. People tend to discount information that does not fit with their preexisting views. Individuals rarely dwell on missed opportunities to make money from an investment; more often they seek to confirm their good judgment by telling how they made money (or did not lose any) on the investments they did make. As you will see when we study social psychology in Chapter 13, reliance on past experience and reluctance to seek information (or listen to it) that might disconfirm one's beliefs leads to stereotypes and prejudices that are often ill-informed and wrong.

Culture and Reasoning

Problem solving, reasoning, and decision making seem like straightforward thought processes. Everybody recognizes difficult situations, complexities, and even barriers to good decision making and problem solving. But people also believe that in the end, all people go about reasoning in the same way. This just isn't so.

It turns out, for example, that the intellectual traditions of the East and the West are quite different, and so are the reasoning and decision-making tendencies of their peoples (Peng & Nisbett, 1999). For example, when given contradictory statements to reason through, people from China prefer compromise solutions; European Americans prefer noncompromising ones. Chinese traditions hold that reality is a process, does not stand still, and is in constant flux. Chinese tradition recognizes contradictions in life and that such contradictions must be embraced. It further argues that all things are in one way or another connected. Western, European, and American traditions use reasoning that is analytical and logical; reality is considered objective, fixed, and identifiable; reality is precise and constant; and many things are isolated and independent of one another.

Such different worldviews affect how people in the East and the West solve problems; they think about problems differently (Peng & Nisbett, 1999). Therefore, when the conclusions of business leaders, politicians, and soldiers of the East puzzle Westerners, it should not be surprising. We have much more to learn about cognition by studying such cultural variation. One potentially illuminating research method will be to study multicultural individuals. What is a person's reasoning like when she is raised in one culture but then moves to another? How long in the new culture will it take for her to realize a new mode of thinking? Is it even possible for people to switch modes of thinking? Tomasello (2000) asserts that culture is learned at very young ages. But Hong and colleagues (2000) have found that people are able to switch modes of thought, especially about a recently evaluated thought. There is much more work to be done concerning multicultural individuals, who constitute a growing segment of the world's population.

Part of your new job for the city of Cambridge is to study the demographics of transportation. You read an existing report on the habits of Cambridge residents that says, people who go to Boston take the subway.

The cards below have information about four Cambridge residents. Each card represents one person. One side of a card tells where a person went, and the other side of the card tells how that person got there. Indicate only those card(s) you definitely need to turn over to see if any of these people violate the rule, "If a person goes into Boston, then that person takes the subway."

Boston	Arlington	Subway	Cab

Solution: Violations occur when people go into Boston without using the subway. To determine whether a violation has occurred, you need to turn over the card that says "Boston" (to check if the person, who went to Boston, failed to take the subway) and the card that says "Cab" (to see if the person, who traveled by cab, went to Boston).

FIGURE 9.6

For the Active Learner: Solving Logic Problems

(Cosmides, 1989)

Evolution and Reasoning

How do evolutionary theorists and researchers account for reasoning? First and foremost, remember that evolutionary psychologists assume that people have specific abilities because those skills have helped them be fit, survive, and reproduce. The world is a complex place, filled with information and many decisions to make. Evolutionary psychologists believe that humans have built-in mechanisms to help them sift through the information and make decisions, concentrating on the decisions that are most relevant for survival and reproduction. Most psychologists believe that cognition is shaped by general mechanisms, cognitive processes, and ways of handling information that apply to a variety of situations. Evolutionary psychologists argue that human brains have specific "programs," specialized ways of handling certain information, that shape our cognitions and reasoning (Cosmides & Tooby, 1997). Thus, some of our reasoning is determined by the type of information processing that our brains are set up to do. This type of cognition and reasoning is easier than other types. For example, certain types of logic problems are difficult for humans. Figure 9.6 presents such a logic problem. Try to solve this problem now before reading further. Leda Cosmides and John Tooby (1997) claim that only around 25% of people solve this type of problem in the most efficient way (see the Solution). Other problems in finding rule violations, however, are much easier: "If a person eats cookies, then the person must wash dishes first." This situation also involves "if-then" logic, but it is framed as a benefit that occurs only when the person performs the required task. If people eat cookies and have not washed dishes first, then they have violated the rule—they have cheated. Cosmides and Tooby argue that people have evolved "cheater detectors" that allow them to detect this type of social contract violation. This specialized mechanism allows people to be good at this type of logic problem.

Evolutionary psychologists argue that cognitive psychology has focused on problems that are difficult for humans rather than studying the types of reasoning that the human brain is programmed to do. Therefore, evolutionary psychologists claim that cognitive psychology has ignored some of the most important problems.

Be an *Active* learner

REVIEW

- Identify and describe several barriers to making good decisions. pp. 309–310
- How do evolutionary psychologists account for reasoning? p. 311

THINK CRITICALLY

- What might be the main reason people are not very good at estimating the probability of real-world events?
- Are problems of daily life well defined? Can you think of ways to help people better define their daily problems so as to minimize problem-solving barriers?
- When do you think that you reason through problems with less clarity than you might like? Why then?

APPLY PSYCHOLOGY

- Can you think of a political situation or crisis during which overconfidence or confirmation bias contributed to questionable decisions?
- Design a plan or training session that will help people avert confirmation bias.

Artificial Intelligence

There was a time—not so long ago—when computers were rare in homes and laboratories; but today they are everywhere and have transformed what we do and how we do it. And because human beings invented computers, it is not surprising that computers handle information in much the same way as the human brain does—though the brain has far more options and strategies for information processing than a computer does. By simulating specific models of the human brain, computers help psychologists understand human thought processes. For example, computers help shape the development of hypotheses about information processing and about perception, assist researchers in investigating how people solve problems, and enable psychologists to test models of certain aspects of behavior, such as memory. Computers also perform many tasks that humans find too time-consuming or complicated. Computer programs that mimic some type of human cognitive activities are said to use *artificial intelligence* (AI).

The Computer as Information Processor

The information-processing approach to perception, memory, and problem solving is a direct outgrowth of computer simulations. Flowcharts showing how information from sensory memory reaches working memory and long-term memory rely implicitly on a computer analogy. Those who study memory extend the computer analogy further by referring to storage areas as "buffers" and information-processing mechanisms as "central processors." The information-processing approach is widely used, although it has come under attack because it tends to reduce memory processes to small mechanistic elements.

The most widely investigated aspect of computer simulation and artificial intelligence is problem solving. And the problem often considered is the game of chess. Researchers use chess for two key reasons. First, the solution is well defined—capture the king—and as such, the scope of the problem is clear. Second, by understanding how humans or machines solve a relatively simple problem like chess they hope to generalize and garner insights into more complex forms of problem solving.

Playing chess was one of the first human activities that researchers tried to duplicate with computers; ever since then, human beings like master chess player Garry Kasparov have been challenging computers for dominance—with some modest successes and some notable failures! Computers have been taught to play other games, such as checkers and backgammon, and to solve simple number-completion tasks. They can also solve complicated problems involving large amounts of memory. The most sophisticated programs mimic aspects of human memory and decision-making systems and have been used to solve a wide array of problems including the design of computer chips and management of human resources (Lawler & Elliot, 1996).

Although computers can be programmed to process information the way human beings do, they lack human ingenuity and imagination. In addition, computers cannot interpret information by referring to or analyzing its context. Computers do not have contexts. Further, they cannot evaluate their own knowledge or improve their own problem-solving abilities by developing heuristics.

student voices

Glenn McMillon, Jr.
Massachusetts Institute of Technology

When I first came to MIT, I was a computer science major wanting to work in artificial intelligence. I thought it would be cool to make a computer that thinks like a real person. But after a few classes, I realized how little is known about how the mind works. I figured the best way to make a computer that thinks is to first understand how humans think. So now I'm studying psychology and cognitive neuroscience.

Neural Networks

The comparison of the brain to a computer is a compelling one, and interesting research has been focusing on the brain's ability to represent information in a number of locations simultaneously. Take a moment and imagine a computer. You may conjure up an image of an IBM or a Macintosh, a laptop or a mainframe. You may also start thinking about programming code, monitor screens, or even your favorite computer game. Your images of a computer or representations of what the

point*counterpoint*

Can Computers Think?

The Issue: Do computers think the way human beings do?

POINT
Computers have problem-solving and decision-making abilities; these abilities correspond to human thinking.

COUNTERPOINT
A computer's ability to store information and answer questions does not constitute thought, and its abilities are exaggerated by those who state that a computer thinks.

The computer has transformed the workplace and the home. Its miniaturization has led to small phones, smart phones, and wireless miniature phones. We have palm devices, robots, and the Internet, which has transformed commerce. But does the computer think, or does it merely process preprogrammed ideas and thoughts that human beings put into it?

Clearly computers know how to solve problems; they also have decision-making abilities. Computers can be given mathematical, economic, social, and weather models and make highly accurate predictions. In fact, when predicting the weather, a computer acts in much the same way human beings do. The computer can take multiple variables into account, factor in subtle potential changes, and be as good as the NBC weatherperson. The truth is computers can be programmed with both general rules and specific ones. They can relate symbols and build organized structures. A computer's capabilities are far-ranging, it does not get tired, it can hold huge amounts of information—theoretically, unlimited amounts—and it will work at blinding speeds 24 hours per day. Computers have already been shown to have reasoning properties in common with thought processes of human beings. Although a computer's processing methods are often clear-cut and repetitive, this is not necessarily a basis for denying computers thinking status.

But computers are not human beings, and they operate differently. They do not use strategies that can be considered perceptual in nature. Their approach tends to be step-by-step rather than intuitive. And once committed to a strategy—usually an algorithm—a computer cannot change its mind. In fact, it has no mind and thus cannot use multiple strategies. People, unlike computers, can interpret language (and the world) not because they run the right computer code, but because they are organisms with a biological structure capable of producing action, purpose, learning, perception, insight, and other planned experiences. Computers do not reflect or think about themselves and their purpose for being. You cannot find a computer that can tease, dream, or fall head over silicon in love.

In the end, the real question is this: can a computer think like a human being? The answer is not entirely clear. Computers are not human, they do not intuit, they do not have imagination, they are not endowed with a spirit that makes them soar when they hear music or become depressed on the demise of another computer; but they compute like crazy, they have nearly infinite memory, and they are able to solve problems, anticipate events, and increasingly behave more and more like human beings. Computer—yes. Human being—no.

computer can do are stored and coded at different places in your brain. No one suggests that you have a "computer corner," where all information about computers is stored. Since various pieces of information are stored in different parts of the brain, the electrical energy representing them must be combined at some point, in some way, for you to use the word *computer*, understand it, and visualize what it stands for.

Because the brain has specific processing areas, in different physical locations, a *convergence zone*, or center, is necessary to mediate and organize the information, according to University of Iowa researcher Antonio Damasio (Adolphs & Damasio, 2000; Damasio, 2000; Parvizi & Damasio, 2001). Signals from widely separated clusters of neuronal activity come together in convergence zones to evoke words and allow a person to develop sentences and fully process ideas and images about the subject at hand. That convergence zones are not located in the same place as specific pieces of information helps explain why some stroke victims and patients with various brain lesions (injuries) can tell you some things about a given topic—say, pianos—but not everything they once knew. For example, a stroke victim may be able to look at a picture of a piano and tell you that it has keys and pedals but be unable to say that it is a picture of a piano. According to Damasio's view, in such a case, a key convergence zone has been corrupted.

The idea of convergence zones has led to the development of models of where and how the brain operates to represent the world, develop concepts, solve problems, and process day-to-day tasks like reading and listening (Posner & Pavese, 1998). It also helps explain why a person whose visual cortex has been damaged can sometimes have knowledge of things that she or he is unaware of having seen. This residual vision—sometimes referred to as *blindsight*—is attributed to secondary, less important visual pathways. Place (2000) and Jackson (2000) reported cases of individuals who demonstrated blindsight. A patient who has incurred localized brain damage is periodically able to discriminate visual information of which they claim to have no visual awareness. They claim to be merely "guessing." Such multistage models of knowledge of the world—with multiple sources of input—suggest convergence zones and multiple levels and layers of processing.

In recent years, mathematicians, physiologists, and psychologists have joined forces to develop specific models of how neural structures represent complicated information (e.g., Crosson, 2000). Their work is often based on the concept of *parallel distributed processing* (PDP), which suggests that many operations take place simultaneously and at many locations within the brain. Most computers can perform only one operation at a time—admittedly very quickly, but still only one at a time. In contrast, the largest of modern computers can operate hundreds or even thousands of processors at once. Today's supercomputers are made up of many powerful computers that operate simultaneously (in parallel) to solve problems. PDP models assert that the brain can similarly process many events simultaneously, store them, and compare them to past events. PDP models also incorporate perception and learning; they combine data from studies of eye movements, hearing, the tactile senses, and pattern recognition to present a coherent view of how the brain integrates information to make it meaningful. PDP models can even account for nodes, units, or (in Damasio's terminology) convergence zones that store different types of information in different ways.

To study parallel distributed processing, researchers have devised artificial neural networks. These networks are typically composed of interconnected units that serve as model neurons. Each unit, or artificial neuron, receives signals of varying and modifiable weight to represent signals that would be received by a real neuronal dendrite. Activity generated by a unit is transmitted as a single outgoing signal to other neural units. Both input and output to units can be varied electronically, as can the interconnections among units. Layers of units can be connected to other layers, and the output of one layer may be the input to another.

A neural network can be a physical entity, but researchers are tending to use computers to create complex electronic representations of neural networks that simulate specific activities. For example, such electronic neural networks have sophisticated pattern-recognition abilities and can be taught to recognize handwritten letters—say, the letter *A*—and other simple patterns. In addition, such a network can learn to recognize a range of forms that look like the letter *A*. In this case, the network has learned a *prototype*. The prototypes may constitute the network's basis of form and letter perception.

An interesting aspect of networks is what happens when one portion of a network is destroyed. The network does not

Be an *Active* learner

REVIEW

- In what ways can the human brain be compared to a computer? pp. 312–313
- How do computers help psychologists understand human thought processes? p. 312
- Describe the fundamental idea of a convergence zone. p. 313
- What is blindsight? p. 314

THINK CRITICALLY

- Think from an evolutionary point of view. What made the brain develop in such a way that it exhibits creativity and humor (which a computer cannot do)?
- What are the implications of Damasio's idea that information is stored all over the brain and brought together in convergence zones for memory and thought to take place? for locating the memory store?

APPLY PSYCHOLOGY

- Do you think that if you give a person extra time, he or she will come up with better solutions to problems? Is this also true for computers?
- People often struggle with decisions–which car to buy, which course to take–do computers go through this? Why or why not?

crash, but it makes some mistakes, much as the brain would. When portions of the brain are surgically destroyed or removed or injured in an accident, the person is still able to complete some tasks. (Remember the split-brain patients who could name an object presented to one hemisphere but could only point to the object presented to the other hemisphere—see page 63.)

Neural networks, such as the brain, learn and remember. A neural network learns by noting changes in the weights or values associated with various connections. Sophisticated networks learn quickly and easily and modify themselves based on experience. The connections between various units within the network change because of experience. Most neural network models suggest that those units that are frequently activated will become more pronounced, have a lower threshold of activation, and be more easily accessed in the future (Posner, DiGirolamo, & Fernandez-Duque, 1997). This access is part of the retrieval process; easy access means easy retrieval, and both are dependent on clear, unambiguous learning.

Although neural networks operate efficiently and can learn to recognize speech and handwriting, chess moves, and spatial layouts, they are subject to error. Furthermore, they do not have the creativity and personality that human beings possess. They lack a sense of humor and the ingenuity that arises from perseverance, motivation, and intelligence. Neural networks help us understand human cognition, but they are not going to take its place.

Language

Someone says the word "cat." How do you know she is referring to a four-legged furry creature? Are you sure she is referring to an animal? Or might she be saying "cap"—as in headgear, or as in a small quantity of explosive enclosed in paper in a toy gun. Perhaps she said "cab," as in taxi? The truth is we know she is referring to a pet because of the context we find the person in. We use our decision-making processes, which are well honed, to decide whether an utterance was *cat* or *cap* or *cab*. They all sound alike but the sentence the word is found in, the discussion that preceded the use of the word, and the setting the word is used in (work or home) help us decide what that utterance actually was. Linguists even have a name for the study of how the social context of a sentence affects its meaning—*pragmatics*.

A **language** is a system of symbols, usually words, that convey meaning; in addition to the symbols, a language also has rules for combining symbols to generate an infinite number of messages (usually sentences). The key elements of this definition are that language is symbolic, it is a structured system, it is used to represent meaning, and it is generative, allowing an infinite number of sentences to be created. We'll examine these key elements in a moment. For now, think about how amazing it is that we can refer to objects and ideas that are not present in time or space; we are able to talk about abstractions such as future career goals, places we want to see, and concepts like justice and creativity that have no distinct physical reality. No other form of communication used by any other animal (not whales, dolphins, bees, or chimps) can do that. And best of all, we are able to process such a system effortlessly, despite its complexity. Languages evolve and grow; they reflect a person's culture; they allow individuals to share ideas and values almost effortlessly. Thus language is a social tool. Language takes place in a context, and the same words can have different meanings depending on who says them and when, whether they are said with a smile, with a grunt, or in a song (Trimble, 2000). Language is often also expressed with gestures. The French and the Italians are well known for speaking with their hands when excited. Second, language is clearly rule governed—the rules we use are called grammar (more on it later). And third, language is a generative system—knowledge of a language's rules allows a user to generate or create an infinite number of meaningful ideas and sentences.

Language
A system of symbols, usually words, that convey meaning and a set of rules for combining symbols to generate an infinite number of messages.

Recognizing that language and culture are intertwined, some researchers have wondered whether two people who speak the same language yet use different expressions to describe the same event or situation actually think about the world in different ways. Does language determine thought, or do all people think alike, regardless of their language? Is language gendered? Ultimately, what is the influence of culture on language? Let's start by looking at one's sex and language.

Language and Gender Stereotypes

In churches, synagogues, and mosques around the country, people are trying out, and getting used to, gender-neutral language. In some liturgies, God is no longer referred to as "father," and "forefathers" are called "ancestors." Research shows that such changes affect listeners' responses to liturgy and sermons (Greene & Rubin, 1991). In general, the English language has evolved in such a way that its words define many roles as male, except for roles that traditionally have been played by women (nurses, teachers) and considered softer and weaker—and less powerful (Lakoff, 2000).

Language with a sexist bias expresses stereotypes and expectations about men and women. For example, men are often described using active, positive words (for example, *successful, strong, independent*, and *courageous*). Women have traditionally been described with words implying passiveness (such as *gentle*, *loving*, or *patient*), or even with negative terms (*the weaker sex*, *timid*, *frail*). When language indicative of strength or courage is applied to a woman, it is often in the context of incongruity—for example, "She thinks like a man."

Lakoff (2000) asserts that people still see the world through a male frame of reference and that this is assumed to be the preferred value system. Research supports the idea that men and women are perceived and treated differently and that they speak differently. Frable (1989) concluded that if people believe in gender-specific abilities, they are likely to apply that belief to their decision making. Frable found that people with strong gender-typed ideas were especially likely to pay attention to the gender of job applicants and then to devalue the interview performance of the women.

Gender differences in language use are usually context-dependent; researchers know that men's and women's language is different and English does appear to have more female-valued terms (Sankis, Corbitt, & Widiger, 1999), but they also know that the differences must be considered within a larger context of ethnicity, class, age, and gender—not to mention social norms and personality (Pennebaker & King, 1999; Wodak & Benke, 1997).

Although gender stereotypes continue to exist, some women and men accept the value of *androgyny*, the state of possessing characteristics traditionally considered masculine as well as those considered feminine. People are becoming more accepting of individuals whose behavior is gender-flexible—for example, men who cook and women who are engineers. Even more important, people are becoming more sensitive to how language shapes their concept of the world and their problem-solving abilities. Research shows that people can adapt their language style depending on whom they talk to; that is, they "gender" their language depending on whether the listener is a man or a woman (Thomson, Murachaver, & Green, 2001).

■ *Walk down any street that is under construction, and you may see the warning sign "Men Working"—even though you are likely to see women as part of the construction crew.*

Thought, Culture, and Language

In the 1950s, researchers thought that language shaped thinking. In some researchers' views, the structure of the language that people speak directly determines their thoughts and perceptions. But even though human beings are very sensitive to odors, they have a limited language structure to describe them. We think about odors, they are easily detected, but they are difficult to describe; descriptions are often based on personal experiences and sometimes reflect a personal biographical event—for example, something might be said to smell like Granddad's pipe tobacco, Mother's perfume, or Aunt Maria's attic. Linguistic processes play a limited role in the processing of smell; the language of odors is determined by factors other than simply olfactory perceptions. Language may influence thought, but language does not determine thought (Lillo-Martin, 1997).

■ *Culture has an important influence on both language and thought.*

Certainly language and thought interact. Culture has a great influence on both language and thought. As was discussed in the previous section, people who believe in role- and gender-specific abilities are likely to apply those beliefs to their language and decision making. In France, for example, fairly rigid linguistic customs reflect hundreds of years of history; so, in the French language, there are formal and informal means of address. The word "you" for friends is *tu*; in more formal settings, one uses *vous*. Japan has even greater culturally determined distinctions in formality of language; who a person is in the workplace—boss, manager, supervisor, worker—affects how he or she is addressed and whether he or she will be shown deference. (In Chapter 17, we will consider workplace psychology in more detail.) Language is thus an expression of ethnic, geographic, cultural, and religious tendencies.

Americans are in a minority, in that most speak only one language; in most other developed countries, people are bilingual, speaking at least two languages. Although bilingualism promotes cognitive flexibility, research shows that when bilingual people are asked to respond to a question, take a personality test, or otherwise interact in the world, they do so in a culturally bound way—depending on the language in which they respond. When responding to a personality inventory, or to a list of symptoms people suffer from, native speakers of Chinese are likely to reflect Chinese values if the test or list is written in Chinese; when they respond to an English version of the same personality test or list, their responses are more likely to reflect Western values (Dinges, Atlis, & Vincent 1997; Dinges & Cherry, 1995).

As Matsumoto (2000) asserts, language and culture are intertwined. Along with studies of culture, we know that language does not determine thought, but rather, subtly influences it. Thoughts about ideas and events help shape language, which is used to express those thoughts. In many ways the language people speak is a manual of the language in which they reflect and reason. The even deeper question of whether the human brain is innately structured so as to facilitate various cognitive and linguistic functions is explored in the Brain and Behavior box.

Linguistics

Linguistics is the study of language, including speech sounds, meaning, and grammar. **Psycholinguistics** is the study of how language is acquired, perceived, understood, and produced. Among other things, psycholinguists seek to discover how children learn the complicated rules necessary to speak correctly.

Linguistics [ling-GWIS-ticks]
The study of language, including speech sounds, meaning, and grammar.

Psycholinguistics
The study of how language is acquired, perceived, understood, and produced.

For most of us language is conveyed through spoken words and then later writing. But other means of communication also exist. For example, many deaf individuals communicate through American Sign Language, or ASL. ASL is visual rather than auditory and is composed of precise hand shapes and movements; interpreters are required to translate spoken English into ASL. It is the native

BRAIN AND BEHAVIOR

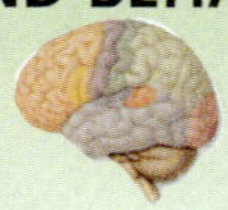

Is Cognition Hardwired in Any Way?

Is the brain hardwired for some cognitive activities? Researchers have conducted EEG studies to see if there are observable differences in the brain waves, brain structures, or neuroanatomical details of young and old people and of individuals while they perform new and well-learned tasks.

Research using brain-imaging techniques and language studies provides some suggestions about brain development and structure. PET and fMRI scans, which trace the distribution and timing of activity in the brain while a person is involved in a cognitive task, show that specific brain areas do seem to be activated while people are performing certain functions (Simpson et al., 2000). The occipital lobe becomes more involved in visual activities, the temporal lobe in more cognitive functions, and the left superior temporal gyrus in auditory language comprehension (e.g., Yancey and Phelps, 2001). Such scan studies thus lend credence to the traditional view that there is correspondence between brain structure and function.

Research is constantly challenging traditional findings, however. Language functions have traditionally been thought to be based solely in the left hemisphere for right-handed people (about 90% of the population). An area on the left side of the brain, called the *sylvian fissure*, has been thought to be responsible for the expression and comprehension of spoken and written language—closely associated activities. But left–right asymmetries disappeared as children grew older and developed more sophisticated language ability (Eliot, 1999). Furthermore, Baynes and others (1998) found that writing functions may be located in the right side of the brain. Baynes found that for a patient who had undergone a surgical split-brain procedure (see Chapter 2, p. 62), in which the left and right sides of the brain are disconnected, the abilities to read and speak were left-brain activities but writing was a right-brain activity. This new finding—that spoken and written language may be controlled by independent hemispheres—has yet to be substantiated, but it raises new questions about brain function (Langdon & Warrington, 2000). Some researchers think that the brain may consist of many more modules, or parts, than previously thought, and that these parts may operate both independently and together to create language.

So, is the brain hardwired for some cognitive activities? Perhaps. We saw in Chapter 2 that the brain is plastic, malleable, and sensitive to experience and that it changes over time in a developmental sequence (Epstein, 2001). The brain may have specific structures and functions that are hardwired, but their proper operation requires sophisticated control and coordination that may depend on experience and even on the context and culture in which people mature (Zhou, 2001). Perhaps it is this coordination that allows each of us to develop unique and potentially creative thought processes.

language of many deaf men and women, as well as some hearing children born into deaf families. Like spoken English or French, ASL is capable of communicating subtle, complex, and abstract ideas. Research shows that ASL is complex and expressive. It has its own distinct grammatical structure that is not a form of English; in fact, ASL shares more with spoken Japanese than it does with English. The rules and grammar of ASL must be mastered in the same way as the grammar of any other language (Siple, 1997).

Children are astonishingly adept at understanding and using the basic rules of spoken language. Even children only 18 months old, who have vocabularies of perhaps 50 words, understand the world around them; psychologists say that their *receptive vocabulary* is greater than their *productive vocabulary*—but that changes quickly. A 3-year-old, noticing that many nouns can be turned into verbs by the addition of a suffix, may say, "It sunned today," meaning it was a sunny day. By the time most English-speaking people reach adulthood, they recognize about 40,000 words.

■ *Children are astonishingly adept at understanding the basic rules of spoken language.*

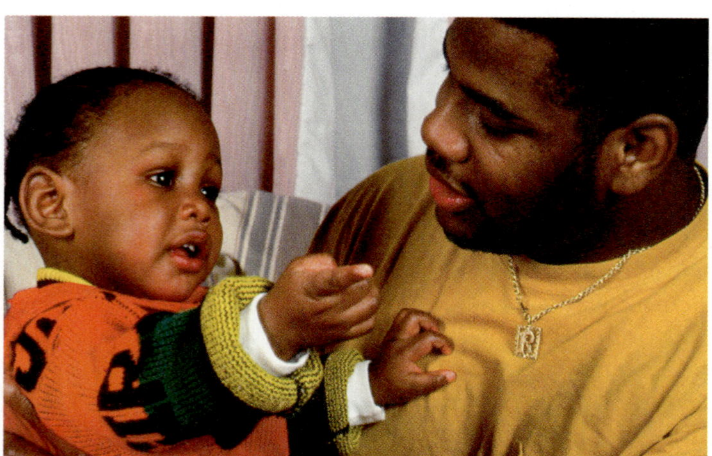

The miracle of language acquisition in children has long fascinated linguists and psycholinguists. Psychological studies since the early 1970s show that children first acquire the simple aspects of language and then learn progressively more complex elements and capabilities. Studies have also revealed *linguistic structures*—the rules and regularities that exist in, and make it possible to learn, a language. We will examine three major areas of psycholinguistic study: *phonology*, the study of the sounds of language; *semantics*, the study of the meanings of words and sentences; and *syntax*, the study of the relationships among words and how they combine to form sentences. In each of these areas, researchers have tried to identify the universal characteristics that exist in all languages, not just English.

Language Structure

The basic components of any language are its sounds, the meaning of the sounds, and its overall organization. Let's consider these elements, known more formally as phonology, semantics, and syntax.

■ **PHONOLOGY**. The gurgling, spitting, and burping noises infants first make are caused by air passing through the vocal apparatus. At about 6 weeks, infants begin to make speechlike cooing sounds. During their first 12 months, babies' vocalizations become more varied and frequent, until eventually they can combine sounds into pronounceable units. As psychologists have studied people's speech patterns, they have helped define the field of **phonology:** the study of the patterns and distribution of speech sounds in a language and the tacit rules for their pronunciation.

The basic units or smallest units of sound that compose the words in a language are called **phonemes.** In English, phonemes are basic sounds, such as *b, p, f,* and *v*, and simple combinations of sounds, such as *th* in *these*. All the sounds in the English language are expressed in 45 phonemes; of those, just 9 make up nearly half of all words. Phonemes are cognitive and perceptual abstractions and are considered separate from and independent of a writing system such as English—so phonemes are not the sounds of letters. Researchers argue that the structure of the mouth, tongue, and throat—the biomechanical properties of speech—play a key role in the initial production of phonemes (MacNeilage & Davis, 2000); when added to the cognitive and social constraints of interactions, more complex combinations develop that lead to words.

Words consist of **morphemes,** the basic units of meaning in a language. A morpheme consists of one or more phonemes combined into a meaningful unit. The morpheme *do*, for example, consists of two phonemes, the sounds of the letters *d* and *o*. Adding prefixes and suffixes to morphemes can form other words. Adding *un-* or *-er* to the morpheme *do*, for example, gives *undo* or *doer*. *Morphology* is the study of these meaningful sound units.

No matter what language people speak, one of their first meaningful utterances is the morpheme *ma*. It is coincidental that *ma* is a word in English. Other frequently heard early words of English-speaking children are *bye-bye*, *dada*, and *baby*. In any language, the first words often refer to a specific person or object, especially food, toys, or animals. At about 1 year of age, children make the first sounds that can be classified as communicative speech. Initially they utter only one word, but soon they are saying as many as four or five words. Once they have mastered 100 or so words, there is a rapid increase in the size of their vocabulary. Interestingly, there is considerable variation in when this "vocabulary spurt" takes place; some children exhibit it far earlier than others (Dromi, 1997). In the second year, a child's vocabulary may increase to more than 200 words, and by the end of the third year, to nearly 900 words. Figure 9.7 on the following page shows vocabulary growth through age 9.

■ **SEMANTICS**. At first, babies do not fully understand what their parents' speech means. But as more words take on meaning, the growing child develops semantic capability. **Semantics** is the analysis of the meaning of language, especially of individual words, the relationships among them, and their significance within particular contexts.

Consider how a 4-year-old child might misconstrue what her mother says to her father: "I've had a terrible day. First, the morning traffic made me a nervous wreck.

Phonology
The study of the patterns and distribution of speech sounds in a language and the tacit rules for their pronunciation.

Phoneme [FOE-neem]
A basic or minimum unit of sound in a language.

Morpheme [MORE-feem]
A basic unit of meaning in a language.

Semantics [se-MAN-ticks]
The analysis of the meaning of language, especially of individual words.

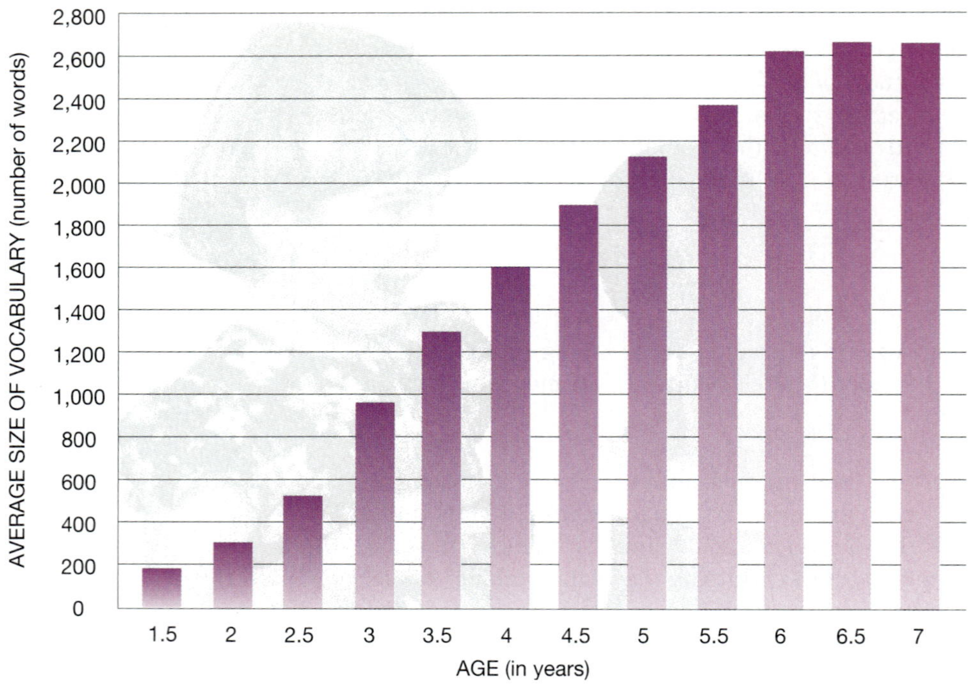

FIGURE 9.7

Vocabulary Changes in Childhood

The average size of children's vocabulary increases rapidly from age 1½ until age 6, when children are fully functional—with a vocabulary of more than 2,500 words. *(Moskowitz, 1978)*

Then, I got into an argument with my boss, and he almost fired me." The child might think her mom got into a car accident and was nearly set on fire. In trying to understand what is being said, a child must decipher not only the meanings of single words but also their relationships to other words. As everyone who has attempted to learn a new language knows, the meaning of a sentence is not always the same as the definitions of the individual words added together. Although children acquire words daily, the words they learn mean different things, depending on their context. Of course, even adults use only a small set of words over and over again; most other words are used rarely. People who learn a new language usually concentrate on the most widely used words. Teachers of French or Spanish rarely attempt to have students learn the words for *aura* or *modality*. The focus tends to be on basic, utilitarian vocabulary and syntax.

■ **SYNTAX.** Young children start out by using single words to represent whole sentences or ideas. They say "peas" or "hungry," and adults understand that they mean they want more peas or that they are hungry. We call such one-word utterances *holophrases*. Eventually, children begin to combine words into short sentences, such as "Mama look" or "Bye-bye, Mama." This kind of slightly expanded, but still reduced, speech in which words are left out is referred to as *telegraphic speech*, or *telegraphese*. Over a period of weeks and months, children show syntactic capability. **Syntax** is the way words and groups of words combine to form phrases, clauses, and sentences. Syntactic capability enables children to convey more meaning. For example, children acquire a powerful new way of making their demands known when they learn to combine the words *I want* or *Give me* with appropriate nouns. Suddenly, they can ask for cookies, toys, or Mommy, without any of them being within pointing range. The rewards that such linguistic behavior bring children are powerful incentives to learn more language. Children do not really need external rewards to want to learn language, though. Children begin to use sentences at different ages; but once they begin, they tend to improve at similar rates (Brown, 1970). Moreover, the average length of sentences increases at a fairly regular rate as children grow older.

Syntax [SIN-tacks]
The way words and groups of words combine to form phrases, clauses, and sentences.

Grammar
The linguistic description of how a language functions, especially the rules and patterns used for generating appropriate and comprehensible sentences.

Early studies of children's short sentences suggested that early speech could be characterized by descriptions of the positions and types of words they used. However, later investigations showed these descriptions to be inadequate and suggested that young children possess an innate grammar and that they use grammatical relationships in much the same ways as adults do (McNeill, 1970). **Grammar** is the linguistic description of how a language functions, especially in terms of the rules and patterns used for generating appropriate and comprehensible sentences. A key point about language—any language—is that with a limited set of units (phonemes, morphemes, plus syntactic rules) an infinite number of novel forms of sentences and ideas can be produced. Table 9.1 summarizes some of the early linguistic milestones in a child's life.

TABLE 9.1

Early Linguistic Milestones

Age	Language Activity
12 weeks	Smiles when talked to; makes cooing sounds spontaneously
16 weeks	Turns head in response to human voices
20 weeks	Makes vowel and consonant sounds while cooing
6 months	Changes from cooing to babbling
12 months	Imitates sounds; understands some words
18 months	Uses from 3 to 50 words (some babies use very few words at this age—as few as 3—while others use as many as 100); understands basic speech
24 months	Uses between 50 and as many as 250 words; uses two-word phrases
30 months	Uses new words daily; has good comprehension of speech; vocabulary of about 500 words
36 months	Has vocabulary of more than 850 words; makes grammatical mistakes, but their number decreases significantly with each passing week

It is important to remember that there are many ways to communicate; think back to American Sign Language. ASL has a very rich and complex grammar. Unlike spoken languages, which present one steady stream of phonemes, sign language can have multiple things going on simultaneously. This makes it a challenging language for linguists to study and a frustrating language for hearing people to learn. ASL has its own morphology (rules for the creation of words), phonetics (rules for hand shapes), and a grammar unlike those in spoken languages.

The Biological and Evolutionary Basis of Language

In 1957, linguist Noam Chomsky began the development of an idea that has found wide support. He suggested that one of the defining characteristics of human beings—language—is innate. He put forward the idea that human beings have an inborn, biologically based, universal grammar that allows them to easily master the language of their caregivers. This universal grammar, he asserted, is an innate word–sound–sentence generational mechanism capable of forming meaningful sentences. You can think of this universal grammar as a set of built-in "super-rules" that are instinctive, unconscious, and innate.

Evidence for the biological readiness of human beings to learn a language comes from physiological brain studies showing that infants—even very young ones—begin to respond physiologically to the language to which they are first exposed (Werker & Vouloumanos, 1999). This means that the infant brain must be prewired, plastic, and ready to adapt to the sounds and meanings of speakers (Bates & Roe, 1999).

Evidence also exists from studies of congenitally deaf infants and children who have never been taught a sign language. For example, Goldin-Meadow and Mylander (1998) found that deaf children in the United States and in the

Be an *Active* learner

REVIEW

- Does the structure of spoken language determine people's thoughts and perception? Explain your answer. pp. 316–317
- Distinguish between a phoneme and a morpheme. p. 319

THINK CRITICALLY

- Do you think that learning two languages as a child facilitates cognitive development? Why or why not?
- Why do you think that American Sign Language shares more with spoken Japanese (or any other language, for that matter) than it does with English?
- If there is one universal grammar, do you think people around the world make the same grammatical mistakes? Why or why not?

APPLY PSYCHOLOGY

- If a person is going to learn a second language, where is the best place to do it, and when? Why?

student voices

Lauren Elizabeth White
Loyola University

Psych has definitely affected the way I look at and respond to people and situations; I find myself using my knowledge of psychology in conversations, when giving advice to a friend with a problem, and when handling my own problems.

Republic of China (Taipei) evoked spontaneous signing—despite the fact that parents tried to communicate through lip reading and speech. Not only did they spontaneously emit signs, but also they did so in a consistent, grammatically coherent pattern that shared commonalities. Their gestures were in gesture sentences rather than single signs, and the sentences did not conform to the grammars of English or Mandarin. This is more evidence for an innate (signing) grammar (Goldin-Meadow, 2000).

Chomsky (1999) and Pinker (1994, 1997, 1999) argue that there is but one grand-grammar, innate and thus biologically based in the human genome, that underpins the specific grammars of English, Swahili, or Hebrew. From a strictly evolutionary point of view, the reasons human beings have language—and animals do not—is a part of the process of natural selection. Language has enormous adaptive value, and those adaptations that help the species survive and prosper will lead to their further development. Pinker (1999) points out that from an evolutionary viewpoint we learn language (be it Spanish or Farsi), but we have an instinctive tendency to speak, babble, and acquire knowledge and words.

Language Acquisition

That human beings acquire language is one of their defining characteristics. Acquiring language is a major achievement in the life of a child, and language continues to define us as adults and separates us from other species (Bickerton, 1998). All our cultural achievements, including the arts and advances in science, technology, and even warfare, depend on the use of language. Language development is an individual achievement, but it is also a social process that involves people communicating with one another. Since language is a unique human gift, a special ability, was there an evolutionary turn of events that set humans apart in this respect (MacWhinney, 1998)? If language were solely an evolutionary unfolding, the story would be simple, but research shows that language and thought are sensitive to both genetic inheritance (nature) and experience (nurture). As in other areas of human behavior, the debate continues about the relative contribution of each factor. If language is based on evolution and biology, two things should be true: (1) many aspects of language ability should be evident early in life, and (2) all children, regardless of their culture or language, should develop grammar (an understanding of language patterns) in a similar way. If environmental factors account for language acquisition, the role of learning should be preeminent. In trying to resolve the nature–nurture debate with respect to language acquisition, researchers use observational studies of infants and children, case histories of sensory-deprived infants, studies of reading-disabled or brain-damaged individuals, and experiments with chimpanzees.

Learning Theories

The learning approach to language acquisition is quite simple. People speak and understand language because specific language behaviors are reinforced and repeated from the moment of birth. Babies attend in a focused way, listening intently and repeating the sounds they hear, especially those they have heard before (Johnson & Jusczyk, 2001).

As parents become better able to untangle a baby's babble and make sense of it, they often repeat the baby's sounds in proper English so that the baby can hear them pronounced correctly. Parents often then reinforce the baby by responding in some way to the baby's utterance. A baby might say, "Daddy, baby, wasue," and the parent may say, "You want Daddy to give you water?" The baby smiles, receives a drink, and the process continues—until eventually, over days and weeks, the baby learns correct pronunciation and proper word order. Thus, learning

introduction to research basics

Acquiring a First Language

In the early 1960s, the process of acquiring a first language was not well understood. Roger Brown (1973) and a group of researchers at Harvard University conducted a study that changed the understanding of language development and how researchers approach this problem.

HYPOTHESIS Children develop language in a sequence of stages that is similar for all children.

DESIGN Brown and his group conducted a naturalistic observation of language development. **Naturalistic observation** is a descriptive research method in which researchers study behavior in its natural context. This method involves no manipulation of variables; indeed, researchers typically do not interact with participants and may attempt to "make themselves invisible" so that their presence will not affect the participants' behavior.

PARTICIPANTS Participants were three children, one of whom was 18 months old, and two of whom were 27 months old when the study began. Two were girls, and one was a boy. The boy was African American, and the girls were European American. The children's parents varied in educational level from high school through graduate school education.

PROCEDURE Brown and his research team obtained the parents' permission and cooperation to go into the childrens' homes and make audio recordings of at least 30 minutes of speech per week for each child. The recordings included not only the children's speech but also people who were interacting with each child at the time, including mothers, fathers, and other visitors in the home. At least one member of Brown's research team was present to take notes about the situation in which the vocalizations occurred. These weekly recordings continued for a year for one of the children and for four years for two of them.

RESULTS The researchers analyzed the progress that the children made in constructing sentences. They found that all three children developed language through a similar series of stages, but age was not a good predictor of this sequence. In fact, the youngest child made the most rapid progress, and her sentence complexity at age 18 months was comparable to that of the other two children at age 27 months.

CONCLUSIONS Children go through a similar process of developing a first language, but they acquire language at different rates. Therefore, age is not a good way to divide children when considering language development; 4-year-olds may differ a great deal in their development. This finding of similarity is consistent with the belief that there is an underlying, universal basis for language acquisition.

approaches use traditional learning (operant conditioning) theories and more modern (social/observational learning) theories to explain the acquisition of language.

Biological Theories

Learning theories emphasize the role of environmental influences, or nurture, in language acquisition. The basic idea is that language is acquired in a process that reflects traditional concepts of learning. But people have the ability to generate an almost infinite number of correctly formed sentences in their native language. Because this ability cannot be acquired solely through imitation or instruction, many researchers, such as psychologist George Miller (1965), assert that human beings are biologically equipped with an innate, unique capacity to acquire and develop language. Such nativist positions assume that human beings are born with a mental *language acquisition device*, or *LAD*, to process and facilitate the learning of language.

Although Miller as well as Chomsky (1957) do not exclude experience as a factor in shaping children's language, they claim that human nature itself, through an LAD, allows children to pay attention to language in their environment and ultimately to use it. Nonetheless, even the strongest proponents of the nature (biological) argument do not contend that a specific language is inborn. Rather, they agree that a predisposition toward language use exists and that human beings are born with a "preprinted" blueprint for language. As a child matures, this blueprint provides the framework through which the child learns a specific language and its rules (e.g., Marcus et al., 1999). Three major sources of evidence support the nature side

Naturalistic observation
A descriptive research method in which researchers study behavior in its natural context.

psychology *in action*

Deaf People and Cochlear Implants

Many deaf and hard-of-hearing individuals straddle both the deaf and hearing worlds and function well. They sign, they read, they lip-read, and they lead successful family and business lives. There is a distinct culture and community among people who are deaf, although this is not well known to the hearing world. Sign language, as has already been pointed out, is one of the main methods of communication and has its own unique structure and grammar. But a recent technological advance—cochlear implants—has created a controversy.

A cochlear implant is a hearing prosthesis designed to help severe to profoundly deaf individuals who gain little or no benefit from hearing aids. Cochlear devices are implanted within the ear structure to help a user perceive sound. The cochlear implant is a prosthetic substitution for the cochlea. The cochlea consists of a bony tube that spirals around a middle "core" that contains the auditory nerve. It bypasses damaged parts of the cochlea and electronically stimulates the auditory nerve. The device is implanted in the skull behind the ear, and electrodes are inserted into the cochlea. The other part of the device is external and has a microphone and a speech processor (to convert sound into electrochemical impulses). The stated goal of implants is to help deaf people—especially children—develop language based on spoken communication by eliciting patterns of nerve activity that imitate those of a normal ear. Ideally, such a system would allow deaf people to recognize all types of sound (including speech) and also allow many children deafened at a young age to acquire speech. Today's devices enable about 10% of those with implants to communicate without lip reading and the majority to communicate well when the sound is combined with lip reading. According to the National Institutes of Health (1995), cochlear implants have a profound impact on hearing and speech reception; most individuals demonstrate significantly enhanced speech-reading capabilities, attaining scores of 90–100% correct on everyday sentence materials. Cochlear implants do not eliminate deafness; they are not a cure. But for a child who has experienced sound and then has become deaf, they work fairly well in helping fill in gaps. About 40,000 people worldwide have had cochlear implants and most consider the results miraculous (Rauschecke, & Shannon, 2002)..

However, the National Association of the Deaf maintains a healthy skepticism about implants, cautioning parents that a decision to forgo implants does not condemn children and later adults to a world of meaningless silence. The organization feels strongly that the deaf world is rich and meaningful and that through other means of communication, deaf and hard-of-hearing people develop language. The National Association of the Deaf sees cochlear implants as an option, but one with attendant surgical risks. Furthermore, not all children benefit from cochlear implants; in addition, knowing that a child has an implant may cause his or her parents and teachers to neglect more traditional methods of deaf education, in the belief that the child can be considered to be "hearing."

Cochlear implants may be a boon to some with hearing impairments; they may also allow researchers to better understand how language processing takes place, when its critical periods occur, and from a clinical point of view, how to best help families become educated about the attendant risks and rewards of cochlear implants. In sum, cochlear implants are not viewed with the same enthusiasm by all—especially segments of the deaf community who assert that deaf and hard-of-hearing people develop language through other means of communication.

of the nature–nurture debate: (1) studies of brain structure, lateralization, and convergence zones; (2) studies of learning readiness; and (3) studies of language acquisition in children and animals such as chimpanzees and dolphins.

■ **BRAIN STRUCTURE, LATERALIZATION, AND CONVERGENCE ZONES.** Even as early as 1800, researchers knew that the human brain was specialized for different functions. At that time, researchers began mapping the brain and discovering that if certain areas were damaged (usually through accidents), the injured person exhibited severe disorders in language abilities. Later work, some of it by Norman Geschwind (1972), led to the idea of *lateralization*—the localization of a particular brain function primarily in one hemisphere. As Chapter 2 showed, considerable evidence suggests that the left and right hemispheres of the brain (normally connected by the corpus callosum) have some distinctly different functions.

Some researchers argue that the brain has unique processing abilities in each hemisphere. For example, important language functions are predominantly, but not exclusively, left-hemisphere functions (Corina, 1999). However, the available data do not make an airtight case; each hemisphere seems to play a dominant role in some functions and to interact with the other hemisphere in the performance of others (Baynes et al., 1998).

■ **LEARNING READINESS.** Researcher Eric Lenneberg (1921–1975) claimed that human beings are born with a grammatical capacity and a readiness to produce language (Lenneberg, 1967). Lenneberg believed that the brain continues to develop from birth until about age 13, with the greatest developmental leap taking place around age 2. During this period, children develop grammar and learn the rules of language. After age 13, there is little room for improvement or change in an individual's neurological structure. Lenneberg supported his argument with the observation that brain-damaged children can relearn some speech and language, whereas brain-damaged adolescents or adults who lose language and speech are unable to regain the lost ability completely. Lenneberg's view is persuasive, but some of his original claims have been seriously criticized—particularly his idea of the role of a critical time period in language development, although this is shown to be the case in some animals, such as birds and fish (e.g., Tchnernichovski et al., 2001).

Some researchers claim that not only human beings but also other animals—for example, chimpanzees—are born with a grammatical capacity and a readiness for language.

Language Studies with Chimpanzees

Clearly, many animals communicate with one another. Whales use clicks and wails, squeaks and groans; monkeys have various sounds to signal one another, especially when predators appear; wolves howl—the examples are nearly endless. But do animals communicate with one another through language? If they do, is that language the same as, similar to, or totally different from the language of human beings? Most important, what can scientists learn from animals about the inborn aspects of language?

The biological approach to language suggests that human beings are "prewired"—born with a capacity for language. Experience is the key that unlocks this existing capacity and allows its development. The arguments for and against the biological approach to language acquisition use studies showing that chimpanzees naturally develop some language abilities. Chimpanzees are generally considered among the most intelligent animals; in addition, they resemble human beings more closely than any other animal does. Playful and curious, chimps share many common physical and mental abilities with human beings. Their brains have a similar organization; and some languagelike functions may even be lateralized (the localization of a particular brain function primarily in one hemisphere) in chimpanzees (Gannon et al., 1998). This is an important and interesting finding, because psychologists have generally believed that only human beings exhibited brain asymmetries related to lateralization of language functions. Researchers are not sure what this lateralization in chimps means, but it will most likely provide some hints into their language abilities. What it does *not* mean is that chimps have human language—a similar structure does not necessarily imply a similar function.

Chimps are especially valuable to study because researchers can control and shape the environment in which chimps learn language, something they cannot do in studies involving human beings. For these reasons, chimpanzees have been the species of choice when psychologists have studied language in animals.

However, all attempts to teach animals to talk have failed. Until recently, this failure had led most psycholinguists to conclude that only human beings have the capacity to acquire language. Three decades ago, however, some major research projects showed that even though chimpanzees lack the physical vocal apparatus necessary to produce speech, they can learn to use different methods to communicate with humans. Scientists have studied chimpanzees both in near-natural environments and in laboratory settings using computer technology. With results from sharply different environments, clear conclusions are emerging.

■ **WASHOE.** From age 1, the chimpanzee Washoe was raised like a human child by Allen and Beatrice Gardner (1969). Rather than being taught to speak words,

Washoe was taught American Sign Language, making signs that stood for words as well as simple concepts and commands (for example, *more, come, give me, flower, tickle*, and *open*). Washoe learned a large number of signs that refer to specific objects or events. She was able to generalize these signs and to combine them in meaningful order to make sentences. There is no proof, however, that she used a systematic grammar to generate novel kinds of sentences.

FIGURE 9.8

Icons Used by Sarah in Premack's Study

Sarah learned to construct sentences using pieces of magnetized plastic that varied in color and shape. *(Premack, 1971)*

■ **SARAH.** The chimp Sarah was raised in a cage, with more limited contact with human beings than Washoe had. Psychologist David Premack (1971) used magnetized and colored plastic icons to teach Sarah words and sentences (see Figure 9.8). Sarah gradually developed a small but impressive vocabulary. She learned to make compound sentences, to answer simple questions, and to substitute words in a sentence construction. There is no evidence, however, that she could generate a new sentence, such as "Where are the apples?"

■ **LANA.** The chimp Lana learned to interact with a computer at the Yerkes Primate Research Center at Emory University. Researchers Rumbaugh, Gill, and Von Glaserfeld (1973) gave Lana 6 months of computer-controlled language training. Lana learned to press a series of keys imprinted with geometric symbols. Each symbol represented a word in an artificial language the researchers called Yerkish. The computer varied the location of each Yerkish word and the color and brightness of the keys. Through conditioning, Lana learned to demonstrate some of the rudiments of language acquisition. Lana did not show that she could manipulate grammatical relations in meaningful and regular ways.

The studies of chimps just described show that their language usage is similar to that of very young children: it is concrete, specific, and limited. However, chimps do not show the ability to generate an unlimited number of grammatically correct sentences, an ability that human beings begin to acquire at a fairly young age.

■ **NIM.** Columbia University psychologist Herbert Terrace reports significant differences between chimp language and the language of young children. Terrace taught his chimp, Nim Chimpski (a play on the name of the famous linguist Noam Chomsky), to communicate using manual signs. Terrace found that Nim's signed communications did not increase in length, as young children's sentences do. Nim acquired many words, but only 12% of Nim's utterances were spontaneous; the remaining 88% were responses to her teacher. Terrace points out that a significantly greater percentage of children's utterances are spontaneous. Terrace also found no evidence of grammatical competence in either his own data or that of other researchers.

■ *Many researchers studied language differences between the chimpanzee and the human and eventually concluded that chimps just do not use language the way humans do.*

■ **CHIMP LANGUAGE?** Unlike young children, who spontaneously learn to name and to point at objects (often called *referential naming*), chimps do not spontaneously develop such communication skills. Terrace (1985) agrees that the ability to name is a basic part of human consciousness. He argues that, as part of socialization, children learn to refer to various inner states: feelings, thoughts, and emotions. Chimps can be taught some naming skills, but the procedure is long and tedious. Children, on the other hand, develop these skills easily and spontaneously at a young age. Accordingly, researchers generally assert that chimps do not interpret the symbols they use in the same way that children do. These researchers question the comparability of human and chimp language.

In the end, chimps do not culturally transmit sign language from ape to ape to ape. Chimps do not have sophisticated referential naming. Chimps do not have the ability to be generative—to form new words, sentences, and ideas. So chimps do not use language the way human beings do. The answers to researchers' questions about language acquisition are far from complete, but the quest is exciting and is being extended to other species, including dolphins (Kuczaj, 1998; Schusterman & Gisiner, 1996).

And What About Dolphins?

It is widely known that dolphins communicate with one another through squeaks and groans. It is also well accepted that dolphins learn quickly and well. But do they have language? Not in a human sense. They have no vocal cords to modulate their speech, and they do not gesture. Nevertheless dolphins do communicate with one another. They repeat signals from other dolphins—a part of language; Vincent Janik (2000) showed that wild bottlenose dolphins listened, learned the whistles of other dolphins, and repeated those signals. This ability is an early part of language.

Researchers Miller and Bain (2000) presented evidence that whales not only communicate with one another, but they do so with flair. He found that whales repeat sounds, like dolphins, but do so with inflections, almost like a tone of voice among human beings. Miller and Bain found that whales, their offspring, and even a third generation of whales possess some calls or sounds that are distinct to their families. Do dolphins or whales have language? The answer is no. Do they have communicative abilities? The answer is surely yes.

Social Interaction Theories: A Little Bit of Each

The debate over language acquisition is a wonderful example of how issues in psychology emerge, grow, and contribute to an understanding of human behavior. Early learning theorists took an unbending view of the role of reinforcement in language development. Later, biologically based researchers assumed that the biological and physical underpinning of language was just too strong to deny the role of physiology in language. But neither view by itself is correct. Children are born with a predisposition to language—there is no doubt about that. And nearly everybody agrees that children are reinforced for their language behavior. But children's use of language takes place within a social setting that changes daily—the child's differing moods and needs may be met by different caretakers with their own moods and needs. So language is in part innate and in part reinforced—and rigid polarized views of innate grammars or reinforced behaviors are probably too limited in their conceptions of language acquisition (Seidenberg, 1997).

Like so many other behaviors, language use is affected by the context in which it occurs. At feeding time, babies are far more likely to express hunger vocally. While playing, babies are far more likely to be self-centered, making utterances that do not necessarily have communicative functions. Parents often use a teaching mode and articulate words, sentences, and emotional expressions especially strongly when talking to a child because they want the child to learn something particular. In the early months of life, infants acquire phonetic properties of their native language by listening to adults speak (a social/observational approach). Interestingly, mothers exaggerate—they produce vowel

Be an *Active* learner

REVIEW

- What is the crucial assumption of biological approaches to language acquisition? p. 323
- Why are studies of lateralization important to studies of language? p. 324
- What is a cochlear implant? How does it work? p. 324
- What important differences between chimp language and the language of human children did Terrace's work point out? p. 326

THINK CRITICALLY

- The two learning approaches to language acquisition–conditioning and social/observational learning–differ with respect to what key underlying principle?
- What is the implication of the finding that chimps do not culturally transmit sign language from ape to ape to ape?

APPLY PSYCHOLOGY

- If you were deaf, would you want to have a cochlear implant? Why or why not?

sounds acoustically more extreme—when talking with infants than when talking to adults (Kuhl et al., 1997).

A key to understanding language acquisition is to consider not only the structure of language, but also its function and the context in which it is learned, expressed, and practiced. Human beings are very much social organisms, and language serves a vital function as a way for children to get attention and make their needs known. So, although a child may be prewired for language acquisition and reinforced for using language correctly, language nearly always is used in a social setting—whose importance cannot be overestimated.

Summary and Review

Cognitive Psychology: An Overview

What is the focus of cognitive psychology?

■ *Cognitive psychology* is the study of the overlapping fields of perception, learning, memory, and thought. Cognitive psychology focuses on how people attend to, acquire, transform, store, and retrieve knowledge. Cognitive psychologists study thinking; they assume that mental processes exist, are systematic, and can be studied scientifically. pp. 300–301

KEY TERM

cognitive psychology, p. 300

Concept Formation: The Process of Forming Mental Groups

What is involved in the process of concept formation?

■ *Concepts* are the mental categories used to classify events or objects according to common properties or features. Concept formation involves classifying and organizing events or objects by grouping them with or isolating them from others on the basis of a shared characteristic. In laboratory studies of concept formation, participants are presented with stimuli that are either positive or negative instances of a concept. They are asked to identify the concept. pp. 301–302

■ A *prototype* is an abstraction, an idealized pattern of an object or idea that is stored in memory and used to decide whether similar objects or ideas are members of the same class of items. p. 302

KEY TERMS

concept, p. 301; prototype, p. 302

Problem Solving: Confronting Situations That Require Solutions

What are the fundamental differences between algorithms and heuristics?

■ *Algorithms* are problem-solving procedures that implement a particular series of steps repeatedly. *Heuristics* are sets of strategies that act as guidelines, not strict rules, for problem solving. p. 304

■ In *subgoal analysis*, a problem is broken down into several smaller steps, each of which has a subgoal. In *means–ends analysis*, the current situation or position is compared with the desired end in order to determine the most efficient means for getting from one to the other. p. 304

What are some barriers to effective problem solving?

■ *Functional fixedness* is the inability to see that an object can have a function other than its stated or usual one. Functional fixedness has been shown to be detrimental to problem solving. pp. 304–305

■ *Creativity* is the ability to develop responses that are original, novel, and appropriate. According to Guilford, creative thinking is divergent thinking. *Divergent thinking* is the process of widening the range of possible solutions. In contrast, *convergent thinking* is the process by which the number of possible options is reduced until one option remains as the answer. To solve problems creatively, some people use the technique of *brainstorming*. pp. 306–307

KEY TERMS

problem solving, p. 303; algorithm, p. 304; heuristics, p. 304; subgoal analysis, p. 304; means–ends analysis, p. 304; backward search, p. 304; functional fixedness, p. 304; creativity, p. 304; convergent thinking, p. 307; divergent thinking, p. 307; brainstorming, p. 307

Reasoning and Decision Making

Differentiate between reasoning and decision making.

■ *Reasoning* is the purposeful process by which a person generates logical and coherent ideas, evaluates situations, and reaches conclusions. The system or principles of reasoning used to reach valid conclusions or make inferences is called *logic. Decision making* is the assessment of alternatives; people make decisions that sometimes involve the probability of occurrence of an event or the expected value of the outcome. p. 308

What is a psychological approach to studying decision making?

■ Psychological factors, especially previous events, affect how people estimate probabilities of behaviors and events. Sometimes a person may ignore key pieces of data and thus make bad (or irrational) decisions not based on probability; also, a person's worldview may affect decision making. pp. 308–309

What is the effect of culture on reasoning?

■ The intellectual traditions of the East and the West are quite different, and so are the reasoning and decision-making tendencies of their peoples—different worldviews affect how people in the East and West solve problems. pp. 310–311

How do evolutionary theorists and researchers account for reasoning?

■ Evolutionary psychologists assert that reasoning is a direct consequence of evolution and adaptations to a complex, even dangerous world—reasoning is an adaptation. p. 311

KEY TERMS

reasoning, p. 308; logic, p. 308; decision making, p. 308

Artificial Intelligence

What is artificial intelligence?

■ Computer programs that mimic some type of human cognitive activities are said to use artificial intelligence (AI). A computer analogy of perception and reasoning has been the model for most studies of AI; this work is often based on the concept of parallel distributed processing (PDP), which suggests that many operations take place simultaneously and at many brain locations. p. 312

Describe how neural networks work.

■ Electronic neural networks simulate specific cognitive activities, including recognizing patterns, recognizing handwriting, planning computer moves, and recognizing spatial layouts. Neural networks learn and remember by noting changes in the weights or values associated with various connections between their units. Those units that are frequently activated become more pronounced, have lower thresholds of activation, and can be more easily accessed. pp. 310–315

Language

How are language, thought, and culture interrelated, and what are the key elements of language?

■ Research shows that language structure alone is unlikely to account for the way people think because culture also influences language and thought. pp. 315–316

■ The English language has evolved in such a way that its words define many roles as male; many people still see the world through a male frame of reference and assume that this is the preferred value system. Although gender stereotypes continue, some women and men are becoming more androgynous. p. 316

■ *Linguistics* is the study of language, including speech sounds, meaning, and grammar. *Psycholinguistics* is the study of how people acquire, perceive, understand, and produce language. *Phonemes* are the basic units of sounds in a language; *morphemes* are the basic units of meaning. *Semantics* is the study of the meaning of language components. *Syntax* is how words and groups of words are related and how words are arranged into phrases and sentences. *Grammar* is the linguistic description of a language, in terms of its rules and patterns for generating comprehensible sentences. pp. 317–320

KEY TERMS

language, p. 315; linguistics, p. 317; psycholinguistics, p. 317; phonology, p. 319; phoneme, p. 319; morpheme, p. 319; semantics, p. 319; syntax, p. 320; grammar, p. 320

Language Acquisition

How do theorists explain language acquisition?

■ Learning plays an important part in language acquisition. However, people have the ability to generate an unlimited number of correctly formed sentences in their native language. This ability cannot be acquired solely through imitation or instruction, which suggests the existence of an innate language ability. p. 322

■ Damasio asserts that the brain has specific language-processing areas, some of which are lateralized. Information about any thing or event may be stored in multiple locations throughout the brain. However, the locations are connected through convergence zones, or centers that mediate and organize the information. p. 324

■ Studies of language ability in chimpanzees have produced some impressive results, although few psychologists are completely convinced that the ways in which chimps use language parallels human use of language. The criticisms, however, do not diminish the chimps' language abilities or accomplishments. pp. 325–326

■ A key to understanding language acquisition is to consider not only the structure of language, but also its function and the context in which it is learned, expressed, and practiced. Communication serves a vital function and nearly always takes place in an interactive, social setting. p. 327

KEY TERM

naturalistic observation, p. 323

10 Intelligence

Lee Krasner, *Composition* (1943)

The admission committee at State U. faced quite a challenge. They had literally thousands of students applying for admission and only 1,500 seats for new students. The truth was that nearly all of the students who applied could do the work and get a college degree. Their task was to find the "best" first-year class possible. But what's best? The situation goes on at every admissions committee: two students have SATs of 1150. Will one student's writing and extracurriculars count more than another's acting and sports activities? Or will the 1150 make them equal in the eyes of the university? It turns out that at Ivy League schools like Harvard, if they took every applicant with a perfect math score on the SAT, they would still have to turn away hundreds of students a year. But the landscape is changing.

Nearly 90% of colleges and universities take SAT scores into consideration for admission. But over 280 schools, including several highly selective ones (such as Bates,

chapter outline

Bowdoin, and Mount Holyoke), have made the SAT optional in the admission process. Schools that are deemphasizing the SAT assert that it doesn't measure the range of intellectual and motivational qualities that educational environments require. The University of California is considering deemphasizing the SAT and even abandoning it—all of this despite the research finding that the SAT, the GRE, and other similar tests are pretty good predictors of future academic performance (Kuncel, Hezlett, & Ones, 2001).

Intelligence tests (which the SAT, by the way, is *not*) do not measure other characteristics that are important to success, such as motivation, creativity, and leadership skills. People demonstrate effective and intelligent behavior in many ways, but not in the same ways. Intelligent behavior for a dancer is very different from intelligent behavior for a scientist, and both of these are different from intelligent behavior for a child with a learning disability.

No single set of test questions—whether they focus on verbal ability, knowledge of English literature, or math skills—provides a clear measure of intelligence. Psychologists therefore use a variety of test results, as well as other data, including interviews, teacher evaluations, and writing and drawing samples, to evaluate an individual's current intellectual status, to make predictions about future performance or behavior, and to offer suggestions for remedial work or therapy. In this chapter, we consider individual differences in intelligence and examine theories, tests, and controversies. We also examine two special populations: those who are gifted and who are mentally retarded. But first, let's begin with that basic but difficult question: what is intelligence?

What Is Intelligence?

Human beings are capable of artistic greatness; think of Michelangelo's frescoes in the Vatican, Yo-Yo Ma's virtuoso cello performances, or Maya Angelou's rich and nuanced poetry. Humans can accomplish enormously difficult tasks—such as building the pyramids with relatively primitive tools, exhibiting great compassion for others (think of Gandhi and Mother Teresa), and communicating effectively with each other, at least now and then. We are an intelligent species capable of thinking about our past, predicting our future, and using our abilities for good—and evil. From a scientist's point of view, quantifying human intelligence so as to make predictions about human behavior is an important task. Pursuing it gave rise to the intelligence test, or as most of us know it, the IQ test. Everyone has heard of IQ tests; but do IQ tests actually measure intelligence? Can any test measure it? Further, why are people so different from one another intellectually?

■ *Maya Angelou's poetry is read around the world, a testimony to human ability to express intelligence through the arts.*

Although most psychologists, and the public, accept the idea that intelligence exists, it has been measured and described quite differently, or not at all, in various societies. Clearly, agricultural societies that depend on skills related to planting and harvesting do not have standard tests that measure the speed or quality of those skills. But today's fast-paced technological society requires specialized computational and linguistic skills, generating a need to evaluate people as good or bad on specific tasks involving that set of skills, which has been named intelligence (Kagan, 1998).

For some psychologists, intelligence concerns mental abilities; for others, it is the basic general factor necessary for all mental activity; for still others, it is a group of specific abilities. Most agree, however, that intelligence is a capacity, not a thing. Reaching this point of agreement involved a convoluted process. Early psychologists sought to separate normal children from mentally retarded children. They developed tests to do so. Later researchers refined the tests and developed elaborate theories of the "factors" that make up intelligence. From the beginning, researchers have sought to know the source of intelligence. Does it come from parents through the genes, or from learning and the environment? The history of psychology has been punctuated with thousands of research papers on intelligence and its nature. Part of the problem is defining what intelligence is and is not. Part is deciding whether intelligence has one or many components. And part is determining whether nature or nurture is primarily responsible for intelligent behavior.

Recognizing these complexities, we can still formulate a working definition of **intelligence** as the overall capacity of an individual to act purposefully, to think rationally, and to deal effectively with the environment. It is a person's ability to learn and understand. By this definition, intelligence is expressed behaviorally. It is shown in a person's actions and abilities to learn new things and to use previously learned knowledge. Most important, intelligence has to do with a person's ability to adapt to the social and cultural environment. Intelligence is thus not a thing but a capacity, which is affected by a person's day-to-day experiences in the world. Intelligence is *not* a person's IQ, which is merely a score derived from a test.

Theories of Intelligence—One Ability or Many?

Clearly, all people do not act intelligently all of the time. The realization of individual differences in behavior has been a problem for psychology from its beginnings. Psychologists want to study individual behavior and how it varies over time and in different circumstances, but they also want to make generalizations about human behavior.

A key issue has been, and continues to be, whether there is one intelligence or many. Is intelligence a singular property, or does it consist of many, more or less independent components? Today, the most influential views on this issue are Wechsler's theory, factor theories, Jensen's two-level theory, Vygotsky's view, Gardner's theory of multiple intelligences, and Sternberg's triarchic theory.

■ **WECHSLER'S THEORY.** David Wechsler viewed intelligence from the perspective of a tester. As one of the developers of a widely used and respected intelligence test (which we will examine later), Wechsler knew that such tests are made up of many subparts, each measuring a fairly narrow aspect of a person's functioning and resourcefulness. He argued that intelligence tests involving spatial relations and verbal comprehension reveal little about someone's overall capacity to deal with the world. In Wechsler's view, psychologists need to remember that intelligence is more than simply mathematical or problem-solving ability; it is the broader ability to deal with the world.

■ **FACTOR THEORIES.** Factor theories of intelligence use a correlation technique known as *factor analysis* to explore what makes up intelligence. **Factor analysis** is a statistical procedure designed to discover the independent elements (factors) in any set of data. With regard to intelligence testing, factor analysis attempts to find a cluster of items that measure a common ability. Results of tests of verbal comprehension,

Intelligence
The overall capacity of an individual to act purposefully, to think rationally, and to deal effectively with the environment.

Factor analysis
Statistical procedure designed to discover the independent elements (factors) in any set of data.

spelling, and reading speed, for example, usually correlate highly, suggesting that some underlying attribute of verbal abilities (a factor) determines a person's score on those three tests.

In the early 1900s, Charles E. Spearman (1863–1945) used factor analysis to show that intelligence consists of two parts: a general factor affecting all tasks, which he termed the *g* factor, and specific factors associated with particular tasks. According to Spearman, some amounts of both the general factor and the appropriate specific factor(s) were necessary for the successful performance of any task. This view of intelligence is known as the *two-factor theory of intelligence*. Experts assert that a general factor underlies the diverse cognitive abilities (Brody, 1997), and there is physiological evidence for it (Duncan et al., 2000).

Louis L. Thurstone (1887–1955) further developed Spearman's work by postulating a general factor analogous to Spearman's, as well as seven other basic factors, each representing a unique mental ability: verbal comprehension, word fluency, number facility, spatial visualization, associative memory, perceptual speed, and reasoning. Known as the *factor theory of intelligence*, Thurstone's theory included a computational scheme for sorting out these seven factors. The factor theory is not universally accepted. Many assert that there is a general factor of intelligence and that it cannot be separated into distinct parts that account for specific abilities; rather, the same overall factor accounts for success in both academic work and other pursuits (Kranzler, 1997).

■ **JENSEN'S TWO-LEVEL THEORY.** Arthur Jensen (1969, 1970, 1987) suggests that intellectual functioning consists of associative abilities and cognitive abilities. *Associative abilities* enable people to connect stimuli and events; they involve little reasoning or transformation. Items testing associative abilities might, for example, ask someone to repeat from memory a seven-digit number sequence and to identify geometric shapes or classify them into categories. *Cognitive abilities*, on the other hand, involve reasoning and problem solving. What is novel is Jensen's claim that associative and cognitive abilities are inherited, which adds fuel to the nature–nurture controversy about intelligence (which we'll consider later in this chapter).

■ *Vygotsky held that when children develop problem-solving skills, language, and thought in general, it is done in a cultural and social context.*

■ **VYGOTSKY'S VIEW.** Lev Vygotsky (1896–1934) was a Russian psychologist who saw intellectual development as occurring in a social context that includes communication, with the self and with others. Intelligence is not one task, but many, which are interwoven. Children, for example, engage in private speech to plan their own actions and behavior; when they use such speech, they do better at various intellectual tasks. Vygotsky suggested that private speech helps a child understand his or her world. For Vygotsky (1934/1962), even the earliest speech is essentially social and useful and a key part of intelligence; in fact, he asserted that social speech comes first, followed by egocentric (self-centered) speech, then inner speech.

Vygotsky held that when children are presented tasks that are

TABLE 10.1

Gardner's Multiple Intelligences

Type of Intelligence	Exemplar	Core Components
Linguistic	Poet Journalist	Sensitivity to the sounds, rhythms, and meanings of words; sensitivity to the different functions of language
Logical–mathematical	Scientist Mathematician	Sensitivity to and capacity to discern logical or numerical patterns; ability to handle long chains of reasoning
Musical	Composer Violinist	Ability to produce and appreciate rhythm, pitch, and timbre; appreciation of the forms of musical expressiveness
Spatial	Navigator Sculptor	Capacity to perceive the visual–spatial world accurately and to perform transformations on initial perceptions
Bodily–kinesthetic	Dancer Athlete	Ability to control bodily movements and to handle objects skillfully
Naturalist	Botanist Chef	Ability to make fine discriminations among the flora and fauna of the natural world or the patterns and designs of human artifacts
Interpersonal	Therapist Salesperson	Capacity to discern and respond appropriately to the moods, temperaments, motivations, and desires of other people
Intrapersonal	Person with detailed, accurate, self-knowledge	Access to one's own feelings and the ability to discriminate among them and draw on them to guide behavior; knowledge of one's own strengths, weaknesses, desires, and intelligence

Gardner & Hatch, 1989

beyond their current abilities, they need the help of society to accomplish them. The child eventually incorporates new skills into his or her repertoire of behaviors and thus shows intelligence. Since children solve practical tasks with the help of their own inner speech, psychologists have to watch how and when that speech develops. Vygotsky ultimately believed that psychologists must examine not only the result of intellectual growth, but the process of getting there as well. Since many tasks are involved, intelligence is not so much a product as a process; this argument is supported by a number of contemporary thinkers who assert the existence of multiple intelligences.

■ **GARDNER'S MULTIPLE INTELLIGENCES.** Howard Gardner has proposed that there are multiple types of intelligences and that traditional intelligence tests do not measure them (1983/1993, 1995; Gardner & Hatch, 1989). Gardner argues that human competencies, of which there are many, do not all lend themselves to measurement on a standard test. He maintains that people have multiple intelligences—"an intelligence" being an ability to solve a problem or create a product within a specific cultural setting. Gardner's eight types of intelligences are summarized in Table 10.1.

Gardner's view has been praised for its recognition of the cultural context of intelligence, its consideration of multiple human competencies, and the framework it offers in which to analyze intelligence in school and other applied settings. The criticisms of his multiple intelligences approach focus on terminology—for example, are talents one type of intelligence? Some critics assert that Gardner's "intelligences" are all highly correlated with one another, essentially measuring the same thing. Others claim that the intelligences seem to resemble lists of learning and personality styles, not competencies or intelligence. The scientific jury is still out, but Gardner's work on multiple intelligences has certainly influenced other theorists, including Sternberg.

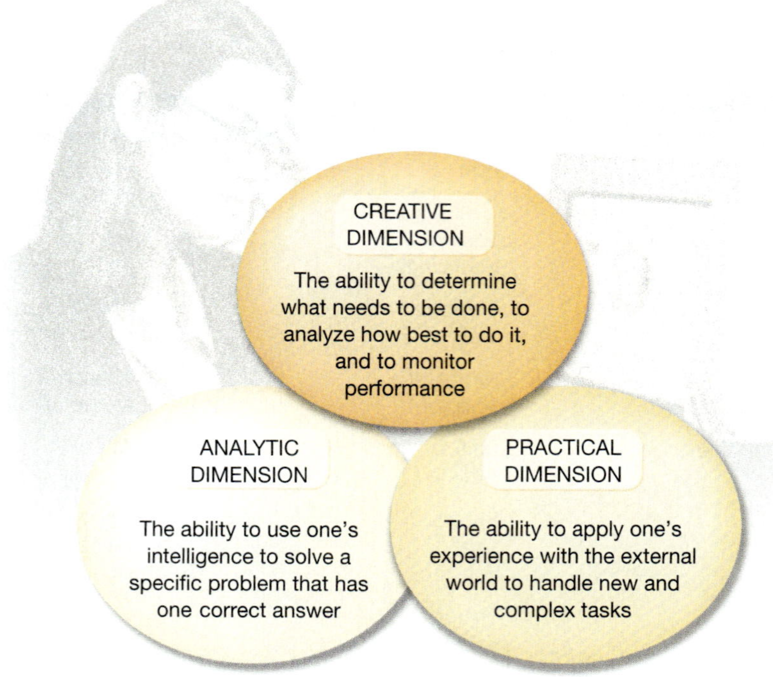

FIGURE 10.1

Sternberg's Triarchic Theory of Intelligence

■ **STERNBERG'S TRIARCHIC THEORY.** Robert J. Sternberg maintains that traditional tests used by colleges to make admissions decisions—including the SAT, the GRE, and even IQ tests—measure only limited aspects of behavior and do not predict future success very well (Sternberg, Grigorenko, & Bundy, 2001; Sternberg & Williams, 1997). He feels that psychologists keep using the same populations and the same tasks in the same contexts and keep drawing the same results—often wrong and not generalizable to all peoples (Sternberg & Grigorenko, 2000b).

Sternberg (1997a) asserts that a solid theory of intelligence must focus on *successful intelligence*, or the ability to adapt to, shape, and select environments to accomplish one's goals and those of society. Sternberg believes psychologists should investigate not how much intelligence people have, but how they use it; this makes his theory highly applicable cross-culturally. Sternberg (1985, 1997a; Sternberg et al., 2001) has proposed a *triarchic theory* in which intelligence has three dimensions: analytic, practical, and creative (see Figure 10.1).

The *analytic dimension* of intelligence involves an individual's ability to use intelligence for problem solving in specific situations where there is one right answer. This part of the triarchic theory focuses on how people shape their environments so that their competencies can be used to best advantage. In Western societies, analytical intelligence is measured on tests and valued in classrooms. For example, a person might organize a situation in a meaningful way, perhaps by grouping similar items together. However, the analytic dimension does not refer to any mental operations required to carry out problem solving, and thus it is likely to be culture-free. It may be used by an African herdsman weaving leaves to build walls for a dwelling, a machinist cleaning a well-used lathe, or a student solving a problem in long division.

The *practical dimension* has to do with a person's application of his or her experience with the external world and with everyday tasks. According to this part of Sternberg's theory, a test measures intelligence if it assesses a person's ability both to handle novel tasks and to master tasks so that they can be performed in an automatic manner. An example of such mastery through experience is memorizing verb forms in a foreign language or troubleshooting malfunctioning electronic equipment. Initially, such tasks are usually difficult and tedious, but practice makes them nearly automatic (Sternberg & Grigorenko, 2000a).

The *creative dimension* of Sternberg's triarchic intelligence is the glue that holds the other two dimensions together. It describes the mental mechanisms underlying what are commonly considered intelligent behaviors. Creative intelligence includes a person's ability to determine which tasks need to be done, to determine the order in which subtasks should be undertaken, to analyze their subparts, to decide which information should be processed, and to monitor performance. This is the aspect of intelligence necessary to write a love poem or a computer program. Tasks involving analogies, vocabulary, and syllogisms can be used to measure the elements of creative intelligence.

Few behaviors engage all three dimensions of intelligence, so Sternberg asserts that various tasks measure intelligence to a different extent. Thus, from Sternberg's point of view, new batteries of tests are needed to fully analyze the three basic dimensions of intelligent behavior. Good predictors of a person's academic achievement will take into account knowledge of the world—practical intelligence or common sense—in addition to verbal comprehension and mathematical reasoning (Sternberg, 2000b). Too often, children do poorly in school and in life despite having obvious intellectual skills. These individuals often do not know how to allocate their time or how to work effectively with other people. Such skills need to be taught, because some students do not develop them

pointcounterpoint

Are There Many Intelligences?

The Issue: Is the idea of multiple intelligences flawed?

POINT
Intelligence must be considered from multiple vantage points, with many competencies making up intelligence.

COUNTERPOINT
Theories of multiple intelligences, like Howard Gardner's, involve circular reasoning and are misleading.

All people are unique in the way they go about life; while human beings share a common genome, how they express their heredity is affected by a myriad of variables—from prenatal nutrition, playground encounters, and parental exchanges large and small. So it is not surprising that as adults people express their intelligence, and their humanity for that matter, in many ways. Howard Gardner (1998) maintains that people have multiple intelligences—"an intelligence" being an ability to solve a problem or create a product within a specific cultural setting. Gardner ultimately describes eight types of intelligence. Similarly, Sternberg (2000b) boils his "intelligences" down—in his case to three types. Both Gardner's and Sternberg's approaches have had enormous impact on educators' thinking.

However, having intuitive appeal and being widely popular doesn't make the multiple intelligence theories right—or so say critics like Perry Klein (1997), who argue that theories of multiple intelligence do not tell us anything new, that these intelligences are not independent of one another, that the intelligences are so closely related that they cannot really be distinguished from one another, and that telling people that they are high or low in one form of intelligence or another may discourage initiative and do more harm than good.

Gardner and Sternberg argue that we have to keep in mind that people can excel in many ways and that facility on the dance floor is quite different than computer fluency or verbal fluency. They argue that the different kinds of intelligences must be recognized and fostered in the classroom. Klein counters that these "intelligences" are nothing more than special abilities and that labeling them as intelligences does little or nothing to help us understand human intelligence.

The multiple intelligence approach is seen by many as a deeper analysis, a more subtle, nuanced explanation of this thing we call intelligence; yet the unitary approach that argues that there is one general factor called intelligence has been around for decades and has withstood many assaults on its validity. Time—and a great deal of research—will tell. We can't wait to see what the research will say in the next decade.

on their own. As Ceci (2000) asserts, schools foster the learning of specific skills, not necessarily general problem-solving abilities. In addition, schools often promote specific ways of thinking about problems, but researchers and tests need to value alternative modes of thought and creativity. For example, tests—especially IQ tests—should begin to probe for wise responses (Sternberg, 1998). The issue of the multiplicity of intelligence becomes even more complex when emotions enter the equation, as we'll see next.

Emotions–A Different Kind of Intelligence?

Being highly intelligent is no guarantee of success in life. It is true that doing well in school is important for getting ahead. But there is more to success, in work and in life, than superior cognitive ability. You probably know people who are quite bright intellectually but have little common sense, few leadership skills, or insufficient motivation. In 1995, Daniel Goleman published a book titled *Emotional Intelligence*, which claims that one's emotional life can matter much more than one's intellectual abilities.

Goleman holds that traditionally defined intelligence is separate from emotional intelligence. According to Goleman, emotional intelligence seems to be the key to getting ahead in life. Emotional intelligence includes self-awareness, impulse control, persistence, self-motivation, ability to recognize emotions in others, and social agility. Goleman gives credit to psychologists such as Gardner and Sternberg, who stress the multiplicity of intelligence, but he believes their theories don't go far enough.

Cognitive ability and emotional intelligence are not mutually exclusive. Highly intelligent people can be outgoing, cheerful, poised, sympathetic, and caring (high in emotional intelligence), but they can also be cold, unresponsive, and detached (that is, low in emotional intelligence). Goleman's assertion is that, all other things being equal, those with high emotional intelligence will nearly always do better than those with low emotional intelligence—regardless of cognitive abilities. Of course, emotional intelligence is not simply either low or high. Like other types of intelligence, emotional intelligence is displayed in a wide range of degrees.

Goleman proposes that people who develop a high emotional intelligence can better manage the difficulties of life, such as inappropriate aggression, eating disorders, depression, and alcoholism. He argues that people can be taught to recognize emotions and understand relationships, to develop greater tolerance of frustration and effective management of anger, to focus better on the task at hand and pay attention (thus becoming less impulsive), and to take another person's perspective. Goleman's point has been emphasized by researchers who assert that only when people can accurately perceive, appraise, and express their emotions can they harness their intellectual capacity. Mayer, Salovey, and Caruso (2000) argue that when people use their emotions to facilitate thought, they can learn to regulate the emotions. They try to separate the effects of emotion and intelligence and assert that each affects the other; they contend that a definition like Goleman's focuses too much on the motivational properties of emotional states and too little on the feeling of emotions.

Psychologists have to ask some critical questions: To what extent are cognitive ability and emotions independent? Are they affected by the same environmental variables? Can emotional intelligence be fostered or enhanced? (You saw in Chapter 3 that Head Start programs have successfully enhanced academic skills. Might the same be done for emo-

Be an *Active* learner

REVIEW

- What is the central and most important part of a definition of intelligence? pp. 332–333
- What did theoreticians mean by a *g* factor? p. 334

THINK CRITICALLY

- What might be the implications for researchers of Vygotsky's claim that scientists must examine the process of intelligence, not just its products?
- Is love an emotionally intelligent feeling? Can a person's feelings and thoughts be separated from his or her intelligence? If so, how?
- What are some key competencies that you think should be in an intelligence test?
- Identify ways that people can keep emotions from determining thoughts.

APPLY PSYCHOLOGY

- What do you think the goal of intelligence testing should be?
- Identify some elements that you would put in a test of emotional intelligence.

tional intelligence?) Shouldn't Goleman's qualities of emotional intelligence be correlated? If so, how can they be measured? Psychologists know a great deal about both intelligence and emotion, but there is little research evidence to support Goleman's emotional intelligence, despite its intuitive appeal (Davies, Stankov, & Roberts, 1998). Until solid, systematic research is done, this idea remains an interesting working hypothesis, one that deserves investigation. It will very likely be tested in longitudinal studies in the coming decades.

The Process of Test Development

You probably have taken one or more intelligence tests during your school years. Whether or not you were aware of the results of these tests, they may have determined your educational track from elementary school onward. But psychologists are among the first to admit that intelligence tests have shortcomings, and researchers continue to revise these tests to correct the inadequacies and to maximize the tests' practical benefits in educational, occupational, and clinical settings (Daniel, 1997).

Intelligence tests have a long history. In the late 19th and early 20th centuries, Frenchman Alfred Binet (1857–1911) became interested in psychology and began to study behavior. He later hired Theodore Simon (1873–1961), a 26-year-old physician, to assist him; their friendship and collaboration became famous. Binet and Simon are best known as the founders of the psychological testing movement. Interestingly, however, their first intelligence tests weren't developed for the general population. In 1904, Binet was commissioned to devise procedures for identifying and educating children in Paris who suffered from mental retardation. Binet was chosen for the task because he had been lobbying for action to help the schools. (French schools had only recently been made public, and retarded children were doing poorly and dropping out.) As Stagner (1988) suggests, this may have been the first government-sponsored psychological research.

■ *Binet and Simon are best known as the founders of the psychological testing movement. In 1904, Binet (shown here) attempted to devise procedures for identifying and educating Parisian children with mental retardation.*

Binet coined the phrase *mental age*, meaning the age level at which a child is functioning cognitively, regardless of chronological age. Binet and Simon applied everyday tasks, such as counting, naming, and using objects, to determine mental age. The scale they developed is widely considered to be the first practical measure of intelligence. A century later, psychologists are still following some of Binet and Simon's recommendations about how tests should be constructed and administered. In fact, one of the most influential intelligence tests in use today is the Stanford–Binet test, a direct descendant of Binet's and Simon's early tests.

Developing an Intelligence Test

Imagine you are a 7-year-old child taking an intelligence test, and you come to this question: "Which one of the following tells you the temperature?" Below the question are pictures of the sun, a radio, a thermometer, and a pair of mittens. Is the thermometer the only correct answer? Suppose there are no thermometers in your home, but you often hear the temperature given on radio weather reports. Or imagine that you estimate the temperature each morning by standing outside to feel the sun's strength, or that you know it's cold outside when your parents tell you to wear mittens. Based on your experiences, any one of the answers to the question might be appropriate.

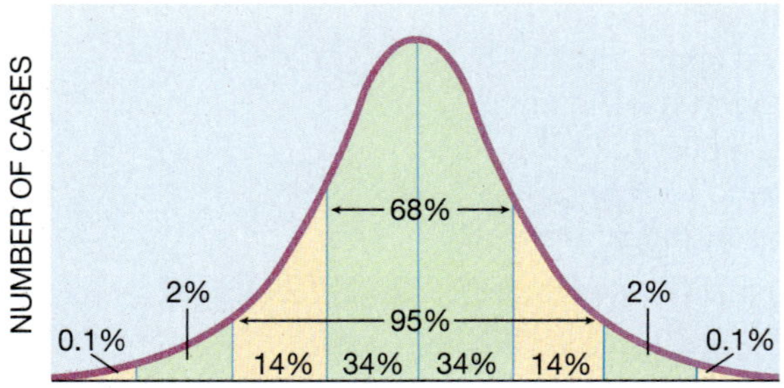

FIGURE 10.2

A Normal Distribution

The bell-shaped curve shows a standard normal distribution. As in normal distributions of height, weight, and even intelligence, very few people are represented at the extremes.

■ **WHAT DOES A TEST MEASURE?** The predisposition to respond to almost any test question based on experiences—social and cultural biases—illustrates the complexity of intelligence test development. In general, a *test* is a standardized device for examining a person's responses to specific stimuli, usually questions or problems. Because there are many potential pitfalls in creating a test, psychologists follow an elaborate set of guidelines and procedures to make certain that questions are properly constructed. First, a psychologist must decide what the test is to measure. For example, will it measure musical ability, knowledge of geography, or math skills? Second, the psychologist needs to construct items for the test such that answering them successfully reflects the kind of ability being measured. Third, the test must be standardized.

■ **STANDARDIZATION.** **Standardization** is the process of developing uniform procedures for administering and scoring a test and for establishing norms. **Norms** are the scores and corresponding percentile ranks of a large and representative sample of individuals from the population for which the test is designed. A **representative sample** is a sample of individuals who match the population with whom they are to be compared with regard to key variables such as socioeconomic status and age. Thus, a test designed for all U.S. college freshmen might be given to a sample of 2,000 freshmen, including an equal number of males and females, between the ages of 16 and 20, who graduated from large and small high schools, come from different areas of the United States, and represent different ethnic groups and socioeconomic levels.

Standardization ensures that there is a basis for comparing all future test results with those of a standard reference group. After a test is designed and administered to a representative sample, the test developers examine the results to establish norms for different segments of the test population. Knowing how people in the representative sample have done allows psychologists and educators to interpret future test results properly. In other words, the scores of those in the representative sample serve as a reference point for comparing individual scores.

Standardization
Process of developing uniform procedures for administering and scoring a test and for establishing norms.

Norms
The scores and corresponding percentile ranks of a large and representative sample of individuals from the population for which a test was designed.

Representative sample
A sample of individuals who match the population with whom they are to be compared with regard to key variables such as socioeconomic status and age.

Normal curve
A bell-shaped graphic representation of data showing what percentage of the population falls under each part of the curve.

Raw score
A test score that has not been transformed or converted in any way.

Standard score
A score that expresses an individual's position relative to the mean, based on the standard deviation.

■ **THE NORMAL CURVE.** Test developers generally plot the scores of the representative sample on a graph that shows how frequently each score occurs. On most tests, some people score very well, some score very poorly, and most score in the middle. Psychologists say that test scores distributed in that way are *normally distributed*, or fall on a normal curve. A **normal curve** is a bell-shaped graphic representation of data that shows the percentage of the population that falls under each part of the curve. As Figure 10.2 shows, most people fall in the middle range, with a few at each extreme. Tests are often devised so that individual scores can be compared to a normal distribution. (The Appendix discusses the normal distribution in detail.)

■ **SCORES.** The simplest score on a test is the **raw score**—the number of correct answers, not converted or transformed in any way. The raw score, however, is seldom a true indicator of a person's ability. Raw scores on many tests, particularly intelligence tests, must be adjusted to take into account a person's age, gender, and grade level. An adjusted score is commonly expressed as a **standard score**—a score that expresses an individual's position relative to those of other test takers, based on the mean score and how scores are distributed around it. If, for example, a 100-item intelligence test is administered to students in the 3rd and 11th grades, test developers expect those in the 11th grade to answer more items correctly than those in the 3rd grade. To adjust for the differences, scoring procedures allow each student's score to be compared to the score typically achieved by other students at the same grade level. Thus, if 11th-graders typically answer 70 questions correctly, an 11th-grader who answers 90 questions correctly has done better than most other students

TABLE 10.2

Traditional Calculation of Intelligence Quotient for Three People

	Person 1	Person 2	Person 3
Mental Age (MA)	6 years	15 years	15 years
Chronological Age (CA)	6 years	18 years	12 years
MA ÷ CA	6 ÷ 6 = 1	15 ÷ 18 = 0.83	15 ÷ 12 = 1.25
(MA ÷ CA) × 100	1 × 100 = 100	0.83 × 100 = 83	1.25 × 100 = 125
IQ	100	83	125

at that grade level. Similarly, if 3rd-graders usually answer 25 questions correctly, a 3rd-grader who answers 15 questions correctly has done worse than most other 3rd-grade students. A standard score is generally a **percentile score**—a score indicating what percentage of the test population obtained a lower score. If, for example, someone's percentile score is 84, then 84% of those taking the test obtained a lower score than that person did.

■ **INTELLIGENCE QUOTIENTS.** Binet and Simon's test to determine mental age clearly qualifies as an intelligence test—even though it was a relatively crude one. In the early 20th century, intelligence was measured by a simple formula. To obtain an intelligence quotient (IQ), a psychologist divided a person's mental abilities, or mental age, by the person's chronological age and multiplied the result by 100. (See Table 10.2 for examples.) Children's mental ages were estimated from the number of correct answers on a series of test items; the higher the number, the higher the mental age.

A problem with the traditional formula—divide mental age by chronological age and multiply the result by 100—is that young children's answers to test items vary far more than do older children's or adults'; it is as if their intelligence were less stable, less repeatable, and more subject to change. This variability makes predictions and comparisons difficult. To simplify measures of IQ, psychologists and testers began using **deviation IQ**—a standard IQ test score whose mean and standard deviation remain constant for all ages. If a child of 9 and an adolescent of 16 each have a deviation IQ of 116, they are in the same percentile relative to others of their respective ages who have taken the same IQ test.

Perhaps the most important goal of developers of IQ tests is to ensure that tests are both reliable and valid. If a student obtains different scores on two versions of the same test, which score is correct? Furthermore, does the test measure what it is supposed to measure and only that?

Reliability

Reliability refers to the consistency of test scores. In general, **reliability** is a test's ability to yield very similar scores for the same individual over repeated testings. (When a researcher says that test scores have consistency, the researcher is assuming that the person taking the test is in approximately the same emotional and physiological state each time the test is administered.) If a test's results are not consistent over several testing sessions or for two comparable groups of people, useful comparisons are impossible. A test is rarely perfectly reliable; the question is, is it *generally* consistent, and does it yield *similar* results on multiple testings?

Among the ways to determine whether a test is reliable, the simplest, termed the *test–retest* method, is to administer the same test to the same person on two or more occasions. If, for example, the person achieves a score of 87 one day and 110 another, the test is probably not reliable (see Table 10.3 on the following page). Of

Percentile score
A score indicating what percentage of the test population would obtain a lower score.

Deviation IQ
A standard IQ test score whose mean and standard deviation remain constant for all ages.

Reliability
Ability of a test to yield very similar scores for the same individual over repeated testings.

TABLE 10.3

Test–Retest Reliability

Test–retest reliability indicates whether people who are given the same or a similar test on repeated occasions achieve similar scores each time.

	Test With High Reliability		Test With Low Reliability	
	First Testing	**Second Testing**	**First Testing**	**Second Testing**
Person 1	92	90	92	74
Person 2	87	89	87	96
Person 3	78	77	78	51

course, the person might have remembered some of the items from the first testing to the next. To avoid that problem, testers use the *alternative-form method* of determining reliability, which involves giving two different versions of the same test. If the two versions test the same characteristic and differ only in the test items used, both should yield very similar results. Another way to evaluate reliability is to use the *split-half method*, which involves dividing a test into two parts; the scores from the two halves of a reliable test yield similar, if not identical, results.

A reliable test has a relatively small standard error of measurement. The *standard error of measurement* is the number of points by which a score varies because of imperfect reliability. Consider an IQ test that has a standard error of measurement of 3. If someone scores 115 on that test, the test developer can state with a high degree of confidence that the individual's real IQ is between 112 and 118—within 3 points above or below the score obtained.

Validity

If a psychology exam included questions such as "What is the square root of 647?" and "Who wrote *The Grapes of Wrath*?" it would not be a valid measure of the students' knowledge of psychology. That is, it would not be measuring what it is supposed to measure. To be useful, a test must have not only reliability, but also **validity**—the ability to measure only what it is supposed to measure and to predict only what it is supposed to predict.

■ **TYPES OF VALIDITY.** *Content validity* is a test's ability to measure the knowledge or behavior it is intended to measure, which is based upon a detailed examination of the contents of the test items. A test designed to measure musical aptitude should not include items that assess mechanical aptitude or personality characteristics.

In addition to content validity, a test should have *predictive validity*—the ability to predict a person's future achievements with at least some degree of accuracy. Critics of tests like to point out that scores on tests are not always accurate predictors of people's performance. Tests cannot take into account high levels of motivation or creative abilities. Nevertheless, many colleges use standard scores to decide which high school students should be accepted for admission—thus assuming that the scores accurately predict ability to do college-level work.

Two additional types of validity are *face validity*, the extent to which a test's appropriateness can be gauged by reading or examining the test items, and *construct validity*, the extent to which a test actually does measure the particular quality or trait it is supposed to measure, such as intelligence, anxiety, or musical ability.

Validity
Ability of a test to measure what it is supposed to measure and to predict what it is supposed to predict.

■ **CRITICISMS OF INTELLIGENCE TEST VALIDITY.** Critics cite six basic problems concerning the validity of intelligence tests. The first is that there is no way to measure intelligence because no clear definition of intelligence has been agreed on. The defense against this argument is that although different intelligence tests seem to measure different abilities, the major tests have face validity.

The second criticism is that because intelligence test items usually refer to *learned information*, they reflect the quality of a child's schooling rather than the child's actual intelligence. The response to this challenge is that most vocabulary items on intelligence tests are learned in the child's general environment, not only in school; moreover, the ability to learn vocabulary terms and facts seems to depend on a general ability to reason verbally. Further, scores on other measures of ability seem independent of schooling and correlate highly with traditional intelligence test scores (Richardson, 2000).

Halo effect
The tendency for one characteristic of an individual to influence a tester's evaluation of other characteristics.

The third criticism is that the administration of intelligence tests in school settings may adversely affect test scores—not only because the tests are often administered inexpertly, but also because of the halo effect (e.g., Darley and Gross, 2000). The **halo effect** is the tendency for one particular or outstanding characteristic about an individual (or a group) to influence the evaluation of other characteristics. A test administrator can develop a positive or negative feeling about a person, a class, or a group of students that may influence the administration of tests or the interpretation of test scores. People who defend intelligence testing against this charge acknowledge that incorrectly administered tests are likely to result in inaccurate scores, but they claim that this occurs less often than opponents think.

Two other criticisms of intelligence tests are less directly related to the issue of validity. One of these is that some people are *test-wise*. These individuals make better use of their time than others do, guess the tester's intentions, and find clues in the test. The usual responses to this criticism are that the items on intelligence tests are unfamiliar even to experienced test takers and that the effects of previous practice are seldom or never evident in test scores. Another criticism is that test takers' scores often depend on their *motivation to succeed* rather than on actual intelligence. Claude Steele (1999; Steele & Aronson, 2000) has argued that whenever members of ethnic or other minorities concentrate explicitly on a scholastic task, they worry about confirming negative stereotypes of their group. This extra burden may drag down their performance, through what Steele calls *stereotype threat*—people fear being reduced to a stereotype and then do worse because of the fear. Stereotype threat probably occurs in part because of subtle instructional differences and in part because of situational pressure that may undermine a test taker's self-confidence; unless members of minority groups (African Americans, older adults) are resilient to such threats, their performance is likely to suffer (Steele, 1999). (We will discuss this issue further in Chapter 16.) Defenders of intelligence tests agree that examinees' motivation and attitudes toward being tested are important; however, they deny that the tests themselves may influence motivation.

Last, success in the United States—economic and social—is heavily influenced by one's academic achievement and the ensuing opportunities that emerge from completing college. But entry into college is determined by success on standardized tests (Sternberg, 2000b), and standardized tests are affected by schooling. Thus, the system is self-reinforcing and circular. So the criticism is that the society *creates* the correlation between academic success and intelligence test scores. The defense against this criticism, again, is that the test scores also correlate with measures of intelligence that seem independent of schooling.

Critics of intelligence tests are concerned about the interpretation of scores. It is important to remember that intelligence

Be an *Active* learner

REVIEW

- Describe a normal curve. p. 340
- What fundamental assumption underlies the use of a representative sample? p. 340
- Why is the normal curve an essential part of the process of standardization? pp. 340–341
- What is a standard error of measurement? p. 342
- What is a key problem with the traditional formula for IQ tests? pp. 342–343
- Intelligence tests are criticized on what key grounds? pp.342–343

THINK CRITICALLY

- Which of the criticisms of intelligence tests and testing is most significant, in your opinion? Why?
- Is it true there is *no* way to measure intelligence? Can you devise a unique scheme?
- If society *creates* the correlation between academic success and intelligence test scores, how might it undo this creation without undoing our very successful higher education system?
- Why might a psychologist not want parents to know their child's IQ score?

APPLY PSYCHOLOGY

- Make a list of things about you an intelligence test would measure—other than your intelligence.
- If you were devising your own IQ test, what kinds of items would you place on it?

TABLE 10.4

Some Misconceptions About Intelligence Tests and Testing

Misconception	Reality
Intelligence tests measure innate intelligence.	IQ scores measure some of an individual's interactions with the environment; they never measure only innate intelligence.
IQs never change.	People's IQs change throughout life, but especially from birth through age 6. Even after this age, significant changes can occur.
Intelligence tests provide perfectly reliable scores.	Test scores are only estimates. Every test should be reported as a statement of probability, such as "There is a 90% chance that the test taker's IQ falls within a 6-point range of the reported score (from 3 points above to 3 points below)."
Intelligence tests measure all aspects of a person's intelligence.	Most intelligence tests do not measure the entire spectrum of abilities related to intellectual behavior. Some stress verbal and nonverbal intelligence but do not adequately measure other areas, such as mechanical skills, creativity, or social intelligence.
A battery of tests reveals everything necessary to make judgments about a person's competence.	No battery of tests can give a complete picture of any person. A battery can only illuminate various areas of functioning.

Sattler, 1992

tests are generally made up of different subtests or subscales, each yielding a score. There may also be one general score for the entire test. All these scores require knowledgeable interpretation; that is, test scores must be put into a context that is relevant to the situation of the person who took the test (Daniel, 2000). Without such a context, a score is little more than a number. The interpretation of test scores is the key; without such interpretation, a single score can be biased, inaccurate, or misleading. Table 10.4 summarizes some misconceptions about intelligence tests and testing.

Four Important Intelligence Tests

What is the best intelligence test? What does it measure? Can you study for an intelligence test and get a higher score? As in other areas of science, theory leads to application; many theorists applied their ideas to the development of intelligence tests. The four tests we examine here—the Stanford–Binet Intelligence Scale, the Wechsler scales, the Kaufman Assessment Battery for Children, and Woodcock–Johnson–III—are all widely used. They were developed by well-known and respected researchers, and they predict performance well. Their results all correlate well with one another, and research shows that they are reliable and valid. We'll begin by examining the first real IQ test, the Stanford–Binet Intelligence Scale.

The Stanford–Binet Intelligence Scale

Most people associate the beginning of intelligence testing with Alfred Binet and Theodore Simon. As noted earlier, the two men collaborated to develop the Binet–Simon Scale in 1905. The original test was actually 30 short tests arranged in order of difficulty and consisting of tasks such as distinguishing food from nonfood and pointing to objects and naming them. The Binet–Simon Scale leaned heavily toward verbal questions and was not well standardized.

From 1912 to 1916, Lewis M. Terman revised the scale and developed the test now known as the Stanford–Binet Intelligence Scale. (Terman was teaching at Stanford University when he revised the test.) With the Stanford–Binet, a child's mental age (intellectual ability) is divided by chronological age and multiplied by

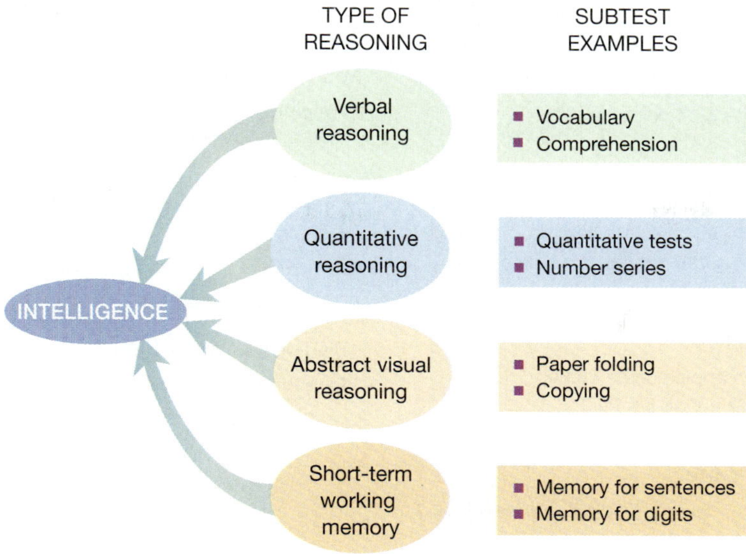

FIGURE 10.3

The Modern Stanford–Binet Intelligence Scale

The most recent version of the Stanford–Binet Intelligence Scale measures intelligence with a composite score made up of four scores on broad types of mental activity: verbal reasoning, quantitative reasoning, abstract visual reasoning, and short-term memory. Each score is obtained through a series of subtests that measure specific mental abilities.

100 to yield an intelligence quotient (IQ). This test has traditionally been a good predictor of academic performance, and many of its simplest subtests correlate highly with one another.

A newer version of the Stanford–Binet Intelligence Scale, published in 1986, contains items designed to avoid favoring either men or women or stressing ethnic stereotypes. It is composed of four major subscales that test verbal reasoning, quantitative reasoning, abstract visual reasoning, and short-term memory. Within the four major subscales, there are 15 possible subtests, which vary greatly in content (see Figure 10.3). The Stanford–Binet can be used to test anyone from age 2 through age 23, yielding one overall IQ score. The test administration time varies with the examinee's age, because the number of subtests given is determined by age. All examinees are first given a vocabulary test; along with their age, this test determines the level at which all other tests begin. Each of the subtests consists of a series of levels, with two items at each level. The tester begins by using entry-level items and continues until a higher level on each subscale is established (until the test taker fails a prescribed number of items).

Raw scores, determined by the number of items passed, are converted to a standard score for each age group. The new Stanford–Binet Intelligence Scale is a potent test; one of its great strengths is that it can be used over a wide range of ages and abilities. The new Stanford–Binet correlates well with the old one, as well as with the Wechsler scales and the Kaufman Assessment Battery for Children.

■ *The Wechsler Intelligence Scale for Children groups test items by content. The score on each subtest is calculated and converted to a standard score, adjusted for the test taker's age.*

The Wechsler Scales

David Wechsler (1896–1981), a Rumanian immigrant who earned a PhD in psychology from Columbia University, was influenced by Charles Spearman and Karl Pearson, two English statisticians with whom he studied. In 1932, Wechsler was appointed chief psychologist at Bellevue Hospital in New York City; there, he began making history. Wechsler recognized that the Stanford–Binet Intelligence

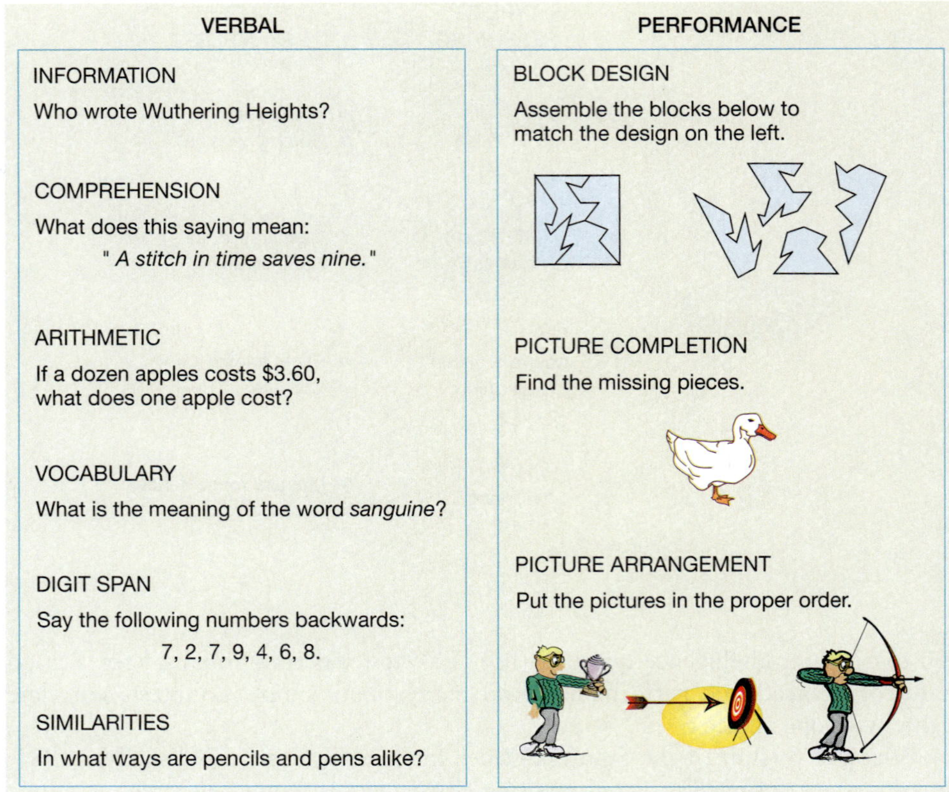

FIGURE 10.4
Items from the WAIS–III Verbal and Performance Subtests

Scale was inadequate for testing adults. He also maintained that some of the Stanford–Binet items lacked validity. In 1939, Wechsler developed the Wechsler–Bellevue Intelligence Scale to test adults. In 1955, the Wechsler Adult Intelligence Scale (WAIS) was published; it eliminated some technical difficulties inherent in the Wechsler–Bellevue scale. The most recent revision of the test is the WAIS–III. Figure 10.4 shows some sample items from the WAIS.

Wechsler also developed the Wechsler Intelligence Scale for Children (WISC), which covers children of ages 6 through 16. It was revised in 1974, becoming the WISC–R; the 1991 revision is the WISC–III. Table 10.5 shows some typical subtests included. In 1967, the Wechsler Preschool and Primary Scale of Intelligence (WPPSI) was developed for children of ages 4 through 6½; it was revised, becoming the WPPSI–R.

The Wechsler scales group test items by content; for example, all the information questions are presented together, all the arithmetic problems are presented together, and so on. The score on each subtest is calculated and converted to a standard (or scaled) score, adjusted for the test taker's age. The scaled scores allow for a comparison of scores across age levels. Thus, an 8-year-old's scaled score of 7 is comparable to an 11-year-old's scaled score of 7. An overall IQ score is reported, as well as subscale scores. Thousands of studies have confirmed the reliability and validity of the Wechsler scales.

The Kaufman Assessment Battery for Children

Alan and Nadeen Kaufman contend that their Kaufman Assessment Battery for Children (K–ABC) uses tasks that tap the experiences of all individuals, regardless of background. A memory task in the K–ABC, for example, might ask a child to

TABLE 10.5

Typical Subtests of the WISC–R Performance test

Verbal Test		Performance Test	
Subtest	**Type of Task**	**Subtest**	**Type of Task**
Information	When questioned, recall a general fact that has been acquired in a formal or informal school setting	Picture completion	Point out the part of an incomplete picture that is missing
Similarities	Use another concept in describing how two ideas are alike	Picture arrangement	Put a series of pictures that tell a story in the right sequence
Arithmetic	Solve a word problem without pencil and paper	Block design	Use real blocks to reproduce a picture of a block design
Digit span	Recall an orally presented string of digits	Object assembly	Put the pieces of a jigsaw-like puzzle together to form a complete object
Vocabulary	Define a vocabulary word	Coding	Given a key that matches numbers to geometric shapes, fill in a form with the shapes that go with the listed numbers
Comprehension	Answer a question requiring practical judgment and common sense		

look at a picture of a face and, a few moments later, to pick it out from among pictures of other faces. The K-ABC examines intelligence of participants ages 3–18 and was revised in 2001.

The K–ABC was designed especially for assessment of school problems. School psychologists, who are the primary users of the K–ABC, evaluate scores on the K–ABC and act as consultants to families and schools, helping them set and achieve appropriate educational goals for particular children. The K–ABC consists of four global scales. Three measure mental processing abilities (sequential processing, simultaneous processing, and a composite of the two); the fourth assesses achievement. A sequential task requires the manipulation of stimuli in sequential order; for example, a child might be asked to repeat a series of digits in the order in which the examiner presented them. A simultaneous-processing task involves organizing and integrating many stimuli presented at the same time; for example, a child might be asked to recall the placement of objects on a page that was presented only briefly. The K–ABC assesses not only how a child solves problems on each task, but how well she or he does so; the test thus minimizes the role of language and of acquired facts and skills. The Kaufmans believe that the sequential- and simultaneous-processing scales measure abilities synonymous with intelligence—that is, the ability to process information and the ability to solve problems (Kaufman, 1983).

The Woodcock-Johnson

There are thousands of tests and hundreds of intelligence tests. The Stanford–Binet, Wechsler, and K–ABC are widely used, but many practitioners have used the Woodcock–Johnson for many years. The Woodcock–Johnson–III is a test for measuring general intellectual ability, specific cognitive abilities, scholastic aptitude, oral language, and academic achievement. It consists of several subparts, and it is one of the most comprehensive test batteries available. Recently revised, this widely used test is given to children in kindergarten through adults in graduate school. Its strengths are that it measures and evaluates domain-specific skills with related cognitive abilities as well as traditional ability/achievement discrepancies; it is a useful diagnostic tool and can be used across the life span.

introduction to research basics

Seeing What You Expect to See

Scores on IQ tests are important, especially in the school setting. Children's scores influence educational and career decisions. Test administrators are supposed to be fair and objective in giving and interpreting the tests, but other opportunities for bias are possible in how test scores are used. Possibilities for bias arise through the **self-fulfilling prophecy,** the creation of a situation that unintentionally allows personal expectancies to influence participants. This effect is also called the *experiment expectancy effect*, and Robert Rosenthal and Lenore Jacobson (1966) investigated how this effect applies in classroom situations involving intelligence and intelligence testing.

DESIGN This study was an **experimental design** in which the researchers manipulated the information that they furnished to teachers about their students' IQs in order to produce different expectancies about students' abilities. The difference in expectation was the *independent variable*, and the *dependent variable* was students' scores on an IQ test. (See Chapter 1 for more details on experimental designs.)

HYPOTHESIS Rosenthal and Jacobson hypothesized that teachers' expectancies would influence students' performance—that is, the information about IQ would produce a self-fulfilling prophecy.

PARTICIPANTS Participants were 18 teachers (16 women and 2 men) who taught grades 1 through 6 in an elementary school.

METHOD Rosenthal and Jacobson conducted their study in an elementary school that had administered an IQ test to all students in grades 1 through 6. This situation allowed the researchers to manipulate the information that teachers received about their students' scores on the IQ test. They told the teachers that some students' scores were in the top 20%, indicating that these students would "bloom" within the next year and show big gains in their learning ability. This group was the experimental group. Rosenthal and Jacobson said that students whose scores were low would continue to make progress, but they would not experience a spurt in intellectual growth. This group was the control (comparison) group.

These stories were both untrue, but the false feedback allowed the researchers to create differential expectancies in the teachers by manipulating the information received. In fact, Rosenthal and Jacobson randomly assigned which students were "bloomers" and which were not.

RESULTS Examining students' scores on the IQ test at the end of the academic year, Rosenthal and Jacobson found that teacher expectancies made a significant difference for student performance. The students who were supposed to intellectually "bloom" did so, showing significantly higher IQ scores than the comparison students who were not expected to make dramatic gains. The effect was much stronger for grades 1 and 2 than for grades 3 through 6.

CONCLUSIONS Self-fulfilling prophecy applies to teachers in classroom situations. The effect can be powerful, accounting for gains in IQ of up to 30 points. This effect probably occurs through the ways that teachers communicate with and encourage students; teachers give more attention and encouragement to those students for whom they have high expectations. The results highlight one of the ways that information about IQ can be used to perpetuate discrimination. This study has many implications for teachers, counselors, and supervisors whose expectations can affect the behavior of students, clients, and workers.

Environmental and Biological Factors in Intelligence

The political, cultural, and scientific issues involved in the debate about what intelligence is and what intelligence tests actually measure are complicated. Ethnic and other minority groups have joined some psychologists and educators in challenging the usefulness of IQ tests. Underlying public concern and scientific debate is the fundamental issue of how much of intelligence is due to heredity and how much is due to a person's upbringing and culture. Further, if culture is a major factor, are tests biased?

Experimental design
A design in which researchers manipulate an independent variable and measure a dependent variable to determine a cause-and-effect relationship.

Self-fulfilling prophecy
The creation of a situation that unintentionally allows personal expectancies to influence participants.

Cultural Biases?

A major argument against IQ testing is that the tests are culturally biased and thus effectively discriminate against people who do not resemble the test makers, who are usually White, male, middle-class suburbanites. A test item or subscale is considered culturally biased if, with all other factors held constant, its content is more difficult for members of one group than for those of other groups. To understand how a test can be culturally biased, imagine that the child of an impoverished migrant worker is given the temperature problem posed earlier. If the child is unfamiliar with thermometers and radios, the child might choose the sun as the best answer. But if the test designer has deemed "thermometer" the correct answer, the migrant child's answer would be counted wrong.

■ *Cross-cultural differences in IQ scores, SAT scores, and other measures of achievement are narrowing. In addition—and especially important—differences among individuals within a group are often greater than differences between groups.*

Clearly, those who interpret IQ test scores must be particularly sensitive to any potential biases in the tests. Nonetheless, although researchers find differences among the IQ scores of various racial, ethnic, and cultural groups, they have found no consistent and conclusive evidence of bias in the tests themselves. Differences between siblings are usually as great as differences between ethnic groups; there is as great a variability between individuals as between groups. It is simply not the case that tests such as the WISC–R involve systematic discrimination on the basis of ethnicity. It is possible that any bias that appears to exist in an IQ test actually arises from how the results are used (a point to be examined shortly).

IQ tests cannot predict or explain all types of intellectual behavior. They test a small sample of a restricted range of cognitive activities. Intelligence can be demonstrated in many ways; an IQ test tells little about someone's ability to be flexible in new situations or to function maturely and responsibly. Intelligence tests do reflect many aspects of people's environments—how much they are encouraged to express themselves verbally, how much time they spend reading, and the extent to which they are encouraged to engage in academic pursuits (e.g., Barrett & Depinet, 1991).

Since the early 1970s, educators and psychologists have scrutinized the weaknesses of IQ tests and have attempted to eliminate cultural biases in testing by creating better tests and establishing better norms for comparison. The tests have attempted to control for the influences of different cultural backgrounds. In isolation, IQ scores mean little. Information about an individual's home environment, personality, socioeconomic status, and special abilities is crucial to understanding intellectual functioning.

Cultural Dimensions of Intelligence

Differences in IQ scores, SAT scores, and other measures of achievement or ability are narrowing for various ethnic groups within the United States (Fan, Chen, & Matsumoto, 1997; Williams & Ceci, 1997). This narrowing may be due to a variety of factors, including more equal opportunities under the law, intervention programs for at-risk children, and more equal academic preparation for ethnic minority students. As ethnic minority students' enrollment in advanced mathematics courses rises, these students' scores on achievement tests also increase. Historical and cultural background has a significant effect on people's patterns of mental ability and achievement (Geary, 1996). The culture of a child from Texas or California is clearly different from that of a child from New Guinea, and so the instrument used to test any child must be culturally relevant (Greenfield, 1997). Furthermore, differences among individuals within a group are often greater than differences between groups, a situation that minimizes the importance of between-group differences and highlights the importance of considering the individual rather than the ethnic group (Zuckerman, 1990).

■ *One type of adoptive study compares the intellectual abilities of adopted identical twins who were separated at birth; because such twins share the same genetic heritage, any differences in IQ must be the result of environmental influences.*

One conclusion is strikingly clear: *Rather than measuring innate intellectual capacity, IQ tests measure the degree to which people adapt to the culture in which they live.* In many cultures, to be intelligent is to be socially adept. In Western society, because social aptitude is linked with schooling, the more schooling you have, the higher your IQ score is likely to be (Ceci & Williams, 1997). All individuals have special capabilities (not necessarily intellectual ones), and how those capabilities are regarded depends on the social environment. Being a genius in traditional African cultures may include being a good storyteller; in the United States, it may mean being astute and aggressive (Eysenck, 1995). In the United States, however, the concept of genius is too often associated solely with high academic achievement. Concern about the implications of this limited conception of intelligence is one reason why some educators are placing less emphasis on IQ scores.

Researchers now assert that the typical intelligence test is too limited because it does not take into consideration the many forms of intelligent behavior that occur outside the testing situation, within the diverse culture of the United States (Sternberg, 2000b). Real-life problem situations might be used to supplement the usual psychological tests—intelligence must be evaluated on many levels, including the environment in which a person lives and works. Yet, in spite of all the limitations of IQ scores, research continues to show that they are the best overall predictor of school performance (Kuncel, Hezlett, & Ones, 2001). This situation should be no surprise—Binet and Simon developed the first IQ test for the Paris school system.

Environmental and Genetic Impact

If you came from a well-bred, upper-class family and had access to schooling and appropriate family connections, you would likely be smart. Or so thought Sir Francis Galton in the 19th century. Galton was among the first to speculate that genetics was a factor in intelligence, arguing that intelligence—a measurable trait or ability—is passed from generation to generation. Today, psychologists recognize that both the genetic heritage established before birth (nature) and a person's life experiences (nurture) play an important role in intelligence.

■ **HERITABILITY.** Few would debate the idea that the environment, and especially schooling, has a potent effect on performance of intellectual tasks (Ceci & Williams, 1997). Certainly, persistent poverty clearly has detrimental effects on children (McLoyd, 1998); still, Ramey, Ramey, and Lanzi (2001) assert that children from impoverished homes can achieve more on standardized tests if cognitive training begins early in life and continues for an extended period. But efforts to unravel the fixed genetic component from the environmental impact have required some sophisticated research and statistical techniques. The main goal of such studies has been to determine various traits' **heritability,** the genetically determined proportion of a trait's variation among individuals in a population. The heritability of some traits is fairly obvious; for example, height is a highly heritable trait. Children who have two tall parents have a strong likelihood of being tall—the heritability of height is high, and thus scientists say that heredity is a key factor in determining height. When scientists say that a trait is heritable, especially when they attach a percentage to that heritability—for example, 50%—they mean that 50% of the variation (differences) among *a group* of people is attributable to heredity. Note that this is *not* the same as saying that 50% of a

Heritability
The genetically determined proportion of a trait's variation among individuals in a population.

specific person's intelligence, height, or any other variable is determined by heredity. One last caution: although heritability is a biological phenomenon, even highly heritable traits, such as height, can be modified by the environment. Deprive the child of tall parents of a nutritious diet during the growth years, and the child will be less likely to be tall. So even highly heritable traits are modifiable by the environment.

Estimates of the heritability of intelligence have varied widely, as have research techniques that attempt to measure it. To establish how much of intelligence is heritable, several researchers have studied adopted children, who are raised apart from their biological parents (e.g., Finkel et al., 2000; McGue & Bouchard, 2000). Researchers compare an adopted person's intelligence test scores and other measures of cognitive ability with those of biological parents, adoptive parents, biological siblings, and adoptive siblings. The goal is to see if scores later in life more greatly resemble those of biological relatives or adoptive relatives. A French adoption study showed a 14-point increase in IQ scores for children from impoverished homes after they were adopted into families in a higher socioeconomic class (Schiff et al., 1982). This study demonstrated that the environment in the adoptive home had a strong effect on intellectual abilities. Other data, however, strongly suggest that the biological mother's IQ score has a more important effect than the adoptive home environment on an adopted child's IQ score. In fact, as time passes, the correlation between the IQ of an adopted child and those of the adoptive parents decreases, and the correlation with the IQ of the child's biological parents increases (Plomin & DeFries, 1999; Plomin et al., 1997; Stoolmiller, 1999). Eysenck (1998) explains this finding by asserting that when an adopted child is young, his or her environment is determined solely by the adopted parents, leading to a correlation between their IQs. But as the child grows older and makes more life choices, he or she becomes less subject to restrictive parental environmental influences. His or her biological predispositions become more evident, and the result is a greater correlation between the child's IQ and the biological parents' IQ.

One type of adoptive study compares the intellectual abilities of adopted identical twins who were separated at birth; because the twins share the same genetic heritage, any differences in IQ scores *must* be the result of environmental influences. Figure 10.5 summarizes the correlation between the IQ scores of related and unrelated children and parents in different studies. If genetics were the sole determinant of IQ scores, the correlation for identical twins would be 1.00 whether they were reared together or apart. However, identical twins, whether raised together or apart, do not have identical IQ scores—although their scores are similar. In general researchers conclude that about 50% of the similarities in IQ test scores of identical twins can be accounted for by genetics. Interestingly, most of the data about IQ scores and the role of genetics come from studies of identical twins and their performance early in life; only recently have data emerged from studies of older identical twins, who have lived full lives and had a wide range of experiences (Finkel et al., 1998; McClearn et al., 1997). These data confirm the idea that about half of the similarity in scores of identical twins—even into old age—can be accounted for by genetics (Petrill et al., 1998).

FIGURE 10.5

Correlations Between IQ Scores of Persons of Varying Relationships

The closer the biological relationship of two individuals, the more similar their IQ scores—strong support for a genetic component to intelligence.
(Based on data from Bouchard & McGue, 1981, and Erlenmeyer-Kimling & Jarvik, 1963.)

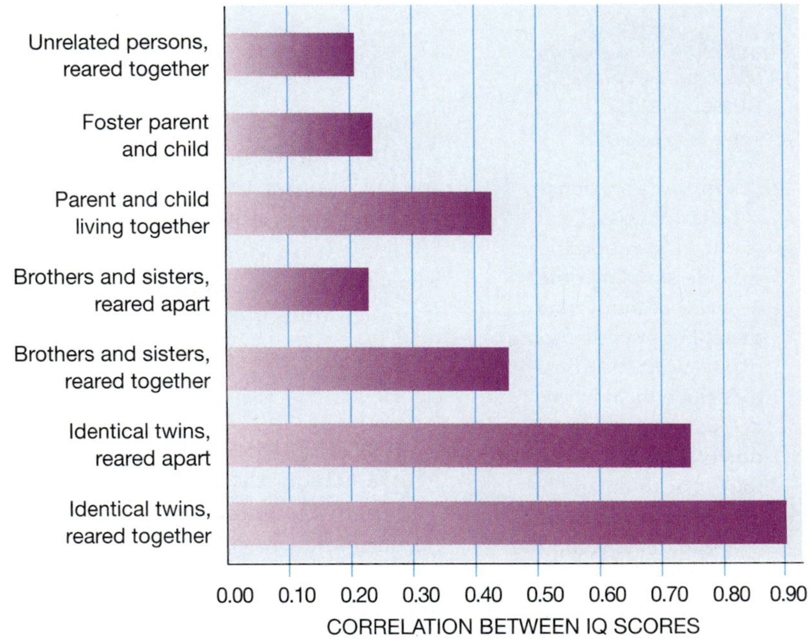

Evolution and Intelligence

It is important to remember that a fundamental assumption of evolutionary psychology is that human behavior can be explained in terms of striving to fulfill some evolutionary goal. Intelligent human behavior can be seen as an adaptation (see p. 84) whose purpose is to increase the chances for reproduction. From an evolutionary perspective then, intelligence develops because smart human beings were able to avoid predators, developed the use of tools, and planted crops that provided nutrition; ultimately, over the course of generations, smarter people predominated. In this way, over hundreds of generations, the elements of complex intellectual functioning are acquired.

But not all scientists agree with this view of evolution and natural selection. Scientists like Stephen Jay Gould (1997) assert that the evolutionary perspective has failed to appreciate other principles of evolutionary change such as accidental genetic changes due to catastrophic events that might wipe out a city or country. Furthermore, he contends, by identifying a genetic origin for intelligence, the evolutionary perspective would have us believe that human behaviors are far more absolute than they really are. The evolutionary perspective argues that most of our intelligence has been crafted over thousands of generations by natural selection, whereas theorists like Gould believe that human attributes as basic as human intelligence may, in fact, be accidental. Gould would say that human intelligence is just not the end result of predictable evolutionary progress.

John Tooby and Leda Cosmides (1997), among the foremost intellectual leaders of evolutionary psychology, argue that Gould misrepresented evolutionary theory and that he overstated its assumptions. They contend that intelligence and other adaptations do not determine our destiny but are affected by both random and purposeful events in people's lives. Has evolution helped human beings develop their intelligence? Certainly it has. Is it the only determinant? Certainly not.

In the end, volumes of arguments from evolutionary theorists as well as data from child-rearing studies attempt to demonstrate the genetic and environmental components of intelligence. However, to frame the argument as a debate with a winner and a loser is a mistake; nature and nurture work together in a partnership. The idea that a genetically influenced behavior or characteristic cannot be changed is a myth. Genes do not fix behavior; instead, they establish a range of possible reactions. Environments determine the extent to which the range of genetic potential will be expressed (Ceci & Williams, 1997). Thus, the study of nature and nurture together is essential to an understanding of intelligence.

student voices

Russell Fields
Texas Tech University

In my organizational behavior class, I learned the importance of understanding others as a way of motivating them. For example, some people want their boss to include them in the decision-making process; others just want to be told what to do and be left alone. A good manager can understand the difference.

The Bell Curve

Publication in 1994 of *The Bell Curve*, by Richard J. Herrnstein and Charles Murray, stirred up a whirlpool of controversy. Among its controversial positions, the book makes the argument that IQ is largely genetically determined; that U.S. minority groups, especially African Americans, are trapped in an IQ-lowering environment from which they are unlikely to emerge; and that any attempts to reverse this situation are doomed to failure. Let's take a look at the authors' claims and see if critical thinking supports them.

The Bell Curve asserts that the United States is ruled by a cognitive elite whose members are selected by IQ tests, SAT scores, and admission to prestigious colleges. This elite is said to occupy the top of the socioeconomic ladder, while the rest of society is assigned to inferior and subordinate status—and, Herrnstein and Murray claim, the situation is likely to stay that way. Herrnstein and Murray suggest that unless something is done to alter the present trends, the United States will be permanently split between a ruling cognitive elite and an ever-increasing and powerless underclass made up primarily of low-IQ blacks, Whites, Latinos/Latinas, and immigrants. Yet Herrnstein and Murray consider it futile to attempt to raise the poor, the disadvantaged, and the cognitively impaired above the limits of their own genetics.

Not surprisingly, others hold the opposite point of view. For example, Myerson and his colleagues (1998) argue that people are most likely to take tests of academic ability at the point in life when ability differences are most pronounced; Blacks gain more from college educations than do Whites, and if students were given IQ tests as they finished college, the gap between scores would be much smaller. Flynn (1999) convincingly shows that average IQs of groups of individuals can change over time and that ethnic- or race-based arguments about genetically rooted differences just do not follow from the data. Hout (2002) presents additional evidence that social factors, for example, schools, the family, and labor markets, are the main determinants of social inequality. Crane (1996; Phillips et al., 1998) and Hall (2001) assert that there is simply no evidence that the race gap in cognitive test scores is caused by genetically determined differences. He argues that, in contrast, there is a good deal of evidence that supports an environmental explanation.

It is crucial to remember that the concept of race is fraught with issues; Fish (2002) cautions that the human species does not have "races" in the biological sense, although cultures have a variety of folk concepts of "race." Although any debate about race, ethnicity, IQ, and genetics is inherently controversial, Herrnstein and Murray present data in a way that makes careful critical analysis especially difficult. For example, they omit much historical data, fail to separate the effects of nature and nurture in some early childhood data, present limited new data, and make a series of questionable claims and assumptions (Horn, 2002). In addition, heritability is a concept that deals with groups of people, and their recommendations about education focus on individuals—a classic flaw in scientific thinking. Among their weak assumptions are that IQ represents a general quality, that IQ largely or solely reflects genetics, that IQ is fixed and immutable, and that there is a cause and

psychology *in action*

The Abecedarian Intervention

In this section we saw that *The Bell Curve* argued that there is no way out for the poor and disadvantaged; no matter how many early educational programs are introduced, children will be held back by cognitive disabilities created by their genetics. But research that began in 1972 shows evidence to the contrary (Ramey & Campbell, 1984, 1992; Ramey, Ramey, & Lanzi, 2001). The *Abecedarian Project* was a carefully controlled study in which 57 infants from low-income families were randomly assigned to receive early intervention in a high-quality child-care setting and 54 were placed in a no-treatment control group. All of the infants were considered at risk for delayed and poor intellectual development because of issues of poverty, for example. The children who received care had full-time, high-quality educational intervention from infancy through age 5; each child had an individualized scheme of educational activities that usually consisted of "games" built into the child's day. The activities focused on social, emotional, and cognitive areas of development but gave special emphasis to language activities. Progress was monitored over time, with follow-up studies conducted at ages 12, 15, and 21.

The results showed that children who participated in the program had higher cognitive test scores from the toddler years to age 21. Academic achievement in both reading and math was higher. Not only that, but those treated completed more years of education and were more likely to attend a four-year college. Enhanced language development appears to have been especially influential in raising cognitive test scores.

In the end, young adults who received *early* educational intervention had significantly higher mental test scores from toddlerhood through age 21 than did untreated participants. The truth is that large gains in IQ test scores can be obtained with intensive early intervention programs, especially when the program is sustained for long periods of time (Ramey & Sackett, 2000; Ramey et al., 2000). Instead of poor children lagging behind even in the early school years, the Abecedarian Project shows that early intervention works and works well. Ed Zigler's Project Head Start (see p. 91) would take no issue with these findings, and students who do service learning activities in early intervention provide first-hand testimony.

student voices

Heather Pettit
Iowa State University

In a psychological measurement class we learned how to write good test questions and how to recognize bad ones. Now on all my tests, I look for bad questions that give away the answer.

effect reltionship between low IQ and problematic social behaviors. Average differences between groups more likely reflect the environment than genetics—remember again, differences within groups are usually greater than differences between groups. Psychologists, however, recognize the multidimensional nature of intelligence, the modifiability of intelligence, and the fact that IQ is neither the only predictor of performance on a job or in life, nor always a very good one.

The Stability of Intelligence Test Scores

Nearly every American has taken an intelligence test at some time. Was the test you took in grade 2 a good predictor of your academic ability when you were a sophomore in high school? Does an IQ score remain stable over a long period of time? Early examinations of IQ score stability showed that the IQ scores of infants did not correlate well with their IQ scores when they were school age (Bayley, 1969). Researchers quickly realized that it is not possible to measure the same capabilities in infants and in older children and adults. Further, correlations of the IQ scores of school-age children and adults show that such scores can change, sometimes substantially. Yet some research indicates that to a certain extent infant IQ can predict school-age IQ (DiLalla et al., 1990; Rose & Feldman, 1995). Note that the items included on tests vary quite substantially over the years; first-graders are asked quite different questions than are sophomores in high school. What remains stable is a person's score in relation to those of his or her peers of the same age.

What about the IQ scores of adults? Do IQ scores remain stable throughout adulthood? In general, psychologists have shown that intelligence and achievement test scores at first increase with age, then level off in adulthood, only to decline in late adulthood. The results of a 40-year study of IQ showed that, in general, the intellectual functioning of men increased a bit around age 40 and then gradually declined to its earlier level when the men were in their 50s (Schwartzman et al., 1987). In other words, despite the passage of years, cognitive performance remained relatively stable. The effect of aging on IQ scores is difficult to assess because some aspects of the scores decrease more with age than others. For example, scores on numerical portions of IQ tests tend to show a more significant decrease with advancing age than do scores on verbal portions. In addition, not everyone shows age-related IQ declines; people who continue their education throughout their lives show relatively small decreases.

There is now ample evidence that IQ scores remain relatively stable once test subjects reach adulthood. However, the scores of infants and children are so prone to change that they are not reliable predictors of later IQ scores. Of course, a child who achieves a high score on an IQ test at age 9 is likely to do well or perhaps even better at age 10. The data show enough fluctuation, though, especially at younger ages, to make predictions uncertain.

Are There Gender Differences in Intelligence?

Many psychologists believe there are gender differences in verbal ability, with girls surpassing boys in most verbal tasks during the early school years. However, most differences have been found to be due to the expectations of parents and teachers. For example, parents and teachers have long encouraged boys to engage in spatial, mechanical tasks. Two interesting trends have been observed in the United States in recent decades, though. First, many parents have been encouraging both girls and boys to acquire math, verbal, and spatial skills; that is, they have endeavored to avoid gender stereotyping. Second, the observed cognitive differences between boys and girls have been diminishing each year (American Association of University Women, 1998).

In fact, the old consensus about gender differences is at least exaggerated, if not simply wrong (Halpern, 1997). Janet Shibley Hyde has investigated and explored the results of thousands of studies on sex differences in a variety of domains—self-esteem, mathematics, stress, and cognitive ability—these studies had tested more than 1 million individuals (Hyde, 1996; Jaffee & Hyde, 2000; Plant et al., 2000). Although Hyde and Linn (1988) found a gender difference in verbal ability in favor of women, it was exceedingly small. They further argued that more refined tests and theories of intelligence are needed to examine any gender differences that may exist. The differences found today exist only in certain special populations; for example, among the very brightest mathematics students, boys continue to outscore girls, although the boys' scores vary more than girls' scores (Hedges & Nowell, 1995). Boys are motivated to achieve more and strive harder at math, in part because more of them have career aspirations that involve mathematical skills. As a consequence of these aspirations, boys tend to take more math courses and more advanced ones—this puts them still further ahead on standardized tests. It is important to remember the small gender differences (and ethnic differences) that do exist are based on group averages and say nothing about individual abilities (Halpern, 1997; Suzuki & Valencia, 1997). In general, differences between the test scores of males and those of females are disappearing, and this trend has been observed in many cultures (Geary, 1998).

In 1998, under pressure from the federal government, the SAT and the PSAT underwent revision intended to narrow the gap between the genders as much as possible. The government got involved because merit scholarships based on SAT scores were more likely to go to men than women; it was assumed that biases in the test favored men. An outcome of the Hyde analysis is the realization that since verbal ability tests provide gender-unbiased measures of cognitive ability, perhaps they should be used to select students for academic programs. Sound selection procedures are especially important for academic programs for special students, such as the gifted (Halpern, 1997).

Be an *Active* learner

REVIEW

- What are the chief differences between the Kaufman Assessment Battery for Children (K-ABC) and the Stanford-Binet, Wechsler, and Woodcock-Johnson scales? pp. 346–347
- If IQ tests do not examine innate ability, what do they measure? p. 350
- What is the main goal of heritability studies? p. 350
- Gould believes that human attributes as basic as human intelligence may, in fact, be accidental rather than a result of natural selection. How might this occur? p. 352

THINK CRITICALLY

- What conclusions about nature versus nurture can be drawn from data on correlations between IQ scores and child-rearing environments for both related and unrelated children?
- What is a possible explanation for an over-representation of ethnically diverse students in special education classes?

APPLY PSYCHOLOGY

- If you had to design a series of selection procedures for a college or a program for gifted students, what procedures would you choose?
- If you were designing an early intervention project, what features would you consider absolutely essential to having an impact on intelligence?

Exceptionality and Education

The American educational system is oriented toward testing for and teaching special or exceptional children. As early as the first weeks of grade 1, most children take some kind of reading readiness test; by the end of grade 4, students are usually classified and labeled as to their projected future development, again largely on the basis of tests. Educators often use the term *exceptional* to refer to individuals who are gifted or those who experience learning disabilities, physical impairments, and mental retardation.

Giftedness

Gifted individuals represent one end of the continuum of intelligence and talent. The phenomenon of giftedness has been recognized and discussed for centuries. Some display their genius musically, like Wolfgang Mozart, Duke Ellington, or Billie Holiday. Others, like Tiger Woods, display it in athletics; still others display their giftedness in science; many great scientists, like Albert Einstein, made their most important theoretical discoveries very early in their careers. We often study giftedness first in the young, so as to optimize their development. Although there is no universally accepted definition of giftedness (just as there is no universally agreed-on definition of intelligence), Section 902 of the federal government's Gifted and Talented Children's Act of 1978 provides the following:

> The term *gifted and talented* means children and, whenever applicable, youth who are identified at the preschool, elementary, or secondary level as possessing demonstrated or potential abilities that give evidence of high performance responsibility in areas such as intellectual, creative, specific academic or leadership ability, or in the performing or visual arts and who by reason thereof require services or activities not ordinarily provided by the school.

Defining who is gifted and what gifted behaviors are turns out to be a complicated task. As soon as people invoke the concept of intelligence as part of the definition, the debate ensues. Furthermore, giftedness often refers to creative talents that are not easily addressed with simple IQ test scores; also, the gifted often develop more quickly than others and show their abilities in one domain, but not others (Winner, 2000). Renzulli (1998) argues that you have to consider three key factors to determine giftedness: above-average ability, creativity, and task commitment. *Ability* for Renzulli refers to both specific abilities as well as general capacity—and this does not just mean IQ test scores but rather high levels of abstract thinking and rapid accurate, automatic thinking processes. *Task commitment* refers to a focused form of motivation—persistence, a drive to achieve, and a capacity for perseverance and dedicated practice (Winner, 2000). The third factor is *creativity*—this refers to originality of thought, flexibility, curiosity, and an ability to set aside established well-used ideas (Sternberg, 2001a). Renzulli argues that it is the convergence and joining together of these three factors that creates the gifted individual. You can think of these factors as overlapping abilities—and when a person possesses all three, you are most likely to see a person we say is truly gifted.

student voices

Jessica E. Brown
Boston College

BC is 5,000 miles away from my home in Hawaii. I've experienced many bouts of homesickness leading to depression. What surprised me during these times was that I wrote and thought better than I had before. Then I took a course called Psychology of Art and Creativity. Studying creativity and mood disorder relationships helped me approach my problems and deal with being far from home.

Among children, the gifted may have superior cognitive, leadership, or performing arts abilities. Very gifted students need special opportunities to fully develop their abilities. Most take advantage of such opportunities, earning advanced placement and college credit during high school (Lubinski et al., 2001). Indeed, very gifted students usually experience academic success, attaining college and advanced degrees. Their success depends on the availability of special programs and assistance in helping them cope with being so "different." Their instruction needs to be individualized (Detterman & Thompson, 1997), but in truth, all children may be in need of individualized instruction because most of them—but especially the gifted—are underchallenged by school (Winner, 1997).

Nearly every state has a special program for the gifted; however, some local school systems have none, and others provide special instruction only in brief periods or to small groups and still do not challenge the extraordinarily gifted. Some school districts provide special schools for children with superior cognitive abilities, performing talents, or science aptitude—most do not offer gifted programs for all grades. The special needs of gifted students and of those with special needs should not be addressed only 1 day a week or only in grades 1 through 6, or with traditional teaching techniques.

Special Education–IDEA

The law guarantees a free appropriate public education to children with disabilities; the Individuals with Disabilities Education Act (IDEA), Public Law 102–119, provides the guarantee. Evaluations are given to the "whole child" by a multidisciplinary team, which may include a school psychologist, speech pathologist, classroom teacher, and occupational therapist. Parents, the school, or a doctor may request an

BRAIN AND BEHAVIOR

Art, Creativity, and Intelligence

People's intelligence, their creativity, and ultimately their humanity have a neurological basis. It's an easy thing to forget because we think of such capacities as special and almost ethereal. Barry Bond's abilities at bat, Michael Jordan's grace on the basketball floor, or any number of talented writers, actors, and singers can transfix us with their abilities to bring us to a different place or time through their writings, theater, song, or dance.

What becomes intriguing, but difficult to resolve, is the relationship between these states or activities, which are hard to define and measure, and other states of being. Consider various mental illnesses. We know that people who have bipolar disorder (you will later see that this is the proper term for what is often called manic-depression) are often creative and exceptionally intelligent. Sometimes the long-lasting mood swings are accompanied by wild bursts of intelligence, exuberance, and creativity. Think historically for a moment. Mozart, Beethoven, Van Gogh, Edgar Allan Poe, and William Styron all were expansively creative and brilliant; they also suffered from depression and perhaps bipolar disorder. They combined new ideas, were creative, and were unhappy. Is there a common theme here? Was it their heightened distractibility? Was their chronic unhappiness at the crux of their creativity? Kay Redfield Jamison (1993, 1996) thinks so, and she makes the case that the artistic temperament and bipolar disorder in many cases are inextricably woven together.

The conclusion that Jamison leads to is the idea that physiologically—underpinning the disorder and creative intelligence—is one process, or at least one set of crossed connections. In reality there is little *experimental* evidence for this assertion, and critics argue that Jamison takes too narrow a view of mental disorders (Sass, 2001). But there is much anecdotal and correlational evidence. Enough data exist to make many psychologists and psychiatrists like Jamison ask how we can study the brains of the exceptionally intelligent, the creative, and those who suffer from various psychological disorders to learn more about human thought, so as to maximize our human potential. Whether the two states of being—mental illness and creativity—are tied together is yet to be determined. Jamison asks probing questions, but the evidence that will firmly connect maladjustment with creativity is yet to ascertained.

evaluation of a student with the ultimate aim of developing an Individualized Education Program (IEP). A child's IEP is a written statement of the child's educational program; IEPs establish learning goals and state the methods that a school district will implement to help the child meet those goals. Parents have to be involved in the development of IEPs and can take an active role in tracking their child's progress.

Fundamental to understanding IDEA is the basic assumption that children can achieve, that schools still have high expectations for all children, that parents should and must be involved in the education of children, that special programs be provided for teachers to build skills for working with special needs children, and that local municipalities provide for the education of children with disabilities. These disabilities include mental retardation (see page 358), hearing impairments, speech impairments, visual impairments including blindness, emotional impairments, orthopedic impairments, autism, and specific learning disabilities, as well as delayed development.

Prior to the 1980s, thousands of children received a substandard education after doing poorly on an intelligence test. Labeled as slow learners or perhaps even as mentally retarded, these children received neither special education nor special attention. Today under IDEA all school-age children must be provided with an appropriate, free public education. After testing, children with special needs are not to be grouped separately unless their conditions necessitate it. Tests for identification and placement must be unbiased. Further, educational programs for special needs children must be arranged to make them as close to normal as possible, considering the unique needs of each child. The law also mandates that schools must follow specific procedures for conducting evaluation procedures and regular reevaluations and explaining to parents their child's rights and any changes in the child's status. IDEA has significantly increased the amount of testing done in public school systems, leading to more classification and labeling. Many see this as a disadvantage. However, the law has also guaranteed that thousands of children with special needs will

■ *Since IDEA, there has been a shift toward mainstreaming—the integration of all children with special needs into regular classroom settings, whenever appropriate.*

receive an appropriate education. This is costly for local school districts; but when students need a special education, they can rely on the courts to make sure that the school system provides it. The services may include special education provided by a teacher and focused on the needs of the child; counseling; occupational, physical, or language therapy; recreational activities; school health services; transportation services; and parent training or counseling. These services should be provided in the least restrictive setting, for example, a regular preschool program, a Head Start center, or the child's home.

Since the passage of laws protecting people with disabilities, there has been a shift toward **mainstreaming**—the integration of all children with special needs into regular classroom settings, whenever appropriate, with the support of professionals who provide special education services. Technically, the law requires students to be placed in the least restrictive or least unusual environment feasible. The purpose is to make life as normal as possible for children with mental retardation by requiring that they and their teachers and classmates cope with their current skill levels while trying to expand them as much as possible. In mainstreaming, children are assigned to a regular class for at least half of the school day. For the rest of the day, they participate in special education classrooms or in vocational training situations. Although research studies have produced conflicting data on the effectiveness of mainstreaming, psychologists and educators generally support it (Zigler & Hodapp, 1991).

Although real progress has been made, mainstreaming has been problematic in many school settings. Too often, children are mainstreamed not into the academic (classroom) aspects, but only into the social side of school life (athletics, lunch). One consequence is a lack of adequate special academic services delivered to children who require them (Zigler & Hodapp, 1991). Because of such problems, some schools now keep students with special education needs in regular classrooms and bring support to them rather than bringing the children to supportive services—an approach called *inclusion*. Not without its critics, the inclusionary approach focuses on the needs of individual children in new ways; research on its success is yet to be conducted.

Mainstreaming
Practice of placing children with special needs in regular classroom settings, with the support of professionals who provide special education services.

Mental Retardation

The term *mental retardation* covers a wide range of behaviors, from slow learning to severe mental and physical impairment. Mental retardation is a state of functioning that begins in childhood and is characterized by limitation in both intelligence and adaptive skills. Many people with mental retardation are able to cope well. Mental retardation cuts across the lines of racial, ethnic, educational, social, and economic backgrounds. It can occur in any family. The impact of mental retardation varies considerably, just as the range of aptitudes varies considerably among those who do not have mental retardation. Most mentally retarded people learn to walk and to feed and dress themselves; many learn to read and are able to work. According to data reported to the U.S. Department of Education, in the 1998–99 school year, about 610,000 students of ages 6–21 were classified as having mental retardation and were provided with special education by the public schools.

■ *Individuals with mental retardation often have functional limitations; however, many participate and succeed in many activities including sports.*

■ **DEFINITION.** In 1992, the American Association on Mental Retardation adopted a new formal definition of mental retardation:

> **Mental retardation** refers to substantial limitations in present functioning. It is characterized by significantly subaverage intellectual functioning, existing concurrently with related limitations in two or more of the following applicable adaptive skill areas: communication, self-care, home living, social skills, community use, self-direction, health and safety, functional academics, leisure, and work. Mental retardation manifests before age 8.

Psychologists and other practitioners who work with mentally retarded people must consider (1) the community's cultural and linguistic diversity, (2) how a person's adaptive skills interact with the community setting, (3) the fact that specific skills often exist but have limitations, and (4) the likelihood that life functioning will generally improve with age.

There are a variety of causes for mental retardation—from deprived environments (especially among those with mild retardation) to genetic abnormalities, infectious diseases, and physical trauma (including that inflicted on a fetus by drugs taken during pregnancy). Three of the major known causes of mental retardation are the genetic conditions of Down syndrome and fragile X, as well as fetal alcohol syndrome, the result of alcohol consumption during pregnancy.

■ **LEVELS OF RETARDATION.** A diagnosis of mental retardation involves three criteria: a lower-than-normal (below 70) IQ score on a standardized test such as the WISC–R or the WAIS–R, difficulty adapting to the environment, and the presence of such problems before age 8. There are four basic levels of mental retardation: mild, moderate, severe, and profound—each corresponding to a different range of scores on a standardized IQ test (see Table 10.6 on the following page).

Mental retardation
Below-average intellectual functioning, as measured on an IQ test, accompanied by substantial limitations in functioning that originate before age 8.

Mild Retardation. Approximately 90% of those classified as mentally retarded have mild mental retardation (Wechsler IQ score of 55–69). (See Figure 10.6 on the following page.) Through special programs, they are able to acquire academic and occupational skills, but they generally need extra supervision of their work (e.g., Allington and McGill-Franzen, 1995). As adults, people with mild mental

TABLE 10.6

Mental Retardation as Measured on the Wechsler Scales

Classification	Wechsler IQ Score	Percentage of the Mentally Retarded
Mild	55–69	90
Moderate	40–54	6
Severe	25–39	3
Profound	Below 25	1

retardation function intellectually at about the level of 10-year-olds. Thus, with some help from family and friends, most people with mild mental retardation can cope successfully with their environment.

Moderate Retardation. People with moderate mental retardation (Wechsler IQ score of 40–54) account for approximately 6% of those classified as mentally retarded. Most moderately retarded people live in institutions or as dependents of their families. Those who are not institutionalized need special classes; some can hold simple jobs, although few are employed. People with moderate mental retardation are able to speak, write, and interact with friends, but their motor coordination, posture, and social skills are clumsy. Their intellectual level is equivalent to that of 5- to 6-year-olds.

Severe Retardation. Only about 3% of people with mental retardation are severely retarded (Wechsler IQ score of 25–39). People with severe mental retardation show great motor, speech, and intellectual impairment and are almost totally dependent on others to take care of their basic needs. Severe retardation often results from birth disorders or traumatic injury to the brain.

Profound Retardation. Only 1% of people with mental retardation are classified as profoundly retarded (Wechsler IQ score below 25). These people are unable to master even simple tasks and require total supervision and constant care. Their motor and intellectual development is minimal, and many are physically underdeveloped or have physical deformities or other congenital defects (such as deafness, blindness, and seizures).

■ **MAINSTREAMING.** It turns out that mainstreamed students with retardation can turn out to be good workers. Companies are realizing that if individuals with mild

FIGURE 10.6

Mental Retardation in the Population

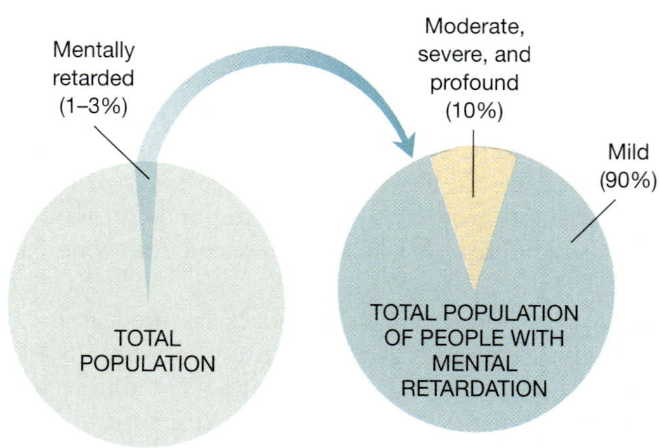

mental retardation are placed in the right job, are properly trained, and are effectively motivated, they can be counted on to be good workers. There are some drawbacks to hiring such workers, however. One is that training them often requires extra patience. Even a relatively simple task may have to be broken down into 30 or 40 individual steps. Workers with mental retardation sometimes need help to remain focused on their job. Nonetheless, there are many great successes. Those workers who have been through training programs do exceptionally well. Workers with mental retardation are likely to stay with jobs others tire of. They may be more dependable, motivated, and industrious than other workers.

The federal government has taken an extensive role in the education and support of individuals with mental retardation. Advocates for people with mental retardation are concerned because the costs of such support programs are rising very quickly. Some states are directing funds formerly used for institutionalizing the retarded to businesses and colleges to pay for training mentally retarded workers.

Be an *Active* learner

REVIEW

- What is an Individualized Education Program (IEP)? p. 357
- What are the requirements of IDEA? pp. 356–357
- Define *mental retardation.* pp. 358–359
- What is mainstreaming? p. 358

THINK CRITICALLY

- A diagnosis of mental retardation involves a lower-than-normal IQ score. What does this imply about IQ tests as predictors of behavior?
- If gifted children often develop more quickly than others, how do you distinguish early developers from the gifted?

APPLY PSYCHOLOGY

- What might a practitioner do to diagnose mental retardation differently?
- Identify five individuals whom you consider gifted and explain why they are gifted.

Summary and Review

What Is Intelligence?

Identify the key features of a definition of intelligence.

- *Intelligence* is the overall capacity of an individual to act purposefully, to think rationally, and to deal effectively with the environment. p. 333

Describe several different approaches to intelligence.

- Wechsler examined the components of intelligence and argued that intelligence tests made up of subparts involving spatial relations and verbal comprehension reveal little about someone's overall capacity to deal with the world. p. 333
- A *factor analysis* approach to evaluating intelligence uses correlational techniques to determine which tasks are involved in intellectual ability. In factor analysis, the assumption is that tasks with high correlations test similar aspects of intellectual functioning. p. 333
- Vygotsky argued that the most significant moment in the course of intellectual development occurs when speech and practical activity, two previously completely independent lines of development, converge. Thus, researchers need to study the processes of intelligence in a social context, not just the products of intelligence. p. 334
- Gardner maintains that people have multiple intelligences (at least eight). An intelligence is an ability to solve a problem or create a product within a specific cultural setting. He argues that not all human intelligences, or competencies, lend themselves to measurement by a test, and he criticizes IQ tests because they place so much emphasis on linguistic and logical–mathematical skills. p. 335
- Sternberg takes an information-processing view of intelligence. Like Gardner's view that intelligence has many parts, Sternberg's triarchic theory divides intelligence into three dimensions: analytic, practical, and creative. Sternberg's theory focuses on adaptation to the world. p. 336

KEY TERMS

intelligence, p. 333; factor analysis, p. 333

The Process of Test Development

Why were Binet and Simon significant in the development of intelligence tests?

- Binet coined the phrase *mental age*, meaning the age level at which a person is functioning cognitively, regardless of chronological age. He and Simon applied everyday tasks, such as counting, naming, and using objects, to determining mental age. The scale they developed can be considered the first useful and practical test of intelligence. p. 339

What criteria must be addressed in order to develop a fair and accurate intelligence test?

- *Standardization* is the process of developing uniform procedures for administering and scoring a test. This includes developing *norms*—the scores and corresponding percentile ranks of a large and representative sample of test takers from the population for which the test was designed. A *representative sample* is a sample of individuals who match the population with whom they are to be compared, with regard to key variables such as socioeconomic status and age. pp. 339–340

■ A *normal curve* is a bell-shaped graphic representation of data, showing what percentage of the population falls under each part of the curve. The simplest score on a test is the *raw score*—the number of correct answers unconverted or transformed in any way. Scores are commonly expressed in terms of a *standard score*—a score that expresses an individual's position relative to those of others and based on the mean and how scores are distributed around it. A standard score is generally a *percentile score*—a score indicating what percentage of the test population would obtain a lower score. A *deviation IQ* is a standard IQ test score whose mean and standard deviation remain constant for all ages. pp. 340–341

■ There are several types of *reliability*. A test is considered reliable if it yields a very similar score for the same individual over repeated testings. All tests are unreliable to some degree. The standard error of measurement is the number of points by which a score varies because of the imperfect reliability of a test. A test's *validity* is its ability to measure what it is supposed to measure; if a test does not have validity, no inferences can be drawn from test results. pp. 341–342

■ There are several basic criticisms of—and defenses of—the validity of intelligence tests and testing. The first is that there is no agreed-on definition of intelligence. The second is that intelligence tests measure learned information rather than intelligence. The third is that school settings may adversely affect IQ test results. Another criticism of testing is that some people may be test-wise, which improves performance. A fifth criticism is that IQ test scores may depend on people's motivation to succeed. Finally, some claim that society helps create the correlation between academic success and IQ test scores. pp. 342–343

■ Critics of IQ tests are concerned about the interpretation of scores. Intelligence tests are generally made up of different subtests or subscales, each yielding a score; there may also be one general score for the entire test. All these scores require knowledgeable interpretation; that is, test scores must be given a context that is meaningful to the person who receives the information—without such a context, a test score is little more than a number. pp. 342–343

KEY TERMS

standardization, p. 340; norms, p. 340; representative sample, p. 340; normal curve, p. 340; raw score, p. 340; standard score, p. 340; percentile score, p. 341; deviation IQ, p. 341; reliability, p. 341; validity, p. 342; halo effect, p. 343

Four Important Intelligence Tests

Describe the Stanford–Binet Intelligence Scales, the Wechsler scales, and the Kaufman Assessment Battery for Children (K–ABC), and the Woodcock–Johnson–III.

■ The Stanford–Binet Intelligence Scale consists of four major subscales and one overall IQ test score. It has been a good predictor of academic performance, and many of its tests correlate highly with one another; its newer items minimize gender and racial characteristics. pp. 344–345

■ The Wechsler scales group test items by content. The score on each subtest is converted to a standard (or scaled) score, adjusted for the subject's age. The test yields verbal, performance, and overall IQ scores. pp. 345–346

■ The K–ABC consists of four global scales. Three measure mental processing abilities—sequential and simultaneous processing, and a composite of the two; the fourth assesses achievement. p. 346

■ The Woodcock–Johnson–III measures general intellectual ability, specific cognitive abilities, scholastic aptitude, oral language, and academic achievement. p. 347

KEY TERM

self-fulfilling prophecy, p. 348

Environmental and Biological Factors in Intelligence

What is the effect of cultural variables and gender on intelligence test scores?

■ Although researchers find differences among the IQ test scores of various ethnic groups, they find little or no consistent and conclusive evidence of bias in the tests themselves. The evidence of many studies of a variety of intelligence tests used with ethnic minority groups indicates that intelligence tests are not culturally biased. But IQ test scores in isolation mean little. Intelligence can be demonstrated in many ways, including through mature and responsible behavior. pp. 348–349

■ Cross-cultural differences are evident in IQ test scores; for this reason, many psychologists (1) deemphasize overall test scores, (2) focus on interpretation of test results, (3) remember that IQ test scores do not measure innate ability, and (4) focus on intellectual functioning in the context of real-life situations. pp. 349–350

■ Proponents of the environmental (nurture) view of intelligence believe that intelligence tests do not adequately measure a person's adaptation to a constantly changing environment. Many researchers claim that the question of nature versus nurture will never be resolved because factors such as family structure, family size, and other environmental variables are important and impossible to measure accurately. The *heritability* of a trait is the genetically determined proportion of a trait's variation within a population of individuals. Heredity (nature) does not fix a person's intelligence; it sets a framework within which intelligence is shaped by the environment. pp. 350–351

- The extent of gender differences in verbal and mathematical abilities has been exaggerated; gender differences in verbal ability are so small that they can be ignored. pp. 354–355

KEY TERM
heritability, p. 350

Exceptionality and Education

Describe the ends of the continuum of intelligence–giftedness and mental retardation–and their implications for educational settings.

- Giftedness means having superior cognitive, leadership, or performing arts abilities. Gifted children represent one end of a continuum of cognitive and other abilities. Such individuals need special schooling to meet their needs. pp. 355–356
- *Mainstreaming* is the integration of all children with special needs into regular classroom settings wherever appropriate, with the support of special services. The purpose of mainstreaming is to help normalize the life experiences of children with special needs; unfortunately, mainstreaming is most often done with regard to the social aspects of school rather than academic ones. p. 358
- *Mental retardation* is below-average intellectual functioning, together with substantial limitations in adaptive behavior, originating before age 8. Retardation can affect communication, self-care, home living, social skills, self-direction, health and safety, leisure activities, and work. There are four basic levels of mental retardation; each corresponds to a specific range of scores on a standardized intelligence test. The behaviors associated with mental retardation vary from slow learning to an inability to care for oneself because of impaired physical, motor, and intellectual development. pp. 358–359

KEY TERMS
mainstreaming, p. 358; mental retardation, p. 359

11 Motivation and Emotion

Ruby Pearl, *Solitude,* 1998

On September 17, 2001, CBS news reporter Dan Rather cried on *The Late Show with David Letterman*. And Letterman cried, too. This show was Letterman's first broadcast after the terrorist attacks on the World Trade Center and the Pentagon, and no one was in the mood for comedy, especially Letterman's typical irony (Lippert, 2001). Rather than comedy, two men—both with reputations for being tough—wept on national television.

Their display of emotion was not unusual for that week; millions of people cried over the destruction and loss of life. Rather had spent 16-hour days broadcasting the news about the attacks and their aftermath. He had experienced a variety of emotions, but these were not an issue in his news reports; he focused on the story. But on the Letterman show, Rather let his emotions show in a way that is not typical for newscasters or for men.

chapter outline

■ *CBS newsman Dan Rather and talk show host David Letterman both cried on the air on September 17, 2001, expressing their emotions about the September 11th terrorist attacks.*

He was the subject of criticism for his tears; some said he was losing his professionalism by his display of emotionality (Brioux, 2001). Others noted the double standard for the display of emotion, saying that Diane Sawyer would not have received similar criticism if she had cried on the air (*Pittsburgh Post-Gazette*, 2001). This observation is valid: we expect and allow different displays of emotions from women and men. Gender stereotypes differ sharply concerning emotion: women are allowed to cry, and men are often criticized for any display of emotion (except anger). Sometimes emotion overrules the rules—many men openly displayed their fear and sadness following the September 11th tragedies.

In this chapter we explore the topics of motivation and emotion, including the rules that apply to the display of emotion and how those rules vary by gender and culture. First we examine motivation—why people do the things they do.

Theories of Motivation

Researchers have always sought to discover what impels people to take various actions—from simple, biologically based actions such as eating to complex actions such as learning to juggle or compete in world-class athletic events. The word *motivation* derives from the Latin *movere*, meaning "to move." **Motivation** can be defined as any condition, although usually an internal one, that initiates, activates, or maintains an organism's goal-directed behavior.

Let's examine the four basic parts of this definition of motivation. First, motivation is usually an *internal condition*, which means that it cannot be directly observed. Regardless of whether the motivation develops from physiological needs and drives or from complex desires, such as the desire to help others, to obtain approval, or to earn a higher income, the source for motivation is internal. Second, motivation is *inferred* to be the link between a person's internal conditions and external behaviors; an observer can only infer its presence from the behavioral effects. Third, motivation *initiates, activates*, or *maintains* behavior. If a person wants to make a good grade in a college class, that motivation will require the person to maintain class attendance, studying, and good test-taking behaviors. Finally, motivation generates *goal-directed behavior*. Individuals' goals vary widely. Some are concrete and immediate—for example, to get up and eat something, to remove a painful stimulus, or to finish an assignment. Other goals are more abstract—the behavior of someone who studies hard, for example, may be motivated by a desire to learn more, to obtain good grades, or to get a good job.

Motivation
Any internal condition, although usually an internal one, that initiates, activates, or maintains an organism's goal-directed behavior.

The study of motivation can be considered the study of what people choose to do, why they choose to do it, and how much energy they spend doing it (Edwards,

1999). Many theories of motivation have been developed to explain human behavior, and these theories fall into five broad categories, each of which has generated research activity: evolutionary theories, drive theory, arousal theory, cognitive theory, and humanistic theory. Let's examine each of these categories in turn and then look at some basic types of motivation, before turning to how emotions and motivation are intertwined.

Evolutionary Theories

In the early days of psychology, instinct was a popular explanation for motivation. *Instinct* is a fixed behavioral pattern that occurs throughout a species and appears without learning or practice. Psychologists made lists of instincts, and the length of the lists grew, but the explanation of motivation in terms of instinct faded when behaviorism began to dominate psychology because behaviorists believe that learning controls motivation.

Evolutionary psychology has brought back the concept of instinct, claiming that the behavior of humans and other animals is motivated by many instincts. Rather than hypothesizing that humans are less controlled by instinct than other animals, evolutionary psychologists believe that humans have *more* instincts. These instincts give humans a variety of built-in, complex programs that automatically deploy behaviors that were adaptive in our evolutionary history. However, many of these built-in behavior sequences occur automatically and thus without conscious thought or decision making. These programs endow humans with natural competencies, and their automatic activation makes such responses rapid. This view of many automatic behaviors is contrary to the view of much of psychology, but Leda Cosmides and John Tooby (1997) claim that the rest of psychology is "instinct blind" because other psychological orientations cannot see how prominent and important instincts are.

In the evolutionary view, motivation and emotion are inseparable (Pinker, 1997). Motivation pushes people toward a number of behaviors, possibly simultaneously, but emotion sets priorities about what to do at any particular time. A person may be motivated to eat, even moving toward food, but a threatening noise in the next room will change that motivated behavior to another very quickly.

Evolutionary psychologists examine motivations in the framework of understanding how they help organisms survive and reproduce. According to the evolutionary view, things that produce pleasure or pain will be motivating because these feelings relate to survival. Thus, eating, drinking, pain avoidance, temperature regulation, and reproductive behaviors are all of interest to evolutionary psychologists, who assume that these behaviors have built-in bases.

Drive Theory

Some of the most influential and best-researched motivation theories are forms of drive theory, which arose as part of the behaviorist approach. **Drive theory** is an explanation of behavior that assumes that an organism is motivated to act because of a need to attain, reestablish, or maintain some goal. Stimuli such as hunger and pain energize and initiate such behavior. A person who is hungry is *driven* to seek food.

A **drive** is an internal aroused condition that directs an organism to satisfy some need. Drive theory focuses on **need**—a state of physiological imbalance usually accompanied by arousal. (The arousal component prompted the development of an alternative view of motivation, which we explore in the next section.) Physiological needs are said to be *mechanistic*, because an organism is pushed and pulled by them, almost like a machine. The organism motivated by a need is said to be in a *drive state*. Both animals and human beings in such a state show goal-directed behavior. The ultimate goal is **homeostasis**—maintenance of a constant state of inner stability or balance. The processes by which organisms seek homeostasis are a key part of

Drive theory
An explanation of behavior that assumes that an organism is motivated to act because of a need to attain, reestablish, or maintain some goal that helps with survival.

Drive
An internal aroused condition that directs an organism to satisfy a physiological need.

Need
State of physiological imbalance usually accompanied by arousal.

Homeostasis
Maintenance of a constant state of inner stability or balance.

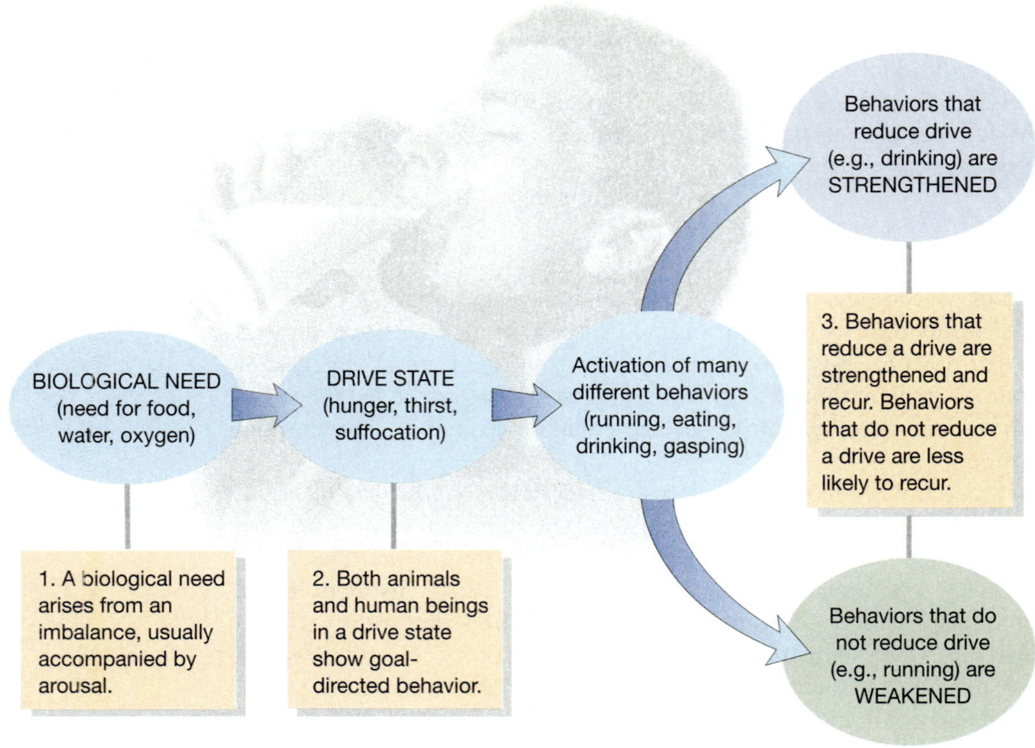

FIGURE 11.1

An Overview of Drive Theory

drive theory. For example, a thirsty animal will seek out water to reestablish its body fluid balance. (Psychologists refer to any normally maintained level as a *steady state*.) Motivation theorists often refer to the goal that satisfies a need as an *incentive*. Incentives can be positive and lure us, as does food or a sexually attractive person; they can also repel us and cause us to act to avoid a painful situation or someone we dislike. Behaviors such as eating or drinking, which reduce biological needs (and promote homeostasis), are reinforced when the goal is attained and the drive is reduced; such behaviors are therefore especially likely to recur. Behaviors such as yodeling, which do not reduce a biological need, are less likely to recur. (See Figure 11.1 for an overview and examples of drive theory.)

Physiologically based behaviors such as eating and drinking offer clear examples of motivation according to the drive reduction point of view. In the 1950s, drive reduction theorist Clark Hull asserted that the actions of reinforcers in developing stimulus–response associations were in part determined by the motivational drive state of the organism. In his elaborate, and mechanistic, theory of motivation and learning, Hull argued that only hungry organisms find food a good reinforcer and are thus motivated to engage in tasks that lead to food. Organisms are also motivated to avoid pain, and escaping from situations with negative consequences can be strong motivation. The possibility that a person can experience drives both toward and away from certain goals can result in conflict.

■ **CONFLICT.** When people (or other animals) face competing motives, they may experience a state of conflict. **Conflict** is the state or condition that arises when a person must make a choice about two or more competing motives, behaviors, or impulses. Consider the difficult situation facing a student who must choose between two equally desirable academic courses, both of which are required for graduation but which meet at the same time. This person experiences conflict.

Conflict
The emotional state or condition that arises when a person must choose between two or more competing motives, behaviors, or impulses.

One of the first psychologists to describe and quantify such conflict situations was Neal Miller (1944, 1959). Miller developed hypotheses about how animals and human beings behave in situations that have both positive and negative aspects. In general, he described three types of conflicts that result when situations involve competing goals or demands: (1) approach–approach conflict, (2) avoidance–avoidance conflict, and (3) approach–avoidance conflict. **Approach–approach conflict** results when a person must choose between two attractive alternatives (for example, receiving acceptance notices from two good universities creates this type of conflict). Approach–approach conflict generates distress, but people can usually tolerate it because either alternative is pleasant. **Avoidance–avoidance conflict** results from having to choose between two distasteful alternatives (for example, mowing the lawn or cleaning the garage). **Approach–avoidance** conflict results from having to choose an alternative that has both attractive and unappealing aspects. For example, a young woman is good at math and science and wants to be an engineer because she finds this field interesting, but her friends maintain that engineers are nerds. As Figure 11.2 shows, the three types of conflict situations lead to different degrees of distress. Miller developed principles to predict behavior in conflict situations, particularly in approach–avoidance conflicts: (1) The closer a person is to achieving a goal, the stronger the tendency is to approach the goal. (2) When two incompatible responses are available, the stronger one will be expressed. (3) The strength of the tendency to approach or avoid is correlated with the strength of the motivating drive. (The young woman may become an engineer when she learns about the starting salaries for engineers.)

Drive theory does not explain all, or even most, motivated behavior; besides, concepts such as need and hunger are difficult to define and vary from person to person. Although Hull's theory influenced the study of learning and motivation for decades, his ideas were too mechanistic and numerically precise to account for diverse human behaviors. We can all think of examples of conflicts such as those Miller hypothesized, but motivation understood in terms of drives came to be viewed as too mechanistic, and theorists began to concentrate on the arousal component of motivation.

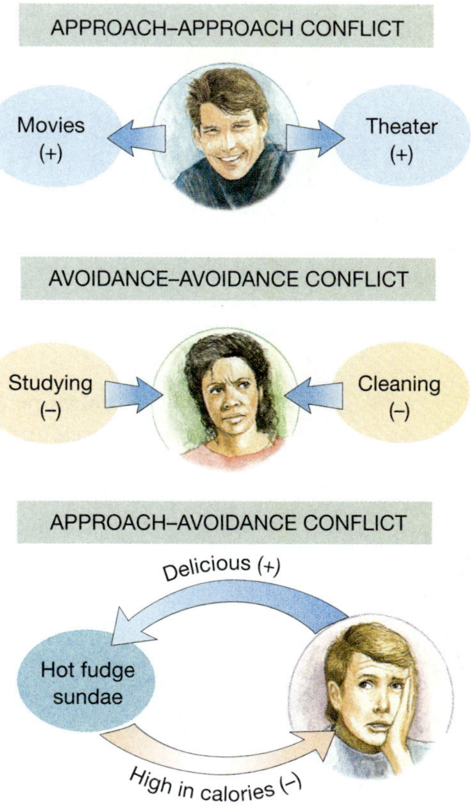

FIGURE 11.2

Three Types of Conflict

In approach–approach conflict, people have to choose between equally appealing alternatives. In avoidance–avoidance conflict, people have to choose between equally distasteful alternatives. In approach–avoidance conflict, people are faced with a single alternative that is both appealing and distasteful.

Arousal Theory

According to drive theory, arousal is a component of all motivational systems. **Arousal** is generally thought of as physical activation, including the central nervous system, the autonomic nervous system, and the muscles and glands. The evolution of drive theory into arousal theory was prompted by findings that deprivation or conflict is not necessary for motivated behavior; an animal does not have to be need-deprived to seek a goal. For example, if you have ever had a hamster or gerbil as a pet, you noticed that it had a strong motivation to explore its environment and to run, climb, and play in the tunnels, wheels, and chambers of its home cage. These behaviors were not all oriented toward seeking food or water—it looks very much as if the animals are playing. The motivation to seek novel stimulation applies to humans as well as hamsters—the amusement parks allow us to play in tunnels, wheels, and chambers. Some motivational theorists have concentrated on this finding and suggest that organisms seek to maintain optimal levels of arousal by actively varying their exposure to sensory stimuli.

Unlike hunger and thirst, the lack of sensory stimulation does not result in a physiological imbalance; yet both human beings and animals seem motivated to seek such stimulation. When deprived of a normal amount of visual, auditory, or tactile stimulation, some people become irritable and consider their situation or environment intolerable ("I'm so bored"). This motivation is not unique to humans; kittens like to explore their environment; young monkeys investigate mechanical devices and play with puzzles.

Approach–approach conflict
Conflict that results from having to choose between two attractive alternatives.

Avoidance–avoidance conflict
Conflict that results from having to choose between two distasteful alternatives.

Approach–avoidance conflict
Conflict that results from having to choose an alternative that has both attractive and unappealing aspects.

Arousal
Activation of the central nervous system, the autonomic nervous system, and the muscles and glands.

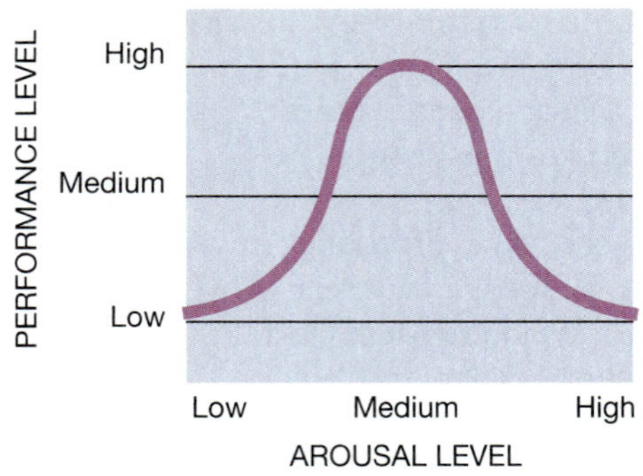

FIGURE 11.3

Performance and Arousal

Performance is at its peak when arousal is at moderate levels; too much or too little arousal results in low performance levels.

Arousal theory attempts to explain the link between a behavior and a state of arousal. R. M. Yerkes and J. D. Dodson first scientifically explored the link between performance and arousal in 1908. They described a relationship involving arousal and performance that has become known as the *Yerkes–Dodson principle.* This law suggests that arousal and level of task difficulty are related: on easy tasks, moderate to high levels of arousal produce maximum performance, but on difficult tasks, low levels of arousal yield better performance and high arousal decreases performance. For example, if the task is stepping on a pedal as quickly as possible when a light comes on, a high state of arousal will be a benefit. But if the task is driving a car, too much arousal may yield poor decision-making, for example, by causing oversteering and braking too soon. Contemporary researchers have refined the Yerkes–Dodson principle by suggesting that when a person's level of arousal is either too high or too low, performance will be poor, especially on complex tasks. Optimal performance requires matching the level of arousal to the task's requirements. The curve in Figure 11.3 shows this relationship between level of arousal and level of performance.

Thus, people who do not care about what they are doing have little anxiety but also have low arousal and therefore usually perform poorly. If arousal increases to the point of high anxiety, performance also suffers. The Yerkes–Dodson principle explains why some baseball players have very good batting records during the regular season, when pressure is only moderately high, and then hit poorly during the playoffs, when the pressure is high (the Houston Astros have provided an excellent example of this phenomenon). It also explains why essentially the same task brings different levels of arousal at different times. Many people find it very easy to answer the questions on *Who Wants to Be a Millionaire?* when they are sitting in the living room, but if they were contestants on the show with millions of people watching, answering those same questions would not be so easy.

Building Table 11.1

Evolutionary, Drive, and Arousal Theories of Motivation

Theory	Theorist	Principally Explains	Key Idea	View of Behavior
Evolutionary	Cosmides and Tooby	Motivation as instincts that benefit survival and reproductive ability	Instincts apply to humans even more than to other animals.	Strongly influenced by evolutionary history
Drive	Hull	Learning through stimulus–response associations and drive reduction	*Homeostasis*—the organism seeks physiological balance.	Largely mechanistic
	Miller	Conflict among motivations	Conflicts can be categorized as approach–approach, avoidance–avoidance, and approach–avoidance.	Largely mechanistic
Arousal	Hebb	Optimal arousal	Performance depends on level of arousal.	Determined by the level of physiological arousal

Researcher Donald Hebb (1904–1985) suggested that behavior varies from disorganized to effective, depending on a person's level of arousal. He argued that human functioning is most efficient when people are at an optimal level of arousal (Hebb, 1955). It is important to realize that the stimulus itself (for example, the SAT, the World Series, or a date on Saturday night) does not produce arousal; it is the internal response to a stimulus that determines how a person behaves. Hebb's idea shifted researchers' focus from stimuli, drives, and needs to the idea that arousal energizes behavior but does not direct it. The development of optimal-arousal theories helped psychologists explain the variation in people's responses in terms of a state of internal arousal rather than solely in terms of responses to stimuli. This shift in emphasis marked a subtle but important transition from a strictly mechanistic drive reduction theory toward learning, expectancy, and more cognitive theories. (See Building Table 11.1 for a comparison of evolutionary, drive, and arousal theories.)

As early as 1949, Donald Hebb anticipated how cognitive theory would influence psychology by suggesting that it is unsatisfactory to equate motivation with biological need. Other factors, such as arousal and attention, are also important determinants of motivation. Moving away from mechanistic views of motivation and behavior, contemporary researchers consider, and many emphasize, the role of active decision making and the human capacity for abstract thought.

Cognitive Theories

In the study of motivation, **cognitive theories** focus on goals that people actively determine and how they achieve them. For these theorists, thought is an initiator and determinant of behavior. For some cognitive theorists, expectation about reaching a goal is a key factor in motivation.

■ **EXPECTANCY THEORIES.** Explanations of behavior that focus on people's expectations about reaching a goal and their need for achievement can be described as **expectancy theories.** Such theories connect thought and motivation. A key element of these theories, as expressed by achievement researcher David McClelland (1961), among others, is that people's thoughts, their expectations, guide their behaviors. A **motive** is a specific (usually internal) condition, typically involving some form of arousal, which directs an organism's behavior toward a goal. Unlike a drive, which always has a physiological origin, a motive does not necessarily have a physiological basis. The motives and needs people develop are not initiated because of some physiological imbalance. Rather, people learn through their interactions in the environment to have needs for mastery, affiliation, and competition. These needs are based on their expectations about the future and about how their efforts will lead to various rewarding outcomes.

Expectations are based on experience that occurs in a social context, and some expectancies originate in social needs. A **social need** is an aroused condition that directs people to behave in ways that allow them to feel good about themselves and others and to establish and maintain relationships. The needs for achievement and affiliation are determined by many factors, including socioeconomic status and ethnicity. For example, Asian American families often stress school achievement even more strongly than families from other ethnic groups, so Asian American children fulfill both needs for achievement and acceptance by their families for doing well in school. The need to feel good about oneself often leads to specific behaviors that the individual hopes will be evaluated positively by others (Geen, 1991). We will explore this topic in more detail when we discuss achievement later in this chapter and when we consider social psychology in Chapter 13.

■ **INTRINSIC AND EXTRINSIC MOTIVATION.** A child may love doing puzzles, coloring in coloring books, or playing video games yet need to be coaxed or ordered to

Cognitive theories
In the study of motivation, an explanation of behavior that asserts that people actively and regularly determine their own goals and the means of achieving them through thought.

Expectancy theories
Explanations of behavior that focus on people's expectations about reaching a goal and their need for achievement as energizing factors.

Motive
A specific (usually internal) condition, usually involving some form of arousal, which directs an organism's behavior toward a goal.

Social need
An aroused condition that directs people to behave in ways that allow them to feel good about themselves and others and to establish and maintain relationships.

■ *People are motivated to engage in some activities that offer intrinsic motivation.*

practice the piano or do homework. Why do some activities seem like fun, and others seem like work? What are the critical variables?

In general, psychologists find that some activities are intrinsically fun—people like to do them because they provide their own reward. Other activities, however, are not nearly as much fun; people need to be motivated to perform them, either with reinforcers or with threats of punishment. Psychologists talk about these two types of motivation as *intrinsic* and *extrinsic* motivation. **Extrinsic motivation** comes from the external environment in the form of rewards. Praise, a high grade, and money given for a particular behavior are extrinsic rewards. Such rewards can strengthen existing behaviors, provide people with information about their performance, and increase feelings of self-worth and competence. In contrast, behaviors engaged in for no apparent reward except the pleasure and satisfaction of the activity itself arise from **intrinsic motivation.** Edward Deci (1975) suggests that people engage in such behaviors for two reasons: to obtain cognitive stimulation and to gain a sense of accomplishment, competence, or mastery over the environment. Individuals vary widely with respect to the need for cognitive stimulation; each person's experiences and genetic makeup affect the strength of this need (Cacioppo et al., 1996).

A typical study on intrinsic motivation contrasts two groups of people. One group receives a reward for performing a task that is intrinsically interesting, such as solving puzzles, and the other group receives no reward for performing the same task (Deci, Koestner, & Ryan, 1999). The participants can be college students or children; the rewards can be money or any other tangible reward. After receiving tangible rewards for performing an intrinsically interesting activity, participants are *less* motivated to perform the activity than the participants who received no rewards. This effect is known as the **overjustification effect,** which is the decrease in likelihood that an intrinsically motivated task, after having been extrinsically rewarded, will be performed when the reward is no longer given.

Research on the overjustification effect has been extensive and controversial. The earliest research focused on the basic finding that extrinsic rewards can have detrimental effects; however, later research suggests that these detrimental effects occur only in restricted situations (Eisenberger & Cameron, 1996; Pittenger, 1997; Snelders & Lea, 1996). These researchers argue for the benefits of rewards on motivation. More recent research criticized those advocates, saying that reward has drawbacks in a number of situations, not only in laboratories but also in classroom and workplace settings; children are more strongly affected than adults (Deci et al., 1999). When a task is interesting, tangible rewards can decrease the intrinsic motivation for that task, and this effect applies to a variety of tangible rewards, from candy to dollar bills.

Keep in mind that the overjustification effect is limited. Verbal reinforcement does not have the same effect as tangible reward; verbal reinforcement can act as positive feedback, which increases intrinsic motivation. When rewards increase feelings of mastery and control, they can be effective in boosting intrinsic motivation (Cialdini et al., 1998). In addition, the overjustification effect applies only to inherently *interesting* tasks—activities that people would do even without reward. The value of reward as a factor in performance of uninteresting tasks is not part of this controversy. Reward is a way to get both children and adults to work at a task they

Extrinsic [ecks-TRINZ-ick] motivation
Motivation supplied by rewards that come from the external environment.

Intrinsic [in-TRINZ-ick] motivation
Motivation that leads to behaviors engaged in for no apparent reward except the pleasure and satisfaction of the activity itself.

Overjustification effect
Decrease in likelihood that an intrinsically motivated task, after having been extrinsically rewarded, will be performed when the reward is no longer given.

Building Table 11.2

Evolutionary, Drive, Arousal, and Cognitive Theories of Motivation

Theory	Theorist	Principally Explains	Key Idea	View of Behavior
Evolutionary	Cosmides and Tooby	Motivation as instincts that benefit survival and reproductive ability	Instincts apply to humans even more than to other animals.	Strongly influenced by evolutionary history
Drive	Hull	Learning through stimulus–response associations and drive reduction	*Homeostasis*—the organism seeks physiological balance.	Largely mechanistic
	Miller	Conflict among motivations	Conflicts can be categorized as approach–approach, avoidance–avoidance, and approach–avoidance.	Largely mechanistic
Arousal	Hebb	Optimal arousal	Performance depends on level of arousal.	Determined by the level of physiological arousal
Cognitive	McClelland	Achievement motivation	Humans learn the need to achieve.	Learned, based on expectation of outcome
	Deci	Intrinsic motivation	Intrinsic motivation is self-rewarding because it makes people feel competent.	Inherent motivation for interesting tasks, but extrinsic rewards can decrease it.

find inherently uninteresting or dull. However, reward becomes the motivation, and people do not have the opportunity to develop internal self-regulation for those rewarded behaviors. When parents offer their child money for making good grades, they may be focusing on the goal of good grades too much to realize that their child needs to develop a sense of accomplishment by mastering the school subjects. The money can become the motivation, which may decrease the child's motivation to learn. (See Building Table 11.2 for a comparison of cognitive theories with evolutionary, drive, and arousal theories.)

Humanistic Theory

Humanistic theory is an explanation of behavior that emphasizes the entirety of life rather than individual components of behavior. It focuses on human dignity, individual choice, and self-worth. One of the appealing aspects of humanistic theory is that it recognizes the interplay among behavioral theories and incorporates some of the best elements of the drive, arousal, and cognitive approaches for explaining motivation and behavior. Humanistic psychologists believe that a person's behavior must be viewed within the framework of the person's environment and values.

As you learned in Chapter 1, one of the founders and leaders of the humanistic approach was Abraham Maslow (1908–1970), who assumed that people are essentially good—that they possess an innate inclination to develop their potential and to seek beauty, truth, and harmony. Maslow believed that people are born open and trusting and can experience the world in healthy ways. In his words, people are naturally motivated toward self-actualization. **Self-actualization** is the final

Humanistic theory
An explanation of behavior that emphasizes the entirety of life rather than individual components of behavior and focuses on human dignity, individual choice, and self-worth.

Self-actualization
In humanistic theory, the final level of psychological development, in which one strives to realize one's uniquely human potential—to achieve everything one is capable of achieving.

FIGURE 11.4

Maslow's Hierarchy of Needs

Physiological needs are at the base of the ladder. Successively higher levels represent needs that are increasingly learned social ones.

level of psychological development, in which a person strives to realize his or her uniquely human potential—to achieve everything he or she is capable of. This includes attempts to minimize ill health, to attain a superior perception of reality, and to feel a strong sense of self-acceptance.

Maslow's influential theory conceives of motives as forming a hierarchy, which can be represented as a ladder, with fundamental physiological needs at the bottom, followed by the needs for safety, love and belongingness, esteem, and self-actualization near the top (see Figure 11.4). According to Maslow, as lower-level needs are satisfied, people begin to be motivated by the next higher level needs; the ladder culminates in self-actualization. Maslow believed that a small percentage of people

Building Table 11.3

Evolutionary, Drive, Arousal, Cognitive, and Humanistic Theories of Motivation

Theory	Theorist	Principally Explains	Key Idea	View of Behavior
Evolutionary	Cosmides and Tooby	Motivation as instincts that benefit survival and reproductive ability	Instincts apply to humans even more than to other animals.	Strongly influenced by evolutionary history
Drive	Hull	Learning through stimulus–response associations and drive reduction	*Homeostasis*—the organism seeks physiological balance.	Largely mechanistic
	Miller	Conflict among motivations	Conflicts can be categorized as approach–approach, avoidance–avoidance, and approach–avoidance.	Largely mechanistic
Arousal	Hebb	Optimal arousal	Performance depends on level of arousal.	Determined by the level of physiological arousal
Cognitive	McClelland	Achievement motivation	Humans learn the need to achieve.	Learned, based on expectation of outcome
	Deci	Intrinsic motivation	Intrinsic motivation is self-rewarding because it makes people feel competent.	Inherent motivation for interesting tasks, but extrinsic rewards can decrease it.
Humanistic	Maslow	Learned needs for fulfillment and feelings of self-actualization	Humans can seek self-actualization, the highest level of psychological development, after basic needs for food and security are fulfilled.	Cognitive

attained this level of motivation, mostly because their circumstances prevent others from making this progress: people who are hungry or in danger cannot be motivated by the drive to achieve their fullest potential, to go the extra mile, because they must instead focus on their very survival—their most basic needs. Although Maslow's theory provides an interesting way to organize aspects of motivation and behavior, its global nature makes experimental verification difficult.

Building Table 11.3 adds Maslow's humanistic theory to the comparative summary of motivation theories.

Be an *Active* learner

REVIEW

- What are the necessary components of a homeostatic system? pp. 367–368
- What is the difference between the concepts of drive and motive? p. 371
- How do cognitive theories of motivation differ from arousal theory? pp. 370–371

THINK CRITICALLY

- How comprehensive is the concept of homeostasis; that is, to how many different motivations can this concept apply? What are the problems with this broad application?
- Why are humanistic theories difficult to test experimentally?

APPLY PSYCHOLOGY

- Can you think of an example from your life of the overjustification effect–when receiving a reward for a behavior decreased your motivation?
- At what level on Maslow's hierarchy are you motivated?

Hunger: A Physiological Need

Now that you understand how theorists have looked at motivation, let's look at a few specific examples of motivation. All of us have been hungry, felt sexually aroused, and experienced the need for achievement. These three motivators—food, sex, and accomplishment—illustrate how motivation includes a variety of behaviors, from motives with a clear biological foundation to those with complex cultural contributions. Let's begin with hunger, which would seem to have a straightforward biological basis. You will see that for this motivation, like other areas of psychology, a complex interplay of biology and learning occur; even hunger and eating are not as simple as they seem.

The Physiological Determinants of Hunger

The basis of eating and hunger may seem very clear—we need energy to fuel our bodies, and eating furnishes this fuel. When depleted of energy, our bodies send out signals that prompt us to seek food and consume it. The first part is correct: we need energy in the form of calories to fuel our bodies, and we get that energy as well as other nutrients from food. But the explanation of hunger as energy depletion and eating as the automatic response to low fuel levels is too simple to be correct. In addition, this biologically based motivation has learned and cultural influences.

Food intake is only one factor in the weight maintenance equation. To maintain weight, the energy expenditures must equal the energy intake. Those expenditures include physical activity and basal metabolism, maintenance of basic cellular and body functions. Physiological explanations of hunger have focused on the concept of *homeostasis*, which we encountered earlier in this chapter (p. 367). Applied to weight maintenance, homeostasis is a balance of energy intake and output that results in a stable weight. When you eat as many calories as you burn, your weight remains the same.

Many people maintain a relatively stable weight over many years, which led researchers to look for a homeostatic mechanism for weight control. Weight stability is consistent with the concept of a *set point* for weight—a predetermined weight that the body maintains. Such a system requires a mechanism to set the weight and some way to signal when body weight gets out of line with the set point. Richard Nisbett (1972) proposed that fat cells are the basis of the body's set point. Fat cells vary both with genetic and environmental factors; the number of fat cells an infant has can increase during the first several years of life. Have you noticed the similarity in body shape among family members? This similarity is a result of the inheritance of fat cell distribution on the body, creating similar body shapes. Recent research has supported the possibility that body fat provides a basis for weight regulation. The other component for a homeostatic weight control system is a signaling system that notes nutritional excess or deficit and sends signals that prompt the increase or decrease of food intake. Researchers have considered several possibilities. One hypothesis involved the level of glucose that circulates in the blood, and another hypothesis concentrated on fat metabolism. Digestion and metabolism produce both glucose and fats that circulate through the blood and thus could be part of the signaling system that prompts eating. However, blood levels of neither glucose nor fat fall low enough to initiate eating or rise rapidly enough after a meal to terminate eating (Woods et al., 2000). Therefore, some of the obvious possibilities for a homeostatic mechanism to regulate eating are not the key factors.

Two hormones appear to be important in maintaining a weight balance. These two hormones are *insulin*, which is produced by the pancreas and allows glucose to be taken into body cells and used, and *leptin*, which is produced by fat cells. The discovery that fat cells produce a hormone prompted a rush to research the effects of this hormone and resulted in a better understanding of weight regulation. Both of these hormones furnish signals to the brain, which contains receptors for these hormones. The complex chain of events in the brain has not yet been established, but the hypothalamus (see Chapter 2, p. 56) is important in receiving the signals that insulin and leptin send and in forming connections with other brain structures involved in the control process. It's really difficult to develop a picture of how these factors function because they happen on a cellular level in your brain and body. You know about feeling hungry or full, but you generally don't know how your hormone levels change in relation to food metabolism.

Researchers have known for years that the hypothalamus is involved in eating because surgery to this brain structure alters eating; surgery that damages the ventromedial hypothalamus produces extreme overeating, and surgery that damages the lateral hypothalamus produces a drastic decrease in eating (see Figure 11.5). The actions of insulin and leptin on the neural pathways in the brain produce a complex cascade of events that appear to signal hunger and satiation.

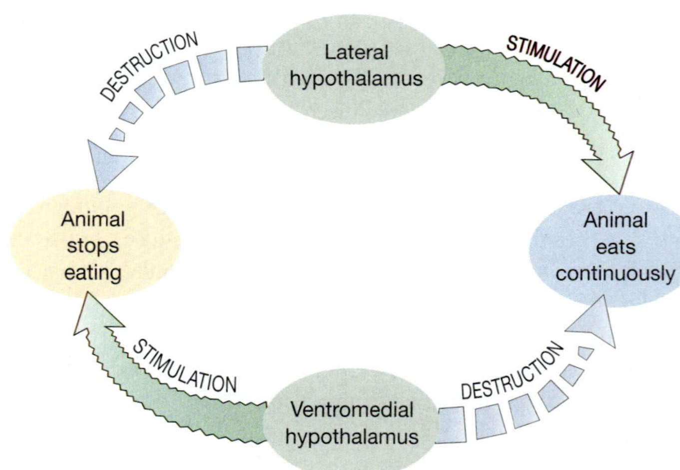

FIGURE 11.5

The Effects of the Hypothalamus on Eating Behavior

The stimulation or destruction (ablation) of a rat's hypothalamus alters the rat's eating behavior; the location of the hypothalamic stimulation or destruction—ventromedial or lateral—affects the results.

People (and other animals) do not begin eating a meal because their blood glucose or fat levels have fallen to low levels. Instead, eating begins *before* bodies actually need food (Woods et al., 2000). This arrangement prevents energy levels from falling too low, which seems like an excellent adaptation. Animals that protect themselves against starvation are much more likely to survive and reproduce than those that were on the verge of starvation before they felt the urge to eat. This conceptualization of eating brings up a question: if energy deficit is not the reason why people start eating, what is?

Learning to Be Hungry: Environmental and Cultural Influence

The physiological mechanisms that underlie eating are not the whole story of hunger and eating. People do not eat because they are energy deficient; they eat *before* they are. But we *feel* hungry, and that feeling prompts us to seek food. Research shows that learning and experience are important in feeling hungry. Stimuli in the environment associated with food can be the signal to eat (Sclafani, 1997). One of those powerful stimuli is time of day. Most of us feel hungry at specified times. You have probably missed a meal and had the experience of feeling very hungry for an hour or so, but then your hunger diminishes. This experience shows how eating at regular times leads to hunger at those times. Both rats and humans are susceptible to training to eat on a schedule.

We also learn what to eat, and the enormous cultural variations in desirable and forbidden foods reflect the strength of this experience. Almost every substance that has nutritional value is eaten by the people of some culture in some part of the world (Rozin, 1999). Refried beans and tortillas are foods that most Americans know, but until fast-food restaurants began marketing breakfast burritos, most non-Latino/Latina Americans did not consider them appealing breakfast foods. Fried grasshoppers—or other insects—are not considered desirable foods by most college students in the United States, but in some cultures, insects are a favorite. American favorites are not accepted worldwide; an extensive advertising campaign attempted to market corn flakes to Spanish children, but this effort was not very successful because in general the Spanish do not pour milk over any foods before eating them. Indeed, milk is not a staple in the Spanish diet as it is in the United States, so the marketing campaign was pitted against a cultural tradition that made corn flakes a hard sell in Spain (Visser, 1999). Cereal products are certainly not considered repulsive or forbidden foods in the way that insects might be, but still corn flakes are somewhat foreign to the cultural tradition of Spanish food.

■ *Fried grasshoppers are considered repulsive by many people in the U.S., but people in some cultures find insects delectable.*

Cultural experiences are not the only learned factor in food preferences; individuals also develop food likes and dislikes. Those preferences are guided by some innate preferences and some family, peer, and advertising influences. Examining the foods that were available in human prehistory, those with sweet or salty tastes were usually safe and nutritious, whereas bitter foods often contained poisonous toxins, which has led to an inborn preference for sweet and salty foods and a tendency to avoid bitter foods (Rozin, 1999). Another component of taste preference is sensitivity to various tastes, and some taste sensitivities have a genetic component (Tepper, 1998). For example, vegetables in the broccoli and cabbage family contain a chemical to which people have varying genetic sensitivities that may relate to their preferences for this taste. So, if you dislike broccoli, it may be in your genes. Early family experiences, peer pressure, and advertising also play a role in individual food choices, creating a wide range of variation in liked and disliked foods (Nestle et al., 1998).

Sometimes hunger is not even a factor in eating; people eat for pleasure, and pleasure is an important factor in eating. When tasty food is available, people eat, even if they are not hungry. Almost everyone has had the experience of yielding to the temptation of a luscious dessert after eating a large meal. Despite being full (perhaps uncomfortably so) from the meal, a person finds the dessert just too good to resist. We would not be as tempted to eat more of the same food that we had just consumed, but a different food can prompt additional eating. This situation suggests that variety is a factor in eating, and research and personal experience support this view (Sokolov, 1999). A variety of tasty food can produce overeating in both rats and humans, and variety is a key factor in the pleasure of eating. Even your favorite food—turkey with dressing, pepperoni pizza, a ripe peach, chocolate—would eventually become unappealing if it were the only thing you could eat.

Is the great variety of food available to many people in the United States a factor in overeating and obesity, or is obesity due to inherent factors?

Eating and Obesity

Despite widespread signs of health-consciousness (low-fat foods, health clubs, strong sales of sports gear), it seems there is an ever-growing tendency for Americans to be ever growing. Over one-third of Americans are overweight, and 22.5% of the population is clinically obese—a rate almost twice as high as it was two decades ago (Taubes, 1998). No one tries to be obese—indeed, most people want to be slim. Is it the ever-increasing variety of junk food, time spent watching television, not enough exercise? What is the underlying reason for obesity? Both physiological and psychological explanations have been offered to account for it.

■ **EVOLUTIONARY AND PHYSIOLOGICAL EXPLANATIONS OF OBESITY.** One type of explanation for obesity comes from an examination of evolutionary history. For humans and other animals, food scarcity and potential starvation were serious threats. A good fat supply was one way to diminish that threat, so animals with a tendency to develop fat stores had a survival advantage. This interpretation suggests that humans and other animals have a tendency to get fat when food is readily available. That hypothesis is confirmed by obesity rates in industrialized countries. In the United States and many other countries, the food supply is steady and plentiful, and these countries have a much higher obesity rate than poorer countries. Yet the evolutionary explanation of obesity leaves some unanswered questions. For one, why are most people, even in circumstances with lots of food, able to maintain a stable weight? For another, why is there such variation among people, with some individuals getting fat and others staying slim?

One possibility for individual variation comes from an inherited tendency to store fat, which varies among people. Some researchers insist that obesity has a genetic basis and that behavioral and biological patterns for the distribution of body fat are inherited (Bar-Or et al., 1998; Comuzzie & Allison, 1998). If you have an overweight parent, your likelihood of being overweight as an adult increases dramatically, even if your weight was normal as a youngster. The possibility of a genetic predisposition for obesity is based partly on the observation that fat runs in families, but additional evidence is necessary because eating habits also run in families. The other piece of evidence for the genetics of obesity comes from research on rats and mice. During the 1990s, researchers discovered a genetic mutation in mice and another in rats that affected the hormone leptin, the hormone that we discussed as one of the substances that forms a brain-level signaling system related to eating (see p. 376). Mice that do not produce leptin and rats that have faulty brain receptors for this hormone are obese, leading researchers to hypothesize that some genetically determined problem with leptin may be involved in human obesity (Woods et al., 2000).

■ *Hunger is not always a factor in eating; people eat for pleasure.*

Further, some studies suggest that people can inherit both a tendency to overeat and a slow (or low) metabolism. A slow metabolism has a lower basal metabolic rate, which uses available energy (calories) from food efficiently and stores unused calories as fat. This type of metabolism is an advantage in protecting against starvation but tends to result in obesity when people with a low metabolism eat what would otherwise be a normal diet. For example, the Pima Indians of Arizona are prone to obesity; 80–90% of the tribe's young adults are dangerously overweight. According to Ravussin and his colleagues (Norman et al., 1998; Ravussin et al., 1988; Tataranni et al., 1997), who have studied these Native Americans extensively, the Pima have unusually low metabolic rates. During any 24-hour period, the typical Pima (who is as active as the average European American) burns about 80 calories less than an average European American. Ravussin's view is that the Pima, whose ancestors spent generations in a desert environment where they went through periods of famine, developed a metabolism that adapted to this on-again, off-again pattern of food availability. But in the 20th century, the Pima abandoned their traditional low-fat diet and began to eat like other Americans. Their metabolisms, which had developed a disposition to be "thrifty" and store fat, became a liability as the proportion of fat in their diet increased.

■ *Some groups are prone to obesity in which over 80% are overweight.*

■ **PSYCHOLOGICAL EXPLANATIONS OF OBESITY.** Even people with low metabolic rates are not destined to be obese. They can balance their food intake to their metabolic rate or increase their energy output by exercising. Nor are people with a normal metabolic rate guaranteed lifelong thinness. All of us are bombarded with food-oriented messages that have little to do with nutritional needs. Advertisements proclaim that merriment can be found at a restaurant or a supermarket. Parents coax good behavior from their children by promising them desserts or snacks. Thus, eating acquires a significance that far exceeds its role in satisfying physiological needs: it serves as a center for social interaction, a means to reward good behavior, and a way to fend off unhappy thoughts and reduce stress (Greeno & Wing, 1994). Eating has many meanings beyond nutrition. In addition to promoting excessive food intake, the American environment both encourages physical activity and offers multiple opportunities to avoid it.

■ *Thinness is the current ideal, especially for women, and dieting is a way of life.*

The problem is that the human body has developed effective mechanisms for gaining weight and weak ones for shedding pounds that are no longer needed (Hill & Peters, 1998). Researchers through the past five decades have identified four key factors that contribute to overeating. First, food is readily available—from drive-through windows and vending machines, restaurants and street vendors, at home, at work, and everywhere in between. Second, portion sizes are growing ever bigger—fast-food restaurants have supersize meals. Third, the average person's diet is higher in fat than ever before—fat provides nearly twice the calories per gram as protein or carbohydrates. Fourth, most children and adults do not engage in regular, sustained physical activity. Put all of this together—low physical activity, eating too much, too often, of the wrong things—and the result is an overweight population that has trouble losing weight.

To make the situation even worse, being thin has become increasingly desirable, especially for women. So dieting has become a way of life for many Americans who hope to be thin. Indeed, more

Be an *Active* learner

REVIEW

- What brain structures and hormones are related to hunger and eating? pp. 375–376
- What cultural and psychological factors influence eating? p. 377

THINK CRITICALLY

- How does obesity fit with the concept of set point? Why should some people have a set point that is set at obesity?
- Why might the one-food diet described below be an effective (if not pleasant) weight reduction strategy?

APPLY PSYCHOLOGY

- Choose a favorite food, and make it your personal diet. Eat only this one food for every meal and every snack. Keep a diary of your eating and your feelings about the experience. How long did it take for you to become tired of this favorite food? Do you think you could lose weight on this diet?

people are dieting than are overweight; most dieters are in the normal weight range, but not all overweight people are dieting (U.S. Bureau of the Census, 2000). The majority of normal-weight dieters are women who want to attain the very thin body that has become the ideal in modern America. This ideal has led to chronic dieting and other eating disorders, which are more common among women than men (see Chapter 4 for a discussion of eating disorders). In recent years, an increasing number of men are developing eating disorders (Lakkis, Ricciardelli, & Williams, 1999).

The quest for thinness is most often unsuccessful; most dieters gain back the weight they lose. People who are obese are not often successful in losing enough weight to enter the normal weight range. If they do, they too are likely to gain it back. The same factors that make obesity increasingly likely push the newly thin toward weight gain. This evidence supports the notion of a set point for weight, to which people return when they lose. However, increasing obesity is evidence against set points as the only factor in weight maintenance: if people gain weight, they should also return to the set point. The increasing number of obese Americans is evidence for psychological and social factors in weight gain.

Obviously, there is no simple answer to this nature-versus-nurture question with respect to obesity. Research from the 1990s, especially the discovery of the hormone leptin, has led to a renewed excitement about the possibilities of understanding how the brain experiences hunger and the ways that these brain signals initiate eating and the feeling of being satiated (Woods et al., 2000). This research has led to the view that obesity is a chronic health problem that requires treatment (Mokdad et al., 2000). The active research in the molecular biology of eating and its behavioral implications may lead to the development of effective treatments for obesity in the near future.

Sexual Behavior: Physiology plus Thought

Sex is often in the news. Prince Charles and his mistress, Camilla Parker-Bowles, President Bill Clinton and Monica Lewinsky, Gary Condit and Chandra Levy. People's preoccupation with the sex lives of national figures indicates that they are fascinated by sexuality. As fascinating and powerfully motivating as sex is, it is not physiologically necessary to sustain a person's life. You won't die if you don't have sex (no matter what your dates tell you). Thus, there is an important difference between sexual behavior and food seeking. In many animals, sexual behavior is controlled largely by physiological and hormonal systems. In human beings, the degree of hormonal control is less clear because ideas, past behaviors, emotions, expectations, and goals all enter into the sexual behavior of human beings. The relative contributions of these factors vary, depending on an array of variables. For some people, sights, sounds, and smells are triggers for sexually motivated behavior. For others, thoughts, feelings, and fantasies either initiate or, in many cases, satisfy sexual needs. Sexual behavior varies with age, gender, religion, and cultural background. The diversity among cultures is enormous—what one culture considers forbidden, another deems necessary. For example, the British find sexual indiscretions among politicians primarily titillating—in contrast to Americans, who generally find sexual misbehavior in the White House, Congress, and similar political venues difficult to condone. Recognizing this diversity, let's look at some of the initiators of human sexual behavior, at the physiology of that behavior, and then at its range.

What Initiates the Sex Drive?

Hardly a day goes by when you are not bombarded with sexually suggestive advertisements. Ads for everything from toothpaste to automobiles, sports equipment to orange juice, feature attractive, half-clad models to sell the product. Advertisers use learning principles to pair attractive people and situations with products in the hope that the products will take on an arousing glamour—and to hint that if you use the product, you may become as alluring as the models. The advertisers are seeking to initiate buying activity by activating the sexual drive. They know, of course, that people's thoughts direct buying behavior. But sexual behavior is affected by hormones as well as by thoughts.

■ **SEX HORMONES.** Sex hormones are important for sexual behavior in humans, beginning before birth. Both males and females produce both androgens (the "male" hormones) and estrogens (the "female" hormones), but in different proportions. In males, the testes are the principal producers of androgens. In females, the ovaries are the principal producers of estrogens. During prenatal development, the presence of testosterone prompts the development of the male reproductive system; their absence allows development of the female system. The release of androgens and estrogens initiates the onset of the secondary sex characteristics in developing teenagers (see Chapter 4, p. 114). The presence of these hormones is important for the development of sexual desire, and their regulation is essential for the development and maintenance of fertility. Women's levels of sex hormones vary according to their menstrual cycles and then decrease at menopause, whereas men's levels of sex hormones do not vary as much or in a cyclic fashion. However, men's levels of testosterone also decline as they age. For humans, hormone levels are involved in but not directly responsible for sexual behavior.

In the animal kingdom, the relationship between sex hormones and sexual behavior is clear. Female rats, for example, are sexually responsive only when they are fertile, and both sexual receptivity and fertility are regulated by a complex series of hormones released into the bloodstream (when they are "in heat"). If the testes of male rats are removed, the animals show a marked decrease in sexual interest and performance. Most sexual responses in nonhuman animals do not occur without hormonal activation. Human beings, on the other hand, can choose whether or not to respond sexually at any given time. In human beings, the removal of hormone-generating organs has a much less drastic effect on sexual interest and behavior.

■ **SIGHTS, SOUNDS, SMELLS, AND FANTASY.** In animals, a receptive female may show her receptivity by releasing pheromones; the pheromones trigger sexual activity in the male (see Chapter 5, p. 177). A specific movement or set of actions may also signal female receptivity and trigger sexual behavior from the male animal. But human beings, because they are not so directly under hormonal control, can be aroused by the sight or sound of something with erotic associations or the smell of a familiar perfume. Thought plays an enormous role in human sexuality; people's thoughts, fantasies, and emotions initiate and activate sexual desire and behavior. And PET studies have recently located specific areas of the brain that are activated when people are experiencing sexual arousal (Stoléru et al., 1999).

The Sexual Response Cycle

When human beings become sexually aroused, they go through a series of four phases (stages). Together known as the *sexual response cycle*, they include the excitement, plateau, orgasm, and resolution phases.

student voices

Glenda Smith
Carson-Newman College

After battling eating disorders as a teenager, I wanted to study about them in college. Classroom study, research, and fieldwork experiences in psychology have now become practical to me. As a camp counselor, I worked with two campers with eating disorders. I also have mentored middle-school girls with body image and self-esteem issues.

The **excitement phase** is the first phase of the cycle, during which there are increases in heart rate, blood pressure, and respiration. A key characteristic of this phase is **vasocongestion**—engorgement of the blood vessels, particularly in the genital area, due to increased blood flow. In women, the breasts and clitoris swell, the vaginal lips expand, and vaginal lubrication increases; in men, the penis becomes erect. The excitement phase may last from a few minutes to a few hours.

The **plateau phase** is the second phase of the sexual response cycle, during which physical arousal continues to increase as the partners' bodies prepare for orgasm. Autonomic nervous system activity increases, causing a faster heart rate. In women, the clitoris withdraws, the vagina becomes engorged and fully extended; in men, the penis becomes fully erect, turns a darker color, and may secrete a bit of fluid, which may contain sperm.

The **orgasm phase** is the third phase of the sexual response cycle, during which autonomic nervous system activity reaches its peak and muscle contractions occur in spasms throughout the body, especially in the genital area. An *orgasm* is the peak of sexual activity. In men, muscles throughout the reproductive system contract to help expel semen; in women, muscles surrounding the vagina contract. An orgasm lasts only a few seconds and is an all-or-none activity; once the threshold for orgasm is reached, the orgasm occurs. Although men experience only one orgasm during each sexual response cycle, women are capable of multiple orgasms.

The **resolution phase** is the fourth phase of the sexual response cycle following orgasm, during which the body returns to its resting, or normal, state. This return takes from one to several minutes; the time required varies considerably from person to person. During this phase, men are usually unable to achieve an erection for some amount of time, called the *refractory period*.

Like many other physiological events, the sexual response cycle is subject to considerable variation, with longer or shorter phases and different signs of arousal, depending on the person and his or her age.

Excitement phase
The first phase of the sexual response cycle, during which there are increases in heart rate, blood pressure, and respiration.

Vasocongestion
In the sexual response cycle, engorgement of the blood vessels, particularly in the genital area, due to increased blood flow.

Plateau phase
The second phase of the sexual response cycle, during which physical arousal continues to increase as the partners' bodies prepare for orgasm.

Orgasm phase
The third phase of the sexual response cycle, during which autonomic nervous system activity reaches its peak and muscle contractions occur in spasms throughout the body, but especially in the genital area.

Resolution phase
The fourth phase of the sexual response cycle, following orgasm, during which the body returns to its resting, or normal, state.

Human Sexual Behavior

While American culture is saturated with sexually suggestive advertisements and sexually explicit movies, it also shows considerable reluctance to examine and talk about sexual behavior scientifically. Efforts to examine sexuality in a systematic way are often viewed with skepticism; in 1994, Congress even sought to ensure that a federally funded sex survey was not conducted.

■ **STUDYING SEXUALITY.** Despite this reluctance to look at sex objectively, various researchers have studied sex, mostly by conducting sex surveys. One of the first and most famous was conducted by a biologist, Alfred Kinsey, and his colleagues. For years, the Kinsey surveys were the main source of information about sexual attitudes and behavior, but contemporary researchers such as Morton Hunt (1974), Masters, Johnson, and Kolodny (1994), and Edward Laumann and his colleagues (1994; Michael et al., 1998) have conducted more recent and more representative sex surveys (see the *Introduction to Research Basics* on page 383). Comparisons of the results from these surveys allow conclusions to be drawn about how sexual behavior has changed over the past 50 years.

When Kinsey and his colleagues conducted their sex surveys, the results showed differences between women's and men's sexual behavior. Later surveys have revealed a decrease in those differences; the percentage of women and men who engage in masturbation, premarital sex, and extramarital sex are now more similar than in the 1950s. Men and women are more likely today than in the 1950s to have intercourse before marriage, and there has been a slow and steady decrease in the age of first intercourse for both boys and girls (see also Feldman et al., 1997; Wadsworth et al., 1995). Today, people express their sexuality more often and more

introduction to research basics

Sex Surveys

The most common approach to studying sexuality has been to survey or interview people about their sexual behavior. A **survey** is one of the descriptive methods of research; it requires construction of a set of questions to administer to a group of participants. Analysis of the responses enables researchers to understand their topic. This method has a built-in limitation: people do not always tell the truth when asked about their behavior. All survey researchers must deal with the challenge of obtaining truthful answers from their research participants.

Despite this limitation, several groups of researchers have surveyed people about their sexual behavior. The early sex surveys of Alfred Kinsey and his colleagues (Kinsey et al., 1948, 1953) and Morton Hunt (1974) were limited in the people whom they questioned. To be accurate, surveys must include a **representative sample,** a sample that reflects the composition of the population from which it is drawn. In this case, the population is American adults, and obtaining a representative sample of this group is a major challenge. Working for the National Opinion Research Center, Edward Laumann and his colleagues (1994) claim that they conducted the first sex survey in the United States that achieves this goal.

DESIGN The study was a survey that included an extensive list of questions, which participants answered during a personal interview.

PARTICIPANTS Participants were 3,432 adults between 18 and 59 years old living in the United States. They were selected to be representative of the adult population.

PROCEDURE Teams of trained interviewers conducted face-to-face interviews, a situation that makes some people uncomfortable and may lead participants to distort the truth. Failures to be truthful are a drawback of the survey method and may have affected this survey.

RESULTS Many behavioral scientists found the results of the Laumann study predictable—but there were some surprises. The results of this survey revealed a picture of sex in America that varies from media portrayals. Despite the image of "swinging singles," the report found that married couples had sex more frequently than others. The image of extramarital sex is commonplace, but 86% of women and 75% of men said that they were sexually faithful to their spouses. The most frequent and the most appealing form of sexuality for both women and men was vaginal intercourse. A very low percentage—1.4% of women and 2.8% of men—said that their sexual orientation was primarily gay or lesbian. The results did include some surprising findings. For example, 25% of women said that they had been forced to do something sexually that they did not want to do, and only 4% of the perpetrators were strangers. These results mean that most forced sex is done by acquaintances—most commonly boyfriends and husbands. In addition, 12% of men and 17% of women report that they had some type of sexual experience during childhood that qualifies as sexual abuse.

CONCLUSIONS This survey included a representative sample of adults in the United States, which allows generalization to that population. The picture of sexuality in America includes some very conventional behaviors, such as monogamy, a low percentage of homosexuality, and little attraction to "kinky" sex. The survey also revealed a surprisingly high percentage of women who had experienced forced sex and both men and women who were sexually abused as children.

LIMITATION Like all survey research, the main limitation of this survey is its reliance on self-reports. People have a tendency to present themselves in a positive way, and this tendency is especially strong when the topic is so intimate. These results may be the best sex survey, but they are not necessarily the full picture of sexuality in America.

openly—and seek to understand their own feelings and behaviors. Laumann's team (Michael et al., 1998) reports a wide variety in sexual behaviors among Americans, compared with other cultures, and a decline in the differences between male and female sexuality. The incidence of masturbation and the acceptance of casual sex remain substantially higher for men than women in the United States, but differences in other sexual attitudes and behavior are small or do not exist (Oliver & Hyde, 1993).

In general, reports about sexual practices show that individuals engage in sexual behaviors more when they are younger than when they are older. For example, the frequency of intercourse decreases from the early 20s to the 50s or 60s (Call, Sprecher, & Schwartz, 1995). Similarly, the duration of any specific sexual activity decreases with increasing age. Older people are less happy with their sex lives, and

Survey
One of the descriptive methods of research; it requires construction of a set of questions to administer to a group of participants.

Representative sample
A sample that reflects the characteristics of the population from which it is drawn.

many older women have no sexual partners (Laumann et al., 1994). For all ages, sexuality occurs within a context, and the most common context is a relationship. Laumann and his colleagues (1994) found that most individuals have sex with someone they know and live with (usually a spouse) and that people who are sexually active think about and desire sex more than do individuals who are not sexually active. Further, when people do engage in an extramarital affair, it is usually not a casual encounter but a relationship with one person they know (Wadsworth et al., 1995).

The picture of sexuality in the United States is not completely happy, and American sexuality has negative aspects. Compared with other industrialized countries, individuals in the United States begin sexual activity at younger ages, and although pregnancy rates have fallen among American adolescents, the pregnancy rate is substantially higher than that in other developed countries (Singh & Darroch, 2000). Other negative factors include a high incidence of sexually transmitted diseases, the continuing spread of AIDS (discussed in Chapter 14), and the continuation of risky sexual behaviors, such as not using condoms (Downey & Landry, 1997). The rates of *sexual dysfunction*—the term for sexual problems—are high: 43% for women and 31% for men. Young women and older men are more likely to suffer from sexual dysfunction, including inability to experience orgasm, low sexual desire, problems attaining an erection in men, and painful intercourse in women. These problems have both health-related and psychological components (Laumann, Paik, & Rosen, 1999). Unfortunately, embarrassment prevents many people from seeking treatment. Despite the problems, most people report their sex lives as being satisfactory (Laumann et al., 1994).

■ **SEXUAL ORIENTATION.** One's sexual orientation is the direction of one's sexual interest. A person with a *heterosexual orientation* has an erotic attraction and preference for members of the other sex; a person with a *homosexual orientation* has an erotic attraction to and preference for members of the same sex. A *bisexual orientation* is an erotic attraction to members of both sexes. Kinsey introduced the idea of a continuum of sexual behaviors ranging from exclusively homosexual behaviors through some homosexual behaviors, to mostly heterosexual behaviors, to exclusively heterosexual behaviors. Kinsey also recognized that a same-sex sexual experience does not make a person homosexual. In addition, a person may have a homosexual or bisexual orientation without ever having had a sexual experience with someone of the same sex. It is thus an overgeneralization to define a person's sexual orientation based solely on a single, or even on multiple, sexual encounters (Haslam, 1997).

The Kinsey survey of male sexual behavior reported that 37% of men had at least one same-sex sexual experience and that 10% of men were primarily homosexual in orientation. Other surveys reported lower rates, and most sex researchers consider the Kinsey statistics to be overestimates. The Laumann study (1994) found that 2.8% of men and 1.4% of women identified themselves as primarily homosexual, and other studies confirm these low figures (Cameron & Cameron, 1998; Sell, Wells, & Wypij, 1995). Regardless of the percentages, people who are not heterosexual experience discrimination and censure. Americans, perhaps more than people in other cultures, still have great difficulty with homosexuality as an acceptable sexual orientation. For example, having gays in the military causes intense debate, and an important part of this debate is the basis of homosexuality (see *Point/Counterpoint*).

Be an *Active* learner

REVIEW

- What are the phases of the human sexual response cycle? pp. 381–382
- What changes in sexual behavior have occurred over the past 50 years in the United States? pp. 382–383
- Summarize the evidence supporting each side of the debate about the determination of sexual orientation. pp. 384–385

THINK CRITICALLY

- Do you think the federal government should study sexual behavior? Why or why not?
- Many people argue that homosexual orientation is a matter of choice, but heterosexual orientation is innate. How can both be true?

APPLY PSYCHOLOGY

- When you read the statistics on different sexual behaviors presented by sex researchers, which ones surprised you? Which ones did not? What is the basis for your reactions?

point*counterpoint*

The Basis of Homosexuality

The Issue: Is sexual orientation determined by biological factors?

POINT
Sexual orientation is determined by nature: innate, biological factors produce homosexuality.

COUNTERPOINT
Sexual orientation is determined by nurture: social experiences determine homosexuality.

The causes of homosexuality have been debated for decades, and the argument has developed into a classic nature-versus-nurture one. Those on the nature side of the debate assert that biological factors determine sexual orientation, and most see genetics as the determining factor. They cite data showing that homosexual men and women knew when they were young children that they were "different." Studies have pointed to genes, prenatal events, and brain structures as possible biological contributors to homosexual orientation. Many studies have confirmed the family association of homosexuality; studies of twins and adopted children confirm that sexual orientation runs in families (Pillard & Bailey, 1998). Gay men tend to come from extended families that have included other gay men. Further, Dean Hamer and his colleagues (Hamer et al., 1993; LeVay & Hamer, 1994) reported that they found unique DNA markers on the X chromosomes of gay men—that is, a "gay gene," but other researchers (Rice et al., 1999) failed to confirm this location for this gene. Thus, the location of the gene remains uncertain, and the search is still in progress. Another possibility for a physiological basis for sexual orientation lies within the brain. Research found differences between gay and heterosexual men in a specific area within the hypothalamus (LeVay, 1991; Swaab & Hofman, 1995). More recent research has not contradicted these findings, but no one has replicated these differences, either.

The nurture side of the debate asserts that homosexuality is a choice and under voluntary control, which means that it can change through therapy. Daryl Bem (1996; 2000) developed a theory that explains the development of sexual orientation through the interaction of innate personality traits and experience. Bem suggests that children develop feelings of familiarity for those with whom they associate, but the unfamiliar is exotic and exciting. During preadolescence, the exotic becomes erotic through association with heightened autonomic activity, leading to sexual attraction. Most children associate with same-sex peers and develop feelings of familiarity for them, thus never developing erotic feelings for individuals of the same sex. Other children associate with other-sex peers, which makes those of the same sex the exotic ones; these individuals are likely to develop homosexual orientation. Bem (2000) cited evidence from surveys of gay men and lesbian women that, he argues, confirm his theory. However, other researchers contend that Bem's interpretation of these survey results is incorrect (Krisel, 2001).

The level of debate increased when Robert Spitzer presented a paper at the American Psychiatric Association convention that asserted that homosexuals can change to a heterosexual orientation (Kluger, 2001). Spitzer based this conclusion on telephone interviews with 143 men and 57 women who had sought counseling (often religious counseling) to help them change their sexual orientation, asking them if they had achieved good sexual functioning as heterosexuals. Sixty-six percent of the men and 44% of the women said that they had. Critics pointed to problems with the biased sample (only people who sought therapy to change their sexual orientation) and the subjective nature of the question (personal opinion rather than objective measurements of sexual arousal). This study has added to, rather than settled, the controversy over the basis of sexual orientation.

Achievement: A Social Need

Do you consider yourself an overachiever? What sacrifices have you made to achieve the goals you have reached? Do you believe that something in your personality has pushed you toward these achievements, or has the motivation come from your parents, teachers, and friends? Personality psychologists such as Henry Murray assert that individual needs interact with key events and situations in a person's environment to prompt behavior. Murray used the word *press* to indicate how environmental situations may motivate a person (Murray, 1938): the environment may press an individual to excel at sports, to be a loving caregiver to a grandparent, or to achieve great wealth. The press of poverty may produce a social need for financial security; it may therefore cause a person to work hard and become educated so as to earn a comfortable living.

The most useful theories for measuring these kinds of motivation are expectancy theories that focus specifically on the **need for achievement**—a social need that directs a person to strive constantly for excellence and success. According to such achievement theories, people engage in behaviors that satisfy their desires for success, mastery, and fulfillment. Tasks that do not further these goals are less motivating for people with high need for achievement, and these individuals either do not undertake these tasks or perform them with less energy or commitment. Many people bicycle for fun but do not race; few racers are motivated to train and enter the Tour de France, but Lance Armstrong is.

Need for achievement
A social need that directs a person to strive constantly for excellence and success.

Self-efficacy
The belief that a peson can successfully engage in and execute a specific behavior.

One of the leaders in studies of achievement motivation was David C. McClelland (1917–1998), whose early research focused on the idea that people have strong social motives for achievement (McClelland, 1958). McClelland showed that a person learns achievement motivation in the home environment during childhood. People with a high need for achievement had parents who stressed excellence and who provided physical affection and emotional rewards for high achievement. Such people also generally walked early, talked early, and had a high need for achievement even in elementary school (e.g., Teevan & McGhee, 1972). A high need for achievement is strongest for firstborn children, perhaps because parents typically have more time to give them direction and praise. Culture is also a factor in achievement motivation. Many Asian cultures, for example, stress the value of achievement (Eaton & Dembo, 1997). However, factors related to achievement in Asian cultures vary from those of Western cultures. One difference is independence, which is positively related to achievement in Western cultures but not in Asian cultures, which are more collectivist than individualist. Interdependence is highly valued in Asia, and need for achievement and need for affiliation are positively related there (Ang & Chang, 1999). In Western cultures, factors emphasizing the individual are more strongly related to achievement needs, including a willingness to leave family and country. The need for achievement was found to be positively related to willingness to immigrate for students in Albania, the Czech Republic, and Slovenia (Boneva et al., 1998). Not surprisingly, these achievement-oriented students had lower affiliation needs than those less willing to leave their countries. Therefore, need for achievement occurs in Asian and European cultures, but the other characteristics that relate to this need vary among these cultures.

■ *The Thematic Apperception Test (TAT) is used to measure achievement motivation.*

Achievement motives are often measured by analyzing the thought content of imaginative stories. Early studies of people's need for achievement used the *Thematic Apperception Test (TAT)*. In this test, people are shown pictures of scenes in which what is happening is unclear, making the pictures open to interpretation. Test takers are instructed not to think in terms of right or wrong answers but to answer four basic questions for each scene:

1. What is happening?
2. What has led up to this situation?
3. What are those in this situation thinking?
4. What will happen next?

In the picture on page 386, a young man is responding to a TAT scene and answering the four questions above. The TAT involves a complex scoring system and some researchers criticize it as being too subjective. The researchers assert that despite clear scoring criteria, different clinicians deduce different results from the same responses. In general, researchers analyzing participants' descriptions of each scene in the TAT have found that persons with a high need for achievement tell stories that stress success, getting ahead, and competition (Spangler, 1992). Claims of culture bias in the TAT have led to an alternative assessment of achievement motivation. John Oshodi (1999) created an alternative to the TAT, the Oshodi Sentence Completion Index (OSCI), which asks participants to complete a series of sentences to assess their achievement needs. The scoring of this test is based on an African worldview, which Oshodi believes to be a more valid assessment of achievement motivation in African Americans.

With tests such as the TAT or the OSCI, a researcher can differentiate individuals with a high need for achievement from those with a low need. Lowell (1952) found that when he asked participants to rearrange scrambled letters (such as *wtse*) to construct a meaningful word (*west* or *stew*), those with a low need for achievement improved only slightly at the task over successive testing periods. In contrast, participants who scored high in the need for achievement showed increasing improvement over several periods of testing (see Figure 11.6). The researchers reasoned that, when presented with a complex task, persons with a high need for achievement find new and better ways of performing the task as they practice, whereas those with a low need for achievement try no new methods. People with a high need for achievement constantly strive toward excellence and better performance; they have developed a belief in the importance of effort in determining performance (Carr, Borkowski, & Maxwell, 1991; McClelland, 1961).

Those people with high need for achievement also tend to be high in **self-efficacy,** the belief that they can successfully engage in and execute a specific behavior. The relationship between self-efficacy and achievement motivation was demonstrated in a study of children's occupational aspirations (Bandura et al., 2001). This study measured self-efficacy for both academics and occupations in girls and boys around age 12. These researchers found that parents convey achievement-related messages to their children, and these messages influence children's occupational aspirations, mediated through feelings of academic self-efficacy. Children with higher academic self-efficacy were more likely to choose occupations that require higher achievement, regardless of the type of occupation. For example,

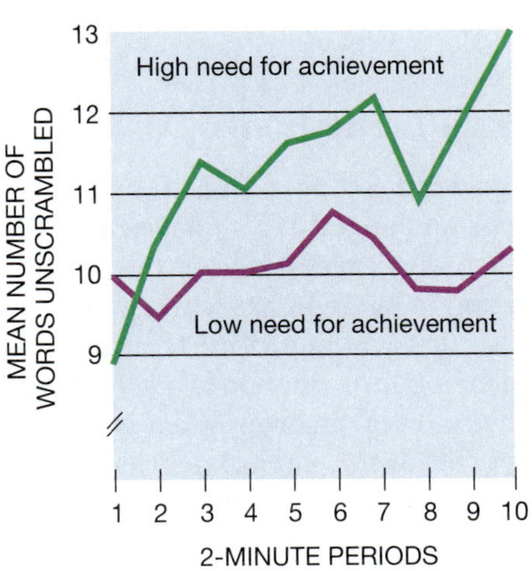

FIGURE 11.6

Performance on a Scrambled-Letter Task

The graph shows performance on a scrambled-letter task for successive 2-minute periods. Performance is affected by a person's overall approach to achievement-related tasks. Participants with a low need for achievement improved overall; however, those with a high need for achievement improved even more. *(Based on data from Lowell, 1952.)*

Be an *Active* learner

REVIEW

- Define *need for achievement,* and explain how psychologists measure it. p. 386
- What is self-efficacy, and how does it relate to the need for achievement? pp. 387–388

THINK CRITICALLY

- Do you think that second- and third-born children have needs that are different from or greater than those of firstborn children? What might those needs be?
- What cultural components shape women and men to have different achievement needs?

APPLY PSYCHOLOGY

- As a parent, what would you do to build achievement needs in your child?

children with high academic self-efficacy for scientific careers were more likely to choose the occupational activities of scientists rather than scientific assistants.

The study about self-efficacy and career development also considered the factor of gender and the differences between career achievement for women and men, relating those differences to self-efficacy beliefs (Bandura et al., 2001). The results showed no overall gender difference in self-efficacy for occupations, but boys were attracted to careers in the military and technology and girls to occupations involving social services and caregiving—traditional gender differences. This continuing pattern prevents men and women from considering some types of achievement, and those who do not consider possibilities do not pursue them. Self-efficacy is not the only factor that influences achievement motivation, but the expectations of parents, teachers, and peers influence a person's belief in his or her ability to be successful in various activities, which makes self-efficacy an important concept in the need for achievement.

Emotion

On February 11, 2000, Sara McBurnett was involved in a fender-bender. The man whose car she hit was furious, got out of his sport-utility vehicle, and confronted her. As he yelled at her, her dog jumped into her lap, and the man grabbed the dog and threw it out of the car into oncoming traffic, where it was killed (*People Weekly*, 2001). The man fled the scene and was not apprehended for 14 months, but people around the country were infuriated. In April 2001, Andrew Burnett was arrested for this offense. He was later convicted of animal cruelty and sentenced to 3 years in prison. His motivation for such a cruel and unwise action was clear: he was angry, but so were thousands of people who heard or read about Burnett's actions. Indeed, many felt so strongly that they donated money to a fund that grew to $120,000 to help find the dog's killer.

That motivation and emotion are interconnected should come as no surprise. Anger can cause you to lash out at a friend and to hurl an object across a room (although few people hurl dogs). When a loud noise startles you, you may freeze up. Happiness can make you smile all day or stop to help a motorist with a flat tire. Although emotions, including love, joy, and fear, can motivate behavior, emotional categories remain difficult to define (Panksepp, 2000).

What Is Emotion?

Emotion
A subjective response, usually accompanied by a physiological change, which is interpreted in a particular way by the individual and often leads to a change in behavior.

The word *emotion* refers to a wide range of subjective states, such as love, fear, sadness, and anger. We all have emotions, talk about them, and possibly even agree on what represents them; but this agreement is not scientific. The psychological investigation of emotion has led to a more specific definition. Most psychologists acknowledge that emotion consists of three elements: feelings, physiological responses, and behaviors. An **emotion** is a subjective response (a feeling), usually accompanied by a physiological change, which is interpreted in a particular way by the individual and often leads to a change in behavior. The elements often fit together, but they are separable. If a person comes across a large bear while hiking in the woods, that person is likely to experience fear. This situation is likely to be accompanied by faster breathing, sweating, and decreased salivation (dry mouth) on the physiological level. The person would likely admit to being afraid or at least startled (although I [LB] have a friend who never admits to fear; he says, "That got my attention" instead). Despite these physical experiences and feelings, people who encountered the bear might mask the experience of emotion by maintaining control of facial expression and restraining the impulse to run. The person might feel fear without showing behaviors associated with fear. These three components of emotion have resulted in a variety of approaches to understanding and studying emotion.

Psychologists focus on different aspects of emotional behavior. The earliest researchers attempted to catalogue and describe basic emotions (Bridges, 1932; Wundt, 1896). Others focused on the physiological bases of emotion (Bard, 1934) and created theories based on their conceptualization of emotion.

Physiological Theories of Emotion

Researchers who take a physiological orientation feel that happiness, rage, and even romantic love are physiologically based. They argue that the wide range of emotions that human beings experience and express is in large part controlled by neurons located in an area deep within the brain, the limbic system. The *limbic system* is composed of cells in the hypothalamus, the amygdala, and other cortical and subcortical areas. Studies of these crucial areas began in the 1920s, when Bard (1934) found that the removal of portions of the cortex of cats produced sharp emotional reactions to simple stimuli such as a touch or a puff of air. The cats would hiss, claw, bite, arch their backs, and growl—but their reactions did not seem directed at any specific person or target. Bard referred to this behavior as *sham rage*, a behavior sequence that showed the signs of rage but without appropriate motivation. Later researchers stimulated portions of the brain with electrical current and found that many brain centers were involved in the experiencing of emotions—they deduced that the cortex was integrating information. Two major biological approaches to the study of emotion dominated psychology for decades: the James–Lange theory and the Cannon–Bard theory. Both are concerned with the physiology of emotions and with whether physiological change or emotional feelings occur first. More recent theories have questioned whether the limbic system is the foundation of

■ *Watching the World Trade Center attacks, people displayed a variety of emotions.*

emotion, focusing on specific brain structures. Another recent approach goes back to the beginning—the evolutionary theory of emotion.

THE JAMES–LANGE THEORY. According to a theory proposed by both William James (1842–1910) and Carl Lange (1834–1900) (who are given joint credit because their approaches were so similar), people experience physiological changes and *then* interpret them as emotional states. People do not cry because they feel sad; they feel sad because they cry. People do not run because they are afraid; they feel afraid after they run. In other words, the James–Lange theory says that people do not experience an emotion until after their bodies become aroused and begin to respond with physiological changes; feedback from the body produces feelings or emotions (James, 1884; Lange, 1922). For this approach, in its most simplified form, *feeling* is the essence of emotion. Thus, James (1890, p. 1006) wrote, "Every one of the bodily changes, whatsoever it be, is felt, acutely or obscurely, the moment it occurs."

A modern physiological approach suggests that facial movements, by their action, can create emotions. Called the *facial feedback hypothesis*, this approach suggests that sensations from the face provide cues or signals to the brain that act as feedback to help a person determine an emotional response. In some ways, this approach derives from the James–Lange theory. As William James said, "We don't cry because we are sad, but rather, we are sad because we cry." According to this theory, a facial movement such as a smile or an eye movement may release the appropriate emotion-linked neurotransmitters (Ekman, 1993; Izard, 1990; Neumann & Strack, 2000). Crying, for example, is associated with a mixture of sympathetic, parasympathetic, and somatic activation (Gross, Fredrickson, & Levenson, 1994). Facial action is not necessary for the experience of emotion, but facial expression may influence the occurrence of emotions, actually creating an emotion that would not have otherwise occurred (Kleinke, Peterson, & Rutledge, 1998; McIntosh, 1996). That is, putting on a happy face may actually make you happier.

THE CANNON–BARD THEORY. Some physiologists, notably Walter Cannon (1871–1945), were critical of the James–Lange theory. Cannon and colleague Philip Bard argued that the physiological changes associated with many emotional states are identical. They reasoned as follows: if increases in blood pressure and heart rate accompany feelings of both anger and joy, how can people determine their emotional state simply from their physiological state? Cannon spoke of undifferentiated arousal—the physiological response underlying the fight-and-flight response (the body's response to emergency situations that includes activating resources needed for energy to fight or flee) is the same.

Cannon argued that when a person is emotional, two areas of the brain—the thalamus and the cerebral cortex—are stimulated simultaneously (he did not know the whole story about the limbic system). Stimulation of the cortex produces the emotional component of the experience; stimulation of the thalamus produces physiological changes in the sympathetic nervous system. According to Cannon (1927), emotional feelings *accompany* physiological changes; they neither produce nor result from such changes. Building Table 11.4 presents a contrast of these two physiological approaches to emotion.

When Cannon and Bard were formulating their theory, they knew relatively little about how the brain operates. For example, physiological changes in the brain do not happen exactly simultaneously. Further, people report that they often have an experience and then have physiological and emotional reactions to it. Neither the James–Lange nor the Cannon–Bard approach considered how a person's thoughts about a situation might alter physiological reactions and emotional responses. But the James–Lange and Cannon–Bard approaches provided a conceptual bridge to newer approaches. One of those approaches concentrates on the role of a brain structure called the amygdala (see *Brain and Behavior*), and the other approach considers the evolutionary value of emotions.

Building Table 11.4

Physiological Theories of Emotion

Theory	Theorist	The Role of Physiology	The Role of Cognition	The Role of the Situation
Physiological	James and Lange	Arousal precedes interpretation of events.	People interpret bodily arousal as emotion.	Not a factor
	Cannon and Bard	Physiological arousal and interpretation occur simultaneously.	Cognition supplies an interpretation, which occurs at the same time as arousal.	Not a factor

■ **EVOLUTIONARY THEORY.** Evolutionary psychologists see complex behavior as a series of specialized subprograms that are called into action by specific situations (Cosmides & Tooby, 2000). Emotions have a prominent role in evolutionary psychology, furnishing the coordination and ordering of many different specialized programs. Repeated situations in human evolutionary history organized these programs around emotions, so when specific situations arise, emotions occur, and along with them, the behaviors governed by these programs. In this view, emotional responses are hardwired into the brain's circuits, and subjective feelings follow them. Fear responses—such as freezing up at the sight of a natural predator—occur automatically without thought and have adaptive advantages that caused these behavioral sequences to become part of evolutionary biology. LeDoux's view of fear (see *Brain and Behavior*) is very much an evolutionary one; evolution has prepared humans (and other animals) to respond in certain basic emotional ways to some stimuli

BRAIN AND BEHAVIOR

Experiencing and Recognizing Fear

Joseph LeDoux (1995, 1996; LeDoux & Phelps, 2000) has investigated the physiological bases of emotions, concentrating on the emotion of fear. His research has centered on one brain structure—the amygdala and its connections. In his popular book *The Emotional Brain*, LeDoux asserts that a person's feelings and subjective experiences are initiated through a trail to the amygdala.

For LeDoux, emotional experiences are determined by stimulation of two routes. The first route is a fast system that makes use of subcortical structures, including the amygdala, and results in the ability to react quickly. These reactions include arousal in various other brain structures and automatic responses in the body—release of hormones, sweating, and facial changes. The other route involves the cerebral cortex as well as the amygdala. This route allows an evaluation of the situation and the inclusion of thoughts and past experiences in the assessment of the situation and decisions about what steps to take. For example, an unexpected touch is often enough to produce a quick fear reaction, but the experience of fear will be different if the touch occurs in your home by a friend versus in a dimly lighted corridor by a stranger. In the end, LeDoux (1996) asserts that there seem to be two routes for fear, one subcortical and one cortical, but both involving the amygdala.

The amygdala is also important for forming memories related to fear, probably through its connections to the neighboring hippocampus (LeDoux & Phelps, 2000). Studies using brain imaging techniques show that the amygdala is active when people see photos of fearful faces. Humans with damage to the amygdala show altered perceptions of fear (Davidson, Jackson, & Kalin, 2000); they have difficulty identifying a photograph as expressing fear (but can recognize other emotions). One patient with damage to the amygdala has problems in recognizing but not in showing fear (Anderson & Phelps, 2000). This problem is not restricted to facial expressions; people with damage to the amygdala also have problems in recognizing vocal signs of fear.

People with psychological problems related to fear also show increased activity in the amygdala (Davidson et al., 2000). Brain imaging studies of people with anxiety disorders and phobias (unreasonable fears) show that these individuals' amygdalas react more strongly to their feared situations than the amygdalas of comparison participants.

Building Table 11.5

Physiological and Evolutionary Theories of Emotion

Theory	Theorist	The Role of Physiology	The Role of Cognition	The Role of the Situation
Physiological	James and Lange	Arousal precedes interpretation of events.	People interpret bodily arousal as emotion.	Not a factor
	Cannon and Bard	Physiological arousal and interpretation occur simultaneously.	Cognition supplies an interpretation, which occurs at the same time as arousal.	Not a factor
Evolutionary	LeDoux	Physiological changes occur in the amygdala and subcortical structures first.	Subjective interpretation is mediated by a different, slower pathway to the brain.	Can affect the emotion through access to memories and interpretation
	Cosmides and Tooby	The brain contains a series of specialized programs for basic emotions.	Cognition follows the reactions of the brain and body.	Brings forth the appropriate programs

(1996; LeDoux & Phelps, 2000). Through the process of natural selection, the human brain has evolved the ability to be very sensitive to fear-inducing situations and to respond rapidly to avoid such situations (see Building Table 11.5). Indeed, the situations that elicit such an alert do not have to produce fear—any new or unusual stimulus should provoke a response orienting the animal to this new element. The new element could be trouble, or alternatively, it could be food (Cacioppo & Gardner, 1999).

Fear of heights, snakes, or insects has an evolutionary basis; encountering any of these situations can be dangerous, and built-in responses to these stimuli can be adaptive. Of course, the modern world is drastically different from that of our ancestors, and such fears today may be unreasonable phobias—tall buildings are typically safe, and people see snakes more often in zoos or as pets than in the street. Thus, some of our programs from prehistory are not nearly as adaptive in the modern world as they were in the past. Indeed, this discrepancy may be one source of discontent with modern life (Buss, 2000). Our evolutionary history has prepared us to perceive fear and to be competitive, and enacting these tendencies can produce major problems. Evolutionary psychology also explains that humans have the capacity to experience a range of positive emotions (Buss, 2000). Humans lived in groups during prehistory, and their history of living in small groups and forming close, mating relationships gives humans the evolutionary predisposition to form close personal relationships and to derive great satisfaction from them. That is, evolutionary psychology sees love and friendship as part of our evolved history. Indeed, these close relationships should be the basis for many people's most satisfying experiences, and studies of happiness confirm this view (Myers, 2000).

Evolutionary psychologists have been interested in identifying "basic" emotions and determining if these emotions are evident among all humans, and even all primates. Facial expressions have provided a means to this goal. Facial expressions are easily observed and interpreted by others. Paul Ekman and his colleagues (1992; Keltner & Ekman, 2000) conducted cross-cultural studies of the perception of emotion, finding a great deal of consistency among cultures in people's ability to interpret facial expressions. In addition, people are extremely good at detecting changes in facial expressions (Edwards, 1998; Farah et al., 1998). But the claims

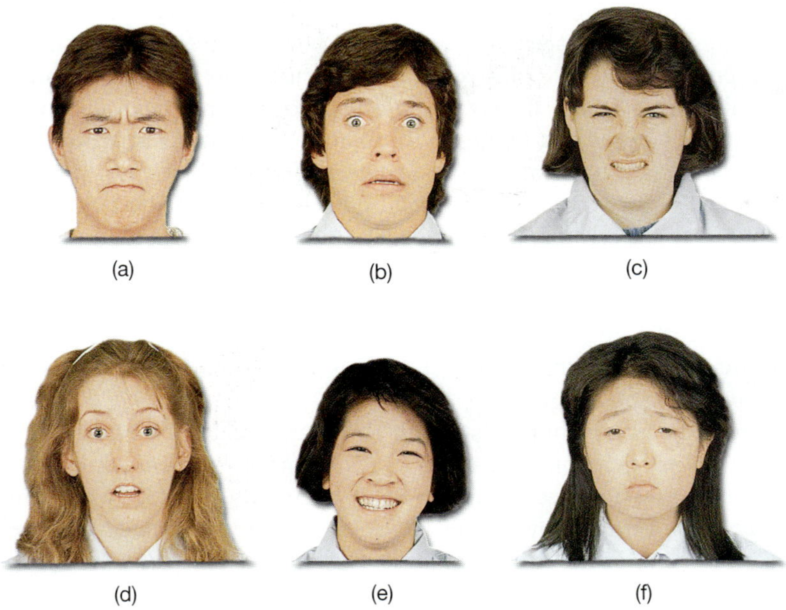

FIGURE 11.7

For the Active Learner: Recognizing and Naming Emotions

Look carefully at the six photographs. Which of the following six emotions is portrayed in each photo?

1. Happiness
2. Sadness
3. Fear
4. Anger
5. Surprise
6. Disgust

Answers:
(a) 4; (b) 3; (c) 6; (d) 5; (e) 1; (f) 2

for universality of facial expressions are the target of criticism (Russell, 1994), and in addition, facial expressions do not always reflect people's feelings. People can "put on a happy face" to mask sadness. In addition, some cultural variations exist in both the interpretation of expressions and the situations that elicit them (Keltner & Ekman, 2000). For example, laughter is common at funerals in some cultures but very unusual in others, and individuals from Southeast Asia show a wider variety of facial expressions to reflect embarrassment than do people in the United States. For a demonstration that emotions are both easy and difficult to read, see Figure 11.7.

Cognitive Theories of Emotion

Fear, sadness, rage, and excitement all have readily recognizable emotional and physiological manifestations, but these emotions also are accompanied by thoughts and feelings. And what about more complex emotions? Consider, for example, pride, embarrassment, or guilt. All of these require a far more subtle and complex analysis—one that focuses on thought (Lewis, 1995). Cognitive theories of emotion focus on mental interpretation as well as physiology.

■ **THE SCHACHTER–SINGER APPROACH.** The Schachter–Singer view of emotion is a cognitive approach that focuses on emotional activation and incorporates elements of both the James–Lange and the Cannon–Bard theories. Stanley Schachter and Jerome Singer observed that people do indeed interpret their emotions, but not solely from bodily changes. They argued that people interpret physical sensations within a specific context. They knew that bodily states, including chemically induced states brought on by alcohol or other drugs, can change moods. But observers cannot interpret what a person's emotional behavior means unless they know the situation in which it occurs. If a man cries at a funeral, observers suspect he is sad; if he cries at his daughter's wedding, they suspect he is joyful. Thus, according to the Schachter–Singer view, an emotion is created by cognitive factors as a person tries to account for a state of perceived activation (Lang, 1994).

To demonstrate their contention, Schachter and Singer (1962) designed a complex but clever experiment in which they manipulated participants' level of physiological arousal plus the emotional climate of their surroundings. To manipulate arousal, Schachter and Singer injected volunteers with epinephrine (adrenaline), a powerful stimulant that increases physiological arousal in areas such as heart rate, blood pressure, and even sensations of butterflies in the stomach. These participants were compared to a group who received a saline injection, which has no physiological effects. To see if they could affect how participants interpreted their aroused state, Schachter and Singer manipulated the settings in which the volunteers experienced their arousal. The researchers hired confederates, undergraduate students trained to act either happy or angry. The hired confederates pretended that they were volunteers in the drug study, but they were actually behaving according to a script; their emotional behavior was strictly an act. The "happy" confederates had a great time in the experiment; they shot wads of paper into a wastebasket and flew paper airplanes around the room. The "angry" ones complained about the questionnaire they had to fill out and voiced their dissatisfaction with the experiment.

Schachter and Singer found that both their manipulations were successful. All the experimental participants who received epinephrine injections showed increased physiological arousal when compared to the participants who received saline. Those who interacted with the happy stooges reported that the drug made them feel good; those who interacted with the angry ones reported feeling anger. Schachter and Singer reasoned that when people have no label for the cause of their physiological arousal (especially when arousal levels are low), they will label their feelings in terms of the thoughts available to them—in this case, thoughts stimulated by their interactions with the confederates.

Schachter and Singer had the kernel of an important idea: arousal does intensify emotions. However, it does not work alone. People don't live in an experiential vacuum. For example, when people first smoke marijuana or take other psychoactive drugs, they tend to approach the experience with definite expectations. If told the drug produces feelings of hunger, new users report feeling hungry; if told the drug is a downer, new users often interpret their bodily sensations as depressed. In Schachter and Singer's view, people experience internal arousal, become aware of the arousal, seek an explanation for it, identify an external cue, and then label the arousal. In an important way, arousal provides the fuel—the energy—for the physiological reaction, but the labeling determines the feeling.

These findings have been the target of criticism of several types, including both relying too much and too little on physiological arousal to explain emotion. That is, some critics believe that thoughts alone are sufficient to produce emotion (Reisenzein, 1983). And the physiological theorists argue that brain arousal or excitation of the autonomic nervous system is the controlling factor in the experience of emotion.

■ **THE LAZARUS APPROACH.** Richard Lazarus (1991) formulated a theory of emotion that also relies heavily on cognition. Like Schachter and Singer, Lazarus considered both physiology and cognition important in emotion, and he also believes that the situation is critical in people's experience of emotion. Lazarus argues that cognition affects emotion through people's appraisal of the situation and its impact on them. **Appraisal** is the evaluation of the significance of a situation or event for a person's well-being. Thus, people's evaluation of a situation in personal terms is important for emotion. For example, a hiker will not always appraise the sighting of a bear as threatening. I [LB] once saw two bears while hiking, but they were babies that were running away from the group of hikers, so I felt no fear (although I did give some thought to the location of their mother, and I was watchful for a while). Lazarus's cognitive theory of emotion is controversial, but his insistence on the importance of thoughts and personal appraisal in the experience of emotion fits well with the varieties of emotional experience that occur. Building Table 11.6 allows you to contrast the key elements of physiological, evolutionary, and cognitive theories of emotion.

Appraisal
The evaluation of the significance of a situation or event as it relates to a person's well-being.

Building Table 11.6

Physiological, Evolutionary, and Cognitive Theories of Emotion

Theory	Theorist	The Role of Physiology	The Role of Cognition	The Role of the Situation
Physiological	James and Lange	Arousal precedes interpretation of events.	People interpret bodily arousal as emotion.	Not a factor
	Cannon and Bard	Physiological arousal and interpretation occur simultaneously.	Cognition supplies an interpretation, which occurs at the same time as arousal.	Not a factor
Evolutionary	LeDoux	Physiological changes occur in the amygdala and subcortical structures first.	Subjective interpretation is mediated by a different, slower pathway to the brain.	Can affect the emotion through access to memories and interpretation
	Cosmides and Tooby	The brain contains a series of specialized programs for basic emotions.	Cognition follows the reactions of the brain and body.	Brings forth the appropriate programs
Cognitive	Schachter and Singer	Physiological arousal requires a cognitive interpretation before it is experienced as emotion.	Cognitive labels determine the experience of emotion.	Key determinant of emotion because situation affects how people interpret their experience
	Lazarus	Physiological reaction is less important than cognition.	Cognition affects emotion through appraisal of the situation.	Must be appraised before people experience emotion

Varieties of Emotional Experience

Over the years, researchers have tried to identify the "basic" emotional expressions of feeling. One noted researcher (Izard, 1997) isolated ten such basic emotions (joy, interest, surprise, sadness, anger, disgust, contempt, fear, shame, and guilt). But such cataloguing is difficult because of the enormous variations in emotional expression. Research can be seen as finding basic emotions in the kinds of emotions people experience, but other factors vary, including intensity, quality, and situation. Emotional responses are also molded by strong cultural expectations. Fear, for example, can be praised or punished, depending on the culture, and children may learn to hide some emotions. One person's sense of joy may differ from another's, and the ways of expressing joy differ from individual to individual and from culture to culture.

The experience of emotion is private and personal, but the expression of emotion is observable behavior. Thus, people may experience similar emotions but behave differently. *Display rules* are the rules that govern the display of emotion, and these rules vary according to age, culture, and gender, creating wide differences in emotional expression. For example, in the United States we consider temper tantrums unacceptable behavior, but these displays are more expected and accepted for 3-year-olds than for 30-year-olds. A 3-year-old throwing a tantrum in a restaurant will probably receive attention (possibly positive or negative) from the parents, but a 30-year-old behaving similarly may receive attention (almost certainly negative) from the police.

■ **CULTURE AND EMOTION.** Most emotions are expressed in most cultures, indicating some type of commonality across cultures. But the expressions vary in degree and especially in the circumstances under which they occur, indicating some variation. Thus, emotions show both consistency and variation among cultures. Questions about cultural variation in emotion are important to those theorists who argue that emotions are universal and biologically based. Research indicates that even for "basic" emotions such as disgust, fear, and happiness, some cultural and individual variation exists (Keltner & Ekman, 2000; Scherer, 1997; Scherer, Walbott, & Summerfield, 1986). Individuals from different cultures vary in how they interpret the underlying meaning of facial expressions and how intense people judge the underlying emotion. In addition, different cultures allow the display of very different emotions in very similar situations. For example, Japanese children are taught to smile when an elder scolds or corrects them (they should be grateful for this useful information). Children in the United States are not taught to frown and pout, but they learn that these responses are expected and accepted when they are scolded.

Culture is not specific to national boundaries, and culture can vary within a country, for example, between different ethnic groups living in the same country. Culture can also be shared across countries, and one survey (Scherer, 1997) found that the greatest differences among cultures came from people's evaluations of the situations and events that provoke emotion. This survey revealed differences among geopolitical regions but similarities within these regions. For example, people in Latin America had opinions about morality, fairness, and justice that varied from those of people in Africa, and both differed from those in western Europe. These differences in judgments of such events might produce substantial differences in the emotions and reactions that people experience. For example, if a person believes that an action is unfair, then the person would be justified in feeling angry, whereas if someone from another region evaluated the same situation, he or she could interpret the situation and emotion quite differently, with implications for international travelers, politicians, and diplomats.

One of the most frequently assessed variables in cross-cultural research is the distinction between individualist and collectivist cultures. Individualist cultures stress the individual, whereas collectivist cultures stress how the individual fits within a group and within the entire society. People living within these different cultures show some variations in emotionality (Mesquita, 2001). Contrasting people from collectivist cultures in Surinam and Turkey with those from the individualist culture of Holland showed that people from collectivist cultures were more likely than those from the individualist culture to see emotion as reflecting reality rather than their own individual experience. In addition, the collectivist cultures tended to foster the attitude that emotion resides in the interaction between people rather than within the person.

Emotions are also differently valued by collectivist and individualist cultures. In a study of people in 61 countries (Suh et al., 1998), the relationship between positive emotions and life satisfaction was stronger in individualist than in collectivist cultures. In collectivist cultures, life satisfaction was more closely related to achieving the culture's norm for happiness. This result suggests that people in individualist cultures use their own emotions as the standard to judge their happiness, whereas people in collectivist cultures use social standards to make that judgment. People in individualist cultures are not necessarily more satisfied with life or happier than those in collectivist cultures, but the life situations and feelings that relate to happiness varies for these two cultural patterns (Diener, 2000). For example, self-esteem and self-respect are more strongly related to happiness in individualistic than in collectivist cultures. One factor that does not vary with happiness is gender (Myers, 2000), but women and men show other differences in emotion.

GENDER AND EMOTION. In this society, it is widely believed that women are more emotional than men, but that assumption requires that people concentrate on some emotions and overlook others. People are thinking of sympathy, fear, and sadness when they associate women with emotion, but they are overlooking anger when they consider men unemotional (Plant et al., 2000). These beliefs about men and women are widely accepted. However, research shows that the degree to which these stereotypes reflect reality may be due to the power of the stereotypes to shape that reality. People who do not conform to generally held beliefs might be punished through social rejection, and people who do conform are rewarded for such behaviors. People have a tendency to notice and recall examples that conform to their stereotypes and to ignore and forget examples that do not. This tendency helps to shape and perpetuate these gender stereotypes of emotionality. In addition, people interpret situations that are not clear in stereotypical terms. All these tendencies perpetuate gender stereotypes of emotion and limit both men's and women's full expression of their emotionality.

Consider, for example, the gender stereotype that men experience more anger than women. This stereotype is largely inaccurate because it focuses on the behavioral expression of anger through aggression but ignores the experience of anger and anger expressed in other ways. Research on the experience of anger indicates that few gender differences exist in feelings of anger (Larson & Pleck, 1999). Considering other expressions of anger, women often verbalize more intense anger and for longer periods of time than do men—especially women who are in close heterosexual relationships. Men in a similar situation more frequently "stonewall" by inhibiting facial expressions and minimizing listening behaviors as well as eye contact (Gottman, 1998). Yet the physiological reactions of men and women in these situations are much more similar than their behaviors indicate. Even in less personally involving situations, such as viewing an emotion-arousing movie, the physiological reactions of women and men are similar (Kring & Gordon, 1998). Thus, the experience and feelings of anger are probably very similar for men and women.

Even when their experience of emotion is similar, men and women differ in their expression of emotions (Kring & Gordon, 1998). A great deal of this difference is due to display rules. Gender stereotypes of emotionality hold that women are more emotional, giving them the freedom to express a wider variety of emotions than men can. However, women are restricted in their expression of anger, so even though they feel anger as frequently and as intensely as men, they display their anger verbally or indirectly rather than in direct, physical confrontations. Men are similarly restricted in their expressions of sadness, fear, affection, and most emotions except anger. Women and men learn to conform to the display rules deemed appropriate to their gender, and this learning suggests that people can learn to control their emotions. But if one component of emotion comes from brain and nervous system arousal, how can emotions be controlled?

CAN WE CONTROL EMOTIONS? Whether or not we can control our emotions depends on which of the three components of emotion we mean—physiology, feelings, or behaviors. If we are concentrating on the physiological component of emotion, then control is quite difficult. The changes that occur in brain structures and the resulting activity of the peripheral nervous system and changes to hormone levels happen automatically and largely outside the level of conscious thought. Controlling these physiological reactions is possible but difficult (see Chapter 6 and the discussion on biofeedback, p. 206). A controversial example of the difficulty of controlling emotional reactions is the use of those physiological responses to detect emotionality with polygraphs (see the *Psychology in Action* on the following page).

Changing feelings and behavior holds more promise in the management of emotion. If cognitions are an important component of emotional experience, then changes in how people think about a situation should produce alterations in the

student voices

Josh Levenson
University of Miami-Coral Gables

After learning about the ambassadors of psychology—ambassadors in the sense that each has blazed a new trail in the psychological field—like Maslow, Erikson, and Freud, it amazes me to see how each view can be applied to situations we all experience in life.

psychology *in action*

Lie Detectors and Emotion

Would you take a job if one of the conditions for employment was taking a polygraph examination whenever the employer asked? How would you feel if you were actually asked to take such an examination? How nervous would you be? Would you feel guilty, even if you hadn't done anything wrong? Thousands of employees are put into this position because some employers attempt to guard against employee dishonesty by administering "lie detector" tests. The accuracy of this type of testing is the subject of intense debate, but the basis for the procedure is the nervous system and its responses to emotional situations. Many physiological changes associated with emotion are caused by an increase in activity in the sympathetic branch of the autonomic nervous system. When the sympathetic nervous system is activated, many different responses take place almost simultaneously. For example, arousal of the sympathetic nervous system slows or halts digestion, increases blood pressure and heart rate, deepens breathing, dilates the pupils, decreases salivation, and tenses the muscles. Recognition that the autonomic nervous system provides direct, observable, measurable responses that can be quantified in a systematic manner led to the development of the *polygraph device*, commonly called the *lie detector*.

A polygraph test involves recording many physiological responses that indicate changes in the activity of the sympathetic branch of a person's autonomic nervous system. Most autonomic nervous system activity is involuntary, and lying is usually associated with an increase in autonomic activity. A trained polygraph operator compares a person's physiological responses while answering a series of relatively neutral questions to the person's responses while answering questions about the issue being explored. During neutral questioning (such as requesting the person's name or address), autonomic nervous system activity remains at what is considered the baseline level. During critical questioning (such as asking whether the person used a knife as a holdup weapon or took money from the cash register), however, a person with something to hide usually shows a dramatic increase in autonomic nervous system activity.

Polygraphs do not measure lying and are far from perfect in allowing operators to conclude who is telling the truth and who is not. Critics argue that even well-trained operators do not use polygraphs as standardized tests but as interrogation devices (Frater, 2000). In addition, critics claim that polygraphs are little better than flipping a coin in deciding about truth telling (Phillipps, 1999). However, the results may not be random, but worse—some people show little or no change in autonomic activity when they lie (Honts, 1994). Such people seem to able to lie without becoming emotionally aroused and thus can systematically "beat the machine." Equally important is the finding that some people who tell the truth may register changes in autonomic nervous system activity because of anxiety. If you believe that you would be so nervous by being hooked up to the machine that your testing would not be valid, you may be correct. Lie detectors are subject to significant errors in both directions.

The American Psychological Association has also expressed strong reservations about polygraph tests, asserting that their use may inflict psychological damage on innocent persons. A survey of members of APA and the Society for Psychophysiological Research reflected doubts about the theoretical basis and the validity of polygraph use as well as the belief that polygraphs can be fooled easily (Iacono & Lykken, 1997). Thus, these professionals advocate against the use of polygraphs in court cases.

Today, most states do not accept the results of lie detector tests as valid evidence in court, especially in criminal cases. A federal law restricts businesses from using the polygraph to test prospective employees. Ironically, several branches of the U.S. federal government use polygraphs to test their employees (Frater, 2000). Employees object and morale suffers, but the federal government, like many other employers, is anxious to know about drug use and theft, and unlike other employers, national security is an issue. If psychologist Paul Ekman (1996) is correct, these problems have no easy solution because lying is difficult to detect. He claims that our evolutionary heritage has left us poorly equipped to detect liars, but our current social structure has made this problem an urgent one.

emotions. Indeed, the notion that cognitions can change emotions is the basis for one type of psychotherapy, rational–emotive therapy (see Chapter 16, p. 593). When people learn to think about their problems and situations in different ways, they can change their feelings about their lives. This process is not easy, but it is possible. An easier approach involves changing the situations that provoke emotions, preventing the unwanted emotions from occurring (Gross, 1999). People can elect to avoid certain situations, modify some component of the situation, or attend to some other aspect of the situation. For example, if you had to work with someone whom you found annoying, you might try to avoid the person, change the way you interact, or attend to some positive aspect of the person's behavior. Any of these strategies could be successful in managing your emotions.

■ *Polygraph recordings measure the physiological responses that indicate changes in the activity of the sympathetic nervous system. They do not directly measure lying and are far from completely accurate in allowing operators to conclude who is telling the truth and who is not.*

Of the three components of emotion, changing the behaviors associated with emotion are the easiest. We can "put on a happy face," "turn the other cheek," or use our "poker face" rather than expressing our true feelings. We also have the option of behaving in some way that is different from our first impulse. When we are angry with someone, our first impulse may be to lash out, either verbally or physically, but people have been taught since childhood to control these behaviors. Some people have more trouble with this type of control than others. For example, Andrew Burnett, who threw Sara McBurnett's dog into oncoming traffic, has a history of legal problems associated with his "bad temper," including trying to kick out the window of a police car and taunting police officers who stopped him for speeding.

Although it may seem that some people cannot control their emotions, research indicates that their problems are not a matter of inability to exert control. Such behavior may be more attributable to immediate, personal priorities. Dianne Tice and her colleagues (2001) studied breakdowns of impulse control to attempt to understand the origin of these (often problem) behaviors. Rather than imagining that people with impulse control problems are self-destructive or poor at self-regulation, these researchers considered the possibility that people indulge themselves in some behaviors that may be unacceptable as a strategy to make themselves feel better in times of emotional distress. When people feel bad, they want to do something to feel better, which may include behaviors that are unwise, socially inappropriate, or even dangerous. In this study of impulse control, Tice and her colleagues found that people who feel bad are more likely to indulge in eating unhealthy snacks, to choose an immediate rather than a delayed gratification, and put off a tedious task than people who are in a better mood. Ethical restrictions kept the researchers from testing violence or other serious emotional reactions, but the results from this study imply that inappropriate and even dangerous emotional reactions are not beyond control. Rather, people make choices to behave in ways that they believe will make them feel better immediately (if you feel bad, do it). Thus, we can control our emotional reactions, but we do not always do so.

Be an *Active* learner

REVIEW

- Identify the fundamental ideas that distinguish the James-Lange from the Cannon-Bard view of emotion. How does the evolutionary view differ from other physiological theories of emotion? pp. 390–392
- What finding from Schachter and Singer's study prompted them to give cognitions such a prominent role in emotion? p. 394
- What findings from cross-cultural and gender research argue against universal experience of certain emotions? pp. 395–397

THINK CRITICALLY

- Do you think using lie detectors should be permitted in the public or private sector? Why or why not?
- How do domestic violence issues relate to gender differences in emotional expressiveness?

APPLY PSYCHOLOGY

- Design a program to help people control anger, targeting the components of physiology, feelings, and behavior.

Summary and Review

Theories of Motivation

Distinguish between a motivation and a need.

■ A *motivation* is any internal condition that can be inferred to initiate, activate, or maintain an organism's goal-directed behavior. Motivation is inferred from behavior and is caused by needs, drives, or desires. A *need* is a state of physiological imbalance that is usually accompanied by arousal. pp. 366–367

Differentiate among the various theories of motivation.

■ Evolutionary psychologists believe that humans have many instincts, innate behavior sequences, that motivate them. These motivations are the result of evolutionary history and have produced people motivated by forces that relate to survival and reproduction. p. 367

■ *Drive theory* is an explanation of behavior that assumes that an organism is motivated to act because of a need to attain, reestablish, or maintain some goal. A *drive* is an internal arousal condition related to a need. A drive explanation of behavior is said to be mechanistic, viewing the organism as being pushed and pulled, almost like a machine. The goal of many drives is *homeostasis*, the maintenance of a constant state of inner stability or balance. Goals can also cause *conflict. Approach–approach conflict* arises when a person must choose between two equally pleasant alternatives, such as two wonderful jobs. *Avoidance–avoidance conflict* occurs when a choice involves two equally distasteful alternatives, such as mowing the lawn or painting the garage. *Approach–avoidance conflict* results when an alternative has both attractive and undesirable aspects, such as eating a delicious but fattening dessert. pp. 367–368

■ According to *arousal theory,* individuals seek an optimal level of stimulation. The Yerkes–Dodson law asserts that behavior varies from disorganized to effective to optimal, depending on the person's level of *arousal.* Contemporary researchers have extended the idea by suggesting that when a person's level of arousal and anxiety is too high or too low, performance will be poor, especially on complex tasks. Performance peaks when arousal is at a moderate level. pp. 369–370

■ *Cognitive theory* is an explanation of behavior that emphasizes the role of thoughts and active decision making regarding life goals and the means of achieving them. *Expectancy theories* are cognitive theories of motivation that focus on people's expectations about reaching a goal and their need for achievement. A *motive* is typically an internal condition that directs an organism's behavior toward a goal, but a motive is not based on physiology. Needs are also learned, and a *social need* directs people to behave in ways that establish and maintain relationships. p. 371

■ *Intrinsic motivation* gives rise to behaviors that a person performs in order to obtain cognitive stimulation and a sense of competence and accomplishment. *Extrinsic motivation* is supplied by rewards that come from the external environment. The *overjustification effect* is the decrease in likelihood that an intrinsically motivated task will be performed once it has been extrinsically rewarded and then the reward is no longer given. pp. 371–373

■ *Humanistic theory* emphasizes that people are drawn toward *self-actualization,* fulfilling their full human potential. Theorists such as Maslow describe how motivation can be arranged in a hierarchy, ranging from physiological need to self-actualization. This theory focuses on human dignity, individual choice, and self-worth, but such concepts are difficult to verify experimentally. pp. 373–375

KEY TERMS

motivation, p. 366; drive theory, p. 367; drive, p. 367; need, p. 367; homeostasis, p. 367; conflict, p. 368; approach–approach conflict, p. 369; avoidance–avoidance conflict, p. 369; approach–avoidance conflict, p. 369; arousal, p. 369; cognitive theories, p. 370; expectancy theories, p. 370; motive, p. 370; social need, p. 370; extrinsic motivation, p. 372; intrinsic motivation, p. 372; overjustification effect, p. 372; humanistic theory, p. 373; self-actualization, p. 373

Hunger: A Physiological Need

What causes hunger?

■ People do not eat because their energy levels are low; they eat before energy deficits occur. The hormones insulin and leptin provide signals to the brain, including the hypothalamus, where a complex series of events signal hunger and satiation. pp. 375–376

■ Learning is also important for hunger and eating. The initiation of eating is affected by habit and learning, and food preferences are strongly influenced by cultural and individual factors. pp. 377–378

Why are people obese?

■ There is no clear, convincing answer to the question of whether nature or nurture is a more important determinant of obesity. Genetics plays a role, but a person's history with food and current weight also influence the likelihood of recurrence or development of obesity. pp. 378–380

Sexual Behavior: Physiology plus Thought

What are the roles of hormones and thought in human sexual behavior?

■ Sexual behavior in human beings is in part under

homonal control, and the hormones are different in men and women. In men, the androgens produced by the testes predominate, and in women, estrogens produced by the ovaries do. These sex hormones control prenatal development of the reproductive systems and prompt the development of sexual behavior and fertility during puberty. pp. 380–381

■ Thought plays an enormous role in the sexual behavior of human beings; thoughts, fantasies, and images can initiate and activate sexual desire and activity. p. 381

What are the phases in the sexual response cycle?

■ When human beings become sexually aroused, they go through a series of four phases, which together are known as the sexual response cycle: *excitement* (characterized by *vasocongestion*), *plateau, orgasm,* and *resolution.* p. 382

How have Americans' sex lives changed over the past 40 years?

■ The Laumann study, the most recent and comprehensive study of sexual behavior, has shown that the sex lives of Americans are predictable and not as active as many assume, but most Americans are satisfied with their sex lives. In contrast with the Kinsey reports, the Laumann study showed that men and women are more likely today than they were 40 years ago to have had intercourse before marriage and that there has been a slow and steady decrease in the age of first intercourse. Men think about sex more than women do, and married men and women have more sex than do unmarried people. pp. 383–384

■ A person with a heterosexual orientation has an erotic attraction and preference for members of the other sex; a person with a homosexual orientation has an erotic attraction and preference for members of the same sex. According to the Laumann study, only 2.8% of men and 1.4% of women identify themselves as exclusively homosexual in orientation. These figures are substantially lower than Kinsey reported in the 1950s. pp. 384–385

KEY TERMS

excitement phase, p. 382; vasocongestion, p. 382; plateau phase, p. 382; orgasm phase, p. 382; resolution phase, p. 382; survey, p. 383; representative sample, p. 383

Achievement: A Social Need

How does expectancy theory explain the need for achievement?

■ *Need for achievement* is a social need that directs a person to strive constantly for excellence and success. According to expectancy theories, people engage in behaviors that satisfy their desires for success, mastery, and fulfillment. Tests such as the TAT have been used to measure need for achievement. Achievement values vary among and within cultures, and personal *self-efficacy* is related to the need for achievement. pp. 386–388

KEY TERMS

need for achievement, p. 386; self-efficacy, p. 387

Emotion

What is an emotion, and what are the components of emotion?

■ An *emotion* is a subjective response (a feeling), usually accompanied by a physiological change, which is interpreted in a particular way by the individual and often leads to a change in behavior. Thus, the three components of an emotion are feelings, physiological responses, and behavior. These components usually function together but are separable. pp. 388–389

Identify the fundamental ideas that distinguish various theories of emotion.

■ Physiological theories of emotion include the James–Lange theory, the Cannon-Bard theory, and evolutionary theory. The James–Lange theory states that people experience physiological changes and then interpret those changes as emotions. The Cannon–Bard theory states that when people experience emotions, two areas of the brain are stimulated simultaneously, one creating an emotional response and the other creating physiological changes. Evolutionary theory, including LeDoux's view of the emotional brain, views emotion as preparing people to adapt to situations and to increase their survival and reproductive advantages. Facial expressions have been used as a way to assess universal emotional experience, which the evolutionary theory hypothesizes. pp. 389–391

■ According to cognitive theories of emotion, for example, the Schachter–Singer approach and Lazarus's approach, thoughts and an appraisal of the situation are an important, even a determining component of emotion. pp. 393–394

What factors relate to varieties of emotional experience?

■ Culture and display rules affect the expression of emotion.

■ Gender may not produce differences in the feelings or physiological reactions involved in emotion, but women and men are governed by different display rules that lead to different behavioral expression of emotion. p. 397

KEY TERMS

emotion, p. 388; appraisal, p. 394

12 Personality and Its Assessment

Margarett Sargent, *Beyond Good and Evil* (self-portrait), 1930

Harry Potter's first encounter with Severus Snape, the Potions Master at Hogwarts School of Witchcraft and Wizardry, left Harry with the impression that the Potions Master was an unpleasant man who disliked him. After the second meeting, Harry believed that *hated* would be a more accurate description of Snape's feelings, and Harry formed some negative opinions of Snape's personality, too. Subsequent encounters led Harry (and other students) to consider Snape suspicious, malicious, and vengeful. Snape seemed to enjoy belittling Harry and finding opportunities to make trouble for Harry and his friends. In her best-selling Harry Potter series, J. K. Rowling highlights the evil in Snape, making his motivation unclear but his character one-dimensional.

Such an emphasis on one dimension of a personality is consistent with the personality theory of Gordon Allport, who said that some people have a *cardinal trait* that is so dominant that a person's entire personality revolves around that one trait. According to Allport, most people do not have a cardinal trait, but those who do have personalities that are unmistakable. Indeed, people

chapter outline

■ *To Harry Potter and his friends, Professor Snape's personality was characterized by malice.*

with a cardinal trait often become associated with that trait. Harry Potter fans associate Snape with malice.

Of course, Snape's personality was created by J. K. Rowling, so it could be as one-dimensional as the story demanded. But what do real people have in common with such characters? What is necessary to understand the personalities of real people, and are those personalities subject to the extremes that appear in Severus Snape? To explore those questions, we turn to a definition of personality and an examination of theories and assessment of human personality.

What Is Personality?

Although personality psychologists may disagree on the meaning of the word *personality,* most agree that the term originated from the Latin *persona,* that is, the theatrical mask worn by Roman actors in Greek dramas. Despite the original meaning of the word, psychologists now speak of personality as something more than simply the role people play. **Personality** is a pattern of relatively permanent traits, dispositions, or characteristics that give some consistency to people's behavior. More specifically, personality includes traits or dispositions that lead you to behave at least somewhat consistently in different environmental situations. But the definition of personality must also allow for some inconsistency of behavior. For example, you may behave quite aggressively in one situation but rather submissively in another, depending on the presence of other people, the behavior of those people, and your own mood and motivation.

The traits, dispositions, or characteristics that make up your personality may be unique to you, common to your particular social group, or shared with all other people. Thus, you are identical to no other person, similar to others in your cultural group, and akin to all other people in some ways.

What causes people to have certain personality dimensions? Personality theorists differ in their answer to this question. Some, such as Freud, focus on unconscious conflicts that originated during childhood; others, such as Skinner, see human personality as largely learned from the environment. Yet others, such as Allport, emphasize the *pattern* of personal traits that characterize people; still others, such as Cattell and Eysenck, look for genetic influences that motivate behavior and shape personality. Another group of theorists, such as Rogers and Maslow, see humans as moving toward fulfillment or self-actualization, and finally, some personality theorists, such as Bandura, emphasize a variety of cognitive factors that influence personality development and functioning.

Personality
A pattern of relatively permanent traits, dispositions, or characteristics that give some consistency to people's behavior.

Like all theories, personality theories should generate research as well as organize, explain, and predict data. These data help psychologists answer questions such as these:

- Does nature or nurture play a greater role in personality development?
- Do unconscious processes direct behavior?

- What accounts for the development of stable behavior patterns in humans?
- Does a person's behavior depend on the situation?
- Do people behave consistently throughout their lives?

Psychodynamic Theories

We begin our discussion of personality theories by examining psychodynamic theory—an approach to personality that focuses on how unconscious processes direct day-to-day behavior. The most famous and perhaps the most widely disputed of these approaches is the psychoanalytic theory of Sigmund Freud. We follow Freud's theory with a discussion of two other psychodynamic theories, namely, the individual psychology of Alfred Adler and the analytical psychology of Carl Jung.

The Psychoanalytic Theory of Sigmund Freud

Sigmund Freud developed psychoanalytic theory.

Sigmund Freud (1856–1939) was an Austrian physician whose influence on psychology was so great that some of his basic concepts are now taken for granted. Such terms as *ego*, *oral fixation*, *death wish*, *anal retentive*, *Freudian slip*, *unconscious motivation*, and *Oedipus complex* are part of everyday language. However, when Freud introduced his ideas, he was seen as strange and radical. Freud's exploration of the unconscious and his suggestion that children have sexual experiences were, to say the least, revolutionary ideas.

Freud developed his theory by treating people with mental problems. Freud used hypnosis and later a process known as *free association* to treat people with physical and emotional problems. (We will discuss free association in Chapter 16.) Most of his patients were from the middle and upper classes of Austrian society. Many were married women of wealth and position who, because they lived in a repressive society, had limited opportunities for the release of anxiety and tension. Freud noticed that many of them needed to discuss their problems and often felt better after having done so. From his therapeutic work with these patients, Freud began to formulate a theory of behavior that centered on early childhood experiences and fantasies. Originally, Freud believed that the neurotic symptoms of his adult patients sprang from their experiences of being sexually seduced by an older person, often a parent. However, he soon abandoned this seduction theory and replaced it with the *Oedipus complex*, a concept that places responsibility for childhood sexual experiences on fantasies of the child rather than the behavior of the parent. Over time, Freud developed an elaborate theory of personality and an accompanying approach to therapy called *psychoanalysis*.

Psychoanalytic theory rests on several key assumptions:

1. Human experience takes place on three *levels of consciousness*—conscious, preconscious, and unconscious, with the unconscious dominating the other two.
2. Human functioning is influenced by three basic *structures of the mind*—id, ego, and superego.
3. The foundation of personality is shaped mostly by *early childhood experiences*.
4. Parental punishment of a child's *sexual and aggressive* behaviors results in repression of at least part of these experiences and leads to psychological conflict.

5. Unconscious psychological conflict creates anxiety, and all people learn to protect themselves against anxiety by adopting a variety of *defense mechanisms*.

LEVELS OF MENTAL LIFE. Freud assumed that mental life can take place on three levels: conscious, preconscious, and unconscious. **Consciousness** occupies a relatively minor place in psychoanalytic theory. It simply refers to those experiences that we are aware of at any given time. It is the only level of mental life directly available to us. The **preconscious** is that level of the mind that contains those experiences that are not currently conscious but may become so with varying degrees of difficulty. You can probably become aware of your social security number very easily, but you may have much difficulty recalling some date in history that you learned four years ago. Both the social security number and the history date are in your preconscious, but one is easily recalled whereas the other is quite difficult or perhaps impossible to remember.

The **unconscious** contains experiences that, by definition, are beyond the realm of awareness. They are not like the history date, which is simply forgotten; they must remain unconscious to prevent us from experiencing too much anxiety. However, unconscious urges can become preconscious, or even conscious, by adopting a disguise that prevents us from recognizing their true nature. For example, thoughts about harming a despised rival may be too anxiety provoking, so we disguise these thoughts by behaving in an overly friendly manner toward that person. This façade may slip, and we may say or do something that reflects our true feelings of hostility. These *Freudian slips* reveal our true but unconscious thoughts.

Consciousness
Freud's level of mental life that consists of those experiences that we are aware of at any given time.

Preconscious
Freud's level of the mind that contains those experiences that are not currently conscious but may become so with varying degrees of difficulty.

Unconscious
Freud's level of mental life that consists of mental activities beyond people's normal awareness.

Id
In Freud's theory, the source of a person's instinctual energy, which works mainly on the pleasure principle.

Ego
In Freud's theory, the part of personality that seeks to satisfy instinctual needs in accordance with reality.

THE STRUCTURE OF THE MIND. According to Freud's theory, the primary structural elements of the mind and personality are three mental forces (not physical structures of the brain) that reside, fully or partially, in the unconscious: the id, the ego, and the superego. Each force accounts for a different aspect of functioning (see Table 12.1).

The **id** is the source of a person's instinctual energy, which, according to Freud (1933/1964), is either sexual or aggressive. The id works mainly by the *pleasure principle*; that is, it tries to maximize immediate gratification through the satisfaction of raw impulses. Residing deep within the unconscious, the demanding, irrational, and selfish id seeks pleasure—without regard for reality or morality.

While the id seeks to maximize pleasure and obtain immediate gratification, the **ego** (which grows out of the id) is the part of the personality that seeks to satisfy the

TABLE 12.1

Comparison of Freud's Three Systems of Personality

	Id	Ego	Superego
Nature	Represents biological aspect	Represents psychological aspect	Represents societal and parental aspect
Level	Unconscious	Conscious, preconscious, and unconscious	Conscious, preconscious, and unconscious
Principle	Pleasure	Reality	Moralistic and idealistic
Purpose	Seek pleasure and avoid pain	Adapt to reality while controlling the id and superego	Represent right and wrong
Aim	Immediate gratification	Safety, compromise, and delayed gratification	Perfection

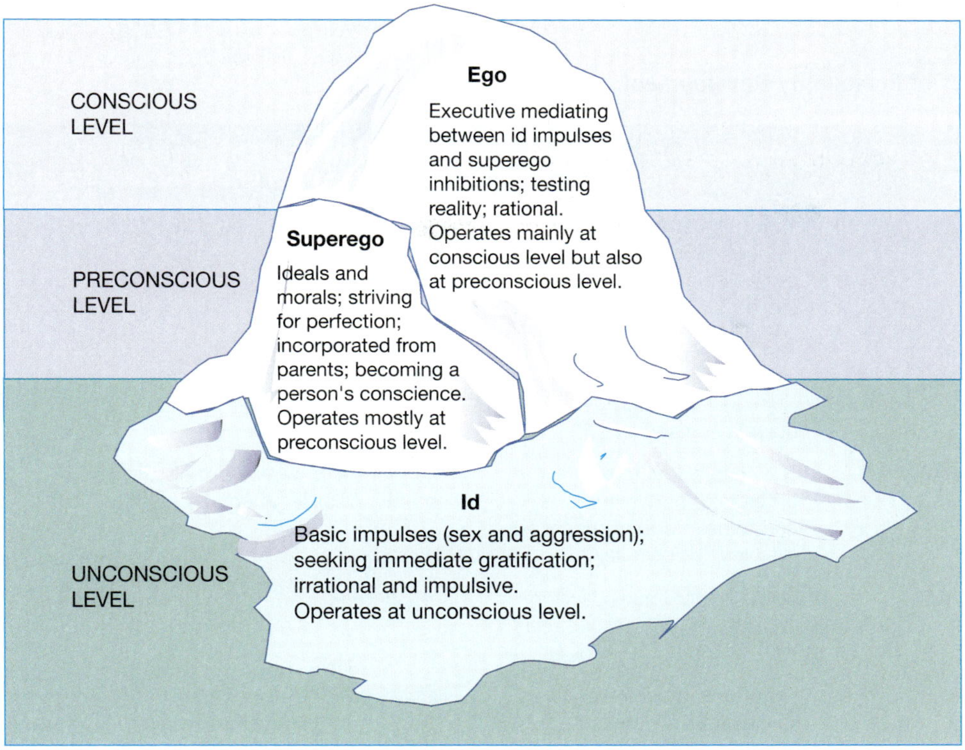

FIGURE 12.1

Freud's View of Mental Forces

Freud viewed consciousness as having three levels: the conscious, the preconscious, and the unconscious. Freud theorized that just as the greater part of an iceberg is hidden beneath the surface of the sea, most of the contents of the mind are below the level of conscious awareness. The *ego* is mainly a conscious and preconscious mental force. The *superego* operates mostly as a preconscious mental force. The *id* operates solely at an unconscious level.

individual's instinctual needs in accordance with reality; that is, it works by the *reality principle*. Whereas the id strives to achieve immediate gratification, the ego attempts to check the power of the id and delay gratification. The ego acts as a manager, adjusting cognitive and perceptual processes to balance the person's functioning, to control the id, and to keep the person in touch with reality. For example, a 4-year-old boy who is in a grocery store sees candy; his id says, "Take the candy." However, his ego may recognize that he is likely to be caught and punished. His decision to leave the candy alone is NOT based on morality but on reality. Reality says, "If I take the candy, I will be caught and punished."

As children grow older, their **superego** develops and provides them with both an *ego ideal* and a *conscience*. A developed superego would provide a somewhat older child in the grocery store two additional reasons for not taking the candy. First, stealing candy is not consistent with the ego ideal, and second, the child's conscience does not permit stealing. The child's id may say, "Take the candy. It tastes good," and the ego may say, "I won't get caught. No one is looking," but the ego ideal says, "I'm not a person who steals candy" and the conscience says, "I would feel guilty if I took something that did not belong to me." The ego and superego thus attempt to moderate the demands of the id and direct it toward appropriate ways of behaving.

The superego in Freud's theory has something in common with the id—neither is in touch with reality. In other ways, however, they are direct opposites. The id seeks instant pleasure without regard for what is wise or possible, while the superego tells a person not to do anything that would be pleasurable. (See Figure 12.1 for an illustration of Freud's levels of consciousness and structure of the mind.)

Superego [sue-pur-EE-go]
In Freud's theory, the moral aspect of mental functioning, comprising the ego ideal (what a person would ideally like to be) and the conscience and taught by parents and society.

■ **DEVELOPMENT OF PERSONALITY.** Freud strongly believed that if people looked at their past, they could gain insight into their current behavior. This belief led him to create an elaborate psychosexual stage theory of personality development. Freud believed that the core aspects of personality are established early, remain relatively stable throughout life, and are changed only with great difficulty. He argued that all people pass through five critical stages of personality development:

TABLE 12.2

Freud's Five Psychosexual Stages of Personality Development

Stage	Erogenous Zone	Conflicts/Experiences	Adult Traits (Especially Fixations) Associated with Problems at a Stage
Oral (birth to 2 years)	Mouth	Infant achieves gratification through oral activities, such as feeding, thumb sucking, cooing.	Optimism, gullibility, passivity, hostility, substance abuse
Anal (2 to 3 years)	Anus	The child learns to respond to some parental demands (such as for bladder and bowel control).	Excessive cleanliness, orderliness, messiness, rebelliousness
Phallic (4 to 7 years)	Genitals	The child learns to realize the differences between males and females and experiences the Oedipus complex.	Flirtatiousness, vanity, promiscuity, chastity, disorder in gender identity
Latency (7 to puberty)	None	The child continues developing but sexual urges are relatively quiet.	Not specified
Genital (puberty onward)	Genitals	The growing adolescent shakes off old dependencies and learns to deal maturely with the other sex.	Not specified

oral, anal, phallic, latency, and genital (see Table 12.2). At each of these stages, Freud (1933/1964) asserted, people experience conflicts and issues associated with *erogenous zones*—areas of the body that give rise to erotic or sexual sensations when they are stimulated.

Freud believed that these stages began at birth and that babies experienced sexual feelings and impulses. His concept of infantile sexuality was quite controversial when he first began writing about the sexual life of young children. However, Freud had an expanded view of sexuality. To him, sexual pleasure was not limited to the genital areas of the body but included the mouth, anus, and other erogenous zones.

The concept of the **oral stage** is based on the fact that the instincts of infants (from birth to about age 2) are focused on the mouth as the primary pleasure center. Infants receive oral gratification through feeding, thumb sucking, and cooing during the early months of life, when their basic feelings about the world are being established. Relying heavily on symbolism, Freud contended that adults who consider the world a bitter place (referring to the mouth and taste senses) probably had difficulty during the oral stage of development and may have traits associated with passivity and hostility. Their problems tend to focus on their need for nurturing, warmth, and love.

Oral stage
Freud's first stage of personality development, from birth to about age 2, during which the instincts of infants are focused on the mouth as the primary pleasure center.

Anal stage
Freud's second stage of personality development, from about age 2 to about age 3, during which children learn to control the immediate gratification they obtain through defecation and to become responsive to the demands of society.

Adults who continue to remain attached to the oral stage or who revert to this stage during times of intense anxiety will display the traits of an "oral" personality. They may take pleasure in biting objects (or making biting comments); smoking cigarettes, cigars, or pipes; overeating; or using the mouth for sexual pleasure.

The **anal stage** is Freud's second stage of personality development, from age 2 to about age 3, during which children learn to control the immediate gratification they obtain through defecation and to become responsive to the demands of society. At about age 2 or 3, children learn to respond to some of parents' and society's demands. One parental demand is that children control their bodily functions of urination and defecation and become toilet trained. Most 2- and 3-year-olds experience pleasure in moving their bowels. This stage therefore establishes the basis for conflict between the id and the ego—between the desire for immediate gratification of physical urges and the demand for controlled behavior. Freud claimed that during the anal stage, children may develop certain lasting personality characteristics related to control. Children who are able to rebel against the parents' demands for cleanliness and control may develop the anal expulsion personality and become exceedingly sloppy, messy, and rebellious. On the other hand, children who do not successfully rebel against parents' attempts to toilet train them may acquire an anal retentive personality pattern characterized by compulsive needs for orderliness, miserliness, and stubbornness. Thus, adults who had difficulty in the anal stage tend to have problems that focus on orderliness (or lack of it) and also might be compulsive in many behaviors.

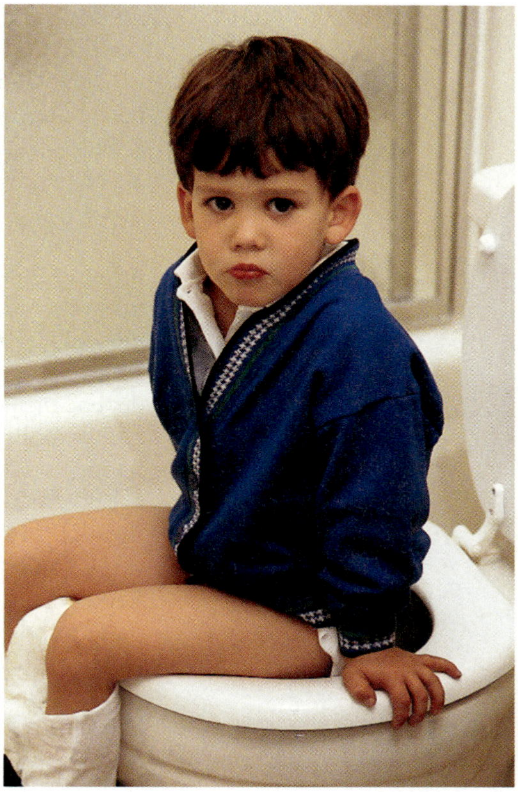

■ *Toilet training often presents a conflict between parents and the child.*

The **phallic stage** is Freud's third stage of personality development, from about age 4 through 7, during which children obtain gratification primarily from the genitals. At about age 4 or 5, children become aware of their genitals and the pleasure that comes from them. During the phallic stage, children pass through what Freud termed the **Oedipus complex.** According to Freud, this complex is a group (or complex) of unconscious wishes to have sexual intercourse with one parent and to kill or "remove" the other parent. Freud derived the term *Oedipus complex* from the story of Oedipus as told by the Greek playwright Sophocles. Oedipus unknowingly killed his father and married his mother.

The male Oedipus complex usually involves feelings of rivalry toward the father and sexual love for the mother. The boy develops feelings of hostility toward his father and believes that his attraction to his mother makes his father jealous. This rivalry produces *castration anxiety*, the fear that his father will remove the boy's penis as a punishment. This castration anxiety resolves the Oedipus complex. Freud argued that the Oedipus complex follows a slightly different course for girls than it does for boys. The female Oedipus complex typically involves hostile feelings for the mother and sexual love for the father. Freud held that when a girl realizes that she has no penis, she develops what he called *penis envy* and the desire to acquire a penis. Freud suggested that the little girl could symbolically acquire a penis by forming a relationship with her father. A young girl might ask her father to marry her so that they can raise a family together. Thus, the action of children during the Oedipus complex produces uneasiness within the family and causes anxiety for the children.

For both genders, the Oedipus complex is resolved through identification with the parent of the same sex and the acquisition of a developing superego, one based on the child's perception of the same-sex parent's morals and ideals. When the Oedipus complex is properly resolved, children will accept the authority of the same-sex parent and surrender the sexual nature of their love for the other-sex parent. In this way, a young boy begins to model his behavior after that of his father, and the young girl takes her mother as a role model. For both boys and girls, the critical component in resolving the Oedipus complex is the development of identification with the parent of the same sex. Adult traits associated with problems at this stage usually involve sexuality and may include vanity, promiscuity, or excessive worry about chastity.

Phallic [FAL-ick] stage
Freud's third stage of personality development, from about age 4 through age 7, during which children obtain gratification primarily from the genitals.

Oedipus [ED-i-pus] complex
Feelings of rivalry with the parent of the same sex and sexual desire for the parent of the other sex, occurring during the phallic stage and ultimately resolved through identification with the parent of the same sex.

Whether the Oedipus complex explains behavior is controversial and widely debated, especially because many people find the idea insulting to women. There is no doubt about Freud's view of women; he saw them as morally weaker and inferior to men. Most researchers now believe that Freud's notion of penis envy was imaginative but unconvincing, overdrawn, and lacking credibility (Breger, 2000; Webster,

1995). Is it a good explanation of the dynamics of 4- and 5-year-olds with their parents? Again, most researchers think not.

The **latency stage** follows the phallic stage and lasts from about age 7 until puberty. During this period, children develop physically, but sexual urges are inactive (latent). Much of children's energy is channeled into social or intellectual activities. Some psychoanalysts believe that this stage has nearly disappeared from the development of American children because of their rapid maturation into adolescence.

Freud's last stage of personality development, the **genital stage,** begins at the onset of puberty and continues through adolescence into adulthood. When individuals reach this stage, sexuality re-emerges, along with the fears and repressed feelings of earlier stages. Repressed sexual feelings toward one's parents may also resurface at puberty. Over the course of the genital stage, the adolescent shakes off dependence on parents and learns to deal with members of the other sex in socially and sexually mature ways. Members of the other sex, who were ignored during the latency stage, are now seen as attractive. Many unresolved conflicts and repressed urges affect behavior during this stage. Ideally, if people have passed successfully through previous stages of development, they will develop heterosexual relationships. If not, they may continue to have unresolved conflicts within their unconscious throughout their adult life.

As children proceed from one developmental stage to the next, they adjust their views of the world. Successfully passing through a stage requires resolution of that stage's principal conflict. Freud likened the process to military troops moving from battle to battle—a failure to successfully resolve one conflict weakens an army at its next.

■ **SEX AND AGGRESSION: THE TWO GREAT DRIVES.** Freud also theorized that people are energized to act the way they do because of two basic instinctual drives: the drive toward *life*, which is expressed through sex and sexual energy, and the drive toward *death*, which is expressed through aggression. These instincts are buried deep within the unconscious, and their expression is not always socially acceptable. Freud wrote little about aggression until late in his life; he focused mainly on energy from the sexual instinct, which he termed the **libido**—the instinctual (and sexual) life force that, working on the pleasure principle and seeking immediate gratification, energizes the id.

When people exhibit socially unacceptable behaviors or have feelings they consider socially unacceptable, especially sexual feelings, they often experience self-punishment, guilt, and anxiety—all forms of inner conflict. Freud's theory thus describes a conflict between a person's instinctual (often unconscious) need for gratification and society's demand that each individual be socialized. In other words, it paints a picture of human beings caught in a conflict between basic sexual and aggressive desires and socialization. Personality functions as a delicate balancing act, with sexual and aggressive desires weighed against the demands of society, and the person attempting to satisfy both.

■ **DEFENSE MECHANISMS.** To defend itself against the anxiety brought about by sexual and aggressive drives, the ego adopts one or more **defense mechanisms.** Freud made several key assumptions about defense mechanisms:

1. They are normal and universal reactions.
2. When carried to extremes, they may lead to compulsive, unhealthy behaviors.
3. They operate on an unconscious level.
4. They protect the ego against anxiety.
5. They are helpful to the individual and generally harmless to society.
6. They all have some elements of repression.

Latency [LAY-ten-see] stage Freud's fourth stage of personality development, from about age 7 until puberty, during which sexual urges are inactive.

Genital [JEN-it-ul] stage Freud's last stage of personality development, from the onset of puberty through adulthood, during which the sexual conflicts of childhood resurface (at puberty) and are often resolved (during adolescence).

Libido [lih-BEE-doe] In Freud's theory, the instinctual (and sexual) life force that, working on the pleasure principle and seeking immediate gratification, energizes the id.

Defense mechanism An unconscious way of reducing anxiety by distorting perceptions of reality.

Thus, **repression**, or the forcing of unwanted anxiety-laden experiences into the unconscious, is the basic Freudian defense mechanism.

What types of experiences are most likely to be repressed? Freud believed that childhood experiences with sex and aggression are often unacceptable to the parents and eventually are denied or repressed by the child. For example, the Oedipal feelings of sexual attraction toward one parent and aggression toward the other are not acceptable to most parents in Western countries. After parents suppress their child's sexual and aggressive behaviors by either punishing or withholding reward for these behaviors, the child begins to develop anxiety about certain sexual and aggressive impulses and therefore forces them into the unconscious.

In addition to repression, Freud identified several other defense mechanisms:

- **Rationalization** is the defense mechanism by which people reinterpret undesirable feelings or behaviors in terms that make them seem acceptable. For example, a shoplifter may rationalize that no one will miss the things she steals or that she needs the things more than other people do. A student may cheat, asserting to himself that failing the course would hurt his parents far too much for them to bear.

- **Fixation** is a defensive mechanism by which a person develops an excessive attachment to another person or object that was appropriate only at an earlier stage of development. For example, with an oral fixation, a person continues to receive pleasure from talking, biting, drinking, eating, smoking, and other oral functions. Examples of anal fixation would be anal retentive people who hold on to their money or opinions in the same manner that they originally held on to their feces.

- **Regressions** are related to fixations, except they take place after a person has progressed through the various stages of development. During periods of extreme anxiety, a person may regress or move backward to an earlier state, typically the oral stage. For example, college students during final exam week may increase their talking, eating, or smoking as a means of handling test anxiety.

- **Projection** is a defense mechanism by which people attribute their own undesirable traits to others. A friend who inexplicably asks, "Are you mad at me?" may actually be mad at you but afraid to admit it to himself; instead, he sees *your* behavior as angry. Similarly, a person with deep aggressive tendencies may see other people as acting in an excessively hostile way.

- **Reaction formation** is the defense mechanism by which people behave in a way opposite to what their true but anxiety-provoking feelings would dictate. A classic example of reaction formation is the behavior of a person who has strong sexual urges but who becomes extremely chaste. Similarly, a person with strong but unconscious hostile feelings for her boss may behave in an overly friendly manner to him or her. Reaction formations can be detected by other people because they produce behavior that is exaggerated or overly dramatic.

- **Displacement** is the defense mechanism by which people divert sexual or aggressive feelings for one person onto another person. For example, a woman who is mistreated by her employer may repress her hostility for her boss but take out her anger on her husband, children, pets, or even a stuffed animal. Displacement differs from reaction formation in that the behaviors are not exaggerated or overdone.

- **Denial** is the defense mechanism by which people refuse to accept reality or recognize the true source of their anxiety. For example, someone with strong sexual urges may deny any interest in sex rather than deal with those urges. Or a person with drinking or drug problems may deny that these behaviors are causing problems.

Repression
Defense mechanism by which anxiety-provoking thoughts and feelings are forced to the unconscious.

Rationalization
Defense mechanism by which people reinterpret undesirable feelings or behaviors in terms that make them appear acceptable.

Fixation
An excessive attachment to some person or object that was appropriate only at an earlier stage of development.

Regression
A return to a prior stage after a person has progressed through the various stages of development; caused by anxiety.

Projection
Defense mechanism by which people attribute their own undesirable traits to others.

Reaction formation
Defense mechanism by which people behave in a way opposite to what their true but anxiety-provoking feelings would dictate.

Displacement
Defense mechanism by which people divert sexual or aggressive feelings for one person onto another person.

Denial
Defense mechanism by which people refuse to accept reality or recognize the true source of their anxiety.

- **Sublimation** differs from the other defense mechanisms in that it can be helpful to society; other defense mechanisms help the person but do little or nothing to enhance society. With sublimations, people redirect socially unacceptable impulses toward acceptable goals. Thus, a man who has sexual desire for someone he knows is off limits (perhaps a cousin) may channel that desire into working 14-hour days for his church. Similarly, a student who wants to drop out of school may throw himself into artistic endeavors or athletics.

FREUD TODAY. When Freud's psychosexual theory of development was first proposed, around 1900, it received a great deal of unfavorable attention. It was considered outrageous to suggest that young children had sexual feelings, especially toward their parents. Opinion changed, and Freud's theory became popular. If you watch how young children respond to and identify with their parents, you will see that there are elements of truth in Freud's conception of how personality development proceeds. Little girls do tend to idolize their fathers, and little boys often become strongly attached to their mothers. And it is widely accepted that individuals use projection and other defense mechanisms (Newman, Duff, & Baumeister, 1997).

Despite these observations, Freud's theory has been sharply criticized. Some psychologists object to Freud's basic conception of human nature—his emphasis on sexual urges toward parents and his idea that human behavior is so biologically determined. Others reject his predictions about psychosexual stages and fixations. Still others assert that his theory does not account for changing situations and differing cultures. His case histories are seen by many today as "clinical romances" and intellectually contrived (Webster, 1995). At a minimum, his ideas are controversial, and many psychologists do not regard them as valid (Schatzman, 1992). *Point/Counterpoint* summarizes the continuing controversy over Freud within psychology.

Adler and Individual Psychology

Although Alfred Adler (1870–1937) was one of the original members of Freud's Vienna Psychoanalytic Society, his differences with Freud led him to resign and to formulate an alternative personality theory. His theory, now called *individual psychology*, is quite different from Freud's in almost all aspects. Adler chose the term *individual* to suggest that personality is indivisible and must not be divided into various levels of consciousness or different regions of the mind.

In Adler's individual psychology, each concept relates to all others, making division of personality terms somewhat arbitrary. Nevertheless, we discuss the following concepts separately: striving for superiority or success, unity of personality, social interest, creative power, family constellations, and early recollections.

STRIVING FOR SUPERIORITY OR SUCCESS. According to Adler, people are motivated, or energized, by natural feelings of inferiority, which lead them to strive for superiority or success. We all begin life with small and fragile bodies. At the same time, we possess an innate striving force that combines with our inferior bodies to create *feelings* of inferiority. The criterion of successful striving is a matter of how we handle these inevitable feelings of inferiority. By the time we are 3 or 4 years old, we have adopted a *style of life* that may either lead us toward unhealthy striving for personal gain (superiority) or toward completion and psychological health (success). Thus, feelings of inferiority are not necessarily detrimental to personal development; they may lead to either a self-centered style of life or to a desire to improve the human condition. Although we all strive as a *compensation* for feelings of incompleteness, many people *overcompensate* and strive in a fixed and rigid manner.

Sublimation [sub-li-MAY-shun]
Defense mechanism by which people redirect socially unacceptable impulses toward acceptable goals.

point*counterpoint*

Freud's Continuing Relevance to Psychology

The Issue: Is Freud still relevant to psychology?

POINT
Freud's theory is outdated and unscientific, making it irrelevant to contemporary psychology.

COUNTERPOINT
Freud has left an important legacy to contemporary culture and to scientific psychology.

Freud's detractors have leveled many criticisms against him and his theory. These criticisms have ranged from the sexism of his theory to the difficulties of subjecting it to empirical testing. During the first half of the 20th century, Freud went from obscurity to controversy to widespread acceptance. During the last half of the 20th century, psychology moved in different directions, and the Freudian view was no longer prominent. Freud's theory depicts women in very derogatory ways, and the growing number of women in psychology was a factor in this theory's diminishing popularity.

Another type of criticism comes from problems in scientific testability. That is, critics cite Freud's use of poorly defined terms, his failure to distinguish between his observations and the inferences he made from them, and his reliance on the unconscious to explain any possible behavior. Good scientific theories make specific predictions about behavior, such as people with fixations at the oral stage will enjoy drinking beer from bottles more than from glasses. Freud's theory explains *any* possible behavior, not just the ones that occur.

Thus, the theory's comprehensiveness is actually a drawback. Other psychologists argue that psychology moved beyond Freud, leaving unscientific personality theories behind and developing better alternatives. Summarizing the view of many psychologists, Frederick Crews (1996, p. 63) said, "[T]here is literally nothing to be said, scientifically or therapeutically, to the advantage of the entire Freudian system or any of its component dogmas."

Other psychologists argue that Freud has exerted a greater influence on psychology and Western culture than any other personality theorist. Proponents like Drew Westen (1998, p. 333) explain that "Freud, like Elvis, has been dead for a number of years but continues to be cited with regularity." Westen criticizes Freud's critics, claiming that psychoanalytic thought has evolved into a theory that contributes to contemporary scientific knowledge. Westen argues that psychoanalytic thought is consistent with the beliefs of a wide variety of psychology researchers. These shared assumptions include the existence of the unconscious and its influence on behavior, the importance of early childhood in personality formation, and the appropriate emphasis on sexuality and aggression. Westen claims that the belief in the unconscious is part of the renewed interest in consciousness among neuroscientists. In addition, Westen argues that support for the existence of the unconscious comes from experimental evidence for unconscious emotional processing. Westen also discusses the research on personality development, saying that most research highlights the importance of childhood as important for adult personality formation and functioning. In addition, a great deal of research indicates that childhood abuse and neglect produce psychological damage that persists into adulthood. Although personality development consists of more than controlling sexuality and aggression, these two tasks are important in forming socially responsible adults. Thus, contemporary psychoanalytic theorists argue that this theoretical view is far from dead; it has contributed to mainstream psychology research as well as Western thought and popular culture.

Adler recognized that people seek to express their need for superiority in different areas of life. Some seek to be superior artists; others seek to be superior parents or corporate executives. Thus, each person develops a unique style of life, in which attitudes and behaviors express a specific life *goal* or an ideal approach to achieving superiority.

■ **UNITY OF PERSONALITY.** Adler believed in the essential unity of personality. All of our thoughts, feelings, and actions serve a single purpose, one that is consistent with the *final goal* we set at about age 4 or 5 years. One person may set a final goal as achieving an overdependent relationship with his mother. As a child, he feels frightened when his mother is out of sight and fusses when his mother spends time with other children. As an adult, he looks for a woman to take care of him and allow him to continue his goal of having a dependent relationship with a mother figure.

According to Adler, inconsistent behavior does not exist; a close look at another person's final goal reveals the unity of seemingly inconsistent behaviors. For example, our overly dependent boy might alternate between submissive and aggressive behaviors toward his mother. With both behaviors, he is attempting to solidify his dependency on his mother.

■ **SOCIAL INTEREST.** The pinnacle of Adlerian theory is the notion of **social interest,** or a feeling of oneness with all humanity. Adler (1927) regarded social interest as the "sole criterion" of human values, or the primary gauge for judging the worth of people's actions. The potential for social interest is acquired during the early parent–child relationship. Everyone who has survived infancy has received at least minimum care from an adult who has demonstrated some measure of social interest. However, children who are pampered or neglected will develop little social interest. These children strive for personal gain and grow up to believe that people cannot be trusted, living in "enemy territory" and feeling overly suspicious of people. They may get along with others on a superficial level, but their deficit of social interest leads them to believe that people can't be trusted.

Adler believed the effects of the early parent–child relationship may have a lasting influence on later development. By the time children are 5 or 6 years old, Adler said, their experiences with social interest (or lack of social interest) is sufficiently powerful to blur the effects of heredity. People with high levels of social interest are generally motivated by normal feelings of incompleteness, whereas those with low levels of social interest develop exaggerated feelings of inferiority and attempt to compensate for their incompleteness by setting personal goals and by striving for personal superiority.

■ **CREATIVE POWER.** Adler acknowledged that heredity and environment furnish the building material of personality, but he insisted that each of us is our own architect, freely deciding how we wish to use the building materials. Adler called this ability to shape our own personality the *creative power*. Our creative power permits us to freely choose our final goal and to select our manner of striving toward that goal, generally placing us in control of our lives. Thus, we are much more than an interaction of heredity and environment; we are creative beings who not only react to our environment but also act on it and cause it to react to us. We can create either a healthy style of life or an unhealthy one; the choice is ours.

■ **FAMILY CONSTELLATIONS.** Adler believed that psychologists can learn about people's personality from an understanding of their *family constellation*. Family constellation is not the same as birth order. Birth order is simply one's rank order among siblings, whereas family constellation considers the gender and health of siblings as well as the age difference between siblings. Adler and others have observed some typical traits of four family positions: only child, firstborn, second-born, and last-born. (See Table 12.3.) A firstborn child, for example, is likely to have a different relationship with people than a second-born child does and is thus likely to develop a different style of life. Only children may be socially mature but may demand to be the center of attention. Firstborns are pushed by parents toward success, leadership, and independence and so tend to have a high need for achievement. Their early experiences make it likely that they will choose careers reflecting that need for achievement, such as corporate executive or politician. Second-born children, on the other hand, are usually more relaxed about achievement. If they feel competitive with an older sibling (as Adler did toward his older brother Sigmund), however, they may develop a strong need for achievement that will drive

Social interest
In Adler's theory, a feeling of oneness with all humanity.

TABLE 12.3

Some of Adler's Hypotheses About Birth Order

Birth Order	Hypothesis
Only child	The center of attention, dominant; often spoiled because of parental timidity and anxiety
Firstborn	Driven to success; independent; high need for achievement; high levels of anxiety; protective toward others
Second-born	Actively struggling to surpass others; often competitive (especially with older sibling)
Last-born	The most pampered (the smallest and weakest); dependent on others; may excel by being different

them toward public success. Youngest children are often pampered and allow older siblings to take care of them.

■ **EARLY RECOLLECTIONS.** Adlerian therapists are much more likely to use *early recollections* rather than birth order to reveal a person's style of life. With this technique, they simply ask the people to describe the earliest experience they can remember. The objective validity of the memory is of no importance; the crucial factor is people's interpretation of the event.

Although Adler believed that early recollections yield clues for understanding people's current style of life, he did not believe that the early event is the cause for present style of life. Rather, people reconstruct their early experiences to make them consistent with some theme that runs through their life. To illustrate this point, Adler (1929/1964, p. 123) reported the case of one of his patients, a young man who was about to be married but who deeply and inexplicably distrusted women, including his fiancée. When asked his earliest recollection, the young man recalled that he was "going with my mother and little brother to market. Suddenly it began to rain and my mother took me in her arms, and then, remembering that I was the older, she put me down and took up my younger brother." This seemingly insignificant memory related to the man's current distrust of women. Having first gained the favorite position with his mother, he quickly lost it to his younger brother. Although women may initially love him, they cannot be trusted to continue their love. In the Adlerian interpretation, the man's present style of life continues to reshape the way he perceives his early experiences.

Jung and Analytical Psychology

The second important theorist to break from Freud's psychoanalytic theory was Carl Gustav Jung (1875–1961), a Swiss psychiatrist. Jung, a brilliant thinker, had an intense personal relationship with

■ *Carl Jung broke with Freud and formulated an alternative theory of personality.*

Freud but ultimately left the Freudian group over several key issues. Compared to Freud, Jung placed relatively little emphasis on sex. He saw people's behavior as less rigidly fixed and determined than Freud described. Jung also emphasized the search for meaning in life and focused on religiosity. By 1911, he and Freud were exchanging angry letters; in 1913, when Jung declared publicly his disagreements with Freud, the two severed their relationship—Freud was intolerant of followers who deviated too much from his positions.

Like Freud's *psychoanalytic approach*, Jung's *analytical psychology* emphasized unconscious processes as determinants of behavior. Jung believed that people are ultimately motivated to attain self-realization or perfection and that our journey toward self-realization is an exceedingly difficult one, including many obstacles and several tests of courage.

Like Freud, Jung believed in an unconscious. However, his version of the unconscious was somewhat different from Freud's in that he added a collective unconscious. The **collective unconscious** is a shared storehouse of primitive ideas and images that reside in the unconscious and are inherited from one's ancestors. Called **archetypes**, these inherited ideas and images are emotionally charged and rich in meaning and symbolism. The archetypes of the collective unconscious emerge in art, in religion, and especially in dreams.

One important archetype is the shadow, or the dark side of our personality. The shadow represents those personal experiences we find distasteful and attempt to hide from ourselves and others. For example, we may enjoy reading about serial killers and other criminals because it allows us to deny parts of ourselves and to project our shadow onto other people. On our quest for self-realization, our first test of courage is to recognize our shadow; that is, to come to grips with the darkness and ugliness within ourselves. The second test of courage for men is to recognize their anima, or feminine side of their personality, and for women to make peace with their animus, or masculine side of their personality. Many men, and especially young men, have difficulty coming to grips with their feminine side. Often, they behave in ultra-masculine ways to convince themselves and others that they are totally masculine.

Collective unconscious
In Jung's theory, a shared storehouse of primitive ideas and images that reside in the unconscious and are inherited from one's ancestors.

Archetypes [AR-ki-types]
In Jung's theory, the emotionally charged ideas and images that are rich in meaning and symbolism and exist within the collective unconscious.

Two other archetypes are the *great mother* and the *wise old man*. The great mother is the archetype of nourishment and destruction. Just as "mother nature" and our own mother can either nourish us or destroy us, the great mother archetype includes these two qualities. In fairy tales and legends, the great mother may appear as a fairy godmother, a witch, or Mother Earth. The wise old man is the archetype of wisdom, but this wisdom is often shallow, with no substance. The wizard in the Wizard of Oz is a good example—he seemed to be quite wise, but his wisdom, at

The mandala is a mystical symbol that holds significance in many religions.

best, was merely common sense. The wise old man is seen in dreams and legends as a father, grandfather, philosopher, doctor, priest, or rabbi.

The most important archetype is the *self*, the archetype of completion and wholeness. The self encompasses all other archetypes as well as the opposing sides of personality, such as extraversion and introversion, masculinity and femininity, conscious and unconscious, light and dark forces, and so on. Our final test of courage on the road to completeness is to realize the self—to bring all the opposing forces of personality together. As an archetype, the self is symbolized by a person's ideas of perfection, completion, and wholeness, but its ultimate symbol is the mandala. The *mandala* is a mystical symbol, generally circular in form, that in Jung's view represents a person's inward striving for unity. Jung pointed out that many religions have mandala-like symbols; indeed, Hinduism and Buddhism use such symbols as aids to meditation.

Jung's ideas are widely known but not widely accepted by mainstream psychologists. Although their impact on psychodynamic theory is important, Jung's ideas never achieved prominence in leading psychological thought because they are so difficult to verify. Some theorists even view them as mere poetic speculation; others see them as attractive but untestable hypotheses.

Be an *Active* learner

REVIEW

- How do the id, ego, and superego develop through the psychosexual stages? pp. 408–409
- In Freud's view, why is the unconscious so important in personality development? pp. 406–407
- Summarize the common function of all of Freud's defense mechanisms. In what ways do they differ? pp. 410–411
- What elements of Freud's theory did Adler and Jung object to? pp. 412, 416

THINK CRITICALLY

- Freud initially believed that seduction by a parent was an important cause of mental disorders, but he abandoned this theory and accepted the Oedipus complex in its place. Considering current statistics on child abuse, was Freud correct in his decision?
- What societal forces can shape a personality theorist's point of view?

APPLY PSYCHOLOGY

- Rent any of the Star Wars movies (*Star Wars* itself provides the best examples), and analyze the characters based on Jung's archetypes.

Skinner and Behavioral Analysis

We often speculate about what goes on "inside" the minds of our favorite movie stars, athletes, or other famous figures; we try to guess what their personal and professional lives might be like and infer things about their personalities. But B. F. Skinner would have argued that such an exercise is a waste of time—you cannot see inside people's minds. Skinner (1904–1990), a leader of American behaviorism, applied the principles of learning to all facets of behavior, including personality. Behaviorists argue that speculating about private, unobservable behavior is fruitless. They further assert that inner drives, psychic urges, and levels of consciousness are concepts that are impossible to define.

The Power of Learning

Behaviorists look at personality very differently than do any of the theorists described so far. They generally do not look within the psyche; they look only at overt behavior. Behavioral approaches are often viewed as a reaction to the conceptual vagueness of traditional psychodynamic personality theories. Behavioral personality theorists assert that personality develops as people learn from their environments. The key word is *learn*. According to behaviorists, personality characteristics are not fixed traits; instead, they are learned and subject to change. Thus, for behaviorists, personality is the sum of a person's learned tendencies.

How do people learn? The concept of *operant conditioning* is critical in a behavioral analysis of personality. The principles of operant conditioning come from experiments with nonhuman animals, mostly rats and pigeons, but these laboratory experiences can be generalized to humans. People (and other animals) learn mostly as a result of their experiences with reinforcement. As we saw in Chapter 7, *reinforcement* is any condition within the environment that strengthens a behavior. Both positive reinforcement and negative reinforcement strengthen behavior. Positive reinforcement is synonymous with reward. More technically, a *positive reinforcer* is any positively valued condition that, when added to a situation, increases the probability that a given behavior will occur. A child who receives a cookie for cleaning her room is being positively reinforced. A *negative reinforcer*, on the other hand, is any aversive stimulus that, when removed from a situation, increases the probability that a given behavior will occur. If you take an aspirin when you have a headache and your headache goes away, then you have been negatively reinforced and you are more likely to use this same technique in the future. Negative reinforcement must not be confused with punishment, which does not strengthen behavior; punishment weakens behavior. There are also two types of punishment: (1) adding an aversive stimulus to a situation and (2) taking away a positive valued stimulus. An example of the first type would be embarrassing a person telling a sexist joke by walking away before the story is finished. An example of the second type of punishment might be finding that your car has been stolen because you neglected to lock it.

How can you tell the difference between reinforcement and punishment? Behaviorists are very empirical, relying on observation. If any given behavior increases in frequency, then we know that it has been reinforced. For example, if a teacher scolds a child for misbehaving in class, and the child's rowdy behavior increases, then we know the admonishment is a reward for that child, not a punishment. The teacher may have meant to punish, but that was not the result. If a 12-year-old boy hides when his overly affectionate aunt comes for a visit, then we know that the aunt's affectionate behaviors serve as a punishment for the boy, not reinforcement.

Acquiring a Personality

Theorists who take the behavioral analysis point of view believe that, in addition to the individual's experiences with reinforcement, personality is acquired through natural selection and cultural evolution (Skinner, 1987). As a species, our behaviors are partially shaped by the contingencies of survival. Throughout human history, those behaviors that were helpful to the species tended to survive, whereas those that were merely beneficial to an individual tended not to survive. For example, natural selection has favored people who formed cooperative communities to protect themselves from outside forces. Today, cooperation remains an important human behavior.

The evolution of cultures is also responsible for at least some human behavior. Perhaps the two strongest contributors to modern life are the development of symbolic language and the continuing evolution of technology. Thus, your facility with

Building Table 12.1

Psychodynamic and Behavioral Approaches to Personality

Approach	Major Proponent	Core of Personality	Structure of Personality	Development	Cause of Problems
Psychodynamic	Sigmund Freud	Maximizes gratification while minimizing punishment or guilt; instinctual unconscious urges direct behavior	Id, ego, superego	Five stages: oral, anal, phallic, latency, genital	Imbalances between the id, ego, and superego, resulting in fixations
Behavioral	B. F. Skinner	Patterns of behaviors learned through experience with the environment	Responses	Process of learning new responses	Faulty or inappropriate behaviors learned through experience with the environment

language contributes at least some measure to your personality. Similarly, your experiences with important inventions, especially since the industrial revolution, have greatly shaped your life, making you a much different person than your ancestors of a thousand years ago.

Skinner and others who take the behavioral analysis view reject many of the concepts that other personality theorists use. Skinner emphasized learning, and personal learning history was the foundation of his approach to personality. Through experiences, people form stable tendencies to behave in similar ways over time. These tendencies, not underlying dimensions of personality, are the basis for behavior. This approach is a sharp contrast with the psychodynamic view, as Building Table 12.1 shows.

Trait and Type Theories: Stable Behavioral Dispositions

Ancient philosophers and medieval physicians believed that the proportions of various fluids (called *humors*) in the body determine a person's temperament and personality. Cheerful, healthy people, for example, were said to have a *sanguine* (hopeful and self-confident) personality because blood was their primary humor; those who had a preponderance of yellow bile were considered hot-tempered.

Longitudinal study
A research approach that follows a group of people over time to determine change or stability in behavior.

introduction to research basics

Are Personality Traits Stable?

Most personality theorists conceptualize personality as stable over time and resistant to change, but relatively few studies have measured the stability of personality. The main reason for this lack is the difficulty of performing the required research. The method required is a **longitudinal study,** which is a research approach that follows a group of people over time to determine change or stability in behavior. The process of making multiple measurements over a span of time makes this method difficult and expensive. Thus, relatively few researchers have been able to perform longitudinal studies, especially projects that span many years.

DESIGN Susan Charles and her colleagues (2001) conducted a longitudinal study of personality stability, concentrating on positive and negative affect, which can be defined as having either a positive and optimistic outlook or a negative and pessimistic viewpoint.

HYPOTHESIS Charles and her team hypothesized that the characteristic of negative outlook would decrease over the life span, whereas positive outlook would be stable.

PARTICIPANTS Researchers recruited over 2,000 participants in 1971 and later added younger family members from these original families. A total of 2,804 people responded on at least two of the five testings, furnishing the necessary data for a longitudinal analysis. The participants represented four generations from the cooperating families. Participants varied in age from 15 to 90 years old at the time of their first testing.

PROCEDURE The researchers measured positive and negative affect using a self-report measure in which participants responded to a set of standardized questions. Researchers collected data at 5 times over 23 years. At one testing, the researchers also assessed the personality dimensions of extraversion and neuroticism, using the Eysenck Personality Inventory.

RESULTS Charles and her colleagues performed an analysis that allowed them to determine the patterns of change over time. As hypothesized, these researchers found both change and stability in personality over time. As expected, positive affect and feelings of optimism showed a stable pattern over the time of the study, but negative affect decreased with age. Individuals with high neuroticism scores (anxious, emotional, reactive) tended to score higher on negative affect, and those with high extraversion scores (sociable, impulsive, adventurous) tended to also have high scores on positive affect.

CONCLUSIONS The personality trait of positive affect is stable over many years, whereas the factor of negative affect decreases over time. These effects are not due to differences in time periods in history but rather represent patterns that occurred for each of the age groups in the sample. These trends paint a picture of positive personality changes over time. However, individual differences were large, and not all people experienced these positive trends.

Cheerful and hot-tempered could be considered as traits. A **trait** is any readily identifiable stable quality that characterizes how an individual differs from other individuals. Someone might characterize one political figure as energetic and forward-looking and another as tough and patriotic, for example. Such characterizations present specific ideas about a person's *disposition*—the way that person is likely to behave across a wide range of circumstances and situations as well as over time (see the *Introduction to Research Basics* on page 419). Traits can be placed on a continuum, so a person can be extremely shy, very shy, shy, or mildly shy, for example. For some personality theorists, traits are the elements of which personality is made.

Types emerge when personality theorists combine several related traits into one category. **Types,** therefore, are personality categories in which broad collections of traits are loosely tied together and interrelated.

We'll examine the trait and type theories of Gordon Allport, Raymond Cattell, and Hans Eysenck, as well as a newer model of traits—the Five Factor Model.

Allport's Personal Disposition Theory

The distinguished psychologist Gordon Allport (1897–1967) suggested that each individual has a unique set of personality traits, which he called *personal dispositions*. Allport counted several thousand trait names in an English language dictionary, and these traits have formed the bases for the way Allport and other people have studied traits.

■ *Woody Allen's film persona is usually high in neuroticism.*

Allport divided traits into three categories: cardinal, central, and secondary. *Cardinal traits* are so dominant that a person's entire life revolves around that trait, like Snape in the Harry Potter books. Most people do not have a cardinal trait, but those who do are guided by a single ruling passion. For example, a clergyman's cardinal trait may be intense belief in and devotion to God. His entire life revolves around this passion. Some words in the English language stem from people (real or fictional) who possessed a cardinal trait, for instance, *sadism* (from the Marquis de Sade), *narcissism* (from Narcissus), and *Scrooge* (from Dickens's character).

Although most people do not have a cardinal trait, each of us has about 5 to 10 *central traits*, or qualities that characterize our daily interactions. To understand a person, we should look at the *pattern* of that person's central traits. Two people could possess the same set of traits, such as self-control, apprehension, tension, self-assertiveness, forthrightness, and practicality, but the manner in which one woman's self-control relates to her apprehension, tension, and so on may be quite different from the way another woman's self-control relates to these other central traits.

Trait
Any readily identifiable stable quality that characterizes how an individual differs from other individuals.

Types
Personality categories in which broad collections of traits are loosely tied together and interrelated.

Secondary traits are characteristics that are exhibited in response to specific situations. For example, a person may have a secondary trait of xenophobia—a fear and intolerance of strangers or foreigners. Secondary traits are more easily modified than central traits and are not necessarily exhibited daily. Also, people have many more secondary traits than central traits.

Everyone has different combinations of traits, which is why Allport claimed that each person is unique. To identify a person's traits, Allport recommended an in-depth study of that individual through an analysis of personal diaries, letters, and interviews over a lengthy period of time.

Cattell's Trait Theory

Allport's study of traits was based mostly on nonmathematical procedures, including common sense. In contrast, Raymond B. Cattell (1905–1998) used the technique of *factor analysis*—a statistical procedure in which psychologists analyze groups of variables (factors) to detect which are related—to show that groups of traits tend to cluster together. Thus, researchers find that people who describe themselves as warm and accepting also tend to rate themselves as high in nurturance and tenderness and low in aggression, suspiciousness, and apprehensiveness. Researchers also see patterns within professions: for example, artists may see themselves as creative, sensitive, and open; accountants may describe themselves as careful, serious, conservative, and thorough-minded. Cattell termed obvious, day-to-day traits *surface traits,* and he called higher-order, "deep" traits *source traits.*

Cattell used the factor analysis process to extract 35 specific traits. These 35 can be broken down into 23 normal and 12 abnormal primary source traits. (Sixteen of the normal traits are the basis for Cattell's personality test, which is described on p. 436.) By additional factor analysis, Cattell identified eight second-order traits. The most powerful of these is the extraversion–intraversion dimension, which also appears in Eysenck's theory and in the Five Factor Model.

Eysenck's Factor Theory

Whereas Allport and Cattell focused on traits, Hans Eysenck (1916–1997) focused on higher levels of trait organization, or what he called **types.** Each type incorporates lower-level elements (traits), and each trait incorporates still-lower-order qualities (habits). Eysenck (1970) argued that all personality traits could be grouped under three basic bipolar dimensions: extraversion–introversion (E), neuroticism–emotional stability (N), and psychoticism–superego function (P).

Extraverts are sociable and impulsive, and they enjoy new and exciting experiences, including meeting new people. In contrast, *introverts* are unsociable and cautious, prefer routine activities, and do not enjoy meeting new people. People who score high on *neuroticism* (N) are not necessarily pathological, but they do have high levels of anxiety, tend to overreact emotionally, and experience difficulty calming down after emotional arousal. They frequently complain of physical difficulties, such as headache or back pain, and are often overconcerned about matters they cannot change. People who score low on this scale are *emotionally stable* and are able to control their feelings. They are often spontaneous, genuine, and warm. Eysenck's third factor, psychoticism, is sometimes called tough- or tender-mindedness. Again, high scores on *psychoticism* (P) do not necessarily indicate psychopathology, but they do suggest a person who is cold, self-centered, nonconforming, hostile, aggressive, and suspicious. People who score low on this dimension (toward the superego function) tend to be altruistic, highly socialized, caring, cooperative, and conventional.

Eysenck argued that personality has a biological basis; he also believed that learning and experience help shape an individual's behavior. For example, he said that introverts and extraverts experience different levels of arousal in the cortex of the brain. Accordingly, persons of each type seek the amount of stimulation necessary to achieve their preferred level of arousal. For example, a person who prefers a low level of arousal, in which stimulation is less intense, might become a librarian; a person who prefers a high level of arousal might become a race-car driver. Many people who prefer high levels of arousal might be characterized as sensation seekers; they climb mountains, ride dirt bikes, gamble, and take drugs.

student voices

Bethany Carter
Texas Tech University

As an actress, I constantly studied the characters and tried to make my portrayals truthful. That's why I liked learning about personality types in psychology. I remember playing the part of a young girl whose influences weren't helping her be the best person she could be. I found it hard to relate to her, so when I thought of why she was the way she was, it helped me bring the character to life.

The Five Factor Model

Because trait and type theories follow a common-sense approach, researchers today still find them attractive. However, rather than speaking of hundreds of traits or of a few types, many theorists agree that there are five broad trait categories. These categories have become known as the Five Factor Model or the Big Five (McCrae & Costa, 1999):

- Sensation seekers strive to maintain a high level of arousal by stimulating (and even dangerous) activities.

- *Extraversion–introversion*, or the extent to which people are social or unsocial, talkative or quiet, affectionate or reserved
- *Agreeableness–antagonism*, or the extent to which people are good-natured or irritable, courteous or rude, flexible or stubborn, lenient or critical
- *Conscientiousness–undirectedness*, or the extent to which people are reliable or undependable, careful or careless, punctual or late, well organized or disorganized
- *Neuroticism–stability*, or the extent to which people are worried or calm, nervous or at ease, insecure or secure
- *Openness to experience*, or the extent to which people are open to experience or closed, independent or conforming, creative or uncreative, daring or timid

Although dozens of traits can describe people, researchers think of the five factors as "supertraits," the important dimensions that characterize every personality (McCrea & Costa, 1999). Research has supported the idea of the Five Factor Model (Busato et al., 1999) and shown the stability of the categories (Borkenau & Ostendorf, 1998); in addition, the Five Factor Model holds up cross-culturally (Costa & McCrea, 1998; McCrea et al., 1998; McCrea et al., 2000; Trull & Geary, 1997). Some research suggests there may be genetic influences on the categories (see *Brain and Behavior*). Finally, the Five Factor Model may help us understand children's personalities (Shiner, 1998), although little research has been conducted on children and personality development.

The Five Factor Model is easily understood (Sneed, McCrae, & Funder, 1998) and has been adapted to psychological assessment (Matthews et al., 1998). However, not all researchers agree on the categories (Almagor, Tellegen, & Waller, 1995; Benet-Martinez & Waller, 1997), and certain elements of personality are not well identified by the Five Factor Model (Schinka, Dye, & Curtiss, 1997).

Like other trait theories, the Five Factor Model is a description but not an explanation of personality. In describing broad traits, these approaches lose some ability to predict behavior and why it occurs. Individual behavior is affected by situation and context (Schmit & Ryan, 1993). Knowing that a person in the Brazilian rain forest and another in London are both high in anxiety is descriptive, but these two people will almost certainly not express their anxiety in similar ways. Therefore, the knowledge of their status on this personality trait will not allow predictions about their behavior.

Be an *Active* learner

REVIEW

- Identify three behavioral concepts used to explain personality development. pp. 417–418
- Distinguish between a *trait* and a *type*. p. 420
- Trace the development of the Five Factor Model, beginning with Cattell's theory and including Eysenck's theory. p.421

THINK CRITICALLY

- Many psychologists accept the basic idea of the Five Factor Model but think the list should include six, seven, or possibly four factors. Does the Five Factor Model have the right number and assortment of factors? Are five dimensions too many or not enough to characterize individual differences in personality? Explain your reasoning.
- How does evolution explain the existence of various personality traits such as neuroticism and psychoticism?

APPLY PSYCHOLOGY

- Describe your best friend and yourself in terms of the five factors from the Five Factor Model of personality. What are the similarities and differences? If you used the same traits to characterize someone whom you dislike, what differences would emerge?

BRAIN AND BEHAVIOR

The Genetics of Personality Traits

The ideal of a biological basis for personality is widely debated, but a growing body of evidence indicates that some traits or dispositions have a genetic basis. Researchers in the area of behavior genetics attempt to identify genetic influences, determining the proportion of a trait that is determined by heredity and what is due to environment (Segal & MacDonald, 1998). Common methods include assessing people with various degrees of biological relationship to determine how much variation in a trait is genetic. For example, a common method involves administering a personality inventory to both identical and fraternal twins. For traits with a genetic basis, the relationship is higher in identical than in fraternal twins.

Research on the heritability of personality traits has concentrated on the traits of the Five Factor Model, and each of these five traits shows some heritability (Loehlin, 1992; Loehlin et al., 1998; Plomin & Caspi, 1999). Heritability is a measure of how much of the variation in a trait is due to genetics and is expressed as a proportion or percentage. Estimates of these numbers vary from study to study, but the studies that examine genetics and personality traits typically show some degree of heritability higher than zero, which suggests some degree of genetic contribution. Figure 12.2 shows the range of estimates for genetics in the personality factors in the Five Factor Model.

Behavior genetics studies do not directly measure genes. To determine the genetic basis for any trait, researchers must establish exactly how genes affect the behaviors in the personality trait. That is, researchers must establish a link between specific gene locations and a given behavior that is part of a personality trait.

Researchers using this approach found an association between the personality trait *novelty seeking* and the gene for a receptor for the neurotransmitter dopamine (Cloninger, Adolfsson, & Svrakic, 1996). This gene is expressed primarily in the limbic system in the brain, a structure that mediates emotion and excitement. In several studies, individuals with a particular type of variation in this gene differed in *novelty seeking* from those with another variant of the gene. These studies in molecular genetics are a necessary component in establishing how genetics influences personality traits.

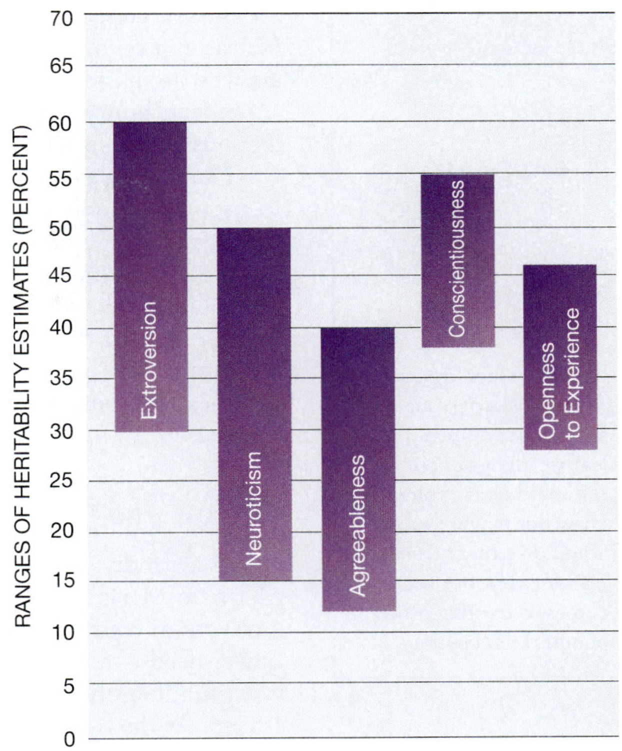

FIGURE 12.2

Estimates for the Heritability of Personality Traits in the Five Factor Model Range from Low to Moderate

Robert Plomin and Avshalom Caspi (1999, p. 262) described the difficulties of the task of finding the genetic basis of personality: "The goal is not to find *the* gene for a particular personality trait, but rather *some* of the many genes that make contributions of varying effect sizes to the variance of the trait." Some genes may make very small contributions, and their effects will be difficult to determine, even with advances in gene mapping, but research has made a promising start in this difficult task.

Humanistic Approaches: The Search for Psychological Health

Some psychologists have objected to psychodynamic, behavioral, and type theories because they believe these approaches have *dehumanized* people, describing them as being a prisoner of their unconscious (Freud and Jung), little different from other animals (Skinner), or best understood by measuring their types and traits (Cattell and Eysenck). These psychologists, led by Abraham Maslow and Carl Rogers, attempted to humanize the study of personality by focusing on humans' unique qualities. Humanistic theorists are interested in people's conceptions of themselves and

student voices

Rhonda Felty
Carson-Newman College

In my psychology class, we took a personality self-evaluation test. I learned things about myself that I kind of already knew but maybe wouldn't admit, like that I trust myself easily, but when it comes to trusting other people, I am cautious.

what they would like to become. In general, *humanistic theories* assume that people are motivated by internal forces to achieve personal goals. Humanistic psychology focuses not on maladjustment or abnormal behavior but on well-adjusted individuals who are basically decent (although some of their specific behaviors may not be). Moreover, humanistic theories enable theoreticians and practitioners to make predictions about specific behaviors.

Humanistic theories usually take a *phenomenological approach* because they focus on the individual's unique experiences with and ways of interpreting the things and people in the world (phenomena). These approaches are more likely to examine immediate experiences than past ones and are more likely to deal with an individual's perception of the world than with a therapist's perception of the individual. Finally, they focus on self-determination; the theories assert that people carve their own destinies, from their own vantage points, and in their own ways. For these reasons, many psychologists regard Alfred Adler as the first humanistic theorist.

Maslow and Self-Actualization

No single individual is more closely associated with humanistic psychology than Abraham Maslow (1908–1970). In Chapter 11, we examined Maslow's theory of motivation, which states that human needs are arranged in a step-by-step hierarchy. Lower needs—for food and water, for example—are powerful and drive people toward fulfilling them. In the middle are the needs for safety, belongingness, and self-esteem. At the top step is **self-actualization,** or the need to realize one's full human potential. The higher a need is in the hierarchy, the more distinctly human it is.

As a humanist, Maslow focused on psychologically healthy people rather than disturbed individuals. He studied both living and historical people who he believed were self-actualizing and found that these people differed from the rest of the population on several important characteristics. Self-actualizing people, who make up a very small percentage of all people, have a more efficient perception of reality—they are not easily fooled by phony people; they accept themselves, others, and nature; they are spontaneous, simple, and natural; they are problem centered rather than person centered—a good idea is a good idea regardless of who thought of it first; they are able to feel comfortable when they are alone, but they genuinely like at least some people; they are autonomous and are unmoved by either flattery and unjust criticism; they are almost childlike in their continual appreciation of the world around them; they have high levels of what Adler called *social interest*, or a genuine concern and caring for all people; they enjoy profound interpersonal relations; they can clearly discriminate between ends and means—they recognize that a desirable end product does not justify unlawful means to attain it; they have a philosophical sense of humor and are not amused by contrived stories; they are creative in the broad meaning of the term—a hand-picked bouquet of flowers may be more creative than a popular work of art; and they have the ability to transcend a particular culture—they don't do things merely because "everyone else is doing it." Maslow believed that each of us has the potential for self-actualization, but to reach that stage of psychological health we must have our lower level needs at least mostly satisfied.

Self-actualization
The process of growth and the realization of individual potential; in the humanistic view, a final level of psychological development in which a person attempts to minimize ill health, be fully functioning, have a superior perception of reality, and feel a strong sense of self-acceptance.

Critics of Maslow find his notions too fuzzy and view his approach to psychology as romantic and not fully developed. Also, his theory is virtually untestable because he provided little explanation of the nature of self-actualizing tendencies. Carl Rogers formulated a more complete and scientific humanistic approach to personality.

Rogers and Self Theory

Carl Rogers (1902–1987) began to formulate his personality theory during the first years of his practice as a clinician in Rochester, New York. He listened to thousands of patients and was among the first psychologists to tape-record and transcribe his interactions with patients. What Rogers's patients said about their experiences, their thoughts, and themselves led him to make three basic assumptions about behavior: (1) behavior is goal-directed; (2) people have the potential for growth; and (3) how individuals see their world determines how they will behave.

Rogers believed that personal experiences provide an individual with a unique and subjective internal frame of reference and worldview. He believed that **fulfillment**—an inborn tendency directing people toward actualizing their essential nature and thus attaining their potential—is the force that motivates personality development. However, people do not move inevitably toward fulfillment. Like a seed that reaches its potential only if certain conditions are present, people attain self-fulfillment only if they have experienced three essential conditions. For a seed, those conditions might be water, fertile soil, and sunlight. For humans the necessary and sufficient conditions for growth are *empathy* and *unconditional positive regard* received in a relationship with a *congruent* partner or therapist. You experience empathy when you perceive that another person accurately senses your feelings; you receive unconditional positive regard when you sense that another person accepts you completely and unconditionally; and both these conditions must be received from a partner who is congruent, or psychologically healthy.

■ **THE SELF-CONCEPT AND THE IDEAL SELF.** Rogers's theory of personality is structured around the concept of the **self**—the view that you have of yourself and of your relationships to other people and to various aspects of life. Your *self-concept* is how you see your own behavior and internal characteristics. In addition to your self-concept, you have a picture of what you would like to be, that is, your **ideal self.** Incongruence, or psychological stagnation, exists when your ideal self is greatly inflated and severely out of line with your self-concept. According to Rogers, people are generally happy when there is agreement between their self-concept and their ideal self. Great discrepancies between the two selves create unhappiness, dissatisfaction, and, in extreme cases, maladjustment. These discrepancies are seen by the individual—not by another person. Rogers stressed that each person evaluates her or his own situation using a personal (internal) frame of reference, not the external framework that would be provided by society or others.

When your self-concept and ideal self are congruent, you will move naturally toward *self-actualization*, that is, toward becoming fully functioning. People who are fully functioning have a clear perception of reality and feel a strong sense of self-acceptance. When your self-concept is not what you would like it to be, you may become anxious. Rogers saw anxiety as useful because it motivates people to try to actualize their best selves, to become all they are capable of being.

■ **PSYCHOLOGICAL STAGNATION.** People with rigid self-concepts guard themselves against potentially threatening feelings and experiences. Rogers suggested that such people become unhappy and psychologically stagnant when they are unable to fit new types of behavior into their existing self-concepts. They then distort their perceptions of their behavior in order to make these perceptions compatible with the self-concept. A man whose self-concept includes high moral principles, rigid religious observance, and strict self-control, for example, might become anxious when he feels greed; such a feeling is inconsistent with his self-concept. To avoid anxiety, he denies or distorts what he is truly experiencing. He may deny that he feels greed, or he may insist that he is entitled to the object he covets.

■ **THE FULLY FUNCTIONING PERSON.** People who have received empathy and unconditional positive regard from a congruent, healthy partner develop healthy self-concepts and will move in a positive direction, toward becoming a fully functioning person. Rogers suggested several characteristics of the fully functioning person.

Fulfillment
In Rogers's theory of personality, an inborn tendency directing people toward actualizing their essential nature and thus attaining their potential.

Self
In Rogers's theory of personality, the perception an individual has of himself or herself and of his or her relationships to other people and to various aspects of life.

Ideal self
In Rogers's theory of personality, the self a person would ideally like to be.

Such people are in a constant state of change; they welcome new experiences and have little reason to deny or distort their view of self. They allow even unpleasant and repugnant experiences to come to awareness, because they see each new experience as an opportunity to learn and to grow. They trust in their organismic self, which means that they act on deeply felt emotions such as love, disgust, joy, anger, fear, and so on. They do not waste time in wishful thinking and have a clear perception of their own values. Finally, fully functional people establish harmonious relations with others. Because they like themselves, they behave in likable ways, which in turn, makes it easier for other people to like them.

Positive Psychology

As humanistic psychologists contend, psychology has tended to concentrate on problems and maladjustment to the neglect of studying positive human qualities. Although humanistic psychology focused on positive factors such as self-actualization, congruence, and fulfillment, the humanistic movement did not generate a body of research to provide confirmation for its contentions (Seligman & Csikszentmihalyi, 2000). The developing field of *positive psychology* attempts to include well-being, contentment, hope, optimism, and happiness, but researchers in this field strive to collect information using scientific research methods. Martin Seligman and Mihaly Csikszentmihalyi (2000, p. 7) explain the emphasis of this developing field: "Psychology is not just a branch of medicine concerned with illness or health; it is much larger. It is about work, education, insight, love, growth, and play. And in this quest for what is best, positive psychology does not rely on wishful thinking, faith, self-deception, fads, or hand waving; it tries to adapt what is best in the scientific method to the unique problems that human behavior presents to those who wish to understand it in all its complexity."

Subjective well-being—happiness—has been a topic of research in the field of positive psychology. Although it surprises some people, results indicate that people are generally happy (Diener, 2000; Myers, 2000). These findings apply to people in countries throughout the world, including people living in conditions of poverty and disease that would seem to make happiness difficult to attain (Diener, 2000). Rather than concentrating on who is happy, positive psychology focuses on the processes that influence subjective well-being. Adaptation is one such process. People adapt to unfortunate circumstances, but they also adapt to prosperity, so personal evaluations of well-being remain fairly stable. Personality is another factor in happiness, and culture also exerts influences in the values and goals people set and are able to attain. Ed Diener (2000) has called for the development of a measurement of subjective well-being that can apply on a national level so that researchers can compare happiness not only among people but also across cultures.

■ *Optimistic people are able to maintain a positive outlook, even under difficult circumstances.*

People tend to be happier when they are involved with family, friends, and community and when they are productive. According to psychologist Mihaly Csikszentmihalyi (1997), when people become deeply engaged in some activity, they may experience the phenomenon of *flow*. Flow occurs when a person's skills are engaged in overcoming a challenge that they can meet. When people are engaged in an activity, they feel less self-conscious, more in control, and more confident. From Csikszentmihalyi's view, happiness follows from flow, from engagement—whether a person is a physician or a clerk in a department store. Csikszentmihalyi argues that each of us can transform our lives, find flow, and then achieve happiness by complete engagement with what we do and those we do it with.

Happiness is only one of the topics in positive psychology. This area also includes research into optimism, wisdom, creativity, and giftedness. At this point, positive psychology has asked important questions but leaves many others without answers. For example, research needs to address the development of engagement, the role of genetics and biology in positive states, and the benefits of positivity.

Be an *Active* learner

REVIEW

- What does self-actualization mean in the context of Maslow's and Rogers's personality theories? pp. 424–425
- How do empathy and unconditional positive regard contribute to fulfillment? p. 425
- How does the area of positive psychology differ from humanistic psychology? What do the two fields share? pp. 426–427

THINK CRITICALLY

- What do you think is the most important way humanistic theory differs from Freudian theory?
- What are the problems and challenges of research investigations of the concept of *flow*?

APPLY PSYCHOLOGY

- Do you know anyone who matches the characteristics of the self-actualizing person? Describe that person.

Cognitive Approaches to Personality

Recently, cognitive approaches to personality theory have gained acceptance among many psychologists. Cognitive theorists generally reject the broad theories of Freud, Adler, and Jung that were based largely on experiences during therapy. Cognitive theorists also find problems with the behaviorists, especially the early behaviorists, who were single-minded in their belief that psychology should limit itself to only observable, measurable behavior. But human beings clearly have an inner mental and psychic life; they think about things and react emotionally, and those thoughts and reactions are not always evident in observable behavior. In important ways, cognitive approaches to personality appeared as a reaction not only to psychodynamic and behavioral theories but also to trait and type theories, as well as to humanistic theories.

Cognitive theories emphasize the interaction of thoughts and behavior. They consider the uniqueness of human beings, especially of their thought processes, and assume that human beings are decision makers, planners, and evaluators of their own behavior. Rather than viewing people as having stable traits, cognitive approaches assume people are fluid and dynamic in their behavior and responses to the world. Many contemporary cognitive therapists claim that people can change their behavior, their conceptions of themselves, and thus their personalities, if they change their thoughts.

Key Cognitive Concepts

From a cognitive point of view, the mere association of stimuli and responses is not enough for conditioning and learning to occur in human beings; thought processes also have to be involved. Thought and behavior affect each other. According to cognitive theory, whether a person exhibits learned behavior depends on the situation and personal needs at a particular time. If thought and behavior are closely intertwined, then when something affects the person's thoughts, it should also affect his or her behavior.

One of the key elements of the cognitive approach to personality is the idea that people develop self-schemata. As we saw in Chapters 3 and 8, a *schema* is a conceptual framework by which people make sense of the world. Self-schemata (*schemata* is the plural of *schema*) are collections of ideas and bits of self-knowledge that organize people's thoughts about themselves. They are often global themes that help individuals define themselves. A man's self-schemata may comprise one self-schema that involves exercise, another that concerns his wife, and still others that are about work, family, and religious feelings. Cognitive researchers assert that people's self-schemata help shape their day-to-day behavior. They may affect people's adjustment, maladjustment, and ability to regulate their own behavior. Thus, someone who has a self-schema for being in control of her emotions may find the death of a loved one a challenge to normal day-to-day coping mechanisms.

Over the years, a number of cognitive theories have been developed, dealing with how people perceive themselves and their relationship with the world. Like their behaviorist colleagues, cognitive psychologists have reacted against psychoanalytic and humanistic theories, which they deem difficult or impossible to verify scientifically. Several cognitive theories have attempted to account for specific behaviors in specific situations. Because these cognitive concepts are far better defined than those in psychodynamic and humanistic theories, they are easier to test. We will consider three such concepts from cognitive personality theories next: Julian Rotter's concept of locus of control, Albert Bandura's concept of self-efficacy, and Walter Mischel's concept of cognitive social learning. Each of these concepts is an integral part of these theorists' cognitive personality theories.

Rotter and Locus of Control

Patients who seek the help of a therapist frequently say they feel "a lack of control." And often the task of therapy is to help clients realize what forces are shaping events and what they can do to gain a sense of control. One widely studied cognitive–behavioral concept that therapists often make use of is locus of control, introduced in the 1950s and systematically developed by Julian Rotter and Herbert Lefcourt. *Locus of control* involves the extent to which individuals believe that a reinforcer or an outcome is contingent on their own behavior or personal characteristics rather than being a function of external events not under their control or simply unpredictable (Lefcourt, 1992; Rotter, 1990). Rotter focused on whether people place their locus of control inside themselves (internal) or in their environments (external). Locus of control influences how people view the world and how they identify the causes of success or failure in their lives. In an important way, locus of control reflects people's personalities—their views of the world and their reactions to it.

To examine locus of control, Rotter developed an inventory consisting of a series of statements about oneself and other people. To determine whether your locus of control is internal or external, ask yourself to what extent you agree with the statements in Table 12.4. People with an internal locus of control (shown by their choice of statements) feel a need to control their environment. They are more likely to engage in proactive behavior, such as preventive health measures and dieting, than are people with an external locus of control. People who endorse most, but not all, of the internal statements have the highest level of health—those who endorse all the internal items feel anxious and guilty because they see themselves as responsible for everything, even the things they actually cannot control, and those who endorse most of the external statements feel little responsibility for their actions.

TABLE 12.4

Statements Reflecting Internal Versus External Locus of Control

Internal Locus of Control		External Locus of Control
People's misfortunes result from the mistakes they make.	*Versus*	Many of the unhappy things in people's lives are partly due to bad luck.
With enough effort, we can wipe out political corruption.	*Versus*	It is difficult to have much control over the things politicians do in office.
There is a direct connection between how hard I study and the grade I get.	*Versus*	Sometimes I can't understand how teachers arrive at the grades they give.
What happens to me is my own doing.	*Versus*	Sometimes I feel that I don't have enough control over the direction my life is taking.

Locus of control is associated with differences in many behaviors, including those important to school and achievement. College students characterized as internal are more likely than others to show high academic achievement (Lefcourt & Davidson-Katz, 1991). In contrast, people with an external locus of control believe they have little control over their lives. A college student characterized as external may attribute a poor grade to a lousy teacher, feeling there was nothing he or she could have done to get a good grade. They are more likely than those with an internal locus of control to procrastinate on a project (Janssen & Carton, 1999). External locus of control is also associated with high levels of competitiveness but lower grade-point averages (Frederick, 2000). Individuals who develop an internal locus of control, on the other hand, feel that hard work will allow them to make their best grades. In general, such people report less stress in their lives (Carton & Nowicki, 1994; Carton, Nowicki, & Balser, 1996).

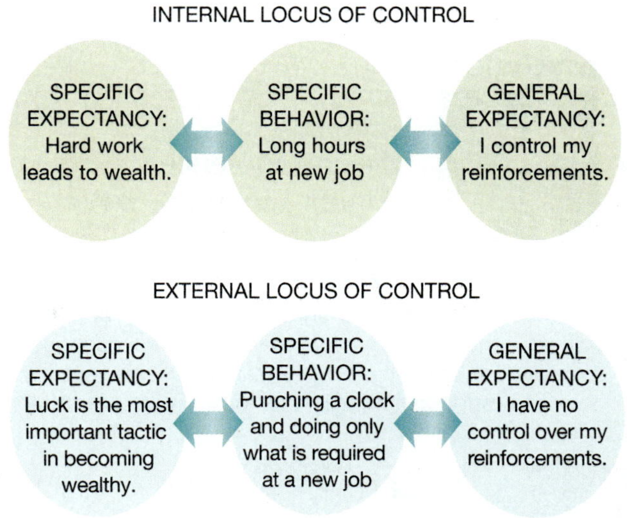

FIGURE 12.3

Locus of Control

A person's general expectations about life are determined in a three-part process: specific expectancies result in specific behaviors, which are reinforced. This cycle eventually leads to a general expectancy about life, which underlies either an internal or an external locus of control.

People develop expectations based on their beliefs about the sources of reinforcement in their environment. These expectations lead to specific behaviors. Reinforcement of these behaviors in turn strengthens expectancy and leads to increased belief in internal or external control (see Figure 12.3). Not surprisingly, in therapeutic situations where self-esteem is an issue, psychologists often seek to bolster a client's self-esteem by helping the person recognize the things she or he can control effectively (Betz, 1992).

Locus of control integrates personality theory, expectancy theories, and reinforcement theory. It describes several specific behaviors but is not comprehensive enough to explain all, or even most, of an individual's behavior.

Bandura and Self-Efficacy

Albert Bandura, a psychology professor at Stanford, developed one of the most influential cognitive theories of personality. His conception of personality began with observational learning theory and the idea that human beings observe, think about, and imitate behavior, which accounts for learning both acceptable and unacceptable behaviors (see *Psychology in Action*). Bandura has played a major role in reintroducing thought processes into learning and personality theory.

Bandura argued that people's expectations of mastery and achievement and their convictions about their own effectiveness determine the types of behaviors they will engage in and the amount of risk they will undertake (Bandura, 1977a). He used the term **self-efficacy** to describe a person's belief about whether he or she can successfully engage in and execute a specific behavior. Judgments about self-efficacy determine how much effort people will expend and how long they will persist in the face of obstacles (Bandura, 2001).

A strong sense of self-efficacy allows people to feel free to influence and even create the circumstances of their own lives. Also, people's perceived self-efficacy in managing a situation heightens their sense that they can control it (Conyers, Enright, & Strauser, 1998). Thus, people who have a high level of self-efficacy are more likely than others to attribute success to variables within themselves rather than to chance factors, making them more likely to pursue their own goals (Bandura, 1999, 2000). Because people can think about their motivation, and even their own thoughts, they can effect changes in themselves, persevere during tough times (Sterrett, 1998), and do better at difficult tasks (Stajkovic & Luthans, 1998).

Self-efficacy
A person's belief about whether he or she can successfully engage in and execute a specific behavior.

Bad luck or nonreinforcing experiences can damage a developing sense of self-efficacy. Observation of positive, prosocial models during the formative years, on

psychology *in action*

Seeing Violence, Doing Violence

You and a group of your friends walk out of a club late one night and see two people involved in a fight in the parking lot. How do you infer the reasons for their behavior? For Freud, aggression was one of the basic drives that underlie personality; he saw aggression as an instinctive force. In Freudian theory, expressing aggression could be cathartic, leading to "getting it out of your system." For Bandura, aggression is learned through observation and thus far from inevitable. In his view, seeing violence leads to doing violence. Rather than getting it out of your system, performing violence makes it more likely that such behavior will be repeated. These two views lead to very different predictions about the influence of observing violence.

In modern society, you have many opportunities to see violence, and the electronic media offer many times more opportunities than does real life. The power of the media to teach violence has been a topic of research since the 1960s (Bandura, Ross, & Ross, 1963). That research has indicated a positive relationship: seeing violence on television and in the movies makes children and adults more likely to do violence (Villani, 2001; Johnson et al., 2002).

The effects of observing violence are stronger for younger than for older children, and preschool children are affected the most strongly (Villani, 2001). Television affects young children more than other media because young children are exposed to television more than any other medium. Children see about 10,000 acts of violence on television each year, and 38% of such acts were committed by an attractive person. According to Bandura, the attractiveness and power of the model are factors in observational learning, so the current television depictions of violence have a great deal of power to do harm.

Another distressing trend in media violence is the connection between violence and sexuality. This connection occurs in movies but is especially prominent in music videos (Villani, 2001) and on the Internet (Barron & Kimmel, 2000). The combination of violence and sex not only connects the two through association but also desensitizes viewers to occurrences of sexual violence. The presentation of sexual violence should lead to a high occurrence of such violence, and this prediction is confirmed by the results of a survey of adolescent girls. This survey showed that dating violence is very common—20% of young women in the survey reported that they had experienced some type of dating violence (Silverman et al., 2001).

Another study offers some hope for a strategy to control the influence of media violence. Reducing the time children spent watching television and playing video games decreased their aggressive behavior (Robinson, 2001). Children in one elementary school participated in a 6-month school program to decrease their television and video game usage. Children were rated by their peers and parents to assess their aggression. Decreased television and video game use was associated with lower peer ratings of aggression and lower ratings of verbal aggression on the playground. This result suggests that seeing less violence leads to doing less violence (Anderson & Bushman, 2002).

And the answer is at the tip of our fingers—turn off the television.

the other hand, can help people to develop a strong sense of self-efficacy that will encourage them in directing their own lives. Bandura's theory allows individual flexibility in behavior. People are not locked into specific responses to specific stimuli, as some strict behaviorists might assert. According to Bandura, people choose the behaviors they will imitate, and they are free to adapt their behavior to any situation. Self-efficacy both determines and flows from feelings of self-worth. Thus, people's sense of self-efficacy may determine how they present themselves to other people. For example, a man whom others view as successful may not share that view, whereas a man who has received no public recognition may nevertheless consider himself a capable and worthy person; each of these men will present himself as he sees himself (as a failure or a worthy person), not as others see him.

Bandura's theory is optimistic. It is a long way from Freud's view, which argues that conflicting biologically based forces determine human behavior. It is also a long way from a strict behavioral theory, which suggests that environmental contingencies shape behavior. Bandura believes that human beings have choices, that they direct the course of their lives. He also believes that society, parents, experiences, and even luck help shape the life course.

■ **GENDER AND SELF-EFFICACY.** In Bandura's view, gender has a major impact on personality through modeling and observational learning. Boys and girls receive different rewards for gender-typed behaviors—girls tend to be reinforced for behaviors considered feminine, boys for behaviors considered masculine. Girls and boys also have the experience of observing women and men who receive rewards for gender-typical behaviors and punishments for behaviors that are not typical of their gender (Bussey & Bandura, 1999). Their environment is filled with stereotypical models in the family, schools, and media. This stereotyping has effects on self-efficacy in women and men.

Self-efficacy is specific to any given activity, and people tend to have higher self-efficacy for activities that are gender-typed for their gender. However, women show lower expectancies for success on a masculine task than on a feminine or neutral task, but this bias does not occur in men (Beyer, 1998). Thus, the many messages that women receive about the limits on their achievement affect their self-efficacy, which may have major effects on their choices in coursework and careers (Bussey & Bandura, 1999). For example, girls who believe that girls are not good at math will not enroll in advanced mathematics courses and will not consider careers in engineering.

Mischel's Cognitive–Affective Personality System

Like Bandura, Walter Mischel claims that thought is crucial in determining human behavior and that both past experiences and current reinforcement are important. But Mischel is an *interactionist*—he focuses on the interaction between people's stable personality traits and the situation (Mischel, 1999). Mischel and other cognitive theorists argue that people respond flexibly to various situations. They change their responses on the basis of their past experiences and their current assessment of the present situation (Brown & Moskowitz, 1998). This process of adjustment is called *self-regulation*. For example, people make subtle adjustments in their tone of voice and overt behavior (aspects of their personality), depending on the context in which they find themselves. Those who tend to be warm, caring, and attentive, for example, can in certain situations become hostile and dismissive.

Mischel believes that behaviors are relatively inconsistent from one situation to another, but they have some consistency over time. He and Yuichi Shoda (Mischel & Shoda, 1998, 1999) suggest that relatively permanent personal dispositions interact with cognitive–affective units to produce behavior. Cognitive–affective personality units include *competencies* (what people know and can do), *encoding strategies* (the way they process, attend to, and select information), *expectancies and beliefs* (their prediction of the outcomes of their actions), *personal goals and values* (the importance they attach to various aspects of life), and *affective responses* (their feelings and emotions as well as the affects that accompany physiological responses).

Mischel has had a great impact on psychological thought because he has challenged researchers to consider the idea that traits alone cannot predict behavior. The context of the situation must also be considered—not only the immediate situation but also the culture in which a person lives and was raised, as well as other variables such as the gender and age of the person whose behavior is being predicted. Day-to-day variations in behavior should not be seen as aberrations, but

Building Table 12.2

Psychodynamic, Behavioral, Trait and Type, Humanistic, and Cognitive Approaches to Personality

Approach	Major Proponent	Core of Personality	Structure of Personality	Development	Cause of Problems
Psychodynamic	Sigmund Freud	Maximizes gratification while minimizing punishment or guilt; instinctual unconscious urges direct behavior	Id, ego, superego	Five stages: oral, anal, phallic, latency, genital	Imbalances between the id, ego, and superego, resulting in fixations
Behavioral	B. F. Skinner	Patterns of behaviors learned through experience with the environment	Responses	Process of learning new responses	Faulty or inappropriate behaviors learned through experience with the environment
Trait and Type	Raymond Cattell Hans Eysenck	Organizes responses in characteristic modes	Traits and types	Genetic factors and learning	Having learned faulty or inappropriate traits
Humanistic	Carl Rogers	Actualizes, maintains, and enhances the experiences of life through the process of self-actualization	Self	Process of cumulative self-actualization and development of sense of self-worth	Incongruence between self and concept of ideal self
Cognitive	Several, including Rotter, Bandura, and Mischel	Ways of thinking and acting in response to a changing environment	Responses determined by thoughts	Process of thinking about new responses	Inappropriate thoughts or faulty reasoning

rather as meaningful responses to changing circumstances (Brown & Moskowitz, 1998). Mischel's view of personality takes situation and culture into account, but most theories of personality do not, making them subject to criticisms of inflexibility and cultural bias. Next, we turn to a consideration of the effects of culture on personality.

Building Table 12.2 presents an overall summary of the theories presented in this chapter.

Personality in Cultural Context

Like other behaviors, personality must be viewed in cultural context. The fact that Freud's patients were primarily from a certain segment of Austrian society has wide implications. Freud developed a theory from dealing with a particular group of patients whose day-to-day behavior, personalities, and problems were shaped by the culture in which they lived. In addition, Freud's own interpretation of his patients' behavior was influenced by the culture. *Culture*, as we have seen, refers to the norms, ideals, values, rules, patterns of communication, and beliefs adopted by a group of people. Within a culture, there may be different social classes, but all of the people have the same basic set of norms.

Cultural differences between countries are still apparent. For example, people in England, Spain, France, Germany, China, and Turkey have distinctly different value systems, lifestyles, and personalities. Modes of dress and attitudes about work, family, and religion all differ. Culture is significant because it shapes how people raise their children, what values they teach, and what family life is like. However, the role of culture in personality is controversial.

Some researchers have focused on the differences among cultures, concentrating on the obvious ones. Western societies value competitiveness, autonomy, and self-reliance, and Western conceptions of personality focus on the individual. In contrast, many non-Western cultures value interdependence and cooperation; they also focus more on group dynamics in constructing conceptions of personality. For developing adolescents, one culture may value conformity to rules, strict adherence to religious values, and obedience to parental authority. Another culture may stress independence of thought, experimentation, and less reliance on parental authority. Even within American culture, there are significant variations in values and social norms among various ethnic and cultural groups.

■ *Collectivist cultures emphasize interdependence and cooperation.*

These sorts of cultural differences have obvious effects on behavior, but do they affect personality? The answer to that question depends in part on the definition of personality. Some researchers have searched for differences in behaviors that relate to cultural variations. For example, the difference between independence and interdependence is consistent with the individualistic versus collectivist difference. Some cultures value conformity and pleasing the family and social group, whereas others emphasize personal achievement and "doing your own thing." Nor are all individualistic or collectivist cultures the same; American individualism varies from Swedish individualism (Triandis & Gelfand, 1998). Differences between individuals in collectivist versus individualist cultures have a great deal of research support. For example, conformity is higher among individuals from collectivist than individualist cultures (Bond & Smith, 1996; Kim & Markus, 1999).

Rather than exploring differences among cultures, some personality researchers contend that culture makes very little contribution to personality traits. These researchers tend to see personality as the expression of biological traits and look for the commonalities across cultures, searching for the underlying dimensions of personality that all humans share (McCrae & Costa, 1997; McCrae et al., 2000). This line of research has also been successful. Using the Five Factor Model as their basis, researchers have found this factor structure in many different cultures around the world.

Do these results mean that people in different cultures have the same personalities? Not exactly. The results mean that people's personalities can be analyzed in terms of the same factors but not that people in different cultures have the same scores on these factors. Indeed, average scores for personality traits vary substantially across cultures (Lynn & Martin, 1997). For example, people in China score much lower on the trait of extraversion than people in the United States; individuals in Italy score in between. In some cultures, women score higher in extraversion than men, but in most,

Be an *Active* learner

REVIEW

- What is locus of control? p. 428
- What is self-efficacy? p. 429
- Why is Mischel called an interactionist? p. 431
- In what sense is personality common across cultures, and in what sense does it vary? p. 433

THINK CRITICALLY

- What are some possible explanations a cognitive psychologist might offer for the constancy of personality?
- What types of problems are risks for a person with an internal locus of control?
- Are there differences in personalities within different ethnic groups in the United States?

APPLY PSYCHOLOGY

- Have you experienced any change in your self-efficacy since beginning college? For what tasks or skills? Has the change been positive?

men's scores are higher than women's. In all cultures, individual variation is large. The search for commonalities does not mean that personality researchers will lose their interest in the individual.

The search for differences and similarities in personality depends on measuring personality and personality traits. This goal has been part of psychology from the early years, and the large variety of personality assessments is our next topic of discussion.

Personality Assessment

When you think to yourself that your neighbor is a fun-loving guy, that your mom is an affectionate person, or that your brother is politically skillful, you are making assessments of their personalities. Most people make these types of evaluations, but psychologists approach assessment in a more thorough and systematic way.

Assessment is the process of evaluating individual differences among human beings by means of tests, interviews, observations, and recordings of physiological processes. Psychologists who conduct personality assessments usually have one of two goals. They either seek to evaluate personality in order to explain behavior or to diagnose and classify people with behavioral problems. Psychologists who are motivated by the first goal have developed hundreds of personality tests, which can be grouped according to the personality theory that prompted their development. Psychologists who want to diagnose psychopathology use some of the same tests that personality researchers do, but they also have other tests that are oriented toward specific types of psychopathologies. Rather than relying on a single test, clinicians often use information from a battery of tests to make their diagnosis. The purpose of the testing determines the types and numbers of tests administered, but personality tests fall into two major types—projective tests and personality inventories.

Projective Tests

Assessment
Process of evaluating individual differences among human beings by means of tests, interviews, observations, and recordings of physiological processes.

Projective tests
Devices or instruments used to assess personality, in which examinees are shown a standard set of ambiguous stimuli and asked to respond to the stimuli in their own way.

The fundamental idea underlying the use of projective assessment techniques is that a person's unconscious motives direct daily thoughts and behavior, a belief that can be traced back to Freud's theory of personality. To uncover a person's unconscious motives, psychologists have developed **projective tests**—devices or instruments used to assess personality by showing examinees a standard set of ambiguous stimuli and asking people being tested to respond to the stimuli in their own way. The examinees are assumed to use the defense mechanism of projection and to impose their unconscious feelings, drives, and motives onto the ambiguous stimuli. Such tests can be used by personality researchers but are more often clinical tools used to diagnose problems, most often by clinicians with a psychodynamic orientation. Projective tests are used when it is important to determine whether an examinee is trying to hide something. They do not have the rigorous

FIGURE 12.4

The Rorschach Inkblot Test

In a Rorschach Inkblot Test, the psychologist asks a person to describe what he or she sees in an inkblot such as this one. From the person's descriptions, the psychologist makes inferences about his or her drives, motivations, and unconscious conflicts.

development on standardized scoring procedures associated with IQ tests, and they are less reliable than personality inventories—nevertheless, they help complete a picture of psychological functioning.

■ **THE RORSCHACH INKBLOT TEST.** A classic projective test is the *Rorschach Inkblot Test* (see Figure 12.4). The test taker sees 10 inkblots, one at a time. The blots are symmetrical, with a distinctive form; five are black and white, two also have some red ink, and three have various pastel colors. Examinees tell the clinician what they see in the design, and a detailed report of the response is made for later interpretation. Aiken (1988, p. 390) reports a typical response:

> My first impression was a big bug, a fly maybe. I see in the background two facelike figures pointing toward each other as if they're talking. It also has a resemblance to a skeleton—the pelvis area. I see a cute little bat right in the middle. The upper half looks like a mouse.

The examiner usually prompts the examinee to give additional information, such as "Describe the facelike figures." Although norms are available for responses, skilled interpretation and good clinical judgment are necessary in order to place an individual's responses in a meaningful context. Long-term predictions can be formulated only with great caution (Exner, Thomas, & Mason, 1985) because of a lack of substantive supporting research (Garb, Florio, & Grove, 1998).

■ **THE THEMATIC APPERCEPTION TEST.** The *Thematic Apperception Test* (TAT) is much more structured than the Rorschach. (The TAT was discussed in Chapter 11 as one way to assess a person's need for achievement.) It consists of black-and-white pictures, each depicting one or more people in an ambiguous situation; examinees are asked to tell a story describing the situation. Specifically, they are asked what led up to the situation, what will happen in the future, and what the people are thinking and feeling. The TAT is particularly useful as part of a battery of tests to assess a person's characteristic way of dealing with others and of interacting with the world.

To some extent, projective tests have a bad reputation among psychologists who are not psychodynamically oriented. Most argue that the interpretation of pictures is too subjective and prone to error. Practicing clinicians, even those who use projective tests, often rely more heavily on personality inventories to assess people with problems, and personality researchers rarely use projective techniques.

Personality Inventories

Next to intelligence tests, the most widely given tests are *personality inventories*, generally consisting of true/false or multiple-choice questions to which people respond. The aims of personality inventories vary, but the major approaches to personality have generated assessments, each tied to its theoretical basis. Well-constructed personality tests turn out to be valid predictors of performance in a wide array of situations, including school, work, and personal interactions; this is true for people of various ethnicities and minority status groups (Hogan, Hogan, & Roberts, 1996).

The Myers–Briggs Type Indicator (MBTI; Myers, 1962) is a test based on Jung's theory of personality. Jung proposed that each individual favors specific modalities, or ways of dealing with and learning about the world; the preferred modalities define personality type. The MBTI asks people to choose between pairs of statements that deal with preferences or inclinations and scores the responses so that the test taker is characterized as predominantly at one pole or another on four distinct dimensions: extraversion–introversion (E or I), sensing–intuition (S or N), thinking–feeling (T or F), and judging–perceptive (J or P). The MBTI is a quick and easy way to gather information about personality, but its uses are limited. This test was developed using students in grades 4 through 12 and is best

TABLE 12.5

For the Active Learner: The Sixteen Personality Factor Assessment

Place an X on each of the lines to indicate where you think you would rate on each of the following dimensions if you took Cattell's Sixteen Personality Factor Test. *(Cattell, 1979)*

Low Description		High Description
Reserved	....	Outgoing
Less intelligent	....	More intelligent
Affected by feelings	....	Emotionally stable
Humble	....	Assertive
Serious	....	Happy-go-lucky
Expedient	....	Conscientious
Shy	....	Venturesome
Tough-minded	....	Tender-minded
Trusting	....	Suspicious
Practical	....	Imaginative
Forthright	....	Astute
Self-assured	....	Apprehensive
Conservative	....	Experimenting
Group-dependent	....	Self-sufficient
Undisciplined self-conflict	....	Controlled
Relaxed	....	Tense

used for individuals in that age range. The MBTI has been used to predict romantic attraction and relationship stability (Hester, 1996) and academic success (Schurr et al., 1997).

Trait theories of personality have generated the majority of personality inventories. These tests require test takers to respond to many items (often over 100 and some over 500) that are measurements of the personality traits in the theory. These items have been created and tested on groups of people such that the responses reflect not only the traits in each theory but also a comparison among individuals. The process allows an assessment of how people vary along these dimensions of personality.

The Sixteen Personality Factor Test (16 PF) was developed by Raymond Cattell (1949). Using the technique of factor analysis, Cattell constructed a test of personality traits that fits with his theory of personality. People taking this test respond to 187 items, choosing one of three choices for each item. The scoring results in a score for each of the 16 factors, so test administrators can compare the person being tested to others on each dimension. Table 12.5 lists the 16 factors included in Cattell's 16 PF and the descriptors for each dimension. In contrast to the many traits in the 16 PF, Hans Eysenck conceptualized personality as consisting of only the three broad factors called types—extraversion, neuroticism, and psychoticism. The Eysenck Personality Questionnaire (Eysenck & Eysenck, 1993) includes scales that measure each of these types.

The Five Factor Model (or Big Five model) of personality has also prompted the development of a personality inventory, the Revised NEO-Personality Inventory (NEO-PI-R; Costa & McCrae, 1995). This personality inventory consists of 240 items, which yield measures on the five factors proposed by the theory as well as six traits related to each of the five factors. The test can be used in research as well as in clinical diagnosis and has generated a large body of research.

Humanistic personality theory prompted the development of the Personal Orientation Inventory (POI), based on Maslow's theory of personality (Shostrom, 1974). This test is oriented toward assessing self-actualization. The POI consists of 150 items to which people must choose one of two alternatives, such as (a) "Two people can get along best if each concentrates on pleasing the other" versus (b) "Two people can get along best if each person feels free to express himself." The items are scored in terms of two major scales and 10 subscales. Higher scores indicate agreement with self-actualizing values.

One of the most widely used and researched personality tests is the Minnesota Multiphasic Personality Inventory–2nd Edition (the MMPI–2). Unlike the personality inventories designed to assess personality in terms of various theories, the MMPI was designed as a diagnostic instrument. The MMPI–2 consists of 567 true/false statements that focus on the test taker's attitudes, feelings, motor disturbances, and bodily complaints.

Generally, the MMPI–2 is used as a screening device or diagnosis for behavior problems or psychopathology. Its norms are based on the profiles of thousands of normal people and smaller groups of psychiatric patients. Each scale compares test takers' responses to those of the normal people and the psychiatric patients. In general, a score significantly above normal may be considered evidence of psychopathology. The test has built-in safeguards to detect people who are not responding truthfully to the items. Interpretation of the MMPI–2 generally involves looking at patterns of scores, rather than at a person's score on a single scale.

Students who want to know about their personalities are often anxious to take the MMPI. I [LB] always discourage my students from doing so; the test is designed to diagnose pathological problems, making it unsuitable for students interested in learning about testing or their own personalities. The other personality tests are typically better choices than the MMPI.

Be an *Active* learner

REVIEW

- What is the goal of a projective test? p. 434
- What are the two major goals of personality assessment? p. 434

THINK CRITICALLY

- Do you think that projective tests such as the TAT and the Rorschach Inkblot Test can achieve their goal? Explain your answer.
- What aspects of personality do you think a personality test might be unable to characterize? Why?

APPLY PSYCHOLOGY

- Lay out the basic plans for constructing a personality test, including the type of test, the format of the questions, and the type of scoring you would use.

Summary and Review

What Is Personality?

How do psychologists define personality?

- *Personality* is a set of relatively enduring behavioral characteristics (including thoughts) and internal predispositions that describe how a person reacts to the environment. p. 404

KEY TERM

personality, p. 404

Psychodynamic Theories

What fundamental assumptions about human behavior and the mind underlie Freud's theory?

- Freud's structure of the mind includes three levels: *conscious*, *preconscious*, and *unconscious*. The primary structural elements of the mind and personality—the id, the ego, and the superego—are three forces that reside, completely or partially, in the unconscious. The *id*, which works through the pleasure principle, is the source of human instinctual energy. The *ego* tries to satisfy instinctual needs in accordance with reality. The *superego* is the moral aspect of mental functioning. pp. 406–407
- Freud described the development of personality in terms of five consecutive stages: oral, anal, phallic, latency, and genital. In the *oral stage*, newborns' and young children's instincts are focused on the mouth—their primary pleasure-seeking center. In the *anal stage*, children learn to control the immediate gratification obtained

through defecation and become responsive to the demands of society. In the *phallic stage*, children obtain gratification primarily from the genitals. During this stage, children pass through the *Oedipus complex*, which occurs somewhat differently in boys and girls, but results in identification with the same-sex parent. In the *latency stage*, sexual urges are inactive. The *genital stage*, Freud's last stage of personality development, is that in which the sexual conflicts of childhood resurface (at puberty) and are resolved (in adolescence). The energy for personality comes from the instincts of sex (*libido*) and aggression. pp. 408–410

What is the fundamental function of all of Freud's defense mechanisms?

■ For Freud, the most important *defense mechanism* (a defense against anxiety caused by drives toward sex and aggression) was *repression*—in which people block anxiety-provoking feelings from conscious awareness and push them into the unconscious. Other defense mechanisms, such as *rationalization, fixation, regression, projection, reaction formation, displacement, denial,* and *sublimation,* are ways to reduce anxiety by distorting one's perceptions of reality. Defense mechanisms allow the ego to deal with anxiety. pp. 410–412

How did Adler and Jung differ from Freud in their views of personality?

■ Adler and Jung modified some of the basic ideas of Freud; these theorists usually attributed a greater influence to cultural and interpersonal factors than did Freud. Adler broke with Freud and argued that Freud overemphasized sex and ignored social issues, formulating the concept of *social interest* as a foundation of his view of personality. Adler theorized that people strive for superiority or success. This tendency is often prompted by feelings of inferiority. According to Adler, individuals develop a lifestyle that allows them to express their goals in the context of human society. pp. 412–414

■ Jung emphasized unconscious processes as determinants of behavior and believed that each person houses past events in the unconscious. The *collective unconscious* is a shared collection of *archetypes*, emotionally charged ideas and images that have rich meaning and symbolism and are inherited from one's ancestors. pp. 415–417

KEY TERMS

conscious, p. 406; preconscious, p. 406; unconscious, p. 406; id, p. 406; ego, p. 407; superego, p. 407; oral stage, p. 408; anal stage, p. 408; phallic stage, p. 409; Oedipus complex, p. 409; latency stage, p. 410; genital stage, p. 410; libido, p. 410; defense mechanism, p. 410; repression, p. 411; rationalization, p. 411; fixation, p. 411; regression, p. 411; projection, p. 411; reaction formation, p. 411; displacement, p. 411; denial, p. 411; sublimation, p. 412; social interest, p. 414; collective unconscious, p. 416; archetypes, p. 416

Skinner and Behavioral Analysis

What are the important aspects of behavioral approaches to personality?

■ The behavioral approach to personality centers on learning principles, such as reinforcement and punishment. These principles allow behavioral researchers to determine which behaviors increase and which behaviors decrease in frequency. For behaviorists, the structural unit of personality is the response. Behavioral psychologists try to discover behavior patterns. pp. 417–418

Describe Skinner's view of personality.

■ According to Skinner, personal learning history is the foundation of stable patterns of behavior, the basis of personality. However, Skinner used not only behavioral learning principles but also the concepts of natural selection and evolution of culture to explain personality. pp. 417–419

Trait and Type Theories: Stable Behavioral Dispositions

Distinguish between a trait and a type.

■ A *trait* is any readily identifiable stable quality that characterizes how an individual differs from others; a *type* is a personality category in which a broad collection of traits are loosely tied together and interrelated. A person can be said to *have* a trait or to *fit* a type. pp. 419–420

Describe the ideas of Allport, Cattell, and Eysenck regarding traits.

■ Allport argued that if you know a person's traits, it is possible to predict how he or she will respond to stimuli. Cardinal traits are enduring characteristics that determine the direction of a person's life. Central traits are the qualities that characterize a person's daily interactions. Secondary traits are characteristics that are exhibited in response to specific situations. Cattell used the technique of factor analysis to show that groups of traits tend to cluster together. Cattell called obvious, day-to-day traits surface traits and higher-order, "deep" traits source traits. Eysenck focused on types, which are higher levels of trait organization. Eysenck argued that all personality traits can be grouped under three basic dimensions: emotional stability, introversion–extraversion, and psychoticism. pp. 420–421

What is the Five Factor Model?

■ Although dozens of traits exist, researchers think of the Five Factor Model as consisting of "supertraits," the important dimensions that characterize every personality. The five dimensions are extraversion–introversion, or the extent to which people are social or unsocial; agreeableness–antagonism, or the extent to which people are good-natured or irritable; conscientiousness–undirectedness, or the extent to which people are reliable or undependable; neuroticism–stability, or the extent to which people are nervous or at ease; and openness to experience, or the extent to which people are independent or conforming. p. 422

KEY TERMS

longitudinal study, p. 419; trait, p. 420; types, p. 420

Humanistic Approaches: The Search for Psychological Health

What are the motivating forces of personality development, according to Maslow's and Rogers's theories?

■ In Maslow's theory, *self-actualization* is the process of realizing one's innate human potential to become the best one can be. The process of realizing potential, and of growing, is the process of becoming self-actualized. pp. 423–424

■ The humanistic approach of Rogers states that *fulfillment* is the motivating force of personality development. Rogers focuses on the concept of *self*; the *ideal self* is the self a person would ideally like to be. For personal growth, people must experience a relationship that includes empathy, congruence, and unconditional positive regard. pp. 424–426

What is positive psychology?

■ Positive psychology is a new movement within psychology that focuses on positive human characteristics such as happiness, optimism, and flow. In contrast to the traditional humanist movement, positive psychology seeks to integrate an emphasis on positive characteristics and behaviors with research that confirms the existence and benefits of these qualities. pp. 426–427

KEY TERMS
self-actualization, p. 424; fulfillment, p. 425; self, p. 425; ideal self, p. 425

Cognitive Approaches to Personality

What are the key ideas of the cognitive approach to personality?

■ The cognitive approach emphasizes the interaction of a person's thoughts and behavior. Cognitive views assert that people make rational choices in trying to predict and manage events in the world. One important concept in the cognitive approach is the idea that people develop self-schemata—collections of ideas and bits of self-knowledge that organize how a person thinks about himself or herself. pp. 427–428

■ Locus of control, according to Rotter, is the extent to which individuals believe that a reinforcement or an outcome is contingent on their own behavior or personal characteristics, rather than not being under their control or being unpredictable. People with an internal locus of control feel in control of their environment and future; people with an external locus of control believe that they have little control over their lives. pp. 428–429

■ *Self-efficacy*, in Bandura's theory, is a person's belief about whether he or she can successfully engage in and execute a specific behavior. Judgments about self-efficacy determine how much effort people will expend to achieve a goal and how long they will persist in the face of obstacles. A strong sense of self-efficacy allows people to feel free to influence and even construct the circumstances of their lives. pp. 429–431

■ Cognitive theories of personality have reintroduced thought into the equation of personality and situational variables. They focus on how people interpret the situations in which they find themselves and then alter their behavior. Mischel argues that people adjust their responses based on their past experiences and their assessment of the current situation. This process of adjustment is called self-regulation. p. 431

KEY TERM
self-efficacy, p. 429

Personality in Cultural Context

What are the effects of culture on personality?

■ Personality theories all developed within a cultural context, but culture was not considered as a factor in personality theory until recently. Some psychologists look for differences in personality from culture to culture, such as variance across the individualistic–collectivist dimension, and others search for the universal traits in personality. pp. 432–433

Personality Assessment

What is the process and what are the uses of personality testing?

■ *Assessment* is the process of evaluating individual differences among human beings by means of tests, interviews, observations, and recordings of physiological processes. Psychologists use personality tests as part of an assessment process. Some psychologists use personality tests to understand personality, and others use these tests to diagnose psychopathology. p. 434

What is a projective test?

■ *Projective tests* such as the Rorschach Inkblot Test and the TAT ask examinees to respond to ambiguous stimuli in their own way. Examinees are thought to project unconscious feelings, drives, and motives onto the ambiguous stimuli. pp. 434–435

What are personality inventories?

■ Personality inventories are tests consisting of questions to which test takers respond. The responses are scored, yielding assessments of personality according to the traits measured by the specific tests. Many tests are based on various theories of personality, such as the 16 PF and the NEO-PI-R. The MMPI–2 is a personality test that is used for diagnosis of psychopathology. pp. 435–437

KEY TERMS
assessment, p. 434; projective tests, p. 434

13 Social Psychology

Edward Hopper, *Nighthawks,* 1942

Jeremy Glick, a passenger on United Airlines flight 93, which crashed near Philadelphia on September 11, called his wife and reported that three men had hijacked the plane. Todd Beamer, another passenger, tried to place a credit card call to his wife but talked to the operator. He told her that a group of passengers were planning "to jump" the hijackers, and the last words the operator heard were "Are you ready guys? Let's roll." These passengers were really a group of strangers who banded together and took on the hijackers. They became heroes—along with others.

When the planes crashed into the World Trade Center towers, some people started to make their way to the stairs, trying to escape. Strangers banded together to render aid, calming and directing frightened people toward the stairwells. Two coworkers carried a paraplegic woman down the stairs. Their actions gave the woman a chance to live but made their own safety less likely. For these two men, their altruism turned out well, and all three escaped safely. Another man's altruism did not have such a happy ending. He stopped to help a man in a wheelchair, but the building collapsed before they could get out. The two men were strangers.

chapter outline

As people fled from the damaged World Trade Center, firefighters and emergency workers rushed toward it, trying to save those who were injured and trapped. Hundreds of them died. Their actions were brave but, in some sense, understandable; rescue was their job. The behavior of the people on flight 93 and people in the World Trade Center and Pentagon is less easy to understand. These people banded together with strangers to perform amazing acts of heroism at the risk of their own lives. What is it about people that makes them heroic and altruistic? That question is part of the area of social psychology.

Single individuals do change the world. Franklin Delano Roosevelt changed the course of World War II; John F. Kennedy forged the U.S. space exploration program and the technology that we derived from it. A. Philip Randolph, a civil rights leader and labor activist, led the way for equality for African American workers. Individuals make a difference because they influence others in profound ways. Since humans are social creatures, their interactions with others are as important as individual characteristics and behavior.

In this chapter, we examine the world of social interactions among individuals and within groups. We will see that people affect one another's attitudes, self-perceptions, and behavior. **Social psychology** is the scientific study of how people think about, interact with, influence, and are influenced by the thoughts, feelings, and behaviors of others. This chapter looks at some of the traditional concepts in social psychology: attitudes, social cognition, and social interactions. These concepts help psychologists understand behavior involving more than one person—that is, of social behavior. We study social psychology because human beings are social organisms; we live with, work with, and seek out others—and those others shape our behavior and we shape theirs. Let's look first at how individual attitudes are affected by other people.

Attitudes: Deeply Held Feelings and Beliefs

When I left home to go to college, I (LL) vowed to stay friends forever with my high school buddies. We had known each other for years and had gone through a lot together. But when I returned after a year away, how much my friends had changed! The close bond, the easy understanding, the shared opinions all seemed to have altered. Our political views and interests were different; even our tastes in music had changed.

My high school buddies were still my friends, but our year away from one another had created distance between us. We had changed how we dressed, how we voted, whom we paid attention to, what we valued. I know now that all these changes were affected by an array of social variables.

Social psychology
The scientific study of how people think about, interact with, influence, and are influenced by the thoughts, feelings, and behaviors of other people.

Attitudes
Patterns of feelings and beliefs about other people, ideas, or objects that are based on a person's past experiences, shape his or her future behavior, and are evaluative in nature.

Attitudes are patterns of feelings and beliefs about other people, ideas, or objects, which are based on a person's past experiences and shape his or her future behavior. They are often long-lasting, usually evaluative, and serve certain functions, such as guiding new behaviors and helping a person interpret the world efficiently. Attitudes are shaped by how a person perceives other people, how others perceive him or her, and how the person *thinks* others see him or her. For example, my college roommate, who I had decided was "with it," initiated my appreciation of jazz. Listening to this music at a club where I met my new girlfriend, who had been a devoted listener for 2 years, also influenced me, as did the reinforcement I received when I announced my new interest to my dad and to an uncle who loved jazz. My friends, my relatives, and their reactions to me changed my attitude.

Dimensions and Functions of Attitudes

Football fans are often fanatical in their attitudes: they know every possible statistic about their favorite team's record, they feel elated or down in the dumps after each game, and they often back up their feelings with visible support for the team. People's feelings and beliefs about football, or any other subject, are a crucial part of their attitudes. Attitudes have three dimensions—cognitive, emotional, and behavioral—each of which serves a specific function.

The *cognitive dimension* of an attitude consists of thoughts and beliefs. When someone forms an attitude about a group of people, a series of events, or a political philosophy, the cognitive dimension of the attitude functions to help the person categorize, process, and remember the people, events, or philosophy. The *emotional dimension* of an attitude involves evaluative feelings, such as liking or disliking. For example, some people like the improvisational abstractions of cool jazz; others prefer the down-to-earth sound of country and western music. The *behavioral dimension* of an attitude determines how the beliefs and evaluative feelings are demonstrated, such as by voting in accordance with one's political beliefs or attending the concerts of a favorite group. Behaviorally, attitudes function to shape specific actions. Individuals do not always express their attitudes in behavior, of course, especially when the attitudes are not yet firmly established or when they hold two attitudes that are inconsistent with each other. For example, many more people cognitively and emotionally support a nuclear arms freeze than give their time, energy, or money to organizations supporting this cause. Similarly, your aunt might give you a gift that you think is hideous or frivolous, but in deference to your affection for her, you express gratitude for the "special" present—your real attitude is not expressed.

When people have strongly held attitudes about a specific topic, they think about it and become identified with it (which makes attitudes long-lasting and resistant to change). For example, despite carbon dating evidence to the contrary, many people still believe that the Shroud of Turin is older than it really is. Once people have formed a belief, it functions to justify a wide range of behaviors and colors their interpretation of new information about events.

What variables determine how attitudes are formed, displayed, or changed? Why are some attitudes much harder to modify than others? We consider these questions in the following sections, beginning with attitude formation.

Do Attitudes Predict Behavior?

Social psychologists can assess people's attitudes, but whether those attitudes predict behavior depends on numerous variables. Some of these are attitude strength, vested interest, specificity of attitudes, and accessibility of attitudes.

Attitudes are better predictors of behavior when they are strong and there are few competing outside influences, such as conflicting advertising appeals or advice from friends. A person who believes strongly in the health hazards of cigarette smoking, even after being bombarded by Camel and Marlboro advertisements, may work actively for an antismoking campaign. Furthermore, attitudes people consider personally important (those in which they have a vested interest) are more likely to be shown in behavior and to stay intact, regardless of how situations change over time. If a parent believes strongly in improving her child's educational

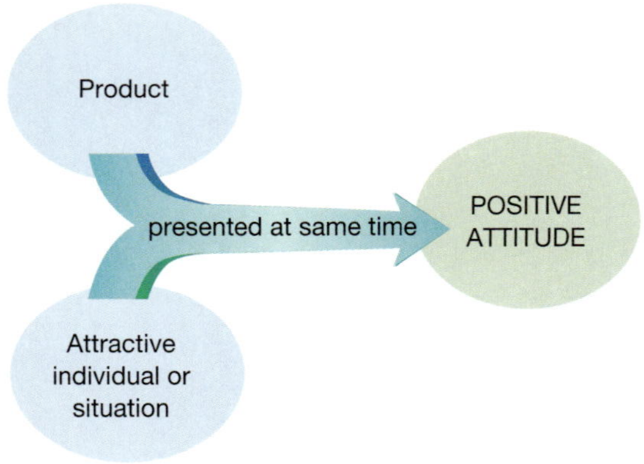

FIGURE 13.1

Classical Conditioning in Attitude Formation

In attempting to create positive attitudes toward a product or idea, advertisers use classical conditioning techniques. They pair the product or idea with an attractive, desirable individual or situation to evoke a positive response.

opportunities, she will be far more likely to attend PTA meetings. The extent to which a belief is tied up with a person's self-concept is also a good predictor of both the strength of the belief and the likelihood that the person will act on it (Pomerantz, Chaiken, & Tordesillas, 1995).

Attitudes are also more likely to foretell behavior when they are specific and the situation requiring a decision closely matches the situation to which the attitude applies. Global attitudes, and even stereotypes about groups of people, do not predict specific behaviors very well. For example, a person may have broadly liberal political beliefs, but only a specific attitude about health care, welfare reform, or government waste will predict whether the person will vote for a specific candidate. Last, attitudes predict behavior best when they are accessible, that is, clearly stated and easily remembered. When people have sharply delineated ideas about a political position, they can easily decide how favorably they rate a new candidate. When they cannot easily remember or articulate their views, making such judgments is more time-consuming and less predictable.

Does Behavior Determine Attitudes?

Is it possible that your attitudes don't determine your behavior, but just the opposite—that your behavior shapes your attitudes? Mounting evidence argues that to a certain extent this is the case. People often develop positive attitudes toward a charity after making a contribution, however small. In weight control programs, alcohol abstinence programs, and many therapy groups, facilitators try to change behaviors (get people to abstain from alcohol, for example) with the idea that positive attitudes about a new life will *follow* changes in behavior.

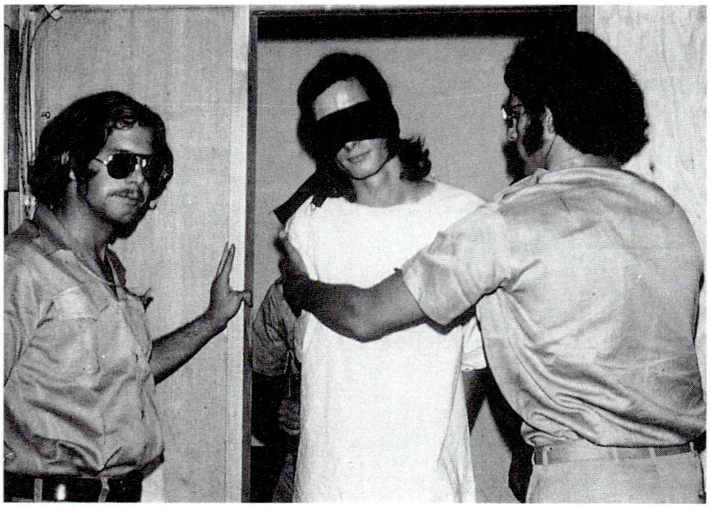

■ *In studies that came to be known as the Stanford Prison Experiment, researchers asked normal, well-adjusted students to dress and act as prisoners and guards.*

A dramatic demonstration of attitudes resulting from behaviors occurred in the 1970s. In studies that came to be known as the Stanford Prison Experiment (Haney, Banks, & Zimbardo, 1973; Zimbardo, Maslach, & Haney, 2000), researchers asked normal well-adjusted college students to dress and act as prisoners or guards. Guards were given uniforms, billy clubs, and whistles; prisoners were given prison jumpsuits and were locked in cells. Within a few days, "guards" were harassing and degrading "prisoners." Prisoners were caving in and becoming obedient, and many were suffering intense psychological pain. The experiment was aborted after a week. This research study, with its shocking result, would not be conducted today because of ethical considerations. The study showed that an individual could play a role—guard or prisoner—and quickly adapt to that role, develop attitudes that were consistent with it, and become actively committed to the attitudes associated with that role.

Persuasion: Changing Attitudes

Television is one of the prime means by which politicians and marketing executives try to change attitudes. They know that since attitudes are learned, they can be changed or replaced. Changed attitudes may impel a person to do almost anything—from voting Democratic, to trying a new brand of soap, to undergoing a religious conversion, to becoming a lover of jazz. In the 1950s, Carl Hovland was one of the first social psychologists to identify key components of attitude change: the communicator, the communication, the medium, and the audience.

■ **THE COMMUNICATOR.** To be persuasive, a communicator—a person trying to effect attitude change—must project integrity, credibility, and trustworthiness. If people don't respect, believe, or trust the communicator, they are unlikely to change their attitudes. Communicators with "mature" faces have more influence (Berry & Landry, 1997). Researchers have also found that the perceived power, prestige, celebrity, prominence, modesty, and attractiveness of the communicator are extremely important (Petty & Wegner, 1998). For example, the Surgeon General is more likely to influence your views about cigarette smoking in the workplace than a doctor who writes a column in the local paper.

Information received from friends is considered more influential than information from the communications media. So the best predictor of whether a person will purchase solar energy equipment is the number of the person's acquaintances who currently own such devices. Similarly, a teenager is more likely to follow a close friend's advice on the use of condoms than that of an unknown public health official.

■ **THE COMMUNICATION.** A clear, convincing, and logical argument is the most effective tool for changing attitudes—especially attitudes with a strong emotional dimension, such as those concerning capital punishment or abortion. This is especially true in Western culture, where appeals to logic and reason are more prevalent than in Japan, for example, where appeals to authority and tradition are common.

Communications that arouse fear are effective in motivating attitude change, especially when they focus on health issues and the communicator does not overdo the fear appeal (Sturges & Rogers, 1996). For example, think of some of the antismoking messages you've seen on television. What techniques do they use to induce fear? Fear works; in fact, research shows that negative information influences people more strongly than positive information (Ito et al., 1998).

If people hear a persuasive message often enough, they begin to believe it, regardless of its validity. Repeated exposure to certain situations can also change attitudes. For example, after seeing numerous TV commercials that show the Energizer battery outperforming another brand, a viewer may change his or her attitude toward the product from neutral to positive. Similarly, a name that is heard often is more likely to be viewed positively than is one heard infrequently; this is called the *mere exposure effect*.

■ *Communications that arouse fear are effective in motivating attitude change, especially when they focus on health issues and the communicator does not overdo the fear appeal.*

■ **THE MEDIUM.** The means by which a communication is presented—its medium—influences people's receptiveness to attitude change. Today, one of the most common avenues for attempts at attitude change is the mass media, particularly television. After all, the goal of TV commercials is either to change or to reinforce people's behavior. Commercials exhort viewers to drink Pepsi instead of Coke, to say no to drugs, or to vote for a Democrat instead of a Republican. Research shows that TV advertising is one of the most influential media for changing attitudes in the Western world; this is not too surprising, given the fact that the television is on for more than 4 hours every day in the average American household.

Nevertheless, face-to-face communication often has more impact than communication through television or in writing. Thus, even though candidates for public office rely heavily on TV, radio, and printed ads, they also try to meet people face to face, sometimes taking bus or train tours to deliver their message directly to the people.

student voices

Amerson H. Lin
Massachusetts Institute of Technology

In psychology, I found the topics that covered cultural differences enlightening. I remember an example that said the ancient Chinese valued family relationships more than anyone else because the Chinese rooming system was such that you had to enter other rooms to reach your room and thus there was this sense of interconnectedness within the family.

■ **THE AUDIENCE.** From time to time, people actually want to have their attitudes changed and seek out alternative views. At other times, they fold their arms and firmly announce, "It's going to take an act of Congress to change my mind." Openness to attitude change is related in part to age and education. People are most susceptible to attitude change in their early years (Ceci & Bruck, 1993). People of high intelligence are less likely to have their opinions changed, and those who have high self-esteem tend to be similarly unyielding (Rhodes & Wood, 1992). A change is far more likely to occur if the person trying to change another's attitude is a friend (Cialdini, 2001).

Attitude change is complicated, and researchers have shown that a wide array of other variables are important as well. For example, attitude change is more likely when the targeted attitude is not too different from an existing one (McCaul, Jacobson, & Martinson, 1998); it is also more likely when the audience is not highly committed to a particular point of view (Johnson & Eagly, 1989). But changing the attitudes of politically involved citizens is more difficult than altering those of non-involved citizens. Research also shows that people who positively anticipate a new idea or who feel that others around them are inclined to change their views are likely to exhibit attitude change (Cialdini, 2001). The extent of attitude change is even affected by prevalent attitudes in the particular region of the country. This effect was seen with the Gore–Bush recount: regional variations predicted voters' attitudes—Southern voters, being more conservative, tended to believe that the Florida vote count was accurate and no recount was needed. Northern voters tended to believe that the Florida vote count was biased and inaccurate.

Changing people's attitudes, and ultimately their behavior, can be difficult if they have well-established habits (which often come with advancing age) or are highly motivated in the direction opposite to the desired change. Consider attitudes toward smoking. Although most people generally believe in the serious health consequences of smoking, 25% of the people in the United States still smoke. Getting someone to stop smoking takes more than fostering positive attitudes about health; it also requires instilling a new habit and removing an old one. Education can be helpful, as can devices to help people remember not to smoke (such as warning buzzers or strings on fingers); nevertheless, because of its addictive properties, smoking is hard to stop.

The next section describes some tried-and-true techniques that have been used for decades to influence attitudes, change behaviors, and obtain favors.

Tactics and Techniques for Inducing Attitude Change

Change a person's attitudes, and you can change his or her behavior—many practitioners believe this and use it in their therapeutic techniques. Many applied psychologists also use this idea to help people do better at work. How do people actually influence one another? What techniques promote attitude change? Bosses, salespeople, parents, and politicians all apply the principles of social psychology. First, they must be credible, and then they influence others by using social psychological techniques such as the foot-in-the-door-technique, the door-in-the-face technique, the ask-and-you-shall-be-given approach, lowballing, modeling, and incentives.

■ **CREDIBILITY.** We suggested earlier that to induce attitude change, a person must project integrity, credibility, and trustworthiness. What does that mean? It suggests that a person must be believable because he or she is knowledgeable, has special training, doesn't hold outlandish or way-out views; further, the person has developed his or her view of the world (or product) through reasonable means and doesn't have a particular vested (personal) interest in the outcome of your decision. So, when a knowledgeable, friendly, helpful clerk in a nutrition store touts

psychology *in action*

Why We Listen to What "They" Say

We listen to our parents, teachers, and spiritual leaders. We listen to our elected leaders, movie star heroes, and environmental icons. We listen to "them"; they are our bosses, pundits, and authorities—both real and imaginary. Douglas Rushkoff (1999) asserts that it is amazing that we listen to "them" because they are often not real authorities and we let them make up our mind for us about details in our lives large and small. They tell us how to feel about clothes, homes, politics, and drugs. "They" are aided and abetted by the media who set the tone for what we believe and when we will believe something. For example, over a short time span news outlets told the public that television was bad for kids, then they told the public that it didn't make much difference, and the same outlets then reverted to their earlier stance that TV violence was detrimental (Bushman & Anderson, 2001). And the public listened.

Not only do we listen, but they change our attitudes. They tell us that "clothes make the man" or "you've come a long way baby" or this is "must-see TV." Atmospheres in malls are set for us; spin doctors—media agents—weave tales and make movie personalities and politicians appear more sympathetic. In 2001, Representative Gary Condit from California hired media consultants to make him appear more believable to the public. Like salespeople, public relations specialists seek to reflect the concerns of the public in order to change their perceptions of truth. So a car dealer may at one minute be folksy with clients who are from the country; the next minute she may be a techno-geek showing a client how the global positioning system of a new sports car works. Media consultants and sales people try to "close the sale," deliver the vote, or change a public's sympathy. So on the Internet we are deluged with junk mail advertisements, pop-up advertisements, and other attempts to grab our attention. Rushkoff argues that we need to be discerning listeners and not let the media, the spin doctors, or Internet advertisers tell us what and how to think.

your use of vitamin E, you are likely to believe the clerk because the views expressed will not benefit the clerk personally (the clerk is on salary), the view has been expressed before (you have read about vitamin E in newspapers), the view is consistent with other expert opinions (vitamins are a good thing), and the clerk doesn't push a view that the vitamin will make you into something that you are not. The clerk appears credible, and being credible is a prerequisite to induce attitude change.

THE FOOT-IN-THE-DOOR TECHNIQUE. To get someone to change an attitude or grant a favor, begin by asking for a small attitude change or a small favor. In other words, get your foot in the door. Ask to borrow a quarter today, next week ask for a dollar, and next month ask for money for your tuition. The essence of the *foot-in-the-door technique* is that a person who grants a small request is likely to comply with a larger request later. It works, however, only if the person first grants the small favor, and it works best if there is some time between the first small request and the later larger one. A person who says no to the first favor may find it even easier to say no to subsequent ones. Although use of the foot-in-the-door technique is relatively common in U.S. society, cross-cultural studies show that it is not as effective in all cultures (Kilbourne, 1989).

THE DOOR-IN-THE-FACE TECHNIQUE. To use the *door-in-the-face technique*, first ask for something outrageous, and then ask for something much smaller and more reasonable. Ask a friend to lend you $100; after being turned down, ask to borrow $5. Your friend may be relieved to give you the smaller amount. The door-in-the-face technique assumes that a person may be more likely to grant a small request after turning down a larger one; it appears to work because people do not want to turn someone down twice, and it works best if there is little time between requests. To look good and maintain a positive self-image, people agree to the lesser of two requests.

THE ASK-AND-YOU-SHALL-BE-GIVEN TECHNIQUE. When people are asked for money for what they perceive as a good cause, whether the request is large or small, they usually will respond positively. If the person has given before, the request is even more likely to be granted, especially if the person is in a good mood (Forgas, 1998). Fund raisers for universities, religious groups, and museums know that asking usually will get a positive response. Research indicates that asking in an unusual way can pique a person's interest, turn the donor aside from his or her well-rehearsed script of saying no, and increase the likelihood of giving (Santos, Leve, & Pratkinis, 1994).

■ **THE LOWBALLING TECHNIQUE.** *Lowballing* is a technique by which a person is influenced to make a decision or commitment because of the low stakes associated with it. Once the decision is made, the stakes may increase; but the person is likely to stick with the original decision. For example, if a man agrees to buy a car for $14,000, he may still buy it even if several options are added on, increasing the price to $15,000. Lowballing works because people tend to stick to their commitments, even if the stakes are raised. Changing one's mind may suggest a lack of good judgment, may cause stress, and may make the person feel as if she or he were violating an (often imaginary) obligation.

■ **THE MODELING TECHNIQUE.** Modeling good behavior for someone increases the likelihood that the person will behave similarly. *Modeling*, which we examined in Chapter 7, is a powerful technique for influencing behaviors and attitudes by demonstrating those behaviors and expressing those attitudes. When well-known athletes exhibit generosity of spirit and act like good sports, they serve as models for youngsters.

Elaboration likelihood model
Theory suggesting that there are two routes to attitude change: the central route, which focuses on thoughtful consideration of an argument for change, and the peripheral route, which focuses on less careful, more emotional, and even superficial evaluation.

■ **THE INCENTIVES TECHNIQUE.** Nothing succeeds better in eliciting a particular behavior than a desired incentive. Offering a 16-year-old unlimited use of the family car for setting the dinner table every day usually results in a neatly set dinner table. Offering a large monetary bonus to a sales agent for achieving higher-than-usual performance usually boosts sales figures. Offering incentives can bring about such behavior changes, but it usually doesn't produce attitude changes—the 16-year-old sets the table, but still hates doing so.

The Elaboration Likelihood Model

Decades of research have identified the basic components of attitude change. But researchers have only recently begun to focus on what happens cognitively to individuals whose attitudes are being changed. Various theories attempt to explain such individuals' thought processes so as to predict attitude change. One such theory, proposed by Richard Petty and John Cacioppo (1985), suggests that people generally want to have attitudes and beliefs that will prove helpful in the face of day-to-day challenges and problems (Petty & Wegener, 1999). This theory is called the **elaboration likelihood model**—a view of attitude change suggesting that it can be accomplished via two routes: central and peripheral. (See Figure 13.2 for an overview of this model.)

FIGURE 13.2
Elaboration Likelihood Model
According to the elaboration likelihood model, attitude change can occur through the central route or the peripheral route.

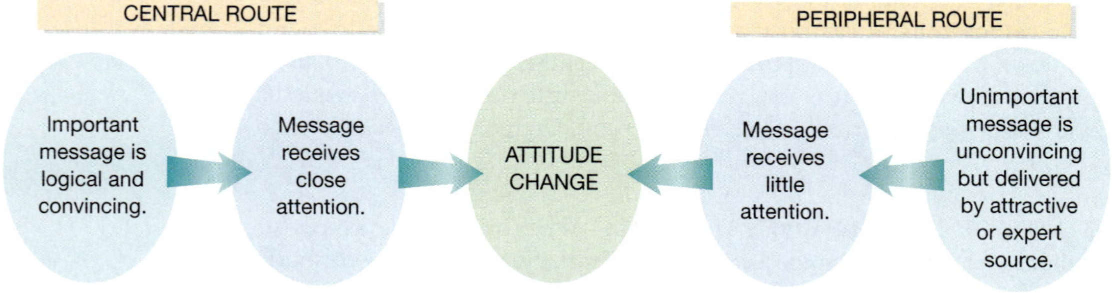

The *central route* emphasizes conscious, thoughtful consideration and elaboration of arguments concerning a given issue. Attitude change via this route depends on how effective, authoritative, and logical a communication is. For example, when confronted with scientific evidence about the effects of secondhand smoke on people's health, especially concerning the prevalence of respiratory diseases, most people are convinced via the central route that secondhand smoke is in fact detrimental to health. That is, unless they are highly motivated to believe otherwise, they conclude that the scientific arguments on this topic are too strong to refute.

The *peripheral route* emphasizes less careful and more emotional, even superficial, evaluation of the message. This route has an indirect but nevertheless powerful effect, especially when there are no logical arguments that can force the use of the central route. This is what happens frequently with political messages (Petty et al., 1993). For example, George W. Bush tried to unite the country behind his antiterrorism views by appealing in emotion-laden terms to what he considered voters' common sense ("I want justice; and there is an old poster out West, I recall, that says, 'Wanted: dead or alive,'" Bush said on September 17, 2001).

Whether a person accepts a message delivered via this route depends on how the person perceives its pleasantness, its similarity to well-established personal attitudes, and the communicator. Think of an "infomercial" on television that attempts to sell exercise equipment. Such commercials often make their pitch while featuring attractive models and an upbeat, eager (and trim) audience. You may believe the evidence presented only because a respected, convincing, and seemingly honest person has expressed the ideas. The attitude change that you may show—desire to buy the product—often stems largely from emotional or personal rather than logical arguments and therefore may not be long-lasting (Petty et al., 1993).

The key idea of the elaboration likelihood model is that people can form or change attitudes because of thoughtful conscious decisions (central route) or because of quick, emotional choices (peripheral route). The central route is used when people have the ability, time, and energy to think through arguments carefully; the peripheral route is more likely to be used when motivation is low, time is short, or the ability to think through arguments is impaired (Petty et al., 1994).

Searching for Cognitive Consistency

People often try to maintain consistency among their various attitudes and between their attitudes and their behavior. *Consistency* refers to a high degree of coherence among elements of behavior and mental processes; such coherence makes day-to-day life go a bit smoother and enables people to make decisions about their future behavior without having to filter out numerous alternatives.

■ **COGNITIVE DISSONANCE.** Imagine the dilemma faced by a scientist who smokes cigarettes and who finds through her research that cigarettes do indeed cause cancer. As a scientist, she must find the research evidence compelling; as a smoker, she can't help pointing out that she feels fine after smoking for years and that her 92-year-old grandmother still smokes. How does she reconcile these opposing facts? Moreover, what further confusion would she suffer if she learned that a chest X-ray showed her grandmother's lungs to be totally clear?

Whenever people's attitudes conflict with one another or with their behavior, they feel uncomfortable. Leon Festinger (1919–1989) termed this feeling **cognitive dissonance**—a state of mental discomfort that arises from a discrepancy between two or more of a person's beliefs or between a person's beliefs and overt behavior. Based on the premise that people seek to reduce such dissonance, Festinger (1957) proposed a *cognitive dissonance theory*. According to the theory, when people experience conflict among their attitudes or between their attitudes and their behavior, they are motivated to change either their attitudes or their behavior (see Figure

Cognitive dissonance [COG-nih-tiv DIS-uh-nents]
A state of mental discomfort arising from a discrepancy between two or more of a person's beliefs or between a person's beliefs and overt behavior.

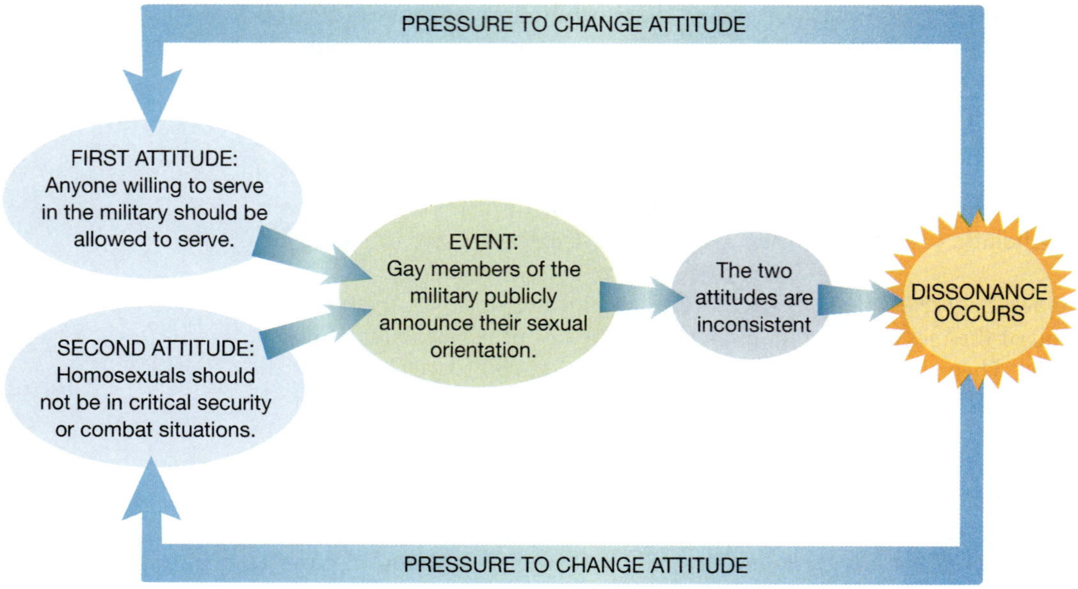

FIGURE 13.3

Cognitive Dissonance

A person often holds conflicting attitudes or behaves in ways that are inconsistent with his or her attitudes. When an event challenges one of those attitudes or the behavior, the person is motivated to change the attitude or behavior because of cognitive dissonance.

13.3). Most psychologists consider cognitive dissonance theory to be a type of motivation theory, because it suggests that people become energized by their cognitive dissonance to do something (Tesser, 2001). As an example of behavior–attitude conflict, suppose you are a strong proponent of animal rights. You support the American Society for the Prevention of Cruelty to Animals (ASPCA) and Greenpeace, refrain from eating meat, and are repulsed by fur coats. Then you win a raffle and are awarded a stylish black leather coat. Wearing the coat goes against your beliefs; but you know it looks great on you, and all your friends admire it. According to cognitive dissonance theory, you are experiencing conflict between your attitudes (belief in animal rights) and your behavior (wearing the coat). To relieve the conflict, you either stop wearing the coat or modify your attitude (leather becomes an acceptable choice). Psychologists acknowledge that not all people are consistent, nor do all psychologists suggest that consistency is important (Stone, 2001).

■ **SELF-PERCEPTION THEORY.** Social psychologist Daryl Bem (1972) claims that people do not change their attitudes because of internal states such as dissonance. He has proposed **self-perception theory**—an approach to attitude formation that assumes that people infer their attitudes and emotional states from their behavior. Bem holds that people don't know what their attitudes are until they stop and examine their behavior. First, they search for an external explanation, such as "someone forced me to do this." If no such explanation is available, they turn to an internal one. That is, people look at their behavior and say, "I must have felt like this if I behaved that way." See Figure 13.4 for a comparison of Bem's view and the traditional view of attitude formation.

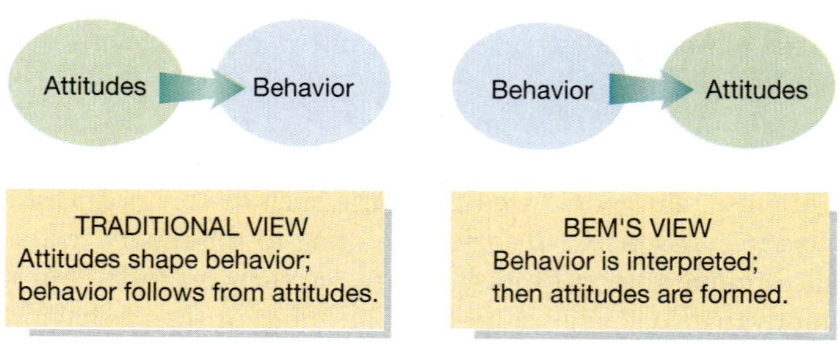

FIGURE 13.4

Two Views of Attitudes

Does behavior follow from attitudes (the traditional view), or do attitudes follow from behavior (Bem's view)?

■ **REACTANCE THEORY.** Our attitudes—and even our deepest beliefs—are often challenged by the behaviors of others. How do we respond to such challenges? Have you ever been ordered (perhaps by a parent) to do something and realized that you wanted to do the exact opposite? According to social psychologist Jack Brehm (1966), whenever people feel their freedom of choice is being unjustly restricted, they are motivated to reestablish it. Brehm terms this form of negative influence *reactance*. **Reactance** is the negative response evoked when there is an inconsistency between a person's self-image as being free to choose and the person's realization that someone is trying to force him or her to choose a particular alternative.

Reactance theory focuses on how people reestablish a feeling that they have freedom of choice. Often, forbidden activities become attractive; choosing the "forbidden fruit" may boost an individual's sense of autonomy. For example, an adolescent who is told he cannot be friends with a member of a minority group may seek out members of that group more often. When coercion is used, resistance follows. According to reactance theory, the extent of reactance is directly related to the extent of the restriction on freedom of choice. If a person does not consider the choice very important and if the restriction is slight, little reactance develops. The wording or delivery of the restriction also affects the extent of reactance. People who are told they *must* respond in a certain way are more likely to react negatively than if they merely receive a suggestion or are given a relatively free choice.

Be an *Active* learner

REVIEW

- Do attitudes predict behavior, or is it the other way around? Explain your answer. pp. 443–444
- What are the most salient qualities of the communicator that can change attitudes? p. 445
- What is the fundamental idea of the elaboration likelihood model? p. 448
- What is reactance theory? p. 451

THINK CRITICALLY

- Under what conditions are attitudes most likely to predict behaviors? Can you think of examples of attitudes that will not predict future behaviors?
- What can people do as individuals to help them avoid the "spin" put on stories from television and print media?

APPLY PSYCHOLOGY

- If you were a sales manager, what would you tell your salespeople to do to appear, and in fact be, more credible to customers?

Social Cognition: The Impact of Thought

On meeting someone for the first time, you might say, "I really like him!" or "I can't put my finger on why, but she irritates me." Often, first impressions are based on nothing more than someone's appearance, body language, and speech patterns. Yet these impressions can have lasting effects. Such individual impressions form one aspect of social cognition—one's view of the entire social milieu.

Social cognition is the process of analyzing and interpreting events, other people, oneself, and the world in general. It focuses on social information in memory, which affects judgments, choices, evaluations, and, ultimately, behavior (Fiske, 1992). Social cognition is a useful and pragmatic process in which people often use mental shortcuts to help them make sense of the world. The process often begins with attempts to form impressions of other people and understand their communications, which can be verbal (words) or nonverbal (looks, gestures, and other means of expression). The process by which people use the behavior and appearance of others to form attitudes about them is known as **impression formation;** sometimes the impressions are accurate, but certainly not always. We'll look at impression formation in more depth later in this section, when we study attribution.

Self-perception theory
Approach to attitude formation that assumes that people infer their attitudes and emotional states from their behavior.

Reactance
The negative response evoked when there is an inconsistency between a person's self-image as being free to choose and the person's realization that someone is trying to force him or her to choose a particular alternative.

Social cognition
The process of analyzing and interpreting events, other people, oneself, and the world in general.

Impression formation
The process by which a person uses the behavior and appearance of others to form attitudes about them.

Organizing the World by Using Mental Shortcuts

You saw earlier that people use their attitudes to help them make decisions and organize their lives. In a related way, using mental shortcuts helps people process information and avoid or reduce information overload. People seek to be "cognitive misers," processing information superficially unless they are motivated to do otherwise. According to Susan Fiske (1992, p. 879), "Social cognition operates in the service of practical consequences." To help themselves make decisions, people develop pragmatic (results-oriented) rules of thumb.

One rule of thumb is *representativeness;* individuals or events that appear to be representative of other members of a group are quickly classified as such, often despite a complete lack of evidence. If you see a 6-foot-6-inch young man, you are likely to assume that he plays basketball—without knowing anything else about him, let alone his interests or abilities. Another rule of thumb is *availability;* the easier it is to bring to mind instances of a category, type, or idea, the more likely it is that the category, type, or idea will be used to describe an event. Politicians count on the availability principle when they associate memorable images and ideas with themselves or their opponents. The more vivid the image, the more likely it will remain available in constituents' memories. Still another rule of thumb is the *false consensus effect;* people tend to think that others hold the same beliefs as they, themselves, do. Finally, *framing,* the way in which information is presented to people, helps determine how easily they accept it. Consider the different impact of two versions of a public health warning: "Ninety-five percent of the population will not be affected by the disease, and only 5% will become seriously ill" versus "Five percent of the population will become seriously ill; the rest of the public will be unaffected."

When other people's behavior fits neatly into your conceptions of the world, you do not need to expend much effort to make judgments about it. One of the most powerful ways of sending easily interpreted signals is nonverbal communication.

Assessing the World by Using Nonverbal Communication

Impression formation often begins with **nonverbal communication,** the communication of information by physical cues or actions that include gestures, tone of voice, vocal inflections, and facial expressions. When a person irritates you, it may be a shrill laugh, a grimace, or an averting of the eyes that generates your bad feelings—not the words the person uses. Nonverbal communication is difficult to suppress and is easily accessible to observers (DePaulo & Friedman, 1998). Three major forms of nonverbal communication are facial expressions, body language, and eye contact.

■ **FACIAL EXPRESSIONS.** Many of the conclusions we draw about other people are based on their facial expressions. Most people, across cultures, can distinguish six basic emotions in the facial expressions of other people: happy, sad, angry, fearful, surprised, and disgusted (Kupperbusch et al., 1999). A simple expression such as a smile, for example, gives others a powerful cue about a person's truthfulness. Research shows that when a person smiles, both the smile and the muscular activity around the eyes help determine if the person is telling the truth or is smiling to mask another emotion (Ekman & Keltner, 1997).

Nonverbal communication
The communication of information by cues or actions that include gestures, tone of voice, vocal inflections, and facial expressions.

Body language
Communication of information through body positions and gestures.

Attribution
The process by which a person infers other people's motives or intentions by observing their behavior.

■ **BODY LANGUAGE.** People also convey information about their moods and attitudes through body positions and gestures—**body language.** Movements such as crossing the arms, lowering the head, and standing rigidly can communicate negative attitudes. On the other hand, when a server in a restaurant moves close to the table and makes direct eye contact, tips increase (Lynn & Mynier, 1993). Aspects of body language differ with culture and gender. For example, in the United States, the energetic and forceful way younger people walk makes them appear sexier, more carefree, and happier than older people (Montepare & Zebrowitz-McArthur, 1988). A pensive, reflective posture or a deferential movement or head position might signal composure, confidence, and status in Japan (Matsumoto & Kudoh, 1993). Gestures also have different meanings in different societies. For example, the

American A-OK sign (a circle formed with the thumb and forefinger) is a rude gesture referring to sexual acts in many cultures. Research also shows that in Western cultures, women are sometimes better than men at communicating and interpreting nonverbal messages, especially facial expressions (Graham & Ickes, 1997). Women are more likely to send nonverbal facial messages but are also more cautious in interpreting nonverbal messages sent to them by men. It turns out, though, that while women may be more accurate than men at interpreting social cues, the advantage is small; furthermore, women cannot intuit, any more than men, the specific content of another person's thoughts (Graham & Ickes, 1997).

■ **EYE CONTACT.** Another form of nonverbal communication is *eye contact*. The eyes convey a surprising amount of information about feelings. A person who is looking at you may glance briefly or stare; you may glance or stare back. You would probably gaze tenderly at someone you were fond of but avoid eye contact with someone you did not trust or like or did not know well. Frequent eye contact between two people may indicate that they are sexually attracted to each other.

People tend to judge others based on the eye contact they engage in, making inferences (attributions) about others' internal motivations from the degree of eye contact. Americans generally prefer modest amounts of eye contact rather than constant eye contact or none at all. Job applicants, for example, are rated more favorably when they make moderate amounts of eye contact; speakers who make more rather than less eye contact are preferred; and witnesses testifying in a court trial are perceived as more credible when they make eye contact with the attorney (DePaulo, 1992). However, all this is true only in Western cultures, which foster an individualistic stance; in some non-Western cultures—for example, Japan—making direct eye contact may be a sign of disrespect, arrogance, or even a challenge.

Inferring the Causes of Behavior: Attribution

If you see people standing in line at a bus stop, you can be fairly certain that they are waiting for a bus. Similarly, if you saw a man at the bus stop reading the Muslim holy book, the Koran, you might infer that he is a devout Muslim. In getting to know others, people often infer the causes of their behavior. When they do, they are making attributions. **Attribution** is the process by which a person infers other people's motives or intentions by observing their behavior. It turns out that attributions are not just cognitive processes but also communicative acts (Malle & Knobe, 1997; Malle et al., 2000). Through attribution, people decide how they will react toward others, in an attempt to evaluate and to make sense of their social world as well as to decide how to respond to it. Attribution may seem like a fairly straightforward process based on common sense. However, it must take into account internal as well as external causes of behavior. Someone making an *internal attribution* thinks the behavior being observed comes from within the person, arising somehow from the individual's personality. Someone making an *external attribution* believes that the person's behavior is caused by outside events, such as the weather or luck.

■ *In some non-Western cultures, making direct eye contact may be a sign of disrespect, arrogance, or even a challenge.*

People can be mistaken when they infer the causes of another person's behavior. Suppose that the man you saw reading the Koran is actually a Catholic taking a class in world religions that uses the book as a text. In that case, your original attribution (that he is a Muslim) is wrong. It is also easy to see that culture shapes attributions; Morris

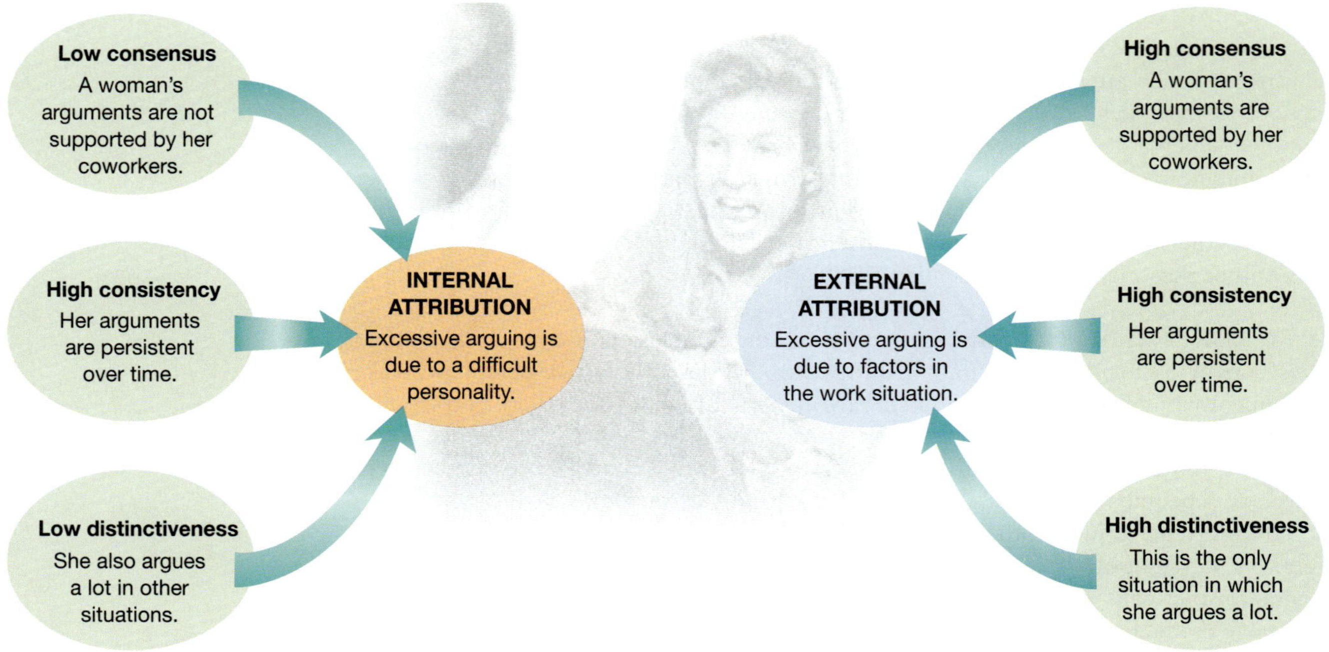

FIGURE 13.5

Attributional Thinking

Kelley's attributional model outlines three criteria for determining the causes of behavior: consensus, consistency, and distinctiveness. According to the theory, assigning an internal attribution to a person's behavior is usually the result of low consensus, high consistency, and low distinctiveness. When a person's behavior shows high consensus, consistency, and distinctiveness, others tend to attribute the causes of the behavior to external reasons.

and Peng (1994) found that accounts of certain crimes in English-language newspapers focused on character, but that Chinese newspapers were more situational in their explanations of the same crimes.

To learn more about attribution, researchers have attempted to conceptualize the process. Harold Kelley's (1972, 1973) theory of attribution suggests that people decide whether the causes of a behavior are internal or external based on three criteria: *consensus, consistency*, and *distinctiveness* (see Figure 13.5). According to Kelley, to infer that someone's behavior is caused by internal characteristics, you must believe that (1) few other people in the same situation would act in the same way (low consensus), (2) the person has acted in the same way in similar situations in the past (high consistency), and (3) the person acts in the same way in different situations (low distinctiveness). To infer that a person's behavior is caused by external factors, you must believe that (1) most people would act that way in that sort of situation (high consensus); (2) the person has acted that way in similar situations in the past (high consistency); and (3) the person acts differently in other situations (high distinctiveness).

To see how Kelley's theory works, suppose that a man in an office gets into an argument with his supervisor, but other people in the same office do not enter into the discussion (low consensus). Also, suppose that the man has argued about the same issue on other occasions (high consistency). Finally, assume that he argues with everybody (low distinctiveness). In such a case, people will no doubt attribute the argument with the supervisor to the man's personality; he is simply argumentative. Now, suppose that many of the man's coworkers join in and support him in the debate (high consensus), that the man has argued about the same issue in the past (high consistency), but that he does not argue in other situations (high distinctiveness). People will be more likely in this case to attribute the argument with the supervisor to situational factors, such as the supervisor's incompetence.

■ **WHY PEOPLE MAKE ATTRIBUTIONS.** Why do people make attributions? What motivates a person to want to know the causes of other people's behavior? The accepted explanation is that people use the process of attribution to maintain a sense of control over their environment. Attribution helps people feel competent and masterful because they think that knowledge about the causes of behavior will help them control and predict similar events in the future. People also make attributions in order to make sense of the world quickly. If a person's behavior fits in with a pattern you have seen before, why analyze it in depth? People are quick to make causal attributions if the behavior being observed is not unusual. It is not surprising that one's cultural viewpoint will shape how people make attributions and when. An Asian mother will attribute a disrespectful remark from a teenager as a much more serious offense than an American mother would, as Asian cultures tend to place high value on respect for elders. Part of this is due to their collectivist culture. (See Table 13.1.)

TABLE 13.1

Attributions in Different Cultural Contexts

Individualist cultures stress personal rather than group goals and value individual freedom and autonomy; *collectivist cultures* stress group needs (including those of family, coworkers, religious and political groups). Collectivist cultures value a tightly knit social fabric, and they also stress a willingness to go along with the group. A representative group of individualist and collectivist cultures is shown below.

Individualist	Collectivist
United States	Hong Kong
Australia	Taiwan
Great Britain	Pakistan
Italy	Panama
France	Guatemala

■ **ASYMMETRIES: ERRORS IN ATTRIBUTION.** The residents of Lake Wobegon are strong women, good-looking men, and above-average children. Like the fictional characters of Garrison Keillor, most of us tend to see ourselves in flattering ways—we often have unrealistic and positive perceptions of our abilities and of our control of our world. Like Lake Wobegoners, we tend to see ourselves and the rest of our peer group as above average (Klar & Giladi, 1997). These perceptions are self-enhancing and even egocentric (Farwell & Wohlwend-Lloyd, 1998). Social psychologists have found that people can be especially error-prone or biased in their attributions concerning the behaviors of others. Sometimes they make errors because they use mental shortcuts that are not accurate. Two of the most common attribution errors are the fundamental attribution error and the actor–observer effect.

When people commit the **fundamental attribution error,** they assume that other people's behavior is caused by their internal dispositions and underestimate situational influences. A man in a restaurant loses his temper, for example, and you assume he is "hot tempered"; but the truth is he was kept waiting for his table, treated rudely by the staff, served the wrong entrée, and then overcharged for his meal. We often observe a behavior and tend to discount or not pay attention to the circumstances (Sabini, Siepmann, & Stein, 2001).

The **actor–observer effect** is the tendency to attribute the behavior (especially the failings) of others to internal character causes but to attribute one's own behavior to situational causes. Individuals know themselves and know that their own day-to-day behavior varies; as observers, on the other hand, they have less information to go on and are more likely to make dispositional or internal attributions. A young child who falls off his bike may say, "The sidewalk was bumpy." When a friend does the same thing, however, the same child may say, "You're clumsy."

Errors in attribution are often judgments made in a limited context, with limited knowledge—and they tend to focus solely on the person or the situation. But attributions must also consider whether a behavior is intentional or unintentional to be thorough (Malle et al., 2000). Often, attributions do not help people understand others (or themselves) better—they simply assign blame (Weisberg et al., 2001). Errors in attribution cause people to blame rape victims rather than rapists, for example. Some errors in attribution come from the fact that people generally perceive themselves as having more positive traits than others do and as being more flexible and adaptable. This tendency has been seen cross-culturally, but it does not exist to the same extent or have the same meaning in every culture (Bersoff & Miller, 1993; Takaku, 2000). This has important implications in business relationships, where goodwill and trust are important. If a businessperson tends to see others as less (or more) flexible than the people in his or her company, this attribution error may affect a negotiation in a fundamental way (Menon et al., 1999).

Fundamental attribution error
The tendency to attribute other people's behavior to dispositional (internal) causes rather than situational (external) causes.

Actor–observer effect
The tendency to attribute the behavior of others to dispositional causes but to attribute one's own behavior to situational causes.

Self-serving bias
People's tendency to ascribe their positive behaviors to their own internal traits, but their failures and shortcomings to external, situational factors.

■ **SELF-SERVING BIAS.** The **self-serving bias** is people's tendency to ascribe their positive behaviors to their own internal traits and characteristics but to blame their failures and shortcomings on external, situational factors. People may develop a self-serving bias because it helps meet their need for self-esteem. This bias can be seen as an adaptive response that helps people deal with their limitations and gives them the courage to venture into areas they normally might not explore. People also develop this bias to help maintain a sense of balance by resolving inconsistencies between old and new information about themselves (Higgins & Snyder, 1990). Often, a person who makes an excuse about some negative personal behavior mentally shifts the cause of the behavior to a less central element of personality or to situational factors. This results in an enhanced self-image and a sense of control. Furthermore, a self-serving bias allows people to present themselves to others in a positive light (Celuch & Slama, 1995). The self-serving bias is more common in men than in women, and in Western than in non-Western cultures (Higgins & Bhatt, 2001).

Errors in attribution contribute to the self-serving bias. People tend to take credit for their successes but to blame others for their failures; that is, people assume that good things happen to them because they deserve them and that bad things happen to them because they have bad luck. The combination of attribution errors and self-serving bias helps *some* people maintain self-esteem and appear competent. Such an attitude, however, may inhibit people from having realistic goals, thus setting them up for disappointment.

The truth is that people are concerned about how they appear to others. And this is especially true if they are somewhat different from other people. For example, Claude Steele has asserted that whenever members of minority groups concentrate on scholastic tasks, they worry about the risk of confirming negative stereotypes about their group (Aronson, Quinn, & Spencer, 1998; Steele, 1997). This burden may drag down their performance, through what Steele calls *stereotype threat*. Stereotype threat probably occurs in part because situational, academic pressure threatens self-esteem; people fear being reduced to a stereotype, so they stop trying and ultimately do worse because of the fear (van Laar, 2001). This behavior (no longer trying) is referred to as *disidentification*; it suggests that there was once a relationship between academic success and self-esteem, but it no longer exists. It turns out that African American boys are especially affected by stereotype threat—they stop trying (they disidentify) because they are no longer uplifted by academic success (Osborne, 1997). Unless minorities (African Americans, older adults, gang members) are resilient to stereotype threat, their performance is likely to suffer (Steele, 1997). The flip side of stereotype threat is positive stereotyping. When people are stereotyped positively—for example, Asian Americans as having superior quantitative skills—their individual performance is enhanced. Shih, Pittinsky, and Ambady (1999) assert that it is the stereotype itself that positively influences performance.

People constantly assess the reasons for other people's behavior in order to make judgments about them. Most people also regularly reflect on their own behavior and in doing so form self-perceptions. Of course, not everyone forms attributions in the same way, and some people, especially in some cultures, are more likely to be sensitive to situational causes of behavior. For example, people in East Asian cultures are less likely to attach traits to an individual and thus consider situational variables more than people in Western cultures do (Choi, Nisbett, & Norenzayan, 1999; Hinton, 2000). Recent research by Greenwald shows that people's views of others and themselves are modifiable. If you change the social context, change the associations, and present to individuals examples of people or situations that are admired or valued and tie those to neutral or even negatively viewed people or events, the new associations tend to take hold (Dasgupta & Greenwald, 2001; Greenwald et al., 2001). Greenwald concludes that people's near-automatic attitudes can be modified and can help buffer them from the negative effects of disappointment or failure (Greenwald & Farnham, 2001). This becomes important in studying prejudice, our next topic.

Prejudice

■ *Children are less often the focus of racial bias.*

People's ideas about themselves and others help define who they are, how they view the world, and ultimately how they behave. But what happens when the ideas, values, or activities of another person or another group of people are different from yours? What happens when you do not know the other group of people well, or at all? Why do some people form negative evaluations of certain groups, such as Arab Americans, African Americans, Asians, Jews, or lesbians and gay men? In this section, we explore prejudice—the shadowy side of attitudes and attributions about others—and how it can be prevented.

Prejudice is a negative evaluation of an entire group of people that is typically based on unfavorable (and often wrong) stereotypes about the group. It is usually based on a small sample of experience, with an individual from the group being evaluated, or even on no experience. **Stereotypes** are fixed, overly simple, and often erroneous ideas about traits, attitudes, and behaviors of groups of people; stereotypes assume that all members of a given group are alike. Stereotypes exist about Native Americans, Catholics, women, and city dwellers, among others; such stereotypes, often shared by many people, can lead to prejudice.

Prejudice, as an attitude, is composed of a cognitive belief (all *X*s are stupid), an emotional element (I hate those *X*s), and often a behavior (I am doing everything I can to keep those *X*s out of my neighborhood). When prejudice is translated into behavior, it is called **discrimination**—behavior targeted at individuals or groups and intended to hold them apart and treat them differently. Stereotyping promotes prejudice, and prejudice promotes discrimination. You can think of discrimination as prejudice in action. It occurs in organizations and companies (Operario & Fiske, 2001) but is most often seen in evaluating other individuals. For example, one common type of discrimination is *sexism* (arising from prejudice based on gender), which involves accepting the strong and widely held beliefs of rigid gender-role stereotyping. Overt discrimination based on sex is illegal, but it still exists, and many people's expectations for women are still based on old stereotypes about gender (Eagly & Steffen, 2000; Goodwin & Fiske, 2001). In fact, Fiske asserts that gender—with all that goes with one's views of gender—dominates perception of another person (Zemore, Fiske, & Kim, 2000).

Sometimes people are prejudiced but do not show that attitude in their behavior; that is, they do not discriminate. Merton (1949) referred to such people as *cautious bigots* (unlike true bigots, who *do* discriminate). Also, people sometimes show *reverse discrimination*, bending over backward to show favoritism to someone from a group that is otherwise discriminated against, in order to counter preexisting biases or stereotypes common in society (Chidester, 1986). That is, someone who deplores prejudice toward African Americans may treat an African American person oversolicitously and may evaluate the person favorably on the basis of standards different from those used for others. This, too, is discrimination. In the end, people who hold stereotypes and discriminate are at risk for maladaptive behaviors that are often at odds with society (Wheeler, Jarvis, & Petty, 2001).

A related behavior is *tokenism*, in which the actions of prejudiced people toward members of a group they dislike are only superficially positive. A male executive may make a token gesture toward a woman on his staff by assigning her to coordinate a project that is of no importance; a manager may hire one token Latino/Latina so as to appear not to discriminate against that group. By engaging in tokenism, a person often attempts to avoid taking more important

Prejudice
Negative evaluation of an entire group of people, typically based on unfavorable (and often wrong) stereotypes about the group.

Stereotypes
Fixed, overly simple, and often erroneous ideas about traits, attitudes, and behaviors of groups of people; stereotypes assume that all members of a given group are alike.

Discrimination
Behavior targeted at individuals or groups and intended to hold them apart and treat them differently.

TABLE 13.2

Prejudice and Discrimination

Prejudice and discrimination interact in such a way that one can be evident without the other.

	Presence of Prejudice	Absence of Prejudice
Presence of Discrimination	An employer believes that non-Whites cannot do quality work and does not promote them, regardless of their performance.	An employer believes that all people can do quality work but does not promote minorities because of long-held company policies.
Absence of Discrimination	An employer believes that non-Whites cannot do quality work but promotes them on the basis of their performance rather than following preconceived ideas.	An employer believes that all people can do quality work and promotes people on the basis of their performance on the job.

actions, such as changing overall personnel or hiring practices. The trivial behavior signifies that he or she has done something for the disliked group. Tokenism has negative consequences for the self-esteem of the person it is applied to, and it perpetuates discrimination.

■ **WHAT CAUSES PREJUDICE?** The causes of prejudice cannot be summarized with a single explanation. Like so many other human behaviors, prejudice is a cross-cultural phenomenon (Pettigrew et al., 1998); it has multiple causes and can be examined within an individual, between individuals, within a group, or within society (Duckitt, 1992). We'll consider four theories to explain prejudice: social learning theory, motivational theory, cognitive theory, and personality theory.

According to *social learning theory*, children *learn* to be prejudiced: they watch parents, other relatives, and neighbors engaged in acts of discrimination, which often include stereotyped judgments and racial slurs; they then incorporate those ideas into their own behavioral repertoire. After children have observed such behaviors, they are reinforced (operant conditioning) for exhibiting similar behaviors. Thus, through imitation and reinforcement, a prejudiced view is transmitted from one generation to the next.

We saw in Chapter 11 that people are motivated to succeed, to get ahead, and to provide for basic as well as high-level emotional needs. If people are raised to compete against others for scarce resources, the competition can foster negative feelings about those competitors. *Motivational theory* asserts that individuals learn to dislike specific individuals (competitors) and then generalize that dislike to whole classes of similar individuals (races, religions, or cultures). Gordon Allport claimed that the arousal of competition followed by erroneous generalizations creates specific prejudice toward minority groups (Allport, 1954/1979; Gaines & Reed, 1995). This helps make minorities that are seen as economic competitors into scapegoats—for example, every new wave of immigrants that has come to the United States (the Italians, Chinese, and Irish in the early part of the 20th century and Mexicans and people from Central America today) have faced being cast as scapegoats. Research with children, adolescents, and adults shows that people who are initially seen as friends or as neutral are sometimes treated badly if they become competitors.

Cognitive theorists assert that people think about individuals and their groups of origin as a way of organizing the world. Cialdini (1993) argues that so many events, circumstances, and changing variables exist in their lives that people cannot easily analyze all the relevant data about any one thing. People thus devise mental shortcuts to help them make decisions. One of those shortcuts is to stereotype individuals and the groups they belong to—for example, all Latinos/Latinas, all homeless people, all men, all lawyers. Research shows that people use such shortcuts to categorize individuals according to traits such as athleticism, intelligence, gender, and ethnicity and that they develop illusory correlations between social groups and their behaviors (Schaller, 1991; Spears & Haslam, 1997; Stone, Perry, & Darley, 1997). An *illusory correlation* is an unsubstantiated and incorrect connection between two events or situations that appear to be related. By devising such shortcuts in thinking, people develop ideas about who is in an *in group*—that is, who is a member of a group to which they belong or want to belong. The division of the world into groups labeled "in" versus "out" or "us" versus "them" is known as **social categorization.** Not only do people divide the world into in groups and out groups, but they tend to see themselves and other members of an in group in a favorable light; doing so bolsters their self-esteem and occurs almost automatically (Fiske, 1998).

As we saw earlier in this chapter, when judging other people, individuals often make fundamental attribution errors. They assume that other people's behavior is caused by their internal dispositions—which may not be true—and that other people are all alike, at least most of the time (Lambert, 1995). They use other people's behaviors as evidence for their own attitudes (prejudices). Thus, for example, hostilities between Arabs and Israelis in the Middle East and between Catholics and Protestants in Ireland are perpetuated.

Researchers such as Susan Fiske (1998) assert that when people develop stereotypes about groups—who's in and who's out—the stereotype and the prejudice that follow from it are more complex than previously thought. This duality of liking/respecting may translate into complex social behaviors such as sexism or racism in which individual members of a given group are treated benevolently while the group as a whole is treated with hostility (Glick & Fiske, 1997; Glick et al., 1997).

Personality psychologists and *evolutionary approaches* have their supporters as well. Fiske (2000) argues that we must not only pay attention to cultural factors but potential evolutionary ones, as well, that assert a person who develops prejudices has a "prejudice-prone personality." In fact, some personality tests examine the extent to which people are likely to be prejudiced. For example, one common personality type is the *authoritarian personality*. Authoritarian individuals may have been fearful and anxious as children and may have been raised by cold, unloving parents who regularly used physical punishment. To gain control and mastery as adults, such individuals become aggressive and controlling over others. They see the world in absolutes—good versus bad, Black versus White. They also tend to blame others for their problems and to become prejudiced toward those they blame (Adorno et al., 1950). Ideas about the relationship between personality and prejudice have roots in psychoanalytic theory and are hotly debated.

student voices

Aimee Mark

University of Kentucky

After taking two courses, Psychology of Oppression and Psychology of Women, I saw the impact society has over groups with little power. I feel compelled to understand how such animosity happens in the hopes of figuring out how society can move beyond petty differences.

■ **IS PREJUDICE AN AUTOMATIC PROCESS?** Social category features (e.g., race, gender) that are normally outside awareness can have commanding influences on thought and behavior. In particular, research shows that there can be an unconscious operation of stereotypes in consciously unprejudiced individuals. Research aimed at providing an understanding of the subtle yet important manner in which stereotyped judgments are produced shows that a person may not be aware of automatic negative reactions to a racial group and may even regard such negative feelings as objectionable when expressed by others; nevertheless they may possess automatic negative feelings.

Research on such unconscious effects is shown in demonstrations inside and outside of the laboratory (Banaji & Greenwald, 1995; Greenwald & Banaji, 1995). Here is a demonstration: participants are asked to rapidly classify (by tapping their left or right knee) each of a list of names (shown on a projector screen) into those that are most often considered Black (such as Malik and Lashonda) and those that are most often seen as White (such as Tiffany and Peter). Next they are asked to quickly classify each of a list of words as pleasant in meaning or unpleasant.

Social categorization
The process of dividing the world into "in" groups and "out" groups.

TEST ITEM 1

I prefer other people over Arab Muslims.	I have no preference.	I prefer Arab Muslims over other people.
☐ Strongly ☐ Moderately ☐ Somewhat ☐ Slightly	☐	☐ Slightly ☐ Somewhat ☐ Moderately ☐ Strongly

Please rate how warm or cold you feel toward the following groups.
(0 coldest feelings, 5 neutral feelings, 10 warmest feelings)

Arab Muslims ________

Other peoples ________

Please rate your agreement or disagreement with the following statements.

It should be against the law to allow security personnel to search passengers in their ethnic group.

☐ Strongly ☐ Moderately ☐ Somewhat ☐ Slightly

Law enforcement officers should pay particular attention to those social groups more heavily involved in crime.

☐ Strongly ☐ Moderately ☐ Somewhat ☐ Slightly

TEST ITEM 2

I prefer Black children over White children.	I have no preference.	I prefer White children over Black children.
☐ Strongly ☐ Moderately ☐ Somewhat ☐ Slightly	☐	☐ Slightly ☐ Somewhat ☐ Moderately ☐ Strongly

Please rate how warm or cold you feel toward the following groups.
(0 coldest feelings, 5 neutral feelings, 10 warmest feelings)

White children ________ White adults ________

Black children ________ Black adults ________

FIGURE 13.6

Self-Report Items Used in Conjunction with the Implicit Association Test

The Implicit Association Test helps assess an individual's level of prejudice. Test questions, used in conjunction with this test, are similar to the items presented here. *(Implicit Association Test Corporation and www.tolerance.org website)*

Then participants classify a randomly ordered list that include all of the Black names, White names, pleasant words, and unpleasant words. First, they are asked to tap their left knee for any Black name or unpleasant-meaning word and their right knee for any White name or pleasant-meaning word. Then the instructions are changed—participants are asked to tap their left knee for White names and unpleasant words and their right knee for Black names and pleasant words. Appropriate controls were made between participants to control for the order of presentation of "White," "pleasant," and so forth.

The result is that it takes about twice as long to respond to the second task, even though the tasks were of equal difficulty. The greater difficulty of giving the same response to Black names and pleasant words provides a measure of automatic preference for the White names. This effect—the speed difference between the two tasks—is very large. Banaji and Greenwald think unconscious prejudice may occur despite people's wishes and results from the culture they live in and the culture's attitudes toward stigmatized groups. Various tests have been developed for assessing prejudice; a sample is shown in Figure 13.6.

■ **SUBTLE PREJUDICE FOR MODERN TIMES.** In the late 1970s and 1980s, researchers began to look at *symbolic racism*—the expression by Whites, in terms of day-to-day behaviors, of the feeling that Blacks violate certain cherished American values (McConahay & Hough, 1976). Kinder and Sanders (1996) argue that Whites adopt a socially acceptable and ostensibly nonprejudicial reason to reject minorities—Blacks have supposedly violated the cherished American value of being independent and self-sufficient by accepting welfare payments. This less blatant but still overt form of racism is expressed by voting against all Black candidates and opposing busing, integration, and affirmative action. Today, proponents of this idea, especially Donald Kinder (Kinder & Sanders, 1996), call it *racial resentment* and assert that it features indignation as a central emotional theme, provoked by the idea that minorities—in this case, African Americans—are getting more than their fair share economically. Racial resentment is thought to be at the heart of White American feelings toward Blacks. Although not all researchers agree, Kinder argues that racial resentment colors Whites' views of Blacks and fuels their prejudiced and discriminatory behaviors.

HOW TO REDUCE AND ELIMINATE PREJUDICE. To reduce and eliminate prejudice, people can teach rational thinking, try to judge others based on their behavior, promote equality, and avoid labels that perpetuate stereotypes (Jussim et al., 1995). Research shows that once people have worked on a community project with a member of a different culture, lived with a person of another race, or prayed with members of a different church, their emotional views of them as individuals change (Pettigrew, 1997). While some individuals use race or ethnicity as a categorizing variable, it turns out that as little as a few minutes exposed to an individual who is grouped by some other category—such as religion, political party, or which side of a social issue a person aligns—can change an individual's use of social categorization (p. 459) and ultimately their definition of "us" and "them." (Kurzban, Tooby, & Cosmides, 2001)

A society can pass laws that mandate equal treatment for all people. Voters can elect officials on the basis of their competence, throw them out on the basis of their incompetence, and make gender-neutral judgments of performance. The administrator of the U.S. Environmental Protection Agency, Christine Todd Whitman, should be judged by her performance, not by her gender. *Washington Post* publisher Katherine Graham was respected for her courage and style. And General Colin Powell, who is widely perceived to have integrity and a strong character, has the ability to transform people's views of the role of African Americans in U.S. society (Sigelman, 1997).

Be an *Active* learner

REVIEW

- Identify key characteristics of nonverbal communication. pp. 450–453
- Describe the fundamental difference between internal and external attribution in interpreting the causes of behavior. pp. 453–454
- Describe the actor-observer effect. p. 455
- How do psychological theories explain the development of prejudice? p. 458
- How do you describe social categorization? p. 459
- What are symbolic racism and racial resentment? p. 460

THINK CRITICALLY

- Can you describe any useful functions that errors in attribution have served for you or a friend in the last few months? Have such errors helped someone feel more intelligent, more worthwhile, or less at fault?
- Negative behaviors, especially in a small group, are high in distinctiveness. What does this suggest will happen when the negative behaviors occur in a minority ethnic group?

APPLY PSYCHOLOGY

- In the United States, prejudice has led to unfair treatment of African Americans, Arab Americans, women, the aged, gay people, and many minority groups. What are some effective techniques (not necessarily governmental policies) that could help eliminate prejudice, right previous injustices, and make for a more tolerant society?
- Devise a program that could be run in a club, house of worship, or social group that could help break down the idea of "us" versus "them."

Social Interactions

How to start a conversation with someone you haven't met before is a problem all of us have faced. When people interact, new realms of possible behaviors open up. Day-to-day social interactions can be exceedingly complex, affected by many variables.

Social Influence

Parents try to instill specific values in their children. An adolescent admires the hairstyle or mannerisms of an attractive peer and decides to adopt them. Adoring fans emulate the behavior or appearance of a rock star or top athlete. Religious leaders exhort their followers to live in certain ways. Social interactions affect individual behavior in profound ways; when people are members of a group, their social interactions are often even more noticeable than their individual behavior.

Social influence refers to the ways people alter the attitudes or behaviors of others, either directly or indirectly. Two important topics studied by researchers on social influence are conformity and obedience.

Social influence
The ways people alter the attitudes or behaviors of others, either directly or indirectly.

■ **CONFORMITY.** When someone changes her or his attitudes or behaviors so that they are consistent with those of other people or with social norms, the person is exhibiting **conformity**, or trying to fit in. An individual may adopt positive, prosocial behaviors such as wearing seat belts, volunteering time and money to a charity, or buying only products that are safe for the environment. Sometimes, however, conformity leads to counterproductive, antisocial behaviors, such as drug abuse, fraternity hazing, or mob violence.

■ *Groups strongly influence conformity; Solomon Asch found that people in a group tend to adopt its standards.*

People conform to the behaviors and attitudes of their peer or family groups. A young executive may wear conservative dark suits and drive a BMW in order to fit in with office colleagues. Similarly, the desire to conform can induce people to do things they might not do otherwise. An infamous example is the My Lai massacre, in which American soldiers slaughtered Vietnamese civilians during the Vietnam War. Although several factors account for the soldiers' behavior (including combat stress, hostility toward the Vietnamese, and obedience to authority), the soldiers also yielded to extreme group pressure. The few soldiers who refused to kill civilians hid that fact from their comrades. One soldier even shot himself in the foot to avoid taking part in the slaughter.

Groups strongly influence conformity. Solomon Asch (1907–1996) found that people in a group adopt its standards. Examples of conformity to group standards range from an individual's refraining from speaking during a public address to a whole nation's discriminating against a particular ethnic group. Studies also show that individuals conform to group norms even when they are not pressured to do so. Consider what happens when an instructor asks a class of 250 students to answer a relatively simple question, but no one volunteers. When asked, most of the students will report that they did not raise their hand because no one else did. Asch (1955, p. 6) stated: "The tendency to conformity in our society [is] so strong that reasonably intelligent and well-meaning young people [being] willing to call white black is a matter of concern. It raises questions about our ways of education and about the values that guide our conduct."

Imagine this situation: You have agreed to participate in an experiment. You are seated at a table with four other students. The experimenter holds up a card with two straight lines printed on it and asks each of you to pick which of the two lines is longer, A or B. You quickly discover that the task is simple. The experimenter holds up successive cards showing pairs of lines; in each case, every participant correctly identifies the longer line. After several rounds, you notice that the first person has chosen line A instead of line B, though B is obviously longer. You are surprised when the second person also chooses line A, then the third, then the fourth. Your turn is next. You are sure that line B is longer. What do you do?

FIGURE 13.7

Asch's Classic Study of Conformity

Participants were shown cards like these and asked to choose the line on the lower card that was the same length as the line on the upper card. The confederates deliberately chose incorrect answers to see if the unsuspecting participant (fifth from the left in the photo) would go along with the majority.

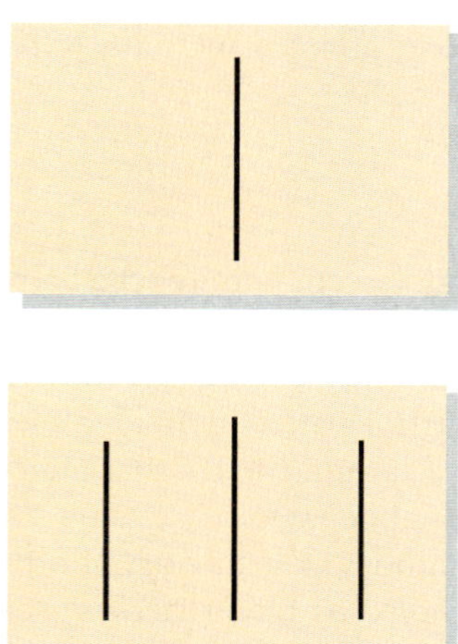

In 1951, Asch performed an experiment like this to explore conformity. Seven to nine people were brought together and asked to judge which of three lines matched a standard line (see Figure 13.7). However, only one group member—the naive participant—was unaware of the purpose of the study. The others were confederates of the researcher, and they deliberately gave false answers to try to influence the naive participant. Asch found that some naive participants would go along with the group, even though the majority answer was obviously wrong and even though the group exerted no explicit pressure to conform.

It turns out that the number of confederates a researcher uses is a critical variable in such situations. When 1 or 2 individuals collaborate with the researcher, the naive participant shows considerably less tendency to conform than when 10 do. Another important variable is the existence of dissenting votes. If even 1 of 15 people disagrees with the other collaborating participants, the naive participant is more likely to choose the correct line.

How do groups influence individuals to conform? One conformity variable is the *amount of information* provided when a decision is to be made. When people are uncertain of how to behave in ambiguous situations, they seek the opinions of others. For example, people who are unsure of how they should vote in an election will often ask trusted friends for advice.

Another important variable that affects the degree of conformity is the *relative competence* of the group. People are more likely to conform to the decision of a group if they perceive its members as being more competent than they are. This pressure becomes stronger as group size increases. A first-year student in a large class, for example, may not answer even a simple question if no one else speaks up, because he assumes that his classmates are more competent than he is.

Position within a group also affects individual behavior. A person who confidently believes that a group holds her in high esteem will respond independently. If she feels insecure about her status, she may respond as the group does in order not to worsen her position within the group.

The *public nature of behavior* also determines people's responses. Individuals are more willing to make decisions that are inconsistent with those of a group when the behavior is private. In a democracy, for example, citizens vote privately so as to minimize group pressure on how individuals vote.

Why do people tend to conform? Several theories have attempted to explain this phenomenon. The *social conformity approach* states that people conform to avoid the stigma of being wrong, deviant, or different from others. According to this view, people want to do the right thing, and they define "right" as whatever is generally accepted (Festinger, 1954). Another explanation for why individuals in a group conform—or don't conform—is *attribution*. When a person can identify causes for the behavior of others in a group and strongly disagrees with those causes, conformity disappears (Ross, Bierbrauer, & Hoffman, 1976). The issue of *independence* also helps explain conformity (or the lack of it). Although most people would like to be independent, independence is risky. People in a group may have to face the consequences of their independence, such as serious disapproval, peer pressure to conform, being seen as deviant, becoming less powerful, or simply being left out. Last, conformity is partly a matter of *expediency*; conforming conserves mental energy. Recall Cialdini's (1993) argument that people face too many events, circumstances, and changing variables to be able to analyze all the relevant data. People therefore need shortcuts to help them make decisions. It is efficient and easy for people to go along with others whom they trust and respect, especially if the basic elements of a situation fit in with their views.

It is important to recognize that not everyone conforms to group pressures all the time. Both everyday experience and research show that *dissenting opinions* help counteract group influence and conformity. Even one or two people in a large group can seriously influence decision making. Moreover, when group decision making occurs, a consistent opposing voice (think of South African leader Nelson Mandela) can exert substantial influence and foster a sense of liberation, even when the opposition has little power or status (Kitayama & Burnstein, 1994). Not surprisingly, analysis of cross-cultural studies shows that people in countries with collectivist

Conformity
People's tendency to change attitudes or behaviors so that they are consistent with those of other people or with social norms.

cultures exhibit more conformity than do people in countries with individualistic cultures (Cialdini et al., 2001).

OBEDIENCE AND MILGRAM'S STUDY. **Obedience** is compliance with the orders of another person or group of people. The studies on obedience by Stanley Milgram (1933–1984) are classic, and his results and interpretations still generate debate. Milgram's work focused on the extent to which an individual will obey a significant person. His studies showed that ordinary people were remarkably willing to comply with the wishes of others, especially if they saw the others as legitimate authority figures.

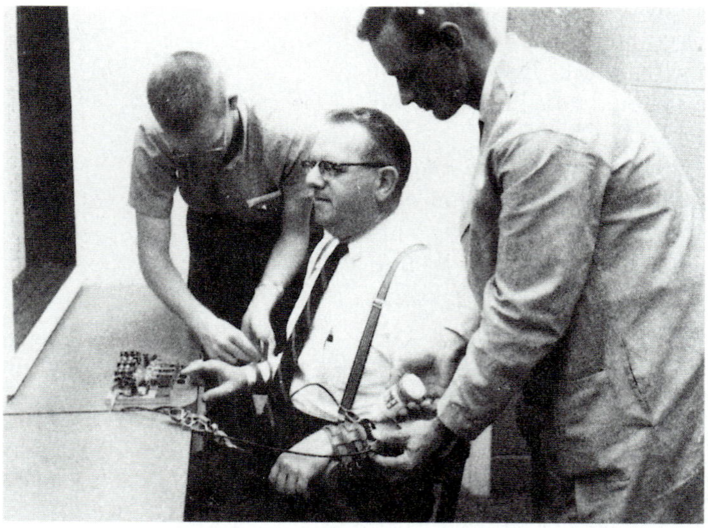

Milgram's work focused on the extent to which an individual will obey. His studies showed that ordinary people were remarkably willing to comply with the wishes of others, especially if they saw the others as legitimate authority figures.

Imagine that you are one of the participants in Milgram's 1963 study at Yale University. You and a man you do not know are brought into a laboratory and are told that you will be participating in an experiment on the effect of punishment on paired-associate learning. You draw lots to determine who will be the teacher and who will be the learner. Unbeknownst to you, the drawing is actually rigged so that you will be the teacher and the man, who is collaborating with the experimenter, will be the learner.

The learner/collaborator is taken to an adjoining room. You are shown a shock-generating box containing 30 switches, with labels that range from "Slight Shock" to "Danger: Severe Shock." You are told that the shock-generating equipment is connected to the learner in the other room. The learner will be given a test, and you will listen to his answers and punish him when he is incorrect. Your job is to shock the learner by flipping one of the switches every time he makes an error on the test.

As the test continues, the experimenter and an assistant, both wearing white lab coats, encourage you to increase the shock voltage by one level each time the learner makes a mistake. As the shock level rises, the learner/collaborator screams as if he is suffering increasing pain. When the shocks reach a certain intensity, the learner stops responding vocally and instead pounds on the walls of the booth. The experimenter tells you to treat the learner's lack of vocal response as an error and to continue increasing the levels of shock. What would you do?

This was the basic scenario of the Milgram study. As you may have guessed by now, the learner/collaborators were not actually receiving shocks; they were only pretending to be in pain, but the participants believed they were delivering actual shocks. As Figure 13.8 shows, 65% of the participants in the study continued to shock the learner until they had delivered shocks at all levels. However, not all of Milgram's participants were obedient. Moreover, in a follow-up study, the presence of another "teacher" who refused to participate reduced the probability of obedience to as little as 10% (Milgram, 1965; Powers & Geen, 1972). These data suggest that obedience is sensitive to both authority and peer behavior. The fact that an individual's ability to resist coercion improves in the presence of an ally who also resists indicates the importance of other social influences on behavior.

Obedience
Compliance with the orders of another person or group of people.

Did conducting the study at the prestigious Yale University influence the participants? Milgram (1965) suggested that his experiment might have involved a particular type of experimental bias—*background authority*. To investigate the issue, Milgram conducted a second study in an office building in Bridgeport, Connecticut. Participants were contacted by mail and had no knowledge that Milgram or his associates were from Yale. In this second study, 48% of the participants delivered the

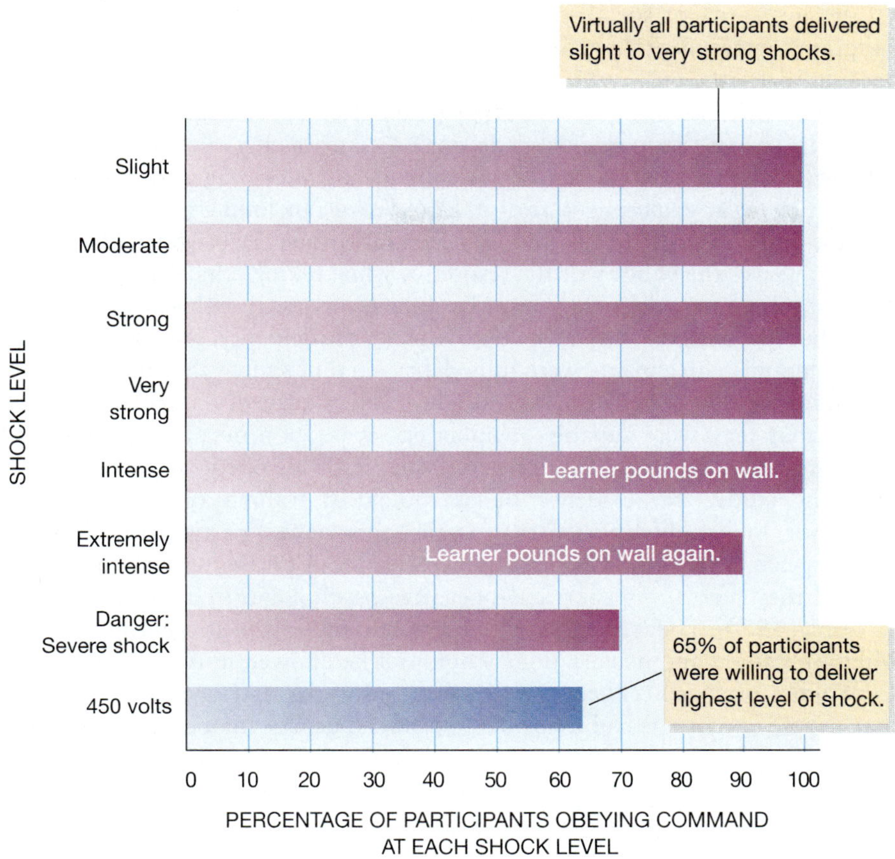

FIGURE 13.8

Milgram's Obedience Study

(Milgram, 1963.)

maximum level of shock, as compared with the 65% of those who participated at Yale. Although this was not a huge difference, Milgram inferred that the perceived authority of an institution could induce obedience in participants. Moreover, an institution's qualitative position within a category (for example, a prestigious university versus a little-known one) may be less important than the simple fact that it is some type of institution (for example, a university rather than an office building) (Rochat, Maggioni, & Modigliani, 2000).

Why did so many participants in Milgram's experiments obey the wishes of the authority figure? One reason is that they were volunteers. Volunteers often bring undetected biases to an experimental situation, and one such bias is a willingness to go along with authority. When instructed to deliver a shock, Milgram's participants did what they were told (Blass, 2000). Another explanation derives from learning theories. Children learn that authority figures, such as teachers and parents, know more than they do and that taking their advice generally proves beneficial. As adults, they maintain those beliefs and apply them to authority figures such as employers, judges, government leaders, and so on. Cialdini (1993) also notes that obedience has practical advantages, such as helping people make decisions quickly: "It is easy to allow ourselves the convenience of automatic obedience. . . . We don't have to think, therefore we don't" (p. 178).

Other researchers repeated Milgram's methods, and the results of one study suggest that obedience to authority is not specific to Western cultures (Shanab & Yahya, 1978). People tend to obey those in authority, and such obedience is even more highly valued in many non-Western cultures. Students at the University of Jordan participated in a study similar to Milgram's; as in the original Milgram study, about 65% were willing to give high levels of shock to other students. Milgram's findings apply to men and women, old and young; they show that people's interactions within the social world are strongly affected by others.

In any study of social influence, researchers worry about ethical issues, and Milgram's experimental methods certainly raised such issues. The primary issue was deception; another involved potential harm to those who participated. Obtaining unbiased responses in psychological research often requires deceiving naive participants. To ensure that participants do not have any lasting ill effects, researchers debrief them after the experiment. **Debriefing** means informing participants about the true nature of an experiment after its completion, including an explanation of hypotheses, methods, and expected or potential results. Debriefing *after* the experiment preserves the validity of the responses while taking ethical considerations into account. Of course, debriefing must be done clearly and with sensitivity, especially in studies like Milgram's, which could affect a participant's self-esteem.

Milgram's participants were fully debriefed and shown that they had not actually harmed the other person. Nevertheless, critics argued, the participants came to realize that they were capable of inflicting severe pain on other people. Milgram therefore had a psychiatrist interview a sample of his obedient participants a year after the study. No evidence of psychological trauma or injury was found. Moreover, one study reported that participants viewed participation in the obedience experiment as a positive experience. They did not regret having participated, nor did they report any short-term negative psychological effects (Ring, Wallston, & Corey, 1970). Today, because more stringent ethical constraints are now in place, Milgram's study and its variations would not be allowed in research laboratories.

Studies of social influence, especially conformity and obedience studies, show that people exert powerful influences on others, gender matters little, and those influences are greater when they are exerted by a group (Blass, 1999, 2000). Let's look next at the effects of groups on individual behavior and how individuals behave within groups.

Groups: Sharing Common Goals

"Visa—it's everywhere you want to be," according to Visa. In appealing to people's desire to be part of an in group, Visa is employing psychological principles to sell its product and engender loyalty. To make the group of Visa cardholders as attractive as possible, the company has run magazine ads featuring famous athletes, actors, politicians, and businesspeople who are cardholders and who travel to the most exotic, desirable places—everywhere you want to be.

Membership in any group—even holding a Visa card conveys such group membership—does confer certain advantages, which is why people belong to all kinds of groups. There are formal groups, such as the American Association of University Students, and informal ones, such as a lunch group of coworkers. A **group** can be any number of people who are working with a common purpose or have some common goals, characteristics, or interests. By joining a group, people indicate that they agree with or have a serious interest in its purpose. For example, a major function of the American Cancer Society is to raise money for cancer research, and a person's membership indicates an interest in finding a cure for cancer. It has generally been thought that groups enhance individual performance; research shows, however, that this effect is modest and that the larger effect that emanates from a group is a sense of cohesion, solidarity, and commitment to a task (Mullen & Copper, 1994).

■ **SOCIAL FACILITATION.** Individual behavior is affected not only by membership in a group but also by the mere presence of a group. **Social facilitation** is a change in behavior that occurs when people are (or believe they are) in the presence of other people. For example, an accomplished person who is playing a sport may do even better when other people are watching. A person who is less accomplished, however, may do worse when other people are around. Research studies that examine people's performance at various tasks—for example, keyboard data entry—show this effect (Aiello & Kolb, 1995).

Debriefing
Informing participants about the true nature of an experiment after its completion.

Group
Two or more individuals who are working with a common purpose or have some common goals, characteristics, or interests.

Social facilitation
Change in behavior that occurs when people believe they are in the presence of other people.

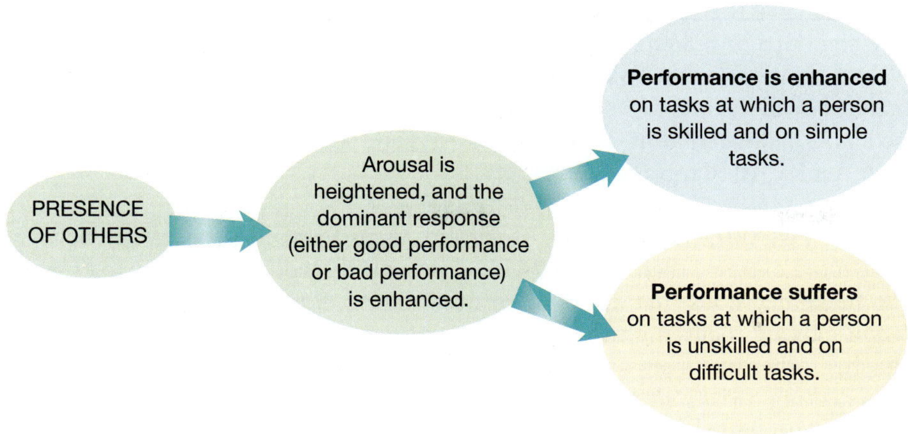

FIGURE 13.9

Social Facilitation

The presence of others may either help or hinder a person's performance. The presence of others heightens arousal, and heightened arousal leads to better performance on tasks a person is good at and worse performance on difficult tasks.

Whether the presence of others is likely to change a person's behavior for better or worse is illustrated in Figure 13.9. This figure is based on Robert Zajonc's (1965) drive theory of social facilitation. According to Zajonc, the presence of others produces heightened arousal, which leads to a greater likelihood that an individual will exhibit a particular response (Jackson & Latané, 1981; Zajonc, 1965).

But just what is the nature of the heightened arousal? This is a source of some debate. One theory of social facilitation suggests that fear of evaluation—not the mere presence of people—brings about changes in performance (Innes & Young, 1975). If an auto mechanic knows that a customer is watching him repair an engine, he is likely to increase his work speed to demonstrate his efficiency and professionalism. Bond and Titus (1983) suggest that the effects of social facilitation are often overestimated and the effects of believing oneself to be observed are often underestimated. They caution that studies of social facilitation must take into account the actual and believed presence of observers, as well as the perceived importance of the evaluation by the observers. Being evaluated by a friend has a different effect than being evaluated by a stranger (Buck et al., 1992).

■ **SOCIAL LOAFING.** A decrease in an individual's effort and productivity as a result of working in a group is known as **social loafing.** Suppose you and your friends join forces in a club effort to win a tug of war. Do you expend as much effort as a member of the group as you would have if you had to win the tug of war alone? Research confirms the social loafing effect. In an experiment in which participants were instructed to clap their hands and cheer, they clapped and cheered less loudly when they were part of a group (Latané, Williams, & Harkins, 1979).

Most psychologists claim that social loafing occurs when individual performance within a group cannot be evaluated—that is, when poor performance may go undetected and exceptional performance may go unrecognized. Consequently, people feel less pressure to work hard or efficiently. The general idea is that, as group size increases, individual members believe their efforts are more dispensable—the group can function without their help. "Let someone else do it" becomes the prevailing view. Such findings are evident cross-culturally; for example, Japanese students, who come from a society that stresses cohesion and group cooperation, worked less hard when they were working together than when working alone (Kugihara, 1999).

Social loafing is minimized when the task is attractive and rewarding and when the group is cohesive and committed to task performance (Karau & Williams, 2001). It is also less apparent when the group is small, when the members know one another well, and when a group leader calls on individuals by name or lets it be known that individual performance may be evaluated (Williams, Harkins, & Latané, 1981). Some researchers have observed decreased social loafing when

Social loafing
Decrease in effort and productivity that occurs when an individual works in a group instead of alone.

individuals have the opportunity to assess their own performance relative to an objective standard or relative to other people's performance, even though no one else is evaluating them (Szymanski & Harkins, 1993). As with so many other social phenomena, a wide array of variables can alter the extent of social loafing, yet researchers conclude that it occurs across a wide variety of tasks and situations (North, Linley, & Hargraeves, 2000).

GROUP POLARIZATION. People in groups may be willing to adopt behaviors slightly more extreme than their individual behavioral tendencies. They may be willing to make decisions that are risky or even daring. Some early research on group decision making focused on the willingness of individuals to accept riskier alternatives when other members of the group did so; this research described such individuals as making a *risky shift* in decisions.

In a group, individuals initially perceive themselves as being more extreme than the other members of the group. They also believe they are fairer, more right-minded, more liberal, and so on. When they discover that their positions are not very different from those of others in the group, they shift, or become *polarized*, to show that they are even more right-minded, fairer, or more liberal. They also may become more assertive in expressing their views. Shifts or exaggerations in group members' attitudes or behaviors that take place after group discussion are referred to as **group polarization;** in an individual, such a shift is known as a *choice shift* (Zuber, Crott, & Werner, 1992).

Another explanation of the polarization phenomenon, *persuasive argument*, asserts that people tend to become more extreme after hearing views similar to their own. A person who is mildly liberal on an issue becomes even more liberal, more polarized. This explanation suggests that people in a group often become more wedded to their initial views instead of becoming more moderate. If other people in the group hold similar views, that may polarize individual members even more. The effects of group polarization are particularly evident among juries. After group discussion, jury members are likely to return to their initial views and argue for them more strongly. Thus, individual jury members who initially have doubts about a witness will have even deeper doubts after group discussion.

Another explanation for group polarization is *diffusion of responsibility*—the feeling of individual members of a group that they cannot be held responsible for the group's actions. If a group makes a decision to invest money, for example, no single individual is responsible. Diffusion of responsibility may allow the members to make far more extreme investment decisions as a group than they would individually.

■ *Groups such as the military, prisons, and cults encourage their members to conform and behave as members of the larger group.*

Social comparison may also play a role in group polarization. People compare their views with the ideas of others whom they respect and who may hold more extreme attitudes than theirs. Feeling as right-minded as their colleagues, they become at least as liberal or as conservative as their peer group—they polarize their views.

GROUPTHINK: COLLECTIVE WISDOM? Studies of decision making in government have often focused on **groupthink**—the tendency of people in a group to seek concurrence with one another when reaching a decision, rather than effectively evaluating the options. Groupthink occurs when group members reinforce shared beliefs in

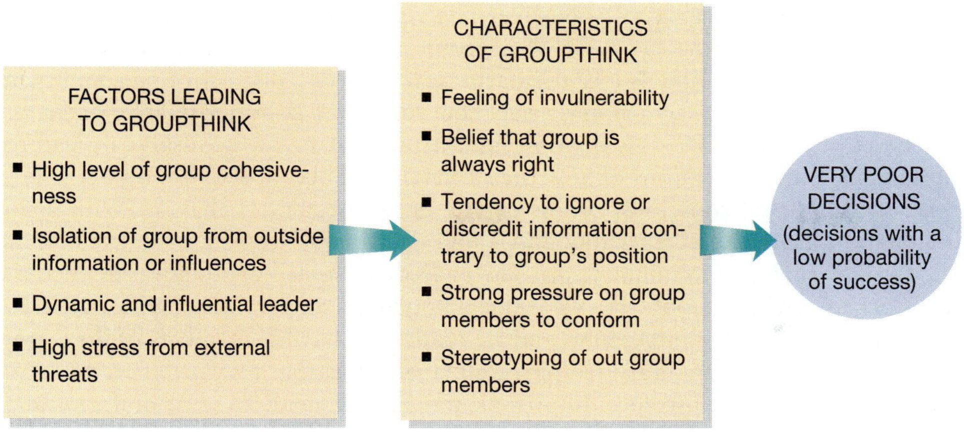

FIGURE 13.10
Groupthink: Development and Results

the interest of getting along. The group does not allow its members to disagree, to accept dissenting opinions, or to evaluate options realistically (Janis, 1983). Groupthink discredits or ignores information not held in common, and thus cohesive groups are more likely to exhibit it (Mullen et al., 1994). Figure 13.10 summarizes the factors leading to groupthink.

Studies of history and government offer several examples of groupthink resulting in defective decision making, including the ill-fated decision to launch the space shuttle *Challenger* in 1986 (Moorhead, Ference, & Neck, 1991). Another example is the Bay of Pigs invasion, cited by Janis (1982). In April 1961, President John F. Kennedy decided to go ahead with a CIA plan to use U.S.-trained anti-Castro exiles to invade Cuba and bring down the regime of Fidel Castro. When the president asked for counsel from his advisers—an impressive group with wide political experience—no one voted against the plan, and the mission was launched. The Bay of Pigs invasion was a result of the unwillingness of group members to upset each other (or the boss), and it turned out to be a major military and political fiasco that nearly resulted in war between the United States and the Soviet Union (an ally of Cuba).

Groupthink occurs when members' overriding concern is to maintain group cohesiveness and harmony. Cohesiveness helps individuals believe that the group cannot make mistakes. In addition, strong leaders often insulate a group from outside information to keep the group thinking along the same line (Pratkinis and Turner, 1999; Raven, 1998).

Despite the intuitive appeal of the groupthink concept, however, research support for it is limited (Paulus, 1998). Nevertheless, groupthink *can* happen and researchers continue to study it; it is a defective process that people should guard against, and leaders, committees, and technology experts need to focus on the variables that may create groupthink, as well as factors that help defend against it (Shelton, 2000).

■ **UNRESTRAINED GROUP BEHAVIOR.** The presence of other people can arouse people (social facilitation), can make them less active (social loafing), can cause them to take extreme views (group polarization), or can lead to poor decisions (groupthink). When placed in a group, normally thoughtful people have been known to make bad decisions and even to exhibit irrational behaviors. Consider mob violence. When people engage in a riot, looting, or other violent behavior, individuals explain their participation not in terms of individual responsibility but as a group decision.

A key component of unrestrained behavior such as mob violence is *anonymity*. Anonymity produces a lack of self-awareness and self-perception that leads to decreased concern with social evaluation. When people have fewer concerns about being evaluated, they are more willing to engage in inappropriate or irrational behaviors. When there is violence or illegal drug use among a crowd at a rock concert,

Group polarization
Shifts or exaggeration in group members' attitudes or behavior as a result of group discussion.

Groupthink
The tendency of people in a group to seek concurrence with one another when reaching a decision, rather than effectively evaluating the options.

for example, people feel less responsible. The view that no single individual can be held responsible for the behavior of a group arises out of **deindividuation**—the process by which individuals lose their self-awareness and distinctive personality in the context of a group, which may lead them to engage in antinormative behavior (Diener et al., 1980). Deindividuation (and its accompanying arousal) can lead to shifts in people's perceptions of how their behavior will be viewed—and thus to less controlled, less self-conscious, or less careful decisions about behavior. With deindividuation, people alter their thoughts about decisions.

Groups such as the military, prisons, and cults use deindividuation to encourage their members to conform. With their unique personality stripped away, they are no longer treated as individuals and are made to behave as members of the larger group. In boot camp, military recruits are made to feel that they are there to serve the group, not their conscience. In prisons, inmates are made to wear uniforms and are assigned numbers. A cult persuades members to go along with group beliefs and acquire a sense of obligation to the group by asking individual members to perform increasingly difficult acts on the group's behalf. In the end, an individual's behavior in a group often becomes distorted, more extreme, and less rational; the group makes members feel less accountable for their own actions. Researchers are increasingly asserting that people's interpretation of the setting in which they find themselves holds the key to understanding deindividuated behavior.

Aggression and Violence: The Threatening Side of Human Behavior

Terrorism and teenagers' violence have dominated the news in the past few years. Terrorism in the United States and in Israel is a part of people's daily awareness. No traveler here or abroad can fail to be aware of the potential violence of terrorism. And no one will ever know for sure what went so wrong in the lives of Eric Harris and Dylan Klebold, the two high school students who planned and executed the devastating 1999 Columbine High School massacre. While trying to help the traumatized families and friends of the victims, psychologists became aware, yet again, of how little we really know about one another, about how our actions and words influence others. What were key domestic and world events or interactions that shaped the attitudes and behaviors of both international and teenage terrorists? Many questions like these will be asked again and again as the families and friends of the victims try to recover from their shock and grief.

Social interactions are sometimes quite inconsequential—briefly saying hello to others we pass in school or on the street, for example. Other social interactions affect important relationships—such as when your teacher or boss makes a point to commend your good work. But social interactions also include the violent side of people's behaviors, including aggressive and brutal acts—children, adolescents, and adults terrorize, hurt, and even kill each other. Often, the cause is not apparent or does not justify the act.

When people feel unable to control situations that affect their lives, they may become frustrated, angry, and aggressive. Social psychologists define **aggression** as any behavior intended to harm another person or thing. An aggressive person may attempt to harm others physically through force, verbally through rumors or irritating comments, or emotionally by withholding attention or love. On a larger scale, whole countries attempt to harm others by acts of war. Three major theoretical explanations for aggressive behavior focus on acquired drives, cognitive psychology, and biological influences.

Deindividuation
The process by which individuals lose their self-awareness and distinctive personality in the context of a group, which may lead them to engage in antinormative behavior.

Aggression
Any behavior intended to harm another person or thing.

■ **ACQUIRED DRIVES.** An explanation for aggressive behavior is that it results when goal-directed behavior has been frustrated—this is the *frustration–aggression hypothesis*, initially proposed by John Dollard and colleagues (1939). This theory

TABLE 13.3

A Tendency to Violence Is Not Inherited

Scientific groups, including the American Psychological Association, have adopted a statement called the Seville Statement on Violence, which asserts that the use of scientific data to support war is wrong and is based on erroneous assumptions.

The following statements are scientifically incorrect:
We have inherited a tendency to make war from our animal ancestors.
War or any other violent behavior is programmed into our human nature.
Through the course of human evolution, aggression, more than any other characteristic, has been programmed into human behavior.
Humans have a violent brain.
War is caused by instinct or any other specific inborn motivation.

Adapted from the Seville Statement on Violence (APA, 1994)

relies on observations demonstrating that people involved in everyday goal-oriented tasks often become aggressive or angry when frustrated. For example, ordinarily, you may be unlikely to become very upset if another car pulls into traffic in front of you. However, if you are late for work, you might honk or mutter angrily at the other driver. On a larger scale, the violence between Catholics and Protestants in Northern Ireland is fueled in part by intense competition for decent jobs in a depressed economy.

Berkowitz (1964) examined the evidence for the frustration–aggression hypothesis and proposed a modified version of it. He suggested that frustration creates a *readiness* for aggressive acts rather than producing actual aggression. He showed that even when frustration is present, certain events must occur or certain conditions must exist before aggression results; for example, someone embroiled in a heated argument might be more likely to become aggressive if there is a weapon lying on a nearby table. In a later reformulation, Berkowitz (2000) suggested that frustrations generate aggressive inclinations to the extent that they arouse negative feelings in the frustrated individual (Berkowitz, 1990). Berkowitz's conception accounts for the instances when frustrated people don't become aggressive. Although many psychologists find the frustration–aggression hypothesis too simplistic, it is useful, in part because it has led to other research that helps describe behavior—for example, cognitive theory.

■ **COGNITIVE PSYCHOLOGY.** A tendency to violence is not inherited (see Table 13.3); rather people actively engage in thoughts that lead them to violent behaviors, according to cognitive psychologists. What thoughts go through people's minds when they engage in road rage? What possesses people to engage in mob violence? Leonard Eron (1987) conducted a 22-year longitudinal study of aggression. He tracked the entire third-grade population (870 students) of Columbia County, a semirural area in New York State. Eron's work probed the influences in children's lives that cause them to *interpret* the world in a way that makes them aggressive. He reasoned that an aggressive child responds to the world with combativeness because the child has internalized aggressive ideas. These children saw the world as a violent place and responded accordingly. Eron (1987, p. 441) argued: "It was what the subjects were saying to themselves about what they wanted . . . what might be an effective or appropriate response . . . that helped determine how aggressive they are today."

Researchers today are examining how stimuli in an individual's environment may bring forth thoughts and emotional responses that lead to aggressive behavior (Bushman & Geen, 1990). Stimuli that have been examined include difficult personal situations and frustrating social conditions. Such views have led researchers to believe that harsh, punitive parenting leads to aggressiveness and negativity. Aggressive children see others as hostile to them, and they respond in kind.

A key cognitive variable that may predispose people to aggression is their self-esteem. Conventional wisdom has held that people with low self-esteem—unfavorable overall impressions of themselves—are more likely to be violent and aggressive. But a review of research shows that crime, violence, and aggression are not *caused by* low self-esteem (or, for that matter, by high self-esteem). According to Roy Baumeister (Bushman & Baumeister, 1998), aggression is caused by *threats* to a person's level of self-esteem. When their views of themselves (however high or low) are threatened or contradicted, people become aggressive. This view suggests that those who fail to adjust their self-appraisal—despite evidence of the correctness of the new view—may become aggressive. There are some strong direct implications of such an

point*counterpoint*

Rating Program Content: Do the Systems Work?

The Issue: Do rating systems used by the media help parents?

POINT
Media rating systems are ineffective, badly conceived, and poorly executed.

COUNTERPOINT
Media rating systems are necessary, can be useful, and are desired by parents and the public at large.

If you accept the idea that media violence and sex are prevalent and have negative effects (Cantor, 2000; Villani, 2001), then you have to ask what can people do about it. Tipper Gore, wife of former vice president Al Gore, had an idea back in 1984 to label music as being violent or sexual in nature. In 1984, Gore was chastised by the press, media executives, and noninterventionists who value the free expression of any idea. Today some people embrace such labeling. We see labels on movies and television programs. But do they work?

The movie rating system has been in effect for more than 30 years; the television rating system began in 1997 but was mired in controversy from day one. Parents—and the rating systems are aimed at them—want advice about the content of the show so that they can decide whether to let their kids see movies. They do not want age-based rating systems but rather want to how much violence, sex, or coarse language is in a show.

Opponents of the current systems argue that age-based systems (such as PG-13 or TV-Y7, directed at children older than age 7) do not reflect a program's level of sex, violence, or coarse language. The warnings are visual only—there is no voice-over announcement—and so they are easy to miss. Opponents also argue that the labels make the content more desirable—a forbidden fruit like an R-rating makes something interesting. Research shows that parents are critical of the age-based systems, and such rating systems do indeed make the shows more attractive to younger children when the ratings are restrictive (Ableman, 1999; Cantor, 2000).

But labels are good advisories; the research also shows that labels such as "parental discretion advised" do not tantalize younger children; further, when content ratings such as MA (mature audiences), L (coarse language), and V (violence) are used, parents take note and try to do the right thing for their children. Parents and the public at large clearly want advice, and they insist that they do, in fact, take that advice.

Yet problems continue to exist. Despite the presence of these more descriptive systems, media outlets still use euphemisms rather than describing content clearly and accurately. Parents' views are being heard, but the newer systems, with multiple labels and euphemisms, are still hard to decode. Parents want to be told the content of the show so they can judge if their child is ready for it—they do not want to hear whether it is "appropriate for young children" or a network's opinion of the content's suitability. As the police are often heard to say, "Just the facts, please."

idea. Western society places a strong emphasis on helping develop individuals' self-esteem. But development of self-esteem doesn't protect individuals from threats to it. Baumeister suggests that societal pursuit of high self-esteem for everyone may end up doing considerable harm, given the fact that it is impossible to insulate everyone from threats to self-esteem! As yet there is little research on how threats to self-esteem affect aggression, but the idea has considerable interest. Perhaps it derives from previous experience and people are set up to be aggressive.

What happens when you are provoked by a coworker at the office and then go immediately home? Do you argue with a housemate? If you go to a rousing, exciting football game and are then confronted by road rage on the way home, how do you respond? Zillman (1994) proposed the excitation transfer theory. He argued that excitation (arousal) dissipates slowly and that excitation that is stirred up in a specific situation can transfer to situations afterward. He reasoned that emotional reactions may come from a previous event. He claimed that aggression is most likely to occur when we are not aware of surplus (leftover) arousal and we misattribute the source of our current arousal to present events rather than previous ones. So when someone cuts you off while you drive home from an exciting game, you misattribute your current arousal to the bad driver and get aggressive.

Excitation transfer theory also relates to the effects of television violence. A stimulus such as high-violence television programs produces a high level of excitation, and it may take a long time for the excitation to decay or lessen. The outcome: aggressive behavior—let's look at the evidence.

■ **TELEVISION VIOLENCE.** Exposure to television, with its stylized view of the world, may have negative consequences. Exposure to violence on television has been likened to a public health epidemic; violence is portrayed on city streets, in rural communities, and on the worldwide stage. Its presence is almost commonplace; nowhere are violence and aggression, especially sexual aggression, more prevalent than on television (MacKay & Covell, 1997). And most children of ages 2–11 spend more hours watching television (an average of almost 22 hours a week) than in any other activity except sleep; they are also often indiscriminate viewers (Grossman, 2000).

The fact that television portrays so much aggressive behavior concerns parents and educators as well as social psychologists. Half of all prime-time TV characters are involved in violent activity of some kind; about one-tenth kill or are killed; the perpetrators of these crimes go unpunished in nearly three-quarters of violent scenes. Sixty percent of television programs contain violence—and that violence is often glamorized (Bushman & Phillips, 2001; Smith et al., 1998). Moreover, about 20% of males appearing on TV shows are employed in law enforcement, whereas less than 1% of adult men are so employed in the real world. Although the overall amount of violence shown on television is staggering, some programs clearly account for a disproportionate number of violent acts.

Research generally supports the contention that viewers who frequently watch violent programs on television are more likely to be aggressive than are viewers who see less TV violence (Anderson & Bushman, 2002; Johnson et al, 2002; Villani, 2001). Further, children exposed to large doses of TV violence are less likely to help a real-life victim of violence, and viewers of violence are less sympathetic to victims than are nonviewers (Villani, 2001). Viewers of violence also are more fearful of becoming victims of violent acts. Children who play violent video games also seem to act more aggressively at later ages (Anderson & Dill, 2000; Brooks, 2000), and even infants can become fearful from watching television (Meltzoff, 1988). According to Stacy Smith and her colleagues (1998), who conducted the National Television Violence Study, violence on television hasn't changed appreciably in decades—neither its overall prevalence nor how it is presented has changed much. How does watching violence on television affect viewers? Smith and her colleagues describe some of the key effects of viewing violence on television:

- It weakens viewers' inhibitions.
- It may suggest new ideas and techniques to the uninitiated.
- It may activate or stimulate existing aggressive ideas and behaviors.
- It desensitizes people, reducing their overall emotional sensitivity to violence.
- It introduces a fear of being a victim of violence.

Of course, television can also have positive effects on children (Henry et al., 2000). Children exposed to shows such as *Sesame Street* and *Mister Rogers' Neighborhood*, which focus on topics such as sharing and caring, are thought to encourage more prosocial behavior with other children. Still, watching too much television has a deleterious impact on children's reading comprehension skills (Koolstra, van der Voort, & van der Kamp, 1997).

BRAIN AND BEHAVIOR

Biological Aspects of Human Aggression

When we watch the Academy Award–winning movie *Gladiator,* are we fulfilling a basic human need? Is Russell Crowe exhibiting an inborn biological tendency when he battles for freedom in the Coliseum? It is widely held by many people that human beings are aggressive and that this is an inborn, biologically based capacity. It is our human nature. Or is it? Can we blend social psychology and brain science? The joining together of social psychology and brain science hopes to make sense of how the brain controls cognitive processes such as memory and attention, which in turn influence social behaviors such as self-control, aggression, and attitudes. In the end social psychologists are developing what some call *social cognitive neuroscience* and it speaks directly to aggressive behaviors.

Some psychologists believe that many aspects of behavior, including aggression, are inborn (DiLalla & Gottesman, 1991), but most psychologists and the American Psychological Association (1990) do not agree. Evolutionary theorists support this biological view—at least to some extent. They argue that sexual jealousy, for instance, is a factor in homicidal violence among young men (Starzomki & Nussbaum, 2000). The jealousy of a young man is a consequence of his evolved tendencies to be proud of his offspring of his chosen mate (Wilson & Daly, 1998). While there is anecdotal evidence for male pridefulness, little firm evidence shows an evolutionary link to all types of violence because indiscriminate violence is more of a problem than a benefit—both to individuals and to the groups to which they belong.

But wait. Studies of genetics and monozygotic twins show that reported aggressiveness is a heritable trait. Identical twin brothers, of whom one is aggressive, show that the other twin is also aggressive. Yet not all research in this field shows consistent results (Miles & Carey, 1997). Geen (1998) argues that there are just too many conflicting results and too many definitions of aggression to make firm conclusions possible. How much aggression does one have to show to be considered aggressive? Hitting, kicking, cursing, spitting, frowning, killing . . . where does one draw the line? Nevertheless, Niehoff (1999) concludes that heritability, along with neurochemistry, plays a role in human aggression.

What about raging hormones? We know that in animals, hormones such as testosterone organize and activate aggressive behaviors. For humans the data are a bit murkier. Many investigators argue that testosterone plays an important or significant role in human aggression; other research shows that it produces only some activation effects (McCaul, Gladue, & Joppa, 1992). So in some cases we find that teenage boys who are viewed as *rebellious* often have higher levels of testosterone than other boys; but concerning *aggression,* testosterone levels do not vary among aggressive and nonaggressive boys (Constantino et al., 1993). It also turns out that testosterone often rises *after* (not before) competitive or aggressive behavior—that is, rising testosterone may be a result rather than a cause of competitive and aggressive behavior. Thus, no simple causal relationship exists between aggression and androgens in human males. Hormonal activity may predispose individuals to competition and aggression, but it does not determine this behavior.

Whether aggression is inhibited or expressed depends on the organism's previous experiences and current social context—for example, whether it has been raised in a hostile environment or is currently being provoked (Lore & Schultz, 1993). While most social psychologists are attempting to sort out the cultural variables that prompt aggression—such as viewing or listening to violence portrayed by the media—those who study brain and behavior find links in biology. Evolutionary history, genetic inheritance, and hormones may contribute to the base level of aggressiveness in human beings (Miczek et al., 2001). That means it may determine the type and even the magnitude of responses. It is generally accepted that there is some biological predisposition for violence among people (Dobash & Dobash, 1998). But in the end, the research does not show—by any stretch of the imagination—that biology *determines*, or causes, aggressive behavior in human beings.

Research on the effects of television and other media is tricky. Often the effects are subtle because potential influences—violence, sex, and education—are sometimes combined in one program. Some assert that children are "protected" from the effects of violence by knowledge that what they see is not real (Davies, 1997); research, however, indicates that even adults blend the fictional portrayals of characters on television into their views of real people (Murphy, 1998). In the end, the data are fairly clear: TV programming, for better or worse, can affect children (and adults). How, when, and how often information is conveyed to children ultimately have important social implications (Calvert, 1998). Social psychologists interested in public policy suggest requiring that every TV station broadcast at least a certain amount of educational programming for children and establishing controls to protect children from advertising that exploits their special vulnerability (Smith et al., 1998).

PREJUDICE AND AGGRESSION. Muslim and Arab American leaders have condemned the terrorist attacks on the World Trade Center and the Pentagon and have appealed to the American public not to take out its anger on their peaceful communities. An estimated 3 million U.S. inhabitants trace their roots to an Arab country, and 82% of Arab Americans are U.S. citizens. Yet in the final months of 2001, many of them feared retaliation for the events of September 11. In a telephone conversation on September 13 with New York City Mayor Rudolph Giuliani and New York State Governor George Pataki, George W. Bush warned Americans not to blame Arab Americans for the terrorist attacks that destroyed the World Trade Center and the Pentagon. Bush said, "We must be mindful that, as we seek to win the war, we treat Arab Americans with the respect they deserve." He went on to say, "There are thousands of Arab Americans who live in New York City who love their flag. We should not hold one who is a Muslim responsible for an act of terror."

Unfortunately, people with limited knowledge of others often fall into the trap of relying on their sometimes prejudiced view of people—and research shows that they know that they are prejudiced (Gordijn, Koomen, & Stapel, 2001). Even when they try to be neutral, prejudice exerts its effects (Wheeler, Jarvis, & Petty, 2001). As we saw earlier, prejudice is typically based on overly simple, often erroneous ideas about traits, attitudes, and behaviors of groups of people. This prejudice—in this case, potentially concerning Arab Americans—often leads to discriminatory treatment, and this treatment is often aggressive in nature.

GENDER DIFFERENCES IN AGGRESSION. Many people believe that men are naturally more aggressive than women. They refer to aggressive contact sports such as football and boxing, the aggressive behavior of men in business, the overwhelming number of violent crimes committed by men, and the traditional view that men are more likely than women to be ruthless and unsympathetic. It is also generally accepted that "more masculine" people (whether men or women) are more aggressive, and this attitude is reflected in children's toys (Dietz, 1998), on television (Browne, 1998), and in viewing behavior (Wright et al., 2001). But are men really more aggressive than women?

Many have observed that men are more *physically* aggressive than women (Harris & Knight-Bohnhoff, 1996). But Crick and Rose (2000) found that both men and women use *psychological* aggression such as verbal abuse and angry gestures. For example, some girls use indirect aggression with peers; they instigate fights and conflicts among friends or family members

Men are more physically aggressive than women but both men and women use verbal aggression and threats. Women in many cultures have been raised with values that make them feel guilty if they cause physical pain; men have not been raised with these values, at least not to the same extent.

Be an *Active* learner

REVIEW

- What are the key findings of Milgram's study? pp. 464–465
- How do social facilitation and social loafing differ? p. 466
- Identify the social variables that are important in explaining unrestrained group behavior. pp. 469–470
- Why might not getting what one wants sometimes lead to aggression? pp. 470–471

THINK CRITICALLY

- Is it possible to shape society to make people less aggressive?
- Some advertisers and local television stations dropped ABC's *Politically Incorrect* after host Bill Maher referred to some past U.S. military actions as "cowardly." Did his dissent influence society?

APPLY PSYCHOLOGY

- Devise a system, a program, or a plan to help people feel less pressure to conform to group norms and more likely to make choices based on their own conscience.

or perhaps spread false stories (Owens, Shute, & Slee, 2000; Walker, Richardson, & Green, 2000). One interpretation of this finding suggests that the differences in aggression that appear between boys and girls, and men and women, are directly related to the perceived consequences of the aggression. Women in many cultures have been raised with values that make them feel especially guilty if they cause physical pain; men have not been raised with those values, at least not to the same extent. In addition, women are more vulnerable to physical retaliation than men are. So women are more likely than men to use relationship or indirect aggression, which does harm but carries less risk of physical retaliation. However, situations involving insults and condescending treatment provoke women more than men (Bettencourt & Miller, 1996), and when women feel justified and protected from retaliation, they can be as aggressive as men (Brannon, 2002).

Research supports the idea that the context and situation in which people find themselves alter the nature and extent of aggression in men and women toward individuals of their own and the other gender (Crick & Rose, 2000). The research picture is complicated, and some important and subtle effects occur. For example, research shows that the age at which aggression occurs varies in men and women; girls develop aggressive behaviors in adolescence, while boys do so earlier (Werner & Crick, 1999). Furthermore, early-maturing girls are at higher risk for psychological problems and aggressive behaviors (Loeber & Stouthamer-Loeber, 1998). Some social behaviors may be genetically programmed and may have an evolutionary basis, but the weight of the evidence leans toward socialization by society. Psychologists are just beginning to assess the important issues involving gender and the developmental course of aggression.

Prosocial Behavior

On September 11, 2001, hundreds of people in and around the World Trade Center helped others escape. Some of these individuals were helping coworkers, but many rendered aid to strangers, often risking their own lives to do so. Psychologists have long studied less dramatic instances of people rendering help. For example, if you are walking down the street with a bag of groceries and you drop them, what is the likelihood that someone will help you pick them up? Psychologists who try to find out when, and under what conditions, someone will help a stranger are examining the likelihood of **prosocial behavior**—behavior that benefits someone else or society but that generally offers no obvious benefit to the person performing it and may even involve some personal risk or sacrifice.

Prosocial behavior
Behavior that benefits someone else or society but that generally offers no obvious benefit to the person performing it and may even involve some personal risk or sacrifice.

Altruism
Behaviors that benefit other people and for which there is no discernible extrinsic reward, recognition, or appreciation.

■ **ALTRUISM: HELPING WITHOUT REWARDS.** Why did the passengers—all of whom we think of as heroes—on the September 11 flight that crashed in Pennsylvania sacrifice their own lives by rushing the terrorists? Why does Peter Beneson, the founder of Amnesty International, devote so much time and effort to helping "prisoners of conscience" around the world? What compelled Mother Teresa to wander Calcutta's streets and attend to the wounds and diseases of people no one else would touch? Why did Oskar Schindler risk his life to save 1,100 Jews from the Nazi death camps during World War II?

Altruism consists of behaviors that benefit other people and for which there is no discernible extrinsic reward, recognition, or appreciation (Toch, 2001). The key is that rewards are not part of the altruism equation. Although many prosocial behaviors involve rewards and altruistic behaviors are prosocial, altruistic behaviors are done without any expectation of reward. But isn't the feeling of well-being after performing an altruistic act a type of reward?

Many behaviorists contend that some element of personality directs people to seek social approval by helping. According to this view, people with a high need for achievement are more likely than others to be helpful, and people may continue to be helpful because the positive consequences of their actions are self-reinforcing (Batson et al., 1991). From a behavioral view, intrinsically rewarding activities become powerful behavior initiators; thus, for example, when you have a relationship with a person, the person's affection and approval make you more likely to be caring and helpful (Batson, 1990). Further, once kindness and helpfulness become well established and even routine, individuals are more likely to help others, such as the homeless, disadvantaged senior citizens, and orphans.

Other theorists argue that biological drives underlie altruistic behavior. Consider the following scenario: an infant crawls into a busy street as a truck is approaching. The mother darts in front of the oncoming vehicle and carries her child to safety. Most people would say that love impels the mother to risk her life to save the child. Sociobiologists and evolutionary psychologists would argue that the mother commits her brave deed so that her genes will be passed on to another generation.

The idea that people are genetically predisposed toward certain behaviors was described by Edward Wilson, a Harvard University zoologist, in his book *Sociobiology: A New Synthesis* (1975). Wilson argued that genetic factors underlie all behavior. But he went one step further. He founded a new field, **sociobiology,** based on the premise that even day-to-day behaviors are determined by the process of natural selection—that social behaviors that contribute to the survival of a species are passed on via the genes from one generation to the next. Evolutionary psychologists have accepted this point of view, asserting that natural selection accounts for the mechanisms that have evolved to produce altruistic behaviors (Crawford & Anderson, 1989). For the sociobiologist, genetics is the key to daily behavior.

Psychologists hotly debate sociobiological theory because it places genetics in a position of primary importance and minimizes the role of learning. Most psychologists feel strongly that learning plays a key role in the day-to-day activities of human beings. People *learn* to love, to become angry, to help or hurt others, and to develop relationships with others. But although sociobiology is too fixed and rigid for most psychologists, it does raise interesting questions about the role of biology and genetics in social behavior.

Behavioral theories and sociobiology are two ways of explaining why people help others. People don't always help, however. One important area of research seeks to explain why.

■ **THE BYSTANDER EFFECT.** The study of helping behavior has taken some interesting twists and turns. For example, psychologists have found that in large cities, where potentially lethal emergencies (accidents, thefts, stabbings, rapes, and murders) occur frequently, people often watch but do not help. This unwillingness increases with the number of observers, a fact that has been termed the **bystander effect.** In a well-known incident in New York City in 1964, Kitty Genovese was walking home when a man approached her with a knife. A chase ensued, during which she screamed for help. He stabbed her, and she continued screaming. When lights came on in nearby buildings, the attacker fled. But when he saw that no one was coming to his victim's aid, he returned and stabbed her again. The assault lasted more than 30 minutes and was heard by dozens of neighbors; yet no one came to the victim's aid. This is a classic case of bystander effect.

Bibb Latané and John Darley (1970) investigated the bystander effect in a long series of studies. They found that people must decide whether to introduce themselves into a problematic situation, especially when there are other bystanders. But

Sociobiology
A discipline based on the premise that even day-to-day behaviors are determined by the process of natural selection—that social behaviors that contribute to the survival of a species are passed on via the genes from one generation to the next.

Bystander effect
Unwillingness to help exhibited by witnesses to an event, which increases when there are more observers.

FIGURE 13.11

The Bystander Effect

In a classic bystander effect study, as the number of people in the group increased, the willingness of the naive participant to inform the experimenter that the victim had suffered a seizure decreased. *(From Latané & Darley, 1970.)*

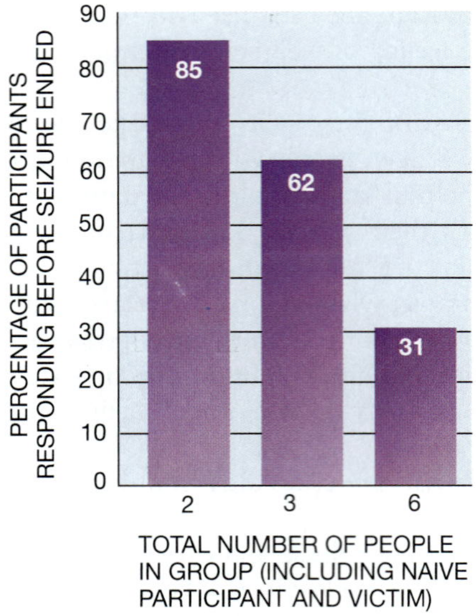

first they have to decide what is going on (whether or not there is an emergency), and they are often misled by the *apparent* lack of concern among other bystanders to conclude that nothing really bad is going on after all—so they don't help. Latané and Darley reasoned that when people are aware of other bystanders in an emergency situation, they may also be less likely to help because they experience *diffusion of responsibility* (the feeling that they cannot be held responsible). To test their hypothesis, the researchers brought college students to a laboratory and told them they were going to be involved in a study of people who were interested in discussing college life in New York City. The researchers explained that in the interest of preserving people's anonymity, a group discussion would be held over an intercom system rather than face to face, and that each person in the group would talk in turn. In fact, there was only one actual participant in each experimental session. Assistants who worked for the researchers prerecorded all the other conversations.

The independent variable was the number of people the naive participant thought were in the discussion group. The dependent variable was whether and how fast the naive participant reported as an emergency an apparently serious seizure affecting one of the other "participants." The future "seizure victim" spoke first; he talked about his difficulties getting adjusted to New York and mentioned that he was prone to seizures, particularly when studying hard. Next, the naive participant spoke. Then came the prerecorded discussions by assistants. Then the "seizure victim" talked again. After a few relatively calm remarks, his speech became increasingly loud and incoherent; he stuttered and indicated that he needed help. At this point, the experimenters began timing the speed of the naive participant's response.

Each naive participant was led to believe that his or her discussion group contained two, three, or six people. That is, participants in the two-person group believed they were the only bystanders when the "victim" suffered his seizure; participants in the three-person group thought there was one other bystander. Eighty-five percent of participants who thought they were the only bystanders responded before the end of the seizure; 62% of the participants who thought there was only one other bystander responded by the end of the seizure. When participants thought there were four additional bystanders, only 31% responded by the end of the seizure (see Figure 13.11).

In general, research has shown that bystanders will help under some conditions—so much has to do with the character and characteristics of the bystander (Laner, Benin, & Ventrone, 2001). For one thing, people's self-concepts and previous experiences affect their willingness to intercede. Bystanders who see themselves as being especially competent in emergencies (such as doctors and nurses) are likely to help a victim regardless of the number of people present (Pantin & Carver, 1982). If the person who needs help has a relationship with the person who can offer help, help is more likely to be given (Batson, 1990). Research in cities of various sizes shows that people who live in smaller communities are more likely to help (Levine et al., 1994). Also, personality characteristics of the individual involved in a bystander situation are important. Men respond more often than women (Salminen & Glad, 1992). Tice and Baumeister (1985) found, however, that participants with a high degree of masculinity were less likely to respond. They contended that highly

Interpersonal attraction
The tendency of one person to evaluate another person (or a symbol or image of another person) in a positive way.

masculine participants might be especially fearful of embarrassment. In U.S. society, the ideal personality characteristics for men, in general, emphasize strength and aggression rather than sensitivity and nurturing. This finding is supported by work showing that women are more likely than men to help friends, and that when women do so, they do it in a nurturing rather than a problem-solving way (Belansky & Boggiano, 1994).

Relationships and Attraction

Some people feel that life is predetermined and that their relationships with others—especially love relationships—are a part of their personal destiny. It turns out that people who believe in romantic destiny—that members of a couple are meant for each other—tend to have long relationships, if they let a relationship get started in the first place (Knee, 1998). But relationships with friends, lovers, and spouses are intricate. What is it about people that attracts you and makes you want to maintain a relationship with them in the first place? We saw in Chapter 11 that people develop relationships to fulfill their needs for warmth, understanding, and emotional security. Social psychologists also know that people are attracted to those who live or work near them, whom they consider good-looking, who share their attitudes, and with whom they spend time. These factors are related to **interpersonal attraction,** the tendency of one person to evaluate another person (or a symbol or image of another person) in a positive way.

■ **PROXIMITY.** People are more likely to develop a relationship with a neighbor than with someone who lives several blocks or miles away. Three decades of research show that the closer people are geographically, the more likely they are to become attracted. A simple explanation is that they are likely to see each other more often, and repeated exposure leads to familiarity, which leads to attraction. Another reason is that attraction is facilitated by the anticipation of a relationship with someone one encounters frequently. In addition, people who are members of the same group, such as a club, a volunteer organization, or a class, perceive themselves as sharing the same feelings, attitudes, and values as others in the group. That perception leads to attraction.

■ **PHYSICAL ATTRACTIVENESS.** Within seconds of seeing a person, you probably decide if they are attractive to you. Attractiveness is affected by subtle but powerful variables. For example, in one study both men and women were shown images of the faces of Caucasian and Japanese females and males; the shapes of the faces had been "feminized" or "masculinized" using a computer (Perrett et al., 1998). Both Caucasian and Japanese participants preferred and rated as most attractive the faces that were feminized. Interestingly, both men and women tend to find more appealing men who are more feminine looking than rugged. The researchers suggested that computer alteration of men's faces to make them slightly feminine makes them appear less menacing and softens other features that are associated with negative traits. The researchers assert that more feminine faces appear younger and that people's preferences for young faces are correlated with their preference for feminized faces. Such results are probably no surprise to Leonardo DiCaprio's agent.

■ Look at these four sets of faces. In each group, which appeals to you more? The feminized or the masculinized?

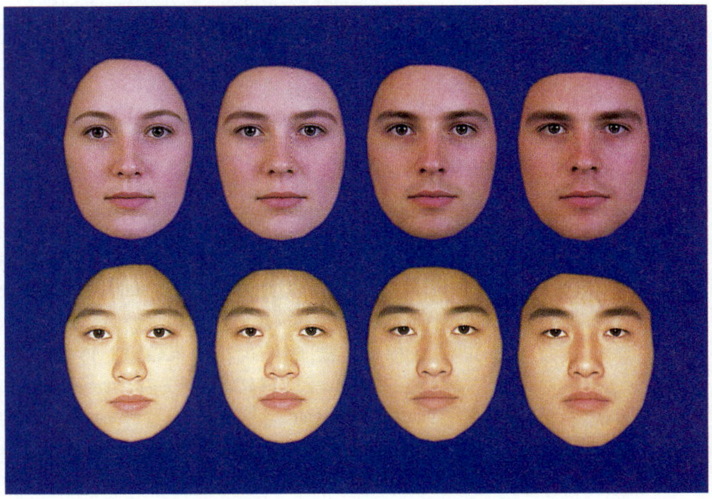

Volumes of research show that people are attracted romantically, at least at first, to those whom they find physically attractive (Langlois,

student voices

David Jackel
Brandeis University

Social psychology has taught me to recognize the thinking patterns people fall into in groups, and therefore to question my own decisions and assumptions. While working in a recording studio, I realized that, to preserve group unity, we were all agreeing on a final mix that none of us truly liked. I decided to end the session and meet up several days later—this time with an outside person to give us another opinion.

Roggman, & Musselman, 1994). People judge an attractive individual to have more positive traits and characteristics than an unattractive one, especially when appearance is the first information provided (DeSantis & Kayson, 1997). People feel more personal regard for and ascribe more power, status, and competence to individuals they find physically attractive than to those they don't; this affects who can best change people's attitudes (Feingold, 1992a; Fiske, 2001). Attractive people are granted more freedom and are perceived as being fairer and healthier than unattractive people (Cherulnik, Turns, & Wilderman, 1990; Kalick et al., 1998). For example, attractive college professors are seen as better teachers and are less likely to be blamed by a student who receives a failing grade in a course (Romano & Bordieri, 1989). But such findings about attractiveness are a distinctly Western phenomenon; ideas about attractiveness may differ cross-culturally (Matsumoto & Kudoh, 1993). For over a thousand years Chinese women endured the suffering of footbinding in the name of beauty. Yet a study by Cunningham and colleagues (1995) found that Asian, Latino/Latina, and White judges of what was attractive were consistent in their judgments: faces with neonate large eyes, greater distance between eyes, and small noses; sexually mature, narrower female faces with smaller chins; expressive, higher eyebrows, dilated pupils, larger lower lips, larger smiles, and well-groomed, full hair. Yet some cultural differences persist, while some change over time. In our culture, thin is the standard. In Hawaiian culture of the past century, fat was considered desirable. A few hundred years ago, European culture held a similar view. Westerners wear earrings; many women in India also wear nose-rings. Thus, though some standards of beauty appear consistent throughout the world, certain elements can vary according to place and time period.

How important is physical attractiveness when it comes to dating? Do people always select the best-looking person to date? Research shows that people prefer attractive dates, and some studies show that people seek out those of their own level of attractiveness. But other variables also seem to play an important role; educational level, intelligence, socioeconomic status, and similarity of previous experiences all weigh heavily in the choice of whom to date or marry. Men and women are more selective when choosing a long-term rather than a short-term relationship partner (Regan et al., 2000; Stewart, Stinnett, & Rosenfeld, 2001). Although physical attractiveness and youthfulness are initially important in the selection of dates and mates (especially among men), appearance is just one variable among many (Freederick & Morrison, 1999). Among those variables, according to evolutionary theorists, are facial symmetry and hip-to-waist ratios. For example, men prefer a hip-to-waist ratio of 7 to 10—hips not exaggerated relative to the waist. A female figure with low hip-to-waist ratio is judged by men to be more desirable in a marriage partner than either underweight or overweight figures with very high or very low hip-to-waist ratios. Though in some generations relatively thin partners are preferred and at other times, relatively chubby partners are preferred, across cultures the well-known hourglass figure seems universally favored.

In a typical physical attractiveness experiment, participants receive two identical job résumés, each with a different picture attached to it. Results show that people will evaluate the résumé of the person they find physically attractive more positively than that of the other person, even though the qualifications of the "applicants" are the same. Attractive people are preferred as coworkers and as friends; they are also thought to be less menacing (Eagly et al., 1991)

■ **LIKING THOSE WHO SHARE THE FEELING AND WHO HOLD SIMILAR ATTITUDES.** Learning theorists contend that people are attracted to and form relationships with those who give them positive reinforcement and that they dislike those who punish them. The basic idea is simple: you like the people who like you

(Katz & Beach, 2000). Moreover, if you like someone, you tend to assume (sometimes incorrectly) that the other person likes you in return and that the two of you share similar qualities.

Another attribute that affects the development of relationships is real or perceived similarity in attitudes and opinions. If you perceive someone's attitudes as being similar to your own, this perception increases the probability that you will like that person. Having similar values, interests, and backgrounds is a good predictor of a friendship or romantic relationship (Katz & Beach, 2000). Similarly, voters who agree with the views of a particular candidate tend to rate that person as more honest, friendly, and persuasive than the candidates with whom they disagree. Researchers have also found that, conversely, if you already like someone, you will perceive that person's attitudes as being similar to your own. For example, voters who like a particular candidate, perhaps because they perceive the candidate as warm-hearted or physically attractive, will tend to minimize their attitudinal differences.

That you like those who like you is explained by cognitive consistency theory, which suggests that sharing similar attitudes reduces cognitive dissonance (a phenomenon we examined earlier). Given a natural inclination to avoid dissonance, you feel attracted to those you believe share similar attitudes; shared attitudes in turn lead to attraction and liking. Learning theories also suggest that you like people with similar attitudes because similar attitudes are reinforcing to you.

■ **FRIENDSHIPS AND THE ROLE OF EQUITY.** Liking each other and sharing ideas and values have been the basis of many friendships and romantic relationships (Katz & Beach, 2000). *Friendship* is a special two-way relationship between people. According to one influential group of researchers, if two people's behaviors, emotions, and thoughts are similar, and the people are dependent on one another, a close relationship exists (Kelley et al., 1983). Closeness is a key variable that defines a friendship, although *close* must be defined so that all researchers mean the same thing when they use the word.

As we discussed in Chapter 3, ideally, friends participate as equals, are intimate, and share confidences. Reciprocity and commitment are essential to friendship; close friends interact frequently across a wider range of settings, are more exclusive, and offer each other more benefits (Hays, 1989). Elementary school children tend to form same-gender friendships; cross-gender friendships are rare. With youngsters, friendships lead to cooperation rather than competition, at least more than with nonfriends (Hartup, 1989). Furthermore, children who have friends in the classroom do better in school (Ladd, 1990). Adolescent friendships sometimes provide an arena for sharing and intimacy, although they can also be filled with conflict over social or political issues, drugs, gangs, and sexual behavior (Berndt, 1992). Western cultural expectations for specific gender-based behaviors often control male–female interactions in friendship. Women talk more about family, personal matters, and doubts and fears than men do; men talk more than women about sports and work.

Equity plays an important role in close relationships. **Equity theory** states that people attempt to maintain stable, consistent interpersonal relationships in which the ratio of members' contributions is balanced. People in a close relationship usually feel a sense of balance in the relationship and believe it will last for a long time.

According to equity theory, one way people maintain a balanced relationship is to make restitution when it is demanded. Apologies help restore a sense of autonomy and fairness in an injured individual. Similarly, people who do favors expect favors in return, often using the principle of equity unconsciously in day-to-day life. If a friend helps you move into your new apartment, you may be expected to lend her a hand when she has to take an old refrigerator to the dump.

Equity theory
Social psychological theory that states that people attempt to maintain stable, consistent interpersonal relationships in which the ratio of members' contributions is balanced.

Liking each other and sharing ideas and values have been the basis of many friendships and romantic relationships.

INTIMATE RELATIONSHIPS AND LOVE. People involved in a close relationship may be intimate with one another. **Intimacy** is a state of being or feeling in which each person in a relationship is willing to self-disclose and to express important feelings and information to the other person; in response, the other person usually acknowledges the first person's feelings, a process that makes each feel valued and cared for (Katz & Beach, 2000). Research shows that self-disclosure tends to be reciprocal; people who disclose themselves to others are usually recipients of intimate information. When people self-disclose, they validate each other; that is, they accept each other's positive and negative attributes.

Research on intimate relationships concentrates on marriage rather than friendship, but some research exists on communication, affection, consideration, and self-disclosure between friends. However, important individual and gender differences in friendships have been identified (Reeder, 2000). For example, women, more than men, incorporate close relationships into their view of themselves and let those views affect their thoughts and behaviors (Cross & Madson, 1997). Women also evaluate same-sex friendships more positively than men do (Veniegas & Peplau, 1997). Furthermore, in general, men are less likely to be self-disclosing and intimate than are women (Dindia & Allen, 1992), but men are more self-disclosing with a woman than they are with another man. On the whole, however, psychologists know much more about intimate relationships that involve sex, love, and marriage (Stewart, Stinnett, & Rosenfeld, 2000).

Love, emotional commitment, and sex are the parts of relationships that most people think of when they hear the word *intimacy*. People in love relationships often express feelings in unique ways—they give flowers, take moonlit walks, write lengthy letters, and have romantic dinners. According to psychologists, love has psychological, emotional, biochemical, and social factors. Consider this array of definitions of *love*:

- Fromm (1956) focused on the idea that mature love is possible only if a person achieves a secure sense of self-identity. He said that when people are in love, they become one and yet remain two individuals.
- Heinlein (1961) wrote that love "is a condition in which the happiness of the other person is essential to your own."
- Branden (1980) suggested that love is "a passionate spiritual, emotional, sexual attachment . . . that reflects a high regard for the value of each other's person."
- Tennov (1981) believed that the ultimate state of romantic love is one called "limerance": a head-over-heels involvement and preoccupation with thoughts of the loved one.

Intimacy
A state of being or feeling in which each person in a relationship is willing to self-disclose and to express important feelings and information to the other person.

PASSIONATE AND COMPANIONATE LOVE. Many classifications of love have been suggested, and all have some overlapping components. One early classification designates two types of love: *passionate love,* which involves continuously thinking about the loved one and warm, even searing sexual feelings and potent emotional reactions; and *companionate love,* which involves having trusting and tender feelings for someone with whom close friendship is shared, as well as a deep sense of being intertwined (Hatfield & Rapson, 1993). Passionate and companionate love

TABLE 13.4

Six Varieties of Love

Variety of Love	Sample Test Items
Passionate love	My lover and I were attracted to each other immediately after we first met.
	My lover and I became emotionally involved rather quickly.
Game-playing love	I have sometimes had to keep two of my lovers from finding out about each other.
	I can get over love affairs pretty easily and quickly.
Friendship love	The best kind of love grows out of a long friendship.
	Love is really a deep friendship, not a mysterious, mystical emotion.
Logical love	It is best to love someone with a similar background.
	An important factor in choosing a partner is whether or not he (she) will be a good parent.
Possessive love	When my lover doesn't pay attention to me, I feel sick all over.
	I cannot relax if I suspect that my lover is with someone else.
Selfless love	I would rather suffer myself than let my lover suffer.
	Whatever I own is my lover's to use as he (she) chooses.

Hendrick & Hendrick, 1986

are not completely separate processes. As people become more intimate and intertwined in a relationship, their level of passion may also rise and wane—this view accounts for a range of behaviors in long-term relationships including varying frequency of sexual encounters as well as gender differences in intimate behaviors (Baumeister & Bratslavsky, 1999).

This two-level classification system seemed unfinished to Robert Sternberg (1986b; Barnes & Sternberg, 1997), who sees love as having three components: intimacy, commitment, and passion. *Intimacy* is a sense of emotional closeness. *Commitment* is the extent to which a relationship is permanent and long-lasting. *Passion* is arousal, partly sexual, partly intellectual, and partly inspirational. When all three components are present, the highest type of love—*consummate love*—results. Another view of love (Hendrick & Hendrick, 1986) identifies six distinct varieties: passionate, game-playing, friendship, logical, possessive, and selfless. Table 13.4 shows a series of statements that are used on a test to measure the way people relate in a love relationship.

Different as all of the classifications may be, researchers have nonetheless identified some common elements in love relationships. Love usually involves the idealization of another person; people see their loved ones in a positive light. It also involves caring for another person and being fascinated with that person. Love includes trust, respect, liking, honesty, companionship, and (sometimes) sexual attraction. A central element is commitment; however, researchers disagree as to whether love and commitment can be separated, because one usually follows from, or is part of, the other (Fehr & Russell, 1991).

For couples that stay together, love grows over time (Sprecher, 1999). But what happens when love disappears? People in a close emotional relationship, whether married or not, experience emotional distress when they break up. Sadness, anger, loss, and despair are among the emotions experienced by people at the end of a close relationship. However, research shows that the extent of those feelings is determined by an individual's level of security. If you lose a lover

introduction to research basics

Internet Use and Sociability

Most people think of themselves as social beings. In fact among adolescents you often hear the statement "I'm a people person." With the widespread availability of computers, is the Internet changing all that? What happens to our sense of relationship and self-esteem when people use the Internet a great deal? Does sitting in front of a computer screen rather than interacting with human beings make a difference? Tiffany Field and her colleagues explored the relationship between Internet use and social isolation among adolescents (Sanders, Field, Diego, & Kaplan, 2000).

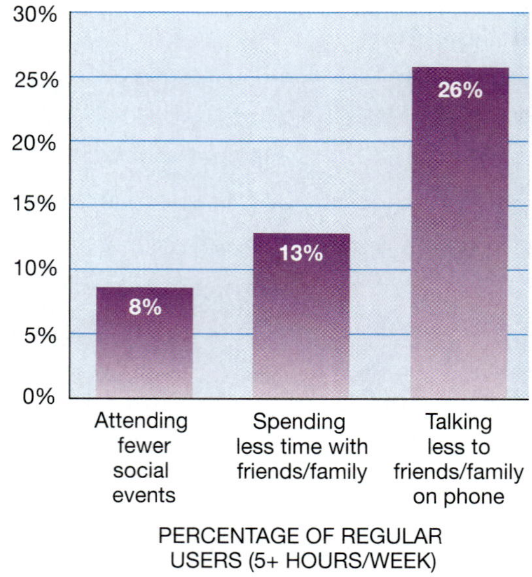

FIGURE 13.12

Internet Users Spend Less Time in Social Activities
(Nie, 2002)

DESIGN The study was an **ex post facto design,** a type of design that contrasts groups of people who differ on some variable of interest to the researcher. The participants in this study differed in how much time they spent per week on the Internet. The researchers assessed how many hours per week participants spent on the Internet and in other activities—especially social ones.

HYPOTHESIS The researchers hypothesized that a high level of Internet use would relate to lower ratings on relationships and higher ratings on depression.

PARTICIPANTS Eighty-nine seniors (52 girls, 37 boys), mostly Caucasian (76%) middle-class high school students, participated.

PROCEDURE The students responded to a series of 181 questions about psychological aspects of adolescence, including the quality of their relationships with parents and friends. Participants responded to questions such as "How much do you go to your mother for support?" The researchers also administered a depression scale and asked how many hours a day they spent on the Internet. The researchers used the information about Internet use to divide participants into a high-use group, which they contrasted with a low-use group.

RESULTS The low-use and high-use groups were similar in proportion of boys and girls, ethnicity, and socioeconomic levels. But adolescents who used the Internet for less than one hour per day, when compared with teens who used the Internet for more than two hours per day, had significantly better relationships with mothers and friends. The level of Internet use was not related to depression.

CONCLUSIONS The researchers argued that high Internet use is related to weaker social ties and that low Internet use was related to better relationships with mothers and friends (Sanders et al., 2000). The obvious implication is that Internet use may increase social isolation, a finding also supported by other research; for example, Nie (2002) found heavy Internet users are spending less time with family, friends, and in social activities, as shown in Figure 13.12 (Weiser, 2001).

This study by field was limited in a number of ways. The choice of the ex post facto study, rather than an experimental design, prevents researchers from drawing conclusions about causality. The participants may be more socially isolated because they use the Internet more, or alternatively, they may resort to Internet use because of their social isolation. That is, this research design does not reveal this information. In addition, the participants were not a random selection of high school seniors—they were either high or low in the level of Internet use. Participants were disproportionately female and Caucasian.

Nevertheless, the study points to the need for further research on the role of the Internet as a factor in social isolation for teens. This relationship between Internet use and social isolation is important because social support from family and friends is crucial in dealing with stress, and adolescence is often a time of change and stress (McKenna & Bargh, 2000).

or spouse, your reaction will be determined not only by the loss of the relationship but also by your own basic feelings of security, attachment, and anxiety (Simpson, 1990).

Love is a state, but it is also a series of behaviors. Thus, although a person may be in love, most psychologists think of love in terms of the behaviors that demonstrate it, including remaining faithful sexually and showing caring (Buss, 1988). Yet researchers also wish to know whether love has a biological basis.

Love is expressed differently in every culture, and there are enormous variations in its expression even within a single culture. When Susan Sprecher and her colleagues (1992) compared love attitudes and experiences among Japanese, Americans, and Russians, they found distinct cultural differences. For example, the Japanese were less romantic than the other groups; the Americans were more likely to associate love with marriage than were the other groups; the Russians were the most excitable and had the most difficulty staying calm when in love.

Cultural differences in love relationships arise in part because of the nature of marriage. In cultures where marriages are arranged by parents, love comes about slowly over time. In cultures where passionate love is equated with happiness, such as in the United States, love is often seen to wane over time; in cultures where romantic, passionate love is valued less, the depth of relationships and the waning of passion are viewed differently and have a different time course. Even within American culture, there are differences in decisions to marry among ethnic groups; for example, African American women are more likely than White women to insist on having economic supports, such as a steady job, in place before marriage (Bulcroft & Bulcroft, 1993). Psychologists know far too little about love relationships in various cultures; yet love is a basic human emotion that is nurtured from birth to death and is seen in every culture. As psychologists discern the key elements of friendship, they will be better prepared to tackle the even more complicated subject of love.

Ex post facto design
A type of design that contrasts groups of people who differ on some variable of interest to the researcher.

Evolution and Social Psychology

Throughout this chapter we have been considering the various personal and situational variables that create social behaviors. But evolutionary theory argues that this is only part of the story; our genes have changed over time (adapted) to reflect environmental and breeding dynamics. From an evolutionary view, our social behavior reflects smart adaptations to survive in groups both large and small. Remember that evolutionary theory asserts that behavior is a product of the mix between evolved psychological mechanisms and social and physical environments. The adaptations that people make are meant to solve problems of survival and reproduction, and getting along in groups and forming interpersonal relationships are important for survival. Thus men are attracted to those women whom they see as fertile, good reproductive hosts; and women are attracted to men who will be good providers (Hinsz, Matz, & Patience, 2001). Indeed, social relationships are at the core of evolved psychological mechanisms because friendships, alliances, close relationships, and sexual behavior are at the root of reproduction. It follows that men and women differ genetically, and in social behaviors, because of evolved psychological adaptations, and evolutionary psychologists hold that men and women value different characteristics in mates. As Buss and Kenrick (1998) put it, beauty is in the eyes and adaptations of the beholder. And so are violence and aggression; when a man sees a threat to his spouse or family, his natural evolved instinct gives rise to aggression and protective mechanisms, but people must restrain their aggressive impulses toward members of their families and others in their social group.

Be an *Active* learner

REVIEW

- What is the primary explanation for the bystander effect? pp. 477–478
- Are bystanders indifferent or inhibited? Why? p. 478
- Distinguish between a casual friendship and a close relationship. p. 482

THINK CRITICALLY

- Provide a psychological explanation of why you probably will like someone whose attitudes you perceive as similar to your own. Why might that person be able to influence you to do things that you might otherwise not do?
- Do you think that some people create situations that make them ultimately feel lonely? Explain your answer.

APPLY PSYCHOLOGY

- Psychologists know that people like those who are like themselves. What psychological principles could you call on to increase the likelihood that you will get a job or be promoted in the job you are in?
- Make a list of those things that would attract you to someone else romantically. Then make a list of those things that you would see as a turn-off. Are they polar opposites, for example, good-looking versus ugly? Which dimensions are opposites? Why?

In the end, evolutionary psychology may be a unifying theory for social psychological phenomena. The research is still being done, and evolutionary theory is hard to test, but data from many areas come together to support this approach.

Summary and Review

Attitudes: Deeply Held Feelings and Beliefs

What is social psychology?

■ *Social psychology* is the scientific study of how people think about, interact with, influence, and are influenced by the thoughts, feelings, and behaviors of others. p. 442

What is the relationship between attitudes and behavior?

■ *Attitudes* are long-lasting patterns of feelings and beliefs about other people, ideas, or objects, which are based in people's experiences and shape their future behavior. Attitudes are usually evaluative and have cognitive, emotional, and behavioral dimensions, each of which serves a function. Attitudes are formed early in life, through learning processes. Social psychologists can assess people's attitudes, but whether those attitudes predict behavior depends on a number of variables including attitude strength, vested interest, specificity of attitudes, and accessibility of attitudes. pp. 443–444

What are the key components of attitude change?

■ There are four key components of attitude change: the communicator, the communication, the medium, and the audience. Each of these affects the extent of change that may take place. The *elaboration likelihood model*, proposed by Petty and Cacioppo, asserts that there are two routes to attitude change: central and peripheral. The central route emphasizes rational decision making; the peripheral route, which is more indirect and superficial, emphasizes emotional and motivational influences. pp. 444–446

■ Cognitive explanations of attitudes and attitude change include cognitive dissonance and reactance theory. *Cognitive dissonance* is the state of mental discomfort that results when an individual maintains two or more beliefs, attitudes, or behaviors that are inconsistent with one another. *Reactance* is the negative response evoked when there is an inconsistency between a person's self-image as being free to choose and the person's realization that someone is trying to force him or her to choose a particular alternative. pp. 449–451

KEY TERMS

social psychology, p. 442; attitudes, p. 442; elaboration likelihood model, p. 448; cognitive dissonance, p. 449; self-perception theory, p. 451; reactance, p. 451

Social Cognition: The Impact of Thought

What is social cognition?

■ *Social cognition* is the process of analyzing and interpreting events, other people, oneself, and the world in general. Often, to save time, people use mental shortcuts to make sense of the world, developing rules of thumb. p. 451

What are nonverbal communication and attribution theory?

■ *Nonverbal communication* is the communication of information by cues or actions that include gestures, tone of voice, vocal inflections, and facial expressions. These sources of information help people make judgments about other people and about events in the world. pp. 452–453

■ *Attribution* is the process by which someone infers other people's attitudes, beliefs, motives, or intentions from observing their behavior and deciding whether the causes of the behavior are dispositional (internal) or situational (external). Attribution helps people make sense of the world, organize their thoughts quickly, and maintain a sense of control over the environment. It helps people feel competent and masterful because it helps them predict similar events in the future. pp. 453–456

Describe the most common attribution errors.

■ Two of the most common errors in attribution are the fundamental attribution error and the actor–observer effect. The *fundamental attribution error* is the tendency to attribute other people's behavior to dispositional rather than situational causes. The *actor–observer effect* is the tendency to attribute the failings of others to dispositional causes but to attribute one's own failings to situational causes. Sometimes these errors occur because of a *self-serving bias,* that is, people's tendency to ascribe their positive behaviors to their own internal traits but their failures and shortcomings to external, situational factors. pp. 455–456

Define prejudice, and identify the theories that explain it.

■ *Prejudice* is a negative evaluation of an entire group of people. Prejudice is typically based on *stereotypes*—fixed, overly simple, and often erroneous ideas about traits, attitudes, and behaviors of groups of people; members of a group are assumed to be all alike. Prejudice often leads to *discrimination*, behavior targeted at individuals or groups with the aim of holding them apart and treating them differently. Prejudice has multiple causes and can be accounted for, at least to some extent, by social learning theory, motivational theory, cognitive theory, and personality theory. pp. 457–461

KEY TERMS

social cognition, p. 451; impression formation, p. 451; nonverbal communication, p. 452; body language, p. 452; attribution, p. 452; fundamental attribution error, p. 455; actor–observer effect, p. 455; self-serving bias, p. 455; prejudice, p. 457; stereotypes, p. 457; discrimination, p. 457; social categorization, p. 459

Social Interactions

Explain social influence and conformity.

■ *Social influence* refers to the ways people alter the attitudes or behavior of others, either directly or indirectly. Social influence is easily seen in studies of conformity. *Conformity* occurs when a person changes attitudes or behaviors so that they are consistent with those of other people or with social norms. pp. 461–463

What is obedience, and what did Milgram's studies of obedience demonstrate?

■ *Obedience* is compliance with the orders of another person or group of people. Milgram's studies demonstrated that an individual's ability to resist coercion is limited, although the presence of an ally who refuses to participate reduces obedience, which underscores the importance of social influences on behavior. p. 464–466

What are social facilitation and social loafing?

■ *Social facilitation* is a change in a person's behavior that occurs when people believe they are in the presence of other people. The change can be either positive or negative. *Social loafing* is a decrease in an individual's effort and productivity as a result of working in a group. pp. 467–468

Identify three processes that may occur in group decision making that may or may not be helpful.

■ Processes that may affect group decision making, positively or negatively, include *group polarization*, the exaggeration of preexisting attitudes as a result of group discussion; *groupthink*, the tendency of people in a group to seek concurrence with one another; and *deindividuation*, the process by which the individuals in a group lose their self-awareness, self-perception, and concern with evaluation and ultimately may engage in antisocial, antinormative behavior. pp. 468–469

Describe aggression, prosocial behavior, and the bystander effect.

■ *Aggression* is viewed by social psychologists as any behavior intended to harm another person or thing. *Prosocial behavior* exhibits itself in *altruism*, behaviors that benefit someone else or society but that generally offer no obvious benefit to the person performing them. In contrast, the *bystander effect* is the unwillingness of witnesses to an event to help, especially when there are numerous observers. pp. 470, 477–478

Define interpersonal attraction.

■ *Interpersonal attraction* is the tendency of one person to evaluate another person (or a symbol or image of another person) in a positive way. The process of attraction involves the characteristics of both the people involved and the situation. People give more personal regard and ascribe more power, status, and competence to people they find attractive than to those they don't. pp. 479–481

Define friendship and love, and distinguish between them.

■ Reciprocity, closeness, and commitment between people who see themselves as equals are essentials of friendship. *Equity theory* holds that people attempt to maintain stable, consistent relationships in which the ratio of members' contributions is balanced. Love usually involves the idealization of another person. People see their loved ones in a positive light, care for them, and are fascinated with them; love also involves trust and commitment. According to Sternberg, love has three components: intimacy (a sense of emotional closeness), commitment (the extent to which a relationship is permanent), and passion (arousal, some of it sexual, some intellectual, and some inspirational). pp. 481–484

KEY TERMS

social influence, p. 461; conformity, p. 463; obedience, p. 464; debriefing, p. 466; group, p. 466; social facilitation, p. 466; social loafing, p. 469; group polarization, p. 468; groupthink, p. 469; deindividuation, p. 470; aggression, p. 470; prosocial behavior, p. 476; altruism, p. 476; sociobiology, p. 477; bystander effect, p. 477; interpersonal attraction, p. 479; equity theory, p. 481; intimacy, p. 482; ex post facto design, p. 485

14 Stress and Health Psychology

George Tooker, *Government Bureau,* 1956

Michael Jordan is widely regarded as the most successful basketball player of all time. He led his team to six championships and demonstrated how the game can be played. Then he retired from basketball at the height of his career. But superstars are not the only ones who walk away. Andrea Galambos, a 16-year-old high school junior in Westport, Connecticut, was captain of the volleyball team, played the flute in the school orchestra, played on the tennis team, and took singing and art classes (Noonan, 2001). Andrea also walked away from her involvement in athletics (and music and art). The reason each of these motivated, successful individuals made drastic changes in their lives may be similar: burnout. In applying that term to these two people, two slightly different definitions were used, and both vary from the definition that psychologists use to discuss this concept.

chapter outline

Andrea was certainly overloaded with activities. She said she didn't want to get up in the morning because she faced a day full of tasks and no time for herself (Noonan, 2001). She had stopped enjoying the activities in her full schedule and wanted to do less. When enrichment activities become chores, it's time to cut back, and parents are often more understanding and supportive than adolescents imagine they will be.

Michael Jordan's position was somewhat different. He, too, was working hard but was not necessarily overloaded. Steven Berglas (2001) identified Jordan's problem as burnout, arguing that many successful people become prisoners of their own success—trapped in careers that they no longer find fulfilling because they have met every challenge. The view from the top is not as good as they had imagined, and they become burned out. Few walk away like Michael Jordan did (and he did not stay away, making a comeback in 2001).

The concept of burnout originated as a description for what happens to some people involved in human services careers (Maslach, Schaufeli, & Leiter, 2001). **Burnout** is a state of emotional and physical exhaustion, lowered productivity, and feelings of isolation, often caused by work-related pressures. Since its origin in the 1970s, the concept has generated a great deal of research indicating that people in a variety of job situations experience burnout. When the job requires some emotional commitment to people, such as counseling, health care, and teaching, burnout is more common. But people in all types of occupations have the potential to experience burnout, and some writers have extended the definition so that Michael Jordan and Andrea Galambos are included in it. Neither of them experienced the lowered productivity or feelings of isolation that are part of the definition for burnout that psychologists use, but both definitely felt exhausted and stressed by the demands of their lifestyles.

The notion that stress is a problem for modern life is not even controversial—everyone accepts the inevitability of stress. You face a variety of stressors: studying for multiple exams in the same week, juggling studies and a part-time job, getting along with a difficult roommate in cramped quarters. Stressors, from the hassles of filing tax returns to the traumas of loss of loved ones, are a reality for everyone. People can deal with stressors in either positive or negative ways; unfortunately, many don't cope effectively, and some take their frustrations out on others.

In this chapter, we examine the nature of stress, discuss how to cope with it, and look at the interrelationship of health and stress. We also look into how learned skills and personality work together to influence the ability to cope with stress in day-to-day life.

Burnout
State of emotional and physical exhaustion, lowered productivity, and feelings of isolation, often caused by work-related pressures.

Stress

Launching into tirades at coworkers or friends, pounding their fists on a table, refusing to discuss a problem, and downing cocktails each night are signs and symptoms of stress caused by jobs, families, or financial burdens. Others manage stress in more positive ways, such as scheduling time more effectively, getting enough sleep, or exercising. One person may have a high-pressure job that affects her social life and causes regular migraines. A coworker may manage the same amount of stress in more positive ways, without suffering negative health consequences. Such examples illustrate an important point: different people evaluate and handle stress in different ways.

What Is Stress?

The definition of stress depends on whose theory you follow. Theorists and researchers have defined stress in terms of external forces, internal responses, and an interaction of the two. According to Hans Selye, one of the first researchers to consider its effects, **stress** is a nonspecific response to real or imagined challenges or threats. Theorists who consider stress as a response define a **stressor** as an environmental stimulus that affects an organism, producing physical and psychological effects such as physical arousal and psychological tension and anxiety. According to Richard Lazarus, stress results from a cognitive appraisal of situations involving challenges or threats. According to this view, not all people view a situation in the same way; *a person must appraise a situation as stressful for it to be stressful.* Each of these views of stress has been important in guiding psychologists' research. Let's examine them.

■ SELYE'S GENERAL ADAPTATION SYNDROME. In the 1930s, Canadian Hans Selye (1907–1982) began a systematic study of stressors and stress. He investigated the physiological changes in animals and people who were experiencing various amounts of stress. Selye conceptualized people's responses to stress in terms of a *general adaptation syndrome* (1956, 1976). (A *syndrome* is a set of responses; in the case of stress, these responses include behaviors and physical symptoms.) Selye's work initiated thousands of studies on stress and stress reactions, and Selye himself published more than 1,600 articles on the topic.

According to Selye, people respond to any stressor similarly, regardless of the type of stressor. This response occurs in three stages: (1) an initial short-term stage of alarm, (2) a longer period of resistance, and (3) a final stage of exhaustion (see Figure 14.1). During the *alarm stage*, people experience increased physiological arousal. They become excited, anxious, or frightened. Bodily resources are mobilized. Metabolism speeds up dramatically, heart rate increases, and blood is diverted

Stress
A nonspecific emotional response to real or imagined challenges or threats; a result of a cognitive appraisal by the individual.

Stressor
An environmental stimulus that affects an organism in physically or psychologically injurious ways, usually producing anxiety, tension, and physiological arousal.

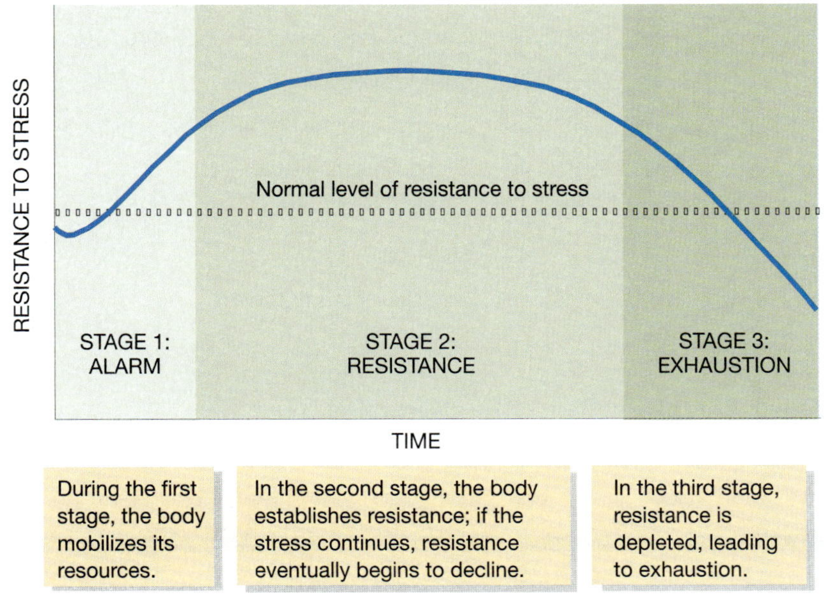

FIGURE 14.1
Selye's General Adaptation Syndrome
According to Hans Selye, a person's response to a stressor can be divided into three stages: alarm, resistance, and exhaustion. (*Selye, 1976*)

from the skin and extremities to the brain and internal organs. (The responses involve activation of the sympathetic nervous system; see Chapter 2.)

When stress continues, people's responses change. Because people cannot remain highly aroused for very long, *resistance* occurs. During this stage, physiological and behavioral responses become more moderate (but still elevated) and sustained. People in the resistance stage may appear normal, but their physiological responses are not. They continue to operate at a heightened level, and they are often irritable, impatient, and easy to anger; they may experience loss of appetite, sleep problems, headaches, or hormone imbalances. This stage can persist for a few hours, several days, or even years, although eventually resistance begins to decline.

TABLE 14.1

For the Active Learner:
A Portion of the Holmes–Rahe Social Readjustment Rating Scale

Check the events that have happened to you within the past 18 months.

Rank	Life Event	Value	Rank	Life Event	Value
□ 1	Death of spouse	100	□ 23	Son or daughter leaving home	29
□ 2	Divorce	73	□ 24	Trouble with in-laws	29
□ 3	Marital separation	65	□ 25	Outstanding personal achievement	28
□ 4	Jail term	63	□ 26	Wife begins or stops work	26
□ 5	Death of close family member	63	□ 27	Begin or end school	26
□ 6	Personal injury or illness	53	□ 28	Change in living conditions	25
□ 7	Marriage	50	□ 29	Revision of personal habits	24
□ 8	Fired at work	47	□ 30	Trouble with boss	23
□ 9	Marital reconciliation	45	□ 31	Change in work hours or conditions	20
□ 10	Retirement	45	□ 32	Change in residence	20
□ 11	Change in health of family member	44	□ 33	Change in schools	20
□ 12	Pregnancy	40	□ 34	Change in recreation	19
□ 13	Sex difficulties	39	□ 35	Change in church activities	19
□ 14	Gain of new family member	39	□ 36	Change in social activities	18
□ 15	Business readjustment	39	□ 37	Loan for lesser purchase (under $10,000)	17
□ 16	Change in financial state	38	□ 38	Change in sleeping habits	16
□ 17	Death of a close friend	37	□ 39	Change in number of family get-togethers	15
□ 18	Change to different line of work	36	□ 40	Change in eating habits	15
□ 19	Change in number of arguments with spouse	35	□ 41	Vacation	13
□ 20	Mortgage or loan for major purchase	31	□ 42	Christmas	12
□ 21	Foreclosure of mortgage or loan	30	□ 43	Minor violations of the law	11
□ 22	Change in responsibilities at work	29			

Add the points for each of the events you checked. Totals of more than 300 elevate the risk of health problems; totals below 150 reflect low risk.

Holmes & Rahe, 1967

The final stage is *exhaustion*. Stress saps psychological and physical energy; adaptability is depleted. If people don't reduce their level of stress, they can become so exhausted physically, mentally, and emotionally that they give up. Selye believed that serious illness or even death could occur in the exhaustion stage.

This view of stress predicts that any event that requires adaptation is stressful and that illness and stress are linked; that is, stress can make people sick. To test the link between stress and illness, researchers must have ways to measure stress, and several assessments of stress have been created.

■ THE HOLMES–RAHE SCALE. Among the many researchers inspired by Selye to study stressors and refine the theory were Thomas Holmes and Richard Rahe. Their basic assumption was that stressful life events, especially those occurring in combination, damage health (Holmes & Rahe, 1967; Rahe, 1989). *Stressful life events* are prominent events in a person's life that necessitate change; this change requires adaptation, which is the source of stress. Even positive events, such as getting a new job, can produce stress.

To test their assumption, the researchers devised the Social Readjustment Rating Scale—basically a list on which individuals circle significant life events (changes) that they've recently experienced (Table 14.1 shows part of this scale). Holmes and Rahe developed a rating for each of the life events. The death of a spouse, divorce, and serious illness rate high as stressors; changes in eating or sleeping habits or vacations rate lower but still require some adaptation. A person taking the test indicates the number of events experienced, typically within the past year. A person's total score reflects the cumulative impact of stressful life events, and according to Holmes and Rahe, provides an index of the likelihood of the person suffering stress-related illness in the next 2 years. According to Holmes and Rahe, a person who scores above 300 points will be much more likely to suffer a stress-induced physical illness than a person whose score is below 150.

Although widely used, the Holmes–Rahe scale has been sharply criticized for a number of reasons. First, most people whose scores are high do not get sick. Even people who accumulate many points are not destined to develop any illness, and most do not. That is, the relationship between life events and illness is far from perfect. Another criticism stems from the fact that the scale was based on a study of young male Navy personnel, whose characteristics do not necessarily match those of the general U.S. population, especially older people, women, and low-income individuals (Shalowitz et al., 1998). In addition, the inclusion of major life events is not a comprehensive way to conceptualize stress. The Undergraduate Stress Questionnaire (Crandall, Preisler, & Aussprung, 1992) is an alternative that includes events common in the lives of college students. The Undergraduate Stress Questionnaire appears in Table 14.2 on the following page.

As many items on the Undergraduate Stress Questionnaire reflect, the stressors faced by most people are seldom major events or crises; people experience stress from day-to-day irritation and difficulties. These irritations and their effects are more closely related to the conceptualization of stress put forth by Richard Lazarus.

■ LAZARUS AND STRESS. This broad definition recognizes that everyone experiences stress at times, but also that stress is an interpreted state; it is a response by an individual. Richard Lazarus (1993), a leader in the study of emotion and stress, asserts that people *actively negotiate* between the demands of the environment (stressors) and personal beliefs and behaviors. Therefore, stress is the result of an interaction of events and people's evaluation of those events. Cognitive researchers refer to this active negotiation as *cognitive appraisal*. Sometimes the arousal that stressors bring about initiates positive actions; sometimes its effects are detrimental. Thinking "I can't possibly handle this!" is likely to lead to a less positive response than is thinking "This is my chance to really show my stuff!" (Lyubomirsky &

Tucker, 1998). See Figure 14.2 for an overview of the responses that occur after a cognitive appraisal has identified an event as a stressor.

What influences an individual's cognitive appraisal, determining whether a particular event will be stressful? The answer lies in the extent to which the person is familiar with the event, how much she or he has anticipated the event, and how

TABLE **14.2**

For the Active Learner: Undergraduate Stress Questionnaire

Has this stressful event happened to you at any time during the last two weeks?
If it has, please check the space next to it. If it has not, then please leave it blank.

- □ Lack of money
- □ Someone broke a promise
- □ Death (family member or friend)
- □ Dealt with incompetence at the Registrar's office
- □ Can't concentrate
- □ Had a lot of tests
- □ Thought about unfinished work
- □ Someone did a "pet peeve" of yours
- □ It's finals week
- □ Living with boy-/girlfriend
- □ No sleep
- □ Applying to graduate school
- □ Felt need for transportation
- □ Sick, injury
- □ Bad haircut today
- □ Victim of a crime
- □ Had a class presentation
- □ Job requirements changed
- □ Applying for a job
- □ Assignments in all classes due the same day
- □ Fought with boy-/girlfriend
- □ No time to eat
- □ Have a hard upcoming week
- □ Felt some peer pressure
- □ Lots of deadlines to meet
- □ Went into test unprepared
- □ Working while in school
- □ Arguments, conflict of values with friends
- □ Have a hangover
- □ Problems with your computer
- □ Lost something (especially wallet)
- □ Death of a pet
- □ Bothered by having no social support of family
- □ Performed poorly at a task
- □ Did worse than expected on test
- □ Problem getting home from bar when drunk
- □ Used a fake ID
- □ Had an interview
- □ Had projects, research papers due
- □ Did badly on a test
- □ Can't finish everything you needed to do
- □ Heard bad news
- □ No sex for a while
- □ Someone cut ahead of you in line
- □ Had confrontation with an authority figure
- □ Maintaining a long-distance boy-/girlfriend
- □ Crammed for a test
- □ Parents getting divorce
- □ Dependent on other people
- □ Feel unorganized
- □ Breaking up with boy-/girlfriend
- □ Trying to decide on major
- □ Feel isolated
- □ Having roommate conflicts
- □ Checkbook didn't balance
- □ Visit from a relative and entertaining them
- □ Decision to have sex is on your mind
- □ Car/bike broke down, flat tire, etc.
- □ Parents controlling with money
- □ Couldn't find a parking space
- □ Noise disturbed you while trying to study
- □ Someone borrowed something without permission
- □ Had to ask for money
- □ Got a traffic ticket
- □ Talked with a professor
- □ Change of environment (new doctor, dentist, etc.)
- □ Exposed to upsetting TV show, book, or movie
- □ Got to class late
- □ Erratic schedule
- □ Found out boy-/girlfriend cheated on you
- □ Can't understand your professor
- □ Trying to get into your major or college
- □ Missed your period and waiting
- □ Coping with addictions
- □ Registration for classes
- □ Stayed up late writing a paper
- □ Property stolen
- □ Someone you expected to call did not
- □ Holiday
- □ Sat through a boring class
- □ Favorite sporting team lost
- □ Thoughts about future

Count the number of check marks. Student with higher scores are more likely to need health care (as measured by going to the student health center or infirmary) than students with lower scores.

Did this stress inventory do a better job of capturing the stress in your life than Holmes and Rahe's Social Readjustment Rating Scale?

Crandall, Preisler, & Aussprung, 1992

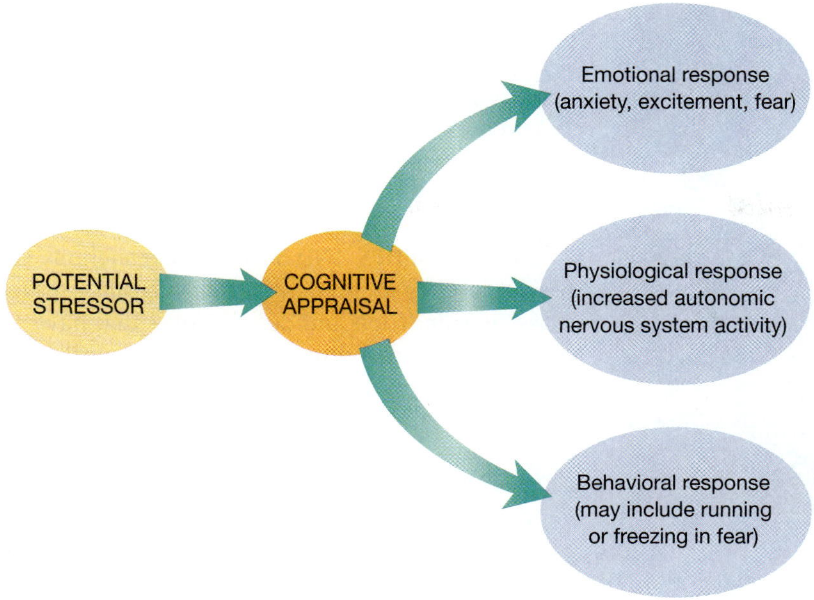

FIGURE 14.2

The Effect of Cognitive Appraisal on Responses to Stressors

Depending on how a potential stressor (for example, entering a tied game in overtime) is evaluated, its impact can vary emotionally, physiologically, and behaviorally.

much control she or he has over the event and the response to it. For example, the first day of a new course brings excitement and some apprehension about the instructor's expectations and whether the time commitments for the course will be burdensome; the second or third time the class meets is usually much less worrisome. When people can predict events and are familiar with them, they feel more in control, more confident that they can have some impact on the future. That is, when people appraise that they have the resources to cope with an event, that event is not a threat. When people believe that they lack the resources to cope with a threat, then they experience stress. This view of stress includes a wider variety of potential stressors plus individual evaluation of these events. The concept of hassles—inconveniences and annoyances in everyday life—captures this view better than major life events and has led to the development of an alternative assessment.

■ **THE HASSLES SCALE.** Even routine life events can cause stress. Indeed, Lazarus and his colleagues propose that routine events are more closely related to the experience of stress and physical problems than are major life events. Lazarus and his colleagues (Kanner et al., 1981) developed an assessment, the Hassles Scale, that is oriented toward measuring these events. People completing this assessment respond to 117 potential hassles, rating each according to how much the situation is a hassle. Table 14.3 presents the 10 daily hassles most frequently cited as sources of stress. A later, streamlined revision of this scale contains only 53 items (DeLongis, Folkman, & Lazarus, 1988). According to research, daily hassles are more strongly correlated with physical and psychological health than are major life events. Both major life events and daily hassles relate to health, but in somewhat different ways (Cassidy, 2000). In addition, hassles affect the quality of intimate relationships (Tesser & Beach, 1998) and symptoms such as headaches (Fernandez & Sheffield, 1996). Therefore, the concept of hassles adds to the explanation of the relationship between stress and health.

TABLE 14.3

Life's Little Hassles—The Top Ten

1. Concerns about weight
2. Health of a family member
3. Rising prices of common goods
4. Home maintenance
5. Too many things to do
6. Misplacing or losing things
7. Yard work or outside home maintenance
8. Property, investments, or taxes
9. Crime
10. Physical appearance

Kanner, Coyne, Schaefer & Lazaras, 1981

■ *After the September 11 attacks on the WTC, many people were traumatized.*

Sources of Stress

Researchers have taken both life events and hassles approaches to studying the impact of stressors. As a result, researchers have examined a variety of situations, ranging from war and earthquakes to traffic congestion and deadlines.

■ **CATASTROPHES AND STRESS.** Throughout U.S. history, there have been many *catastrophes*—events of massive proportion and destruction—that have affected people and communities profoundly. Catastrophes can be either natural disasters, such as earthquakes and hurricanes, or events with a human origin, such as airplane crashes and terrorist attacks. No catastrophe influenced the nation so strongly as the terrorist attacks on the World Trade Center towers and the Pentagon on September 11, 2001. The nation watched as the attacks took place and continued to watch as rescue workers frantically searched for survivors.

How do people respond to catastrophes? How do people cope with stressors of such magnitude? It turns out that people are amazingly resilient (a topic we'll consider later), but the impact of a catastrophe—of a natural disaster, war, or traumatic

psychology ***in action***

Psychology and the Aftermath of September 11, 2001

When terrorists attacked the World Trade Center and the Pentagon on September 11, 2001, Americans were stunned, horrified, and traumatized. Psychologists responded immediately, both personally and professionally. For example, Sharon Brennan was working at her clinical practice in New York City when the attack occurred (APA Monitor Staff, 2001). She is a member of the American Psychological Association's Disaster Response Network, which was established in 1992 and includes over 2,000 psychologists who have received training for disaster intervention (Daw, 2001). Like Brennan, members in New York reported to the Red Cross and helped set up the disaster response center. Brennan arrived with the first emergency response team that included mental health workers; they worked throughout the night of September 11 to provide support for the emergency workers. Brennan continued for several weeks, helping people search for missing relatives and friends, and she went to schools to talk to children about the attacks.

Members of the APA's Disaster Response Network came from all over the country to help in New York and Washington, DC. However, the terrorist attacks on September 11, 2001, affected people throughout the United States. They not only saw the attacks on television but also reexperienced these feelings over the next few days, during television replays of the explosions and the WTC collapse. Psychologists knew that the problems would affect a far larger group than those who were directly involved. The extensive media coverage brought the attacks into most people's homes.

After the initial shock, people began trying to cope with the situation and to explain the events to their children. For a few days, psychologists saw no increase in the number of people seeking counseling for problems related to the attacks, but after a week, the number of people consulting mental health professionals began to rise. Psychologists were prepared for these reactions and began to offer services to help people cope and explain the situation to children in ways that helped diminish their fears.

The National Association of School Psychologists (www.nasponline.org) offered information for teachers and parents to help children understand and deal with the attacks. The American Psychological Association marshaled an extensive effort to provide counseling and also to make information available on their website (www.helping.apa.org). MTV broadcasted the website's address, publicizing the help offered by psychologists. This information includes papers about the effects of traumatic experiences, how to talk to children about the attacks, what symptoms to look for as signs of serious problems, and where to find professional help. Psychologists' expertise helped many people deal with this tragedy. Psychologist Sally Singer Horwatt (APA Monitor Staff, 2001, p. 25) expressed the view of many of these volunteers when she said, "In a crisis, it's not our insights or theories that count. It's our support."

event—can be long lasting (see *Psychology in Action* on the following page). Mental health practitioners see many clients who continue to suffer long after an event that has changed their lives. For example, in 1989, a group of U.S. Army veterans returned with several therapists to Vietnam, where they had waged war more than two decades earlier. This time, however, their mission was not to fight an enemy but to heal their own psychological wounds. One veteran reported that he had been haunted for years by nightmares of his combat experiences. This severe stress-related disorder is termed **posttraumatic stress disorder (PTSD)**—a psychological disorder that may become evident after a person has undergone severe stress caused by some type of disaster.

PTSD was recognized in military veterans who experienced combat, and the diagnosis became common among Vietnam veterans. Common symptoms of PTSD are vivid, intrusive recollections or reexperiencing of the traumatic event and occasional lapses of normal consciousness (Morgan et al., 1998). People may develop anxiety, depression, or exceptionally aggressive behavior; they may avoid situations that resemble the traumatizing events. Such behaviors may eventually interfere with daily functioning, family interactions, and health.

Although most veterans of the Vietnam War did not develop the disorder, thousands did. Decades later, these individuals still endure sleep problems, the reliving of painful experiences, difficulty in concentrating, and feelings of panic and alienation (Kagan et al., 1999). Initially, combat veterans were diagnosed with PTSD, and the disorder was considered to be confined mostly to men. But others who experienced traumatic events were considered and found to suffer from similar symptoms. Now a wide variety of experiences are recognized to raise the risk for PTSD. Veterans are at elevated risk (Hankin et al., 1999; Keane, 1998; Rosebush, 1998; Ursano et al., 1995), but victims of all types of trauma, especially those who are the victims of violence, are at risk (Dohrenwend, 2000).

An increasing number of studies are focusing on the psychological aftermath of natural disasters such as earthquakes, tornadoes, and floods (Wang et al., 2000), as well as the impact on survivors of traumatic events such as the Holocaust of World War II (Yehuda et al., 1998), the displacement of refugees (Weine et al., 2001) and refugee children (Ajdukovic & Ajdukovic, 1998), severe accidents (Schnyder et al., 2000), and even cancer (Kahana, Deimling, & Bowman, 2000).

Despite the initial emphasis on men, women have been found to be more susceptible to PTSD than men (Stein, Walker, & Forde, 2000). Rape, violence at the hands of intimate partners such as boyfriends or husbands, and sexual abuse during childhood are all experiences that elevate the risk for PTSD, and women are more likely than men to have such experiences (Golding, 1999). The likelihood that a person will experience PTSD at some time during his or her life is about 8% (Kessler et al., 1995).

■ **UNHEALTHY ENVIRONMENTS AND STRESS.** Some environments may be hazardous to people's health. A neighborhood environment may contain many factors that contribute to stress. Certainly toxins and pollution are stressors that also carry health risks, but even without such obvious health threats, certain neighborhoods contain elements that produce stress. Many of these factors revolve around poverty and the communities in which poor people live. People in *low socioeconomic groups* often live in overcrowded and substandard housing, lack access to services such as banks and stores, experience high noise levels, and live with the threat of crime and violence (Taylor, Repetti, & Seeman, 1997). These situations often combine to produce the type of stressors called hassles, such as having trouble cashing a check, and the type of life events that are related to PTSD, such as witnessing or being the victim of violence. Research indicates that the chances of witnessing violence are high especially for children living in a poor, inner-city neighborhood, and this experience is related to stress and anxiety (Cooley-Quille et al., 2001).

Posttraumatic stress disorder (PTSD)
Psychological disorder that may become evident after a person has undergone extreme stress caused by some type of disaster; common symptoms include vivid, intrusive recollections or reexperiences of the traumatic event and occasional lapses of normal consciousness.

Even people who are wealthy do not escape the stresses of urban living. Eric Graig (1993) formulated the term *urban press* to describe the multitude of factors that combine in modern urban life. These factors include crowding, pollution, noise, commuting stress, and fear of crime. Graig argues that these factors are a constant presence for city dwellers, and their combination produces a level of stress that is not accounted for by each stressor considered individually.

These environments can be detrimental in several ways—when safety is threatened, when the environment prevents people from forming social ties, and when conflicts occur in schools, in families, and on the street. Any or all of them can affect physiology and health. Thus, people who live in poverty are at higher risk for stress, anxiety, and associated health consequences.

Although unhealthy environments produce stress, the evolutionary point of view hypothesizes that environmental stress may not be all bad. In this view, environmental stress is a force for selection and evolution (Hoffmann & Hercus, 2000). For example, the presence of chemical pesticides has produced changes in some insect species so that they are resistant to these chemicals. The environmental stressors in modern city life may act similarly, providing a means of rapid evolution as a way to adapt to these stressful conditions.

■ **DISCRIMINATION AND STRESS.** Discrimination is an all too common experience, and people perceive that they are discriminated against on the basis of ethnicity, sex,

introduction to research basics

Racism and Reactivity

Research has established that racial discrimination is an important source of stress. In addition, African Americans have a higher rate of heart disease than other ethnic groups, and researchers are investigating how such discrimination may translate into higher rates of heart disease in African Americans. Carolyn Fang and Hector Myers (2001) conducted a study to determine the effect of racist remarks on reactivity of the cardiovascular system. *Reactivity* is how strongly the body, in this case, the heart and vascular system, reacts to stimulation.

DESIGN The design was an *experimental design* that manipulated the independent variable, type of stimuli, by choosing three different types of movie scenes: emotionally neutral, anger-provoking, and racist clips. The researchers measured several dependent variables, but their measures of reactivity were blood pressure and heart rate. In addition, the researchers compared African Americans to Caucasians, but of course, this variable was not manipulated; rather, the researchers selected groups of participants from the two ethnic groups.

HYPOTHESIS Fang and Myers hypothesized that participants would show greater reactivity in response to racist film clips than to anger-provoking ones.

PARTICIPANTS Healthy African American and Caucasian male undergraduates (31 in each ethnic group) participated in this study. Their family histories of heart disease and blood pressure scores were assessed and shown to be similar, and all were between 18 and 25 years old.

PROCEDURE Participants were monitored for blood pressure and heart rate while they saw the three different types of film clips. They always viewed the emotionally neutral clip first; the anger-provoking and racist clips were *counterbalanced*; that is, half of the group saw the anger-provoking clip followed by the racist clip, whereas the other half saw the racist clip first and then the anger-provoking scene. This procedure prevents the order of viewing from biasing the participants' responses.

RESULTS As predicted, the emotionally charged film segment provoked greater reactivity than the emotionally neutral one. Contrary to prediction, the anger-provoking and racist stimuli prompted similar blood pressure changes, and the African Americans and Caucasians reacted similarly. However, individuals who were high in hostility showed prolonged reactivity.

CONCLUSIONS Experiencing racist stimuli caused blood pressure reactions in both African American and Caucasian college men. Because the experience of racism is more common for African Americans, they may experience more serious effects from these episodes. In addition, the trait of hostility increases reactivity for both ethnic groups, putting African American men high in hostility at potential risk from discrimination as well as other emotion-provoking stimuli.

and sexual orientation. A survey of people in the United States showed that 33.5% of participants said they had been the target of some major incident of discrimination (Kessler, Mickelson, & Williams, 1999). In addition, there was a substantial relationship between perception of discrimination and mental health problems.

Discrimination and unfair treatment are factors in feeling stressed, and the combination of discrimination with poverty showed a potent effect in producing distress in a study of African Americans (Schultz et al., 2000). Indeed, racism has been identified as a significant factor in the experience of stress for African Americans (Hendryx & Ahern, 1997; see *Introduction to Research Basics* for how stress from discrimination may be damaging for African Americans). Latinas/Latinos and Asian Americans are also influenced by racist discrimination; those who have immigrated to the United States experience stressors involved with adapting to a new culture (Guarnaccia, 1997; Prelow & Guarnaccia, 1997). Language problems and the lack of familiarity with the culture can make daily tasks into hassles. Immigrants are more likely than native-born people to be poor and affected by the stressors related to poverty. All ethnic groups are affected by life events and daily hassles, but racial discrimination is a source of stress that adds to the stress for members of ethnic minorities.

Sexist discrimination is also a stressor. Women are the targets of sexist discrimination and harassment much more often than men are, and these experiences produce stress (Klonoff, Landrine, & Campbell, 2000). Indeed, women who experience a high level of sexist discrimination feel its effects in terms of physical symptoms, whereas women whose experience of sexist discrimination is low report stress levels similar to men's. For some women, discrimination is a significant factor in their lives.

Gays, lesbians, and bisexuals also experience discrimination because of their sexual orientation (DiPlacido, 1998). Indeed, having any sexual orientation other than heterosexual is a stigma in our culture. Gays, lesbians, and bisexuals are a minority group and subject to stress from discrimination. Any such individuals who decide to reveal their sexual orientation often experience conflict; research indicates that this conflict may have no stress-free resolution. Revealing a gay or lesbian sexual orientation puts a person in a position of facing discrimination, but being "in the closet" is also stressful (Cole et al., 1996). For those who are not heterosexual, either choice potentially brings stress.

■ *For traders the day-to-day fluctuation of the stock market, often caused by crises in other parts of the world, make it a high-stress occupation.*

■ **PERSONAL FACTORS AND STRESS.** People who experience catastrophic events and the stressors associated with poverty may also face stress from personal factors. People who experience no catastrophe and only minor stress from the environment still have stress from the workplace, personal relationships, and time pressure. Stress is an unavoidable part of life.

Workplaces are environments and may contain environmental stressors such as toxins, noise, and crowding. However, work presents an additional array of stressors. People tend to think of executives who make many important decisions as experiencing a great deal of stress, but research indicates that the freedom to make decisions actually *decreases* a job's stress (de Jonge et al., 2000; Karasek, 1979). Instead, high-stress jobs tend to be the ones that impose high demands on workers but give them little latitude to make decisions or to exert control. The types of jobs that are high in stress include middle-level managers, inner-city high school teachers, customer service agents, waiters and waitresses, and emergency workers. These jobs combine high demands and low decision-making power; this combination tends to create stress for workers.

A number of additional factors associated with work can produce stress. Demanding jobs are not necessarily stressful; when workers feel in control of the important aspects of their jobs, they may see high demands as a challenge. Alternatively, when workers experience high demands and low control on the job, they are more likely to feel stressed than challenged (Cheng et al., 2000). Workers who feel many constraints, who work at night, who work a lot of overtime, and who are under constant deadline pressure experience increased stress (Ettner & Grzywacz, 2001). When workers feel adequately rewarded for their job performance, they are less likely to feel stressed than workers who feel that their rewards are not proportional to their efforts on the job (de Jonge et al., 2000).

The dangers of low-level jobs apply to men as well as women (Wamala et al., 2000). A specific comparison of female managers and female clerks showed that the clerks evaluated stressors as more severe, less controllable, and more distressing than did the managers (Long, 1998). These results point to low-level rather than high-level jobs as stressful. However, even high-level jobs can be stressful. A study of physicians indicated that both male and female doctors felt stressed by the time pressure of keeping up with scheduled appointments and the amount of work they were required to do (Rout, 1999). Therefore, all types of jobs have stressful components, and very few people escape on-the-job stress. Despite the many possibilities for stress on the job, being without a job or being uncertain about continued employment is even more stressful (Ferrie et al., 2001).

■ *Deadlines, exams, and schoolwork may be sources of stress for adolescents.*

Personal relationships are a potential source of stress, both at work and at home. At work, interactions with coworkers can be sources of satisfaction or stress (Monnier et al., 1998). Support from supervisors and coworkers can make a critical difference in the experience of stress on the job; supportive relationships are positive factors in work and life satisfaction. Coworkers who are harassing or violent create workplace problems that produce stress not only for the targets of these unacceptable behaviors but also for the entire staff (Bennett & Lehman, 1999).

Work stress and personal relationships also intersect in the challenge of balancing job and family commitments. This balancing act is a major source of stress, especially for women. Traditionally, women have been the primary caregivers for children and family. As women have entered the workforce, they have also kept the caregiver role, creating difficulties in fulfilling both roles (Hochschild, 1997; Williams, 2000). Men who work long hours sacrifice family time, and their children feel this choice even more sharply than their wives do (Crouter et al., 2001). Men who have become more involved in family life and wish to devote more time to home and family experience problems in justifying this choice to their employer (Hochschild, 1997). These men are in a position similar to that of employed women who feel the time bind and conflict of balancing family and work demands.

Marriage is celebrated as a positive event in many cultures. Nonetheless, adjusting to married life means becoming familiar with new experiences, responding in new ways, and having less control over many aspects of day-to-day life—all of which can be stressful. Even among couples married for years, daily hassles increase stress between partners (Harper, Schaalje, & Sandberg, 2000). Also, at times, marriage involves interpersonal conflict, which may produce stress. One partner may not be fulfilling obligations or may be preoccupied in some way, causing the spouse to feel left out; both possibilities may bring about stress and even health problems (Tesser & Beach, 1998). One prominent source of stress for many couples is conflict over household chores; men's lower contribution to household work is a significant source of stress for women (Bird, 1999). Stresses in marriage are certainly problems, but ending a marriage creates even more stress (McKelvey & McKenry, 2000).

Lack of time is another common source of stress. Everyone faces deadlines: students must complete tests before class ends, auto workers must keep pace with the assembly line, and taxpayers must file their returns by April 15. People have only a limited number of hours each day in which to accomplish tasks, and people who work long hours often have no time for leisure and family. If people do not handle time pressure successfully, they may begin to feel overloaded and stressed. Employees mention time pressure constraints as a source of stress in several different work settings (Rout, 1999; Teuchmann, Totterdell, & Parker, 1999). One possibility for more time is flexible or fewer hours spent working, but most people are unwilling to take that option, even when their workplace offers it (Fast & Frederick, 1996).

Stress affects children as well as adults. Children are much less able to change or control the circumstances in which they find themselves (Band & Weisz, 1988). They often experience stress in school, and an abusive or neglectful home life may produce symptoms of PTSD in children. Like adults, children often show their stress response in physical symptoms, and physical symptoms are a common manifestation of stress in children (Walker et al., 2001). Therefore, both children and adults must show specific responses to stress that produce physical symptoms.

Responses to Stress

People respond to stress on physiological as well as behavioral and psychological levels, and individuals vary in their responses on each of these levels. The basic idea underlying the work of many researchers is that stress activates physiological responses that can result in disease. Psychologists who study stress typically divide the stress reaction into physiological and behavioral components.

■ *Stress can affect a person's behavior, making their responses disorganized and ineffective.*

■ **THE PHYSIOLOGY OF STRESS.** Researchers such as James, Lange, and Cannon (discussed in Chapter 11) studied emotions, focusing on when an emotion was felt in response to a stressful incident—during or after the actual event. *Physiologically*, the stress response is characterized by arousal of the sympathetic division of the autonomic nervous system (see Chapter 2, p. 52). This arousal consists of a host of changes, including increased heart rate, faster but shallower breathing, higher blood pressure, sweating palms, and dilation of the pupils. This array of physiological changes begins in the brain, with the activation of the pituitary gland and the hypothalamus. This action produces the release of a hormone that stimulates the adrenal glands,

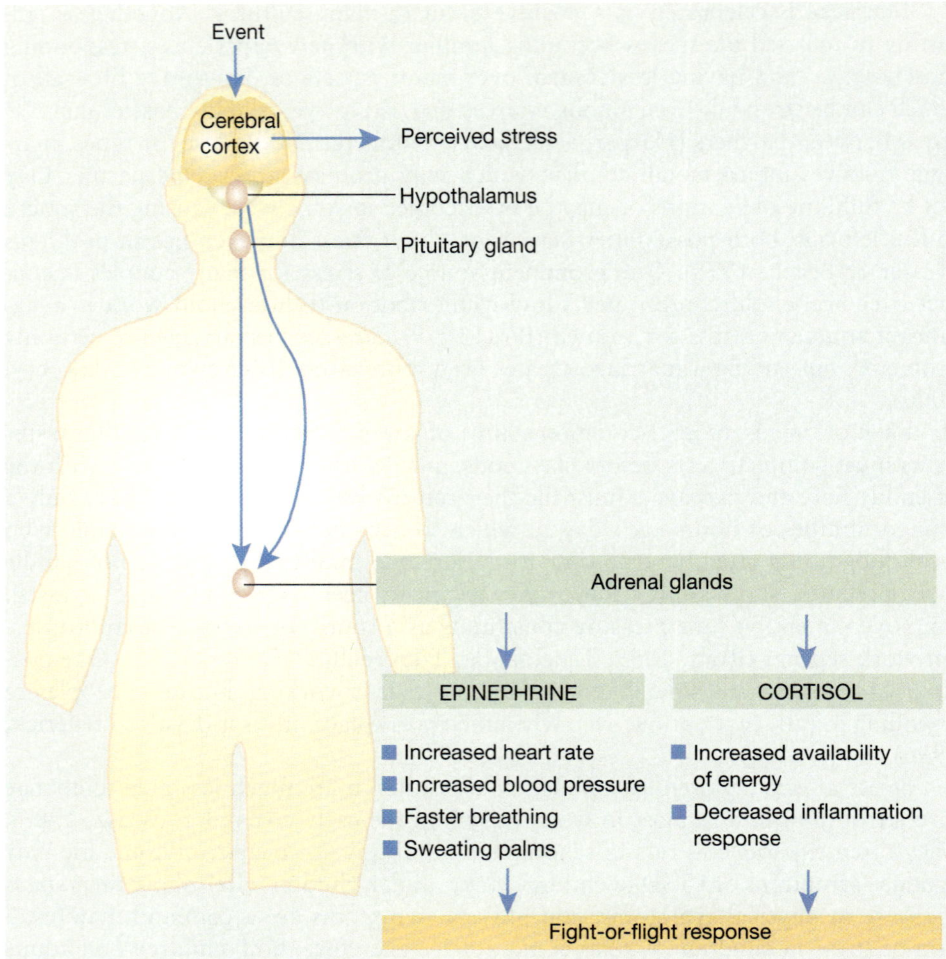

FIGURE 14.3

Physiological Reactions to Stress

Perceiving stress initiates a cascade of effects, including the nervous system and hormones.

located above the kidneys. These glands release several hormones related to stress, including cortisol and epinephrine, each of which produces specific effects. The action of epinephrine produces the variety of physiological reactions associated with stress. Cortisol allows for the mobilization of energy reserves and decreases in inflammation. Figure 14.3 shows these responses. This arousal of the sympathetic division of the autonomic nervous system mobilizes the body for fight or flight, preparing for a physiological response to a stressor. It may be that this response was more adaptive in our evolutionary history than it is today; cortisol and epinephrine and the reactions they provoke have been implicated in the health risks related to stress.

■ **BEHAVIOR AND STRESS.** *Behaviorally*, stress and arousal are related. As we saw in Chapter 11, psychologist Donald Hebb (1972) has argued that effective behavior depends on a person's state of arousal. When people are moderately aroused, they behave with optimal effectiveness. When they are underaroused, they lack the stimulation to behave effectively. Overarousal tends to produce disorganized and ineffective behavior, particularly if the tasks people undertake are complex. (Figure 14.4 shows the effects of arousal on task performance.)

A moderate level of stress and the arousal that accompanies it may be unavoidable and even desirable. Arousal keeps people active and involved. It impels students to study, athletes to excel during competition, and workers to perform better on the job. In short, some levels of stress and arousal can be beneficial, helping people achieve their potential. Some levels of stress are related to a variety of diseases.

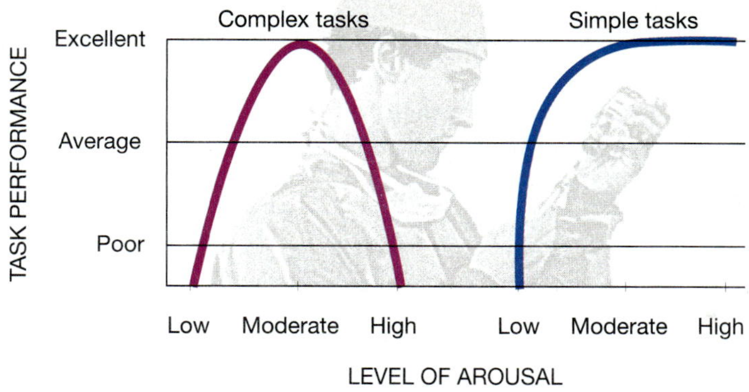

FIGURE 14.4

Effects of Arousal on Task Performance

When arousal is low, task performance is poor or nonexistent. Performance is usually best at moderate levels of arousal. High levels of arousal usually improve performance on simple tasks but impair performance on complex tasks (such as surgery).

Stress and Health

Mothers and self-help books have long advised people to reduce their levels of stress to keep from getting sick, and research now supports their advice. Stress prompts a variety of physical responses, but its effect on the development of disease is not direct; rather, stress responses cause a range of physiological reactions that can initiate various disease processes. Therefore, stress has a relationship to many diseases, including the five major causes of death in the United States: heart disease, cancer, stroke, lung disease, and accidental injuries. However, researchers have been most interested in the link between stress and heart disease.

Many people assume that there is a clear relationship between stress and heart disease; they know that stress elevates blood pressure and that high blood pressure creates a risk for heart disease. Therefore, they assume that stress causes chronic high blood pressure (hypertension) and elevates the risk of heart attack. This explanation is incorrect. Stress does elevate blood pressure, but that increase is temporary; the underlying cause of hypertension is currently unknown. Stress can be a problem for people with hypertension, but it is not the cause of hypertension. Therefore, the link between stress and heart disease turns out to be less obvious and more complex than most people imagine.

■ **HEART DISEASE AND STRESS.** Heart disease is the number one killer of both men and women in the United States. Each year, more than 450,000 Americans die of heart attacks caused by coronary heart disease (American Heart Association, 2000). The coronary arteries furnish the blood supply to the heart muscle, and when those arteries are blocked, the heart muscle no longer gets blood, precipitating a heart attack. The most common underlying cause is the buildup of deposits inside the coronary arteries, which restricts blood flow.

The behavioral factors related to this physiological condition have been the subject of intensive research, and several behaviors relate to the disease process that results in coronary artery blockage. Therefore, both physicians and psychologists accept that lifestyle factors are important to the development of heart disease. One of the first attempts to link behavior and heart disease was the formulation of the Type A behavior pattern.

In the late 1950s, physicians Meyer Friedman and Ray Rosenman identified a pattern of behavior that they believe contributes to heart disease; they called it Type A behavior (Friedman & Rosenman, 1974). **Type A behavior** is the behavior pattern of individuals who are competitive, impatient, hostile, and always striving to do more in less time. **Type B behavior** is the pattern exhibited by people who are calmer, more patient, less hurried, and less hostile.

Type A behavior
Behavior pattern characterized by competitiveness, impatience, hostility, and constant efforts to do more in less time.

Type B behavior
Behavior pattern exhibited by people who are calmer, more patient, and less hurried than Type A individuals.

Early studies of the Type A behavior pattern showed a positive association with heart disease; that is, Type A individuals were more likely than Type B individuals to have heart attacks. The concept became well known, and people accepted that the combination of behaviors significantly increased the risk for heart disease. More recent research, however, casts doubt on the concept. This research suggests that the overall Type A behavior pattern is not a risk for heart disease (Johnson, Espnes, & Gillard, 1998; Lilla et al., 1998). Criticisms include the applicability of the concept to Western culture and to men more than to other groups. Heart disease is a leading cause of death across the world, but the Type A behavior pattern fits middle-aged North American businessmen better than other people. Women exhibit Type A behavior, but some evidence suggests that this behavior pattern does not relate to heart disease in women (Orth-Gormér, 1998).

Researchers began to examine components of the Type A behavior pattern for their toxic effects and found that hostility and anger relate to the development of heart disease (Madigan, Dale, & Cross, 1997; Morren, 1998). Feelings of suspiciousness, mistrust of others, and thinking the worst of people are associated with increased risk for coronary heart disease. Anger is associated with increased blockage of arteries in women (Matthews et al., 1998) and in African Americans (Iribarren et al., 2000). Anger and anxiety are also associated with death from cardiovascular disease (Suinn, 2001). In addition, both the experience of anger and its expression are related to heart disease. That is, even people who only experience the emotion of anger and do not express it are at increased risk. To examine your own behaviors and attitudes that relate to heart disease risk, answer the questions in Figure 14.5.

The link between anger and heart disease may come about through the physiological changes that occur in response to this emotion, which is the same as the stress response—activation of the sympathetic division of the autonomic nervous system. However, hostility and anger are not the same as stress. Therefore, the experience of stress relates to the development of heart disease, but the relationship is complex. For people who have coronary heart disease, however, the experience of stress increases the chances of sudden heart attack (Bosma et al., 1998) and fatal heart attack (Zoler, 2001). Therefore, several lines of research have linked stress and heart disease.

Another link between heart disease and stress has become apparent from a situation generated by world politics. Following the collapse of the Soviet Union, heart disease deaths skyrocketed in Russia and in countries that had been under the control of the Soviet Union. Stress has been implicated in this epidemic (Stone, 2000; Weidner, 2000). Some researchers argue that when communism collapsed, people felt optimistic for a better life that did not happen. Instead, people experienced uncertainty and economic turmoil that translated into feelings of stress, pessimism, and depression. The incidence of heart disease rose dramatically and life expectancy decreased, especially among middle-aged men. Researchers examined other behavioral factors that related to heart disease, such as diet and smoking, but found few differences between people in eastern and western Europe. Yet their heart disease death rates were dramatically different. Now researchers are concentrating on stress and depression as a source of difference. This emphasis highlights the involvement of stress and psychological factors in the development of heart disease and the importance of considering the cultural context of health and disease.

■ **STRESS AND INFECTIOUS DISEASE.** Does it seem as if you always get a cold just after final exams are over? Do you feel as though the stress makes you vulnerable to all types of infections? That feeling may be correct. Stress is related to the development of disease through its effect on the immune system, the body's defense against infection. The immune system is a complex network of specialized cells and organs that has evolved to defend the body against attacks by "foreign invaders"—bacteria, viruses, and fungi. These specialized cells and organs are able to distinguish these foreign invaders from the body's own cells and tissues. The recognition of cells that are not part of the body prompts immune system reactions that locate, identify, and obliterate the invaders. As part of the immune response, the system acquires a

Rate the following statements according to how each applies to you. Write the number that represents your rating in the blank to the left of each statement. Use the same scale for both sets of questions.

1	2	3	4	5	6	7
Not at all			Sometimes			All the time

Set 1

___ I get impatient when people do things slowly.

___ I experience a lot of time pressure.

___ I feel the pressure to get ahead and succeed.

___ I do many things fast—talking, walking, eating, and so forth.

___ People consider me short-tempered.

___ I work long hours.

___ I often want to (and sometimes actually do) finish other people's sentences.

___ I think that it is important to acquire a lot of money and possessions.

___ I often lose my temper.

___ I hate to stand in line.

___ It is not necessary for others to impose deadlines; I set them for myself.

Set 2

___ People seem to annoy me intentionally.

___ I often raise my voice.

___ Many situations make me angry.

___ I expect the worst from people, and that's what usually happens.

___ Although I often feel angry, I try to hide these feelings.

___ I have a "short fuse" when it comes to tolerating incompetence.

___ Being caught in slow traffic frustrates me so much that I want to yell at the other drivers (and sometimes, I do).

___ It's not wise to trust people.

___ Sometimes I think people single me out for bad treatment.

___ I try to control my temper, but I often lose it.

___ I express my anger physically by hitting, kicking, slapping, or throwing things.

If you rated many of the statements in Set 1 with 6s or 7s, then you have characteristics consistent with the Type A behavior pattern.

If you marked 6s or 7s to many of the items in Set 2, your responses indicate that you experience a lot of hostility and anger, and you tend to express or suppress these feelings.

Although the Type A behavior pattern is popularly associated with the development of heart disease, the experience and expression of anger have a much stronger relationship. So, indications of Type A behavior based on the first set of questions do not elevate your behavioral risk of coronary heart disease as much as high ratings on the second set.

FIGURE 14.5

For the Active Learner:
Estimating Risk Factors for Heart Disease

way to fight against reinfection, called immunity. Thus, exposure to the same infectious agent causes a rapid immune system response and protection against reinfection—the body has acquired immunity against that specific infectious agent. For example, there are hundreds of variations on the virus that produces colds; we never get the same cold twice, but we can get a new version any time. The immune system also has cells that fight infection in more general ways, protecting against a wide range of infections.

We are exposed to many infectious agents daily, and sometimes our immune systems are not 100% effective. When they are not, we can get sick. The reason that some people get sick and others do not may relate to the efficiency of their immune systems. When researchers discovered that the immune system responds to behaviors and events through connections with the nervous system, the field of psychoneuroimmunology was born (Ader & Cohen, 1975). **Psychoneuroimmunology** is an interdisciplinary area of study that includes behavioral, neurological, and immune factors and their relationship to the development of disease (see *Brain and*

Psychoneuroimmunology (PNI) [SYE-ko-NEW-ro-IM-you-NOLL-oh-gee]
An interdisciplinary area of study that includes behavioral, neurological, and immune factors and their relationship to the development of disease.

BRAIN AND BEHAVIOR

Psychoneuroimmunology

The immune system is responsible for fighting foreign invaders in the body, much like an army defending against bacteria, viruses, and fungi that should not cross the border—the skin—and enter the body. For many years, experts believed that the immune system operated independently of the nervous and endocrine systems, performing its functions under its own directions rather than communicating with any other system. However, researchers demonstrated that the immune system can be conditioned by pairing an unconditioned stimulus (an injection of a drug that decreases immune system response) and a conditioned stimulus (the presentation of a water and saccharine solution) (Ader & Cohen, 1975). The result of the injection was an unconditioned response (a decrease in immune function) in the rats that received the immune-suppressant drug, and the conditioning was demonstrated when the immune suppression response appeared in response to the saccharine solution. This finding suggests that the immune and nervous systems interact.

The suggestion of an interaction between the immune and nervous systems prompted the development of psychoneuroimmunology (PNI), an interdisciplinary area of study that includes behavioral, neurological, and immune factors and their relationship to the development of disease. The endocrine system was soon included in the area, and researchers began to investigate this interaction among systems. One pathway is through chemicals called cytokines, which are messenger molecules in the immune system (Glaser et al., 1999). The hormones released by sympathetic nervous system arousal produce changes in cytokines, so activity in the brain affects both sympathetic nervous system activity and the messenger system for the immune system.

Research in the area of psychoneuroimmunology indicates that stressors decrease a wide variety of immune system responses and affect the risk for infectious disease (Cohen, 1996), wound healing (Marucha, Kiecolt-Glaser, & Favagehi, 1998), and recovery from surgery (Kiecolt-Glaser et al., 1998). The degree of change is typically small, which suggests that stressors are not a major source of decrease in immune system response (Ader, 2001). However, many people have immune system problems, including people under chronic stress and those who have immune disorders such as HIV. For people with compromised immune systems, additional stressors could make a significant difference for immune system functioning and the ability to fight disease (Glaser et al., 1999). For people with healthy immune systems, chronic stress can have a cumulative effect, which may explain the increased number of visits to the infirmary at the end of the semester.

Behavior). A basic finding from this field shows that events affecting the immune system make people more vulnerable to disease (Herbert et al., 1994; Sher, 1998).

Sheldon Cohen and his colleagues (Cohen, 1996; Cohen et al., 1998) have demonstrated that stress makes people more vulnerable to infection from the common cold. Cohen conducted a series of experiments in which he assessed the level of people's stress and their moods, made sure they were healthy, and then exposed them to a combination of cold viruses. Only one-third of the people developed colds, but those who reported high stress and negative moods were much more likely to get sick than those who reported low levels of stress and positive moods.

The participants' perceptions were important, but their experience of stressful life events was an independent risk. In addition, Cohen's studies indicate that the duration of the stress may be more important than the severity in decreasing immune system function. A study on the same topic, using a naturalistic setting, confirmed the relationship between stress and vulnerability to infection with cold viruses (Takkouche, 2001). Therefore, the amount, duration, and perception of stress are all important factors in vulnerability to infection.

Coping
Process by which a person takes some action to manage, master, tolerate, or reduce environmental or internal demands that cause or might cause stress and that tax the individual's inner resources.

Resilience
The extent to which people are flexible and respond adaptively to external or internal demands.

■ **STRESS AND HEALTH-RELATED BEHAVIORS.** Stress has another route through which it can influence health—through behaviors that increase the risk for disease and death. We examined how stress may be related to the development of heart disease through responses mediated by activation of the sympathetic nervous system and the development of infectious disease through its effect on the immune system. However, stress also affects how people behave, including behaviors that can damage or enhance health (Schneiderman et al., 2001). For example, many people claim that smoking helps them cope with stress. Whether or not this belief is accurate, smoking is related to the development of heart disease, cancer, and chronic lung disease. These three diseases are among the leading causes of death in the United States and many other countries. Thus, this indirect link between stress and disease takes a substantial health toll.

Relief from stress is also one of the reasons people give for drinking alcohol, and alcohol is a risk for some types of cancer as well as a significant risk for accidents. Stress also influences eating, which can be either a positive or negative factor for health. Stressed people tend to eat a less healthy diet, and dietary factors are involved in heart disease and many types of cancers (Baum & Posluszny, 1999). Therefore, stress has several routes through which it can affect health. The extent to which stress will result in disease is moderated by successful coping.

Be an *Active* learner

REVIEW

- How do Selye's and Lazarus's views of stress differ? p. 493
- What are the symptoms of posttraumatic stress disorder, and what types of events produce this disorder? pp. 496–497
- How can stress cause disease? pp. 503–504
- What connection exists among the immune system, behavior, and health? pp. 505–506

THINK CRITICALLY

- Are children or adults more vulnerable to posttraumatic stress disorder?
- Evaluate the sources of stress experienced by a 24-year-old single African American factory worker who is the mother of two preschool children.

APPLY PSYCHOLOGY

- Assess the amount of stress in your life and how you think it relates to your health. Does the concept of hassles or of life events best define your stress?

Coping

Everyone needs a way to cope with stress, and most people use a variety of strategies. People may not be aware that they choose among various ways to cope, but they do. However, most people imagine that they could choose ways to cope more effectively, and they are correct. Coping strategies need to be tailored to the individual and the situation—and some strategies are better than others.

What Is Coping?

In general, *coping* means dealing with a situation. However, for a psychologist, **coping** is the process by which a person takes some action to manage, master, tolerate, or reduce environmental and internal demands that cause or might cause stress and that will tax the individual's inner resources. This definition of coping involves five important assumptions. First, coping is constantly changing and being evaluated and is therefore a process or a strategy. Second, coping involves managing situations, not necessarily bringing them under complete control. Third, coping is effortful; it does not happen automatically. Fourth, coping aims to manage cognitive as well as behavioral events. Finally, coping is learned.

■ *Social skills are personal resources that influence coping.*

There are many types of coping strategies, and people tend to use a variety. Coping begins with the reaction to stress at the physiological level. People's bodies respond to stress with specific reactions, including changes in hormone levels, in autonomic nervous system activity, and in the levels of neurotransmitters in the brain. Effective coping strategies are developed when people learn new ways of dealing with their vulnerabilities.

Factors That Influence Coping

People vary enormously in their ability to cope with stressors, and some of that variation is due to personal resources that contribute to **resilience**, the extent to which people are flexible and respond adaptively to external or internal demands.

A person who is resilient is said to be less vulnerable to stressors (Zuckerman, 1999). Factors that influence coping include personal resources, a sense of control, and social support.

Personal resources include a variety of factors, ranging from money to good health. Money and other material resources can be an important factor in dealing with both daily hassles, such as car problems, and with life events, such as changing residence. Social skills and knowledge are also personal resources that affect coping. People who are socially skilled are better at getting along with others and are at ease in social situations. These individuals are less likely to feel stressed by having to attend a social gathering or make a speech than individuals who are less socially skilled. Knowledge is an important resource, and people who know about automobile transmissions may not need the money that someone with less knowledge requires to get the transmission fixed. Being healthy is an obvious advantage in coping with stressors; healthy people have more energy and are able to endure the physical demands imposed by the stress response.

A sense of being in control is also important in resilience and coping. People who believe that they can control important factors in their lives have an internal (rather than an external) locus of control. As we explored in Chapter 12, people who have an internal locus of control have advantages over those who have an external locus of control, and coping with stress is one of those advantages. People who believe that they can exert control over important events and conditions in their lives have advantages, even if the things they control are minor and even if the control is only an illusion and not real.

Two classic experiments demonstrated the importance of control, over even minor details. Ellen Langer and Judith Rodin (1976) demonstrated how important control could be by manipulating the amount of control residents exerted over their new rooms in a retirement home. The new residents of one floor were asked about their schedules, were encouraged to arrange the furniture to their liking, and were given a plant, which they were told was their responsibility to care for. The new residents of another floor lived in similar rooms but were not given choices or encouraged to make decisions. They also received a plant, but the staff cared for it. Those residents who had more control were happier and healthier than the comparison residents, and these advantages persisted over time (Rodin & Langer, 1977). These studies show that controlling even small details can be beneficial.

Feeling in control is a positive state of mind that leads to optimism, which has a positive relation to health. Even more interesting, the feeling of being in control does not have to be reality based to be effective; even the *illusion of control* can exert a positive effect on mental and physical health (Taylor, Kemeny, et al., 2000). When people feel in control of their health and factors that relate to their health, they adopt more healthy behaviors, maintain better social relationships, and possibly have healthier immune systems. The personal belief in control, even if it is not entirely reality based, is healthy when this belief prompts people to behave in health-promoting ways (Peterson, 2000).

Feeling in control is the opposite of learned helplessness. People who experience learned helplessness find that rewards and punishments are not contingent on their behavior, and they learn not to try to cope. Because they are young, children are less likely to have well-developed coping skills and are especially vulnerable to learned helplessness (Hilsman & Garber, 1995). Faced with poor coping skills and a loss of control, both children and adults stop responding (Job & Barnes, 1995). (We examined learned helplessness in Chapter 7.)

Exposure to stressful conditions is not sufficient to produce a stressed individual. Some children are separated from their parents by war and live among strangers who are suspicious of them and yet grow up to be healthy, happy adults (Palmer, 2000). Some adolescents live in poverty with the threat of violence and manage to function effectively (D'Imperio, Dubow, & Ippolito, 2000). Some people are re-

Social support
The comfort, recognition, approval, and encouragement available from other people, including friends, family members, and coworkers.

Coping strategies
The techniques people use to deal with the stress of changing situations.

silient to trauma and stress. The feelings of control, self-worth, and optimism are related to resilience (Dumont & Provost, 1999).

Studies focusing on the development of resilience have focused on children and adolescents, and those studies tend to show that children often experience many short-term problems when they are separated from their parents under traumatic circumstances, but they may still grow up to be well adjusted and capable (Palmer, 2000). One key factor in resilience is a close, supportive relationship. The experience of good parenting early in life conveys some protection against stress, but other types of supportive experiences may also be important. For example, a group of Native American students who were attending college related their stories about the factors in their lives that allowed them to go to college (Montgomery et al., 2000). For many, tribal traditions and feeling that they were part of the Indian community were related to their resiliency and success. Social support is a repeated theme in developing a sense of resiliency, and it is also an important coping resource.

Social support consists of the comfort, recognition, approval, and encouragement available from other people, including friends, family members, and coworkers. Even animals can provide social support (Siegel, 1990). People provide social support in the form of emotional support, but they can also contribute material resources such as money and knowledge and advice. All of these forms of social support enhance the ability to deal with stress.

People receive social support from friends and family, but being part of a network includes obligations to provide support as well as opportunities to receive support. Providing social support can be stressful, so being part of a social network has costs as well as benefits. The benefits outweigh the costs, but not always equally for women and men. Women tend to have larger social networks, which may overburden them with providing support (Orth-Gomér, 1998), but which offers the benefits of variety and accessibility.

In addition to (and sometimes in place of) friends and family, group therapy (to be examined in Chapter 16) and support groups can be effective in managing stress. In group therapy and in support groups, other people who are in a similar situation can offer concern, advice, and emotional support. Therefore, people who do not have social support can find ways to obtain it, which suggests that people can find ways to develop coping skills and strategies.

■ *Writing about stress and trauma is an emotion-focused coping technique that can be effective.*

Coping Strategies

Stress is a universal experience, and everyone uses some techniques to make the levels of stress more manageable. All people do not use the same techniques, even if they find themselves in similar situations, and some people are much more effective in coping than others are. That is, some people use coping strategies more effectively than other people do.

Coping strategies are the techniques people use to deal with the stress of changing situations. Effective coping requires that people

student voices

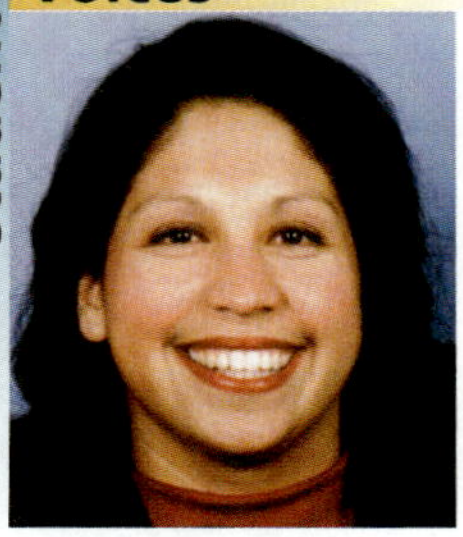

Piilani Koonce

Texas A&M University

When I entered the psychology program, I was like so many other people who want to go into the field to 'help other people.' One of the most interesting aspects of psychology is the realization of the change that takes place within you while you are busy helping those around you. It is an incredibly rewarding experience to help people discover and develop skills that can help them live more healthy and positive lives.

have a variety of strategies and make appropriate choices about when to use them. No single strategy is bad or good, but some strategies tend to be more effective than others. For example, some coping strategies involve actively dealing with the stressor, whereas other strategies are more passive. Passive coping strategies include refusing to accept the reality of the problem, trying to ignore the problem, avoiding the situation, engaging in distracting activities, or sleeping more than usual.

These approaches sound ineffective and even potentially dangerous, but under some circumstances, they can work. For example, avoiding an unpleasant person may be an effective way to cope with that person. However, this coping strategy is effective in a limited number of situations and will be disastrous in others. For example, avoiding a person with whom one must work is not an effective way to deal with a difficult colleague. Also, failing to accept the possibility that one is ill and avoiding medical care can be fatal.

Psychologists usually accept active coping strategies as more effective than passive ones, but some types of active coping are not necessarily the best choices. For example, using drugs or alcohol requires active effort, but this activity is not oriented toward solving the problem. Thus, this type of active coping is not a good strategy. One way to conceptualize active coping is to divide the strategies into emotion-focused strategies and problem-focused strategies. Both are active ways to deal with stressful situations, but the two types of strategies are very different. *Emotion-focused coping* concentrates on managing the feelings that accompany stress and trying to find ways to feel better, including focusing on and expressing emotions, reinterpreting the event in a positive way, finding comfort in religion, and seeking social support. *Problem-focused coping* concentrates on doing something about the situation, including taking action to get rid of the problem, making a plan about what to do, and putting aside other activities to concentrate on the problem. Researchers initially believed that some people tend to choose one approach and use that strategy in many situations. Researchers hypothesized that women choose emotion-focused strategies and men select problem-focused approaches. This stereotypical view is not accurate. Both women and men use both emotion-focused and problem-focused strategies.

In the selection of coping strategy, situation is more important than gender. For example, a woman who deals with problems with her husband by emotional confrontations might be less likely to deal with problems with her supervisor in the same way. Following nationality stereotypes, researchers hypothesized that Indian and Canadian students would differ in their levels of stress, attitudes about life, and preferred coping strategies (Sinha, Willson, & Watson, 2000). The students living in India did prefer emotion-focused coping more than the Canadian students did, especially in their tendency to reappraise their stresses in a positive way. Otherwise, the students in both countries were similar in levels of stress and attitudes about life, demonstrating both the influence of culture and the importance of situation in stress and coping—the situation of being a student involves similar stressors in many cultures.

■ **EMOTION-FOCUSED COPING.** When you have a problem (or just a bad day), is your first thought to talk to a friend or partner to help you ease those feelings of stress? If so, you are using emotion-focused coping. Women tend to use the strategy of seeking social support more than men do, but this tendency may relate to their relationship styles and the availability of support in their social network. In addition, seeking social support can be an adaptive strategy (Taylor, Klein, et al., 2000).

In addition to seeking social support, another emotion-focused technique that can be very effective is writing about stresses and trauma. James Pennebaker (1997; Pennebaker & Graybeal, 2001) has researched the benefits of writing about problems. Pennebaker asked students to write about a traumatic event for 20 minutes for three consecutive days and compared these participants to other students who wrote about trivial events. Those students who wrote about stresses and problems experienced better health; these findings prompted additional research, which confirmed the benefits of writing about emotional events. Improvements include a wide variety of benefits, from better immune system functioning to better grades. Pennebaker believes that the benefits come from helping people think differently about their stresses and traumas and not from merely "getting it out in the open." Talking about problems is the basis for many psychological treatments (see Chapter 16), but writing as a coping technique has a much shorter history but comparable effectiveness (Pennebaker & Graybeal, 2001).

Therefore, some emotion-focused coping strategies are effective ways to deal with some stressors. However, problem-focused coping is usually a better choice as a coping strategy.

■ **PROBLEM-FOCUSED COPING.** Most psychologists recommend problem-focused coping for managing stress. This strategy has the goal of solving or managing the problem that is producing stress, and includes approaches for planning and resolving problems, gathering information, making decisions, and obtaining resources to deal with the problem (Folkman & Moskowitz, 2000).

These strategies require an active, task-oriented approach, which is associated with effective problem solving and decision making in many domains other than stress. People who use these strategies tend to feel that they can effectively solve a problem with a stressor, so they have a high sense of self-efficacy for the problem. As we saw in Chapter 12 (p. 429), a sense of self-efficacy is important, and this concept applies to stress situations (Ingledew, Hardy, & Cooper, 1997). In addition, people with an internal locus of control tend to choose problem-focused coping; such individuals believe that they can control important aspects of their lives (see Chapter 12, pp. 428–429) and attempt to control their stress. Thus, some individuals are more likely to use problem-focused coping, at least in some situations, and these individuals tend to be effective problem solvers.

Not only do problem-focused strategies tend to be more likely to solve stress-related problems, but some research indicates that people who use this strategy tend to have a more positive outlook (Folkman & Moskowitz, 2000), experience fewer symptoms of illness (Soderstrom et al., 2000), and show better immune system functioning (Stowell, Kiecolt-Glaser, & Glaser, 2001). Therefore, this approach has advantages over emotion-focused coping. Figure 14.6 on the following page compares the two approaches and also includes another strategy—proactive coping.

■ **PROACTIVE COPING.** If you know that you are going to have a challenging semester next fall, you might try to get a full-time job over the summer so that you'll only need to work part-time when school starts. By doing so (whether you think of it that way or not), you are already coping with your tough fall semester. You are practicing **proactive coping;** you are anticipating a problem and taking action to avoid or decrease its impact.

Lisa Aspinwall and Shelley Taylor (1997) have described proactive coping as a five-stage process. First, we accumulate resources, mustering time, money, and social support and managing current situations. Next, we recognize that a stressful event is coming. Third, we appraise the event for its difficulty and its potential impact. Fourth, we engage in preliminary coping, to see what we can do now to prevent or minimize a threat. And last, we elicit and use feedback to assess whether or not we have averted a future stressor.

Using this active approach, some stressors can be avoided and others can be modified so that they are not so stressful; thus, people can avoid stress. However, the process of proactive coping requires effort, so people need to be reasonable in choosing which situations to manage and which to allow to develop. Therefore, choosing a strategy is important for effectively managing stress.

Proactive coping
Taking action in advance of a potentially stressful situation to prevent it, modify it, or prepare for it before it occurs.

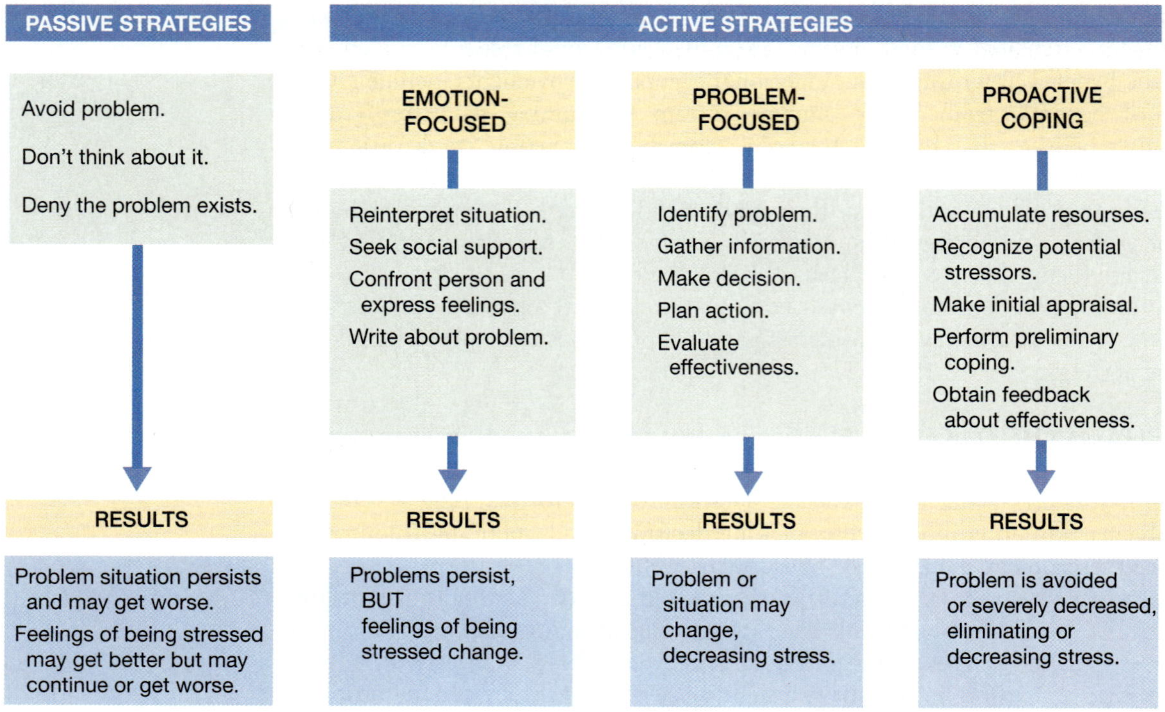

FIGURE 14.6

Coping Strategies and Their Effects

■ **EFFECTIVE COPING.** Both emotion-focused and problem-focused coping can be successful, and both can fail. Proactive coping can prevent or decrease stress but requires time and effort. Therefore, selecting the appropriate strategy is critically important for managing stress. Emotional confrontation is obviously a strategy that needs to be chosen with much care; inappropriate choices may be not only ineffective but also dangerous. Seeking social support or writing about a distressing experience are better choices to manage the emotions generated by stress. Some research indicates that people who have to deal with chronic pain as a daily stressor rely first on problem-focused coping, but when that strategy fails, they resort to emotion-focused efforts to manage the stress (Tennen et al., 2000). Their approach may be similar to the one used by many people—use a variety of strategies; if the first strategy is not effective, change to an alternative.

This picture portrays people as flexible and effective in dealing with the stressors in their lives, but this picture is not true for everyone, and some people need help in learning to cope with stress. Biofeedback, relaxation techniques, and meditation are effective for some people in helping manage the physical responses that accompany stress (see Chapter 6, pp. 206–210, for a description of biofeedback and meditation).

The process of **stress inoculation** is a therapeutic technique developed to help people cope with stress. This approach combines cognitive and behavioral techniques to improve coping (Meichenbaum & Cameron, 1983). Stress inoculation is based on the same principle as inoculation against a disease: it introduces a low, harmless level of stress and provides people with practice in using coping skills so that when threatening stress comes along, they will know how to cope—they have become immune to stressors. This process involves three stages:

1. *Conceptualization.* People develop an understanding of the stress process and their specific problems.
2. *Skills acquisition and rehearsal.* People learn relaxation and imagery techniques that are incompatible with stress and anxiety; they learn how to reinterpret stressors and regulate their feelings.

Stress inoculation [in-OK-you-LAY-shun]
Procedure of teaching people ways to cope with stress and allowing them to practice in realistic situations so they will develop "immunity" to stress.

3. *Follow-through.* People apply their acquired coping skills to problems in a natural context; that is, they practice the techniques they have learned in the second stage.

This program provides training in a number of coping techniques, giving people a variety of strategies to manage stress. It can help people who have not devised effective strategies on their own.

In addition to having a variety of strategies to manage stress, people are better equipped to deal with the inevitable stressors of life if they lead a healthy lifestyle. However, a healthy lifestyle is important for much more than effective coping. Behaviors that relate to health are part of the area of health psychology, a relatively new field within psychology, which we will discuss next.

Be an *Active* learner

REVIEW

- What factors influence coping in a beneficial way, and what factors diminish the ability to cope? pp. 508–509
- What are the advantages and disadvantages of emotion-focused and problem-focused coping? pp. 510–511
- What is proactive coping? p. 511

THINK CRITICALLY

- In what types of situations will emotion-focused coping be the best strategy?
- Contrast women's and men's styles of emotion-focused coping.

APPLY PSYCHOLOGY

- Keep a stress diary for a week to record your stressors and how you coped with each one, and then analyze how you could improve your coping strategies.

Health Psychology

At least half of all the premature deaths in the United States are the result of unhealthy lifestyles. In the past, infectious diseases such as influenza, tuberculosis, and pneumonia were among the leading causes of death. Today, the leading causes of death in the United States—heart disease, cancer, stroke, lung disease, and accidents—relate to behavioral and environmental variables. Psychologists believe that there is a direct relationship between people's health and their behavior. **Health psychology** is the subfield of psychology concerned with the use of psychological ideas and principles to enhance health, prevent illness, diagnose and treat disease, and improve rehabilitation. It is an action-oriented discipline that assumes that people's ideas and behaviors contribute to the onset and prevention of illness. A closely related field, behavioral medicine, integrates behavioral science with biomedical knowledge and techniques; it is narrower in focus than health psychology.

Traditionally, physicians have considered health to be the absence of disease. A person who was not experiencing adverse effects from an infection, injury, or abnormal condition of some kind was considered healthy. Now, however, physicians and psychologists acknowledge that health is not just the absence of disease but must take into account a person's total social, physical, and mental well-being. This new orientation gives health psychology a focus on the positive—health promotion. Health and wellness are seen as conditions people can actively pursue by eating well, exercising regularly, and managing stress effectively (Baum & Posluszny, 1999). Unlike medicine, which focuses on specific diseases, health psychology looks at the broad effects of thoughts and behaviors on fundamental psychosocial mechanisms that affect health and disease. In addition, researchers focus on the positive effects of health-promoting behaviors as well as the dangers of risky behaviors.

Variables That Affect Health and Illness

We can set a positive tone for our lives, enhance feelings of belonging, and see the bright side of things. We can laugh at things and wear "rose-colored glasses" to help ward off the impact of negative or difficult life events (Kuiper & Martin, 1998). Our attitudes and outlook affect health and illness, and they in turn are affected by complex interrelationships among many events (Cohen, 1996; Lefcourt & Thomas, 1998). But health is also affected by behaviors. Research has demonstrated that health-related behaviors have a large influence not only on health but also on life expectancy.

Health psychology
Subfield concerned with the use of psychological ideas and principles to enhance health, prevent illness, diagnose and treat disease, and improve rehabilitation.

■ *Positive experiences and outlook can be important in health, illness, and recovery.*

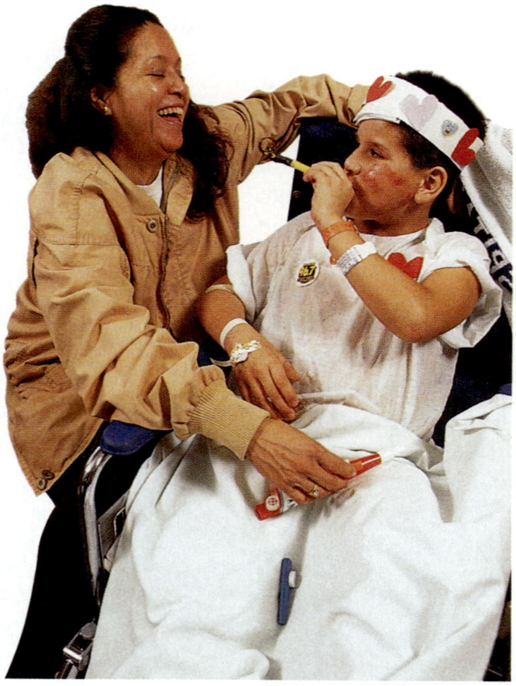

■ **HEALTH-RELATED BEHAVIORS.** In 1965 researchers in Alameda county, California, began a study on health practices and social variables that continues today (Berkman & Breslow, 1983). The study began with nearly 7,000 adults who were questioned about their health practices. Results indicated that five of those behaviors showed a strong relationship to health and life expectancy: (1) getting 7 or 8 hours of sleep daily, (2) drinking alcohol in moderation or not at all, (3) not smoking cigarettes, (4) exercising regularly, and (5) maintaining a weight near the prescribed ideal.

Follow-ups over the years have indicated that people who practice zero to two of the five behaviors are about three times more likely to be sick or die than people who practice all five. These behaviors reflect typical advice for maintaining a moderate and healthy lifestyle, and the Alameda County Study demonstrated the validity of such advice—how important behavior can be in determining health. Since the beginning of that study, research evidence has grown that connects the failure to perform these behaviors to the leading causes of death in the United States.

For example, people engage in a whole range of self-destructive, health-impairing behaviors. About 23% of Americans still smoke cigarettes, despite massive evidence that smoking causes and ultimately leads to premature deaths (U.S. Bureau of the Census, 2000). Cigarette smoking is related to increased risks for heart disease, cancer, stroke, and lung disease—the four leading causes of death in the United States. Indeed, tobacco use is the most damaging health habit, related to more preventable deaths than any other single behavior. Health psychologists are involved in research concerning why people begin to smoke and the difficulties they have in quitting so that they can devise more effective programs to help decrease this health-threatening behavior.

Americans also eat too much of the wrong things, and a high-fat diet contributes to heart disease, cancer, and stroke (U.S. Department of Health and Human Services, 2000). The typical American diet is too high in fat and protein and too low in fruits, vegetables, and grains. This typical diet is a factor in obesity, which affects over 30% of Americans and relates to a number of other health problems (Taubes, 1998). Health psychologists also research eating and weight control as well as devise programs to help individuals and communities adopt healthier eating habits.

Health psychologists also recognize the value of exercise in promoting health, recognizing that Americans are too sedentary to be healthy. A sedentary lifestyle is related to heart disease and stroke as well as some types of cancers and, of course, obesity. People who exercise regularly have better overall health and more effective immune systems, are better at coping with stress, and live longer than people who are sedentary (Baum & Posluszny, 1999). Over the past 10 years, Americans have become more sedentary. As computers and video games become preferred entertainment for children, the trend toward a sedentary lifestyle applies to children as well as adults. Finding ways to boost physical activity is one challenge that faces health psychologists.

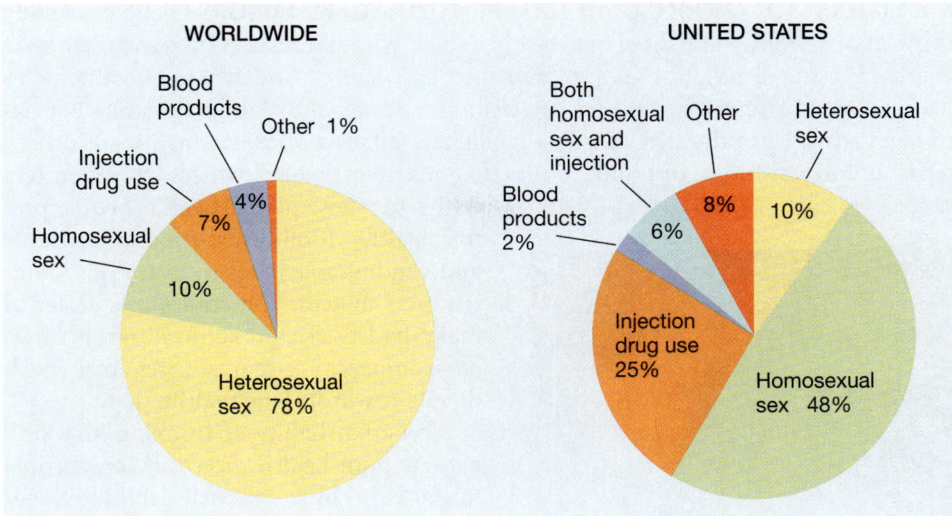

FIGURE 14.7

Sources of HIV Infection in Adults

Worldwide figures based on information from Communicable Disease Prevention Service (2001); U.S. figures based on USDHHS (2000).

■ **PREVENTING AIDS.** Educating people about prevention and wellness and discovering the variables that affect health are central goals of health psychologists. The focus on disease prevention led health psychologists to be involved in the AIDS (acquired immune deficiency syndrome) epidemic from its beginning. AIDS is caused by the human immunodeficiency virus (HIV), which is an infectious disease transmitted through bodily fluids. The serious worldwide AIDS epidemic is still continuing, and the disease kills thousands of people in the United States each year. (See Figure 14.7 for U.S. and worldwide mortality rates.) Despite the developing knowledge about the virus and its methods of infection, no vaccine exists to prevent its transmission. A combination of drugs can help infected people manage the disease, but no cure exists.

The primary modes of transmission of the virus are behavioral; that is, risky behaviors spread HIV infection. High-risk behaviors are those that directly expose a person to the blood or semen of others who are likely to have been exposed to the virus—in other words, to others who are likely to have engaged in high-risk behaviors. Those behaviors include having sex with many partners, having sex with a man who has had sex with other men, and injection drug use. During the early years of the epidemic, AIDS was associated with gay men, and many people developed the belief that heterosexuals were not at risk. That belief is incorrect; heterosexuals who have had sexual contact with carriers of AIDS are at significant risk.

In the United States, about 18% of known cases of AIDS are contracted through heterosexual sex. But according to the Centers for Disease Control and Prevention, heterosexual sex accounts for 75% of reported AIDS cases in other parts of the world. Everywhere, adolescents are at especially high risk because they, more than adults, are likely to engage in unprotected sexual activity, and they have some of the highest rates of sexually transmitted diseases, including HIV.

Health psychologists are involved in preventing the spread of HIV infection through attempts to change risky behaviors. An extensive education campaign transmitted information about HIV infection and the dangers of high-risk behaviors, but this campaign was not sufficient to alter risky behaviors. People who understand the risks still engage in risky behavior (Helweg-Larsen & Collins, 1997). Additional strategies are necessary to change behavior. An example of such a strategy involves condom use. Research shows that the most effective way to get men and women to use condoms is not through fear but through engendering positive attitudes about condoms—that others will accept and like condoms and that carrying and using condoms are positive and rewarding behaviors (Sheeran, Abraham, & Orbell, 1999).

■ BARRIERS TO ADOPTING HEALTH-PROMOTING BEHAVIORS. People usually know about healthy lifestyles, but they are stuck with habits that increase their risks for disease and death. It's easy to fall into bad habits, and it's often difficult to change. Social circumstances and personal attitudes make change difficult. For example, eating a healthy diet can be a challenge. Billions of dollars are spent on advertising for fast foods and junk foods (that are poor dietary choices) to generate a desire for these foods. Even if people prefer healthy foods, fast-food restaurants and vending machines offer few good nutritional choices. Sometimes it is easier to make bad choices than good ones. Thus, environmental circumstances can push people toward an unhealthy diet.

■ *Vending machines are often a barrier to healthy eating.*

Personal habits of thinking also perpetuate poor health choices. Many people mistakenly think that self-destructive behaviors are likely to affect other people but not them. That is, people have an *optimistic bias*; they believe that risky behaviors will harm others but not them (Weinstein, Rothman, & Sutton, 1998). This biased way of thinking allows people to continue risky behavior, even if they have an intellectual understanding of the dangers. This "magical thinking" resembles teenagers' belief in the personal fable—they are so special and unique that risky behaviors (unsafe sex or alcohol consumption or cigarette smoking) that might harm other people will not harm them. These cognitive distortions allow people to continue unsafe behaviors. Health psychologists must work against these thought patterns in helping people adopt healthier behaviors.

The Psychology of Being Sick

When people experience symptoms that may indicate illness, they must decide what to do. Should they continue with their regular activities, treat the symptoms themselves, or seek medical care? Most people prefer not to be sick, and the thought of a disease that impairs day-to-day functioning is threatening. These factors make people reluctant to seek medical care, and being sick changes many factors in people's lives. Health psychologists are concerned not only with the links between stress and illness but with how people cope with illness when it occurs.

■ SEEKING MEDICAL CARE. When do people seek medical care? What variables prompt a person to get help? Most people avoid medical care and advice except when they judge it to be necessary. The presence of visible symptoms (rashes, cuts, swellings, or fever) that are threatening, painful, or persistent are all important factors in the decision to seek professional help. Painful symptoms alone will not necessarily motivate people to seek medical care. For example, a cut or burn can be very painful, but if the injury is not judged to be serious, people tend to treat themselves rather than seek help. Visible symptoms, rather than those not readily visible, are more likely to prompt a search for medical care. However, if the symptom does not persist or if the person believes that the symptom does not indicate a serious condition, the person will not seek medical care.

People are more willing to seek medical help when they believe it will lead to a cure, and they are especially reluctant when the potential diagnosis is a dreaded one. For example, people avoid cancer screenings, partly because cancer is such a dreaded disease. In addition, people try to find the least threatening explanation for a symptom—the headache must be due to a stressful day and not to brain cancer. All these tendencies point to a great deal of personal reluctance in seeking medical care (Brannon & Feist, 2000).

There are gender differences in people's willingness to seek medical attention. The female gender role is more compatible with seeking help, and women seek medical help more than men do (Waldron, 1997). Women often visit physicians not for reasons of ill health but for consultation regarding birth control, pregnancy, and childbirth; women do, however, report more distress and symptoms of illness than men do.

Being strong and invincible is part of the male gender role, and they may perceive seeking health care as a sign of weakness or vulnerability. Ironically, men have a shorter life span than women do, so their tendency to avoid health care may not serve them well. A dramatic gender difference in life expectancy comes from men's higher rate of heart disease during middle age, leading to premature death. (Women also die of heart disease, but at older ages.) Heart disease may produce few noticeable symptoms, and men's avoidance of health care allows their heart disease to go undiagnosed and untreated—a potentially fatal situation.

Major cultural differences exist in making decisions about seeking health care, and people tend to do so in a manner that is consistent with their cultural conceptions of appropriate care. Most people in the United States and other Western countries have beliefs about the causes of and cures for disease that are compatible with Western medicine and expect to seek help from physicians and go to the hospital for certain treatments. Other views of health and disease vary drastically from those of traditional Western medicine, leading people to seek different practitioners and health-care settings. For example, traditional Chinese medicine is oriented toward understanding the body's vital energy, blood, and body fluids and maintaining a balance in the flow of these essential elements (Takeichi & Sato, 2000). This holistic concept of health has become attractive to a growing number of people in the United States and Great Britain. They are seeking health care from alternative sources, and the *Point/Counterpoint* feature on the following page presents the controversy over choosing between traditional and alternative medicine.

Large, ethnically diverse societies such as the United States, Canada, and Great Britain are faced with providing health care to people who have a variety of beliefs about the nature of health and illness, some of which differ sharply from the views of traditional practitioners (McLaughlin & Braun, 1998). For example, European Americans do not often seek the services of a Native American shaman or Latin American *curanderos,* but Native Americans and Latinos/Latinas do. Indeed, these practitioners provide health care that is compatible with the beliefs of those who seek their care, thus producing situations that boost healing: patients trust and will follow the directions of these health care providers (Applewhite, 1995; Kim & Kwok, 1998; Lowery, 1998).

Seeking health care from practitioners associated with specific ethnic groups is more common among immigrants and older people (Applewhite, 1995), but people tend to hold beliefs about health and illness that include what constitutes appropriate treatment. These beliefs may continue, even among those who accept the cultural values of their adopted countries. In such situations, people often seek health care from a combination of practitioners—those traditional to their society plus traditional Western physicians (Applewhite, 1995; Kim & Kwok, 1998). This combination of sources for health care is similar to individuals who seek alternative healthcare.

■ **THE SICK ROLE.** When people seek medical care and receive a diagnosis, they are expected to follow medical advice and try to get well. When they try to recover, they are adopting a *sick role.* For most people, this means taking specific steps to get well, relieving themselves of normal responsibilities, and realizing that they are not at

pointcounterpoint

Using Alternative Medicine

The Issue: Does the use of alternative medicine prevent people from seeking effective traditional care?

POINT

There is a lack of evidence that alternative medicine is effective.

COUNTERPOINT

Alternative medicine offers valuable benefits that have advantages over traditional medicine.

The growing popularity of alternative medicine has sparked a heated debate. On one side of the debate is traditional medicine, which represents the majority of treatment in developed countries. Traditional practitioners believe that modern medicine offers the best treatments for medical problems (Ziel, 1999). Indeed, medical advances

have resulted in treatment that is more effective than that of any time in the past. Modern medicine is much more than bedside manner, and more than at any point in history, medicine promises cures for diseases that have been disabling and even fatal in the past. Advocates of traditional medicine believe that the best chances for recovery come through diagnosis, drugs, and surgery and that alternative treatments are unproven or even dangerous.

However, the advent of technological medicine and the growth of managed medical care have resulted in the loss of personal relationships and trust between patient and physician. This loss is seen as the main reason that prompts people to seek alternative medical care; people who feel that their doctor doesn't listen to or care about them seek care that seems more accessible and personal (Holland, 1999).

Alternative medicine encompasses a wide variety of treatments. Exercise and dietary programs are considered alternative but are part of traditional medical recommendations for many conditions such as diabetes. Other treatments such as herbal remedies, massage therapy, and meditation fit into the alternative category but have many adherents (Ernst, 2000). Indeed, the number of people who seek alternative medical care has grown in recent years, not only in the United States but also in many countries.

Research on people who seek alternative care reflects a picture of users who are well educated with high incomes—people who could afford any type of care but choose alternative therapies (Astin, 1998). But they also seek traditional medical care and use alternative sources in addition to traditional ones in a pattern than can be described as *complementary* rather than *alternative*. Only 4.4% use alternative medicine exclusively. People who seek alternative care are more likely to have problems that are resistant to traditional medical care, such as back pain, chronic pain, allergies, and headaches. Those who seek alternative treatment tend to be satisfied with the treatment and report relief from their symptoms. Some who use alternative medicine fit the "new age" stereotype of having belief in the power of holistic healing and herbal medicine, but most who seek alternative medicine pick and choose among available treatments and do not limit their care to traditional medicine.

fault for their illness. When they are in the hospital, they give the responsibility for their care to physicians and nurses. The situation of relinquishing personal control may create a feeling of helplessness that adds stress to the experience of being ill.

Sickness is generally seen as a temporary state, so people are expected to work toward getting well—taking medication, sleeping, and, especially, complying with medical advice. This view fits well with diseases from infection, which are typically temporary. Chronic diseases, on the other hand, do not have cures. These diseases include heart disease, diabetes, most types of cancer, asthma, and many other conditions that can be managed but not cured. This difference creates problems for people with these disorders—they cannot get well, they may have to (or want to) continue with normal responsibilities, but following medical advice is critically important. To manage their chronic illness, they must comply with medical advice.

■ **COMPLIANCE WITH MEDICAL ADVICE.** Getting people to adhere to health regimens or to follow their physicians' advice has long been a focus of health psychologists because it is a persistent problem for medical treatment. People have trouble in following all types of medical recommendations. Some problems originate in communication problems between practitioner and patient—when patients do not understand practitioners' recommendations, they cannot follow them (Baum & Posluszny, 1999). Other problems occur when patients stop taking their medications when they begin to feel better. Another type of noncompliance problem comes from the failure to follow a healthy lifestyle, including eating a healthy diet, getting enough exercise, avoiding tobacco, drinking alcohol in moderation or not at all, getting enough sleep, and having medical check-ups and screening tests.

People are more likely to comply with recommendations about treatments designed to cure a disease than with prevention efforts (DiMatteo, 1994). That is, people will comply with specific recommendations such as "Take three tablets a day for 10 days," but they are less likely to adhere to general recommendations aimed at improving overall health conditions, such as quitting smoking or getting more exercise. Overall, noncompliance is around 50%, which means that half of all people who receive medical advice fail to follow it in some way.

Compliance with medical advice has some relationship with the severity of the problem, but the patient's perception of the severity is what matters, not the medical practitioner's view. If an illness causes pain or discomfort, people are more likely to comply with a regimen of treatment to alleviate the discomfort. People are more receptive to medical treatment when it is specific, simple, and easy to do, when it has minimal side effects, and when it brings relief they can see quickly (Ley, 1997).

Compliance with a health-care regimen is increased when the regimen is tailored to the person's lifestyle and habits. Patients are more likely to follow the advice of a practitioner whom they like and trust than one whom they find uncaring and uncommunicative. Written agreements between practitioners and clients can be helpful in detailing the responsibilities and commitments of each; clients who sign such an agreement are more likely to adhere to their commitment than clients who agree but do not sign an agreement.

Health psychologists have found clients more likely to adhere to treatments when a physician's influence and the family support systems are substantial. Social support from family and friends turns out to be especially effective in getting even very sick people to comply with guidelines for treatment (DiMatteo & DiNicola, 1982). However, compliance is far from perfect, even under the best conditions, and this problem remains persistent for health psychologists who want to help practitioners provide better health care.

Health Psychology and Healthier Lifestyles

Health psychologists focus on research to help them understand health-related behaviors, and they devise and implement interventions to bring about changes for healthier lifestyles. The interventions may take the form of individual programs for people with health-impairing behaviors or health problems, but some interventions are aimed at groups and even entire communities.

Health psychologists recommend preventive programs in the workplace to educate people about ways to manage stress and about other positive behaviors that can enhance and prolong life. They frequently conduct stress management workshops to help managers and workers cope with increasing pressures and heavy workloads; they are also involved in helping people quit smoking, control their alcohol intake, follow exercise programs, make healthy dietary choices, and practice safer sex. Let's examine three ways of dealing with health problems: pain management, workplace stress management, and the nationwide campaign to promote condom use.

■ **PAIN MANAGEMENT.** We all experience pain, but that experience is usually brief and does not present a problem for daily functioning. People with chronic headache, arthritis, back problems, or many types of cancers must live with pain that does cause problems for their daily lives. Psychologists work to help such individuals manage this pain. Severe and disabling pain can take three forms: (1) *chronic pain* is long-lasting and ever present, such as the pain caused by arthritis; (2) *periodic pain* comes and goes, such as headache pain; (3) *progressive pain* is ever present and increases in severity as the illness progresses, such as cancer-related pain. Drugs, surgery, or other medical interventions are usually part of treatment for chronic pain, but behavioral techniques can also offer relief.

Pain management programs usually work on two fronts: they try to reduce suffering, the negative emotional experience that accompanies pain, while also decreasing the physical aspects of pain. A number of behavioral treatments have been used to manage pain, including hypnosis and biofeedback (examined in Chapter 6), behavior modification, and cognitive therapy. Behavior modification uses learning principles (see Chapter 7) to teach people new effective behaviors, to help them unlearn maladaptive behaviors, and to train those around them not to reward pain behaviors (McCracken, 1997). For example, a person with back pain might be rewarded for performing normal activities and ignored for complaining about how bad his back hurts. In addition, the person might be taught to relax as a coping strategy rather than becoming tense, focusing on the pain, and thus making it worse.

A review of studies on behavior modification for back pain indicates that these techniques are effective in increasing the level of patients' physical activity and in decreasing use of medications (Compas et al., 1998). Chapter 15 looks into the use of cognitive therapy to help people acquire new thoughts, beliefs, and values, which can also be helpful in managing pain.

■ **WORKPLACE WELLNESS PROGRAMS.** People care about stress management, and health psychologists have devised many techniques that can be applied to stress management. Employers are concerned about the effects of stress on their employees. Work site stress is one of the major sources of stress (see p. 500), and it decreases work effectiveness and increases health-care costs to employers (Stein, Karel, & Zuidema, 1999). Employers are interested in having healthier employees in order to decrease the payments that they make for employees' health care, so some companies offer employees workplace wellness programs.

Such programs may include one or many components; smoking cessation programs are a common choice because smoking relates to so many health problems. However, relaxation or other stress management techniques are also common (Hobfoll & Shirom, 2001). The programs usually involve inducements for employee participation, and effective programs are voluntary rather than required. The results are fewer workdays lost to illness and lower health-care costs. An example of such a program targeted secondary school teachers, who participated in a work site stress management program (Lapp & Attridge, 2000). The program had educational, stress management, and strategy-building components and lasted 9 months. Before the program, one-third of the teachers reported high levels of stress, and the intervention had a positive impact in helping these teachers to reduce their levels of stress.

■ **COMMUNITY INTERVENTIONS.** To manage existing health problems and help prevent disease, behavioral interventions are necessary and important. Individual and workplace programs can reach many people, but wide-scale campaigns are necessary to reach enough people to improve life expectancy for a community or for a nation. Health psychologists know that many problem behaviors can be modified, but they also know that traditional information campaigns are not very effective in changing behavior.

The "safer-sex" campaign is an example of an attempt to change behavior in order to decrease health risks. Such campaigns use a variety of approaches that target the entire society as well as smaller risk groups. When researchers discovered that HIV infection was transmitted through contact with blood or semen, one of the prevention strategies was to increase condom use. Initially, the targets were gay men because their rate of HIV infection was very high compared to that of other groups (Centers for Disease Control and Prevention [CDC], 2001). That campaign took many forms, educating people about the dangers of HIV infection and the behaviors that are risky. As psychologists know, education is not an adequate intervention, and the campaign was extended to using persuasive techniques to increase condom use and to overcome the barriers to it (Perloff, 2001). This campaign was at least somewhat successful. Indeed, gay men changed their sexual behavior and condom use, and their rate of HIV infection slowed more than that of other groups (CDC, 2001).

Other groups, including heterosexuals, became the targets of the campaign to increase condom use. Messages about condom use appeared in a variety of settings, from school-based sexuality education programs that provided condoms to TV public service announcements in which entertainment personalities advocated condom use. Teenagers and young adults were the primary targets because their rate of infection from sexually transmitted diseases is higher than that of older individuals (Kaplan et al., 2001). Among adolescents, condom use has increased significantly over the past two decades, suggesting that a massive nationwide health campaign oriented toward changing behavior can have some success.

Unfortunately, recent research has shown that continued efforts are required to maintain condom use. Heterosexuals encounter a number of relationship issues, such as trust and suspicion, that make requests for condom use difficult (Gavin, 2000), and the growing availability of treatment for HIV-infected people has created a climate of acceptance of risky sex among gay men (Williams, Elwood, & Bowen, 2000).

Therefore, continued efforts are required to maintain behavior changes, even when people understand and accept the value of their health-protective behaviors. Condom use and sexual behavior are not exceptions; people have a tendency to quit exercise programs, regain lost weight, and relapse into smoking after they have quit. Maintaining a healthy lifestyle is a personal challenge, also creating a challenge for health psychologists.

■ *A national campaign to prevent the spread of HIV infection was successful in changing some risky behaviors.*

Health Psychology and the Future

At the beginning of this chapter, we considered the idea that stress has biological, psychological, and social components, but so does health. A number of biological, behavioral, and social factors intersect to determine each person's state of wellness, including genetics, biological endowment, education, social support, health habits, and medical care.

Be an *Active* learner

REVIEW

- What behaviors have a positive relationship to health and increased life expectancy? p. 519
- Under what conditions do people tend to comply with medical advice? p. 519
- How do health psychologists help individuals and communities lead healthier lives? pp. 520–521

THINK CRITICALLY

- The Alameda County Study originally included seven rather than five behaviors, but two of those behaviors did not relate to improved health or longer life expectancy. These behaviors were snacking between meals and eating breakfast. Why do you think that these behaviors failed to show a relationship to health?
- A great deal of the increase in life expectancy in the United States and other industrialized nations is due to the decrease in infectious illness, but these decreases occurred primarily before the development of effective drugs to treat infection. In what ways might behavior play a role in the decline of infectious disease and the increase in life expectancy?

APPLY PSYCHOLOGY

- Create a behavioral health plan for yourself that you can follow while attending school. Make this plan realistic and attainable, yet include some improvements over your current health-related behaviors.

Whether studying stress and its causes and treatment or looking at ways to improve health, psychologists are taking a prosocial, action-oriented approach. In many ways, the study of stress and health can be considered the future of the discipline. If people can learn to manage their stressors and adopt a healthy lifestyle, they may be able to avoid many psychological and physical problems, function at a higher and more effective level, and live longer and healthier lives.

Created in the 1970s, health psychology has a short history, but during this time it has managed to draw from research and applied areas of psychology, including biopsychology, learning, motivation, emotion, personality, developmental, social, and clinical psychology (Brannon & Feist, 2000). In addition, health psychology has integrated information from disciplines outside psychology, such as sociology and various areas of medicine, including neurology and immunology. This integration has moved psychology to a more prominent place in health care. As practitioners in health care come to accept the value of psychological contributors to health and disease and psychologically based interventions, the field of health psychology will continue to grow.

Summary and Review

Stress

How has stress been defined and measured?

- *Stress* was defined by Selye as a nonspecific emotional response to real or imagined challenges or threats. He characterized stress responses as a general adaptation syndrome with three stages: alarm, resistance, and exhaustion. Physiological arousal is heightened during alarm and resistance. If people do not relieve their stress, they experience exhaustion. *Stressors* are environmental stimuli that affect an organism in either physically or psychologically injurious ways. Life events scales, such as the Holmes–Rahe scale, measure stress as life events that require change and adaptation. pp. 491–493
- According to Lazarus, stress is an interaction of stressors and a cognitive appraisal of threat in the situation. Whether a situation is stressful or not depends on a person's appraisal of the situation. The Hassles Scale is an alternative way to assess stress based on the concept that everyday annoyances are more important stressors than life events. pp. 493–495

What are the major sources of and responses to stress?

- Stress can come from catastrophes, such as natural disasters and events of human origin, that may produce *posttraumatic stress disorder* (*PTSD*). Stress can also originate in unhealthy environments such as poverty, or in discrimination based on ethnicity, gender, or sexual orientation. Personal factors such as jobs and relationships can produce satisfaction or stress. pp. 496–501
- Responses to stress occur on the physiological level in terms of arousal of the sympathetic nervous system and on the behavioral level. pp. 501–502

How is stress related to disease?

- *Type A behavior* is the behavior pattern of individuals who are competitive, impatient, hostile, and always striving to do more in less time. The overall Type A behavior pattern is not related to the development of heart disease, but the elements of anger and hostility seem to be. pp. 503–509
- The field of *psychoneuroimmunology* studies how stress can decrease the function of the immune system,

which increases vulnerability to infectious disease. In addition, stress tends to alter behavior in ways that affect health-related behaviors. pp. 504–507

KEY TERMS

burnout, p. 490; stress, p. 491; stressor, p. 491; posttraumatic stress disorder (PTSD), p. 497; Type A behavior, p. 503; Type B behavior, p. 503; psychoneuroimmunology, p. 505

Coping

What factors influence coping?

■ A sense of personal control, even if it is an illusion, is a positive factor in coping. Social support also increases coping ability. People who cope, despite a great deal of stress, have a high level of *resilience*. pp. 507–508

Distinguish various forms of coping.

■ *Coping* is the process by which a person takes some action to manage, master, tolerate, or reduce environmental and internal demands that cause or might cause stress and that tax the individual's inner resources. *Social support* can provide a buffer against stress. *Coping strategies* are the techniques people use to change stressful situations. pp. 509–510

■ People use both passive and active strategies to cope. Active coping strategies can be emotion-focused or problem-focused. *Proactive coping* is taking action in advance of a potentially stressful situation to prevent it or modify it before it occurs. Typically, active strategies are better than passive ones, and problem-focused strategies are more effective than emotion-focused ones, but all coping strategies can be effective in some situations. Therefore, people must learn a variety of coping strategies and how to effectively employ them. *Stress inoculation* is a therapy technique that teaches people how to cope more effectively. pp. 510–512

KEY TERMS

coping, p. 507 resilience, p. 507; social support, p. 508; coping strategies, p. 508; proactive coping, p. 511; stress inoculation, p. 512

Health Psychology

What is the role of health psychology?

■ *Health psychology* uses psychological ideas and principles to help enhance health, prevent illness, diagnose and treat disease, and rehabilitate people. Health psychology is an action-oriented discipline that emphasizes preventive health measures as well as interventions directed at existing conditions. pp. 513–516

■ Health psychologists also work to help people who are ill, trying to understand the factors that relate to seeking medical care and compliance with medical advice. pp. 516–519

■ Health psychologists are involved in promoting healthy behavior for individuals, such as pain management programs; for workplaces, such as stress management programs; and for communities, such as the AIDS prevention campaign that focuses on condom use and safe sex. pp. 519–521

KEY TERM

health psychology, p. 513

15 Psychological Disorders

Stanton MacDonald-Wright, *The Prophecy—Sleep Suite 2,* 1955

Pop singing star Mariah Carey checked into a psychiatric hospital in late July 2001. Press reports said that she had a "nervous breakdown," and her publicist described her as having "an emotional and physical breakdown" (Goehner & Tyrangiel, 2001). In the weeks before Carey entered the hospital, her life was filled with stress, pressure, and a demanding work schedule, and she broke up with her boyfriend of several years. Her behavior became increasingly erratic. She posted rambling messages on her website; she began talking about "positivity" at an appearance to promote a new record; she began taking off her clothes on MTV. The people close to her became concerned, but no one intervened to help her until her mother called 911 and had her taken to the hospital. She left the hospital after a short stay, but returned, canceling scheduled interviews and appearances. She clearly was experiencing problems that were reflected in her behavior.

"Nervous breakdown" and "emotional exhaustion" are terms that many people find meaningful, but neither is a psychiatric diagnosis. Most people, however, have a concept of what constitutes a nervous breakdown, which they see as a mental disorder that has symptoms of

chapter outline

■ *During the weeks before her "nervous breakdown," Mariah Carey's behavior reflected the problems she was experiencing.*

depression and anxiety, lasts for a limited time, and is brought on by stressors (Rapport et al., 1998). These symptoms could reflect any of several actual diagnoses, and press reports do not furnish sufficient information to formulate an accurate diagnosis for Mariah Carey's problems. In this chapter, we explore behaviors that reflect mental disorders and symptoms that signal various diagnoses. In order for a person to be labeled as having a mental disorder, that person must show symptoms of a problem; that is, the person's behavior must be abnormal.

What Is Abnormal Behavior?

The first time I (LB) visited San Francisco, the number of homeless people surprised me. In the cities in which I had lived, I had never seen anyone walking down the street, talking out loud to himself, with no one paying much attention. These homeless people kept their belongings in shopping carts or bags and lived in cardboard boxes. Starting in the 1970s, many people who were diagnosed as mentally ill were deinstitutionalized (released from hospitals). Lacking resources and coping skills, they became the core of today's homeless population. With their shopping carts in tow, these people have their own communities and lifestyles. Not all homeless people have mental disorders or behave bizarrely, of course. But isn't walking down the street while talking out loud to oneself abnormal behavior? To some extent, the answer depends on the culture; every society has its own definition of abnormal behavior. In Russia, for example, people were once regularly placed in mental institutions for homelessness or political dissent. Generally, however, behavior classified by psychologists as abnormal is more than odd. Abnormal behavior, however, is not uncommon. In any single year, between 15% and 25% of adults in the world meet the criteria for having a mental disorder; that is, they exhibit symptoms of abnormality (Kessler, 2000). These figures make mental disorders a significant source of disability for the world's population.

A Definition

Abnormal behavior is behavior characterized as (1) not typical, (2) socially unacceptable, (3) distressing to the person who exhibits it or to the person's friends and family, (4) maladaptive, and/or (5) the result of distorted cognitions. Let's consider these five distinguishing characteristics in turn.

First, abnormal behavior is *not typical*. Many behaviors are unusual; however, abnormal behaviors tend to be so unusual as to be statistically rare. For example, taking one's clothing off is not all that unusual on MTV, but when Mariah Carey did so without notice or prior planning, people considered her behavior abnormal. Of course, some behavior that is not typical is still not abnormal. Mariah Carey is not a typical 31-year-old in a number of ways: she sold more records than any other female singer during the 1990s, made a recording deal for $117 million dollars, and has some of the eccentricities associated with being a diva (Goehner & Tyrangiel, 2001). But in July 2001, she began to show signs of behavior that was beyond eccentric.

Abnormal behavior
Behavior characterized as atypical, socially unacceptable, distressing to the individual or others, maladaptive, and/or the result of distorted cognitions.

Second, abnormal behavior is also often *socially unacceptable.* To some degree, ideas about what is normal and abnormal vary according to cultural values. What is acceptable in one culture may be labeled unacceptable in another; what is unacceptable for one person may be allowed for another. For example, pop singers are allowed to dress and behave in ways that others are not. Similarly, behavior that was considered unacceptable 25 years ago, such as a man wearing earrings, may be considered acceptable today. A behavior that is judged abnormal, however, is one that is unacceptable to society in general.

■ *Abnormal behavior is atypical and often unacceptable.*

Third, a person's abnormal behavior often causes *distress* to the person or to those around the person. While feelings of anxiety or distress are normal in many situations, prolonged anxiety (distress) may result from abnormal behavior. Singers often feel anxious before a concert, but they find ways to manage these feelings. Mariah Carey's anxiety and distress seemed out of control, and she finally agreed to enter a psychiatric hospital.

Fourth, abnormal behavior is usually *maladaptive*, or self-defeating to the person exhibiting it. Maladaptive behavior, such as smashing dishes and walking in the broken shards, is harmful. Such an incident occurred, involving Mariah Carey, in the hours before her mother persuaded her to seek professional help (Goehner & Tyrangiel, 2001).

Last, abnormal behavior is often the result of *distorted cognitions* (thoughts). Mariah Carey hired a private detective to investigate her recording executive former husband, whom she believed was waging a campaign within the music business to ruin her career. Their divorce was bitter, so her cognitions may not be distorted, but the belief that others are trying to harm one is a common type of cognitive distortion.

In recent years, psychologists have begun to describe behavior in terms of *maladjustment* rather than *abnormality.* The distinction is important because it implies that maladaptive behavior can, with treatment, be adjusted—and become adaptive and productive. The term *maladjustment* also emphasizes specific behaviors rather than labeling the entire person as abnormal.

Using the sociocultural approach (described on pp. 529–530), researchers such as Thomas Szasz go so far as to say that maladjustment and mental illness are socially constructed and defined—abnormal behaviors are whatever the society fails to accept. Szasz argues that there is, in fact, a myth of mental illness; according to him, once a practitioner labels a person as "abnormal," the person starts to act that way (Szasz, 1984, 1987). The patient confirms the therapist's expectations about his or her abnormality, even when the expectations may not reflect the patient's real condition. In Szasz's view, a patient in therapy creates situations that lead to behaviors that the therapist has predicted. This phenomenon is called the *self-fulfilling prophecy*, the creation by the therapist of the expected behaviors. The phenomenon of the self-fulfilling prophecy is one of the drawbacks of diagnosis and labeling. Giving a person or the person's behavior a label or tag rarely helps; in Szasz's view, "mental illness" is a label that serves no good purpose. However, people *do* suffer from behavior problems, and labeling is part of the process of diagnosis and treatment. Labels have negative consequences, but they also have the advantage of allowing researchers to categorize and research these problems and allowing people who receive a diagnosis to identify and understand their behavior.

To summarize, abnormal behavior is not typical; it is socially unacceptable, distressing, maladaptive, and may be the result of distorted cognitions. There are, of course, exceptions to this definition. For example, most people would not hesitate to label drug abuse as abnormal behavior, but it is more typical than it once was. Nevertheless, this definition provides psychologists with a solid framework from which to explore abnormal behavior and its treatment.

Perspectives on Abnormality

■ *Andrea Yates believed that she was possessed by the devil and drowned her five children.*

On June 20, 2001, Andrea Yates killed her five children by drowning them in the bathtub of her suburban home. She had a history of mental problems, including a suicide attempt after the birth of her fourth child, and additional problems after giving birth to her fifth child. She told her brother than she believed she was possessed by the devil, and some observers say that she is clearly not in touch with reality. Many women experience the "baby blues" after giving birth, but these feelings do not lead to murder. Yates's behavior seems not only maladjusted but also contradictory: she said she loved her children, yet she killed them.

Mental health practitioners want to know why such a person is maladjusted and understand the origins of the problem because establishing the cause of a disorder is important in defining the problem and formulating a treatment plan (and possibly preventing tragedy before it happens). Therefore, practitioners often turn to theories and models that attempt to explain the causes of abnormality. A **model** is an analogy or a perspective that helps scientists discover relationships among data; it uses a structure from one field to help describe data in another. Psychologists use models to make predictions about behavior. Models of maladjustment help form the basis of **abnormal psychology,** the field of psychology concerned with the assessment, treatment, and prevention of maladaptive behavior. Several models help explain abnormal behavior: medical–biological, psychodynamic, humanistic, behavioral, cognitive, sociocultural, evolutionary, and biopsychosocial.

■ **THE MEDICAL–BIOLOGICAL MODEL.** Thousands of years ago, people believed that abnormal behavior was caused by demons that invaded an individual's body. The "cure" often involved a surgeon performing *trephination*—drilling a hole into the skull to allow the evil force to escape. Even as recently as a few hundred years ago, people with psychological disorders were caged, like animals. Early reformers, such as Philippe Pinel, advocated the medical model and proposed that abnormal behavior could be treated and cured, like an illness. When scientists showed that syphilis could cause mental disorders, the medical model gained even greater acceptance and led to more humane treatment and better conditions for those with psychological disorders.

The *medical–biological model* of abnormal behavior focuses on the physiological conditions that initiate and underlie abnormal behaviors. This model adequately deals with a range of mental ailments, such as those caused by mercury poisoning or viral infections. It focuses on genetic abnormalities, problems in the central nervous system, and hormonal changes. It also helps explain and treat substance abuse problems, bipolar disorder, and schizophrenia—disorders that have a biological component. Proponents of the medical–biological model might explain a homeless person's ramblings as the result of a problem with neurotransmitters that alters brain chemistry and thus behavior.

Many of the terms and concepts used in psychology and psychiatry are borrowed from medicine—among them *treatment, case, symptom, patient,* and *syndrome*, as well as *mental illness*. The medical model assumes that abnormal behavior, like other illnesses, can be diagnosed, treated, and cured or managed. This approach has not gone unchallenged, however. Its critics say that it does not take advantage of modern psychological insights, such as those of learning theory. A major—but not surprising—disadvantage of the medical model is that it emphasizes hospitalization and drug treatment rather than psychological insights into mental problems. Use of the medical model also has fostered the incorrect notion that abnormal behavior can be contagious, like an infectious disease.

Model
An analogy or a perspective that uses a structure from one field to help scientists describe data in another field.

Abnormal psychology
The field of psychology concerned with the assessment, treatment, and prevention of maladaptive behavior.

■ **THE PSYCHODYNAMIC MODEL.** The *psychodynamic model* of abnormal behavior is loosely rooted in Freud's theory of personality (discussed in Chapter 12). This model assumes that psychological disorders result from anxiety produced by unresolved conflicts and forces that lie outside a person's awareness. It asserts that maladjustment occurs when a person's ego is not strong enough to balance the demands of the id, the superego, and the outside world. According to the psychodynamic model, maintaining a healthy, functioning personality is a careful balancing act of satisfying these often conflicting demands. Thus, even seemingly healthy people are vulnerable to maladjustment. A homeless person's talking to himself might be explained as loneliness, despair, or anger turned inward, traceable to personality development during childhood.

■ **THE HUMANISTIC MODEL.** Like the psychodynamic model, the *humanistic model* of abnormal behavior assumes that inner psychic forces are important in establishing and maintaining a fulfilling lifestyle. Unlike psychodynamic theorists, however, humanists believe that people have a good deal of control over their lives. The humanistic model focuses on individual uniqueness and decision making. Maladjustment occurs when people's needs are not met; either they are unable to fulfill their needs or some circumstance prevents them from doing so. In the case of a homeless person, many needs may be unfulfilled; the person may lack food and shelter, putting the person in the situation of concentrating on these needs. Thus, a homeless person's abnormal behavior may be determined by the circumstances of living on the street rather than by internal, personal factors.

■ **THE BEHAVIORAL MODEL.** The *behavioral model* of abnormal behavior states that such behavior is learned. Behavioral theorists assume that events in a person's environment selectively reinforce or punish various behaviors and, in doing so, shape personality and may create maladjustment. They thus contend, for example, that an abusive husband may have learned to assert dominance over women through physical abuse because physical force has been effective in allowing him to dominate women. Two fundamental assumptions of behavioral (learning) theorists are that disordered behavior can be reshaped and that more appropriate, worthwhile behaviors can be substituted through traditional learning techniques (see Chapter 7). Proponents of the behavioral model might explain a man's homelessness by hypothesizing that he did not find significant reinforcers in the work world and felt he could take care of himself and manage better by living on the streets.

■ **THE COGNITIVE MODEL.** The *cognitive model* of abnormal behavior asserts that human beings engage in both prosocial and maladjusted behaviors because of their thoughts. As thinking organisms, people decide how to behave; abnormal behavior is based on false assumptions or unrealistic coping strategies. Practitioners with a cognitive perspective treat people with psychological disorders by helping them develop different ways of thinking about problems and new values. A cognitive theorist might assume that maladjusted people have developed ideas about the world that made them want to withdraw; these ideas might be irrational and might have led to abnormal behaviors.

■ **THE SOCIOCULTURAL MODEL.** According to the *sociocultural model* of abnormal behavior, people develop abnormalities within and because of a context—the context of the family, the community, and the society. Cross-cultural researchers have shown that personality development and psychological disorders reflect the culture and the stressors in the society. Relying heavily on the learning and cognitive frameworks, the sociocultural model focuses on cultural variables as key determinants of maladjustment.

As researchers examine the frequency and types of disorders that occur in different societies, they also note some sharp differences between societies. In China, for example, depression is relatively uncommon, but stress reactions manifested in the form of physical ailments are frequent. Americans and Europeans report guilt and shame when they are depressed; depressed individuals in Africa, on the other hand, are less likely to report these symptoms but more likely to report somatic (physical) complaints. Certain disorders seem highly culture-specific; for example, *amok* (as in "running amok") is a disorder that is characterized by sudden rage and homicidal aggression and is seen in some Asian countries, including Malaysia and Thailand. Brought on by stress, sleep deprivation, and alcohol consumption, the behavior can be broken down into a series of stages. Researchers now recognize that some disorders are specific to a culture.

■ **THE EVOLUTIONARY MODEL.** According the *evolutionary model*, abnormal behavior may arise from several types of circumstances. The evolutionary view hypothesizes that humans evolved in a specific type of environment, and humans are best suited to function in similar environments. Modern societies are not like that ancestral environment, so maladjustments may represent behavior that was normal at some point in evolutionary history but is not today (Cosmides & Tooby, 1999). Some behavior problems are adaptive behaviors taken too far, such as fear of heights or snakes. These fears were likely to keep people out of trouble in the distant past, but today, they may produce problems. Another source of maladjustment comes from the many genetic defects that all humans have; these defects do not produce problems in all environments, but in some circumstances, they do. When built-in mechanisms do not perform their adaptive function, they may instead produce harmful dysfunctions (Wakefield, 1999). The criterion of producing harm is one that evolutionary psychologists use to identify a behavior as abnormal.

■ **WHICH MODEL IS BEST?** Each of the models we've examined—medical–biological, psychodynamic, humanistic, behavioral, cognitive, sociocultural, and evolutionary—looks at maladjustment from a different perspective. Some psychologists hold to one model and use it to analyze all behavior problems, but other psychologists believe that different models seem to explain different disorders. For phobias (unreasonable fears), learning theory explains the cause and prescribes an effective course of treatment. For schizophrenia, medical–biological theory clarifies a significant part of the problem. Consequently, many psychologists use an *eclectic approach,* choosing the model that seems to fit the problem. Other psychologists prefer a *biopsychosocial approach*, which acknowledges that a combination of biological, psychological, and social factors shape behavior. This approach differs from an eclectic approach in its combination of influences; the eclectic approach promotes a selection among discrete models.

■ **BE A CRITICAL THINKER.** People have developed a whole range of ideas about abnormality, and a veil of misunderstanding still surrounds mental illness in many people's minds. For example, many individuals still think that a mental illness is "forever" and incurable. They sometimes worry that those diagnosed as mentally ill are dangerous, violent, or out of control, behaving bizarrely and wildly different from normal people. The truth is, of course, that more people recover from mental illness than do not, few people with mental illness are violent, and most people with mental illnesses suffer quietly and bear their pain privately. Treatment with therapy, drugs, and love and care from family members and friends helps in managing these illnesses.

As you examine each psychological disorder presented in this chapter, think about whether you favor one model of maladjustment over another. Do you have a cognitive bent, or do you favor a more psychodynamic approach? Perhaps you take a more behavioral view, or the biopsychosocial model represents a combination you

Prevalence
The percentage of a population displaying a disorder during any specified period.

like. Regardless of a practitioner's predispositions, it is important that symptoms be carefully evaluated so proper diagnoses can be made. People who are suffering need appropriate help, and a wide variety of treatments are available.

Next, we consider a system that has been developed to help practitioners make diagnoses. The system is presented in *The Diagnostic and Statistical Manual of Mental Disorders*.

Diagnosing Psychopathology: The *DSM*

If you ask psychologists and psychiatrists to explain homeless people, they are likely to say that homeless people may be odd but not necessarily abnormal. This distinction underscores the fact that diagnosing maladjusted behavior is a complicated process.

■ ***THE DIAGNOSTIC AND STATISTICAL MANUAL OF MENTAL DISORDERS.*** The American Psychiatric Association has devised a system for diagnosing maladjusted behavior—*The Diagnostic and Statistical Manual of Mental Disorders,* usually called the *DSM*. The current edition of the manual is a text revision (TR) of the fourth edition, the *DSM–IV–TR*, published in 2000. The goals of the *DSM* are to provide a system for diagnosing disorders according to observable behaviors, to improve the reliability of diagnoses, and to make diagnoses consistent with research evidence and practical experience (Widiger et al., 1991), but many critics claim that the system is less successful than intended (Kutchins & Kirk, 1997).

The *DSM* designates 16 major categories of disorders and more than 200 subcategories. Table 15.1 lists some of the major classifications. In this chapter, we will explore a selection of these disorders, but we obviously cannot cover all of them. The selection includes disorders that are common and thus relevant to many people as well as disorders that are well known but also popularly misunderstood.

The *DSM* also cites the **prevalence** of each disorder—the percentage of the population displaying the disorder during any specified period. For most psychological disorders, the *DSM* also indicates the lifetime prevalence—the statistical likelihood that a person will develop the disorder during his or her lifetime. So, a typical *DSM* statement might read, "Community-based studies reveal a lifetime prevalence for Posttraumatic Stress Disorder of approximately 8% of the adult population of the United States. . . . Studies of at-risk individuals (i.e., groups exposed to specific traumatic incidents) yield variable findings, with the highest rates (ranging between one-third and more than half of those exposed) found among survivors of rape, military combat and captivity, and ethnically or politically motivated internment and genocide" (APA, 2000, p. 466). The symptoms and disorders described in the *DSM* have existed for years, but the *DSM* system of classification assigns names to the disorders consistent with current thought. The behaviors associated with

TABLE 15.1

Major Classifications of *The Diagnostic and Statistical Manual of Mental Disorders*, Fourth Edition, Text Revision

Disorders first diagnosed in infancy, childhood, and adolescence
Delirium, dementia, and other cognitive disorders
Mental disorders due to a general medical condition
Substance-related disorders
Schizophrenia and other psychotic disorders
Mood disorders
Anxiety disorders
Somatoform disorders
Factitious disorders
Dissociative disorders
Sexual and gender identity disorders
Eating disorders
Sleep disorders
Impulse control disorders
Adjustment disorders

Note: Each classification is further broken down into subtypes.

depression, schizophrenia, or attention-deficit/hyperactivity disorder have been around for years—but those names are part of the current *DSM*.

An important feature of the *DSM* is that diagnostic information for any disorder is laid out on five different dimensions. The *DSM* refers to these dimensions as *axes*; the manual thus uses what is called a *multiaxial system*, and an individual receives a diagnosis on each of the five axes. Axis I describes the *clinical disorders* themselves. Axis II describes *personality disorders and mental retardation*. Axis III describes *current medical conditions* that might be pertinent to understanding or managing the individual's mental disorder—for example, heart disease may be a relevant factor in depression. Other relevant medical conditions include diseases of the endocrine, digestive, and respiratory systems. Axis IV, *psychosocial or environmental problems*, refers to life stresses (including economic or educational problems) and familial support systems that may or may not facilitate a person's treatment or recovery. Finally, Axis V comprises a *global assessment of functioning*, which reports the clinician's overall assessment of the person's functioning in the psychological, social, and occupational domains. For example, a client might be said to have some mild symptoms such as insomnia and occasional truancy from school but to be generally functioning pretty well, with some meaningful personal relationships. These five axes, when viewed together, help a clinician fully describe the nature of a person's maladjustment. It is important to note that a clinician might not diagnose a client on a particular axis. So, for example, there may be no medical condition to report on Axis III. Table 15.2 describes the axes of the *DSM–IV–TR*.

You might think that such a diagnostic manual would be straightforward, like an encyclopedia of mental disorders. However, because it was written by committees, the *DSM* represents various points of view, biases, and compromises; therefore, it has met with resistance and engendered controversy. Some take issue with the way the *DSM* groups disorders based on symptoms rather than causes. This feature results in a diagnostic system without a theoretical basis. Others argue that it is too complex, with too many categories and symptoms that overlap among the categories. Some say that, despite its complexity, questions remain about the reliability of its diagnoses for many disorders (Nathan & Langenbucher, 1999). Some have criticized those who formulated the *DSM* for using political rather than scientific criteria in determining what disorders are included (Kutchins & Kirk, 1997). Some have concerns about potential gender bias against women (e.g., Hartung & Widiger, 1998). Many psychologists are unhappy with the use of psychiatric terms that perpetuate a medical rather than a behavioral model. Finally, a few psychologists maintain that the *DSM* pathologizes everyday behaviors and allows some practitioners to take advantage of its legitimization of the psychiatric terms for political and mon-

TABLE 15.2

The Axes of the *DSM*

Axis	Description
Axis I	Clinical disorders—symptoms that cause distress or significantly impair social or occupational functioning
Axis II	Personality disorders—personality patterns that are so pervasive, inflexible, and maladaptive that they impair interpersonal or occupational functioning
Axis III	Medical conditions that may be relevant to the understanding or treatment of a psychological disorder
Axis IV	Psychosocial and environmental problems (such as negative life events and interpersonal stressors) that may affect the diagnosis, treatment, and prognosis of psychological disorders
Axis V	Global assessment of functioning—the individual's overall level of functioning in social, occupational, and leisure activities

Adapted from American Psychiatric Association, 2000.

etary gain (Kutchins & Kirk, 1997). Therefore, the *DSM* is the most widely accepted classification system for mental disorders, but many object to its widespread use.

This Latina woman is experiencing *ataque de nervios*, which she will later not remember. This disorder exists mainly in the cultural context of Latin America.

DIVERSITY AND DIAGNOSES. The *DSM* is by no means the final word in diagnosing maladjustment; it is a developing system of classification, and the American Psychiatric Association is always engaged in debate over new diagnoses and revisions to existing categories. *DSM–IV–TR* includes instructions to clinicians to become more sensitive to issues of diversity and examples of syndromes that are specific to various cultures. Some psychologists, however, feel that these instructions are not sufficient to assure fair diagnoses.

Research shows that the likelihood of a specific diagnosis is related to ethnicity and culture. In the United States, diagnosis of African Americans, Latinos/Latinas, Asian Americans, and Native Americans differs from that of whites for some diagnostic categories in the *DSM*. The stigma of seeking mental health care is stronger in some cultures than others, preventing individuals from seeking care until their maladjustment is severe. Thus, people from some groups are more severely pathological when they are diagnosed (Takeuchi, & Cheung, 1998). In addition, different rates of diagnoses may be due to how clinicians interpret symptoms presented by various people, but evidence indicates that culture makes a difference in how people express maladjustment (Whaley, 1997).

For example, in Latino/Latina cultures in the Caribbean, some individuals experience *ataque de nervios* (literally, "attack of nerves"), symptomized by screaming, crying, trembling, and often verbal or physical aggression (Lopez & Guarnaccia, 2000). When the *ataque* has passed, individuals may have no memory of the experience. Between 16% and 23% of people in Puerto Rico report having an *ataque de nervios*, and divorced, middle-aged women from lower socioeconomic

Be an *Active* learner

REVIEW

- If you accept the medical-biological model of abnormal behavior, what factors would you take seriously that those who accept the behavioral model would find unimportant? pp. 528–529
- What are the differences in the psychodynamic, humanistic, and evolutionary views of abnormal behavior? Are there any similarities? pp. 529–530
- What are the goals of the DSM, and what are its potential advantages and disadvantages? pp. 531–532

THINK CRITICALLY

- Try to "think outside the box" of your culture and analyze what behaviors are accepted as normal that might be considered abnormal for a visitor from another country or another world.
- A medical model assumes that people who suffer from a psychological disorder have no more control over their problem than do people who suffer from cancer. What do you think are the implications of such an assumption for the diagnosis and treatment of mental illnesses?

APPLY PSYCHOLOGY

- Make a list of behaviors that you consider abnormal but have observed on your campus. Keep this list and try to classify these behaviors according to the *DSM*.

introduction to research basics

Cross-Cultural Factors in a Diagnosis

A mother brought her 12-year-old daughter to the emergency room of a hospital because the girl seemed ill. Her diagnosis and treatment constituted an interesting case that Jason Takeuchi (2000) presented as a case study to illustrate the influence that culture has on abnormal behavior and the diagnosis of mental disorders.

DESIGN A **case study** is a descriptive study that includes an intensive study of one person. This approach allows an intensive examination of a single case, usually chosen for its interesting or unique characteristics.

HYPOTHESIS Ethnicity has an impact on the expression of abnormal behavior as well as on diagnosis and the types of treatment approaches that are successful.

PARTICIPANT Takeuchi described the case of this 12-year-old girl, whom he called C, because of her ethnic background and how it affected her behavior. C's father was from the United States and her mother was from Tonga, in the South Pacific. C was born and lived in the United States, but her mother maintained close ties with her family and the cultural traditions of Tonga.

HISTORY During the two weeks prior to the emergency room visit, her mother said that C became progressively preoccupied, isolated, and "spacey." Before that time, her mother had been in Tonga taking care of her father, who had died.

PROCEDURE During the initial interview, C expressed a fear that she would harm herself, and subsequent conversations revealed hallucinations and claims that ghosts were after her, trying to harm her, including the ghost of her recently deceased grandfather. Her thought processes were disorganized, and her emotional reactions were not always appropriate to the situation.

The interpretation of C's symptoms varies according to the cultural perspective of the person making the diagnosis. According to psychiatric diagnosis in the United States, she exhibited seriously abnormal behavior, which would likely result in prolonged treatment with psychoactive drugs and possibly psychotherapy. According to the cultural beliefs of Tonga, her grandfather's ghost could be haunting C. The condition is known as *fakamahaki*, which includes hearing the voices of dead relatives. Both her mother and grandmother reported that they had experienced *fakamahaki* and were cured by native healers who applied a specified course of herbs and rituals.

OUTCOME An interesting part of this case study was that C received both diagnoses and both treatments. She was confined to a psychiatric facility and treated with psychoactive drugs and psychotherapy, which were only partially effective in bringing about a decrease in her symptoms. Then her mother took her to Tonga, where she underwent treatment from a native healer. This treatment was more effective. C's acceptance of the treatment, belief in its effectiveness, and her family's cultural values were important in its success.

In many ways, C appeared to be completely acculturated to U.S. society, but her close relationship with her Tongan relatives and acceptance of Tongan cultural values made a difference for both the expression of her symptoms and the effectiveness of her treatment. This case study provides a valuable lesson to psychiatrists and psychologists about the importance of taking culture into account in decisions concerning diagnosis and treatment. However, the uniqueness of the case does not allow generalization of these findings to others, which is a limitation of the case study method.

groups are most vulnerable to it. People with *ataque de nervios* may also have disorders listed in the *DSM*, but this disorder exists in the cultural context of Latin America. The prevalence rate of a specific disorder in a particular country probably reflects racial, religious, and cultural situations; it especially reflects the specific culture-bound behavior patterns that a society considers abnormal as well as normal. As suggested earlier, various cultures allow for, and perhaps encourage, the experience of specific symptoms such as those of *ataque de nervios*.

The effect of culture on clinical diagnosis and treatment plans is underresearched and constitutes an important area of concern for practicing psychologists. The American Psychological Association (1993) suggests that practitioners should recognize cultural diversity, understand the role of culture and ethnicity in development, and understand how culture, race, gender, and sexual orientation affect behavior. Understanding cultural factors in the expression of abnormal behavior is a continuing challenge for clinicians involved in making diagnoses (see *Introduction to Research Basics*).

Case study
A descriptive study that includes an intensive study of one person and allows an intensive examination of a single case, usually chosen for its interesting or unique characteristics.

The remainder of this chapter explores some of the disorders described in the *DSM*. We discuss some disorders that are common (such as phobias) as well as some that are not common but are well known yet misunderstood (such as multiple personality disorder). We begin with a classification of disorders that are common—anxiety disorders.

Anxiety Disorders

Everyone experiences anxiety. Most people feel anxious in specific situations, such as before taking an examination, competing in a swim meet, or delivering a speech. Although anxiety can be a positive, motivating force, its effects can also be debilitating; left untreated, chronic anxiety may eventually impair a person's health. Those who have had anxiety problems serious enough to cause them to be hospitalized are at increased risk for suicide (Allgulander, 1994). Anxiety disorders as a whole are common in the general population. Research into them, however, is not extensive, and there is an even more serious lack of research on specific populations—for example, Asian Americans (Lee, Lei, & Sue, 2001). In recent years, researchers have found that at least some anxiety-related traits may have a genetic basis, and that symptoms may be alleviated through various drugs that facilitate serotonin transmission (Lesch et al., 1996).

Defining Anxiety

Karen Horney (pronounced HORN-eye), a neo-Freudian renowned for her work on anxiety, described it as the central factor in both normal and abnormal behavior (Horney, 1937). **Anxiety** is a generalized feeling of fear and apprehension that may be related to a particular situation or object and is often accompanied by increased physiological arousal. Horney considered it a motivating force, an intrapsychic urge, and a signal of distress. She also argued that anxiety underlies many forms of maladjustment. She believed that maladjustment occurs when too many defenses against anxiety pervade the personality.

■ *Karen Horney conceptualized anxiety as a central factor in both normal and abnormal behavior.*

Freud, in contrast, saw anxiety as the result of constant conflict among the id, ego, and superego; he called nearly all forms of behavior associated with anxiety *neurotic*. Freud's term *neurosis* has made its way into everyday language, to the point where nonpsychologists tend to describe any quirky or annoying behavior as neurotic. Anxiety (and what Freud called neurotic behavior) refers to a wide range of symptoms, including fear, apprehension, inattention, heart palpitations, respiratory distress, and dizziness. The term *neurosis* was once part of the *DSM* and diagnostic terminology, but it was removed and is no longer part of the official terminology that describes abnormal behavior. People also use the term *free-floating anxiety* to describe persistent anxiety not clearly related to any specific object or situation and accompanied by a sense of impending doom. This term also dates back to psychodynamic theories of abnormal behavior and is not part of current terminology.

Psychologists recognize that anxiety is an important symptom of maladjustment—not necessarily the cause. Thoughts, environmental stimuli, or perhaps some long-standing and as yet unresolved conflict causes apprehension, fear, and its accompanying autonomic nervous system arousal. Feelings of not being able to control a situation are common to both children's and adults' anxiety. Some researchers speculate that childhood anxiety and a perceived sense of lack of control may lead to similar, if not identical, feelings in adulthood, which may result in a disorder (Chorpita & Barlow, 1998).

Anxiety
A generalized feeling of fear and apprehension that may be related to a particular situation or object and is often accompanied by increased physiological arousal.

student voices

Tanya Short
Lynn University

When I started learning about disorders in my Intro to Psych class, I began to think things like, 'Maybe he's a little depressed because he's lost interest in things and hasn't been eating' or 'That girl seems anxious and fidgety all the time. Those would be symptoms for general anxiety disorder.' This made me realize I was learning a lot in class.

During the 1980s, research on anxiety disorders increased dramatically, partially prompted by the recognition that these disorders were very common and not always diagnosed (Cox & Taylor, 1999). Several different types of anxiety disorders appear in the *DSM*, including generalized anxiety disorder, phobias, and obsessive–compulsive disorder.

Generalized Anxiety Disorder

Generalized anxiety disorder is an anxiety disorder characterized by persistent anxiety occurring on more days than not for at least 6 months, sometimes with increased activity of the autonomic nervous system, apprehension, excessive muscle tension, and difficulty in concentrating. In addition to such excessive anxiety, people with generalized anxiety disorder find it difficult to control the anxiety they experience, so anxiety is a persistent problem in their lives. In addition, people with generalized anxiety disorder show impairment in at least three of six areas of functioning. These areas include three types of symptoms related to vigilance—restlessness or feeling "on edge," difficulty in concentrating, and irritability or impatience. Other symptoms include being easily fatigued, but another symptom is sleep difficulties or disturbances. Muscle tension and the inability to relax are the last set of symptoms. The *DSM* states that a person must show persistent anxiety that is not specific to one situation to be diagnosed with generalized anxiety disorder.

People with generalized anxiety disorder feel anxious almost constantly, even though nothing specific seems to provoke their anxiety. Expressed fears often revolve around health, money, family, or work. Unable to relax, they have trouble falling asleep; they tend to feel tired and have trouble concentrating. They often report excessive sweating, headaches, and insomnia. They are tense and irritable, have difficulty making decisions, and may hyperventilate (Kendall, Krain, & Treadwell, 1999).

Phobic Disorders

Do you know someone who avoids crowds at all cost, who is petrified at the thought of flying in a plane, or who shudders at the sight of a harmless garter snake? That person may suffer from a **phobic disorder**—an anxiety disorder involving excessive irrational fear of, and consequent avoidance of, specific objects or situations. Unlike people who feel anxious almost constantly, the anxiety of those who suffer from phobic disorders is focused on some specific object or situation. People with a phobic disorder exhibit avoidance and escape behaviors, show increased heart rate and irregular breathing patterns, and report thoughts of disaster, severe embarrassment, or both. Many psychologists agree that once a phobia is established, it is maintained by the relief a person derives from escaping or avoiding the feared situation. Phobic disorders are common, affecting over 10% of the people in the United States (Kessler et al., 1994).

One key to diagnosing phobic disorders is that the fear must be excessive and disproportionate to the situation, enough to induce a person to avoid the situation altogether. Most people have fears, some of which can be adaptive. Phobias, however, are not normal fears, and they are not adaptive. For example, many people fear heights, but this fear is not usually phobic—heights can be dangerous. Most people who fear heights would not avoid visiting a friend who lived on the top floor of a tall building; however, a person with a phobia of heights would. Their fears are unreasonable and disproportionate to the situation. Fear alone does not distinguish a phobia; both fear and avoidance must be evident. An almost infinite number of objects and situations inspire fear in people. Because of the diversity and number of phobias, the *DSM* classifies three basic kinds: agoraphobia, social phobia, and specific phobia. We consider these next.

Generalized anxiety disorder
An anxiety disorder characterized by persistent anxiety occurring on more days than not for at least 6 months, sometimes with increased activity of the autonomic nervous system, apprehension, excessive muscle tension, and difficulty in concentrating.

Phobic disorders
Anxiety disorders characterized by excessive and irrational fear of, and consequent attempted avoidance of, specific objects or situations.

■ **AGORAPHOBIA.** **Agoraphobia** is an anxiety disorder characterized by marked fear and avoidance of being alone in a place from which escape might be difficult or embarrassing. This phobia is accompanied by avoidance behaviors that may eventually interfere with normal activities. It can become so debilitating that it prevents the individual from going into a space from which escape might be difficult or awkward (for example, airplanes or tunnels) or from being in crowds. People with severe cases may decide never to leave their homes, fearing that they will lose control, panic, or cause a scene in a public place. An episode of agoraphobia is often brought on by stress, particularly interpersonal stress. It is far more common in women than in men (5.8% versus 2.8%; Kessler et al., 1994).

Symptoms of agoraphobia are hyperventilation, extreme tension, and even cognitive disorganization. Agoraphobia may occur alone, but people with agoraphobia often suffer from severe panic attacks. **Panic attacks** are characterized as acute anxiety, accompanied by sharp increases in autonomic nervous system arousal, that is not triggered by a specific event. Persons who experience such attacks often avoid the situations that are associated with them, thus perpetuating the agoraphobia. Some cognitive psychologists think of a panic attack as a "fear of fear." People attempt to avoid anxiety because they are so sensitive to it and its symptoms and may panic while trying to avoid the symptoms of being fearful (McNally et al., 1997; Zuckerman, 1999). About 24% of people who experience panic disorders (including those with agoraphobia) also have some type of depressive disorder, and about 10% and 20% have alcohol problems (Cox & Taylor, 1999).

Agoraphobia is complicated, can be incapacitating, and remains extraordinarily difficult to treat. According to Freud and other psychoanalysts, traumatic childhood experiences may cause people to avoid particular objects or situations that produce anxiety. Freudians speculate that agoraphobics may have feared abandonment by a cold or nonnurturing mother when they were young children, and the fear became generalized to a fear of abandonment or helplessness. Most researchers today find Freudian explanations of phobic behavior unconvincing. Contemporary researchers have searched for the events that initiate panic attacks and the development of agoraphobia in individual learning history, family experiences, and genetics (Zuckerman, 1999). Despite much research, no simple cause for the disorder has been found.

■ **SOCIAL PHOBIA.** A person with a social phobia tends to avoid situations involving possible exposure to close attention from other people. A **social phobia** is an anxiety disorder characterized by fear of, and desire to avoid, situations in which one might be exposed to scrutiny by others and might behave in an embarrassing or humiliating way. A person with a social phobia avoids eating in public, for example, or speaking before other people. Such a person also avoids evaluation by refusing to enter into situations in which evaluation and a lowering of self-esteem might occur (Hackmann, Clark, & McManus, 2000). The most common social phobia is a fear of speaking in public, although going to parties where many unknown people will be is also associated with a high level of anxiety. Social phobia is more than being shy; shy individuals don't actually avoid circumstances that make them uncomfortable or self-conscious. Social phobia disrupts normal living and social relationships. The dread of speaking to a group or attending a social function can begin weeks in advance and lead to debilitating symptoms.

■ **SPECIFIC PHOBIA.** A **specific phobia** is an anxiety disorder characterized by irrational and persistent fear of a particular object or situation, along with a compelling desire to avoid it. Most people are familiar with specific phobias; see Table 15.3 on the following page for some examples. Among specific phobias are *claustrophobia* (fear of closed spaces), *hematophobia* (fear of blood), and *acrophobia* (fear of heights). Many specific phobias develop in childhood, adolescence, or early adulthood. Most people who have fears of heights, small spaces, water, doctors, or

Agoraphobia [AG-or-uh-FOE-bee-uh]
Anxiety disorder characterized by marked fear and avoidance of being alone in a place from which escape might be difficult or embarrassing.

Panic attacks
Anxiety disorders characterized as acute anxiety, accompanied by sharp increases in autonomic nervous system arousal, that is not triggered by a specific event.

Social phobia [FOE-bee-uh]
Anxiety disorder characterized by fear of, and desire to avoid, situations in which the person might be exposed to scrutiny by others and might behave in an embarrassing or humiliating way.

Specific phobia
Anxiety disorder characterized by irrational and persistent fear of a particular object or situation, along with a compelling desire to avoid it.

TABLE 15.3

Some Common Specific Phobias

Acrophobia (fear of high places)	Hematophobia (fear of blood)
Ailurophobia (fear of cats)	Mysophobia (fear of contamination)
Algophobia (fear of pain)	Nyctophobia (fear of darkness)
Anthropophobia (fear of men)	Pathophobia (fear of disease)
Aquaphobia (fear of water)	Pyrophobia (fear of fire)
Astraphobia (fear of storms, thunder, and lightning)	Thanatophobia (fear of death)
Claustrophobia (fear of closed spaces)	Xenophobia (fear of strangers)
Cynophobia (fear of dogs)	Zoophobia (fear of animals)

flying can calm themselves and deal with their fears; but those who cannot—true phobics—often seek the help of a psychotherapist when the phobia interferes with their health or with day-to-day functioning. Treatment using behavior therapy is typically effective.

Obsessive–Compulsive Disorder

Being orderly and organized is usually an asset, especially in today's fast-paced, complex society. However, when orderliness becomes an overriding concern, a person may be suffering from obsessive–compulsive disorder. **Obsessive–compulsive disorder** is an anxiety disorder characterized by persistent and uncontrollable thoughts and irrational beliefs that cause the performance of compulsive rituals that interfere with daily life. The unwanted thoughts, urges, and actions of people with obsessive–compulsive disorder focus on maintaining order and control. About 2.5% of the U.S. population suffers from obsessive–compulsive disorder, and the rate is similar for women and men (Zuckerman, 1999). Of those with the disorder, about 20% have only obsessions or compulsions; about 80% have both.

People with obsessive–compulsive disorder combat anxiety by carrying out ritual behaviors that reduce tension; they feel they have to *do* something. Their thoughts have extraordinary power to control actions. For example, a man obsessed with avoiding germs may wash his hands a hundred times a day and may wear white gloves to avoid touching contaminated objects. If he does not perform these compulsive acts, he may develop severe anxiety. A woman obsessed with punctuality may become extremely anxious if she might arrive late for a dinner date. Adolescents with obsessive–compulsive disorder tend to wash and rewash, check, count, touch, and straighten items in their environment (March, Leonard, & Swedo, 1995). A person may compulsively write notes about every detail of every task before permitting herself or himself to take any action. Here is an account of extreme obsessive–compulsive behavior:

> I used to write notes to remind myself to do a particular job, so in my mind there was a real risk that one of these notes might go out of the window or door. . . . My fear was that if one of these papers blew away, this would cause a fatality. . . . I found it difficult to walk along the street, as every time I saw paper I wondered if it was some of mine. I had to pick it

Obsessive–compulsive disorder
Anxiety disorder characterized by persistent and uncontrollable thoughts and irrational beliefs that cause the performance of compulsive rituals that interfere with daily life.

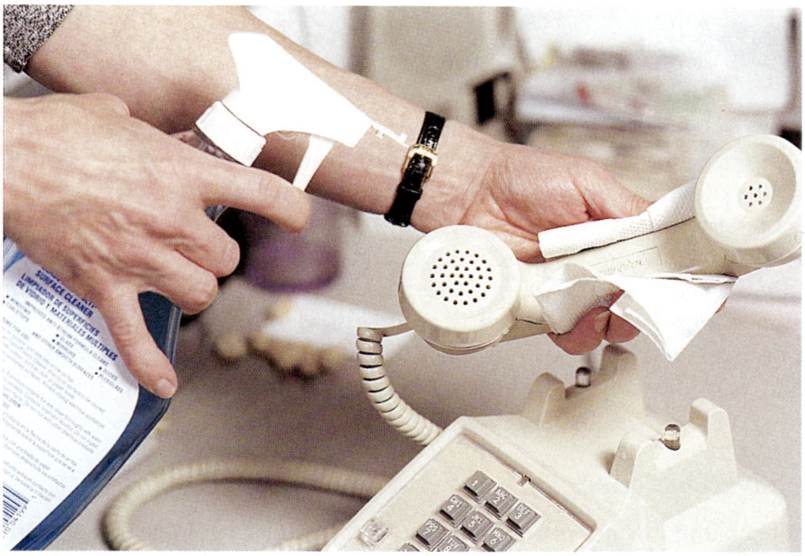

An obsession with avoiding "germs" and a compulsion to disinfect is a common form of obsessive-compulsive disorder.

all up, unless it was brown chocolate paper, or lined paper, which I didn't use. And before I got on my bike, I checked that nothing was sticking out of my pockets and got my wife to recheck. . . . I couldn't smoke a cigarette without taking it to bits and checking there was no document between the paper and tobacco. I couldn't even have sex because I thought a piece of paper might get intertwined into the mattress. (Melville, 1977, pp. 66–67)

Freud and other psychodynamic theorists believed that obsessive–compulsive disorder stems largely from difficulties during the anal stage of development, when orderliness and cleanliness are often stressed. Learning theorists argue that bringing order to the environment reduces uncertainty and risk and thus is reinforcing. Because reinforced behaviors tend to recur, these behaviors become exaggerated during times of stress. Biopsychologists have identified brain structures involved with obsessive–compulsive disorder. Studies that involve imaging the brain indicate that several parts of the brain are involved, including parts of the frontal lobe of the cerebral cortex, the basal ganglia, and the amygdala (Szeszko et al., 1999). Both the functioning and the structure of the area of the frontal lobes just behind the eyes and the amygdala (under the temporal lobes) are affected in individuals with obsessive–compulsive disorder. This evidence leads some neurologists to define obsessive–compulsive disorder as a brain disorder with behavioral symptoms (Micallef & Blin, 2001).

Practitioners report that full-blown cases of obsessive–compulsive disorder are relatively rare. Treatment often includes drugs such as Anafrinil, Prozac, or Zoloft (see Chapter 16) combined with relaxation exercises (March et al., 1995) and cognitive behavior therapy (Abramowitz, 1998). Such treatment helps change ideas about stress and the consequences of anxiety. Family support and family psychotherapy are also helpful; families are taught that they should neither encourage the behaviors nor participate in the person's rituals. Today, self-help groups are also part of successful treatments. People who develop obsessive–compulsive disorder before age 20 are less likely to improve over time; most people improve, even without treatment, over a period of five years or more (Skoog & Skoog, 1999).

Be an *Active* learner

REVIEW

- How does agoraphobia differ from the other phobias? p. 537
- Identify the central elements of obsessive–compulsive disorder. pp. 538–539

THINK CRITICALLY

- Evolutionary psychologists argue that a value for cleanliness and disgust over filth are adaptive. How would evolutionary psychology explain obsessive-compulsive disorder, which is clearly not adaptive?

APPLY PSYCHOLOGY

- What situations do you fear? How do your fears differ from phobias?

Mood Disorders

Everyone experiences dark moods at one time or another. Ending a long-term intimate relationship, feeling overwhelmed during final exams, mourning the death of a close friend, and experiencing serious financial problems can all be sources of bad moods. We often refer to *depression* as feeling bad. But when people become so depressed or sad that a change occurs in their outlook and overt behavior, they may be suffering from *clinical depression*, a term that has a specific meaning for psychologists. Depression is considered to be a type of mood disorder. Mood disorders, which include bipolar disorder and depressive disorders, may sometimes be triggered by a specific event, although for many individuals the symptoms develop with no apparent cause.

Depressive Disorders

Bonnie Strickland, former president of the American Psychological Association, said during the 1988 APA annual meeting, "Depression has been called the common cold of psychological disturbances . . . which underscores its prevalence, but trivializes its impact." Strickland noted that at any time, about 14 million people are suffering from this disabling disorder. And many of those people are misdiagnosed or undiagnosed and are not receiving treatment, despite its availability (Hirschfeld et al., 1997).

In his 1990 memoir, *Darkness Visible*, American novelist and Pulitzer Prize winner William Styron described his state of mind during a period of depression:

> He [a psychiatrist] asked me if I was suicidal, and I reluctantly told him yes. I did not particularize—since there seemed no need to—did not tell him that in truth many of the artifacts of my house had become potential devices for my own destruction: the attic rafters (and an outside maple or two) a means to hang myself, the garage a place to inhale carbon monoxide, the bathtub a vessel to receive the flow from my opened arteries. The kitchen knives in their drawers had but one purpose for me. Death by heart attack seemed particularly inviting, absolving me as it would of active responsibility, and I had toyed with the idea of self-induced pneumonia—a long frigid, shirt-sleeved hike through the rainy woods. Nor had I overlooked an ostensible accident, à la Randall Jarrell, by walking in front of a truck on the highway nearby. . . . Such hideous fantasies, which cause well people to shudder, are to the deeply depressed mind what lascivious daydreams are to persons of robust sexuality. (p. 52)

Depressed people are more than simply blue or sad. As Styron reveals, depression is debilitating, overwhelming, and dangerous. **Depressive disorders** are mood disorders in which people show extreme and persistent sadness, despair, and loss of interest in life's usual activities on a day-to-day basis. **Major depressive disorder** (or clinical depression) is characterized by loss of interest in almost all of life's usual activities; a sad, hopeless, or discouraged mood; sleep disturbance; loss of appetite; loss of energy; and feelings of unworthiness and guilt. Someone experiencing major depressive disorder is not merely experiencing fleeting anxiety or sadness, although this disorder may be triggered by a specific event, such as the loss of a loved one, a job, or a home. Sufferers show at least some difficulties with social and occupational functioning, although their behavior is not necessarily bizarre.

Depressive disorders
General category of mood disorders in which people show extreme and persistent sadness, despair, and loss of interest in life's usual activities.

Major depressive disorder
Depressive disorder characterized by loss of interest in almost all of life's usual activities; a sad, hopeless, or discouraged mood; sleep disturbance; loss of appetite; loss of energy; and feelings of unworthiness and guilt.

■ **SYMPTOMS.** The symptoms of major depressive disorder include poor appetite, insomnia, weight loss, loss of energy, feelings of worthlessness and intense guilt, inability to concentrate, and sometimes thoughts of death and suicide (Zuckerman, 1999). Depressed people have a gloomy outlook on life, an extremely distorted view of their problems, a tendency to blame themselves, and low self-esteem. They often withdraw from social and physical contact with others. Every task seems to require a great effort, thought is slow and unfocused, and problem-solving abilities are impaired. Individuals may display certain physical problems as well; for example, decrease in bone density and heightened risk of osteoporosis occur in those who suffer from depression, and depression is associated with abnormal brain activity in the frontal lobes and with immune system problems (Leonard, 2001; Schweiger et al., 1994; Videbech, 2000).

■ *Depressed people are more than sad—depression is a debilitating disorder.*

Depressed people may also have **delusions**—false beliefs that are inconsistent with reality but are held in spite of evidence that disconfirms them. Delusions may induce feelings of guilt, shame, and persecution. Seriously disturbed people show even greater disruptions in thought and motor processes and a total lack of spontaneity and motivation. Such people typically report that they have no hope for themselves or the world; nothing seems to interest them. They are often extremely self-critical (Blatt, 1995). Some feel responsible for serious world problems such as economic depression, disease, or hunger. They report strange diseases and may insist that their body is disintegrating or that their brain is being eaten from the inside out. Most people who exhibit symptoms of major depressive disorder can describe their reasons for feeling sad and dejected; however, they may be unable to explain why their response is so deep and so prolonged.

Psychologists say that many people suffering from major depressive disorder are poor at reality testing. *Reality testing* is a person's ability to judge the demands of the environment accurately and to deal with those demands. People who are poor at reality testing are unable to cope with the demands of life in rational ways because their reasoning ability is grossly impaired.

■ **ONSET AND DURATION.** A major depressive episode can occur at any age, but most people who experience these episodes usually undergo the first one before age 40. Symptoms are readily apparent and may last for days, weeks, or even months. Because so many different circumstances can be involved, the extent of depression varies dramatically from individual to individual. Episodes may occur once or many times. Sometimes a depressive episode may be followed by years of normal functioning—followed by two or three brief incidents of depression a few weeks apart. Stressful life events are sometimes predictors of depression (Mazure et al., 2000). Major depressive disorder is not exclusively an adult disorder; researchers find evidence of it in children and adolescents (Lewinsohn et al., 1999). When children suffer from depression, they often have other symptoms, especially anxiety and loneliness.

■ **PREVALENCE.** According to the National Institute of Mental Health, major depressive disorder strikes about 14 to 15 million Americans each year; around the world, depression imposes an enormous burden of disease to additional millions (Kessler, 2000). Women are twice as likely as men to be diagnosed as depressed and are more likely to express feelings of depression openly (Culbertson, 1997; Sprock & Yoder, 1997). In the United States, about 19%–23% of women and 8%–11% of men have experienced a major depressive episode at some time. About 6% of women and 3% of men have experienced episodes severe enough to require hospitalization. Women's higher rate of depression appears in many (but not all) cultures around the world. The reasons for this gender difference are not clear, but Susan Nolen-Hoeksema and her colleagues (Nolen-Hoeksema, 2000; Nolen-Hoeksema,

Delusions
False beliefs that are inconsistent with reality but are held in spite of evidence that disproves them.

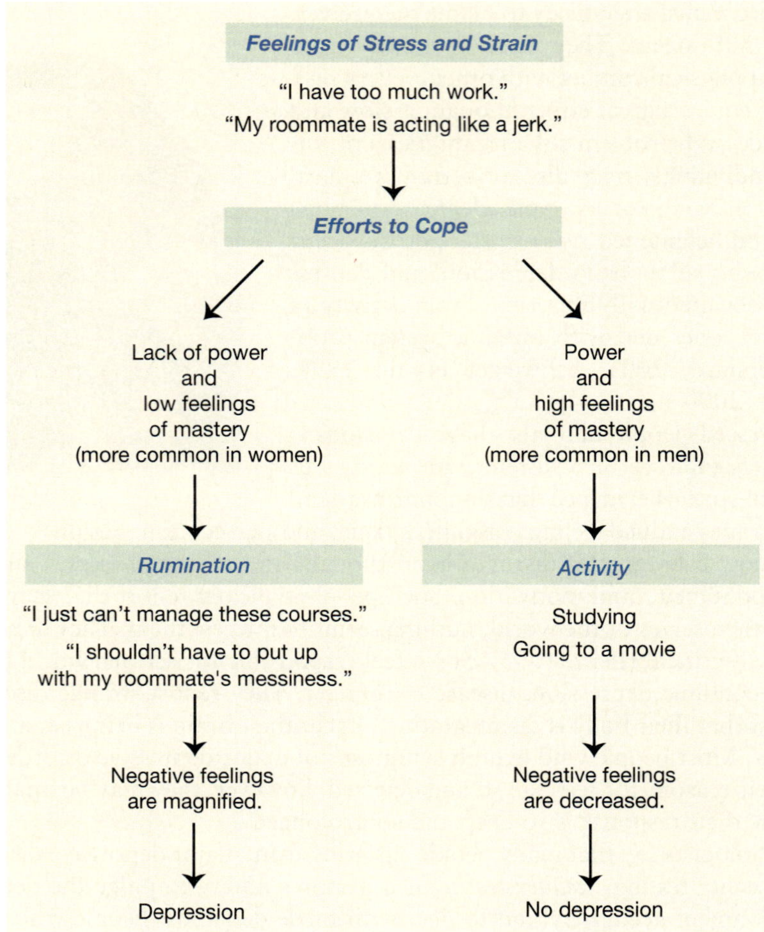

FIGURE 15.1

How Stress, Feelings of Mastery, and Rumination Influence Depression

Susan Nolen-Hoeksema and her colleagues hypothesize that rumination increases feelings of depression. Women are more likely than men to experience low power and feelings of low mastery, which magnify rumination and depression.

Larson, & Grayson, 1999) hypothesize that girls and women have more negative experiences as well as lower feelings of mastery, and they engage in rumination in response to negative events and feelings. *Rumination* is the process of dwelling on and analyzing problems and negative feelings. As Figure 15.1 shows, this coping style tends to prolong negative feelings and to increase depression.

Depression varies with age, and people between ages 25 and 45 are most vulnerable (Ingram, Scott, & Siegle, 1999). According to several studies, Americans born since 1950 are more likely to be depressed than their grandparents or great-grandparents were (Lewinsohn et al., 1993). These changes may be due to changes in diagnosis or reporting frequency, but the difference may be mostly due to the method of study rather than increases in the risks for depression (Stassen, Ragaz, & Reich, 1997). Martin Seligman (1988) suggests that the increased incidence of depression in the United States stems from too much emphasis on the individual, coupled with a loss of faith in supportive institutions such as family, country, and religion. Some research (Oliver & Novak, 1993) supports the notion that the type of alienation Seligman describes is related to depression. Examining the rates of mood disorders in countries around the world, industrialized countries show higher rates than developing countries (WHO International Consortium in Psychiatric Epidemiology, 2000), but this difference may reflect better access to mental health services in developed countries. However, depression is a worldwide problem not restricted to industrialized, individualistic cultures. It is a leading cause of disability worldwide, affecting more than 300 million people (Holden, 2000).

■ **CLINICAL EVALUATION.** How does a practitioner know if a person is suffering from major depressive disorder? Diagnosis for depression (or any other mental disorder) should include a complete clinical evaluation, which comprises three parts: a physical examination, a psychiatric history, and a mental status examination. The *physical examination* is done to rule out thyroid disorders, viral infection, and anemia—all of which cause a slowing down of behavior. A neurological check of coordination, reflexes, and balance is part of this exam, to rule out brain disorders. The *psychiatric history* attempts to trace the course of the apparent disorder, genetic or family factors, and past treatments. Finally, the *mental status examination* scrutinizes thought, speaking processes, and memory; it includes interviews and may include tests for psychiatric symptoms (such as the MMPI–2) and projective tests (such as the TAT) (see Chapter 12 for information about these tests).

One reason for the extensive clinical evaluation is the importance of distinguishing between major depressive disorder and dysthymic disorder. In *dysthymic disorder*, people experience a chronic depressed mood for more days than not for a period of at least 2 years, but this reaction is mild compared to major depressive disorder. Along with depressed mood, people with dysthymic disorder experience poor appetite, insomnia, low self-esteem, and feelings of hopelessness. This disorder often goes undiagnosed and untreated; people begin to accept this mood as part of their typical personality. Dysthymic disorder spreads a thin veil of sadness over a person's life; individuals with the disorder are less likely to marry and more likely to divorce and are often underemployed or unemployed. They report being self-critical, take little interest in life's activities, and show occupational and social impairment. Dysthymic disorder is not as severe as major depressive disorder but lasts longer and often occurs alongside it; clinicians often diagnose dysthymic disorder in persons who were initially seeking help for a major depressive episode.

Causes of Major Depressive Disorder

Although major depression is "the common cold of mental disorders," its cause is not understood. Identifying the cause is difficult because several different theories exist, and all have research support. However, the research does not present a coherent picture; instead, results are complex and mixed, leading prominent researcher Marvin Zuckerman (1999) to propose that more than one theory may be necessary to explain all cases of depression. Let's consider the leading theories and the research support and problems with each, bearing in mind that Zuckerman may be correct, and depression may have more than one cause.

■ **BIOLOGICAL THEORIES.** Both genetics and neurotransmitters have been implicated as biological factors that underlie depression. Children of depressed parents are more likely than other children to be depressed; further, twin studies indicate that genetic factors play a substantial role in depression (Barondes, 1998; Kendler et al., 1992; Kendler, Neale, Kessler, et al., 1993). However, depression is not caused by a single gene, and finding multiple gene locations is a complex task (Zuckerman, 1999). In addition, the process through which genes affect behavior must be demonstrated. In the case of depression, genetics may affect neurotransmitters (Dikeos et al., 1999).

Neurotransmitters held within vesicles in one neuron are released, move across the synaptic space, and attach themselves at a binding site at an adjacent neuron (see Chapter 2). The receptors have binding sites for particular neurotransmitters. This is an important point, because a specific neurotransmitter can and will influence only those neurons that have receptors for it. Four of the key neurotransmitters in the brain are dopamine, norepinephrine, epinephrine, and serotonin, all of which are categorized chemically as *monoamines*.

When monoamines are released but do not bind to the next neuron, researchers find that people report feeling depressed. Such neurotransmitters are then either neutralized or taken back up by the neuron that released it, in a process called *reuptake*. (Again, see Chapter 2 for a review of this process.) When a person is given drugs that do not allow the neurotransmitters to be neutralized or restored to the releasing cell, the neurotransmitter is more likely to bind, and depression lifts. The *monoamine theory of depression* suggests that major depression results from a deficiency of monoamines or inefficient monoamine receptors (Mann et al., 1996; Soares & Mann, 1997). This theory is supported by the effectiveness of antidepressant drugs, which affect the availability of monoamines.

But part of the problem in accepting neurotransmitters as the underlying cause of depression is the length of time required for these drugs to take effect—depressed people must take antidepressant drugs for several weeks before they start to feel relief of their symptoms, but blood tests show that the drugs are available in the body after a few days. In addition, these drugs are not effective for some individuals, and researchers are beginning to question the adequacy of the monoamine theory of depression (Hindmarch, 2001). The inconsistency of findings points to the possibility that Zuckerman (1999) mentioned: multiple causes of depression. Another type of explanation for depression comes from learning and distorted ways of thinking.

■ **LEARNING AND COGNITIVE THEORIES.** Learning and cognitive theorists argue that learning and thoughts underlie depression. Peter Lewinsohn (1974) developed a view that people who fail to receive reinforcement are deprived of pleasure and thus become depressed. Other people find them unpleasant to be with and avoid them, thus perpetuating an environment with little reinforcement (Lewinsohn & Talkington, 1979). Lewinsohn stresses that depressed people often lack the social skills needed to obtain reinforcement, such as asking a neighbor or friend for help with a problem. See Figure 15.2 for details of Lewinsohn's view. A modification of this view incorporates the impact of stressful life events and cognition, making the model no longer strictly a learning explanation of depression (Ingram et al., 1999).

Psychiatrist Aaron Beck proposed another influential theory that explains depression in terms of thought processes. Beck (1967) suggested that depressed people already have negative views of themselves, the environment, and the future, and these views cause them to magnify their errors. This way of thinking forms a schema that is the basis for depression. Depressed people compare themselves to other people, usually unfairly; when they come up short, they see the difference as disastrous. They see the human condition as universally wretched and view the world as a place

FIGURE 15.2

Lewinsohn's View of Depression

According to Lewinsohn, some people have few reinforcers available in the environment. This lack of reinforcers causes depression, which then leads to even fewer reinforcers.

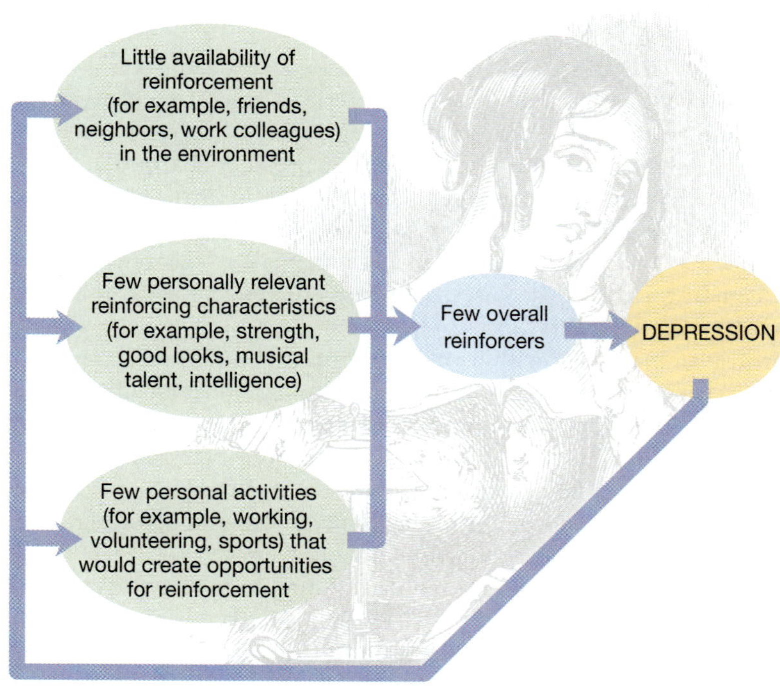

that defeats positive behavior. Their poor self-concept and negative expectations about the world lead to depression.

These cognitive distortions may occur in adolescents as well as adults, and research indicates that adolescents who have a negative, fatalistic view of the world are at greatly increased risk for depression (Roberts, Roberts, & Chen, 2000). Research also supports Beck's view that depressed people have more negative thoughts about themselves, the future, and the world in general and that this tendency to interpret the world in negative terms is a stable way to process information (Ingram et al., 1999). These tendencies exist and are activated under situations of stress.

According to Beck, cognitions underlie depression and perpetuate it by causing poor judgments, which feed back into negative cognitions. Beck's theory is influential among psychologists for two reasons: First, it is consistent with the notion that depression stems from ways of thinking. Second, it acknowledges the interaction of the cognitive schema that underlies depression with environmental variables such as stress.

■ **LEARNED HELPLESSNESS.** What would you do if you failed every exam you took, regardless of your efforts? What happens when a person's hopes and dreams are constantly thwarted, regardless of her or his behavior? The result may be **learned helplessness**—the behavior of giving up or not responding, exhibited by people and animals exposed to negative consequences or punishment over which they feel they have no control.

Seligman (1976) has suggested that people's beliefs about the causes of their failures determine whether they will become depressed. When they attribute their failures to unalterable conditions within themselves ("my own weakness, which is unlikely to change"), their self-esteem is diminished (Maddux & Meier, 1995). People who develop learned helplessness feel that they cannot change highly aversive life events (Abramson, Metalsky, & Alloy, 1989). That is, when people come to believe that outcomes are unrelated to anything under their control, they develop learned helplessness and become pessimistic rather than optimistic. For example, a man who comes to believe that his effort to meet new people by being outgoing and friendly never works may stop trying. Eventually, he will choose not to respond to the environment because he has learned that his behavior makes no difference (Peterson & Seligman, 1984). According to Seligman, the major cause of learned helplessness is a person's (or animal's) belief that its response will not affect what happens to it in the future. The result of this belief is anxiety, depression, and, eventually, nonresponsiveness. The opposite of learned helplessness is *learned optimism*—a sense that the world has positive outcomes, which leads people to see happy things in their lives (Seligman, 1991; Seligman & Csikszentmihalyi, 2000). Seligman asserts that *learning* is key to developing a sense of hopelessness or optimism. Seligman (1988) argues that the environment, not genetics, is the cause of pessimism, depression, and helplessness, especially when people believe that they are responsible for long-standing failures in many areas of their lives.

■ **THE BIOPSYCHOSOCIAL MODEL.** Many variables determine whether an individual will develop depression, or any other disorder, for that matter. Some factors, including genetic history, brain chemistry, cognitions, stress, and family environment, make some people more vulnerable than others. **Vulnerability** is a person's diminished ability to deal with demanding life events. The more vulnerable a person is, the less environmental stress or other factors (such as anxiety) are needed to initiate depression. This is the vulnerability–stress hypothesis, sometimes termed the *diathesis–stress model.*

The diathesis–stress model hypothesizes that mental disorders occur when people with vulnerability encounter stressful situations. That is, disorders develop from

Learned helplessness
The behavior of giving up or not responding, exhibited by people and animals exposed to negative consequences or punishment over which they feel they have no control.

Vulnerability
A person's diminished ability to deal with demanding life events.

Bipolar disorder
Mood disorder originally known as manic–depressive disorder because it is characterized by behavior that vacillates between two extremes: mania and depression.

the combination of factors. The vulnerability may be due either to biological factors or learned tendencies, but vulnerable people develop problems at lower levels of stress than do less vulnerable people (Zuckerman, 1999). For example, a person with a genetic vulnerability for depression will not necessarily become depressed, but experiences such as parental divorce or death will be more likely to result in depression for this individual than for one with no genetic vulnerability for depression. The concept of vulnerability also applies to another type of mood disorder—bipolar disorder.

Bipolar Disorder

Movie directors Francis Ford Coppola and Tim Burton, actors Jean-Claude Van Damme, Linda Hamilton, Margot Kidder, and Carrie Fisher, and musicians Axl Rose and Sting all have at least two things in common: artistic talent and a diagnosis of bipolar disorder. People who suffer from bipolar disorder experience depression similar to major depression, but they also experience the opposite feelings—excitement, confidence, and euphoria. **Bipolar disorder,** which was originally known as *manic–depressive disorder*, gets its name from the fact that people with this disorder experience behavior that varies between two extremes: mania and depression. The *manic phase* is characterized by rapid speech, inflated self-esteem, impulsiveness, euphoria, and decreased need for sleep. People in the manic phase are easily distracted, get angry when things do not go their way, and seem to have boundless energy. A person in the *depressed phase* is moody and sad, with feelings of hopelessness. People with bipolar disorder cycle between these two mood extremes.

Bipolar disorder is much less common than major depression. Only about 1.6% of the population develops this disorder, but that percentage means that about 2 million Americans suffer from bipolar disorder. Men and women are equally likely to be affected. People who suffer from bipolar disorder are often in their late 20s before they begin to manifest the symptoms, and the disorder often continues throughout their lives. Bipolar disorder may go unrecognized and be underdiagnosed in children and adolescents (Geller & Luby, 1997).

People with bipolar disorder may be relatively stable for a few days, weeks, or months between episodes of excitement and depression, or they may rapidly cycle between the two moods. The key component of bipolar disorder is the shift from excited states to depressive states of sadness and hopelessness. The disorder seems to have a biological basis with a substantial genetic component (Zuckerman, 1999). People with bipolar disorder often respond fairly well to drug treatment, especially to lithium and other newer drugs, which we'll discuss in Chapter 16 (Barondes, 1998; Post et al., 1998). Although those who take the appropriate medications for the disorder respond fairly well, many refuse to medicate themselves because it means forgoing the "highs" of the manic episodes. As many as 50% of individuals who suffer from bipolar disorder also exhibit maladaptive behaviors or personality traits, such as obsessions and compulsions or extreme dependence or narcissism (Peselow, Sanfilipo, & Fieve, 1995). Table 15.4 lists the signs and symptoms of mania and depression in bipolar disorder.

Depressive and bipolar disorders leave people unable to cope effectively on a day-to-day basis. Dissociative disorders, which will be discussed next, can be even more disruptive.

Be an *Active* learner

REVIEW

- What are the essential characteristics of major depression? pp. 540–541
- What evidence supports each of the theories of depression? pp. 543–545
- Identify the characteristics that distinguish bipolar disorder from major depression. p. 546

THINK CRITICALLY

- Women are diagnosed with major depression at a 2-to-1 ratio compared to men in the United States and many other countries. In some societies, however, rate of diagnosis is similar for men and women. What are the implications of these differing rates of diagnoses for major depression?
- People often believe that mental disorders lead to unusual thought processes, which boost creativity. Most people diagnosed with mental disorders are not as creative as normal people, but a disproportionate number of creative people have been diagnosed with bipolar disorder. What characteristics of this disorder might relate to creativity?

APPLY PSYCHOLOGY

- Visit the website for the National Depression and Manic Depressive Association at http://www.ndmda.org to learn more about these disorders. The website includes a screening for bipolar disorder. Complete this screening to help you understand how your behavior matches (and fails to match) the symptoms of bipolar disorder.

TABLE 15.4

Bipolar Disorder: Cycles of Mania and Depression

	Manic Behavior	Depressive Behavior
Emotional Characteristics	Elation, euphoria Extreme sociability, expansiveness Impatience Distractibility Inflated self-esteem	Gloominess, hopelessness Social withdrawal Irritability
Cognitive Characteristics	Desire for action Impulsiveness Talkativeness Grandiosity	Indecisiveness Slowness of thought Obsessive worrying about death Negative self-image Delusions of guilt Difficulty in concentrating
Motor Characteristics	Hyperactivity Decreased need for sleep Sexual indiscretion Increased appetite	Fatigue Difficulty in sleeping Decreased sex drive Decreased appetite Decreased motor activity

Dissociative Disorders

If you watch daytime TV dramas, you see dissociative disorders more often than psychologists and psychiatrists do. These disorders are much more common in fictional plots than in reality. **Dissociative disorders** are psychological disorders characterized by a sudden but temporary alteration in consciousness, identity, sensorimotor behavior, or memory. Although relatively rare, these disorders are easily identifiable. They include dissociative amnesia and dissociative identity disorder.

Dissociative Amnesia

Dissociative amnesia (formerly called *psychogenic amnesia*) is a dissociative disorder characterized by the sudden and extensive inability to recall important personal information, usually information of a stressful or traumatic nature. The memory loss is too extensive to be explained as ordinary forgetfulness; it may be loss of all information about personal identity or only selective portions.

Dissociative amnesia is not the same as amnesia due to head injury. When people receive a blow to the head or an electric shock severe enough to produce unconsciousness, they often experience some memory loss. This organically based memory loss typically occurs from the point of injury backward and may include loss of all personal memory. People with this type of memory loss typically find that their memories return gradually, and memory loss rarely persists for more than a few days or weeks. Dissociative memory, on the other hand, may be selective, only affecting certain types of memory; it is usually associated with traumatic events, but often not an injury. Just as it does on daytime television, dissociative amnesia can suddenly disappear, and the person's memory returns. Often, dissociative amnesia is brought on by a traumatic incident involving the threat of physical injury or death. Unlike its portrayal on daytime television, dissociative amnesia occurs most often during wars or natural disasters.

Dissociative disorders
Psychological disorders characterized by a sudden but temporary alteration in consciousness, identity, sensorimotor behavior, or memory.

Dissociative amnesia
Dissociative disorder characterized by the sudden and extensive inability to recall important personal information, usually of a traumatic or stressful nature.

point*counterpoint*

Multiple Personality Disorder—Is It Real?

The Issue: Is multiple personality disorder a legitimate diagnosis of mental disorder?

POINT

Multiple personality disorder is created by therapists and is not a naturally occurring mental disorder.

COUNTERPOINT

Multiple personality disorder is a legitimate diagnosis that identifies people with a specific mental disorder.

The publication of *The Three Faces of Eve* and *Sybil* and the movies based on these books caught the imagination of the public and sparked interest in multiple personality disorder. The disorder was considered rare, and most therapists had never seen a client whom they identified as having multiple personalities. That situation changed during the 1980s, when thousands of cases were identified and treated (Acocella, 1999). This explosion of cases coincides with the recognition of the problem of child sexual abuse, and most cases of multiple personality disorder were identified as people who had been abused as children. Sybil is the most famous psychiatric patient in history and provides a model for multiple personality disorder. Her history includes physical and sexual abuse, leading to the hypothesis that abuse was a risk factor for multiple personality disorder. Some therapists identified dozens.

Some researchers contend that the thousands of people (mostly women) who were diagnosed with multiple personality disorder received invalid diagnoses; these women did not have this disorder. Instead, these patients exhibited symptoms suggested by their therapists and created by hypnosis and psychoactive drugs administered by therapists (Acocella, 1999), or these patients enacted the role of multiple personality learned from the media (Lilienfield et al., 1999; Spanos, 1994). Either view casts doubt on the validity of multiple personality disorder, contending that the symptoms are either implanted by therapists or created by patients playing a role.

Other researchers consider multiple personality disorder (now called dissociative identity disorder) a legitimate diagnosis and contend that the critics are doing a disservice to people with this disorder (Gleaves, 1996). These authorities consider multiple personality disorder as a response to traumatic experiences during childhood that lead to the creation of separate facets of personality, each of which functions independently to cope with specific types of stressors. They propose that the disorder is often misdiagnosed, and it is not as rare as researchers initially believed (Murray, 1994). Some researchers who hold this view acknowledge that it is possible for therapists to create symptoms of multiple personality disorder, but the disorder is also real in some cases (Ross, 1999). These researchers argue that multiple personality consists of more than patients' acting or therapists' suggestions.

In a survey of mental health care professionals (Hayes & Mitchell, 1994), 24% expressed skepticism about the diagnosis of multiple personality disorder. In addition, these professionals said that multiple personality disorder poses more of a diagnostic problem than other disorders, such as schizophrenia. These findings suggest that the controversy over multiple personality disorder has affected psychologists and psychiatrists, and the prevailing belief is that more research is necessary to resolve this controversy.

Dissociative Identity Disorder: Multiple Personality

Dissociative identity disorder
Dissociative disorder characterized by the existence within an individual of two or more distinct personalities, each of which is dominant at different times and directs the individual's behavior at those times; commonly known as *multiple personality disorder*.

Another form of dissociative disorder, often associated with dissociative amnesia but presenting a dramatically different kind of behavior, is **dissociative identity disorder,** more commonly known as *multiple personality disorder*. Dissociative identity disorder is characterized by the existence within an individual of two or more distinct personalities, each of which is dominant at different times and directs the individual's behavior at those times. The person with the disorder often gives the various personalities different names, and their identities may differ quite sharply from the person's principal identity. A person with dissociative identity disorder usually cannot recall what occurs when one of the alternate personalities is controlling his or her behavior. Each personality has unique traits, memories, and behavioral patterns. For example, one personality may be adaptive and efficient at coping with life, while another may exhibit immature, maladaptive behavior. Some people's alternate personalities are of the other sex. Each of the alternate personalities is sometimes aware of the other ones (Putnam & Carlson, 1998; Steinberg, 1995). Each personality, when active, acknowledges that time has passed but cannot account for it. The switch from one personality to another is usually brought on by stress.

Cases of dissociative identity disorder began to receive a great deal of publicity during the 1950s, but symptoms consistent with this disorder appeared in a case reported in 1815 (Hacking, 1997). The disorder was not recognized as a diagnosis in the *DSM* until 1980, and it was considered very rare. During the 1980s, thousands of cases were identified, and controversy ensued (see *Point/Counterpoint* on page 548). Despite its common portrayal in fiction, dissociative identity disorder remains poorly understood and controversial.

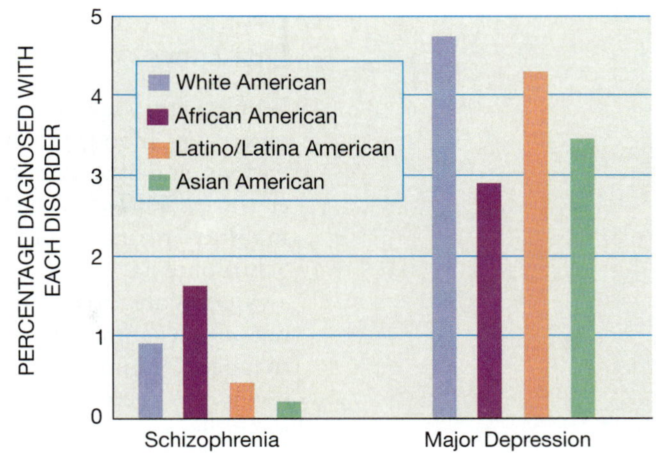

FIGURE 15.3

Cultural Factors in the Diagnosis of Schizophrenia and Mood Disorders

African Americans are more likely than Whites to be diagnosed as suffering from schizophrenia. In contrast, Whites and Latinos/Latinas are more likely than African Americans to be diagnosed as depressed. *(Based on data from Zhang & Snowden, 1999)*

Schizophrenia

Schizophrenia is considered the most devastating, puzzling, and frustrating of all mental disorders; people with this disorder lose touch with reality and are often unable to function in a world that makes no sense to them. The word *schizophrenia* comes from two Greek words that together mean "split mind," and the split refers to the fragmentation of thought processes. (A caution—schizophrenia is *not* split or multiple personality. People sometimes confuse the notion of a "split mind" with dissociative identity disorder, which is characterized by the existence of two or more distinct personalities within one person. We discussed this disorder in the previous section.) In 1911, when one of the most influential psychiatrists of the time, Eugen Bleuler, coined the term *schizophrenia,* he recognized that the symptoms include seriously disorganized thinking, perceptions, emotions, and actions.

A person with schizophrenia is said to have a schizophrenic disorder; this is because schizophrenia is really a variety of disorders. **Schizophrenic disorders** are a group of disorders characterized by a lack of reality testing and by deterioration of social and intellectual functioning. The symptoms must begin before age 45, and some disturbances in behavior must last at least 6 months, with symptoms persisting for at least 1 month. People diagnosed as having a schizophrenic disorder often show serious personality disintegration. They match the definition of **psychotic**—suffering from a gross impairment in reality testing that is wide-ranging and interferes with their ability to meet the ordinary demands of life.

Schizophrenia usually begins slowly, with more symptoms developing as time passes. It affects 1 out of every 100 people in the United States, which means that in any given year, about 2.2 million people in the United States have schizophrenia (National Institute of Mental Health, 2001). Women and men are equally likely to be affected. The disorder is associated with more lengthy hospital stays than most conditions are, so people with schizophrenia account for a larger percentage of people in mental hospitals than those with other mental disorders (Cano et al., 1996). The diagnosis is applied more frequently to those in lower socioeconomic groups, especially to African Americans, even when symptoms are similar (Cano et al., 1996; Nathan & Langenbucher, 1999). This finding suggests that diagnosis is biased, and a study of bias among clinicians making diagnoses confirms this view (Trierweiler et al., 2000). As Figure 15.3 shows, African Americans are more likely than Whites to be diagnosed as schizophrenic.

Schizophrenic [SKIT-soh-FREN-ick] disorders
A group of psychological disorders characterized by a lack of reality testing and by deterioration of social and intellectual functioning and personality, beginning before age 45 and lasting at least 6 months.

Psychotic [sye-KOT-ick]
Suffering from a gross impairment in reality testing that interferes with the ability to meet the ordinary demands of life.

Essential Characteristics of Schizophrenic Disorders

People with schizophrenic disorders display sudden significant changes in thought, perception, mood, and overall behavior. How they think about themselves, social situations, and other people—their social cognition—becomes seriously distorted (Penn et al., 1997). Those changes are often accompanied by distortions of reality and an inability to respond with appropriate thoughts, perceptions, or emotions. Schizophrenia is characterized by both positive and negative symptoms. *Positive symptoms* are those that people with schizophrenia experience and normal people do not—for example, delusions or hallucinations. *Negative symptoms* are behaviors that occur normally but are absent in people with schizophrenia—for example, an inability to experience pleasure. Not all of the symptoms of a schizophrenic disorder are necessarily present in any given person, although many are often seen together.

■ **THOUGHT DISORDERS.** One of the first signs of schizophrenia is difficulty maintaining logical thought and coherent conversation. People with schizophrenic disorders show disordered thinking and impaired memory (Hooley & Candela, 1999). They may also suffer from *delusions,* incorrect beliefs. For example, delusions of persecution cause the person to believe that someone or something is trying to harm him or her. Such delusions are often accompanied by delusions of grandeur, which cause the person to believe that he or she is particularly important—important enough to be the target of persecution. Some people with schizophrenia take on the role of an important character in history (for example, Jesus Christ or the Queen of England) and imagine that people are conspiring to harm them. Delusional thought is often apparent in schizophrenics' speech, in which sentence structure, words, and ideas become jumbled and disordered, creating a "word salad" of thoughts. Thus, a schizophrenic person might be heard to say, "Your highness, may I more of some engine to my future food, for his lowness." Memory is seriously disturbed, especially working memory (Schooler et al., 1997). Recall that working memory holds information for a brief period so that further processing can take place and allow a person to respond as a task demands. It is not surprising that when a system that is so important to thought and language fails, both thought and speech patterns become disorganized and often incoherent.

■ **PERCEPTUAL DISORDERS.** Another sign of schizophrenic disorders is the presence of *hallucinations*—compelling perceptual (visual, tactile, olfactory, or auditory) experiences that occur without any actual physical stimulus. Auditory hallucinations are the most common. Hallucinations have a biological basis; they are caused by abnormal brain responses (Shergill et al., 2000). The person reports hearing voices originating outside his or her head, which may comment on the person's behavior or direct the person to behave in certain ways. For example, convicted murderer David Berkowitz (known to the media as "Son of Sam") claimed that he was following the orders of his neighbor's dog, which told him to kill.

■ **EMOTIONAL DISORDERS.** One of the most striking characteristics of schizophrenia is the display of *inappropriate affect*—emotional responses that are not appropriate in the circumstances. A person with schizophrenia may become upset and cry when her favorite food falls on the floor, yet laugh hysterically at the death of a close friend or relative. Some people with schizophrenia display no emotion (either appropriate or inappropriate) and seem incapable of experiencing a normal range of feeling. Their affect is constricted, or *flat.* Their faces are blank and expressionless, even when they are presented with a deliberately provocative remark or situation. Other people with schizophrenia exhibit *ambivalent* affect. They go through a wide range of emotional behaviors in a brief period, seeming happy one moment and dejected the next.

Paranoid [PAIR-uh-noid] type of schizophrenia
Type of schizophrenia characterized by hallucinations and delusions of persecution or grandeur (or both), and sometimes irrational jealousy.

Catatonic [CAT-uh-TONN-ick] type of schizophrenia
Type of schizophrenia characterized either by displays of excited or violent motor activity or by stupor.

TABLE 15.5

Types and Symptoms of Schizophrenia

Type	Symptoms
Disorganized	Frequent incoherence; disorganized behavior; blunted, inappropriate, or silly affect
Paranoid	Delusions and hallucinations of persecution or grandeur (or both) and sometimes irrational jealousy
Catatonic	Stupor in which there is a negative attitude and marked decrease in reactivity to the environment, or an excited phase in which there is agitated motor activity not influenced by external stimuli and which may appear or disappear suddenly
Residual	History of at least one previous episode of schizophrenia with prominent psychotic symptoms but at present a clinical picture without any prominent psychotic symptoms; continuing evidence of the illness, such as inappropriate affect, illogical thinking, social withdrawal, or eccentric behavior
Undifferentiated	Prominent delusions, hallucinations, incoherence, or grossly disorganized behavior, which do not meet the criteria for any other types or which meet the criteria for more than one type

Types of Schizophrenia

People with schizophrenia display a variety of symptoms, but the *DSM* classifies schizophrenia into five types: paranoid, catatonic, disorganized, residual, and undifferentiated. Each of these has different symptoms and diagnostic criteria (see Table 15.5).

■ **THE PARANOID TYPE.** People with the **paranoid type of schizophrenia** may seem quite normal, but their thought processes are characterized by hallucinations and delusions of persecution or grandeur (or both). Their delusions are often organized around a theme, and the hallucinations (which are most often auditory) are typically related to this theme. For example, a paranoid schizophrenic may have the delusion that Martians have implanted a radio receiver in his brain and may hallucinate hearing messages telling him to stop those who are polluting the environment or Martians will destroy the earth. They may believe certain world events are particularly significant to them. If, for example, the president of the United States makes a speech deploring pollution, the paranoid schizophrenic person may believe that the president is referring specifically to his behavior and confirming the messages from the Martians to act against polluters.

■ *Russell Crowe portrays the mathematician John Nash in the movie* A Beautiful Mind. *Professor Nash has battled schizophrenia for many years.*

Paranoid schizophrenics may be alert, intelligent, and responsive. In addition, they may be secretive concerning their delusions and hallucinations, which makes them difficult to detect and diagnose. However, their delusions and hallucinations impair their ability to deal with reality, and their behavior is often unpredictable and sometimes hostile. The relatively low level of cognitive impairment leads people with the paranoid type of schizophrenia to have a better chance of recovery than do people with other types of schizophrenia.

■ **THE CATATONIC TYPE.** The **catatonic type of schizophrenia** is characterized either by displays of excited or violent motor activity or by stupor. That is, there are actually two subtypes of the catatonic type of schizophrenia—excited and withdrawn—both of which involve extreme overt behavior. *Excited* catatonic schizophrenics show excessive activity. They may talk and shout almost continuously and engage in seemingly uninhibited, agitated, and aggressive motor activity. These episodes usually appear and disappear suddenly. *Withdrawn* catatonic schizophrenics tend to appear stuporous—mute and basically unresponsive. Although they occasionally exhibit some signs of the excited type, they usually show a high degree of muscular rigidity. They are not immobile, but they speak, move, and respond very little, although they are usually aware of events around them. Withdrawn catatonic schizophrenics may use immobility and unresponsiveness to maintain control over their environment; their behavior relieves them of the responsibility of responding to external stimuli.

THE DISORGANIZED TYPE. The **disorganized type of schizophrenia** is characterized by severely disturbed thought processes, frequent incoherence, disorganized behavior, and inappropriate affect. People with this type of schizophrenia may exhibit bizarre emotions, with periods of giggling, crying, or irritability for no apparent reason. Their behavior can be silly or even obscene. They show a severe disintegration of normal personality, a total lack of reality testing, and often poor personal hygiene.

RESIDUAL AND UNDIFFERENTIATED TYPES. People who show symptoms attributable to schizophrenia but who remain in touch with reality are said to have the

BRAIN AND BEHAVIOR

"It's All In Your Brain"

People who show evidence of psychological distress are sometimes told to "snap out of it" because "it's all in your mind." The development of brain imaging technology and the study of brain function in people with various mental disorders have led to a revision of the old saying "It's all in your brain."

Brain imaging studies of people with obsessive–compulsive disorder have found some structural differences in the frontal lobes of the cerebral cortex, but larger functional differences (Szeszko et al., 1999). The areas most strongly affected are the frontal lobes, in the area just behind the eyes; the anterior cingulate, the front part of a structure just underneath the cerebral cortex; and the basal ganglia, a group of forebrain structures underneath the cerebral cortex. These structures appear in Figure 15.4. These areas show increased metabolism when people with this disorder are provoked into showing symptoms, for example, when someone with an obsession with germs is holding a dirty towel. Metabolism becomes more normal with treatment.

Many structures implicated in obsessive–compulsive disorder are believed to be involved in major depression (Videbech, 2000). Brain imaging studies show that parts of the prefrontal cortex, the anterior cingulate, and parts of the basal ganglia are involved in depression, but blood flow and metabolic activity levels are lower in depressed than nondepressed people (whereas activity is higher in people with obsessive–compulsive disorder). When depressed people are treated with drugs in psychotherapy, similar changes occur in their brains, which suggests that

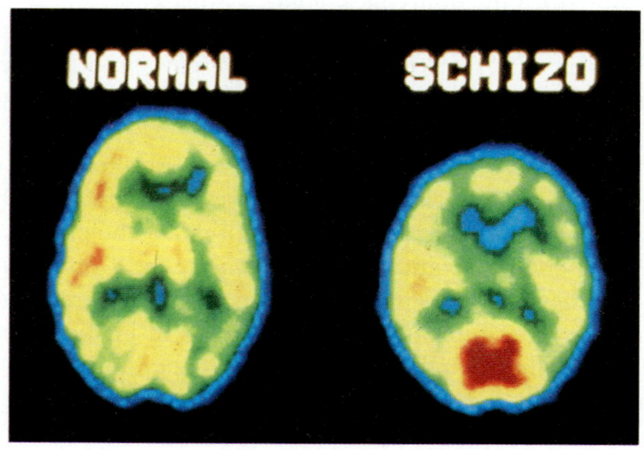

both types of treatments are similar at the brain level (Sackeim, 2001).

Brain imaging and autopsy studies show physical differences associated with schizophrenia. For example, the *ventricles* (hollow areas in the brain that are normally filled with fluid) are enlarged in some people with schizophrenia (Cornblatt et al., 1999; Raz & Raz, 1990). People with schizophrenia also have larger spaces (sulci) between the ridges (gyri) in their brains. Furthermore, some brain structures, notably the frontal lobes, show reduced blood flow and functioning in schizophrenics (Longworth, Honey, & Sharma, 1999). These differences were interpreted to indicate degeneration of the brain, but more recent views cast these differences as developmental differences in the brains of schizophrenics. That is, these brain structures exist before the diagnosis of schizophrenia (Cornblatt et al., 1999). The underlying cause of these structural differences in the brains of people with schizophrenia is not clear; genetics could be the cause, but prenatal exposure to viruses and birth trauma have also been implicated.

In some specific ways, the brains of people with mental disorders function differently than those of people without

residual type of schizophrenia. Such people show inappropriate affect, illogical thinking, eccentric behavior, or some combination of these symptoms. They have a history of at least one previous schizophrenic episode.

Sometimes it is difficult to determine which category a specific person best fits into (Gift et al., 1980). Some people exhibit all the essential features of schizophrenia—prominent delusions, hallucinations, incoherence, and grossly disorganized behavior—but do not fit neatly into the category of paranoid, catatonic, disorganized, or residual. Individuals with these characteristics are said to have the **undifferentiated type of schizophrenia.**

Causes of Schizophrenia

What causes people with schizophrenia to lose their grasp on reality with such devastating results? Are people born with schizophrenia, or do they develop it as a result of painful childhood experiences? Researchers take markedly different positions on these questions. Biologically oriented psychologists focus on genetics, brain structures, and chemicals in the brain; their basic argument is that schizophrenia is a brain disease. Psychodynamic and learning theorists argue that a person's environment and

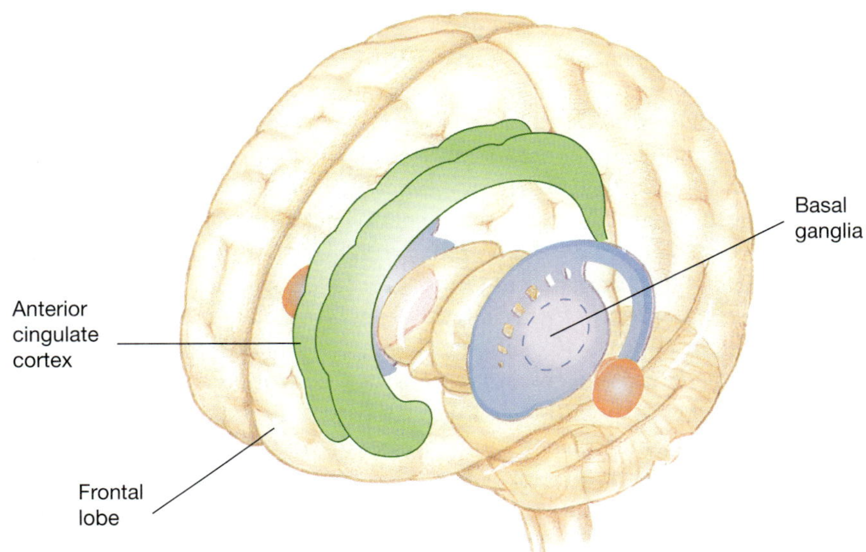

FIGURE 15.4

Brain Structures Involved in Anxiety and Mood Disorders

Several brain structures are involved in both anxiety and mood disorders, but their activation levels differ from these disorders. The anterior cingulate and basal ganglia are more active during anxiety reactions but less active during depression.

disorders. However, these findings do not indicate that mental disorders are all "in your brain." That is, these differences in brain function are not necessarily the underlying basis of these disorders. To understand mental disorders, researchers must learn how genetic factors affect brain structure and function as well as how stressors, personal learning history, and culture interact with biological factors to produce problems. These mental disorders involve both nurture and nature.

Disorganized type of schizophrenia
Type of schizophrenia characterized by severely disturbed thought processes, frequent incoherence, disorganized behavior, and inappropriate affect.

Residual type of schizophrenia
A schizophrenic disorder in which the person exhibits inappropriate affect, illogical thinking, and/or eccentric behavior but seems generally in touch with reality.

Undifferentiated type of schizophrenia
A schizophrenic disorder that is characterized by a mixture of symptoms and does not meet the diagnostic criteria of any one type.

early experiences cause schizophrenia. The arguments for each approach are compelling, but most theorists adopt a *diathesis–stress model*, asserting that schizophrenia is the result of a combination of genetic predisposition or biological vulnerability, which interacts with life situations to produce schizophrenia. Let's look at the evidence.

■ **BIOLOGICAL FACTORS.** Substantial evidence suggests that biological factors play some role in schizophrenia, producing a predisposition to develop the disorder. People born with that predisposition have a greater probability of developing schizophrenia than do other people, given similar circumstances.

When one parent has schizophrenia, the probability that an offspring will develop the disorder is between 3% and 14%. If both parents have schizophrenia, their children have about a 35% probability of developing this disorder. It is now generally accepted that schizophrenia runs in families; the children and siblings of people with schizophrenia are more likely to exhibit maladjustment and schizophrenic symptoms than are other people (Kety et al., 1994). Researchers have been looking for a gene that might carry specific traits associated with schizophrenia, but no single gene seems likely to be the cause of schizophrenia (Zuckerman, 1999).

If schizophrenia were totally genetic, the likelihood would be 100% that identical (monozygotic) twins, who have identical genes, would both manifest the disorder if one did. This kind of estimate of the degree to which a condition or trait is shared by two or more individuals or groups is referred to as a **concordance rate.** But studies of schizophrenia in identical twins show concordance rates that range from 15% to 86%, averaging around 48% (Gottesman, 1991). This figure suggests that factors other than genetics are involved. In one important study, analysis of brain structures showed subtle but important brain abnormalities in a schizophrenic individual whose identical twin did not show the abnormality. Such studies support the hypothesis that nongenetic factors must exert an important influence related to schizophrenia and are critical in its development (DiLalla & Gottesman, 1995). Nevertheless, most researchers agree that genetic background is a fundamental factor in the disorder. The concordance rate for schizophrenia in identical twins is 48%, compared to 17% for fraternal twins. Moreover, identical twins reared apart from their natural parents and from each other show a higher concordance rate than do fraternal twins or controls (Cornblatt, Green, & Walker, 1999).

The development of antischizophrenic drugs contributed to a better understanding of the biochemistry of the disorder. Researchers today readily acknowledge that neurotransmitters and their actions are involved in schizophrenia. An early view of neurotransmitter involvement was the *dopamine theory of schizophrenia*. This theory asserts that too much of the neurotransmitter dopamine or too much activity at dopamine receptors causes schizophrenia. Neuroleptic drugs, the drugs that control symptoms of schizophrenia, block dopamine sites and decrease the disturbed thought processes and hallucinations characteristic of schizophrenia; drugs that stimulate the dopamine system (such as amphetamines) aggravate existing schizophrenic disorders. Dopamine receptors are considered to be major sites of biochemical disturbances in the brain (Fang, 1996; Masotto & Racagni, 1995). Further research revealed that there are subtypes of dopamine receptors and neuroleptic drugs that bind to the specific receptors that most likely inhibit schizophrenic symptoms, especially positive symptoms (O'Connor, 1998). Neuroleptic drugs also affect other neurotransmitters, and the neurotransmitters glutamate and GABA have both been implicated in schizophrenia (Cornblatt et al., 1999).

Biochemistry is not the whole story—if it were, drugs would fully control symptoms of schizophrenia. Unfortunately, this is not the case, and researchers have also looked for differences in brain structures between people with and without schizophrenia (see *Brain and Behavior* on pages 552–553).

Concordance rate
The degree to which a condition or trait is shared by two or more individuals or groups.

In sum, researchers now assert that genetic, biochemical factors and brain abnormalities are all associated with schizophrenia. While many stress factors (which

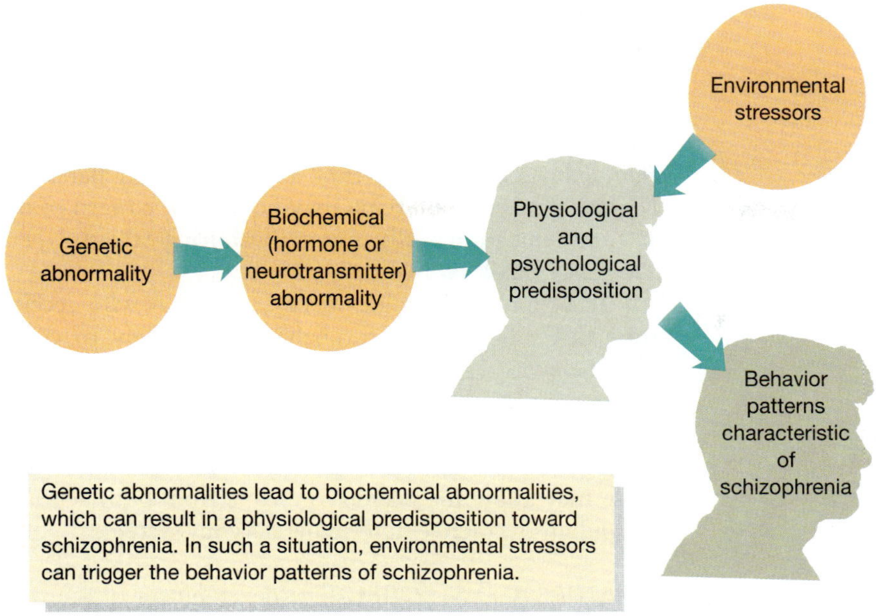

FIGURE 15.5

The Vulnerability–Stress View of Schizophrenia

According to the vulnerability–stress view of schizophrenia, the environment triggers behaviors in people who are predisposed to schizophrenia.

are the focus of environmental researchers) may contribute to schizophrenia, a biological component seems to be essential.

■ **ENVIRONMENTAL FACTORS.** Some psychologists believe that, in addition to genetic factors, environmental interactions determine the onset and development of schizophrenia (see Figure 15.5). Behavioral explanations of schizophrenia are based on traditional learning principles (explored in Chapter 7). The behavioral approach argues that faulty reinforcement and extinction procedures, as well as social learning processes, can account for schizophrenia. Imagine a child brought up in a family where the parents constantly argue, where the father or the mother is alcoholic, and where neither parent shows much affection for the other parent or for anyone else. Lidz (1973) argues that children who grow up in homes where they receive no reinforcement for showing interest in events, people, and objects in the outside world may become withdrawn and begin to exhibit schizophrenic behavior. Growing up in such an emotionally fragmented environment may predispose individuals to emotional disorders and even schizophrenia (Miklowitz, 1994; Walker et al., 1983).

Even in families in which there is no alcoholism or much marital conflict, parents sometimes confuse their children or have difficulty communicating effectively. Research indicates that the emotional tone in families affects the developmental course and severity of a member's schizophrenia. When families have an interaction style characterized by hostility, criticism, emotional overinvolvement, and a lack of boundaries (overintrusiveness), their level of *expressed emotions* is said to be high. People with schizophrenia who return to families in which there are high levels of expressed emotion have a higher relapse rate than that those from families with low levels of expressed emotion (Widiger & Sankis, 2000). In addition, parents can place their children in a situation that offers inconsistent messages, a **double bind.** Initially described by Bateson as an explanation for the causes of schizophrenia (Bateson et al., 1956), double bind usually occurs between individuals with a strong emotional attachment, such as a child and a parent (Mishler & Waxler, 1968). For example, a parent may present a gift and teasingly say, "No, you may not have this," while smiling and giving other nonverbal assurances that the individual may have the gift. Most children understand that the parent is teasing. However, not all children will understand, and not all situations are so clearly cued. And research

Double bind
A situation in which an individual is given two different and inconsistent messages.

Be an *Active* learner

REVIEW

- What symptoms allow a diagnosis of dissociative identity disorder rather than dissociative amnesia? pp. 547–549
- What are the thought, perceptual, and emotional disorders associated with schizophrenia? p. 550
- What are the different types of schizophrenia? p. 551
- What biological factors contribute to vulnerability for schizophrenia? What environmental factors contribute? pp. 554–555

THINK CRITICALLY

- People tend to confuse dissociative personality disorder (multiple personality) with schizophrenia, probably because schizophrenia is often described as "split personality." In what sense is the personality "split" in schizophrenia?
- How likely would it be for a homeless person to be diagnosed as schizophrenic? Explain.

APPLY PSYCHOLOGY

- Watch an episode of The X-Files, and analyze character Fox Mulder for symptoms of the paranoid type of schizophrenia.

shows that people with schizophrenia are less accurate at interpreting emotional communications than are control participants (Fagan & Silverthorn, 1998). Games and ineffective communication of this kind, if frequent, may shape an environment of confusion conducive to the development and maintenance of schizophrenia. However, what Bateson saw as a cause of schizophrenia may be more a pattern of a lack of communication skills, especially during stressful periods (Docherty, Hall, & Gordinier, 1998).

According to learning theory, a person who receives a great deal of attention for behaviors is likely to continue those behaviors, even bizarre ones. People who fail to develop effective social skills are more at risk for bizarre behaviors (Mueser et al., 1990). Other learning theories suggest that bizarre behavior and thoughts are themselves reinforcing because they allow the person to escape from both acute anxiety and an overactive autonomic nervous system.

■ **NATURE AND NURTURE.** The development of schizophrenia does not occur through any simple mechanism—both biology and environment are involved. Some people, because of family environment, genetic history, or brain chemistry, are more vulnerable than others. As with mood disorders, *vulnerability* is a person's diminished ability to deal with demanding life events. The more vulnerable a person is, the more likely the person will experience a schizophrenic episode as a reaction to difficult events.

To summarize, although the exact causes of schizophrenia are still unknown, the development of this disorder is likely to be due to a set of factors. These factors include a genetic component. This component may underlie the neurochemical functions associated with schizophrenia. These biological vulnerabilities do not produce schizophrenia by themselves; environmental events contribute to the development of the disorder. Early childhood relationships filled with mixed emotional messages, poor communication, and even abuse may leave biologically vulnerable children at high risk for schizophrenia.

Personality Disorders

Disorders such as phobias, obsessive–compulsive disorder, depression, dissociative personality disorder, and schizophrenia are among the disorders classified on Axis I of the *DSM* classification system. The disorders on Axis II are **personality disorders.** These disorders apply to people who exhibit inflexible and long-standing maladaptive behaviors that typically cause stress and social or occupational difficulties. Often these disorders begin in childhood or adolescence and persist throughout adulthood. People with personality disorders are easy to spot but difficult to treat. Although they were never diagnosed, Eric Harris and Dylan Klebold, the two young men who murdered classmates at Columbine High School, have been analyzed as having a personality disorder (Black, 1999).

Categorizations of personality disorders are more controversial than those of the disorders on Axis I of *DSM*, both in terms of their reliability and their validity. The line separating normal from abnormal behavior, as well as the characteristics of each class of disorder, sometimes can be blurry, which may lead to problems in reliably placing an individual in one category (Nathan & Langenbucher, 1999).

Consistent with this view, a person with a personality disorder is often at high risk for other disorders; thus it is not uncommon for an individual to exhibit symptoms of two disorders simultaneously.

People with personality disorders are divided into three broad classes: (1) those whose behavior appears odd or eccentric, (2) those whose behavior is dramatic, emotional, and erratic, and (3) those who are fearful or anxious. We'll consider six specific personality disorders: paranoid, borderline, histrionic, narcissistic, antisocial, and dependent.

Personality disorders
Psychological disorders characterized by inflexible and longstanding maladaptive behaviors that typically cause stress and/or social or occupational problems.

Antisocial personality disorder
Personality disorder characterized by egocentricity, behavior that is irresponsible and that violates the rights of other people, a lack of guilt feelings, an inability to understand other people, and a lack of fear of punishment.

People with *paranoid personality disorder* experience odd or eccentric behavior with unwarranted feelings of persecution; they mistrust almost everyone. They are hypersensitive to criticism and have a restricted range of emotional responses. They have strong fears of being exploited and of losing control and independence. Sometimes they appear cold, humorless, and even scheming. As you might expect, people with paranoid personality disorder are suspicious and seldom able to form close, intimate relationships with others.

Fitting into the second behavior classification, individuals with *borderline personality disorder* have trouble with relationships; they show a pattern of instability in interpersonal relationships, self-image, and affect. In addition, they are often impulsive. They are sometimes suicidal; they report feelings of emptiness and are sometimes inappropriately angry. Easily bored and distracted, such individuals fear abandonment. Individuals with borderline personality disorder often sabotage or undermine themselves just before a goal is to be reached—for example, by dropping out of school just before graduation.

Fitting into the second broad class, because of their dramatic, emotional, and erratic behaviors, are those people with *histrionic personality disorder*. Individuals with this disorder seek attention by exaggerating situations in their lives. They have stormy personal relationships, are excessively emotional, and demand constant reassurance and praise.

Closely related to histrionic personality disorder, and also classified in the second class, is *narcissistic personality disorder*. People with this disorder have an extremely exaggerated sense of self-importance, expect favors, and need constant admiration and attention. They show little concern for others, and they react to criticism with rage, shame, or humiliation.

Perhaps the most widely recognized personality disorder in the second class is antisocial personality disorder. People with **antisocial personality disorder** are self-centered and irresponsible, violate the rights of other people (through lying, theft, cheating, or other violations of social rules), lack guilt feelings, are unable to understand other people, and do not fear punishment. Individuals with this disorder may be superficially charming, but their behavior is destructive and often reckless.

As many as 3% of all individuals may be candidates for diagnosis with antisocial personality disorder. Men are much more likely than women to receive this diagnosis, even when they both show similar symptoms (Nathan & Langenbucher, 1999). Researchers are exploring the possibility of a biological component in antisocial personality disorder, and some evidence for brain differences and genetic influence has appeared. A brain imaging study showed that people with antisocial personality disorder have less brain tissue in their frontal lobes (Raine et al., 2000). This structure is involved in planning and impulse control, abilities that present problems for people with antisocial personality disorder. This study also confirmed a difference in nervous system response;

Be an *Active* learner

REVIEW

- Identify the distinguishing characteristics of a person diagnosed with an antisocial personality disorder. p. 557

THINK CRITICALLY

- Some critics have argued that personality disorders seem like exaggerations of gender and ethnic stereotypes. Think about these six personality disorders according to both kinds of stereotypes. Do you think that these stereotypes influence clinicians who make these diagnoses?

APPLY PSYCHOLOGY

- You probably know someone who, if diagnosed, would meet the criteria for antisocial personality disorder. Think of this person, and decide what behaviors lead you to this diagnosis. What harm has this person done to others? How has this person avoided punishment?

people with antisocial personality disorder do not show normal autonomic nervous system reactions to fear and surprise. As a result of experiencing abnormal reactions to these emotions, people with antisocial personality disorder do not learn to associate fear or anxiety with unacceptable behavior (Patrick, 1994). Thus their biological differences interact with the environment to produce these symptoms of the disorder.

Interaction between biology and environment may also occur through parents' interactions with children. Parental neglect and abuse are important risks for antisocial personality disorder, and one study suggests that children with an antisocial parent interacted with their adoptive parents in more negative ways than children with no genetic risk (Ge et al., 1996). The biological roots of antisocial personality disorder clearly interact with family and social circumstances to prompt the development of antisocial personality disorder.

Fitting into the third behavioral classification are those acting fearful or anxious—individuals with *dependent personality disorder*. Such people are submissive and clinging; they let others make all the important decisions in their lives. They try to appear pleasant and agreeable at all times. They act meek, humble, and affectionate in order to keep their protectors. Battered wives often receive diagnoses of dependent personality disorder, which may result from the mistreatment they receive and their strategy for coping (or possibly because of stereotyping and diagnostic bias). Overprotective, authoritarian parenting seems to be a major initiating cause of dependency (Bornstein, 1992).

Violence and Mental Disorders

The media have linked mental disorders and violence. Movies show mentally disturbed individuals who "snap" and go on homicidal rampages. Television presents stories of seemingly ordinary people who are, in reality, crazed killers. News stories about Andrea Yates, the depressed woman who drowned her five children, are examples of the extensive, sensationalized coverage that the media give to people with mental disorders who have committed crimes (Smellie, 1999). These images are powerful in shaping opinions about people with mental disorders and add to the stigma of having such a problem (Link, Phelan, et al., 1999). Is there any truth to the association of mental disorders and violence? Was Andrea Yates an unusual case, or are people with mental disorders more likely than others to be violent?

Andrea Yates was a very unusual case. Most people who have mental disorders are not violent, and most people who commit violence do not have a mental disorder. However, some mental disorders are associated with a greater likelihood of committing violent acts.

Diagnoses Associated with Violence

Several diagnoses are associated with increased risk for violence. In general, the more serious disorders carry a greater risk, and people who have delusions may be at specific risk (Nathan & Langenbucher, 1999). For example, in the manic phase of bipolar disorder, people can be impatient and easily angered. This anger may become violence. People who question the plans and capabilities of a person experiencing a manic episode may be the target for a violent reaction.

People with schizophrenia are also risks for violence, especially those with the paranoid type. An extreme example of violence among schizophrenics is Theodore Kaczynski, the serial killer called the Unabomber, who was diagnosed as paranoid schizophrenic. His paranoia focused on technology, and his violence was directed toward those who were involved with technology. Such delusions of persecution make people with paranoid schizophrenia suspicious, and they feel the need to protect themselves against what they see as real danger (Link, Monahan, et al., 1999). When paranoid schizophrenics react to these "dangers," their actions are difficult for others to understand and anticipate because the danger is a delusion. Nevertheless, the actions that they take for protection may be harmful, even deadly, to someone who has accidentally said or done the wrong thing. Research on people discharged from mental institutions indicates that the threat of violence is elevated, but not as strongly related to the experience of threatening delusions as previously believed (Appelbaum, Robbins, & Monahan, 2000).

Most schizophrenics who are violent are not killers, but young adults with schizophrenia account for a disproportionate amount of community violence (Arseneault et al., 2000). However, young adults with alcohol- or drug-dependency problems are more likely than schizophrenics to be involved in violent crimes. Substance abuse alone is a risk for violence, but the combination of alcohol or drug use with other mental disorders additionally elevates risks for violence (Nathan & Langenbucher, 1999).

Individuals with antisocial personality disorder may be violent; in addition, they do a great deal of damage by nonviolent criminal and amoral behavior (Zuckerman, 1999). Their disregard for the welfare of others and their resistance to change make people with antisocial personality disorder risks to others. When these individuals are violent, they feel no compassion or remorse. Extreme examples of antisocial personality disorder are Dylan Klebold and Eric Harris, who shot classmates at Columbine High School in April 1999, and Kip Kinkel, who shot his parents and then his classmates in Springfield, Oregon, in May 1998. These young men showed little emotion as they shot classmates, and Kinkel killed both parents and sat in the room with his mother's body as he casually conversed on the telephone with friends.

Despite the possibility that killers such as Kinkel, Klebold, and Harris meet the criteria for antisocial personality disorder, they would not meet the legal definition of insanity. Indeed, most people with mental disorders who commit violence do not meet that definition. The concept of insanity is not a psychological one; its definition is legal. *Insanity* refers to a condition that excuses people from responsibility and protects them from punishment. From the legal point of view, a person cannot be held responsible for a crime if, at the time of the crime, the person lacked the capacity to distinguish right from wrong or to obey the law.

For example, a jury declared John W. Hinckley Jr., the man who attempted to assassinate former president Ronald Reagan, "not guilty by reason of insanity," and he was acquitted of attempted murder charges. During the public outcry that followed, states sought to prohibit the insanity plea because people perceived defendants as "getting away with murder." At least half the states changed their insanity pleas, 12 adopted the new plea "guilty but mentally ill," and 3 chose to eliminate the insanity plea altogether.

Most people overestimate how often such pleas are made. The truth is that only about 1% of all felony defendants use an insanity defense—and the plea is successful only about one-quarter of the time (Lymburner & Roesch, 1999). Despite media portrayals of the insanity defense as a mainstay of the legal system that frees guilty people, people who "get away with murder" by using the insanity plea are more common in fiction than in courtrooms. Even when the insanity plea is successful, the person rarely walks out of the courtroom a free person; John Hinckley is currently confined to a mental hospital.

People with mental disorders are more likely to be a danger to themselves than to others. That is, violence among people with mental disorders is more likely to be suicide or a suicide attempt than assault or homicide. Depressed people feel hopeless, and their feelings of endless misery lead to thoughts of and attempts at suicide. Each

student voices

Courtney O'Neil

Lynn University

In fall 1999, my mother committed suicide. I fell apart and was left to pick up the pieces. I enrolled in my first psychology class the following year. It gave me the foundation to understand so much more about myself, the people around me, and most importantly, my mother.

TABLE 15.6

Myths and Facts about Suicide

Myth	Core Components
1. Suicide happens without warning.	1. Suicidal individuals give many clues; 80% have to some degree discussed with others their intent to commit suicide.
2. Once people become suicidal, they remain so.	2. Suicidal persons remain so for limited periods—thus the value of restraint.
3. Suicide occurs almost exclusively among affluent or very poor individuals.	3. Suicide tends to occur in the same proportion at all economic levels of society.
4. Virtually all suicidal individuals are mentally ill.	4. This is not so, although most are depressed to some degree.
5. Suicidal tendencies are inherited or run in families.	5. There is no evidence for a direct genetic factor.
6. Suicide does not occur in primitive cultures.	6. Suicide occurs in almost all societies and cultures.
7. In Japan, ritual suicide is common.	7. In modern Japan, ritual suicide is rare; the most common method is barbiturate overdose.
8. Writers and artists have the highest suicide rates because they are "a bit crazy to begin with."	8. Physicians and police officers have the highest suicide rates; they have access to the most lethal means, and their work involves a high level of frustration.
9. Once a person starts to come out of a depression, the risk of suicide dissipates.	9. The risk of suicide is highest in the initial phase of an upswing from the depth of depression.
10. People who attempt suicide fully intend to die.	10. People who attempt suicide have diverse motives.

Meyer & Salmon, 1988

day, more than 80 people in the United States commit suicide, which means that over 30,000 people each year take their own lives (National Institute of Mental Health, 2001). However, many more people attempt than commit suicide. *Attempters* try to commit suicide but are unsuccessful. They tend to be young, impulsive, more often women than men, and more likely to make nonfatal attempts such as making only shallow cuts on the wrists. *Completers* succeed in taking their lives. They tend to be White, male, and older, and they use highly lethal techniques of self-destruction, such as guns. Alcohol or drug abuse increases the risk for violence associated with mental disorders, and this increase applies to suicide. Although estimates vary with age and gender, there are an estimated 10–25 attempted suicides for every completion. Table 15.6 presents some of the many myths about suicide and counters them with facts.

Although only 15% of depressed people are suicidal, most people who commit suicide are depressed (Gustafsson & Jacobsson, 2000). Adolescent suicide has received a great deal of attention because it is the second leading cause of death for this age group. Negative moods are common among this age group. For college students, feelings of depression are a common experience, and thoughts of suicide are not unusual; 53% of college students report that they have experienced depression, and 9% say they have considered suicide during their college years (Furr et al., 2001). However, the group at the greatest risk for suicide is White men over age 85 (National Institute of Mental Health, 2001). Preventing suicide has become a national priority involving all age groups and an increased attention to depression, which is the underlying cause of most suicides and attempts (see *Psychology in Action*).

psychology *in action*

Preventing Suicide

Most individuals who attempt suicide really want to live. However, their sense of hopelessness about the future tells them that death is the only way out. Feelings of despair underlie suicide attempts, but alcoholism and alcohol use, drug abuse, emotional isolation, and the ready availability of guns increase the risk (Maris & Silverman, 1995). In April 2001, U.S. Surgeon General Dr. David Satcher introduced the National Strategy for Suicide Prevention. This initiative includes 11 goals aimed at decreasing suicide through increases in research and in the availability of suicide prevention services and decreases in access to means of committing suicide and in the stigma attached to seeking mental health care (U.S. Department of Health and Human Services, 2001b).

People who attempt or complete suicide typically give some warnings before their attempts. Knowing these signs permits family and friends to understand the depth of pain the person is experiencing and allows them to intervene. People who have made a suicide attempt in the past are at especially high risk, as are lesbian and gay adolescents (Lock & Steiner, 1999). The following warning signs are signals of danger for anyone, especially when appearing in combination:

- Depression
- Verbal threats such as "You'd be better off without me" or "Maybe I won't be around anymore . . ."
- Expressions of hopelessness, helplessness, or a combination of the two
- Daring and risk-taking behavior that is not typical of the person
- Personality changes such as withdrawal, aggression, or moodiness
- Giving away prized possessions
- Lack of interest in the future

Direct threats are the most serious signal, and *when a person makes a suicide threat, always take that threat seriously*. If you know someone you think may be considering suicide, here are some steps you can take:

- Remember that the most important thing is to listen. Say that you understand the person's feelings but do not agree with the suicide plans.
- Talk with the person about your concerns, and show that you care and want to help.
- Do not act shocked or judge the person.
- Ask the person direct questions. The more detailed their plan, the greater the immediate risk.
- Do not leave the person alone.
- Do not agree to secrecy. Resist the person's attempts to force you to remain quiet, and tell relatives, friends, or a counselor.
- Get professional help—even if the person resists. One source is 800-SUICIDE, but assist the person in finding a psychologist, psychiatrist, or counselor who can help.

Violence as a Risk for Developing Mental Disorders

Only a few mental disorders increase the likelihood that a person will be violent, but being the target of violence increases the risk for many disorders. The experience of violence that has the greatest potential for harm is violence toward children. **Child abuse** is the physical, emotional, or sexual mistreatment of a child. This problem is a large one—over 820,000 children in the United States are the victims of abuse or neglect each year (U.S. Department of Health and Human Services, 2001a). Girls are more often targets than are boys, especially of sexual abuse (Molnar, Buka, & Kessler, 2001). Children who are the victims of sexual abuse are at elevated risk for posttraumatic stress disorder (PTSD; see Chapter 14), depression, suicide, and sexual problems

- *Often perpetrators of child abuse appear to be quite normal socially; however, their behavior can produce both short-term and long-term problems for the abused children.*

Child abuse
Physical, emotional, or sexual mistreatment of a child.

during adulthood as well as for growing up to be abusers themselves (Oddone-Paolucci, Genuis, & Violato, 2001). Childhood victims of abuse and neglect are at greater risk of developing mood disorders and antisocial personality disorder than are children who are not abused (Horwitz et al., 2001). Abused girls show an increased risk for alcohol abuse problems as adults, but abused boys do not.

Child abusers usually do not have any diagnosable mental disorder; only about 5% of child abusers exhibit symptoms of very disturbed behavior. Most abusive parents seem quite normal by typical social standards, and sometimes they are prominent members of their communities. Most psychologists and social workers consider child abuse an interactive process involving incompetent parenting, environmental stress, and poor child management techniques. Although their behavior does not necessarily signal mental disorders for the abusers, it can produce both short-term and long-term problems for the abused children.

Other forms of violence within families also create mental health problems, such as violence between intimate partners (husbands and wives or boyfriends and girlfriends). *Intimate partner violence* is also known as spouse abuse and domestic violence. This type of violence is a common occurrence throughout the world (Heise, Ellsberg, & Gottemoeller, 1999). Both men and women do violence to each other, but women are more likely than men to be harmed—about one-third of all women in the world have been physically abused in some way. Partner violence is more likely to occur in couples and in societies in which gender roles are rigid and inflexible and when women have little power and few resources. Partner violence poses a substantial risk for PTSD and depression. Indeed, some researchers believe that women's higher rate of depression is largely due to their victimization by childhood sexual abuse, partner violence, and rape (Golding, 1999).

These negative effects are not limited to violence between spouses; a survey of teenage girls (Silverman et al., 2001) found that 20% reported some experience of violence from a boyfriend. Those girls were at increased risk for a variety of problems, including suicide, eating disorders, and substance abuse. Those who perpetrate partner violence may have some mental disorder, but most do not; they are exerting rational and often effective attempts to control their partners.

Rape is also a form of violence that women experience more often than men. **Rape** is forcible sexual assault on an unwilling partner. The legal definition of rape varies from state to state, but it is generally being broadened to include any sexual assault (usually intercourse) that occurs without freely given consent. People tend to think of rape as a violent attack by a stranger, but most cases of rape involve individuals who are acquainted. That is, *date rape* or *acquaintance rape* is more common than stranger rape. Studies of high school girls (Silverman et al., 2001), college women (Koss, Gidycz, & Wisniewski, 1987), and women from the general U.S. population (Tjaden & Thoennes, 2000) indicate that around 20% have been the targets of some type of sexual violence; around 15% have been raped. In some ways, knowing the person who commits rape is an additional trauma—the person is known and trusted. A survey of women in the United States indicated that only 17% were raped by strangers. For 62%, an intimate partner (husband, boyfriend, date) was the perpetrator; for another 21%, an acquaintance was the rapist. Rape perpetrated by intimate partners and acquaintances is less likely to be reported and less likely to be prosecuted than stranger rape (Koss, 2000). Thus, rape victims may feel victimized by the experience of rape and again by the failure of the justice system. Men are victims of sexual violence less often than women; around 3% of men are the victims of attempted or completed rape (Tjaden & Thoennes, 2000). When men are the victims of sexual violence, their experience is similar: they are likely to be raped by an intimate, they are not likely to report the incident, and they are likely to feel additionally victimized by their experience with the justice system.

Rape
Forcible sexual assault on an unwilling partner.

The most common effect of rape on victims' mental health is posttraumatic stress disorder. Indeed, the *DSM* mentions rape as one of the events that may cause

PTSD. In addition, rape victims are at increased risk for anxiety disorders, depression, suicide, and substance abuse disorders (Boudreaux et al., 1998).

Similar to other perpetrators, rapists are not likely to have a disorder that fits into any diagnostic category in the *DSM*. Men (and women) with antisocial personality disorder are more likely than other men to do harm to others, including sexual violence, but the majority of rapists does not fit into this classification. Ten percent of men admit that they have committed acquaintance rape, and 24% of men admit that they have used force or other tactics that would meet the criteria for rape (Rubenzahl & Corcoran, 1998); these percentages are much higher than the estimates for antisocial personality disorder, indicating that most men who commit acquaintance rape do not have this disorder.

Circumstances, social setting, and attitudes can be factors in rape. For example, substance use and abuse increase the risk. Men who admit to perpetrating acquaintance rape are more likely than sexually active, nonaggressive men to use drugs or alcohol (Ouimette, 1997). Alcohol use also makes women more vulnerable to acquaintance rape (Ullman, Karabatsos, & Koss, 1999). Thus, substance use is a risk for rape for both victim and perpetrator. Men who commit acquaintance rape are also more likely than other men to find sexual aggression attractive, to have attitudes that support violence, to have many sexual partners, and to see relationships with women as a contest (Malamuth, 1996). Their attitudes differ from other men in ways that allow them to commit sexual violence, but most are not mentally ill.

Be an *Active* learner

REVIEW

- What diagnoses are associated with an increased risk for violence? pp. 558–559
- How does the legal definition of insanity differ from the psychological definition of mental disorders? p. 559
- What diagnoses are more likely for people who are the victims of violence? pp. 561–562

THINK CRITICALLY

- Analyze the role of the media in the connection between mental illness and violence. How could the media become a positive factor in decreasing the stigma associated with mental disorders?
- Describe the key aspects of a preventive program to help decrease child abuse.

APPLY PSYCHOLOGY

- Make a plan for the action you would take if a friend or relative showed the warning signs of suicide. Think about specific things you would say, and find sources for professional help on your campus and in your community.
- Most colleges have a rape prevention program, but what steps can colleges take to make these programs more effective?

Summary and Review

What Is Abnormal Behavior?

Define abnormal behavior, and describe the major perspectives that try to explain it.

- *Abnormal behavior* is behavior that is not typical but is socially unacceptable, distressing, maladaptive, and/or the result of distorted cognitions, and *abnormal psychology* is the field of psychology concerned with the assessment, treatment, and prevention of maladaptive behavior. pp. 526–527
- Different *models* provide alternatives for understanding abnormal behavior. The medical–biological model focuses on the biological and physiological conditions that initiate abnormal behaviors. The psychodynamic model focuses on unresolved conflicts and forces of which a person may be unaware. The humanistic model assumes that people naturally move toward health, so maladaptive behavior is the result of some force that prevents this movement. The behavioral model states that abnormal behavior is caused by faulty or ineffective learning. The cognitive model looks at people's ideas and thoughts. The sociocultural model examines abnormalities within the context of culture, the family, the community, and society. The evolutionary model sees abnormal behavior as potentially adaptive in evolutionary history but not in modern society. The biopsychosocial model holds that biological, personal, and social forces all influence the expression of abnormal behavior. pp. 528–530

What are the goals of the *DSM*, and what are its advantages and disadvantages?

- The *DSM–IV–TR* is the latest edition of the *Diagnostic and Statistical Manual of Mental Disorders*, the manual that mental health practitioners use to diagnose and classify mental disorders. It describes behavior in terms of its characteristics and its *prevalence* and uses what is called a multiaxial system. Its goals are to improve the reliability of diagnoses and to provide a standardized system for diagnosis. Some psychologists applaud the *DSM* for its recognition of social and environmental influences on behavior; others take issue with how it creates diagnoses based on political rather than research or theoretical criteria. pp. 531–534

KEY TERMS

abnormal behavior, p. 526; model, p. 528; abnormal psychology, p. 528; prevalence, p. 530; case study, p. 533

Anxiety Disorders

What are the chief characteristics of anxiety disorders?

■ *Anxiety* is a generalized feeling of fear and apprehension, which is often accompanied by increased physiological arousal and may or may not be related to a specific event or object. p. 535

■ *Generalized anxiety disorder* is characterized by persistent anxiety of at least 6 months' duration. It can include increased physiological arousal, excessive muscle tension, and vigilance. Irrational fear and avoidance of certain objects or situations characterize a *phobic dis–order,* including *agoraphobia* (with and without *panic attack*), *social phobia,* and *specific phobia.* pp. 536–537

■ Individuals with *obsessive–compulsive disorder* have persistent and uncontrollable thoughts and irrational beliefs, which cause them to perform compulsive rituals that interfere with normal daily functioning. The focus of these behaviors is often on maintaining order and control. pp. 538–539

KEY TERMS

anxiety, p. 535; generalized anxiety disorder, p. 536; phobic disorders, p. 536; agoraphobia, p. 537; panic attacks, p. 537; social phobia, p. 537; specific phobia, p. 537; obsessive–compulsive disorder, p. 538

Mood Disorders

What are the characteristics of the major mood disorders, and what theories account for these disorders?

■ People diagnosed with *depressive disorders* such as *major depressive disorder* have a gloomy outlook on life, slow thought processes, loss of appetite, sleep problems, *delusions* such as an exaggerated view of current problems, loss of energy, and a tendency to blame themselves. pp. 540–541

■ The monoamine theory of depression suggests that major depression results from deficient monoamines or inefficient monoamine receptors. This theory is based on the finding that antidepressant drugs work by blocking reuptake of monoamines, thus keeping people from being depressed. Learning theorists argue that reinforcement patterns and social interactions determine the course and nature of depression. Cognitive theorists hypothesize that depressed people have thoughts that perpetuate their negative mood. *Learned helplessness* produces feelings consistent with the experience of depression. pp. 543–545

■ *Vulnerability* is a person's diminished ability to deal with demanding life events. The more vulnerable a person is, the fewer environmental stressors are needed to initiate a depressive episode. pp. 545–546

■ *Bipolar disorder* gets its name from the fact that people with this disorder show behavior that vacillates between two extremes: mania and depression. p. 546

KEY TERMS

depressive disorders, p. 540; major depressive disorder, p. 540; delusions, p. 541; learned helplessness, p. 545; vulnerability, p. 545; bipolar disorder, p. 546

Dissociative Disorders

Characterize dissociative disorders.

■ *Dissociative disorders* are disorders characterized by a sudden but temporary alteration in consciousness, identity, sensorimotor behavior, or memory. These disorders include *dissociative amnesia* and *dissociative personality disorder*. These disorders are not well understood and are controversial, with some authorities believing that they do not actually exist. pp. 547–548

KEY TERMS

dissociative disorders, p. 547; dissociative amnesia, p. 547; dissociative identity disorder, p. 548

Schizophrenia

Identify the essential characteristics of the major types of schizophrenia.

■ Schizophrenia is a group of disorders characterized by a lack of reality testing and by deterioration of social and intellectual functioning. Individuals with *schizophrenic disorders* often show serious personality disintegration, with significant changes in thought, mood, perception, and behavior, which matches the definition of *psychotic.* Positive symptoms are those present in people with schizophrenia but not in normal people, for example, hallucinations; negative symptoms relate to behaviors that people with schizophrenia lack but normal people have, for example, an inability to experience pleasure. pp. 549–550

■ People with the *paranoid type of schizophrenia* experience delusions of persecution—beliefs that there are plots to harm them. They also often experience delusions of grandeur as well as hallucinations. Their paranoia may make them secretive, so their behavior may seem normal, but their thought processes are not. There are actually two subtypes of the *catatonic type of schizophrenia*: excited and withdrawn. Severely disturbed thought processes characterize the *disorganized type of schizophrenia.* People with this type of schizophrenia have hallucinations and delusions and are frequently incoherent. People who show symptoms attributable to schizophrenia but who remain in touch with reality are diagnosed as having the *residual type of schizophrenia.* Some people exhibit all the essential features of schizophrenia but do not fall clearly into any one of the other categories; these individuals are classified as suffering from the *undifferentiated type of schizophrenia.* pp. 551–553

What has research revealed about the causes of schizophrenia?

■ The *concordance rate* is the likelihood that two groups or biologically related individuals show the same trait. Research into schizophrenia shows higher concordance rates for identical twins than for fraternal twins, which suggests that schizophrenia has a genetic component. p. 554

■ The dopamine theory of schizophrenia asserts that too much dopamine or too much activity at dopamine receptors causes schizophrenia. The effectiveness of antischizophrenic drugs that decrease dopamine activity supports this view. p. 554

■ A family environment that lacks good communication and sends mixed messages can create a *double bind,* which is one situation that increases vulnerability for schizophrenia. Other factors include genetic history and brain chemistry. In vulnerable individuals, low levels of environmental stress or other disorders can precipitate a schizophrenic episode. p. 555

KEY TERMS

schizophrenic disorders, p. 549; psychotic, p. 550; paranoid type of schizophrenia, p. 550; catatonic type of schizophrenia, p. 550; disorganized type of schizophrenia, p. 552; residual type of schizophrenia, p. 553; undifferentiated type of schizophrenia, p. 553; concordance rate, p. 554; double bind, p. 555

Personality Disorders

What are the chief characteristics of six key personality disorders?

■ People who have unwarranted feelings of persecution and who mistrust almost everyone are said to be suffering from the type of *personality disorder* called paranoid personality disorder. Those with borderline personality disorder have unstable interpersonal relationships, self-image, and affect and are often impulsive and easily distracted. Dramatic, emotional, and erratic behaviors are characteristic of the histrionic personality disorder. The narcissistic personality disorder is characterized by an extremely exaggerated sense of self-importance, an expectation of special favors, and a constant need for attention; people with the disorder show a lack of concern for others and react to criticism with rage, shame, or humiliation. The *antisocial personality disorder* is characterized by behavior that is irresponsible and destructive and violates the rights of others; persons with antisocial personality disorder experience little guilt or empathy for others. Submissive and clinging behaviors are characteristic of people with a dependent personality disorder. p. 557

KEY TERMS

personality disorders, p. 556; antisocial personality disorder, p. 557

Violence and Mental Disorders

What diagnoses are associated with increased risk for violence?

■ The association between mental disorders and violence is not as strong as the popular perception of it, but some disorders increase the risk for violence. More serious disorders are the highest risks, including schizophrenia, bipolar disorder, depression, and antisocial personality disorder. People with mental disorders are more likely to harm themselves than others. pp. 558–559

■ Most depressed people do not attempt suicide, but most people who attempt suicide are depressed. Many people think about suicide, but most do not make an attempt. Many more people attempt suicide than commit suicide. Over 30,000 people commit suicide each year in the United States, and all of these deaths are preventable. pp. 560–561

How does violence relate to the risk of developing mental disorders?

■ Victims of child abuse, domestic violence, and rape are at increased risk for a variety of mental disorders, including posttraumatic stress disorder, depression, substance abuse, and anxiety disorders. pp. 561–562

■ People who commit violence may have mental disorders, but most do not fit into any of the current diagnostic categories. pp. 562–563

KEY TERMS

child abuse, p. 561; rape, p. 562

16 Therapy

Claude Fourel, *Fish,* 2000

There was a time when Tony Soprano, the fictional head of a New Jersey mafia family depicted on HBO's *The Sopranos*, would never have thought about treatment through psychotherapy. Yet this violent mobster's therapy is the recurring theme of the hit show. Tony has conflicts in his family life (his wife knows he is unfaithful); he has work pressures (rival gangs seeking power); he has issues with his family, including his dead father and mother, assorted uncles and cousins, and a scheming, extremely dislikable sister. The pressures and conflicts affect Tony in fairly predictable ways—he has anxiety attacks, he has a brutal, hair-trigger temper, and he acts out in ways that most of us never even think about. His anxiety attacks lead him to need the assistance of a therapist, Dr. Melfi. The therapist is appropriate, warm, and accepting of Tony's antisocial ways of earning a living—gambling, extortion, drugs, and in general being a crook. She assesses Tony's issues, helps him evaluate his condition, prescribes medication—it turns out she is a psychiatrist—and guides him through his life crises.

chapter outline

In HBO's hit series *The Sopranos*, mobster Tony Soprano turns to psychological and drug therapy to cope with life's pressures.

Tony is prescribed Prozac, and he undergoes regular therapy sessions. And his life improves. To a great extent Dr. Melfi's recurring role in the program shows how therapy progresses. And it shows how a therapist uses many techniques to help a patient—even a mobster—gain some control over his or her life, without letting the therapist's value system or ideas judge or overdirect the person into becoming a carbon copy of the therapist.

Tony improved; was it the psychological therapy that helped Tony, or was it the drug? The truth is that it was probably a combination of the two that helped him move ahead. Would one have worked without the other? Perhaps—but the combination turned out to be extremely effective. Many researchers think that combining medication and talking is the key to effective therapy; others insist on approaches involving only talking therapies or only drug therapies. A great deal depends on the type of problem a client is having.

The causes of people's disorders—the initiators of psychological distress—are not usually biological. When people have marital problems, workplace stress or conflicts, or other psychological difficulties, help from a therapist—not a drug—is usually the order of the day. Today, mental health and therapy efforts are complicated by two facts: first, HMOs are putting pressure on practitioners to find fast, efficient cures that are less costly; second, some disorders, such as depression, are often left undiagnosed and untreated, which leads to greater problems later on. Let's look at the available therapies to try to determine what works best, and when.

Therapy Comes in Many Forms

Psychotherapy [SYE-ko-THER-uh-pee]
The treatment of emotional or behavior problems through psychological techniques.

Placebo [pluh-SEE-bo] effect
A nonspecific improvement that occurs as a result of a person's expectations of change rather than as a direct result of any specific therapeutic treatment.

Many sources and types of treatment are available to people who are having difficulty coping with their problems (see Figure 16.1). When a person seeks help from a physician, mental health counseling center, or drug treatment center, an initial working diagnosis is necessary. Does the person have medical problems? Should the person be hospitalized? Is the person dangerous? If talking therapy is in order, what type of practitioner is best suited for the person? There are two broad types of therapies: biologically based therapy and psychotherapy.

Biologically based therapy has traditionally been called *somatic therapy*; this term refers to treating psychological disorders by treating the body, often using therapy that affects hormone levels and the brain. For example, severely depressed individuals may need antidepressants; those diagnosed with schizophrenia may need antipsychotic drugs; those with less severe disorders may be advised to change their diet and to exercise more, because exercise has mood-enhancing effects (Tkachuk &

Martin, 1999). We'll examine some biological therapies later in this chapter, after we explore the broad array of psychological therapies that are available for people suffering from life problems or maladjustment.

Psychotherapy is the treatment of emotional or behavioral problems through psychological techniques. It is a change-oriented process, sometimes a fairly emotional one, whose goal is to help individuals cope better with their problems and achieve more emotionally satisfying lives. Psychotherapy accomplishes its goal by teaching people how to relieve stress, improve interpersonal communication, understand previous events in their lives, and/or modify their faulty ideas about the world. Psychotherapy helps people improve their self-image and adapt to new and challenging situations.

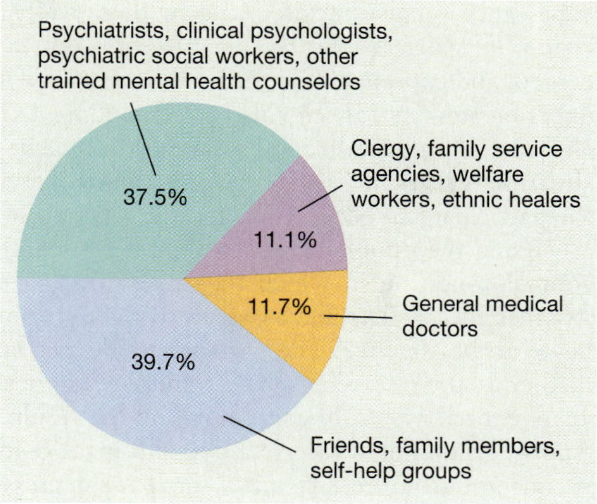

FIGURE 16.1

Types of Treatment

A 1993 study of nearly 23 million people with mental health or substance abuse problems showed that such people seek help from a variety of sources. *(Adapted from Narrow et al., 1993.)*

Of course, different cultures perceive different outcomes as optimal. Thus, in the United States, enhancing a client's self-esteem through some personal accomplishment may be seen as an optimal goal of psychotherapy. In Asia, a desired outcome may be improving family harmony, which may enhance self-esteem but involves working for a collective rather than a client's personal good. This difference is recognized by professional organizations such as the American Psychological Association and the American Psychiatric Association.

Is Psychotherapy Necessary and Effective?

The images presented to the public by the mass media often shape the public's perception of psychotherapy. Talk-show psychologist Frasier Crane of the TV series *Frasier* bumbles through his own life. Images like this, as well as talk-show pop psychology, make many ask, "Is psychotherapy really necessary or effective?" Some researchers note that many clients could outgrow or otherwise find relief from their symptoms without psychotherapy. Others assert that psychotherapy is more art than science. Still others believe psychotherapy provides only temporary relief. Let's consider some of the arguments.

■ *Talk-show psychologist Frasier Crane of the TV series* Frasier *bumbles through his own life. These images presented by the mass media often shape the public's perception of psychotherapy.*

■ **PLACEBO EFFECTS.** A **placebo effect** is a nonspecific improvement that occurs as a result of a person's expectations of change rather than as a result of any specific therapeutic treatment. Is the benefit of psychotherapy largely a placebo effect? Physicians report that sometimes people experience relief from their symptoms when they are given sugar pills and are told that the pills are medicine. Similarly, some patients in psychotherapy may show relief from their symptoms simply because they have entered therapy and expect change. For some people, just the attention of a therapist and the chance to express their feelings can be therapeutic.

The placebo effect complicates research on therapy effectiveness. Researchers must determine if the improvements they observe are the result of people's expectancy or real benefits of the therapy. The double-blind technique allows researchers to distinguish between improvement produced by expectancy versus that produced by therapy. The **double-blind technique** is a procedure in which neither the experimenter nor the participants know who is in the control and experimental groups. It helps eliminate any potential bias on the part of experimenters or participants by reducing the experimental **demand characteristics,** elements of an experimental situation that might cause a participant to perceive the situation in a certain way or become aware of the purpose of the study and thus bias the participant to behave in a certain way and in so doing distort results.

Using the double-blind technique, a researcher assigns some participants to a control condition in which they receive a placebo rather than actual treatment, whereas the participants assigned to the experimental group receive treatment believed to be effective. The participants do not know which group they are in, and neither do the researchers. This "blinding" of both participants and researchers prevents expectancy from contaminating the results. For example, participants in the control group might receive a pill with inactive ingredients whereas those in the experimental group receive a new drug for depression. Both groups receive pills that look the same, so the placebo effect and demand characteristics apply to both equally; they have similar expectancies for effectiveness. The researchers who dispense the pills have no way to convey different expectancies to the participants in the experimental group because they too are "blind" to the conditions. Thus, any improvement that the experimental group shows can be attributed to the treatment effect rather than placebo effect. Double-blind studies are the best technique for demonstrating therapy effectiveness. Research studies that compare traditional psychotherapies with placebo treatment show that the therapies are consistently more effective (Kazdin, 2001).

■ **RESEARCH ON PSYCHOTHERAPY.** In 1952, an important paper by Hans Eysenck challenged the effectiveness of psychotherapy, claiming that it produces no greater change in maladjusted individuals than do naturally occurring life experiences. Thousands of studies attempting to investigate the effectiveness of therapy followed. These studies showed what clients and therapists have known for decades: Eysenck was wrong. Analyses of large amounts of data using sophisticated statistical techniques found psychotherapy effective (Bachar, 1998; Smith, Glass, & Miller, 1980; Tritt et al., 2000). Although some psychologists challenge the data, techniques, and conclusions of these analyses, most are still convinced that psychotherapy is effective with a wide array of clients (e.g., Kazdin, 2000). The effectiveness of therapy and the client's speed of response do vary with the type of problem—anxiety and depression respond more rapidly to psychotherapy than do personality disorders. Table 16.1 presents some generally recognized signs of good progress in therapy.

Is one type of therapy more effective than another? Many researchers contend that most psychotherapies are equally effective; that is, regardless of the approach a therapist uses, the results are often the same (Wampold et al., 1997). Some newer and trendier approaches—the kinds that often appear in popular magazines—tend to be less reliable and to reflect a culture that is fascinated with novelty. Some therapists do not pay attention to known data, and some therapists—often those with little training—do their clients a disservice by ignoring the facts and looking for the exotic or easy way out. But if most of the traditional therapies are effective, there must be some common underlying component that makes them successful. The American Psychological Association and many individual researchers are seeking to systematize research strategies so as to investigate the effectiveness of therapies; this research will lead to a clearer picture of which approaches are best for certain disorders and for clients of various ages and different ethnic groups (Chambless & Hollon, 1998; Kazdin, 2001). Furthermore, researchers are suggesting ways to validate therapy findings in the laboratory and in the real world (Goldfreid & Wolfe, 1998) for problems as diverse as family conflict and cocaine addiction (Van Horn & Frank, 1998).

Double-blind technique
A research technique in which neither the experimenter nor the participants know who is in the control and experimental groups.

Demand characteristics
Elements of an experimental situation that might cause a participant to perceive the situation in a certain way or become aware of the purpose of the study and thus bias the participant to behave in a certain way, and in so doing, distort results.

TABLE 16.1

Signs of Good Progress in Therapy

The client is providing personally revealing and significant material.
The client is exploring the meanings of feelings and occurrences.
The client is exploring material avoided earlier in therapy.
The client is expressing significant insight into personal behavior.
The client's method of communicating is active, alive, and energetic.
There is a valued client–therapist working relationship.
The client feels free to express strong feelings toward the therapist—either positive or negative.
The client is expressing strong feelings outside of therapy.
The client is moving toward a different set of personality characteristics.
The client is showing improved functioning outside of therapy.
The client indicates a general state of well-being, good feelings, and positive attitudes.

Mahrer & Nadler, 1986

Which Therapy, Which Therapist?

Before 1950, there were about 15 types of psychotherapies; today, there are hundreds. Some focus on individuals, some on groups of individuals (group therapy), and others on families (family therapy). Some psychologists even deal with whole communities; these *community psychologists* focus on helping members of communities develop more action-oriented approaches to individual and social problems. A therapist's training usually determines the type of treatment approach he or she takes. Rather than using just one type of psychotherapy, many therapists take an *eclectic approach*—that is, they combine several different techniques when treating clients.

A number of systematic psychotherapeutic approaches are in use today. Each can be applied in several formats—with individuals, couples, or groups—and each will be defined and examined in greater detail in later sections of this chapter. Some practitioners use *psychodynamically based approaches*, which follow Freud's basic ideas to varying degrees. These therapists' aim is to help patients understand the motivations underlying their behavior. They assume that maladjustment and abnormal behavior occur when people do not understand themselves adequately. Practitioners of *humanistic therapy* assume that people are essentially good—that they have an innate disposition to develop their potential and to seek beauty, truth, and goodness. This type of therapy tries to help people realize their full potential and find meaning in life. In contrast, *behavior therapy* is based on the assumption that most behaviors, whether normal or abnormal, are learned. Behavior therapists encourage their clients to learn new adaptive behaviors. Growing out of behavior therapy and cognitive psychology (see Chapters 1 and 9) is *cognitive therapy*, which focuses on changing a client's behavior by changing her or his thoughts and perceptions.

In most of the therapy approaches we will discuss, practitioners adopt a point of view that guides both research and practice. A clear example is psychoanalysis, which prescribes a strict set of guidelines for therapy. But a new approach, called *psychotherapy integration*, is emerging. Psychotherapy integration is not a single-school

student voices

Adam J. Guilmino
University of North Dakota

As a child, I attended counseling sessions to deal with my depression over my parents' divorce. This event in my life affected my career decision to enter the counseling field. I figured I can help children who are in the same situation I was in.

introduction to research basics

Prevention Instead of Treatment?

Smoking is a major health problem in the United States and causes disease and death. But people smoke, try to quit, and go through relapses, and many become quite disturbed about their own smoking behaviors. Even the best smoking prevention programs have high relapse rates. Are there prevention techniques that researchers can devise to help prevent relapses? Prevention research focuses on learning how the risk of developing a disorder (or relapse) can be reduced and what protective factors people can develop against a given disorder (or relapse). Prevention science offers the possibility of new insights into the development of disorders, the mechanisms that cause disorders, and the social context in which disorders develop.

A team of researchers headed by Thomas Brandon (Brandon et al., 2000) examined two modest interventions to see if they could prevent relapses in smokers. They sought to know if mailings and hot lines could be an aid.

DESIGN The design was an *experimental design*. The researchers manipulated the type of intervention participants received as their *independent variable* and measured continued abstinence from smoking as their *dependent variable*.

HYPOTHESIS The researchers hypothesized that minimal interventions such as repeated mailings or access to a telephone hot line in times of smoking crisis would prevent relapses among former smokers.

PARTICIPANTS Participants were recruited through newspapers and had to have abstained from smoking for at least one week. Out of 804 inquiries from ex-smokers, 466 individuals met various criteria to be included as participants.

PROCEDURE The participants were randomly assigned to one of four groups. The *hot-line* group received a booklet with material about relapse prevention and a hot-line number that instructed them to call if they were experiencing a smoking crisis. A *mailing group* received the same booklet and then got a series of eight additional pamphlets over a year's period. A *combination condition* received a hot-line number and the frequent mailings; and last, a *control group* received only the single booklet at the beginning of the study (no hot line, no mailings).

RESULTS The use of hot lines helped participants, but not a lot. The mailings, however, were helpful. Self-reports of abstinence from cigarette smoking were affected by the frequent mailings. Overall there was a two-thirds lower likelihood that participants would be smoking one year later if they received a series of booklets compared with participants who received only a single booklet.

CONCLUSIONS The use of a prevention technique to help cigarette smokers abstain is effective. The frequent mailing technique helped people abstain from smoking. So, on the simplest level this study showed that prevention techniques are effective. But the researchers, being careful and cautious, noted several potential limitations of the study. The sample was small. The dependent measures were self-reports. The time frame was only a year. The sample of participants was self-selected—that is, they volunteered in response to advertisements for a free program. What if there was a charge? Would the result be better? Would the hot-line condition or the combination condition be more effective? These questions are still unresolved. Because of its very nature, this study did not use the double-blind technique, and the different amount of attention to the groups may have been a factor in improvement.

Despite its limitations, this study was one among many showing that prevention works; policy makers must think about therapy, in its many forms, as a prevention technique as well as a treatment technique. This mind-set differs from the idea of simply "fixing" people who are suffering—it suggests planning ahead and avoiding disorders before they develop (or recur).

approach, but rather is open to using diverse theories and techniques. Psychotherapy integration is more than an eclectic approach because the goal is to integrate theories into a new approach to solving problems. Research on psychotherapy integration is relatively scarce, however, because it is difficult to generate testable hypotheses from the new points of view that are created by integrating theories. Arkowitz (1997) argues that psychotherapy integration does not try to develop one overarching view of therapy; he suggests that it is a way of thinking about and doing psychotherapy that

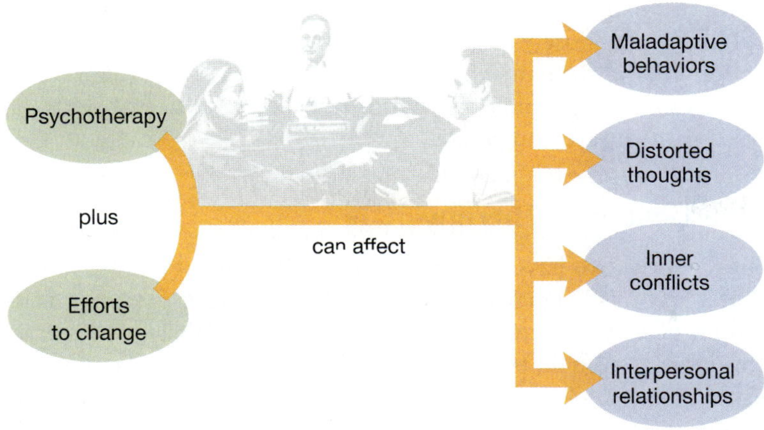

FIGURE 16.2

Goals of Psychotherapy

An important goal of psychotherapy is engaging the client in the process of change. Once initiated, psychotherapy, along with efforts to change, can affect a host of problems, including specific maladaptive behaviors, distorted thoughts, inner conflicts, and interpersonal relationships.

reflects an openness to points of view other than the one with which a therapist is most familiar. In some important ways, psychotherapy integration is an ongoing process that may help define the future of psychotherapy. Another ongoing development that may prove a better avenue to explore is research on prevention of disorders, discussed in *Introduction to Research Basics.*

The effectiveness of the different kinds of therapies varies with the type of disorder being treated and the goals of the client. Research to discover the best treatment method often focuses on specific disorders, such as depression. Conclusions from such studies are usually limited to recommending a specific method as effective for a specific problem. For example, cognitive behavior therapy has a good success rate for people with phobias or depression, but it is less successful for those with schizophrenia. Long-term group therapy is more effective than short-term individual therapy for people with personality disorders. Behavior therapy is usually the most effective approach with children, regardless of the disorder.

An individual can receive effective treatment from a variety of therapists. One therapist might focus on the root causes of maladjustment. Another might concentrate on eliminating symptoms: sadness, anxiety, or alcohol abuse. Besides the therapeutic approaches, personal characteristics of the therapists themselves can affect treatment; among these characteristics are ethnicity, personality, level of experience, and degree of empathy.

Although there are differences among the various psychotherapies and therapists, there are also some commonalities. No matter which therapy they experience, clients usually expect a positive outcome, which helps them strive for change. (Figure 16.2 presents an overview of outcomes when psychotherapy is combined with efforts to change.) In addition, clients receive attention, which helps them maintain a positive attitude. Moreover, no matter what type of therapy is involved, certain characteristics must be present in both therapist and client for therapeutic changes to occur. For example, good therapists communicate interest, understanding, respect, tact, maturity, and ability to help. They respect clients' ability to cope with their troubles. They use suggestion, encouragement, interpretation, examples, and perhaps rewards to help clients change or rethink their situations. But clients must be willing to make some changes in their lifestyle and ideas. A knowledgeable, accepting, and objective therapist can facilitate behavior changes, but the client is the one who must make the changes.

In general, the therapist and client must form an alliance to work together purposefully; such alliances are formed more readily if the therapist and client share some values (Howe, 1999). Because psychoanalysis is based on the development of a unique relationship between the therapist and the patient, compatibility is especially critical to the success of that type of therapy.

To clarify the main issues involved in psychotherapy, further sections of this chapter will look more closely at the four major psychotherapeutic approaches and some variations: psychodynamic, humanistic, behavior, and cognitive therapies. Then we will examine the biologically based approaches. But first, let's look at the crucial variables of culture and gender.

Culture and Gender in Therapy

Throughout this book we have been emphasizing the role of culture in psychology, stressing that a person's vantage point and worldview affect his or her thoughts and behavior. In no place is this more vital than in therapy. When a person seeks help for problems large and small, both the therapy process and the outcome are affected by the client's ethnicity. To be effective, care must be culturally congruent—there must be a sensitivity and match between the therapist and client (Zoucha & Hustead, 2000).

At a minimum psychologists respect *multiculturalism*—the acceptance and celebration of distinct cultural heritages—and it continues to be the prevailing organization through which ethnic identity and social problems are examined. But practitioners and scholars also know that therapists must see beyond the distinct margins of a specific culture (such as Vietnamese, French, Bosnian) and see individuals as made up of a confluence of different influences. This view, *transculturalism*, recognizes that a woman with an Asian family heritage may embrace Western values of independence and individuality and be a single mother who runs a business. Transculturalism reflects changes that have occurred through the world due to globalization, increased mobility, improved communications systems (including the Internet), and intermarriage. Therapists need to be well informed about clients' backgrounds and provide interventions based upon and using cultural symbols, rituals, and metaphors that are meaningful to the client (Witzum & Buchbinder, 2001).

So, for example, in traditional Asian cultures, the *family* is the primary source of emotional support. The most important family relationship is not the husband–wife–children relationship but rather the parent–child relationship. A person is defined by her or his roles in the family, including parent roles, grandparent roles, and child roles. Children of any age, including adult children, are expected to maintain a deferential and respectful relationship to their elders. These roles and the consequent responsibilities provide emotional support for individual family members. The therapeutic alliance must respect the family, its life cycle, and its traditions and recognize the types of problems presented to practitioners (Tempo & Saito, 1996). Often, emphasizing family bonds—perhaps through family therapy—is an effective technique, as is relying on traditional and familiar Asian American philosophical traditions. Not all Americans have the same needs.

■ *In traditional Asian cultures, the family is the primary source of emotional support. The most important family relationship is the parent-child relationship.*

Within a culture, therapists need to recognize that culture, even popular culture, is powerful and can be used as a tool to influence clients and help them explore their values and goals (Oliver,

2000). It also helps therapists to realize that various communities have constraints and prohibitions against self-disclosure, or toward control or an acceptance of domestic violence (Thomas, 2001). Some Arab cultures are strongly patriarchal and resistant to emotional exploration and more likely to value and adapt to therapies that are cognitive in nature (Chaleby, 2001). Cultural mistrust of therapy situations is also common among African Americans (Whaley, 2001). By contrast, among the Latino/Latina community many are from cultures with deep-seated notions of social order, clear authoritarian social roles, and a high regard for experts like therapists (de-Leff & Espejel, 2001). Expectations for the therapist and client often follow these orientations—so, for example, a Latina woman may expect her therapist to be highly orderly and specific. Because most Latino/Latina cultures place high value on respect and dignity for every person, they will expect the therapist to treat them in an especially caring, confidential, and kind style, however directive.

Interestingly, the therapist's ethnicity is a variable—LatinoLatina, African American, and Asian American therapists are viewed differently by clients than are European American therapists (Tang & Gardner, 1999). And client variables are also potent—evidence shows that there are both gender and ethnic differences in the way people respond to drugs that treat anxiety and depression (Lin, 2001; Melfi et al., 2000; Smith, Mendoza, & Lin, 1999) as well as cultural effects on maintaining commitment to medical advice and therapeutic drug usage (Kemppainen et al., 2001). Men and women respond to therapy differently (Philpot, 2001; Scher, 2001), and one's ethnicity—the therapist's and the client's—is an important variable and must be studied, valued, and taken into account in the therapeutic milieu (LaRoche, 1999). And last, culture is dynamic, contextual, and even political; stereotypes and oversimplifications abound (Romero, 2000). Therapists must recognize that all Asian men, Orthodox Jews, feminists, or Creoles are not the same and that therapists' own cultural values and preconceived ideas may be oppressive to their clients and constrain the effectiveness of therapy (Laird, 2000).

Not only is ethnicity important, but a person's gender turns out to be significant. Women seek out therapy more often than do men, and they respond differently to talking therapy (Romans, 2000) and to drug therapy (Martenyi et al., 2001). Therapists need to be aware of gender roles and expectations related to gender roles (Papp, 2000; Scher, 2001). For example, therapists must also consider the way men and women talk about themselves, others, and situations. Linguist Deborah Tannen (2001) has studied language and social interactions among men and women and convincingly argues that men and women talk differently; while both try to be open and communicative, men tend to give *reports* while women try to establish *rapport*. She further argues that people in therapeutic and family relationships feel an ability to say things that are heard quite differently than they are intended. So she argues mothers who offer help are often heard to be offering criticism. "Oh, your hair would be so cute if it were short" may be heard by a daughter as "You look terrible." In a therapeutic relationship, a therapist must hear what clients say and the messages that they actually intend to deliver. They must also realize that they and their clients may have experienced gender bias in their families that affect their gender assumptions (Atwood, 2001). This is compounded by ethnicity—Asian men view masculinity differently than do European or American men (Sue, 2001), as do Latinos (Casas et al., 2001), and women view it differently still. Gay men and lesbians bring still another view to gender roles and the therapeutic situation (Biaggio et al., 2000; Gainor, 2000).

Differences occur between men and women in a variety of domains; for example, men and women tend to report similar alcohol-related psychosocial problems, but women are more likely to be diagnosed as suffering from depression and men diagnosed with antisocial personality disorder (Parks, 2001). Again, the differences between men and women become compounded by ethnicity; African American women are seen first as women, and then considered as African American—with each designation connected to certain biases (Williams, 2000). As with ethnicity,

student voices

Juan M. Viator
Loyola University

I remember sitting down in eighth grade and counseling everyone in my class on the problems they were having with their families, friends, boyfriends, etc. Now I am starting to actually be able to give advice backed up by psychological principles.

psychology *in action*

Choosing a Therapist

You might think that with over 100,000 therapists in the United States, choosing one would be an easy task. But the reality is that a whole range of practitioners do therapy, and each one uses a slightly different approach consistent with his or her training and view of emotional problems. So just like all medical doctors have specialties—and within specialties we have preferences for one doctor over another—so it is with therapists.

The best place to begin looking for a therapist is through friends and relatives. Ask around. Talk to your doctor. Many family practitioners work with a team of health-care providers, including psychologists, and they can refer you to someone they know who is effective. Consult the psychology department of a local college or the staff at a community mental health center.

Table 16.2 presents an overview of the major types of psychotherapeutic practitioners, including the degrees they most likely have earned and their activities. The table lists some practitioners who do not have as much training in psychotherapy as do psychologists—for example, psychiatric nurses and social workers. These types of practitioners often work with a clinical psychologist or a psychiatrist, as part of a team that delivers mental health services to clients.

Once you have the names of several practitioners, ask if they are licensed psychologists and how long they have been practicing. Ask what kinds of treatment procedures they like to use and if they have a specialty—for example, working with children or teenagers, or dealing with eating disorders or depression. Don't be shy about asking about fees or about insurance issues. In the end you must choose a psychologist with whom you feel secure and comfortable.

therapists must come to understand how their own personal gender socialization affects therapy (Brooks, 2000), avoid stereotypes, and recognize the diversity of men's and women's experiences (McMahon & Luthar, 2000).

Managed Care and Therapy

The term *managed care* is used to describe a variety of different insurance and health care delivery arrangements. It emphasizes active coordination and arrangement of services and usually involves three key components: oversight of the care given, contractual relationships with and organization of the providers giving care, and the covered benefits. A principal aim is to control costs. You may hear consumers complaining about managed care. Is this a problem for psychologists? The answer from most practitioners is yes.

There are two major difficulties with managed care; both deal with access to timely and effective treatment. The first problem is that insurance companies, looking out for profits, will seek to limit either the duration or type of psychotherapeutic services a person may access. The second problem is that they limit choices in whom a client can see (Grohol, 1995). Not only that, but many HMOs (health maintenance organizations) require reapproval of the therapy every 6 sessions, which tends to make the course of therapy shorter (Liu, Sturm, & Cuffel, 2000). It also means the psychologists need to continually justify the treatment a patient is receiving. Edward (1999) asserts that the practitioner–client alliance is thus compromised. You either play by the managed care rules or pay higher premiums for a different insurance plan that might offer a bit more flexibility in choice of doctors and length of stay in therapy (Grohol, 1995).

Managed care has led to *brief therapy*, a therapeutic approach based on a blend of psychotherapeutic orientations and skills (Cummings, 1986). A basic goal is to give clients what they need; the therapy therefore focuses on treating clients' problems efficiently and getting them back on their own as quickly as possible. The time frame varies from therapist to therapist, client to client, and HMO to HMO, but 6

TABLE 16.2

Psychotherapy Practitioners and Their Activities

Type of Practitioner	Degree	Years of Education Beyond Undergraduate Degree	Activities
Clinical or counseling psychologist	PhD (Doctor of Philosophy) or PsyD (Doctor of Psychology)	5–8	Diagnosis, testing, and treatment using a wide array of techniques, including insight and behavior therapy
Psychiatrist	MD (Doctor of Medicine)	8	Biomedical therapy, diagnosis, and treatment, often with a psychoanalytic emphasis
Social worker	MSW (Master of Social Work)	2	Family therapy or behavior therapy, often in community-based settings such as hospitals
Psychiatric nurse	BSN (Bachelor of Science in Nursing) or MA (Master of Arts)	0–2	Inpatient psychiatric care, supportive therapy of various types
Counselor	MA (Master of Arts, often in counseling)	2	Supportive therapy, family therapy, vocational readjustment, alcoholism and drug abuse counseling

weeks is common; anything more than 16 weeks is considered lengthy. One of the objectives is to save clients time and money. Although HMOs or insurance companies may place limits on the number of sessions, clients may remain in therapy longer if they feel the need and are willing and able to continue to pay. They can also return if they need help in the future. This approach's primary effect on therapy is that more and more therapists are thinking in terms of *planned* short-term treatments (Messer & Wachtel, 1997).

The therapist makes sure that treatment begins in the first session of brief therapy. He or she strives to perform an *operational diagnosis* that answers this question: why is the client here today instead of last week, last month, last year, or next year? The answer helps the therapist pinpoint the specific problem for which the client is seeking help. Also, in the first session, "every client makes a therapeutic contract with every therapist" (Cummings, 1986). The goals of therapy are established and agreed on by the client and the therapist, and the therapy is precise, active, and directive, with no unnecessary steps.

Research on and using brief therapy is encouraging, suggesting that the therapy is effective and that the effects are long-lasting (Kush & Flemming, 2000). Research has been limited to relatively few clients with a narrow range of problems. Nonetheless, researchers have found brief therapy to be effective when treatment goals and procedures are tailored to the client's needs and the time. It can be especially effective with couples and when combined with cognitive restructuring (Donovan, 1998).

Brief therapy is not a cure-all, however. Like all therapies, its aim is to help relieve clients' suffering, and it is effective with some clients and with some problems some of the

Be an Active learner

REVIEW

- What is the essential difference between biologically based therapy and psychotherapy? pp. 568–569
- What is transculturalism? p. 574

THINK CRITICALLY

- Imagine that you are undergoing treatment for anxiety or depression. What would you expect to gain, lose, or change during therapy?
- Why do you think some disorders respond more quickly to therapy than others?
- Why do you think ethnicity is an important variable in therapy?

APPLY PSYCHOLOGY

- What are the implications for society of the fact that the rich and the poor have access to dramatically different mental health services? What could be done to alter this situation?
- If you were training individuals to be therapists, what steps could you initiate to ensure culture sensitivity in therapy?

time (Hemphill & Littlefield, 2001; Stalker, Levene, & Coady, 1999). Further research on brief therapy is being conducted, and its future will depend on the results of that research.

To suggest that no one gets appropriate care—often of short duration—from managed care is inaccurate and misleading (Cummings, Budman, & Thomas, 1998). But most practitioners worry that care is terminated too quickly and is managed by people with little or no training and who never meet patients. In some ways, the issue is a social policy question, focusing on whether we as a society want to provide psychotherapy for those who are in need (Gilford, 2000). Psychologists answer in the affirmative, but many argue that managed care limits our ability to do so.

Psychoanalysis and Psychodynamic Therapies

Psychoanalysis is a lengthy insight therapy that was developed by Freud and aims at uncovering conflicts and unconscious impulses through special techniques, including free association, dream analysis, and transference. There are about 3,300 practicing psychoanalysts in the United States. Many other psychologists use a therapy loosely connected to or rooted in Freudian theory. These psychologists refer to their therapies as **psychodynamically based therapies**—therapies that use approaches or techniques derived from Freud, but that reject or modify some elements of Freud's theory.

Sigmund Freud believed that the exchange of words in psychoanalysis causes therapeutic change. According to Freud (1920/1966):

> The patient talks, tells of his past experiences and present impressions, complains, and expresses his wishes and his emotions. The physician listens, attempts to direct the patient's thought-processes, reminds him, forces his attention in certain directions, gives him explanations and observes the reactions of understanding or denial thus evoked. (p. 21)

Freud's therapy is an **insight therapy**—a therapy that attempts to discover relationships between unconscious motivations and current abnormal behavior. Any insight therapy has two basic assumptions: (1) becoming aware of one's motivations helps one change and become more adaptable, and (2) the causes of maladjustment are unresolved conflicts that the person was unaware of and therefore unable to deal with. The goal of insight therapy is to treat the causes of abnormal behaviors rather than the behaviors themselves. In general, insight therapists try to help people see life from a different perspective so that they can choose more adaptive behaviors.

Psychoanalysis [SYE-ko-uh-NAL-uh-sis]
A lengthy insight therapy that was developed by Freud and aims at uncovering conflicts and unconscious impulses through special techniques, including free association, dream analysis, and transference.

Psychodynamically [SYE-ko-dye-NAM-ick-lee] based therapies
Therapies that use approaches or techniques derived from Freud, but that reject or modify some elements of Freud's theory.

Insight therapy
Any therapy that attempts to discover relationships between unconscious motivations and current abnormal behavior.

Goals of Psychoanalysis

Many individuals who seek psychotherapy are unhappy with their behavior but are unable to change it. As we saw in the discussion of Freud's theory of personality (Chapter 12), Freud believed that conflicts among a person's unconscious thoughts produce maladjusted behavior. The general goal of psychoanalysis is to help patients understand the unconscious motivations that direct their behavior. Only when they become aware of those motivations can they begin to choose behaviors that lead to more fulfilling lives. In psychoanalysis, patients are encouraged to express healthy impulses, to strengthen day-to-day functioning based on reality, and to perceive the world as a positive rather than a punishing place.

To illustrate the psychoanalytic approach, suppose that a person seeks the help of a psychologist who uses a psychodynamically based therapy. The psychologist might attempt to discover the source of the patient's problems by asking him to describe how he relates to his parents.

Techniques of Psychoanalysis

■ *In traditional psychoanalysis, the patient lies on a couch and the therapist sits in a chair out of the patient's view. This is a photo of Freud's office where he saw patients.*

In general, psychoanalytic techniques are geared toward the exploration of early experiences. In traditional psychoanalysis, the patient lies on a couch and the therapist sits in a chair out of the patient's view. Freud used this arrangement in his office in Vienna because he believed it would allow the patient to be more relaxed and feel less threatened than if the therapist was in view. Today, however, many followers of Freud prefer face-to-face interactions with patients.

Two major techniques used in psychoanalysis are free association and dream analysis. In **free association,** the patient is asked to report whatever comes to mind, regardless of how disorganized it might be, how trivial it might seem, or how disagreeable it might sound. A therapist might say, "I can help you best if you say whatever thoughts and feelings come to your mind, even if they seem irrelevant, immaterial, foolish, embarrassing, upsetting, or even if they're about me, even very personally, just as they come, without censoring or editing" (Lewin, 1970, p. 67). The purpose of free association is to help patients learn to recognize connections and patterns among their thoughts and to allow the unconscious to express itself freely.

In **dream analysis,** patients are asked to describe their dreams in detail; the dreams are interpreted so as to provide insight into unconscious motivations. Sometimes lifelike, sometimes chaotic, sometimes incoherent, dreams may at times replay a person's life history and at other times venture into the person's current problems. Freud believed that dreams represent some element of the unconscious seeking expression. Psychodynamically oriented therapists believe that dreams are full of symbolism; they assert that the content of a dream hides its true meaning. The goal of dream analysis is to help therapists reveal patients' unconscious desires and motivations by discovering the meaning of their dreams.

Both free association and dream analysis involve the therapist's interpretation. **Interpretation,** in Freud's theory, is the technique of providing a context, meaning, or cause for a specific idea, feeling, or set of behaviors; it is the process of tying a set of behaviors to its unconscious influence. With this technique, the therapist tries to find common threads in a patient's behavior and thoughts. Patients' use of *defense mechanisms* (ways of reducing anxiety by distorting reality, described in Chapter 12) is often a sign pointing to an area that may need to be explored. For example, if a male patient avoids the subject of women, invariably deflecting the topic with an offhand remark or a joke, the therapist may wonder if the man is experiencing some kind of denial. The therapist may then encourage the patient to explore his attitudes and feelings about women in general and about his mother in particular.

Two processes are central to psychoanalysis: resistance and transference. **Resistance** is an unwillingness to cooperate, which a patient signals by showing a reluctance to provide the therapist with information or to help the therapist understand or interpret a situation. Resistance can sometimes reach the point of belligerence. For example, a patient disturbed by her analyst's unsettling interpretations might become angry and start resisting treatment by missing appointments or failing to pay for therapy. Analysts usually interpret resistance as meaning either that the patient wishes to avoid discussing a particular subject or that an especially difficult stage in psychotherapy has been reached. To minimize resistance, analysts try to accept patients' behavior. When a therapist does not judge but merely listens, a patient is more likely to describe feelings thoroughly.

Free association
Psychoanalytic technique in which a person is asked to report to the therapist his or her thoughts and feelings as they occur, regardless of how trivial, illogical, or objectionable their content may appear.

Dream analysis
Psychoanalytic technique in which a patient's dreams are described in detail and interpreted so as to provide insight into the individual's unconscious motivations.

Interpretation
In Freud's theory, the technique of providing a context, meaning, or cause for a specific idea, feeling, or set of behaviors; the process of tying a set of behaviors to its unconscious determinant.

Resistance
In psychoanalysis, an unwillingness to cooperate, which a patient signals by showing a reluctance to provide the therapist with information or to help the therapist understand or interpret a situation.

Transference is a psychoanalytic phenomenon in which a therapist becomes the object of a patient's emotional attitudes about an important person in the patient's life, such as a parent. For example, if a patient's therapist is a man, and he becomes hostile toward him, a psychoanalyst would say that the patient is acting as though the therapist were his father; that is, he is directing attitudes and emotional reactions from that earlier relationship toward the therapist (Butler & Strupp, 1991). The importance of transference is that the psychotherapist will respond differently so the patient can experience the conflict differently, which will lead him to a better understanding of the issue. By permitting transference, a therapist gives patients a new opportunity to understand their feelings and can guide them in the exploration of repressed or difficult material. The examination of thoughts or feelings that were previously considered unacceptable (and therefore were often repressed) helps patients understand and identify the underlying conflicts that direct their behavior.

Psychoanalysis, with its slowly gained insights into the unconscious, is a gradual and continual process. Through their insights, patients learn new ways of coping with instinctual urges and develop more mature means of dealing with anxiety and guilt. The cycle of interpretation, resistance to interpretation, and transference occurs repeatedly in the process of psychoanalysis and is sometimes referred to as **working through.**

Criticisms of Psychoanalysis

Freud's theory has not been universally accepted; even his followers have often disagreed with him. One group of psychoanalysts, referred to as *ego analysts*, or *ego psychologists*, have modified some of Freud's basic ideas. *Ego analysts* are psychoanalytic practitioners who assume that the ego has greater control over behavior than Freud suggested and who focus more on a patient's reality testing and control over the environment than on unconscious motivations and processes. Like Freud, ego analysts believe that psychoanalysis is the appropriate method for treating patients with emotional problems. Unlike Freud, however, they assume that people have voluntary control over whether, when, and in what ways their biological urges will be expressed.

A major disagreement between ego analysts and traditional psychoanalysts has to do with the role of the id and the ego. (Recall from Chapter 12 that the id operates on the pleasure principle, while the ego operates on the reality principle and tries to control the id's impulsivity.) A traditional Freudian asserts that the ego grows out of the id and controls it—but an ego analyst asserts that the ego is independent of the id, controls memory and perception, and is not in constant conflict with the id. Whereas traditional psychoanalysts begin by focusing on unconscious material in the id and only later try to increase the patient's ego control, ego analysts begin by helping clients develop stronger egos. They may ask a client to be assertive and take control of a situation—to let reason, rather than feeling, guide a specific behavior pattern. From an ego analyst's point of view, a weak ego may cause maladjustment through its failure to perceive, understand, and control the id. Thus, by learning to master and develop their egos—including moral reasoning and judgment—people gain greater control over their lives.

Critics of psychoanalysis contend that the approach is unscientific, imprecise, and subjective; they assert that psychoanalytic concepts such as id, ego, and superego are not linked to reality or to day-to-day behavior. Other critics object to Freud's biologically oriented approach, which suggests that a human being is a mere bundle of energy caught in conflict and driven toward some hedonistic goal. These critics ask, Where does human free will enter the picture? Also, elements of Freud's theory are untestable, and some are sexist. Freud conceived of men and women in prescribed roles; most practitioners today find this idea objectionable.

Aside from these criticisms, the effectiveness of psychoanalysis is open to question. Research shows that psychoanalysis is more effective for some people than for

Transference
Psychoanalytic phenomenon in which a therapist becomes the object of a patient's emotional attitudes about an important person in the patient's life, such as a parent.

Working through
In psychoanalysis, the repetitive cycle of interpretation, resistance to interpretation, and transference.

Building Table 16.1

Key Components of Psychoanalytic Therapy

Therapy	Nature of Psycho-pathology	Goal of Therapy	Role of Therapist	Role of Unconscious Material	Role of Patient's Insights	Techniques
Psychoanalytic	Maladjustment reflects inadequate conflict resolution and fixation in early development.	Attainment of maturity, strengthened ego functions, reduced control by unconscious or repressed impulses	An *investigator,* uncovering conflicts and resistances	Primary in classical psychoanalysis; less emphasized in ego analysis	Includes not solely intellectual understanding but also emotional experiences	Analyst takes an active role in interpreting the dreams and free associations of patients.

others. It is more effective, for example, for people with anxiety disorders than for those diagnosed as schizophrenic. In addition, younger patients improve more than older ones. In general, studies show that psychoanalysis can be as effective as other therapies, but no more so (Kazdin, 2000, 2001). Psychoanalysis does have certain inherent disadvantages. The problems it addresses are difficult, and a patient must be highly motivated and articulate to grasp the complicated and subtle relationships being explored. Further, because traditional psychoanalysis involves meeting with the analyst for an hour at a time, 5 days a week, for approximately 5 years, psychoanalysis is typically extremely expensive. Many people who seek therapy cannot afford the money or the time for this type of treatment, nor will most insurance companies foot the bill.

Building Table 16.1 presents a summary of the key components of the psychoanalytic view of therapy. Humanistic therapies, which we'll examine next, are neither as time-consuming nor as comprehensive in their goals as psychoanalysis.

Humanistic Therapies

Humanistic therapies, unlike psychoanalytic therapies, emphasize the uniqueness of the human experience, the human ability to reflect on conscious experience, and the idea that human beings have free will to determine their destinies. Humanistic psychologists tend to focus on the present and the future rather than on the past, and they assert that human beings are creative and born with an innate desire to fulfill themselves. To some extent, humanistic approaches, being insight-oriented, are an outgrowth of psychodynamically based insight therapies. Humanistic therapies focus on helping basically healthy people understand the causes of their behavior—both normal and maladjusted—and take responsibility for their future by promoting growth and fulfillment. Client-centered therapy is a humanistic therapy that centers on self-determination.

Client-centered therapy, or *person-centered therapy*, is an insight therapy that seeks to help people evaluate the world and themselves from their own perspective. Carl Rogers (1902–1987) first developed client-centered therapy. He was a quiet, caring man who turned the psychoanalytic world upside-down when he introduced his approach. He focused on the person, listening intently to his clients and encouraging them to define their own "cures." Rogers saw people as having the potential to grow and, with a nourishing environment, to become mature, fulfilled individuals.

Client-centered therapy
An insight therapy, developed by Carl Rogers, that seeks to help people evaluate the world and themselves from their own perspective by providing them with a nondirective environment and unconditional positive regard; also known as *person-centered therapy*.

TABLE 16.3

Rogers's Assumptions About Human Beings

1. People have an innate tendency to move toward fulfillment of their potentials.
2. People have a concept of their ideal self and a self-concept; when these two are very discrepant, problems arise.
3. Healthy people are aware of all their behavior; they choose their behavior patterns.
4. A client's behavior can be understood only from the client's point of view. Even if a client has misconstrued events in the world, the therapist must understand how the client sees those events.
5. Effective therapy occurs only when a therapist creates conditions of unconditional positive regard, congruence, and empathy, allowing the client to become more congruent, less defensive, and more open to experiences.

He believed that to reach one's full potential, a person must be involved in a relationship that includes unconditional positive regard, congruence, and empathy (to be discussed in a few paragraphs). When people lack this experience in their lives, client-centered therapy can provide it.

Rogerian therapists hold that problem behaviors occur when the environment prevents a person from developing his or her own innate potential. If children are given love and reinforcement only for their achievements, for example, then as adults, they may see themselves almost solely in terms of their achievements. Rogerian treatment involves helping people improve their self-regard and see themselves more accurately. To this end, a Rogerian therapist might treat a client by first encouraging him to explore his past goals, current desires, and expectations for the future. This places his current behavior and problems in a framework. It also allows the therapist to then ask this client whether he can achieve what he wants through his current emphasis on achievement, or if some other strategy would be more effective. Table 16.3 presents the basic assumptions underlying Rogers's approach to treatment.

■ *Carl Rogers' client-centered therapy, or person-centered therapy, is an insight therapy that seeks to help people evaluate the world and themselves from their own perspective.*

Techniques of Client-Centered Therapy

The goal of client-centered therapy is to help clients discover their ideal selves and reconcile this ideal with their real selves. The use of the word *client* rather than *patient* is a key aspect of Rogers's approach to therapy (*patient* connotes a medical model). In psychoanalysis, the therapist *directs* the "cure" and helps patients understand their behavior; in client-centered therapy, the therapist *guides* clients and helps them realize what they feel is right for themselves. Clients are viewed as the experts concerning their own experience.

The therapist must have certain characteristics for therapy to be successful. The three essential characteristics are unconditional positive regard, congruence, and empathy (Rogers, 1957). A basic tenet of client-centered therapy is that the therapist must show *unconditional positive regard*—be an accepting person who projects positive feelings toward clients. To counteract clients' negative experiences with people who were unaccepting, and who thus have taught them to think they are bad or unlikable, client-centered therapists accept clients as they are, with good and bad points; they respect them as individuals.

Congruence is the second necessary component of client-centered therapy. This term refers to being real or genuine. Rogers believed that therapists must be more than accepting; they must be honest and aware of their own feelings. Counselors' congruence allows them to communicate more effectively and to help clients become more aware and open.

Empathic listening, whereby therapists sense how their clients feel and communicate these feelings to clients, is a final condition for client growth. Therapists help clients organize their thoughts and ideas simply by asking the right questions, by giving neutral responses to encourage the client to continue, and by reflecting back the clients' feelings. (That is, the therapist may *paraphrase* a client's ideas, ask the client to clarify and *restate* ideas and feelings in other words, or *reflect* back what the client has just said so that the person can hear his or her own words again.) Even a small physical movement, such as a nod or gesture, can help clients stay on the right track. The client learns to evaluate the world from a personal vantage point, with little interpretation by the therapist.

The combination of acceptance and recognition of clients' emotions, expression of genuine feelings, and listening to clients' problems with empathy form the essentials of the therapeutic relationship. Client-centered therapy can be viewed as a consciousness-raising process that helps people expand their awareness so as to construct new meanings.

Initially, clients tend to express the attitudes and ideas they have adopted from other people, are defensive, and show ineffective, disorganized behavior. A client might say, "I should be making top sales figures," implying "because my father expects me to be a success." As therapy progresses and he experiences the empathy, congruence, and unconditional positive regard of the therapist, the client will begin to use his own ideas and standards when evaluating himself (Rogers, 1951). As a result, he may adjust his ideal self so that it is more in line with his own (rather than his father's) goals, or his behavior may change so that his sales figures climb. Such change allows him to begin to talk about himself in more positive ways and to try to please himself rather than others, part of the process of constructing new meanings. He may say, "I'm satisfied with my sales efforts," or "Since I've started rethinking my goals, my sales figures have improved," reflecting a more positive, more accepting attitude about himself. Successful therapy results in clients who are less defensive, more congruent, and more open to new experiences (Rogers, 1980). As this client begins to feel better about himself, he will eventually suggest to the therapist that he feels ready to deal with the world and may be ready to leave therapy.

Criticisms of Client-Centered Therapy

Client-centered therapy is acclaimed for its focus on the therapeutic relationship. No other therapy makes clients feel so warm, accepted, and safe. These are important characteristics of any therapy, but critics argue that they may not be enough to bring about long-lasting change. And some critics assert that lengthy discussions about past problems do not necessarily help people with their present difficulties. They believe that this therapy may be making therapeutic promises that cannot be fulfilled and that it focuses on concepts that are hard to define, such as self-actualization.

Be an *Active* learner

REVIEW

- Define *resistance* and *transference*. p. 579
- What basic criticism of psychoanalysis do ego analysts offer? p. 580
- Identify the disadvantages of psychoanalysis. p. 580
- What is the major disagreement between ego analysts and traditional psychoanalysts on the roles of the id and the ego? p. 580
- Why is Rogers's form of therapy called *client-centered*? p. 581
- What is the fundamental aim of client-centered therapy? pp. 581–583

THINK CRITICALLY

- Why do you think most practitioners feel that psychoanalysis is not the most appropriate treatment for marital problems?
- What are the implications of a theory of therapy based on the assumption that people are drawn toward growth fulfillment, as Rogers assumed?
- Why do you think client-centered therapy might be viewed as a consciousness-raising process?

APPLY PSYCHOLOGY

- If you were a psychologist training others, how might you help them communicate acceptance and recognition of clients' emotions?

Building Table 16.2

Key Components of Psychoanalytic and Humanistic Therapies

Therapy	Nature of Psychopathology	Goal of Therapy	Role of Therapist	Role of Unconscious Material	Role of Patient's Insights	Techniques
Psychoanalytic	Maladjustment reflects inadequate conflict resolution and fixation in early development.	Attainment of maturity, strengthened ego functions, reduced control by unconscious or repressed impulses	An *investigator,* uncovering conflicts and resistances	Primary in classical psychoanalysis; less emphasized in ego analysis	Includes not solely intellectual understanding but also emotional experiences	Analyst takes an active role in interpreting the dreams and free associations of patients.
Humanistic	Incongruity exists between real self and potential, desired self; overdependence on others for gratification and self-esteem is also present.	Self-determination; release of human potential; expanded awareness	An *empathic person,* in honest encounter with client, sharing experience	Emphasis on conscious experience	More emphasis on *how* and *what* questions than on *why* questions	Therapist helps client to see the world from a different perspective and focus on the present and the future instead of the past.

Building Table 16.2 presents a summary of the key components of the psychoanalytic and humanistic views of therapy.

Behavior Therapy

Behavior therapy has assumptions and goals that differ from those of psychodynamic and humanistic therapies. It has become especially popular in the past three decades for three principal reasons. First, people sometimes have problems that may not warrant an in-depth discussion of early childhood experiences, an exploration of unconscious motivations, a lengthy discussion about current feelings, or a resolution of inner conflicts. Examples of such problems are fear of heights, anxiety about public speaking, marital conflicts, and sexual dysfunction. In these cases, behavior therapy may be more appropriate than psychodynamically based or humanistic therapies. Second, behavior therapy has become popular because HMOs and other insurance organizations are seeking quicker, less expensive solutions to everyday problems. Last, behavior therapy can be very effective. As you will see, this type of therapy is very focused on changing current behavior and on designing solutions to problems.

Behavior therapy
A therapy that is based on the application of learning principles to human behavior and that focuses on changing overt behaviors rather than on understanding subjective feelings, unconscious processes, or motivations; also known as *behavior modification*.

Goals of Behavior Therapy

Behavior therapy is a therapy based on the application of learning principles to human behavior. Also called *behavior modification*, it focuses on changing overt behaviors rather than on understanding subjective feelings, unconscious processes, or motivations. It uses learning principles to help people replace maladaptive behaviors with more effective ones. Behavior therapists assume that changes in people's environment affect the way they respond to that environment and the way they interact with other people—their behavior. Unlike psychodynamically based therapies, behavior therapy does not aim to discover the origins of a behavior; it works only to alter it. For a person with a nervous twitch, for example, the goal would be to eliminate the twitch. Thus, behavior therapists treat people by having them first "unlearn" faulty behaviors and then learn more acceptable or effective ones.

Behavior therapists do not always focus on the problem that caused the client to seek therapy. If they see that the client's problem is associated with some other situation, they may focus on changing that situation. For example, a man may seek therapy because of a faltering marriage. However, the therapist may discover that the marriage is suffering because of the client's frequent and acrimonious arguments with his wife, each of which is followed by a period of heavy drinking. The therapist may then discover that both the arguments and the drinking are brought on by stress at work, aggravated by the client's unrealistic expectations regarding his performance. In this situation, the therapist may focus on helping the client develop standards that will ease the original cause of the problem—the tension experienced at work—and will be consistent with the client's capabilities, past performance, and realistic likelihood of future performance.

Unlike psychodynamic and humanistic therapies, behavior therapy does not encourage clients to interpret past events to find their meaning. Although a behavior therapist may uncover a chain of events leading to a specific behavior, that discovery will not generally prompt a close examination of the client's early experiences.

When people enter behavior therapy, many aspects of their behavior may change, not just those specifically being treated. Thus, a woman being treated for extreme shyness may find not only that the shyness decreases, but also that she can engage more easily in discussions about emotional topics and can perform better on the job. Behaviorists argue that once a person's behavior has changed, it may be easier for the person to manage attitudes, fears, and conflicts.

Behaviorists are dissatisfied with psychodynamic and humanistic therapies for three basic reasons: (1) those therapies use concepts that are almost impossible to define and measure (such as the id and self-actualization); (2) some studies show that patients who do not receive psychodynamic and humanistic therapies improve anyway; and (3) once a therapist has labeled a person as abnormal, the label itself may lead to maladaptive behavior. (Although this is true of any type of therapy, psychodynamic therapy tends to use labels more than behavior therapy does.) Behavior therapists assume that people display maladaptive behaviors not because they are abnormal but because they are having trouble adjusting to their environment; if they are taught new ways of coping, the maladjustment will disappear. A great strength of behavior therapy is that it provides a coherent conceptual framework.

However, behavior therapy is not without its critics. Most insight therapists, especially those who are psychodynamically based, believe that if only overt behavior is treated, symptom substitution may occur. **Symptom substitution** is the appearance of one overt symptom to replace another that has been eliminated by treatment. Thus, insight therapists argue that if a therapist eliminates a nervous twitch without examining its underlying causes, the client will express the underlying disorder by developing some other symptom, such as a speech impediment. Behavior therapists, on the other hand, contend that symptom substitution does not occur if the treatment makes proper use of behavioral principles. Research shows that behavior therapy is at least as effective as insight therapy and in some cases more effective (Kazdin, 2000, 2001).

Behavior therapists use an array of techniques, often in combination, to help people change their behavior; chief among these techniques are operant condition-

student voices

Jennifer Felty
Carson-Newman College

As an education major, I've certainly seen how these theorists have come up with their ideas just by watching and studying children's behaviors. When you start to notice how children can learn vicariously or by modeling, it causes you as a person to check your own behavior since you're never sure who's watching you.

Symptom substitution The appearance of one overt symptom to replace another that has been eliminated by treatment.

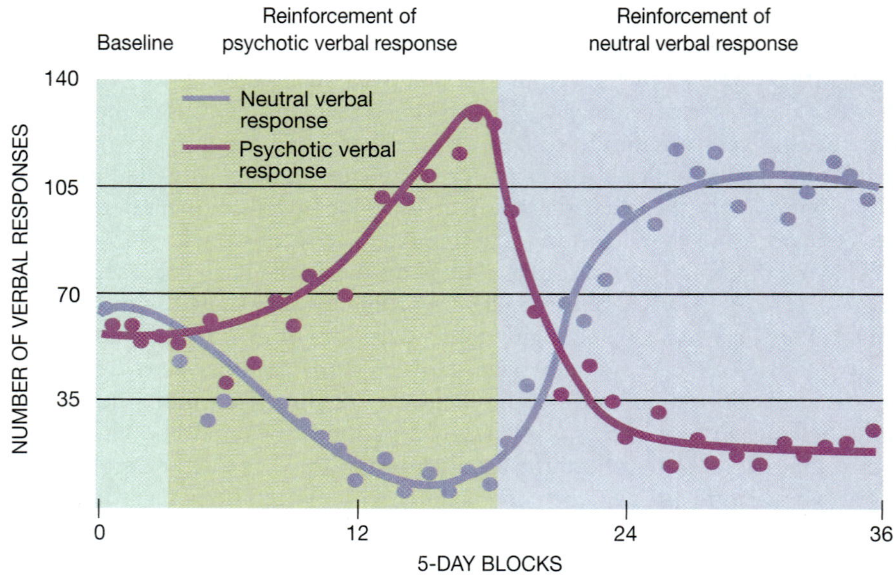

FIGURE 16.3

Reinforcement Increases Desired Behaviors

A study by Ayllon and Haughton (1964) found that reinforcement affected the frequency of psychotic and neutral verbal behavior in hospitalized patients.
(Ayllon & Haughton, 1964)

ing, counterconditioning, and modeling. A good therapist will use whatever combination of techniques will help a client most efficiently and effectively—so, in addition to using several behavioral techniques, a behavior therapist may use some insight techniques. The more complicated the disorder being treated, the more likely it is that a practitioner will use a mix of therapeutic approaches.

Behavior therapy usually involves three general procedures: (1) identifying the problem behavior and its frequency by examining what people actually do; (2) treating a client with treatment strategies that are individually tailored to the client, perhaps by reeducation, communication training, or some type of counterconditioning; and (3) continually assessing whether there is a behavior change. If the client exhibits a new behavior for several weeks or months, the therapist concludes that treatment was effective. Let's now explore the three major behavior therapy techniques: operant conditioning, counterconditioning, and modeling.

Operant Conditioning

Operant conditioning procedures are used with various people in different settings to achieve a wide range of desirable behaviors, including increased reading speed, improved classroom behavior, and the maintenance of personal hygiene. As we saw in Chapter 7, operant conditioning to establish new behaviors often depends on a *reinforcer*—an event or circumstance that increases the probability that a particular response will recur. A client could employ operant conditioning to help herself adopt more positive responses toward herself. For example, she could ask her boyfriend to acknowledge her effort every time she tries to express her feelings openly.

One of the most effective uses of operant conditioning is with children who are antisocial, slow to learn, or in some way maladjusted. Operant conditioning is also effective with patients in mental hospitals. Ayllon and Haughton (1964), for example, instructed hospital staff members to reinforce patients for psychotic, bizarre, or meaningless verbalizations during one period and for neutral verbalizations (such as comments about the weather) during another. As expected, the relative frequency of each type of verbalization increased when it was reinforced and decreased when it was not reinforced (see Figure 16.3).

Token economy
An operant conditioning procedure in which individuals who display appropriate behavior receive tokens that they can exchange for desirable items or activities.

■ **TOKEN ECONOMIES.** One way of rewarding adaptive behavior is with a **token economy**—an operant conditioning procedure in which individuals who display ap-

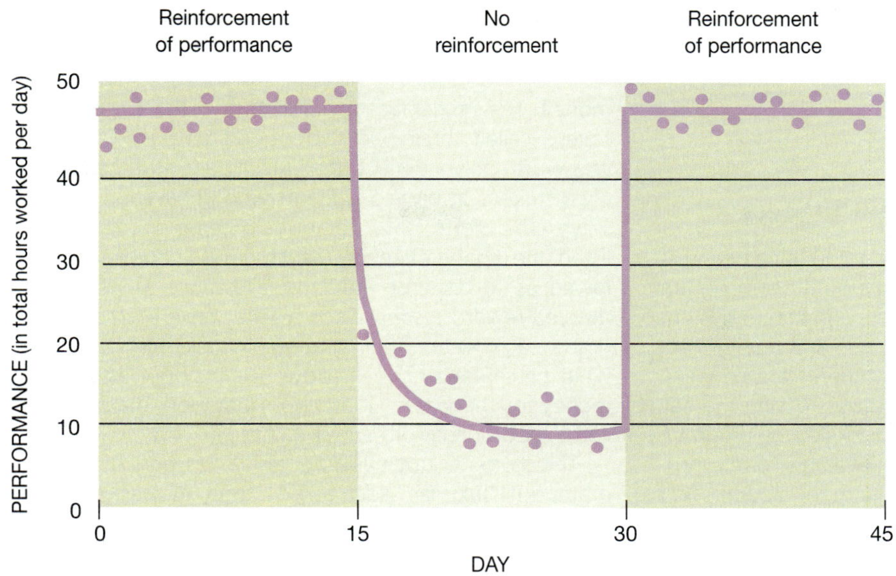

FIGURE 16.4

Token Economies Change Performance Effectively

Ayllon and Azrin (1965) found that tokens increased the total number of hours worked per day by a group of 44 patients. *(Ayllon & Azrin, 1965)*

propriate behavior receive tokens that they can exchange for desirable items or activities. In a hospital setting, for example, some rewards might be candy, new clothes, games, or time with important people in the patients' lives; the more tokens individuals earn, the more items or activities they can obtain. Token economies have also been effective in school settings. Teachers who use a token economy often keep track of tokens publicly and reward students with some fanfare.

Token economies are used to modify behavior in social settings; they aim to strengthen behaviors that are compatible with social norms. For example, a patient in a mental hospital might receive tokens for cleaning tables, helping in the hospital laundry, or maintaining certain standards of personal hygiene and appearance. The level of difficulty of the behavior or task determines the number of tokens earned. Thus, patients might receive 3 tokens for brushing their teeth but 40 tokens for engaging in helping behaviors.

Ayllon and Azrin (1965) monitored the performance of a group of hospitalized patients who were involved in doing simple tasks for 45 days. They found that when tokens (reinforcement) were contingent on performance, the patients worked about four times as long each day as when tokens were not delivered. (See Figure 16.4, which presents some of the results of the research.) Token economies become especially effective when combined with other behavioral techniques as discussed in *Psychology in Action* on the following page. We examine three of these techniques next—extinction, punishment, and time-out.

■ **EXTINCTION.** As we saw in Chapter 7, if reinforcers are withheld, extinction of a behavior will occur. Suppose a 6-year-old girl refuses to go to bed at the designated time. When she is taken to her bedroom, she cries and screams violently. If the parents give in and allow her to stay up, they are reinforcing the crying behavior: the child cries and the parents give in. A therapist might suggest that the parents stop reinforcing the crying behavior by insisting that their daughter go to bed and stay there. Chances are that the child will cry loudly and violently for two or three nights, but the behavior will eventually be extinguished (Williams, 1959).

■ **PUNISHMENT.** Another way to decrease the frequency of an undesired behavior is to punish it. Punishment often involves the presentation of an aversive stimulus. In the laboratory, researchers might use slight electric shocks to get adult participants to stop performing a specific behavior. As we saw in Chapter 7, a serious limitation of punishment as a behavior-shaping device is that it suppresses only existing

psychology *in action*

A Token Economy

For many years, I (LB) have been associated with a summer program for gifted adolescents. This program is a comprehensive enrichment program that includes academic and fine arts activities in a residential program. The students are between ages 12 and 16; they attend various classes during the day and stay in a campus dorm for the 7 weeks of the program. Counselors (who are most often college-age former students of the program) live in the dorm with the students and supervise them when students are not in class. These gifted students are bright and creative—not only academically and artistically but also in terms of getting into trouble. Behavior problems are a continual concern. One misbehaving child is a problem; 80 gifted children living together and thinking of creative ways to break the rules is a real challenge.

Five years ago, the director of the program asked me to design a token economy to help manage the problem behavior. For a psychologist, this challenge was a terrific opportunity to put principles of operant conditioning into action. Token economies have been used in schools and in mental hospitals to help teachers and therapists control undesirable behaviors. This system works best when the people in charge control the rewards. Our program for gifted students seemed ideal.

We designed a system with immediate and delayed rewards, using an important source of reinforcement—money. The immediate rewards involve the dispensing of tokens (called "brain bucks") for good behavior. Each token was worth only a dime, but all faculty and staff kept a supply of tokens to give to students who behaved in desirable ways. (The motto was "Catch them being good.") We enlisted the cooperation of the students' parents, who allowed us to dispense students' allowance as part of the delayed reward system. Each teacher gave each student a grade each week. Their grade-point average determined what percentage of their allowance they got as spending money for the week. Good classroom work maximized income; good behavior earned tokens.

The students got basic necessities as part of the program, but "luxuries" such as junk food, movies, and other entertainment came out of their allowance. Thus, the students became motivated to do their work and behave in acceptable ways. This system has been quite successful, especially in controlling misbehavior in the dorm.

Two years ago, I had a classroom experience that showed me the power of the token economy system. Another instructor and I were team-teaching—an ideal situation in which I could dispense tokens while he lectured—on the first day of classes. This day is devoted to getting acquainted, and little work gets done, but my coteacher started to lecture the students about the plan for the session. When he did, I decided to get out the tokens. I got the bag of tokens out of my briefcase and set them on the desk. The students immediately became quiet, focused on the lecturer, and sat straight in their seats. The visible presence of the tokens prompted them to behave like good students.

behaviors; it cannot be used to establish new, desired behaviors. Thus, punishment for undesired behaviors is usually combined with positive reinforcement for desired behaviors.

Research also shows that people, especially young people, imitate aggression. Thus, a child (or institutionalized person) in therapy may strike out at the therapist who administers punishment in an attempt to eliminate the source of punishment, sometimes inflicting serious injury. Punishment can also bring about generalized aggression. This is especially true for prison inmates, whose hostility is well recognized, and for class bullies, who are often the children most strictly disciplined by their parents or teachers. Skinner (1988) believed that punishment is harmful; he advocated nonpunitive therapeutic techniques, which might involve developing strong bonds between clients and therapists and reinforcing specific prosocial activities. In general, procedures that lead to a perception of control on the part of a client are much more likely to lead to the extinction of undesired behavior.

Time-out
An operant conditioning procedure in which a person is physically removed from sources of reinforcement to decrease the occurrence of undesired behaviors.

■ **TIME-OUT.** As we saw in Chapter 7, one effective operant conditioning procedure is **time-out,** the physical removal of a person from sources of reinforcement in order to decrease the occurrence of undesired behaviors. Suppose a boy regularly throws a temper tantrum each time he wants a piece of candy, an ice cream cone, or his little brother's toys. With the time-out procedure, whenever the child misbehaves, he is taken to a restricted area (such as a chair or a room) away from the rest of the family, without sweets, toys, or other people, or any type of reinforcer. He is made to stay in the restricted area for a short period, say, 5 or 10 minutes; if he leaves, more time is added. The procedure ensures that the child not only does not get what he wants, but that he is also removed from any potential source of reinforcement. Time-out is principally used with children; it is especially effective when it is combined with positive reinforcers for appropriate behavior and is administered by a knowledgeable parent or child-care specialist (Crespi, 1988).

Counterconditioning

A second major technique of behavior therapy is **counterconditioning,** a process of reconditioning in which a person is taught a new, more adaptive response to a familiar stimulus. For example, anxiety in response to any of a number of stimuli is one of the main reasons people seek therapy. If a therapist can condition a person to respond to a stimulus with something other than anxiety—that is, if the therapist can *countercondition* the person—a real breakthrough will be achieved, and the person's anxiety will be reduced.

Joseph Wolpe (1915–1997) was one of the initial proponents of counterconditioning. His work in classical conditioning, especially in situations in which animals show conditioned anxiety responses, led him to attempt to inhibit or decrease anxiety as a response in human beings. His therapeutic goal was to replace anxiety with some other response, such as relaxation, amusement, or pleasure.

Behavior therapy using counterconditioning begins with a specific stimulus (S1), which elicits a specific response (R1). After the person undergoes counterconditioning, the same stimulus (S1) should elicit a new response (R2) (Wolpe, 1958). There are two basic approaches to counterconditioning: systematic desensitization and aversive counterconditioning.

■ **SYSTEMATIC DESENSITIZATION.** **Systematic desensitization** is a three-stage counterconditioning procedure in which people are taught to relax when confronting stimuli that formerly elicited anxiety. The client first learns how to relax, then describes the specific situations that arouse anxiety, and finally, while deeply relaxed, imagines increasingly vivid scenes of the situations that elicit anxiety. In this way, the client is gradually, step by step, exposed to the source of anxiety, usually by imagining (while relaxed) a series of progressively more intense fear- or anxiety-provoking situations. With each successive experience, the client learns relaxation rather than fear as a response. Eventually, the client confronts the real-life situation.

Flying in an airplane, for example, is a stimulus situation (S1) that can bring about a fear response (R1). With systematic desensitization therapy, the idea of flying (S1) can eventually elicit a response of curiosity or even relaxation (R2). The therapist might first ask the relaxed client to imagine sitting in an airplane on the ground, then to imagine the airplane taxiing down a runway, and eventually to imagine flying though the billowing clouds. As the client practices relaxation while imagining the scene, he or she becomes able to tolerate more stressful imagery and may eventually perform the behavior that previously elicited anxiety—in this case, flying in an airplane. Eventually, practicing and becoming desensitized in real-world situations produce the most lasting effects. If systematic desensitization is combined with efforts to change a person's ideas about the world—cognitive therapy, which we examine in the next section—the person can cope better. Through systematic desensitization and cognitive therapy, people can lose their fear of flying, which has traditionally been a major problem for 25 million Americans and many more since the World Trade Center attacks.

Counterconditioning
Process of reconditioning in which a person is taught a new, more adaptive response to a familiar stimulus.

Systematic desensitization
A three-stage counterconditioning procedure in which people are taught to relax when confronting stimuli that formerly elicited anxiety.

Aversive counterconditioning A counterconditioning technique in which an aversive or noxious stimulus is paired with a stimulus that elicits an undesirable behavior so that the person will cease responding to the familiar stimulus with the undesirable behavior.

Systematic desensitization is most successful for people who have problems such as impulse control or who exhibit particular forms of anxiety such as phobias. It is not especially effective for people who exhibit serious psychotic symptoms; nor is it the best treatment for situations involving interpersonal conflict.

■ **AVERSIVE COUNTERCONDITIONING.** Clients often have problems because they do not avoid a stimulus that prompts inappropriate behavior. This is where aversive counterconditioning can be used. **Aversive counterconditioning** is a counterconditioning technique in which an aversive or noxious stimulus is paired with a stimulus that elicits an undesirable behavior so that the person will cease responding to the familiar stimulus with the undesirable behavior. As with systematic desensitization, the objective is to teach a new response to the original stimulus. A behavior therapist might use aversive counterconditioning to teach an alcoholic client to avoid alcohol. The first step might be to teach the person to associate alcohol (the original stimulus) with the sensation of nausea (a noxious stimulus). If having the client simply imagine the association is not enough, the therapist might administer a drug that causes the client to feel nauseous whenever he or she consumes alcohol. The goal is to make drinking alcohol unpleasant. Eventually, the treatment will make the client experience nausea just at the *thought* of consuming alcohol, thus causing the client to avoid alcohol.

Modeling

Both children and adults learn behaviors by watching and imitating other people—in other words, by observing models. Children learn a whole host of behaviors—from table manners to toileting behavior to appropriate responses to animals—by observing and imitating their parents and other models. Similarly, the music you listen to, the clothing styles you wear, and the social or political causes you support are determined, in part, by the people around you.

According to Albert Bandura (1977a), modeling is a behavior therapy technique that is most effective for (1) teaching new behavior, (2) helping to eliminate fears, especially phobias, and (3) enhancing already existing behavior. By watching the behavior of others, people learn to exhibit more adaptive and appropriate

■ *Children learn a host of behaviors by observing and imitating their parents and other models.*

point*counterpoint*

Controlled Drinking and Alcoholism

The Issue: Can alcoholics become controlled drinkers?

POINT
Alcoholism is a disease that can be treated only through complete and total abstinence.

COUNTERPOINT
Some people with alcohol-related disorders can be taught to control their drinking; abstinence is not required.

Alcohol and drug abuse problems are among the most common that practitioners face, and they are not all of one voice when it comes to treatment goals.

On one hand, some psychologists argue that the goal of treatment must be total, complete, and permanent abstinence from alcohol. This position has been popularized by Alcoholics Anonymous (AA) and has become the most prominent approach among those therapists who treat alcoholism. From AA's point of view, once a person has crossed the line from heavy drinking to irresponsible alcoholic drinking, there seems to be no turning back—an alcoholic will never be able to control his or her drinking for any significant duration. Alcoholics must become abstinent—staying away from alcohol completely. Abstinence is a difficult treatment goal; only 15% of all alcoholics seen in treatment facilities are abstinent for at least 5 years.

Some therapists, on the other hand, contend that controlled, moderate drinking is an attainable treatment goal. Through training oriented toward teaching problem drinkers to pace their drinking and limit their alcohol intake, proponents argue that problem drinkers can become social drinkers.

Is controlled drinking an attainable goal for problem drinkers? Many individuals who develop drinking problems modify their alcohol abuse habits without professional help, which suggests that people can learn to control their problem drinking (Sobell, Cunningham, & Sobell, 1996). Controlled drinking becomes less likely the more severe the degree of alcohol-related problems; people who have been heavy, long-term drinkers are not good candidates for controlled drinking. The duration and extent of abusive drinking predict who best can control their drinking (Rosenberg, 1993).

If a person is a long-term alcoholic, the likelihood that controlled drinking will be attainable is unlikely—abstinence is the most reliable goal. Others who have experienced problems with alcohol may be able to learn to be moderate drinkers, and for these individuals, controlled, moderate drinking is a reasonable treatment goal.

behavior. Bandura, Blanchard, and Ritter (1969), for example, asked people with snake phobia to watch other people handling snakes. Afterward, the watchers' fear of snakes was reduced.

One problem with modeling is that people may observe and imitate the behavior of inappropriate models. As we saw in Chapter 12, people imitate violent behaviors they have observed on television and in movies. Further, many adolescents abuse alcohol and other drugs because they imitate their peers. Such imitation often occurs because of faulty thinking about situations, people, or goals.

Building Table 16.3

Key Components of Psychoanalytic, Humanistic, and Behavior Therapies

Therapy	Nature of Psycho-pathology	Goal of Therapy	Role of Therapist	Role of Unconscious Material	Role of Patient's Insights	Techniques
Psychoanalytic	Maladjustment reflects inadequate conflict resolution and fixation in early development.	Attainment of maturity, strengthened ego functions, reduced control by unconscious or repressed impulses	An *investigator*, uncovering conflicts and resistances	Primary in classical psychoanalysis; less emphasized in ego analysis	Includes not solely intellectual understanding but also emotional experiences	Analyst takes an active role in interpreting the dreams and free associations of patients.
Humanistic	Incongruity exists between real self and potential, desired self; overdependence on others for gratification and self-esteem is also present.	Self-determination; release of human potential; expanded awareness	An *empathic person*, in honest encounter with client, sharing experience	Emphasis on conscious experience	More emphasis on *how* and *what* questions than on *why* questions	Therapist helps client to see the world from a different perspective and focus on the present and the future instead of the past.
Behavior	Symptomatic behavior stems from faulty learning or learning of maladaptive behaviors.	Relief of symptomatic behavior by suppressing or replacing maladaptive behaviors	A *helper*, helping client unlearn old behaviors and learn new ones	Not concerned with unconscious processes	Irrelevant and unnecessary	Clients learn new responses; purpose is to establish new behaviors and eliminate faulty or undesirable ones.

Building Table 16.3 summarizes the key components of the psychoanalytic, humanistic, and behavioral views of therapy.

Be an *Active* learner

REVIEW

- Identify the fundamental reasons behaviorists are dissatisfied with psychodynamic and humanistic therapies. p. 584
- For what disorders is the behavior therapy technique of operant conditioning especially effective? pp. 584–586
- Explain what happens in time-out. p. 588

THINK CRITICALLY

- How would a behavior therapist's approach to assisting a person suffering from low self-esteem differ from that of a humanistic therapist?
- Why do you think modeling is especially effective in the treatment of phobias?
- Do you think that the appearance of one overt symptom to replace another that has been eliminated by treatment—symptom substitution—is a sufficient reason to discredit behavior therapy? Explain your answer.

APPLY PSYCHOLOGY

- To achieve optimal results, in what ways should HMOs be permitted to determine the best type and duration of therapy for a client?
- Is it possible to design a time-out procedure for an adolescent who will not keep his or her clothes clean? What specific procedures might you put in place?

Cognitive Therapy

Behavior therapy and cognitive therapy have been heavily influenced by HMOs and managed care. A managed care organization usually controls the reimbursement of therapists and thus intervenes between a client and a therapist to make rulings about questions such as these: Does this problem qualify for reimbursement? What technique should be used to treat this client? Is this clinician the appropriate therapist for this client? Many psychologists see managed care as a crisis, a nightmare, and the downfall of psychotherapy (Fishman & Franks, 1997). Behavior therapists and cognitive therapists, however, more than other therapists, have become allies of managed care organizations because of the close alignment of their shared goals, especially the goal of efficiency.

According to cognitive therapists, wrong, distorted, or underdeveloped ideas and thoughts often prevent a person from establishing effective coping strategies. Growing out of behavior therapy and the developing study of cognitive psychology, *cognitive therapy* focuses on changing a client's behavior by changing his or her thoughts and perceptions. Cognitive therapy is derived from three basic propositions: (1) cognitive activity affects behavior, (2) cognitive activity can be monitored, and (3) behavior changes can be effected through cognitive changes. Cognitive psychologists have had a profound impact in many areas of psychology, especially in therapy. In the past, behavior therapists were concerned only with overt behavior; today, many incorporate thought processes into their treatments. For this reason, their work is often called *cognitive behavior therapy*. Researchers now suggest that thought processes may hold the key to managing many forms of maladjustment, including disorders such as obsessive–compulsive disorder (Abramowitz, 1998).

Therapists who use *cognitive restructuring* (cognitive therapy) are interested in modifying the faulty thought patterns of disturbed people (Mahoney, 1977). This type of therapy is effective for people who have attached overly narrow or otherwise inappropriate labels to certain behaviors or situations; for example, such a person may believe that sex is dirty or that assertiveness is unwomanly. Whenever presented with a situation that involves sex or assertiveness, the person will respond in a way that is determined by his or her thoughts about the situation rather than by the facts of the situation.

Cognitive therapy typically focuses on current behavior and current thoughts. It is not especially concerned with uncovering forgotten childhood experiences, although it can be used to alter thoughts about those experiences. It has been used effectively to assist in weight loss and to treat depression, bulimia, excessive anger, and adolescent behavior problems (e.g., Bruce, Spiegel, & Hegel, 2000; Mohr et al., 2000). When cognitive restructuring is combined with other psychological techniques, such as reinforcement, which help a person make behavioral changes, results are even more impressive (Wilson et al., 1999).

Three Therapies

Cognitive therapy has gone through three decades of development, and its future looks promising (Beck et al., 1994; Brown & Barlow, 1995; Gaffan, Tsaousis, & Kemp-Wheeler, 1995). Let's look at three such therapies.

■ **RATIONAL–EMOTIVE THERAPY.** The best-known cognitive therapy is **rational–emotive therapy**, a cognitive behavior therapy that emphasizes the importance of logical, rational thought processes. Researcher Albert Ellis developed this therapy more than 30 years ago. Most behavior therapists assume that abnormal behavior is caused by faulty and irrational *behavior* patterns. Ellis and his colleagues, however, assume that it is caused by faulty and irrational *thinking* patterns (Ellis, 1970, 1999a; Dryden & Ellis, 2001). They believe that if faulty thought processes can be replaced with rational ones, maladjustment and abnormal behavior will disappear.

Rational–emotive therapy
A cognitive behavior therapy that emphasizes the importance of logical, rational thought processes.

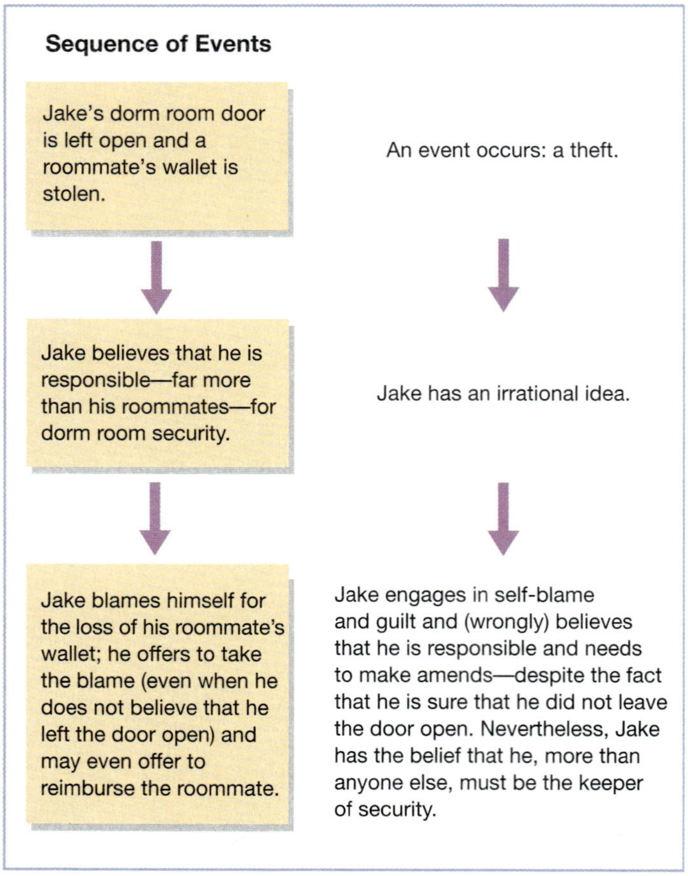

FIGURE 16.5

The Foundations of Irrational Behaviors

From Albert Ellis's view, irrational beliefs about events in people's lives cause emotional distress and maladjustment. Jake has a careless roommate (or even a careless friend) who leaves a dorm room open; a roommate's wallet disappears. Jake's wrongheaded belief that he alone has to take responsibility for dorm room security leads to unhappiness and anxiety.

According to Ellis, psychological disturbance is a result of events in a person's life that give rise to irrational beliefs leading to negative emotions and behaviors. Moreover, these beliefs are a breeding ground for further irrational ideas (Dryden & Ellis, 1988). Ellis (1999b) argues that people make demands on themselves and on other people, and they rigidly hold on to them no matter how unrealistic and illogical they are. See Figure 16.5 to see this sequence of events.

Thus, a major goal of rational–emotive therapy is to help people examine the past events that produced the irrational beliefs (Ellis, 2001). Ellis, for example, tries to focus on a client's basic philosophy of life and determine if it is self-defeating. He thus tries to uncover the client's thought patterns and help the client recognize that the underlying beliefs are faulty. Table 16.4 lists ten irrational assumptions that, according to Ellis, cause emotional problems and maladaptive behaviors. They are based on people's needs to be liked, to be competent, to be loved, and to feel secure. When people assign irrational or exaggerated value to fulfilling these needs, the needs become maladaptive and lead to emotional disturbance, anxiety, and abnormal behavior. If rational–emotive therapy is successful, the client adopts different behaviors based on more rational thought processes. Research supports the effectiveness of the approach (Abrams & Ellis, 1994; Haaga & Davison, 1993), and Ellis (2001) asserts that rational–emotive therapy has broad applications in both therapeutic and classroom settings.

■ **BECK'S APPROACH.** Another cognitive therapy that focuses on irrational ideas is that of Aaron Beck (1963). As we saw in Chapter 15, Beck's theory assumes that depression is caused by people's distorted thoughts about reality, which lead to negative views about the world, themselves, and the future, and often to gross overgeneralizations. For example, people who think they have no future—that all of their options are blocked—and who undervalue their intelligence are likely to be depressed. Such individuals form appraisals of situations that are distorted and based on insufficient (and sometimes wrong) data. The goal of therapy, therefore, is to help them develop realistic appraisals of the situations they encounter and solve their problems (Beck, 1991). The therapist acts as a trainer and coinvestigator, providing data to be examined and guidance in understanding how cognitions influence behavior (Beck & Weishaar, 1989).

According to Beck (1976), a successful client passes through four stages in the course of correcting faulty views and moving toward improved mental health: "First, he has to become aware of what he is thinking. Second, he needs to recognize what thoughts are awry. Then he has to substitute accurate for inaccurate judgments. Finally, he needs feedback to inform him whether his changes are correct" (p. 217).

■ **MEICHENBAUM'S APPROACH.** Some researchers, among them Donald Meichenbaum, believe that what people say to themselves determines what they will do. Therefore, a key goal of therapy is to change the things people say to themselves. According to Meichenbaum, the therapist has to change the client's appraisal of

TABLE 16.4

Ellis's Outline of Ten Irrational Assumptions

1. It is a necessity for an adult to be loved and approved of by almost everyone for virtually everything.
2. A person must be thoroughly competent, adequate, and successful in all respects.
3. Certain people are bad, wicked, or villainous and should be punished for their sins.
4. It is catastrophic when things are not going the way one would like.
5. Human unhappiness is externally caused. People have little or no ability to control their sorrows or to rid themselves of negative feelings.
6. It is right to be terribly preoccupied with and upset about something that may be dangerous or fearsome.
7. It is easier to avoid facing many of life's difficulties and responsibilities than it is to undertake more rewarding forms of self-discipline.
8. The past is all-important. Because something once strongly affected someone's life, it should continue to do so indefinitely.
9. People and things should be different from the way they are. It is catastrophic if perfect solutions to the grim realities of life are not immediately found.
10. Maximal human happiness can be achieved by inertia and inaction or by passively and without commitment "enjoying oneself."

Ellis & Harper, 1961.

stressful events and the client's use of self-instructions, thus normalizing her or his reactions (Meichenbaum, 1993).

A strength of Meichenbaum's theory is that self-instruction can be used in many settings for many kinds of problems. It can help people who are shy or impulsive, people with speech impediments, and even those who are schizophrenic (Meichenbaum, 1974; Meichenbaum & Cameron, 1973). Rather than attempting to change their irrational beliefs, clients learn a repertoire of activities they can use to make their behavior more adaptive. For example, they may learn to conduct a private monologue in which they work out adaptive ways of coping with situations. They can then discuss with a therapist the quality and usefulness of these self-instructional statements. They may learn to organize their responses to specific situations in an orderly set of steps that can be easily carried out.

Building Table 16.4 on the following page provides an overall summary of the psychoanalytic, humanistic, behavioral, and cognitive approaches to individual therapy.

Cognitive therapy in its many forms has been used with adults and children and with groups having particular characteristics, such as women and the elderly. It can be applied to problems such as anxiety disorders, marital difficulties, chronic pain, and (as is evident from Beck's work) depression. Cognitive therapy continues to make enormous strides. It is influencing an increasing number of theorists and practitioners who conduct both long-term therapy and brief therapy.

Be an *Active* learner

REVIEW

- What is the basic idea behind cognitive therapy? pp. 593–594
- According to Ellis, what are the consequences of developing irrational beliefs? p. 593
- Compare and contrast rational-emotive therapy and Beck's approach to cognitive therapy. pp. 594–595

THINK CRITICALLY

- What do you think that people say to themselves that brings about dysfunctional behavior? How can therapy change that conversation?

APPLY PSYCHOLOGY

- What irrational belief can you identify in a friend or family member who suffers from some psychological condition? Make a list of the top three things that you think guide this person's behavior in maladaptive ways.

Building Table 16.4

Key Components of Psychoanalytic, Humanistic, Behavior, and Cognitive Therapies

Therapy	Nature of Psychopathology	Goal of Therapy	Role of Therapist	Role of Unconscious Material	Role of Patient's Insights	Techniques
Psychoanalytic	Maladjustment reflects inadequate conflict resolution and fixation in early development.	Attainment of maturity, strengthened ego functions, reduced control by unconscious or repressed impulses	An *investigator,* uncovering conflicts and resistances	Primary in classical psychoanalysis; less emphasized in ego analysis	Includes not solely intellectual understanding but also emotional experiences	Analyst takes an active role in interpreting the dreams and free associations of patients.
Humanistic	Incongruity exists between real self and potential, desired self; overdependence on others for gratification and self-esteem is also present.	Self-determination; release of human potential; expanded awareness	An *empathic person,* in honest encounter with client, sharing experience	Emphasis on conscious experience	More emphasis on *how* and *what* questions than on *why* questions	Therapist helps client to see the world from a different perspective and focus on the present and the future instead of the past.
Behavior	Symptomatic behavior stems from faulty learning or learning of maladaptive behaviors.	Relief of symptomatic behavior by suppressing or replacing maladaptive behaviors	A *helper,* helping client unlearn old behaviors and learn new ones	Not concerned with unconscious processes	Irrelevant and unnecessary	Clients learn new responses; purpose is to establish new behaviors and eliminate faulty or undesirable ones.
Cognitive	Maladjustment occurs because of faulty, irrational thought patterns.	Change in the way clients think about themselves and the world	A *trainer* and *coinvestigator,* helping the client learn new, rational ways to think about the world	Little or no concern with unconscious processes	Irrelevant to therapy but may be used if they do occur	Clients learn to think situations through logically and to reconsider many of their irrational assumptions

Group Therapy

Group therapy
Psychotherapeutic process in which several people meet as a group with a therapist to receive psychological help.

When several people meet as a group to receive psychological help from a therapist, the treatment is referred to as **group therapy.** This technique was introduced in the early 1900s and has become increasingly popular since World War II. One reason for its popularity is that in the United States the demand for therapists exceeds the number available. Individually, a therapist can generally see up to 40 clients a week for 1 hour each. But in a group, the same therapist might see 8 to 10 clients in just 1 hour. Another reason for the popularity is that the therapist's fee is shared among the members of the group, making group therapy less expensive than individual therapy.

Group therapy can also be more effective than individual therapy (Barlow, Burlingame, & Nebeker, 2000; McRoberts, Burlingame, & Hoag, 1998) because the social pressures that operate in a group can help shape the members' behavior. In addition, group members can be useful models of behavior for one another, and they can provide mutual reinforcement and support.

■ *When several people meet as a group to receive psychological help from a therapist, the treatment is referred to as group therapy.*

Techniques and Formats

The techniques used in group therapy are determined largely by the nature of the group and the orientation of its therapist—psychoanalytic, client-centered, behavioral, or other. No two groups are alike, and no two therapists deal with individual group members in the same way.

In traditional group therapy, 6 to 12 clients meet regularly (usually once a week) with a therapist in a clinic, a hospital, or the therapist's office. Generally, the therapist selects members on the basis of what they can gain from and offer to the group. The goal is to construct a group whose members are compatible (though not necessarily identical) in terms of age, needs, and problems. The duration of group therapy varies; it usually takes longer than 6 months, but there are a growing number of short-term groups that meet for fewer than 12 weeks (Rose, 1999; Rycroft, 2001). The format of traditional group therapy varies, but generally each member describes her or his problems to the other members, who in turn relate their experiences with similar problems and how they coped with them. This gives individuals a chance to express their fears and anxieties to people who are accepting; each member eventually realizes that everyone has emotional problems. Group members also have opportunities to role-play (try out) new behaviors in a safe environment. In a mental health center, for example, a therapist might help group members relive past traumas and cope with their continuing fears. Sometimes the therapist directs the group in addressing a problem. At other times, the therapist allows the group to resolve a problem independently. Members can also exert pressure on an individual to behave in more appropriate ways.

Family Therapy

Family therapy is a special form of group therapy in which two or more people who are committed to each other's well-being are treated together in an effort to change the ways they interact. (Marital, or couples, therapy is thus a subcategory of family therapy.) A *family* is defined as any group of people who are committed to one another's well-being, preferably for life (Bronfenbrenner, 1989, 1999). Today's therapists recognize that families are often nontraditional; blended families and single-parent families are very common, for example. Different kinds of families are shaping the way people respond to the world and must be considered as part of the cultural context in which psychologists view behavior. And even for traditional families, life has grown more complicated by the increasing need to juggle work and family responsibilities and cope with societal problems.

With families facing new kinds of problems, family therapy is now used by a large number of practitioners, especially social workers. In today's world of managed care and HMOs, brief family therapy is the order of the day, and symptom relief is usually the first, but certainly not the only, goal. From a family therapist's point of view, the real focus of family therapy is the family's structure and organization. While family members may identify one person—perhaps a delinquent child—as the problem, family therapists believe that in many cases, that person may

Family therapy
A type of therapy in which two or more people who are committed to one another's well-being are treated at once, in an effort to change the ways they interact.

simply be a scapegoat. The so-called problem member diverts the family's attention from structural problems that are difficult to confront. Any clinician who works with a person who has some type of adjustment problem must also consider the impact of this problem on the people that individual interacts with.

Sometimes family therapy is called *relationship therapy* because relationships are often the focus of the intervention, especially with couples (Jacobson et al., 2000; Johnson & Lebow, 2000; Lawrence et al., 1999). Research indicates that, like other forms of therapy, family therapy and marital (couples) therapy are effective (Behr, 2001). However, because of the myriad of variables operating within families, such research is complicated, to say the least (Villeneuve, 2001).

Family therapists often attempt to change *family systems*. This means that treatment takes place within the dynamic social system of the marriage or the family (Fraenkel & Pinsof, 2001; Hoffman, Fruzzetti, & Swenson, 1999). Therapists assume that there are multiple sources of psychological influence: individuals within a family affect family interactions, and family interactions affect individuals; the family is thus an interactive system (Sturges, 1994). For example, when a mother labels a son "lazy" because he doesn't have a job, the son may feel shame but may act out his feeling as anger. He may lash out at his father's poor work habits and lack of success. This reaction may be followed by a squabble over who "brings home the bacon," and so forth. The mother's attitude thus leads to a clash among all the individuals within the family system. The family systems approach has become especially popular in colleges of social work, in departments of psychology, and even in colleges of medicine, where patients are often seen in a family setting. A useful technique in family therapy is to *restructure* the family's interactions. If a son is responding passively to his domineering mother, for example, the therapist may suggest that the son be assigned chores only by his father.

An issue that often emerges in family therapy is how all members of the family can become enmeshed in one member's problem—for example, depression, alcoholism, drug abuse, or anxiety disorder. Such involvement often becomes devastating for the whole family. This problem is termed *codependence*. Practitioners often see patients with alcoholism or cocaine addiction whose friends or family members are codependent. Codependence is not a disorder in the *DSM*. In fact, the families of people with problems such as substance abuse have gone relatively unnoticed. But practitioners who treat whole families, not just the person suffering from maladjustment, view codependence as an additional type of adjustment problem—not for the patient but for the patient's family and friends.

The codependents—the family members or friends—are often plagued by intense feelings of shame, fear, anger, and pain; they cannot express those feelings, however, because they feel obligated to care for the person suffering from the disorder or addiction. Codependent children may believe their job is to take care of their maladjusted parents. Codependent adults may strive to help their maladjusted spouses, relatives, or friends with their problems. They often think that if they were perfect, they could help the maladjusted individual. In some cases, people actually *need* the person to stay disordered; family members sometimes unconsciously want a member with a problem to remain dependent on them so that they can remain in a controlling position.

Some researchers believe the family systems approach to be as effective as individual therapy—and more effective in some situations (Ford et al., 1998). Not all families profit equally from such interventions, however. Family therapy is

Be an *Active* learner

REVIEW

- Why do therapists feel that group therapy can sometimes be more effective than individual therapy? pp. 576–577
- What is a codependent person? p. 578

THINK CRITICALLY

- Why do you think that having several people in treatment together makes such a difference? Isn't getting a great deal of one-on-one attention—individual therapy—likely to produce superior results? Explain your answer.
- Why do you think that researchers believe the family systems approach is as effective, or even more effective, than other approaches to therapy?
- Why do you think that codependent people are often plagued by intense feelings of shame, fear, anger, and pain, and they cannot express those feelings?

APPLY PSYCHOLOGY

- As an adult, is group therapy for you? Why do you think it would be more or less influential in your life than individual therapy?

difficult with families that are disorganized. Younger couples and families seem to have better outcomes. When depression is evident, outcomes are not as good (Lebow & Gurman, 1995). In addition, some family members may refuse to participate or drop out of therapy; this almost always has negative consequences (Prinz et al., 2001).

Family therapy is eclectic, borrowing from many schools of therapy and treating a broad range of families and problems (Guerin & Chabot, 1997). Family therapists join with families in helping them change because they acknowledge and recognize that change of one sort or another is inevitable in a dynamic system. They further assert that only a small change for the better is necessary to make a big difference. Most family therapists assert that clients have the strength and resources to change and that people don't need to understand the origins of a problem to solve it. Last, there is no *one* solution to family problems—especially given today's complicated families (Selekman, 1993).

Biologically Based Therapies

Do some people have preexisting brain abnormalities that make them susceptible to alcohol or other drug abuse? Are there inborn mechanisms that create such drug abuse? Are these evolved mechanisms? Evolutionary psychologists think that they are evolved mechanisms gone awry. Indeed, evolutionary psychologists assert that in therapy one must take into consideration the way the brain has evolved and consider both drug and talking therapies to overcome the limitations that may have developed (Bailey, 2001; Troisi & McGuire, 2000).

When a person seeks a therapist for help with a psychological problem—whether it has a biological basis or not—the usual approach involves some form of talking therapy that may be based on psychodynamic, humanistic, behavioral, or cognitive theories. For some patients, however, talking therapy is not enough. Some may be too profoundly depressed; others may be exhibiting symptoms of bipolar disorders (manic depression) or schizophrenia; still others may need hospitalization because they are suicidal. This is where biologically based therapies enter the picture. These therapies often involve medication, hospitalization, and physicians. They are generally used in combination with traditional forms of psychotherapy. Most practitioners and theoreticians believe that the most effective treatment is drugs in combination with psychotherapy (Guimon et al., 2001). Biologically based therapies exist as drug therapy (often used), electroconvulsive therapy (occasionally used), and psychosurgery (rarely used).

Drug Therapy

In this fast-paced society, people seem to want quick fixes. Every few years, politicians promise a new plan to eliminate poverty or a simple solution to racial tension. Similarly, people often want to take drugs to alleviate emotional problems. Drug therapy is an important form of treatment, especially for anxiety, depression, and schizophrenia. (See Figure 16.6 for recent trends in the use of drugs in treating depression.) It is the most widely used biologically based therapy, and it is effective when used correctly and carefully. Drug therapy is sometimes used in combination with traditional talking therapy. Clinicians who recommend drug therapy must be aware of several key issues. Dosages are especially important and must be monitored; too much or too little of certain drugs is dangerous. Long-term use of many drugs is ill advised. Further, no drug will permanently cure the maladjustment of people who are

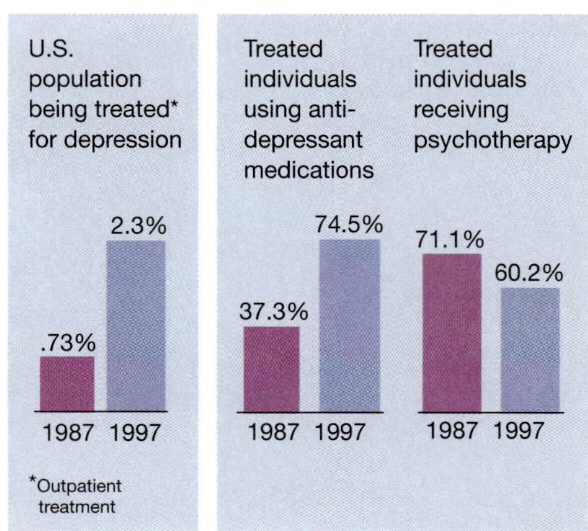

FIGURE 16.6

Trends in Treatment of Depression

More people receive drug treatment for depression than ever before. Note the decline in psychotherapy (Olson, 2002).

Source: Journal of the American Medical Association.

not coping well. Last, physicians and psychiatrists must be sensitive to the issues of overmedication and long-term dependency on drugs.

In the past decade, clinical psychologists have been lobbying for the legal right to write prescriptions for a limited class of drugs. The argument is that patients would benefit by the better integration of medications and psychological techniques (Hines, 1997; Tuckman, 1996), but this is a controversial proposition even among psychologists (Tasman, Riba, & Silk, 2000). Those who do support the idea recognize that additional training would be necessary and licensing authority would need to be instituted (Klusman, 1998). This debate continues among physicians and psychologists as well as state licensing boards.

When physicians (often psychiatrists) do administer drugs, people may experience relief from symptoms of anxiety, mania, depression, and schizophrenia. Drugs for the relief of mental problems are sometimes called *psychotropic drugs*; they are usually grouped into four classes: antianxiety drugs, antidepressant drugs, antimania drugs, and antipsychotic drugs.

ANTIANXIETY DRUGS. Antianxiety drugs, or tranquilizers (technically, *anxiolytics*), are mood-altering substances. Librium, Xanax, and Valium are trade names of the most widely prescribed antianxiety drugs. Widely used in the United States (and probably overprescribed), these drugs reduce feelings of stress, calm patients, and lower excitability. When taken occasionally to help a person through a stressful situation, such drugs are useful. They can also help moderate anxiety in a person who is extremely anxious, particularly when the person is also receiving some form of psychotherapy. However, long-term use of antianxiety drugs without some adjunct therapy is usually ill advised. Today, physicians are wary of patients who seek antianxiety drugs for management of daily stress; they worry about substance abuse and an overreliance on drugs to get through the day.

ANTIDEPRESSANT DRUGS. As their name suggests, antidepressants (technically, *thymoleptics*) are sometimes considered mood elevators. They work by altering the level of neurotransmitters in the brain. With the wide availability of antidepressants, it is surprising that half of those who have been depressed for more than 20 years have never taken an antidepressant (Hirschfeld et al., 1997). Depression often goes undiagnosed and is definitely undertreated.

One kind of antidepressant, selective serotonin reuptake inhibitors (SSRIs), blocks the reuptake of serotonin. SSRIs work by prolonging the time that serotonin stays in a synapse. According to researchers, when a key neurotransmitter like serotonin is released but does not bind to receptors on the next neuron, the person experiences symptoms of depression. After release, the neurotransmitter is either neutralized in the synapse or taken back up by the neuron that released it, in the process called *reuptake*. SSRIs do not allow the neurotransmitter to be neutralized or restored to the releasing cell; thus, it stays in the synapse longer, where it is more likely to bind, and depression is averted.

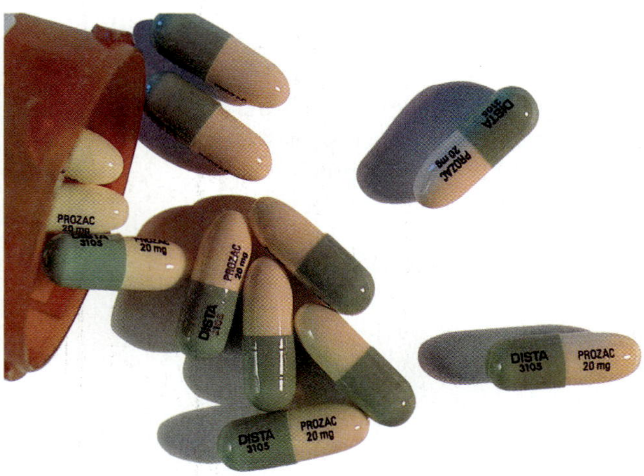

■ *Drug therapy is an important form of treatment, especially for anxiety, depression, and schizophrenia.*

Drugs such as Prozac, Zoloft, and Paxil are SSRIs. These drugs account for 60% of antidepressant sales in the United States. *Brain and Behavior* discusses the

BRAIN AND BEHAVIOR

A Best-Selling Medication—Prozac

Since its introduction in 1987, about 31 million people have taken the drug Prozac. Along with two other drugs, Zoloft and Paxil, which are similar to Prozac in chemical makeup, this "wonder drug" is so popular that pharmacies need whole shelves to stock the supply necessary for a week. Prozac is a member of the serotonin reuptake inhibitor (SSRI) family, as are Zoloft (sertraline) and Paxil (paroxetine). Yearly sales of such drugs bring in more than $4 billion.

Many people who take Prozac and its sister medications feel better—symptoms of depression lift, appetite returns, and the outlook seems less bleak (Rahola, 2001). People who take the drug feel so much better that they do better in their work and their relationships, and life seems to turn around. The drugs decrease the likelihood of new episodes of depression and work well for older adults, adolescents, and even children (Geller et al., 2001; Schmitz et al., 2001; Yohannes, Connolly, & Baldwin, 2001).

The number of side effects from drugs like Prozac is small compared to drugs used earlier. Those drugs had potent side effects—increased heart rate, increased blood pressure, nausea, and sleepiness, to name a few. So one reason why Prozac has been so successful is that it is relatively free of serious side effects. But it is not totally without them.

Researchers have long known that drugs that affect the reuptake of monoamines (serotonin, dopamine, norepinephrine, and epinephrine) can lighten some depressive symptoms. But the runaway success of Prozac has startled practitioners and researchers alike. They are also puzzled because not everyone who takes Prozac feels better. Furthermore, Prozac does have side effects, including a diminution of sexual appetite. Originally intended to be taken for short durations—6 months or so—Prozac is now being taken for years on end. Are people staying on the drug too long? Researchers are wondering if the drug (like many others) is being overprescribed and not especially effective (Glenmullen, 2001; Kirsch & Sapirstein, 1999). How many people who take the drug actually need it? How many were not properly diagnosed?

The effects of this class of drugs are so quickly evident, and the side effects so few, that psychologists worry that the original problems—low self-esteem or depression over a bad relationship, for example—may not get the attention they deserve. SSRIs have an important place in the treatment of people with various disorders, but most psychologists feel they should be part of a full treatment program that also involves short-term or perhaps even long-term psychotherapy.

Some researchers have questioned whether depression, schizophrenia, and a host of other disorders can be explained solely on the basis of brain chemistry (Valenstein, 1998). They argue that easy explanations and quick fixes with drugs are rarely the complete answer to psychological problems. Will new drugs evolve that will be better, more refined, and more potent than today's SSRIs? The answer is undoubtedly yes. Will drugs alone solve people's psychological problems? The answer is surely no. Are they part of a solution for some people? The answer is unquestionably yes.

success of Prozac. Extremely depressed people who take such antidepressants often become more optimistic and redevelop a sense of purpose in their lives after taking antidepressants for about 4 weeks. These medications allow many people to function outside a hospital setting.

Antidepressants also include two other major categories of drugs: tricyclics and monoamine oxidase (MAO) inhibitors. Both types of drugs are potent. The tricyclics (named for their chemical structure) act like SSRIs to block neurotransmitter reuptake, but MAO inhibitors work by breaking down monoamine oxidase, an enzyme that destroys the neurotransmitters. Tricyclics are prescribed much more often than MAO inhibitors because they pose less danger of medical complications. (Patients on MAO inhibitors have to adhere to special diets and some other restrictions to prevent adverse physical reactions to the drugs.) To help a patient suffering from a severe bout of depression, a physician might prescribe a commonly used tricyclic such as imipramine (Tofranil) or amitriptyline (Elavil), which has fewer serious side effects and can alleviate symptoms of most people with depressive problems.

Research on the effectiveness of antidepressant drugs is contradictory. Some researchers assert that these drugs have strong effects; others report only modest help from the drugs (Greenberg et al., 1992; Schulberg & Rush, 1994). Research using double-blind procedures and carefully controlled conditions continues, especially with drugs that have specific actions on depressive behaviors (Palatnik et al., 2001;

Schmitz et al., 2001). The impact of new research findings will be profound because there are a great number of people with depressive disorders.

■ **ANTIMANIA DRUGS.** Lithium carbonate has long been used as an effective antimania drug (like antidepressants, technically, a *thymoleptic*) and has come into wide use for patients with bipolar (manic–depressive) disorder because it relieves the manic symptoms. Psychiatrists find that when clients take a daily maintenance dose, lithium is especially helpful in warding off episodes of mania. The dosage of any drug is important, but in the case of lithium it is vital. Too much produces noxious side effects; too little has no effect. No drug will cure all individuals with bipolar disorder of all their symptoms and solve all their problems (for example, lithium is less effective with young patients); in general, however, lithium allows some patients to cope better, to control their symptoms, and to seek other therapies that allow them to manage their lives in the most productive way possible (Moncrieff, 1997). The same is true of other drugs in this class, including valproic acid, or valproate.

■ **ANTIPSYCHOTIC DRUGS.** Antipsychotic drugs (technically, *neuroleptics*) are used mainly for people who suffer from the disabling disorder schizophrenia. These drugs reduce hostility and aggression in violent patients. They also reduce delusions and allow some patients to manage life outside a hospital setting.

TABLE 16.5

Drugs Commonly Used to Treat Psychiatric Disorders

Effect Group	Chemical Group	Generic Name	Trade name
Antianxiety (anxiolytic)	Benzodiazepines	Diazepam Chlordiazepoxide Alprazolam Clonazepam	Valium Librium Xanax Klonapin
	Nonbenzodiazepine	Buspirone	Buspar
Antidepressant (thymoleptic)	Tricyclics	Amitriptyline Imipramine Nortriptyline Desipramine Doxepin Clomipramine	Elavil Tofranil Pamelor Norpramin Sinequan Anafranil
	Monoamine oxidase inhibitors	Phenelzine Tranylcypromine	Nardil Parnate
	Selective serotonin reuptake inhibitors	Fluoxetine Sertraline Paroxetine Fluvoxamine	Prozac Zoloft Paxil Luvox
Antimanic (thymoleptic)	Lithium carbonate	Lithium	Eskalith Lithonate Lithobid
	GABA agonist	Valproic acid	Depakene
Antipsychotic (neuroleptic)	Phenothiazines	Chlorpromazine Trifluoperazine Fluphenazine Thioridazine	Thorazine Stelazine Prolixin Mellaril
	Atypical antipsychotic	Clozapine Risperidone	Clozaril Risperdal

Most of the antipsychotic drugs prescribed are phenothiazines; one of the most common is chlorpromazine (Thorazine). However, a number of other antipsychotic drugs (sometimes called "atypical antipsychotics") have been introduced in the past decade. One of these, clozapine (Clozaril), has been shown to be especially effective but can have severe side effects. Even newer antipsychotic drugs, such as risperidone (Risperdal), are safer than either chlorproazine or clozapine, and they also may be tolerated better.

Antipsychotic drugs are often very effective in treating certain symptoms of schizophrenia, particularly hallucinations and delusions; unfortunately, they may not be as effective for other symptoms, such as reduced motivation and emotional expressiveness. As with antidepressants, dosages of antipsychotic drugs are crucial. Further, if patients are maintained on antipsychotic drugs for too long, other problems can emerge. One such problem is *tardive dyskinesia*—a central nervous system disorder characterized by involuntary, spasmodic movements of the upper body, especially the face and fingers, and including leg jiggling and tongue protrusions, facial tics, and involuntary movements of the mouth and shoulders (Fleischacker, Lemmens, & van Baelen, 2001). See Table 16.5 for a detailed listing of some common drugs used to treat psychiatric disorders.

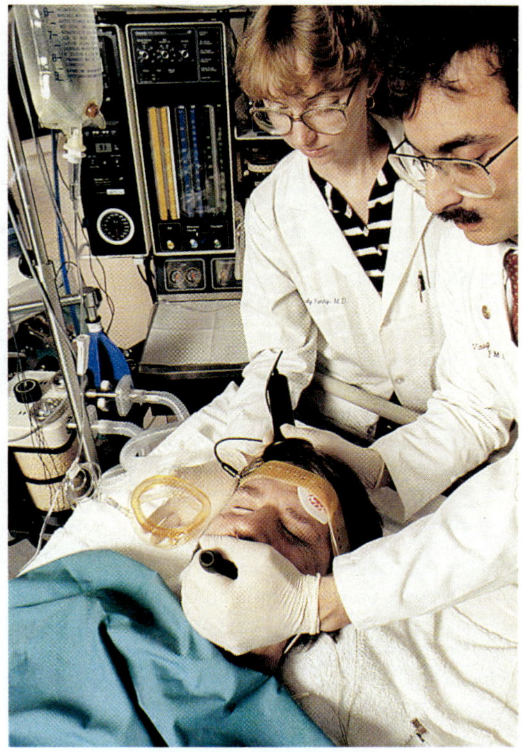

■ *Electroconvulsive therapy, once widely used with depressed patients, is a treatment for severe mental illness in which an electric current is briefly applied to the head to produce a generalized seizure.*

Psychosurgery and Electroconvulsive Therapy

Psychosurgery is brain surgery; it was used in the past to alleviate symptoms of serious mental disorders. A particular type of psychosurgery commonly performed in the 1940s and 1950s was the *prefrontal lobotomy*, in which the surgeon would sever parts of the brain's frontal lobes from the rest of the brain. The frontal lobes were thought to control emotions; their removal destroyed connections within the brain, making patients calm and passive. Patients lost the symptoms of their mental disorders, but they also became unnaturally calm and completely unemotional. Some became unable to control their impulses, and an estimated 1%–4% of patients died from the operation.

Today, despite advances in technology and in the precision of the operation, psychosurgery is rare, for three reasons: first, drug therapy has proved more effective than surgical procedures. Second, the long-term effects of psychosurgery are questionable. Third, and most important, the procedure is irreversible and therefore morally objectionable to most practitioners and to patients and their families. Its widespread use during the 1940s and 1950s is considered by many to have been a serious mistake.

Electroconvulsive therapy (ECT), once widely employed to treat depressed individuals, is a therapy for severe mental illness in which an electric current is briefly applied to the head in order to produce a generalized seizure (convulsion). The duration of the shock is less than a second, and patients are treated in 3 to 12 sessions over several weeks. In the 1940s and 1950s, ECT was routinely given to severely disturbed patients in mental hospitals. Unfortunately, it was often used on patients who did not need it or administered by physicians who wished to control difficult patients. Today, ECT is not a widely used treatment. According to the National Institutes of Health, fewer than 2.5% of all psychiatric hospital patients are treated with ECT.

Is ECT at all effective? Could drug therapy or traditional psychotherapy be used in its place? ECT is effective in the short-term management of severely depressed individuals, those suffering from extreme episodes of mania, and people with psychotic depression (Flint & Rifat, 1998; Rohland, 2001); it is sometimes used when

Psychosurgery
Brain surgery used in the past to alleviate symptoms of serious mental disorders.

Electroconvulsive [ee-LECK-tro-con-VUL-siv] therapy (ECT)
A treatment for severe mental illness in which an electric current is briefly applied to the head in order to produce a generalized seizure.

Be an *Active* learner

REVIEW

- What are the major classes of psychotropic drugs, and for which disorders or conditions is each effective? pp. 599–600
- What are selective serotonin reuptake inhibitors? How do they work? p. 600

THINK CRITICALLY

- Drugs take a while before they start to work. What does this imply for individuals who take the drugs? How might the delay impede performance in therapy?
- If drug therapy is so effective, why aren't more people being treated in this way?
- What are the ethical implications of the use of psychosurgery and electroconvulsive therapy (ECT)?

APPLY PSYCHOLOGY

- Devise a policy solution to the problem of the overprescription of medications, especially antidepressants.

a particular patient is at risk of suicide (Cohen, Tyrrell, & Smith, 1997). It is effective and safe (Glass, 2001; McCall et al., 2001); however, its effects are only temporary if it is not followed by drug therapy and psychotherapy (American Psychiatric Association, 2001). Generally speaking, ECT should be used as a last option, when other forms of treatment have been ineffective and when a patient does not respond to medications (Prudic, Olfson, & Sackheim, 2001). ECT is not appropriate for treating schizophrenia or for managing unruly behaviors associated with other psychological disorders.

The risk of death during the administration of ECT is low (Coffey et al., 1991). But there are side effects including memory loss (Lisanby et al., 2000; Prudic, Peyser, & Sackheim, 2000). In addition, ECT frightens some patients. If practitioners determine that ECT is warranted, the law requires (and medical ethics demand) that the patient be given the option to accept or reject the treatment—as is true for *any* treatment.

Summary and Review

Therapy Comes in Many Forms

What is the essential difference between biologically based therapy and psychotherapy?

■ Two broad types of therapy are biologically based therapy and psychotherapy. Biologically based therapy refers to treatment of emotional or behavioral problems by treating the body. *Psychotherapy* is treatment through psychological techniques. pp. 568–569

What is the placebo effect in therapy?

■ A *placebo effect* is a nonspecific therapeutic change that occurs as a result of a person's expectations of change rather than as a direct result of a certain treatment. However, any long-term therapeutic effects come from the client's and therapist's efforts. pp. 568–570

KEY TERMS

psychotherapy, p. 568; placebo effect, p. 568; double-blind technique, p. 570; demand characteristics, p. 570

Psychoanalysis and Psychodynamic Therapies

According to psychoanalytic theory, what causes maladjustment, and what processes are involved in treatment?

■ *Insight therapies*, which include *psychodynamically based therapies*, assume that maladjustment and abnormal behavior are caused by people's failure to understand their own motivations and needs. Insight therapists believe that once patients understand the motivations that produce maladjusted behavior, the behavior can be changed. p. 578

■ According to Freud, conflicts among a person's unconscious thoughts and processes produce maladjusted behavior. Classical Freudian *psychoanalysis* often involves a process of *free association, dream analysis, interpretation, resistance*, and *transference*; the repetitive cycle of interpretation, resistance, and transference is referred to as *working through*. pp. 578–580

What are the basic criticisms of psychoanalysis?

■ Ego analysts are psychoanalytic practitioners who are often critical of classical Freudian analysis and believe that the ego has greater control over behavior than Freud suggested. They are more concerned with a client's reality testing and control over the environment than with unconscious motivations and processes. p. 580

■ Some critics of psychoanalysis contend that the approach is unscientific, imprecise, and subjective. Other critics object to Freud's biologically oriented approach, which suggests that a human being is a mere bundle of energy caught in conflict and driven toward some hedonistic goal. Further, many elements of Freud's theory are sexist or untestable. pp. 580–581

KEY TERMS

psychoanalysis, p. 578; psychodynamically based therapies, p. 578; insight therapy, p. 578; free association,

p. 579; dream analysis, p. 579; interpretation, p. 579; resistance, p. 579; transference, p. 580; working through, p. 580

Humanistic Therapies

Briefly describe the focus of client-centered therapy.

■ *Client-centered therapy* aims to help clients realize their full potential by forming a therapeutic relationship with a counselor. To be effective, the therapist must convey unconditional positive regard, show congruence, and practice empathic listening so that clients can become less defensive, more open to new experiences, and more fulfilled. pp. 581–583

KEY TERMS

client-centered therapy, p. 581

Behavior Therapy

Identify the basic assumptions and techniques of behavior therapy.

■ *Behavior therapy*, or behavior modification, is a therapy based on the application of learning principles to human behavior. It focuses on changing overt behaviors rather than on understanding subjective feelings, unconscious processes, or motivations. It attempts to replace undesirable behaviors with more adaptive ones. p. 584

■ Techniques of behavior therapy include *token economies, time-out*, and *counterconditioning*. *Systematic desensitization* is a three-stage counterconditioning procedure in which a person is taught to relax while imagining increasingly fearful situations. pp. 586–587

■ As part of behavior therapy, modeling is especially effective in three areas: (1) teaching new behavior, (2) helping to eliminate fears, especially phobias, and (3) enhancing already existing behavior. pp. 590–591

KEY TERMS

behavior therapy, p. 584; symptom substitution, p. 585; token economy, p. 586; time-out, p. 588; counterconditioning, p. 589; systematic desensitization, p. 589; aversive counterconditioning, p. 590

Cognitive Therapy

What are the basic propositions that guide cognitive therapy?

■ The three basic propositions of cognitive therapy are that (1) cognitive activity affects behavior, (2) cognitive activity can be monitored, and (3) behavior changes can be effected through cognitive changes. p. 593

■ *Rational–emotive therapy* emphasizes the role of logical, rational thought processes in behavior. It assumes that faulty, irrational thinking patterns are the cause of abnormal behavior. p. 593

KEY TERM

rational–emotive therapy, p. 593

Group Therapy

What is group therapy, and what is the function of family therapy?

■ *Group therapy* is therapy used to treat several people simultaneously for emotional and behavior problems. The techniques used in a therapy group are determined by the nature of the group and the orientation of its therapist. pp. 596–597

■ *Family therapy* attempts to change family systems, because individuals affect family processes and family processes affect individuals. Treatment takes into account that a family is a dynamic social system. p. 597

KEY TERMS

group therapy, p. 596; family therapy, p. 597

Biologically Based Therapies

What are the major types of biologically based therapies and the major classes of psychotropic drugs?

■ Drugs for the relief of mental problems are usually grouped into four classes: antianxiety drugs, antidepressant drugs, antimania drugs, and antipsychotic drugs. Such drugs often work by altering the level of a key neurotransmitter in the brain. pp. 599–600

■ The major biologically based therapies are psychosurgery, electroconvulsive therapy, and drug therapy. *Psychosurgery* (brain surgery) is an infrequently used method of treatment used to alleviate symptoms of serious mental disorders. *Electroconvulsive therapy* (ECT) is a treatment for severe mental illness in which a brief application of electricity to the head is used to produce a generalized seizure. pp. 603–604

KEY TERM

psychosurgery, p. 603; electroconvulsive therapy (ECT), p. 603

17 Psychology in Action

Joseph Stella, *The Voice of the City of New York Interpreted: The Bridge,* 1920–1922

Rick Ankiel is one of the best left-handers in the world of baseball. He's especially tough against left-handed hitters, who hit only one homer off him in 95 at-bats in a recent season. He received a $2.5 million bonus for signing with the Cardinals. He is young, athletic, and focused on one thing and one thing only—winning. But Ankiel isn't always consistent and can throw wild pitches. In one playoff game he threw five wild pitches in one inning—a record.

Ankiel now realizes it's all about attitude. Ankiel got his groove back after some rest, relaxation with family, and a lot of talking about the game. Ankiel has tried to put behind him a bad season and a couple of really bad games. He has been heard to say, "Let's turn the page"; he means, "Let's get on with the future" and is confident that everything will come up fastballs. He is going to focus on each day, one day at a time—he's not going to ponder the past or what went wrong.

chapter outline

■ *Rick Ankiel is one of the best lefthanders in baseball, but he isn't always consistent. In one playoff game he threw five wild pitches in one inning—a record.*

Psychologists know that Rick Ankiel is right. Much of top performance in sports is about attitude—and preparation, skill, and a little luck. But having a proper frame of mind turns out to be a key component of success. Performance may be improved through mental strategies that either refine the practices of successful athletic performers or help unsuccessful athletes overcome obstacles.

Applied psychology is the branch of psychology that uses psychological principles to help solve practical problems of everyday life—whether those problems come up on the job, at school, or on the playing field. Consider baseball, for example. Applied psychologists examine how the basics of behavior, such as learning and memory, affect athletic activities. They also consider how coaches can motivate athletes to perform their best by using common psychological concepts to help them visualize possibilities, overcome obstacles, and achieve fulfillment. To a great extent, applied psychologists help people manage their own behavior better. Whether you are the coach of the Chicago Bulls, the regional director of the Red Cross, or a corporate manager making human resources decisions, the principles of applied psychology go a long way.

In this chapter, we consider an array of fields that apply psychology to modern life. We begin with the workplace because that is where psychological principles have been studied and applied longest and most systematically—going as far back as John B. Watson, who applied psychology to a Maxwell House coffee advertising campaign in 1915.

Industrial/Organizational Psychology

In recent seasons of *The Drew Carey Show,* Carey played the role of an assistant director of personnel who had to, from time to time, endure his sadistic boss's ways of handling employees. He got himself caught in wacky triangles involving employees, new employees, and friends. He led a sitcom life that was about as unlike the life of a personnel manager as one can be. Human resources managers—the people who assist corporations in hiring new employees—play key roles in the workforce. Work consumes a high proportion of our waking hours, and how we work, where we work, and why we work are important questions. Increased global competition, new information technology, and industrial re-engineering are changing the world of work. As productivity has become increasingly important to businesses, industrial/organizational psychology has grown in importance. **Industrial/organizational (I/O) psychology** is the study of how individual behavior is affected by the work environment, by coworkers, and by organizational practices. It is the study of people not only in industry but in government and in nonprofit organizations such as hospitals and universities.

I/O psychology grew out of two fields: the study of individual differences often in industry (the I part of the equation) and social psychology's study of group dynamics and organizational behavior (the O part of the equation). The two fields still study different topics, but they often overlap. Today, I/O psychologists pay close

Applied psychology
The branch of psychology that uses psychological principles to help solve practical problems of everyday life.

Industrial/organizational (I/O) psychology
The study of how individual behavior is affected by the work environment, by coworkers, and by organizational practices.

attention to the type of company they work or consult for because companies vary widely in the people they hire and their organizational structures.

Given today's global economy, I/O psychologists must take into account *cultural differences* among organizations. Many companies adopt an organizational structure that reflects aspects of their society. Asian companies—in Korea, for example—often have a family orientation, in which people work hard for the good of the entire family and focus on interdependence. A saying that might reflect the Asian work ethic is *The nail that stands above the rest invites being hammered down.* This orientation affects hiring decisions, firing, promotions, hierarchies, and the general work ethic. Culture especially affects how management decisions are made; in Japan, for example, new ideas often filter from the bottom up, rather than emanating from higher levels of an organization, as they often do in the United States. Some companies, especially those in Latin American countries, are extremely hierarchical in nature, according high respect to authority figures; some companies in third world countries are more loosely organized in terms of who does what; in the United States, roles tend to be more rigid, although there is often some flexibility as to who is allowed to assume various roles; independent thought and entrepreneurial ability are valued. Sayings that reflect the U.S. work ethic are *The squeaky wheel gets the grease,* or perhaps *Nice guys finish last;* in the end, getting results is more important than how you get them.

■ *In past seasons,* The Drew Carey Show *poked fun at the human resources profession, as Drew Carey portrayed an assistant director of personnel whose sole job was to endure his sadistic boss's way of handling employees. Real-life human resources professionals use psychology for much more important tasks.*

In general, I/O psychology can be divided into four broad areas: human resources psychology, motivation of job performance, job satisfaction, and leadership. *Human resources psychology* focuses on the ongoing personnel functions of placing people in jobs, training and promoting them, determining benefits, and evaluating performance. *Motivation and job performance* are key areas for I/O psychologists; they study not only how rewards relate to successful performance, but also the relationships between management and employees and management's self-assessment. *Job satisfaction* is a top concern of workers and employers alike. Last, the study of *leadership* focuses on the defining attributes of leaders—people who influence other people's behavior to attain agreed-upon goals.

Human Resources Psychology

Human resources psychologists, or personnel psychologists, are involved in a broad array of activities related to employment—helping employers choose among prospective job candidates, determining compensation packages, facilitating on-the-job training, and arranging termination programs when businesses must downsize. To help organizations succeed, human resources psychologists must consider both internal conditions (the organization's size, structure, and business strategies) and external conditions (legal, social, political, and cultural factors) (Jackson & Schuler, 1995). Among the most important tasks is helping organizations select qualified candidates for specific positions. Today, finding the right people for jobs is part of an organization's *strategic planning.* This high-level planning, which is finalized at the top levels of the organization, includes forecasting the organization's future needs, establishing specific objectives, and implementing programs to ensure that qualified job candidates will be available when needed (Jackson & Schuler, 1990).

Job analyses
Detailed descriptions of the various tasks and activities that comprise each job, as well as the knowledge, skills, and abilities necessary to do it.

■ **JOB ANALYSES.** An important step in the strategic planning process is ensuring that there are well-qualified personnel to fill all the company's needs. Companies often prepare **job analyses**—detailed descriptions of the various tasks and activities that comprise each job, as well as the knowledge, skills, and abilities necessary to do it. Such an analysis specifies *what* gets done and *how* it gets done. It spells out performance criteria—behaviors—that are required of employees. For example, a computer programmer might be expected to write code, debug the code of other programmers, and evaluate the efficiency of the code. A job analysis also enumerates the qualifications for employment. For example, a computer programmer might need a college degree in computer science, 2 or 3 years of experience, and top-notch computing skills.

The federal government has taken a leading role in preparing what it terms a *functional job analysis,* or *FJA,* that describes each type of job in some detail. An FJA is appealing to I/O psychologists because—like an operational definition of behavior in a research study—it is concrete, observable, and measurable. An FJA has three hierarchies of worker functions: how workers deal with data (information), people (coworkers, subordinates, or customers), and things (objects). For example, employees may have to compare, contrast, or copy data; on a more complex level, they may also have to analyze or synthesize data from different sources. Employees may have to take instructions from some people or help others; on a more complex level, they may have to supervise, instruct, negotiate with, or mentor others. Employees may handle, carry, sort, or tend things; on a more complex level, they may be altering, preparing, or fixing them.

There are other ways to quantify what a job entails. For example, the *position analysis questionnaire* is a widely used instrument that asks those who know a job best to analyze it. It is used to record the duties, responsibilities, qualifications, and fiscal impact of employees. On this questionnaire, workers complete up to 194 statements describing the job they do (Jeanneret, 1992). The position analysis questionnaire covers six major areas: information sources (where the worker gets data), mental processes (what decision making is required), work output (what physical work is required), relationships with others (communication skills), job context (physical working conditions), and other (licensing, criticality of position, special clothes required, and so on).

Although the FJA and the position analysis questionnaire are widely used, there are many other such tests and analysis instruments, and most of them work well. All have a similar goal: employers need to ensure that jobs are well defined and doable. A job should not be too big or encompass too many tasks; nor should it be too limiting and so focused that it becomes boring and repetitive. Ideally, jobs should allow employees some level of responsibility for and control over how they do their work. Two of the main tasks of an I/O psychologist are balancing the scope and complexity of jobs and helping employers make jobs as motivating as possible.

■ **SELECTION PROCEDURES.** Imagine you are applying for a job; will an employer find you an attractive applicant? Employers want to hire individuals who will enjoy their work, suit the company's needs, and be productive. I/O psychologists develop specific selection procedures, including tests, to produce the best match between jobs and employees. The selection procedures at large firms are often complicated and time-consuming.

Selection procedures have one basic goal—assessing the suitability of job candidates in order to help an employer determine which ones to hire. Employers and researchers use application forms, interviews, work samples, and tests to make comparisons between job candidates. Subtle factors can be at work in selection procedures, and evaluators have to pay particular attention to these factors—for example, to guard against being influenced by their own moods (Baron, 1993), by an applicant's expensive clothes or unattractive looks, or by other non-job-related characteristics that have nothing to do with an applicant's true capabilities (Forsythe, 1990).

Companies use a wide range of selection methods that involve everything from tests of mental ability to peer rating, examination of experience, interests, and even handwriting. But research shows that the best measures to help employers make hiring decisions are mental ability tests, work samples, and integrity tests—and when these are combined, employers are even more likely to choose the best candidates (Schmidt & Hunter, 1998).

Employers want to hire individuals who will enjoy work, suit the company's needs, and be productive.

Tests of general mental ability come in many forms and focus on general abilities; most are paper-and-pencil tests that can be administered either to groups or individually. Intelligence tests are widely used as part of the selection procedures for jobs that require high-level cognitive skills. However, an important question for I/O psychologists is whether such tests (or any tests, for that matter) are the *best* predictors of job performance.

Work samples are hands-on simulations of all or some of a job's tasks. Depending on the job, work samples may include tests of spatial abilities (for air traffic controllers), perceptual accuracy (stenographers, proofreaders), or motor abilities (firefighters). Work samples help employers determine whether a job candidate's abilities match the job's requirements. Tests of managerial ability, which sometimes present the applicant with a simulated in-box to sort through, have also been devised that have proved effective in evaluating managerial potential (Berman & Miner, 1985).

One type of test that is being used for many kinds of jobs is the *test of integrity*. Some of these tests focus on attitudes about theft, including rationalizations about "acceptably" small amounts of on-the-job theft. Other tests examine integrity more indirectly by assessing such characteristics as dependability, conscientiousness, and thrill seeking. Department store managers routinely query applicants about ethical values, often ruling out candidates who answer in the wrong direction (even after telling them that there is no "right" answer!). Finally, tests such as the MMPI–2, which screens for maladjustment, are also used to evaluate candidates' integrity. Although such tests are controversial—many believe there is a danger that prospective employees will be wrongly classified as lacking in integrity—some employers see them as an alternative that is better than not testing at all (Camara & Schneider, 1994).

In addition many businesses in today's service-based economy want their employees to be able to provide high-quality service to customers and to be creative, adaptable, resilient, empathic, and understanding with them—but also to be technologically adept. Since such qualities are now considered important as job qualifications (Cascio, 1995), it is not surprising that the use of tests to measure elements of personality in the workplace has increased markedly in the last decade. Several million such tests are administered yearly. Personality tests tend to be used to find specific behavior patterns that are well suited to a type of job rather than to screen out people who may be abnormal (Hogan, Hogan, & Roberts, 1996). For example, some people who exhibit Type A behavior patterns (discussed in Chapter 14) may do better at some types of high-pressure jobs, such as being a commodities trader, than at others, such as meticulously checking a manuscript for typographical errors (Lee, Ashford, & Bobko, 1990). Tests of personality and interests, however, are difficult to correlate with job performance; for example, outgoing individuals may be good salespeople, but quiet, introspective individuals can often be just as persuasive.

Tests are just one way to gather information about applicants. Biographical data can help paint an accurate picture of an individual, as can letters of recommendation, and interviews in which job candidates take part in general discussions about work. Interviews can be important in evaluating the fit between an applicant and a position—but research shows that interviewers often make decisions about an applicant within the first minutes of an interview! Also, sometimes interviewers base their judgments more on any negative information provided than on positive information. Structured interviews—in which each applicant is asked the same questions in a certain way, in a certain order, and in the same manner—work better than unstructured interviews (Arvey & Campion, 1982).

Surprisingly little is known about ethnicity and interview outcomes. What evidence there is suggests that African Americans receive slightly lower ratings in interviews than Whites do. Most research has been done with college students, with simulated interviews and questionnaires, rather than observations of real-life interviews.

Huffcutt and Roth (1998) reviewed research studies on ethnicity and employment interviews and did a statistical analysis of all of the results. They found several things: first, African Americans Latino/Latinas and scored lower than Whites did on ability tests. The score on such a test is strongly affected by a candidate's educational background, the school she or he attended, and other similar socioeconomic variables. Second, for complex jobs, ethnic differences disappeared; in fact, applicants for very technical jobs were so highly sought after that minorities and Whites were recruited equally vigorously. Third, most important, and counter to expectations, group differences on *structured* interviews were small. A structured, carefully worded interview, in which the phrasing of questions and their sequence are specified in advance, limits bias. Finally, differences in overall ability between an ethnic group and a White majority tend to be exaggerated when the minority pool is sufficiently large to allow comparisons and there is more variability among candidates.

What all this boils down to is that to be fair and hire the best possible candidates, employers should make sure that their human resources departments use structured interviews because they are a more reliable and valid selection procedure (Campion, Palmer, & Campion, 1998).

■ **EDUCATION AND TRAINING.** Imagine you landed a new job; now you are faced with "learning the business." It is a process of training and education whereby organizations systematically teach employees skills to improve their job performance. Most corporations offer systematic training, which typically begins by educating employees about the organization and its goals. Walt Disney World's Disney University offers world-class training ranging from computer applications to culinary arts. Using first-tier faculty, self-paced courses, and distance education, Disney U. trains its workers to be top flight, upbeat, and service oriented. They recognize that people are at the core of their business, and a well-educated workforce is essential (including when asked "How many Mickeys are in the park?" to act confused and insist that there is only one). Disney, like all employers, recognizes that a new employee may also need to learn specific skills, such as how to use a particular computer animation program. The increasing amount of information required in today's fast-changing workplace makes employers especially concerned that employees have the necessary knowledge to perform their jobs. To help ensure this, knowledge must be defined in job-relevant terms, a classification of knowledge areas that are relevant to the job must be identified, and evidence of the comprehensiveness of the new knowledge system must be gathered (Fleishman, Costanza, & Marshall-Mies, 1999).

■ *Surprisingly little is known about ethnicity and interview outcomes.*

A variety of methods are available for education and training. Among the most common are lectures, films, and videotapes. Self-paced instructional materials are often used. Training programs may also include discussion groups, simulations, and on-the-job demonstrations. Letting employees observe others so that they can imitate them is particularly effective. However, some people respond better than others to any training method. A training program can involve an apprenticeship or a mentoring relationship, with regular performance appraisals made by a more experienced or higher-ranking employee. Finding female mentors for women has sometimes been difficult because of smaller numbers of women in upper management.

Even seasoned employees need education and retraining. In large organizations, education is an ongoing process, as new products and technologies are introduced. I/O psychologists typically break down a training program into a series of learning objectives. Because it provides very specific goals for knowledge and skill acquisition, this method of training can be a particularly effective way to help employees identify their strengths and weaknesses. It also helps employees pinpoint specific obstacles to overcome and opportunities for improvement.

Training may be as simple as reviewing a new tool or procedure—as in introducing an executive to the Internet, teaching a secretary a new word-processing program, or working with custodians to promote recycling efforts. It may also be an elaborate process that takes place on the job and involves the employee's active participation—perhaps in programming a robot or pitching a product to clients. Training may include repetitive practice, particularly with highly technical equipment. It often involves moving from a classroom or meeting room to the actual workplace. Last, good training usually includes feedback, so that employees can learn whether they have successfully acquired the new skill or knowledge.

I/O psychologists assign great importance to education and training because business or organizational success requires well-informed employees. To help ensure good education and training, researchers attempt to determine what constitutes good work performance. That is, they begin with the desired outcome and work backward to determine how employees should be trained. I/O psychologists evaluate the effectiveness of recent training by examining employees' work products or test results immediately after the training procedure. Results are, after all, what employers are interested in. Effective education and training produce improvements in employees' ability to deliver results, whether in the form of better-quality products, clearer communications, or more effective supervision.

■ **PERFORMANCE APPRAISAL.** Have you ever been evaluated by an employer or supervisor? Bosses are sometimes good at appraising work, but they may overlook your best efforts and remember your mistakes, or they may not accurately convey how they feel about your performance. What makes someone good at evaluating employees?

The process by which a supervisor periodically evaluates the job-relevant strengths and weaknesses of a subordinate is called **performance appraisal.** Performance appraisals are important because they are often used to determine salaries, layoffs, firings, transfers, and promotions (Harris, Gilbreath, & Sunday, 1998). Researchers have tried to find ways to do these appraisals systematically and effectively.

Evaluating other people in the work setting is uncomfortable for many people. Supervisors generally report that they dislike conducting appraisals—especially face-to-face ones (Kikoski, 1998). They don't like to review their subordinates, and many acknowledge that they do not have strong evaluative skills. Further, supervisors have just as many inappropriate biases as anyone else (Swim et al., 1989), including the tendency to make attribution errors (pointed out in Chapter 13). And even when performance appraisals are done well, research shows that people's pay is more often associated with the quantity of their work than with its quality (Jenkins et al., 1998). So a potential problem with performance appraisals is that they are sometimes done inaccurately by people with few evaluative skills and diagnostic aids.

Performance appraisal
The process by which a supervisor periodically evaluates the job-relevant strengths and weaknesses of a subordinate.

There are ways to do appraisals well. The first thing to consider is the criteria, or standards, on which a worker should be judged. There is usually no single performance criterion, no comprehensive yardstick, by which to evaluate a worker.

Second, a worker's quantity of work is often important, but so is the quality. Also, relationships with other workers often affect performance. Researchers have devised scales to measure performance variables such as sales volume, relationship with customers, and quality of interworker communication; these scales can be helpful diagnostic tools. But because skills often overlap, composite scales have had to be devised. None has proved totally satisfactory.

Because of the "soft" nature of some performance criteria, such as how well people "get along," most I/O psychologists recommend focusing on the best available criteria. This means giving first attention to those elements that *best* describe satisfactory performance, recognizing that many criteria can be used. For example, a manager would look first at "measurables," such as a salesperson's sales volume, a keyboarder's number of words or characters typed, a bank teller's number of shortages, or a nursery worker's number of saplings planted. The manager would then assess other elements of performance that may be important, such as customer relations or coworker communication.

Performance appraisals need objective measures. Managers often compare employees, ranking them from best to worst or rating them in percentile groups (the top 10%, the next 20%, and so on). Such ratings help differentiate among employees, but they sometimes fall short of fairness. What if workers doing the same job are evaluated by different supervisors, one of them easygoing and the other demanding? What if supervisors use, even if unintentionally, subjective, "soft" criteria, such as how friendly they feel employees are? Might that discriminate against workers who don't have personal interests in common with the supervisors?

Even when using objective measures, certain problems arise; these include leniency, central tendency, the halo effect, and lack of reliability. Some raters always judge people with *leniency,* giving them higher evaluations than they actually deserve. The rater may simply want to be liked, may want to avoid confrontation, or may want to have the employee's positive evaluation reflect well on himself or herself. Other raters always judge people "about average," giving them a *central* rating. These raters are unwilling to rank people very high or very low but give "safe" judgments that are unlikely to raise eyebrows. The *halo effect* occurs in job performance appraisals when a rater is unable to discriminate among the many discrete parts of a job. Thus, a good first impression or good work on one part of a job may lead to a high rating on later work or on other parts of the job—regardless of the quality of performance in that case. *Reliability* refers to the consistency of observations. Good raters consistently rate similar work in similar ways; others, however, deviate in their ratings from one occasion to the next and from one employee to the next, based on factors that are hard to quantify, such as a worker's unique ability to work well in a team.

Most companies require periodic evaluations, so if a reluctant manager does them as infrequently as possible and in a cursory manner, they must be taught how do them objectively and with skill. Good-faith evaluations leave employees feeling appreciated and comfortable with the system (Tziner & Murphy, 1999).

Motivation and Job Performance

What would motivate you more, money or long vacations? Young, new lawyers are often faced with such choices about careers that involve sometimes tedious work with very high pay and exceedingly long hours, or public interest work that is often of low pay but personally quite satisfying.

I/O psychologists help people work together in organizations; they seek ways to make jobs more satisfying, to improve work environments, and to help organizations motivate employees. One obvious motivator is an employee's paycheck—people need money to live. But both employers and psychologists know that people are motivated by different things. Monetary rewards are important, of course—but so is the likelihood of praise for success. Motivators are culturally determined. The

introduction to research basics

Sex Discrimination in Employment Interviews

The law explicitly forbids discrimination on the basis of sex, yet there is evidence of continuing intentional discrimination in the workplace. In 1997, there were 25,000 charges filed with the Equal Opportunity Employment Commission. It has long been known that men are favored over women in interview settings and that when discrimination occurs there is less information gathered overall, but more gender-relevant information. Two researchers from Tulane University, Heather Davison and Michael Burke (2000), decided to take a broad look at sex discrimination in employment contexts. They wondered whether across an array of studies, evidence of discrimination still exists.

DESIGN Davison and Burke used a meta-analysis technique. A **meta-analysis** is a set of statistical procedures designed to gather experimental and correlational results across multiple and separate studies that address a related set of research questions. A meta-analysis ultimately consists of a careful literature search and a calculation of research effect sizes.

HYPOTHESIS The researchers predicted that an applicant's sex, the sex of the evaluator, and amount of job-relevant information gathered would affect the extent of gender-related discrimination.

PROCEDURE The researchers searched the psychological literature and identified over 160 studies that examined sex discrimination in employment. The studies were categorized to ensure that they were empirical (based on observation and experiment rather than theory and speculation) and were asking the right types of questions. The data from the studies were subjected to the statistical procedures of meta-analysis, which include calculating how big an effect was observed, if any, for the relevant variables under study.

RESULTS Overall, men received higher ratings than women in employment interviews. Gender-related characteristics stereotypically associated with the job also made a difference in ratings: when the job was one stereotypically associated with women (such as nurse), women received higher ratings; men received higher ratings for jobs stereotypically associated with men (such as plumber). The sex of the interviewer was not as strong a predictor of ratings as the researchers had hypothesized. However, as hypothesized, Davison and Burke found that women were subject to greater discrimination when less job-relevant information about applicants was available.

CONCLUSIONS Generally, the hypotheses concerning job sex-type and job-relevant information were supported. Female and male applicants received lower ratings when being considered for a job typically associated with the other sex; the difference between ratings decreased as more job-relevant information was provided.

Discrimination tended to occur when people being interviewed failed to match gender-stereotyped job characteristics. This is important because a relatively large number of jobs are consistently characterized as gender-typed, suggesting that job-related gender discrimination is common and applies to both men and women.

value placed on hard work varies from culture to culture. Some cultures stress a person's duty to contribute to society; others stress a person's right to meaningful work; still others stress a person's need for happiness at work. I/O psychologists are especially interested in studying the impact of rewards and success within the context of culture.

When Hofstede (1983) examined attitudes in more than 50 countries, he found that organizations and cultures vary on four main dimensions. *Power distance* is the extent to which there is a rigid hierarchy, or "pecking order," in a company, limiting employees' independence of action. *Uncertainty avoidance* is a lack of tolerance for ambiguity or vagueness about rules and expectations in the workplace; this uncertainty avoidance occurs especially frequently in risk-averse countries such as Japan and Greece. In such cultures it is never good to break laws or get around the chain of command, whatever the motive. Cultures vary in the extent to which they value *individualism* as opposed to the collective good. Finally, Hofstede found that emphasis on work goals as opposed to interpersonal goals, a trait he labeled *masculinity,* also varies from culture to culture. Not surprisingly, Hofstede found that most Western companies foster a combination he called independent individualism, while most Asian companies foster collectivism. Companies in some other societies foster unique combinations. Those in Israel, for instance, foster dependent collectivism (high power distance, low individualism). Such cultural values will affect people's

Meta-analysis
A set of statistical procedures designed to gather experimental and correlational results across multiple and separate studies that address a related set of research questions; it ultimately consists of a careful literature search and a calculation of research effect sizes.

■ *Most Western companies foster a sense of independent individualism, while most Asian companies foster collectivism.*

needs and goals, what they consider equitable, and how they can most effectively be managed. Interestingly, small shared activities—even eating lunch together in a group—can stimulate group cohesion and willingness to work toward shared goals.

In American culture at least, job performance is to some degree affected by whether the job is *intrinsically motivated behavior*—engaged in because it brings pleasure. (We examined intrinsic and extrinsic motivation in Chapters 7 and 11.) Recall that when intrinsically motivated behaviors are reinforced with direct external rewards (such as money), productivity often drops. Money is often not that important to job performance. A well-paid computer programmer may find plumbing work tedious and unfulfilling, whereas a lower-paid clerical worker who finds the job important and challenging will perform well. With the help of I/O psychologists' theoretical work, employers can find ways to motivate their employees to be more productive (and thus to increase profits).

■ **GOAL-SETTING THEORY.** Workers often perform difficult tasks for long hours, not for pay or for praise, but merely to reach a goal or to compare their present performance with new performance. Mountain climbers tackle a new peak "because it's there." In business and in personal life, people often set goals that involve specific activities needed to accomplish a larger vision or ultimate purpose. When people set goals, they often try to make them SMART—Specific, Motivational, Attainable, Relevant, and Trackable. **Goal-setting theory** asserts that setting specific, clear, attainable goals for a given task leads to better performance. For example, I (LL) challenge myself to ride my mountain bike harder and longer, not to break records for middle-aged men but to meet goals I have set for myself.

FIGURE 17.1
Goal-Setting Theory

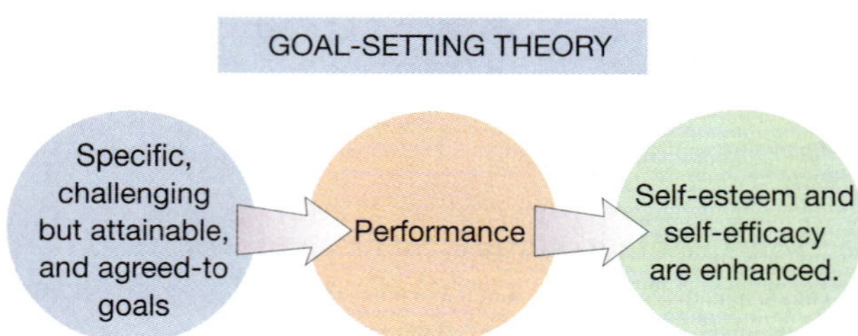

Goal-setting theory states that the best job goals are those that are somewhat challenging but attainable and that a worker has agreed to. Goals work especially well when they enhance a worker's sense of self-esteem or self-efficacy. For example, if a sales manager and her staff agree to generate a 50% increase in annual sales, rather than an unrealistic 200% increase, chances are that they will perform well (see Figure 17.1).

Goal-setting theory can account for some work behaviors, but it will not explain why people will work on projects for years, at low pay or under difficult conditions. More fully developed expectancy theories take the next step—explaining the motivation for this type of performance.

Goal-setting theory
Theory that asserts that setting specific, clear, attainable goals for a given task leads to better performance.

Expectancy theories
Theories that suggest that a worker's effort and desire to maintain goal-directed behavior (to work) are determined by expectations regarding the outcomes of behavior.

■ **EXPECTANCY THEORIES.** A successful employer–employee relationship relies on many factors beyond economic motivation. **Expectancy theories,** which we discussed in Chapter 11, suggest that a worker's effort and desire to maintain goal-directed behavior (in other words, to work) are determined by expectations regarding the outcomes of that behavior.

One expectancy theory, proposed by Victor Vroom (1964), suggests that both motivation and ability determine job performance. Vroom's proposal is considered an expectancy theory because it states that motivation is determined by what people expect to experience in performing a task—a rewarding outcome or a frustrating one. Vroom's theory holds that motivation results from a three-part equation made up of expectancy, instrumentality, and valence. *Expectancy* is the belief that hard or extra work will lead to good or improved performance; *instrumentality* refers to a worker's belief that good performance will be rewarded; *valence* refers to the value placed on the rewards that are offered. A person who gets a big raise but later gets the cold shoulder from coworkers because of it may give the raise lower valence.

It turns out that ability, effort, *and* role perceptions—the ways people believe they should be doing their jobs—are the key variables that determine performance (see Figure 17.2). Edward Lawler and Lyman Porter (1967) believed that workers must fully understand the nature of their positions and exactly what is required of them. Too often, people fail not because of lack of effort or ability, but because they do not know what is expected of them or how to achieve a sense of control or power in the organization. So an employee may burn a great deal of midnight oil, but if he or she has misread what it really takes to succeed in the organization (say, teamwork rather than long hours), performance may not be rated highly.

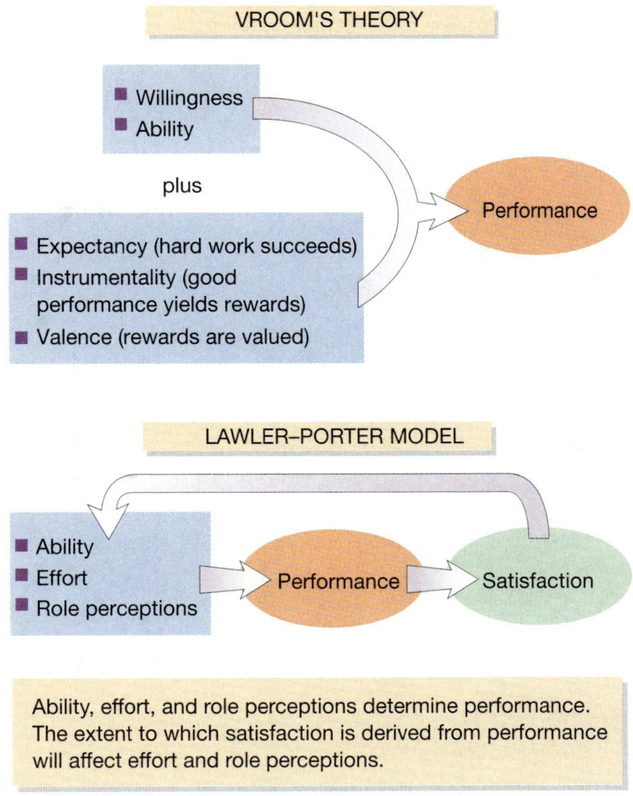

FIGURE 17.2
Expectancy Theories

Today, researchers claim that the motivation to work can be explained more by integrative theories that focus on goals, experiences, and thoughts (Locke & Latham, 1990a). When people receive incentives, when they think their contributions are important, and when the effort required of them is not excessive, productivity tends to be high (Shepperd, 1993). When performance is high, job satisfaction is likely; job satisfaction then increases the employee's commitment to the organization and its goals.

■ **EQUITY THEORY**. People want to be compensated for their work and to earn as much as they can, but most people feel that they are worth more than they are paid. What happens when people feel that they aren't being treated fairly?

In I/O psychology, **equity theory** asserts that what people bring to a work situation should be balanced by what they receive compared with other workers; that is, workers' input (what they do) should be balanced by their compensation (what they receive). If input and compensation are not balanced, people will adjust their work level, and their job satisfaction and performance may be affected. According to equity theories, each individual privately assesses the balance between her or his own input and compensation and compares this ratio to other people's input/compensation ratio. When the ratios are similar, people are relatively happy. Thus, if my workload and compensation are at certain levels and other faculty members seem to have similar levels, our input/compensation ratios are about equal.

Equity theory
The theory in I/O psychology that asserts that what people bring to a work situation should be balanced by what they receive compared with other workers; that is, input should be balanced by compensation.

But what if a person feels that his or her ratio is way out of balance? In such cases (especially in cases of underpayment), people may slow down their efforts and gripe and groan, causing the quality of their work to decrease (see Figure 17.3 on the following page). If people perceive inequities, they will choose one of several alternatives to alter the situation (Berg, 1991; Greenberg, 1990, 1996; Hellriegel & Slocum, 1992; Summers & Hendrix, 1991):

- They can increase their inputs to justify higher rewards (when they feel overrewarded).
- They can decrease their inputs (loaf on the job or leave work early) to compensate for low rewards.

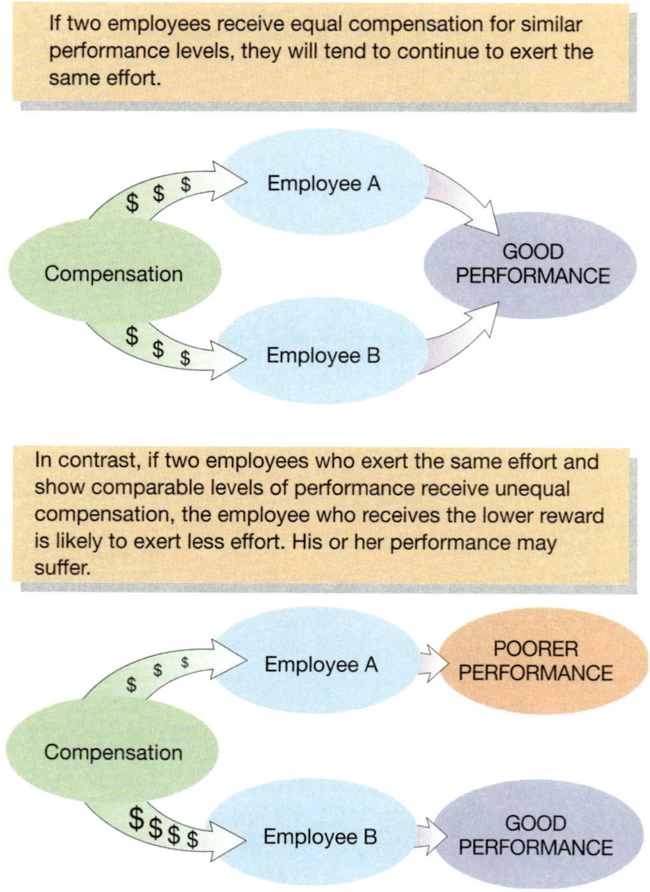

FIGURE 17.3
Equity Theory

- They can change their rewards through legal actions or illegal ones (stealing company assets).
- They can distort reality by rationalizing inequities, and thus feel better.
- They can quit.

There are hidden costs of inequity in pay and benefits. When Greenberg (1990) examined employee theft rates in manufacturing plants, he found that rates of theft increased after pay reductions. When supervisors explained the basis for pay cuts to workers, the theft rate decreased. Thus, when management explains the causes of pay shifts, the perception of unfairness is minimized.

■ SELF-EFFICACY AND WORK. How well you expect to execute a series of actions required to deal with a situation is a measure of your belief in your abilities, or *self-efficacy*. People who view themselves as competent tend to do better at work than others (but this effect is especially true on easier tasks). This leads researchers to some practical suggestions for employers: managers should provide accurate descriptions of work to be performed; managers should indicate to employees what techniques should be used to complete tasks; employers should provide tasks that employees can accomplish to enhance their self-efficacy; rewards should be timed to enhance workers' self-efficacy. Knowing what the goals are—and the rewards associated with them—can match employees to tasks and enhance self-esteem and ultimately, effectiveness (Audia, Kristof-Brown, & Locke, 1996; Latham, Daghighi, & Locke, 1997).

■ MOTIVATION MANAGEMENT: THREE APPROACHES. Recognizing the complexity of motivation management, I/O psychologists have observed three basic approaches to motivation in the workplace: paternalistic, behavioral, and participatory. The fundamental idea underlying the *paternalistic approach* to motivation is that a company takes care of its employees' needs and desires as a protective father would. Early in this century, this approach was common in the company mining towns of Appalachia and in the mills of Massachusetts; the company owners provided housing, schools, recreation, and churches for employees. This approach is still followed in some Japanese companies, which promote lifelong employment and fill employees' needs, from recreation to drug rehabilitation. However, this approach is contrary to many American psychologists' views on behavior. Instrumental (operant) conditioning studies show that for a behavior (such as good performance of job tasks) to be established and maintained—at least in Western cultures—reinforcement must be contingent on performance. In a paternalistic system all employees, productive as well as nonproductive, are reinforced. As equity theory predicts, reinforcement without the need for performance does not encourage people to work hard.

The *behavioral approach* to motivation assumes that people will work only if they receive tangible rewards for specific task performance. Examples include paying a factory worker by the piece and a typist by the page. In such a system, hardworking employees obtain more rewards—commissions, salary increases, bonuses, and so on—because they produce more. However, little attention is paid to the emotional needs of workers. Goal-setting theory and, to some extent, expectancy theory thus argue that the behavioral approach to motivation is incomplete.

The *participatory approach* to motivation is based on the belief that individuals who have a say in the decisions that affect their work lives are motivated to work harder and smarter. Participation, it is argued, allows managers and employees to exchange information to solve problems (Tjosvold, 1987). Supporters of this approach believe that a sense of competence and self-determination is likely to increase individuals' levels of motivation (Deci, 1975). *Quality circles,* in which workers at all levels meet to discuss ways to improve product quality and promote excellence, constitute one technique employers use to involve workers in the management process (Matsui & Onglatco, 1990).

Many variables affect the success of participatory programs: the work setting, the individuals involved, the kinds of decisions to be made, and the company's hiring policies, for example. Truly participatory programs have positive effects on workers' values, thoughts, and motivation. These changes lead to less conflict among workers, increased productivity, and better overall job performance (see Figure 17.4). When workers feel comfortable with and involved in their work and their organization, they are more likely to be spontaneous, to help coworkers, to look out for the organization's best interests, and so on. Many of these behaviors depend on the employee's feeling positive about the work environment and having a good job attitude (George & Brief, 1992). So in many firms, when workers feel a

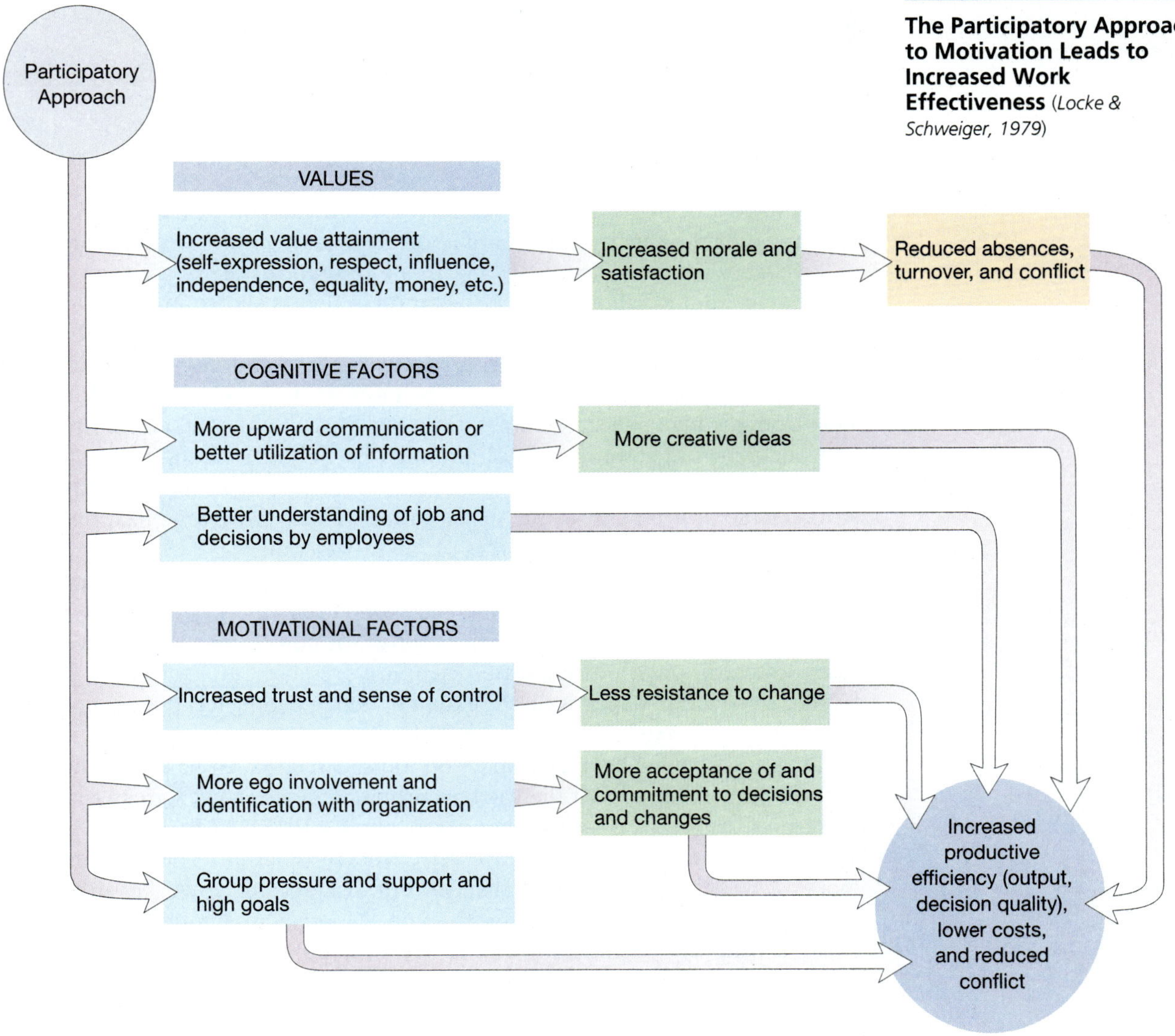

FIGURE 17.4

The Participatory Approach to Motivation Leads to Increased Work Effectiveness (*Locke & Schweiger, 1979*)

lack of participatory management, the result is low self-esteem among them—and a resulting lack of a good work ethic. By contrast, workers could be told that they are capable of designing the best precision-drilling-systems device because of the specialized knowledge they have about machine drilling operations.

■ *The participatory approach to motivation is based on the belief that individuals who have a say in the decisions that affect their work lives are motivated to work harder and smarter.*

Job Satisfaction

If you have a positive view of your abilities and feel competent and in control (at least most of the time), chances are good that you will like your job and that you will feel satisfied (Judge et al., 1998). It is important to realize that job satisfaction is different from job motivation. Motivation is always shown in behavior; job satisfaction (a person's attitude about the work and workplace) may not be shown in behavior. A tired, bored, overworked electrician may feel discouraged and angry—and may even hate her job—but still be motivated to work. Her motivation may stem from the high pay she receives, from her sense of obligation to get the job done, or from some other source. Thus, although her job satisfaction is low, it does not affect her performance. In general, however, a satisfied worker is a high-performing worker who will remain in the organization. This is why organizations want I/O psychologists to identify the sources of job satisfaction.

There are probably more sources of job satisfaction than can be listed here, but they cluster in five basic categories: the work itself, the perceived rewards of the work, the quality of supervision, the support of coworkers, and the work setting. These categories, with examples of each, are presented in Table 17.1. The overall level of satisfaction depends on the extent to which people feel their expectations for satisfaction are matched by their actual feelings of satisfaction.

Pay and benefits have an impact on job satisfaction, to be sure. But workplace support and feelings about the work environment have an even greater impact. And a person's dispositions—his or her personality—also affect job satisfaction. Mood and emotions experienced at work affect job satisfaction. The key here is that a mood, a bad day, a difficult challenge, or a disagreeable coworker may—but also may not—affect a person's job satisfaction. Moods and emotions at work are not equated with job satisfaction (Brief & Weiss, 2002).

One potential way to maximize and foster job satisfaction is having people work in teams. Today, more than ever before, companies are relying on teams of workers to accomplish complex tasks. Surprisingly, as teamwork has increased,

TABLE 17.1

Key Factors Related to Job Satisfaction

Area	Factors
The work itself	The work is interesting.
	The work is perceived to be challenging.
	There are opportunities to apply one's own judgment.
	There is some degree of autonomy.
Perceived rewards	There is adequate recognition.
	The pay is adequate and equitable.
	The work contributes to self-esteem and self-efficacy.
	There are opportunities for advancement.
Quality of supervision	Supervisors offer encouragement, support, and help.
Support from coworkers	There are opportunities to interact socially and in teams.
	Coworkers are supportive and compatible.
The work setting	There is job security.
	The work environment is viewed positively (it is seen as pleasant, attractive, and comfortable).
	There are opportunities to influence company policy and procedures.
	Adequate information and equipment are available.

research on what makes a good team, how teams work, and how to best utilize teams has decreased (Ilgen, 1999). Teams are groups of two or more people who work interdependently toward some common goal. The idea behind teams is that many tasks cannot be accomplished by a single person but require the skills and abilities of more than one person (Cannon-Bowers & Salas, 1998). When teams are put together carefully, job satisfaction is bound to increase. Workers enjoy collaborating with their colleagues toward a shared goal. Identifying the shared goals—such as developing the best precision-drilling-systems device—and setting up the teams often require the leadership that comes from managers.

Leadership

A company president who announces a new program and suggests that "resistance is futile" is bound to fail. Such a person is interested not in leading, but in dominating. In real-life organizations, large and small, however, leaders are needed, and instead of dominating, they try to persuade, encourage, and inspire. They try to build cohesion and goal-oriented teamwork. In every organization, some individuals emerge as *leaders*—people who influence other people's behavior toward the attainment of agreed-upon goals. But there is no "right" type of leader; in fact, leadership styles fluctuate widely, from autocratic leaders, who say, "My way or the highway," to democratic leaders, whose motto is "Let's decide this together."

In any work setting, informal leaders may emerge spontaneously; higher management may also choose them formally. Leaders are expected to help further the purposes of their organizations. Thus, one of their primary roles is to persuade and motivate employees to perform well. Note, however, that not all managers are leaders; nor are all leaders managers. Truly effective leadership is so close to being an art that it should come as no surprise that I/O psychologists have made intensive efforts to understand it.

Psychologists know a great deal about leadership. Yet there are a number of questions still pending: Can people choose a good leader? Is it possible to predict who will provide effective leadership? Why do some leaders succeed and others fail? The study of leadership has gone through three major phases, each with a different focus: traits, behaviors, or situations. The right combination of these elements ultimately produces an effective leader.

■ **TRAIT THEORIES OF LEADERSHIP.** The specific personality traits of individual organizational leaders were studied intensively in the early 1950s and are receiving renewed attention. This research tries to isolate the characteristics that make individuals good or poor leaders; for example, are good leaders assertive, directive, or authoritarian? But the trait approach troubles some researchers. Leaders cannot be universally characterized by traits such as assertiveness, self-confidence, or drive. Many good business leaders are assertive, but many equally good ones are not. In fact, although an individual leader's personality traits will tell psychologists something about leadership, the differences among leaders tend to be greater than the similarities. One reason that studies are unable to find a common denominator is that each leader and each organization have different goals. Today, researchers also recognize that a defining trait of effective business leaders is *flexibility*—the ability to adapt to a rapidly changing work environment and global economy. Other key traits are intelligence, maturity, inner motivation, and employee orientation.

■ **LEADERSHIP BEHAVIORS.** Another focus of research on leadership is specific behaviors of leaders. Many research studies try to find characteristic ways in which leaders interact with other members of their organizations. Some of the pioneering work on leadership was done at the University of Michigan's Institute for Social Research. The Michigan studies (as they are often called) found that many business leaders tend to be either employee- or task-oriented—but many have both orientations. Whether a leader is principally employee- or task-oriented has to do with how the leader chooses to influence behavior. An employee-oriented leader acts to maintain and enhance individual employees' feelings of self-worth or self-esteem. Such leaders try to empower employees and coworkers and make them feel valued and important. A task-oriented leader focuses on getting the job done as efficiently and quickly as possible.

Leadership styles are sometimes related to gender; generally, women are more employee-oriented, and men are more task-oriented (Eagly & Johnson, 1990). Recent studies show that the gender of the leader has other important effects. For example, female leaders or managers tend to be evaluated as positively as their male counterparts. However, when they behave in alpha male, dominating ways (physical, aggressive, forceful), female leaders are devalued—especially if the evaluators are men (Eagly, Makhijani, & Klonsky, 1992).

Other research has confirmed that behavioral differences among leaders are sometimes determined by the group of people being led. Some groups of individuals have characteristics that demand an employee orientation on the leader's part. For example, an underpaid, overworked, but dedicated social worker may have a great need to maintain a high level of self-esteem, to feel that his work is worthwhile. A supervisor must motivate this person not with task-oriented directions but with concern for his sense of self-worth. Highly paid executives, however, may be more easily motivated by a task-oriented approach because they assume that their salaries reflect their higher levels of ability, creativity, and/or productivity. Job performance, job satisfaction, and the way a worker is treated are closely related. In motivating workers, leaders must consider their own personal traits, the various possible behaviors they might use to influence others, and the conditions in which they and their coworkers work.

■ **SITUATIONAL LEADERSHIP THEORY.** Many researchers have shifted from investigating leaders' behaviors to investigating the *situations* in which these behaviors are performed. Some situations lend themselves to leadership, and even to specific forms of leadership; others call for little leadership. Thus, a warm, friendly, employee-oriented leader (or supervisor) is generally very useful for a group of service workers. But if the organization encounters financial trouble and decides to lay off some employees, and if the supervisor has no control over who is let go, the climate of uncertainty may undermine the effects of the warmth and friendliness.

President Franklin D. Roosevelt was a transformational leader who acted daringly and decisively and was an empowering inspiration to others.

THEORIES OF LEADERSHIP EFFECTIVENESS. A number of interacting factors determine the most effective style of leadership for a given situation. Effective leaders may simply be those who are best at perceiving the current goals and needs of their organization and fitting their style to those needs. A major theory that accounts for leadership effectiveness is *Vroom's leadership model.*

Victor Vroom and his colleagues Phillip Yetton and Arthur Jago focused on the various ways in which leaders may make decisions in organizations. As part of this leader-participation model, Vroom created a flowchart for determining the amount of advice a leader should seek, depending on the task to be accomplished. A leader can make an authoritarian decision and simply announce it; a leader can present a problem, solicit advice, and then make the final decision; or a leader can allow other people to make the decision. As a leader's use of authority increases, the freedom of others in the group decreases. That is, when a manager makes a decision and announces it, subordinates and coworkers have little freedom of choice; this style of leadership is called *boss-centered* (Vroom, 1974; Vroom & Jago, 1995; Vroom & Yetton, 1973). According to Vroom's leadership model, each time a decision is to be made, managers can ask themselves a series of questions to arrive at the best possible leadership approach for the situation. For example, a prototypical question is "Is the quality of the final result important?" (The answer had better be yes!)

The strength of Vroom's model is that it recognizes that leaders have options—that they can choose how to behave in light of their previous experiences and knowledge and the current situation or conditions (Vroom, 1997). Vroom's model has received some research support, but its practical implications in the workplace have not been evaluated systematically. It emphasizes the important role of situational variables in determining which leadership approach is most appropriate at any given time.

TRANSFORMATIONAL LEADERSHIP. If a person took charge of a faltering organization and provided it with direction, a new vision, and a sense of purpose, that person would be considered a first-rate leader. Such leaders are hard to find, but occasionally someone emerges who is charismatic and has extraordinary effects on others. These leaders are often called **transformational leaders;** they provide inspiration, intellectual stimulation, and individual attention to followers and are able to draw extra effort out of organization members (Bass, 1985, 1990, 1997). Often such individuals do not have formal authority; because of their personality, style, and interpersonal skills, however, they seem to be able to influence and empower others. Transformational leaders have a strong sense of moral purpose and an aura of authority and dignity; they define people's roles in terms of their own ideological values. Such leaders often use unconventional techniques or novel ideas to frame their vision for the future, and they communicate extreme confidence in their own abilities to lead and to solve problems. Lee Iacocca, formerly of Chrysler, is one.

Transformational leader
Charismatic leader who can change an organization dramatically by inspiring and providing intellectual stimulation and individual attention to followers, who respond with extra effort.

So is GE's Jack Welch. They both led their companies through good and bad times, never lacked confidence, and always inspired commitment and loyalty in employees. In the political arena, Abraham Lincoln and Franklin D. Roosevelt were both transformational leaders who acted daringly and decisively in spite of contrary public opinion and political opposition.

Transformational leaders often take advantage of organizational weaknesses and create opportunities to transform an organization and its employees or constituents. Transformational leaders are often able to instill in others a willingness to go along with their ideas and a reluctance to criticize their ideas or themselves by creating situations that allow them to be seen as charismatic—they manage impressions well (Gardner & Avolio, 1998). A transformational leader inspires followers to rank organizational goals above self-interest. Some researchers assert that charisma isn't needed but that transformational leaders can be effective using inspiration, intellectual stimulation, and individual consideration (Barbuto, 1997). With such leadership, the members of an organization adopt new values, ideas, and ways of operating (Sosik, Kahai, & Avolio, 1998). When new values are adopted, new levels of performance are often expected. Many feel that transformational leaders are born, not made, and are individually unique. Bernard Bass (2001) asserts that the unique combination of three types of intelligence—cognitive, social, and emotional—contributes to transformational leadership. In the end, we still are not sure that transformational skills can be learned.

WHAT CONSTITUTES EFFECTIVE LEADERSHIP? Psychologists' knowledge of how people influence and manage others has grown dramatically. Researchers now know that effective leadership depends not only on personal traits and on specific techniques or behaviors, but also on the situation. Workers may exaggerate a boss's leadership effectiveness if they are productive and happy (Shamir, 1992). Thus, leadership, workers' perceptions of leadership, and motivation are interrelated.

Although the research is complex and not unanimous, several ideas are widely agreed on (Bass, 1998; McGill & Slocum, 1998; Ross & Offermann, 1997). To be an effective leader, follow these guidelines:

- Know the job, and be practical in decision making.
- Be an active leader—passive leadership is not effective.
- Set up effective personnel selection policies—good selection procedures help establish a favorable working situation.
- Act in ways consistent with the organization's vision—this builds a strong organization.
- Foster listening among all levels of employees.
- Create an organization that allows for choices.
- Be sensitive to worker motivation, satisfaction, and performance—be nurturing.

Through carefully conducted I/O research, psychologists can help organizations more effectively meet their goals by seeking out effective leaders who can persuade, motivate, build confidence, and create a better workplace with more satisfied workers and stockholders (Hogan, Curphy, & Hogan, 1994).

Be an *Active* learner

REVIEW

- Discuss the focus and scope of the work of an I/O psychologist. pp. 608–609
- What is a job analysis? pp. 609–610
- What are the goals of selection procedures in human resources departments? pp. 610–611
- What are performance appraisals? pp. 613–614
- Describe the elements of transformational leadership. p. 623

THINK CRITICALLY

- Ability, effort, *and* role perceptions are supposed to be the key variables that determine job performance. Can you think of any others?
- If you were the boss of a corporation, how would you determine workplace dress codes? Why?
- In what ways might a company benefit from assigning employees to work in teams rather than independently?
- If you became a transformational leader, would you have to create a "new" organization, that is, redefine the current one from scratch?

APPLY PSYCHOLOGY

- Imagine you have been assigned to develop a training manual to help employees learn about a particular company's culture and ways of operating. Write a paragraph to motivate employees to become part of the company culture.
- If you were the head of human resources and had to choose a new corporate president, do you think you would choose someone very different from one whom stockholders, who are concerned about profits, would choose? Why or why not?

Human Factors

When I (LL) sit at my computer paying bills, I often recall how frustrating it used to be to write checks, address envelopes, buy stamps, and mail the bills. Now I can pay bills at my convenience with a computer. In addition, I can check my bank balance and move money between accounts all rather easily. Applied psychologists who study human factors have played an important role in streamlining banking procedures as well as many other day-to-day routines. Donald Norman, a psychologist who has studied applied issues, wrote a best-selling book that I regularly recommend to my students: *Design of Everyday Things* (1990). Entertaining and enlightening, it focuses on how cleverly designed machines and software are making life easier.

Human factors (sometimes called *ergonomics*) is the study of the relationship of human beings to machines and to workplaces and other environments. A human factors psychologist might focus on the creation of health-care products for use by handicapped people, the design of cooking utensils or educational products, or the interaction between robots and people. The photos show various controls that adjust automobile seats. As you can see, not all are equally well designed. From a human factors view, the controls in photo (b) are the most effective; those in photo (d), the least effective. Most human factors research focuses on the work environment, especially on the issues of efficiency and safety.

Efficiency

Earning money is an everyday task for most people; getting at it used to be much harder. When I (LL) stand at an ATM (automatic teller machine), I often recall how exasperating it used to be to see a teller in a bank and wait in line for 10 to 15 minutes to get 20 dollars. At first, banks designed "more efficient," roped-off waiting lines. Now we can all bank at our convenience at ATMs. Researchers have examined workers' ability to operate machines effectively. Much of this research centers on the study of the fit between human anatomy or physiology, the demands of a particular task or piece of equipment, and the environment in which the task occurs. Human factors researchers seek to develop person–machine interfaces that minimize frustration and errors, maximize output, and are reliable. (Person–machine interfaces are devices, often computer screens, that provide the links between a human user and a machine, often a computer.) Such researchers study how machines are used to ensure that speed and accuracy of work are optimized and that workers' fatigue and stress are minimized (Westgaard, 2001).

■ *Not all automobile adjusters are equally well-designed.*

A key difference between a human factors psychologist and an I/O psychologist is that the I/O psychologist tends to focus on what can be done to human beings to change their behavior to improve efficiency. A human factors psychologist, on the other hand, looks at how the equipment or tools used by workers can be improved

Human factors
The study of the relationship of human beings to machines and to workplaces and other environments.

to increase efficiency. It is often easier to change a machine than to change a human being!

In the early part of the 20th century, working with machinery meant reading dials, turning wheels, and lifting equipment. Today, working with machinery often means operating a computer, monitoring computer-controlled devices, or programming them. To a great extent, *controlling* equipment, rather than operating it, has become a focus of human factors research. If equipment is to be properly controlled, dials, computer screens, and display devices have to be designed to minimize errors. For example, a pilot must be able to read a computer screen accurately, under all possible conditions, in order to land a plane safely; a nuclear power plant operator must be able to read the temperature of nuclear devices.

Computer displays are everywhere. You often use a computer at work or school, pay a restaurant bill at a computerized cash register, and bank at ATMs. Well-designed computer interfaces minimize errors, but the ability to create good interfaces depends on knowledge of how human beings perceive and interact with machines. This means studying perception, human information processing, and complex decision making (Sommerich, Joines, & Psihogios, 2001). The ATM is an example of an interface that has been studied extensively by human factors researchers. My local bank has an ATM that is easy to operate—I have never made a mistake there. But the ATM at the bank next door to mine has a confusing, overly complicated interface, and I have seen many users kick or curse it and lose their cards. It is usually a human factors psychologist who can take the credit for a well-designed interface that minimizes errors, confusion, and anger on the part of customers.

Even the tools of carpenters, tailors, and data-entry operators can be designed using the principles of human factors. For example, what is the best weight for a hammer? How tall should a drill press be? Today, computer keyboards have been designed to be easy to type on, to minimize typing errors, and to reduce carpal tunnel syndrome. The human factors psychologists who help design such keyboards are attempting to meet the important human considerations of accuracy, productivity, and safety. (Interestingly, keyboard designs that rearrange the letters on the keyboard, putting frequently used letters together, facilitate typing more than the standard keyboard does.)

student voices

Kevin L. Youngblood
Wright State University

Human factors or engineering psychology is what interests me. Human factors psychologists help in the design of [everything from] the F-16 fighter jets' cockpit to something as simple as a hammer. I like knowing I am making life easier for everyone.

Behavior-Based Safety

The goal of any safety practice is injury prevention. In *behavior-based safety,* effective safety management refers to a wide range of programs that focus on changing the behavior of workers *and* companies to prevent occupational injuries and illnesses. A good safety culture within a company minimizes shortcuts and rule violations, encourages open communication among workers and management, and thus reduces the probability of on-the-job injuries. In fact, the failure of employees and management to communicate about safety issues is in itself a safety issue—safety is more than just common sense, and it is more than just a way to shift responsibility to workers alone (Geller, 2001a, 2001b).

Geller (2001c) argues that corporations must develop cultures that value and reinforce safety; that safety has to be part of the work ethic; that it is a process of continuous development; and that companies must develop a total safety culture. Human factors research can contribute to making work environments not only efficient but also safe. Many industrial accidents occur despite attempts to protect workers' safety; human factors research can help reduce accidents through design improvements. Human factors psychologists can also help estimate how quickly people become fatigued and then can design work schedules that optimize the safe use of potentially dangerous equipment. Such psychologists can help promote safety through programs that improve people's attitudes about safety and therefore promote safer work behavior. Only when workers believe that the company values their safety are they likely to make safety-promoting changes.

It is often easier to design a safe, or nearly safe, work environment than to influence workers to work safely. Researchers classify efforts to design safe work environments into three categories (Sanders & McCormick, 1993): *exclusion designs* make it impossible for a specific error to occur; *prevention designs* make it difficult though not impossible for an error to happen; *fail-safe designs* do not reduce the likelihood of an accident, but do lessen its consequences should it occur. For a nuclear power plant, human factors psychologists might develop prevention designs that greatly decrease the likelihood of a nuclear accident (or so they hope). In efforts to ensure safe work environments, the federal government has enacted the Occupational Safety and Health Act (OSHA), which established standards for health and safety in the workplace. These standards function as prevention designs. Workers must accept safety standards before they can be effective, and the government really does not have adequate staff to regulate, enforce, or inspect all places of business. Since OSHA was enacted, however, the death rate from workplace accidents has been cut in half.

Be an *Active* learner

REVIEW

- What does "human factors" mean? p. 625
- What is the most effective approach for ensuring that people will take safety precautions? p. 626
- What steps can a company or a management team take to help ensure the safety of employees? pp. 626–627

THINK CRITICALLY

- What might community organizations do to facilitate the health, safety, and effectiveness of shift workers?

APPLY PSYCHOLOGY

- Imagine you are the boss of a company who is developing safety manuals to help employees learn to operate machinery safely. Write a paragraph to motivate an employee to become part of a safety team.
- If you were designing a new kind of scanner at a supermarket checkout, what would you do to make it efficient *and* accurate?

Research in several other subdisciplines in psychology has also helped establish and maintain workplace safety. *Perceptual research* investigates topics such as which light levels are appropriate for reading computer screens. Which color is most visible in the dark? (Yellow.) Is it easier to see white letters on a dark background, or the reverse? (White letters on dark backgrounds are easier.) *Environmental research* (which we'll examine in more detail later) has focused on variables such as temperature and noise. When the temperature or noise level is too high, performance decreases. Moderate temperatures and noise levels improve both efficiency and safety. Warnings, labels, and compliance techniques are also helpful in establishing safety. Environmental research reveals that signs and warnings help motivate people to follow regulations. Specific instructions for a specific user—for example, using that person's name as part of the instructions—work better still. Labels are especially effective when the user has to remove a warning label before using a machine (Duffy, Kalsher, & Wogalter, 1993). Even if people are given specific warnings about equipment safety and clear directions, incentives and proper reinforcements boost compliance; this is the domain of learning and social psychologists, who study how reinforcements and social influence can be used to induce worthwhile and helpful behaviors.

Psychology and the Law

Ally McBeal, the dizzy but likable attorney on the show that bears her name, uses a mix of psychology and the law to win her cases. Often dealing with employment law—discrimination, harassment, wrongful dismissal—McBeal understands psychology and the law, despite the fact that she often has little insight into her own psyche. In the workplace and elsewhere, the laws that govern society help regulate both public and private behavior. People's thoughts and behaviors shape laws, and laws in turn shape people's behaviors; there is a reciprocal relationship between the two.

The interaction between the fields of psychology and law has greatly increased over the past few decades. *Legal psychology* is the field that conducts empirical research on psychological issues important to the legal system, such as eyewitness accuracy, police selection, decision making in juries, and assumptions about human behavior relevant to the legal rights of defendants, victims, children, and mental patients. *Forensic psychology* focuses on legal issues on which clinical psychologists can act as expert witnesses and consultants, such as the insanity defense, competence to stand trial, and commitment to mental hospitals. Forensic psychologists might help a judge decide which parent should have custody of a child or evaluate the victim of an accident to determine if he or she suffered psychological or neurological damage. Some forensic psychologists counsel prison inmates; others counsel the victims of crimes and help them prepare to testify, cope with emotional distress, and resume their normal activities. *Psychological jurisprudence* is the study of efforts to develop a philosophy of law and justice based on psychological principles.

Psychologists in the Legal System

Psychologists play several roles in the legal system: researchers, policy or program evaluators, advocates, and expert witnesses. As *researchers,* they look at legal issues from a psychological perspective (for example, how juries decide cases) and psychological questions in a legal context (for example, how jurors assign blame or responsibility for a crime). They also help determine why individuals behave in ways that are unacceptable to society. For instance, psychologists do basic research on intelligence, personality, and the role of genetics in determining aggressiveness, to name just a few areas. This basic research often helps solve some very practical problems. For example, some psychologists develop tests to determine who is mentally ill or to evaluate the truthfulness and integrity of defendants and witnesses. Other psychologists look for the causes of aggressiveness in order to develop programs to avert it or to help people channel their aggressive impulses productively.

Psychologists often serve as *policy or program evaluators,* helping governments and other institutions determine whether various policies, agencies, or programs actually work. For example, psychologists interpret what remedial education has accomplished and whether IQ testing has been valid. When legislators wondered whether Head Start programs were making a difference, they turned to psychologists. When new laws calling for equal educational opportunities for handicapped people were being considered, lawyers and judges turned to psychologists for insight into how well various programs might work. Psychologists advise government agencies at all levels on how to help those who suffer posttraumatic stress after a flood, earthquake, or other disaster and on how to respond more effectively to such disasters in the future. Psychologists were inundated with clients suffering from anxiety, fear, and grief after the World Trade Center attacks in 2001.

■ *Legal psychology conducts empirical research on psychological issues relavant to the legal system, such as the legal rights of defendants, victims, children, and mental patients.*

Psychologists are also often asked to be *advocates,* helping to shape social policy on issues such as education of minorities or the gifted and remedial education. When state and federal governments seek to trim budgets of social programs affecting children, they turn to psychologists to ascertain what the impact of such acts might be. Boards of education consult psychologists to determine how best to mainstream students with disabilities.

Finally, psychologists often serve as *expert witnesses,* bringing their knowledge to the courts as consultants. They do not try to address legal issues directly or to make decisions for the courts. Rather, they help the courts in their area of competence—psychology. Psychologists might be asked to determine who is a good eyewitness (we examined this topic in Chapter 8). They also address specific questions: Is this person insane? What are the implications of a divorce for this child? Is this woman competent to stand trial? Psychologists can help determine whether there is a

BRAIN AND BEHAVIOR

Forensic Psychology–DNA and the Law

A man serving two consecutive life terms for the rape of an elderly northern Missouri woman hopes for exoneration through DNA evidence. The man long thought to be the Boston Strangler has also been exonerated for the Massachusetts crimes. No longer are individuals convicted (or released) solely on testimony of others, their state of mind, or "motivation." In some ways forensic psychologists are being asked to step aside. Now our brain and biology are often on trial, and DNA is the expert witness.

DNA, or deoxyribonucleic acid, is the primary building block of an individual's genetic makeup. Testing can establish the identity of the person from whom cellular material is taken. DNA is contained in blood, semen, skin cells, tissue, organs, muscle, brain cells, bone, teeth, hair, saliva, mucus, perspiration, and fingernails, among other things. DNA analysis is a powerful tool because every person's DNA is different from every other individual's (except for the DNA of identical twins). DNA analysis can be likened to fingerprint analysis. If enough of the identifying features are the same between the DNA of a suspect and some evidence found on an injured person or at the scene of a crime, the DNA fingerprint is determined to be a match. And so today police and district attorneys are preserving biological evidence such as hairs and mucus to prove a defendant's guilt. Police and prosecutors routinely take into account evidence that may contain DNA. So the saliva on the stamp of a letter containing anthrax can be compared with a potential perpetrator's saliva sample.

On a practical side, DNA helps prosecutors. States are in the process of implementing a DNA index of individuals convicted of certain crimes—rape, murder, and child abuse, to name three—that can help them find and identify criminals or suspects. Eyewitnesses are no longer as essential, motivation and state of mind can be sometimes put aside, and forensic psychologists are similarly asked to step aside when DNA evidence is available.

link between a person's mental state or problem and the crime the person committed. From a legal standpoint, a person who deliberately plans a crime is more accountable for it than one who accidentally commits one. In many states, when an accused person is convicted of a serious crime, a jury can judge the person "guilty, but mentally ill." This verdict is seen by many as a reasonable alternative because it reduces the number of outcomes of "not guilty by reason of insanity" (a finding that many find unsatisfying), encourages treatment for people with serious mental illness, and takes a potentially dangerous offender off the street.

Psychologists may also be hired as expert witnesses by individuals who file suit against their employer; in this capacity, they help the aggrieved individuals establish that an employer engaged in bias, discrimination, unfair practices, or some combination of these. They may question the validity of a particular employment criterion (such as attractiveness and youthfulness for flight attendants). Of course, employers hire their own expert witnesses. In court, these I/O psychologists testify to the validity, reliability, and predictability of various tests and selection procedures.

Crime and Punishment

An example of the type of issue that links psychology and the law directly is whether capital punishment is a deterrent to crime—especially violent crimes like murder. The majority of countries in western Europe, North America, and South America—more than 95 nations worldwide—has abandoned capital punishment. In contrast, support for capital punishment for convicted murderers has grown in the United States since the 1960s, and "three-strikes" laws for repeat felons have become increasingly common at the state level. These get-tough approaches have resulted in a growing U.S. prison population, as more criminals are jailed than ever before (Shaw et al., 1998).

The murder rate (the number of murders per 100,000 residents) in the United States in 2001 was its lowest in 35 years. Across the United States, the murder rate was 5.5 per 100,000 people—a 3% drop from the 1999 rate. It also turns out that annual murder rates in states with the death penalty are significantly higher than

Be an
Active learner

REVIEW

- What is forensic psychology? p. 628
- What do program evaluators do? p. 628

THINK CRITICALLY

- Do you think DNA analysis will put forensic psychologists out of work? Or is DNA analysis a fad? Explain your answer.
- Do you think capital punishment is a deterrent to some crimes and not other ones? Why?

APPLY PSYCHOLOGY

- If you were to try to teach lawyers about psychology, what topics do you think would be most crucial for you to stress?

those in states that have abolished it. For example, the 1993 murder rate per 100,000 residents was 9.35 for states with the death penalty and 5.22 for states without the death penalty. In 1997, the average murder rate in states without the death penalty was 3.5 per 100,000 residents; in Texas (with capital punishment), the rate was nearly twice that at 6.8 per 100,000 residents. When researchers examined states that had capital punishment, abolished it, and then reinstated it, the results were identical—the annual murder rates were higher when the death penalty was in force. In fact, in the 12 states that do not have the death penalty, there is a lower or identical homicide rate to that of states that do have it. In the states that instituted capital punishment after the Supreme Court reestablished it in 1976, homicide rates have gone up (Costanzo, 1997; Lester, 2000).

The fact is that most murders are crimes of passion—committed because of rage, hatred, or jealousy. Psychologists have tried to help the courts understand that deterrence of violent crime through capital punishment depends on uncertain assumptions. Interestingly, Acker (1993) argues that the courts have often ignored such research studies. One faulty assumption is that capital punishment actually deters crime (e.g., Bailey & Peterson, 1999); another is that violent criminals will view the possibility of execution in the future as a substantially harsher punishment than life imprisonment.

An Uneasy Alliance

The psychologists who conduct research on controversial social issues such as capital punishment are, to be sure, in the eye of a storm. Most people's views on capital punishment—and other similar issues—are informed by data, theory, religion, their own anecdotal experiences, media portrayals, and their own common sense. Psychologists try to provide the judicial system with data and theory to make predictions about criminals a more exact process. There is an uneasy alliance between the legal and the psychological professions. Lawyers assert that psychology is an inexact, or "fuzzy," science and that psychologists should not be allowed to testify as expert witnesses. Psychologists argue that lawyers always want simple answers to complicated human questions and insist on seeking facts even when theories may best describe the truth. For example, a psychologist might be asked to testify in a capital punishment case as to whether a defendant understood the consequences of his or her actions. Far more commonly, because divorce is so widespread, a clinical psychologist might be asked to testify as to which of the divorcing parents should have custody of the children and what the psychological consequences of living with one parent or the other would be for a child. Yet because the legal system is adversarial, each side is likely to have a psychologist testifying that the children will do best with that parent. In fact, there may be no right or wrong answer in some cases. Unfortunately, the legal system cannot generally tolerate such ambiguity.

Environmental Psychology

Neighbors and neighborhoods are amazingly resilient and responsive. A few years ago a toxic waste spill contaminated a stream that flowed into a small lake in my neighborhood (LL). Children occasionally swam in this lake, and people regularly caught fish there. The reaction of the neighborhood was swift; people became alarmed about their health and welfare. Signs went up warning people to stay away from the lake, and property owners began to worry about the value of their homes.

My neighbors feared cancer and worried about monetary losses from the damage. The phone lines hummed, the press was brought in, and the local environmental control agency sprang into action. In the end, the spill turned out to be very localized, the levels of toxins were low, and no one was hurt. There were some small legal claims against the chemical company that had spilled the waste. From an applied psychologist's point of view, however, the mobilization of the residents in my neighborhood was classic. Within a neighborhood group, people became energized, and discussions ensued. Individuals who had never met one another started sharing ideas, and people who had never given much thought to hazardous waste became knowledgeable and outspoken on the subject.

Environmental psychology
The study of how physical settings affect human behavior and how people change their environment.

A particular group of applied psychologists, known as *environmental psychologists,* studies how physical settings such as people's homes and neighborhoods affect behavior. They are interested in issues such as the effects of crowding, how personal space can be changed to meet changing needs, and group reactions to environmental threats. **Environmental psychology** is the study of how physical settings affect human behavior and how people change their environment, often to make it more comfortable and acceptable. Today, the field of environmental psychology has expanded to embrace the idea that, to a great extent, human beings can maintain environmental quality for future generations. Behavioral interventions are being designed to preserve and protect the environment (Dwyer et al., 1993; Porter, Leeming, & Dwyer, 1995). Because of the large number of variables that enter into studies in environmental psychology, the field has become a multidisciplinary one, encompassing research from many other fields, including architecture, geography, and sociology (Stokols, 1995).

Environmental psychologists often conduct studies and act as consultants to institutions such as governments, schools, hospitals, churches, and museums. For example, consider a nursing station, which is the center of activity on each floor in a hospital. In traditional hospital floor plans, it is usually placed at the junction of two long corridors. An alternative is to place it at the hub of corridors arranged like the spokes of a wheel (a radial design). Most of the patients' rooms will then be closer to the nursing station, and nurses can reach them faster. When Trites and his coworkers (1970) investigated nurses' satisfaction with different hospital designs, they found a distinct preference for the radial design. That result led to the redesigning of many hospital floors (Proshansky & O'Hanlon, 1977) with positive results (Ortega-Andeane, 1989). The work space of a hospital or any semi-public space is crucial. When museums are redesigned to allow for dynamic displays that promote interactivity and multisensory stimulation, visitors become more immersed in the exhibits—again, design affects how people use and appreciate space (Harvey et al., 1998).

Environmental psychology is the study of how physical settings affect human behavior. Environmental psychologists are interested in issues such as group reactions to environmental threats.

Environmental Variables

The environment not only includes the layout of a hospital floor or a dormitory or the arrangement of buildings in a housing development or shopping mall—it also includes furniture and light fixtures, climate, noise level, and the number of people per square foot. Environmental psychologists study the relationships among many such variables. Whether a room is perceived as crowded, for example, depends not only on the number of people in it but also on the room's size and shape, furniture layout, ceiling height, number of windows, wall colors, and lighting. Researchers who look at larger environmental systems such as cities and neighborhoods must consider all these variables and more. The three environmental variables that are easiest to control in order to promote people's well-being are temperature, noise, and environmental toxins.

TEMPERATURE. Very hot or very cold climates can cause behavioral effects that range from annoyance to inability to function. New England industrial workers, for example, would never survive the winter without proper shelter, heating, and warm clothes; Southern workers would be far less productive without air conditioning during the summer.

Environmental variables that impair work performance are considered stressors. As we saw in Chapter 14, a *stressor* is a stimulus that affects an organism in physically or psychologically injurious ways and usually elicits feelings such as anxiety, tension, and physiological arousal. Temperature can be a stressor that affects many behaviors, including academic performance, driving an automobile, and being attracted toward others. In general, performance is optimal at moderate temperatures and becomes progressively worse at high or low temperatures.

When the temperature rises and people become uncomfortable, they are more likely to make risky decisions and to behave erratically, and less likely to perform tasks accurately (Kudoh et al., 1991). Research shows that as temperature rises, aggressive feelings and aggression increase (Anderson, Anderson, & Deuser, 1996). In hotter regions of the world, people show more aggression; hotter years, months, and days have all been associated with more aggressive behaviors, such as murders, riots, and spouse abuse (Anderson, 1989). Laboratory research on temperature can never duplicate situations in a real-life setting; therefore, ongoing field-based research is likely to provide better evidence about the exact nature of the relationship between heat and aggression (Anderson & Anderson, 1998; Anderson & DeNeve, 1992).

NOISE. Another environmental variable that often affects human behavior is *noise*—unwanted sound. Noise is a stressor that can overstimulate people, making them too aroused, and it often leads to poor work performance and social functioning.

Some noises are almost always present: the buzzing of fluorescent lights, the humming of refrigerators, the banging of doors as they open or close, the chirping of birds, the sounds of moving cars, the murmur of people talking. Although some of these sounds may be unwanted, they are usually not too disruptive; nor are they stressors. They rarely raise levels of arousal or interfere with daily activities.

However, an unpredictable and intermittent noise of moderate intensity, such as a train whistle, can impair performance on tasks that involve sustained attention or memory. And if noise raises physiological arousal to very high levels, it may impair performance in general and even cause hearing damage (see Chapter 5). Thus, noise acts as a stressor when it interferes with communication, raises physiological arousal, or is so loud that it causes pain. More commonly, noise simply interferes with the ability to concentrate, learn, and remember—thus, it induces stress (Evans, Hygge, & Bullinger, 1995).

ENVIRONMENTAL TOXINS (POLLUTANTS). As you drive into a congested city such as Los Angeles, Detroit, or New York, it is distressing to see how the skyline's beauty is blurred by air pollution. Cities continue to become more congested; crowding continues to be a problem; people continue to drive big gas-guzzling cars; industries continue to develop new products made from new chemicals. Adding to all of this is the array of substances such as carbon monoxide and sulfur that fill the air from the burning of high-sulfur coal and oil in industrial cities. Nearly any airborne substance, whether a chemical emitted by an industrial plant or a naturally occurring substance such as pollen, can trigger respiratory problems and result in diminished work performance and health consequences. Airborne toxins, which are breathed in and absorbed by the lungs, can impair motor tasks that involve reaction time and affect long-term health; for example, even in cities that meet federal standards for clean air, the risk of premature death is 3%–8% higher than in the areas with the cleanest air.

Crowding
The perception that one's personal space is too restricted.

While smokestacks have been made taller and in some communities have even been banned, the automobile is not becoming any less common. Thus, pollution from cars continues to be a major urban problem. Another pollutant that has received enormous attention in the past few years is cigarette smoke. Smoking in restaurants, bars, and the urban workplace has come under great criticism because of the damaging effects of secondhand smoke; increasingly, local governments are making buildings smoke-free (Gostin, 1997). Although individuals tend to support such laws, enforcement is difficult. Psychologists work with community, state, and local governments to help individuals and agencies combat pollution in its various forms. This is a daunting task because businesses and individuals have grown used to polluting the environment with few consequences.

Crowding

The large prison and jail populations have produced crowded conditions in state, local, and federal correctional facilities. In 2002 there were nearly 1 million state prisoners, more than 620,000 local jail inmates, and more than 150,000 federal prisoners. The correctional facilities housing these individuals are bursting at the seams, despite the fact that the rate of growth in prisons has slowed a bit. A crucial environmental variable that has a profound impact on individual and group behavior is simply the number of people that are around. In some situations that involve many people, you may feel closed in and crowded. In other situations, the excitement of a crowd may be exhilarating. It is generally not the size of a space or the number of people that causes a feeling of being crowded; rather, **crowding** is the *perception* that personal space is too limited. Thus, crowding is a psychological state. One person may feel crowded and uncomfortable in a mall filled with Christmas shoppers; someone else may feel that the throngs are part of the holiday ambiance. When people feel crowded, their sense of well-being is threatened, and day-to-day behaviors may be affected—a typical response is social withdrawal (Evans et al., 2001).

■ *Crowding is the perception that personal space is too limited. Thus, crowding is a psychological state.*

■ **SOCIAL DENSITY AND SPATIAL DENSITY.** Both social density and spatial density contribute to crowding. *Social density* is the number of people in a given space; *spatial density* is the amount of space allocated to a fixed number of people. For example, in an empty theater, a person might feel lonely; if the theater is full, or even half-full, the person might feel crowded (social density). In contrast, eight people may feel comfortable in a large modern elevator but

FIGURE 17.5

Social Density and Spatial Density

Manipulations of *social density* are manipulations of the number of people in the same size space. Manipulations of *spatial density* are manipulations of the size of the space, with the number of people held constant.

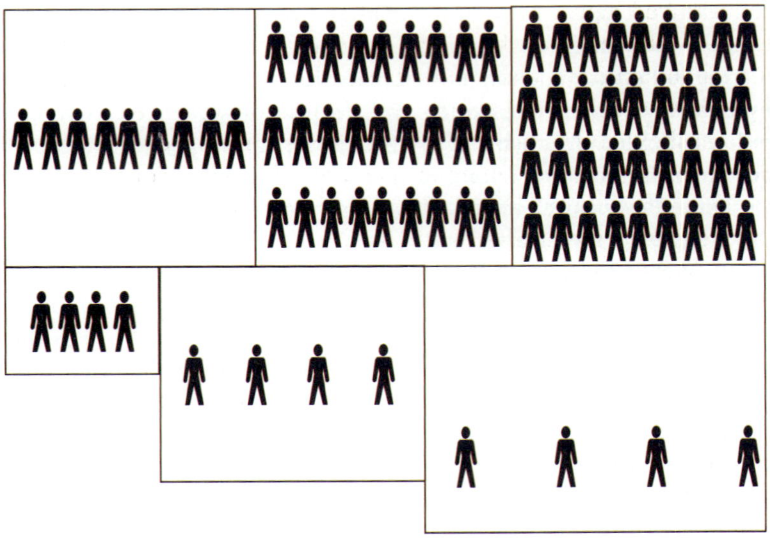

intolerably cramped in a small old-fashioned elevator (spatial density). Researchers must be careful to separate the variables of social and spatial density as it affects satisfaction with various space constraints (Kaya & Erkip, 2001). See Figure 17.5.

Valins and Baum did a study in 1973 on how the architectural design of college dormitories affected students. The dormitories had two designs: either long hallways, or corridors, having rooms on either side, with 2 people per room, 34 people per floor, and a shared bathroom and lounge, or suites, with 4 or 6 students sharing a bathroom and lounge; and several suites per floor (see Figure 17.6). The actual square footage per student was about the same in both types of dormitories, but 67% of corridor residents found their living space crowded, compared with only 25% of suite residents. Corridor residents reported too many people on their floor and too many unwanted interactions. Valins and Baum concluded that corridor designs promoted "excessive social interaction and that such interaction is associated with the experience of crowding" (p. 249).

If some dormitories produce feelings of crowding, as Valins and Baum have suggested, these feelings should be evident in people's behavior. In a classic study, Bickman and colleagues (1973) compared the helping behavior shown by students living in housing of different densities. They used a measure called the *lost-letter technique,* in which unmailed letters were purposely dropped in dormitory corridors, in areas near stairwells and elevators, with no more than one letter per corridor. The letters were addressed, sealed, and stamped but had no return addresses. The researchers reasoned that someone finding a letter would assume that a person living in the dormitory had dropped it by mistake on the way to the mailbox. The dependent variable was the number of "lost" letters that were subsequently mailed. The independent variable was the density of housing. The

FIGURE 17.6

The Psychological Effects of Architectural Design

A corridor dorm and a suite have different psychological effects on students, even when actual space per student is about the same. Valins and Baum reported that students living in corridor dorms complained about being crowded more than students living in suites did. *(Baum & Valins, 1977)*

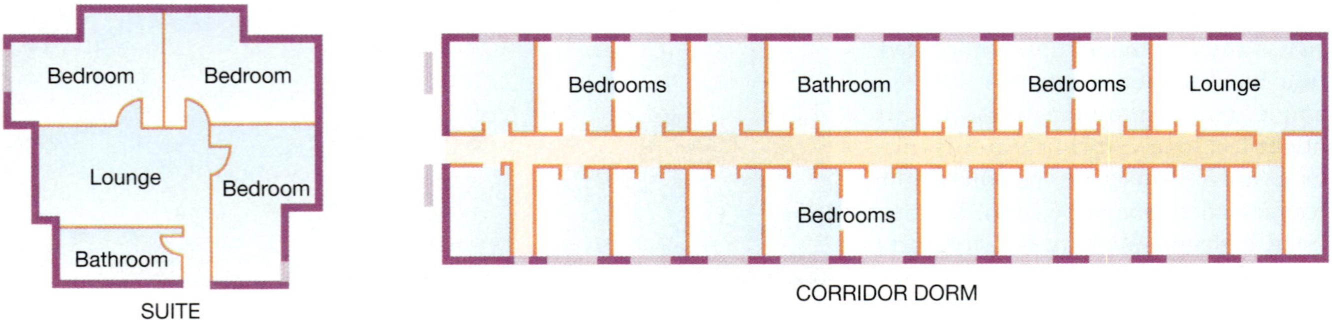

experiment involved high-density dorms (high-rise, 22-story towers, each housing more than 500 students), medium-density dorms (4- to 7-story buildings, each housing about 165 students), and low-density dorms (2- to 4-story buildings, with about 58 students each).

The results showed that helping behavior (putting the "lost" letter into a mailbox) occurred for 63% of the letters dropped in high-density dorms, 87% of those dropped in medium-density dorms, and 100% of those dropped in low-density dorms. And when questionnaires were distributed to the students in the various dorms, the answers generally reflected attitudes related to the kind of housing in which the students lived. For example, students in high-density dorms reported feeling less trust, cooperativeness, and responsibility toward their fellow residents than did students in lower-density dorms. The researchers concluded that the students living in the high-density dormitories behaved in a less socially responsible manner toward other dormitory residents. Baum believes that high-density situations tend to make people feel stressed, out of control, and crowded. All of this contributes to potential problems in such situations—for example, in prisons (Fleming, Baum, & Weiss, 1987).

Although many of the effects of crowding are not consistent across all situations or populations, certain ones seem to be universal (Sinha & Nayyar, 2001). In high-density situations, people feel stressed and sometimes overaroused (Ruback, Pandey, & Begum, 1997). They may feel alone or anonymous, and they may withdraw from the situation. They may become apathetic, exhibit impaired task performance, and even become hostile (Malik & Batra, 1998). Maintaining a sense of control and of personal space seems to be a crucial variable in preventing such reactions (Evans et al., 1998; Morgan & Stewart, 1998).

■ **PERSONAL SPACE.** To help assert their individuality and maintain a sense of personal control, human beings generally try to establish appropriate degrees of personal space. **Personal space** is the area around an individual that the person considers private and that is enclosed by an invisible psychological boundary. Encroachment on that space causes displeasure and often withdrawal.

The size of your personal space can change, depending on the situation and the people near you. For example, you may walk arm in arm with a family member, but you will avoid physical contact with a stranger. You may stand close to a friend and whisper in her ear, but you will keep a certain distance from an elevator operator or a store clerk.

Anthropologist Edward Hall (1966) suggested that personal space is a mechanism by which people communicate with others. He proposed that people adhere to established norms of personal space that are learned in childhood. Hall observed that the use of personal space also varies from culture to culture. In the United States, especially in suburban and rural areas, people are used to large homes and generous personal space. In Japan, on the other hand, people are used to small homes that provide little personal space. In general, Western cultures insist on a fair amount of space for people, reserving proximity for intimacy and close friends, while Arab and some Eastern cultures allow much smaller distances between strangers (Rustemli, 1991).

To explain the concept of personal space in the United States, Hall classified four *spatial zones,* or distances, used in social interactions with other people: the intimate, the personal, the social, and the public. An *intimate distance* (from 0 to 18 inches) is maintained between people who have great familiarity with one another. It is an acceptable distance for comforting someone who is hurt or for interactions between lovers, physicians and patients, and athletes. The closeness enables someone to hold another person, look into the other's eyes, and hear the other's breath. An acceptable distance between friends and acquaintances is *personal distance* (1.5 to 4 feet); this is the distance used for most social interactions. At 1.5 to 2 feet, someone might tell a secret to a close friend; at 2 feet,

Personal space
The area around an individual that the person considers private and that is enclosed by an invisible psychological boundary.

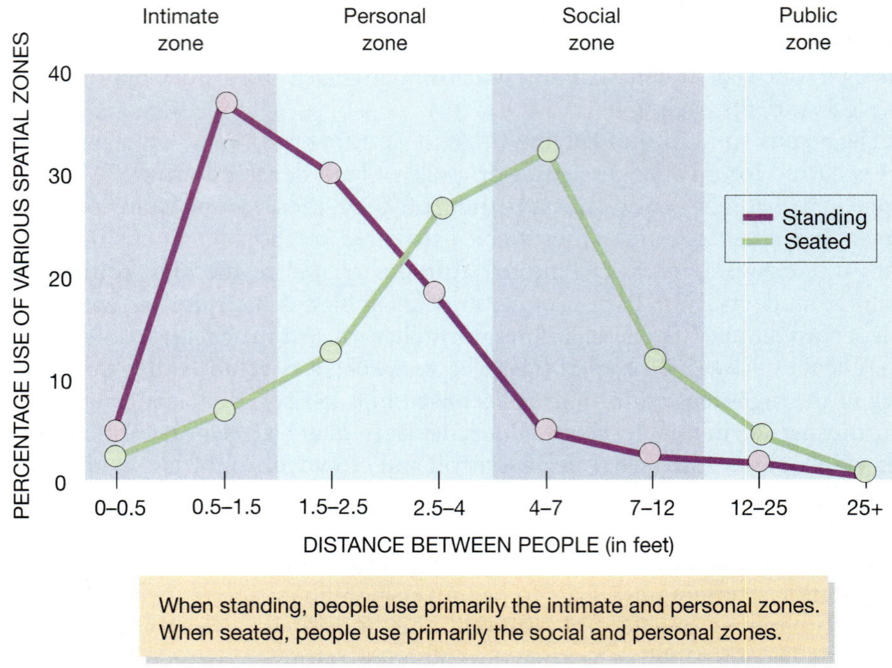

FIGURE 17.7

People's Use of Personal Space When Seated and Standing *(Altman & Vinsel, 1977)*

people can walk and talk together; at 2 to 4 feet, a person can maintain good contact with a coworker without seeming too personal or too impersonal. *Social distance* (4 to 12 feet) is used for business and for interactions with strangers. At 4 to 6 feet, people are close enough to communicate their ideas effectively but far enough away to remain separated. Physical barriers, such as a desk to separate a clerk, receptionist, or boss from the people with whom the person interacts, may control personal space in the social zone. *Public distance* (12 to 25 feet or more) minimizes personal contact. It is the distance maintained between politicians and audiences, teachers and students, and actors or musicians and their audiences. Public distance is sufficiently great to eliminate personal interaction between individuals.

Of course, determining personal space is a tricky endeavor, and researchers are trying to sort out distance estimations (Zakay, Hayduk, & Tsal, 1992) for adults and children (Roques et al., 1997) and for men and women (Idehen, 1997). Figure 17.7 presents generally accepted estimates of the spaces people use when seated and when standing.

■ **TERRITORIALITY.** If you have ever lived in a dormitory, you may have experienced a lack of privacy, and the less personal space you had, the more stressful you may have found dormitory life (Sinha & Mukherjee, 1996). Irwin Altman (1975) has suggested that the key to understanding why people feel crowded and need personal space is their need for privacy. **Privacy** is the freedom from intrusion that results from controlling boundaries between oneself and other people so that access is limited. Everyone needs privacy. According to Altman, privacy allows people to develop and nurture a sense of self. People who lack privacy feel they have no control over who and what can intrude on them. This sense of helplessness can lead to low self-esteem and poor social adaptation. Understanding the need for privacy is central to understanding the behavior of human beings.

Privacy
The freedom from intrusion that results from controlling the boundaries between oneself and other people so that access is limited.

One way people maintain a sense of privacy is to change their immediate environment. When a teenage girl goes into a room and shuts the door, she closes herself off from other people; she limits their access to her. The teenager has set up a boundary—a closed door—behind which she can do what she wants when she wants to.

Maintaining a sense of privacy is closely related to territoriality, another important aspect of many people's lives. **Territorial behavior** is behavior involved in establishing, maintaining, personalizing, and defending a delineated space. One or more persons regulate the exclusive use of a specific space by marking it as a private area where intruders are not welcome. Homeowners put up fences and signs that say NO TRESPASSING, street gangs defend their turf, and nations wage war in defense of their national boundaries. Like personal space, territoriality is a privacy-regulating mechanism.

Territorial behavior
Behavior involved in establishing, maintaining, personalizing, and defending a delineated space.

Preserving the Environment

Elementary school children often come home from school reminding parents of the need to recycle, reuse, and cut back on waste. Starting with the youngest, people are being encouraged to do their part to preserve this fragile planet—and some high-profile companies like Ben & Jerry's are leading the way. An emerging area of environmental research focuses on doing something to actually control people's behavior in the environment. For example, research by Scott Geller at Virginia Polytechnic Institute and State University found that littering can be significantly reduced if people are given instructions for proper disposal of trash; the more specific the instructions are, the less littering occurs (Geller, 1975; Geller, Witmer, & Tuso, 1977). But more important is integrating specific procedures and changing attitudes to increase environmentally responsible behavior (Geller, 1995).

Aside from their children's reminders, what makes people want to preserve the environment—to conserve energy and reduce pollution by recycling, by driving smaller, more fuel-efficient cars, and by investing in solar panels for their homes? Research on these issues has shown that tax laws that reward energy savings, signs about energy conservation, and new energy-saving equipment help people adopt more energy-saving behaviors. As with littering, when people are given specific energy-saving instructions and prompts, they are more likely to comply. And when the task is made easier, for example, with recycling—recycling bins, convenient drop-offs, payments for recycling—the likelihood of recycling increases.

Some tremendous worldwide environmental problems must be solved. Geller (1989, 1992) suggests that information science, marketing principles, and behavioral analysis be combined to solve problems such as preserving the earth's rain forests, managing waste, and conserving energy. First, environmentally beneficial behaviors must be proposed; this helps move people to the point where they at least *intend* to engage in such behaviors. Environmentally safe products can be promoted as being affordable, accessible, easy to use, and desirable (Burn, 1991). Psychologists must then analyze the wants, needs, and perceptions of the people being targeted for attitude change. After these steps have been taken, researchers should evaluate the results of efforts to change attitudes and behavior to see whether strategies have been effective. Geller calls for a collaboration of social action research and scholarship to preserve the quality of the environment. Many interventions are not as effective as they might be (Needleman & Geller, 1992); once people stop being reinforced for recycling or other beneficial behaviors, such as wearing seat belts, they often discontinue the behavior (Geller et al., 1989). Wide-ranging social change begins at the local level, and community psychologists, considered next, attempt to foster such change.

Be an *Active* learner

REVIEW

- How does a stressor affect behavior? pp. 631–633
- Distinguish between social density and spatial density. pp. 633–634
- What is personal space? p. 635

THINK CRITICALLY

- What are the results of the lost-letter experiments? Do you think the same results would happen with students that attend your school? Why or why not?
- How does personal space help people maintain a sense of privacy?
- What are the implications of studying the effects of environmental variables for architectural firms, window designers, and companies that provide heating, ventilation, and air conditioning systems?

APPLY PSYCHOLOGY

- Sketch a diagram or a blueprint of a home that is small and still allows people intimacy and personal space.

Community Psychology

If you have ever lived in a community that faced a challenge—high unemployment, a toxic spill, a hurricane, or racial upheaval—you know that communities can be mobilized. They can take on a school board or vote a mayor in or out of office, and their members do so by pooling their resources, using their collective talent, and reaching out. Some communities are more proactive than others and seek to prevent problems before they occur. They address school problems, restore decaying sections of town, and lobby legislators for new funds for community centers. Many psychologists today are studying not only individuals, but also whole communities—they seek to influence individuals, families, and the entire social structure

point*counterpoint*

The Internet and Social Isolation

The Issue: Has the Internet left people with fewer meaningful social contacts?

POINT
The Internet is a positive, prosocial way of helping people communicate quickly and efficiently.

COUNTERPOINT
Frequent use of the Internet adversely affects social involvement and psychological well-being.

There is no doubt that the Internet is fast and inexpensive and has transformed communication. But is it also changing our lives in harmful ways? Are people cutting themselves off from others as they hunker down over their terminals, communicating with anonymous strangers, or buying anything and everything online? Has the Internet left people with fewer social contacts, seeking entertainment and relationships through a medium that is asocial and anonymous and that promotes a solitary activity?

The Internet is having enormous effects on society. It is accessible to nearly everyone. More than 9.8 billion emails are delivered every day. This technology gives people greater opportunities to meet, communicate, catch up, get acquainted with new people, develop chat relationships, and share ideas with diverse individuals all over the world at rapid-fire speed. People form new bonds, exchange information, and increase their social contacts. The Internet is a major medium of communication. Some think the Internet is great—at least that is one side of the story.

But some researchers assert that greater use of the Internet is associated with small but reliable increases in loneliness, declines in social involvement, and increases in depression. They assert that using the Internet adversely affects social involvement and psychological well-being. The time people spend on the Internet has displaced other social activities. The new online relationships are mostly superficial or enhance existing friendships at school, work, or house of worship.

The Internet is not all bad or good—for example, people learn computer skills while accessing the Internet, and it provides a quick way to gather information, helping with schoolwork. But are these benefits worth the trade-off? Can accessing the Internet be entertaining and useful, without causing disengagement from real life? Can psychologists help design Internet applications that enhance social interactions so as to benefit society? Can the Internet become a more social medium? The research jury is still out.

(Levine, 1998). They hope to help people develop resilience and a sense of purpose and nurture what is essential for survival and personal growth (Sonn & Fisher, 1998). Access to information, communication within a community, and a sense of social involvement are necessary for the work of these psychologists. The *Point/Counterpoint* looks at the effect of the Internet on these kinds of variables.

The beginnings of this movement in psychology can be traced to the 1960s. In that decade, many psychologists recognized that individual therapy was at best imprecise and at worst inefficient for treating large numbers of people. Researchers and practitioners, as well as politicians, sought a more efficient and effective approach. President John F. Kennedy's 1963 message to Congress called for "a bold new approach" to the treatment of mental illness; it was followed by legislation and funding for community mental health centers. Community psychology has emerged in response to a widespread desire for a more action-oriented approach to individual and social adjustment. **Community psychology** is the branch of psychology that seeks to reach out to society by providing services such as community mental health centers and especially to effect social change through empowerment of individuals.

The general aims of community psychology are to strengthen existing social support networks and to stimulate the formation of new networks to meet new challenges (Gonzales et al., 1983). Psychologists with a community orientation conduct community-based research and interventions in a society with a complex mix of religions, ethnicities, and political inclinations. Practitioners are aware of the community needs and how both qualitative and quantitative practices can be employed to address complex social problems like drug abuse, teen pregnancy, and decaying family structures. A crucial element in accomplishing these goals is community involvement. A group at a church, synagogue, or mosque, for example, could mobilize its senior citizens to participate in a foster grandparent program. The focus of community psychology is often on solving applied behavior problems. For example, a community psychologist might help a group of residents develop better fire safety procedures in public housing. A key element of community psychology is **empowerment**—helping people in the community enhance their existing skills and develop new ones and acquire knowledge and motivation so that they can gain control over their own lives (Rappaport, 1987). Community psychologists work with schools, with religious groups, on planning commissions, and in prisons. They plan and set up programs to bring psychological skills and knowledge into the community. Community psychologists work especially hard at prevention of psychological problems. Their efforts often take the form of developing neighborhood organizations to work on preventing and solving mental health problems (Wandersman & Nation, 1998). Prevention operates at three levels: primary, secondary, and tertiary.

Primary prevention means reducing the risk of *new* cases of a disorder and counteracting harmful circumstances before they lead to maladjustment. Primary prevention usually targets groups rather than individuals. It may focus on an entire community, on moderate-risk groups (such as children from families of low socioeconomic status), or on high-risk groups (such as children of schizophrenic parents). Community psychologists may seek to establish drug prevention centers, safe houses for battered women, or suicide hot lines. For example, Nathaniel Donson (1999) has a primary prevention model for day care. He asserts that since 5 million young children are cared for by adults other than their parents and since affordable high-quality day care is very hard to find for those who need it most, community psychologists should take action.

In response to growing public awareness of mental health problems, a special kind of primary prevention service agency—the *neighborhood clinic*—came into being. Such clinics help communities cope with problems that may be created by mental illness, unemployment, and lack of education. They offer consultation, educational programs, and lectures and literature on topics such as therapy, family planning, and drug rehabilitation.

Community psychology
The branch of psychology that seeks to reach out to society by providing services such as community mental health centers and especially to effect social change through empowerment of individuals.

Empowerment
Facilitating the development of skills, knowledge, and motivation in individuals so that they can act for themselves and gain control over their own lives.

Secondary prevention involves identifying new cases of a mental health problem in the early stages. Community psychologists offer secondary prevention services in *crisis intervention centers*, which help people deal with short-term stressful situations requiring immediate therapeutic attention. Often the crisis is a specific event; for example, a person may be contemplating suicide, or a woman may have been raped. The focus of crisis intervention is on the immediate circumstances, not on past experiences.

Tertiary prevention focuses on the treatment of full-blown psychological problems. There is considerable overlap between secondary and tertiary prevention, as sometimes issues and problems that are treated in the short term or in their early stages may have a long-standing underlying source. Community psychologists offer help to eliminate or reduce a problem as well as to strengthen existing family or community resources. The emphasis is on utilizing existing community resources and empowering individuals to manage their own lives more effectively.

An important aim of community psychology is to serve all members of a community, including people who might not otherwise be able to afford the services of a psychotherapist or counselor. Community psychologists seek to develop individuals' sense of community, which has a clear psychological benefit (Brodsky, 1996). Community psychologists are change-oriented. Because they believe that some so-

psychology *in action*

Who Is at Risk for Excessive Drinking?

If there is an area of intervention where community psychologists can make a difference, it's unquestionably in helping to get excessive drinking under control. College campuses have long been known as places where students indulge and

overindulge in alcohol. Every year there are reports of deaths from binge drinking; every year thousands of college students are hurt or hurt others in alcohol-related automobile accidents.

Many factors have been implicated in college students' drinking, including increased risk taking, a sense of invulnerability, and immaturity among young people. One factor that seems to stand out is self-esteem—a global evaluation about one's personality and the extent to which self-evaluations are favorable or not. Some research has reported a relationship between low self-esteem and excessive drinking such that people with low self-esteem drink more.

One team of researchers (Glinerman, Geller, & Fortney, 1999) assessed a group of college students' self-esteem and then measured their actual level of intoxication with a Breathalyzer after a fraternity party. It turned out that students with lower self-esteem had much higher levels of blood alcohol than students with higher self-esteem. The effect was the same for men and women.

The researchers point out that Greek-life students are considered to be among the heaviest drinkers on college campuses, and their parties and events contribute disproportionately to drinking-related problems on campus. Student service divisions of universities can—and should—work with fraternities in education programs, treatment programs, and health programs to help students enhance self-esteem, realize that alcohol is neither a solution nor a cure for negative feelings about self-esteem, and recognize that alcohol—especially binge drinking—will not cure loneliness or feelings of isolation. Can community psychologists make a difference? You bet. Here is a place in college campuses where a practitioner can reach out to help stop problems before they begin.

Is this an area where the problem and the solution are obvious? Yes and no. We have long suspected that self-esteem is a key variable, but research studies have been contradictory. Here is an opportunity where research can be put into action to help save lives—let's help students develop higher levels of self-esteem, and then let's measure their drinking behavior. This research is yet to be done, but should be.

cial conditions and organizational procedures result in maladjusted behavior, they often advocate changes in community institutions. For example, they seek to improve the court system, develop programs to prevent drug use in schools, consult with industry about reducing stress on the job, help religious organizations develop volunteer programs to aid the homeless, help hospitals set up preventive medicine programs, and foster community involvement in educational issues.

Educational Psychology

When I was in elementary school, most students were grouped according to ability, but that ability was often inferred only from the teacher's observations of classroom behavior rather than through ability testing. Those who acted out in any way (as I [LL] unfortunately did, far too often) were assigned seats in the seventh row. Occupants of the seventh row received little attention.

Things have changed. Today, accrediting bodies and state legislators are requiring that virtually all teachers have undergraduate college degrees; most have advanced degrees. Teachers are now required to be trained not only in the content areas but also in sophisticated educational techniques. History teachers need to know history and how to teach it, as well as how to manage classrooms and help individual students meet particular challenges. This is where educational psychology comes in.

Educational psychology is the systematic application of psychological principles to learning and teaching. Psychology has a long tradition of studying learning principles; psychological researchers have thoroughly explored how people learn and forget. Educators have long focused on instructional techniques and principles of classroom management. *Educational psychologists* bring these two disciplines together. They show how psychological theories and methods can be applied to improve learning in individual students and in whole classrooms and to improve the process of teaching itself. In short, they help create better classroom managers (Fox, 1993). Note that there is a distinction between educational psychologists and school psychologists, although they share many concerns. Educational psychologists are likely to focus on strategies to improve overall learning and classroom techniques. School psychologists are more likely to focus on interventions for specific individuals—such as diagnoses of individual psychological and learning problems and consultations with parents and educators about an individual child's progress or plans.

Problems Studied by Educational Psychologists

Educational psychologists need to know a great deal about how children develop intellectually and socially to help promote effective teaching strategies. For example, they seek normative information about how students interact with other students and how they solve problems. Educational psychologists usually do research in five broad areas of inquiry in order to put theory into practice. You will recognize these areas from earlier chapters, because educational psychologists apply the lessons of many psychological subdisciplines—from learning, to developmental psychology, to social psychology.

A key focus for educational psychologists is *developmental change*—how and when individuals develop physically, socially, and intellectually. In children, these processes are rapid and dramatically affect the ways a child or adolescent learns and interacts with teachers and other students.

Educational psychologists also study students' backgrounds to learn how *environmental conditions* can affect the learning process. Socioeconomic status is but one of those conditions; parental marital status, use of drugs in the home, and how

Educational psychology
The systematic application of psychological principles to learning and teaching.

learning is valued in the home are other important environmental factors. Classroom learning styles are important to educational psychologists, who study *behavioral principles of learning* to ensure that the classroom routine is organized appropriately. They also study *cognitive processes* to learn how students learn and process new information, and they examine *social interactions* to find out how students are influenced by others and how they can be influenced in positive ways. Applying research findings in each of these areas plus a knowledge of children makes for effective teaching.

Putting Theory into Practice: Classroom Management

Studying the principles of psychology is obviously a prerequisite for developing effective classroom techniques. But what are effective classroom techniques? Educational psychologists try to bridge the gap between theory and practice by developing approaches to learning and instruction that optimize student outcomes. For example, educational psychologists have focused on developing individualized educational plans to personalize instruction; they work to develop mastery learning—breaking learning down into a series of discrete steps for students to master one at a time. They also encourage immediate feedback, establish clearly defined objectives, and develop effective classroom management techniques.

Educational psychologists are both theoreticians and practitioners. They try to implement instructional techniques in innovative ways that have measurable outcomes. What if a student acts out in class by verbally abusing another child? Such situations arise throughout the school day, and there are dozens of things an instructor can do. Should a teacher *scold* the child, *ignore* the child, *banish* the child to the school office, *punish* the child for classroom misbehavior, or *instruct* the child on respect for peers? The answers lie in psychological principles: scolding, ignoring, and banishment are forms of punishment, but the most effective instruction tries to focus on positive behaviors—including how to get along with other people, the value of ideas, and the dignity and power individuals gain from knowledge.

Let's look at some specific classroom management techniques. There is a difference between how long a class period lasts and how much time students actually engage in learning. Both time allocation and management of engaged time are important skills for teachers. Establishing clear classroom rules and pacing a class effectively are important. When teachers who are modern and "reform-minded" participate in development programs to enhance classroom effectiveness, the result is usually quite positive for students (Stipek et al., 1998).

■ *Establishing clear classroom rules and pacing a class effectively are important in classroom management.*

■ **TIME ALLOCATION.** Because teachers have such small amounts of time with students, they must allocate time effectively. How much time is actually spent on learning? In many elementary schools, only about 60% of classroom time is spent on the tasks at hand (Karweit & Slavin, 1981). Researchers have found that carefully dividing up the allocated class time is essential. Other recommendations are to avoid starting class periods late and finishing early. Late starts signal to students that the lesson is not important. This leads to further delays by students and a general lackadaisical attitude. A teacher should avoid interruptions at all costs; interruptions break a lesson's momentum and steal substantial time from engaged learning. When students are actively engaged in learning, they are said to be *on task*. To encourage on-task behaviors, effective teachers minimize time spent on routine procedures by ensuring that those are handled smoothly and efficiently. Cooperative learning, with children working in teams, facilitates achievement and increases on-task time (Ross, Haimes, & Hogaboam-Gray, 1998). Finally, efficient teachers minimize time spent on discipline by quickly and efficiently imposing penalties in private and then seeking to reestablish a positive relationship with the offender (Weinstein & Mignano, 1993).

If time is well allocated, students are more likely to maximize their on-task time. Effective teachers try to maintain momentum and smoothness of instruction by setting up a meaningful sequence of instructional ideas. Managing transitions from one topic to the next helps keep students engaged and focused.

Maintaining an entire class's focus is also an important task. Letting students know that the teacher is aware of the activities of the class keeps students on task; praising students for their good work is vital (Craft, Alber, & Heward, 1998). Instructors who can juggle many tasks at one time and can work well with both individuals and small groups provide effective on-task instruction (Charles, 1985). Teachers who make the basics clear, monitor work in progress, and give frequent feedback are more effective in engaging students.

■ **CLASSROOM RULES.** When a teacher starts the year with a clear set of guidelines for students, which systematically introduces them to the procedures and the teacher's expectations, students are more likely to stay on task and remain engaged. When rules are limited in number, they are far more likely to be enforceable. In addition, when students are asked to help establish ground rules, such as not talking without raising one's hand, offenders know that they are breaking their own rules, not arbitrary regulations. Educational psychologists assert that it is necessary to "let the punishment fit the crime" (Notterman & Drewry, 1993), that students themselves may be the best judges of appropriate punishments, and that students can be helpers in the process of reducing disruptions (Arceneaux & Murdock, 1997).

■ **PACING.** The tempo of a class is like the tempo of a symphony. A conductor does not want the musicians to play everything quickly or slowly or with enthusiasm all the time. Effective classrooms, like successful concerts, include quiet times as well as high-energy moments. Repetition is minimized, and a good teacher holds students' attention with her or his voice. The pace is varied—short segments are more likely to hold attention than long ones.

Pacing is determined by the age, development level, and temperament of the students, the material to be covered, and the instructor's personal style. But combined with classroom rules and effective allocation of time to ensure on-task behavior, pacing is an important element of effective instruction.

Each of these elements—time allocation, classroom rules, and pacing—helps establish effective instruction. There are other important tactics, too, of course: summarizing, using feedback, encouraging student interaction, and even planning seating arrangements (Fenwick, 1998). And one of the most important elements of managing a classroom is caring for students and the learning process; research supports the idea that caring is a key characteristic of the master teacher and classroom manager (Agne, 1999). All of

Be an *Active* learner

REVIEW

- What do community psychologists mean by *empowerment*? pp. 638–639
- What is primary prevention? p. 640
- What are some of the issues studied by educational psychologists? pp. 641–642

THINK CRITICALLY

- How can community psychologists focus on helping groups of people in neighborhoods and even whole communities to change? How do they do it?
- Why is primary prevention so important to psychologists?
- As a psychologist, what do you think would be the most important part of instruction?
- How do you think teaching should vary according to grade level and subject matter (think Piaget—Chapter 3)?

APPLY PSYCHOLOGY

- If you were to design a program to help ensure that children did not become adolescent drinkers, what community psychology techniques would you employ?
- Many schools use the concept of block scheduling, in which two periods are joined to provide one long class. What might be some advantages and disadvantages of block scheduling, compared with traditional classes of shorter duration?

these topics are important to educational psychology. Each has been explored in depth by learning researchers, classroom teachers, and educational psychologists.

Sport Psychology

Imagine lining up a shot—any kind of shot will do. You picture the ball, you think about its final destination, you visualize its trajectory. You take your shot. When tennis players such as Venus Williams, basketball players such as Vince Carter, and quarterbacks such as Brian Griese prepare to take their shots, they usually imagine them first. In using mental imagery, they are applying the principles of sport psychology.

Sport psychology is the systematic application of psychological principles to sports. Sport psychologists are interested in how participating in sports or any physical activity may enhance a person's well-being. These psychologists work to help athletes in a number of areas; first and foremost, they help *improve sports performance*. In general, performance may be enhanced through mental strategies that either refine the practices of effective performers or help ineffective performers overcome obstacles. Second, sport psychologists try to *enhance the sports experience for young participants*. Third, they provide *assistance with injury rehabilitation*.

Sport psychologists, like any psychologists, recognize that behavior (in this case, athletic performance) is affected by the individual athlete, the athlete's team, the team leader or coach, and the environment in which these individuals interact. The characteristics of athlete, coach, and environment are multidimensional; people's personal characteristics, how they interact with others, and how the environment affects them are all influenced by past events, relationships, and successes or failures. Nevertheless, sport psychologists have tried to bring some order to the study of athletic performance.

To obtain certification from the Association for the Advancement of Applied Sport Psychology, sport psychology professionals may be trained primarily in the sport sciences with additional training in counseling or clinical psychology *or* primarily in clinical psychology with supplemental training in the sport sciences. Sport psychologists study the behaviors associated with sports in the traditional ways that psychologists go about things: some do basic research on sports performance; others take an educational role, teaching about sport psychology; still others are applied practitioners who help athletes overcome obstacles to achieve their highest potential. Researchers consider a whole range of sports topics, among which are those we consider here: motivation, activation and arousal, anxiety and performance, and intervention strategies (Cox, Qiu, & Liu, 1993).

Activation and Arousal in Athletic Performance

The discussion of motivation in Chapter 11 revealed that, given moderate levels of arousal and moderately difficult tasks, as arousal increased, performance also increased. Arousal is generally viewed as stimulation and excitement—a performance enhancer. But excessive levels of arousal are associated with poor performance. Yerkes and Dodson characterized such a learning curve as an inverted U (see p. 370 for a review of the Yerkes–Dodson principle). You don't need to be a psychologist to recognize that when people are extremely frightened or aroused, performance suffers. This is certainly true in sports; dozens of research studies have shown that being activated and aroused increases athletic performance—but only up to a point.

Sport psychology
The systematic application of psychological principles to sports.

The inverted U relationship between arousal and performance is not always consistent, especially in sports situations that involve intensive cognitive activity, such as quarterbacking in football or catching in baseball. Researchers know that for every increase in a person's arousal, a corresponding increase (or decrease) in performance is not necessarily evident. Sometimes a small increase in arousal can push some people "over the top" to acute anxiety and poor performance. Young children are less affected by pressure; older children, in contrast, think about options ("Our second baseman doesn't catch very well, so it makes more sense to throw to first") and are more affected by pressure (French, Spurgeon, & Nevett, 1995). How then is arousal distinct from anxiety?

■ *Professional tennis player Venus Williams visualizes her shots before making them.*

Anxiety and Sports Performance

Think back to Rick Ankiel, the terrific left-hander described at the chapter's opening. Ankiel tried to put a bad season and a few bad games behind him by focusing on each day, one day at a time—for Ankiel, it's all about attitude. Ankiel recognizes that it is never good to overtrain or overanalyze, either physiologically or psychologically—such overtraining can lead to intense anxiety (Kreider, Fry, & O'Toole, 1998). When an athlete is tense and apprehensive and such feelings are associated with arousal, the athlete is experiencing anxiety. Some people, including some athletes, feel this way most of the time—trait personality theorists would say that such people have a strong, or dominant, anxiety trait. A whole range of tests has been developed to measure anxiety in athletes and to discern whether anxiety is related to specific events or is a trait of a given athlete.

Unlike weekend or casual sports enthusiasts, competitive athletes often reach their peak of anxiety significantly before an athletic event begins, and their levels of anxiety may diminish immediately before the event. As they step up to the plate or onto the court or field, professional athletes often become cool, collected, and in control. Three hours earlier, they may have felt overwhelmed by their anxiety, but when they have to perform, it is gone.

If the relationship between anxiety and performance were predictable, psychologists wouldn't be quite so interested in precompetitive anxiety. But like so many other psychological phenomena, anxiety is affected by many aspects of an athlete's performance and life (Ferraro, 2001). If an athlete's arousal exceeds the level needed for effective performance, anxiety can take over. Similarly, an underaroused athlete may also become anxious and stay anxious through an event. So arousal and anxiety are closely related and hard to separate. But separation can be achieved through good intervention strategies.

Intervention Strategies

When an athlete's level of anxiety is sufficiently high that arousal leads to lower performance, interventions can be put in place to help relieve the anxiety. Stress management approaches described in Chapter 14 have proved to be effective. There are a broad array of such anxiety-reducing techniques (Humara, 2001).

One widely used technique is *progressive relaxation,* in which athletes are taught to relax slowly and progressively. Relaxation of individual muscles, focusing on progressively deeper muscle groups, is the goal. Typically, the trainer or

student voices

Nixon Daniel Dodd
Northeast Mississippi Community College

Psychology is big in sports, and if you can understand how to use it to your advantage then you can really excel. Many times coaches tend to ride players and put them in certain scenarios to test their mental toughness. I have found this evident through my basketball career.

psychologist instructs the person to relax in steps: to relax the limbs, to feel heaviness or warmth in the arms and legs, to feel a reduced heart rate, and to sense coolness on the forehead.

Hypnosis, which can facilitate uncritical acceptance of suggestions, has been widely used to help athletes achieve deep relaxation, as well as to help them focus their energy and attention. Closely associated with hypnosis is *meditation,* a technique that can help an athlete relax and gain focus. Meditation involves focusing one's attention on a single thought, idea, sound, or object. (Hypnosis and meditation can help athletes relax and focus, of course, but they will never make a bad athlete into a good one.) Closely associated are the physical and mental techniques involved in yoga. Practitioners of yoga claim that it is capable of causing profound physiological and psychological changes. When Phil Jackson was head coach of the Chicago Bulls, he made his team attend mandatory yoga sessions!

Using *mental imagery* to promote relaxation has been shown to be worthwhile in many sports activities (Overby, 1990), and combining mental imagery with other relaxation strategies has proved especially effective (Murphy & Jowdy, 1992). As described earlier, athletes also use mental imagery to "psyche themselves up" or practice a sports activity mentally (Murphy, 1990).

Cognitive interventions that focus on changing thought patterns about a sport, an event, one's abilities, or one's strategies have been especially helpful (Boutcher, 1992). Cognitive strategies often focus on education about aspects of the sport in combination with training in relaxation, such as thinking calm thoughts just before a pole vault. Cognitive interventions may teach athletes to think positively, block out distractions, and focus on the one part of their body that is crucial in their sport (Eubank, Collins, & Smith, 2000).

How Do You Motivate Athletes?

In the end, what factors ultimately energize, direct, and sustain athletic performance? To understand what motivates a person to perform well at a sport, you have to ask a number of key questions:

1. *What is the goal?* Is the person striving to compete in the sport, or is the goal to master the sport for personal satisfaction? Is the goal to play squash in national competition, or to have a friendly game, feel competent, and have fun?
2. *Is the motivational climate set by friends, parents, and coaches geared toward competition or mastery?* When the motivational climate is geared toward mastery, the athlete's energy level is usually much lower, and so is anxiety.
3. *How does the athlete perceive his or her abilities—as high, low, or not relevant?* When people feel confident about their abilities, they do better in sports. As we saw in Chapter 12, when people have a positive sense of self-efficacy, they do much better at a task.
4. *Is the athlete's behavior adaptive or maladaptive?* Does the athlete set up realistic goals, practice schedules, and training routines, or does he or she engage in self-defeating behaviors?

To a great extent, this four-step analysis of motivation looks at what energizes and sustains an athlete (Roberts, 1992). But human beings are not always rational or goal-directed and do not always behave consistently. People's behavior is affected by their health, love life, family situation, and financial status—to name just a few variables.

Enhancing motivation is part of the picture. In various sports, high achievers also do several other things:

- Set realistic goals.
- Announce their goals to others.
- Chart their progress toward goals.
- Vary workout regimes.
- Take days off so as to not experience burnout and boredom.
- Try to find workout partners.
- Try to keep their sports activity fun.

You can see that the complexity of these situations makes the psychology of sport resistant to easy explanations, but also more intriguing. Researchers have much to learn, especially about the energizing of behavior through activation and arousal.

Be an *Active* learner

REVIEW

- What is the role of motivation in sport psychology? pp. 644–645
- Why does high arousal lead to lower performance in sports? p. 645

THINK CRITICALLY

- Do you think that behavior management in sports raises any ethical problems for sport psychologists? Explain.
- When psychologists say that much of top sports performance is about attitude, what do they mean? Why?

APPLY PSYCHOLOGY

- When athletes say they are going to focus on each day, one day at a time—how do they go about doing this? Can you devise five specific things that they might do to stay on task?

Sport Psychology: The Future

As sport psychologists gain a stronger sense of the variables that affect athletic performance, more comprehensive theories will emerge to help explain success in various sports. Specialization will increase, as psychologists begin to focus on areas such as motivation, personality variables, coaching, specific behavioral training, relaxation, imagery, and aggression. And since people all over the world play sports, there will be significant growth in cross-cultural research in sport psychology. Sport behavior cannot be examined in isolation—coaches, environments, and cultural expectations in each country shape athletic performance in different ways. For example, Chinese athletes see the causes of their failures as more internal and controllable than do German athletes (Si, Rethorst, & Willimczik, 1995). Researchers need to understand how factors such as locus of control (discussed in Chapter 12) operate in sports, how the family environment affects an athlete's development, and how such factors vary cross-culturally (Hellstedt, 1995). Such research may begin to reveal why Russian athletes are such wonderful ice dancers, why Canadians play hockey so well, and why rugby and soccer are not the national sports of the United States.

Summary and Review

Industrial/Organizational Psychology

What is I/O psychology?

- *Industrial/organizational (I/O) psychology* is the study of how individual behavior is affected by the work environment, coworkers, and organizational practices. It can be divided into four broad areas: human resources psychology, motivation of job performance, job satisfaction, and leadership. pp. 608–609

What are the goals of job analyses, selection procedures, and training efforts in today's workplace?

- The functional job analysis and the position analysis questionnaire are instruments that have been developed by I/O psychologists for *job analyses*. All such analyses have a similar goal: to ensure that jobs are well defined and doable. Two important tasks of an I/O psychologist are to balance the scope and complexity of jobs and to help employers create jobs that will be motivating. pp. 609–610
- Selection procedures have the basic goal of evaluating job candidates in order to help an employer determine which ones to hire. Application forms, interviews, samples of work, and ability tests are some of the instruments

used in selection. Training is the process by which organizations systematically teach employees skills to improve their job performance. pp. 610–611

What is performance appraisal?

■ *Performance appraisal* is the process whereby a supervisor periodically evaluates the job-relevant strengths and weaknesses of subordinates. The problem with performance appraisals is that they are often done inaccurately by people with few evaluative skills and with few diagnostic aids. Multiple performance criteria must enter into an appraisal. pp. 613–614

How have psychologists tried to help managers motivate workers?

■ I/O psychologists help employers find ways to motivate employees to be more productive. *Goal-setting theory* asserts that setting specific, clear, attainable goals for a given task leads to better performance. pp. 614–615

■ *Expectancy theories* assert that a worker's effort and desire to work are determined by expectations about the outcome of the work. Vroom suggested that work motivation is determined by expectancy (the belief that hard or extra work will lead to good or improved performance); instrumentality (the belief that good performance will be rewarded); and valence (the value put on rewards that are offered). Lawler and Porter contended that performance is determined by ability, effort, and role perceptions—the ways people believe they should be doing their jobs. pp. 616–617

How have psychologists analyzed worker performance and job satisfaction?

■ The view that what people bring to a work situation should be balanced by what they receive there compared with others constitutes *equity theory*. Thus, workers' input (what they do) should be balanced by the rewards they receive. If input is not balanced with compensation, people will adjust their work input accordingly. p. 617

■ I/O psychologists have identified three basic approaches to motivation management: paternalistic, behavioral, and participatory. pp. 618–619

■ There are many sources of job satisfaction, including the work itself, the perceived rewards of the work, the quality of supervision, the support of coworkers, and the work setting. In the end, the overall level of satisfaction depends on the extent to which people feel their expectations for satisfaction are matched by their actual satisfaction. p. 620

What makes a good leader?

■ A leader is a person who influences other people's behavior toward the attainment of agreed-upon goals. Business leaders can be employee-oriented or task-oriented; the situation or the organization is a key determinant of which type of leader will be more effective. *Transformational leaders*—charismatic leaders who inspire and provide intellectual stimulation—create opportunities to transform an organization, often by empowering employees. pp. 621–623

KEY TERMS

applied psychology, p. 608; industrial/organizational (I/O) psychology, p. 608; job analyses, p. 609; performance appraisal, p. 613; meta-analysis, p. 615; goal-setting theory, p. 616; expectancy theories, p. 616; equity theory, p. 617; transformational leader, p. 623

Human Factors

Describe the field of human factors.

■ *Human factors* is the study of the relationship of human beings to machines and to workplaces and other environments. It involves the study of the fit between human anatomy or physiology, the demands of a particular task or piece of equipment, and the environment in which the task occurs. Human factors research can help design work environments that are both efficient and safe. Warnings, labels, and compliance techniques are all helpful in improving safety. pp. 625–626

What is behavior-based safety?

■ In behavior-based safety, effective safety management refers to a wide range of programs that focus on changing the behavior of workers *and* companies to prevent occupational injuries and illnesses. pp. 626–627

KEY TERM

human factors, p. 625

Psychology and the Law

What key roles do psychologists play in the legal system?

■ As researchers, psychologists help determine why individuals behave in ways that are unacceptable to society. Psychologists also act as policy or program evaluators, helping governments and other institutions determine whether various policies, agencies, or programs actually work. Psychologists work as advocates for individuals and society, helping shape social policy in areas such as minority, remedial, and gifted education. Finally, psychologists often serve as expert witnesses, bringing their knowledge to court as consultants. pp. 629–630

What is the new role of DNA in relationship to the law?

■ DNA analysis can be likened to fingerprint analysis—if enough of the identifying features are the same between the DNA of a suspect and some evidence found on an injured person or at the scene of a crime, the DNA profile is determined to be a match. p.629

Environmental Psychology

What do environmental psychologists study?

■ *Environmental psychology* is the study of how physical settings and aspects of the environment affect human behavior, as well as how people can change their environment to meet their psychological needs. *Crowding* is the perception that one's personal space is too limited. Social density is the number of people in a given space; spatial density is the amount of space allocated to a fixed number of people. *Personal space,* as defined by Hall, is the immediate area around an individual that the person considers *private.* Four spatial zones, or distances, that can be observed in social interactions in the United States are intimate, personal, social, and public. pp. 635–636

KEY TERMS
environmental psychology, p. 631; crowding, p. 633; personal space, p. 635; privacy, p. 636; territorial behavior, p. 637

Community Psychology

What are the goals of community psychology, and what do community psychologists mean by *empowerment*?

■ *Community psychology* seeks to reach out to society by providing psychological services to people who might not otherwise receive them. The general aims of community psychologists are to empower people and to use three levels of prevention strategies to help ward off, treat, or stop psychological problems in the community. pp. 638–639

■ *Empowerment* refers to helping people enhance existing skills and develop new skills, knowledge, and motivation so that they can gain control over their own lives. p. 639

Has the Internet left people with fewer social contacts?

■ The Internet is not all bad or good—people learn computer skills while accessing the Internet, and it helps with schoolwork; but use of the Internet is associated with small but reliable increases in loneliness, declines in social involvement, and increases in depression. p. 638

KEY TERMS
community psychology, p. 639; empowerment, p. 639

Educational Psychology

What are the goals of and the problems studied by educational psychologists?

■ *Educational psychology* is the systematic application of psychological principles to learning and teaching. To help create effective teaching, educational psychologists seek to understand students' backgrounds, interests, abilities, and past learning; how they interact with other students and other teachers; and how they solve problems. Key areas of study for educational psychologists are developmental changes (how and when individuals grow physically, socially, and intellectually), environmental conditions that affect the learning process, and classroom learning styles. Time allocation and classroom management are key skills of effective teachers. pp. 641–644

KEY TERM
educational psychology, p. 641

Sport Psychology

What is sport psychology?

■ *Sport psychology* is the systematic application of psychological principles to sports. Sport psychologists recognize that athletic performance is affected by the athlete, the team leader or coach, and the environment. Sport psychologists study factors such as arousal and performance and have found that Yerkes and Dodson's inverted U-shape relationship between arousal and performance is not always consistent in sports; that is, as arousal increases, performance may or may not increase or decrease smoothly. When anxiety is too high and arousal lowers performance, interventions can help lower arousal and relieve anxiety. pp. 644–645

Identify four levels of analysis used to understand what motivates a person to perform a sport well.

■ The four levels of analysis ask the following questions: What is the goal? Is the motivational climate set by friends, parents, and coaches geared toward competition or mastery? How does the athlete perceive his or her abilities? And, is the athlete's achievement behavior adaptive or maladaptive—does the athlete set realistic goals? pp. 645–646

Identify some intervention strategies that can help athletes improve their performance.

■ One widely used technique to improve sports performance is progressive relaxation, in which athletes are taught to relax individual muscles slowly and progressively. Another technique, hypnosis, has been widely used to help athletes achieve deep relaxation, as well as to help them focus their energy and attention. Closely associated with hypnosis is meditation. Last, mental imagery to promote relaxation and focus is worthwhile in many sports activities. pp. 645–646

KEY TERM
sport psychology, p. 644

Appendix
Statistical Methods

appendix outline

Scientific progress is in many ways directly linked to researchers' ability to measure and quantify observations; that is, to collect data. **Statistics** is the branch of mathematics that deals with classifying and analyzing data. To rule out coincidence and discover the true causes of behavior, psychologists control the variables in experiments (as discussed in detail in Chapter 1) and then use statistics to describe, summarize, and present results. These methods and procedures for analyzing data are the topics of this appendix.

Descriptive Statistics

Researchers use statistics to evaluate and organize data. Specifically, they use **descriptive statistics**—procedures used to summarize, condense, and describe sets of data. Descriptive statistics make it possible for researchers to interpret the results of their experiments. For example, your professors use descriptive statistics to interpret exam results. A statistical description of a 100-point midterm exam may show that 10% of a class scored more than 60 points, 70% scored between 40 and 60 points, and 20% scored fewer than 40 points. On the basis of this statistical description, the professor might conclude that the test was exceptionally difficult and might arrange the grading so that anyone who earned 61 points or more would receive an A. But before inferences can be drawn or grades assigned, the data from a research study or the scores on a test must be organized in a meaningful way.

Organizing Data: Frequency Distributions

When psychologists do research, they often produce large amounts of data that must be assessed. Suppose a social psychologist asked parents to monitor the number of hours their children watch television. The parents might report between 0 and 20 hours of TV watching a week. Here is a list of the actual number of hours of TV watching by 100 children in a particular week:

11	18	5	9	6	20
9	7	15	3	6	11
6	1	10	3	4	4
8	8	9	10	13	12
16	1	15	9	4	3
10	5	6	12	8	2
14	12	6	9	8	12
10	7	3	14	13	7
10	17	11	13	16	7
15	11	9	11	16	8
14	7	10	10	12	8
11	1	12	7	6	0
19	18	9	8	2	5
9	14	7	10	9	2
10	4	13	8	5	4
9	8	5	17	15	17
5	13	10	11		

The first step in making these numbers meaningful is to arrange them in a chart or array, organized from the highest to the lowest, showing the number of times each number occurs; this type of organization is known as a **frequency distribution.** As the frequency distribution in Table A.1 on the following page shows, 10 children were reported to have watched 9 hours of television in a week—a greater number of children than for any other number of hours of TV watching.

Researchers often construct graphs from the data in frequency distributions. Such graphs, called **frequency polygons,** show the range of possible results or scores (for example, numbers of hours of TV watching) on the horizontal axis, or *abscissa,* and the frequency of each score (for example, the number of children who watched

Statistics
The branch of mathematics that deals with collecting, classifying, and analyzing data.

Descriptive statistics
A general set of procedures used to summarize, condense, and describe sets of data.

Frequency distribution
A chart or array of scores, usually arranged from the highest to the lowest, showing the number of instances for each score.

Frequency polygon
Graph of a frequency distribution that shows the number of instances of obtained scores, usually with the data points connected by straight lines.

TABLE A.1

A Frequency Distribution of the Number of Hours of Television Watched in a Week by 100 Children

Number of Hours of Television Watched	Individuals Watching Each Number of Hours	Total Number of Individuals Watching
0	I	1
1	III	3
2	III	3
3	IIII	4
4	IIIII	5
5	IIIIII	6
6	IIIIIII	7
7	IIIIIIII	8
8	IIIIIIIII	9
9	IIIIIIIIII	10
10	IIIIIIIII	9
11	IIIIIII	7
12	IIIIII	6
13	IIIII	5
14	IIII	4
15	IIII	4
16	III	3
17	III	3
18	II	2
19	I	1
20	I	1
		100

Note: Few individuals score very high or very low—most score in the middle range.

FIGURE A.1

A Frequency Polygon Showing Hours of Television Watched in a Week by 100 Children

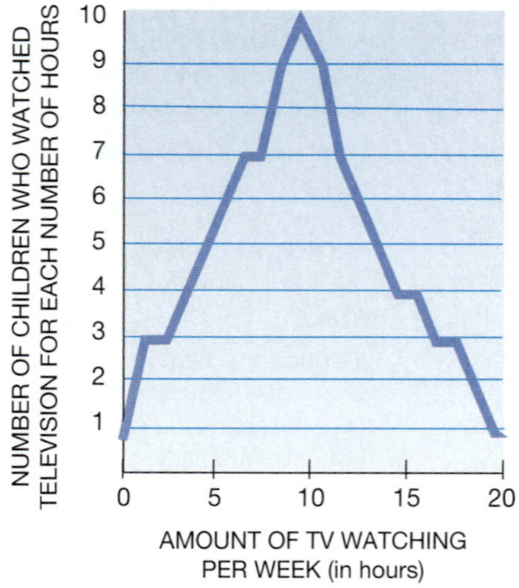

television for each number of hours) on the vertical axis, or *ordinate.* Figure A.1 is a frequency polygon of the data from the frequency distribution in Table A.1. Straight lines connect the data points.

Measures of Central Tendency

A descriptive statistic that tells which result or score best represents an entire set of scores is a **measure of central tendency.** It is used to summarize and condense data; all the numbers in the distribution are condensed into one number. Also, because almost every group has members who score higher or lower than the rest of the group, researchers often use a measure of central tendency to describe the group *as a whole.*

People often use the word *average* in a casual way to describe a variety of traits or tendencies. A woman asks a clerk to help her find a sweater for her "average-sized" husband. The owner of a new sedan boasts that his car "averages" 40 miles to a gallon of gasoline. A doctor tells her patient that his serum cholesterol level is "average" because it falls halfway between low and high measurements. In each of these cases, the person is using *average* to depict a type of norm, and others understand what the person means, even though not all of these examples are technically "averages." Consider this statement: men are taller than women are. Because you know that some women are taller than some men are, you assume that the statement means: *on the average,* men are taller than women are. In other words, comparing the heights of all the men and all the women in the world would show that, *on the average,* men are taller.

Let's look more closely at three measures of central tendency: mean (arithmetic average), mode, and median.

■ **MEAN.** How could a researcher investigate the truth of the statement that men are taller than women are? One way would be to measure the heights of thousands of men and women, taking a careful sample from each country, ethnic group, and age group. The researcher could then calculate the average heights of the men and the women in the sample and plot the results on a graph. Table A.2 lists height data from a small sample of men and women. For each group, the measured heights were added together and divided by the number of people in the group. The resulting number is the **mean,** or *arithmetic average,* the measure of central tendency calculated by dividing the sum of scores (the total of all heights) by the total number of scores (in this case, number of heights). The mean is the most frequently used measure of central tendency.

TABLE A.2

Calculation for Mean Height for 20 Men and 20 Women

Men	Height (in inches)	Women	Height (in inches)
Davis	62	Leona	58
Baird	62	Golde	59
Jason	64	Marcy	61
Ross	67	Mickey	64
David	68	Sharon	64
Cary	68	Rozzy	66
Mark	69	Bonnie	66
Evan	70	Dianne	66
Michael	70	Cheryl	66
Davey	70	Carol	67
Steven	70	Iris	67
Morry	70	Nancy	67
Alan	70	Theresa	67
Bernie	70	Sylvia	67
Lester	70	Jay	68
Al	70	Linda	68
Arnold	73	Elizabeth	71
Andrew	79	Jesse	75
Corey	79	Gabrielle	76
Stephen	79	Sarah	77
Total height	**1400**	**Total height**	**1340**
Mean: $\frac{\sum S}{N} = \frac{1400}{20} = 70$ inches		Mean: $\frac{\sum S}{N} = \frac{1340}{20} = 67$ inches	

Note: $\sum S$ means add up the scores; N means number of scores.

Measure of central tendency
A descriptive statistic that tells which result or score best represents an entire set of scores.

Mean
The measure of central tendency that is calculated by dividing the sum of the scores by the total number of scores; also known as the arithmetic average.

TABLE A.3

The Mode for Men's and Women's Heights

The mode is 70 inches, the most frequently observed height.

Height (in inches)	Number of Individuals of Each Height
58	I
59	I
60	
61	I
62	II
63	
64	III
65	
66	IIII
67	IIIIII
68	IIII
69	I
70	IIIIIIII **Mode**
71	I
72	
73	I
74	
75	I
76	I
77	I
78	
79	III

TABLE A.4

The Median of Men's and Women's Heights

The median is the height in the middle of the range of heights measured—half of the heights are above the median and half are below.

Height (in inches)
58
59
61
62
62
64
64
64
66
66
66
66
67
67
67
67
67
67
68
68 ← **Median**
68
68
69
70
70
70
70
70
70
70
70
70
71
73
75
76
77
79
79
79

■ **MODE.** Another statistic used to describe the central tendency of a set of data is the mode. The **mode** is the most frequently observed data point. Table A.3 shows the frequencies of all the different heights from Table A.2. It shows, for example, that only one person is 58 inches tall, three are 79 inches tall, and more people are 70 inches tall than are any other single height. The mode of the heights of this group is therefore 70 inches.

■ **MEDIAN.** The **median** is the 50% point: half the observations (or scores) fall above it, and the other half fall below it. Table A.4 presents all the heights of men and women given in Table A.2, arranged from lowest to highest. It shows that half the heights fall above 68 and half fall below 68. The median of the data set, therefore, is 68. You have probably read news reports that refer to medians, for example: "According to the U.S. Census Bureau, the median family income in the United States rose to $36,000 this year." What this means is that half of U.S. families earned more than this amount and half earned less.

Table A.5 presents a set of data from an experiment on memory. The scores are the numbers of items correctly recalled. There are three groups of participants: a control group, which received no special treatment; one experimental group, which received task-motivating instructions (such as "Think hard," "Focus your attention"); and a second experimental group, whose members were hypnotized and told under hypnosis that they would have good recall. The results of the study show that the task-motivated group did slightly worse than the control group, with a mean of 10.3 words recalled, compared with the control group's mean of 10.6. But the

TABLE A.5

Calculations of Mean and Median Memory Scores for Three Groups (with 10 People in Each Group)

Person	Scores of Control Group	Scores of Task-Motivated Group	Scores of Hypnosis Group
1	10	11	16
2	12	13	14
3	14	14	16
4	10	12	12
5	11	12	10
6	9	8	9
7	5	10	15
8	12	5	12
9	16	10	18
10	7	8	32
Total	106	103	154
Mean	10.6	10.3	15.4
Median	10.5	10.5	14.5

Control Group (scores are reordered lowest to highest)

$$\text{Mean} = \frac{5 + 7 + 9 + 10 + 10 + 11 + 12 + 12 + 14 + 16}{10} = \frac{106}{10} = 10.6$$

Median = 5 7 9 10 [10 11] 12 12 14 16

↓

10.5

The point at which half the scores fall above and half the scores fall below is 10.5; that is, 10.5 is the median.

Task-Motivated Group (scores are reordered lowest to highest)

$$\text{Mean} = \frac{5 + 8 + 8 + 10 + 10 + 11 + 12 + 12 + 13 + 14}{10} = \frac{103}{10} = 10.3$$

Median = 5 8 8 10 [10 11] 12 12 13 14

↓

10.5

The point at which half the scores fall above and half the scores fall below is 10.5; that is, 10.5 is the median.

Hypnosis Group (scores are reordered lowest to highest)

$$\text{Mean} = \frac{9 + 10 + 12 + 12 + 14 + 15 + 16 + 16 + 18 + 32}{10} = \frac{154}{10} = 15.4$$

Median = 9 10 12 12 [14 15] 16 16 18 32

↓

14.5

The point at which half the scores fall above and half the scores fall below is 14.5; that is, 14.5 is the median.

hypnosis group did better, recalling 15.4 words on average, compared with the control group's average recall of 10.6 words—a difference of 4.8 words. Hypnosis therefore *seemed* to have a positive effect on memory, but we need to do some additional analysis before coming to that conclusion.

The medians for the control group and the task-motivated group were equal—10.5 words. The difference between the median of the control group and the median of the hypnosis group was 4 words. Hypnosis still seems to have had a positive

Mode
The measure of central tendency that is the most frequently observed data point.

Median
The measure of central tendency that is the data point with 50% of all the observations (scores) above it and 50% below it.

effect, but the difference between the medians (4 words) is smaller than the difference between the means (4.8 words)—because the median discounts very high and very low scores. For example, if you get a test score of 0 after obtaining five other scores whose average is about 70, the sixth score will drop that *average* substantially; averaging in a sixth score of 60 would not have as large an impact. But with a median, a single extreme score (such as 0 or 120) counts as much as all the other scores. For a sample as small as this one, where a single score can have a big impact, the median is often a better measure of central tendency.

The mean, mode, and median are descriptive statistics that measure central tendency. Each tells researchers something about the average (or typical) person, score, or data item. Sometimes the mean, the mode, and the median are the same; but more often, there is enough variability in a sample (one very tall or very short person in a group of height measurements, for example) that each central tendency measure yields a slightly different result and will be used for different purposes. If you had to guess the height of a woman you had never met, a good guess would be the mean, or average, height for women. If you were a buyer for a clothing store and had to pick one dress size or one shoe size to order, you might be more likely to pick the modal size—the size that occurs more often than any other.

Measures of Variability

A measure of central tendency is a single number that describes a hypothetical "average." In real life, however, people do not always reflect the central tendency because they vary so much. Consequently, knowledge of an average data item or score is more useful when accompanied by knowledge of how all the items or scores in the group are distributed relative to one another. If you know that the mean of a group of numbers is 150, you still do not know how widely dispersed are the numbers that were averaged to calculate that mean. In other words, the mean on the final examination in your psychology class may be 150, and you may have scored 170 (above the mean), but you still do not know how much you can celebrate. Are there few other scores above your score? If there are many others, how much better than you did they do?

Statistics that describe the extent to which scores in a distribution differ from one another are called *measures of variability*. **Variability** is the extent to which scores differ from one another, especially the extent to which they differ from the mean. If all scores obtained are the same, there is no variability; this, however, is unlikely to occur. It is more usual that in any group of people being tested or measured in some way, personal and situational characteristics will cause some to score high and some to score low. If researchers know the extent of the variability, they can estimate the extent to which participants differ from the mean, or "average," person. Two important and useful measures of variability are range and standard deviation.

■ **RANGE.** The **range** shows the spread of scores in a distribution; it is calculated by subtracting the lowest score from the highest score. If the lowest score on a test is 20 points and the highest is 85, the range is 65 points. The range is unaffected by the mean. In this example, whether the mean is 45, 65, or 74 points, the range remains 65; that is, there is a 65-point spread from the lowest score to the highest.

The range is a relatively crude measure of the extent to which participants vary within a group. In a group of 100 students, for example, the mean score might be 80, and nearly all the students might have scored within 10 points of that mean. But if the lowest score is 20 and the highest is 85, the range is 65. More precise measures of the spread of scores within a group are available, however. They indicate how scores are distributed as well as the extent of their spread.

Variability
The extent to which scores differ from one another, especially the extent to which they differ from the mean.

Range
A measure of variability that describes the spread between the highest and the lowest scores in a distribution.

■ **STANDARD DEVIATION.** Consider a reaction-time study that measures how fast people press a button when a light flashes. The following list gives the number of milliseconds (thousandths of a second) it took each of 30 randomly chosen 10th graders to press the button when the light flashed; clearly, the reaction times vary.

450	490	500	610	520	470
480	492	585	462	600	490
740	700	595	500	493	495
498	455	510	470	480	540
710	722	575	490	495	570

If you knew only that the mean reaction time is 540 milliseconds, you might conclude that 540 is the best estimate of how long it takes a 10th-grader to respond to the light. But of course, not everyone reacted in 540 milliseconds; some took more time and some took less. Psychologists say that the data are variable, or that variability exists.

To find out how much variability exists among data, and to quantify it in a meaningful manner, researchers use a statistic called the standard deviation. A **standard deviation** is a descriptive statistic that measures the variability of data from the mean of the sample—that is, the extent to which each score differs from the mean. The calculations for a standard deviation are shown in Table A.6. Here is the general procedure: First, subtract the mean from each score, and then square that difference. Next, add up the squared differences and divide by the number of scores minus 1. (For a small sample, to get a better estimate of the sample's standard deviation, researchers typically divide by 1 less than the number of scores.) Last, take the square root of the answer. You have now calculated a standard deviation.

TABLE A.6

Computation of the Standard Deviation for a Small Distribution of Scores

Score	Score − Mean	(Score − Mean)^2
10	10 − 6 = 4	16
10	10 − 6 = 4	16
10	10 − 6 = 4	16
5	5 − 6 = −1	1
4	4 − 6 = −2	4
4	4 − 6 = −2	4
4	4 − 6 = −2	4
1	1 − 6 = −5	25
48		86

Standard deviation = $\sqrt{\frac{\Sigma(X - \overline{X})^2}{N - 1}}$, where Σ means "sum up," X is a score, $\overline{X}$ is the mean of the scores, and N is the number of scores.

Sum of scores = 48.

$\overline{X}$ = sum of scores ÷ 8 = 6.

Sum of squared differences from mean = 86.

Average of square differences from mean (dividing by the number of scores − 1) = 86 ÷ 7 = 12.3.

Square root of average square difference from the mean = 3.5.

Standard deviation = 3.5.

Standard deviation
A descriptive statistic that measures the variability of data from the mean of the sample.

TABLE A.7

Reaction Times, Mean Reaction Times, and Standard Deviations for Responses to a Light

Group 1 shows a wider range of scores and thus great variability. Group 2, in contrast, shows a narrow range of scores and little variability.

Times for Group 1 (in milliseconds)	Times for Group 2 (in milliseconds)
380	530
400	535
410	540
420	545
470	550
480	560
500	565
720	570
840	575
935	580
Mean = 555	Mean = 555
Standard deviation = 197	Standard deviation = 17

A standard deviation gives information about all the members of a group, not just an average member. Knowing the standard deviation—that is, the variability associated with a mean—enables a researcher to make more accurate predictions. Table A.7 shows the reaction times for two groups of participants responding to a light. The mean is the same for both groups, but group 1 shows a large degree of variability, whereas group 2 shows little variability. The standard deviation (the estimate of variability) for group 1 participants is substantially higher than that for group 2 participants because the scores differ from the mean much more in the first group than in the second. Since the standard deviation for participants in group 2 is small, a researcher can more confidently predict that any one individual in that group will respond to the light in about 555 milliseconds (the mean response time). However, the researcher cannot make the same prediction for individuals in group 1 with the same confidence, since that group's standard deviation is high.

The Normal Distribution

The **normal distribution** is the approximate distribution of scores expected when a sample is drawn from a large population; it is drawn as a frequency polygon that takes the form of a bell-shaped curve, known as a *normal curve*. Normal distributions usually have few scores at each extreme and progressively more scores toward the middle. Height, for example, is approximately normally distributed: more people are of average height than are very tall or very short (see Figure A.2). Weights, shoe sizes, IQs, and scores on psychology exams also tend to be normally distributed.

FIGURE A.2

A Normal Curve for Height

A normal curve for height shows that many more people are of average height than are at the extremes.

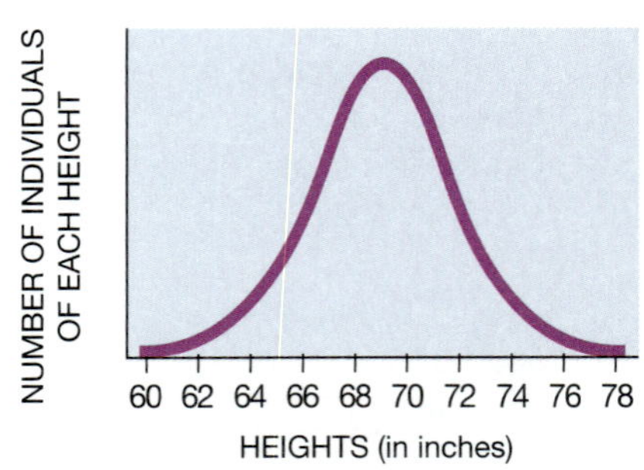

FIGURE A.3

Percentages of Population for a Normal Curve

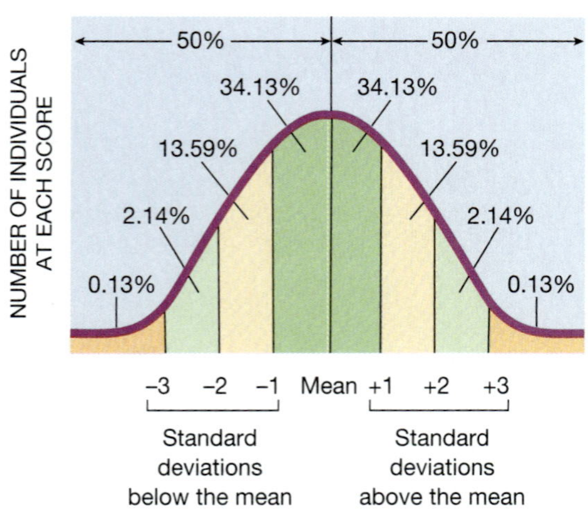

On a normal curve, most individuals score within 6 standard deviations, 3 on either side of the mean.

■ **CHARACTERISTICS OF A NORMAL CURVE.** A normal curve has certain characteristics. The mean, mode, and median are the same; the distribution of scores around that central point is symmetrical. Also, most individuals have a score that occurs within 6 standard deviations—3 above the mean and 3 below it (see Figure A.3).

To understand this phenomenon, look at Figure A.4, which shows a normal curve for test scores. The mean is 50, and the standard deviation is 10 points. Note how each increment of 10 points above or below the mean accounts for fewer and fewer individuals: scores between 50 and 60 account for 34.13% of those tested; scores between 60 and 70 account for 13.59%; scores above 70 account for under 2.5%. The sum of these percentages (34.13 + 13.59 + 2.14 + 0.13) represents 50% of the scores.

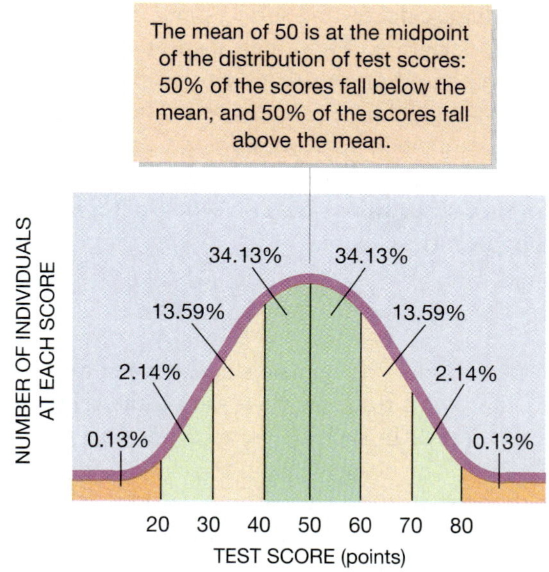

FIGURE A.4

A Normal Curve with a Standard Deviation of 10 Points

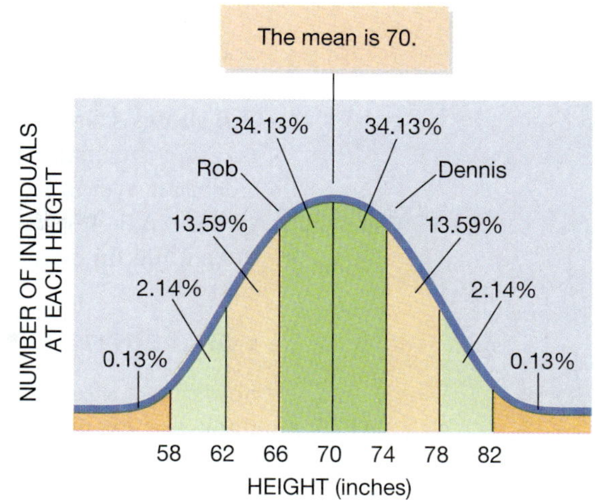

FIGURE A.5

A Normal Curve with a Mean of 70 and a Standard Deviation of 4 Inches

On this normal curve, Dennis's height of 74 inches is 1 standard deviation above the mean height of 70 inches. Rob's height is 66 inches, which is 1 standard deviation below the mean.

When you know the mean and standard deviation of a set of data, you can estimate where an individual in the sample population stands relative to others. Figure A.5 shows a normal curve representing heights of a sample of men. Dennis is 74 inches tall. His height is 1 standard deviation above the mean, which means that he is taller than 84% of the population (0.13 + 2.14 + 13.59 + 34.13 + 34.13 = 84.12%). Rob, who is 66 inches tall, is taller than only 16% of the population. His height is 1 standard deviation below the mean.

Normal distribution
The approximate distribution of scores expected when a sample is taken from a large population, drawn as a frequency polygon that often takes the form of a bell-shaped curve, known as a normal curve.

■ **NORMAL CURVES: A PRACTICAL EXAMPLE.** Your grade on an examination is often determined by how other members of the class do. This is what instructors mean when they say that grades are calculated using a "sliding scale" or a "curve." If the average student in a class answers only 50% of the questions correctly, a student who answers 70% correctly has done a good job in comparison to the rest of the class. But if the average student scores 85%, then someone who scores only 70% has not done so well.

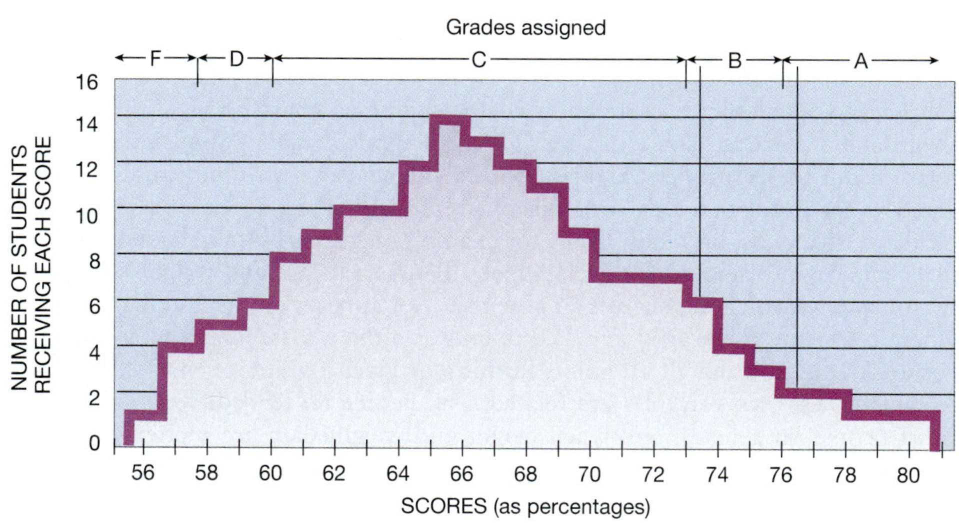

FIGURE A.6

Grading on a Sliding Scale

To calculate grades on a sliding scale, instructors often draw a graph like this one, showing the number of individuals who received each score. They then figure out the cutoff points for assigning letter grades (A, B, C, D, and F).

Before they assign grades on a sliding scale, testing services and instructors generally calculate a mean and standard deviation. They then inspect the scores and "slide the scale" to an appropriate level based on those descriptive statistics. Figure A.6 shows scores achieved and grades assigned on a calculus test. The average score is 65%; the instructor decides to give students who score 65% a C, which she considers an average grade. Those students who do better get an A or a B, depending on how much better than the mean they score; those who do worse get a D or an F, depending on how much below the mean they score.

Correlation

Sometimes a researcher wants to know about the relationship between two sets of data. For example, an instructor might want to know how strong the relationship was between the scores on test 1 and test 2. In such cases, a correlation will show the strength of this relationship.

A correlation exists when an increase in the value of one variable is regularly accompanied by an increase or a decrease in the value of a second variable. The degree and direction of relationship between two variables is expressed by a numerical value called the **correlation coefficient.** Correlation coefficients range from –1, through 0, to +1. Any correlation coefficient greater or less than 0, regardless of its sign, indicates that the variables are somehow related. When two variables are perfectly correlated, they are said to have a correlation coefficient of 1. Correlation coefficients close to 1 indicate stronger relationships than those close to 0.

When knowing the value of one variable allows a researcher to predict *precisely* the value of the second, the variables are perfectly correlated; a perfect correlation is, of course, a rare occurrence in psychological research. But strong correlations allow predictions (although not perfect ones). This characteristic of correlation allows researchers to predict the occurrence of one variable if they know the other and know that the correlation between the two is strong. For example, there is a correlation between scores on the SAT and grade-point average during the first year in college. The correlation is not perfect (1.00), but it is high enough to allow colleges and universities to use the SAT as a way to select students; they choose students with high SAT scores because those students are more likely to do well in college.

Most variables are not perfectly correlated, and SAT scores and first-year college grade point averages are no exception. Some students receive high scores on the SAT but do poorly in college because they party too much, have trouble adapting to the college routine, become distracted by extracurricular activities, and so forth. Other students get lower SAT scores and still succeed in college because they are disciplined students who work hard. The correlation between SAT scores and college grades is high but not perfect. Only when the correlation is perfect is the prediction perfect. College admission committees know that they need to look at more than SAT scores in making admission decisions. However, the correlation between scholastic ability tests and college grades allows for their use in predicting behavior.

Before calculating a correlation coefficient, researchers often plot, or graph, their data in a scatter plot. A *scatter plot* is a diagram of data points that shows the relationship between two variables. An individual's score on one variable is measured on the horizontal axis, or x axis; the score on the second variable is measured on the vertical axis, or y axis. Thus, for example, a scatter plot might show 10 people's heights and weights; for each person, there is a height and weight pair. If one person is 6 feet tall and weighs 170 pounds, a dot appears on the graph at the point where 6 feet (on the x axis) and 170 pounds (on the y axis) intersect, as shown in Figure A.7(a). Plotting all 10 points in this way gives a graphic sense of the extent to which these two variables are related. Tall people do tend to weigh more than short people, in general, and when height and weight data are plotted, the graph usually shows that as height increases, so does weight (at least most of the time), indicating a correlation.

Correlation coefficient
A number that expresses the degree and direction of a relationship between two variables, ranging from –1 (a perfect negative correlation) to +1 (a perfect positive correlation).

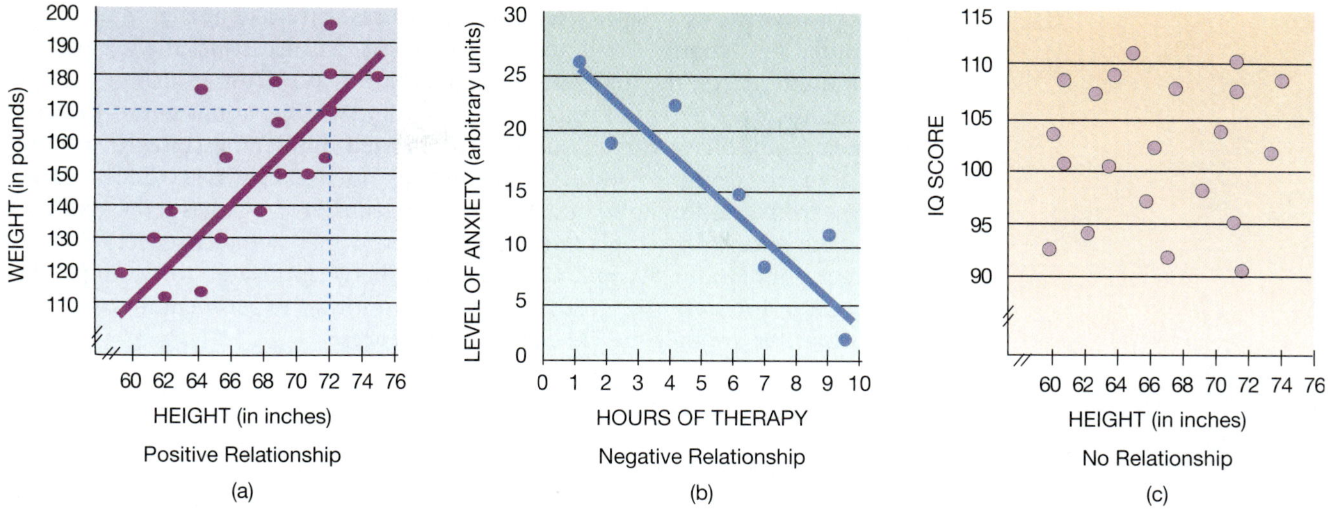

FIGURE A.7

Three Types of Correlations: A Summary

(a) In a positive correlation, an increase in one variable is associated with an increase in the other variable. (b) In a negative correlation, an increase in one variable is associated with a decrease in the other variable. (c) No correlation exists when changes in one variable are not associated in any systematic way with changes in the other variable.

When one variable shows an increase in value and a second also shows an increase, the two variables are said to be positively related, and the relationship is known as a *positive correlation.* Height and weight show a positive correlation: generally, as height increases, so does weight—although knowing a person's height does not allow someone to predict his or her weight precisely. The scatter plot in Figure A.7(a) shows a positive direction overall—upward and to the right. These two variables have a correlation coefficient of about 0.65.

On the other hand, if one variable decreases as the other increases, the variables are said to be negatively correlated, and the relationship is known as a *negative correlation.* For example, the relationship between the number of hours of therapy and the extent of anxiety shows a negative correlation—that is, as the number of hours of therapy increases, anxiety decreases; see Figure A.7(b). The scatter plot shows a corresponding movement downward and to the right. These two variables have a negative correlation of about –0.6 or –0.7.

A correlation coefficient of +0.7 is no stronger than one of –0.7. That is, the plus or minus sign changes the *direction,* but not the strength, of a relationship. The strength is shown by the number: the larger the number, the greater the strength of the correlation. A correlation coefficient of –0.8 is stronger than one of +0.7; a correlation coefficient of +0.6 is stronger than one of –0.5.

Some variables show absolutely no correlation; absence of correlation is expressed by a correlation coefficient of 0. Figure A.7(c) plots data for IQ and height. There is no pattern in the scatter plot and thus no correlation between IQ and height; the two variables have a correlation coefficient of 0.

As we saw in Chapter 2, a correlation in no way implies a cause-and-effect relationship. A correlation between two variables simply indicates that if there is an increase in one variable, there will probably be an increase (or decrease) in the other variable. It is only through experimental studies that researchers can make cause-and-effect statements. Many of the studies cited and described in this text are correlational, but far more are experimental. Whenever possible, researchers wish to draw causal inferences. To do so, they use a different type of statistic—inferential statistics.

Inferential Statistics

Researchers perform experiments so that they can draw causal inferences. Researchers want to be able to tell whether a difference between a control group and an experimental group is due to manipulation of the independent variable, to extraneous variables, or to one or two deviant scores. It turns out that many of the manipulations and controls that researchers devise are necessary if they wish to make sound inferences, the topic we consider next.

Researchers use inferential statistics in making decisions about data—to determine if their studies have turned out as hypothesized. **Inferential statistics** are procedures used to draw reasonable conclusions (generalizations) about larger populations from small samples of data. There are usually two issues to be explored: First, does the mean of a sample (a small group of people) actually reflect the mean of the larger population? Second, are differences between means (for example, between the mean for a control group and the mean for an experimental group) real and important, or are they merely chance occurrences?

Significant Differences

Psychologists hope to find a **significant difference**—a difference that is statistically unlikely to have occurred because of chance alone and thus is more likely to be due to the experimental conditions. To claim that a difference is significant, a researcher must show that a performance difference between two or more groups is not a result of chance variations and can be repeated experimentally. Generally, psychologists assume that a difference is statistically significant if the likelihood of its occurring by chance is less than 5%—that is, if it would occur by chance fewer than 5 out of 100 times. But many researchers assume a difference is significant only if the likelihood of its occurring by chance is less than 1%.

Inferential statistics
Procedures used to draw reasonable conclusions (generalizations) about larger populations from small samples of data.

Significant difference
An experimentally obtained statistical difference that is unlikely to have occurred because of chance alone.

It is difficult to decide if a difference is significant by looking at the scores. Look back at Table A.5, which shows calculations for a set of memory scores. The results showed that the task-motivated group recalled slightly fewer words, on average, than the control group did. The hypnosis group recalled 4.8 more words, on average, than the control group. Since the hypnosis group did better than the control group, can the researcher conclude that hypnosis is a beneficial memory aid? Did the hypnosis group do significantly better than the control group? Is a 4.8-word difference significant? It is easy to see that if the difference in recall between the two groups had been 10 words, and if the variability within each group had been very small, the difference would be considered significant. Similarly, a 1- or 2-word difference would not be considered significant if the variability within each group was large. In the present case, a 4.8-word difference is not significant; the scores were highly variable, and the study included only a small sample of people. When scores are variable (widely dispersed), both statistical analysts and researchers are unlikely to view a small difference between two groups as significant or important. (See Figure A.8 for an illustration of this point.)

Even if they obtain statistically significant differences, researchers often repeat an experiment and hope that the results will be the same. Repeating an experiment to verify a result is called *replicating* the experiment. If the results of a replicated experiment are the same as the original experiment, a researcher can generally say that the observed difference between the two groups is statistically significant, showing a reliable pattern of difference between control and experimental groups.

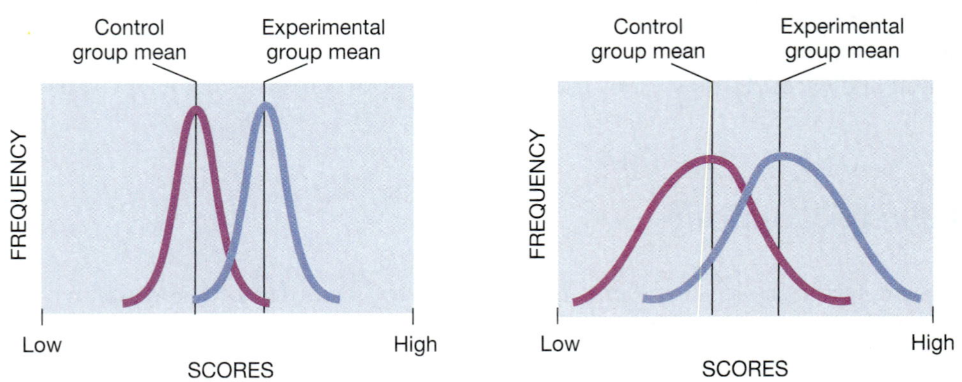

FIGURE A.8

The Possible Outcomes of Experiments Whose Means Are Identical

In the first graph, the observed scores all cluster around the means—there is little variability. The difference between the means in the first graph is therefore likely to be significant. The means in the second graph (although identical to the ones in the first graph) are unlikely to be deemed significantly different—the scores are too widely distributed. Here, there is too much variability; the means may be affected by extreme scores. Thus, a scientist is less likely to accept these means as different from one another.

Summary and Review

Statistics

■ *Statistics* is the branch of mathematics that deals with classifying and analyzing data. Researchers use statistics to help them understand and interpret the data they gather. p. 651

Descriptive Statistics

How do descriptive statistics help researchers organize data?

■ Researchers use *descriptive statistics* to summarize, condense, and describe sets of data. A *frequency distribution* is a way of organizing data to show the number of times each item occurs; the graphic version of a frequency distribution is a *frequency polygon.* pp. 651–652

How are measures of central tendency used?

■ *Measures of central tendency* are descriptive statistics that indicate which single score best represents an entire set of scores. The most frequently used measure of central tendency is the *mean,* or arithmetic average of all the scores. Also used are the *mode,* the most frequently observed score, and the median, the data point that has 50% of the scores above it and 50% below it. pp. 652–656

What is a measure of variability?

■ A measure of *variability* is any statistic that describes the extent to which scores in a distribution differ from one another. One such measure, the *range,* shows the spread of scores in a distribution. Another measure of variability, the *standard deviation,* shows the extent to which individual scores in a distribution vary from the mean. pp. 656–658

What are the key characteristics of a normal distribution?

■ The mean, mode, and median of a *normal distribution,* or normal curve, are generally assumed to be the same, and the scores are distributed symmetrically around that central point. pp. 658–659

What is correlation, and how is it used?

■ A *correlation coefficient* is a number that expresses the degree of relationship between two variables. Correlation coefficients range from +1 to –1. When two variables are perfectly correlated, they are said to have a correlation coefficient of 1. A plus or minus sign in front of the correlation coefficient indicates the direction, not the strength, of a correlation relationship. The strength is shown by the number: The closer the number is to 1, the greater the strength of the correlation. pp. 660–661

Compare correlational and experimental studies with regard to cause and effect.

■ Correlational studies make no statements about cause and effect. They simply show that if there is an increase in one variable, there will probably be an increase or decrease in another variable. This property allows researchers to make predictions based on strong correlations, but only experimental studies allow researchers to make cause-and-effect statements. p. 661

KEY TERMS

statistics, p. 651; descriptive statistics, p. 651; frequency distribution, p. 651; frequency polygon, p. 651; measure of central tendency, p. 652; mean, p. 653; mode, p. 654; median, p. 654; variability, p. 656; range, p. 656; standard deviation, p. 657; normal distribution, p. 658; correlation coefficient, p. 660

Inferential Statistics

What is the role of inferential statistics?

■ Researchers use *inferential statistics* to determine whether two or more groups differ from one another and whether the difference is a result of chance. A *significant difference* is one that most likely did not occur by chance and that can be repeated experimentally with similar groups of people. Repeating an experiment to verify a result is called replicating the experiment. p. 662

KEY TERMS

inferential statistics, p. 662; significant difference, p. 662

References

Abelman, R. (1999). Preaching to the choir: Profiling TV advisory ratings users. *Journal of Broadcasting and Electronic Media, 43,* 529–550.

Abbott, L. F., Varela, J. A., Sen, K., & Nelson, S. B. (1997). Synaptic depression and cortical gain control. *Science, 275,* 220–224.

Abramowitz, J. S. (1998). Does cognitive–behavioral therapy cure obsessive–compulsive disorder? A meta-analytic evaluation of clinical significance. *Behavior Therapy,* 29, 339–355.

Abrams, M., & Ellis, A. (1994). Stress management and counselling: Rational emotive behaviour therapy in the treatment of stress. *British Journal of Guidance and Counselling, 22,* 39–50.

Abramson, L. Y., Metalsky, G. I., & Alloy, L. B. (1989). Hopelessness depression: A theory-based subtype of depression. *Psychological Review, 96,* 358–372.

Acker, J. R. (1993). A different agenda: The Supreme Court, empirical research evidence, and capital punishment decisions, 1986–1989. *Law & Society Review, 27,* 65–88.

Acocella, J. (1999). *Creating hysteria: Women and multiple personality disorder.* San Francisco: Jossey-Bass.

Ader, R. (1997). The role of conditioning in pharmacotherapy. In A. Harrington (Ed.), *The placebo effect: An interdisciplinary exploration* (pp. 138–165). Cambridge, MA: Harvard University Press.

Ader, R. (2000). True or false: The placebo effect as seen in drug studies is definitive proof that the mind can bring about clinically relevant changes in the body: The placebo effect: If it's all in your head, does that mean you only think you feel better? *Advances in Mind-Body Medicine, 16,* 7–11.

Ader, R. (2001). Psychoneuroimmunology. *Current Directions in Psychological Science, 10,* 94–98.

Ader, R., & Cohen, N. (1975). Behaviorally conditioned immunosuppression. *Psychosomatic Medicine, 37,* 333–340.

Ader, R., & Cohen, N. (1993). Psychoneuroimmunology: Conditioning and stress. *Annual Review of Psychology, 44,* 53–85.

Adler, A. (1927). *Understanding human nature.* New York: Greenberg.

Adler, A. (1964). *Problems of neurosis.* New York: Harper Torchbooks. (Original work published 1929)

Adolphs, R., & Damasio, A. R. (2000). Neurobiology of emotion at a systems level. In J. C. Borod (Ed.), *The neuropsychology of emotion: Series in affective science* (pp. 194–213). New York: Oxford University Press.

Adorno, T., Frenkel-Brunswick, E., Levinson, D., & Sanford, R. (1950). *The authoritarian personality.* New York: Harper and Row.

Agne, K. J. (1999). Caring: The way of the master teacher. In R. P. Lipka & T. M. Brinthaupt (Eds.), *The role of self in teacher development. SUNY Series, Studying the Self* (pp. 165–188). Albany: State University of New York Press.

Aiello, J. R., & Kolb, K. J. (1995). Electronic performance monitoring and social context: Impact on productivity and stress. *Journal of Applied Psychology, 80,* 339–353.

Aiken, L. R. (1988). *Psychological testing and assessment* (6th ed.). Boston: Allyn and Bacon.

Ajdukovic, M., & Ajdukovic, D. (1998). Impact of displacement on the psychological well-being of refugee children. *International Review of Psychiatry, 10,* 186–195.

Alkon, D. L. (1989, July). Memory storage and neural systems. *Scientific American,* 42–50.

Allen, G. L. (2000). Men and women, maps and minds: Cognitive bases of sex-related differences in reading and interpreting maps. In S. O. Nuallain (Ed.), *Spatial cognition: Foundations and applications: Selected papers from Mind III, Annual Conference of the Cognitive Science Society of Ireland, 1998: Advances in Consciousness Research* (pp. 3–18). Amsterdam: John Benjamins Publishing Company.

Allen, G. L., Kirasic, K. C., & Spilich, G. J. (1997). Children's political knowledge and memory for political news stories. *Child Study Journal, 27,* 163–177.

Allen, G. L., & Willenborg, L. J. (1998). The need for controlled information processing in the visual acquisition of route knowledge. *Journal of Environmental Psychology, 18,* 419–427.

Allen, W. (1983). *Without feathers.* New York: Ballantine.

Allington, R. L., & McGill-Franzen, A. (1995). Individualized planning. In M. C. Wang, M. C. Reynolds, & H. J. Walberg (Eds.), *Handbook of special and remedial education: Research and practice* (2nd ed, pp. 5–35). Oxford, UK: Elsevier Science Publishing.

Allison, T., Ginter, H., McCarthy, G., Nobre, A. C., Puce, A., Luby, M., & Spencer, D. D. (1994). Face recognition in human extrastriate cortex. *Journal of Neurophysiology, 71,* 821–825.

Allport, G. W. (1979). *The nature of prejudice.* Cambridge, MA: Addison-Wesley. (Original work published in 1954)

Almagor, M., Tellegen, A., & Waller, N. G. (1995). The big seven model: A cross-cultural replication and further exploration of the basic dimensions of natural language trait descriptors. *Journal of Personality and Social Psychology, 69,* 300–307.

Altman, I. (1975). *The environment and social behavior.* Monterey, CA: Brooks/Cole.

Amaral, D. G. (2000). The functional organization of perception and movement. In E. R. Kandel., J. H. Schwartz, & T. M. Jessell (Eds.), *Principles of neural science.* (337–348). New York: McGraw-Hill.

Ambady, N., & Rosenthal, R. (1993). Half a minute: Predicting teacher evaluations from thin slices of nonverbal behavior and physical attractiveness. *Journal of Personality and Social Psychology, 64,* 431–441.

American Association of University Women Educational Foundation. (1998). *Gender gaps: Where schools still fail our children [Special report].* Washington, DC: Author.

American Heart Association. (2000). *2001 heart and stroke statistical update.* Dallas, TX: Author.

American Psychiatric Association. (2000). *Diagnostic and statistical manual of mental disorders* (4th ed., text revision). Washington, DC: Author.

American Psychiatric Association. (2001). *The practice of electroconvulsive therapy: Recommendations for treatment, training, and privileging: A task force report of the American Psychiatric Association* (2nd ed.). Washington, DC: Author

American Psychological Association. (1992). Ethical principles of psychologists and code of conduct. *American Psychologist, 47,* 1597–1611.

American Psychological Association. (1993). Guidelines for providers of psychological services to ethnic, linguistic, and culturally diverse populations. *American Psychologist, 48,* 45–48.

American Psychological Association. (2001). Gender of full-time faculty in U.S. graduate departments of psychology: 1985–2000. *Survey of Graduate Departments of Psychology, 1984–1985 through 1999–2000, American Psychological Association and Council of Graduate Departments of Psychology.* Data Compiled by APA Research Office.

Anderson, A. K., & Phelps, E. A. (2000). Expression without recognition: Contributions of the human amygdala in emotional communication. *Psychological Science, 11,* 106–111.

Anderson, C. A. (1989). Temperature and aggression: Ubiquitous effects of heat on occurrence of human violence. *Psychological Bulletin, 106,* 74–96.

Anderson, C. A., & Anderson, K. B. (1998). Temperature and aggression: Paradox, controversy, and a (fairly) clear picture. In R. G. Geen & E. Donnerstein (Eds.), *Human aggression: Theories, research, and implications for social policy* (pp. 247–298). San Diego, CA: Academic Press.

Anderson, C. A., Anderson, K. B., & Deuser, W. E. (1996). Examining an affective aggression framework: Weapon and temperature effects on aggressive thoughts, affect, and attitudes. *Personality and Social Psychology Bulletin, 22,* 366–376.

Anderson, C. A., & DeNeve, K. M. (1992). Temperature, aggression, and the negative affect escape model. *Psychological Bulletin, 111,* 347–351.

Anderson, C. A. & Bushman, B. J. (2002). The effects of media violence on society. *Science Magazine, 295,* 2377–2379.

Anderson, C. A., & Dill, K. E. (2000). Video games and aggressive thoughts, feelings, and behavior in the laboratory and in life. *Journal of Personality and Social Psychology, 67,* 772–790.

Anderson, J. R., & Schooler, L. J. (2000). The adaptive nature of memory. In E. Tulving & F. I. Craik (Eds.), *The Oxford handbook of memory* (pp. 557–570). New York: Oxford University Press.

Anderson, J. S., Lampl, I., Gillespie, D. C., & Ferster, D. (2000). The contribution of noise to contrast invariance of orientation tuning in cat visual cortex. *Science, 290,* 1968–1972.

Anderson, N. D., Iidaka, T., Cabeza, R., Kapur, S., McIntosh, A. R., & Craik, F. I. M. (2000). The effects of divided attention on encoding- and retrieval-related brain activity: A PET study of younger and older adults. *Journal of Cognitive Neuroscience 12,* 775–792.

Andreasen, N. C. (1997). Neuroimaging techniques in the investigation of schizophrenia. *Journal of Clinical Psychiatry Monograph Series, 15*(3), 16–19.

Andresen, J. (2000). Meditation meets behavioural medicine: The story of experimental research on meditation. *Journal of Consciousness Studies, 7*(11–12), 17–73.

Ang, R. P., & Chang, W. C. (1999). Impact of domain-specific locus of control on need for achievement and motivation. *The Journal of Social Psychology, 139,* 527–529.

Anstey, K. J., Luszcz, M. A., Giles, L. C., & Andrews, G. R. (2001). Demographic, health, cognitive, and sensory variables as predictors of mortality in very old adults. *Psychology and Aging 16,* 3–11.

Appelbaum, P. S., Robbins, P. C., & Monahan, J. (2000). Violence and delusions: Data from the MacArthur Violence Risk Assessment Study. *American Journal of Psychiatry, 157,* 566–572.

Applewhite, S. L. (1995). Curanderismo: Demystifying the health beliefs and practices of elderly Mexican Americans. *Health and Social Work, 20,* 247–253.

Apter, T. (1995). *Secret paths: Women in the new midlife.* New York: Norton.

Arceneaux, M. C., & Murdock, J. Y. (1997). Peer prompting reduces disruptive vocalizations of a student with developmental disabilities in a general eighth-grade classroom. *Focus on Autism and Other Developmental Disabilities, 12,* 182–186.

Archibald, A. B. (2000). Moody girls: Is puberty to blame? *Dissertation Abstracts International: Section B: The Sciences & Engineering, 60*(12-B), 6394.

Ariely, D. (2001). Seeing sets: Representation by statistical properties. *Psychological Science, 12,* 157–162.

Arkowitz, H. (1997). Integrative theories of therapy. In P. L. Wachtel & S. B. Messer, (Eds.), *Theories of psychotherapy: Origins and evolution* (pp. 227–288). Washington, DC: American Psychological Association.

Armel, K. C., & Ramachandran, V. S. (1999). Acquired synesthesia in retinitis pigmentosa. *Neurocase: Case Studies in Neuropsychology, Neuropsychiatry, and Behavioural Neurology, 5,* 293–296.

Arnedt, J. T., Wilde, G. J. S., Munt, P. W., & MacLean, A. W. (2001). How do prolonged wakefulness and alcohol compare in the decrements they produce on a simulated driving task? *Accident Analysis and Prevention, 33,* 337–344.

Arnett, J. J. (1999). Adolescent storm and stress, reconsidered. *American Psychologist, 54,* 317–326.

Aronson, J., Quinn, D. M., & Spencer, S. J. (1998). Stereotype threat and the academic underperformance of minorities and women. In J. K. Swim & C. Stangor (Eds.), *Prejudice: The target's perspective* (pp. 83–103). San Diego, CA: Academic Press.

Arseneault, L., Moffitt, T. E., Caspi, A., Taylor, P. J., & Silva, P. A. (2000). Mental disorders and violence in a total birth cohort: Results from the Dunedin Study. *Archives of General Psychiatry, 57,* 979–986.

Arvey, R. D., & Campion, J. E. (1982). The employment interview: A summary and review of recent research. *Personnel Psychology, 35,* 281–322.

Asch, S. E. (1955, November). Opinions and social pressure. *Scientific American,* 31–35.

Aserinsky, E., & Kleitman, N. (1953). Regularly occurring periods of eye motility, and concomitant phenomena, during sleep. *Science, 118,* 273–274.

Aspinwall, L. G., & Taylor S. E. (1997). A stitch in time: Self-regulation and proactive coping. *Psychological Bulletin, 121,* 417–436.

Astin, J. A. (1998). Why patients use alternative medicine: Results of a national study. *Journal of the American Medical Association, 279,* 1548–1553.

Atwood, N. C. (2001). Gender bias in families and its clinical implications for women. *Social Work, 46,* 23–36.

Aube, J., Fichman, L., Saltaris, C., & Koestner, R. (2000). Gender differences in adolescent depressive symptomatology: Towards an integrated social–developmental model. *Journal of Social & Clinical Psychology, 19,* 297–313.

Audia, G., Kristof-Brown, K. G., & Locke, E. A. (1996). Relationship of goals and micro-level work processes to performance on a multipath manual task. *Journal of Applied Psychology, 81,* 483–497.

Avis, N. E. (1999). Women's health at midlife. In S. L. Willis & J. D. Reid (Eds.), *Life in the middle: Psychological and social development in middle age.* (pp. 105–146). San Diego, CA: Academic Press.

Ayllon, T., & Azrin, N. H. (1965). The measurement and reinforcement behavior of psychotics. *Journal of the Experimental Analysis of Behavior, 8,* 357–383.

Ayllon, T., & Haughton, E. (1964). Modification of symptomatic verbal behavior of mental patients. *Behavior Research and Therapy, 2,* 87–97.

Bachar, E. (1998). Psychotherapy—an active agent: Assessing the effectiveness of psychotherapy and its curative factors. *Israel Journal of Psychiatry and Related Sciences, 35,* 128–135.

Baddeley, A. (2000). Short-term and working memory. In E. Tulving & F. I. M. Craik (Eds.), *The Oxford handbook of memory* (pp. 77–92). New York: Oxford University Press.

Baddeley, A. D., & Hitch, G. (1974). Working memory. In G. Bower (Ed.), *Recent advances in learning and motivating* (Vol. 8). New York: Academic Press.

Baddeley, A. D., & Hitch, G. J. (1994). Developments in the concept of working memory. *Neuropsychology, 6,* 485–493.

Bahrick, H. P. (1984). Semantic memory content in permastore: Fifty years of memory for Spanish learned in school. *Journal of Experimental Psychology: General, 113,* 1–29.

Bahrick, H. P. (2000). Long-term maintenance of knowledge. In E. Tulving and F. I. Craik (Eds.), *The Oxford handbook of memory* (pp. 347–362). New York: Oxford University Press.

Bailey, W. C., & Peterson, R. D. (1999). Capital punishment, homicide, and deterrence: An assessment of the evidence and extension to female homicide. In M. D. Smith, M. Zahn, (Eds.), *Homicide: A sourcebook of social research* (pp. 257–276). Thousand Oaks, CA: Sage.

Baird, J. C., Wagner, M., & Fuld, K. (1990). A simple but powerful theory of the moon illusion. *Journal of Experimental Psychology: Human Perception and Performance, 16,* 675–677.

Balay, J., & Shevrin, H. (1988). The subliminal psychodynamic activation method. *American Psychologist, 3,* 161–174.

Ball, K., & Lee, C. (2000). Relationship between psychological stress, coping and disordered eating: A review. *Psychology & Health, 14,* 1007–1035.

Balota, D. A., Dolan, P. O., & Duchek, J. M. (2000). Memory changes in healthy older adults. In E. Tulving & F. I. M. Craik (Eds.), *The Oxford handbook of memory* (pp. 395–409). New York: Oxford University Press.

Banaji, M. R., & Greenwald, A. G. (1995). Implicit gender stereotyping in judgments of fame. *Journal of Social and Personality Psychology, 68,* 181–198.

Band, E. B., & Weisz, J. R. (1988). How to feel better when it feels bad: Children's perspectives on coping with everyday stress. *Developmental Psychology, 24,* 247–253.

Bandura, A. (1969). *Principles of behavior modification.* New York: Holt, Rinehart & Winston.

Bandura, A. (1977a). Self-efficacy: Toward a unifying theory of behavioral change. *Psychological Review, 84,* 191–215.

Bandura, A. (1977b). *Social learning theory.* Englewood Cliffs, NJ: Prentice-Hall.

Bandura, A. (1999). Social cognitive theory of personality. In L. A. Pervin & O. P. John (Eds.), *Handbook of personality: Theory and research* (pp. 154–196). New York: Guilford Press.

Bandura, A. (2000). Exercise of human agency through collective efficacy. *Current Directions in Psychological Science, 9,* 75–78.

Bandura, A. (2001). Social cognitive theory: An agentic perspective. *Annual Review of Psychology, 52,* 1–26.

Bandura, A., Blanchard, E. B., & Ritter, B. (1969). Relative efficacy of desensitization and modeling approaches for inducing behavioral, affective, and attitudinal changes. *Journal of Personality and Social Psychology, 13,* 173–199.

Bandura, A., & Menlove, F. L. (1968). Factors determining vicarious extinction of avoidance through symbolic modeling. *Journal of Personality and Social Psychology, 8,* 99–108.

Bandura, A., Ross, D., & Ross, S. A. (1963). Imitation of film-mediated aggressive models. *Journal of Abnormal and Social Psychology, 66,* 3–11.

Baptista, M. A. S., Siegel, S., MacQueen, G., & Young, L. T. (1998). Pre-drug cues modulate morphine tolerance, striatal c-Fos, and AP-1 DNA binding. *Neuroreport: An International Journal for the Rapid Communication of Research in Neuroscience, 9,* 3387–3390.

Bar-Or, O., Foreyt, J., Bouchard, C., Brownell, K. D., Dietz, W. H., Ravussin, E., Salbe, A. D., Schwenger, S., St. Jeor, S., & Torun, B. (1998). Physical activity, genetic, and nutritional considerations in childhood weight management. *Medicine and Science in Sports and Exercise, 30,* 2–10.

Barash, D. P. (2001, April 20). Deflating the myth of monogamy. *Chronicle of Higher Education, 47*(32), Section 2, B16–17.

Barber, J. (1991). The locksmith model: Accessing hypnotic responsiveness. In S. J. Lynn & J. W. Rhue (Eds.), *Theories of hypnosis: Current models and perspectives* (pp. 241–274). New York: Guilford Press.

Barbuto, J. E., Jr. (1997). Taking the charisma out of transformational leadership. *Journal of Social Behavior and Personality, 12,* 689–697.

Bard, P. (1934). Emotion: The neuro-humoral basis of emotional reactions. In C. Murchison (Ed.), *Handbook of general experimental psychology.* Worcester, MA: Clark University Press.

Barlow, S. H., Burlingame, G. M., & Nebeker, R. S. (2000). Meta-analysis of medical self-help groups. *International Journal of Group Psychotheraprу, 50,* 53–69.

Barnes, M. L., & Sternberg, R. J. (1997). A hierarchical model of love and its prediction of satisfaction in close relationships. In R. J. Sternberg, & M. Hojjat (Eds), *Satisfaction in close relationships* (pp. 79–101). New York: Guilford Press.

Barnier, A. J., & McConkey, K. M. (1998). Posthypnotic responding away from the hypnotic setting. *Psychological Science, 9,* 256–262.

Baron, R. A. (1993). Interviewers' moods and evaluations of job applicants: The role of applicant qualifications. *Journal of Applied Social Psychology, 23,* 253–271.

Barondes, S. H. (1998). *Mood genes: Hunting for origins of mania and depression.* New York: Freeman.

Barrett, G. V., & Depinet, R. L. (1991). A reconsideration of testing for competence rather than for intelligence. *American Psychologist, 46,* 1012–1024.

Barron, M., & Kimmel, M. (2000). Sexual violence in three pornographic media: Toward a sociological explanation. *The Journal of Sex Research, 37,* 161–168.

Bartoshuk, L. M. (2000). Comparing sensory experiences across individuals: Recent psychophysical advances illuminate genetic variation in taste perception. *Chemical Senses, 25,* 447–460.

Bartoshuk, L. M., Duffy, V. B., Reed, D., & Williams, A. (1996). Supertasting, earaches, and head injury: Genetics and pathology alter our taste worlds. *Neuroscience and Biobehavioral Reviews, 20,* 79–87.

Bass, B. M. (1985). *Leadership and performance beyond expectations.* New York: Free Press.

Bass, B. M. (1990). From transactional to transformational leadership: Learning to share the vision. *Organizational Dynamics, 18,* 19–31.

Bass, B. M. (1997). Does the transactional–transformational leadership paradigm transcend organizational and national boundaries? *American Psychologist, 52,* 130–139.

Bass, B. M. (1998). *Transformational leadership: Industrial, military, and educational impact.* Mahwah, NJ: Erlbaum.

Bass, B. M. (2001). Cognitive, social, and emotional intelligence of transformational leaders. In R. E. Riggio & S. E. Murphy (Eds). *Multiple intelligences and leadership. LEA's organization and management series* (pp. 105–118). Mahwah, NJ: Erlbaum.

Bates, E., & Roe, K. (1999). Language development in children with unilateral brain injury. In C. A. Nelson & M. Luciana (Eds.), *Handbook of developmental cognitive neuroscience* (pp. 269–280). Cambridge, MA: The MIT Press.

Bateson, G., Jackson, D. D., Haley, J., & Weakland, J. (1956). Toward a theory of schizophrenia. *Behavioral Science, 1,* 251–264.

Batson, C. D. (1990). How social an animal? *American Psychologist, 45,* 336–346.

Batson, C. D., Batson, J. G., Slingsby, J. K., Harrell, K. L., Peekna, H. M., & Todd, R. M. (1991). Empathic joy and the empathy–altruism hypothesis. *Journal of Personality and Social Psychology, 61,* 413–426.

Baudry, M. (1998). Synaptic plasticity and learning and memory: 15 years of progress. *Neurobiology of Learning & Memory, 70,* 113–118.

Baum, A., & Posluszny, D. M. (1999). Health psychology: Mapping biobehavioral contributions to health and illness. *Annual Review of Psychology, 50,* 137–164.

Baumeister, R. F., & Bratslavsky, E. (1999). Passion, intimacy, and time: Passionate love as a function of change in intimacy. *Personality & Social Psychology Review, 3,* 49–67.

Baumeister, R. F., & Tice, D. M. (2001). *The social dimension of sex.* Boston: Allyn and Bacon.

Bavelier, D., Tomann, A., Hutton, C., Mitchell, T., Corina, D., Liu, G., & Neville, H. (2000). Visual attention to the periphery is enhanced in congenitally deaf individuals. *The Journal of Neuroscience, 20* (RC93), 1–6.

Bayley, N. (1969). Consistency and variability in the growth of intelligence from birth to eighteen years. *Journal of Genetic Psychology, 25,* 165–196.

Baynes, K., Eliassen, J. C., Lutsep, H. L., & Gazzaniga, M. S. (1998). Modular organization of cognitive systems masked by interhemispheric integration. *Science, 280,* 902–905.

Bayster, P. G., & Ford, C. M. (2000). The impact of functional issue classification on managerial decision processes: A study in the telecommunications industry. *Journal of Managerial Issues, 12,* 468–483.

Beaulieu, C., & Colonnier, M. (1989). Number and size of neurons and synapses in the motor cortex of cats raised in different environmental complexities. *Journal of Comparative Neurology, 289,* 178–181.

Beck, A. T. (1963). Thinking and depression: 1. Idiosyncratic content in cognitive distortions. *Archives of General Psychiatry, 9,* 324– 333.

Beck, A. T. (1967). *Depression: Clinical, experimental, and theoretical aspects.* New York: Hober.

Beck, A. T. (1976). *Cognitive therapy and emotional disorders.* New York: International Universities Press.

Beck, A. T. (1991). Cognitive therapy. *American Psychologist, 46,* 368–375.

Beck, A. T., & Weishaar, M. (1989). Cognitive therapy. In A. Freeman, K. M. Simon, L. E. Beutler, & H. Arkowitz (Eds.), *Comprehensive handbook of cognitive therapy.* New York: Plenum.

Beck, J. (1966). Effects of orientation and of shape similarity on perceptual grouping. *Perception and Psychophysics, 1,* 311–312.

Beck, J. G., Stanley, M. A., Baldwin, L. E., Deagle, E. A., III, & Averill, P. M. (1994). Comparison of cognitive therapy and relaxation training for panic disorder. *Journal of Consulting and Clinical Psychology, 62,* 818–826.

Beech, H., Buia, C., Ganguly, M., Fulton, G., Hasnain, G., Horn, R., Johnson, K., Kan, W., Kim, S., Macintyre, D., Park, A., Ramakrishnan, M., Shannon. E., Thompson, D., Sindayen, N., & Tedjasukmana, J. (2000, November 13). The lure of Ecstacy. *Time International, 156*(19), 40+.

Beers, T. M. (2000). Flexible schedules and shift work: Replacing the "9-to-5" workday? *Monthly Labor Review, 123,* 33–40.

Begg, I. M., Needham, D. R., & Bookbinder, M. (1993). Do backward messages unconsciously affect listeners? No. *Canadian Journal of Experimental Psychology, 47,* 1–14.

Behr, H. (2000). Families and group analysis. In D. Brown & L. Zinkin, (Eds.). *The psyche and the social world: Developments in group-analytic theory.* International Library of Group Analysis (pp. 163–179). London, UK: Jessica Kingsley Publishers, Ltd.

Belansky, E. S., & Boggiano, A. K. (1994). Predicting helping behaviors: The role of gender and instrumental/expressive self-schemata. *Sex Roles, 30,* 647–662.

Belgrave, F. Z., Brome, D. R., & Hampton, C. (2000). The contribution of africentric values and racial identity to the prediction of drug knowledge, attitudes, and use among African American youth. *Journal of Black Psychology, 26,* 386–401.

Bell, B. E., & Loftus, E. F. (1989). Trivial persuasion in the courtroom: The power of (a few) minor details. *Journal of Personality and Social Psychology, 56,* 669–679.

Bem, D. J. (1972). Self-perception theory. In L. Berkowitz (Ed.), *Advances in experimental social psychology.* New York: Academic Press.

Bem, D. J. (1996). Exotic becomes erotic: A developmental theory of sexual orientation. *Psychological Review, 103,* 320–335.

Bem, D. J. (2000). Exotic becomes erotic: Interpreting the biological corelates of sexual orientation. *Archives of Sexual Behavior, 29,* 531–548.

Bem, S. L. (1985). Androgyny and gender schema theory: A conceptual and empirical integration. In T. B. Sonderegger (Ed.), *Nebraska symposium on motivation* (pp 179–226). Lincoln, NE: University of Nebraska Press.

Bem, S. L. (1993). *The lenses of gender.* New Haven, CT: Yale University Press.

Bender, S. T. (1999). Attachment style and friendship characteristics in college students. *Dissertation Abstracts International: Section B: The Sciences & Engineering, 60* (5-B), 2407.

Benet-Martinez, V., & Waller, N. G. (1997). Further evidence for the cross-cultural generality of the Big Seven Factor model: Indigenous and imported Spanish personality constructs. *Journal of Personality, 65,* 567–598.

Bennett, J. B., & Lehman, W. E. K. (1999). The relationship between problem co-workers and quality of work practices: A case study of exposure to sexual harassment, substance abuse, violence, and job stress. *Work and Stress, 13,* 299–311.

Berg, T. R. (1991). The importance of equity perception and job satisfaction in predicting employee intent to stay at television stations. *Group and Organizational Studies, 16,* 268–284.

Berglas, S. (2001). *Reclaiming the fire: How successful people overcome burnout.* New York: Random House.

Berkley, K. J. (1997). Sex differences in pain. *Behavioral and Brain Sciences, 20,* 371–380.

Berkman, L. F., & Breslow, L. (1983). *Health and ways of living: The Alameda County Study.* New York: Oxford University Press.

Berkowitz, L. (1964). *The effects of observing violence.* San Francisco: Freeman.

Berkowitz, L. (1990). On the formation and regulation of anger and aggression. *American Psychologist, 45,* 494–503.

Berkowitz, L. (2000). *Causes and consequences of feelings: Studies in emotion and social interaction.* New York: Cambridge University Press.

Berman, F. E., & Miner, J. B. (1985). Motivation to manage at the top executive level: A test of the hierarchic role-motivation theory. *Personnel Psychology, 38,* 377–391.

Bernal, G., & Berger, S. M. (1976). Vicarious eyelid conditioning. *Journal of Personality and Social Psychology, 34,* 62–68.

Berndt, T. J. (1992). Friendship and friends' influence in adolescence. *Psychological Science, 1,* 156–159.

Bernstein, D., & Ebbesen, E. (1978). Reinforcement and substitution in humans: A multiple-response analysis. *Journal of the Experimental Analysis of Behavior, 30,* 243–253.

Bernstein, I. L. (1988, September). *What does learning have to do with weight loss and cancer?* Paper presented at a science and public policy seminar sponsored by the Federation of Behavioral, Psychological, and Cognitive Sciences, Washington, DC.

Bernstein, I. L. (1991). Aversion conditioning in response to cancer and cancer treatment. *Clinical Psychology Review, 11,* 185–191.

Bernstein, K. S. (2000). The experience of acupuncture for treatment of substance dependence. *Journal of Nursing Scholarship, 32,* 267–272.

Berry, D. S., & Landry, J. C. (1997). Facial maturity and daily social interaction. *Journal of Personality and Social Psychology, 72,* 570–580.

Bersoff, D. M., & Miller, J. G. (1993). Culture, context, and the development of moral accountability judgments. *Developmental Psychology, 29,* 664–676.

Bettencourt, B. A., & Miller, N. (1996). Gender differences in aggression as a function of provocation: A meta-analysis. *Psychological Bulletin, 119,* 422–447.

Betz, N. E. (1992). Counseling uses of career self-efficacy theory. *Career Development Quarterly, 41,* 22–26.

Bexton, W. H., Heron, W., & Scott, T. H. (1954). Effects of decreased variation in the sensory environment. *Canadian Journal of Psychology, 8,* 70–76.

Beyer, S. (1998). The accuracy of academic gender stereotypes. *Sex Roles, 41,* 297–306.

Biaggio, M., Roades, L. A., Staffelbach, D., Cardinali, J., & Duffy, R. (2000). Intracultural and intercultural. Dialogue in psychoanalytic psychotherapy and psychoanalysis. *Journal of Applied Social Psychology, 30,* 1657–1669.

Bickerton, D. (1998). The creation and re-creation of language. In C. B. Crawford & D. L. Krebs (Eds.). *Handbook of evolutionary psychology: Ideas, issues, and applications* (pp. 613–634). Mahwah, NJ: Erlbaum.

Bickman, L., Teger, A., Gabriele, T., McLaughlin, C., Berger, M., & Sunaday, E. (1973). Dormitory density and helping behavior. *Environment and Behavior, 5,* 465–466.

Bird, C. E. (1999). Gender, household labor, and psychological distress: The impact of the amount and division of housework. *Journal of Health and Social Behavior, 40,* 32–45.

Blagrove, M. (1996). Problems with the cognitive psychological modeling of dreaming. *The Journal of Mind and Behavior, 17,* 99–134.

Blakemore, C., & Campbell, F. W. (2000). On the existence of neurons in the human visual system selectively sensitive to the orientation and size of retinal images. In S. Yantis, *Visual perception: Essential readings: Key readings in cognition* (pp. 172–189). Philadelphia: Psychology Press/Taylor & Francis.

Blass, T. (1999). The Milgram Paradigm after 35 years: Some things we now know about obedience to authority. In T. Blass (Ed.), *Obedience to authority: Current perspectives on the Milgram paradigm* (pp. 35–59). Mahwah, N.J.: Erlbaum.

Blatt, S. J. (1995). The destructiveness of perfectionism. *American Psychologist, 50,* 1003–1020.

Bleak, J. L., & Frederick, C. M. (1998). Superstitious behavior in sport: Levels of effectiveness and determinants of use in three collegiate sports. *Journal of Sport Behavior, 21,* 1–15.

Bleske, A. L., & Buss, D. M. (2000). Can men and women be just friends? *Personal Relationships, 7,* 131–151.

Blount, S., & Larrick, R. P. (2000). Framing the game: Examining frame choice in bargaining. *Organizational Behavior & Human Decision Processes, 81,* 43–71.

Blum, K., Braverman, E. R., Holder, J. M., Lubar, J. F., Monastra, V. J., Miller, D., Lubar, J. O., Chen, T. H., & Comings, D. E. (2000). Reward deficiency syndrome: A biogenetic model for the diagnosis and treatment of impulsive, addictive, and compulsive behaviors. *Journal of Psychoactive Drugs, 32,* 1–68.

Bobo, L., & Kluegel, J. R. (1997). Status, ideology, and dimensions of whites' racial beliefs and attitudes: Progress and stagnation. In S. A. Tuch & J. K. Martin (Eds.), *Racial attitudes in the 1990s: Continuity and change.* Westport, CT: Praeger.

Bodnar, A. G., Ouellette, M., Frolkis, M., Holt, S. E., Chiu, C. P., Morin, G. B., Harley, C. B., Shay, J. W., Lichtsteiner, S., &

Wright, W. E. (1998). Extension of life-span by introduction of telomerase into normal human cells. *Science, 279,* 349–352.

Bogren, L., Boren, I., & Thorell, L. (1998). Defense mechanism test and electrodermal activity. *Perceptual & Motor Skills, 87,* 279–290.

Boivin, D. B., Duffy, J. F., Kronauer, R. E., & Czeisler, C. A. (1996). Dose-response relationships for resetting of human circadian clock by light. *Nature, 379,* 540–542.

Bolanowski, S. J., Maxfield, L. M., Gescheider, G. A., & Apkarian, A. V. (2000). The effect of stimulus location on the gating of touch by heat- and cold-induced pain. *Somatosensory & Motor Research, 17,* 195–204.

Bond, C. F., Jr., & Titus, L. J. (1983). Social facilitation: A meta-analysis of 241 studies. *Psychological Bulletin, 94,* 265–292.

Bond, R., & Smith, P. B. (1996). Culture and conformity: A meta-analysis of studies using Asch's (1952b, 1956) line judgment task. *Psychological Bulletin, 119,* 111–137.

Boneva, B., Frieze, I. H., Ferligoj, A., Pauknerová, D., & Orgocka, A. (1998). Achievement, power, and affiliation motives as clues to (e)migration desires: A four-countries comparison. *European Psychologist, 3,* 247–254.

Borg, E., & Counter, S. A. (1989, August). The middle-ear muscles. *Scientific American,* 74–80.

Borkenau, P., & Ostendorf, F. (1998). The Big Five as states: How useful is the five-factor model to describe intraindividual variations over time? *Journal of Research in Personality, 32,* 202–221.

Bornstein, R. F. (1992). The dependent personality: Developmental, social, and clinical perspectives. *Psychological Bulletin, 112,* 3–23.

Boronat, C. B., & Logan, G. D. (1997). The role of attention in automatization: Does attention operate at encoding, or retrieval, or both? *Memory and Cognition, 25,* 36–46.

Borrie, R. A. (1991). The use of restricted environmental stimulation therapy in treating addictive behaviors. *International Journal of the Addictions, 25,* 995–1015.

Bosma, H., Richard, P., Siegrist, J., & Marmot, M. (1998). Two alternative job stress models and the risk of coronary heart disease. *American Journal of Public Health, 88,* 68–74.

Botschner, J. V. (1996). Reconsidering male friendships: A social-development perspective. In C. W. Tolman, F. Cherry, R. Van Hezewijk, & I. Lubek (Eds.), *Problems of theoretical psychology* (pp. 242-253). North York, Ontario: Captus Press.

Boudreaux, E., Kilpatrick, D. G., Resnick, H. S., Best, C. L., & Saunders, B. E. (1998). Criminal victimization, posttraumatic stress disorder, and comorbid psychopathology among a community sample of women. *Journal of Traumatic Stress, 11,* 665–678.

Bourtchuladze, R., Frenguelli, B., Blendy, J., Cioffi, D., Schutz, G., & Silva, A. J. (1994). Deficient long-term memory in mice with a targeted mutation of the camp-responsive element-binding protein. *Cell, 79,* 59–68.

Boutcher, S. H. (1992). Attention and athletic performance: An integrated approach. In T. S. Horn (Ed.), *Advances in sport psychology* (pp. 251–265). Champaign, IL: Human Kinetics.

Bower, B. (1999, September 25). Slumber's unexplored landscape. *Science News, 156,* 205.

Bower, G. H. (1981). Mood and memory. *American Psychologist, 36,* 126–148.

Boynton, R. M. (1988). Color vision. *Annual Review of Psychology, 39,* 69–101.

Bradley, C. L., & Marcia, J. E. (1998). Generativity-stagnation: A five-category model. *Journal of Personality, 66*(1), 39–44.

Braffman, W., & Kirsch, I. (1999). Imaginative suggestibility and hypnotizability: An empirical analysis. *Journal of Personality and Social Psychology, 77,* 578–587.

Branden, N. (1980). *The psychology of romantic love.* Los Angeles: Tarcher.

Brandon, T. H., Collins, B. N., Juliano, L. M., & Lazev, A. B. (2000). Preventing relapse among former smokers: A comparison of minimal interventions through telephone and mail. *Journal of Consulting and Clinical Psychology, 68,* 103–113.

Brannon, L. (2002). *Gender: Psychological perspectives* (3rd ed.). Boston: Allyn and Bacon.

Brannon, L., & Feist, J. (2000). *Health psychology: An introduction to behavior and health* (4th ed.). Belmont, CA: Wadsworth.

Braun, A. R., Balkin, T. J., Wesensten, N. J., Gwadry, F., Carson, R. E., Varga, M., Baldwin, P., Belenky, G., & Herscovitch, P. (1998). Dissociated pattern of activity in visual cortices and their projections during human rapid eye movement sleep. *Science, 279,* 91–96.

Breger, L. (2000). *Freud: Darkness in the midst of vision.* New York: Wiley.

Brehm, J. W. (1966). *A theory of psychological reactance.* New York: Academic Press.

Bretschneider, J. G., & McCoy, N. L. (1988). Sexual interest and behavior in healthy 80- to 102-year-olds. *Archives of Sexual Behavior, 17,* 109–129.

Bridges, K. M. B. (1932). Emotional development in early infancy. *Child Development, 3,* 324–341.

Brief, A. P., & Weiss, H. M. (2002). Organizational behavior: Affect in the workplace. *Annual Reviews Psychology,* 53, 279–307.

Brioux, B. (2001, October 19). A human reponse to an inhumane deed: Dan Rather shows personal pain as anthrax hits his office. *Toronto Sun,* E5.

Brodsky, A. E. (1996). Resilient single mothers in risky neighborhoods: Negative psychological sense of community. *Journal of Community Psychology, 24,* 347–363.

Brody, L. R. (1997). Gender and emotion: Beyond stereotypes. *Journal of Social Issues, 53*(2), 369–392.

Bronfenbrenner, U. (1989, September). Who cares for children? Invited address, UNESCO, Paris.

Bronfenbrenner, U. (1999). Environments in developmental perspective: Theoretical and operational models. In S. L. Friedman & T. D. Wachs (Eds.). *Measuring environment across the life span: Emerging methods and concepts* (pp. 3–28). Washington, DC: American Psychological Association.

Brooks, G. R. (2001). Developing gender awareness: When therapist growth promotes family growth. In S. H. Daniel & D. D. Lusterman, (Eds.), *Casebook for integrating family therapy: An ecosystemic approach* (pp. 265–274). Washington, DC: American Psychological Association.

Brooks, M. C. (2000). Press start: Exploring the effects of violent video games on boys. In *Dissertation Abstracts International: Section B: The Sciences & Engineering, 60*(12B), 6419.

Brown, G. M. (1994). Light, melatonin and the sleep–wake cycle. *Journal of Psychiatry & Neuroscience, 19,* 345–353.

Brown, K. W., & Moskowitz, D. S. (1998). Dynamic stability of behavior: The rhythms of our interpersonal lives. *Journal of Personality, 66,* 105–108.

Brown, L. M. (1998). *Raising their voices: The politics of girls' anger.* Cambridge, MA: Harvard University Press.

Brown, R. (1970). The first sentences of child and chimpanzee. In R. Brown (Ed.), *Psycholinguistics: Selected papers* (pp. 208–231). New York: Free Press.

Brown, R. (1973). *A first language: The early stages.* Cambridge, MA: Harvard University Press.

Brown, R., & Kulik, J. (1977). Flashbulb memories. *Cognition, 5,* 73–99.

Brown, S. C., & Craik, F. I. M. (2000). Encoding and retrieval of information. In E. Tulving & F. I. M. Craik (Eds.), *The Oxford handbook of memory* (pp. 93–107). New York: Oxford University Press.

Brown, T. A., & Barlow, D. H. (1995). Long-term outcome in cognitive–behavioral treatment of panic disorder: Clinical predictors and alternative strategies for assessment. *Journal of Consulting and Clinical Psychology, 63,* 754–765.

Bruce, T. J., Spiegel, D. A., & Hegel, M. T. (1999). Cognitive–behavorial therapy helps prevent relapse and recurrence of panic disorder following alprazolam discontinuation: A long-term follow-up of the Peoria and Dartmouth studies. *Journal of Consulting & Clinical Psychology, 67,* 151–156.

Brzustowicz, L. M., Hodgkinson, K. A., Chow, E. W. C., Honer, W. G., & Basstee, A. S. (2000). Location of major susceptibility locus for familial schizophrenia on chromosome 1q21-q22. *Science, 288,* 678–682.

Buck, R., Losow, J. I., Murphy, M. M., & Costanzo, P. (1992). Social facilitation and inhibition of emotional expression and communication. *Journal of Personality and Social Psychology, 6,* 962–968.

Bukowski, W. M., Sippola, L. K., & Hoza, B. (1999). Same and other: Interdependency between participation in same- and other-sex friendships. *Journal of Youth & Adolescence, 28,* 439–459.

Bukowski, W. M., Sippola, L. K., Newcomb, A. E. (2000). Variations in patterns of attraction of same- and other-sex peers during early adolescence. *Developmental Psychology, 36,* 147–154.

Bulcroft, R. A., & Bulcroft, K. A. (1993). Race differences in attitudinal and motivational factors in the decision to marry. *Journal of Marriage and the Family, 55,* 338–355.

Burn, S. M. (1991). Social psychology and the stimulation of recycling behaviors: The block leader approach. *Journal of Applied Social Psychology, 21,* 611–629.

Bushman, B. J., & Anderson, C. A. (2001). Media violence and the American public: Scientific facts versus media misinformation. *American Psychologist, 56,* 477–489.

Bushman, B. J., & Baumeister, R. F. (1998). Threatened egotism, narcissism, self-esteem, and direct and displaced aggression: Does self-love or self-hate lead to violence? *Journal of Personality & Social Psychology, 75,* 219–229.

Bushman, B. J., & Geen, R. G. (1990). Role of cognitive–emotional mediators and individual differences in the effects of media violence on aggression. *Journal of Personality and Social Psychology, 58,* 156–163.

Bushman, B. J., & Phillips, C. M. (2001). If the television program bleeds, memory for the advertisement recedes. *Current Direction in Psychological Science, 10,* 43–47.

Buss, D. M. (1988). Love acts: The evolutionary biology of love. In R. J. Sternberg & M. L. Barnes (Eds.), *The psychology of love.* New Haven, CT: Yale University Press.

Buss, D. M. (1999). *Evolutionary psychology.* Boston: Allyn and Bacon.

Buss, D. M. (2000a). *The dangerous passion: Why jealousy is as necessary as love and sex.* New York: Free Press.

Buss, D. M. (2000b). The evolution of happiness. *American Psychologist, 55,* 15–23.

Buss, D. M., & Kenrick, D. T. (1998). Evolutionary social psychology. In D. T. Gilbert, S. T. Fiske, & G. Lindzey (Eds.), *The handbook of social psychology* (pp. 982–1019). Boston, MA: The McGraw-Hill Company.

Bussey, K., & Bandura, A. (1999). Social cognitive theory of gender development and differentiation. *Psychological Review, 106,* 676–713.

Butler, S. F., & Strupp, H. H. (1991). Psychodynamic psychotherapy. In M. Hersen, A. E. Kazdin, & A. S. Bellack (Eds.), *The clinical psychology handbook* (2nd ed., pp. 519–533). New York: Pergamon Press.

Cabeza, R., & Nyberg, L. (2000). Imaging cognition II: An empirical review of 275 PET and fMRI studies. *Journal of Cognitive Neuroscience, 12,* 1–47.

Cabeza, R., Rao, S. M., Wagner, A. D., Mayer, A. R., & Schacter, D. L. (2001). Can medial temporal lobe regions distinguish true from false? An event-related functional MRI study of veridical and illusory recognition memory. *Proceedings of the National Academy of Sciences of the United States, 98,* 4805–4810.

Cacioppo, J. T., Berntson, G. G., Sheridan, J. F., & McClintock, M. K. (2000). Multilevel integrative analyses of human behavior: Social neuroscience and the complementing nature of social and biological approaches. *Psychological Bulletin, 126,* 829–843.

Cacioppo, J. T., & Gardner, W. L. (1999). Emotion. *Annual Review of Psychology, 50,* 191–214.

Cacioppo, J. T., Petty, R. E., Feinstein, J. A., & Jarvis, W. B. G. (1996). Dispositional differences in cognitive motivation: The life and times of individuals varying in need for cognition. *Psychological Bulletin, 119,* 197–253.

Cairns, R. B., & Cairns, B. D. (1994). *Lifelines and risks: Pathways of youth in our time.* Cambridge, UK: Cambridge University Press.

Cairns, R. B., & Cairns, B. D. (2000). The natural history and developmental functions of aggression. In A. J. Sameroff, M. Lewis, S. M. Miller (Eds.), *Handbook of developmental psychopathology* (pp. 403–429). New York: Kluwer/Plenum.

Call, V., Sprecher, S., & Schwartz, P. (1995). The incidence and frequency of marital sex in a national sample. *Journal of Marriage and the Family, 57,* 639–652.

Calvert, S. L. (1998). *Children's journeys through the information age.* New York: McGraw-Hill.

Camara, W. J., & Schneider, D. L. (1994). Integrity tests: Facts and unresolved issues. *American Psychologist, 49,* 112–119.

Cameron, P., & Cameron, K. (1998). "Definitive" University of Chicago sex survey overestimated prevalence of homosexual identity. *Psychological Reports, 82*(3, Pt.1), 861–862.

Campbell, S. S., & Murphy, P. J. (1998). Extraocular circadian phototransduction in humans. *Science, 279,* 396–399.

Campion, M. A., Palmer, D. K., & Campion, J. E. (1998). Structuring employment interviews to improve reliability, validity, and users' reactions. *Current Directions in Psychological Science, 7,* 77–82.

Cannon, T. D., Kaprio, J., Lönnqvist, J., Huttunen, M., & Koskenvuo, M. (1998). The genetic epidemiology of schizophrenia in a Finnish twin cohort: A population-based modeling study. *Archives of General Psychiatry, 55,* 67–74.

Cannon, W. B. (1927). The James–Lange theory of emotion: A critical examination and an alternative theory. *American Journal of Psychology, 39,* 106–124.

Cannon-Bowers, J. A., & Salas, E. (1998). Team performance and training in complex environments: Recent findings from applied research. *Current Directions in Psychological Science, 7,* 83–87.

Cano, C., Hennessy, K. D., Warren, J. L., & Lubitz, J. (1996). Medicare part A: Utilization and expenditures for psychiatric services: 1995. *Health Care Financing Review, 18,* 177–193.

Cantor, J. (2000). Media violence. *Journal of Adolescent Health, 27S,* 30–34.

Caporael, L. R. (2001). Evolutionary psychology: Toward a unifying theory and a hybrid science. *Annual Review of Psychology, 52,* 607–628.

Carlson-Radvansky, L. A., Covey, E. S., & Lattanzi, K. M. (1999). "What" effects on "Where": Functional influences on spatial relations. *Psychological Science, 10,* 516–521.

Carr, M., Borkowski, J. G., & Maxwell, S. E. (1991). Motivational components of underachievement. *Developmental Psychology, 27,* 108–118.

Carstensen, L. L., & Charles, S. T. (1998). Emotion in the second half of life. *Psychological Science, 7,* 144–149.

Carter, B. L., & Tiffany, S. T. (1999). Meta-analysis of cue-reactivity in addiction research. *Addiction, 94,* 327–340.

Carton, J. S., & Nowicki, S. (1994). Antecedents of individual differences in locus of control of reinforcement: A critical review. *Genetic, Social, and General Psychology Monographs, 120,* 31–81.

Carton, J. S., Nowicki, S., & Balser, G. M. (1996). An observational study of antecedents of locus of control of reinforcement. *International Journal of Behavioral Development, 19,* 161–175.

Casagrande, M., Violani, C., Lucidi, F., & Buttinelli, E. (1996). Variations in sleep mentation as a function of time of night. *International Journal of Neuroscience, 85,* 19–30.

Casas, J. M., Turner, J. A., Ruiz, de, E., & Christoper, A. (2001). Machismo revisited in a time of crisis: Implications for understanding and counseling Hispanic men. In G. R. Brooks, R. Gary, G. E. Good (Eds.). *The new handbook of psychotherapy and counseling with men: A comprehensive guide to settings, problems, and treatment approaches,* 1 & 2 (pp. 754–779). San Francisco: Jossey-Bass.

Cascio, W. F. (1995). Whither industrial and organizational psychology in a changing world of work? *American Psychologist, 50,* 928–939.

Casey, B. J., Giedd, J. N., & Thomas, K. M. (2000). Structural and functional brain development and its relation to cognitive development. *Biological Psychology, 54,* 241–257.

Cassidy, T. (2000). Stress, healthiness, and health behaviours: An exploration of the role of life events, daily hassles, cognitive appraisal, and the coping process. *Counselling Psychology Quarterly, 13,* 293–311.

Cattell, R. B. (1949). *Manual for forms A and B: Sixteen personality factors questionnaire.* Champaign, IL: IPAT.

Cavalier, A. R., Ferretti, R. P., & Hodges, A. E. (1997). Self-management within a classroom token economy for students with learning disabilities. *Research in Development Disabilities, 18,* 167–178.

Cavanagh, P., & Leclerc, Y. G. (1989). Shape from shadows. *Journal of Experimental Psychology: Human Perception and Performance, 15,* 3–27.

Ceci, S. J. (2000). So near and yet so far: Lingering questions about the use of measures of general intelligence for college admission and employment screening. *Psychology, Public Policy, & Law, 6,* 233–252.

Ceci, S. J., & Bruck, M. (1993). Suggestibility of the child witness: A historical review and synthesis. *Psychological Bulletin, 113,* 403–439.

Ceci, S. J., & Williams, W. M. (1997). Schooling, intelligence, and income. *American Psychologist, 52,* 1051–1058.

Celuch, K., & Slama, M. (1995). Getting along and getting ahead as motives for self-presentation: Their impact on advertising effectiveness. *Journal of Applied Social Psychology, 25,* 1700–1713.

Centers for Disease Control and Prevention. (2001). HIV and AIDS—United States, 1981–2000. *Morbidity and Mortality Weekly Report, 50,* 430–433.

Chaleby, K. (1999). Psychotherapy with Arab patients, toward a culturally oriented technique. *Arab Journal of Psychiatry, 3,* 16–27.

Chalmers, D. J. (1996). *Conscious mind: In search of a fundamental theory.* New York: Oxford University Press.

Chambless, D. L., & Hollon, S. D. (1998). Defining empirically supported therapies. *Journal of Consulting and Clinical Psychology, 66,* 7–18.

Channouf, A. (2000). Subliminal exposure to facial expressions of emotion and evaluative judgements of advertising messages. *European Review of Applied Psychology, 50,* 19–25.

Charles, C. M. (1985). *Building classroom discipline: From models to practice* (2nd ed.). New York: Longman.

Charles, S. T., Reynolds, C. A., & Gatz, M. (2001). Age-related differences and change in positive and negative affect over 23 years. *Journal of Personality and Social Psychology, 80,* 136–151.

Chase, V. M. (2000). Where to look to find out why: Rational information search in causal hypothesis testing. *Dissertation Abstracts International: Section B: The Sciences & Engineering, 60*(11-B), 5800.

Chen, H., & Lan, W. (1998). Adolescents' perception of their parents' academic expectations: Comparison of American, Chinese-American, and Chinese high school students. *Adolescence, 33,* 385–390.

Cheng, Y., Kawachi, I., Coakley, E. H., Schwartz, J., & Colditz, G. (2000). Association between psychosocial work characteristics and health functioning in American women: Prospective study. *British Medical Journal, 320,* 1432–1435.

Cherulnik, P. D., Turns, L. C., & Wilderman, S. K. (1990). Physical appearance and leadership: Exploring the role of appearance-based attribution in leader emergence. *Journal of Applied Social Psychology, 20,* 1530–1539.

Chidester, T. R. (1986). Problems in the study of interracial interaction: Pseudo-interracial dyad paradigm. *Journal of Personality and Social Psychology, 50,* 74–79.

Choi, I., Nisbett, R. E., & Norenzayan, A. (1999). Causal attribution across cultures: Variation and universality. *Psychological Bulletin, 125,* 47–63.

Chomsky, N. (1999). On the nature, use, and acquisition of language. In W. Ritchie & T. Bhatia (Eds.), *Handbook of child language acquisition.* New York: Academic Press.

Chorpita, B. F., & Barlow, D. H. (1998). The development of anxiety: The role of control in the early environment. *Psychological Bulletin, 124,* 3–21.

Christenfeld, N., Gerin, W., Linden, W., & Sanders, M. (1997). Social support effects on cardiovascular reactivity: Is a stranger as effective as a friend? *Psychosomatic Medicine, 59,* 388–398.

Cialdini, R. B. (1993). *Influence* (3rd ed.). New York: HarperCollins.

Cialdini, R. B. (2001). Influence: Science and practice. (4th ed.). Boston: Allyn and Bacon.

Cialdini, R. B., Eisenberg, N., Green, B. L., Rhoads, K., & Bator, R. (1998). Undermining the undermining effect of reward on sustained interest. *Journal of Applied Social Psychology, 28,* 249–263.

Claxon, G. (1975). Why we can't tickle ourselves. *Perceptual and Motor Skills, 41,* 335–338.

Cloninger, C. R., Adolfsson, R., & Svrakic, D. M. (1996). Mapping genes for human personality. *Nature Genetics, 12,* 3–4.

Clutton-Brock, T. H., & Parker, G. A. (1995). Punishment in animal societies. *Nature, 373,* 209–216.

Coffey, C. W., Weiner, R. D., Djang, W. T., Figiel, G. S., Soady, S. A. R., Patterson, L. J., Holt, P. D., Spritzer, C. E., & Wilinson, W. E. (1991). Brain anatomic effects of electroconvulsive therapy. *Archives of General Psychiatry, 48,* 1013–1021.

Cohen, S. (1996). Psychological stress, immunity, and upper respiratory infections. *Current Directions in Psychological Science, 5,* 86–90.

Cohen, S., Frank, E., Doyle, W. J., Skoner, D. P., Rabin, B. S., & Gwaltney, J. M., Jr. (1998). Types of stressors that increase susceptibility to the common cold in healthy adults. *Health Psychology, 17,* 214–223.

Cohen, S., Tyrrell, D. A. J., & Smith, A. P. (1997). Psychological stress in humans and susceptibility to the common cold. In T. W. Miller et al. (Eds.), *Clinical disorders and stressful life events* (pp. 217–235). Madison, CT: International Universities Press.

Cohn, L. (1991). Sex differences in the course of personality development: A meta-analysis. *Psychological Bulletin, 109,* 252–266.

Cole, S. W., Kemeny, M. E., Taylor, S. E., Visscher, B. R., & Fahey, J. L. (1996). Accelerated course of human immunodeficiency virus infection in gay men who conceal their homosexual identity. *Psychosomatic Medicine, 58,* 219–231.

Coley, R. L., & Chase-Lansdale, P. L. (1998). Adolescent pregnancy and parenthood: Recent evidence and future directions. *American Psychologist, 53,* 152–166.

Collins, W. A., & Laursen, B. (2000). Adolescent relationships: The art of fugue. In C. Hendrick & S. S. Hendrick (Eds.), *Close relationships: A sourcebook* (pp. 59–69). Thousand Oaks, CA: Sage.

Collins, W. A., Maccoby, E. E., Steinberg, L., Hetherington, E. M., & Bornstein, M. H. (2000). Contemporary research on parenting: The case for nature and nurture. *American Psychologist, 55,* 218–232.

Colman, H., Nabekura, J., & Lichtman, J. W. (1997). Alterations in synaptic strength preceding axon withdrawal. *Science, 275,* 356–361.

Comer, J. P., & Woodruff, D. W. (1998). Mental health in schools. *Child & Adolescent Psychiatric Clinics of North America, 7,* 499–513.

Compas, B. E., Haaga, D. A., Keefe, F. J., Leitenberg, H., & Williams, D. A. (1998). Sampling of empirically supported psychological treatment from health psychology: Smoking, chronic pain, cancer, and bulimia nervosa. *Journal of Consulting and Clinical Psychology, 66,* 89–112.

Comuzzie, A. G., & Allison, D. B. (1998). The search for human obesity genes. *Science, 280,* 1374–1377.

Constantino, J. M., Grosz, D., Saenger, P., Chandler, D. W., Nandi, R., & Earls, F. J. (1993). Testosterone and aggression in children. *Journal of the American Academy of Child and Adolescent Psychiatry, 32,* 1217–1222.

Conway, M. A., Anderson, S. J., Larsen, S. F., Donnelly, C. M., McDaniel, M. A., McClelland, A. G. R., Rawles, R. E., & Logie, R. H. (1994). The formation of flashbulb memories. *Memory & Cognition, 22,* 326–343.

Conyers, L. M., Enright, M. S., & Strauser, D. R. (1998). Applying self-efficacy theory to counseling college students with disabilities. *Journal of Applied Rehabilitation Counseling, 29,* 25–30.

Cooley-Quille, M., Boyd, R. C., Frantz, E., & Walsh, J. (2001). Emotional and behavioral impact of exposure to community violence in inner-city adolescents. *Journal of Clinical Child Psychology, 30,* 199–206.

Corbetta, D., & Vereijken, B. (1999). Understanding development and learning of motor coordination in sport: The contribution of dynamic systems theory. *International Journal of Sport Psychology, 30,* 507–530.

Coren, S., & Previc, F. H. (1996). Handedness as a predictor of increased risk of knee, elbow, or shoulder injury, fractures, and broken bones. *Laterality, 1,* 139–152.

Corina, D. P. (1999). On the nature of left hemisphere specialization for signed language. *Brain and Language, 69,* 230–240.

Cornblatt, B. A., Green, M. F., & Walker, E. F. (1999). Schizophrenia: Etiology and neurocognition. In T. Millon, P. H. Blaney, & R. D. Davis (Eds.), *Oxford textbook of psychopathology* (pp. 277–310). New York: Oxford University Press.

Cosmides, L. (1989). The logic of social exchange: Has natural selection shaped how humans reason? Studies with the Wason selection task. *Cognition, 31,* 187–276.

Cosmides, L., & Tooby, J. (1997). Evolutionary psychology: A primer. Retrieved May 13, 2001 from the World Wide Web: http://www.psych.ucsb.edu/research/cep.

Cosmides, L., & Tooby, J. (1999). Toward an evolutionary taxonomy of treatable conditions. *Journal of Abnormal Psychology, 108,* 453–464.

Cosmides, L., & Tooby, J. (2000). Evolutionary psychology and the emotions. In M. Lewis & J. M. Haviland-Jones (Eds.), *Handbook of emotions* (2nd ed., pp. 91–115). New York: Guilford Press.

Costa, P. T., & McCrae, R. R. (1995). Domains and facets: Hierarchical personality assessment using the Revised NEO Personality Inventory. *Journal of Personality Assessment, 64,* 21–50.

Costa, P. T., Jr., & McCrae, R. R. (1998). Trait theories of personality. In D. F. Barone, M. Hersen, & V. B. Hassett (Eds.), *Advanced personality. The Plenum series in social/clinical psychology* (pp. 103–121). New York: Plenum.

Costanzo, M. (1997). *Just revenge.* New York: St. Martin's Press.

Courthout, E., Uttl, B., Walsh, V., Hallet, M., & Cowey, A. (2000). Plasticity revealed by transcranial magnetic stimulation of early visual cortex. *Neuroreport: An International Journal for the Rapid Communication of Research in Neuroscience, 11,* 1565–1569.

Courtney, S. M., Petit, L., Maisog, J. M., Ungerleider, L. G., & Haxby, J. V. (1998). An area specialized for spatial working memory in human frontal cortex. *Science, 279,* 1347–1351.

Cowan, N., & Wood, N. L. (1997). Constraints on awareness, attention, processing, and memory: Some recent investigations with ignored speech. *Consciousness & Cognition: An International Journal, 6,* 182–203.

Cox, B. J., & Taylor, S. (1999). Anxiety disorders: Panic and phobias. In T. Millon, P. H. Blaney, & R. D. Davis (Eds.), *Oxford textbook of psychopathology* (pp. 81–113). New York: Oxford University Press.

Cox, R. H., Qiu, Y., & Liu, Z. (1993). Overview of sport psychology. In R. N. Singer, M. Murphey, & L. K. Tennant (Eds.), *Handbook of research on sport psychology* (pp. 3–31). New York: Macmillan.

Coyne, Jerry A. (2000, April 3). Of vice and men—the fairy tales of evolutionary psychology. *New Republic, 222,* 27–34.

Craft, M. A., Alber, S. R., & Heward, W. L. (1998). Teaching elementary students with developmental disabilities to recruit teacher attention in a general education classroom: Effects on teacher praise and academic productivity. *Journal of Applied Behavior Analysis, 31,* 399–415.

Craik, F. I. M. (2001). Effects of dividing attention on ecoding and retrieval process. In H. L. Roediger, J. S. Nairne, I. Neath, & A. M. Surprenant (Eds.), *The nature of remembering: Essays in honor of Robert G. Crowder. Science Conference Series* (pp. 55–68). Washington, DC: American Psychological Association.

Craik, F. I. M., & Lockhart, R. S. (1972). Levels of processing: A framework for memory research. *Journal of Verbal Learning and Verbal Behavior, 11,* 671–784.

Craik, F. I. M., Moroz, T. M., Moscovitch, M., Stuss, D. T., Winocur, G., Tulving, E., & Kapur, S. (1999). In search of the self: A positron emission tomography study. *Psychological Science, 10,* 26–34.

Crane, J. (1996). Effects of home environment, SES, and maternal test scores on mathematics achievement. *Journal of Educational Research, 89,* 305–314.

Crawford, C. B., & Anderson, J. L. (1989). Sociobiology. *American Psychologist, 44,* 1449–1459.

Crawford, H. J. (1994). Brain dynamics and hypnosis: Attentional and disattentional processes. *The International Journal of Clinical and Experimental Hypnosis, 42,* 204–232.

Creem, S. H., & Proffitt, D. R. (2001). Grasping objects by their handles: A necessary interaction between cognition and action. *Journal of Experimental Psychology: Human Perception and Performance, 27,* 218–228.

Crespi, T. D. (1988). Effectiveness of time-out: A comparison of psychiatric, correctional, and day-treatment programs. *Adolescence, 23,* 805–811.

Crews, F. (1996). The verdict on Freud. *Psychological Science, 7,* 63–68.

Crick, F., & Koch, C. (1998). Contraints on cortical and thalamic projections: The no-strong-loops hypothesis. *Nature, 391,* 245–250.

Crick, F., & Mitchison, G. (1983). The function of dream sleep. *Nature, 304,* 111–114.

Crick, N. R., & Rose, A. J. (2000). Toward a gender balanced approach to the study of social emotional development: A look at relational aggression. In P. H. Miller, E. Kofsky Scholnick (Eds.). *Toward a feminist developmental psychology* (pp. 153–168). Florence, KY: Taylor & Francis/Routledge.

Cross, S. E., & Madson, L. (1997). Models of the self: Self-construals and gender. *Psychological Bulletin, 122,* 5–37.

Crosson, B. (2000). Systems that support language processes: Verbal working memory. In S. E. Nadeau, L. J. Gonzalez Rothi, & B. Crosson (Eds.), *Aphasia and language: Theory to practice. The science and practice of neuropsychology* (pp. 399–418). New York: Guilford Press.

Crouter, A. C., Bumpas, M. F., Head, M. R., & McHale, S. M. (2001). Implications of overwork and overload for the quality of men's family relationships. *Journal of Marriage and the Family, 63,* 404–416.

Csikszentmihalyi, M. (1997). *Finding flow: The psychology of engagement with everyday life.* New York: Basic Books.

Csikszentmihalyi, M. (2000). *Beyond boredom and anxiety.* San Francisco: Jossey-Bass.

Csikszentmihalyi, M. (2001). The context of creativity. In W. Bennis, G. M. Spreitzer, & T. G. Cummings (Eds.), *The future of leadership: Today's top leadership thinkers speak to tomorrow's leaders* (pp. 116–124). San Francisco: Jossey-Bass.

Culbertson, F. M. (1997). Depression and gender: An international review. *American Psychologist, 52,* 25–31.

Cummings, N. A. (1986). The dismantling of our health system: Strategies for the survival of psychological practice. *American Psychologist, 41,* 426–431.

Cummings, N. A., Budman, S. H., & Thomas, J. L. (1998). Efficient psychotherapy as a viable response to scarce resources and rationing of treatment. *Professional Psychology, Research, and Practice, 29,* 460–469.

Cunningham, C. L., Dickinson, S. D., Grahame, N. J., Okorn, D. M., & McMullin, C. S. (1999). Genetic differences in cocaine-induced conditioned place preference in mice depend on conditioning trial duration. *Psychopharmacology, 146,* 73–80.

Curran, H. V. (2000). Psychopharmacological approaches to human memory. In M. S. Gazzaniga (Ed.), *The new cognitive neurosciences* (pp. 797–804). Cambridge, MA: The MIT Press.

D'Imperio, R. L., Dubow, E. F., & Ippolito, M. F. (2000). Resilient and stress-affected adolescents in an urban setting. *Journal of Clinical Child Psychology, 29,* 129–142.

Dadds, M. R., Bovbjerg, D. H., Redd, W. H., & Cutmore, T. R. (1997). Imagery in human classical conditioning. *Psychological Bulletin, 122,* 89–103.

Damasio, A. R. (1999). *The feeling of what happens.* New York: Harcourt Brace & Company.

Damasio, A. R. (2000). A neurobiology for consciousness. In T. Metzinger (Ed.), *Neural correlates of consciousness: Empirical and conceptual questions* (pp. 111–120). Cambridge, MA: The MIT Press.

Damasio, A. R., & Damasio, H. (2000). Aphasia and the neural basis of language. In M. Mesulam, *Principles of behavioral and cognitive neurology* (2nd ed., pp. 294–315). New York: Oxford University Press.

Damian, M. F. (2001). Congruity effects evoked by subliminally presented primes: Automaticity rather than semantic processing. *Journal of Experimental Psychology: Human Perception and Performance, 27,* 154–165.

Daniel, M. H. (1997). Intelligence testing. *American Psychologist, 52,* 1038–1045.

Daniel, M. H. (2000). Interpretation of intelligence test scores. In R. J. Sternberg (Ed.). *Handbook of intelligence* (pp. 477–491). New York: Cambridge University Press.

Darley, J. M., & Gross, P. H. (2000). A hypothesis-confirming bias in labeling effects. In C. Stangor (Ed.), *Stereotypes and prejudice: Essential readings, Key Readings in Social Psychology* (pp. 212–225). Philadelphia: Psychology Press/Taylor & Francis.

Dasgupta, N., & Greenwald, A. G. (2001). On the malleability of automatic attitudes: Combating automatic prejudice with images of admired and disliked individuals. *Journal of Personality and Social Psychology, 81,* 800–814.

Davidson, R. J., Jackson, D. C., & Kalin, N. H. (2000). Emotion, plasticity, context, and regulation: Perspectives from affective neuroscience. *Psychological Bulletin, 126,* 890–909.

Davies, M. M. (1997). *Fake, fact, and fantasy: Children's interpretations of television reality.* Mahwah, NJ: Erlbaum.

Davies, M., Stankov, L., & Roberts, R. D. (1998). Emotional intelligence: In search of an elusive construct. *Journal of Personality and Social Psychology, 75,* 989–1015.

Davis, K. D. (2001). Studies of pain using functional magnetic resonance imaging. In K. Casey & C. Bushnell (Eds.), *Pain imaging: Progress in pain research and management* (pp. 195–210). Seattle, WA: IASP Press.

Davis, K. D., Kiss, Z. H. T., Luo, L., Tasker, R. R., Lozano, A. M., & Dostrovsky, J. O. (1998). Phantom sensations generated by thalamic microstimulation. *Nature, 391,* 385–387.

Davison, H. K., & Burke, M. J. (2000). Sex discrimination in simulated employment contexts: A meta-analytic investigation. *Journal of Vocational Behavior, 56,* 225–248.

de Jonge, J., Bosma, H., Peter, R., & Siegrist, J. (2000). Job strain, effort-reward imbalance, and employee well-being: A large-scale cross-sectional study. *Social Science & Medicine, 50,* 1317–1327.

De La Casa, L. G., & Lubow, R. E. (2000). Super-latent inhibition with delayed conditioned taste aversion testing. *Animal Learning & Behavior, 28,* 289–399.

Deci, E. L. (1975). *Intrinsic motivation.* New York: Plenum.

Deci, E. L., Koestner, R., & Ryan, R. M. (1999). A meta-analytic review of experiments examining the effects of extrinsic rewards on intrinsic motivation. *Psychological Bulletin, 125,* 627–668.

Deco, G., & Schurmann, B. (2000). A neuro-cognitive visual system for object recognition based on testing of interactive attentional top-down hypotheses. *Perception, 29,* 1249–1264.

DeLongis, A., Folkman, S., & Lazarus, R. S. (1988). The impact of daily stress on health and mood: Psychological and social resources as mediators. *Journal of Personality and Social Psychology, 54,* 486–495.

Dement, W. C., with C. Vaughan. (1999). *The promise of sleep.* New York: Delacorte Press.

Dement, W. C., & Wolpert, E. A. (1958). The relation of eye movements, body motility, and external stimuli to dream content. *Journal of Experimental Psychology, 55,* 543–553.

Dennett, D. C. (1991). *Consciousness explained.* Boston: Little, Brown.

Dennett, D. C. (1996). *Kinds of minds: Toward an understanding of consciousness.* New York: Basic Books.

DePaulo, B. M. (1992). Nonverbal behavior and self-presentation. *Psychological Bulletin, 111,* 230–243.

Depaulo, B. M., & Friedman, H. S. (1998). Nonverbal communication. In D. T. Gilbert & S. T. Fiske (Eds.). *The handbook of social psychology* (4th ed., pp. 3–40). New York: McGraw-Hill.

Dershowitz, A. M. (1986). *Reversal of fortune: Inside the von Bulow case.* New York: Random House.

DeSantis, A., & Kayson, W. A. (1997). Defendants' characteristics of attractiveness, race, and sex and sentencing decisions. *Psychological Reports, 81,* 679–683.

Detterman, D. K., & Thompson, L. A. (1997). What is so special about special education? *American Psychologist, 52,* 1082–1090.

DeValois, R. L., & Jacobs, G. H. (1968). Primate color vision. *Science, 162,* 533–540.

Devoto, A., Lucidi, F., Violani, C., & Bertini, M. (1999). Effects of different sleep reductions on daytime sleepiness. *Sleep, 22,* 336–343.

Diener, E. (2000). Subjective well-being: The science of happiness and a proposal for a national index. *American Psychologist, 55,* 34–43.

Diener, E., Lusk, R., DeFour, D., & Flax, R. (1980). Deindividuation: Effects of group size, density, number of observers, and group member similarity on self-consciousness and disinhibited behavior. *Journal of Personality and Social Psychology, 39,* 449–459.

Dietz, T. L. (1998). An examination of violence and gender role portrayals in video games: Implications for gender socialization and aggressive behavior. *Sex Roles, 38,* 425–428.

Dikeos, D. G., Papadimitriou, G. N., Avramopoulos, D., Karadima, G., Daskalopoulou, E. G., Souery, D., Mendlewicz, J., Vassilopoulos, D., & Stefanis, C. N. (1999). Association between the dopamine D3 receptor gene locus (DRD3) and unipolar affective disorder. *Psychiatric Genetics, 9,* 189–195.

DiLalla, L. F., & Gottesman, I. I. (1991). Biological and genetic contributors to violence: Wisdom's untold tale. *Psychological Bulletin, 109,* 125–129.

DiLalla, L. F., Thompson, L. A., Plomin, R., Phillips, K., Fagan, J. F., III, Haith, M. M., Cyphers, L. H., & Fulker, D. W. (1990). Infant predictors of preschool and adult IQ: A study of infant twins and their parents. *Development Psychology, 26,* 759–769.

DiMatteo, M. R. (1994). Enhancing patient adherence to medical recommendations. *Journal of the American Medical Association, 217,* 79, 83.

DiMatteo, M. R., & DiNicola, D. D. (1982). *Achieving patient compliance: The psychology of the medical practitioner's role.* New York: Pergamon.

Dindia, K., & Allen, M. (1992). Sex differences in self-disclosure: A meta-analysis. *Psychological Bulletin, 112,* 106–124.

Dinges, N. G., Atlis, M. M., & Vincent, G. M. (1997). Cross-cultural perspectives on antisocial behavior. In D. M. Stoff, J. Breiling, & J. Wohl (Eds.), *Handbook of antisocial behavior* (pp. 463–473). New York: Wiley.

Dinges, N. G., & Cherry, D. (1995). Symptom expression and the use of mental health services among American ethnic minorities. In J. F. Aponte, R. Y. Rivers, & J. Wohl (Eds.), *Psychological interventions and cultural diversity* (pp. 40–56). Boston: Allyn and Bacon, Inc.

DiPlacido, J. (1998). Minority stress among lesbians, gay men, and bisexuals: A consequence of heterosexism, homophobia, and stigmatization. In G. M. Herek (Ed.), *Stigma and sexual orientation: Understanding prejudice against lesbians, gay men, and bisexuals: Vol. 4. Psychological perspectives on lesbian and gay issues* (pp. 138–159). Thousand Oaks, CA: Sage.

Dishion, T. J., McCord, J., & Poulin, F. (1999). When interventions harm. *American Psychologist, 54,* 755–764.

Division 44/Committee on Lesbian, Gay, and Bisexual Concerns Joint Task Force on Guidelines for Psychotherapy with Lesbian, Gay, and Bisexual Clients. (2000). Guidelines for psychotherapy with lesbian, gay, and bisexual clients. *American Psychologist, 55,* 1440–1451.

Dobash, R. E., & Dobash, R. P. (1998). Cross-border encounters: Challenges and opportunities. In C. M. Renzetti & J. L. Edleson (Series Eds.), *Rethinking violence against women* (Vol. 9, pp. 1–21). Thousand Oaks, CA: Sage.

Docherty, N. M., Hall, M. J., & Gordinier, S. W. (1998). Affective reactivity of speech in schizophrenia patients and their nonschizophrenic relatives. *Journal of Abnormal Psychology, 107,* 461–467.

Dohrenwend, B. P. (2000). The role of adversity and stress in psychopathology: Some evidence and its implications for theory and research. *Journal of Health and Social Behavior, 41,* 1–19.

Dollard, J., Doob, L. W., Miller, N. E., Mowrer, O. H., & Sears, R. R. (1939). *Frustration and aggression.* New Haven, CT: Yale University Press.

Donovan, J. M. (1998). Brief couples therapy: Lessons from the history of brief individual treatment. *Psychotherapy: Theory, Research and Practice, 35,* 116–129.

Donson, N. (1999). Caring for day care: Models for early intervention and primary prevention. In T. B. Cohen, M. H. Etezady, B. L. Pacella (Eds.), *The vulnerable child* (Vol. 3, pp. 181–212). Madison, CT: International Universities Press.

Downey, V. W., & Landry, R. G. (1997). Self-reported sexual behaviours of high school juniors and seniors in North Dakota. *Psychological Reports, 80*(3, Pt. 2), 1357–1358.

Dromi, E. (1997). Early lexical development. In M. Barerett (Ed.), *The development of language* (pp. 99–131). London: UCL.

Drummond, D. C. (2001). Theories of drug craving, ancient and modern. *Addiction, 96,* 33–46.

Dryden, W., & Ellis, A. (2001). Rational emotive behavior therapy. In K. S. Dobson (Ed.). *Handbook of cognitive–behavioral therapies* (2nd ed.), (pp. 295–348). New York: Guilford Press.

Duckitt, J. (1992). Psychology and prejudice. *American Psychologist, 47,* 1182–1193.

Duffy, R. D., Kalsher, M. J., & Wogalter, M. S. (1993). The effectiveness of an interactive warning in a realistic product-use situation. *Proceedings of the Human Factors and Ergonomics Society, 37th Annual Meeting,* 935–939.

Duman, R. S., Malberg, J., Nakawaga, S., & D'Sa, C. (2000). Neuronal plasticity and survival in mood disorders. *Biological Psychiatry, 48,* 732–739.

Dumont, M., & Provost, M. A. (1999). Resilience in adolescents: Protective role of social support, coping strategies, self-esteem, and social activities on experience of stress and depression. *Journal of Youth and Adolescence, 28,* 343–363.

Duncan, J., Seitz, R. J., Kolodny, J., Bor, D., Herzog, H., Ahmed, A., Newell, F. N., and Emslie, H. (2000). A neural basis for general intelligence. *Science, 289,* 457–460.

Dunn, B. R., Hartigan, J. A., & Mikulas, W. L. (1999). Concentration and mindfulness meditations: Unique form of consciousness? *Applied Psychophysiology and Biofeedback, 24,* 147–165.

Dupont, S., Van de Moortele, P. F., Samson, S., Hasboun, D., Poline, J. B., Adam, C., Lehericy, S., Le Bihan, D., Samson, Y., & Baulac, M. (2000). Episodic memory in left temporal lobe epilepsy: A functional MRI study. *Brain, 123,* 1722–1732.

Dwyer, W. O., Leeming, F. C., Cobern, M. K., Porter, B. E., & Jackson, J. M. (1993). Critical review of behavioral interventions to preserve the environment: Research since 1980. *Environment and Behavior, 25,* 275–321.

Eagly, A. H., Ashmore, R. D., Makhijani, M. G., & Longo, L. C. (1991). What is beautiful is good, but . . . : A meta-analytic review of research on the physical attractiveness stereotype. *Psychological Bulletin, 110,* 109–128.

Eagly, A. H., & Johnson, B. T. (1990). Gender and leadership style: A meta-analysis. *Psychological Bulletin, 108,* 233–256.

Eagly, A. H., Makhijani, M. G., & Klonsky, B. G. (1992). Gender and the evaluation of leaders: A meta-analysis. *Psychological Bulletin, 111,* 1, 3–22.

Eagly, A. H., & Steffen, V. J. (2000). Gender stereotypes stem from the distribution of women and men into social roles. In C. Stangor (Ed.), *Stereotypes and prejudice: Essential reading. Key Readings in Social Psychology* (pp. 142–160). Philadelphia: Psychology Press/Taylor & Francis.

Eaton, M. J., & Dembo, M. H. (1997). Differences in the motivational beliefs of Asian American and non-Asian students. *Journal of Educational Psychology, 89,* 433–440.

Edward, J. (1999). Is managed mental health treatment psychotherapy? *Clinical Social Work Journal, 27,* 87–102.

Edwards, D. C. (1999). *Motivation and emotion: Evolutionary, physiological, cognitive, and social influences.* London: Sage.

Edwards, K. (1998). The face of time: Temporal cues in facial expressions of emotion. *Psychological Society, 9,* 270–276.

Ehrlich, P. R. (2000). *Human natures: Genes, cultures, and the human prospect.* Washington, DC: Island Press.

Eich, E. (1995). Searching for mood dependent memory. *Psychological Science, 6,* 67–75.

Eisenberger, R., & Cameron, J. (1996). Detrimental effects of reward. *American Psychologist, 51,* 1153–1166.

Ekman, P. (1992). Facial expressions of emotion: New findings, new questions. *Psychological Science, 3,* 34–38.

Ekman, P. (1996). Why don't we catch liars? Truth-telling, lying and self-deception. *Social Research, 63,* 801–817.

Ekman, P. (1993). Facial expression and emotion. *American Psychologist, 48,* 384–392.

Ekman, P., & Keltner, D. (1997). Universal facial expressions of emotion: An old controversy and new findings. In U. C. Segerstrale & P. Molnar (Eds.), *Nonverbal communication: Where nature meets culture* (pp. 27–46). Mahwah, NJ: Erlbaum.

Eliot, L. (1999). *What's going on in there? How the brain and mind develop in the first five years of life.* New York: Bantam Books.

Elkind, D. (1999). Authority of the brain. *Journal of Developmental & Behavioral Pediatrics, 20,* 432–433.

Ellis, A. (1970). *The essence of rational psychotherapy: A comprehensive approach to treatment.* New York: Institute for Rational Living.

Ellis, A. (1999a). Early theories and practices of rational emotive behavior therapy and how they have been augmented and revised during the last three decades. *Journal of Rational Emotive and Cognitive Behavior Therapy, 17,* 69–93.

Ellis, A. (1999b). Reasons why rational emotive behavior therapy is relatively neglected in the professional and scientific literature. *Journal of Rational Emotive and Cognitive Behavior Therapy, 19,* 67–74.

Ellis, A., & Harper, R. A. (1961). *A guide to rational living.* North Hollywood, CA: Wilshire.

Engel, S. A. (1999). Using neuroimaging to measure mental representations: Finding color-opponent neurons in visual cortex. *Psychological Science, 8,* 23–26.

Engen, T., & Engen, E. A. (1997). Relationship between development of odor perception and language. *Enfance, 1,* 125–140.

Epstein, H. T. (2001). An outline of the role of brain in human cognitive development. *Brain & Cognition, 45*(1), 44–51.

Erikson, E. H. (1963). *Childhood and society* (2nd ed.). New York: Norton.

Erikson, E. H. (1968). *Identity: Youth and crisis.* New York: Norton.

Ernst, E. (2000). Prevalence of use of complementary/alternative medicine: A systematic review. *Bulletin of the World Health Organization, 78,* 252–257.

Eron, L. D. (1987). The development of aggressive behavior from the perspective of a developing behaviorism. *American Psychologist, 42,* 435–442.

Ettner, S. L., & Grzywacz, J. G. (2001). Workers' perceptions of how jobs affect health: A social ecological perspective. *Journal of Occupational Health Psychology, 6,* 101–113.

Eubank, M., Collins, D., & Smith, N. (2000). The influence of anxiety direction on processing bias. *Journal of Sport and Exercise Psychology, 4,* 292–306.

Evans, G. W., Hygge, S., & Bullinger, M. (1995). Chronic noise and psychological stress. *Psychological Science, 6,* 333–338.

Evans, G. W., Lepore, S. J., Shejwal, B. R., & Palsane, M. N. (1998). Chronic residential crowding and children's well-being: An ecological perspective. *Child Development, 69,* 1514–1523.

Evans, G. W., Rhee, E., Forbes, C., Allen, K. M., & Lepore, S. J. (2000). The meaning and efficacy of social withdrawal as a strategy for coping with chronic residential crowding. *Journal of Environmental Psychology, 4,* 335–342.

Exner, J. E., Jr., Thomas, E. A., & Mason, B. (1985). Children's Rorschachs: Description and prediction. *Journal of Personality Assessment, 49,* 13–14.

Eysenck, H. J. (1970). *The structure of human personality* (3rd ed.). London: Methuen.

Eysenck, H. J. (1995). *Genius: The natural history of creativity.* Cambridge, UK: Cambridge University Press.

Eysenck, H. J. (1998). *A new look at intelligence.* London: Transaction Publishers.

Eysenck, H. J., & Eysenck, S. B. G. (1993). *The Eysenck Personality Questionnaire–Revised.* London: Hodder & Stoughton.

Ezzo, J., Berman, B., Hadhazy, V. A., Jadad, A. R., Lao, L., & Singh, B. B. (2000). Is acupuncture effective for the treatment of chronic pain? A systematic review. *Pain, 86,* 217–225.

Fabiani, M., Stadler, M. A., & Wessels, P. M. (2000). True but not false memories produce a sensory signature in human lateralized brain potentials. *Journal of Cognitive Neuroscience, 12,* 941–949.

Fagan, J., & Silverthorn, A. S. (1998). Research on communication by touch. In E. W. Smith (Ed.), *Touch in psychotherapy: Theory, research, and practice* (pp. 59–73). New York: Guilford Press.

Fagot, B. I., Rodgers, C. S., & Leinbach, M. D. (2000). Theories of gender socialization. In T. Eckes & H. M. Trautner (Eds.), *The developmental social psychology of gender* (pp. 65–89). Mahwah, NJ: Erlbaum.

Faludi, S. (1999). *Stiffed: The betrayal of the American man.* New York: Morrow.

Fang, C. Y., & Myers, H. F. (2001). The effects of racial stressors and hostility on cardiovascular reactivity in African American and Caucasian men. *Health Psychology, 20,* 64EN70.

Fang, H. (1996). Dopamine receptor studies in human postmortem brain by radioreceptor binding. *International Medical Journal, 3,* 265–272.

Farah, M. J., Wilson, K. D., Drain, M., & Tanaka, J. N. (1998). What is special about face perception? *Psychological Review, 105,* 482–498.

Farmer-Dougan, V. (1998). A disequilibrium analysis of incidental teaching: Determining reinforcement effects. *Behavior Modification, 22,* 78–95.

Farwell, L., & Wohlwend-Lloyd, R. (1998). Narcissistic processes: Optimistic expectations, favorable self-evaluations, and self-enhancing attributions. *Journal of Personality, 66,* 65–67.

Fast, J. E., & Frederick, J. A. (1996). Working arrangements and time stress. *Canadian Social Trends, 43,* 14–19.

Fehr, B., & Russell, J. A. (1991). The concept of love viewed from a prototype perspective. *Journal of Personality and Social Psychology, 60,* 425–438.

Feingold, A. (1992). Gender differences in mate selection preferences: A test of the parental investment model. *Psychological Bulletin, 112,* 125–139.

Feldman, L., Holowaty, P., Harvey, B., Rannie, K., Shortt, L., & Jamal, A. (1997). A comparison of the demographic, lifestyle, and sexual behaviour characteristics of virgin and non-virgin adolescents. *The Canadian Journal of Human Sexuality, 6*(3), 197–209.

Fenwick, D. T. (1998). Managing space, energy, and self: Junior high teachers' experiences of classroom management. *Teaching & Teacher Education, 14,* 619–631.

Fernald, R. D., & White, S. A. (2000). Social control of brains: From behavior to genes. In M. S. Gazzaniga (Ed.), *The new cognitive neurosciences* (pp. 1193–1208). Cambridge, MA: The MIT Press.

Fernandez, E., & Sheffield, J. (1996). Relative contributions of life events versus daily hassles to the frequency and intensity of headaches. *Headache, 36,* 595–602.

Ferraro, T. (1999). A psychoanalytic perspective on anxiety in athletes. *Athletic Insight: Online Journal of Sport Psychology* (2). Retrieved from the World Wide Web, www.athleticinsight.com/vol1lssw/Psychoanalytic-Anxiety.htm.

Ferrie, J. E., Martikainen, P., Shipley, M. J., Marmot, M. G., Stansfeld, S. A., & Smith, G. D. (2001). Employment status and health after privatisation in white collar civil servants: Prospective cohort study. *British Medical Journal, 322,* 647–651.

Festinger, L. (1954). A theory of social comparison processes. *Human Relations, 7,* 117–140.

Festinger, L. (1957). *A theory of cognitive dissonance.* Evanston, IL: Row, Petersen.

Finkel, D., Pedersen, N. L., Berg, S., & Johansson, B. (2000). Quantitative genetic analysis of biobehavioral markers of aging in Swedish studies of adult twins. *Journal of Aging & Health, 12,* 47–68.

Finkel, D., Pedersen, N. L., Plomin, R., & McClearn, G. E. (1998). Longitudinal and cross-sectional twin data on cognitive abilities in adulthood: The Swedish Adoption/Twin Study of Aging. *Developmental Psychology, 34,* 1400–1413.

Fischer, A. R., & Good, G. E. (1998). New directions for the study of gender role attitudes. *Psychology of Women Quarterly, 22,* 371–384.

Fischhoff, B., Downs, J., & de Bruin, W. B. (1998). Adolescent vulnerability: A framework for behavioral interventions. *Applied and Preventive Psychology, 9,* 77–94.

Fish, J. M. (2002). The myth of race. In J. M. Fish (Ed.), *Race and intelligence: Separating science from myth* (pp. 113–141). Mahwah, NJ: Erlbaum.

Fishbain, D. A. (2000). Non-surgical chronic pain treatment outcome: A review. *International Review of Psychiatry, 12,* 170–180.

Fisher, C. B., & Fryberg, D. (1994). Participant partners: College students weigh the costs and benefits of deceptive research. *American Psychologist, 49,* 417–427.

Fishman, D. B., & Franks, C. M. (1997). The conceptual evolution of behavior therapy. In P. L. Wachtel & S. B. Messer (Eds.), *Theories of psychotherapy: Origins and evolution* (pp. 131–180). Washington, DC: American Psychological Association.

Fiske, S. T. (1992). Thinking is for doing: Portraits of social cognition from daguerreotype to laserphoto. *Journal of Personality and Social Psychology, 63,* 877–889.

Fiske, S. T. (1998). Stereotyping, prejudice, and discrimination. In D. T. Gilbert, S. T. Fiske, & G. Lindzey (Eds.), *The handbook of social psychology* (pp. 357–411). New York: McGraw-Hill.

Fiske, S. T. (2000). Stereotyping, prejudice, and discrimination at the seam between the centuries: Evolution, culture, mind, and brain. *European Journal of Social Psychology, 30,* 299–322.

Fiske, S. T. (2001). Effects of power on bias: Power explains and maintains individual, group, and societal disparities. In A. Y. Lee-Chai & J. A. Bargh (Eds.). *The use and abuse of power: Multiple perspectives on the causes of corruption* (pp. 181–193). Philadelphia: Psychology Press/Taylor & Francis.

Fivush, R. (2001). Owning experience: Developing subjective perspective in autobiographical narratives. In C. Moore & K. Lemmon (Eds.), *The self in time: Developmental perspectives* (pp. 35–52). Mahwah, NJ: Erlbaum.

Fleischhacker, W. W., Lemmens P., & van Baclen, B. (2001). A qualitative assessment of the neurological safety of antipsychotic drugs: An analysis of risperidone database. *Pharmacopsychiatry, 34,* 104–110.

Fleischman, D. A., Vaidya, C. J., Lange, K. L., & Gabrieli, J. D. E. (1997). A dissociation between perceptual explicit and implicit memory processes. *Brain & Cognition, 35,* 42–57.

Fleming, I., Baum, A., & Weiss, L. (1987). Social density and perceived control as mediators of crowding stress in high-density residential neighborhoods. *Journal of Personality and Social Psychology, 52,* 899–906.

Flint, A. J., & Rifat, S. L. (1998). The treatment of psychotic depression in later life: A comparison of pharmacotherapy and ECT. *International Journal of Geriatric Psychiatry, 13,* 23–28.

Flinton, C. A. (1998). The effects of meditation techniques on anxiety and locus of control in juvenile delinquents. *Dissertation Abstracts International, 59*(2B), 0871.

Flynn, J. R. (1999). Searching for justice: The discovery of IQ gains over time. *American Psychologist, 54,* 5–20.

Folkman, S., & Moskowitz, J. T. (2000). Positive affect and the other side of coping. *American Psychologist, 55,* 647–654.

Ford, J. D., Chandler, P., Thacker, B., Greaves, D., Shaw, D., Sennhauser, S., & Schwartz, L. (1998). Family systems therapy after operation Desert Storm with European-theater veterans. *Journal of Marital and Family Therapy, 24,* 243–250.

Forest, G., & Godbout, R. (2000). Effects of sleep deprivation on performance and EEG spectral analysis in young adults. *Brain and Cognition, 43,* 195–200.

Forgas, J. P. (1998). Asking nicely? The effects of mood on responding to more or less polite requests. *Personality and Social Psychology Bulletin, 24,* 173–185.

Fornai, F., & Orzi, F. (2001). Sexual pheromone or conventional odors increase extracellular lactate without changing glucose utilization in specific brain areas of the rat. *Neuroreport: An International Journal for the Rapid Communication of Research in Neuroscience, 12,* 63–69.

Forsythe, S. M. (1990). Effect of applicant's clothing on interviewer's decision to hire. *Journal of Applied Social Psychology, 20,* 1579–1595.

Fosshage, J. L. (1997). The organizing functions of dream mentation. *Contemporary Psychoanalysis, 33,* 429–458.

Foulkes, D. (1985). *Dreaming: A cognitive-psychological analysis.* Hillsdale, NJ: Erlbaum.

Foulkes, D. (1990). Dreaming and consciousness. *European Journal of Cognitive Psychology, 2,* 39–55.

Foulkes, D. (1996). Dream research. *Sleep, 19,* 609–624.

Foulkes, D., & Kerr, N. H. (1994). Point of view in nocturnal dreaming. *Perceptual and Motor Skills, 78,* 690.

Foulkes, D., Meier, B., Strauch, I., & Kerr, N. H. (1993). Linguistic phenomena and language selection in the REM dreams of German–English bilinguals. *International Journal of Psychology, 28,* 871–891.

Fox, M. (1993). *Psychological perspectives in education.* New York: Cassell Educational.

Foxhall, K. (2000, January). Suddenly, a big impact on criminal justice. *Monitor on Psychology, 31*(1), 36–37.

Frable, D. E. (1989). Sex typing and gender ideology: Two facets of the individual's gender psychology that go together. *Journal of Personality and Social Psychology, 56,* 95–108.

Fraenkel, P., & Pinsof, W. M. (2001). Teaching family therapy-centered integration: Assimilation and beyond. *Journal of Psychotherapy Integration, 11,* 59–85.

Frankenberger, K. D. (2000). Adolescent egocentrism: A comparison among adolescents and adults. *Journal of Adolescence, 23,* 343–354.

Franks, J. J., Bilbrey, C. W., Lein, K. G., & McNamara, T. P. (2000). Transfer-appropriate processing (TAP) and repetition priming. *Memory and Cognition, 28,* 1140–1151.

Frater, E. (2000). Polarized over polygraphs: Polygraph testing in federal government. *National Journal, 32,* 2800–2801.

Frederick, C. M. (2000). Competitiveness: Relations with GPA, locus of control, sex, and athletic status. *Perceptual and Motor Skills, 90,* 413–414.

Frederick, C. M., & Morrison, C. S. (1999). Date selection choices in college students: Making a potential love connection. *North American Journal of Psychology, 1,* 41–50.

French, K. E., Spurgeon, J. H., & Nevett, M. E. (1995). Expert–novice differences in cognitive and skill execution components of youth baseball performance. *Research Quarterly for Exercise and Sport, 66,* 194–201.

Freud, S. (1964). *New introductory lectures on psychoanalysis.* New York: Norton. (Original work published 1933).

Freud, S. (1966). *A general introduction to psychoanalysis* (J. Riviere, Trans.). New York: Washington Square (Original work published 1920).

Frey, B. J., & Hinton, G. E. (1999). Variational learning in nonlinear gaussian belief networks. *Neural Computation, 11,* 193–213.

Frezza, M., di Padova, C., Pozzato, G., Terpin, M., Baraona, E., & Lieber, C. S. (1990). High blood alcohol levels in women. *New England Journal of Medicine, 322,* 95–99.

Friedman, M., & Rosenman, R. H. (1974). *Type A behavior and your heart.* Greenwich, CT: Fawcett.

Friedrich, R. W., & Laurent, G. (2001). Dynamic optimization of odor representations by slow temporal patterning of mitral cell activity. *Science, 291,* 889–894.

Friel, P. N., Logan, B. K., O'Malley, D., & Baer, J. S. (1999). Development of dosing guidelines for reaching selected target breath alcohol concentrations. *Journal of Studies on Alcohol, 60,* 555–565.

Frieze, I. H., Olson, J. E., & Russell, J. (1991). Attractiveness and income for men and women in management. *Journal of Applied Social Psychology, 21,* 1039–1057.

Fromm, E. (1956). *The art of loving.* New York: Harper and Row.

Fulbright, R. K., Shaywitz, S. E., Shaywitz, B. A., Pugh, K. R., Skudlarski, P., Constable, R. T., et al. (1997). Neuroanatomy of reading and dyslexia. *Child & Adolescent Psychiatric Clinics of North America, 6,* 431–445.

Furr, S. R., Westefeld, J. S., McConnell, G. N., & Jenkins, J. M. (2001). Suicide and depression among college students: A decade later. *Professional Psychology: Research and Practice. 32,* 97–100.

Furstenberg, F. F., Jr., & Hughes, M. E. (1995). Social capital and successful development among at-risk youth. *Journal of Marriage and the Family, 57,* 580–592.

Gabriel, M., & Talk, A. C. (2001). A tale of two paradigms: Lessons learned from parallel studies of discriminative instrumental learning and classical eyeblink conditioning. In J. E. Steinmetz, M. A. Gluck, & P. R. Solomon (Eds.), *Model systems and the neurobiology of associative learning: A festschrift in honor of Richard F. Thompson* (pp. 149–185). Mahwah, NJ: Erlbaum.

Gabrieli, J. D. E., Brewer, J. B., Glover, G. H., & Desmond, J. E. (1997). Separate neural bases of two fundamental memory processes in the human medial temporal lobe. *Science, 276,* 264–266.

Gaffan, E. A., Tsaousis, J., & Kemp-Wheeler, S. M. (1995). Researcher allegiance and meta-analysis: The case of cognitive therapy for depression. *Journal of Consulting and Clinical Psychology, 63,* 960–980.

Gaines, S. O., Jr., & Reed, E. S. (1995). Prejudice: From Allport to DuBois. *American Psychologist, 50,* 96–103.

Gainor, K. A. (2000). Including transgender issues in lesbian, gay, and bisexual psychology: Implications for clinical practice and training. In B. Greene & G. L. Croom (Eds.), *Education, research, and practice in lesbian, gay, bisexual, and transgendered psychology: A resource manual, 5* (pp. 131–160). Thousand Oaks, CA: Sage.

Galambos, N. L., & Tilton-Weaver, L. C. (2000). Adolescents' psychosocial maturity, problem behavior, and subjective age: In search of the adultoid. *Applied Developmental Science, 4*(4), 178–192.

Gallopin, T., Fort, P., Eggerman, E., Cauli, B., Luppi, P-H., Rossier, J., Audinat, E., Muhlethaler, M., & Serafin, M. (2000). Identification of sleep-promoting neurons in vitro. *Nature, 404,* 992–995.

Galotti, K. M., Clinchy, B. M., Ainsworth, K. H., Lavin, B., Annick, F., & Mansfield, A. F. (1999). A new way of assessing ways of knowing: The Attitudes Toward Thinking and Learning Survey (ATTLS). *Sex Roles, 40,* 745–766.

Gannon, P. J., Holloway, R. L., Broadfield, D. C., & Braun, A. R. (1998). Asymmetry of chimpanzee planum temporale: Humanlike pattern of Wernicke's brain language area homolog. *Science, 279,* 220–222.

Garb, H. N., Florio, C. M., & Grove, W. M. (1998). The validity of the Rorschach and the Minnesota Multiphasic Personality Inventory: Results from meta-analyses. *Psychological Science, 9,* 402–404.

Garcia, J., Gustavson, C. R., Kelly, D. J., & Sweeney, M. (1976). Prey-lithium aversions: I. Coyotes and wolves. *Behavioral Biology, 16,* 61–72.

Garcia, J., & Koelling, R. A. (1971). The use of ionizing rays as a mammalian olfactory stimulus. In H. Autrum, R. Jung, W. R. Loewenstein, D. M. MacKay, & H. L. Teuber (Eds.), *Handbook of sensory physiology: Vol. 4. Chemical senses (Pt. 1).* New York: Springer-Verlag.

Gardner, H. (1993). *Frames of mind: The theory of multiple intelligences.* New York: Basic Books. (Original worked published in 1983).

Gardner, H. (1995). Multiple intelligences as a catalyst. *English Journal, 84*(8), 16–18.

Gardner, H. (1998). A reply to Perry D. Kleins multiplying the problems of intelligence by eight. *Canadian Journal of Education, 23,* 96–102.

Gardner, H., & Hatch, T. (1989). Multiple intelligences go to school: Educational implications of the theory of multiple intelligences. *Educational Researcher, 18,* 6.

Gardner, R. A., & Gardner, B. T. (1969). Teaching sign language to a chimp. *Science, 165,* 664–672.

Gardner, W. L., & Avolio, B. J. (1998). The charismatic relationship: A dramaturgical perspective. *Academy of Management Review, 23,* 32–58.

Garry, M., & Loftus, E. F. (1994). Pseudomemories without hypnosis. *The International Journal of Clinical and Experimental Hypnosis, 42,* 363–378.

Gatchel, R. J., & Turk, D. C. (1999). Interdisciplinary treatment of chronic pain patients. In R. J. Gatchel & D. C. Turk (Eds.), *Psychosocial factors in pain: Critical perspectives* (pp. 435–444). New York: Guilford Press.

Gavin, J. (2000). Arousing suspicion and violating trust: The lived ideology of safe sex talk. *Culture, Health, and Sexuality, 2,* 117–134.

Gazzaniga, M. S. (2000). Right hemisphere language following brain bisection: A 20-year perspective. In M. S. Gazzaniga (Ed.), *Cognitive neuroscience* (pp. 411–430). Malden, MA: Blackwell Publishers.

Ge, X., Conger, R. D., Cadoret, R. J., Neiderhiser, J. M., Yates, W., Troughton, E., et al. (1996). The developmental interface between nature and nurture: A mutual influence model of child antisocial behavior and parent behaviors. *Developmental Psychology, 32,* 574–589.

Ge, X., Conger, R. D., & Elder, G. H. (1996). Coming of age too early: Pubertal influences on girls' vulnerability to psychological distress. *Child Development, 67,* 3386–3400.

Geary, D. C. (2000). Evolution and proximate expression of human paternal investment. *Psychological Bulletin, 126,* 55–77.

Geary, D. C. (1996). Biology, culture, and cross-national differences in mathematical ability. In R. J. Sternberg & T. Ben-Zeev, (Eds.), *The nature of mathematical thinking: The studies in mathematical thinking and learning series* (pp. 145–171). Mahwah, NJ: Erlbaum.

Geary, D. C. (1998). *Male, female: The evolution of human sex differences.* Washington, DC: American Psychological Association.

Geary, D. C., Liu, F., Chen, G., Saults, S. J., & Hoard, M. K. (1999). Contributions of computational fluency to cross-national differences in arithmetical reasoning abilities. *Journal of Educational Psychology, 91,* 716–719.

Geen, R. G. (1991). Social motivation. *Annual Review of Psychology, 42,* 377–399.

Geen, R. G. (1998). Aggression and antisocial behavior. In D. T. Gilbert, S. T. Fiske, & G. Lindzey (Eds.), *The handbook of social psychology* (4th ed., pp. 317–347). Boston: McGraw-Hill.

Geller, B., & Luby, J. (1997). Child and adolescent bipolar disorder: A review of the past 10 years. *Journal of the American Academy of Child and Adolescent Psychiatry, 36,* 1168–1176.

Geller, E. S. (1975). Increasing desired waste disposals with instructions. *Man–Environment Systems, 5,* 125–128.

Geller, E. S. (1989). Applied behavior analysis and social marketing: An integration for environmental preservation. *Journal of Social Issues, 45*(1), 17–36.

Geller, E. S. (1992). It takes more than information to save energy. *American Psychologist, 47,* 814–815.

Geller, E. S. (1995). Integrating behaviorism and humanism for environmental protection. *Journal of Social Issues, 51*(4), 179–195.

Geller, E. S. (2001a). *The psychology of safety handbook* (2nd ed.). Boca Raton, FL: CRC Press LLC.

Geller, E. S. (2001b). Sustaining participation in a safety improvement process: 10 relevant principles from behavioral science. *American Society of Safety Engineers,* 24–29.

Geller, E. S., Kalsher, M. J., Rudd, J. R., & Lehman, G. R. (1989). Promoting safety belt use on a university campus: An integration of commitment and incentive strategies. *Journal of Applied Social Psychology, 19,* 3–19.

Geller, E. S., Witmer, J. F., & Tuso, M. E. (1977). Environmental intervention for litter control. *Journal of Applied Psychology, 62,* 344–351.

Geller, E. S. (2001). The future of safety: From conversation to commitment. *Occupational Health & Safety, 1,* 58–63.

George, J. M., & Brief, A. P. (1992). Feeling good—doing good: A conceptual analysis of the mood at work—organizational spontaneity relationship. *Psychological Bulletin, 112,* 310–329.

German, T. P., & Defeyter, M. A. (2001). Immunity to functional fixedness in young children. *Psychonomic Bulletin & Review, 7,* 707–712.

Geschwind, N. (1972, April). Language and the brain. *Scientific American, 226*(4), 76–83.

Gherovici, P. (2000). Why do people take Prozac? Anxiety, symptom, and the inhibition of responsibility. In K. R. Malone & S. R. Friedlander (Eds.), *The subject of Lacan: A Lacanian reader for psychologists* (pp. 279–295). Albany: State University of New York Press.

Gift, T. E., Strauss, J. S., Ritzler, B. A., Kokes, R. F., & Harder, D. W. (1980). How diagnostic concepts of schizophrenia differ. *Journal of Nervous and Mental Disease, 168,* 3–8.

Gilbert, C. D., Das, A., Ito, M., Kapadia, M., & Westheimer, G. (2000). Spatial integration and cortical dynamics. In M. S. Gazzaniga (Ed.), *Cognitive neuroscience* (pp. 224–240). Malden, MA: Blackwell Publishers.

Gilford, P. (1999). The normalizing effects of managed care on psychotherapy. In K. Weisgerber (Ed.), *The traumatic bond between the psychotherapist and managed care* (pp. 199–216). Northvale, NJ: Aronson.

Gillies, R. M., & Ashman, A. F. (1996). Teaching collaborative skills to primary school children in classroom-based work groups. *Learning and Instruction, 6,* 187–200.

Gingerich, W. J., & Eisengart, S. (2000). Solution focused brief therapy: A review of the outcome research. *Family Process, 39,* 477–498.

Glaser, R., Rabin, B., Chesney, M., Cohen, S., & Natelson, B. (1999). Stress-induced immunomodulation: Implications for infectious diseases? *Journal of the American Medical Association, 281,* 2268–2270.

Glass, R. M. (2001). Electroconvulsive therapy: Time to bring it out of the shadows. *Journal of the American Medical Association, 285* (10), special issue.

Gleaves, D. H. (1996). The sociocognitive model of dissociative identity disorder: A reexamination of the evidence. *Psychological Bulletin, 120,* 42–59.

Glenmullen, J. (2001). *Prozac backlash: Overcoming the dangers of Prozac, Zoloft, Paxil, and other antidepressants with safe, effective alternatives.* New York: Touchstone Books/Simon & Schuster, Inc.

Glick, P., Diebold, J., Bailey-Wexner, B., & Zhu, L. (1997). The two faces of Adam: Ambivalent sexism and polarized attitudes toward women. *Personality and Social Psychology Bulletin, 23,* 1323–1334.

Glick, P., & Fiske, S. T. (1997). Hostile and benevolent sexism: Measuring ambivalent sexism toward women. *Psychology of Women Quarterly, 21,* 119–135.

Goehner, A. L., & Tyrangiel, J. (2001, August 13). A diva takes a dive: She strips on MTV! Has nervous breakdown! For Mariah Carey, it's what becomes a legend most. *Time, 158,* 56+.

Goldfried, M. R., & Wolfe, B. E. (1998). Toward a more clinically valid approach to therapy research. *Journal of Consulting and Clinical Psychology, 66,* 143–150.

Goldin-Meadow, S. (2000). Learning with and without a helping hand. In B. Landau, J. Sabini, J. Jonides, & E. L. Newport (Eds.), *Perception, cognition, and language: Essays in honor of Henry and Lila Gleitman* (pp. 121–137). Cambridge, MA: The MIT Press.

Goldin-Meadow, S., & Mylander, C. (1998). Spontaneous sign systems created by deaf children in two cultures. *Nature, 39,* 279–281.

Golding, J. (1999). Intimate partner violence as a risk factor for mental disorders: A meta-analysis. *Journal of Family Violence, 14,* 99–101.

Goldstein, A. P. (2001). Low-level aggression: New targets for zero tolerance. In J. N. Hughes, A. M. La Greca, & J. C. Conoley (Eds.), *Handbook of psychological services for children and adolescents* (pp. 161–181). New York: Oxford University Press.

Gonzales, L. R., Hays, R. B., Bond, M. A., & Kelly, J. G. (1983). Community mental health. In M. Hersen, A. E. Kazdin, & A. S. Bellack (Eds.), *The clinical psychology handbook.* New York: Pergamon Press.

Goodwin, S. A., & Fiske, S. T. (2001). Power and gender: The double-edged sword of ambivalence. In R. K. Unger (Ed.), *Handbook of the psychology of women and gender* (pp. 358–366). New York: Wiley.

Gordijn, E. H., Koomen, W., & Stapel, D. A. (2001). Level of prejudice in relation to knowledge of cultural stereotypes. *Journal of Experimental Social Psychology, 37,* 150–157.

Gostin, L. O. (1997). The legal regulation of smoking (and smokers): Public health or secular morality? In A. Brandt & P. Rozin (Eds.), *Morality and health* (pp. 331–357). New York: Routledge.

Gottesman, I. I. (1991). *Schizophrenia genesis: The origins of madness.* New York: Freeman.

Gottman, J. M. (1998). Psychology and the study of marital processes. *Annual Review of Psychology, 49,* 169–187.

Gould, S. J. (1996). *The mismeasure of man* (rev. ed.). New York: Norton.

Gould, S. J. (1997). Darwinian fundamentalism. *New York Review of Books,* 34–37.

Gould, S. J. (1997, January–February). Interview by Michael Krasny. *Mother Jones,* 60–63.

Graber, J. A., Britto, P. R., & Brooks-Gunn, J. (1999). What's love got to do with it? Adolescents' and young adults' beliefs about sexual and romantic relationships. In W. Furman, B. B. Brown, & C. Feiring (Eds.), *Self, social identity, and physical health: Interdisciplinary explorations. Rutgers Series on Self and Social Identity* (pp. 364–395). New York: Cambridge University Press.

Grachev, I. D., & Apkarian, A. V. (2000). Chemical mapping of anxiety in the brain of healthy humans: An in vivo–sup-1H-MRS study on the effects of sex, age, and brain region. *Human Brain Mapping, 11,* 261–272.

Graham, T., & Ickes, W. (1997). When women's intuition isn't greater than men's. In W. Ickes (Ed.), *Empathic accuracy* (pp. 117–143). New York: Guilford Press.

Graig, E. (1993). Stress as a consequence of the urban physical environment. In L. Goldberger & S. Breznitz (Eds.), *Handbook of stress: Theoretical and clinical aspects* (2nd ed., pp. 316–332). New York: Free Press.

Gray, R., & Regan, D. (2000). Risky driving behavior a consequence of motion adaptation for visually guided motor action. *Journal of Experimental Psychology: Human Perception and Performance, 26,* 1721–1732.

Graziano, M. S. A., & Gross, C. G. (1994). Mapping space with neurons. *Current Directions in Psychological Science, 3,* 164–167.

Graziano, M. S., Hu, X. T., & Gross, C. G. (1997). Coding the locations of objects in the dark. *Science, 277,* 239–240.

Greenberg, J. (1990). Employee theft as a reaction to underpayment inequity: The hidden cost of pay cuts. *Journal of Applied Psychology, 75,* 561–568.

Greenberg, R. P., Bornstein, R. F., Greenberg, M. D., Fisher, S., & Seymour, F. (1992). A meta-analysis of antidepressant outcome under "blinder" conditions. *Journal of Consulting and Clinical Psychology, 60,* 664–669.

Greene, K., & Rubin, D. L. (1991). Effects of gender inclusive/exclusive language in religious discourse. *Journal of Language and Social Psychology, 10,* 81–98.

Greenfield, P. M. (1997). You can't take it with you: Why ability assessments don't cross cultures. *American Psychologist, 52,* 1115–1124.

Greeno, C. G., & Wing, R. R. (1994). Stress-induced eating. *Psychological Bulletin, 115,* 444–464.

Greenough, W. T., Black, J. E., Klintsova, A., Bates, K. E., & Weiler, I. J. (1999). Experience and plasticity in brain structure: Possible implications of basic research findings for developmental disorders. In S. H. Broman & J. M. Fletcher (Eds.), *The changing nervous system: Neurobehavioral consequences of early brain disorders* (pp. 51–70). New York: Oxford University Press.

Greenwald, A. G., & Banaji, M. R. (1995). Implicit social cognition: Attitudes, self-esteem, and stereotypes. *Psychological Review, 102,* 1–27.

Greenwald, A. G., Banaji, M., Rudman, R., Laurie, A., Farmham, S. D., Nosek, B., & Mellott, D. S. (2002). A unified theory of implicit attitudes, stereotypes, self-esteem, and self-concept. *Psychological Review, 109,* 3–25.

Greenwald, A. G., Farnham, S. D. (2000). Using the Implicit Association Test to measure self-esteem and self-concept. *Journal of Personality and Social Psychology, 79,* 1022–1038.

Grilo, C. M. (2001). Pharmacological and psychological treatments of obesity and binge eating disorder. In M. T. Sammons & N. B. Schmidt (Eds.), *Combined treatment for mental disorders: A guide to psychological and pharmacological interventions* (pp. 239–269). Washington, DC: American Psychological Association.

Griffin, Z. M., & Bock, K. (2000). What the eyes say about speaking. *Psychological Science, 11,* 274–279.

Grigson, P. S. (2000). Drugs of abuse and reward comparison: A brief review. *Appetite, 35,* 89–91.

Groffman, S. (2000). Seeing a sound, hearing a sight. *Journal of Optometric Vision Development, 30,* 177–180.

Grohol, J. M. (1995). Why managed care hurts you. *PsychCentral.* Retrieved from the World Wide Web: www.apa.org.

Gross, J. J. (1999). Emotion and emotional regulation. In L. A. Pervin & O. P. John (Eds.), *Handbook of personality: Theory and research* (pp. 525–552). New York: Guilford Press.

Gross, J. J., Fredrickson, B. L., & Levenson, R. W. (1994). The psychophysiology of crying. *Psychophysiology, 31,* 460–463.

Grossman, D. (2000). Teaching kids to kill. In R. S. Moser & C. E. Frantz (Eds.), *Shocking violence: Youth perpetrators and victims—A multidisciplinary perspective* (pp. 17–32). Springfield, IL: Thomas.

Grusec, J. F., Goodnow, J. J., & Kuczynski, L. (2000). New directions in analyses of parenting contributions to children's acquisition of values. *Child Development, 71,* 205–211.

Guarnaccia, P. J. (1997). Social stress and psychological distress among Latinos in the United States. In I. Al-Ihsan & M. Tousignant (Eds.), *Ethnicity, immigration, and psychopathology. The Plenum Series on stress and coping* (pp. 71–94). New York: Plenum Press.

Guerin, P. J., Jr., & Chabot, D. R. (1997). Development of family systems theory. In P. L. Wachtel & S. B. Messer (Eds.), *Theories of psychotherapy: Origins and evolution* (pp. 181–226). Washington, DC: American Psychological Association.

Guilford, J. P. (1967). *The nature of human intelligence.* New York: McGraw-Hill.

Guimon, J., Goerg, D., Zbinden, E., & Fischer, W. (2001). Combining pharmacotherapy and psychotherapy: A Swiss survey. *European Journal of Psychiatry, 15,* 13–21.

Gulevich, G., Dement, W., & Johnson, L. (1966). Psychiatric and EEG observations on a case of prolonged (264 hours) wakefulness. *Archives of General Psychiatry, 15,* 29–35.

Gustafsson, L., & Jacobsson, L. (2000). On mental disorder and somatic disease in suicide: A psychological autopsy study of 100 suicides in northern Sweden. *Nordic Journal of Psychiatry, 54,* 383–395.

Haaga, D. A. F., & Davison, G. C. (1993). An appraisal of rational–emotive therapy. *Journal of Consulting and Clinical Psychology, 61,* 215–220.

Hacking, I. (1997). *Rewriting the soul: Multiple personality and the sciences of memory.* Princeton, NJ: Princeton University Press.

Hackmann, A., Clark, D. M., & McManus, F. (2000). Recurrent images and early memories in social phobia. *Behaviour Research and Therapy, 38,* 601–610.

Hall, E. T. (1966). *The hidden dimension.* Garden City, NY: Doubleday.

Hall, R. E. (2001). The bell curve: Calculated racism and the stereotype of African American men. *Journal of Black Studies, 32,* 104–119.

Halpern, D. (1997). Sex differences in intelligence: Implications for education. *American Psychologist, 52,* 1091–1102.

Halpern, D. F., & Coren, S. (1991). Handedness and life span [Letter to the editor]. *New England Journal of Medicine, 324,* 998.

Hambrick, D. Z., Salthouse, T. A., & Meinz, E. J. (1999). Predictors of crossword puzzle proficiency and moderators of age-cognition relations. *Journal of Experimental Psychology: General, 128,* 131–164.

Hamer, D. H., Hu, S., Magnuson, V. L., Hu, N., & Pattatucci, A. M. L. (1993). A linkage between DNA markers on the X chromosome and male sexual orientation. *Science, 261,* 321–327.

Haney, C., Banks, W., & Zimbardo, P. (1973). Interpersonal dynamics in a simulated prison. *International Journal of Criminology and Penology, 1,* 69–97.

Hankin, C. S., Spiro, A., III, Miller, D. R., & Kazis, L. (1999). Mental disorders and mental health treatment among U.S. Department of Veterans Affairs outpatients: The Veterans Health Study. *American Journal of Psychiatry, 156,* 1924–1930.

Harmer, C. J., Thilo, K. V., Rothwell, J. C., & Goodwin, G. M. (2001). Transcranial magnetic stimulation of medial–frontal cortex impairs the processing of angry facial expressions. *Nature Neuroscience, 4,* 17–18.

Harper, J. M., Schaalje, B. G., & Sandberg, J. G. (2000). Daily hassles, intimacy, and marital quality in later life marriages. *American Journal of Family Therapy, 28,* 1–17.

Harris, C. R., & Christenfeld, N. (1997). Humor, tickle, and the Darwin–Hecker hypothesis. *Cognition and Emotion, 11,* 103–110.

Harris, J. R. (1998). *The nurture assumption: Why children turn out the way they do.* New York: Free Press.

Harris, M. B., & Knight-Bohnhoff, K. (1996). Gender and aggression: Personal aggressiveness. *Sex Roles, 35,* 27–42.

Harris, M. M., Gilbreath, B., & Sunday, J. A. (1998). A longitudinal examination of a merit pay system: Relationships among performance ratings, merit increases, and total pay increases. *Journal of Applied Psychology, 83,* 825–831.

Harrison, J. R., & Barabasz, A. F. (1991). Effects of restricted environmental stimulation therapy on the behavior of children with autism. *Child Study Journal, 21,* 153–166.

Hartmann, E. (1995). Making connections in a safe place: Is dreaming psychotherapy? *Dreaming, 5,* 213–228.

Hartmann, E. (1996). Outline for a theory on the nature and functions of dreaming. *Dreaming, 6,* 147–170.

Hartung, C. M., & Widiger, T. A. (1998). Gender differences in the diagnosis of mental disorders: Conclusions and controversies of the *DSM-IV. Psychological Bulletin, 123,* 260–278.

Hartup, W. W., & Stevens, N. (1997). Friendships and adaptation in the life course. *Psychological Bulletin, 121,* 355–370.

Harvey, M. (2000, July). Sleepless in America: A lack of rest reaches epidemic proportions. *American Demographics, 22,* 9–10.

Harvey, M. L., Loomis, R. J., Bell, P. A., & Marino, M. (1998). The influence of museum exhibit design on immersion and psychological flow. *Environment and Behavior, 30,* 601–627.

Haslam, N. (1997). Evidence that male sexual orientation is a matter of degree. *Journal of Personality and Social Psychology, 73,* 862–870.

Hatfield, E., & Rapson, R. L. (1993). *Love, sex, and intimacy: Their psychology, biology, and history.* New York: HarperCollins.

Haveman, R. B., Wolf, K., Wilson, & Peterson, E. (1997). *Do teens make rational choices? The case of teen nonmarital childbearing.* Discussion Paper 1137–97. Institute for Research on Poverty, University of Wisconsin, Madison.

Hayes, J. A., & Mitchell, J. C. (1994). Mental health professionals' skepticism about multiple personality disorder. *Professional Psychology: Research and Practice, 25,* 410–425.

Hayflick, L. (1996). *How and why we age.* New York: Ballantine Books, Inc.

Healy, A. F., & McNamara, D. S. (1996). Verbal learning and memory: Does the modal model still work? *Annual Review of Psychology, 47,* 143–172.

Hebb, D. O. (1949). *Organization of behavior.* New York: Wiley.

Hebb, D. O. (1955). Drives and the C. N. S. (conceptual nervous system). *Psychological Review, 62,* 243–254.

Hebb, D. O. (1972). *Textbook of psychology* (3rd ed.). Philadelphia: Saunders.

Hedges, L. V., & Nowell, A. (1995). Sex differences in mental test scores, variability, and numbers of high-scoring individuals. *Science, 269,* 41–45.

Heeger, D. J. (1999). Linking visual perception with human brain activity. *Current Opinion in Neurobiology, 9,* 474–479.

Heinlein, R. (1961). *Stranger in a strange land.* New York: Putnam.

Heise, L., Ellsberg, M., & Gottemoeller, M. (1999). Ending violence against women. *Population Reports,* Series L, No. 11, Baltimore, MD: Johns Hopkins University School of Public Health, Population Information Program.

Hellriegel, D., & Slocum, J. (1992). *Management* (6th ed.). Reading, MA: Addison-Wesley.

Hellstedt, J. C. (1995). Invisible players: A family systems model. In S. M. Murphy (Ed.), *Sport psychology interventions* (pp. 117–146). Champaign, IL: Human Kinetics.

Helweg-Larsen, M., & Collins, B. E. (1997). A social psychological perspective on the role of knowledge about AIDS in AIDS prevention. *Current Directions in Psychological Science, 6,* 23–26.

Hemphill, S. A., & Littlefield, L. (2001). Evaluation of a short-term group therapy program for children with behavior problems and their parents. *Behavior Research & Therapy, 39*(7), 823–841.

Hendrick, C., & Hendrick, S. S. (1986). A theory and method of love. *Journal of Personality and Social Psychology, 50,* 392–402.

Hendryx, M. S., & Ahern, M. M. (1997). Mental health functioning and community problems. *Journal of Community Psychology, 25,* 147–157.

Henry, D., Guerra, N., Huesmann, R., Tolan, P., VanAcker, R., & Eron, L. (2000). Normative influences on aggression in urban elementary school classrooms. *American Journal of Community Psychology, 28,* 59–81.

Herbert, T. B., Cohen, S., Marsland, A. L., Bachen, E. A., et al. (1994). Cardiovascular reactivity and the course of immune response to an acute psychological stressor. *Psychosomatic Medicine, 56,* 337–344.

Hermann, D. J., Crawford, M., & Holdsworth, M. (1992). Gender-linked differences in everyday memory performance. *British Journal of Psychology, 83,* 221–231.

Herz, R. S., & Engen, T. (1996). Odor memory: Review and analysis. *Psychonomic Bulletin & Review, 3,* 300–313.

Hester, C. (1996). The relationship of personality, gender, and age to Adjective Check List profiles of the ideal romantic partner. *Journal of Psychological Type, 36,* 28–35.

Hetherington, E. M., & Kelly, J. (2002). For better or for worse. In E. M. Hetherington & J. Kelly (Eds). *Divorce reconsidered* (pp. 1–293). New York: W.W. Norton & Company.

Hicks, R. A., Johnson, C., Cuevas, T., Deharo, D., & Baustista, J. (1994). Do right-handers live longer? An updated assessment of baseball player data. *Perceptual and Motor Skills, 78,* 1243–1247.

Higgins, N. C., & Bhatt, G. (2000). Culture moderates the self-serving bias: Etic and emic features of casual attributions in India and in Canada. *Social Behavior and Personality, 29,* 49–61.

Higgins, R. L., & Snyder, C. R. (1990). Self-handicapping from a Heiderian perspective: Taking stock of "bonds." In R. L. Higgins (Ed.), *Self-handicapping: The paradox that isn't. The Plenum Series in social/clinical psychology* (pp. 239–273). New York: Plenum.

Hilgard, E. R. (1965). *Hypnotic susceptibility.* New York: Harcourt, Brace & World.

Hilgard, E. R. (1994). Neodissociation theory. In S. J. Lynn & J. W. Rhue (Eds.), *Dissociation: Clinical and theoretical perspectives* (pp. 32–51). New York: Guilford Press.

Hill, J. O., & Peters, J. C. (1998). Environmental contributions to the obesity epidemic. *Science, 280,* 1371–1374.

Hilsman, R., & Garber, J. (1995). A test of the cognitive diathesis–stress model of depression in children: Academic stressors, attributional style, perceived competence, and control. *Journal of Personality and Social Psychology, 69,* 370–380.

Hindmarch, I. (2001). Expanding the horizons of depression: Beyond the monoamine hypothesis. *Human Psychopharmacology: Clinical and Experimental, 16,* 203–218.

Hines, D. (1997). Arguments for prescription privileges for psychologists. *American Psychologist, 52,* 270–271.

Hinsz, V. B., Matz, D. C., & Patience, R. A. (2001). Does women's hair signal reproductive potential? *Journal of Experimental Social Psychology, 37,* 166–172.

Hinton, P. R. (2000). *Stereotypes, cognition, and culture.* Philadelphia: Psychology Press/Taylor and Francis.

Hiramoto, R. N., Rogers, C. F., Demissie, S., Hseuh, C., Hiramoto, N. S., Lorden, J. F., & Ghanta, V. K. (1997). Psychoneuroendocrine immunology: Site of recognition, learning, and memory in the immune system and the brain. *International Journal of Neuroscience, 92,* 259–286.

Hirsch, H. V. B., & Spinelli, D. N. (1971). Modification of the distribution of receptive field orientation in cats by selective exposure during development. *Experimental Brain Research, 13,* 509–527.

Hirschfeld, R. M. A., Keller, M. B., Panico, S., Arons, B. S., Barlow, D., Davidoff, F., Endicott, J., Froom, J., Goldstein, M., Gorman, J. M., Guthrie, D., Marek, R. G., Maurer, T. A., Meyer, R., Phillips, K., Ross, J., Schwenk, T. L., Sharfstein, S. S., Thase, M. E., & Wyatt, R. J. (1997). The National Depressive and Manic Depressive Association consensus statement on the undertreatment of depression. *Journal of the American Medical Association, 277,* 333–340.

Hobfoll, S. E., & Shirom, A. (2001). Conservation of resources theory: Application to stress and management in the workplace. In R. T. Golembiewski (Ed.), *Handbook of organizational behavior* (2nd ed., pp. 57–80). New York: Marcel Dekker.

Hobson, J. A. (1989). *Sleep.* New York: Freeman.

Hobson, J. A. (1999). *Consciousness.* New York: Freeman.

Hochschild, A. (1997). *The time bind.* New York: Metropolitan Books.

Hodges, J. R. (2000). Memory in the dementias. In E. Tulving & F. I. M. Craik (Eds.), *The Oxford handbook of memory* (pp. 441–459). New York: Oxford University Press.

Hoffmann, A. A., & Hercus, M. J. (2000). Environmental stress as an evolutionary force. *BioScience, 50,* 217–226.

Hofstede, G. (1983). National cultures revisited. *Behavior Science Research, 18,* 285–305.

Hogan, R., Curphy, G. J., & Hogan, J. (1994). What we know about leadership: Effectiveness and personality. *American Psychologist, 49,* 493–504.

Hogan, R., Hogan, J., & Roberts, B. W. (1996). Personality measurement and employment decisions. *American Psychologist, 51,* 469–477.

Holden, C. (2000, April 7). Global survey examines impact of depression. *Science, 288,* 39–40.

Holland, J. C. (1999). Use of alternative medicine—a marker for distress? *New England Journal of Medicine, 340,* 1758–1759.

Hollis, K. L. (1997). Contemporary research on Pavlovian conditioning: A "new" functional analysis. *American Psychologist, 52,* 956–965.

Holloway, F. A. (1977). State-dependent retrieval based on time of day. In B. Ho, D. Chute, & D. Richards (Eds.), *Drug discrimination and state-dependent learning.* New York: Academic Press.

Holmes, T. H., & Rahe, R. H. (1967). The Social Readjustment Rating Scale. *Journal of Psychosomatic Research, 11,* 213–218.

Hong, Y., Morris, M., Chiu, C., & Benet-Martinez, V. (2000). Multicultural minds: A dynamic constructivist approach to culture and cognition. *American Psychologist, 55,* 709–720.

Honts, C. R. (1994). Psychophysiological detection of deception. *Current Directions in Psychological Science, 3,* 77–82.

Hooley, J. M., & Candela, S. F. (1999). Interpersonal functioning in schizophrenia. In T. Millon, P. H. Blaney, & R. D. Davis (Eds.), *Oxford textbook of psychopathology* (pp. 311–338). New York: Oxford University Press.

Horn, J. L. (2001). Selections of evidence, misleading assumptions, and oversimplifications: The political message of *The Bell Curve.* In J. M. Fish (Ed.), *Race and intelligence: Separating science from myth* (pp. 297–325). Mahwah, NJ: Erlbaum.

Horney, K. (1937). *The neurotic personality of our time.* New York: Norton.

Hornstein, G. A. (1992). The return of the repressed. *American Psychologist, 47,* 254–263.

Horwitz, S. M., Leaf, P. J., Leventhal, J. M., Forsyth, B., & Speechley, K. N. (1992). Identification and management of psychosocial and developmental problems in community-based primary care pediatric practices. *Pediatrics, 89,* 480–485.

Hout, M. (2002). Test scores, education, and poverty. In J. M. Fish (Ed.), *Race and intelligence: Separating science from myth* (pp. 329–354). Mahwah, NJ: Erlbaum.

Howes, C., & Tonyan, H. (1999). Peer relations. In L. Balter & C. S. Tamis-LeMonda (Eds.), *Child psychology: A handbook of contemporary issues* (pp. 143–157). Philadelphia: Psychology Press/Taylor & Francis.

Hrdy, S. B. (1981). *The woman that never evolved.* Cambridge, MA: Harvard University Press.

Hubel, D. H., & Wiesel, T. N. (1962). Receptive fields, binocular interaction, and functional architecture in the cat's visual cortex. *Journal of Physiology, 160,* 106–164.

Hubel, D. H., & Wiesel, T. N. (2000). Receptive fields and functional architecture of monkey straite cortex. In S. Yantis (Eds.), *Visual perception: Essential readings, key readings in cognition* (pp. 147–167). Philadelphia: Psychology Press/Taylor & Francis.

Hudak, M. A. (1993). Gender schema theory revisited: Men's stereotypes of American women. *Sex Roles, 28,* 279–293.

Hudspeth, A. J. (1983, January). The hair cells of the inner ear. *Scientific American,* 54–73.

Huff, D. J. (1997). *To live heroically: Institutional racism and American Indian education.* New York: State University of New York.

Huffcutt, A. I., & Roth, P. L. (1998). Racial group differences in employment interview evaluations. *Journal of Applied Psychology, 83,* 179–189.

Hultsch, D. F., Hertzog, C., Small, B. J., & Dixon, R. A. (1999). Use it or lose it: Engaged lifestyle as a buffer of cognitive decline in aging? *Psychology and Aging, 14,* 245–263.

Humara, M. (1999). The relationship between anxiety and performance: A cognitive–behavioral perspective. *Athletic Insight: Online Journal of Sport Psychology, 1*(2). Retrieved from the World Wide Web, www.athleticinsight.com/vol1lss2/cognitive_Behavioral_Anxiety.htm.

Hunt, M. (1974). *Sexual behavior in the 1970s.* New York: Dell.

Hurvich, L., & Jameson, D. (1974). Opponent processes as a model of neural organization. *American Psychologist, 30,* 88–102.

Hyde, J. S. (1996). Gender and cognition: A commentary on current research. *Learning & Individual Differences, 8,* 33–38.

Iacono, W. G., & Lykken, D. T. (1997). The validity of the lie detector: Two surveys of scientific opinion. *Journal of Applied Psychology, 82,* 426–433.

Idehen, E. E. (1997). The influence of gender and space sharing history on the conceptions of privacy by undergraduates. *Ife Psychologia: An International Journal, 5,* 59–75.

Ilgen, D. R. (1999). Teams embedded in organizations: Some implications. *American Psychologist, 54,* 129–139.

Impey, S. (1999). The role of CREB-dependent gene expression in neuronal plasticity and memory formation. *Dissertation Abstracts International: Section B: The Sciences & Engineering, 60*(1-B), 0081.

Ingledew, D. K., Hardy, L., & Cooper, C. L. (1997). Do resources bolster coping and does coping buffer stress? An organizational study with longitudinal aspect and control for negative affectivity. *Journal of Occupational Health Psychology, 2,* 118–133.

Ingram, R. E., Scott, W., & Siegle, G. (1999). Depression: Social and cognitive aspects. In T. Millon, P. H. Blaney, & R. D. Davis (Eds.), *Oxford textbook of psychopathology* (pp. 203–226). New York: Oxford University Press.

Inhelder, B., & Piaget, J. (1958). *The growth of logical thinking from childhood to adolescence.* New York: Basic Books.

Inhoff, A. W., Starr, M., & Shindler, K. L. (2000). Is the processing of words during eye fixations in reading strictly serial? *Perception & Psychophysics, 62,* 1474–1484.

Innes, J. M., & Young, R. F. (1975). The effect of presence of an audience, evaluation apprehension, and objective self-awareness on learning. *Journal of Experimental Social Psychology, 11,* 35–42.

Inzlicht, M., & Ben-Zeev, T. (2000). A threatening intellectual environment: Why females are susceptible to experiencing problem-solving deficits in the presence of males. *Psychological Science, 11,* 365–371.

Ionescu, M. D. (2000). Sex differences in memory estimates for pictures and words. *Psychological Reports, 87,* 315–322.

Iribarren, C., Sidney, S., Bild, D., Liu, K., Markovitz, J., Rosenman, J., & Matthews, K. (2000). Association of hostility with coronary artery calcification in young adults: The CARDIA Study (Coronary Artery Risk Development in Young Adults). *Journal of the American Medical Association, 283,* 2546–2551.

Ito, T. A., Larsen, J. T., Smith, N. K., & Cacioppo, J. T. (1998). Negative information weighs more heavily on the brain: The negativity bias in evaluative categorizations. *Journal of Personality and Social Psychology, 75,* 887–900.

Ito, T. A., Miller, N., & Pollock, V. E. (1996). Alcohol and aggression: A meta-analysis on the moderation effects of inhibitory cues, triggering events, and self-focused attention. *Psychological Bulletin, 120,* 60–82.

Izard, C. E. (1990). Facial expressions and the regulation of emotions. *Journal of Personality and Social Psychology, 58,* 487–498.

Izard, C. E. (1997). Emotions and facial expressions: A perspective from differential emotions theory. In J. A. Russell & J. M. Fernandez-Dols (Eds.), *The psychology of facial expression. Studies in emotion and social interaction, 2nd series* (pp. 57–77). New York: Cambridge University Press.

Izquierdo, I., & Medina, J. H. (1997). The biochemistry of memory formation and its regulation by hormones and neuromodulators. *Psychobiology, 25,* 1–9.

Jackson, J. M., & Latané, B. (1981). All alone in front of all those people: Stage fright as a function of number and type of co-performers and audience. *Journal of Personality and Social Psychology, 40,* 73–85.

Jackson, S. E., & Schuler, R. S. (1990). Human resource planning: Challenges for industrial/organizational psychologists. *American Psychologist, 45,* 223–239.

Jackson, S. E., & Schuler, R. S. (1995). Understanding human resource management in the context of organizations and their environments. *Annual Review of Psychology, 46,* 237–264.

Jackson, S. R. (2000). Perception, awareness, and action: Insights from blindsight. In Y. Rossetti & A. Revonsuo (Eds.), *Beyond dissociation: Interaction between dissociated implicit and explicit processing: Advances in consciousness research* (pp. 73–98). Amsterdam: John Benjamins Publishing Company.

Jacob, S., & McClintlock, M. K. (2000). Psychological state and mood effects of steroidal chemosignals in women and men. *Hormones & Behavior, 37,* 57–78.

Jacobsen, P. B., Bovbjerg, D. H., Schwartz, M. D., Andrykowski, M. A., Futterman, A. D., Gilewski, T., Norton, L., & Read, W. H. (1993). Formation of food aversions in cancer patients receiving repeated infusions of chemotherapy. *Behavior Research & Therapy, 31,* 739–748.

Jacobson, N. S., Christensen, A., Prince, S. E., Cordova, J., & Eldridge, K. (2000). Integrative behavioral couple therapy: An acceptance-based, promising new treatment for couple discord. *Journal of Consulting & Clinical Psychology, 68,* 351–355.

Jaffee, S., & Hyde, J. S. (2000). Gender differences in moral orientation: A meta-analysis. *Psychological Bulletin, 126,* 703–726.

James, W. (1884). What is an emotion? *Mind, 9,* 188–205.

James, W. (1890). *Principles of psychology.* New York: Dover.

Jamison, K. R. (1993). *Touched with fire: Manic-depressive illness and the artistic temperament.* New York: Simon & Schuster.

Jamison, K. R. (1996). Mood disorders, creativity, and the artistic temperament. In J. J. Schildkraut & A. Otero. *Depression and the spiritual in modern art: Homage to Miró* (pp. 15–32). Oxford, UK: Wiley.

Janik, V. M. (2000). Whistle matching in wild bottlenose dolphins. *Science, 289,* 1355–1357.

Janis, I. L. (1983). *Groupthink* (2nd ed.). Boston: Houghton Mifflin.

Janssen, T., & Carton, J. S. (1999). The effects of locus of control and task difficulty on procrastination. *Journal of Genetic Psychology, 160,* 436–442.

Jazwinski, S. M. (1996). Longevity, genes, and aging. *Science, 273,* 54–59.

Jeanneret, R. P. (1992). Applications of job component/synthetic validity to construct validity. *Human Performance, 5,* 81–96.

Jeffery, R. W., Epstein, L. H., Wilson, G. T., Drewnowski, A., Stunkard, A. J., & Wing, R. R. (2000). Long-term maintenance of weight loss: Current status. *Health Psychology, 19,* 5–16.

Jenkins, G. D., Jr., Mitra, A., Gupta, N., & Shaw, J. D. (1998). Are financial incentives related to performance? A meta-analytic review of empirical research. *Journal of Applied Psychology, 83,* 777–787.

Jensen, A. R. (1969). How much can we boost IQ and scholastic achievement? *Harvard Educational Review, 39,* 1–123.

Jensen, A. R. (1970). Can we and should we study race differences? In J. Hellmuth (Ed.), *Disadvantaged child* (Vol. 3). New York: Brunner/ Mazel.

Jensen, A. R. (1987). Psychometric g as a focus on concerted research effort. *Intelligence, 11,* 193–198.

Job, R. F. S., & Barnes, B. W. (1995). Stress and consumption: Inescapable shock, neophobia, and quinine finickiness in rats. *Behavioral Neuroscience, 109,* 106–116.

Johnsen, K., Espenes, G. A., & Gillard, S. (1998). The associations between Type A/B behavioural dimension and Type 2/4 personality patterns. *Personality and Individual Differences, 25,* 937–945.

Johnson, B. T., & Eagly, A. H. (1989). Effects of involvement on persuasion: A meta-analysis. *Psychological Bulletin, 106,* 290–314.

Johnson, E. K., & Jusczyk, P. W. (2001). Word segmentation by 8-month olds: When speech cues count more than statistics. *Journal of Memory and Language, 44,* 548–567.

Johnson, J. G., Cohen, P., Smailes, E. M., Kasen, S., & Brook, J. S. (2002). Television viewing and aggressive behavior during adolescence and adulthood. *SCIENCE Magazine, 295,* 2468–2471.

Johnson, L. C., Slye, E. S., & Dement, W. (1965). Electroencephalographic and autonomic activity during and after prolonged sleep deprivation. *Psychosomatic Medicine, 27,* 415–423.

Johnson, S. H. (1998). Cerebral organization of motor imagery: Contralateral control of grip selection in mentally represented prehension. *Psychological Science, 9,* 219–222.

Johnson, S., & Lebow, J. (2000). The "coming of age" of couple therapy: A decade review. *Journal of Marital & Family Therapy, 26,* 23–38.

Jonas, E., Schulz-Hardt, S., Frey, D., & Thelen, N. (2001). Confirmation bias in sequential information search after preliminary decisions: An expansion of dissonance theoretical research on selective exposure to information. *Journal of Personality and Social Psychology, 80,* 557–571.

Jones, C. J., & Meredith, W. (2000). Developmental paths of psychological health from early adolescence to later adulthood. *Psychology and Aging, 15,* 351–360.

Jones, T. A., Klintsova, A. Y., Kilman, V. L., Sirevaag, A. M., & Greenough, W. T. (1997). Induction of multiple synapses by experience in the visual cortex of adult rats. *Neurobiology of Learning & Memory, 68,* 13–20.

Jonides, J., Schumacher, E. H., Smith, E. E., & Lauber, E. J. (1997). Verbal working memory load affects regional brain activation as measured by PET. *Journal of Cognitive Neuroscience, 9,* 462–475.

Jouvet, M. (1999). *The paradox of sleep: The story of dreaming* (L. Garey, Trans.). Cambridge, MA: The MIT Press.

Judge, T. A., Locke, E. A., Durham, C. C., & Kluger, A. N. (1998). Dispositional effects on job and life satisfaction: The role of core evaluations. *Journal of Applied Psychology, 83,* 17–34.

Jussim, L., Nelson, T. E., Manis, M., & Soffin, S. (1995). Prejudice, stereotypes, and labeling effects: Sources of bias in person perception. *Journal of Personality and Social Psychology, 68,* 228–246.

Kaas, J. H. (2000). The reorganization of sensory and motor maps after injury in adult mammals. In M. S. Gazzaniga (Ed.), *The new cognitive neurosciences* (pp. 223–236). Cambridge, MA: The MIT Press.

Kagan, B. L., Leskin, G., Haas, B., Wilkins, J., & Foy, D. (1999). Elevated lipid levels in Vietnam veterans with chronic posttraumatic stress disorders. *Biological Psychiatry, 45,* 374–377.

Kagan, J. (1998). *Three seductive ideas.* Cambridge, MA: Harvard University Press.

Kahana, B., Deimling, G., & Bowman, K. (2000, October 15). Post traumatic stress reactions among elderly long-term cancer survivors. *The Gerontologist,* p. 354.

Kail, R., & Hall, L. K. (2001). Distinguishing short-term memory from working memory. *Memory and Cognition, 29,* 1–9.

Kalick, S. M., Zebrowitz, L. A., Langlois, J. H., & Johnson, R. M. (1998). Does human facial attractiveness honestly advertise health? Longitudinal data on an evolutionary question. *Psychological Science, 9,* 8–13.

Kandel, E., & Abel, T. (1995). Neuropeptides, adenyl cyclase, and memory storage. *Science, 268,* 825–826.

Kanner, A. D., Coyne, J. C., Schaefer, C., & Lazarus, R. S. (1981). Comparison of two modes of stress measurement: Daily hassles and uplifts versus major life events. *Journal of Behavioral Medicine, 4,* 1–39.

Kaplan, D. W., Feinstein, R. A., Fisher, M. M., Klein, J. D., Olmedo, L. F., Rome, E. S., & Yancy, W. S. (2001). Condom use by adolescents. *Pediatrics, 107,* 1463–1469.

Karabenick, S. A., & Collins, E. J. (1997). Relation of perceived instructional goals and incentives to college students' use of learning strategies. *Journal of Experimental Education, 65,* 331–341.

Karasek, R. A. (1979). Job demands, job decision latitude, and mental strain: Implications for job redesign. *Administrative Science Quarterly, 24,* 285–308.

Karau, S. J., & Williams, K. D. (2000). Understanding individual motivation in groups: The collective effort model. In M. E. Turner (Ed.), *Groups at work: Theory and research. Applied social research* (pp. 113–141). Mahwah, NJ: Erlbaum.

Karweit, N., & Slavin, R. E. (1981). Measurement and modeling choices in studies of time and learning. *American Educational Research Journal, 18,* 157–171.

Kastner, S., De Eerd, P., Desimone, R., & Ungerleider, L. G. (1998). Mechanisms of directed attention in the human extrastriate cortex as revealed by functional MRI. *Science, 282,* 108–111.

Katsuki, Y. (1961). Neutral mechanisms of auditory sensation in cats. In W. A. Rosenblith (Ed.), *Sensory communication.* Cambridge, MA: The MIT Press.

Katz, J., & Beach, S. R. H. (2000). Looking for love? Self-verification and self-enhancement effects on initial romantic attraction. *Society for Personality and Social Psychology, 26,* 1526–1539.

Kaufman, A. S. (1983). Some questions and answers about the Kaufman Assessment Battery for Children (K–ABC). *Journal of Psychoeducational Assessment, 1,* 205–218.

Kaya, N., & Erkip, F. (2001). Satisfaction in a dormitory building: The effects of floor height on the perception of room size and crowding. *Environment and Behavior, 1,* 35–53.

Kazdin, A. E. (2000). *Psychotherapy for children and adolescents: Directions for research and practice.* New York: Oxford University Press.

Kazdin, A. E. (2001). Bridging the enormous gaps of theory with therapy research and practice. *Journal of Clinical Child Psychology, 30,* 59–66.

Keane, T. M. (1998). Psychological effects of military combat. In B. P. Dohrenwend (Ed.), *Adversity, stress, and psychopathology* (pp. 52–65). New York: Oxford University Press.

Keefe, F. J., & France, C. R. (1999). Pain: Biopsychosocial mechanisms and management. *Current Directions in Psychological Science, 8,* 137–140.

Keefe, K., & Berndt, T. J. (1996). Relations of friendship quality to self-esteem in early adolescence. *Journal of Early Adolescence, 16,* 110–129.

Kelley, H. H. (1972). Attribution in social interaction. In E. E. Jones et al. (Eds.), *Attribution: Perceiving the causes of behavior.* Morristown, NJ: General Learning Press.

Kelley, H. H. (1973). Process of causal attribution. *American Psychologist, 28,* 107–128.

Keltner, D., & Ekman, P. (2000). Facial expressions and emotion. In M. Lewis & J. M. Haviland-Jones (Eds.), *Handbook of emotions* (2nd ed., pp. 236–249). New York: Guilford Press.

Kempermann, G., & Gage, F. H. (1999). Experience-dependent regulation of adult hippocampal neurogenesis: Effects of long-term stimulation and stimulus withdrawal. *Hippocampus, 9,* 321–332.

Kemppainen, J. K., Levine, R. E., Mistal, M., & Schmidgall, D. (2001). HAART adherence in culturally diverse patients with HIV/AIDS: A study of male patients from a Veterans Administration hospital in Northern California. *AIDS Patient Care and STD's, 15,* 117–127.

Kendall, P. C., Krain, A., & Treadwell, K. R. H. (1999). Generalized anxiety disorder. In R. T. Ammerman, M. Hersen, & C. J. Last (Eds.), *Handbook of prescriptive treatments for children and adolescents* (2nd ed., pp. 155–171). Boston: Allyn and Bacon.

Kendler, K. S., Neale, M., Kessler, R., Heath, A., & Eaves, L. (1992). A population-based twin study of major depression in women. *Archives of General Psychiatry, 49,* 257–266.

Kendler, K. S., Neale, M., Kessler, R., Heath, A., & Eaves, L. (1993). A twin study of recent life events and difficulties. *Archives of General Psychiatry, 50,* 789–796.

Kennedy, M. B. (2000, October 27). Signal-processing machines at the postsynaptic density. *Science, 290,* 750–754.

Kerns, K. A. (1998). Individual differences in friendship quality: Links to child-mother attachment. In W. M. Bukowski, A. F. Newcomb, & W. W. Hartup (Eds.), *The company they keep: Friendship in childhood and adolescence* (pp. 137–157). New York: Cambridge University Press.

Kessler, R. C. (2000). Psychiatric epidemiology: Selected recent advances and future directions. *Bulletin of the World Health Organization, 78,* 464–474.

Kessler, R. C., McGonagle, K. A., Zhao, S., Nelson, C. B., Hughes, M., Eshleman, S., Wittchen, H-U., & Kendler, K. S. (1994). Lifetime and 12-month prevalence of *DSM-III-R* psychiatric disorders in the United States. *Archives of General Psychiatry, 51,* 8–19.

Kessler, R. C., Mickelson, K. D., & Williams, D. R. (1999). The prevalence, distribution, and mental health correlates of perceived discrimination in the United States. *Journal of Health and Social Behavior, 40,* 208–230.

Kessler, R. C., Sonnega, A., Bromet, E., Hughes, M., & Nelson, C. B. (1995). Posttraumatic stress disorder in the National Comorbidity Survey. *Archives of General Psychiatry, 52,* 1048–1060.

Ketelaar, T., & Ellis, B. J. (2000). Are evolutionary explanations unfalsifiable? Evolutionary psychology and the Lakatosian philosophy of science. *Psychological Inquiry, 11,* 1–21.

Kety, S. S., Wender, P. H., Jacobsen, B., Ingraham, L. J., Jansson, L., Faber, B., & Kinney, D. K. (1994). Mental illness in the biological and adoptive relatives of schizophrenic adoptees: Replication of the Copenhagen study in the rest of Denmark. *Archives of General Psychiatry, 51,* 442–455.

Kiecolt-Glaser, J. K., Page, G. G., Marucha, P. T., MacCallum, R. C., & Glaser, R. (1998). Psychological influences on surgical recovery: Perspectives from psychoneuroimmunology. *American Psychologist, 53,* 1209–1218.

Kikoski, J. F. (1998). Effective communication in the performance appraisal interview: Face-to-face communication for public managers in the culturally diverse workplace. *Public Personnel Management, 27,* 491–513.

Kilbourne, B. K. (1989). A cross-cultural investigation of the foot-in-the-door compliance induction procedure. *Journal of Cross-Cultural Psychology, 20,* 3–38.

Kilgard, M. P., & Merzenich, M. M. (1998). Cortical map reorganization enabled by nucleus basalis activity. *Science, 279,* 1714–1718.

Kilpatrick, D. G., Acierno, R., Saunders, B., Resnick, H. S., Best, C. L., & Schnurr, P. P. (2000). Risk factors for adolescent substance abuse and dependence data from a national sample. *Journal of Consulting and Clinical Psychology, 68,* 19–30.

Kim, C., & Kwok, Y. S. (1998). Navajo use of native healers. *Archives of Internal Medicine, 158,* 2245–2249.

Kim, H., & Markus, H. R. (1999). Deviance or uniqueness, harmony or conformity? A cultural analysis. *Journal of Personality and Social Psychology, 77,* 785–800.

Kinder, D. R., & Sanders, L. M. (1996). *Divided by color: Racial politics and democratic ideals.* Chicago: The University of Chicago Press.

King, M. S. (2000). Individual empowerment as a goal of sentencing: The Enlightened Sentencing Project: The use of transcendantal meditation as a rehabilitation tool in criminal justice. *Alternative Law Journal, 25,* 112–115.

Kinsey, A. C., Pomeroy, W. B., & Martin, C. E. (1948). *Sexual behavior in the human male.* Philadelphia: Saunders.

Kinsey, A. C., Pomeroy, W. B., Martin, C. E., & Gebhard, P. H. (1953). *Sexual behavior in the human female.* Philadelphia: Saunders.

Kirsch, I., & Sapirstein, G. (1999). Listening to Prozac but hearing placebo: A meta-analysis of antidepressant medications. In I. Kirsch (Ed.), *How expectancies shape experience* (pp. 303–320). Washington, DC: American Psychological Association.

Kirshnit, C. E., Richards, M. H., & Ham, M. (1988, August). *Athletic participation and body-image during early adolescence.* Paper presented at the 96th Annual Convention of the American Psychological Association, Atlanta.

Kitayama, S., & Burnstein, E. (1994). Social influence, persuasion, and group decision making. In S. Shavitt & T. C. Brock (Eds.), *Persuasion: Psychological insights and perspectives* (pp. 175–194). Boston: Allyn and Bacon.

Kivilu, J. M., & Rogers, W. T. (1998). A multi-level analysis of cultural experience and gender influences on causal attributions to perceived performance in mathematics. *British Journal of Educational Psychology, 68,* 25–37.

Klar, A. J. S. (1996). A single locus, RGHT, specifies preference for hand utilization in humans. *Cold Spring Harbor Symposium for Quantitative Biology, 61, 59–65.*

Klar, Y., & Giladi, E. E. (1997). No one in my group can be below the group's average: A robust positivity bias in favor of anonymous peers. *Journal of Personality and Social Psychology, 73,* 885–901.

Klein, P. D. (1997). Multiplying the problems of intelligence by eight: A critique of Gardner's theory. *Canadian Journal of Education, 22,* 377–394.

Kleinke, C. L., Peterson, T. R., & Rutledge, T. R. (1998). Effects of self-generated facial expressions on mood. *Journal of Personality and Social Psychology, 74,* 272–279.

Kliegl, R., Philipp, D., Luckner, M., & Krampe, R. (2001). Face memory skill acquisition. In N. Charness, D. C. Parks, & B. A. Sable (Eds.), *Communication, technology, and aging: Opportunities and challenges for the future* (pp. 169–186). New York: Springer.

Kling, K. C., & Hyde, J. S. (1996, August). *Gender differences in self-esteem: A meta-analysis.* Paper presented at the 104th annual convention of the American Psychological Association,Toronto, Canada.

Klinke, R., Kral, A., Heid, S., Tillein, J., & Hartmann, R. (1999). Recruitment of the auditory cortex in congenitally deaf cats by long-term cochlear electrostimulation. *Science, 285,* 1729–1733.

Klonoff, E. A., Landrine, H., & Campbell, R. (2000). Sexist discrimination may account for well-known gender differences in psychiatric symptoms. *Psychology of Women Quarterly, 24,* 93–99.

Kluger, J. (2001, May 21). Can gays switch sides? *Time, 157,* 62.

Kluger, R. (1996). *Ashes to ashes: America's hundred-year cigarette war, the public health and the unabashed triumph of Philip Morris.* New York: Knopf.

Klusman, L. E. (1998). Military health care providers' views on prescribing privileges for psychologists. *Professional Psychology: Research and Practice, 29,* 223–229.

Knapp, S., & VandeCreek, L. (2000). Recovered memories of childhood abuse: Is there an underlying professional consensus? *Professional Psychology: Research and Practice, 31,* 365–371.

Knee, C. R. (1998). Implicit theories of relationships: Assessment and prediction of romantic relationship initiation, coping, and longevity. *Journal of Personality and Social Psychology, 74,* 360–368.

Knight, K. H., Elfenbein, M. H., & Martin, M. B. (1997). Relationship of connected and separate knowing to the learning styles of Kolb, formal reasoning, and intelligence. *Sex Roles, 37,* 401–414.

Knoblich, G., & Ohlsson, S. (1999). Constraint relaxation and chunk decomposition in insight problem solving. *Journal of Experimental Psychology: Learning, Memory, & Cognition, 25,* 1534–1555.

Kohn, A. (1993). *Punished by rewards: The trouble with gold stars, incentive plans, A's, praise, and other bribes.* Boston: Houghton Mifflin.

Kolb, B. (1999). The twentieth century belongs to neuropsychology. *Brain Research Bulletin, 50,* 409–410.

Kolb, B., & Gibb, R. (1999). Neuroplasticity and recovery of function after brain injury. In D. T. Stuss, G. Winocur, & I. H. Robinson (Eds.), *Cognitive neurorehabilitation* (pp. 9–25). New York: Cambridge University Press.

Koob, G. F. (2000). Neurobiology of addiction: Toward the development of new therapies. In S. D. Glick & I. M. Maisonneuve (Eds.), *New medications for drug abuse. Annals of the New York Academy of Sciences* (pp. 170–185). New York: New York Academy of Sciences.

Koob, G. F., Wall, T. L., & Bloom, F. E. (1989). Nucleus accumbens as a substrate for the aversive stimulus effects of opiate withdrawal. *Psychopharmacology, 98,* 530–534.

Koolstra, C. M., van der Voort, T. H., & van der Kamp, L. J. (1997). Television's impact on children's reading comprehension and decoding skills: A 3-year panel study. *Reading Research Quarterly, 32*(2), 128–152.

Koriat, A., Goldsmith, M., & Pansky, A. (2000). Toward a psychology of memory accuracy. *Annual Review of Psychology, 51,* 481–537.

Koski, L., & Petrides, M. (2001). Time-related changes in task performance after lesions restricted to the frontal cortex. *Neuropsychologia, 39,* 268–281.

Koss, M. P. (2000). Blame, shame, and community justice reponses to violence against women. *American Psychologist, 55,* 1332–1343.

Koss, M. P., Gidycz, C. A., & Wisniewski, N. (1987). The scope of rape: Incidence and prevalence of sexual aggression and victimization in a national sample of higher education students. *Journal of Consulting and Clinical Psychology, 55,* 162–170.

Koulack, D. (1991). *To catch a dream.* Albany: State University of New York Press.

Kozyk, J. C., Touyz, S. W., & Beumont, P. J. (1998). Is there a relationship between bulimia nervosa and hazardous alcohol use? *International Journal of Eating Disorders, 24*(1), 95–99.

Kranzler, J. H. (1997). Educational and policy issues related to the use and interpretation of intelligence tests in the schools. *School Psychology Review, 26,* 150–162.

Kreider, R. B., Fry, A. C., & O'Toole, M. L. (1998). Overtraining in sport. *International Journal of Sport Psychology, 27,* 269–285.

Kreiman, G., Koch, C., & Fried, I. (2000). Imagery neurons in the human brain. *Nature, 408,* 357–361.

Kremen, A. M., & Block, J. (1998). The roots of ego-control in young adulthood: Links with parenting in early childhood. *Journal of Personality and Social Psychology, 75,* 1062–1075.

Kring, A. M., & Gordon, A. H. (1998). Sex differences in emotion: Expression, experience, and physiology. *Journal of Personality and Social Psychology, 74,* 686–703.

Krisel, W. (2001). Letter to the editor. *Archives of Sexual Behavior, 30,* 457.

Kruley, P., Sciama, S. C., & Glenberg, A. M. (1994). On-line processing of textual illustrations in the visuospatial sketchpad: Evidence from dual-task studies. *Memory and Cognition, 22,* 261–272.

Kubicek, E. B. (2000). Women in middle management: The impact of an involuntary job change. *Dissertation Abstracts International, A (Humanities and Social Sciences), 60*(9-A), 3235.

Kuczaj, S. A. (1998). Is an evolutionary theory of language play possible? *Cahiers de Psychologie Cognitive, 17,* 135–154.

Kudoh, N., Tajima, H., Hatayama, T., Maruyama, K., Shoji, Y., Hayashi, T., & Nakanishi, M. (1991). Effects of room environment on human cognitive activities. *Tohoku Psychologica Folia, 50,* 45–54.

Kugihara, N. (1999). Gender and social loafing in Japan. *Journal of Social Psychology, 139,* 516–526.

Kuhl, P. K., Andruski, J. E., Chistovich, I. A., Chistovich, L. A., Kozhevnikova, E. V., Ryskina, V. L., Stolyarova, E. I., Sundberg, U., & Lacerda, F. (1997). Cross-language analysis of phonetic units in language addressed to infants. *Science, 277,* 684–686.

Kuiper, N. A., & Martin, R. A. (1998). Laughter and stress in daily life: Relation to positive and negative affect. *Motivation and Emotion, 22,* 133–153.

Kuncel, N. R., Hezlett, S. A., & Ones, D. S. (2001). A comprehensive meta-analysis of the predictive validity of the graduate record examinations: Implications for graduate student selection and performance. *Psychological Bulletin, 127,* 162–181.

Kupperbusch, C., Matsumoto, D., Kooken, K., Loewinger, S., Uchida, H., Wilson-Cohn, C., & Yrizarry, N. (1999). Cultural influences on nonverbal expressions of emotion. In P. Philippot & R. S. Feldman (Eds.), *The social context of nonverbal behavior: Studies in emotion and social interaction* (pp. 17–44). New York; Paris, France: Cambridge University Press: Editions de la Maison des Sciences de l'Homme.

Kush, R. R., & Fleming, L. M. (2000). An innovative approach to short-term cognitive therapy in the combined treatment of anxiety and depression. *Group Dynamics: Theory, Research, and Practice, 4,* 176–183.

Kutchins, H., & Kirk, S. A. (1997). *Making us crazy. DSM: The psychiatric bible and the creation of mental disorders.* New York: Free Press.

LaBerge, S., & Gackenbach, J. (2000). Lucid dreaming. In E. Cardeña, S. J. Lynn, & S. Krippner (Eds.), *Varieties of anomalous experience: Examining the scientific evidence* (pp. 151–182). Washington, DC: American Psychological Association.

Lachter, J., Durgin, F., & Washington, T. (2000). Disappearing percepts: Evidence for retention failure in metacontrast masking. *Visual Cognition, 7,* 269–279.

Laird, J. (2000). Culture and narrative as central metaphors for clinical practice with families. In D. H. Demo, K. R. Allen, & M. A. Fine (Eds.). *Handbook of family diversity* (pp. 338–358). New York: Oxford University Press.

Lakkis, J., Ricciardelli, L. A., & Williams, R. J. (1999). Role of sexual orientation and gender-related traits in disordered eating. *Sex Roles, 41,* 1–16.

Lakoff, R. T. (2000). *The language war.* Los Angeles: University of California Press.

Lambert, A. J. (1995). Stereotypes and social judgment: The consequences of group variability. *Journal of Personality and Social Psychology, 68,* 388–403.

Laner, M. R., Benin, M. H., & Ventrone, N. A. (2001). Bystander attitudes toward victims of violence: Who's worth helping? *Deviant Behavior, 22,* 23–42.

Lang, P. J. (1994). The varieties of emotional experience: A meditation on James–Lange theory. *Psychological Review, 101,* 211–221.

Langdon, D., & Warrington, E. K. (2001). The role of the left hemisphere in verbal and spatial reasoning tasks. *Cortex, 36,* 691–702.

Lange, C. G. (1922). *The emotions* (English translation). Baltimore: Williams & Wilkins. (Original work published 1885)

Langer, E. J. (1992). Matters of mind: Mindfulness/mindlessness in perspective. *Consciousness and Cognition: An International Journal, 1,* 289–305.

Langer, E. J., & Moldoveanu, M. (2000). Mindfulness research and the future. *Journal of Social Issues, 56*(1), 129–139.

Langer, E. J., & Rodin, J. (1976). The effects of choice and enhanced personal responsibility for the aged: A field experiment in an institutional setting. *Journal of Personality and Social Psychology, 34,* 191–198.

Langlois, J. H., Roggman, L. A., & Rieser-Danner, L. A. (1990). Infants' differential social responses to attractive and unattractive faces. *Developmental Psychology, 26,* 153–159.

Lapp, J., & Attridge, M. (2000). Worksite interventions reduce stress among high school teachers and staff. *International Journal of Stress Management, 7,* 229–232.

LaRoche, M. J. (2000). Culture, transference, and countertransference among Latinos. *Psychotherapy: Theory, Research, Practice, and Training, 36,* 389–397.

Larson, R. W. (2000). Toward a psychology of positive youth development. *American Psychologist, 55,* 170–183.

Larson, R., & Pleck, J. (1999). Hidden feelings: Emotionality in boys and men. In D. Bernstein (Ed.), *Nebraska Symposium on Motivation, 1999: Gender and motivation* (pp. 25–74). Lincoln: University of Nebraska Press.

Latané, B., & Darley, J. M. (1970). *The unresponsive bystander: Why doesn't he help?* New York: Meredith.

Latané, B., Williams, K., & Harkins, S. (1979). Many hands make light work: The causes and consequences of social loafing. *Journal of Personality and Social Psychology, 37,* 822–832.

Latest News. (2001). Enlightened sentencing. *Latest News, 11.* Retrieved July 17, 2001 from the World Wide Web: www.tmscotland.org/stoppress.shtml.

Latham, G. P., Daghighi, S., & Locke, E. A. (1997). Implications of goal-setting theory for faculty motivation. In J. L. Bess (Ed.), *Teaching well and liking it: Motivating faculty to teach effectively* (pp. 125–142). Baltimore, MD: Johns Hopkins University Press.

Laumann, E. O., Gagnon, J. H., Michael, R. T., & Michaels, S. (1994). *The social organization of sexuality: Sexual practices in the United States.* Chicago: The University of Chicago Press.

Laumann, E. O., & Michael, R. T. (1994). Setting the scene. In E. O. Laumann & R. T. Michael (Eds). *Sex, love, and health in America: Private choices and public policies* (pp. 1–37). Chicago: University of Chicago Press.

Laumann, E. O., Paik, A., & Rosen, R. C. 1999. Sexual dysfunction in the United States: Prevalence and predictors. *Journal of the American Medical Association, 281,* 537–544.

Laurent, G. (1999). A systems perspective on early olfactory coding. *Science, 286,* 723–728.

Lavie, P. (2001). Sleep-wake as a biological rhythm. *Annual Review of Psychology, 52,* 277–303.

Lawler, E. E., & Porter, L. W. (1967). Antecedent attitudes of effective managerial performance. *Organizational Behavior and Human Performance, 2,* 122–142.

Lawler, J. J., & Elliot, R. (1996). Artificial intelligence in HRM: An experimental study of an expert system. *Journal of Management, 22,* 85–111.

Lawrence, E., Eldridge, K., Christensen, A., & Jacobson, N. S. (1999). Intergrative couple therapy: The dyadic relationship of acceptance and change. In J. M. Donovan (Ed.), *Short-term couple therapy, The Guilford Family Therapy Series* (pp. 226–261). New York: Guilford Press.

Lazarus, R. S. (1991). *Emotion and adaptation.* New York: Oxford University Press.

Lazarus, R. S. (1993). From psychological stress to the emotions: A history of changing outlooks. *Annual Review of Psychology, 44,* 1–21.

Lebow, J. L., & Gurman, A. S. (1995). Research assessing couple and family therapy. *Annual Review of Psychology,* 46, 27–57.

LeDoux, J. E. (1995). Emotion: Clues from the brain. *Annual Review of Psychology, 46,* 209–235.

LeDoux, J. E. (1996). *The emotional brain: The mysterious underpinnings of emotional life.* New York: Simon & Schuster.

LeDoux, J. E., & Phelps, E. A. (2000). Emotional networks in the brain. In M. Lewis & J. M. Haviland-Jones (Eds.), *Handbook of emotions* (2nd ed., pp. 157–172). New York: Guilford Press.

Lee, C., Ashford, S. J., & Bobko, P. (1990). Interactive effects of "Type A" behavior and perceived control on worker performance, job satisfaction, and somatic complaints. *Academy of Management Journal, 33,* 870–881.

Lee, D. M. (1999). Reinventing the university: From institutions to communities of higher education. *Journal of Adult Development, 6,* 175–184.

Lee, M., Lei, A., & Sue, S. (2001). The current state of mental health research on Asian Americans. *Journal of Human Behavior in the Social Environment, 3,* 159–178.

Lefcourt, H. M. (1992). Durability and impact of the locus of control construct. *Psychological Bulletin, 112,* 411–414.

Lefcourt, H. M., & Davidson-Katz, K. (1991). Locus of control and health. In C. R. Snyder & D. R. Forsyth (Eds.), *Handbook of social and clinical psychology* (pp. 246–266). New York: Pergamon.

Lefcourt, H. M., & Thomas, S. (1998). Humor and stress revisited. In W. Ruch (Ed.), *The sense of humor: Explorations of a personality characteristic; Humor research: 3* (pp. 179–202). Berlin: Walter De Gruyter.

Leibowitz, H. W. (1971). Sensory, learned, and cognitive mechanisms of size perception. *Annals of the New York Academy of Sciences, 1988,* 47–62.

Leikin, R., & Zaslavsky, O. (1997). Facilitating student interactions in mathematics in a cooperative learning setting. *Journal for Research in Mathematics Education, 28*(3), 331–354.

Lemonick, M. D. (2000, December 11). Downey's downfall: The actor's latest arrest supports the idea that drugs rewire the brain. *Time, 156*(24), 97.

Lenneberg, E. H. (1967). *Biological foundations of language.* New York: Wiley.

Leonard, B. E. (2001). The immune system, depression, and the action of antidepressants. *Progress in Neuro-Psychopharmacology and Biological Psychiatry, 25,* 767–780.

Lesch, K. P., Bengel, D., Heils, A., Sabol, S. Z., Greenberg, B. D., Petri, S., Benjamin, J., Müller, C. R., Hamer, D. H., & Murphy, D. L. (1996). Association of anxiety-related traits with a polymorphism in the serotonin transporter gene regulatory region. *Science, 274,* 1527–1531.

Lester, D. (2000). Executions as a deterrent to homicide. *Perceptual and Motor Skills, 91,* 696.

LeVay, S. (1991). A difference in hypothalamic structure between heterosexual and homosexual men. *Science, 253,* 1034–1037.

LeVay, S., & Hamer, D. H. (1994, May). Evidence for a biological influence in male homosexuality. *Scientific American,* 44–49.

Levin, D. (2000). Race as a visual feature: Using visual search and perceptual discrimination tasks to understand face categories and the cross-race recognition deficit. *Journal of Experimental Psychology: General, 129,* 559–574.

Levine, M. (1998). Prevention and community. *American Journal of Community Psychology, 26*(2), 189–206.

Levine, R. L., & Stadtman, E. R. (1992). Oxidation of proteins during aging. *Generations, 16,* 39–42.

Levine, R. V., Martinez, T. S., Brase, G., & Sorenson, K. (1994). Helping in 36 U.S. cities. *Journal of Personality and Social Psychology, 67,* 69–82.

Levinson, D. J. (1978). *The seasons of a man's life.* New York: Knopf.

Levinson, D. J. (1996). *The seasons of a woman's life.* New York: Knopf.

Levitt, J. B. (2001). Function following dorm. *Science, 292,* 231–233.

Levy, G. D. (1999). Gender-typed and non-gender-typed category awareness in toddlers. *Sex Roles, 41,* 851–873.

Lewin, K. K. (1970). *Brief psychotherapy.* St. Louis, MO: Warren H. Green.

Lewinsohn, P. M. (1974). Classical and theoretical aspects of depression. In I. S. Calhoun, H. E. Adams, & K. M. Mitchell (Eds.), *Innovative treatment methods in psychopathology.* New York: Wiley Interscience.

Lewinsohn, P. M., Rohde, P., Klein, D. N., Seeley, J. R., & Fischer, S. A. (1993). Age-cohort changes in the lifetime occurrence of depression and other mental disorders. *Journal of Abnormal Psychology, 102,* 110–120.

Lewinsohn, P. M., Rohde, P., Klein, D. N., & Seeley, J. R. (1999). Natural course of adolescent major depressive disorder: I. Continuity into young adulthood. *Journal of the American Academy of Child and Adolescent Psychiatry, 38,* 56–63.

Lewinsohn, P. M., & Talkington, J. (1979). Studies on the measurement of unpleasant events and relations with depression. *Applied Psychological Measurement, 3,* 83–101.

Lewis, M. (1995). Self-conscious emotions. *American Scientist, 83,* 68–78.

Ley, P. (1997). Compliance among patients. In A. Baum, S. Newman, J. Weinman, R. West, & C. McManus (Eds.), *Cambridge handbook of psychology, health, and medicine* (pp. 281–284). Cambridge, UK: Cambridge University Press.

Li, T-K. (2000). Pharmacogenetics of responses to alcohol and genes that influence alcohol drinking, *Journal of Studies on Alcohol, 61,* 5–12.

Lidz, T. (1973). *The origin and treatment of schizophrenic disorders.* New York: Basic Books.

Lilienfield, S. O., Lynn, S. J., Kirsch, I., Chaves, J. F., Sarbin, T. R., Ganaway, G. K., & Powell, R. A. (1999). Dissociative identity disorders and the sociocognitive model: Recalling the lessons of the past. *Psychological Bulletin, 125,* 507–523.

Lilla, I., Szikriszt, E., Ortutay, J., Berecz, M., Gyoergy, F., & Attila, N. (1998). Psychological factors contributing to the development of coronary artery disease—a study of rigidity and the A-type behaviour pattern. *Psychiatria Hungarica, 13*(2), 169–180.

Lillo-Martin, D. (1997). The modular effects of sign language acquisition. In M. Marschark, P. Siple, D. Lillo-Martin, R. Campbell, & V. Everhart (Eds.), *Relations of language and thought* (pp. 62–109). New York: Oxford University Press.

Lilly, J. C. (1956). Mental effects of reduction of ordinary levels of physical stimuli in intact, healthy persons. *Psychiatric Research Reports, 5,* 1–28.

Lin, K. M. (2001). Biological differences in depression and anxiety across races and ethnic groups. *Journal of Clinical Psychiatry, 62* (Suppl. 13), 13–19.

Lin, Y., McKeachie, W. J., & Naveh-Benjamin, M. (1999). Motivation and student's cognitive structure. *Chinese Journal of Psychology, 41*(2), 121–130.

Linberg, M. A., Beggs, A. L., Chezik, D. D., & Ray, D. (1982). Flavor–toxicosis associations: Tests of three hypotheses of long delay learning. *Physiology and Behavior, 29,* 439–442.

Link, B. G., Monahan, J., Stueve, A., & Cullen, F. T. (1999). Real in their consequences: A sociological approach to understanding the association between psychotic symptoms and violence. *American Sociological Review, 64,* 316–332.

Link, B. G., Phelan, J. C., Bresnahan, M., Stueve, A., & Pescosolido, B. A. (1999). Public conceptions of mental illness: Labels, causes, dangerousness, and social distance. *American Journal of Public Health, 89,* 1328–1333.

Lippert, B. (2001, September 24). Corps values: One message not wrapped in the flag. *AdWeek,* 16.

Lisanby, S. H., Maddox, J. H., Prudic, J., Devanand, D. P., & Sackeim, H. A. (2000). The effects of electroconvulsive therapy on memory of autobiographical and public events. *Archives of General Psychiatry, 57,* 581–590.

Liu, X., Sturm, R., Cuffel, B. J. (2000). The impact of prior authorization on outpatient utilization in managed behavioral health plans. *Medical Care and Review, 57,* 182–195.

Lock, J., & Steiner, H. (1999). Gay, lesbian, and bisexual youth risks for emotional, physical, and social problems: Results from a community-based survey. *Journal of the American Academy of Child and Adolescent Psychiatry, 38,* 297–304.

Locke, E. A., & Latham, G. P. (1990). Work motivation: The high performance cycle. In U. Kleinbeck, H. Quast, H. Thierry, & H. Hacker (Eds.), *Work motivation* (pp. 3–25). Hillsdale, NJ: Erlbaum.

Loeber, R., & Stouthamer-Loeber, M. (1998). Development of juvenile aggression and violence: Some common misconceptions and controversies. *American Psychologist, 53,* 242–259.

Loehlin, J. C. (1992). *Genes and environment in personality development.* Newbury Park, CA: Sage.

Loehlin, J. C., McCrae, R. R., Costa, P. T., Jr., & John, O. P. Heritabilities of common and measure-specific components of the Big Five personality factors. *Journal of Research in Personality, 32,* 431–453.

Loftus, E. F. (1975). Leading questions and the eyewitness report. *Cognitive Psychology, 7,* 560–572.

Loftus, E. F. (2000). Remembering what never happened. In E. Tuvling (Ed.), *Memory, consciousness, and the brain: The Tallinn conference* (pp. 106–118). Philadelphia: Taylor & Francis.

Loftus, E. F. (1979). *Eyewitness testimony.* Cambridge, MA: Harvard University Press.

LoLordo, V. M., & Taylor, T. L. (2001). Effects of uncontrollable aversive events: Some unsolved puzzles. In R. R. Mowrer & S. B. Klein (Eds.), *Handbook of contemporary learning theories* (pp. 119–154). Mahwah, NJ: Erlbaum.

Long, B. C. (1998). Coping with workplace stress: A multiple-group comparison of female managers and clerical workers. *Journal of Counseling Psychology, 45,* 65–78.

Longworth, C., Honey, G., & Sharma, T. (1999). Functional magnetic resonance imaging in neuropsychiatry. *British Medical Journal, 319,* 1551–1554.

Lopez, S. R., & Guarnaccia, P. J. J. (2000). Cultural psychopathology: Uncovering the social world of mental illness. *Annual Review of Psychology, 51,* 571–598.

Lore, R. K., & Schultz, L. A. (1993). Control of human aggression. *American Psychologist, 48,* 16–25.

Losa, E. G. (1999). Self-conditioned suppression in parenteral opiate drug addicts. *Psiquis: Revista de Psiquiatria, Psicologia Medica y Psicosomatica, 20,* 47–50.

Louie, K., & Wilson, M. A. (2001). Temporally structured replay of awake hippocampal ensemble activity during rapid eye movement sleep. *Neuron, 29,* 145–156.

Low, B. (2000). *Why sex matters.* Princeton, NJ: Princeton University Press.

Lowe, M. R., Gleaves, D. H., & Murphy-Eberenz, K. P. (1998). The relation of dieting and bingeing in bulimia nervosa. *Journal of Abnormal Psychology, 107,* 263–271.

Lowell, E. L. (1952). The effect of need for achievement on learning and speed of performance. *Journal of Psychology, 33,* 31–40.

Lubart, T. I. (1999). Creativity across cultures. In R. J. Sternberg (Ed.), *Handbook of creativity* (pp. 339–350). Cambridge, MA: Cambridge University Press.

Lubinski, D., Webb, R. M., Morelock, M. J., & Benbow, C. P. (2001). Top 1 in 10,000: A 10-year follow-up of the profoundly gifted. *Journal of Applied Psychology, 86,* 718–729.

Lundin, R. W. (1961). *Personality: An experimental approach.* New York: Macmillan.

Luus, C. A. E., & Wells, G. L. (1994). The malleability of eyewitness confidence: Co-witness and perseverance effects. *Journal of Applied Psychology, 79,* 714–723.

Lynn, M., & Mynier, K. (1993). Effect of server posture on restaurant tipping. *Journal of Applied Social Psychology, 23,* 678–685.

Lynn, R., & Martin, T. (1997). Gender differences in extraversion, neuroticism, and psychoticism in 37 nations. *Journal of Social Psychology, 137,* 369–373.

Lyubomirsky, S., & Tucker, K. L. (1998). Implications of individual differences in subjective happiness for perceiving, interpreting, and thinking about life events. *Motivation and Emotion, 22,* 155–186.

Macaluso, E., Frith, C. D., & Driver, J. (2000). Modulation of human visual cortex by crossmodal spatial attention. *Science, 289,* 1206–1208.

Maccoby, E. E. (1998). *The two sexes: Growing up apart, coming together.* Cambridge, MA: Harvard University Press.

Maccoby, E. E. (2000). Perspectives on gender development. *International Journal of Behavioral Development, 24,* 398–406.

Machado, L., & Rafal, R. D. (2000). Strategic control over saccadic eye movements: Studies of the fixation offset effect. *Perception & Psychophysics, 62,* 1236–1242.

Mack, A., & Rock, I. (1998). *Inattentional blindness.* Cambridge, MA: The MIT Press.

MacKay, N. J., & Covell, D. (1997). The impact of women in advertisements on attitudes toward women. *Sex Roles, 36,* 573–576.

MacLeod, C. M. (1991). Half a century of research on the Stroop effect: An integrative review. *Psychological Bulletin, 109,* 163–203.

MacWhinney, B. (1998). Models of the emergence of language. *Annual Review of Psychology, 49,* 199–227.

Maddux, J. E., & Meier, L. J. (1995). Self-efficacy and depression. In J. E. Maddux (Ed.), *Self-efficacy, adaptation, and adjustment: Theory, research, and application* (pp. 143–169). New York: Plenum.

Madigan, M. F., Jr., Dale, J. A., & Cross, J. D. (1997). No respite during sleep: Heart-rate hyperreactivity to rapid eye movement sleep in angry men classified as Type A. *Perceptual and Motor Skills, 85*(3, Pt. 2), 1451–1454.

Maguire, E. A., Burgess, N., Donnett, J. G., Frackowiak, R. S. J., Frith, C. D., & O'Keefe, J. (1998). Knowing where and getting there: A human navigation network. *Science, 280,* 921–924.

Mahoney, M. J. (1977). Reflections on the cognitive–learning trend in psychotherapy. *American Psychologist, 32,* 5–13.

Mahrer, A. R., & Nadler, W. P. (1986). Good moments in psychotherapy: A preliminary review, a list, and some promising research avenues. *Journal of Consulting and Clinical Psychology, 54,* 10–15.

Maier, N. R. F., & Klee, J. B. (1941). Studies of abnormal behavior in the rat: 17. Guidance versus trial and error and their relation to convulsive tendencies. *Journal of Experimental Psychology, 29,* 380–389.

Maier, S. F., Peterson, C., & Schwartz, B. (2000). From helplessness to hope: The seminal career of Martin Seligman. In J. E. Gillham (Ed.), *The science of optimism and hope: Research essays in honor of Martin E. P. Seligman. Laws of Life Symposia Series* (pp. 11–37). Philadelphia: Templeton Foundation Press.

Malamuth, N. M. (1996). The confluence model of sexual aggression: Feminist and evolutionary perspectives. In D. M. Buss & N. M. Malamuth (Eds.), *Sex, power, conflict: Evolutionary and feminist perspectives* (pp. 269–295). New York: Oxford University Press.

Malik, A., & Batra, P. (1998). Effect of crowding on a complex task. *Journal of Personality and Clinical Studies, 13,* 87–91.

Malinowski, J. C. (2001). Mental rotation and real-world wayfinding. *Perceptual and Motor Skills, 92,* 19–30.

Malle, B. F., & Knobe, J. (1997). Which behaviors do people explain? A basic actor–observer asymmetry. *Journal of Personality and Social Psychology, 72,* 288–304.

Malle, B. F., Knobe, J., O'Laughlin, M. J., Pearce, G. E., & Nelson, S. E. (2000). Conceptual structure and social functions of behavior explanations beyond person–situation attributions. *Journal of Personality and Social Psychology, 79,* 309–326.

Manlove, J. (1998). The influence of high school dropout and school disengagement on the risk of school-age pregnancy. *Journal of Research on Adolescence, 8,* 187–220.

Mann, J. J., Oquendo, M., Underwood, M. D., & Arango, V. (1999). The neurobiology of suicide risk: A review for the clinician. *Journal of Clinical Psychiatry,* 60 (Suppl. 2), 7–11.

March, J. S., Leonard, H. L., & Swedo, S. E. (1995). Obsessive–compulsive disorder. In J. S. March (Ed.), *Anxiety disorders in children and adolescents* (pp. 251–275). New York: Guilford Press.

Marcus, G. F., Vijayan, S., Bandi, R., & Vishton, P. M. (1999). Rule learning by seven-month-old infants. *Science, 283,* 77–79.

Maris, R., & Silverman, M. M. (1995). *Suicide prevention: Toward the year 2000.* New York: Guilford Press.

Markowitsch, H. J. (2000). Neuroanatomy of memory. In E. Tulving & F. I. M. Craik (Eds.), *The Oxford handbook of memory* (pp. 465–484). New York: Oxford University Press.

Marks, L. E. (2000). Synesthesia. In E. Cardena, S. J. Lynn, & S. Krippner (Eds.), *Varieties of anomalous experience: Examining the scientific evidence* (pp. 121–149). Washington, DC: American Psychological Association.

Marks, W. B., Dobell, W. H., & MacNichol, J. R. (1964). The visual pigments of single primate cones. *Science, 142,* 1181–1183.

Marquis, D. P. (1931). Can conditioned responses be established in the newborn infant? *Journal of Genetic Psychology, 39,* 479–492.

Martenyi, F., Dossenbach, M., Mraz, K., & Metcalfe, S. (2001). Gender differences in the efficacy of fluoxetime and maprotiline in depressed patients. A double-blind trial of antidepressants with serotonergic reuptake inhibition profile. *European-Neuropsychopharmacology, 11,* 227–232.

Martin, C., Hill, K. K., & Welsh, R. (1998). Adolescent pregnancy, a stressful life event: Cause and consequence. In T. W. Miller (Ed.), *Children of trauma: Stressful life events and their effects on children and adolescents* (pp. 141–160). Madison, CT: International Universities Press.

Martin, K. C., Bartsch, D., Bailey, C. H., & Kandel, E. R. (2000). Molecular mechanisms underlying learning-related long-lasting synaptic plasticity. In M. S. Gazzaniga (Ed.), *The new cognitive neurosciences* (pp. 121–137). Cambridge, MA: The MIT Press.

Martin, R., & Haroldson, S. (1977). Effect of vicarious punishment on stuttering frequency. *Journal of Speech and Hearing Research, 20,* 21–26.

Martino, G., & Marks, L. E. (2000). Cross-modal interaction between vision and touch: The role of synesthetic correspondence. *Perception, 29,* 745–754.

Martino, G., & Marks, L. E. (2001). Synesthesia: Strong and weak. *Current Directions in Psychological Science, 10,* 61–65.

Marucha, P. T., Kiecolt-Glaser, J. K., & Favagehi, M. (1998). Mucosal wound healing is impaired by examination stress. *Psychosomatic Medicine, 60,* 362–365.

Masia, C. L., & Chase, P. N. (1997). Vicarious learning revisited: A contemporary behavior analytic interpretation. *Journal of Behavior Therapy and Experimental Psychiatry, 28,* 41–51.

Maslach, C., Schaufeli, W. B., & Leiter, M. P. (2001). Job burnout. *Annual Review of Psychology, 52,* 397–422.

Masotto, C., & Racagni, G. (1995). Biological aspects of schizophrenia. *Rivista di Psichiatria, 30*(4), 34–46.

Masters, W. H., Johnson, V. E., & Kolodny, R. C. (1994). *Heterosexuality.* New York: HarperCollins.

Matsui, T., & Onglatco, M. L. U. (1990). Relationships between employee quality circle involvement and need fulfillment in work as moderated by work type: A compensatory or a spillover model? In U. Kleinbeck, H. Quast, H. Thierry, & H. Hacker (Eds.), *Work motivation* (pp. 191–199). Hillsdale, NJ: Erlbaum.

Matsumoto, D. (2000). Culture and self: An empirical assessment of Markus and Kitayama's theory of independent and interdependent self-construal. *Asian Journal of Social Psychology, 2,* 289–310.

Matsumoto, D., & Kudoh, T. (1993). American–Japanese cultural differences in attributions of personality based on smiles. *Journal of Nonverbal Behavior, 17,* 231–243.

Matthews, K., Owens, J., Kuller, L., Sutton-Tyrell, K., & Jansen-McWilliams, L. (1998). Are hostility and anxiety associated with carotid atherosclerosis in healthy postmenopausal women? *Psychosomatic Medicine, 60,* 633–638.

Max, D. T. (2001, May 6). To sleep no more. *New York Times.* Retrieved May 10, 2001 from the World Wide Web: www.nytimes.com/2001/05/06/magazine/06INSOMNIA.html.

Mayer, J. D., Salovey, P., & Caruso, D. (2000). Models of emotional intelligence. In R. J. Sternberg (Ed.). *Handbook of intelligence* (pp. 396–420). New York: Cambridge University Press.

Mazure, C. M., Bruce, M., Maciejewski, P. K., & Jacobs, S. C. (2000). Adverse life events and cognitive-personality characteristics in the prediction of major depression and antidepressant response. *American Journal of Psychiatry, 157,* 896–903.

McBurney, D. H., Gaulin, S. J. C., Devineni, T., & Adams, C. (1997). Superior spatial memory of women: Stronger evidence for the gathering hypothesis. *Evolution & Human Behavior, 18,* 165–174.

McCall, V. W., Reboussin, B. A., Cohen, W., & Lawton, P. (2001). Electroconvulsive therapy is associated with superior symptomatic and functional change in depressed patients after psychiatric hospitalization. *Journal of Affective Disorders, 63,* 17–25.

McCandliss, B. D., Posner, M. I., & Givón, T. (1997). Brain plasticity in learning visual words. *Cognitive Psychology, 33,* 88–110.

McCaul, K. D., Gladue, B. A., & Joppa, M. (1992). Winning, losing, mood, and testosterone. *Hormones and Behavior, 26,* 486–504.

McCaul, K. D., Jacobson, K., & Martinson, B. (1998). The effects of a state-wide media campaign on mammography screening. *Journal of Applied Social Psychology, 28,* 504–515.

McClearn, G. E., Johansson, B., Berg, S., Pedersen, N. L., Ahern, F., Petrill, S. A., & Plomin, R. (1997). Substantial genetic influence on cognitive abilities in twins 80 or more years old. *Science, 276,* 1560–1563.

McClelland, D. C. (1958). Methods of measuring human motivation. In J. W. Atkinson (Ed.), *Motives in fantasy, action, and society.* Princeton, NJ: Van Nostrand.

McClelland, D. C. (1961). *The achieving society.* Princeton, NJ: Van Nostrand.

McClelland, D. C. (1998). Identifying competencies with behavioral-event interviews. *Psychological Science, 9,* 331–339.

McClintock, M. K. (1971). Menstrual synchrony and suppression. *Nature, 229,* 244–245.

McConahay, J. B., & Hough, J. C. (1976). Symbolic racism. *Journal of Social Issues, 32*(2), 23–45.

McCormick, L., Nielsen, T., Ptito, M., & Hassainia, F. (1997). REM sleep dream mentation in right hemispherectomized patients. *Neuropsychologia, 35,* 695–701.

McCracken, L. M. (1997). "Attention" to pain in persons with chronic pain: A behavioral approach. *Behavior Therapy, 28,* 271–284.

McCrae, R. R., & Costa, P. T., Jr. (1997). Personality trait structure as a human universal. *American Psychologist, 52,* 509–516.

McCrae, R. R., & Costa, P. T. (1999). A Five Factor theory of personality. In L. A. Pervin & O. P. John (Eds.). *Handbook of personality theory and research* (pp. 139–153). New York: Guilford Press.

McCrae, R. R., Costa, P. T., Jr., Del Pilar, G. H., Rolland, J. P., & Parker, W. D. (1998). Cross-cultural assessment of the five-factor model: The revised NEO personality inventory. *Journal of Cross-Cultural Psychology, 29,* 171–188.

McCrae, R. R., Costa, P. T., Jr., Hrebickova, M., Ostendorf, F., Angleitner, A., Avia, M. D., Sanz, J., Sanchez-Bernardos, M. L., Kusdil, M. E., Woodfield, R., Saunders, P. R., & Smith, P. B. (2000). Nature over nurture: Temperament, personality, and life span development. *Journal of Personality and Social Psychology, 78,* 173–186.

McDonald, J. J., & Ward, L. M. (2000). Involuntary listening aids seeing: Evidence from human electrophysiology. *Psychological Science, 11,* 167–171.

McGill, M. E., & Slocum, J. W., Jr. (1998). A little leadership, please? *Organizational Dynamics, 26*(3), 39–49.

McGinn, C. (1999). *The mysterious flame: Conscious minds in a material world.* New York: Basic Books.

McGue, M. (1999). The behavioral genetics of alcoholism. *Current Directions in Psychological Science, 8,* 109–115.

McGue, M., & Bouchard, T. J. (2000). Genetic and environmental influences on human behavioral differences. *Annual Review of Neuroscience, 21,* 1–24.

McGuffin, P., Riley, B., & Plomin, R. (2001, February 16). Toward behavioral genomics. *Science, 291,* 1232–1249.

McGuire, S., & Clifford, J. (2000). Genetic and environmental contributions to loneliness in children. *Psychological Science, 11,* 487–491.

McHale, S., Updegraff, K. A., Helms-Erikson, H., & Crouter, A. C. (2001). Sibling influences on gender development in middle childhood and early adolescence: A longitudinal study. *Developmental Psychology, 37,* 115–125.

McIntosh, D. N. (1996). Facial feedback hypotheses: Evidence, implications, and directions. *Motivation and Emotion, 20,* 121–147.

McKelvey, M. W., & McKenry, P. C. (2000). The psychosocial well-being of black and white mothers following marital dissolution. *Psychology of Women Quarterly, 24,* 4–14.

McKenna, K. Y., & Bargh, J. A. (2000). Plan 9 from cyberspace: The implications of the Internet for personality and social psychology. *Personality and Social Psychology Review, 4*(1), 47–75.

McLaughlin, L. A., & Braun, K. L. (1998). Asian and Pacific islander cultural values: Considerations for health care decision making. *Health and Social Work, 23,* 116–126.

McLoyd, V. C. (1998). Socioeconomic disadvantage and child development. *American Psychologist, 53,* 185–204.

McLynn, F. (1997). *Carl Gustav Jung: A biography.* New York: St. Martin's Press.

McMahon, T. J., & Luthar, S. S. (2000). Women in treatment: Within gender differences in the clinical presentation of opioid-dependent women. *Journal of Nervous and Mental Disease, 88,* 679–687.

McNally, R. J., Hornig, C. D., Otto, M. W., & Pollack, M. H. (1997). Selective encoding of threat in panic disorder: Application of a dual priming paradigm. *Behaviour Research and Therapy, 35,* 543–549.

McNeil, J. E., & Warrington, E. K. (1993). Prosopagnosia: A face-specific disorder. *The Quarterly Journal of Experimental Psychology, 46A*(1), 1–10.

McNeill, D. (1970). Explaining linguistic universals. In J. Morton (Ed.), *Biological and social factors in psycholinguistics.* London: Logos.

McRoberts, C., Burlingame, G. M., & Hoag, M. J. (1998). Comparative efficacy of individual and group psychotherapy: A meta-analytic perspective. *Group Dynamics, 2,* 101–117.

Mecklinger, A. (2000). Interfacing mind and brain: A neurocognitive model of recognition memory. *Psychophysiology, 37,* 565–582.

Mehlhorn, G., Holborn, M., & Schliebs, R. (2000). Induction of cytokines in glial cells surrounding cortical beta-amyloid plaques in transgenic Tg2576 mice with Alzheimer pathology. *International Journal of Developmental Neuroscience, 18,* 423–431.

Meichenbaum, D. (1974). *Cognitive behavior modification.* Morristown, NJ: General Learning.

Meichenbaum, D., & Cameron, R. (1973). Training schizophrenics to talk to themselves: A means of developing attentional controls. *Behavior Therapy, 4,* 515–534.

Meichenbaum, D., & Cameron, R. (1983). Stress inoculation training: Toward a general paradigm for training coping skills. In D. Meichenbaum & M. E. Jaremko (Eds.), *Stress reduction and prevention* (pp. 115–154). New York: Plenum.

Meinz, E. J., & Salthouse, T. A. (1997). The effects of age and experience on memory for visually presented music. *Journals of Gerontology Series B—Psychological Sciences and Social Sciences, 53B*(1), P60–P69.

Melfi, C. A., Croghan, T. W., Hanna, M. P., & Robinson, R. L. (2000). Racial variation in antidepressant treatment in a Medicaid population. *Journal of Clinical Psychiatry, 61,* 16–21.

Melville, J. (1977). *Phobias and compulsions.* New York: Penguin.

Melzack, R. (1999). From the gate to the neuromatrix. *Pain* (Suppl. 6), S121–S126.

Menon, T., Morris, M.W., Chiu, C., & Hong, Y. (1999). Culture and the construal of agency attribution to individual versus group dispositions. *Journal of Personality and Social Psychology, 76,* 701–717.

Merckelbach, H., Muris, P., de Jong, P. J., & de Jongh, A. (1996). Disgust sensitivity, blood-injection-injury fear, and dental anxiety. *Clinical Psychology & Psychotherapy, 6,* 279–285.

Merrill, S. S., & Verbrugge, L. M. (1999). Health and disease in midlife. In S. L. Willis & J. D. Reid (Eds.), *Life in the middle: Psychological and social development in middle age* (pp. 77–103). San Diego, CA: Academic Press.

Merton, R. K. (1949). Merton's typology of prejudice and discrimination. In R. M. MacIver (Ed.), *Discrimination and national welfare.* New York: Harper and Row.

Merzenich, M. M., Jenkins, W. M., Johnston, P., Schreiner, C., Miller, S. L., & Tallal, P. (1996). Temporal processing deficits of language-learning impaired children ameliorated by training. *Science, 271,* 77–81.

Mesquita, B. (2001). Emotions in collectivist and individualist contexts. *Journal of Personality and Social Psychology, 80,* 68–74.

Messer, S. B., & Wachtel, P. L. (1997). The contemporary psychotherapeutic landscape: Issues and prospects. In P. L. Wachtel & S. B. Messer (Eds.), *Theories of psychotherapy: Origins and evolution* (pp. 1–27). Washington, DC: American Psychological Association.

Metcalfe, J., Funnell, M., & Gazzaniga, M. S. (1995). Right-hemisphere memory superiority: Studies of a split-brain patient. *Psychological Science, 6,* 157–164.

Meyers-Levy, J., & Maheswaran, D. (1991). Exploring differences in males' and females' processing strategies. *Journal of Consumer Research, 18,* 63–70.

Micallef, J., & Blin, O. (2001). Neurobiology and clinical pharmacology of obsessive–compulsive disorder. *Clinical-Neuropharmacology, 24,* 191–207.

Michael, R. T., Wadsworth, J., Feinleib, H., Johnson, A. M., Laumann, E. O., & Wellings, K. (1998). Private sexual behavior, public opinion, and public health policy related to sexually transmitted diseases: A U.S.–British comparison. *American Journal of Public Health, 88,* 749–754.

Miczek, K. A., Mirsky, A. F., Carey, G., Debold, J., & Raine, A. (2001). An overview of biological influences on violent behavior. In D. P. Barash (Ed.), *Understanding violence* (pp. 31–46). Boston: Allyn and Bacon.

Middleton, B., Arendt, J., & Stone, B. M. (1997). Complex effects of melatonin on human circadian rhythms in constant dim light. *Journal of Biological Rhythms, 12,* 467–477.

Miklowitz, D. J. (1994). Family risk indicators in schizophrenia. *Schizophrenia Bulletin, 20,* 137–150.

Miles, D. R., & Carey, G. (1997). Genetic and environmental architecture of human aggression. *Journal of Personality and Social Psychology, 72,* 207–217.

Milgram, S. (1965). Liberating effects of group pressure. *Journal of Personality and Social Psychology, 1,* 127–134.

Miller, G. A. (1965). Some preliminaries to psycholinguistics. *American Psychologist, 20,* 15–20.

Miller, J. (2000). Measurement error in subliminal perception experiments: Simulation analyses of two regression methods. *Journal of Experimental Psychology: Human Perception & Performance, 26,* 1461–1477.

Miller, J. G., & Bersoff, D. M. (1999). Development in the context of everyday family relationships: Culture, interpersonal morality, and adaptation. In M. Killen & D. Hart (Eds.). *Morality in everyday life: Developmental perspectives* (pp. 259–282). New York:

Miller, J. J., Fletcher, K., & Kabat-Zinn, J. (1995). Three year follow-up and clinical implications of a mindfulness meditation-based stress reduction intervention in the treatment of anxiety disorders. *General Hospital Psychiatry, 17,* 192–200.

Miller, N. E. (1944). Experimental studies of conflict. In J. M. Hunt (Ed.), *Personality and behavioral disorders* (Vol. 1). New York: Ronald Press.

Miller, N. E. (1959). Liberalization of basic S–R concepts: Extensions to conflict behavior, motivation, and social learning. In S. Koch (Ed.), *Psychology: A study of a science* (Vol. 2). New York: McGraw-Hill.

Miller, N. E. (1969). Learning of visceral and glandular responses. *Science, 163,* 434–445.

Miller, P. J. O., & Bain, D. E. (2000). Whining-pod variation in the sound production of a pod of killer whales, *Orcinus orca. Animal Behavior, 60,* 617–628.

Milner, B. (1966). Amnesia following operation on the temporal lobes. In C. W. M. Whitty & O. L. Zangwill (Eds.), *Amnesia.* London: Butterworth.

Mischel, W. (1999). Personality coherence and dispositions in a cognitive-affective personality system (CAPS) approach. In D. Cervone & Y. Shoda (Eds.), *The coherence of personality: Social–cognitive bases of consistency, variability, and organization* (pp. 37–66). New York: Guilford Press.

Mischel, W., & Shoda, Y. (1998). Reconciling processing dynamics and personality dispositions. *Annual Review of Psychology, 49,* 229–258.

Mischel, W., & Shoda, Y. (1999). Integrating dispositions and processing dynamics within a unified theory of personality: The cognitive–affective personality system. In L. A. Pervin & O. P. John (Eds.), *Handbook of personality: Theory and research* (pp. 197–218). New York: Guilford Press.

Mishler, E. G., & Waxler, N. E. (1968). Family interaction processes and schizophrenia: A review of current theories. In E. G. Mishler & N. E. Waxler (Eds.), *Family processes and schizophrenia.* New York: Science House.

Mitchell, K. J., Johnson, M. K., Raye, C. L., & D'Esposito, M. (2000). FMRI evidence of age-related hippocampal dysfunction in feature binding in working memory. *Cognitive Brain Research, 10*(1–2), 197–206.

Mitler, M. M., Miller, J. C., Lipsitz, J. J., & Walsh, J. K. (1997). The sleep of long-haul truck drivers. *New England Journal of Medicine, 337,* 755–761.

Mohr, D., Likosky, W., Bertagnolli, A., Goodkin, D., Van Der Wende, J., Dwyer, P., & Dick, L. (2000). Telephone administered cognitive–behavioral therapy for the treatment of depressive symptoms in multiple sclerosis. *Journal of Consulting and Clinical Psychology, 68,* 356–361.

Mokdad, A. H., Serdula, M. K., Dietz, W. H., Bowman, B. A., Marks, J. S., & Kaplan, J. P. (2000). The continuing epidemic of obesity in the United States. *Journal of the American Medical Association, 284,* 1650–1651.

Molnar, B. E., Buka, S. L., & Kessler, R. C. (2001). Child sexual abuse and subsequent psychopathology: Results from the National Comorbidity Survey. *American Journal of Public Health, 91,* 753–760.

Monahan, J. L., Murphy, S. T., & Zajonc, R. B. (2000). Subliminal mere exposure: Specific, general, and diffuse effects. *Psychological Science, 11,* 462–466.

Moncrieff, J. (1997). Lithium: Evidence reconsidered. *British Journal of Psychiatry, 171,* 113–119.

Mondloch, C. J., Lewis, T. L., Budreau, D. R., Maurer, D., Dannemiler, J. L., Stephens, B. R., & Kleiner-Gathercoal, K. A. (1999). Face perception during early infancy. *Psychological Science, 10,* 419–422.

Monnier, J., Stone, B. K., Hobfoll, S. E., & Johnson, R. J. (1998). How antisocial and prosocial coping influence the support process among men and women in the U.S. Postal Service. *Sex Roles, 39,* 1–19.

Monteleone, P., Luisi, M., Colurcio, B., Casarosa, E., Monteleone, P., Ioime, R., Genazzani, A. R., & Maj, M. (2001). Plasma levels of neuroactive steroids are increased in untreated women with anorexia nervosa or bulimia nervosa. *Psychosomatic Medicine, 63,* 62–68.

Montello, D. R., Lovelace, K. L., Golledge, R. G., & Self, C. M. (1999). Sex-related differences and similarities in geographic and environmental spatial abilities. *Annals of the Association of American Geographers, 89,* 515–534.

Montepare, J. M., & Zebrowitz-McArthur, L. (1988). Impressions of people created by age-related qualities of their gaits. *Journal of Personality and Social Psychology, 55,* 547–556.

Montgomery, D., Miville, M. L., Winterowd, C., Jeffries, B., & Baysden, M. F. (2000). American Indian college students: An exploration into resiliency factors revealed through personal stories. *Cultural Diversity and Ethnic Minority Psychology, 6,* 387–398.

Montgomery, G. H., & Bovbjerg, D. H. (1997). The development of anticipatory nausea in patients receiving adjuvant chemotherapy for breast cancer. *Psychology & Behavior, 61,* 737–741.

Montgomery, G. H., Tomoyasu, N., Bovbjerg, D. H., Andrykowski, M. A., Currie, V. E., Jacobsen, P. B., & Redd, W. H. (1998). Patients' pretreatment expectations of chemotherapy-related nausea are an independent predictor of anticipatory nausea. *Annals of Behavioral Medicine, 20,* 104–108.

Moore, T. E. (1995). Subliminal self-help auditory tapes: An empirical test of perceptual consequences. *Canadian Journal of Behavioral Science, 27,* 9–20.

Moorhead, G., Ference, R., & Neck, C. P. (1991). Group decision fiascoes continue: Space shuttle *Challenger* and a revised groupthink framework. *Human Relations, 44,* 539–550.

Morgan, C. A., III, Kingham, P., Nicolaou, A., & Southwick, S. M. (1998). Anniversary reactions in Gulf War veterans: A naturalistic inquiry 2 years after the Gulf War. *Journal of Traumatic Stress, 11,* 165–171.

Morgan, D. G., & Stewart, N. J. (1998). High versus low density special care units: Impact on the behaviour of elderly residents with dementia. *Canadian Journal on Aging, 17,* 143–165.

Morin, C. M., Stone, J., McDonald, K., & Jones, S. (1994). Psychological management of insomnia: A clinical replication series with 100 patients. *Behavior Therapy, 25,* 291–309.

Morren, M. (1998). Hostility as a risk factor for coronary heart disease. *Psycholoog, 33,* 101–108.

Morris, C. D., Bransford, J. D., & Franks, J. J. (1977). Levels of processing versus transfer appropriate processing. *Journal of Verbal Learning and Verbal Behavior, 16,* 519–533.

Morris, M. W., & Peng, K. (1994). Culture and cause: American and Chinese attributions for social and physical events. *Journal of Personality and Social Psychology, 67,* 949–971.

Moser, E. I., Krobert, K. A., Moser, M. B., & Morris, R. G. (1998). Impaired spatial learning after saturation of long-term potentiation. *Science, 281,* 2038–2042.

Most, S. B., Simons, D. J., Scholl, B. J., Jimenez, R., Clifford, E., & Chabris, C. F. (2001). How not to be seen: The contribution of similarity and selective ignoring to sustained inattentional blindness. *Psychological Science, 12,* 9–17.

Mueser, K. T., Bellack, A. S., Morrison, R. L., & Wade, J. H. (1990). Gender, social competence, and symptomatology in schizophrenia: A longitudinal analysis. *Journal of Abnormal Psychology, 99,* 138–147.

Mullen, B., Anthony, T., Salas, E., & Driskell, J. E. (1994). Group cohesiveness and quality of decision making: An integration of tests of the groupthink hypothesis. *Small Group Research, 25,* 189–204.

Mullen, B., & Copper, C. (1994). The relation between group cohesiveness and performance: An integration. *Psychological Bulletin, 115,* 210–227.

Mumford, M. D., Feldman, J. M., Hein, M. B., & Nagao, D. J. (2001). Tradeoffs between ideas and structure: Individuals versus group performance in creative problem solving. *Journal of Creative Behavior, 35*(1), 1–23.

Murphy, L. R. (1996). Stress management in work settings: A critical review of the health effects. *American Journal of Health Promotion, 11,* 112–135.

Murphy, S. M. (1990). Models of imagery in sport psychology: A review. *Journal of Mental Imagery, 14,* 153–172.

Murphy, S. M., & Jowdy, D. P. (1992). Imagery and mental practice. In T. S. Horn (Ed.), *Advances in sport psychology* (pp. 221–250). Champaign, IL: Human Kinetics.

Murphy, S. T. (1998). The impact of factual versus fictional media portrayals on cultural stereotypes. *The Annals of the American Academy of Political and Social Sciences, 560,* 165–178.

Murray, H. A. (1938). *Explorations in personality.* New York: Oxford University Press.

Murray, J. B. (1995). Evidence for acupuncture's analgesic effectiveness and proposals for the physiological mechanisms involved. *Journal of Psychology, 129,* 443–461.

Murray, J. G. (1994). Dimensions of multiple personality disorder. *Journal of Genetic Psychology, 155,* 233–246.

Musso, M., Weiller, C., Kiebel, S., Mueller, S. P., Buelau, P., & Rijntjes, M. (1999). Training-induced brain plasticity in aphasia. *Brain, 122,* 1781–1790.

Myers, D. G. (2000). The funds, friends, and faith of happy people. *American Psychologist, 55,* 56–67.

Myers, I. B. (1962). *Myers-Briggs type indicator manual.* Princeton, NJ: Educational Testing Service.

Myerson, J., Rank, M. R., Raines, F. Q., & Schnitzler, M. A. (1998). Race and general cognitive ability: The myth of diminishing returns to education. *Psychological Science, 9,* 139–142.

Nadel, L., & Bohbot, V. (2001). Consolidation of memory. *Hippocampus, 11,* 56–60.

Nair, E. (2000). Health and aging: A perspective from the Far East. *Journal of Adult Development, 7,* 121–126.

Napholz, L. (2000). Balancing multiple roles among a group of urban midlife American Indian working women. *Health Care for Women International, 21,* 255–266.

Nash, R. A. (1996). The serotonin connection. *Journal of Orthomolecular Medicine, 11,* 35–44.

Nathan, P. E., & Langenbucher, J. W. (1999). Psychopathology: Description and classification. *Annual Review of Psychology, 50,* 79–108.

Nathans, J. (1989, February). The genes for color vision. *Scientific American,* 42–49.

National Center for Health Statistics. (2000). *Health United States, 2000.* Hyattsville, MD: U.S. Government Printing Office.

National Council on Aging. (1998, September 28). Half of older Americans report they are sexually active; 4 in 10 want more sex, says new survey. Washington, DC: NCOA [On-line press release]. Retrieved from the World Wide Web: http://www.ncoa.org/press/sexsurvey.htm

National Institutes of Mental Health. (2001). The numbers count. Retrieved from the World Wide Web, October 12, 2001: www.nimh.nih.gov/publicat/numbers.cfm

Needleman, L. D., & Geller, E. S. (1992). Comparing interventions to motivate work-site collection of home-generated recyclables. *American Journal of Community Psychology, 20,* 775–785.

Neisser, U., & Libby, L. K. (2000). Remembering life events. In E. Tulving & F. I. M. Craik (Eds.), *The Oxford handbook of memory* (pp. 315–332). New York: Oxford University Press.

Nelson, D. L., McKinney, V. M., & Gee, N. R. (1998). Interpreting the influence of implicitly activated memories on recall and recognition. *Psychological Review, 105,* 299–324.

Nesse, R. M. (1997, October 3). Psychoactive drug use in evolutionary perspective. *Science, 278,* 63–66.

Nestle, M., Wing, R., Birch, L., DiSogra, L., Drewnowski, A., Middleton, S., Sigman-Grant, M., Sobal, J., Winston, M., & Economos, C. (1998). Behavioral and social influences on food choices. *Nutrition Reviews, 56,* S50–71.

Neumann, R., & Strack, F. (2000). Experiential and nonexperiential routes of motor influence on affect and evaluation. In H. Bless & J. P. Forgas (Eds.), *The message within: The role of subjective experience in social cognition and behavior* (pp. 52–68). Philadelphia: Psychology Press/Taylor & Francis.

Neumark-Sztainer, D., Story, M., Hannan, P. J., Beuhring, T., & Resnick, M. D. (2000). Disordered eating among adolescents: Associations with sexual/physical abuse and other familial/psychosocial factors. *International Journal of Eating Disorders, 28,* 249–258.

Neville, H. J., & Bavelier, D. (2000). Specificity and plasticity in neurocognitive development in humans. In M. S. Gazzaniga (Ed.), *The new cognitive neurosciences* (pp. 83–98). Cambridge, MA: The MIT Press.

Newman, L. S., Duff, K. J., & Baumeister, R. F. (1997). A new look at defensive projection: Thought suppression, accessibility, and biased person perception. *Journal of Personality and Social Psychology, 72,* 980–1001.

Ng, V. W. K., Eslinger, P. J., Williams, S., Brammer, M., Bullmore, E. T., Andrew, C. M., Suckling, J., Morris, R. G., & Benton, A. L. (2000). Hemispheric preference in visuospatial processing: A complementary approach with fMRI and lesion studies. *Human Brain Mapping, 10,* 80–86.

Niehoff, D. (1999). *The biology of violence: How understanding the brain, behavior, and environment can break the vicious circle of aggression.* New York: Free Press.

Nisbett, R. E. (1972). Hunger, obesity, and the ventromedial hypothalamus. *Psychological Review, 79,* 433–453.

Nolen-Hoeksema, S. (2000). The role of rumination in depressive disorders and mixed anxiety/depressive symptoms. *Journal of Abnormal Psychology, 109,* 504–511.

Nolen-Hoeksema, S., Larson, J., & Grayson, C. (1999). Explaining the gender difference in depressive symptoms. *Journal of Personality and Social Psychology, 77,* 1061–1072.

Noonan, D. (2001, January 29). Stop stressing me. *Newsweek, 137*(4), 54–55.

Norman, R. A., Tataranni, P. A., Pratley, R., Thompson, D. B., Hanson, R. L., Prochazka, M., Baier, L., Ehm, M. G., Sakul, H., Foroud, T., Garvey, W. T., Burns, D., Knowler, W. C., Bennett, P. H., Bogardus, C., & Ravussin, E. (1998). Autosomal genomic scan for loci linked to obesity and energy metabolism in Pima Indians. *American Journal of Human Genetics, 62,* 659–668.

Notterman, J. M., & Drewry, H. N. (1993). *Psychology and education: Parallel and interactive approaches.* New York: Plenum.

Nyberg, L., & Cabeza, R. (2000). Brain imaging of memory. In E. Tulving and F. I. Craik (Eds.), *The Oxford handbook of memory* (pp. 501–519). New York: Oxford University Press.

Nyberg, L., Cabeza, R., & Tulving, E. (1996). PET studies of encoding and retrieval: The HERA model. *Psychonomic Bulletin and Review, 3,* 135–148.

O'Brien, C. P., Childress, A. R., Ehrman, R., & Robbins, S. J. (1998). Conditioning factors in drug use: Can they explain compulsion? *Journal of Psychopharmacology, 12*(1), 15–22.

O'Brien, E. J., Jeffreys, D., Leitzel, J., O'Brien, J. P., Mensky, L., & Marchese, M. (1996, August). *Gender differences in the self-esteem of adolescents: A meta-analysis.* Paper presented at the 104th annual convention of the American Psychological Association, Toronto, Canada.

O'Connor, F. L. (1998). The role of serotonin and dopamine in schizophrenia. *Journal of the American Psychiatric Nurses Association, 4*(4), S30–S34.

O'Connor, T., & Plomin, R. (2000). Developmental behavioral genetics. In A. J. Sameroff, M. Lewis, & S. M. Miller (Eds.), *Handbook of developmental psychopathology* (pp. 217–235). New York: Kluwer Academic/Plenum Publishers.

Oddone-Paolucci, E., Genuis, M. L., & Violato, C. (2001). A meta-analysis of the published research on the effects of child sexual abuse. *Journal of Psychology, 135,* 17–36.

Okuda-Ashitaka, E., Minami, T., Tachibana, S., Yosihara, Y., Nishiuchi, Y., Kimura, T., & Ito, S. (1998). Nocistatin, a peptide that blocks nociceptin action in pain transmission. *Nature, 392,* 286–289.

Olausson, B., & Sagvik, J. (2000). Pain threshold changes following acupuncture, measured with cutaneous argon laser and electrical tooth pulp stimulation, a comparative study. *Progress in Neuro-Psychopharmacology & Biological Psychiatry, 24,* 385–395.

Olds, J., & Milner, P. (1954). Positive reinforcement produced by electrical stimulation of septal area and other regions of rat brain. *Journal of Comparative and Physiological Psychology, 47,* 419–427.

Olivardia, R., Pope, H. G., Jr., Mangweth, B., & Hudson, J. L. (1995). Eating disorders in college men. *American Journal of Psychiatry, 152,* 1279–1283.

Oliver, J. M., & Novak, B. B. (1993). Depression, Seligman's "modernity" hypothesis, and birth cohort effects in university students. *Journal of Social Behavior and Personality, 8,* 99–110.

Oliver, M. B., & Hyde, J. S. (1993). Gender differences in sexuality: A meta-analysis. *Psychological Bulletin, 114,* 29–51.

Oliver, W. (2000). Preventing domestic in the African American community: The rationale for popular culture interventions. *Violence Against Women, 6,* 533–549.

Olness, K. (1993). Hypnosis: The power of attention. In D. Goleman & J. Gurin (Eds.), *Mind/body medicine: How to use your mind for better health* (pp. 277–290). Yonkers, NY: Consumer Reports Books.

Olsen, R. A. (1997). Desirability bias among professional investment managers: Some evidence from experts. *Journal of Behavioral Decision Making, 10,* 65–72.

O'Mara, S. M., Commins, S., & Anderson, M. (2000). Synaptic plasticity in the hippocampal area CA1-subiculum projection: Implications for theories of memory. *Hippocampus, 10,* 447–456.

Operario, D., & Fiske, S. T. (2001). Causes and consequences of stereotypes in organizations. In M. London (Ed.), *How people evaluate others in organizations: Applied in psychology* (pp. 45–62). Mahwah, NJ: Erlbaum.

Ortega-Andeane, A. P. (1989). User participation in an environmental evaluation in the remodeling of hospital facilities. *Revista Mexicana de Psycologia, 6*(1), 45–54.

Orth-Gomér, K. (1998). Psychosocial risk factor profile in women with coronary heart disease. In K. Orth-Gomér, M. Chesney, & N. K. Wenger (Eds.), *Women, stress, and heart disease* (pp. 25–38). Mahwah, NJ: Erlbaum.

Osborne, J. W. (1997). Race and academic disidentification. *Journal of Educational Psychology, 89,* 728–735.

Oshodi, J. E. (1999). The construction of an Africentric sentence completion test to assess the need for achievement. *Journal of Black Studies, 30,* 216–231.

Otto, L. B. (2000). Youth perspectives on parental career influence. *Journal of Career Development, 27*(2), 111–118.

Ouimette, P. C. (1997). Psychopathology and sexual aggression in nonincarcerated men. *Violence and Victims, 12,* 390–395.

Overby, L. Y. (1990). A comparison of novice and experienced dancers' imagery ability. *Journal of Mental Imagery, 14,* 173–184.

Owens, L., Shute, R., & Slee, P. (2000). Guess what I just heard: Indirect aggression amongst teenage girls. *Aggressive Behavior, 26,* 67–83.

Oyserman, D., Coon, H. M., & Kemmelmeier, M. (2002). Rethinking individualism and collectivism: Evaluation of theoretical assumptions and meta-analyses, *Psychological Bulletin, 128,* 3–72.

Paikoff, R. L., Parfenoff, S. H., Williams, S. A., & McCormick, A. (1997). Parenting, parent-child relationships, and sexual possibility situations among urban African American preadolescents: Preliminary findings and implications for HIV prevention. *Journal of Family Psychology, 11,* 11–22.

Palatnik, A., Frolov, K., Fux, M., & Benjamin, J. (2001). Double-blind, controlled, crossover trial of inositol versus fluvoxamine for the treatment of panic disorder. *Journal of Clinical Psychopharmacology, 21,* 335–339.

Palmer, G. (2000). Resilience in child refugees: An historical study. *Australian Journal of Early Childhood, 25*(3), 39+.

Pan, C., Morrison, R. S., Ness, J., Fugh-Berman, A., & Leipzig, R. M. (2000). Complementary and alternative medicine in the management of pain, dyspnea, and nausea and vomiting near the end of life: A systematic review. *Journal of Pain & Symptom Management, 20,* 374–387.

Panksepp, J. (2000). Emotions as natural kinds within the mammalian brain. In M. Lewis & J. M. Haviland-Jones (Eds.), *Handbook of emotions* (2nd ed., pp. 137–156). New York: Guilford Press.

Pantin, H. M., & Carver, C. S. (1982). Induced competence and the bystander effect. *Journal of Applied Social Psychology, 12,* 100–111.

Papp, P. (2000). Gender differences in depression: His or her depression. In P. Papp (Ed.). *Couples on the fault line: New directions for therapists* (pp. 130–551). New York: Guilford Press.

Park, H. S., Bauer, S. C., & Sullivan, L. M. (1998). Gender differences among top-performing elementary school students in mathematical ability. *Journal of Research and Development in Education, 31,* 133–141.

Park, J., & Liao, T. F. (2000). The effect of multiple roles in South Korean married women professors: Role changes and the factors which influence potential role gratification and strain. *Sex Roles, 43,* 571–591.

Parkin, A. J. (2001). The structure and mechanisms of memory. In B. Rapp (Ed.), *The handbook of cognitive neuropsychology: What deficits reveal about the human mind* (pp. 399–422). Philadelphia: Psychology Press/Taylor & Francis.

Parks, C. A., Hesselbrock, M. N., Hesselbrock, V. M., & Segal, B. (2001). Gender and reported health problems in treated alcohol-dependent Alaska natives. *Journal of Studies on Alcohol, 62,* 286–293.

Parvizi, J., & Damasio, A. (2001). Consciousness and the brainstem. *Cognition, 79,* 135–159.

Patrick, C. J. (1994). Emotion and psychopathy: Startling new insights. *Psychophysiology, 31,* 319–330.

Paulesu, E., Demonet, J., Faxio, F., McCrory, E., Chanoine, V., Brunswick, N., Cappa, S. F., Cossu, G., Habib, M., Frith, C. D., & Frith, U. (2001). Dyslexia: Cultural diversity and biological unity. *Science, 16,* 2165–2167.

Pavlov, I. P. (1927). *Conditioned reflexes.* London: Oxford University Press.

Payne, D. G., Neuschatz, J. S., Lampinen, J. M., & Lynn, S. J. (1997). Compelling memory illusions: The characteristics of false memories. *Current Directions in Psychological Science, 6,* 56–60.

Pedersen, D. M., & Wheeler, J. (1983). The Müller–Lyer illusion among Navajos. *Journal of Social Psychology, 121,* 3–6.

Pedersen, N. L., & Reynolds, C. A. (1998). Stability and change in adult personality: Genetic and environmental components. *European Journal of Personality, 12,* 365–386.

Pedersen, N. L., & Svedberg, P. (2000). Behavioral genetics, health, and aging. *Journal of Adult Development, 7,* 65–71.

Pelli, D. G. (1999). Close encounters—an artist shows that size affects shape. *Science, 285,* 844–846.

Peltonen, L., & McKusick, V. (2001, February 16). Dissecting human disease in the postgenomic era. *Science, 291,* 1224–1229.

Pendergrast, M. (1997). Memo to Pope: Ask the real questions, please. *American Psychologist, 52,* 989–990.

Peng, K., & Nisbett, R. (1999). Culture, dialectics, and reasoning about contradiction. *American Psychologist, 54,* 741–754.

Penn, D. L., Corrigan, P. W., Bentall, R. P., Racenstein, J. M., & Newman, L. (1997). Social cognition in schizophrenia. *Psychological Bulletin, 121,* 114–132.

Pennebaker, J. W. (1997). *Opening up: The healing power of expressing emotions* (rev. ed.). New York: Guilford Press.

Pennebaker, J. W., & Graybeal, A. (2001). Patterns of natural language use: Disclosure, personality, and social integration. *Current Directions in Psychological Science, 10,* 90–93.

Pennebaker, J. W., & King, L. A. (1999). Linguistic styles, language use, and an individual difference. *Journal of Personality and Social Psychology, 77,* 1296–1312.

People Weekly. (2001, April 30). Collared: Fourteen months after the road-rage killing of a dog named Leo, a tenacious detective brings in a suspect. *People Weekly, 55*, 48+.

Perkins, D. N., & Grotzer, T. A. (1997). Teaching intelligence. *American Psychologist, 52*, 1125–1133.

Perloff, R. M. (2001). *Persuading people to have safer sex: Applications of social science to the AIDS crisis.* Mahwah, NJ: Erlbaum.

Perrett, D. I., Lee, K. J., Penton-Voak, I., Rowland, D., Yoshikawa, S., Burt, D. M., Henzi, S. P., Castles, D. L., & Akamatsu, S. (1998). Effects of sexual dimorphism on facial attractiveness. *Nature, 394*, 884–887.

Perry, B. D. (1999). The memories of states: How the brain stores and retrieves traumatic experience. In J. Goodwin & R. Attias (Eds.), *Splintered reflections: Images of the body in trauma* (pp. 9–38). New York: Basic Books.

Peselow, E. D., Sanfilipo, M. P., & Fieve, R. R. (1995). Relationship between hypomania and personality disorders before and after successful treatment. *American Journal of Psychiatry, 152*, 232–238.

Pesut, D. J. (1990). Creative thinking as a self-regulatory metacognitive process: A model for education, training, and further research. *Journal of Creative Behavior, 24*, 105–110.

Peterson, C. (2000). Optimistic explanatory style and health. In J. E. Gillham (Ed.), *The science of optimism and hope: Research essays in honor of Martin E. P. Seligman. Laws of Life Symposia Series* (pp. 145–161). Philadelphia: Templeton Foundation Press.

Peterson, C., & Seligman, M. E. P. (1984). Causal explanations as a risk factor for depression: Theory and evidence. *Psychological Review, 91*, 347–374.

Petrill, S. A., Plomin, R., Berg, S., Johansoon, B., Pedersen, N. L., Ahern, F., & McClearn, G. E. (1998). The genetic and environmental relationship between general and specific cognitive abilities in twins age 80 and older. *Psychological Science, 9*, 183–189.

Petrinovich, L. (1997). Evolved behavioral mechanisms. In M. E. Bouton & M. S. Fanselow (Eds.), *Learning, motivation, and cognition: The functional behavioralism of Robert C. Bolles* (pp. 13–30). Washington, DC: American Psychological Association.

Pettigrew, T. F. (1997). The affective component of prejudice: Empirical support for the new view. In S. A. Tuch & J. K. Martin (Eds.), *Racial attitudes in the 1990s: Continuity and change* (pp. 76–90). New York: Praeger.

Pettigrew, T. F., Jackson, J. S., Brika, J. B., Lemaine, G., Meertens, R. W., Wagner, U., & Zick, A. (1998). Outgroup prejudice in Western Europe. In W. Stroebe & M. Hewstone (Eds.), *European review of social psychology* (Vol. 8, pp. 241–273). Chichester, UK: Wiley.

Petty, R. E., & Cacioppo, J. T. (1985). The elaboration likelihood model of persuasion. In L. Berkowitz (Ed.), *Advances in experimental social psychology* (Vol. 19). New York: Academic Press.

Petty, R. E., Cacioppo, J. T., Strathman, A. J., & Priester, J. R. (1994). To think or not to think: Exploring two routes to persuasion. In S. Shavitt & T. C. Brock (Eds.), *Persuasion: Psychological insights and perspectives* (pp. 113–148). Boston: Allyn and Bacon.

Petty, R. E., Schumann, D. W., Richman, S. A., & Strathman, A. J. (1993). Positive mood and persuasion: Different roles for affect under high- and low-elaboration conditions. *Journal of Personality and Social Psychology, 64*, 5–20.

Petty, R. E., & Wegener, D. T. (1998). Attitude change: Multiple roles for persuasion variables. In D. T. Gilbert, S. T. Fiske, & G. Lindzey (Eds.), *The handbook of social psychology* (pp. 323–371). Boston: McGraw-Hill.

Petty, R. E., & Wegener, D. T. (1999). The elaboration likelihood model: Current status and controversies. In S. Chaiken & Y. Trope (Ed.), *Dual process theories in social psychology* (pp. 37–72). New York: Guilford Press.

Phillipps, M. (1999). Problems with the polygraph. *Science, 286*, 413.

Phillips, M., Brooks-Gunn, J., Duncan, G. J., Klebanov, P., & Crane, J. (1998). Family background, parenting practices, and the Black–White test score gap. In C. Jencks, M. Phillips (Eds.), *The Black–White test score gap* (pp. 103–145). Washington, DC: Brookings Institution.

Philpot, C. L. (2001). Family therapy for men. In G. R. Brooks (Ed.), *The new handbook of psychotherapy and counseling with men: A comprehensive guide to settings, problems, and treatment approaches, 1 & 2* (pp. 622–636). San Francisco: Jossey-Bass.

Pillard, R. C., & Bailey, M. J. (1998). Human sexual orientation has a heritable component. *Human Biology, 70*, 347–365.

Pinker, S. (1994). *The language instinct: How the mind creates language.* New York: Morrow.

Pinker, S. (1997). *How the mind works.* New York: Norton.

Pinker, S. (1999). *Words and rules.* New York: Basic Books.

Pipher, M. (1994). *Reviving Ophelia: Saving the selves of adolescent girls.* New York: Ballantine Books.

Pittenger, D. J. (1997). Reconsidering the overjustification effect: A guide to critical resources. *Teaching of Psychology, 23*, 234–236.

Pitts, C. G. (2000). Women, mental health, and managed care: A disparate system. *Women and Therapy, 22*(3), 27–36.

Pittsburgh Post-Gazette. (2001, October 14). Celebrate folks who "live to the point of tears." Author, G-9.

Place, U. T. (2000). Consciousness and the zombie within: A functional analysis of the blindsight evidence. In Y. Rossetti & A. Revonsuo (Eds.), *Beyond dissociation: Interaction between dissociated implicit and explicit processing. Advances in consciousness research* (pp. 295–329). Amsterdam: John Benjamins Publishing Company.

Plant, E. A., Hyde, J. S., Keltner, D., & Devine, P. G. (2000). The gender stereotyping of emotions. *Psychology of Women Quarterly, 24*, 81–92.

Plomin, R., & Caspi, A. (1999). Behavior genetics and personality. In L. A. Pervin & O. P. John (Eds.), *Handbook of personality: Theory and research* (pp. 251–276). New York: Guilford Press.

Plomin, R., & Crabbe, J. (2000). DNA. *Psychological Bulletin, 126*, 806–828.

Plomin, R., & De Fries, J. C. (1999). The genetics of cognitive abilities and disabilities. In S. J. Ceci & W. M. Williams (Eds.), *The nature-nurture debate: The essential readings. Essential readings in developmental psychology* (pp. 177–195). Malden, MA: Blackwell Publishers.

Plomin, R., Fulker, D. W., Corley, R., & DeFries, J. C. (1997). Nature, nurture, and cognitive development from 1 to 16 years: A parent–offspring adoption study. *Psychological Science, 8*, 442–447.

Pollack, W. (1998). *Real boys: Rescuing our sons from the myths of boyhood.* New York: Random House.

Polonsky, A., Blake, R., Braun, J., & Heeger, D. J. (2000). Neuronal activity in human primary visual cortex correlates with perception during binocular rivalry. *Nature Neuroscience, 3*, 1153–1159.

Pomerantz, E. M., Chaiken, S., & Tordesillas, R. S. (1995). Attitude strength and resistance processes. *Journal of Personality and Social Psychology, 69*, 408–419.

Pope, H. G., Kouri, E. M., & Hudson, J. I. (2000). Effects of supraphysiologic doses of testosterone on mood and aggression in normal men. *Archives of General Psychiatry, 57*, 133–140.

Pope, K. S. (2000). Pseudoscience, cross-examination, and scientific evidence in the recovered memory controversy. *Psychology, Public Policy, and Law, 4*, 1160–1181.

Porter, B. E., Leeming, F. C., & Dwyer, W. O. (1995). Solid waste recovery: A review of behavioral programs to increase recycling. *Environment and Behavior, 27*, 122–152.

Posner, M. I., DiGirolamo, G. J., & Fernandez-Duque, D. (1997). Brain mechanisms of cognitive skills. *Conscious Cognition, 6*, 267–290.

Posner, M. I., & Pavese, A. (1998). Anatomy of word and sentence meaning. *Proceedings of the National Academy of Sciences, 95*, 899–905.

Post, R. M., Frye, M. A., Dnicoff, K. D., Leverich, G. S., Kimbrell, T. A., & Dunn, R. T. (1998). Beyond lithium in the treatment of bipolar illness. *Neuropsychopharmacology, 19*, 206–219.

Powers, P. C., & Geen, R. G. (1972). Effects of the behavior and the perceived arousal of a model on instrumental aggression. *Journal of Personality and Social Psychology, 23*, 175–184.

Powledge, T. M. (1999). Addiction and the brain. *BioScience, 49*, 513–519.

Prados, J., Chamizo, V. D., & Mackintosh, N. J. (1999). Latent inhibition and perceptual learning in a swimming-pool navigation task. *Journal of Experimental Psychology: Animal Behavior Processes, 25*(1), 37–44.

Pratkanis, A. R. (2001). Propaganda and deliberative persuasion: The implications of Americanized mass media for established and emerging democracies. In W. Wosinska, R. B. Cialdini, D. W. Barrett, & J. Reykowski (Eds.), *The practice of social influence in multiple cultures. Applied social research* (pp. 259–285). Mahwah, NJ: Erlbaum.

Pratkanis, A. R., & Turner, M. E. (1999). Groupthink and preparedness for the Loma Prieta earthquake: A social identity maintenance analysis of causes and preventions. In R. Wageman (Ed.),

Research on managing groups and teams: Groups in context (pp. 115–136). Stamford, CT: JAI Press.

Prelow, H. M., & Guarnaccia, C. A. (1997). Ethnic and racial differences in life stress among high school adolescents. *Journal of Counseling and Development, 75,* 442–450.

Premack, D. (1971). Language in chimpanzees? *Science, 172,* 808–822.

Prokopcakova, A. (1998). Drug experimenting and pubertal maturation in girls. *Studia Psychologica, 40,* 287–290.

Proshansky, H. M., & O'Hanlon, T. (1977). Environmental psychology: Origins and development. In D. Stokols (Ed.), *Perspectives on environment and behavior: Theory, research, and application.* New York: Plenum.

Prudic, J., Olfson, M., & Sackeim, H. A. (2001). Electro-convulsive therapy practices in the community. *Psychological Medicine, 31,* 929–934.

Prudic, J., Peyser, S., & Sackeim, H. A. (2000). Subjective memory complaints: A review of patient self-assessment of memory after electroconvulsive therapy. *Journal of ECT, 16,* 121–132.

Punamaki, R. L., & Joustie, M. (1998). The role of culture, violence, and personal factors affecting dream content. *Journal of Cross-Cultural Psychology, 29,* 320–342.

Putnam, F. W., & Carlson, E. B. (1998). Trauma, memory, and dissociation. *Progress in Psychiatry, 54,* 27–55.

Rahe, R. H. (1989). Recent life change stress and psychological depression. In T. W. Miller (Ed.), *Stressful life events* (pp. 5–11). Madison, CT: International Universities Press.

Rahola, J. G. (2001). Antidepressants: Pharmacological profile and clinical consequences. *International Journal of Psychiatry in Clinical Practice, 5* (Suppl. 1), S19–S28.

Raine, A., Lenczk, T., Bihrle, S., LaCasse, L., & Colletti, P. (2000). Reduced prefrontal gray matter volume and reduced autonomic activity in antisocial personality disorder. *Archives of General Psychiatry, 57,* 119–127, 128–129.

Rainville, P., Hofbauer, R. K., Paus, T., Duncan, G. H., Bushnell, M. C., & Price, D. D. (1999). Cerebral mechanisms of hypnotic induction and suggestion. *Journal of Cognitive Neuroscience, 11,* 110–125.

Rajaram, S., Srinivas, K., & Roediger, H. L., III. (1998). A transfer-appropriate processing account of context effects in word-fragment completion. *Journal of Experimental Psychology: Learning, Memory and Cognition, 24,* 993–1004.

Ramachandran, V. S. (2000). Memory and the brain: New lessons from old syndromes. In D. L. Schacter & E. Scarry (Eds.), *Memory, brain, and belief* (pp. 87–114). Cambridge, MA: Harvard University Press.

Ramachandran, V. S., & Hubbard, E. (2001). Psychophysical investigations into the neural basis of synesthesia. Proceedings of the Royal Society of London. Series B. *Biological Sciences, 268,* 979–983.

Ramey, C. T., & Campbell, F. A. (1984). Preventive education for high-risk children: Cognitive consequences of the Carolina Abecedarian Project. *American Journal of Mental Deficiency, 88,* 515–523.

Ramey, C. T., & Campbell, F. A. (1992). Poverty, early childhood education, and academic competence: The Abecedarian experiment. In A. Huston (Ed.), *Children in poverty* (pp. 190–221). New York: Cambridge University Press.

Ramey, C. T., Campbell, F. A., Burchinal, M., Skinner, M. L., Gardner, D. M., & Ramsey, S. L. (2000). Persistent effects of early intervention on high-risk children and their mothers. *Applied Developmental Science, 4,* 2–14.

Ramey, C. T., Ramey, S. L., & Lanzi, R. G. (2001). Intelligence and experience. In R. J. Sternberg & E. L. Grigorenko (Eds.), *Environmental effects on cognitive abilities* (pp. 83–115). Mahwah, NJ: Erlbaum.

Ramey, S. L., & Sackett, G. P. (2000). The early caregiving environment: Expanding views on nonparental care and cumulative life experiences. In A. J. Sameroff, M. Lewis, & S. M. Miller (Eds.), *Handbook of developmental psychopathology* (2nd ed., pp. 365–380). New York: Kluwer/Plenum.

Rappaport, J. (1987). Terms of empowerment/exemplars of prevention: Toward a theory for community psychology. *American Journal of Community Psychology, 2,* 121–148.

Rapport, L. J., Todd, R. M., Lumley, M. A., & Fisicaro, S. A. (1998). The diagnostic meaning of "nervous breakdown" among lay populations. *Journal of Personality Assessment, 71,* 242–252.

Rasmussen, L. E. L., & Krishnamurthy, V. (2000). How chemical signals integrate Asian elephant society: The known and the unknown. *Zoo Biology, 19,* 405–423.

Raven, B. H. (1998). Groupthink, Bay of Pigs, and Watergate reconsidered. *Organizational Behavior and Human Decision Processes, 73,* 352–361.

Ravussin, E., Lillioja, S., Knowler, W. C., Christin, L., Freymond, D., Abbott, W. G. H., Boyce, V., Howard, B. V., & Bogardus, C. (1988). Reduced rate of energy expenditure as a risk factor for body-weight gain. *New England Journal of Medicine, 318,* 467–472.

Rayner, K. (1998). Eye movements in reading and information processing: 20 years of research. *Psychological Bulletin, 124,* 372–422.

Rayner, K., Reichle, E. D., & Pollatsek, A. (2000). Eye movement control in reading: Updating the E-Z reader model to account for initial fixation locations and refixations. In A. Kennedy, R. Radach, D. Heller, & J. Pynte (Eds.), *Reading as a perceptual process* (pp. 701–719). Amsterdam: North-Holland/Elsevier Science Publishers.

Raz, S., & Raz, N. (1990). Structural brain abnormalities in the major psychoses: A quantitative review of the evidence from computerized imaging. *Psychological Bulletin, 208,* 93–108.

Rechtschaffen, A. (1998). Current perspectives on the function of sleep. *Perspectives in Biology and Medicine, 41,* 359–370.

Reed, C. F. (1984). Terrestrial passage theory of the moon illusion. *Journal of Experimental Psychology: General, 113,* 489–516.

Reeder, H. M. (2000). I like you . . . as a friend: The role of attraction in cross-sex friendship. *Journal of Social and Personal Relationship, 17,* 329–348.

Regan, P. C., Levin, L., Sprecher, S., Christopher, F. S., & Cate, R. (2001). Partner preferences: What characteristics do men and women desire in their short-term sexual and long-term romantic partners? *Journal of Psychology and Human Sexuality, 12,* 1–21.

Reichle, E. D., Carpenter, P. A., & Just, M. A. (2000). The neural bases of strategy and skill in sentence-picture verification. *Cognitive Psychology, 40,* 261–295.

Reisenzein, R. (1983). The Schachter theory of emotion: Two decades later. *Psychological Bulletin, 94,* 239–264.

Reiss, D., Neiderhiser, J. M., Hetherington, E. M., & Plomin, R. (2000). *The relationship code.* Cambridge, MA: Harvard University Press.

Renault, B., Signoret, J. L., Debruille, B., Breton, F., & Bolgert, F. (1989). Brain potentials reveal covert facial recognition in prosopagnosia. *Neuropsychologica, 27,* 905–912.

Renzulli, J. S. (1998). The three-ring conception of giftedness. In S. Baum, S. M. Reiss, & L. R. Maxfield (Eds.), *Nurturing the gifts and talents of primary grade students.* Mansfield Center, CT: Creative Learning Press.

Rescorla, R. A. (1977). Pavlovian 2nd-order conditioning: Some implications for instrumental behavior. In H. Davis & H. Herwit (Eds.), *Pavlovian–operant interactions.* Hillsdale, NJ: Erlbaum.

Rescorla, R. A. (1988). Pavlovian conditioning: It's not what you think it is. *American Psychologist, 43,* 151–160.

Rescorla, R. A. (1998). Instrumental learning: Nature and persistence. In M. Sabourin, F. Craik, & M. Robert (Eds.), *Advances in psychological science* (pp. 239–257). Hove, UK: Psychology Press/Erlbaum (UK)/Taylor & Francis.

Rescorla, R. A. (2001a). Experimental extinction. In R. R. Mowrer & S. B. Klein (Eds.), *Handbook of contemporary learning theories* (pp. 119–154). Mahwah, NJ: Erlbaum.

Rescorla, R. A. (2001b). Retraining of extinguished Pavlovian stimuli. *Journal of Experimental Psychology: Animal Behavior Processes, 27,* 115–124.

Resnick, M. D., Bearman, P. S., Blum, R. W., Bauman, K. E., Harris, K. M., Jones, J., Tabor, J., Beuhring, T., Sieving, R. E., Shew, M., Ireland, M., Bearinger, L. H., & Udry, R. (1997). Protecting adolescents from harm: Findings from the National Longitudinal Study on Adolescent Health. *Journal of the American Medical Association, 278,* 823–831.

Restle, F. (1970). Moon illusion explained on the basis of relative size. *Science, 167,* 1092–1096.

Rhode, D. L. (1997). *Speaking of sex: The denial of gender inequality.* Cambridge, MA: Harvard University Press.

Rhodes, N., & Wood, W. (1992). Self-esteem and intelligence affect influenceability: The mediating role of message reception. *Psychological Bulletin, 111,* 156–171.

Rice, G., Anderson, C., Risch, N., & Ebers, G. (1999). Male homosexuality: Absence of linkage to microsatellite markers at Xq28. *Science, 284,* 665–667.

Richardson, K. (2000). *The making of intelligence.* New York: Columbia University Press.
Riegel, B., & Bennett, J. A. (2000). Cardiovascular disease in elders: Is it inevitable? *Journal of Adult Development, 7,* 101–112.
Rieger, E., Touyz, S. W., Swain, T., Beumont, P. J. V. (2001). Cross-cultural research on anorexia nervosa: Assumptions regarding the role of body weight. *International Journal of Eating Disorders, 29,* 205–215.
Riehle, A., Grun, S., Diesmann, M., & Aertsen, A. (1997). Spike synchronization and rate modulation differentially involved in motor cortical function. *Science, 278,* 1950–1953.
Ring, K., Wallston, K., & Corey, M. (1970). Mode of debriefing as a factor affecting subjective reaction to a Milgram-type obedience experiment: An ethical inquiry. *Representative Research in Social Psychology, 1,* 67–88.
Rips, L. J. (1990). Reasoning. *Annual Review of Psychology, 41,* 321–353.
Roberts, G. C. (1992). *Motivation in sport and exercise: Conceptual constraints and convergence* (pp. 3–29). Champaign, IL: Human Kinetics.
Roberts, R. E., Roberts, C. R., & Chen, I. G. (2000). Fatalism and risk of adolescent depression. *Psychiatry: Interpersonal and Biological Processes, 63,* 239–252.
Robinson, T. E., & Berridge, K. C. (2000). The psychology and neurobiology of addiction: An incentive-sensitization view. *Addiction, 95,* 91–117.
Robinson, T. N., Wilde, M. L., Navracruz, L. C., Haydel, K. F., & Varady, A. (2001). Effects of reducing children's television and video game use on aggressive behavior: A randomized controlled trial. *Archives of Pediatrics and Adolescent Medicine, 155,* 17–23.
Rochat, F., Maggioni, O., & Modigliani, A. (1999). The dynamics of obeying and opposing authority: A mathematical model. In T. Blass (Ed.), *Obedience to authority: Current perspectives on the Milgram paradigm* (pp. 161–192). Mahwah, NJ: Erlbaum.
Rock, I., & Palmer, S. (1990). The legacy of Gestalt psychology. *Scientific American, 263*(6), 84–90.
Rodin, J., & Langer, E. J. (1977). Long-term effects of a control-relevant intervention with the institutionalized aged. *Journal of Personality and Social Psychology, 35,* 897–902.
Rodriguez, E., George, N., Lachaux, J. P., Martinerie, J., Renault, B., & Varela, F. J. (1999). Perception's shadow: Long-distance synchronization of human activity. *Nature, 397,* 430–433.
Roediger, H. L., & McDermott, K. B. (1995). Creating false memories: Remembering words not presented in lists. *Journal of Experimental Psychology: Learning, Memory, and Cognition, 21,* 803–814.
Roeser, R. W., Eccles, J. S., & Sameroff, A. J. (2000). School as a context of early adolescents' academic and social-emotional development: A summary of research findings. *Elementary School Journal, 100,* 443–471.
Rogers, C. R. (1951). *Client-centered therapy.* Boston: Houghton Mifflin.
Rogers, C. R. (1957). The necessary and sufficient conditions of therapeutic personality change. *Journal of Consulting Psychology, 21,* 95–103.
Rogers, C. R. (1980). *A way of being.* Boston: Houghton Mifflin.
Rohland, B. M. (2001). Self-report of improvement following hospitalization for electroconvulsive therapy: Relationship to functional status and service use. *Administration and Policy in Mental Health, 28,* 193–203.
Rollmann, S. M. (2000). Courtship pheromone effects on female receptivity in a plethodontid salamander. *Dissertation Abstracts International: Section B: The Sciences & Engineering, 61*(1-B), 144.
Romano, S. T., & Bordieri, J. E. (1989). Physical attractiveness stereotypes and students' perceptions of college professors. *Psychological Reports, 64,* 1099–1102.
Romans, S. E. (2001). Gender issues in psychiatry. *Hong Kong Journal of Psychiatry, 10*(4), 7–11.
Roques, P., Lambin, M., Jeunier, B., & Strayer, F. F. (1997). Multivariate analysis of personal space in a primary school classroom. *Enfance, 4,* 451–468.
Rosch, E. (1978). Principles of categorization. In E. Rosch & B. B. Lloyd (Eds.), *Cognition and categorization* (pp. 27–48). Hillsdale, NJ: Erlbaum.
Rose, S. A., & Feldman, J. F. (1995). Prediction of IQ and specific cognitive abilities at 11 years from infancy measures. *Developmental Psychology, 31,* 685–696.
Rose, S. D. (1999). Group therapy: A cognitive–behavorial interactive approach. In J. R. Price, D. R. Hescheles, & A. R. Price (Eds.), *A guide to starting psychotherapy groups* (pp. 99–113). San Diego, CA: Academic Press.
Rosebush, P. A. (1998). Psychological intervention with military personnel in Rwanda. *Military Medicine, 163*(8), 559–563.
Rosenberg, H. (1993). Prediction of controlled drinking by alcoholics and problem drinkers. *Psychological Bulletin, 113,* 129–139.
Rosenberg, S. D., Rosenberg, H. J., & Farrell, M. P. (1999). The midlife crisis revisited. In S. L. Willis & J. D. Reid (Eds.), *Life in the middle: Psychological and social development in middle age* (pp. 47–73). San Diego, CA: Academic Press.
Rosenbluth, R., Grossman, E. S., & Kaitz, M. (2000). Performance of early-blind and sighted children on olfactory tasks. *Perception, 29,* 101–110.
Rosenthal, R., & Jacobson, L. (1966). Teachers' expectancies: Determinates of pupils' I.Q. gains. *Psychological Reports, 19,* 115–118.
Ross, C. A. (1999). Dissociative disorders. In T. Millon, P. H. Blaney, & R. D. Davis (Eds.), *Oxford textbook of psychopathology* (pp. 466–481). New York: Oxford University Press.
Ross, J. A., Haimes, D. H., & Hogaboam-Gray, A. (1998). Improving student helpfulness in cooperative learning groups. *Journal of Classroom Interaction, 31*(2), 13–22.
Ross, L., Bierbrauer, G., & Hoffman, S. (1976). The role of attribution processes in conformity and dissent. *American Psychologist, 31,* 148–157.
Ross, S. M., & Offermann, L. R. (1997). Transformational leaders: Measurement of personality attributes and work group performance. *Personality and Social Psychology Bulletin, 23,* 1078–1086.
Rossini, P. M., & Pauri, F. (2000). Neuromagnetic integrated methods tracking human brain mechanisms of sensorimotor areas "plastic" reorganisation. *Brain Research Reviews, 33,* 131–154.
Rotter, J. B. (1990). Internal versus external control of reinforcement. *American Psychologist, 45,* 489–493.
Rout, U. (1999). Gender differences in stress, satisfaction, and mental well-being among general practitioners in England. *Psychology, Health, and Medicine, 4,* 345–354.
Rowland, D. L., Greenleaf, W. J., Dorfman, L. J., & Davidson, J. M. (1993). Aging and sexual function in men. *Archives of Sexual Behavior, 22,* 545–558.
Rozin, P. (1999). Food is fundamental, fun, frightening, and far-reaching. *Social Research, 66,* 9–30.
Ruback, R. B., Pandey, J., & Begum, H. A. (1997). Urban stressors in South Asia: Impact on male and female pedestrians in Delhi and Dhaka. *Journal of Cross-Cultural Psychology, 28,* 23–43.
Rubenzahl, S. A., & Corcoran, K. J. (1998). The prevalence and characteristics of male perpetrators of acquaintance rape: New research methodology reveals new findings. *Violence Against Women, 4,* 713–725.
Rudy, D., & Grusec, J. F. (2001). Correlates of authoritarian parenting in individualist and collectivist cultures and implications for understanding the transmission of values. *Journal of Cross-Cultural Psychology, 32,* 202–212.
Ruggieri, V., Milizia, M., Sabatini, N., & Tosi, M. T. (1983). Body perception in relation to muscular tone at rest and tactile sensitivity. *Perceptual and Motor Skills, 56,* 799–806.
Rumbaugh, D. M., Gill, T. V., & Von Glaserfeld, E. D. (1973). Reading and sentence completion by a chimpanzee (Pan troglodytes). *Science, 182,* 731–733.
Rumelhart, D. E. (1997). The architecture of mind: A connectionist approach. In J. Haugeland (Ed.), *Philosophy, psychology, artificial intelligence* (pp. 205–232). Cambridge, MA: The MIT Press.
Rumiati, R. I., & Humphreys, G. W. (1997). Visual object agnosia without alexia or propagnosia: Arguments for separate knowledge stores. *Visual Cognition, 4,* 207–217.
Rushkoff, D. (1999). *Coercion: Why we listen to what "they" say.* New York: Riverhead Books.
Russell, J. A. (1994). Is there universal recognition of emotion from facial expression? A review of the cross-cultural studies. *Psychological Bulletin, 115,* 102–141.
Rustemli, A. (1991). Crowding effects of density and interpersonal distance. *The Journal of Social Psychology, 132,* 51–58.
Rybak, I. A., Gusakova, V. I., Golovan, A. V., Podladchikova, L. N., Shevtsova, N. A. (1998). A model of attention-guided visual perception and recognition. *Vision Research, 38,* 2387–2400.

Rycroft, P. J. (2001). An evaluation of short-term group therapy for battered women. *Dissertation Abstracts International: Section B: The Sciences & Engineering, 61*(7-B). Univ. Microfilms International.

Sabini, J., Siepmann, M., & Stein, J. (2001). The really fundamental attribution error in social psychological research. *Psychological Inquiry, 12*(1), 1–15.

Sackeim, H. A. (2001). Functional brain circuits in major depression and remission. *Archives of General Psychiatry, 58,* 649–650.

Sagrestano, L. M., McCormick, S. H., Paikoff, R. L., & Holmbeck, G. N. (1999). Pubertal development and parent–child conflicts in low-income, urban, African American adolescents. *Journal of Research on Adolescence, 9,* 85–107.

Sakata, S., Shinohara, J., Hori, T., & Sugimoto, S. (1995). Enhancement of randomness by flotation rest (restricted environmental stimulation technique). *Perceptual and Motor Skills, 80*(3, Pt. 1), 999–1010.

Sakitt, B., & Long, G. M. (1979). Cones determine subjective offset of a stimulus but rods determine total persistence. *Vision Research, 19,* 1439–1443.

Salminen, S., & Glad, T. (1992). The role of gender in helping behavior. *The Journal of Social Psychology, 132,* 131–133.

Salthouse, T. A. (1999). Theories of cognition. In V. L. Bengtson & K. W. Schaie (Eds.), *Handbook of theories of aging* (pp. 196–208). New York: Springer.

Salthouse, T. A. (2000). Pressing issues in cognitive aging. In D. C. Park & N. Schwarz (Eds.), *Cognitive aging: A primer* (pp. 43–54). Philadelphia: Psychology Press/Taylor & Francis.

Sammons, M., Gorny, S. W., Zinner, E. S., & Allen, R. P. (2000). Prescriptive authority for psychologists: A consensus support. *Professional Psychology: Research and Practice, 31,* 604–609.

Samoriski, G. M., & Gross, R. A. (2000). Functional compartmentalization of opioid desensitization in primary sensory neurons. *Journal of Pharmacology & Experimental Therapeutics, 294,* 500–509.

Sampson, E. (2000). Reinterpreting individualism and collectivism: Their religious roots and monologic versus dialogic person–other relationship. *American Psychologist, 55,* 1425–1432.

Sanders, C. E., Field, T. M., Diego, M., & Kaplan, M. (2000). The relationship of Internet use to depression and social isolation among adolescents. *Adolescence, 35,* 237–242.

Sanders, M. S., & McCormick, E. J. (1993). *Human factors in engineering and design* (7th ed.). New York: McGraw-Hill.

Sankis, L. M., Corbitt, E. M., & Widiger, T. A. (1999). Gender bias in the English language. *Journal of Personality and Social Psychology, 77,* 1289–1295.

Santos, M. D., Leve, C., & Pratkanis, A. R. (1994). Hey buddy, can you spare seventeen cents? Mindful persuasion and the pique technique. *Journal of Applied Social Psychology, 224,* 755–764.

Sass, L. A. (2001). Schizophrenia, modernism, and the "creative imagination": On creativity and psychopathology. *Creativity Research Journal, 13*(1), 55–74.

Schachter, S., & Singer, J. E. (1962). Cognitive, social, and physiological determinants of emotional state. *Psychological Review, 69,* 379–399.

Schacter, D. L. (1997). False recognition and the brain. *Current Directions in Psychological Science, 6,* 65–70.

Schacter, D. L. (2001). *The seven sins of memory: How the mind forgets and remembers.* Boston: Houghton Mifflin.

Schaie, K. W. (1993). The Seattle longitudinal studies of adult intelligence. *Current Directions in Psychological Science, 2,* 171–175.

Schaie, K. W. (2000). The impact of longitudinal studies on understanding development from young adulthood to old age. *International Journal of Behavioral Development, 24,* 257–266.

Schaller, M. (1991). Social categorization and the formation of group stereotypes: Further evidence for biased information processing in the perception of group-behavior correlations. *European Journal of Social Psychology, 21*(1), 25–35.

Schatzman, M. (1992). Freud: Who seduced whom? *New Scientist,* 34–37.

Scheibel, A. B., Conrad, T., Perdue, S., Tomiyasu, U., & Wechsler, A. (1990). A quantitative study of dendrite complexity in selected areas of the human cerebral cortex. *Brain Cognition, 12,* 85–101.

Scher, M. (2001). Male therapist, male client: Reflections on critical dynamics. In G. R. Brooks & G. E. Good (Eds.), *The new handbook of psychotherapy and counseling with men: A comprehensive guide to settings, problems, and treatment approaches, 1 & 3* (pp. 719–733). New York: Jossey-Bass.

Scherer, K. R. (1997). The role of culture in emotion-antecedent appraisal. *Journal of Personality and Social Psychology, 73,* 902–922.

Scherer, K. R., Wallbott, H. G., & Summerfield, A. B. (1986). *Experiencing emotion: A cross-cultural study.* Cambridge, UK: Cambridge University Press.

Schiff, M., Duyme, M., Dumaret, A., & Tomkiewicz, S. (1982). How much could we boost scholastic achievement and IQ scores? A direct answer from a French adoption study. *Cognition, 12,* 165–196.

Schiller, P. H. (1998). The neural control of visually guided eye movements. In J. E. Richards (Ed.), *Cognitive neuroscience of attention: A development perspective* (pp. 3–50). Mahwah, NJ: Erlbaum.

Schinka, J. A., Dye, D. A., & Curtiss, G. (1997). Correspondence between five-factor and RIASEC models of personality. *Journal of Personality Assessment, 68,* 355–368.

Schlaug, G., Jäncke, L., Huang, Y., Staiger, J. F., & Steinmetz, H. (1995). Increased corpus callosum size in musicians. *Neuropsychologia, 33,* 1047–1055.

Schmidt, D. F., & Boland, S. M. (1986). Structure of perceptions of older adults: Evidence for multiple stereotypes. *Psychology and Aging, 1,* 255–260.

Schmidt, F. L., & Hunter, J. E. (1998). The validity and utility of selection methods in personnel psychology: Practical and theoretical implications of 85 years of research findings. *Psychological Bulletin, 124,* 262–274.

Schmit, M. J., & Ryan, A. M. (1993). The big five in personnel selection: Factor structure in applicant and nonapplicant populations. *Journal of Applied Psychology, 78,* 966–974.

Schmitz, J. M., Averill, P., Stotts, A. L., Moeller, F. G., Rhoades, H. M., & Grabowski, J. (2001). Fluoxetine treatment of cocaine-dependent patients with major depressive disorder. *Drug & Alcohol Dependence, 63,* 207–214.

Schmitz, S. (1999). Gender differences in acquisition of environmental knowledge related to wayfinding ability, spatial anxiety, and self-estimated environmental competencies. *Sex Roles, 41,* 71–94.

Schneiderman, N., Antoni, M. H., Saab, P. G., & Ironson, G. (2001). Health psychology: Psychosocial and biobehavioral aspects of chronic disease management. *Annual Review of Psychology, 52,* 555–580.

Schnyder, U., Moergeli, H., Klaghofer, R., & Buddeberg, C. (2001). Incidence and prediction of posttraumatic stress disorder symptoms in severely injured accident victims. *American Journal of Psychiatry, 158,* 594–599.

Scholl, B. J. (2000). Attenuated change blindness for exogenously attended items in a flicker paradigm. *Visual Cognition, 7,* 377–396.

Schooler, C., Neumann, E., Caplan, L. J., & Roberts, B. R. (1997). A time course analysis of Stroop interference and facilitation: Comparing normal individuals and individuals with schizophrenia. *Journal of Experimental Psychology: General, 126,* 19–36.

Schooler, J. W., & Eich, E. (2000). Memory for emotional events. In E. Tulving and F. I. Craik (Eds.), *The Oxford handbook of memory* (pp. 379–392). New York: Oxford University Press.

Schorow, S. (2000, January 14). Not "interrupted": Treatment of mental illness in adolescent girls has improved dramatically from era depicted in new movie. *Boston Herald,* p. 39.

Schramke, C. J., & Bauer, R. M. (1997). State-dependent learning in older and younger adults. *Psychology and Aging, 12,* 255–262.

Schrauf, R. W. (2000). Bilingual autobiographical memory: Experimental studies and clinical cases. *Culture and Psychology, 6,* 387–417.

Schredl, M., Dombrowe, C., Bozzer, A., & Morlock, M. (1999). Do subliminal stimuli affect dream content? Methodological issues and empirical data. *Sleep & Hypnosis, 1,* 181–185.

Schulberg, H. C., & Rush, A. J. (1994). Clinical practice guidelines for managing major depression in primary care practice: Implications for psychologists. *American Psychologist, 49,* 34–41.

Schultz, A., Williams, D., Israel, B., Becker, A., Parker, E., James, S. A., & Jackson, J. (2000). Unfair treatment, neighborhood effects, and mental health in the Detroit metropolitan area. *The Journal of Health and Social Behavior, 41,* 314–333.

Schultz, G., & Melzack, R. (1999). A case of referred pain evoked by remote light touch after partial nerve injury. *Pain, 81,* 199–202.

Schurr, K. T., Ruble, V., Palomba, C., Pickerill, B., & Moore, D. (1997). Relationships between the MBTI and selected aspects of

Tinto's model for college attrition. *Journal of Psychological Type, 40,* 31–42.
Schwartzman, A. E., Gold, D., Andres, D., Arbuckle, T. Y., & Chaikelson, J. (1987). Stability of intelligence: A 40-year follow-up. *Canadian Journal of Psychology, 41,* 244–256.
Schweiger, U., Deuschle, M., Körner, A., Lammers, C. H., Schmider, J., Gotthardt, U., Holsboer, F., & Heuser, I. (1994). Low lumbar bone mineral density in patients with major depression. *American Journal of Psychiatry, 151,* 1691–1693.
Sclafani, A. (1997). Learned controls of ingestive behavior. *Appetite, 29,* 153–158.
Scott, K., Brady, R., Cravchik, A., Morozov, P., Rzhetsky, A., Zuker, C., & Axel, R. (2001). A chemosensory gene family encoding candidate gustatory and olfactory receptors in *Drosophila. Cell, 104,* 661–673.
Segal, N. L., & MacDonald, K. B. (1998). Behavioral genetics and evolutionary psychology: Unified perspective on personality research. *Human Biology, 70,* 159–174.
Seidenberg, M. S. (1997). Language acquisition and use: Learning and applying probabilistic constraints. *Science, 275,* 1599–1603.
Selekman, M. D. (1993). Solution-oriented brief therapy with difficult adolescents. In S. Friedman (Ed.), *The new language of change: Constructive collaboration in psychotherapy* (pp. 138–157). New York: Guilford Press.
Seligman, M. E. P. (1976). *Learned helplessness and depression in animals and humans.* Morristown, NJ: General Learning.
Seligman, M. E. P. (1988, August). *Learned helplessness.* G. Stanley Hall lecture at the American Psychological Association Convention, Atlanta.
Seligman, M. E. P. (1991). *Learned optimism.* New York: Knopf.
Seligman, M. E. P., & Csikszentmihalyi, M. (2000). Positive psychology. *American Psychologist, 55,* 5–14.
Selkoe, D. J. (1992, September). Aging brain, aging mind. *Scientific American,* 135–142.
Sell, R. L., Wells, J. A., & Wypij, D. (1995). The prevalence of homosexual behavior and attraction in the United States, the United Kingdom, and France: Results of national population-based samples. *Archives of Sexual Behavior, 24,* 235–248.
Selye, H. (1956). *The stress of life.* New York: McGraw-Hill.
Selye, H. (1976). *Stress in health and disease.* London: Butterworth.
Sen, M. G., Yonas, A., Knill, D. C. (2001). Development of infants' sensitivity to surface contour information for spatial layout. *Perception, 30,* 167–176.
Severiens, S., & Ten-Dam, G. (1997). Gender and gender identity differences in learning styles. *Educational Psychology, 17,* 79–93.
Shalowitz, M. U., Berry, C. A., Rasinski, K. A., & Dannhausen-Brun, C. A. (1998). A new measurement of contemporary life stress: Development, validation, and reliability of the CRISYS (Crisis in Family Systems). *Health Services Research, 33,* 1381–1382.
Shamir, B. (1992). Attribution of influence and charisma to the leader: The romance of leadership revisited. *Journal of Applied Social Psychology, 22,* 386–407.
Shanab, M. E., & Yahya, K. A. (1978). A cross-cultural study of obedience. *Bulletin of the Psychonomic Society, 11,* 267–269.
Sharit, J., & Czajia, S. J. (1999). Performance of a computer-based troubleshooting task in the banking industry: Examining the effects of age, task experience, and cognitive abilities. *International Journal of Cognitive Ergonomics, 3,* 1–22.
Shatz, S. M. (2000). The relationship of locus of control and social support to adult nursing home residents. *Dissertation Abstracts International: Section B: The Sciences & Engineering, 61*(3-B), 1655.
Shaw, G. M., Shapiro, R. Y., Lock, S., & Jacobs, L. R. (1998). Trends: Crime, the police, and civil liberties. *Public Opinion Quarterly, 62,* 405–426.
Shaw, J. S., III, Bjork, R. A., & Handal, A. (1995). Retrieval-induced forgetting in an eyewitness-memory paradigm. *Psychonomic Bulletin and Review, 2,* 249–253.
Shaywitz, B. A., Shaywitz, S. E., Pugh, K. R., Constable, R. T., Skudlarski, P., Fulbright, R. K., Bronen, R. A., Fletcher, J. M., Shankweiler, D. P., Katz, L., & Gore, J. C. (1995). Sex differences in the functional organization of the brain for language. *Nature, 373,* 607–609.
Shaywitz, S. E., Shaywitz, B. A., Pugh, K. R., Fullbright, R. K., & Constable, R. T. (1998). Functional disruption in the organization of the brain for reading in dyslexia. *Proceedings of the National Academy of Sciences, 95,* 2636–2641.
Sheehan, P. W., & Robertson, R. (1996). Imagery and hypnosis: Trends and patternings in effects. In R. G. Kunzendorf, N. P. Spanos, & B. Wallace (Eds.), *Hypnosis and imagination* (pp. 1–17). Amityville, NY: Baywood.
Sheeran, P., Abraham, C., & Orbell, S. (1999). Psychosocial correlates of heterosexual condom use: A meta-analysis. *Psychological Bulletin, 125,* 90–132.
Shelton, C. M. (2000). *Achieving moral health: An exercise plan for your conscience.* New York: Crossroad.
Shepperd, J. A. (1993). Productivity loss in performance groups: A motivation analysis. *Psychological Bulletin, 113,* 67–81.
Sher, L. (1998). The role of the immune system and infection in the effects of psychological factors on the cardiovascular system. *Canadian Journal of Psychiatry, 43,* 954–955.
Shergill, S. S., Brammer, M. J., Williams, S. C. R., Murray, R. M., & McGuire, P. K. (2000). Mapping auditory hallucinations in schizophrenia using functional magnetic resonance imaging. *Archives of General Psychiatry, 57,* 1033–1038.
Sherin, J. E., Shiromani, P. J., McCarley, R. W., & Saper, C. B. (1996). Activation of ventrolateral preoptic neurons during sleep. *Science, 271,* 216–219.
Sherrington, R., Rogaev, E. I., Liang, Y., Rogaeva, E. A., Levesque, G., Ikeda, M., et al. (1995). Cloning of a gene bearing missense mutations in early-onset familial Alzheimer's disease. *Nature, 375,* 754–760.
Shih, M., Pittinsky, T. L., & Ambady, N. (1999). Stereotype susceptibility: Identity salience and shifts in quantitative performance. *Psychological Science, 10,* 80–81.
Shiner, R. L. (1998). How shall we speak of children's personalities in middle childhood? A preliminary taxonomy. *Psychological Bulletin, 124,* 308–332.
Shobe, K. K., & Kihlstrom, J. F. (1997). Is traumatic memory special? *Current Directions in Psychological Science, 6,* 70–74.
Shostrom, E. L. (1974). *Manual for the Personal Orientation Inventory.* San Diego, CA: Educational and Industrial Testing Service.
Shum, M. S. (1998). The role of temporal landmarks in autobiographical memory processes. *Psychological Bulletin, 124,* 423–442.
Si, G., Rethorst, S., & Willimczik, K. (1995). Causal attribution perception in sports achievement: A cross-cultural study on attributional concepts in Germany and China. *Journal of Cross-Cultural Psychology, 26,* 537–553.
Siegel, J. M. (1990). Stressful life events and use of physician services among the elderly: The moderating role of pet ownership. *Journal of Personality and Social Psychology, 58,* 1081–1086.
Siegel, S. (1999). Drug anticipation and drug addiction: The 1998 H. David Archibald lecture. *Addiction, 94,* 1113–1124.
Siegel, S., & Allan, L. G. (1996). The widespread influence of the Rescorla-Wagner model. *Psychonomic Bulletin and Review, 3,* 314–321.
Siegel, S., Baptista, M. A. S., Kim. J. A., McDonald, R. V., & Weise-Kelly, L. (2000). Pavlovian psychopharmacology: The associative basis of tolerance. *Experimental & Clinical Psychopharmacology, 8,* 276–293.
Sigelman, L. (1997). Blacks, whites, and the changing of the guard in black political leadership. In S. A. Tuch & J. K. Mart (Eds.), *Racial attitudes in the 1990s: Continuity and change.* Westport, CT: Praeger.
Silverman, I., Choi, J., Mackewn, A., Fisher, M., Moro, J., & Olshansky, E. (2000). Evolved mechanisms underlying wayfinding: Further studies on the hunter-gatherer theory of spatial sex differences. *Evolution & Human Behavior, 21,* 201–213.
Silverman, J. G., Raj, A., Mucci, L. A., & Hathaway, J. E. (2001). Dating violence against adolescent girls and associated substance use, unhealthy weight control, sexual risk behavior, pregnancy, and suicidality. *Journal of the American Medical Association, 286,* 572–579.
Simons, D. J., & Chabris, C. F. (1999). Gorillas in our midst: Sustained inattentional blindness for dynamic events. *Perception, 28,* 1059–1074.
Simons, D. J., Franconeri, S. L., & Reimer, R. L. (2000). Change blindness in the absence of a visual disruption. *Perception, 29,* 1143–1154.
Simpson, J. A. (1990). Influence of attachment styles on romantic relationships. *Journal of Personality and Social Psychology, 59,* 971–980.

Simpson, J. R., Oenguer, D., Akbudak, E., Conturo, T. E., Ollinger, J. M., Snyder, A. Z., Gusnard, D. A., Raichle, M. E. (2000). The emotional modulation of cognitive processing: An fMRI study. *Journal of Cognitive Neuroscience, 12* (Suppl. 2), 157–170.

Singh, S., & Darroch, J. (2000). Adolescent pregnancy and childbearing: levels and trends in developed countries. *Family Planning Perspectives, 32,* 14–23.

Sinha, B. K., Willson, L. R., & Watson, D. C. (2000). Stress and coping among students in India and Canada. *Canadian Journal of Behavioural Science, 32,* 218–225.

Sinha, S. P., & Mukherjee, N. (1996). The effect of perceived cooperation on personal space requirements. *Journal of Social Psychology, 136,* 655–657.

Sinha, S. P., & Nayyar, P. (2000). Crowding effects of density and personal space requirements among older people: The impact of self-control and social support. *Journal of Social Psychology, 140,* 721–728.

Siple, P. (1997). Universals, generalizability, and the acquisition of signed language. In M. Marschark, P. Siple, D. Lillo-Martin, R. Campbell, & V. S. Everhart, *Relations of language and thought: The view from sign language and deaf children* (pp. 24–61). New York: Oxford University Press.

Skinner, B. F. (1987). *Upon further reflection.* Englewood Cliffs, NJ: Prentice-Hall.

Skinner, B. F. (1988, June). Skinner joins aversives debate. *APA Monitor,* p. 22.

Skinner, B. F. (1989). The origins of cognitive thought. *American Psychologist, 44,* 13–18.

Skoog, G., & Skoog, I. (1999). A 40-year follow-up of patients with obsessive–compulsive disorder. *Archives of General Psychiatry, 56,* 121–132.

Smellie, P. (1999). Feeding stereotypes. *The Quill, 87*(2), 25–27.

Smith, E. E. (1997). Working memory: A view from neuroimaging. *Cognitive Psychology, 33,* 5–42.

Smith, E. E., Jonides, J., Koeppe, R. A., & Awh, E. (1995). Spatial versus object working memory: PET investigations. *Journal of Cognitive Neuroscience, 7,* 337–356.

Smith, K. H., & Rogers, M. (1994). Effectiveness of subliminal messages in television commercials: Two experiments. *Journal of Applied Psychology, 79,* 866–874.

Smith, M. L., Glass, G. V., & Miller, T. I. (1980). *The benefits of psychotherapy.* Baltimore: Johns Hopkins University Press.

Smith, M. W., Mendoza, R. P., & Lin, K. M. (1999). Gender and ethnic differences in the pharmacogenetics of psychotropics. In M. Herrera & W. B. Lawson (Eds.), *Cross-cultural psychiatry* (pp. 323–341). New York: Wiley.

Smith, S. L., Wilson, B. J., Kunkel, D., Linz, D., Potter, J., Colvin, C. M., & Donnerstein, E. (1998). *National television violence study. Vol. 3.* London: Sage.

Sneed, C. D., McCrae, R. R., & Funder, D. C. (1998). Lay conceptions of the five-factor model and its indicators. *Personality & Social Psychology Bulletin, 24,* 115–126.

Snelders, H. J., & Lea, S. E. (1996). Different kinds of work, different kinds of pay: An examination of the overjustification effect. *Journal of Socio-Economics, 25,* 517–535.

Soares, J. C., & Mann, J. (1997). The functional neuroanatomy of mood disorders. *Journal of Psychiatric Research, 31,* 393–432.

Sobell, L. C., Cunningham, J. A., & Sobell, M. B. (1996). Recovery from alcohol problems with and without treatment: Prevalence in two population surveys. *American Journal of Public Health, 86,* 966–972.

Soderstrom, M., Dolbier, C., Leiferman, J., & Steinhardt, M. (2000). The relationship of hardiness, coping strategies, and perceived stress to symptoms of illness. *Journal of Behavioral Medicine, 23,* 311–328.

Sokolov, R. (1999). Culture and obesity. *Social Research, 66,* 31–38.

Solomon, P. R., Flynn, D., Mirak, J., Brett, M., Coslov, N., & Groccia, M. E. (1998). Five-year retention of the classically conditioned eyeblink response in young adult, middle-aged, and older humans. *Psychology and Aging, 13,* 186–192.

Sommerich, C. M., Joines, S. M. B., & Psihogios, J. P. (2001). Effects of computer monitor viewing angle and related factors on strain, performance, and preference outcomes. *Human Factors, 43,* 39–55.

Sonn, C. C., & Fisher, A. T. (1998). Sense of community: Community resilient responses to oppression and change. *Journal of Community Psychology, 26,* 457–472.

Sonnenborg, F. A., Anderson, O. K., & Arendt-Nielsen, L. (2000). Modular organization of excitatory and inhibitory reflex receptive fields elicited by electrical stimulation of the foot sole in man. *Clinical Neurophysiology, 11,* 2160–2169.

Sosik, J. J., Kahai, S. S., & Avolio, B. J. (1998). Transformational leadership and dimensions of creativity: Motivating idea generation in computer-mediated groups. *Creativity Research Journal, 11,* 111–121.

Spangler, W. D. (1992). Validity of questionnaire and TAT measures of need for achievement: Two meta-analyses. *Psychological Bulletin, 112,* 140–154.

Spanos, N. P. (1994). Multiple identity enactments and multiple personality disorder: A sociocognitive perspective. *Psychological Bulletin, 116,* 143–165.

Spear, L. P. (2000). Neurobehavioral changes in adolescence. *Current Directions in Psychological Science, 9,* 111–114.

Spears, R., & Haslam, S. A. (1997). Stereotyping and the burden of cognitive load. In R. Spears, P. Oakes, N. Ellemers, & S. A. Haslam (Eds.), *The social psychology of stereotyping and group life* (pp. 171–207). Oxford, UK: Blackwell Publishers.

Speca, M., Carlson, L. E., Goodey, E., & Angen, M. (2000). A randomized, wait-list controlled clinical trial: The effect of a mindfulness meditation-based stress reduction program on mood and symptoms of stress in cancer outpatients. *Psychosomatic Medicine, 62,* 613–622.

Speck, O., Ernst, T., Braun, J., Koch, C., Miller, E., & Chang, L. (2000). Gender differences in the functional organization of the brain for working memory. *Neuroreport: An International Journal for the Rapid Communication of Research in Neuroscience, 11,* 2581–2585.

Sperling, G. (1960). The information available in brief visual presentations. *Psychological Monographs, 74*(11, Whole No. 498).

Spiegel, D. (1998). Hypnosis. *Harvard Mental Health Letter, 15*(3), 5–6.

Sporer, S. L., Penrod, S., Read, D., & Cutler, B. (1995). Choosing, confidence, and accuracy: A meta-analysis of the confidence-accuracy relation in eyewitness identification studies. *Psychological Bulletin, 118,* 315–327.

Sprecher, S. (1999). "I love you more today than yesterday": Romantic partners' perceptions of changes in love and related affect over time. *Journal of Personality and Social Psychology, 76,* 46–53.

Sprecher, S., Aron, A., Hatfield, E., Cortese, A., Potapova, E., & Levitskaya, A. (1992, July). *Love: American style, Russian style, and Japanese style.* Paper presented at the Sixth International Conference on Personal Relationships, Orono, Maine.

Springer, P. J. (2000). The relationship between learned helplessness and work performance in registered nurses. *Dissertation Abstracts International: Section B: The Sciences & Engineering, 60*(12-B), 6407.

Springer, S. P., & Deutsch, G. (1998). *Left brain, right brain: Perspectives from cognitive neuroscience* (5th ed.). New York: Freeman.

Sprock, J., & Yoder, C. Y. (1997). Women and depression: An update on the report of the APA Task Force. *Sex Roles, 36,* 269–303.

Squire, L. R., & Kandel, E. R. (1999). *Memory: From mind to molecules.* New York: Freeman.

Stagner, R. (1988). *A history of psychological theories.* New York: Macmillan.

Stajkovic, A. D., & Luthans, F. (1998). Self-efficacy and work-related performance: A meta-analysis. *Psychological Bulletin, 124,* 240–261.

Stake, J. E. (1997). Integrating expressiveness and instrumentality in real-life settings: A new perspective on the benefits of androgyny. *Sex Roles, 37,* 541–564.

Stalker, C. A., Levene, J. E., & Coady, N. F. (1999). Solution focused brief therapy—one model fits all? *Families in Society, 80,* 468–477.

Stassen, H. H., Ragaz, M., & Reich, T. (1997). Age-of-onset or age-cohort changes in the lifetime occurrence of depression? *Psychiatric Genetics, 7,* 27–34.

Starzomski, A., & Nussbaum, D. (2000). The self and the psychology of domestic homicide–suicide. *International Journal of Offender Therapy and Comparative Criminology, 44,* 468–479.

Steel, G. D., Callaway, M., Suedfeld, P., & Palinkas, L. (1995). Human sleep–wake cycles in the high arctic: Effects of unusual photoperiodicity in a natural setting. *Biological Rhythm Research, 26,* 582–592.

Steele, C. M. (1997). A threat in the air: How stereotypes shape intellectual identity and performance. *American Psychologist, 52,* 613–629.

Steele, C. M. (1999). The psychology of self-affirmation: Sustaining the integrity of the self. In R. F. Baumeister (Ed.), *The self in social psychology, Key Readings in Social Psychology* (pp. 372–390). Philadelphia: Psychology Press/Taylor & Francis.

Steele, C. M., & Aronson, J. (2000). Stereotype threat and the intellectual test performance of African Americans. In C. Stangor (Ed.), *Stereotypes and prejudice: Essential readings, Key Readings in Social Psychology* (pp. 369–389). Philadelphia: Psychology Press/Taylor & Francis.

Stein, A. D., Karel, T., & Zuidema, R. (1999). Carrots and sticks: Impact of an incentive/disincentive employee flexible credit benefit plan on health status and medical costs. *American Journal of Health Promotion, 13,* 260–267.

Stein, M. B., Walker, J. R., & Forde, D. R. (2000). Gender differences in susceptibility to posttraumatic stress disorder. *Behaviour Research and Therapy, 38,* 619–628.

Steinberg, L., Lamborn, S. D., Dornbusch, S. M., & Darling, N. (1992). Impact of parenting practices on adolescent achievement: Authoritative parenting, school involvement, and encouragement to succeed. *Child Development, 63,* 1266–1281.

Steinberg, M. (1995). *Handbook for the assessment of dissociation: A clinical guide.* Washington, DC: American Psychiatric Press.

Stern, K., & McClintock, M. K. (1998). Regulation of ovulation by human pheromones. *Nature, 392,* 126–127.

Sternberg, R. J. (1985). *Beyond IQ.* Cambridge, UK: Cambridge University Press.

Sternberg, R. J. (1986). A triangular theory of love. *Psychological Review, 93,* 119–135.

Sternberg, R. J. (1997). The concept of intelligence and its role in lifelong learning and success. *American Psychologist, 52,* 1030–1037.

Sternberg, R. J. (1998). A balance theory of wisdom. *Review of General Psychology, 2,* 347–365.

Sternberg, R. J. (2000a). Identifying and developing creative giftedness. *Roeper Review, 23,* 60–64.

Sternberg, R. J. (2000b). Implicit theories of intelligence as exemplar stories of success: Why intelligence test validity is in the eye of the beholder. *Psychology, Public Policy, & Law, 6,* 159–167.

Sternberg, R. J. (2001a). Successful intelligence: A unified view of giftedness. In C. F. M. van Lieshout & P. G. Heymans (Eds.), *Developing talent across the life span* (pp. 43–65). Philadelphia: Psychology Press/Taylor & Francis.

Sternberg, R. J. (2001b). What is the common thread of creativity?: Its dialectical relation to intelligence and wisdom. *American Psychologist, 56,* 360–362.

Sternberg, R. J., Castegon, J. L., Prieto, M. D., Hautamaki, J., & Grigorenko, E. L. (2001). Confirmatory factor analysis of the Sternberg Triarchic Abilities Test in three international samples: An empirical test of the triarchic theory of intelligence. *European Journal of Psychological Assessment, 17*(1), 1–16.

Sternberg, R. J., & Grigorenko, E. L. (2000a). Practical intelligence and its development. In R. Bar-On, & J. D. A. Parker (Eds.), *The handbook of emotional intelligence: Theory, development, assessment, and application at home, school, and in the workplace* (pp. 215–243). San Francisco: Jossey-Bass.

Sternberg, R. J., & Grigorenko, E. L. (2000b). Theme-park psychology: A case study regarding human intelligence and its implications for education. *Educational Psychology Review, 12*(2), 247–268.

Sternberg, R. J., Grigorenko, E. L., & Bundy, D. A. (2001). The predictive value of IQ. *Merrill-Palmer Quarterly, 47,* 1–41.

Sternberg, R. J., & Lubart, T. I. (1999). The concept of creativity: Prospects and paradigms. In R. J. Sternberg (Ed.), *Handbook of creativity* (pp. 3–15). New York: Cambridge University Press.

Sternberg, R. J., & Williams, W. M. (1997). Does the Graduate Record Examination predict meaningful success in the graduate training of psychologists? *American Psychologist, 52,* 630–641.

Sterrett, E. A. (1998). Use of a job club to increase self-efficacy: A case study of return to work. *Journal of Employment Counseling, 35*(2), 69–78.

Stewart, A. J., & Ostrove, J. M. (1998). Women's personality in middle age: Gender, history, and midcourse corrections. *American Psychologist, 53,* 1185–1194.

Stewart, A. J., & Vandewater, E. A. (1998). The course of generativity. In D. P. McAdams, E. de St. Aubin, et al. (Eds.), *Generativity and adult development: How and why we care for the next generation* (pp. 75–100). Washington, DC: American Psychological Association.

Stewart, S., Stinnett, H., & Rosenfeld, L. B. (2001). Sex differences in desired characteristics of short-term and long-term relationship partners. *Journal of Social and Personal Relationships, 17,* 843–853.

Stickgold, R., James, L., & Hobson, J. A. (2000). Visual discrimination learning requires sleep after training. *Nature Neuroscience, 3,* 1237–1238.

Stigler, J. W., & Baranes, R. (1988). Culture and mathematics learning. In E. Rothkopf (Ed.), *Review of research in education, 15* (pp. 253–306). Washington, DC: American Educational Research Association.

Stipek, D., Givvin, K. B., Aslmon, J. M., & MacGyvers, V. L. (1998). Can a teacher intervention improve classroom practices and student motivation in mathematics? *Journal of Experimental Education, 66,* 319–337.

Stokols, D. (1995). The paradox of environmental psychology. *American Psychologist, 50,* 821–837.

Stoléru, S., Grégoire, M. C., Gérard, D., Decety, J., Lafarge, E., Cinotti, L., Lavenne, F., LeBars, D., Vernet-Maury, E., Rada, H., Collet, C., Mazoyer, B., Forest, M. G., Magnin, F., Spira, A., & Comar, D. (1999). Neuroanatomical correlates of visually evoked sexual arousal in human males. *Archives of Sexual Behavior, 28,* 1–19.

Stone, J. (2001). Behavioral discrepancies and the role of construal processes in cognitive dissonance. In G. B. Moskowitz (Ed.), *Cognitive social psychology: The Princeton Symposium on the Legacy and Future of Social Cognition* (pp. 41–58). Mahwah, NJ: Erlbaum.

Stone, J., Perry, Z. W., & Darley, J. M. (1997). "White men can't jump": Evidence for the perceptual confirmation of racial stereotypes following a basketball game. *Basic and Applied Social Psychology, 19,* 291–306.

Stone, R. (2000). Stress: The invisible hand in Eastern Europe's death rates. *Science, 288,* 1732–1733.

Stoolmiller, M. (1999). Implications of the restricted range of family environments for estimates of heritability and nonshared environment in behavior-genetic adoption studies. *Psychological Bulletin, 125,* 392–409.

Stowell, J. R., Kiecolt-Glaser, J. K., & Glaser, R. (2001). Perceived stress and cellular immunity: When coping counts. *Journal of Behavioral Medicine, 24,* 323–339.

Striegel-Moore, R. H., & Cachelin, F. M. (1999). Body image concerns and disordered eating in adolescent girls: Risk and protective factors. In N. G. Johnson, M. C. Roberts, & J. Worell (Eds.), *Beyond appearance; A new look at adolescent girls* (pp. 85–108). Washington, DC: American Psychological Association.

Stritzke, W. G. K., Lang, A. R., & Patrick, C. J. (1996). Beyond stress and arousal: A reconceptualization of alcohol–emotion relations with reference to psychophysiological methods. *Psychological Bulletin, 120,* 376–395.

Stroop, J. R. (1935). Studies of interference in serial verbal reactions. *Journal of Experimental Psychology, 18,* 643–662.

Sturges, J. S. (1994). Family dynamics. In J. L. Ronch, W. V. Ornum, & N. C. Stilwell (Eds.), *The counseling sourcebook: A practical reference on contemporary issues* (pp. 358–372). New York: Crossroad.

Sturges, J. W., & Rogers, R. R. (1996). Preventive health psychology from a developmental perspective: An extension of protection motivation theory. *Health Psychology, 15,* 158–166.

Sue, D. (2001). Asian American masculinity and therapy: The concept of masculinity in Asian American males. In G. R. Brooks & G. E. Good (Eds.), *The new handbook of psychotherapy and counseling with men: A comprehensive guide to settings, problems, and treatment approaches, 1 & 2* (pp. 780–795). San Francisco: Jossey-Bass.

Suedfeld, P. (1998). What can abnormal environments tell us about normal people? Polar stations as natural psychology laboratories. *Journal of Environmental Psychology, 18,* 95–102.

Sugihara, Y., & Katsurada, E. (2000). Gender-role personality traits in Japanese culture. *Psychology of Women Quarterly, 24,* 309–318.

Suh, E., Diener, E., Oishi, S., & Triandis, H. C. (1998). The shifting basis of life satisfaction judgments across cultures: Emotions versus norms. *Journal of Personality and Social Psychology, 74,* 482–493.

Suinn, R. M. (2001). The terrible twos—anger and anxiety: Hazardous to your health. *American Psychologist, 56,* 27–36.

Summers, T. P., & Hendrix, W. H. (1991). Modeling the role of pay equity perceptions: A field study. *Journal of Occupational Psychology, 64,* 145–157.

Suzuki, K. (1998). The role of binocular viewing in a spacing illusion arising in a darkened surround. *Perception, 27,* 355–361.

Suzuki, L. A., & Valencis, R. (1997). Race-ethnicity and measured intelligence: Educational implications. *American Psychologist, 52,* 1103–1114.

Swaab, D. F., & Hofman, M. A. (1995). Sexual differentiation of the human hypothalamus in relation to gender and sexual orientation. *Trends in Neuroscience, 18,* 264–270.

Swim, J., Borgida, E., Maruyama, G., & Myers, D. G. (1989). Joan McKay versus John McKay: Do gender stereotypes bias evaluations? *Psychological Bulletin, 105,* 409–429.

Szasz, T. (1984). *The therapeutic state: Psychiatry in the mirror of current events.* Buffalo, NY: Prometheus.

Szasz, T. (1987). *Insanity: The idea and its consequences.* New York: Wiley.

Szeszko, P. R., Robinson, D., Alvir, J. M. J., Bilder, R. M., Lencz, T., Ashtan, M., Wu, H., & Bogerts, B. (1999). Orbital frontal and amygdala column reductions in obsessive–compulsive disorder. *Archives of General Psychiatry, 56,* 913–919.

Szymanski, K., & Harkins, S. G. (1993). The effect of experimenter evaluation on self-evaluation within the social loafing paradigm. *Journal of Experimental Social Psychology, 29,* 268–286.

Takahashi, J. S. (1999). Narcolepsy genes wake up the sleep field. *Science, 285,* 2076–2077.

Takeichi, M., & Sato, T. (2000). Studies on the psychosomatic functioning of ill-health according to Eastern and Western medicine: 4. The verification of possible links between ill-health, lifestyle illness and stress-related disease. *American Journal of Chinese Medicine, 28,* 9–24.

Takeuchi, D. T., & Cheung, M. K. (1998). Coercive and voluntary referrals: How ethnic minority adults get into mental health treatment. *Ethnicity and Health, 3,* 149–158.

Takeuchi, J. (2000). Treatment of a biracial child with schizophreniform disorder: Cultural formulation. *Cultural Diversity and Ethnic Minority Psychology, 6,* 93–101.

Takkouche, B. (2001). A cohort study of stress and the common cold. *Journal of the American Medical Association, 285,* 3070.

Tang, N., & Gardner, J. (1999). Race, culture, and psychotherapy: Transference to minority therapists. *Psychoanalytic Quarterly, 68*(1), 1–20.

Tasman, A., Riba, M. B., & Silk, K. R. (2000). *The doctor–patient relationship in pharmacotherapy: Improving treatment effectiveness.* New York: Guilford Press.

Tataranni, P. A., Young, J. B., Bogardus, C., & Ravussin, E. (1997). A low sympathoadrenal activity is associated with body weight gain and development of central adiposity in Pima Indian men. *Obesity Research, 5,* 341–347.

Tate, D. F., Wing, R. R., & Winett, R. A. (2001). Using Internet-based technology to deliver a behavioral weight loss program. *Journal of the American Medical Association, 285,* 1172–1177.

Taubes, G. (1998). As obesity rates rise, experts struggle to explain why. *Science, 280,* 1367–1368.

Taylor, J., Iacono, W. G., & McGue, M. (2000). Evidence for a genetic etiology of early-onset delinquency. *Journal of Abnormal Psychology, 109,* 634–643.

Taylor, S. E., Kemeny, M. E., Reed, G. M., Bower, J. E., & Gruenwald, T. L. (2000). Psychological resources, positive illusions, and health. *American Psychologist, 55,* 99–109.

Taylor, S. E., Klein, L. C., Lewis, B. P., Gruenwald, T. L., Gurung, R. A. R., & Updegraff, J. A. (2000). Biobehavioral responses to stress in females: Tend-and-befriend, not fight-or-flight. *Psychological Review, 107,* 411–429.

Taylor, S. E., Repetti, R. L., & Seeman, T. (1997). Health psychology: What is an unhealthy environment and how does it get under the skin? *Annual Review of Psychology, 48,* 411–447.

Taylor, W. R., He, S., Levick, W. R., & Vaney, D. I. (2000). Dendritic computation of direction selectivity by retinal ganglion cells. *Science, 289,* 2347–2350.

Tchernichovski, O., Mitra, P. P., Lints, T., & Nottebohm, F. (2001). Dynamics of the vocal imitation process: How a zebra finch learns its song. *Science, 291,* 2564–2569.

Teevan, R. C., & McGhee, P. E. (1972). Childhood development of fear of failure motivation. *Journal of Personality and Social Psychology, 21,* 345–348.

Tempo, P. M., & Saito, A. (1996). Techniques of working with Japanese-American families. In G. Yeo, D. Gallagher-Thompson, et al. (Eds.), *Ethnicity and the dementias* (pp. 109–112). Washington, DC: Taylor & Francis.

Tenenbaum, J. B., de Silva, V., & Langford, J. C. (2000). A global geometric framework for nonlinear dimensionality reduction. *Science, 290,* 2319–2323.

Tennen, H., Affleck, G., Armeli, S., & Carney, M. A. (2000). A daily process approach to coping: Linking theory, research, and practice. *American Psychologist, 55,* 626–636.

Tennov, D. (1981). *Love and limerance.* Briarcliffe Manor, NY: Stein & Day.

Tepper, B. J. (1998). 6-n-propylthiouracil: A genetic marker for taste, with implication for food preference and dietary habits. *American Journal of Human Genetics, 63,* 1271–1276.

Terrace, H. S. (1985). In the beginning was the "name." *American Psychologist, 40,* 1011–1028.

Tesser, A. (2001). On the plasticity of self-defense. *Current Directions in Psychological Science, 10,* 66–69.

Tesser, A., & Beach, S. R. H. (1998). Life events, relationship quality, and depression: An investigation of judgment discontinuity in vivo. *Journal of Personality and Social Psychology, 74,* 36–52.

Teuchmann, K., Totterdell, P., & Parker, S. K. (1999). Rushed, unhappy, and drained: An experience sampling study of relations between time pressure, perceived control, mood, and emotional exhaustion in a group of accountants. *Journal of Occupational Health Psychology, 4,* 37–54.

Thach, W. T. (1998). A role for the cerebellum in learning movement coordination. *Neurobiology of Learning & Memory, 70,* 177–188.

Thomson, R., Murachver, T., & Green, J. (2001). Where is the gender in gendered relationships? *Psychological Science, 12,* 171–175.

Tian, B., Reser, D., Durham, A., Kustov, A., & Rauschecker, J. P. (2001). Functional specialization in rhesus monkey auditory cortex. *Georgetown Institute for Cognitive and Computational Sciences, 292,* 290–293.

Tice, D. M., & Baumeister, R. F. (1985). Masculinity inhibits helping in emergencies: Personality does predict the bystander effect. *Journal of Personality and Social Psychology, 49,* 420–428.

Tice, D. M., Bratslavsky, E., & Baumeister, R. F. (2001). Emotional distress regulation takes precedence over impulse control: If you feel bad, do it! *Journal of Personality and Social Psychology, 80,* 53–67.

Tiggemann, M., & Williamson, S. (2000). The effect of exercise on body satisfaction and self-esteem as a function of gender and age. *Sex Roles, 43,* 119–127.

Tjaden, P. G., & Thoennes, N. (2000). *Full report of the prevalence, incidence, and consequences of violence against women: Findings from the Violence Against Women Survey.* Washington, DC: National Institute of Justice.

Tjosvold, D. (1987). Participation: A close look at its dynamics. *Journal of Management, 13,* 739–750.

Tkachuk, G. A., & Martin, G. L. (1999). Exercise therapy for patients with psychiatric disorders: Research and clinical implications. *Professional Psychology: Research & Practice, 30,* 275–282.

Toch, H. (2001). Altruistic activity as correctional treatment. *International Journal of Offender Therapy and Comparative Criminology, 44,* 270–278.

Tomasello, M. (2000). *Culture and cognitive development: Psychological science* (pp. 37–40). Malden, MA: Blackwell Publishers.

Tooby, J., & Cosmides, L. (1997, June 26). On Stephen Jay Gould's *"Darwinian Fundamentalism" and "Evolution: The Pleasures of Pluralism"* [Letter to the editor]. *The New York Review of Books.*

Trachtenberg, J. T., Trepel, C., & Stryker, M. P. (2000). Rapid extragranular plasticity in the absence of thalamocortical plasticity in the developing primary visual cortex. *Science, 287,* 2029–2032.

Tracy, J. A., Thompson, J. K., Krupa, D. J., & Thompson, R. F. (1998). Evidence of plasticity in the pontocerebellar conditioned stimulus pathway during classical conditioning of the eyeblink response in the rabbit. *Behavioral Neuroscience, 112,* 267–285.

Tracy, R. J., & Barker, C. H. (1994). A comparison of visual versus auditory imagery in predicting word recall. *Imagination, Cognition and Personality, 13,* 147–161.

Trappey, C. (1996). A meta-analysis of consumer choice and subliminal advertising. *Psychology and Marketing, 13,* 517–530.

Triandis, H. C., & Gelfand, M. J. (1998). Converging measurement of horizontal and vertical individualism and collectivism. *Journal of Personality and Social Psychology, 74,* 118–128.

Trierweiler, S. J., Neighbors, H. W., Munday, C., Thompson, E. E., Binion, V. J., & Gomez, J. P. (2000). Clinician attributions associated with the diagnosis of schizophrenia in African American and non–African American patients. *Journal of Consulting and Clinical Psychology, 68,* 171–175.

Trimble, J. E. (2000). Social psychological perspectives on changing self-identification among American Indians and Alaska Natives. In R. H. Dana (Ed.), *Handbook of cross-cultural and multicultural personality assessment. Personality and Clinical Psychology Series* (pp. 197–222). Mahwah, NJ: Erlbaum.

Trites, D., Galbraith, F. D., Sturdavent, M., & Leckwart, J. F. (1970). Influence of nursing-unit design on the activities and subjective feelings of nursing personnel. *Environment and Behavior, 2,* 203–234.

Tritt, K., Loew, T. H., Meyer, M., Werner, B., & Peseschkian, N. (2000). Positive psychotherapy: Effectiveness of an interdisciplinary approach. *European Journal of Psychiatry, 13,* 231–242.

Troisi, A., & McGuire, M. T. (2000). Psychotherapy in the context of Darwinian psychiatry. In P. Gilbert & K. G. Bailey (Eds.), *Genes on the couch: Explorations in evolutionary psychotherapy* (pp. 3–27). Philadelphia: Brunner-Routledge.

Trull, T. J., & Geary, D. C. (1997). Comparison of the Big-Five Factor structure across samples of Chinese and American adults. *Journal of Personality Assesssment, 69,* 324–341.

Tuckman, A. (1996). Isn't it about time psychologists were granted prescription privileges? *Psychotherapy in Private Practice, 15*(2), 1–14.

Tulving, E. (1993). What is episodic memory? *Current Directions in Psychological Science, 2,* 67–70.

Tulving, E., Kapur, S., Craik, F. I. M., Moscovitch, M., & Houle, S. (1994). Hemispheric encoding/retrieval asymmetry in episodic memory: Positron emission tomography findings. *Proceedings of the National Academy of Sciences USA, 91,* 2016–2020.

Turkheimer, E. (2000). Three laws of behavior genetics and what they mean. *Current Directions in Psychological Science, 9,* 160–164.

Turner, G. (1999). Peer support and young people's health. *Journal of Adolescence, 22,* 567–572.

Tziner, A., & Murphy, K. R. (1999). Additional evidence of attitudinal influences in performance appraisal. *Journal of Business and Psychology, 13,* 407–419.

U.S. Bureau of the Census. (2000). *Statistical abstract of the United States: 2000* (120th ed.). Washington, DC: U.S. Government Printing Office.

U.S. Bureau of the Census. (2001). *Statistical abstract of the United States: 2001* (121st ed.). Washington, DC: U.S. Government Printing Office.

U.S. Department of Health and Human Services. (2000). *Health, United States, 2000.* Washington, DC: U.S. Government Printing Office.

U.S. Department of Health and Human Services. (2001). *National strategy for suicide prevention: Goals and objectives for action.* Rockville, MD: U.S. Government Printing Office.

U.S. Department of Justice. (1999). *Eyewitness evidence: A guide for law enforcement.* Rockville, MD: U.S. Government Printing Office.

Udry, J. R. (1990). Biosocial models of adolescent problem behaviors. *Social Biology, 37,* 1–10.

Ullian, E. M., Sapperstein, S. K., Christopherson, K. S., & Barres, B. A. (2001, January 26). Control of synapse number by glia. *Science, 291,* 657–661.

Ungar, M. T. (2000). The myth of peer pressure. *Adolescence, 35,* 167–180.

Ursano, R. J., Fullerton, C. S., Kao, T., & Bhartiya, V. R. (1995). Longitudinal assessment of posttraumatic stress disorder and depression after exposure to traumatic death. *Journal of Nervous and Mental Disease, 183,* 36–42.

Vahava, O., Morell, R., Lynch, E. D., Weiss, S., Kagan, M. E., Ahituv, N., et al. (1998). Mutation in transcription factor POU4F3 associated with inherited progressive hearing loss in humans. *Science, 279,* 1950–1954.

Valenstein, E. S. (1998). *Blaming the brain: The truth about drugs and mental health.* New York: Free Press.

Valins, S., & Baum, A. (1973). Residential group size, social interaction, and crowding. *Environment and Behavior, 5,* 421–435.

Van Horn, D. H. A., & Frank, A. F. (1998). Psychology of addictive behaviors. *Educational Publishing Foundation, 12,* 47–61.

Van Laar, C. (2001). Declining optimism in ethnic minority students: The role of attributions and self-esteem. In F. Salili & C. Chiu (Eds.), *Student motivation: The culture and context of learning. Plenum Series on Human Exceptionality* (pp. 79–104). New York: Kluwer/Plenum.

Vartanian, L. R. (2000). Revisiting the imaginary audience and personal fable constructs of adolescent egocentrism: A conceptual review. *Adolescence, 35,* 639–661.

Vello, J., & Cohen, D. (1999). Patterns of individualism and collectivism across the United States. *Journal of Personality and Social Psychology, 77,* 279–292.

Veniegas, R. C., & Peplau, L. A. (1997). Power and the quality of same-sex friendships. *Psychology of Women Quarterly, 21,* 279–297.

Venter, J. C., Adams, M. D., Myers, G. W., Li, P. W., Mural, R. J., Sutton, G. W., et al. (2001, February 16). The sequence of the human genome. *Science, 291,* 1304–1351.

Vianna, M. R. M., Izquierdo, L. A., Barros, D. M., de Souza, M. M., Rodrigues, C., Sant'Anna, M. K., Medina, J. H., & Izauierdo, I. (2001). Pharmacological differences between memory consolidation of habituation to an open field and inhibitory avoidance learning. *Brazilian Journal of Medical & Biological Research, 34,* 233–240.

Videbech, P. (2000). PET measurements of brain glucose metabolism and blood flow in major depressive disorder: A critical review. *Acta Psychiatrica Scandinavica, 101,* 11–20.

Villani, S. (2001). Impact of media on children and adolescents: A 10-year review of the research. *Journal of the American Academy of Child and Adolescent Psychiatry, 40,* 392–401.

Villeneuve, C. (2001). *Emphasizing the interpersonal in psychotherapy: Families and groups in the era of cost containment.* Philadelphia: Brunner-Routledge.

Visser, M. (1999). Food and culture: Interconnections. *Social Research, 66,* 117–132.

Vogel, G. W. (1991). Sleep-onset mentation. In S. J. Ellman & J. S. Antrobus (Eds.), *The mind in sleep: Psychology and psychophysiology* (2nd ed., pp. 125–142). New York: Wiley.

Von Senden, M. (1932). *Raum- und Gaestaltauffassung bei operierten: Blindgeborernin vor und nach der Operation.* Leipzig, Germany: Barth.

Vroom, V. H. (1964). *Work and motivation.* New York: Wiley.

Vroom, V. H. (1974). A new look at managerial decision making. *Organizational Dynamics, 5,* 66–80.

Vroom, V. H., & Jago, A. G. (1995). Situation effects and levels of analysis in the study of leader participation. *Leadership Quarterly, 6,* 169–181.

Vroom, V. H., & Yetton, P. W. (1973). *Leadership and decision-making.* Pittsburgh: University of Pittsburgh Press.

Vroon, P. (1997). *Smell: The secret seducer.* New York: Farrar, Straus & Giroux.

Vygotsky, L. S. (1962). *Thought and language* (E. Hanfmann & G. Vakar, Eds. and Trans.). Cambridge, MA: The MIT Press. (Original work published in 1934)

Wadsworth, J., McEwan, J., Johnson, A. M., Wellings, K., et al. (1995). Sexual health for women: Some findings of a large national survey discussed. *Sexual and Marital Therapy, 10,* 169–188.

Wakefield, J. C. (1999). Evolutionary versus prototype analyses of the concept of disorder. *Journal of Abnormal Psychology, 108,* 374–399.

Waldie, K., & Mosley, J. L. (2000). Hemispheric specialization for reading. *Brain & Language, 75*(1), 108–122.

Waldron, I. (1997). Changing gender roles and gender differences in health behavior. In D. S. Gochman (Ed.), *Handbook of health behavior research I: Personal and social determinants* (pp. 303–328). New York: Plenum.

Walker, E., Hoppes, E., Mednick, S., Emory, E., & Schulsinger, F. (1983). Environmental factors related to schizophrenia in psychophysiologically labile high-risk males. *Journal of Abnormal Psychology, 90,* 313–320.

Walker, L. S., Garber, J., Smith, C. A., Van Slyke, D. A., & Claar, R. L. (2001). The relation of daily stressors to somatic and emotional symptoms in children with and without recurrent abdominal pain. *Journal of Consulting and Clinical Psychology, 69,* 85–91.

Walker, S., Richardson, D. S., & Green, L. R. (2000). Aggression among older adults: The relationship of interaction networks and gender role to direct and indirect responses. *Aggressive Behavior, 26,* 145–154.

Wall, P. (2000). *Pain: The science of suffering.* New York: Columbia University Press.

Walsh, B. T., & Devlin, M. J. (1998). Eating disorders: Progress and problems. *Science, 280,* 1387–1390.

Wamala, S. P., Mittleman, M. A., Horsten, M., Schenck-Gustafsson, K., & Orth-Gómer, K. (2000). Job stress and the occupational gradient in coronary heart disease risk in women: The Stockholm Female Coronary Risk Study. *Social Science & Medicine, 51,* 481–489.

Wampold, B. E., Monding, G. W., Moody, M., Stich, F., Benson, K., & Ahn, H. (1997). A meta-analysis of outcome studies comparing bona fide psychotherapies: Empirically, "all must have prizes." *Psychological Bulletin, 122,* 203–215.

Wandersman, A., & Nation, M. (1998). Urban neighborhoods and mental health: Psychological contributions to understanding toxicity, resilience, and interventions. *American Psychologist, 53,* 647–656.

Wang, A., Gao, L., Shinfuku, N., Zhang, H., Zhao, C., & Shen, Y. (2000). Longitudinal study of earthquake-related PTSD in a randomly selected community sample in North China. *American Journal of Psychiatry, 157,* 1260–1266.

Webb, W. B., & Agnew, H. W., Jr. (1975). The effects on subsequent sleep of an acute restriction of sleep length. *Psychophysiology, 12,* 367–370.

Webster, R. (1995). *Why Freud was wrong: Sin, science, and psychoanalysis.* New York: Basic Books.

Weidner, G. (2000). Why do men get more heart disease than women? An international perspective. *Journal of American College Health, 48,* 291–294.

Weine, S. M., Kuc, G., Dzudza, E., Razzano, L., & Pavkovic, I. (2001). PTSD among Bosnian refugees: A survey of providers' knowledge, attitudes and service patterns (posttraumatic stress disorder). *Community Mental Health Journal, 37,* 261–272.

Weingartner, H., Adefris, W., Eich, J. E., & Murphy, D. L. (1976). Encoding-imagery specificity in alcohol state-dependent learning. *Journal of Experimental Psychology, 2,* 83–87.

Weinstein, C. S., & Mignano, A. (1993). *Organizing the elementary school classroom: Lessons from research and practice.* New York: McGraw-Hill.

Weinstein, N. D., Rothman, A. J., & Sutton, S. R. (1998). Stage theories of health behavior: Conceptual and methodological issues. *Health Psychology, 17,* 290–299.

Weisberg, R. B., Brown, T. A., Wineze, J. P., & Barlow, D. H. (2001). Casual attributions and male sexual arousal: The impact of attributions for a bogus erectile difficulty on sexual arousal, cognitions, and affect. *Journal of Abnormal Psychology, 110,* 324–334.

Weiser, E. B. (2001). The functions of Internet use and their social, psychological, and interpersonal consequences. *Dissertation Abstracts International: Section B: The Sciences & Engineering, 61*(7-B), 3906.

Weisfeld, G. E. (1993). The adaptive value of humor and laughter. *Ethology and Sociobiology, 14,* 141–169.

Werker, J. F., & Vouloumanos, A. (1999). Speech and language processing in infancy: A neurocognitive approach. In C. A. Nelson & M. Luciana (Eds.), *Handbook of developmental cognitive neuroscience* (pp. 269–280). Cambridge, MA: The MIT Press.

Werner, N. E., & Crick, N. R. (1999). Relational aggression and social psychological adjustment in a college sample. *Journal of Abnormal Psychology, 108,* 615–623.

Westen, D. (1998). The scientific legacy of Sigmund Freud: Toward a psychodynamically informed psychological science. *Psychological Bulletin, 124,* 333–371.

Westgaard, R. H. (2000). Work related musculoskeletal complaints: Some ergonomics challenges upon the start of a new century. *Applied Ergonomics, 6,* 569–580.

Whaley, A. L. (1997). Ethnicity/race, paranoia, and psychiatric diagnoses: Clinician bias versus sociocultural differences. *Journal of Psychopathology and Behavioral Assessment, 19,* 1–20.

Whaley, A. L. (2001). Cultural mistrust and mental health services for African Americans: A review and meta-analysis. *Counseling Psychologist, 29,* 513–531.

Wheeler, M. A. (2000). Episodic memory and autonoetic awareness. In E. Tulving & F. I. M. Craik (Eds.), *The Oxford handbook of memory* (pp. 597–608). New York: Oxford University Press.

Wheeler, S. C., Jarvis, W. B. G., Petty, R. E. (2001). Think unto others: The self-destructive impact of negative racial stereotypes. *Journal of Experimental Social Psychology, 37,* 273–180.

Whicker, K. M., Bol, L., & Nunnery, J. A. (1997). Cooperative learning in the secondary mathematics classroom. *Journal of Educational Research, 91,* 42–48.

White, J. D. (2000). Correlates of children's anxiety in the dental setting. *Dissertation Abstracts International: Section B: The Sciences & Engineering, 60*(12-B), 6388.

WHO International Consortium in Psychiatric Epidemiology. (2000). Cross-national comparisons of the prevalences and correlates of mental disorders. *Bulletin of the World Health Organization, 78,* 413–426.

Widiger, T. A., Frances, A. J., Pincus, H. A., Davis, W. W., & First, M. B. (1991). Toward an empirical classification for the *DSM–IV. Journal of Abnormal Psychology, 100,* 280–288.

Widiger, T. A., & Sankis, L. M. (2000). Adult psychopathology: Issues and controversies. *Annual Review of Psychology, 51,* 377–404.

Wiley, J. (1998). Expertise as mental set: The effects of domain knowledge in creative problem solving. *Memory & Cognition, 26,* 716–730.

Williams, C. B. (1999). African American women, Afrocentrism, and feminism: Implications for therapy. *Women and Therapy, 22,* 1–16.

Williams, C. D. (1959). Case report: The elimination of tantrum behavior by extinction procedures. *Journal of Abnormal and Social Psychology, 59,* 269.

Williams, J. (2000). *Unbending gender: Why family and work conflict and what to do about it.* New York: Oxford University Press.

Williams, M. L., Elwood, W. N., & Bowen, A. M. (2000). Escape from risk: A qualitative exploration of relapse to unprotected anal sex among men who have sex with men. *Journal of Psychology and Human Sexuality, 11,* 25–49.

Willis, S. L., & Schaie, K. W. (1999). Intellectual functioning in midlife. In S. L. Willis & J. D. Reid, *Life in the middle: Psychological and social development in middle age* (pp. 233–247). San Diego, CA: Academic Press.

Wilson, D. A. (2000). Comparison of odor receptive field plasticity in the rat olfactory bulb and anterior piriform cortex. *Journal of Neurophysiology, 84,* 3036–3042.

Wilson, E. O. (1998). *Consilience: The unity of knowledge.* New York: Knopf.

Wilson, G. T., Loeb, K. L., Walsh, B. T., Labouvie, E., Petkova, E., Liu, X., & Waternaux, C. (1999). Psychological treatments of bulimia nervosa predictors and processes of change. *Journal of Consulting and Clinical Psychology, 67,* 451–459.

Wilson, M., & Daly, M. (1985). Competitiveness, risk taking, and violence: The young male syndrome. *Ethology and Socialbiology, 6,* 59–73.

Wilson, M. E. (1992). Factors determining the onset of puberty. In A. A. Gerall, H. Moltz, A. A. Gerall, H. Moltz, & I. L. Ward (Eds.), *Sexual differentiation: Handbook of behavioral neurobiology* (pp. 275–312). New York: Plenum.

Wing, R. R., & Jeffery, R. W. (1999). Benefits of recruiting participants with friends and increasing social support for weight loss and maintenance. *Journal of Consulting & Clinical Psychology, 67,* 132–138.

Winner, E. (1997). Exceptionally high intelligence and schooling. *American Psychologist, 52,* 1070–1081.

Winner, E. (2000). Giftedness: Current theory and research. *Psychological Science, 9,* 153–156.

Winocur, G., McDonald, R. M., & Moscovitch, M. (2001). Anterograde and retrograde amnesia in rats with large hippocampal lesions. *Hippocampus, 11,* 27–42.

Wise, R. A. (1996). Neurobiology of addiction. *Current Opinion in Neurobiology, 6,* 243–251.

Wittrock, M. C. (2000). Knowledge acquisition and education. *Journal of Mind & Behavior, 21,* 205–212.

Witztum, E., & Buchbinder, J. T. (2001). Strategic culture sensitive therapy with religious Jews. *International Review of Psychiatry, 13,* 117–124.

Wodak, R., & Benke, G. (1997). Gender as a sociolinguistic variable: New perspectives on variation studies. In F. Coulmas (Ed.), *The handbook of sociolinguistics.* Oxford, UK: Blackwell Publishers.

Wolpe, J. (1958). *Psychotherapy by reciprocal inhibition.* Stanford, CA: Stanford University Press.

Woods, S. C., Schwartz, M. W., Baskin, D. G., & Seeley, R. J. (2000). Food intake and the regulation of body weight. *Annual Review of Psychology, 51,* 255–278.

Woodward, W. R. (1982). The "discovery" of social behaviorism and social learning theory, 1870–1980. *American Psychologist, 37,* 396–410.

Wright, J. C., Huston, A. C., Vandewater, E. A., Bickham, D. S., Scantlin, R. M., Kotler, J. A., Caplovitz, A. G., Lee, J. H., Hofferth, S., & Finkelstein, J. (2001). American children's use of electronic media in 1997: A national survey. *Journal of Applied Developmental Psychology, 22,* 31–47.

Wright, L. (1997). *Twins and what they tell us about who we are.* New York: Wiley.

Wundt, W. (1896). *Lectures on human and animal psychology.* New York: Macmillan.

Wynn-Dancy, L. M., & Gillam, R. B. (1997). Accessing long-term memory: Metacognitive strategies and strategic action in adolescents. *Topics in Language Disorders, 18,* 32–44.

Wyszecki, G., & Stiles, W. S. (1967). *Color science: Concepts and methods, quantitative data, and formulas.* New York: Wiley.

Yancey, S. W., & Phelps, E. A. (2001). Functional neuroimaging and episodic memory: A perspective. *Journal of Clinical & Experimental Neuropsychology, 23,* 32–48.

Yehuda, R., Schmeidler, J., Wainberg, M., Binder-Brynes, K., & Duvdevani, T. (1998). Vulnerability to posttraumatic stress disorder in adult offspring of Holocaust survivors. *American Journal of Psychiatry, 155,* 1163–1171.

Yeung, R. (1996, November 23). Racing to euphoria. *New Scientist, 152,* 28–31.

Yohannes, A. M., Connolly, M. J., & Baldwin, R. C. (2001). A feasibility study of antidepressant drug therapy in depressed elderly patients with chronic obstructive pulmonary disease. *International Journal of Geriatric Psychiatry, 16,* 451–454.

Youngstedt, S. D., O'Connor, P. J., & Dishman, R. K. (1997). The effects of acute exercise on sleep: A quantitative synthesis. *Sleep, 20,* 203–214.

Youniss, J., McLellan, J. A., & Yates, M. (1999). Religion, community service, and identity in American youth. *Journal of Adolescence, 22,* 243–255.

Zajonc, R. B. (1965). Social facilitation. *Science, 149,* 269–274.

Zakay, D., Hayduk, L. A., & Tsal, Y. (1992). Personal space and distance misperception: Implications of a novel observation. *Bulletin of the Psychonomic Society, 30,* 33–35.

Zangwill, O. L., & Blakemore, C. (1972). Dyslexia: Reversal of eye movements during reading. *Neuropsychologia, 10,* 371–373.

Zarcone, J. R., Crosland, K., Fisher, W. W., Worsdell, A. S., & Herman, K. (1999). A brief method for conduction a negative-reinforcement assessment. *Research in Developmental Disabilities, 20,* 107–124.

Zemore, S. E., Fiske, S., & Hyun-Jeong, K. (2000). Gender stereotypes and the dynamics of social interaction. In T. Eckes & H. S. Hanns (Eds.), *The developmental social psychology of gender* (pp. 207–241). Mahwah, NJ: Erlbaum.

Zhang, A. Y., & Snowden, L. R. (1999). Ethnic characteristics of mental disorders in five U.S. communities. *Cultural Diversity and Ethnic Minority Psychology, 5,* 134–146.

Zhou, Z. (2001). American and Chinese children's knowledge of basic relational concepts. *School Psychology International, 22,* 5–21.

Ziel, H. K. (1999). Complementary alternative medicine: Boon or boondoggle? *Skeptic, 7,* 86–89.

Zigler, E. F., & Hodapp, R. M. (1991). Behavioral functioning in individuals with mental retardation. *Annual Review of Psychology, 42,* 29–50.

Zillmann, D. (1994). Cognition excitation interdependencies in the escalation of anger and angry aggression. In M. Potegal & J. F. Knutson (Eds.), *The dynamics of aggression: Biological and social processes in dyads and groups* (pp. 45–71). Hillsdale, NJ: Erlbaum.

Zimbardo, P. G., Maslach, C., & Haney, C. (2000). *Reflections on the Stanford prison experiment: Genesis, transformations, consequences.* Mahwah, NJ: Erlbaum.

Zimmerman, L. (2000). *The SE switch: Evolution and our self-esteem.* Orlando, FL: Rivercross.

Zola, S. M., & Squire, L. R. (2000). The medial temporal lobe and the hippocampus. In E. Tulving and F. I. Craik (Eds.), *The Oxford handbook of memory* (pp. 485–500). New York: Oxford University Press.

Zoucha, R., & Husted, G. L. (2000). Culturally congruent care to individual patients by health care professional: The differences between transculturalism and multiculturalism are explored. *Issues in Mental Health Nursing, 21,* 324–340.

Zuber, J. A., Crott, H. W., & Werner, J. (1992). Choice shift and group polarization: An analysis of the status of arguments and social decision schemes. *Journal of Personality and Social Psychology, 62,* 50–61.

Zuckerman, M. (1969). Variables affecting deprivation results and hallucinations, reported sensations, and images. In J. P. Zubek (Ed.), *Sensory deprivation.* New York: Appleton-Century-Crofts.

Zuckerman, M. (1990). Some dubious premises in research and theory on racial differences. *American Psychologist, 45,* 1297–1303.

Zuckerman, M. (1999). *Vulnerability to psychopathology: A biosocial model.* Washington, DC: American Psychological Association.

Glossary

Abnormal behavior Behavior characterized as atypical, socially unacceptable, distressing to the individual or others, maladaptive, and/or the result of distorted cognitions.

Abnormal psychology The field of psychology concerned with the assessment, treatment, and prevention of maladaptive behavior.

Absolute threshold The statistically determined minimum level of stimulation necessary to excite a perceptual system.

Accommodation According to Piaget, the process by which existing mental structures and behaviors are modified to adapt to new experiences (see Chapter 3).

Accommodation The change in the shape of the lens of the eye that enables the observer to keep an object in focus on the retina when the object is moved or when the observer focuses on an object at a different distance (see Chapter 5).

Action potential An electrical current that is sent down the axon of a neuron and is initiated by a rapid reversal of the polarization of the cell membrane; also known as a *spike discharge.*

Actor–observer effect The tendency to attribute the behavior of others to dispositional causes but to attribute one's own behavior to situational causes.

Adaptation A trait or inherited characteristic that has increased in a population because it solved a problem of survival or reproduction.

Adolescence [add-oh-LESS-sense] The period extending from the onset of puberty to early adulthood.

Afferent neurons Neurons that send messages to the spinal cord and brain.

Ageism Prejudice against the elderly and the resulting discrimination against them.

Aggression Any behavior intended to harm another person or thing.

Agnosia An inability to recognize a sensory stimulus that should be recognizable because perceptual systems for detecting color, shape, and motion are normal and intact and there are no verbal, memory, or intellectual impairments.

Agonist [AG-oh-nist] Chemical that mimics or facilitates the actions of a neurotransmitter.

Agoraphobia [AG-or-uh-FOE-bee-uh] Anxiety disorder characterized by marked fear and avoidance of being alone in a place from which escape might be difficult or embarrassing.

Algorithm [AL-go-rith-um] Procedure for solving a problem by implementing a set of rules over and over again until the solution is found.

All-or-none Either at full strength or not at all; the basis on which neurons fire.

Altruism [AL-true-ism] Behaviors that benefit other people and for which there is no discernible extrinsic reward, recognition, or appreciation.

Alzheimer's [ALTZ-hy-merz] disease A chronic and progressive disorder of the brain that is the most common cause of degenerative dementia.

Amnesia [am-NEE-zhuh] Inability to remember information (typically all events within a specific period), usually due to physiological trauma.

Amplitude The total energy of a sound wave, which determines the loudness of the sound; also known as *intensity.*

Anal stage Freud's second stage of personality development, from about age 2 to about age 3, during which children learn to control the immediate gratification they obtain through defecation and to become responsive to the demands of society.

Androgynous Having both stereotypically male and stereotypically female characteristics.

Anorexia nervosa [an-uh-REX-ee-uh ner-VOH-suh] An eating disorder characterized by an obstinate and willful refusal to eat, a distorted body image, and an intense fear of being fat.

Antagonist Chemical that opposes the actions of a neurotransmitter.

Anterograde amnesia Loss of memory for events and experiences occurring from the time of injury forward.

Antisocial personality disorder Personality disorder characterized by egocentricity, behavior that is irresponsible and that violates the rights of other people, a lack of guilt feelings, an inability to understand other people, and a lack of fear of punishment.

Anxiety A generalized feeling of fear and apprehension that may be related to a particular situation or object and is often accompanied by increased physiological arousal.

Applied psychology The branch of psychology that uses psychological principles to help solve practical problems of everyday life.

Appraisal The evaluation of the significance of a situation or event as it relates to a person's well-being.

Approach–approach conflict Conflict that results from having to choose between two attractive alternatives.

Approach–avoidance conflict Conflict that results from having to choose an alternative that has both attractive and unappealing aspects.

Archetypes [AR-ki-types] In Jung's theory, the emotionally charged ideas and images that are rich in meaning and symbolism and exist within the collective unconscious.

Arousal Activation of the central nervous system, the autonomic nervous system, and the muscles and glands.

Assessment Process of evaluating individual differences among human beings by means of tests, interviews, observations, and recordings of physiological processes.

Assimilation According to Piaget, the process by which new ideas and experiences are absorbed and incorporated into existing mental structures and behaviors.

Attachment The strong emotional tie that a person feels toward special other persons in his or her life.

Attitudes Patterns of feelings and beliefs about other people, ideas, or objects that are based on a person's past experiences, shape his or her future behavior, and are evaluative in nature.

Attribution The process by which a person infers other people's motives or intentions by observing their behavior.

Autonomic [au-toe-NOM-ick] nervous system The part of the peripheral nervous system that controls the vital and automatic activities of the body, such as heart rate, digestive processes, blood pressure, and functioning of internal organs.

Aversive counterconditioning A counterconditioning technique in which an aversive or noxious stimulus is paired with a stimulus that elicits an undesirable behavior so that the person will cease responding to the familiar stimulus with the undesirable behavior.

Avoidance–avoidance conflict Conflict that results from having to choose between two distasteful alternatives.

Axon A thin, elongated structure that transmits signals from the neuron's cell body to the axon terminals, which pass them on to adjacent neurons, muscles, or glands.

Babinski reflex Reflex in which a newborn fans out the toes when the sole of the foot is touched.

Backward search Heuristic procedure in which a problem solver works backward from the goal or end of a problem to the current position, in order to analyze the problem and reduce the steps needed to get from the current position to the goal.

Behavior therapy A therapy that is based on the application of learning principles to human behavior and that focuses on changing overt behaviors rather than on understanding subjective feelings, unconscious processes, or motivations; also known as *behavior modification*.

Behaviorism The perspective that rejects the study of the contents of consciousness and focuses on describing and measuring only what is observable either directly or through assessment instruments.

Binocular depth cues Cues for depth perception that require the use of both eyes.

Biofeedback A process through which people receive information about the status of a physical system and use this feedback information to learn to control the activity of that system.

Biopsychology perspective The perspective that examines psychological issues in light of how biological factors affect mental processes and behavior and that focuses on how physical mechanisms affect emotions, feelings, thoughts, desires, and sensory experiences; often focusing on the molecular and cellular level it is also known as the neuroscience perspective.

Bipolar disorder Mood disorder originally known as manic–depressive disorder because it is characterized by behavior that vacillates between two extremes: mania and depression.

Blood–brain barrier A mechanism that prevents certain molecules from entering the brain but allows others to cross.

Body language Communication of information through body positions and gestures.

Bonding Special process of emotional attachment that may occur between parents and babies in the minutes and hours immediately after birth.

Brain The part of the central nervous system that is located in the skull and that regulates, monitors, processes, and guides other nervous system activity.

Brainstorming Problem-solving technique that involves considering all possible solutions without making prior evaluative judgments.

Brightness The lightness or darkness of reflected light, determined in large part by the light's intensity.

Bulimia nervosa [boo-LEE-me-uh ner-VOH-suh] An eating disorder characterized by repeated episodes of binge eating (and a fear of not being able to stop eating) followed by purging.

Burnout State of emotional and physical exhaustion, lowered productivity, and feelings of isolation, often caused by work-related pressures.

Bystander effect Unwillingness to help exhibited by witnesses to an event, which increases when there are more observers.

Case study A descriptive study that includes an intensive study of one person and allows an intensive examination of a single case, usually chosen for its interesting or unique characteristics.

Catatonic [CAT-uh-TONN-ick] type of schizophrenia Type of schizophrenia characterized either by displays of excited or violent motor activity or by stupor.

Central nervous system One of the two major parts of the nervous system, consisting of the brain and the spinal cord.

Cerebellum [seh-rah-BELL-um] A large structure that is attached to the back surface of the brain stem and that influences balance, coordination, and movement.

Child abuse Physical, emotional, or sexual mistreatment of a child.

Chromosome Microscopic strands of DNA found in the nucleus of every body cell and carrying the self-replacing genetic information in their basic functional units, the genes.

Chunks Manageable and meaningful units of information organized in such a way that they can be easily encoded, stored, and retrieved.

Circadian [sir-KAY-dee-an] rhythms Internally generated patterns of body functions, including hormonal signals, sleep, blood pressure, and temperature regulation, which have approximately a 24-hour cycle and occur even in the absence of normal cues about whether it is day or night.

Classical conditioning Conditioning process in which an originally neutral stimulus, by repeated pairing with a stimulus that normally elicits a response, comes to elicit a similar or even identical response; also known as *Pavlovian conditioning*.

Client-centered therapy An insight therapy, developed by Carl Rogers, that seeks to help people evaluate the world and themselves from their own perspective by providing them with a nondirective environment and unconditional positive regard; also known as *person-centered therapy*.

Clinical psychologist Mental health practitioner who views behavior and mental processes from a psychological perspective and who assess and treats persons with serious emotional or behavioral problems or conducts research into the causes of behavior.

Cognitive dissonance [COG-nih-tiv DIS-uh-nents] A state of mental discomfort arising from a discrepancy between two or more of a person's beliefs or between a person's beliefs and overt behavior.

Cognitive psychology The study of the overlapping fields of perception, learning, memory, and thought, with a special emphasis on how people attend to, acquire, transform, store, and retrieve knowledge.

Cognitive theories In the study of motivation, an explanation of behavior that asserts that people actively and regularly determine their own goals and the means of achieving them through thought.

Collective unconscious Jung's concept of a storehouse of primitive ideas and images that are inherited from one's ancestors; these inherited ideas and images, called *archetypes,* are emotionally charged and rich in meaning and symbolism.

Color blindness The inability to perceive different hues.

Community psychology The branch of psychology that seeks to reach out to society by providing services such as community mental health centers and especially to effect social change through empowerment of individuals.

Concept Mental category used to classify an event or object according to some distinguishing property or feature.

Concordance rate The degree to which a condition or trait is shared by two or more individuals or groups.

Concrete operational stage Piaget's third stage of cognitive development (lasting from approximately age 6 or 7 to age 11 or 12), during which the child develops the ability to understand constant factors in the environment, rules, and higher-order symbolic systems.

Conditioned response Response elicited by a conditioned stimulus.

Conditioned stimulus Neutral stimulus that, through repeated association with an unconditioned stimulus, begins to elicit a conditioned response.

Conditioning Systematic procedure through which associations and responses to specific stimuli are learned.

Conduction deafness Deafness resulting from interference with the transmission of sound to the neural mechanism of the inner ear.

Conflict The emotional state or condition that arises when a person must choose between two or more competing motives, behaviors, or impulses.

Conformity People's tendency to change attitudes or behaviors so that they are consistent with those of other people or with social norms.

Consciousness The general state of being aware of and responsive to events in the environment, as well as one's own mental processes. Also, Freud's level of mental life that consists of those experiences that we are aware of at any given time.

Conservation Ability to recognize that objects can be transformed in some way, visually or physically, yet still be the same in number, weight, substance, or volume.

Consolidation [kon-SOL-ih-DAY-shun] The process of changing a short-term memory to a long-term one.

Control group In an experiment, the comparison group—the group of participants who are tested on the dependent variable in the same way as those in the experimental group but who do not receive the treatment.

Convergence The movement of the eyes toward each other to keep visual stimulation at corresponding points on the retinas as an object moves closer to the observer.

Convergent thinking In problem solving, the process of narrowing down choices and alternatives to arrive at a suitable answer.

Convolutions Folds in the tissue of the cerebral hemispheres and the overlying cortex.

Coping strategies The techniques people use to deal with the stress of changing situation.

Coping Process by which a person takes some action to manage, master, tolerate, or reduce environmental or internal demands that cause or might cause stress and that tax the individual's inner resources.

Correlation coefficient A number that expresses the degree and direction of a relationship between two variables, ranging from –1 (a perfect negative correlation) to +1 (a perfect positive correlation).

Correlational study A type of descriptive research design that establishes the degree of relationship between two variables.

Cortex The convoluted, or furrowed, exterior covering of the brain's hemispheres, which is about 2 millimeters thick, consists of six thin layers of cells, and is divided into several lobes, or areas, each with characteristic structures; thought to be involved in both sensory interpretation and complex thought processes; also known as the *neocortex*.

Counseling psychologist Mental health practitioner who assists people who have behavioral or emotional problems, through the use of testing, psychotherapy, and other therapies. This profession shares much ground with clinical psychology.

Counterconditioning Process of reconditioning in which a person is taught a new, more adaptive response to a familiar stimulus.

Creativity A feature of thought and problem solving that includes the tendency to generate or recognize ideas considered to be high-quality, original, novel, and appropriate.

Critical Period The time in the development of an organism when it is especially sensitive to certain environmental influences; outside of that period the same influences will have far less effect.

Cross-sectional study A type of research design that compares individuals of different ages to determine how they differ on an important dimension.

Crowding The perception that one's personal space is too restricted.

CT (computerized tomography) scans Computer-enhanced X-ray images of the brain (or any area of the body) in three dimensions—essentially a series of X-rays that show photographic slices of the brain (or other part of the body).

Dark adaptation The increase in sensitivity to light that occurs when the illumination level changes from high to low, causing chemicals in the rods and cones to regenerate and return to their inactive state.

Debriefing A procedure to inform participants about the true nature of an experiment after its completion.

Decay Loss of information from memory as a result of disuse and the passage of time.

Decentration Process of changing from a totally self-oriented point of view to one that recognizes other people's feelings, ideas, and viewpoints.

Decision making Assessing and choosing among alternatives.

Declarative memory Memory for specific information.

Defense mechanism An unconscious way of reducing anxiety by distorting perceptions of reality.

Deindividuation The process by which individuals lose their self-awareness and distinctive personality in the context of a group, which may lead them to engage in antinormative behavior.

Delusions False beliefs that are inconsistent with reality but are held in spite of evidence that disproves them.

Demand characteristics Elements of an experimental situation that might cause a participant to perceive the situation in a certain way or become aware of the purpose of the study and thus bias the participant to behave in a certain way, and in so doing, distort results.

Dementia Impairment of mental functioning and global cognitive abilities in otherwise alert individuals, causing memory loss and related symptoms and typically having a progressive nature.

Dendrites Thin, bushy, widely branching fibers that extend outward from the neuron's cell body and that receive signals from neighboring neurons and carry them back to the cell body.

Denial Defense mechanism by which people refuse to accept reality or recognize the true source of their anxiety.

Dependence The situation that occurs when the drug becomes part of the body's functioning and produces withdrawal symptoms when the drug is discontinued.

Dependent variable The variable in a controlled experiment that is expected to change because of the manipulation of the independent variable.

Depressive disorders General category of mood disorders in which people show extreme and persistent sadness, despair, and loss of interest in life's usual activities.

Descriptive statistics A general set of procedures used to summarize, condense, and describe sets of data.

Descriptive studies A type of research method that allows researchers to measure variables so that they can develop a description of a situation or phenomenon.

Developmental psychology The study of the lifelong, often age-related, processes of change in the physical, cognitive, moral, emotional, and social domains of functioning; such changes are rooted in biological mechanisms that are genetically controlled, as well as in social interactions.

Deviation IQ A standard IQ test score whose mean and standard deviation remain constant for all ages.

Dichromats [DIE-kroe-MATZ] People who can distinguish only two of the three basic colors.

Discrimination Behavior targeted at individuals or groups and intended to hold them apart and treat them differently.

Disorganized type of schizophrenia Type of schizophrenia characterized by severely disturbed thought processes, frequent incoherence, disorganized behavior, and inappropriate affect.

Displacement Defense mechanism by which people divert sexual or aggressive feelings for one person onto another person.

Dissociative amnesia Dissociative disorder characterized by the sudden and extensive inability to recall important personal information, usually of a traumatic or stressful nature.

Dissociative disorders Psychological disorders characterized by a sudden but temporary alteration in consciousness, identity, sensorimotor behavior, or memory.

Dissociative identity disorder Dissociative disorder characterized by the existence within an individual of two or more distinct personalities, each of which is dominant at different times and directs the individual's behavior at those times; commonly known as *multiple personality*.

Divergent thinking In problem solving, the process of widening the range of possibilities and expanding the options for solutions.

Double bind A situation in which an individual is given two different and inconsistent messages.

Double-blind technique A research technique in which neither the experimenter nor the participants know who is in the control and experimental groups.

Dream analysis Psychoanalytic technique in which a patient's dreams are described in detail and interpreted so as to provide insight into the individual's unconscious motivations.

Dream A state of consciousness that occurs during sleep, usually accompanied by vivid visual, tactile, or auditory imagery.

Drive theory An explanation of behavior that assumes that an organism is motivated to act because of a need to attain, reestablish, or maintain some goal that helps with survival.

Drive An internal aroused condition that directs an organism to satisfy a physiological need.

Drug Any chemical substance that, in small amounts, alters biological or cognitive processes or both.

Educational psychology The systematic application of psychological principles to learning and teaching.

Efferent neurons Neurons that send messages from the brain and spinal cord to other structures in the body.

Ego In Freud's theory, the part of personality that seeks to satisfy instinctual needs in accordance with reality.

Egocentrism [ee-go-SENT-rism] Inability to perceive a situation or event except in relation to oneself; also known as *self-centeredness*.

Elaboration likelihood model Theory suggesting that there are two routes to attitude change: the central route, which focuses on thoughtful consideration of an argument for change, and the peripheral route, which focuses on less careful, more emotional, and even superficial evaluation.

Elaborative rehearsal Rehearsal involving repetition and analysis, in which a stimulus may be associated with (linked to) other information and further processed.

Electroconvulsive [ee-LECK-tro-con-VUL-siv] therapy (ECT) A treatment for severe mental illness in which an electric current is briefly applied to the head in order to produce a generalized seizure.

Electroencephalogram [ee-LECK-tro-en-SEFF-uh-low-gram] (EEG) A graphical record of brain-wave activity obtained through electrodes placed on the scalp.

Electromagnetic [ee-LEK-tro-mag-NET-ick] radiation The entire spectrum of waves initiated by the movement of charged particles.

Embryo [EM-bree-o] The prenatal organism from the 5th through the 49th day after conception.

Emotion A subjective response, usually accompanied by a physiological change, which is interpreted in a particular way by the individual and often leads to a change in behavior.

Empiricism The view that knowledge should be acquired through observation and often an experiment.

Empowerment Facilitating the development of skills, knowledge, and motivation in individuals so that they can act for themselves and gain control over their own lives.

Encoding specificity principle Notion that the effectiveness of a specific retrieval cue depends on how well it matches up with the originally encoded information.

Encoding The organizing of information so that the nervous system can process it.

Endocrine [END-oh-krin] glands Ductless glands that secrete hormones directly into the bloodstream, rather than through a specific duct, or opening, into a target organ.

Endorphins [en-DOR-finz] Painkillers produced naturally in the brain and the pituitary gland.

Environmental psychology The study of how physical settings affect human behavior and how people change their environment.

Episodic [ep-ih-SAW-dick] memory Memory of specific, personal events and situations (episodes) tagged with information about time.

Equity theory Social psychological theory that states that people attempt to maintain stable, consistent interpersonal relationships in which the ratio of members' contributions is balanced.

Also, The theory in I/O psychology that asserts that what people bring to a work situation should be balanced by what they receive compared with other workers; that is, input should be balanced by compensation.

Ethics Rules of proper and acceptable conduct that investigators use to guide psychological research; these rules concern the treatment of animals, the rights of human beings, and the responsibilities of investigators.

Ethnocentrism Tendency to believe that one's own group is the standard, the reference point against which other people and groups should be judged.

Evolutionary psychology The psychological perspective that seeks to explain and predict behaviors by analyzing how the human brain developed over time, how it functions, and how input from the social environment affects human behaviors; it seeks to explain human behavior by considering how behavior is affected from the vantage point of evolutionary biology.

Ex post facto design A type of design that contrasts groups of people who differ on some variable of interest to the researcher.

Excitement phase The first phase of the sexual response cycle, during which there are increases in heart rate, blood pressure, and respiration.

Expectancy theories Theories that suggest that a worker's effort and desire to maintain goal-directed behavior (to work) are determined by expectations regarding the outcomes of behavior.

Experiment A procedure in which a researcher systematically manipulates and observes elements of a situation in order to test a hypothesis and make a cause-and-effect statement.

Experimental design A design in which researchers manipulate an independent variable and measure a dependent variable to determine a cause-and-effect relationship.

Experimental group In an experiment, a group of participants to whom a treatment is given.

Explicit memory Conscious memory that a person is aware of, such as a memory of a word in a list or an event that occurred in the past.

Extinction In *classical conditioning,* the procedure of withholding the unconditioned stimulus and presenting the conditioned stimulus alone, which gradually reduces the probability of the conditioned response.

In *operant conditioning,* the process by which the probability of an organism's emitting a response is reduced when reinforcement no longer follows the response.

Extrinsic [ecks-TRINZ-ick] motivation Motivation supplied by rewards that come from the external environment.

Factor analysis Statistical procedure designed to discover the independent elements (factors) in any set of data.

Family therapy A type of therapy in which two or more people who are committed to one another's well-being are treated at once, in an effort to change the ways they interact.

Fetus [FEET-us] The prenatal organism from the 8th week after conception until birth.

Fixation An excessive attachment to some person or object that was appropriate only at an earlier stage of development.

Fixed-interval schedule A reinforcement schedule in which a reinforcer (reward) is delivered after a specified interval of time, provided that the required response occurs at least once in the interval.

Fixed-ratio schedule A reinforcement schedule in which a reinforcer (reward) is delivered after a specified number of responses has occurred.

fMRI (functional magnetic resonance imaging) Imaging technique that allows observation of brain activity as it takes place by registering changes in the metabolism (energy consumption) of cells in various regions of the brain.

Forebrain The largest, most complicated, and most advanced organizationally and functionally of the three divisions of the brain, with many interrelated parts including the thalamus and hypothalamus, the limbic system, the basal ganglia and corpus callosum, and the cortex.

Formal operational stage Piaget's fourth and final stage of cognitive development (beginning at about age 12), during which the individual can think hypothetically, can consider future possibilities, and can use deductive logic.

Fraternal twins Twins that occur when two sperm fertilize two eggs; fraternal twins are only as genetically similar as any brothers or sisters are.

Free association Psychoanalytic technique in which a person is asked to report to the therapist his or her thoughts and feelings as they occur, regardless of how trivial, illogical, or objectionable their content may appear.

Frequency The number of complete changes in air pressure occurring per unit of time; measured in hertz (Hz), or cycles per second.

Frequency distribution A chart or array of scores, usually arranged from the highest to the lowest, showing the number of instances for each score.

Frequency polygon Graph of a frequency distribution that shows the number of instances of obtained scores, usually with the data points connected by straight lines.

Fulfillment In Rogers's theory of personality, an inborn tendency directing people toward actualizing their essential nature and thus attaining their potential.

Functional fixedness Inability to see that an object can have a function other than its stated or usual one.

Functionalism The school of psychological thought that was concerned with how and why the conscious mind works; an outgrowth and reaction to structuralism, its main aim was to know how the contents of consciousness functioned and worked together.

Fundamental attribution error The tendency to attribute other people's behavior to dispositional (internal) causes rather than situational (external) causes.

Gender A socially and culturally constructed set of distinctions between masculine and feminine sets of behaviors that is promoted and expected by society.

Gender identity A person's sense of being male or female.

Gender schema theory The theory that children and adolescents use gender as an organizing theme to classify and interpret their perceptions about the world and themselves.

Gender stereotype A fixed, overly simple, sometimes incorrect idea about traits, attitudes, and behaviors of males or females.

Gene The functional unit of hereditary transmission, consisting of DNA.

Generalized anxiety disorder An anxiety disorder characterized by persistent anxiety occurring on more days than not for at least 6 months, sometimes with increased activity of the autonomic nervous system, apprehension, excessive muscle tension, and difficulty in concentrating.

Genetic mapping Dividing the chromosomes into smaller fragments that can be characterized and ordered (mapped) so that the fragments reflect their respective locations on specific chromosomes.

Genetics The study of heredity, which is the biological transmission of traits and characteristics from parents to offspring.

Genital [JEN-it-ul] stage Freud's last stage of personality development, from the onset of puberty through adulthood, during which the sexual conflicts of childhood resurface (at puberty) and are often resolved (during adolescence).

Genome The total DNA blueprint of heritable traits contained in every cell of the body.

Genotype A person's genetic makeup fixed at conception.

Gestalt [gesh-TALT] psychology The school of psychological thought that argued that behavior cannot be studied in parts but must be viewed as a whole; the focus was on the unity of perception and thinking.

Goal-setting theory Theory that asserts that setting specific, clear, attainable goals for a given task leads to better performance.

Grammar The linguistic description of how a language functions, especially the rules and patterns used for generating appropriate and comprehensible sentences.

Grasping reflex Reflex that causes a newborn to grasp vigorously any object touching the palm or fingers or placed in the hand.

Group polarization Shifts or exaggeration in group members' attitudes or behavior as a result of group discussion.

Group therapy Psychotherapeutic process in which several people meet as a group with a therapist to receive psychological help.

Group Two or more individuals who are working with a common purpose or have some common goals, characteristics, or interests.

Groupthink The tendency of people in a group to seek concurrence with one another when reaching a decision, rather than effectively evaluating the options.

Halo effect The tendency for one characteristic of an individual to influence a tester's evaluation of other characteristics.

Health psychology Subfield concerned with the use of psychological ideas and principles to enhance health, prevent illness, diagnose and treat disease, and improve rehabilitation.

Heritability The genetically determined proportion of a trait's variation among individuals in a population.

Heuristics [hyoo-RISS-ticks] Sets of strategies, rather than strict rules, that act as guidelines for discovery-oriented problem solving.

Higher-order conditioning Process by which a neutral stimulus takes on conditioned properties through pairing with a conditioned stimulus.

Hindbrain The most primitive organizationally of the three functional divisions of the brain, consisting of the medulla, the reticular formation, the pons, and the cerebellum.

Homeostasis Maintenance of a constant state of inner stability or balance.

Hormones Chemicals that are produced by the endocrine glands and regulate the activities of specific organs or cells.

Hue The psychological property of light referred to as color, determined by the wavelengths of reflected light.

Human factors The study of the relationship of human beings to machines and to workplaces and other environments.

Humanistic psychology The perspective that emphasizes the uniqueness of each human being and the idea that human beings have free will to determine their destiny.

Humanistic theory An explanation of behavior that emphasizes the entirety of life rather than individual components of behavior and focuses on human dignity, individual choice, and self-worth.

Hyperopic [HY-per-OH-pick] Able to see objects at a distance clearly but having trouble seeing things up close; farsighted.

Hypothalamus A relatively small structure of the forebrain, lying just below the thalamus, which acts through its connections with the rest of the forebrain and the midbrain and affects many complex behaviors, such as eating, drinking, and sexual activity.

Hypothesis A tentative statement or idea expressing a causal relationship between two events or variables that is to be evaluated in a research study.

Id In Freud's theory, the source of a person's instinctual energy, which works mainly on the pleasure principle.

Ideal self In Rogers's theory of personality, the self a person would ideally like to be.

Identical twins Twins that occur when one zygote splits into two identical cells, which then separate and develop independently; identical twins have exactly the same genetic makeup.

Illusion A perception of a physical stimulus that differs from measurable reality or from what is commonly expected.

Imagery The creation or re-creation of a mental picture of a sensory or perceptual experience.

Imaginary audience A cognitive distortion experienced by adolescents, in which they see themselves as always "on stage" with an audience watching.

Implicit memory Memory a person is not aware of possessing; considered an almost unconscious process, implicit memory occurs almost automatically.

Impression formation The process by which a person uses the behavior and appearance of others to form attitudes about them.

Independent variable The variable in a controlled experiment that the experimenter directly and purposely manipulates to see how the other variables under study will be affected.

Industrial/organizational (I/O) psychology The study of how individual behavior is affected by the work environment, by coworkers, and by organizational practices.

Inferential statistics Procedures used to draw reasonable conclusions (generalizations) about larger populations from small samples of data.

Informed consent The agreement of participants to take part in an experiment and their acknowledgment, expressed through their signature on a document, that they understand the nature of their participation in upcoming research and have been fully informed about the general nature of the research, its goals, and its methods.

Insight therapy Any therapy that attempts to discover relationships between unconscious motivations and current abnormal behavior.

Insomnia Problems in going to sleep or maintaining sleep.

Insulin Hormone that is produced by the pancreas and facilitates the transport of sugar from the blood into body cells, where it is metabolized.

Intelligence The overall capacity of an individual to act purposefully, to think rationally, and to deal effectively with the environment.

Interference Suppression of one bit of information by another received either earlier or later or the confusion of two pieces of information.

Interpersonal attraction The tendency of one person to evaluate another person (or a symbol or image of another person) in a positive way.

Interpretation In Freud's theory, the technique of providing a context, meaning, or cause for a specific idea, feeling, or set of behaviors; the process of tying a set of behaviors to its unconscious determinant.

Intimacy A state of being or feeling in which each person in a relationship is willing to self-disclose and to express important feelings and information to the other person.

Intrinsic [in-TRINZ-ick] motivation Motivation that leads to behaviors engaged in for no apparent reward except the pleasure and satisfaction of the activity itself.

Introspection A person's description and analysis of what he or she is thinking and feeling or what he or she has just thought about.

Job analyses Detailed descriptions of the various tasks and activities that comprise each job, as well as the knowledge, skills, and abilities necessary to do it.

Kinesthesis [kin-iss-THEE-sis] The awareness aroused by movements of the muscles, tendons, and joints.

Language A system of symbols, usually words, that convey meaning and a set of rules for combining symbols to generate an infinite number of messages.

Latency [LAY-ten-see] stage Freud's fourth stage of personality development, from about age 7 until puberty, during which sexual urges are inactive.

Latent content The deeper meaning of a dream, usually involving symbolism, hidden meaning, and repressed or obscured ideas and wishes.

Latent learning Learning that occurs in the absence of direct reinforcement and that is not necessarily demonstrated through observable behavior.

Law of Prägnanz [PREG-nants] The Gestalt notion that when items or stimuli *can* be grouped together and seen as a whole, they *will* be.

Learned helplessness The behavior of giving up or not responding to punishment, exhibited by people or animals exposed to negative consequences or punishment over which they have no control.

Learning Relatively permanent change in an organism that occurs as a result of experiences in the environment.

Levels-of-processing approach Theory of memory that suggests that the brain processes and encodes stimuli (information) in different ways, to different extents, and at different levels.

Libido [lih-BEE-doe] In Freud's theory, the instinctual (and sexual) life force that, working on the pleasure principle and seeking immediate gratification, energizes the id.

Light The small portion of the electromagnetic spectrum that is visible to the human eye.

Limbic system An interconnected group of structures (including parts of the cortex, thalamus, and hypothalamus) located deep within the temporal lobe and influencing emotions, memory, social behavior, and brain disorders such as epilepsy.

Linguistics [ling-GWIS-ticks] The study of language, including speech sounds, meaning, and grammar.

Logic The system or principles of reasoning used to reach valid conclusions or make inferences.

Longitudinal study A research approach that follows a group of people over time to determine change or stability in behavior.

Long-term memory Storage mechanism that keeps a relatively permanent record of information.

Lucid [LOO-sid] dream Dream in which the dreamer is aware of dreaming while it is happening.

Mainstreaming Practice of placing children with special needs in regular classroom settings, with the support of professionals who provide special education services.

Maintenance rehearsal Repetitive review of information with little or no interpretation.

Major depressive disorder Depressive disorder characterized by loss of interest in almost all of life's usual activities; a sad, hopeless, or discouraged mood; sleep disturbance; loss of appetite; loss of energy; and feelings of unworthiness and guilt.

Manifest content The overt story line, characters, and setting of a dream-the obvious, clearly discernible events of the dream.

Mean The measure of central tendency that is calculated by dividing the sum of the scores by the total number of scores; also known as the arithmetic average.

Means–ends analysis Heuristic procedure in which the problem solver compares the current situation with the desired goal to determine the most efficient way to get from one to the other.

Measure of central tendency A descriptive statistic that tells which result or score best represents an entire set of scores.

Median The measure of central tendency that is the data point with 50% of all the observations (scores) above it and 50% below it.

Meditation The use of a variety of techniques including concentration, restriction of incoming stimuli, and deep relaxation to produce a state of consciousness characterized by a sense of detachment.

Medulla [meh-DUH-lah] The most primitive and lowest portion of the hindbrain; controls basic bodily functions such as heartbeat and breathing.

Memory span The number of items that a person can reproduce from short-term memory, usually consisting of one or two chunks.

Memory The ability to recall past events, images, ideas, or previously learned information or skills; the storage system that allows for retention and retrieval of previously learned information.

Mental retardation Below-average intellectual functioning, as measured on an IQ test, accompanied by substantial limitations in functioning that originate before age 18.

Meta-analysis A set of statistical procedures designed to gather experimental and correlational results across multiple and separate studies that address a related set of research questions; it ultimately consists of a careful literature search and a calculation of research effect sizes.

Midbrain The second level of the three organizational structures of the brain, which receives afferent signals from other parts of the brain and from the spinal cord, interprets the signals, and either relays the information to a more complex part of the brain or causes the body to act at once; considered important in the regulation of movement.

Mode The measure of central tendency that is the most frequently observed data point.

Model An analogy or a perspective that uses a structure from one field to help scientists describe data in another field.

Monochromats [MON-o-kroe-MATZ] People who cannot perceive any color, usually because their retinas lack cones.

Monocular [mah-NAHK-you-ler] depth cues Depth cues that do not depend on the use of both eyes.

Morality A system of learned attitudes about social practices, institutions, and individual behavior used to evaluate situations and behavior as right or wrong, good or bad.

Moro reflex Reflex in which a newborn stretches out the arms and legs and cries in response to a loud noise or an abrupt change in the environment.

Morpheme [MORE-feem] A basic unit of meaning in a language.

Motivation Any internal condition, although usually an internal one, that initiates, activates, or maintains an organism's goal-directed behavior.

Motive A specific (usually internal) condition, usually involving some form of arousal, which directs an organism's behavior toward a goal.

MRI (magnetic resonance imaging) Imaging technique that uses magnetic fields instead of X-rays to produce scans of great clarity and high resolution, distinguishing brain parts as small as 1 or 2 millimeters.

Mutations Unexpected changes in the gene replication process that are not always evident in phenotype and create unusual and sometimes harmful characteristics of body or behavior.

Myopic [my-OH-pick] Able to see clearly things that are close but having trouble seeing objects at a distance; nearsighted.

Natural selection The principle that those characteristics and behaviors that help organisms adapt, be fit, and survive will be passed on to successive generations, because flexible, fit individuals have a greater chance of reproduction.

Naturalistic observation A descriptive research method in which researchers study behavior in its natural context.

Nature A person's inherited characteristics, determined by genetics.

Need for achievement A social need that directs a person to strive constantly for excellence and success.

Need State of physiological imbalance usually accompanied by arousal.

Negative reinforcement Removal of a stimulus (usually an aversive one) after a particular response to increase the likelihood that the response will recur.

Nervous system The structures and organs that facilitate electrical and chemical communication in the body and allow all behavior and mental processes to take place.

Neuron The single cell that is the basic building block of the nervous system and comprises dendrites (which receive neural signals), a cell body (which generates electrical signals), and an axon (which transmits neural signals); also known as a *nerve cell.*

Neurotransmitter Chemical substance that resides in the axon terminals within synaptic vesicles and that, when released, moves across the synaptic space and binds to a receptor site on an adjacent cell.

Non–rapid eye movement (NREM) sleep Four distinct stages of sleep during which no rapid eye movements occur.

Nonverbal communication The communication of information by cues or actions that include gestures, tone of voice, vocal inflections, and facial expressions.

Normal curve A bell-shaped graphic representation of data showing what percentage of the population falls under each part of the curve.

Normal distribution The approximate distribution of scores expected when a sample is taken from a large population, drawn as a frequency polygon that often takes the form of a bell-shaped curve, known as a normal curve.

Norms The scores and corresponding percentile ranks of a large and representative sample of individuals from the population for which a test was designed.

Nurture A person's experiences in the environment.

Obedience Compliance with the orders of another person or group of people.

Object permanence The realization of infants that objects continue to exist even when they are out of sight.

Observational learning theory Theory that suggests that organisms learn new responses by observing the behavior of a model and then imitating it; also known as *social learning theory*.

Obsessive–compulsive disorder Anxiety disorder characterized by persistent and uncontrollable thoughts and irrational beliefs that cause the performance of compulsive rituals that interfere with daily life.

Oedipus [ED-i-pus] complex Feelings of rivalry with the parent of the same sex and sexual desire for the parent of the other sex, occurring during the phallic stage and ultimately resolved through identification with the parent of the same sex.

Olfaction [ole-FAK-shun] The sense of smell.

Operant [OP-er-ant] conditioning Conditioning in which an increase or decrease in the probability that a behavior will recur is affected by the delivery of reinforcement or punishment as a consequence of the behavior; also known as *instrumental conditioning*.

Operational definition A definition of a variable in terms of the set of methods or procedures used to measure or study that variable.

Opiates Drugs derived from the opium poppy, including opium, morphine, and heroin.

Opponent-process theory Visual theory, proposed by Herring, that color is coded by stimulation of three types of paired receptors; each pair of receptors is assumed to operate in an antagonistic way so that stimulation by a given wavelength produces excitation (increased firing) in one receptor of the pair and also inhibits the other receptor.

Optic chiasm [KI-azm] Point at which half of the optic nerve fibers from each eye cross over and connect to the other side of the brain.

Oral stage Freud's first stage of personality development, from birth to about age 2, during which the instincts of infants are focused on the mouth as the primary pleasure center.

Orgasm phase The third phase of the sexual response cycle, during which autonomic nervous system activity reaches its peak and muscle contractions occur in spasms throughout the body, but especially in the genital area.

Overjustification effect Decrease in likelihood that an intrinsically motivated task, after having been extrinsically rewarded, will be performed when the reward is no longer given.

Panic attacks Anxiety disorders characterized as acute anxiety, accompanied by sharp increases in autonomic nervous system arousal, that is not triggered by a specific event.

Paranoid [PAIR-uh-noid] type of schizophrenia Type of schizophrenia characterized by hallucinations and delusions of persecution or grandeur (or both), and sometimes irrational jealousy.

Parasympathetic [PAIR-uh-sim-puh-THET-ick] nervous system The part of the autonomic nervous system that controls the normal operations of the body, such as digestion, blood pressure, and respiration.

Participant An individual who takes part in an experiment and whose behavior is observed as part of the data collection process; previously known as a subject.

Percentile score A score indicating what percentage of the test population would obtain a lower score.

Perception Process by which an organism selects and interprets sensory input so that it acquires meaning.

Performance appraisal The process by which a supervisor periodically evaluates the job-relevant strengths and weaknesses of a subordinate.

Peripheral [puh-RIF-er-al] nervous system The part of the nervous system that carries information to and from the central nervous system through spinal nerves attached to the spinal cord and through 12 cranial nerves.

Personal fable A cognitive distortion experienced by adolescents, in which they believe they are so special and unique that other people cannot understand them and risky behaviors will not harm them.

Personal space The area around an individual that the person considers private and that is enclosed by an invisible psychological boundary.

Personality disorders Psychological disorders characterized by inflexible and long-standing maladaptive behaviors that typically cause stress and/or social or occupational problems.

Personality A pattern of relatively permanent traits, dispositions, or characteristics that give some consistency to people's behavior.

PET (positron emission tomography) Imaging technique that tracks radioactive markers injected into the bloodstream, enabling researchers to monitor marked variations in cerebral activity, which are correlated with mental processes.

Phallic [FAL-ick] stage Freud's third stage of personality development, from about age 4 through age 7, during which children obtain gratification primarily from the genitals.

Phenotype A person's observable characteristics shaped by genes and the environment.

Phobic disorders Anxiety disorders characterized by excessive and irrational fear of, and consequent attempted avoidance of, specific objects or situations.

Phoneme [FOE-neem] A basic or minimum unit of sound in a language.

Phonology The study of the patterns and distribution of speech sounds in a language and the tacit rules for their pronunciation.

Photoreceptors The light-sensitive cells in the retina—the rods and the cones.

Pitch The psychological experience that corresponds with the frequency of an auditory stimulus; also known as tone.

Pituitary [pit-YOU-ih-tare-ee] gland The body's master gland, located at the base of the brain and closely linked to the hypothalamus; regulates the actions of other endocrine glands and controls growth hormones.

Placebo [pluh-SEE-bo] effect A nonspecific improvement that occurs as a result of a person's expectations of change rather than as a direct result of any specific therapeutic treatment.

Placenta [pluh-SENT-uh] A mass of tissue that is attached to the wall of the uterus and connected to the developing fetus by the umbilical cord; it supplies nutrients and eliminates waste products.

Plateau phase The second phase of the sexual response cycle, during which physical arousal continues to increase as the partners' bodies prepare for orgasm.

Pons A structure of the hindbrain that provides a link between the medulla and the cerebellum and the rest of the brain; it affects sleep and dreaming.

Positive reinforcement Presentation of a stimulus after a particular response in order to increase the likelihood that the response will recur.

Posttraumatic stress disorder (PTSD) Psychological disorder that may become evident after a person has undergone extreme stress caused by some type of disaster; common symptoms include vivid, intrusive recollections or reexperiences of the traumatic event and occasional lapses of normal consciousness.

Preconscious Freud's level of the mind that contains those experiences that are not currently conscious but may become so with varying degrees of difficulty.

Prejudice Negative evaluation of an entire group of people, typically based on unfavorable (and often wrong) stereotypes about the group.

Preoperational stage Piaget's second stage of cognitive development (lasting from about age 2 to age 6 or 7), during which the child begins to represent the world symbolically.

Prevalence The percentage of a population displaying a disorder during any specified period.

Primacy effect The more accurate recall of items presented at the beginning of a series.

Primary punisher Any stimulus or event that is naturally painful or unpleasant to an organism.

Primary reinforcer Reinforcer (such as food, water, or the termination of pain) that has survival value for an organism; this value does not have to be learned.

Privacy The freedom from intrusion that results from controlling the boundaries between oneself and other people so that access is limited.

Proactive [pro-AK-tiv] interference Decrease in accurate recall of information as a result of the effects of previously learned or presented information; also known as *proactive inhibition*.

Proactive coping Taking action in advance of a potentially stressful situation to prevent it, modify it, or prepare for it before it occurs.

Problem solving The behavior of individuals when confronted with a situation or task that requires insight or determination of some unknown elements.

Procedural memory Memory for skills, including the perceptual, motor, and cognitive skills required to complete complex tasks.

Projection Defense mechanism by which people attribute their own undesirable traits to others.

Projective tests Devices or instruments used to assess personality, in which examinees are shown a standard set of ambiguous stimuli and asked to respond to the stimuli in their own way.

Prosocial behavior Behavior that benefits someone else or society but that generally offers no obvious benefit to the person performing it and may even involve some personal risk or sacrifice.

Prototype An abstraction, an idealized pattern of an object or idea that is stored in memory and used to decide whether similar objects or ideas are members of the same class of items.

Psychedelic drugs Consciousness-altering drugs that affect moods, thoughts, memory, judgment, and perception and that consumed for the purpose of producing those results.

Psychiatrist Physician (medical doctor) specializing in the treatment of patients with mental or emotional disorders.

Psychoactive[SYE-koh-AK-tiv] drug A drug that alters behavior, thought, or perceptions by altering biochemical reactions in the nervous system, thereby affecting consciousness.

Psychoanalysis [SYE-ko-uh-NAL-uh-sis] A lengthy insight therapy that was developed by Freud and aims at uncovering conflicts and unconscious impulses through special techniques, including free association, dream analysis, and transference.

Psychoanalyst Psychiatrist or, occasionally, nonmedical practitioner who has studied the technique of psychoanalysis and uses it in treating people with mental or emotional problems.

Psychoanalytic [SYE-ko-an-uh-LIT-ick] approach The perspective developed by Freud, which assumes that psychological maladjustment is a consequence of anxiety resulting from unresolved conflicts and forces of which a person may be unaware; includes the therapeutic technique known as psychoanalysis.

Psychodynamically [SYE-ko-dye-NAM-ick-lee] based therapies Therapies that use approaches or techniques derived from Freud, but that reject or modify some elements of Freud's theory.

Psycholinguistics The study of how language is acquired, perceived, understood, and produced.

Psychologist Professional who studies behavior and uses behavioral principles in scientific research or in applied settings.

Psychology The science of behavior and mental processes.

Psychoneuroimmunology (PNI) [SYE-ko-NEW-ro-IM-you-NOLL-oh-gee] An interdisciplinary area of study that includes behavioral, neurological, and immune factors and their relationship to the development of disease.

Psychophysics [SYE-co-FIZ-icks] Subfield of psychology that focuses on the relationship between physical stimuli and people's conscious experiences of them.

Psychosurgery Brain surgery used in the past to alleviate symptoms of serious mental disorders.

Psychotherapy [SYE-ko-THER-uh-pee] The treatment of emotional or behavior problems through psychological techniques.

Psychotic [sye-KOT-ick] Suffering from a gross impairment in reality testing that interferes with the ability to meet the ordinary demands of life.

Puberty [PEW-burr-tee] The period during which the reproductive system matures; it begins with an increase in the production of sex hormones, which signals the end of childhood.

Punishment Process of presenting an undesirable or noxious stimulus, or removing a desirable stimulus, to decrease the probability that a preceding response will recur.

Range A measure of variability that describes the spread between the highest and the lowest scores in a distribution.

Rape Forcible sexual assault on an unwilling partner.

Rapid eye movement (REM) sleep Stage of sleep characterized by high-frequency, low-amplitude brain-wave activity, rapid and systematic eye movements, more vivid dreams, and postural muscle paralysis.

Rational–emotive therapy A cognitive behavior therapy that emphasizes the importance of logical, rational thought processes.

Rationalization Defense mechanism by which people reinterpret undesirable feelings or behaviors in terms that make them appear acceptable.

Raw score A test score that has not been transformed or converted in any way.

Reactance The negative response evoked when there is an inconsistency between a person's self-image as being free to choose and the person's realization that someone is trying to force him or her to choose a particular alternative.

Reaction formation Defense mechanism by which people behave in a way opposite to what their true but anxiety-provoking feelings would dictate.

Reasoning The purposeful process by which a person generates logical and coherent ideas, evaluates situations, and reaches conclusions.

Recency effect The more accurate recall of items presented at the end of a series.

Receptive fields Areas of the retina that, when stimulated, produce a change in the firing of cells in the visual system.

Reflex Automatic behavior that occurs involuntarily in response to a stimulus and without prior learning and usually shows little variability from instance to instance.

Refractory period Amount of time needed for a neuron to recover after it fires; during this period, an action potential will not occur.

Regression A return to a prior stage after a person has progressed through the various stages of development; caused by anxiety.

Rehearsal Process of repeatedly verbalizing, thinking about, or otherwise acting on or transforming information in order to keep that information active in memory.

Reinforcer Any event that increases the probability of a recurrence of the response that preceded it.

Reliability Ability of a test to yield very similar scores for the same individual over repeated testings.

Representative sample A sample that reflects the characteristics of the population from which it is drawn.

Repression Defense mechanism by which anxiety-provoking thoughts and feelings are forced to the unconscious.

Residual type of schizophrenia A schizophrenic disorder in which the person exhibits inappropriate affect, illogical thinking, and/or eccentric behavior but seems generally in touch with reality.

Resilience The extent to which people are flexible and respond adaptively to external or internal demands.

Resistance In psychoanalysis, an unwillingness to cooperate, which a patient signals by showing a reluctance to provide the therapist with information or to help the therapist understand or interpret a situation.

Resolution phase The fourth phase of the sexual response cycle, following orgasm, during which the body returns to its resting, or normal, state.

Retinal disparity The slight difference between the visual images projected on the two retinas.

Retrieval Process by which stored information is recovered from memory.

Retroactive [RET-ro-AK-tiv] interference Decrease in accurate recall of information as a result of the subsequent presentation of different information; also known as *retroactive inhibition.*

Retrograde [RET-ro-grade] amnesia Loss of memory of events and experiences that preceded an amnesia-causing event.

Rooting reflex Reflex that causes a newborn to turn the head toward a light touch on lips or cheek.

Saccades [sack-ADZ] Rapid voluntary movements of the eyes.

Sample A group of participants who are assumed to be representative of the population about which an inference is being made.

Saturation The depth and richness of a hue determined by the homogeneity of the wavelengths contained in the reflected light; also known as *purity.*

Schema [SKEEM-uh] A conceptual framework that organizes information and allows a person to make sense of the world (see Chapter 8).

Schema In Piaget's view, a specific mental structure; an organized way of interacting with the environment and experiencing it—a generalization a child makes based on comparable occurrences of various actions, usually physical, motor actions (*schemata* in the plural) (see Chapter 3).

Schizophrenic [SKIT-soh-FREN-ick] disorders A group of psychological disorders characterized by a lack of reality testing and by deterioration of social and intellectual functioning and personality, beginning before age 45 and lasting at least 6 months.

Scientific method In psychology, the techniques used to discover knowledge about human behavior and mental processes; in experimentation, the scientific method involves stating the problem, developing hypotheses, designing a study, collecting and analyzing data (which often includes manipulating some part of the environment to better understand existing conditions that led to a behavior or phenomenon), replicating results, and drawing conclusions and reporting results.

Secondary punisher Any neutral stimulus that initially has no intrinsic negative value for an organism but acquires punishing qualities when linked with a primary punisher.

Secondary reinforcer Any neutral stimulus that initially has no intrinsic value for an organism but that becomes rewarding when linked with a primary reinforcer.

Secondary sex characteristics The genetically determined physical features that differentiate the sexes but are not directly involved with reproduction.

Sedative–hypnotic Any of a class of drugs that relax and calm a user and, in higher doses, induce sleep; also known as a depressant.

Self In Rogers's theory of personality, the perception an individual has of himself or herself and of his or her relationships to other people and to various aspects of life.

Self-actualization The fundamental human need to strive to fulfill one's potential, thus, a state of motivation, according to Maslow; from a humanist's view, the ultimate level of psychological development in which a person attempts to minimize ill health, be fully functioning, have a superior perception of reality, and feel a strong sense of self-acceptance.

Self-efficacy A person's belief about whether he or she can successfully engage in and execute a specific behavior.

Self-fulfilling prophecy The creation of a situation that unintentionally allows personal expectancies to influence participants.

Self-perception theory Approach to attitude formation that assumes that people infer their attitudes and emotional states from their behavior.

Self-serving bias People's tendency to ascribe their positive behaviors to their own internal traits, but their failures and shortcomings to external, situational factors.

Semantic memory Memory of ideas, rules, words, and general concepts about the world.

Semantics [se-MAN-ticks] The analysis of the meaning of language, especially of individual words.

Sensation Process in which the sense organs' receptor cells are stimulated and relay initial information to higher brain centers for further processing.

Sensorimotor stage The first of Piaget's four stages of cognitive development (covering roughly the first 2 years of life), during which the child develops some motor coordination skills and a memory for past events.

Sensorineural [sen-so-ree-NEW-ruhl] deafness Deafness resulting from damage to the cochlea, the auditory nerve, or higher auditory processing centers.

Sensory memory Mechanism that performs initial encoding and brief storage of sensory stimuli; also known as the *sensory register*.

Sex The biologically based categories of male and female.

Shape constancy Ability of the visual perceptual system to recognize a shape despite changes in its orientation or the angle from which it is viewed.

Shaping Selective reinforcement of behaviors that gradually approach (approximate) the desired response.

Signal detection theory Theory that holds that an observer's perception depends not only on the intensity of a stimulus but also on the observer's motivation, on the criteria he or she sets for determining that a signal is present, and on the background noise.

Significant difference In an experiment, a difference that is unlikely to have occurred because of chance alone and is inferred to be most likely due to the systematic manipulations of variables by the researcher.

Size constancy Ability of the visual perceptual system to recognize that an object remains constant in size regardless of its distance from the observer or the size of its image on the retina.

Skinner box Named for its developer, B. F. Skinner, a box that contains a responding mechanism and a device capable of delivering a consequence to an animal in the box whenever it makes the desired response.

Social categorization The process of dividing the world into "in" groups and "out" groups.

Social cognition The process of analyzing and interpreting events, other people, oneself, and the world in general.

Social facilitation Change in behavior that occurs when people believe they are in the presence of other people.

Social influence The ways people alter the attitudes or behaviors of others, either directly or indirectly.

Social interest In Adler's theory, a feeling of oneness with all humanity.

Social loafing Decrease in effort and productivity that occurs when an individual works in a group instead of alone.

Social need An aroused condition that directs people to behave in ways that allow them to feel good about themselves and others and to establish and maintain relationships.

Social phobia [FOE-bee-uh] Anxiety disorder characterized by fear of, and desire to avoid, situations in which the person might be exposed to scrutiny by others and might behave in an embarrassing or humiliating way.

Social psychology The scientific study of how people think about, interact with, influence, and are influenced by the thoughts, feelings, and behaviors of other people.

Social support The comfort, recognition, approval, and encouragement available from other people, including friends, family members, and coworkers.

Sociobiology A discipline based on the premise that even day-to-day behaviors are determined by the process of natural selection—that social behaviors that contribute to the survival of a species are passed on via the genes from one generation to the next.

Somatic [so-MAT-ick] nervous system The part of the peripheral nervous system that carries information from sense organs to the brain and from the brain and spinal cord to skeletal muscles, and thereby affects bodily movement; it controls voluntary, conscious, sensory, and motor functions.

Sound The psychological experience that occurs when changes in air pressure stimulate the receptive organ for hearing; the resulting tones, or sounds, vary in frequency and amplitude.

Specific phobia Anxiety disorder characterized by irrational and persistent fear of a particular object or situation, along with a compelling desire to avoid it.

Spinal cord The portion of the central nervous system that is contained within the spinal column and transmits signals from the sensory organs, muscles, and glands to the brain, controls reflexive responses, and conveys signals from the brain to the rest of the body.

Split-brain patients People whose corpus callosum, which normally connects the two cerebral hemispheres, has been surgically severed.

Spontaneous recovery Recurrence of an extinguished conditioned response, usually following a rest period.

Sport psychology The systematic application of psychological principles to sports.

Standard deviation A descriptive statistic that measures the variability of data from the mean of the sample.

Standard score A score that expresses an individual's position relative to the mean, based on the standard deviation.

Standardization Process of developing uniform procedures for administering and scoring a test and for establishing norms.

Statistics The branch of mathematics that deals with collecting, classifying, and analyzing data.

State-dependent learning The tendency to recall information learned while in a particular physiological state most accurately when one is again in that physiological state.

Stereotypes Fixed, overly simple, and often erroneous ideas about traits, attitudes, and behaviors of groups of people; stereotypes assume that all members of a given group are alike.

Stimulant A drug that increases alertness, reduces fatigue, and elevates mood.

Stimulus discrimination Process by which an organism learns to respond only to a specific stimulus and not to other stimuli.

Stimulus generalization Process by which a conditioned response becomes associated with a stimulus that is similar but not identical to the original conditioned stimulus.

Storage Process of maintaining or keeping information readily available; also, the locations where information is held, or *memory stores.*

Stress inoculation [in-OK-you-LAY-shun] Procedure of teaching people ways to cope with stress and allowing them to practice in realistic situations so they will develop "immunity" to stress.

Stress A nonspecific emotional response to real or imagined challenges or threats; a result of a cognitive appraisal by the individual.

Stressor An environmental stimulus that affects an organism in physically or psychologically injurious ways, usually producing anxiety, tension, and physiological arousal.

Structuralism The school of psychological thought that considered the structure and elements of immediate, conscious experience to be the proper subject matter of psychology.

Subgoal analysis Heuristic procedure in which a problem is broken down into smaller steps, each of which has a subgoal.

Sublimation [sub-li-MAY-shun] Defense mechanism by which people redirect socially unacceptable impulses toward acceptable goals.

Subliminal perception Perception below the threshold of awareness.

Substance abuser A person who overuses and relies on drugs to deal with everyday life.

Sucking reflex Reflex that causes a newborn to make sucking motions when a finger or nipple is placed in the mouth.

Superego [sue-pur-EE-go] In Freud's theory, the moral aspect of mental functioning, comprising the ego ideal (what a person would ideally like to be) and the conscience and taught by parents and society.

Superstitious behavior Behavior learned through coincidental association with reinforcement.

Survey One of the descriptive methods of research; it requires construction of a set of questions to administer to a group of participants.

Sympathetic nervous system The part of the autonomic nervous system that responds to emergency situations by activating bodily resources needed for major energy expenditures.

Symptom substitution The appearance of one overt symptom to replace another that has been eliminated by treatment.

Synapse [SIN-apps] The microscopically small space between the axon terminals of one neuron and the receptor sites of another neuron.

Syntax [SIN-tacks] The way words and groups of words combine to form phrases, clauses, and sentences.

Systematic desensitization A three-stage counterconditioning procedure in which people are taught to relax when confronting stimuli that formerly elicited anxiety.

Temperament Early-emerging and long-lasting individual differences in disposition and in the intensity and especially the quality of emotional reactions.

Teratogen [ter-AT-oh-jen] Substance that can produce developmental malformations (birth defects) during the prenatal period.

Territorial behavior Behavior involved in establishing, maintaining, personalizing, and defending a delineated space.

Thalamus A large structure of the forebrain that acts primarily as a routing station to send information to other parts of the brain but probably also performs some interpretive functions; nearly all sensory information proceeds through the thalamus.

Thanatology The study of the psychological and medical aspects of death and dying.

Theory of mind An understanding of mental states such as feelings, desires, beliefs, and intentions and of the causal role they play in human behavior.

Theory A collection of interrelated ideas and facts put forward to describe, explain, and predict behavior and mental processes.

Time-out An operant conditioning procedure in which a person is physically removed from sources of reinforcement to decrease the occurrence of undesired behaviors.

Token economy An operant conditioning procedure in which individuals who display appropriate behavior receive tokens that they can exchange for desirable items or activities.

Tolerance The characteristic of requiring higher and higher doses of a drug to produce the same effect.

Trait Any readily identifiable stable quality that characterizes how an individual differs from other individuals.

Transduction Process by which a perceptual system analyzes stimuli and converts them into electrical impulses; also known as *coding.*

Transfer-appropriate processing Initial processing of information that is similar in modality or type to the processing necessary in the retrieval task.

Transference Psychoanalytic phenomenon in which a therapist becomes the object of a patient's emotional attitudes about an important person in the patient's life, such as a parent.

Trichromatic [try-kroe-MAT-ick] theory Visual theory, stated by Young and Helmholtz, that all colors can be made by mixing the three basic colors: red, green, and blue; also known as the *Young-Helmholtz theory.*

Trichromats [TRY-kroe-MATZ] People who can perceive all three primary colors and thus can distinguish any hue.

Type A behavior Behavior pattern characterized by competitiveness, impatience, hostility, and constant efforts to do more in less time.

Type B behavior Behavior pattern exhibited by people who are calmer, more patient, and less hurried than Type A individuals.

Types Personality categories in which broad collections of traits are loosely tied together and interrelated.

Unconditioned response Unlearned or involuntary response to an unconditioned stimulus.

Unconditioned stimulus Stimulus that normally produces a measurable involuntary response.

Unconscious Freud's level of mental life that consists of mental activities beyond people's normal awareness.

Undifferentiated type of schizophrenia A schizophrenic disorder that is characterized by a mixture of symptoms and does not meet the diagnostic criteria of any one type.

Validity Ability of a test to measure what it is supposed to measure and to predict what it is supposed to predict.

Variability The extent to which scores differ from one another, especially the extent to which they differ from the mean.

Variable A condition or characteristic of a situation or a person that is subject to change (it varies) within or across situations or individuals.

Variable-interval schedule A reinforcement schedule in which a reinforcer (reward) is delivered after predetermined but varying amounts of time, provided that the required response occurs at least once after each interval.

Variable-ratio schedule A reinforcement schedule in which a reinforcer (reward) is delivered after a predetermined but variable number of responses has occurred.

Vasocongestion In the sexual response cycle, engorgement of the blood vessels, particularly in the genital area, due to increased blood flow.

Vestibular [ves-TIB-you-ler] sense The sense of bodily orientation and postural adjustment.

Visual cortex The most important area of the brain's occipital lobe, which receives and further processes information from the lateral geniculate nucleus; also known as the *striate cortex.*

Vulnerability A person's diminished ability to deal with demanding life events.

Withdrawal symptoms The reactions experienced when a substance abuser stops using a drug with dependence properties.

Working memory Storage mechanism that temporarily holds current or recent information for immediate or short-term use and that is composed of several subsystems: an auditory loop to encode and rehearse auditory information, a visual–spatial "scratch pad" for visual information, and a central processing mechanism, or executive, that balances and controls information flow.

Working through In psychoanalysis, the repetitive cycle of interpretation, resistance to interpretation, and transference.

Zygote [ZY-goat] A fertilized egg.

Name Index

Subject Index

Credits

Chapter Opening Art

Chapter 1: Jacob Lawrence, *The Library,* 1960. Tempera on fiberboard, 24 × 29⅞ in. Copyright Smithsonian American Art Museum, Washington DC/Art Resource, NY. Smithsonian American Art Museum, Washington DC, U.S.A.

Chapter 2: Santiago Hernandez, *Reflector,* 1966. Alkyd on panel. Collection of Kenneth L. Freed.

Chapter 3: Milton Avery, *Child's Supper,* 1945. Oil on canvas, 36 × 48 in. New Britain Museum of American Art, Connecticut. Gift of Roy R. Neuberger. Photo: E. Irving Blomstrann.

Chapter 4: Jonathan Green, *Boy by the Sea,* 1995. Oil on canvas, 18 × 17 in. Collection of Gerhard C. Endler, M.D. Photograph by Tim Stamm.

Chapter 5: Alexander Calder, *Untitled,* 1947. Gouache and ink on paper, 57.6 × 83.8 cm. © Copyright 2002, Estate of Alexander Calder/Artists Rights Society, New York. Copyright Art Resource, NY. Private Collection.

Chapter 6: Andy Warhol, *Marilyn Monroe's Lips,* 1962. Synthetic polymer paint and silkscreen ink on canvas, two panels, each 82 × 80 in. © 2002, The Andy Warhol Foundation for the Visual Arts/Artists Rights Society, New York/Art Resource, NY.

Chapter 7: Lyonel Feininger, *Architecture II, The Man of Potin,* 1921. © Copyright Artists Rights Society, New York/VG Bild-Kunst, Bonn. Copyright Nimatallah/Art Resource, NY. Fundacion Coleccion Thyssen-Bornemisza, Madrid, Spain.

Chapter 8: Jonathan Green, *Colored Clothes,* 1988. Oil on Canvas, 23.5 × 23.5 in. Collection of Carroll Greene, Jr. Photograph by Tim Stamm.

Chapter 9: Stuart Davis, *Abstraction,* 1937. Watercolor and gouache on paper, 17⅞ × 23⅜ in. Copyright Smithsonian American Art Museum, Washington, DC/Art Resource, NY. Smithsonian American Art Museum, Washington, DC, U.S.A. © Estate of Stuart Davis/Licensed by VAGA, New York, NY.

Chapter 10: Lee Krasner, *Composition,* 1943. © Copyright 2002, The Pollock-Krasner Foundation/Artists Rights Society, New York. Copyright Smithsonian American Art Museum, Washington, DC/Art Resource, NY. Smithsonian American Art Museum, Washington, DC, U.S.A.

Chapter 11: Ruby Pearl, *Solitude,* 1998. Courtesy of Gateway Arts, Brookline, Massachusetts, Private Collection.

Chapter 12: Margarett Sargent, *Beyond Good and Evil (self-portrait),* ca. 1930. Oil on canvas, 40 × 23 in. Gift of Honor Moore, Davis Museum and Cultural Center, Wellesley College, Wellesley, Massachusetts. Photograph by Steve Briggs.

Chapter 13: Edward Hopper, *Nighthawks,* 1942. Oil on canvas, 84.1 × 152.4 cm. Friends of American Art Collection, 1942.51. Photo © The Art Institute of Chicago. All Rights Reserved.

Chapter 14: George Tooker, *Government Bureau,* 1956, Egg tempera on wood, 19⅝ × 29⅝ in. The Metropolitan Museum of Art, George A. Hearn Fund, 1956. (56.78) Photograph © 1984 The Metropolitan Museum of Art.

Chapter 15: Stanton MacDonald-Wright, *The Prophecy—Sleep Suite 2,* 1955. AM 1977-610. Copyright CNAC/MNAM/Dist. Réunion des Musées Nationaux/Art Resource, NY. Musee National d'Art Moderne, Centre Georges Pompidou, Paris, France.

Chapter 16: Claude Fourel, *Fish,* 2000. Courtesy of Gateway Arts, Brookline, Massachusetts, Private Collection.

Chapter 17: Joseph Stella, *The Voice of the City of New York Interpreted: The Bridge,* 1920–1922. Oil on and tempera on canvas, 88½ × 54 in.. Collection of The Newark Museum, 37.288e. Copyright The Newark Museum / Art Resource, NY.

Figures and Tables

Chapter 3: Figure 3.2, p. 78: From Berk, Laura (1993). *Infants, children, and adolescents,* 166. Copyright © 1993 by Allyn and Bacon. Reprinted by permission. Figure 3.3, p. 79: From Frankenberg, W. K., & Dobbs, J. B. (1967). The Denver Developmental Screening Tests. *Journal of Pediatrics, 71,* 191. Reprinted by permission of Mosby-Yearbook, Inc. Figure 3.5, p. 83: From Clarke-Stewart, A., Friedman, S., & Koch, J. (1985). *Child development: A topical approach,* 191. Copyright © 1985. Reprinted by permission of John Wiley & Sons, Inc. Figure 3.6, p. 85: From Fox, N.A., Kagan, J., & Weiskopf, S. (1979). The growth of memory during infancy. *Genetic Psychology Monographs, 99,* 91–130. Reprinted with permission of the Helen Dwight Reid Education Foundation. Published by Heldref Publications, 1319 Eighteenth St., NW, Washington, DC 20036-1802. Copyright © 1979. Figure 3.7, p. 87: © Susan Avishai 1995. Reprinted by permission.

Chapter 5: Figure 5.4, p. 151: From Dowling, J. E., & Boycott, B. B. (1966). *Proceedings of the Royal Society (London), B166,* 80–111, Figure 7. Reprinted by permission. Figure 5.5, p. 152: From Pirenne, M. H. (1967). *Vision and the eye,* 32. London: Chapman and Hall, Ltd. Reprinted by permission. Figure 5.13, p. 159: Reprinted from *Vision Research, 4,* MacNichol, Edward F. Jr., Retinal mechanisms of color vision, 119–133, Copyright 1964, with kind permission from Elsevier Science Ltd., The Boulevard, Langford Lane, Kidlington 0X5 1GB, UK. Figure 5.18, p. 168 (bottom right): From Beck, Jacob (1966). Effects of orientation and of shape similarity on perceptual grouping. *Perception and Psychophysics, 1,* 300–302. Reprinted by permission of Psychonomic Society, Inc.

Chapter 6: Figure 6.1, p. 195: From *Some must watch while some must sleep* by Dement, William C., Copyright © 1972 by William C. Dement. Used by permission of the Stanford Alumni Association and William C. Dement. Figure 6.2, p. 197: Reprinted with permission from Roffwarg, Howard P., Muzio, Joseph N., & Dement, William C. (1966). Ontogenetic development of human sleep-dream cycle. *Science, 152,* 604–619. Copyright 1966 American Association for the Advancement of Science. Figure 6.3, p. 212: From Ray, Oakley, & Ksir, Charles (1993). *Drugs, society, and human behavior, ed. 6,* 1993, 192, 194. St. Louis, MO: Mosby-Year Book, Inc. Reprinted by permission.

Chapter 8: Figure 8.9, p. 284 (top): From Kosslyn, Stephen. M. (1975). Information representation in visual images. *Cognitive Psychology, 7,* 341–370. Reprinted by permission of Academic Press, Inc. Figure 8.10, p. 284 (bottom): Reprinted with permission from Shepard, R. N., & Metzler, J. (1971). Mental rotation of three–dimensional objects. *Science, 171,* 701–703. Copyright 1971 by American Association for the Advancement of Science.

Chapter 9: Figure 9.6, p. 311: From Cosmides, Leda (1989). The logic of social exchange: Has natural selection shaped how humans reason? Studies with the Watson Selection Task. *Cognition, 31,* 187–276. Adapted by permission of the author. Figure 9.8, p. 326: Reprinted with permission from Premack, David (1971). Language in chimpanzees? *Science, 172,* 808–822. Copyright 1971 by American Association for the Advancement of Science.

Chapter 10: Table 10.1, p. 335: Adapted from Gardner, H., & Hatch, T. (1989). Multiple intelligences go to school: Educational implications of the theory of multiple intelligences. *Educational Researcher, 18(8),* 6. Reprinted by permission of the authors with adaptation based on personal communication from H. Gardner (1996). Table 10.4, p. 344: From Sattler, Jerome M. (1992). *Assessment of children, revised and updated, 3rd Edition,* 79. Copyright © 1992 Jerome Sattler. Adapted by permission.

Chapter 12: Table 12.5, p. 436: From Cattell, R.B. (1979), *Personality and learning theory, 1,* 61–73. New York: Springer Publishing Company, Inc. Copyright © 1979. Adapted by permission.

Chapter 13: Figure. 13.6, p. 460: Thank you to Implicit Association Test (IAT) Corporation for permission to reprint text appearing on the www.tolerance.org website. Figure 13.8, p. 465: From Milgram, S. (1963). Behavioral study of obedience. *Journal of Abnormal and Social Psychology, 67,* 371–378. Copyright © 1963 by Alexandra Milgram. Adapted by permission. Table 13.4, p. 483: From Hendrick, C., & Hendrick, S. (1986). A theory and method of love. *Journal of Personality and Social Psychology, 50,* 392–402. Copyright © 1986 by the American Psychological Association. Adapted with permission.

Chapter 14: Figure 14.1, p. 491: Figure from Selye, Hans (1976). *The stress of life, Revised Edition.* Copyright 1976. Reproduced with permission of The McGraw-Hill Companies. Table 14.1, p. 492: Reprinted from *Journal of Psychosomatic Research, II,* Holmes, T. H., & Rahe, R. H., Social readjustment rating scale, 213–218, Copyright 1967, with permission from Elsevier Science. Table 14.2, p. 494: From Crandall, C.S., Preisler, J.J., & Aussprung, J. (1992). Measuring life event stress in the lives of college students: The Undergraduate Stress Questionnaire (USQ). *Journal of Behavioral Medicine, 15,* 627–662. Reprinted by pemission of Kluwer Academic/Plenum Publishers. Table 14.3, p. 495 (bottom): From Kanner, A. D., Coyne, J. C., Schaefer, C., & Lazarus, R. S. (1981). Comparison of two modes of stress measurement: Daily hassles and uplifts versus major life events. *Journal of Behavioral Medicine, 4,* 1–39. Reprinted by permission of Kluwer Academic/Plenum Publishers.

Chapter 15: Table 15.6, p. 560: From Meyer, Robert. G., & Salmon, Paul. (1988). *Abnomal psychology, 2nd ed.,* 333 and the work of Edwin Shneidman and Norman Farberow. Copyright © 1988 by Allyn and Bacon. Reprinted by permission.

Chapter 16: Table 16.1, p. 571: From Mahrer, A. R., & Nadler, W. P. (1986). Good moments in psychotherapy: A preliminary review, a list, and some promising research avenues. *Journal of Consulting and Clinical Psychology, 54,* 10–15. Copyright © 1986 by the American Psychological Association. Adapted with permission.

Figure 16.3, p. 586: Reprinted from *Behavior Research and Therapy, 2,* Ayllon, T., & Haughton, T., Modification of symptomatic verbal behavior of mental patients, 87–97, Copyright 1964, with permission from Elsevier Science Ltd., Pergamon Imprint, The Boulevard, Langford Lane, Kidlington 0X5 1GB, UK. Figure 16.4, p. 587 (bottom): From Ayllon, T., & Azrin, N. H. (1965). The measurement and reinforcement of behavior of psychotics. *Journal of the Experimental Analysis of Behavior, 8,* 357–383. Copyright 1965 by the Society for the Experimental Analysis of Behavior, Inc. Reprinted by permission. Table 16.4, p. 595: From Ellis, Albert, & Harper, Robert A. *A guide to rational living.* © 1989, 1961. Reprinted by permission.

Chapter 17: Figure 17.4, p. 619: Reprinted fom Locke, E. A., & Schweiger, D. M. (1979). Participation in decision-making: One more look. In B. M. Staw (Ed.), *Research in organizational behavior, 1.* Copyright © 1979, with permission from Elsevier Science. Figure 17.6, p. 634 (bottom): From Baum, Andrew & Valins, Stuart (1977). Suite-style dorm and traditional corridor dorm figure. *Architecture and social behavior: Psychological studies of social density.* Mahwah, NJ: Lawrence Erlbaum Assoc., Inc. Reprinted by permission. Figure 17.7, p. 636: From Altman, I., & Vinsel, A. M. (1977). Personal space: An analysis of E. T. Hall's proxemics framework. In I. Altman, A. Rapoport, & J. F. Wohlwill (Eds.), *Human behavior and environment: Vol. 2. Advances in theory and research.* New York: Kluwer Academic/Plenum Publishers. Reprinted by permission.

Photos

Box Icon: *Psychology in Action, CORBIS.*

Chapter 1: p. 4, Monty Brinton/CBS. © 2001 CBS Worldwide Inc. All rights reserved; p. 5, Lilo Hess/TimePix; p. 6, Jonathan Nourok/PhotoEdit; p. 15, AP/Wide World Photos; p. 18, A. Ramey/PhotoEdit; p. 21, Freud Museum, London; p. 25, Photofest; p. 31, Prentice Hall, Inc.

Chapter 2: p. 40, CNRI/SPL/Science Source/Photo Researchers; p. 41, Charlyn Zlotnick/Woodfin Camp & Associates; p. 44, Roswell Angier/Stock Boston; p. 47, Andrew Leonard/Science Source/Photo Researchers; p. 48, Omikron/Science Source/Photo Researchers; p. 50, David Madison/Getty Images; p. 51, Kent Miles/Getty Images; p. 54, Brad Markel/Getty Images; p. 59, Wellcome Department of Cognitive Neurology/SPL/Science Source/Photo Researchers; p. 60, Professor K. Ugurbil/Peter Arnold, Inc.

Chapter 3: p. 73, AP/Wide World Photos; p. 77 (top and middle), Petit Format-Nestle/Science Source/Photo Researchers; p. 77 (bottom), J. Stevenson/SPL/Science Source/Photo Researchers; p. 78, Bob Daemmrich/The Image Works; p. 81, Courtesy of J. Campos, B. Bertenthal, and R. Kermoran; p. 83 (top left), SuperStock; p. 83 (top right), Laura Dwight/Peter Arnold, Inc.; p. 83 (middle left), James A. Sugar/Black Star; p. 83 (middle right), Laura Dwight/Peter Arnold, Inc.; p. 83 (bottom left), Andy Cox/ Getty Images; p. 83 (bottom right), Richard Hutchings/ Photo Researchers; p. 90, Robert Brenner/PhotoEdit; p. 91, Paul Conklin/PhotoEdit; p. 96, Jeffrey W. Myers/Stock Boston; p. 99, Ken Cavanagh/Photo Researchers; p. 103, David Lassman/Syracuse Newspapers/The Image Works.

Chapter 4: p. 113, Strauss/Curtis/Off Shoot Stock Special Collections; p. 114, David Young-Wolff/PhotoEdit; p. 115, David Young-Wolff/Getty Images; p. 116, David Young-Wolff/PhotoEdit; p. 122, AP/Wide World Photos; p. 125, Color Day Production/Getty Images; p. 129, Robert W. Ginn/PhotoEdit; p. 131, Michael Newman/PhotoEdit; p. 135 and 137, David Young-Wolff/PhotoEdit.

Chapter 5: p. 144, AP/Wide World Photos; p. 147, Timothy Shonnard/Getty Images; p. 148, Patrick Molnar/Getty Images; p. 149, Benjamin Ailes; p. 152, Ralph C. Eagle, Jr., MD/Science Source/Photo Researchers; p. 156, Arthur Tilley/Getty Images; p. 162, Mike Yamashita/Woodfin Camp & Associates; p. 164 (left), CORBIS; p. 164 (right), Bettmann/CORBIS; p. 165 (top), Ron Pretzer/Luxe; p. 165 (bottom), M.C. Escher's "Relativity" © 1998 Cordon Art B.V.-Baarn-Holland. All rights reserved; p. 166, Richard Lord/The Image Works; p. 176, Omikron/Science Source/Photo Researchers; p. 181, Courtesy of A.V. Apkarian; p. 183, Michael Justice/The Image Works.

Chapter 6: p. 192, AP/Wide World Photos; p. 193, Stuart Cohen/The Image Works; p. 194, HMS/Index Stock Imagery; p. 195, Will and Deni McIntyre/Science Source/Photo Researchers; p. 196, Ted Spagna/Science Source/Photo Researchers; p. 197, UPI/CORBIS; p. 204, The Granger Collection, New York; p. 206, Will & Deni McIntyre/Photo Researchers; p. 208, Brian Phillips/The Image Works; p. 209, Robert Sorbo; p. 213, A. Lichtenstein/The Image Works; p. 216, Getty Images News.

Chapter 7: p. 223, Blair Seitz/Science Source/Photo Researchers; p. 226, Archives of the History of American Psychology/The University of Akron; p. 232, Stan Wayman/Science Source/Photo Researchers; p. 236, AP/Wide World Photos; p. 237, Tony Freeman/PhotoEdit; p. 240 (top left), Brian Smith; p. 240 (top right), Omikron/Science Source/Photo Researchers; p. 240 (bottom left), Kevin Horan/Stock Boston; p. 240 (bottom right), Elizabeth Crews Photography; p. 248, Michael Newman/PhotoEdit; p. 250, Jeff Greenberg/PhotoEdit; p. 253, Will Faller; p. 255, Paul Conklin/PhotoEdit; p. 259, Offshoot Special Collections.

Chapter 8: p. 265, Hulton/Archive/Getty Images; p. 269, Keith Kent/Science Photo Library/Photo Researchers; p. 271, Brian Smith; p. 274, Will Hart; p. 275, Jeff Greenberg/PhotoEdit; p. 277, David Young-Wolff/PhotoEdit; p. 279, Bettmann/CORBIS; p. 281, AP/Wide World Photos; p. 282, Robert E. Daemmrich/Getty Images; p. 286, Archives of the History of American Psychology/The University of Akron; p. 289, Bob Daemmrich/The Image Works; p. 290, Michael Newman/PhotoEdit.

Chapter 9: p. 301 (left), Tim Davis/The National Audubon Society Collection/Photo Researchers; p. 301 (right), Stephen J. Krasemann/The National Audubon Society Collection/Photo Researchers; p. 303, 308, and 309,

AP/Wide World Photos; p. 316, Dana White/PhotoEdit; p. 317, Kal Muller/Woodfin Camp & Associates; p. 318, D. Greco/The Image Works; p. 326, Susan Kuklin/Science Source/Photo Researchers.

Chapter 10: p. 332, AP/Wide World Photos; p. 334, Bill Aron/PhotoEdit; p. 339, Archives of the History of American Psychology/The University of Akron; p. 345, Bob Daemmrich/The Image Works; p. 349, Alan Oddie/PhotoEdit; p. 350, Robert Azzi/Woodfin Camp & Associates; p. 358, Will Faller; p. 359, Bob Daemmrich/The Image Works.

Chapter 11: p. 366, Photofest; p. 372, Ed Lallo/Getty Images; p. 377, Catherine Karnow/Woodfin Camp & Associates; p. 378, Donna Day/Getty Images; p. 379 (top), Jose Galvez/PhotoEdit; p. 379 (bottom), Paul Fenton/Shooting Star; p. 386 and 387, Lew Merrim/Photo Researchers; p. 389, AP/Wide World Photos; p. 393, Copyright David Matsumoto and Paul Ekman; p. 399, Dreamworks/Shooting Star.

Chapter 12: p. 404, Everett Collection; p. 405, National Library of Medicine; p. 409, Tom Prettyman/PhotoEdit; p. 415, National Library of Medicine; p. 416, Alison Wright/Stock Boston; p. 420, Photofest; p. 422, Novastock/PhotoEdit; p. 426, Phil Banko/Getty Images; p. 430, Mary Kate Denny/PhotoEdit; p. 433, Alon Reininger/Contact/Woodfin Camp & Associates.

Chapter 13: p. 444, Philip G. Zimbardo; p. 445, Bob Daemmrich/Stock Boston; p. 453, Charles Gupton/Getty Images; p. 457, Alon Reininger/Contact Press Images/PictureQuest; p. 462, William Vandevert/Scientific American; p. 464, Courtesy of the Milgram Estate; p. 468, Andrew Lichtenstein/The Image Works; p. 475, PhotoDisc, Inc.; p. 479, D. Perrett, I. Penton-Voak, M. Burk/University of St. Andrews/SPL/Science Source/Photo Researchers; p. 482, NBC/Everett Collection.

Chapter 14: p. 496, AP/Wide World Photos; p. 499, John Maier, Jr./The Image Works; p. 500, Kaku Kurita/Getty Images; p. 501, Jon Bradley/Getty Images; p. 507, Peter Scholey/Getty Images; p. 509, David Young-Wolff/PhotoEdit; p. 513, Bob Daemmrich/Stock Boston; p. 516, Michael Newman/PhotoEdit; p. 518, Porter Gifford/Getty Images; p. 520, Rick Strange/Index Stock Imagery.

Chapter 15: p. 526, Frank Ross/CORBIS Sygma; p. 527, Seth Resnick/Stock Boston; p. 528, AP/Wide World Photos; p. 533, Bob Daemmrich/Stock Boston; p. 535, Bettmann/CORBIS; p. 539, Brian Smith; p. 541, Will Hart; p. 551, Everett Collection; p. 552, NIH/Science Source/Photo Researchers; p. 558, Bill Aron/PhotoEdit.

Chapter 16: p. 568, HBO/Newsmakers/Getty Images News; p. 569, Photofest; p. 572, James Wilson/Woodfin Camp & Associates; p. 574, Frank Siteman/Stock Boston; p. 576, Will Hart; p. 579, AP/Wide World Photos; p. 582, Michael Rougier/TimePix; p. 588, Mary Kate Denny/PhotoEdit; p. 590, Lori Adamski Peek/Getty Images; p. 591, Michelangelo Gratton/Getty Images; p. 597, Will Hart; p. 600, Louisa Preston; p. 603, Will and Deni McIntyre/Science Source/Photo Researchers.

Chapter 17: p. 608, AP/Wide World Photos; p. 609, Photofest; p. 611, Michael Newman/PhotoEdit; p. 612, Will Hart; p. 616, Charles Gupton/Stock Boston; p. 620, Charles Gupton/Getty Images; p. 623, Hulton-Deutsch Collection/CORBIS; p. 625, From Anthony D. Andre and Leon D. Segal, "Design Functions," *Ergonomics in Design,* April 1993, p. 5. Copyright 1993 by the Human Factors and Ergonomics Society. Reprinted by permission. All rights reserved.; p. 628, John Chiasson/Getty Images; p. 631, Gary Wagner/Stock Boston; p. 633, Rod Rolle/Getty Images; p. 638, Brian Smith; p. 640, Andrew Lichtenstein/The Image Works; p. 642, Will Faller; p. 645, AP/Wide World Photos.